The Reception of Philo of Alexandria

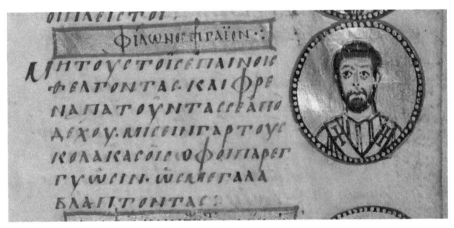

Byzantine portrait of Philo in the manuscript Parisinus graecus 923 (Paris, IX cent.), f. 20r, which contains more than forty such medallians. The crosses on Philo's stole are indicative of the legend of Philo Christianus. Image courtesy of the Bibliothèque National, Paris.

The Reception of Philo of Alexandria

Edited by
COURTNEY J. P. FRIESEN, DAVID LINCICUM, AND
DAVID T. RUNIA

Great Clarendon Street, Oxford, OX2 6DP,
United Kingdom

Oxford University Press is a department of the University of Oxford.
It furthers the University's objective of excellence in research, scholarship,
and education by publishing worldwide. Oxford is a registered trade mark of
Oxford University Press in the UK and in certain other countries

© Oxford University Press 2025

The moral rights of the authors have been asserted

All rights reserved. No part of this publication may be reproduced, stored in
a retrieval system, or transmitted, in any form or by any means, without the
prior permission in writing of Oxford University Press, or as expressly permitted
by law, by licence or under terms agreed with the appropriate reprographics
rights organization. Enquiries concerning reproduction outside the scope of the
above should be sent to the Rights Department, Oxford University Press, at the
address above

You must not circulate this work in any other form
and you must impose this same condition on any acquirer

Published in the United States of America by Oxford University Press
198 Madison Avenue, New York, NY 10016, United States of America

British Library Cataloguing in Publication Data

Data available

Library of Congress Control Number: 2024945810

ISBN 978-0-19-883622-3

DOI: 10.1093/oso/9780198836223.001.0001

Printed and bound by
CPI Group (UK) Ltd, Croydon, CR0 4YY

The manufacturer's authorised representative in the EU for product safety
is Oxford University Press España S.A. of el Parque Empresarial San
Fernando de Henares, Avenida de Castilla,
2 – 28830 Madrid (www.oup.es/en).

Acknowledgments

This book would not exist without the collaboration of the band of remarkable scholars who contributed their expertise to a common project. The editors express our gratitude to them both for their work and for their longsuffering patience as the project was delayed by the global pandemic and by more routine matters. We offer our warm thanks to Tom Perridge at Oxford University Press for his encouragement and for believing in this book from the beginning, and to Karen Raith and Jamie Mortimer for their excellent support. Warren Campbell kindly provided assistance in ascertaining images and permissions, and Maria Sermersheim undertook the laborious task of compiling the final bibliography. Finally, Vinothini Thiruvannamalai and her colleagues at Newgen Knowledge Works assisted skillfully in the production of this volume.

Contents

List of Figures	xi
List of Contributors	xiii
Introduction	1
Courtney J. P. Friesen, David Lincicum, and David T. Runia	

I. THE FIRST CENTURIES

1. Flavius Josephus Katell Berthelot	17
2. The New Testament Torrey Seland	32
3. Apostolic Fathers and Early Christian Apologists James Carleton Paget	47
4. Clement of Alexandria Annewies van den Hoek	65
5. Origen of Alexandria Michael B. Cover	76
6. Gnosticism M. David Litwa	93
7. Ancient Platonic Philosophy Gregory E. Sterling	109
8. Rabbinic Judaism Steven D. Fraade	127

II. LATE ANTIQUITY

9. Eusebius Sabrina Inowlocki	145
10. Didymus the Blind Justin M. Rogers	162
11. The Cappadocians Albert C. Geljon	178

12. Isidore of Pelusium 194
    Madalina Toca and Johan Leemans

13. Ambrose 210
    Maria E. Doerfler

14. Jerome 227
    Matthew A. Kraus

15. Augustine 242
    Ilaria L. E. Ramelli

III. THE MIDDLE AGES

16. The Greek and Latin Manuscript Traditions 259
    James R. Royse

17. Medieval Jewish Philosophy and Mysticism 281
    Elke Morlok and Ze'ev Strauss

18. Armenian Christianity 299
    Olga Vardazaryan

19. Christian Arabic Literature 322
    Alexander Treiger

20. Byzantium 333
    David T. Runia

21. The Latin West from 500 to 1500 CE 347
    David T. Runia and Frans van Liere

IV. THE RENAISSANCE AND EARLY MODERN PERIOD

22. Early Printed Editions of Philo's Writings 367
    David T. Runia, Gregory E. Sterling, and Michael B. Cover

23. The Jewish Rediscovery of Philo in Early Modern Europe 386
    Joanna Weinberg

24. Post-Tridentine Catholic Thought 400
    Eric J. DeMeuse

25. Thomas Mangey and Philonic Scholarship from the Sixteenth to Eighteenth Centuries 414
    Giovanni Benedetto

26. German Philosophy, 1650–1850 429
    Dirk Westerkamp

V. FROM THE EIGHTEENTH TO THE TWENTIETH CENTURIES

27. The Rise of New Testament Criticism 453
    David Lincicum

28. The Jewish Enlightenment (*Haskalah*) 467
    Ze'ev Strauss

29. The *Wissenschaft des Judentums* 484
    Görge K. Hasselhoff

30. Modern Literature from the Nineteenth to the Twenty-First Century 499
    David T. Runia

VI. CONTEMPORARY PERSPECTIVES

31. Contemporary Receptions and Future Prospects among Classicists 517
    Courtney J. P. Friesen

32. Contemporary Receptions and Future Prospects among Historians of Philosophy 532
    Gretchen Reydams-Schils

33. Contemporary Receptions and Future Prospects among Scholars of Judaism 542
    Ellen Birnbaum

34. Contemporary Receptions and Future Prospects among Scholars of Christianity 561
    Mark Edwards

35. Bibliographies on Philo 572
    David T. Runia

Bibliography 587
Index Locorum 639
Subject Index 665

Figures

21.1. Medieval fresco in the chapter house of the Cathedral of Le Puy, France. It depicts the four prophets Isaiah, Jeremiah, Hosea, and Philo. 356

21.2. Close up of the depiction of Philo (written Filo) holding a scroll with the prophetic text drawn from Wisdom of Solomon 2:10, 2:20, and 2:16. The text reads: *dixerunt inpii opprimamus virum iustum / iniuste. morte turpissima condemnemus / eum. tamquam nugaces estimati sumus ab illo* (The ungodly said let us oppress a just man injustly. Let us condemn him to a most disgraceful death. As worthless people we have been regarded by him). 356

21.3. Gilded silver bust of Philo the Prophet in the treasury of the Cathedral of Münster, Germany. The scroll contains the text of Wisdom 2:20, *mortem turpissima contempnemus illum* (let us condemn him to a most disgraceful death). 357

21.4. Second gilded silver bust of Philo the Prophet in the treasury of the Cathedral of Münster, Germany holding the same text. The cap he is wearing may indicate his Jewish status. This bust features a rock crystal containing the relics of the saints Walpurga and Vincent. 357

22.1. Title page of the earliest publication of a Philonic treatise, albeit in an ancient Latin translation, by Augustus Justinianus, Paris: Prelum Ascensianum, 1520. Beinecke Rare Book and Manuscript Library, Yale University. 369

22.2. Title page of the *editio princeps* of Philo's treatises preserved in the original Greek, published by Adrian Turnèbe, Royal Printer of Greek, Paris 1552. Beinecke Rare Book and Manuscript Library, Yale University. 371

22.3. Engraving of Philo accompanied by a Greek poem, by Fédéric Morel in his Latin translation of a Philonic treatise, Paris 1614. (Here is Philo, glory of the Hebrews, image of Plato, / For whom the good was dear (*philon*), the not-good was not dear.) 380

22.4. Title page of *Omnia quae extant opera* of Philo Judaeus, published by the Compagnie du grand navire, Paris, 1640. 382

35.1. The personal bookplate of Howard Lehman Goodhart with the Dutch motto "Beidt uw tijd" (Bide your time). Located on the flyleaf of the 1691 edition of Philo's *opera omnia* in the Beinecke Library, Yale University, New Haven, United States. 580

35.2. Bookplate of the Yale University Library in the same volume, indicating that it was a gift from the Library of Howard Lehman Goodhart. 581

Contributors

Giovanni Benedetto, Professor of Classical Philology and History of Classical Tradition, Università degli Studi di Milano, Italy.

Katell Berthelot, Full Professor of Ancient Judaism at CNRS / Aix-Marseille University, France.

Ellen Birnbaum, Independent Scholar, Cambridge, Massachusetts.

James Carleton Paget, Fellow and Tutor, Peterhouse, and Reader in Ancient Judaism and Early Christianity, University of Cambridge, UK.

Michael B. Cover, Associate Professor of Theology, Marquette University, USA.

Eric J. DeMeuse (PhD Marquette), Headmaster, Chesterton Academy of Milwaukee.

Maria E. Doerfler, Assistant Professor of Religious Studies, Yale University.

Mark Edwards, Professor of Early Christian Studies, Christ Church, Oxford, UK.

Steven D. Fraade, Mark Taper Professor Emeritus of the History of Judaism, Yale University.

Courtney J. P. Friesen, Professor of Religious Studies and Classics, University of Arizona.

Albert C. Geljon, Christelijk Gymnasium Utrecht, Netherlands.

Görge K. Hasselhoff, Adjunct Professor of History of Theology, Technical University Dortmund, Germany.

Annewies van den Hoek, Research Associate of the Harvard Museum of the Ancient Near East.

Sabrina Inowlocki, Research Fellow, Interdisciplinary Center and Genizah Research, eLijah-Lab, University of Haifa, Israel.

Matthew A. Kraus, Associate Professor of Judaic Studies, University of Cincinnati.

Johan Leemans, Professor of Christianity in Late Antiquity, KU Leuven, Belgium.

Frans van Liere, Professor of Medieval History, Calvin University, USA.

David Lincicum, Associate Professor of Theology, University of Notre Dame, USA.

M. David Litwa, Assistant Editor, New Testament Abstracts, Boston College.

Elke Morlok, Postdoctoral Researcher, Goethe University Frankfurt.

Ilaria L. E. Ramelli, Professor of Theology, Durham University and University of Cambridge, UK.

Gretchen Reydams-Schils, Professor in the Program of Liberal Studies at the University of Notre Dame, with concurrent appointments in Classics, Philosophy, and Theology.

Justin M. Rogers, Associate Professor of Biblical Studies, Freed-Hardeman University, USA.

James R. Royse, Retired Professor of Philosophy, Claremont, California.

David T. Runia, Professorial Fellow in School of Historical and Philosophical Studies at the University of Melbourne; and Honorary Professor, Institute of Religion and Critical Inquiry at the Australian Catholic University.

xiv CONTRIBUTORS

Torrey Seland, Professor Emeritus in New Testament Studies, VID Specialized University, Norway.

Gregory E. Sterling, The Reverend Henry L. Slack Dean and the Lillian Claus Professor of New Testament, Yale Divinity School.

Ze'ev Strauss, Assistant Professor of Jewish Religion, University of Hamburg.

Madalina Toca, RSE Saltire Early Career Postdoctoral Fellow, University of Edinburgh; and Free Research Associate, KU Leuven, Belgium.

Alexander Treiger, Professor, Department of Classics with Arabic and Religious Studies, Dalhousie University, Canada.

Olga Vardazaryan, Senior Researcher, Matenadaran, Mesrop Mashtots Institute of Ancient Manuscripts, Armenia.

Joanna Weinberg, Professor Emerita of Early Modern Jewish History and Rabbinics, University of Oxford, UK.

Dirk Westerkamp, Full Professor of Theoretical Philosophy, Christian-Albrechts-Universität zu Kiel, Germany.

Introduction

Courtney J. P. Friesen, David Lincicum, and David T. Runia

It was not to be expected that one of the larger bodies of writing to survive from the ancient world would be the work of a Greek-speaking Jew from Alexandria. Yet this is what occurred. A corpus of nearly fifty treatises remains extant, mostly in the original Greek but also partly in Armenian or Latin translation, the legacy of Philo of Alexandria, who lived and wrote in the eastern Mediterranean metropolis at the beginning of the common era (*c.*15 BCE to 50 CE). His writings are, apart from the Septuagint, the Greek translation of the Hebrew Bible, the only substantial literary remains of the Jewish community of Alexandria, which flourished for a number of centuries until being virtually destroyed in the revolt in 115–17 during the reign of the emperor Trajan. The survival of the corpus Philonicum was a remarkable occurrence, both fortuitous and fortunate.

The present volume, the first to give a comprehensive account of its subject, sets out to delineate the ways in which knowledge about Philo, his writings, and his thought was obtained, utilized, studied, and discussed over a period of nearly two millennia. It is for the most part a diachronic narrative, starting in Philo's own world of the early Empire and moving through the centuries up to contemporary scholarship, when he is studied in distant parts of the globe of which he himself had no knowledge. This narrative consists of a series of stages, each with its own characteristics, which can be summarized in the following list:

1. How Philo's writings and thought related to contemporary Jewish literary production, including the beginnings of what would become Christian literature.
2. How he was valued by the church fathers from the late second century onwards, ensuring the survival of his writings.
3. How his reputation and corpus were not forgotten during the period of late antiquity through to the Byzantine era and the Middle Ages in the west.
4. How with the advent of printing his writings started to spread throughout the early modern world.
5. How for many centuries he virtually disappeared from view in Jewish tradition until rediscovered in the sixteenth century.
6. How aspects of his thought became embroiled in theological and philosophical controversy in the early modern period.
7. How in the nineteenth century study of his writings and thought entered post-enlightenment scholarship in the domains of classics, biblical, and Judaic studies.

8. How in the twentieth century a great expansion of Philonic studies took place.
9. How Philo also gained a presence in literature outside the Academy.

The knowledge and skills required to investigate this long process of reception far exceed the powers of a single individual. For this reason the collaborative mode of scholarship that has been developed in the past decades is particularly suited to the present project. A collective of more than thirty scholars treat a wide range of themes, all forming part of a continuous narrative, with each scholar making contributions based on their own expertise.

It will be evident that in this work we use the term "reception" in a broad and general sense. We take it to include the process of *transmission*. Information about Philo and in particular his corpus of writings have been preserved and disseminated through the written record. Many details about how that occurred are described in the various contributions in this volume. It is fair to say, however, that the primary emphasis of our narrative falls on the aspect of *utilization*: how were Philo's writings and thought used in the process of reception we are describing? The general term utilization covers a broad range of attitudes and practices, and here too a list may be helpful:

1. Approval and appropriation. Philo's writings may contain knowledge and insights that can be taken over and put to use, for example in exegesis of scripture or in theological or philosophical discussion.
2. Historical record. His writings, or what others say about him, can contribute to the recording of historical events, whether real, as in his involvement in Alexandrian politics, or legendary, as in accounts of the beginnings of the Alexandrian church.
3. Disapproval and weaponization. Philo's thought can be associated with religious, philosophical, or theological tendencies which are seen as misguided or deserving of condemnation, such as his use of allegory or his failure to recognize the true nature of the divine Logos.
4. Scholarly study. Philo can be the object of more or less disinterested and objective study, whether for his own sake as a writer and thinker of intrinsic interest, or because he provides information on, or serves as a point for comparison with other fields of study.
5. Religious tradition. Philo can be treated as part of a religious tradition with its own development, notably as illustrated by the slow process of his acceptance in modern Judaism.

It is apparent that, as modern theory emphasizes, reception has everything to do with the recipient, those who in their own context and situation, and with the information available to them, grapple with some aspect of the Philonic legacy. And of course, this also applies to the contributors to this volume, who each approach a limited aspect of the whole subject from their own perspective, both scholarly and personal. The result is a diverse and multi-faceted account, held together by the many-sided figure of the protagonist and the diachronic narrative of how he has been understood and valued throughout two millennia.

As already noted, this is the first book to present a comprehensive account of Philo's reception from its beginnings to the present day. There is only one work that can be regarded as a predecessor. In 1993 David Runia published his study *Philo in Early Christian Literature*, in which he traced Philo's reception in the Christian tradition up to 400 CE, with brief summaries of developments after that date up to the publication of printed texts in the sixteenth century.[1] The subtitle of the work, *A Survey*, is significant. Runia recognized that, scattered among the vast amount of scholarly research on Philo, a good many partial studies had been devoted to this subject, focusing mainly on individual writers but also subjects such as his theology, use of the allegorical method, and so on. But there was no overview of the subject.[2] He decided that the best way to proceed was to provide a survey which would outline the state of our knowledge, making use of existing scholarship, filling in gaps where possible and pointing the way to further research. In the present volume no less than twelve contributions cover the same ground as Runia's monograph, showing how his pioneering work has been a stimulus to further research on this subject. The study also contained an introductory chapter in which Philo's reception (or lack thereof) in the pagan and Jewish traditions was briefly outlined, together with an account of the survival and transmission of his writings up to the appearance of the first printed editions and some brief remarks on Philo's reception in the early modern period up to the nineteenth century.[3] The focus of the book, however, is very much on the period up to 400 CE and the treatment of later periods is fleeting at best. One of the main aims of the present work is to fill that gap, and for this purpose the present volume can take advantage of the considerable amount of research that has taken place in the intervening years.

As much as we have attempted to chart a thorough course through the long history of Philo's reception, we are under no illusion that the current volume is or can be exhaustive in its scope and treatment. Quite apart from the many places where Philonic influence remains to be discovered, there are themes that we could not accommodate within the confines of our project, but which deserve further exploration. For example, as Alexander Treiger's chapter on Philo in Christian Arabic tradition in this volume demonstrates, Philo was often mediated to other linguistic traditions through Eusebius' *Ecclesiastical History*. The same phenomenon can be observed in Syriac, and presumably in other languages that lacked access to a direct transmission of Philo's works.[4]

---

[1] D. T. Runia, *Philo in Early Christian Literature: A Survey* (Van Gorcum: Assen, 1993). It appeared in the series Compendia Rerum Iudicarum ad Novum Testamentum.

[2] On now wholly outdated nineteenth- and early twentieth-century overviews, see Runia, *Philo in Early Christian Literature*, 44–47. Mention should be made of the outstanding article by A. Solignac, "Philon d'Alexandria: II Influence sur les Pères de l'Eglise," *Dictionnaire de spiritualité ascétique et mystique, doctrine et histoire* 12 (Paris: Beauchesne, 1984): 1366–74. But the overview it provides is quite brief. See now also the article by D. T. Runia, "Philon von Alexandria," *RAC* 27 (2015): 605–27.

[3] Runia, *Philo in Early Christian Literature*, 8–33.

[4] For Eusebius' mediation of Philo to Bar Hebraeus, as an example, note P. Druille and D. Asade, "Filón de Alejandría y la embajada a Gayo en el *Chronicon Syriacum* y *Historia Dynasticarum* de Bar Hebraeus. Transmisión, texto y traducción," *Circe de clásicos y modernos* 23.2 (2019): 73–101.

But it is especially after the advent of the printing press that the knowledge of Philo broadens, and has been less intensively studied than the pre-modern period.[5] We have Eric DeMeuse's excellent chapter on Philo in post-Tridentine Catholic thought, but not an equivalent investigation on Protestant traditions in the sixteenth and seventeenth centuries. Philo plays a role in early modern legal discourse, and we find scholars such as the Dutch polymath Hugo Grotius or the German jurist Samuel von Pufendorf engaging Philo's thought.[6] We know that Voltaire (his antisemitism notwithstanding) and the Encyclopédistes made use of Philo, and that use would repay study.[7] Similarly, the early translations of Philo into vernacular languages of Europe and beyond would be worthy subjects of investigation.[8] Although Mark Edwards briefly discusses the appeal to Philo in *nouvelle théologie* in his chapter on the contemporary relevance of Philo for the study of Christianity, it would be possible to mount a dedicated study to the theme. David Runia's chapter on Philo in modern literature breaks new ground in calling attention to Philo's presence in prose works, and such a treatment might be extended by considering those few places where Philo makes an appearance in poetry.[9] While images of Philo are mentioned at a couple of places in this volume, we have not thematized artistic engagement with Philo; there are not abundant sources for such a study, but one or two do exist. For example, the Polish Jewish artist Georges Goldkorn, who emigrated to Paris and became one of a number of Jewish artists in the mid-twentieth century École de Paris, produced a series of etchings and woodcuts interspersed with selections from Philo's writings.[10] We see this volume as opening up a further field of inquiry, rather than being a final word.

I.1 Overview and Summary

While an exhaustive treatment of the history of Philo's reception is not possible, this collection of essays aims toward a comprehensive scope with contributions from specialists in relevant periods, authors, and corpora. Part I treats the first centuries, beginning with the years immediately following Philo's death around 50 CE. The earliest mention of Philo is by Josephus, who notes his role in the Jewish delegation from Alexandria to the emperor Gaius. In her chapter, Katell Berthelot revisits the question

---

[5] In 2018 a conference was organized by Frédéric Gabriel and Smaranda Marcelescu in Lyon, France, on the reception of Philo in Europe in the sixteenth to eighteenth century. This volume will be an important complement to this volume when published.

[6] See e.g. C. Leben, "Hebrew Sources in the Doctrine of the Law of Nature and Nations in Early Modern Europe," *European Journal of International Law* 27.1 (2016): 79–106; M. Jones, "Philo Judaeus and Hugo Grotius's Modern Natural Law," *Journal of the History of Ideas* 74.3 (2013): 339–59.

[7] For Josephus, one might compare M. Hadas-Lebel, "Voltaire lecteur de Flavius Josèphe," *Revue des études juives* 150.3–4 (1991): 529–34.

[8] Note the early translations in H. L. Goodhart, and E. R. Goodenough, "A General Bibliography of Philo Judaeus," in E. R. Goodenough, *The Politics of Philo Judaeus: Practice and Theory* (New Haven: Yale University Press 1938), nos. 462–515.

[9] e.g. N. Dubie, "Simple Philo of Alexandria," in his *Radio Sky* (New York: Norton, 1991); J. G. Whittier, "The Pennsylvania Pilgrim," in his *The Pennsylvania Pilgrim and Other Poems* (Boston: J. R. Osgood and Company, 1872); or the epigraph of H. Smart's collection of poetry, *Pierrot* (London: Faber, 1991).

[10] G. Goldkorn, *Hommage à Philon d'Alexandrie* (Paris: Manuel Bruker, 1964).

of whether Josephus made use of Philo's works. Because the historian does not quote from Philonic treatises, many have concluded that he did not know them directly. Berthelot reevaluates this assessment, arguing, on the contrary, that Josephus appears to have been inspired especially by Philo's apologetic writings which he found conducive to his own advocacy for the Mosaic Law, and he probably also knew Philo's *Legatio ad Gaium*, even though his own version of those events differs in significant ways. Roughly contemporary with Josephus, the writings of the New Testament, the subject of Torrey Seland's chapter, exhibit a much more indirect mode of Philonic reception. Even so, possibilities of influence cannot be ruled out, and Seland explores several areas of overlap, particularly in allegorical interpretation of biblical law and in theologies of Wisdom and Logos. Among the most relevant New Testament books are the Pauline letters, the Epistle to the Hebrews, and the Gospel of John. In the absence of evidence for explicit knowledge of Philo's writings, Seland proposes that correspondences may be accounted for in Philo's common cultural identity with New Testament authors formed in similar religious communities.

Beyond the New Testament and into the second century, evidence for the reception of Philo continues to be largely indirect; yet, the influence of his ideas appears to have taken hold. James Carleton Paget surveys several Christian authors, starting with the epistle of First Clement, where he detects some suggestive verbal parallels. In the Epistle of Barnabas and the apology of Theophilus of Antioch *Ad Autolycum*, allegorical methods are deployed which are closely akin to Philo and his Alexandrian milieu. Justin Martyr's theological reflections on the Logos exhibit clear affinities with concepts developed by Philo, but even so up to this point there are no definitive indications of direct access to Philonic writings. It is not until Clement of Alexandria that a Christian author first explicitly mentions Philo by name and makes extensive use of his writings. Now, at the turn of the third century Philo's treatises appear to have been available to Clement in a Christian library; however, the manner in which he deploys his Alexandrian predecessor is varied and uneven. Annewies van den Hoek helpfully traces the contours of Clement's use of Philo, taking the inventory from her 1988 monograph as a point of departure. She establishes that Clement frequently both quotes from and alludes to Philo, but more than this, he takes over and adapts Philo's intellectual project for his own Christian *paideia*. Along this trajectory, Origen was also intimately acquainted with Philo's writings, and like Clement he deploys them extensively, evident in his numerous references as well as in the appropriation and imitation of Philo's exegetical method. As Michael Cover points out in his contribution, however, the nature of Origen's debt to Philo is dynamic and must be understood in view of his move to Caesarea where he came in close contact with rabbinic scholars, thus diversifying his Jewish intellectual interlocutors. Cover rounds out his discussion with exegetical case studies from Origen's *Commentary on Matthew* and the newly discovered *Homilies on the Psalms*.

Potential influences from Philo's works are also evident in Gnostic traditions, as discussed by David Litwa. This is the case, especially, for the so-called Sethians: while some religious ideas can be accounted for on the basis of a shared milieu of Middle

Platonism, others seem traceable to distinctly Philonic formulations, such as God "the Standing One," theanthropy (the divine form in humanity), Wisdom as God's wife, and a variety of perspectives on the inter-relationship between God, primordial creation, humanity, good, and evil. The transmission of such conceptions from Philo, however, came to be shaped significantly by a growing Christian prejudice against Judaism, and thus it develops in directions that Philo himself would not have approved. Philo's works were also known to a few pagan philosophers, as his intellectual reputation extended beyond Jewish and Christian communities. As Gregory Sterling explores, Greek-speaking intellectuals in the Middle-Platonic tradition were increasingly open to "barbarian" philosophies as embodiments of a common wisdom. Truth was often concealed in myths and riddles, however, and Sterling points to Plutarch's famous exposition of the philosophical import of the mysteries of Isis and Osiris as comparable to Philo's treatment of the writings of Moses. In analyzing another work of Plutarch, *On the E at Delphi*, Sterling demonstrates striking similarities with Philo, for instance, in their understanding of being and becoming and in the schematic division of the stages of human life. Numenius, likewise a Middle Platonist, articulates the self-existence of divinity in a manner that appears to be formulated from Exod 3:14, possibly mediated through Philo. In turn, Plotinus the prominent Neoplatonist, though probably only influenced by Philo by way of Numenius, articulates a metaphysical system resembling Philo's immutable divinity as its First Principle.

As with many of the other authors surveyed in the first centuries, in the final chapter of Part I on ancient Jewish rabbis by Steven Fraade, the reception of Philo is largely oblique. Even so, as Fraade cogently demonstrates, his corpus, along with writings in the Dead Sea Scrolls discovered at Qumran, provides the primary precedent for the midrash produced by the rabbis, that is, line-by-line exposition, with scriptural lemmata followed by interpretation. Like Philo, the rabbis share a common intellectual interest in the Mosaic Law and engage in projects of conceptualizing it topically. That they take up many of the same themes cannot be merely coincidental, even if direct access to the writings of Philo is uncertain with differences of language and geography obscuring the dynamics of influences and borrowings. Nevertheless, the rabbinic corpus provides crucial, albeit indirect and illusive, data for the reception of Philo and attests to the circulation of individuals and texts between the intellectual hubs of Alexandria and Caesarea.

Part II on late antiquity represents a transition in the reception of Philo marked historically by the bourgeoning cultural ascendency of Christians in the post-Constantinian Roman world. Sabrina Inowlocki opens this section with a chapter on Eusebius whose project of reimagining the historical and intellectual significance of Christianity would shape perceptions of Philo for the centuries to follow. Now, with access to the library at Caesarea containing the works of Philo (probably passed down from Origen), Eusebius wrote Philo into his teleological history. As Inowlocki details, Eusebius constructed Philo's *persona* as an idealized and pious "Hebrew" whose expertise in scripture and philosophy both anticipated and contributed to the eventual and inevitable rise of Christianity. Moreover, Philo's account of the Therapeutae in *De vita contemplativa* functions, for Eusebius, as a historical datum for the emergence of the Christian community in Egypt, exemplary for its philosophical and ascetic lifestyle.

The subsequent six chapters in Part II follow the course of Philo's Christian reception and divide evenly between the Greek-speaking east and the Latin west. First, among the former, the celebrated exegete Didymus the Blind, treated by Justin Rogers, refers to Philo explicitly and by name on numerous occasions and views him as a wise man, skilled in the interpretation of scripture. His most involved use of Philo occurs in his *Commentary on Genesis*, where the Jewish writer provides key insights in matters of etymology and arithmology as well as for theological reflections on the nature of God and creation. The Cappadocians, as seen in the chapter by Albert Geljon, were also well acquainted with the Philo. Among them, Gregory of Nyssa's borrowings are the most extensive, though his attitude toward the Jewish exegete is mixed. He appropriates allegorical readings of biblical passages, though without naming Philo, but on other occasions the use of Philo by his theological adversary Eunomius produced a negative association for Gregory and led to a critical response. His brother Basil only mentions Philo once and in Gregory of Nazianzus there are no clear references to Philo's writings, but by this time, as Geljon's analysis makes clear, the exegetical methodologies and theological innovations pioneered by Philo were widely diffuse, even where direct recourse to his writings cannot be established. Next, Madalina Toca and Johan Leemans analyze the writings of Isidore of Pelusium (*c.*360–440 CE), a learned monk, with an extant corpus of more than two thousand letters. Among these, Philo is mentioned by name in four, but Toca and Leemans demonstrate the debt to him as a biblical interpreter is more profound than this might suggest. Indeed, Isidore evokes the Jewish exegete to authorize his own readings, such as in detecting traces of Trinitarian theology in Jewish scripture, justifying the use of allegory, and establishing the precise meaning of a Greek word. Through their survey of Isidore's corpus, Toca and Leemans helpfully draw attention to the methodological challenges inherent in differentiating between direct literary dependence and mediated, oblique reception.

Maria Doerfler's chapter on Ambrose, bishop of Milan in the late fourth century, provides the point of departure for Philo's reception in the Latin west. Though only mentioned once by name in his extant corpus, according to one scholarly estimate Ambrose makes as many as six hundred references to Philo. Doerfler provides context and contours to this material. In the first place, the processes whereby manuscripts of Philo reached Rome or Milan remain obscure, but it appears certain that the bishop read them in Greek. On this basis, Ambrose produced his so-called Philonic treatises, that is, allegorical compositions modeled on counterparts by his predecessor. Extensive influences from Philo are also apparent in many of Ambrose's epistles, which Doerfler helpfully catalogues by specifying epistolary passages that align with particular biblical texts and their corresponding interpretations in Philonic treatises. She closes her chapter by pointing toward new directions to be taken in future research. Jerome, an erudite scholar famed for his philological expertise, takes a primarily historical interest in Philo. As Matthew Kraus notes in his contribution, Jerome bestows lavish praise on him, particularly in a substantial entry in his catalogue *De viris illustribus*. The details are taken over from Eusebius, particularly the account of Philo as an admirer of the first (presumed) Christian community in Egypt (the Therapeutae), and a list of Philo's treatises. There is an apparent discrepancy, however, between the high praise Jerome bestows on Philo, and the degree to which he deploys his writings (nineteen references in all). Kraus suggests that this can be accounted for in part because, while on the one hand Philo's reputation as a learned philosopher and a witness to Christian asceticism appealed to Jerome, on the other, his own philological and exegetical enterprises prioritized Hebrew over Greek and were relatively less occupied with allegory.

Augustine, the subject of Ilaria Ramelli's chapter, as the last author in the Latin west to engage with the legacy of Philo prior to the fall of Rome, provides closure to Part II. As with Ambrose, his spiritual mentor, Augustine mentions Philo only once by name, but the paucity of explicit references similarly belies more extensive influences. His aversion to Greek, however, results in more oblique modes of reception, and accordingly Ramelli argues that Augustine's interest in Philo was prompted by Origen, whose theology he deployed in his writings against the Manicheans. At the same time, Ambrose himself was a significant factor in Augustine's engagements, with the additional possibility there were in circulation some Latin translations that are no longer extant.

Part III turns from individual figures to wider currents of reception in the medieval period, broadly construed. The works of Philo survive because they were copied by scribes in Greek, Latin, and Armenian. James Royse draws on his extensive autopsy of manuscripts to offer an overview of the reception of Philo's works as attested by their Greek and Latin transmission. Noting that Philo's earliest transmission can only be a matter of informed speculation, he nonetheless calls attention to the preservation of four Greek papyrus codices from the third to the seventh centuries, the most important of which, the so-called Coptos Papyrus, survives in forty-four folios. The bulk of Philo's manuscript tradition is medieval, and Royse offers an authoritative survey of the most important of these Greek manuscripts, before going on to consider the indirect tradition of preservation, including Eusebius' substantial quotations, Procopius, Pseudo-Eustathius, and catena and florilegia. The chapter concludes with a consideration of the Latin preservation of Philo's works, which is especially important for the *Quaestiones in Genesim* and *De vita contemplativa*.

Elke Morlok and Ze'ev Strauss pick up the trail of Philo's Jewish reception where Steven Fraade's chapter concludes by analyzing the evidence for medieval Jewish reception. Distancing themselves from some more maximalist claims about the Jewish knowledge of Philo in this period, particularly associated with Harry A. Wolfson, they investigate similarities between Philo and Jewish Neoplatonism and mystical traditions, arguing that midrashic literature forms an important intermediary role in conveying ideas common in Philo to the medieval Hebrew tradition. Even if proof of direct knowledge is impossible to ascertain, the hermeneutical and theological similarities are striking. Medieval Armenian Christianity, by contrast, has clear and direct knowledge of Philo's writings. Olga Vardazaryan chronicles a long and broad, if necessarily selective, engagement with Philo in Armenia. This engagement found an early flourishing in the translation of the Corpus Philoneum Armeniacum in the fifth or sixth centuries CE, consisting of texts whose original survives also in Greek (*Contempl., Abr., Leg.* 1–2, *Decal., Spec.* 1.79–81, 131–61, 285–345; 3.1–7, 8–64) and works preserved only or largely in Armenian (*Prov.* 1–2, *Anim., QG* 1–4, *QE* 1–2, a fragment *Deo* and another on the *Decad*, as well as two pseudo-Philonic sermons *De Sampsone* and *De Jona*). This translation resourced a long series of readings of Philo, and Vardazaryan supplies an expert guide to the shape of Philo's reception, drawing on unpublished manuscript material as well as the edited corpora of medieval Armenian authors. Philo was a source of reflection in the medieval Armenian monastic schools and among those who copied the Corpus, which continued until well into the seventeenth century.

Alexander Treiger turns to Arabic Christian literature, and calls attention to an overlooked stream of Philonic transmission. The eleventh-century Arabic translation of the Dionysian corpus contains an appendix with seven passages from Philo's *De vita contemplativa*. The passages seem to be taken ultimately from Eusebius's *Hist. eccl.* 2.17, perhaps mediated by John of Scythopolis, and were almost certainly translated from Greek into Arabic by a Chalcedonian Orthodox scribe in Damascus in 1009. Treiger supplies an annotated English translation of these passages and their surrounding comments, and also surveys comments on Philo by other Christian authors writing in Arabic who refer to Philo's *Legatio ad Gaium* (again, probably via the mediation of Eusebius) as well as some selections of Philo from Arabic florilegia. Finally, the chapter notes some Pseudo-Philonic citations, in which Philo is made to confess points of Christian orthodoxy.

Next a pair of chapters surveys Philo's reception in the long history of Byzantium (David Runia) and the Latin west (David Runia and Frans van Liere) from roughly 500 to 1500. This period of Philonic reception has been almost entirely neglected until recently, though there is definite evidence of an ongoing interest in the Alexandrian's work and thought. Beginning from a study of places where Philo is named explicitly, but broadening to include implicit references as well, Runia demonstrates deep interest in Philo on the part of John Lydus, Procopius of Gaza, the latter's anonymous predecessor in compiling *Catenae on Genesis* and *Exodus*, and Anastasius of Sinai. Photius explicitly mentions having read six works of Philo and suggests that the Alexandrian's allegorical hermeneutic has shaped the interpretation of the church fathers. Later Byzantine authors—including Arethas of Patras, the encyclopedic *Souda*, Michael Psellus, Theodore Metochites, and others—also evince knowledge of Philo, and find in him a representative of Jewish and classical learning. On the Latin side, Runia and van Liere demonstrate that Philonic knowledge was mediated by his use in the Latin fathers (especially Ambrose, Jerome, and Augustine), by Rufinus' translation of Eusebius' *Historia ecclesiastica*, and three authors of the early medieval period who exerted an influence on subsequent readers: Cassiodorus, Isidore of Seville, and the Venerable Bede. While Philo's works were not translated in full, there did exist a *Liber Philonis* that included a mixture of genuinely Philonic works (*Quaestiones in Genesim* and *De vita contempl.* 1–41), Jerome's brief account of Philo from *Vir. ill.* 11, and the pseudo-Philonic *Liber antiquitatum biblicarum*. Medieval Latin writers draw on Philo for assistance in scriptural interpretation, often ascribe the authorship of the Wisdom of

Solomon to him, and sometimes invoke him in their historical reflections on the first century.

Part IV turns from the late medieval and Byzantine periods to the Renaissance and the early modern period. David Runia, Gregory Sterling, and Michael Cover examine the earliest printed editions of Philo. Initial publication of Philo's writings was slow, with only partial works or minor translations appearing from the invention of the printing press to the mid-sixteenth century. But in 1552 Adrianus Turnebus (or Adrien Turnèbe), Parisian printer and professor, drew on three manuscripts from the Royal Library at Fontainebleau to publish the editio princeps of most of Philo's writings. This edition was translated into Latin almost immediately, first partially by the English divine John Christopherson in 1553, and then in full by the Czech scholar, Sigismund Gelenius in 1554. Philo's works were subsequently published in smaller collections of Latin translations, and in vernacular renderings (English, Italian, French). In 1587, David Hoeschel's *Philonis Iudaei opuscula tria* presented three treatises that had not been included in Turnebus' edition, together with marginal notes and annotations. Hoeschel also published three further Philonic treatises at the end of his life in 1614. In the subsequent century, four large folio volumes with Philo's works in Greek and Latin appeared, though these did not materially improve upon the text of Philo. Joanna Weinberg demonstrates how three Jewish scholars, David Provenzali, Azariah de' Rossi, and Judah Moscato, were responsible for the Jewish rediscovery of Philo in the Italian Renaissance of the sixteenth century. Of these three, de' Rossi's work offers the most searching evaluation, praising Philo on some counts but criticizing him for his use of the Septuagint and ignorance of Hebrew and Aramaic, for his belief in primordial matter, for his allegorical interpretation of scripture, and for being unaware of traditional interpretation of biblical commands. He concludes with the famous verdict that he can call Philo "neither Rav nor sage, heretic nor sceptic. My only name for him shall be Yedidyah the Alexandrian." But David Provenzali begged to differ, as Weinberg shows from a recently discovered manuscript, and sought to counter that Philo was fundamentally rabbinic in outlook. Provenzali's approach was also shared by Judah Moscato, who repeatedly refers to Philo approvingly. In the seventeenth century, Philo is again invoked by Simone Luzzatto to demonstrate the antiquity and nobility of the Jews as a way to combat anti-Jewish sentiment in Venice, and by a number of Karaite authors in eastern and northern Europe.

After the flourishing of interest in Philo in the sixteenth century, Catholic scholars in the post-Tridentine period (after 1563) demonstrate a keen interest in the Alexandrian, as Eric DeMeuse chronicles. A flurry of publications in France and Italy in the latter half of the sixteenth century point to an ongoing concern with Philo, and even ecclesiastical scholars such as Robert Bellarmine extol Philo for his exegesis and his utility in theological argument. Philo also proved useful in anti-Reformation polemic, since his treatise *De vita contemplativa* was taken as a testimony to the antiquity of Christian monastic practice. Philo was not universally admired, however, and DeMeuse also documents some ongoing worries among those who demurred from his philosophical positions or exegetical decisions.

Giovanni Benedetto turns his focus to Thomas Mangey's epochal 1742 edition of the works of Philo, and contextualizes Mangey's project in the landscape of seventeenth- and early eighteenth-century theological disputes. Before Mangey, there was widespread recognition of the need for an improved critical edition of Philo, and his edition marks a notable advance on prior editions by Turnebus, Hoeschel, and Christopherson. Mangey's preface is notable for mentioning two interpretative issues: the nature of Philo's allegorical approach, and his doctrine of the Logos. Both of these points, as Benedetto demonstrates, respond to contemporary currents in Christian debates about the Trinity, and about the extent to which Philo espoused Platonic and Stoic views. In the same period of time, European philosophers were seeking to contextualize Philo's work in the history of the discipline. Dirk Westerkamp demonstrates that Philo proved difficult to categorize. The historiographical holism of the seventeenth- and eighteenth-centuries struggled to decide whether Philo belonged to Greek or Hebrew philosophy. Philo's doctrine of the Logos came in for particular scrutiny, and Westerkamp notes the development of certain associated conventional topoi concerning Philo's role in the history of philosophy. In the German Idealist tradition of the nineteenth-century, Hegel and Schelling look to Philo as the progenitor of important philosophical positions (e.g. God as the Absolute), and Hegel's views in particular find an afterlife with the so-called Jewish Hegelians.

Part V surveys some critical lines of Philonic reception from roughly the eighteenth to the twentieth centuries, with a particular focus on the latter half of the period. Attending to the history of New Testament criticism in this period reveals an ascending interest in Philo and his relevance to the interpretation of the New Testament, as David Lincicum's chapter suggests. Scholarship generally turns from asking comparative questions to asking genealogical ones about the extent to which knowledge of Philo can *explain* the rise of early Christianity, with some scholars arguing for direct knowledge of the Alexandrian on the part of Paul or the Fourth Gospel or the *auctor ad Hebraeos*.

Ze'ev Strauss demonstrates that prominent scholars in the Jewish Enlightenment came to see Philo as a predecessor for their own work, and helped them to root their projects in a lineage that stretched back to antiquity. Both Moses Mendelssohn and Solomon J. L. Rapoport engage Philo substantively, and these engagements, together with the work of their successors like Naḥman Krochmal and Josef Flesch, led to a broader appreciation of the Alexandrian's thought in Jewish circles. In certain ways the fruits of that appreciation came in the nineteenth-century *Wissenschaft des Judentums*. Görge Hasselhoff tells the story of that movement and its engagement with Philo, focusing particularly on the founding of the Jewish Theological Seminary in Breslau. Three major figures in the first generation there—Zacharias Frankel, Heinrich Graetz, Manuel Joel—undertook critical work on Philo and his place in Judaism, and this laid the foundation for subsequent scholars such as Leopold Treitel, Bernhard Loebel Ritter, Hermann Cohen, and others to go further in their analyses. Ultimately this climaxed in one of the great modern achievements of Philonic scholarship, the *editio critica maior* of Leopold Cohn and Paul Wendland.

While much writing on Philo was produced in theological or philosophical works, he also inspired the modern historical imagination, and so found a place in a number of pieces of historical fiction. David Runia surveys ten works of literature that feature Philo, ranging from Charles Kingsley's 1853 novel, *Hypatia, or Old Foes with a New Face*, to the 2018 book by Herman van Praag, translated as *Deference to Doubt: A Young Man's Quest for Religious Identity in First Century Judea*. Runia even discusses a short story by Isaac Bashevis Singer that features a remarkably well-informed scholar of Philo. In the end, Philo emerges as a tantalizing figure for the literary enterprise, living as he did at a time of historical, political, and spiritual importance.

The final part of the volume addresses the reception of Philo among contemporary scholars, and points forward to new horizons of reception to come. Four areas are thematized: classics, ancient philosophy, and the study of Judaism and Christianity respectively. Courtney Friesen argues for the inclusion of Philo in the classical canon and the potential of Philo to contribute to the study of post-classical Greek authors, and goes on to point to three areas of potentially fruitful dialogue between classics and Philonic studies: literary education (*paideia*), Greek identity and Roman imperial politics, and theater and performance. Gretchen Reydams-Schils argues that Philo remains a rich source for the study of ancient philosophy. She chronicles the increasing inclusion of Philo in histories of philosophy, but still points to outstanding lacunae. The role of philosophy in Philo's works, and the precise relationship between Platonist and Stoic elements in his corpus have been ongoing points of discussion, but may also be susceptible to further progress. We need a capacious conception of philosophy to encompass Philo, and to remain flexible in our understanding of the relationship between philosophy and exegesis in his oeuvre.

Ellen Birnbaum analyzes Philo's Jewish identity in important studies from the mid-twentieth century onward. Some scholars (Wolfson, Belkin) sought to harmonize Philonic thought with "normative" Judaism, while others (Goodenough) stressed Philo as a representative of a mystical form of Judaism. More recent work has contextualized Philo and his theology within the landscape of the first century, and we find increasingly as well an attempt to understand the Alexandrian on his own terms, as Birnbaum demonstrates by an analysis of several important scholarly milestones and specific topics. Mark Edwards considers the relevance of Philo to the study of Christianity, finding that the way in which interpreters classified Philo—as a faithful Jew? as a philosopher? as a hybrid produced through Hellenization?—bears on their interpretation of the question. Edwards demonstrates the significant debt that scholars of early Christianity have to Philo, for topics from early mysticism to the deification of Moses.

Finally, David Runia concludes the volume with a chapter on bibliographies devoted to Philo. He demonstrates that bibliographical accumulation is not a modern concern, but goes back at least to the Library of Caesarea and to Eusebius and Jerome. In the early modern period, Fabricius offered an account of Philo in his *Bibliotheca Graeca*, and this was expanded by subsequent scholars. In the nineteenth century, the handbook literature included Philo in its remit, but a new era is reached particularly in Goodhart and Goodenough's 1938 bibliography of Philo. The analytical categorization of works on

Philo was continued in a series of important successors by Feldman, Hilgert, Radice, and especially by Runia himself, in total amounting to some seven thousand items of Philonic scholarship.

To those seven thousand items this book adds one more. We offer it in the spirit of gratitude to our predecessors, ancient and modern, in scholarship, and in the hope that it will stimulate further work on Philo of Alexandria and his reception.

A Note on Abbreviations Used

For abbreviations to works, journals, and series titles relating to ancient and byzantine periods, we have deployed *The SBL Handbook of Style*, 2nd ed. (Atlanta: SBL Press, 2014). The treatises of Philo follow the conventions of the *Studia Philonica Annual* (35 [2023]: 373–81). For further abbreviations, we use the conventions of dictionaries and encyclopedias of the relevant period.

I
THE FIRST CENTURIES

1
Flavius Josephus

Katell Berthelot

In the ever-flourishing academic literature on Second Temple Judaism, and especially in works pertaining to the interpretation of the Bible in ancient Judaism, Philo and Josephus often appear side by side, in separate chapters or articles. Admittedly, their works are often compared, not merely juxtaposed, and this is also true in the case of Philo's so-called historical treatises and the corresponding sections in Josephus' *Jewish Antiquities*.[1] Yet the question of whether Josephus read Philo and used his work in his own writings is not often raised as such, with the exception of Josephus' use of Philo's *Hypothetica* in *Against Apion*.[2] In connection with the only reference to Philo in Josephus' work, *A.J.* 18.259, David T. Runia notes: "This description need not entail that Josephus was acquainted with his work. It is generally agreed, however, that Josephus does show dependence on Philo in certain areas, not only in his account of political events, but also in his paraphrases and exegesis of the Pentateuch."[3] This chapter will argue that there are good reasons to think that Josephus was interested in Philo's works, especially those with an apologetic dimension, and that he read and drew inspiration from some of them.

First, it should be noted that Josephus was born roughly at the time of the crisis in Alexandria that led to the massacre of a large part of the local Jewish community, and was the reason for Philo's embassy to Rome. According to scholarly consensus, Philo died in about 50 CE, when Josephus was still a young man in his early youth. When Josephus wrote his *Antiquities* at the end of the first century, however, he knew about Philo. He mentions him once, precisely in connection with the events in Alexandria and Philo's embassy:

---

[1] See e.g. D. R. Schwartz, "Philo and Josephus on the Violence in Alexandria in 38 C.E.," *SPhiloA* 24 (2012): 149–66. For attempts to compare Philo's and Josephus' interpretations of biblical narratives, see esp. the publications of L. H. Feldman (e.g. "Philo, Pseudo-Philo, Josephus, and Theodotus on the Rape of Dinah," *JQR* 94 [2004]: 253–77), as well as those of C. T. Begg (e.g. "Josephus' and Philo's Retelling of Numbers 31 Compared," *ETL* 83 [2007]: 81–106).

[2] See below. The most systematic attempt to assess whether Josephus used Philo's works is G. E. Sterling, "'A Man of the Highest Repute': Did Josephus Know the Writings of Philo?," *SPhiloA* 25 (2013): 101–13. Sterling considers it "very likely" that "Josephus had not only read but drew from *On the creation of the cosmos* and *The Life of Moses*" (112). According to Sterling, Josephus may also have read other treatises in the "Exposition of the Law," especially *De virtutibus*, as well as the *Quaestiones in Exodum* and *Genesim*, the *In Flaccum*, and the *Legatio* (112). As the following pages will show, I concur with Sterling's conclusions (except in the case of the *Hypothetica*) and will push them a bit further.

[3] D. T. Runia, *Philo in Early Christian Literature* (Assen: Van Gorcum, 1993), 13.

257. Meanwhile, there was civil strife in Alexandria between the Jewish inhabitants and the Greeks. Three delegates were chosen by each of the factions and appeared before Gaius. One of the Alexandrian delegates was Apion, who scurrilously reviled the Jews, asserting, among other things, that they neglected to pay the honours due to the emperor. 258. For while all the subject peoples in the Roman empire had dedicated altars and temples to Gaius and had given him the same attention in all other respects as they did the gods, these people alone scorned to honour him with statues and to swear by his name. 259. And so Apion spoke many angry words by which he hoped that Gaius would be moved, as might be expected. Philo, who stood at the head of the delegation of the Jews, a man held in the highest honour, brother of Alexander the alabarch and no novice in philosophy, was prepared to proceed with the defence against these accusations. 260. But Gaius cut him short, told him to get out of his way, and, being exceedingly angry, made it clear that he would visit some outrage upon them. Philo, having thus been treated with contumely, left the room, saying to the Jews who accompanied him that they should be of good courage, for Gaius' wrath was a matter of words, but in fact he was now enlisting God against himself. (*A.J.* 18.257–60, trans. L. H. Feldman, LCL)

Elsewhere Josephus also tells the reader about Philo's family, especially his brother Alexander, who was chief of customs (*alabarch*) and guardian of the properties of Claudius' mother in Egypt (*A.J.* 19.276), "who surpassed all his contemporaries at Alexandria in ancestry and in wealth" (*A.J.* 20.100), and who was indeed rich enough to lend money to king Agrippa I and his wife (*A.J.* 18.159–60), or to plate the gates of the Temple of Jerusalem in gold and silver (*B.J.* 5.205). Josephus also mentions two sons of Alexander, Marcus Julius Alexander, who married Berenice, the daughter of King Agrippa (*A.J.* 19.276–77), and the famous Tiberius Julius Alexander, who became procurator of Judaea in 46–48 CE and then prefect of Egypt in 66–70 CE. Josephus writes that Tiberius Julius Alexander, in contrast to his father, was not faithful to the ancestral customs of the Jews (*A.J.* 20.100).[4]

Thus, Josephus knew quite a lot about Philo and his family, but he does not tell us much about Philo himself, and even less about his works. As David DeVore emphasizes, insofar as Josephus wanted to present the Jews' glorious deeds and cultural contributions to his readers, he could have made more of the example of Philo, presenting him as an accomplished Jewish philosopher and not merely as someone who was "no novice in philosophy," as *A.J.* 18.259 puts it.[5] DeVore aptly notes that "Josephus' downplaying of a prestigious Judean philosopher may have simply played to the prejudice against philosophers displayed by the Flavians and likely imitated by upper-class

---

[4] See P. Borgen, *Philo of Alexandria: An Exegete for His Time* (Leiden: Brill, 1997), 15; D. R. Schwartz, "Philo, His Family, and His Times," in *The Cambridge Companion to Philo*, ed. A. Kamesar (Cambridge: Cambridge University Press, 2009), 9–31; A. Appelbaum, "A Fresh Look at Philo's Family," *SPhiloA* 30 (2018): 93–114; A. Leonas, "Philo's Chronology and Social Position," *Adamantius* 24 (2018): 334–48.

[5] D. DeVore, "Eusebius' Un-Josephan History: Two Portraits of Philo of Alexandria and the Sources of Ecclesiastical Historiography," *StPatr* 66 (2013): 161–80, esp. 163.

Romans."[6] In the context of Domitian's reign, Josephus may indeed have deliberately avoided presenting Philo's encounter with Caligula as a confrontation between an emperor and a philosopher gifted with *parrēsia*.[7]

A striking point in Josephus' description of Philo is that in *A.J.* 18.260, Philo foretells Caligula's forthcoming punishment at the hands of God (not to the emperor himself, of course, but to "the Jews who accompanied him"). This is very much in line with Philo's discourse in *In Flaccum* and with his theological thought in general, even though such a statement cannot be found in the *Legatio* itself, which in its current state does not contain the announcement or the description of Gaius' subsequent fate. However, since the end of the *Legatio* is lost, the book may have originally mentioned the emperor's death and, logically, have presented it as a divine punishment. In any case, the discourse Josephus attributes to Philo fits both what we know of Philo's theology of history and Josephus' own vision of history in the long run.[8]

This remark brings me to the main thesis of this chapter: Josephus drew inspiration from Philo's writings because he shared some of Philo's views and faced similar challenges. Most scholars who have noticed similarities between the two works, especially as far as *Against Apion* is concerned, have argued that Philo and Josephus relied on a common tradition or source.[9] That Philo and Josephus had access to Jewish traditions presenting "summaries of the Law" or "ethical codes," which circulated both in Judea and in Alexandria is highly probable. However, when Philo and Josephus are the *only* writers known to us who put forward a certain view or a specific argument, the idea of a common source entails some methodological flaws. While one cannot exclude that such a common source existed, its existence cannot be proven either. On the other hand, because Josephus knew about Philo, when *specific* similarities between the works of Philo and Josephus are noticed, they should be interpreted as evidence that the latter knew the writings of the former, even if only in a superficial or limited way.

The main reason this straightforward reasoning has not been adopted by most scholars lies in a narrow understanding of what the use of an author's literary work by another author entails. In other words, because Josephus does not *quote* Philo and because he formulates things in a way that diverges to a great extent from Philo's wording, scholars tend to assume that Josephus did not use Philo. However, when one looks at the way Josephus uses 1 Maccabees, it is clear that although Josephus follows 1 Maccabees rather consistently until chapter 13, he nevertheless re-writes his predecessor's work to a great extent. Moreover, he modifies the text in significant ways, omitting and

---

[6] See DeVore, "Eusebius' Un-Josephan History," 163 n. 4; see also G. Haaland, "Josephus and the Philosophers of Rome: Does *Contra Apionem* Mirror Domitian's Crushing of the 'Stoic Opposition'?" in *Josephus and Jewish History in Flavian Rome and Beyond*, ed. J. Sievers and G. Lembi (Leiden: Brill, 2005), 297–316, which argues that Josephus played down the theme of Judaism as a philosophy in order to take into account Domitian's anti-philosophical tendency. See esp. Cassius Dio, *Roman History* 67.13.

[7] On confrontations between emperors and philosophers, see R. MacMullen, *Enemies of the Roman Order: Treason, Unrest, and Alienation in the Empire* (Cambridge, MA: Harvard University Press, 1966), 46–94.

[8] On Josephus' understanding of God's intervention in history, see T. Rajak, "Friends, Romans, Subjects: Agrippa II's Speech in Josephus' *Jewish War*," in *Images of Empire*, ed. L. Alexander (Sheffield: Sheffield Academic Press, 1991), 122–34; P. Spilsbury, "Flavius Josephus on the Rise and Fall of the Roman Empire," *JTS* 54 (2003): 1–24; for a comparison with Philo, see K. Berthelot, "Philo's Perception of the Roman Empire," *JSJ* 42 (2011): 166–87.

[9] See n. 30 below.

adding things here and there.[10] Yet because of the overlap in terms of content, very few people would deny that Josephus used 1 Maccabees.[11] Now, if one looks at Josephus' account of the events under Caligula for instance, for which Philo's *Legatio* must have been a precious source in Josephus' eyes, one will notice a great deal of overlap, but also very significant differences between the two accounts.[12] Concerning this episode Josephus certainly had access to other sources as well, whereas for the beginning of the Hasmonean period he might have had only 1 Maccabees at his disposal (although this is unlikely, as he seems to know some of the traditions contained in 2 Maccabees). However, it seems hard to believe that Josephus would have eschewed Philo's testimony about Caligula, a testimony written by a Jew who was himself an actor in the events, a Jew who had stayed in Rome and who had been confronted with Roman imperial power, just as Josephus would later be.[13]

Moreover, considering the apologetic dimension of Josephus' work, especially but not exclusively in *Against Apion*, it would be rather surprising if Josephus had not looked at the apologetic works of such a great predecessor as Philo. Josephus' focus on Apion in *Against Apion* and his reference to Apion in *Antiquities* 18.257 are telling in this respect. In *Legatio* 355, Philo mentions Isidorus as the head of the Alexandrian delegation opposing the Jews and the one who accuses the Jews of refusing to sacrifice on behalf of Gaius. By contrast, in *Antiquities* 18.257–59, Josephus attributes this slander to Apion, whom he later depicts as the arch-enemy of the Jews. Moreover, in *Antiquities* what triggers Gaius' decision to have a statue of himself erected in the Jerusalem temple is precisely Apion's slander. This significant detail, together with the efforts Josephus takes in refuting the charges against Judaism formulated by Apion and Lysimachus, as well as a number of specific similarities between *Against Apion* and some Philonic treatises which have a clear apologetic dimension, point to a deep awareness, on Josephus' part, of the challenges that his Alexandrian predecessor had to face. It shows that Josephus' apologetic endeavor was grounded in the Alexandrian context and tradition, even though it had a Roman dimension of its own (linked to a

[10] On Josephus' use of 1 Maccabees, see C. L. W. Grimm, *Das erste Buch der Maccabäer* (Leipzig: S. Hirzel, 1853), xxvii–xxx; H. Bloch, *Die Quellen des Flavius Josephus in seiner Archäologie* (Stuttgart: Teubner, 1879), 80–90; A. Momigliano, *Prime linee di storia della tradizione maccabaica* (Rome: Foro italiano, 1930), 18–48; J. A. Goldstein, *I Maccabees: A New Translation with Introduction and Commentary* (New York: Doubleday, 1976), 55–61 and 558–74; G. Fuks, "Josephus and the Hasmoneans," *JJS* 41 (1990): 166–76; I. M. Gafni, "Josephus and 1 Maccabees," in *Josephus, The Bible, and History*, ed. L. H. Feldman (Leiden: Brill, 1989), 116–31; L. H. Feldman, "Josephus' Portrayal of the Hasmoneans Compared with 1 Maccabees," in *Josephus and the History of the Greco-Roman Period*, ed. F. Parente and J. Sievers (Leiden: Brill, 1994), 41–68; K. Berthelot, *In Search of the Promised Land? The Hasmonean Dynasty between Biblical Models and Hellenistic Diplomacy* (Göttingen: Vandenhoeck & Ruprecht, 2018), 78–80, 86–91, 144–49.
[11] One exception is J. von Destinon, *Die Quellen des Flavius Josephus* (Kiel: Lipsius & Tischer, 1881), 60–80.
[12] See Schwartz, "Philo and Josephus on the Violence in Alexandria in 38 C.E."
[13] Philo may have stayed in Rome for three years and not just a few months. See A. Harker, *Loyalty and Dissidence in Roman Egypt: The Case of the* Acta Alexandrinorum (Cambridge: Cambridge University Press, 2008), 14, 18–19; M. R. Niehoff, "Philo's Exposition in a Roman Context," *SPhiloA* 23 (2011): 1–21 at 2; M. R. Niehoff, *Philo of Alexandria: An Intellectual Biography* (New Haven: Yale University Press, 2018), 3. On both Philo and Josephus as Jewish authors writing in Rome and participating in Roman cultural discourse, see M. R. Niehoff, "Josephus and Philo in Rome," in *A Companion to Josephus*, ed. H. Howell Chapman and Z. Rodgers (Chichester, West Sussex: John Wiley & Sons, 2016), 135–46.

post-70 CE context), as well as its own Josephan flavor.[14] My thesis is that in Josephus' case, this Alexandrian tradition was mainly Philo's work itself, as I shall now attempt to show through a few examples.[15]

1.1 Defensive vs Offensive Wars

In *De virtutibus*, Philo's retelling of the laws of war from Deuteronomy 20 strikingly departs from the biblical narrative. Deuteronomy 20 tackles the case of an Israelite attack against a foreign city, and states:

> 1. Now if you go out to war against your enemies and see horse and rider and a people more numerous than you, you shall not be afraid of them, for the Lord your God is with you, who made you go up from the land of Egypt.... 10. Now if you draw near to a city to fight against it, then you shall call them out with peace. 11. If they respond to you peaceably and open to you, it shall be that all the people found in it shall be bearers of tribute and be subject to you. 12. But if they do not respond to you and make war against you, then you shall besiege it, 13. and the Lord your God will deliver it into your hands, and you shall strike every male in it with slaughter by dagger, 14. except the women and the baggage. And all the livestock and all which is in the city and all the spoil you shall take as plunder for yourself, and you shall eat all the plunder of your enemies, which the Lord your God is giving you. 15. Thus you shall do to all the cities that are very far from you, which are not of the cities of these nations (in Canaan). (Deut 20:1, 10–15, NETS)

In contrast, Philo writes:

> These are the laws that he established regarding the reception they should extend to resident aliens, but there are other kind and most gentle laws regarding wartime enemies. For he does not think it right to consider them as enemies yet—even if they are already at the gates, standing near the walls in full armor and raising their siege towers—until they have sent them envoys making proposals for peace. This way, if they relent they might gain the greatest good, which is friendship, but if they are uncomplying and refuse, the besieged may, having gained the alliance of justice, attack for the purpose of defense (πρὸς ἄμυναν) in the hope of victory. (*Virt.* 109)[16]

---

[14] See already M. Goodman, "Josephus' Treatise *Against Apion*," in *Apologetics in the Roman Empire: Pagans, Jews, Christians*, ed. M. J. Edwards, M. Goodman, and S. Price (Oxford: Oxford University Press, 1999), 45–58 at 55.

[15] If one agrees that the Alexandrian tradition known to Josephus was essentially Philonic, this means that it was in fact a tradition that developed in a *Roman* Alexandrian context.

[16] Trans. W. T. Wilson, *Philo of Alexandria: On Virtues* (Leiden: Brill, 2011), 65.

In the section of *De virtutibus* which contains this passage, *De humanitate* or *Peri philanthrōpias*, Philo's concern is to show the humane character of the Mosaic laws, even concerning enemies.[17] He therefore avoids mentioning the section of Deuteronomy 20 that commands the annihilation of the seven nations of Canaan, and also modifies Deut 20:10–14 in order to present the Jewish nation as merely defending itself vis-à-vis its enemies. Whereas Deut 20:10–14 stipulates how Israel should behave when it attacks a foreign city outside Canaan, Philo describes a wholly different situation, that of a foreign invasion of Israel's land by outsiders. The enemies are described as standing "at the gates," which means that they are besieging an Israelite town. And the words πρὸς ἄμυναν show that the Israelites are only supposed to fight in order to defend themselves. In *De specialibus legibus* 4.219–25, Philo uses the same kind of strategy when dealing with Deut 20:10–19; he again strikingly departs from the biblical text, a phenomenon that is rare when Philo deals with the literal meaning of a given passage. The fundamental message carried by Philo's rewriting is that the children of Israel are a peaceful people.[18]

In Book 4 of the *Antiquities*, Josephus, like Philo, tackles the issue of the Mosaic laws concerning war. In §§296–97, he writes:

> 296. When you are about to wage war (μέλλοντας δὲ πολεμεῖν), send an embassy and heralds to those going to war against you deliberately (παρὰ τοὺς ἑκουσίως πολεμίους). For before taking up arms it is right to carry on discussions with them, revealing that though you have a large army and horses and weapons and, above all, have God who is benevolent and an ally, nevertheless, you do not think it right to be forced to wage war against them, and by removing what is theirs to obtain in addition undesired gain for yourselves. 297. If they agree to be kindly disposed to you, keep the peace....[19]

Josephus' departure from the biblical text is less striking than that of Philo, because his formulation is more ambiguous. The opening words, "When you are about to wage war," can be understood either as referring to a military expedition against an enemy, as in the biblical text, or to a defensive war. That Josephus has the latter in mind is shown by the expression "those going to war against you deliberately" (τοὺς ἑκουσίως πολεμίους), which Thackeray translated as "your aggressive enemy" (LCL). Moreover, as Daniel Schwartz aptly remarks, Josephus "discusses those to be released from army service only in §298, after describing the failed negotiations with the enemy, because for Josephus there would be no war, hence no need for an army, had the enemy not

---

[17] On Philo's apologetic strategy in *De virtutibus*, see K. Berthelot, *Philanthrôpia Judaica: Le débat autour de la "misanthropie" des lois juives dans l'Antiquité* (Leiden: Brill, 2003), 265–300; and below, pp. 27–29.

[18] See I. Heinemann, *Philons griechische und jüdische Bildung: Kulturvergleichende Untersuchungen zu Philons Darstellung der jüdischen Gesetze* (Breslau: M. & H. Marcus, 1932; repr. Hildesheim: G. Olms, 1962), 409–13; K. Berthelot, "Philo and the Conquest of Canaan," *JSJ* 38 (2007): 39–56.

[19] Trans. L. H. Feldman, *Flavius Josephus: Judean Antiquities 1–4* (Leiden: Brill, 2000), slightly modified (πολεμεῖν translated as "wage war" instead of "go to war").

chosen to attack."[20] This contradicts the biblical text, in which the attack is decided right from the outset. So, in the end, Josephus reverses the situation evoked in the biblical text just as Philo does. Moreover, both Philo and Josephus omit to mention the forced labor (or the tribute) imposed upon the enemy who agrees to make peace (Deut 20:11). Josephus also has other issues in mind: he wants to make clear that the Israelites do not negotiate with their enemies because they are weak or fearful, but only because they are just and peaceful.[21] However, Josephus' effort to prove that Jews are not aggressive but merely fight to defend themselves is shown by an additional remark he makes in *Against Apion*: "We have trained our courage not for undertaking wars of self-aggrandizement but for preserving the laws" (*C. Ap.* 2.272).[22]

One could argue that Josephus modified the biblical text independently from Philo, but there are reasons to suppose that he was inspired by the Alexandrian. First, to the best of my knowledge no other Jewish commentator modifies the literal meaning of Deut 20:10–14 the way Philo and Josephus do.[23] Second, there are other indications showing that Josephus knew *De virtutibus*, to which I shall turn below.

Let me, however, formulate one last remark: in connection with *Antiquities* 4.296–98, Louis Feldman notes that "Josephus, in his considerable expansion of the above passage in Deuteronomy, recasts it in accord with … Roman ideals and methods of warfare."[24] On the basis of Cicero's writings, Feldman refers to the idea that the only legitimate objective of war is to live in peace, and to the principle that a war can be just only if declared in a formal way, after the rejection of a demand for redress. Even though one could argue that we are dealing here with a Greco-Roman view of warfare rather than a strictly Roman one, the argument that war is waged in order to achieve peace—the *pax Romana*—was particularly widespread in first-century CE Roman discourses. This Roman background does not undermine the hypothesis that Josephus got his inspiration from Philo. It simply highlights the context in which Josephus' bold exegetical move makes sense, and the reason for which he became interested in Philo's reading of the passage.

Proceeding one step further, one may also argue that this context is relevant for Philo as well, and that he was no less sensitive to Roman rhetorical claims about just warfare than Josephus was. As a matter of fact, Philo too lived in the context of the Roman

---

[20] D. R. Schwartz, *Reading the First Century: On Reading Josephus and Studying Jewish History of the First Century* (Tübingen: Mohr Siebeck, 2013), 10.
[21] Josephus repeatedly emphasizes the courage of the Jews; see e.g. *C. Ap.* 2.232–35.
[22] Trans. J. G. M. Barclay, *Flavius Josephus: Against Apion* (Leiden: Brill, 2007), 323. See also *A.J.* 4.102.
[23] Some rabbinic texts state that Joshua sent heralds to the nations of Canaan and gave them a choice between war, peace and departure from the Land (see Jerusalem Talmud, Shevi'it 6.1 [36c]; Lev. Rab. 17.5–6 [on Lev 14:34]; Deut Rab. 5.14 [on Deut 20:10]; K. Berthelot, "The Canaanites Who 'Trusted in God': An Original Interpretation of the Fate of the Canaanites in Rabbinic Literature," *JJS* 62.2 [2011]: 233–61, at 248–51). However, this tradition represents a re-writing of Deut 20:16–18 (the cities within Canaan), rather than of Deut 20:10–15 (the cities outside Canaan).
[24] Feldman, *Flavius Josephus: Judean Antiquities 1–4*, 461; he refers to Cicero, *Off.* 1.11.34–36 and *Rep.* 3.23.34–35; and to Virgil, *Aen.* 6.852–53. See also L. V. Sementchenko, "On the Two Conceptions of Just War in the 'Jewish Antiquities' of Flavius Josephus," *REA* 103 (2001): 485–95; J. W. van Henten, "Commonplaces in Herod's Commander Speech in Josephus *A.J.* 15.127–146," in *Josephus and Jewish History in Flavian Rome and Beyond*, 183–206 (see 198–203).

Empire.[25] From a methodological point of view, it is interesting to note that while certain aspects of Josephus' argumentation are frequently explained in connection with a Roman background, such an explanation is still rarely advocated in the case of Philo.

1.2 The Humane Character of the Law: A Philonic Theme

Whereas the theme of the benevolence or humane character of the Law of Moses (its *philanthrōpia*) is a recurring theme in Philo's work, the same is not true of Josephus. In the *Jewish War*, for instance, the term *philanthrōpia* exclusively characterizes the Romans.[26] In the *Antiquities*, the single occurrence of *philanthrōpia* pertains to the humane character of the Mosaic Law, in a context (*A.J.* 1.18–25) which is strongly dependent on the beginning of Philo's *De opificio mundi*.[27] It is only in *Against Apion* that Josephus really picks up the theme of the humane character of the Law, and he seems to have found his arguments mainly in Philo's *Peri philanthrōpias* and *Hypothetica*. Again, I have to emphasize that no other Jewish author (such as Pseudo-Phocylides or the author of the Letter of Aristeas, for instance) argues that the Law of Moses teaches *philanthrōpia*.

Let us first look at the evidence indicating that Josephus used Philo's *Hypothetica*. This hypothesis is not new: in an article published in 1911, Bacchisio Motzo already expressed the view that in the last part of *Against Apion*, from 2.145 until the end, Josephus was inspired by the *Hypothetica*.[28] As a matter of fact, the similarity between *Hypothetica* and *Against Apion* was already noticed by Eusebius himself (*Praep. ev.* 8.7.21). While this similarity has been widely acknowledged by scholars, only a few have considered it to imply that Philo was Josephus' source; among them are Salomon Rappaport, Samuel Belkin, Arnaldo Momigliano, Lucio Troiani (with caution), and Tessa Rajak.[29] The majority of

---

[25] On the impact of Roman culture on Philo's writings, see e.g. Niehoff, *Philo of Alexandria: An Intellectual Biography*.
[26] Except for one reference to the "false benevolence" (ὑποκριτὴς φιλανθρωπίας) of John of Gischala (*B.J.* 2.586).
[27] See *A.J.* 1.24. Whether the term *philanthrōpia* in this passage refers to God's *philanthrōpia* or to the human value of *philanthrōpia*, is debated. Together with G. E. Sterling, I consider that the human value of *philanthrōpia* is at stake; see G. E. Sterling, "Recherché or Representative? What Is the Relationship between Philo's Treatises and Greek-Speaking Judaism?" *SPhiloA* 11 (1999): 1–30, at 27–29. On the connection between this passage of the *Antiquities* and *Opif.*, see e.g. Borgen, *Philo of Alexandria*, 64–65 and 78; Berthelot, *Philanthrôpia judaica*, 349–55.
[28] See Motzo, "Le ΥΡΟΘΕΤΙΚΑ di Filone," *Atti della Reale Accademia delle Scienze di Torino* 47 (1911): 556–73; repr. in *Ricerche sulla letteratura e la storia giudaico-ellenistica* (Rome: Centro Editoriale Internazionale, 1977), 581–98. Here I follow the latter's page numbers. Paul Wendland was also among the first scholars who noticed the similarity between the works of Philo and Josephus, but he believed they had a common source (see "Die Therapeuten und die philonische Schrift vom beschaulichen Leben," *Neue Jahrbücher für Philologie und Pädagogik*, Suppl. 22 [1896]: 709–12).
[29] See S. Rappaport, *Agada und Exegese bei Flavius Josephus* (Vienna: Alexander Kohut Memorial Foundation, 1930), 18; S. Belkin, "The Alexandrian Source for *Contra Apionem* II," *JQR* 27 (1936–37): 1–32; A. Momigliano, "Un' apologia del giudaismo: il *Contro Apione* di Flavio Giuseppe," in *Pagine Ebraiche* (Turin: Einaudi, 1987), 63–71, and "Intorno al *Contro Apione*," in *Quinto contributo alla storia degli studi classici e del mondo antico* (Rome: Edizioni di storia e letteratura, 1975), 768–69; L. Troiani, *Commento storico al "Contro Apione" di Giuseppe* (Pisa: Giardini, 1977), 56–60; T. Rajak, "The *Against Apion* and the Continuities in Josephus' Political Thought," in *Understanding Josephus: Seven Perspectives*, ed. S. N. Mason (Sheffield: Sheffield Academic Press, 1998), 227. See also A. Kasher, *Against Apion* (Jerusalem: Zalman Shazar Center, 1997), 2:512 (Hebrew translation with commentary). I have myself defended the view that Josephus used Philo's *Hypothetica* in *Philanthrôpia judaica*, 368–74.

scholars, including George Carras, Gregory Sterling, Peter Borgen, Christine Gerber, and Walter Wilson, have concluded that Philo and Josephus drew on a common Jewish source and that there was no direct literary relationship between them.[30] A new development in this discussion has occurred with John Barclay's claim in his commentary of Josephus' *Against Apion*, that *Hypothetica* had not been written by Philo.[31] I disagree with him for several reasons which cannot be detailed here—for instance the connections between *Hypothetica* and other Philonic treatises, especially *De virtutibus*[32]—and therefore, continue to consider that *Hypothetica* is part of Philo's corpus.

From paragraph 2.145 onwards, the similarities between *Against Apion* and *Hypothetica* are indeed striking. For example, Josephus defends Moses against accusations of γοητεία, "charlatanry" (*C. Ap.* 2.145, 161), just as Philo does in *Hypothetica* (6.2-3) and *De opificio mundi* (2).[33] This motif appears only in the writings of Philo and Josephus. To be sure, they could have included it independently, for the same reason, namely to counter anti-Jewish authors who presented Moses as a charlatan (γόης). But once it is considered alongside other details found only in *Hypothetica* and *Against Apion*, it adds weight to the hypothesis that there is a literary relationship between the two works.[34] John Barclay points to six parallels between *Hypothetica* and *Against Apion* that show a striking degree of similarity, five of which display an "extremely close agreement in citing non-biblical laws, or in reshaping biblical law in non-biblical language."[35]

Among these five cases, the prescription to provide strangers with fire, water, and food has particular significance. Josephus writes in *Against Apion* 2.211: "He (Moses)

---

[30] See Wendland, "Die Therapeuten," 709-12; P. Krüger, *Philo und Josephus als Apologeten des Judentums* (Leipzig: Verlag der Dürr'schen Buchhandlung, 1906), 51-60; Heinemann, *Philons griechische und jüdische Bildung*, 530 and n. 1; Isidore Lévy, *La légende de Pythagore de Grèce en Palestine* (Paris: Champion, 1927), IV.1, 211-12; F. H. Colson, *Philo Volume IX*, LCL 363 (Cambridge, MA: Harvard University Press, 1941), 409 n. a, and 422-37; T. Reinach, *Contre Apion* (Paris: Les belles lettres, 1930, 2nd edn, 1972), 83 n. 1; E. Kamlah, "Frömmigkeit und Tugend: Die Gesetzesapologie des Josephus in C. Apion 2, 145-295," in *Josephus-Studien: Untersuchungen zu Josephus, dem antiken Judentum und dem Neuen Testament*, ed. O. Betz, K. Haacker, and M. Hengel (Göttingen: Vandenhoeck & Ruprecht, 1974), 220-32 (see 220 n. 3); A. Terian, "Some Stock Arguments for the Magnanimity of the Law in Hellenistic Jewish Apologetics," in *Jewish Law Association Studies I*, ed. B. S. Jackson (Chico, CA: Scholars Press, 1985), 141-49; S. J. D. Cohen, "Respect for Judaism by Gentiles According to Josephus," *HTR* 80 (1987): 409-30, at 426; G. E. Sterling, "Philo and the Logic of Apologetics: An Analysis of the *Hypothetica*," *SBL 1990 Seminar Papers*, ed. D. J. Lull (Atlanta: Scholar Press, 1990), 412-30; G. P. Carras, "Philo's *Hypothetica*, Josephus' *Contra Apionem* and the Question of Sources," *SBL 1990 Seminar Papers*, 431-50 (see 447); G. P. Carras, "Dependence or Common Tradition in Philo *Hypothetica* VIII.6.10-7.20 and Josephus *Contra Apionem* 2.190-219," *SPhiloA* 5 (1993): 24-47; Borgen, *Philo of Alexandria*, 58-59; C. Gerber, *Ein Bild des Judentums für Nichtjuden von Flavius Josephus* (Leiden: Brill, 1997), 100-118; W. T. Wilson, *The Sentences of Pseudo-Phocylides* (Berlin: de Gruyter, 2005), 19-22; Sterling, "A Man of the Highest Repute," 107-9.

[31] Barclay, *Flavius Josephus*, 353-61.

[32] For the context of the *Hypothetica*, and the possibility that Philo wrote it in the wake of the events of 38 CE, see Sterling, "Philo and the Logic of Apologetics." Michael Cover argues that the book has a Roman background; see "Reconceptualizing Conquest: Colonial Narratives and Philo's Roman Accuser in the *Hypothetica*," *SPhiloA* 22 (2010): 183-207.

[33] See also *A.J.* 2.286 and 320. See Motzo, "Le ΥΠΟΘΕΤΙΚΑ di Filone," 585; Barclay, *Flavius Josephus*, 248 n. 530. On γοητεία, see R. Bloch, "Mose und die Scharlatane: Zum Vorwurf γόης καὶ ἀπατεών in *Contra Apionem* 2:145.161," in *Internationales Josephus-Kolloquium Brüssel 1998*, Münsteraner Judaistische Studien 4, ed. F. Siegert and J. U. Kalms (Münster: LIT, 1999), 142-57.

[34] Barclay notes that the section of *C. Ap.* that deals with sabbath instruction in the law (2.175-78), "does contain close verbal parallels with *Hypoth*. 7.10-14" (*Flavius Josephus*, 355). For a whole list of the parallels, see Barclay, *Flavius Josephus*, 355-57.

[35] Barclay, *Flavius Josephus*, 356.

prescribed other measures, of which a sample is necessary: to give fire, water, and food to all who request them; to point the way; not to ignore an unburied corpse."[36] These laws (and those toward enemies) illustrate the kindness (ἐπιείκεια) to be shown toward foreigners (πρὸς ἀλλοφύλους, 2.209) as well as the humaneness (φιλανθρωπία) of Moses' teachings (2.213). The passage in the *Hypothetica* is more detailed and runs as follows:

> He must not grudge to give fire to one who needs it or close off running water. If the poor or the cripple beg food of him he must give it as an offering of religion to God. He must not debar dead bodies from burial, but throw upon them as much earth as piety demands, nor disturb in any way the resting places and monuments of the departed. (7.6–7, trans. Colson, LCL)

These ethical commandments were connected in the Greek world with the "curses of Bouzyges," a point made clear by *Hypoth*. 7.8, "What need in heaven's name have we of your Bouzyges and his precepts?" This rhetorical question expresses exasperation with the accusations of misanthropy directed against the Jews, which both Philo and Josephus explicitly addressed in their works.[37] The connection between the non-observance of the Bouzygian precepts and misanthropy is already illustrated by Menander's *Dyskolos* and his famous misanthropic character, Cnemon.[38] Josephus' awareness that the precepts to give fire, water, and so forth were those of Bouzyges, is shown by the fact that he adds to the list found in *Hypothetica* the precept of showing the way to the traveller, which was another Bouzygian precept. This addition was certainly not by chance, in view of what one reads (admittedly later) under Juvenal's pen, who affirms that Jews refuse to show the way to non-Jews.[39] Nor is it by chance that the precepts to give fire, water, etc. are followed by the obligation to bury the dead, yet another Bouzygian precept.[40] Although some of these teachings are also found in biblical or Jewish tradition, the fact that they are listed together and the explicit reference to Bouzyges in *Hypothetica* make clear that both Philo and Josephus had the Bouzygian tradition in mind and tried to show that Judaism matched, and even exceeded, these ethical standards, which were closely associated with the notion of *philanthrōpia*.[41]

---

[36] Τἆλλα δὲ προείρηκεν, ὧν ἡ μετάδοσίς ἐστιν ἀναγκαία· πᾶσι παρέχειν τοῖς δεομένοις πῦρ ὕδωρ τροφήν, ὁδοὺς φράζειν, ἄταφον μὴ περιορᾶν, trans. Barclay, *Flavius Josephus*, 292.

[37] See esp. Philo, *Spec*. 2.167 and *Virt*. 141; but also *Spec*. 1.97, 168, 190; *Mos*. 1.149; *Legat*. 306. For Josephus, see C. Ap. 2.148, 255–61, 291. On the precepts of Bouzyges and *philanthrōpia* (and the corresponding link between the rejection of these basic moral obligations and misanthropy), see Berthelot, *Philanthrôpia judaica*, 54–55; K. Berthelot, *L'"humanité de l'autre homme" dans la pensée juive ancienne* (Leiden: Brill, 2004), 30–31.

[38] See Menander, *Dyskolos* (*The Misanthrope*) 510–11 (he refuses to show the way) and 641–42 (he refuses to give water); T. Williams, "The Curses of Bouzyges: New Evidence," *Mnemosyne* 15 (1962): 396–98.

[39] Juvenal, *Satires* 14.96–107 (see 103). On the popularity of the Bouzygian precepts in Rome, see e.g. Cicero, *Off*. 1.16.51–52; Seneca, *Ben*. 4.29.1; and also E. Courtney, *A Commentary on the Satires of Juvenal* (London: Athlone Press, 1980), 572.

[40] Cf. J. Bernays, "Philon's Hypothetika und die Verwünschungen des Buzyges in Athen," *Gesammelte Abhandlungen* (Berlin: W. Hertz, 1985), 1:262–82, at 279, who quotes a scholia on Sophocles' *Antigone* (v. 255). See also Euripides, *Suppl*. 531; Vergil, *Aen*. 6.365. Dio Chrysostom explicitly links the fact of burying the dead with *philanthrōpia* (*Or*. 76.5).

[41] The obligation to feed the hungry is included by the Stoic philosopher Arius Didymus (first century BCE) among the fundamental precepts of humaneness, between the obligations to show the way and that to indicate a

As a matter of fact, both *Hypothetica* and *Against Apion* argue that the Law of Moses teaches the Jews to behave humanely (*philanthrōpōs*).[42] This context has been disregarded by most scholars, who focus on every individual ethical commandment mentioned by Philo and Josephus or on the commandments as a whole (as a list), but without taking into account the *purpose* for which they are used in both works. For instance, scholars have often argued that because another Jewish author, Pseudo-Phocylides, enumerates several ethical commandments that are also found in *Hypothetica* and *Against Apion* (commandments which are drawn mainly from biblical tradition, but also from popular Greek ethics), a common Jewish tradition must underly the three works.[43] Moreover, according to Barclay, "There is a claim here [*in this tradition*] both to match and to exceed the common expectations of friendliness and humanity, as practiced in the Greek world. Indeed, one further characteristic of this tradition is its comparative mode of discourse."[44] But this is not true of Pseudo-Phocylides! The *Sentences* of Pseudo-Phocylides are not meant to argue anything about Judaism since they are supposed to be read as the work of a Greek poet. The pseudepigraphy worked so well in this case that it was only in the sixteenth century that Joseph Scaliger pointed up its Jewish origin. The *Sentences* were probably meant to show to Jewish readers that Greek and Jewish ethics were compatible, but they cannot have been meant to argue anything concerning the way Jewish teachings matched and even exceeded Greco-Roman ethical standards, including the notion of humaneness (*philanthrôpia*).[45] This purpose is unique to Philo and Josephus, and sheds light on details that are peculiar to them, such as the reference to the Bouzygian precepts. Interestingly enough, Pseudo-Phocylides does not mention at all the commandments to show the way and to give fire or water.[46] In short, there may well have been a common tradition about the core of the Jewish law and its ethical commandments behind the works of Philo, Josephus, and Pseudo-Phocylides, but Philo and Josephus are the only ones who use this tradition in order to elaborate an apology of the Law of Moses as *philanthrōpos*, and they do so in strikingly similar ways.

An analysis of *Against Apion* 2.190–214 in connection with Philo's *Peri philanthrōpias* also corroborates this point. A comparison between the two works shows striking parallels, not in terms of vocabulary but insofar as the structure of the arguments is concerned. Both *De virtutibus* 82–160 and *Against Apion* 2.190–214 argue that the Law of Moses trains its followers to be benevolent or humane (*philanthrōpos*): (1) toward one

---

spring to those who are thirsty; he explicitly associates these precepts with the benevolence (*philanthrōpia*) that must be shown to every human being. See Stobaeus, *Anthology* 2.7.13, ed. Wachsmuth, p. 121.22.

[42] See *Hypoth*. 7.19, 11.2 (in connection with the Essenes); *C. Ap*. 2.146, 213 and 261. For the connection between *C. Ap*. 2.213 and *Virt*. 140, see Berthelot, *Philanthrôpia judaica*, 374–76.

[43] See e.g. Carras, "Philo's *Hypothetica*," 449–50; Sterling, "Philo and the Logic of Apologetics"; Gerber, *Ein Bild des Judentums für Nichtjuden*, 100–118; Wilson, *The Sentences*, 19–22.

[44] Barclay, *Flavius Josephus*, 358.

[45] In this regard, see the very lucid analysis by J. J. Collins, *Jewish Wisdom in the Hellenistic Age* (Edinburgh: T&T Clark, 1998), 175–77.

[46] He refers only to almsgiving, a commandment that has a strong biblical basis, and to the obligation to bury the dead and not disturb the grave (see vv. 22–30, 99–102). He does, however, prescribe to "guide a blind man" (v. 24), a precept that may echo Lev 19:14, Deut 27:18, and Isa 42:16. See Wilson, *The Sentences*, 99.

another (within the Jewish community: *Virt.* 82–101 and *C. Ap.* 2.190–208); (2) toward foreigners (that is, proselytes [*Virt.* 102–8 and *C. Ap.* 2.209–10], but also every human being according to *C. Ap.* 2.211); (3) toward enemies (*Virt.* 109–20 and *C. Ap.* 2.211–12); (4) toward animals (*Virt.* 125–47 and *C. Ap.* 2.213). Philo's treatise is much more detailed and contains two additional sections, pertaining respectively to slaves and to plants. To be sure, Josephus used the work of his predecessor selectively and freely, picking up the main lines of the argumentation but choosing different formulations.[47] In the end, however, *Against Apion* 2.190–214 appears as a nice combination of the arguments found in *De virtutibus* and *Hypothetica*, seasoned in a Josephan sauce.

1.3 The Common Roman Background of Philo and Josephus

In their parallel attempts to defend Judaism against accusations of misanthropy, both Philo and Josephus use the argument that the Law of Moses is *philanthrōpos* because it welcomes proselytes, and they are the only Jewish authors to do so.[48] Although this argument may appear self-evident,[49] it is actually quite strange, because no Greek or Roman author ever accused the Jews of not welcoming proselytes. On the contrary, Roman authors like Tacitus viewed conversions to Judaism as a phenomenon that was too frequent, and despicable. In Tacitus' eyes, the convert joined the Jews in their hostility toward non-Jews.[50] So why did Philo and Josephus use this argument?

Although Josephus probably picked it up from Philo together with the whole framework of Philo's apologetic discourse about the humaneness of the Mosaic Law, in this case the rationale behind the argument is much clearer in Josephus than it is in Philo. In *Against Apion*, Josephus compares the Mosaic *politeia* to those of Athens and Sparta, in a way that is reminiscent of Dionysius of Halicarnassus, who criticizes both cities in order to enhance the superiority of Rome and its exemplary *philanthrōpia*, which consists in welcoming new citizens independently of their ethnic origin.[51] In the same vein, Tacitus has Claudius argue that it is wise to give Roman citizenship to the former enemies of Rome:

> What else proved fatal to Lacedaemon and Athens, in spite of their power in arms, but their policy of holding the conquered aloof as alien-born? But the sagacity of our own founder Romulus was such that several times he fought and naturalized a people in

---

[47] As John Barclay notes, Josephus "selected what he used precisely because it suited his agenda" (*Flavius Josephus*, 361).
[48] See Philo, *Virt.* 102–8; Josephus, *C. Ap.* 2.209–10. See also Philo, *QG* 3.42 and 62 for the idea that Abraham is *philanthrōpos* insofar as he welcomes converts.
[49] See e.g. Borgen, *Philo of Alexandria*, 59: "the acceptance of proselytes by the Jews is seen as a proof of the Jews' equity and love for humanity and their magnanimity."
[50] See Tacitus, *Histories* 5.5.1–2. On Tacitus and the accusations of misanthropy against the Jews, see Berthelot, *Philanthrôpia judaica*, 161–67.
[51] See Dionysius, *Ant. rom.* 2.17.1, 14.6.1–6; Josephus, *C. Ap.* 2.259–61; D. L. Balch, "Two Apologetic Encomia: Dionysius on Rome and Josephus on the Jews," *JSJ* 13 (1982): 102–22. On this issue, see also Berthelot, *Philanthrôpia judaica*, 359–68.

the course of the same day! (*Annals* 11.24, trans. J. Jackson, LCL; cf. Dionysius, *Ant. rom.* 6.55.1)

This discourse can be found again and again in pro-Roman sources from the first and second centuries CE, and Josephus himself reproduces it in *Against Apion* 2:40:

Has not the benevolence of the Romans (ἡ δὲ Ῥωμαίων φιλανθρωπία) ensured that their name has been shared with practically everyone, not only with individuals but with sizeable nations as a whole? Thus, those who were once Iberians, Tyrrhenians, and Sabines are called "Romans." (trans. Barclay, *Flavius Josephus*)

Later, Josephus uses the examples of Athens and Sparta in the same way as Roman or pro-Roman writers did, but this time in order to emphasize the *philanthrōpia* of the Mosaic constitution. In connection with the Lacedemonians, in particular, Josephus writes:

They perhaps might reasonably be criticized for their churlishness:[52] for they would not grant anyone the right of citizenship or of residence among them. 261. We, on the other hand, are not inclined to emulate other people's customs, but gladly welcome those who wish to share ours; and that would be evidence, I take it, of both benevolence and generosity (φιλανθρωπίας ἅμα καὶ μεγαλοψυχίας). (*C. Ap.* 2.260–61)

Like the Romans, the Jews welcome new "citizens," regardless of their birth or rank. In this respect they compare with the Romans, unlike the Greeks. In short, the discourse about Jewish *philanthrōpia* in connection with the integration of proselytes makes sense in a *Roman* context, and tends to present Jews as matching Roman standards.

This was probably already the rationale behind Philo's choice to argue that the Mosaic laws foster *philanthrōpia* because they teach Jews to welcome proselytes. In *De virtutibus* (as well as *Spec.* 1.51–53), Philo describes the proselytes as new citizens in the *politeia* of Moses, using political vocabulary in a metaphorical way. Moreover, in *De virtutibus* 108 he insists that the descendants of former enemies can also become citizens, in accordance with Deut 23:8–9.[53] The peculiar choice of this biblical passage—not the most obvious one to celebrate the Law's *philanthrōpia* toward foreigners—is to be explained by this reference to former enemies, which made Jewish standards look similar to Roman ones. To be sure, in this context Philo does not refer explicitly to Rome. In his time, however, the discourse about Rome's openness to new citizens and

---

[52] The term here is δυσκολία ("misanthropy"), the same as in Menander's play.
[53] See *Virt.* 108: "And if any of them should want to cross over to the Jewish polity (κἂν εἴ τινες ἐθελήσειαν αὐτῶν μεταλλάξασθαι πρὸς τὴν Ἰουδαίων πολιτείαν), they are not to be scorned unyieldingly like the children of enemies, but are to be treated in such a manner that the third generation is invited into the congregation and granted that share of the divine oracles into which the native- and noble-born are also rightfully initiated" (trans. Wilson, *Philo of Alexandria: On Virtues*). See also *Spec.* 1.51–53 for the use of the metaphor of citizenship in connection with proselytes, but without a reference to Deut 23. On Philo's use of Greek political vocabulary, see C. Carlier, *La cité de Moïse: le peuple juif chez Philon d'Alexandrie* (Turnhout: Brepols, 2008), 171–217.

magnanimity toward former enemies was already in vogue, and he probably had such discourses in mind while he was writing *De virtutibus*.⁵⁴

1.4 Conclusion

At the beginning of the *Antiquities*, Josephus writes:

> Some things the lawgiver cleverly denotes symbolically; other things he formulates allegorically with solemnity; but whatever things it was advantageous to set forth with simplicity these things he revealed with utter plainness. For those, however, who wish to consider also the reasons for each thing the inquiry would be deep and very philosophical. I now bypass this, but if God should give us time, I shall try to write the treatise after this one. (*A.J.* 1.24–25, trans. Feldman, *Flavius Josephus: Judean Antiquities*)

While reading these lines, one wonders whether Josephus had the ambition to become another Philo: not only a historian, but also a man with some kind of philosophical expertise in the Law.

In any case, Josephus appears as a vigorous champion of the Mosaic Law, and in so doing he apparently drew heavily on Philo's work, especially *De virtutibus* and *Hypothetica*, Philo's most explicitly apologetic works. One should probably add *De opificio mundi* and *De vita Mosis* to the list. More generally, a good case can be made concerning Josephus' interest in the "Exposition of the Law" as a whole, because all the exegetical details which Philo and Josephus can be shown to have in common come from the "Exposition of the Law" and not from the Allegorical Commentary.⁵⁵ In addition, it is highly probable that Josephus read the *Legatio*, even if his own narrative greatly differs from that of Philo. The important point to grasp is that both authors, while living in different circumstances, shared common interests, perspectives, and challenges. In particular, both Philo and Josephus were confronted with anti-Jewish authors who accused the Jews of being misanthropic. Moreover, they both lived in the context of an all-powerful Roman Empire, and tried to adjust their presentation of the Mosaic Law to Roman standards. In this respect, it must be emphasized that an awareness of Josephus' highly probable dependency upon Philo may in turn help to highlight

---

⁵⁴ The insistence with which both Philo and Josephus praise the Mosaic Law for the severity of its punishments, which is peculiar to these two authors, may also have to do with their Roman context. Tacitus similarly praises the Germans for their courage at war and the severity of the penalties against transgressors (see *Germ.* 7 and 12); see J. M. G. Barclay, "Judaism in Roman Dress: Josephus' Tactics in the *Contra Apionem*," in *Internationales Josephus-Kolloquium Aarhus 1999*, Münsteraner Judaistische Studien 6, ed. J. U. Kalms (Münster: LIT, 2000), 231–45, at 243. See also how Valerius Maximus, in the first century CE, positively evokes the severe laws of the Spartans, which made them akin to the seriousness of the Romans of old (*Memorable Deeds and Sayings* 2.6.1). To be sure, Josephus insists on this aspect of the Mosaic Law to a more considerable extent than Philo; see *C. Ap.* 2.206–7, 214–17, 276–77. Again, the analysis of this theme in Josephus' work may shed light retrospectively on the use Philo made of it.

⁵⁵ See esp. *A.J.* 4.279, 283–84, and 285–86, in connection with *Spec.* 3.93–95, 3.147–49, and 4.30–34.

Philo's Roman context and to understand the implicit background of some aspects of his argumentation.[56]

While dealing with Philo's legacy in Josephus' writings, however, we must keep in mind that Josephus was no servile copyist, but an original author who freely used the work of his predecessor alongside other sources in order to produce his own writings. Moreover, one may suspect that Josephus' ego prevented him from acknowledging the extent of his indebtedness toward the Alexandrian philosopher.

---

[56] For a comparative perspective on Philo and Josephus in their Roman context, see Niehoff, "Josephus and Philo in Rome."

2

The New Testament

Torrey Seland

The works of Philo of Alexandria and the New Testament writings originated in approximately the same century; the latter works, however, emerged after Philo had passed away. Furthermore, Philo and the early Christians lived and traveled in the same social world, the Mediterranean Greco-Roman world. The present contribution will first consider the various possible relationships between Philo's works and the New Testament, and then deal with some texts from the New Testament that have most often been drawn upon in arguing some reception of Philo.

2.1 Philo and the New Testament: Location in Time and Social World

Regrettably, we do not know the exact dates of Philo's span of life, but most scholars locate him in the years between *c.*20 BCE and *c.*50 CE. Hence, as we should most probably not date any of the New Testament works earlier than *c.*50 CE, there is—as far as location in time is concerned—the possibility of a reception of Philo's writings in the New Testament (NT).

Philo grew up, lived, and worked in the same social world as that of the New Testament authors; that is, in the Jewish diaspora settings of the Hellenistic Greco-Roman world. Here they were both subject to its various cultural expressions in religion, philosophy, politics, and other comparable fields of activities. Both Philo and the NT authors are also to be located in the context of the Jewish synagogues. Philo was an expositor of the biblical scriptures. Most of his books are expositions of texts from his holy scriptures, or they deal with themes and topics from these scriptures. He probably "drew on the expository activity in the synagogue,"[1] and he might even have had a school of his own, a "school of the sacred Laws," as Gregory Sterling has suggested.[2] The early Christians' relations to the synagogal milieus of the diaspora are indicated in several parts of the NT as can be drawn from both direct statements of synagogal points of contact (e.g. John 16:1–4; Acts 6:9, 13:5, 14:1, etc.; 2 Cor 11:24), as well as from aspects of comparative views, exegetical methods, and socio-political issues. Furthermore, Philo of Alexandria, as well as the early Christians (of which many were

---

[1] P. Borgen, "Philo of Alexandria: Reviewing and Rewriting Biblical Material," *SPhiloA* 9 (1997): 37–53, at 37.
[2] G. E. Sterling, "The School of the Sacred Laws: The Social Setting of Philo's Treatises," *VC* 53 (1999): 148–64.

Jewish-Christians) all spoke Greek and used their holy scriptures in a Greek translation, a translation most probably very similar to what we have today as the Septuagint. Hence it should be of no surprise if some early Christians came in contact with Philo's writings, and even became interested in some of his ideas and expositions of scripture.

2.2 Possible Personal Points of Contact

We have, for instance, a tradition in Acts 6:9 stating that there were "Alexandrians" living in Jerusalem, probably comprising—or at least being part of—a synagogue in the city. They might have been diaspora Jews who had returned to Jerusalem to spend the last years of their lives in the Holy City. We also know from his work *Prov.* 2.64 that Philo visited Jerusalem at least once in his life to offer prayers and sacrifices in the Temple.

Furthermore, Philo stayed several years in Rome (probably 38–41 CE), as a leader of a Jewish Alexandrian embassy in order to negotiate with the emperor concerning the circumstances of the social and political life of the Jews in Alexandria.[3] Hence there were possibilities of contact between Philo and Christians both in Jerusalem and in Rome.

Then we have the somewhat enigmatic person Apollos from Alexandria, who met Priscilla and Aquila in Ephesus (Acts 18:24–19:1). He is described as ἀνὴρ λόγιος … δυνατὸς ὢν ἐν ταῖς γραφαῖς (i.e. "eloquent" or "learned, cultured" [BDAG], and "well-versed in the scriptures" [NRSV]). Joining Priscilla and Aquila, and receiving further instruction concerning the Christian faith from them, we are told that he later worked in Corinth, and became involved in some schisms in the congregation there (Acts 18:27–19:1; 1 Cor 1:12; 3:4–6:22; 16:12, cf. Tit 3:13). Bruce Winter reads him as a proponent of a Christian sophistic movement in Corinth, but that is still controversial.[4]

Later on, the church historian Eusebius of Caesarea (c.260–339) both uses and describes works of Philo. And he even tells us that he knows traditions stating that Philo went to Rome to talk with Peter, the apostle (εἰς ὁμολίαν ἐλθεῖν Πέτρῳ, *Hist. eccl.* 2.17.1).[5] However, though we know that Philo stayed in Rome for some time, he does not indicate that he met any Christians there, not to mention any of the Christians figuring as authors in the New Testament.

These features, few as they are, leave open many suggestions concerning the possibilities of points of contact between early Christians and influences from Philo, whether

---

[3] Philo describes this in his *Legatio* 181–83, 349–72 (cf. Josephus, *A.J.* 18.257–60). See further S. Gambetti, *The Alexandrian Riots of 38 C.E. and the Persecution of the Jews: A Historical Reconstruction*, JSNTSup 135 (Leiden: Brill, 2009).

[4] B. W. Winter, *Philo and Paul among the Sophists*, SNTSMS 96 (Cambridge: Cambridge University Press, 1997), esp. 177–79.

[5] On the relationships between the early church fathers and Philo, see, in addition to relevant chapters in the present volume, esp. D. T. Runia, *Philo in Early Christian Literature*, CRINT 3.3 (Assen: Van Gorcum, 1993). On Eusebius on Philo, see M. Niehoff, "Eusebius as a Reader of Philo," *Adamantius* 21 (2015): 185–94.

by personal contacts between Christians and Philo, or students and/or works of Philo.[6] We have no hard evidence that Philo of Alexandria ever knew any Christians, or that he even ever had heard about any of them, or of their Messiah, Jesus of Nazareth. At the same time, we have hardly any ways of disproving that he might have had some knowledge of some representatives of the early Christian movement.

We must hasten to add, however, that we have equally few hard facts to use as arguments that any of the early Christian writers represented by the New Testament literature ever knew Philo.[7] No New Testament work mentions him, his literary works, or attributes any ideas dealt with as coming from or being related to him. There might nevertheless be "echoes" of Philo present in the New Testament.

However, the views in the scholarly guild have been varied, and several positions are still around.[8] But a consensus seems to emerge, as we shall see below.

2.3 The New Testament Writings and Philo: A Taxonomy of Possible Relationships

In order to speak confidently of a "reception of Philo" in the New Testament, there must be some similarity between items or issues in his works and the New Testament. As it is difficult to determine what kind of contact there might have been between Philo and what he represented and the New Testament authors and/or their sources, it is hard to make up a taxonomy of possible levels of influence. In presenting what such a taxonomy might look like, I would like to adopt and adapt the one applied by David Lincicum in his study on *Paul and the Early Jewish Encounter with Deuteronomy*.[9] Lincicum differentiates between five different ways of reception, or *modes*, as I would like to call them here:

Mode A: "a quotation or explicit quotation" (a verbatim repetition that is marked with some kind of introductory formula or interpretative comments);

Mode B: "implicit quotation" (a verbatim or near-verbatim quotation, but without any introductory formula or interpretative comments);

---

[6] Cf. K. L. Schenck, who says that "we cannot rule out the possibility that the author (of Hebrews) was aware of Philo's writings. I personally would not be at all surprised if he had some general acquaintance with them"; "Philo and the Epistle to the Hebrews: Ronald Williamson's Study after Thirty Years," *SPhiloA* 14 (2002): 112–35, at 135.

[7] Cf. Runia on Paul: "We have no way of knowing whether he had ever actually heard of Philo" (*Philo in Early Christian Literature*, 67).

[8] Four reviews of Philo's reception in the New Testament may be mentioned here: Runia, *Philo in Early Christian Literature*, 63–86; K. L. Schenck, *A Brief Guide to Philo* (Louisville: Westminster John Knox, 2005), 74–91; F. Siegert, "Philo and the New Testament," in *The Cambridge Companion to Philo*, ed. A. Kamesar (Cambridge: Cambridge University Press, 2009), 175–209; P. J. Bekken, "Philo's Relevance for the Study of the New Testament," in *Reading Philo: A Handbook to Philo of Alexandria*, ed. T. Seland (Grand Rapids: Eerdmans, 2014), 226–67.

[9] D. Lincicum, *Paul and the Early Jewish Encounter with Deuteronomy* (Grand Rapids: Baker Academic, 2013), 13–15. A. van den Hoek operates with a comparable taxonomy concerning Clement's reception of Philo as she distinguishes between "quotation" (a considerable degree of literality), "paraphrase" (containing only a few words from the original source), and "reminiscences" (having no literal correspondences but merely resemblances in theme or thought). See A. van den Hoek, "Techniques of Quotation in Clement of Alexandria: A View of Ancient Literary Working Methods," *VC* 50 (1996): 223–43, esp. 228–29; and in this volume, Chapter 4.

Mode C: "paraphrase or rewriting" (when the substance of an original scriptural account is rendered in other words);

Mode D: "echoes and allusions" (referring to a scriptural precursor text in a manner that is less explicit than a citation); and then

Mode E: the presence of "concepts or ideas" which are not normally supported by a high volume of verbal resonance.

It should be apparent that we here operate with a sliding scale of explicitness, and that the influence of Philo most probably will be at the end of this scale as there is a scholarly consensus that we have no explicit or implicit quotations from Philo in the New Testament texts.

Another possibility or mode perhaps to be mentioned here does not concern a reception of Philo by, for example, Paul but by his opponents. This has been suggested by several as an aspect of some of the conflicts in Corinth,[10] and Peter Borgen[11] has also suggested it as a possible way of reading some of the conflicts dealt with by Paul in his letter to the Galatians. We might call this a Mode F: a possible reflection of influence from Philo which Paul tries to correct or combat. Such cases should be distinguished from those in which Philo primarily is used as a source for relevant social, exegetical, and ideological background information on Paul.[12]

A crucial issue in the discussion of possible influence from Philo is the question: if one can find some influence from Platonic thought in the New Testament, is that indicative of influence from Philo? In former times, this question was often answered in the affirmative; in more recent times, one is more reluctant to draw such conclusions. The Epistle to the Hebrews, for instance, may use some Platonic thought forms without drawing these directly from Philo. It might also have been possible to be influenced by thoughts and ideas very close to, even informed by Philo, without knowing his works, not to say having met him or some of his pupils personally. Folker Siegert pinpoints that "If we assume that more than one teacher like Philo was active in the urban synagogues of antiquity, the diffusion of philonic language and ideas can be explained by an appeal to oral forms of transmission."[13] Hence in more recent years, many have surmised that the similarities that may be found in the New Testament to issues known

---

[10] Cf. Schenck: "Paul seems to interact with some of the same traditions we find in Philo. In many cases, the similarities relate more to those Paul argued against than to Paul's own thinking. In particular, we can make a good case that Paul's opponents in Corinth had come under the influence of interpretations Philo also inherited from his environment" (*A Brief Guide to Philo*, 76).

[11] Cf. P. Borgen, "Observations on the Theme 'Paul and Philo': Paul's Preaching of Circumcision in Galatia (Gal 5:11) and Debates on Circumcision in Philo," in *Die Paulinische Literatur und Theologie*, ed. S. Pedersen (Arhus: Forlaget Aros, 1980), 85–102.

[12] According to P. J. Bekken, Philo is primarily to be used as background information in order to understand the New Testament; see Bekken, "Philo's Relevance," 226: "no direct relationship or influence is plausible, and that as such the Philonic writings represent a rich collection of data providing useful illustration of the Jewish and Greco-Roman background of the New Testament."

[13] Siegert, "Philo and the New Testament," 175.

from the works of Philo may be more due to general influence from Hellenistic synagogal milieus than to specific personal contact.

But in the search for any such features indicating influence, or better, reception, we should remember the warnings set forth by Samuel Sandmel in his famous article on Parallelomania.[14] He defines parallelomania as "that extravagance among scholars which first overdoes the supposed similarity in passages and then proceeds to describe source and derivation as if implying literary connection flowing in an inevitable or predetermined direction."[15] The main thesis and argument in his article is that "detailed study ought to respect the context and not be limited to juxtaposing mere excerpts."[16] Two concepts may seem similar or even close to identical when seen in isolation from their context, but when viewed in context manifest great differences. Hence considering the context of an item in Philo and, for example, Hebrews may demonstrate that the item is used in radically different ways, representing no influence or reception at all. Or as Runia says concerning Philo and Hebrews: "Linguistic, hermeneutical and thematic correspondences are impressive. But the thought worlds are markedly different."[17]

2.4 Reception of Philo in the New Testament: Discussion of Some Cases

The value of the works of Philo for understanding the social world of the New Testament is indisputable; several studies have established the relevance of his works in illuminating both social and ideological issues concerning the world of the New Testament.[18] The question here, however, is to what extent can we talk about a *reception of Philo in* the various works of the New Testament. Having listed some of the historical and methodological problems involved in such a quest above, we shall here present briefly some cases that have been drawn upon in assessing the issue of reception of Philo in the New Testament.

Few scholars suggest any Philonic influence (or reception) in the Synoptic Gospels. The Gospel of John, however, has been in the forefront in the quest for such influence, especially the use of the Logos concept in its first chapter. The author's Midrash-like exegesis of the Old Testament has also been studied in light of Philo.[19]

Several Pauline letters are interesting and have been scrutinized for possible Philonic influence. The most relevant here are 1 Corinthians and Colossians. In studies of 1 Corinthians, Philo has been used in order to understand Paul's

---

[14] Samuel Sandmel, "Parallelomania," *JBL* 81 (1962): 1–13.
[15] Sandmel, "Parallelomania," 1.
[16] Sandmel, "Parallelomania," 2.
[17] Runia, *Philo in Early Christian Literature*, 78.
[18] Cf. several chapters in Torrey Seland, ed., *Reading Philo: A Handbook to Philo of Alexandria* (Grand Rapids: Eerdmans, 2014).
[19] Cf. e.g. the influential study P. Borgen, *Bread from Heaven: An Exegetical Study of the Concept of Manna in the Gospel of John and the Writings of Philo*, 2nd edn, NovTSup 10 (Leiden: Brill, 1981; repr., Eugene, OR: Wipf & Stock Publishers, 2017, orig. 1965). But he does not assume any direct contact between Philo and John.

opponents in Corinth, particularly as the Alexandrian Apollos was active in that city. Concerning Colossians, it has been suggested that its references to false teaching and the so-called Colossian hymn (Col 1:15–20) have—at least some—interesting parallels in Philo's works.[20] In more recent years the letter to the Galatians has come into focus too. But the Epistle to the Hebrews is probably the New Testament letter that has been considered as most closely associated with Philo's works. Hence, we shall here deal with text segments from two of these letters: the letter to the Galatians (4:21–31), and the Epistle to the Hebrews 8:1–6. Then some brief comments on the Gospel of John will be offered.

2.4.1 Hagar and Ishmael in the Letter to the Galatians

There is not much allegorical exposition in Paul's letters; there is, however, a lot in Philo's works as he was an ardent user of allegory (*Migr.* 89–93). In dealing with the story of Hagar and Sarah, they both concur in applying allegorical interpretations. Hence this should be an appropriate place for closer investigation. Though there are similarities in methods in Paul's and Philo's expositions, there are also some dissimilarities. One might thus ask if there are features indicating some reception of Philo in Paul's text.[21]

Galatians 4:24 is the only passage in the New Testament where the word *allegorize* (ἀλληγορέω) is used as a characterization of its own exegesis. Scholars may differ over how to understand this description in light of Alexandrian/Philonic and Palestinian exegetical procedures;[22] here we shall rather focus on Paul's use of the Hagar and Sarah episodes from Genesis.

According to Paul, some agitators had arrived arguing that the believers had to submit to the Law to be saved. They seem in particular to have focused on the necessity of circumcision (2:3, 11–16; 5:2–4; 6:12–15). To Paul, this was to return to a level or a condition they should leave behind, and stay with Christ by believing in Christ, and not trusting in the works of the Law: that is, trusting in the new and not in the old order. A return to the old life under the Law would represent, according to Paul, a return to the condition and status as slaves. But Christ was sent to redeem those under the Law so that they might receive adoption as children (4:4–7).

---

[20] e.g. R. Cox, *By the Same Word: Creation and Salvation in Hellenistic Judaism and Early Christianity*, BZNW 145 (Berlin: de Gruyter, 2007).
[21] See here esp. P. Borgen, "Some Hebrew and Pagan Features in Philo's and Paul's Interpretation of Hagar and Ishmael," in *The New Testament and Hellenistic Judaism*, ed. P. Borgen and S. Giversen (Aarhus: Aarhus University Press, 1995), 151–64; and J. M. Zurawski, "Mosaic Torah as Encyclical Paideia: Reading Paul's Allegory of Hagar and Sarah in Light of Philo of Alexandria's," in *Pedagogy in Ancient Judaism and Early Christianity*, ed. K. Martin Hogan, M. Goff, and E. Wasserman (Atlanta: SBL Press, 2017), 283–308.
[22] See here e.g. the discussion of R. N. Longenecker, *Galatians*, WBC 41 (Dallas: Word, 1998), ad. loc.

2.4.1.1 Hagar and Sarah in Philo

There is much material in Philo's works on the Hagar texts; most of these are in his commentary series called the Allegorical Commentary.[23] A dominating theme in Philo's use of the Hagar-Sarah traditions is the value of the Greek education vis-à-vis Jewish wisdom; that is, Philo has an agenda of education as most clearly set forth in his expositions in the work *On Mating with the Preliminary Studies* (*De congressu eruditionis gratia*).

Again and again Hagar, the handmaid of Sarah, is described as representing the elementary teaching, the encyclical studies (ἐγκύκλιος παιδεία; see *Cher.* 3, 6, 8, 73, 145; *Congr.* 11; *Somn.* 2.240; *Mut.* 255, and elsewhere).[24] They are necessary as the primary learning before advancing to the higher studies represented by Sarah, the study of wisdom, what in Philo's symbolic world is the wisdom of the Jews, the wisdom inherent in the Torah (*Congr.* 64–66, 70). Hence, as Borgen states, "the story about Abraham's family situation is applied by him to the role which encyclical education should play for the Jews."[25] This is so essential to Philo that he can even use himself as an example.[26]

According to Philo, it is necessary to move on from the encyclia to the real wisdom, from Hagar to Sarah, and not remain with her handmaid. Hagar, as an Egyptian, represented the earthly, which here is negative. And as a servant to Sarah, Hagar symbolizes the subordinate role of the encyclica to philosophy, but also that of the body to the mind, the slave to the free, and the handmaid to the mistress.[27]

It is possible that this exposition of Philo to some extent is due to his reception of a similar story of Homer concerning the suitors of Penelope, who, when not able to win Penelope, entertained themselves with her maidens.[28] The more interesting issue for us here, however, is to what extent there might be some influence (or reception) of Philo in the story of Paul in Gal 4:21–31.

2.4.1.2 A Case of Reception?

Such a case has been made by Jason Zurawski. He argues that "Just as Philo sternly warns his readers of the dangers of going back to encyclical paideia once having attained true wisdom, Paul warns the Galatians of the dangers of turning back to the Mosaic Law, as paideia, once having attained true wisdom via Christ." This warning is not directly indicative that Paul was reading Philo (though Zurawski would not

---

[23] A list of the various passages can be seen in Borgen, "Some Hebrew and Pagan Features," 153; see also F. H. Colson, ed. and trans., *Philo*, vol. 10, LCL 379 (Cambridge, MA: Harvard University Press, 1962), 317–19.

[24] On the encyclical studies, see A. Mendelson, *Secular Education in Philo of Alexandria* (Cincinatti: Hebrew Union College Press, 1982).

[25] Borgen, "Some Hebrew and Pagan Features," 153.

[26] See *Congr.* 74–76: "For instance, when first I was incited by the goads of philosophy to desire her I consorted in early youth with one of her handmaids, Grammar, and all that I begat by her, writing, reading and the study of the writings of the poets, I dedicated to her mistress" (*Congr.* 74).

[27] On Hagar as identified with Egypt, a symbol of the body, see S. J. K. Pearce, *The Land of the Body: Studies in Philo's Representation of Egypt*, WUNT 208 (Tübingen: Mohr Siebeck, 2007), 167–77.

[28] See Y. Amir, "The Transference of Greek Allegories to Biblical Motifs in Philo," in *Nourished with Peace: Studies in Hellenistic Judaism in Memory of Samuel Sandmel*, ed. F. E. Greenspahn, E. Hilgert, and B. L. Mack (Chico, CA: Scholars Press, 1984), 15–25; Zurawski, "Mosaic Torah as Encyclical Paideia," 287.

roundly dismiss that possibility), but that he may have been aware of this way of understanding the Genesis account in the Hellenistic diaspora.[29] There are, admittedly, several similarities between Philo's and Paul's expositions, and we should not postulate a too-rigid set of convergences to admit the possibility of some influence here.

Paul is making two significant modifications in his use of the Hagar-Sarah narratives compared to that of Philo: in Galatians 4 the Torah has become a type comparable in its function to Philo's encyclical *paideia*, and the higher wisdom here concerned is that of Christ. The Torah, according to Paul, was a custodian, a preparatory stage, representing slavery (Hagar); one needs to leave that and cling to Sarah, being children of the free. "Paul is adamant in his warning about the dangers of becoming too devoted to the Mosaic pedagogue, particularly because of the second major modification he makes to the Philonic interpretation of the Hagar/Sarah allegory, the fact that Christ has already come and thereby provided the goal to which the Mosaic Law served as preparation."[30]

It is somewhat fascinating that in the only passage where Paul explicitly deals with allegory, he focuses on the roles of Hagar and Sarah, an issue so prominent in the works of Philo. One might wonder if he arrived at this exposition through a reminiscence of the Greek allegorical exegesis of the Homeric Penelope. But after all, some influence from the works of Philo might be more relevant. In light of the various modes of our taxonomy set forth above, I would suggest that we here have a case of echo and allusions to Philo in Paul's handling of Hagar and Sarah (Mode D).

2.4.2 The Epistle to the Hebrews

To many scholars, the influence of Philo is more clearly detectable in the Epistle to the Hebrews than in any other New Testament work. Ceslas Spicq argued that it is more than likely that the writer of Hebrews knew Philo personally and had perhaps listened to his expositions of scripture in the synagogues of Alexandria. He argued that there are similarities in language in the Logos doctrine, the Platonic doctrine of ideas, the concept of faith, and in the use of the Old Testament. Spicq quotes with approval an older scholar (E. Menegoz) who argued that the author of Hebrews was "un philonien converti au christianisme" ("a philonist converted to Christianity").[31] Ronald Williamson,[32] however, after a meticulous investigation of Spicq's arguments, concludes quite the opposite, namely that:

---

[29] Zurawski, "Mosaic Torah as Encyclical Paideia," 286.
[30] Zurawski, "Mosaic Torah as Encyclical Paideia," 293.
[31] The reference is to E. Menegoz, *La théologie de l'Epitre aux Hebreux* (Paris: Librairie Fischbacher, 1894), 198. See further C. Spicq, *L'Epitre Aux Hébreux*, SB (Paris: Libraire Lecoffre, 1977), 13–17; C. Spicq, "Le Philonisme de l'Épitre aux Hébreux," *RB* 56 (1949): 542–72.
[32] Cf. R. Williamson, *Philo and the Epistle to the Hebrews*, ALGHJ 5 (Leiden: Brill, 1970), 493.

the influence of Philo on the Writer of Hebrews was minimal, perhaps even non-existent; that the Writer of Hebrews had never at any time been a Philonist; that he had never come under the personal influence of Philo; and that he had perhaps never read even a single volume of Philo's works. He almost certainly lived and moved in circles where, in broad, general terms, ideas such as those we meet in Philo's works were known and discussed; he drew upon the same fund of cultured Greek vocabulary upon which Philo drew. But this is as much as the evidence allows us to concede.

Kenneth Schenck, on the other hand, who thirty years later carried out an evaluation of Williamson's work, argues that Williamson too overstated his case: "we cannot rule out the possibility that the author was aware of Philo's writings. I personally would not be at all surprised if he had some general acquaintance with them. Yet the author is thoroughly and fundamentally a Christian."[33] In an overview article published in 2009, Siegert airs similar opinions when he states that "The author of Hebrews is likely to have been a Jewish Christian from Rome, and may have heard or met Philo in that city, or have had contacts with others who did."[34] As there were many synagogues in Rome, "we may safely assume that Philo was heard in Roman synagogues during his stay in approximately 38–40 CE."[35] Runia voices the opinion of much research on the Epistle to the Hebrews when he says that:

> Examination of the evidence has shown, to my mind, that the author of the Hebrews and Philo came from the same milieu in a closer sense than was discovered in the case of Paul. I would not be surprised if he had had some form of direct contact with Judaism as it had developed in Philo's Alexandria. Linguistic, hermeneutical and thematic correspondences are impressive. But the thought worlds are markedly different.[36]

There are several aspects of the Epistle to Hebrews that have been singled out as relevant in a search for a reception of Philo in Hebrews, such as language, biblical interpretation, important themes (the Logos, priesthood and cult, dualism, Moses, Melchizedek and perfection).[37] To many, however, the most relevant issue but also the one most discussed in recent research is probably the possible reception of Philo in the descriptions of the heavenly and earthly sanctuaries as found in Hebrews in general and in Heb 8:1–6 in particular.

---

[33] Schenck, "Philo and the Epistle to the Hebrews," 134. Cf. his *A Brief Guide to Philo*, 86.
[34] Siegert, "Philo and the New Testament," at 175; see also 178.
[35] Siegert, "Philo and the New Testament," 178.
[36] Runia, *Philo in Early Christian Literature*, 78; cf. H. W. Attridge, *The Epistle to the Hebrews: A Commentary*, Hermeneia (Philadelphia: Fortress Press, 1989).
[37] See esp. Williamson, *Philo and the Epistle to the Hebrews*.

2.4.2.1 Hebrews 8:5 and Philo

In the text segment of 8:5 the author, on the basis of Exod 25:40 ("See that you make everything according to the pattern that was shown you on the mountain," ποιήσεις πάντα κατὰ τὸν τύπον τὸν δειχθέντα σοι ἐν τῷ ὄρει; cf. Exod 25:9; 26:30; 27:8), describes the earthly sanctuary as a ὑποδείγματι καὶ σκιᾷ ... τῶν ἐπουρανίων, "a copy and shadow of the heavenly one" (8:5), and argues that Jesus, who is now in heaven, has achieved a much better ministry, and is also a mediator of a better covenant (8:6) than the Levitical priests in the earthly sanctuary.

Several descriptions in Hebrews have often been singled out as being very Platonic-like: Christ is "a minister in the sanctuary *and the true tabernacle* (καὶ τῆς σκηνῆς τῆς ἀληθινῆς) that the Lord, not man, set up" (8:2); Christ "passed through the greater and more perfect tent *not made with hands* (σκηνῆς οὐ χειροποιήτου), that is, not of this creation" (9:11); "So it was necessary for the *sketches of the things in heaven* (ὑποδείγματι τῶν ἐν τοῖς οὐρανοῖς) to be purified with these sacrifices, but *the heavenly things* (τὰ ἐπουράνια) themselves required better sacrifices than these. For Christ did not enter a sanctuary made with hands (χειροποίητα)—the *representation of the true sanctuary* (ἀντίτυπα τῶν ἀληθινῶν)—but into heaven itself, and he appears now in God's presence for us" (9:23–24, emphasis added throughout). The main question is, however, to what extent are these features in Hebrews to be read as indicative of a Platonic and Philonic view?

If we then turn to Philo, we find that he rephrases and elaborates on Exod 25:40 thus:

> He saw with the soul's eye the immaterial forms of the material objects about to be made (τῶν μελλόντων ἀποτελεῖσθαι σωμάτων ἀσωμάτους ἰδέας τῇ ψυχῇ θεωρῶν), and these forms had to be reproduced in copies perceived by the senses (νοητῶν παραδειγμάτων αἰσθητὰ μιμήματα), taken from the original draught, so to speak, and from patterns conceived in the mind .... So the shape of the model was stamped upon the mind of the prophet (ὁ μὲν οὖν τύπος τοῦ παραδείγματος ἐνεσφραγίζετο τῇ διανοίᾳ τοῦ προφήτου) ... and then the resulting work was built in accordance with that shape by the artist. (*Mos.* 2.74–76, see also *QE* 2.52, 82, 90; *Leg.* 3.102–3)

Hence both the author of the Epistle to the Hebrews and Philo speak of an earthly and a heavenly sanctuary and interpret and explain this on the basis of Exod 25:40. There are, admittedly, some differences in vocabulary. Most conspicuous is that Heb 8:5 has ὑπόδειγμα instead of παράδειγμα (Exod 25:40; *Mos.* 2.74; *Leg.* 3.102). Some of the most Platonic terms used by Philo in *QE* 2.52, 82, 90 are also lacking. But 8:5 has nevertheless made several scholars state that the use of Exod 25:40 "is so close to Philo that coincidence must be ruled out."[38] The debate, however, goes on.

---

[38] See Runia, *Philo in Early Christian Literature*, 76; S. N. Svendsen, *Allegory Transformed: The Appropriation of Philonic Hermeneutics in the Letter to the Hebrews*, WUNT 2.269 (Tübingen: Mohr Siebeck, 2009), 159. It should be added that the issue is also made more problematic by the fact that we do not have the Greek text of Philo's *QE*.

L. D. Hurst has argued strongly that the term used in Heb 8:5 (ὑπόδειγμα) does not mean "copy"[39] but that it means normally precisely the opposite of "copy," "likeness," or "imitation"—it is something to be copied. But even if this is so, it is hard to make it congruent with the author's use of Exod 25:40 as the proof text, and with his descriptions in 9:23–24 and 10:1.[40] And Hurst's explanation is not without problems.[41] Other scholars find Heb 8:1–6 as "redolent with Platonic terminology,"[42] and as perceiving the Levitical priesthood as a shadow, that is, in a Platonic fashion as a copy (German: *Abbild*). While some try to evade the term "copy," the preferred substitutes[43] demonstrate the problems in translating the ὑποδείγματι καὶ σκιᾷ expression of Heb 8:5 while still retaining the relation between the heavenly and the earthly temple.[44]

A Platonic view is primarily spatial, not temporal, vertical, not horizontal. In Hebrews, however, a Platonic reading has to come to terms with the expressions in the letter that reveal a somewhat different view, namely a temporal, horizontal, and historical perspective. This perspective is evident both in small catchwords as "now" (νυν/ί) in contrasting statements to what was before (8:6; 9:24; 11:16; cf. 8:13), and in direct statements that describe Jesus as priest in the heavenly temple, thus abolishing the need for the present earthly one (8:6–13; 9:11–15; 10:1–18). Observations like these have led scholars to admit that while on the one hand they acknowledge the presence of Platonic and Philonic-like terminology, the author's basic framework is a temporal and historical/eschatological. Hence more recent studies have tried to read the Epistle of Hebrews in light of Jewish apocalyptic hermeneutic and worldview,[45] while some even emphasize the epistle as an apocalyptic word of exhortation, even as "an early Christian expression of Jewish apocalyptic mysticism."[46]

We might conclude that the debate over Hebrews and the possible influence in it from a platonizing Philo is not over. In light of our taxonomy presented above about its possible relationships to the works of Philo, Heb 8:5 could probably be categorized on the scale as being of Mode D to E; that is, as referring to a precursor text in a manner

---

[39] See L. D. Hurst, "How 'Platonic' Are Heb. viii.5 and ix.23f?," *JTS* 34 (1983): 156–68, esp. 156–65; L. D. Hurst, *The Epistle to Hebrews: Its Background of Thought*, SNTSM 65 (Cambridge: Cambridge University Press, 1990), 13–17.

[40] Cf. D. T. Runia, "Ancient Philosophy and the New Testament: 'Exemplar' as Example," in *Method and Meaning: Essays on New Testament Interpretation in Honor of Harold W. Attridge*, ed. A. B. McGowan and K. H. Richards, Resources for Biblical Literature 67 (Atlanta: Society of Biblical Literature, 2011), 347–61.

[41] Hurst tries to explain the author's use of ὑπόδειγμα by arguing that 8:5a and 8:5b should not so easily be run together, "nor is it certain that the author centers his interest in Ex. 25:40 upon the 'make according to' element of the verse" (1990), 15, but that he draws upon Ezek 40–48. This is, however, problematic as Heb 8 also contains the term τύπος, a term drawn from Exod 25:40.

[42] Svendsen, *Allegory Transformed*, 159.

[43] See e.g. "shadowy copy" (Attridge, *The Epistle to the Hebrews*, 219); "a shadowy suggestion" (W. L. Lane, *Hebrews 1–8*, WBC 47A [Dallas: Word, 1998], 199, 206), and "a symbolic foreshadowing" (P. Church, *Hebrews and the Temple: Attitudes to the Temple in Second Temple Judaism and in Hebrews*, NovTSup 171 [Leiden: Brill, 2017], 405).

[44] Runia ("Ancient Philosophy," 357) suggests that the translation (in Heb 8:5) "may have been inspired by the parallels in Wisdom and in Philo, where the term *mimēma* is used."

[45] e.g. Svendsen, *Allegory Transformed*.

[46] J. A. Barnard, *The Mysticism of Hebrews: Exploring the Role of Jewish Apocalyptic Mysticism in the Epistle to the Hebrews*, WUNT 2.331 (Tübingen: Mohr Siebeck, 2012), 284.

that is less explicit than a citation, and more on the level of the presence of concepts and ideas.

2.4.3 The Gospel of John

The social and ideological background of the Gospel of John has been extensively researched, and here the works of Philo have played a significant role too. But when it comes to the quest for possible influence from Philo in the Gospel, it is the first verses of its first chapter, that is the Prologue (John 1:1–18), that have gathered the most interest. And many have narrowed the focus down even further to the Prologue's more hymnic segments: verses 1–5, 10–12b, 14, and 16.[47]

The Prologue may very well be considered as an exposition of Genesis 1, and that even in a midrashic way.[48] Our focus here, however, is on what may have influenced the expositor to use the important term Logos in his exposition; can we talk about a reception of Philo in these verses?

2.4.3.1 Three Fields of Influence?

Basically, there are primarily three fields of influence that have been studied and argued for in recent research: influence from the Old Testament's use of the Word of God, adding later Jewish speculation on the Law; influence from Wisdom traditions in both the Old Testament and other Jewish writings; and influence from Philo of Alexandria, who then again was not only influenced by the writings of Hellenistic philosophies, but also by Jewish Wisdom speculations.

According to Raymond Brown, there is no one Semitic parallel that explains completely the Prologue's use of "the Word," but taken together, several points may make its use quite intelligible. As to the *Word of the Lord* (*debar YHWH*), it had in Hebrew thought a dynamic energy and power; it could be a life-giving factor (Deut 32:46–47), and it could be described as having the power to heal (Ps 107:20). Furthermore, "we see here many of the functions ascribed to the Word in the Prologue: the OT 'word of the Lord' also came, was accepted, was empowered, and gave life. Moreover, the word of God was also described as a light for men (Ps 119:105, 130; 19:8)",[49] and it has a creative function as in the Prologue. The word of God can also be described as almost personal (Isa 40:11; Ps 147:15,18).

As to the second issue, that concerning a possible influence from Wisdom traditions, there are several instances in which Wisdom is described in ways reminding one of the Logos of John 1. The key passages here are above all Job 28; Prov 1:20–23; 8–9; Sirach 24; Baruch 3:9–4:4; Wisdom of Solomon 7–9; and 1 Enoch 42. While there seems to

---

[47] Cf. e.g. T. H. Tobin, "The Prologue of John and Hellenistic Jewish Speculation," *CBQ* 52 (1990): 252–69.

[48] Cf. P. Borgen, "The Prologue of John: An Exposition of the Old Testament," in *Philo, John and Paul: New Perspectives on Judaism and Early Christianity*, ed. P. Borgen, BJS 131 (Atlanta: Scholars Press, 1987), 75–101, who considers, however, John 1:1–18 as a unity.

[49] R. E. Brown, *The Gospel of John I*, AB 29 (Garden City, NY: Doubleday, 1966), 520–24.

be a development in the presentation of Wisdom, the cumulative value of the passages is that "there are good parallels for almost every detail of the Prologue's description of the Word."[50] Most remarkable is the way Wisdom is described as a personalized entity: "The Lord created me at the beginning of his ways, for the sake of his works. Before the present age he founded me, in the beginning. Before he made the earth and before he made the depths, ... he begets me .... When he prepared the sky, I was present with him" (Prov 8:22–24, 27 NETS). However, there are differences that make it difficult to explain the Johannine Logos on the basis of these Jewish wisdom speculations.[51] One aspect is the terminology: In Jewish Wisdom literature, the term Logos was not used as a substitute for the Hebrew *hokmâ* or the Greek *sophia*; another is the fact that the functions and attributes of the Logos in John go beyond what is found in Jewish Wisdom literature.

Proceeding then to the third issue mentioned above, we come to the role of Logos in *the works of Philo*. One viewpoint, which probably most scholars would subscribe to, is that it is almost impossible to sketch the various ways Philo uses the Logos concept as it occurs over 1,400 times in his works.[52] The question is, however, are there examples in Philo's volumes that make it possible that John 1 represents a reception of Philo's presentation of Logos? Tobin provides a list of some very close similarities in Philo and John:

> Both Philo and the hymn use *logos* as the equivalent of *wisdom* in Jewish wisdom literature. In both cases, *logos* overshadows the figure of wisdom in importance. Both Philo (*Op.* 17, 24) and the hymn (John 1:1–2) understand the *logos* as a reality which existed with God before creation. Both Philo (*Somn.* 1.228–30) and the hymn (John 1:1) use the anarthrous *theos* (God) to refer to the *logos*. Both Philo (*Conf.* 146) and the hymn (John 1:1–2) connect the *logos* with the "beginning" (*archē*) of Gen 1:1. Both Philo (*Cher.* 127) and the hymn (John 1:3) think of the *logos* as the instrument through which (*di' hou*) the universe was created. Like the hymn in the Prologue, Philo (*Somn.* 1.75; *Op.* 33; *Conf.* 60–63) associates the *logos* with light. Finally, both Philo (*Conf.* 145–46) and the hymn (John 1:12) connect the *logos* with becoming sons or children of God.[53]

Distinguishing between the early Jewish Wisdom literature of the Hebrew Bible and the writings of the Hellenistic Judaism of the diaspora, it was in this latter world that Logos played a long and increasingly important role, but also that it was in the works

---

[50] Brown, *The Gospel of John I*, 523. For a further presentation of the role of the concept of Wisdom for understanding New Testament christology, see the still valuable description of J. D. G. Dunn, *Christology in the Making: An Inquiry into the Origins of the Doctrine of the Incarnation* (London: SCM Press, 1980), 163–212.

[51] See here Tobin, "The Prologue of John," 254–55.

[52] The most comprehensive, but also probably the most systematized presentation of Logos, is still represented by H. A. Wolfson, *Philo: Foundations of Religious Philosophy in Judaism, Christianity and Islam*, vol. 1 (Cambridge, MA: Harvard University Press, 1948). For a brief, but focused presentation of Logos in the *Allegorical Commentaries*, see H. W. Attridge, "Philo and John: Two Riffs on One Logos," *SPhiloA* 17 (2005): 103–17.

[53] T. H. Tobin, "Logos," *ABD* 4:354.

of Philo that it came into full flowering.⁵⁴ But at the same time Tobin also states that while the similarities of both framework and vocabulary are remarkable, one cannot argue that the author of the Prologue had read Philo, but that "it is difficult to imagine that the two are not part of the same Hellenistic Jewish tradition of interpretation and speculation."⁵⁵

2.4.3.2 Not from Philo, but from a Common Environment?

The concept of Logos had a long and significant history in the world of Hellenistic philosophy and religion. The world of plausibility for both the wisdom speculations referred to above, and Philo's reflections on the Logos, is probably to be located in Hellenistic Jewish interpretation and speculation as carried out in the synagogal milieus in the diaspora. And the descriptions of Logos in the Prologue of John can be viewed as part of that milieu at large. While there are, admittedly, many similarities to be found between Philo's expositions of the Logos and the Prologue, the parallels are not close enough to argue that John had read Philo of Alexandria. Moreover, John's statement that the Logos had become incarnate in Jesus of Nazareth would have been unimaginable for someone like Philo.⁵⁶

Where do we then end up concerning John 1? Maybe John 1 is the closest we have in the New Testament to a reception of Philo. However, while making use of similar structures of thought, and expressing these through similar vocabulary,⁵⁷ the result is different: The Johannine concept of Logos as such, a Logos becoming "incarnated"—becoming σάρξ—is certainly not derived from Philo. Hence, we do not end up in examples of clear reception of Philo in the New Testament, but in milieus in which various ideas thrived, fused, and developed.⁵⁸ And once more, we end up at the lower end of our taxonomy; there is no clear reception of Philo in John in form of explicit or implicit quotations, nor of paraphrases or rewriting, but of echoes, allusions, and the presence of comparable ideas. And Sandmel's warning remains: Beware of parallelomania.

2.5 Conclusion

1. On the basis of location in time, there could very well have been some influence from Philo and his works in the New Testament scriptures as Philo lived from approximately 20 BCE to 50 CE, and the various works of the New Testament came into being after that time.

---

⁵⁴ Tobin, "The Prologue of John," 255–62.
⁵⁵ Tobin, "The Prologue of John," 262.
⁵⁶ Tobin, "The Prologue of John," 268.
⁵⁷ Tobin, "The Prologue of John," 268.
⁵⁸ Compare here the discussion of the "*Sitz im Leben*" of the Epistle to the Hebrews by M.-L. Hermann, *Die 'Hermeneutische Stunde' des Hebräerbriefs: Schriftauslegung in Spannungsfeldern*, Herders Biblische Studien 72 (Freiburg: Herder, 2013).

2. As Philo was traveling to both Jerusalem and Rome, and ideas travel even further, his influence could have been met in several locations.
3. We have, however, no strict evidence in either any of his works or in the New Testament that there was any direct contact between him and any New Testament author.
4. Lacking such strict evidence, we have to look into the New Testament for indirect evidence of influence from forms of various explicit quotations via paraphrase to the presence of echoes and to concepts and comparable ideas.
5. Of all the New Testament works, some letters of Paul, the Epistle of the Hebrews, and the Gospel of John are the writings most often scrutinized and suggested as revealing some influences from Philo.
6. The Epistle to the Hebrews has, for some time, been considered as the most "philonic," and this is still the case, though opinions concerning the degrees of influence vary.
7. Both the production of the works of Philo and of the New Testament had their social locations in some proximity to Jewish diaspora synagogues.
8. The impact of the synagogues and their activities can hardly be overestimated: Here the interpretations and expositions of the Jewish scriptures were central. The influence of the synagogues as spheres of interaction, and the mutual need of Jews, as well as Christians, for social differentiation and identity construction is still to be further researched. Such research may also provide a better picture of the relations of Philo to those groups interested in the messages later to be contained in the New Testament.

3

Apostolic Fathers and Early Christian Apologists

James Carleton Paget

In his pioneering volume on the reception of Philo by Christians, David Runia emphasized the need to resolve "the crucial question of the extent to which Christian writers before Clement were acquainted with Philo."[1] It is the claim of this piece, which concerns itself with early Christian use of Philo outside of the New Testament to Clement of Alexandria, the first Christian author to mention Philo as a source,[2] that the matter is not resolvable in spite of much discussion.[3]

Prima facie, it is reasonable to think that Christians would have found consultation of Philo's works beneficial. As an apologist for the Jews, Philo provided Christians with potentially helpful responses to accusations made against them, numbers of which, understandably, coincided with those made against Jews.[4] Also significant, and connected to the issue of apologetic, is the fact that Philo is primarily an exegete of the Septuagint (in fact a bold defender of its inspired character), a keen expositor of what he understands as the text's profound content, in part in the face of cultured despisers, both Jewish and non-Jewish. His allegorically oriented exegesis, marked by the use of a set of well-known philosophical categories, appropriated in the main from Plato (Philo is often categorized a Middle Platonist), but also from the Stoa and Pythagoras, would have provided Christian writers of the second century, many of whom saw the LXX as a significant factor in the exposition of their beliefs, with an array of exegetical insights and observations. Moreover, Philo's interpretation of scripture presented a vision of God, creation, and providence, which was congenial to some, though not all, of the

---

[1] D. T. Runia, *Philo in Early Christian Literature. A Survey* (Assen: Van Gorcum, 1993), 343.

[2] See Clement, *Strom.* 1.31.1, 1.72.4, 1.151.2, 2.100.3. Passages in which Clement mentions Philo explicitly are far outweighed by ones in which he does not. For a discussion of Clement's use of Philo, see Annewies van den Hoek, Chapter 4 in this volume.

[3] On this, see Runia, *Philo*, 44–60, 87–130. See also J. P. Martín, "Filón y las ideas christianas del siglo II: estado de la cuestión," *RevistB* 50 (1998): 263–94; D. T. Runia, "Philo and the Early Christian Fathers," in *The Cambridge Companion to Philo*, ed. A. Kamesar (Cambridge: Cambridge University Press, 2009), 211–13, still regards the matter as unresolved.

[4] On this, see Monique Alexandre, "Apologétique judéo-hellenistique et premières apologies chretiennes," in *Les apologistes chrétiens et la culture grecque*, ed. B. Pouderon and J. Doré, Théologie historique 105 (Paris: Beauchesne, 1998), 1–40, here discussing the relationship between Jewish and Christian apologetic more generally. See also the interesting comment of F. Knight, "Greek Apologists of the Second Century," in *Apologetics in the Roman Empire*, ed. M. J. Edwards, M. Goodman, and S. Price (Oxford: Oxford University Press, 1999), 81–104, who notes that "Athenagoras' Embassy presupposes a situation analogous to that of Philo when he pleaded on behalf of the Jews of Alexandria. Here is a distinct people with its own politeia, which deserves the same rights as other peoples" (at 103).

developing Christian movement.[5] Indeed there are grounds for saying that the concerns of extant Christian writings from the second century onwards are closer to those of Philo than extant (almost exclusively Rabbinic) Jewish material from a comparable period.[6] This is confirmed by the fact that it is Christians who collect and disseminate his works, certainly from the time of Clement of Alexandria and probably before that.

But before pursuing our investigation, it is necessary to indicate why it is that the subject of this chapter is a complicated one. First, account must be taken of our fragmentary knowledge of the writings of Christians for this period (as well as of Philo's extant works). Many of these are no longer extant.[7] We are better served for the *opera* of Philo where probably two-thirds of his corpus has been preserved.[8] Still our knowledge remains incomplete. Against such a backdrop all conclusions are provisional.

Secondly, we know little that is certain about the dissemination of Philo's works. While Josephus is the first known author to mention Philo (*A.J.* 18.259–60), he does not refer to any of his writings, and scholars continue to argue about the extent of his knowledge of these.[9] Claims, based in part upon Josephus' reference but also upon assumptions about the impact and duration of Philo's visit to Rome in the Principate of Gaius, that his works would have been available in a library there are unproven.[10] Similarly negative comments can be made about our knowledge of his dissemination among Christians before Clement. Gregory Sterling has argued that Philo's library may have become part of a Christian library, either when a single Jewish follower or community of followers became Christian.[11] Annewies van den Hoek argues along similar, but distinct lines, that we should assume transmission through the so-called catechetical school in Alexandria, mentioned by Eusebius, and associated with Pantaenus and then Clement (*Hist. eccl.* 5.10.1–4).[12] Philo's works were rescued by members of the school in the wake of the Trajanic revolt (115–17 CE), and it was there that Clement first read Philo's works.[13] But more recently, the view that Philo's treatises passed directly

---

[5] Often cited are the five "dogmata" referred to by Philo in *Opif.* 170–72, which seem to be echoed in a number of places in early Christian writings. See our discussion of Theophilus below, pp. 56–59. H. A. Wolfson, *The Philosophy of the Church Fathers: Faith, Trinity, Incarnation* (Cambridge, MA: Harvard University Press, 1956), argued that Philo's use of the allegorical method, his subordination of philosophy to scripture, and his advocacy of some scriptural presuppositions including the existence and unity of God, the creation of cosmos, and divine providence, formed the basis of patristic theology, which could be said to begin in the second century.

[6] H. Chadwick, "Philo and the Beginnings of Christian Thought," in *The Cambridge History of Later Greek and Early Medieval Philosophy*, ed. A. H. Armstrong (Cambridge: Cambridge University Press, 1967), 156.

[7] C. Markschies, *Kaiserzeitliche christliche Theologie und ihre Institutionen: Prolegomena zu einer Geschichte der antiken christlichen Theologie* (Tübingen: Mohr Siebeck, 2007), 32, notes that 85 per cent of known second-century texts are no longer available.

[8] G. E. Sterling, "The Place of Philo of Alexandria in the Study of Christian Origins," in *Philo und das Neue Testament, Wechselseitige Wahrnehmungen*, Vol. 1: *Internationales Symposium zum Corpus Judaeo-Hellenesticum*, ed. K.-W. Niebuhr and R. Deines (Tübingen: Mohr Siebeck, 2004), 21–52, esp. 22–23.

[9] For contrasting views on this matter, see G. E. Sterling, "'A Man of the Highest Repute': Did Josephus Know the Writings of Philo?," *SPhiloA* 25 (2013): 101–13; and J. E. Royse, "Did Philo Publish His Works?," *SPhiloA* 25 (2013): 74–100; and Katell Berthelot, Chapter 1 in this volume.

[10] On this, see Sterling, "Highest Repute," 112–13; and M. Niehoff, *Philo of Alexandria: An Intellectual Biography* (New Haven: Yale University Press, 2018). Eusebius, *Hist. eccl.* 2.18.8, states that Philo addressed the Senate "On the Virtues," "and his words were so much admired as to be judged worthy of a place in libraries." The claim remains unsubstantiated.

[11] G. E. Sterling, "Recherché or Representative? What Is the Relationship between Philo's Treatises and Greek-Speaking Judaism?," *SPhiloA* 11 (1999): 1–30.

[12] How old the school was remains unclear. It could have been founded by Pantaenus. See Runia, *Philo*, 132–33.

[13] A. van den Hoek, "The Catechetical School of Early Christian Alexandria and its Philonic Heritage," *HTR* 90 (1997): 59–87, at 39.

"through an unbroken chain of Jewish/'Jewish Christian'/Christian succession," has been questioned.[14] Instead it has been argued that Clement might have received his knowledge of Philo through pagan circles.[15] While knowledge of Philo's dissemination among pagans is similarly scanty,[16] his works could have been known by pagans, given that he was a prominent figure in Alexandrian society, a point Josephus seems to acknowledge; and such a proposal may serve as a partial explanation as to why he is called the Pythagorean by Clement (*Strom.* 1.72.4) rather than the Jew.[17] Whatever view is adopted, reliable evidence of the dissemination of Philo's works in the period with which this essay is concerned is exiguous.

Ignorance surrounding dissemination of Philo's works raises a third problem, namely that of situating Philo within the Judeo-Hellenistic community. For some he is a notable representative of a Jewish Hellenism, which had its origins in the translation of the LXX into Greek, and the subsequent development of a sophisticated form of exegesis, evidenced in a variety of Philo's predecessors, including Demetrius the chronographer, Aristobulus, the author of the Wisdom of Solomon, and other Jewish writers in Greek. Indeed, broad parallels between aspects of what Philo asserts in his writings and other Jewish writings from a variety of places in the Diaspora support this view.[18] Others emphasize the singularity of Philo, not least because of the relatively sparse witnesses to Jewish Hellenism beyond Egypt. This debate is important in the present context because in many instances where scholars have seen Philonic parallels in early Christian works, these are often explained by appealing to a generally disseminated Jewish Hellenism rather than to literary dependence upon Philo. It is this point that J.-P. Martín has emphasized. For him, the positing of such a generally disseminated Jewish Hellenism as an explanation for a piece of Christian writing whose best known parallels are in Philo is a fragile argument from silence.[19] Runia, in his discussion of the relationship between Philo and Theophilus of Antioch, sums up the matter: "The key here lies in the extent to which Judeo-Hellenistic apologetic and exegetical material was disseminated in the Jewish Diaspora in the period after the

---

[14] J. Otto, *Philo of Alexandria and the Construction of Jewishness in Early Christian Writings* (Oxford: Oxford University Press, 2018), 39–40.

[15] Otto, *Philo*, 39–46. Her argument against continuity of transmission from Jews to Christians emerges from (1) the possibly devastating effects of the Trajanic revolt, which renders the precise nature of the relationship of Jewish to Christian communities unclear; (2) the "haphazard nature of textual transmission in antiquity" (once copied a text fell out of the control of its author); and (3) the possibility in a strikingly mobile world in which Alexandria acted as an international hub that Clement read Philo in a city other than Alexandria, a point supported by reference to his knowledge of other Jewish writers through Alexander Polyhistor, who never resided in Alexandria. Clement himself indicates that he travelled (*Strom.* 1.1.11), increasing the chances that he read Philo in a place other than Alexandria. Otto also notes that Alexandria was a place of cultural exchange, implying that the strongly scriptural character of Philo's work would have been no impediment to pagans being interested in it.

[16] See Runia, *Philo*, 8–12; and G. Sterling, Chapter 7 in this volume.

[17] See Otto, *Philo*, 72–74, who leaves the question open as to whether Clement thought Philo a Jew. By associating him with Pythagoras, quite understandable given his exegetical method, Clement associates Philo with someone who comes near to the truth but does not arrive at it, a bit like the Jews (Otto, ibid., 90). See D. T. Runia, "Why Does Clement Call Philo 'the Pythagorean'?," *VC* 49 (1999): 1–22, who explains the term on the basis of intellectual content, but argues that Clement assumes Philo's Jewish origins.

[18] See Sterling, "Recherché," 31: "Philo's treatises are therefore not unique in their orientation and perspective: they are singular in their quantity and quality."

[19] J. P. Martín, "La presencia de Filón en el Exáemeron de Teófilo de Antioquía," *Salamaticensis* 33 (1986): 144–77, at 176: "Pero la gran dificultad consiste en la ausencia de documentación conocida."

Bar Kokhba revolt, and in the extent to which this material would have been accessible to a bishop working in Antioch. If such material was not available, then Martín's hypothesis must hold. If it did and was accessible, then the resemblances are best explained through an appeal to this missing body of Judaeo-Hellenistic thought."[20] Moreover, it should be recognized that for the second century, scholars might agree that something called Jewish Hellenism existed, but it is difficult to speak with any specificity about it because *evidence* for Jewish writings in Greek end with Josephus. If Christian writers had access to such literature, little is known about the latter, though archaeological finds support the view that Greek-speaking Jewish life in the Diaspora continued to flourish well beyond the time of Josephus.[21] Further proof may be provided by Christian writers of the second century and beyond, even if they never refer explicitly to Jewish literary sources in Greek. This is one of the conclusions to draw from Alexandre's essay, referred to in note 4 above, and one which those who eschew a parting of the ways model for the history of Jewish-Christian relations, in favor of something more fluid and blurred, would advocate. The assumption here is that interaction, exchange between those professing faith in Christ and non-Christian Jews, was much more the norm and that using terms like "Jewish" and "Christian" to describe these traditions is unduly prescriptive.

The fourth issue relates to the problem of *demonstrating* knowledge of the Philonic corpus on the part of an author. The best criterion lies with similarity of wording. But there is very little of that.[22] Martín has emphasized shared themes, stating that if the latter are found nowhere else, then we should assume Philonic influence; but this is a crude yardstick, as indicated above. Similar combinations of scriptural texts or exegetical conclusions may also be cited as evidence. Again, for such similarities to be telling, it has to be assumed that such a combination of texts or set of exegetical conclusions was only found in Philo. Moreover, account needs to be taken both of the use of intermediate sources, which know Philo, and of the vexed issue of "secondary orality," stemming from Philonic texts which had been read but became divorced from their original literary context. Into this has to be factored the question of the context and setting of relevant authors. E. R. Goodenough, for instance, emphasized the fact that Justin and Philo entertained different aims in their writing and that this should be taken into account in any comparison of the two.[23] He uses such a difference in aim and setting to support the fact that parallels indicate dependence (these are parallels in spite of difference and so the stronger for that). What is important about Goodenough's point is that it raises the problem of how to calibrate the difference between a Philonic parallel and the Christian text in which it occurs. Can such difference be explained by variant aims?

---

[20] Runia, *Philo*, 116.
[21] J. Carleton Paget, "Judaism in the Second Century," in *Jews, Christians and Jewish Christians*, ed. J. Carleton Paget (Tübingen: Mohr Siebeck, 2010), 383–425.
[22] Runia, *Philo*, 114–16.
[23] "The astonishing thing (about Justin's writing) is that in one so different in spirit and aim from Philo, so much that is recognizably philonic is yet to be found"; E. R. Goodenough, *The Theology of Justin Martyr* (Jena: Biedermann, 1923), 116–17.

And how might one go about proving that?[24] Moreover, the sources under consideration do not seem to hail from a similar social and intellectual setting to Philo, further complicating the situation. Against this background it is striking that the first Christian who explicitly mentions Philo, Clement of Alexandria, shared many of the former's assumptions, even if he is evidently using Philonic ideas to promote different positions from his source.[25] The convergence of educational background and ideological positioning make it more likely that Clement would have used Philo; and the absence of such convergence in the case of many of our extant second-century sources makes the likelihood of Philonic usage less probable.

In what follows discussion has been restricted to four Christian sources. This is partly to accommodate a more in-depth analysis; in part because the figures chosen have the best claim to Philonic influence; in part also because, in different ways, they exemplify some of the difficulties I have outlined above. This does not mean that there are no other Christian authors who could be considered; and in this respect readers are referred to Runia's more comprehensive analysis, which has, when combined with my own judgments, allowed me to make the choices I have.[26]

3.1 First Clement

This text, traditionally attributed to Clement, bishop of Rome, and dated to around the end of the first century CE, is an attempt to resolve a crisis of leadership in the Corinthian Christian community.[27] Most agree that the author betrays knowledge of facets of Greek philosophy, especially Stoicism, and have wondered how such knowledge was mediated to Clement. For some the best answer lies in assuming direct knowledge of Stoic ideas; to others it seems likely that such perspectives were conveyed to him through Jewish-Hellenistic writers, possibly Philo, or traditions associated with him.[28] The latter view gains traction if we note the Jewish atmosphere of the text, seen in the author's intense use of the Septuagint, his apparently positive attitude to temple worship, and the absence of any antipathetic comments about non-Christian Jews.[29]

---

[24] For a recent discussion along similar lines, but here invoking the idea of opposition to Philo (or to Jewish-Hellenistic traditions), see J. M. Hubbard, "Does Justin Argue with Jews? Reconsidering the Relevance of Philo," *VC* 75 (2022): 1–20.

[25] See A. van den Hoek, *Clement of Alexandria and His Use of Philo in the* Stromateis: *An Early Reshaping of a Jewish Model* (Leiden: Brill, 1988).

[26] Runia, *Philo*, 87–131. Perhaps the most significant witness I have omitted is Athenagoras. The work most reliably attributed to him is his so-called *Embassy*. He certainly shares themes in common with Philo, e.g. God's unity, God's power, God's Logos, God's providence, and God's location; but these are not sufficiently close to posit a literary relationship. The work is apologetic and engages in little exegesis, though at one point he refers to Gen 6:1–5, emphasizing the way the fallen angels succumb to flesh, something Runia points out Philo also emphasizes at *Gig.* 19–57, but he rejects evidence for direct dependence (Runia, *Philo*, 107). More importance has been attached to the work *On the Resurrection of the Dead*, though for some this is a work falsely attributed to Athenagoras. For a discussion, see Runia, *Philo*, 107–9.

[27] For introductory questions, see H. E. Lona, *Der erste Clemensbrief* (Göttingen: Vandenhoeck und Ruprecht, 1998), 42–88.

[28] J. P. Martín, "Prima Clementis: estoicismo o filonismo," *Salmanticensis* 41 (1994): 5–11, for the history of discussion. See also Lona, *Clemensbrief*, 267–74.

[29] Lona, *Clemensbrief*, 58–61.

Much of the relevant evidence focuses on chapter 20 where Clement points up the harmonious and ordered workings of the universe in support of retaining order within the community. The latter is God-given and reflected in creation.

Such exemplary use of universal order and harmony is not witnessed in Philo, but individual sentiments find parallels in the latter. For instance, one can compare 1 Clem. 20.2 to *Opif.* 33–35, where both authors describe the way in which God has separated night from day; 1 Clem. 20.3 to *Opif.* 54 and *Agr.* 51 where we find similar interest in the rhythmic movement of the planets; 20.4 to *Opif.* 43, where the fruitfulness of the earth is discussed; and 20.10 to *Somn.* 1.215, where the idea of divine liturgy appears in cosmological discussion.

Verbal parallels also exist. Martín thinks that the use together of the adjectives for spring (ἐαρινοί), summer (θερινοί), autumn (μετοπωρινοί) and winter (χειμερινοί), admittedly for Clement in relation to the seasons, and for Philo in relation to the equinoxes (spring and autumn) and the solstices (summer and winter) (1 Clem. 20.9 and *Her.* 147), is especially striking.[30] The fact that these occur in a section of Philo's *Her.* partially devoted to a discussion of the justice and equality of nature, is possibly significant, though Philo, in contrast to Clement, makes no reference to peace. Perhaps the most interesting of these verbal parallels is found in 20.10, where the reference to ever-flowing springs (ἀέναοί τε πηγαί) finds parallels in a number of places in Philo (*Post.* 150; *Plant.* 121; *Conf.* 182) as well as the metaphorical association of springs with breasts which feed mankind (*Deus* 39; *Aet.* 66; *Virt.* 129; *Somn.* 2.204). It is only, however, in *Aet.* that we have the word μαζοί, as used by Clement, and some hold this to be a quote from Critolaus, leading to the view that both authors are dependent upon a common source.[31]

Martín is right to argue that what some have attributed to Stoicism in 1 Clem. 20 is equally well attested in Philo.[32] But whether he has been able to demonstrate literary dependence is another matter. Two related points are relevant. First, Clement betrays little evidence of knowledge of the context of Philo's interpretation, in particular its strongly scriptural setting (scripture is not discussed in 1 Clem. 20). Secondly, some of the Philonic passages cited as parallels contain sentiments which would have seemed appropriate to 1 Clement but are not mentioned. So at *Opif.* 33, already cited in relation to 1 Clem. 20.1, Philo, in talking about the separation of night and day speaks of the desire on God's part "to prevent discord (στασιάζωσι) arising from perpetual clash" and "war in place of peace prevailing and setting up disorder in an ordered world" (*Opif.* 33), sentiments which Clement may have wanted to articulate explicitly if he had, for instance, known *Opif.*, not least because of the reference to *stasis*, which is such a significant subject for him.

Other parallels could be highlighted. Some of these seem too widely attested to be significant such as the reference to "deep peace" (εἰρήνη βαθεῖα) at 1 Clem. 2.2.[33] Some

---

[30] Martín, "Prima Clementis," 22.
[31] See Lona, *Clemensbrief*, 264.
[32] For the confluence of Stoic vocabulary with 1 Clement and Philo, see Martín, "Prima Clementis," 33.
[33] See J. van Unnik, "'Tiefer Friede' (1 Klemens 2.2)," *VC* 24 (1970): 261–79, for the wide attestation of the idea.

seem only partial like the reference to "the bond of God's love" (δεσμὸν τῆς ἀγάπης) at 49.2.³⁴ Some reflect continuity in vocabulary. For instance, Clement uses a verb widely attested in Philo to describe God's ordering of the universe (διακοσμέω, 1 Clem. 33.3), and associates such ordering with God's incomprehensible wisdom, here using another word attested in Philo (ἀκατάληπτος). On a number of occasions the incomprehensible character of God is associated, as Clement implies, with his ordering of the universe (*Det.* 89; *Post.* 15, 169; *Conf.* 138). Such an association of ideas is suggestive but little more than that. In this respect it is striking that these two words which occur together in 1 Clement, are not associated by Philo, making the possibility of dependence less likely.

At 1 Clem. 33.4–5, Clement expresses the view that the creation of man is the great work of God's intelligence possibly mixing vocabulary found in both Gen 1:26 and 2:7.³⁵ What is striking here is that even if the high opinion of man is exemplified in Philo (*Opif.* 69), and even language of image and "character" play a significant role in his discussion of man's creation, he almost never blends together Gen 1:26 and 2:7—for him the latter is generally the creation of the sensible man, the former the ideal man. Philo did not associate the two types of men in the manner that we find in 1 Clement, and Clement shows no hint of the kind of distinction we find in Philo.³⁶ To some such an observation is insignificant. The author of 1 Clement is not a Platonist and shows no knowledge of Platonist sentiments, particularly as these relate to distinctions between an ideal and a sensible world—he could have plundered Philonic texts for what appealed. Use of a source need not indicate submission to all aspects of its world view. All of this is true, but vague traces of knowledge of such a higher world might be expected, if Philo had been a source. In the same general area, it is striking that 1 Clement shows no interest in allegorical exegesis, an indication, when combined with the previous observation, that his intellectual milieu was different from that in which Philo's writings may have been read.³⁷

3.2 Barnabas

The Epistle of Barnabas was written between approximately 96 and 135 CE.³⁸ Many scholars have argued for an Alexandrian provenance, citing in part parallels with Philo. In contrast to the case of 1 Clement, the most compelling parallels relate to questions of scriptural interpretation, in particular to examples of allegory, though other parallels

---

[34] There are three occasions where Philo names the Logos as the "*desmos*" of God (*Plant.* 9; *Her.* 188; and *Fug.* 112). But it is unclear that Clement is describing Christ with his use of the term, and the word Logos is absent from the relevant passage.

[35] ἔπλασεν recalls Gen 2:7 via Ps 118:73a and Job 10:8a.

[36] See *Opif.* 69, but especially *Leg.* 1.31 and *Virt.* 203. See also Lona, *Clemensbrief*, 357–58. For the view that Philo does combine both texts, see T. Tobin, *The Creation of Man: Philo and the History of Interpretation* (Washington, DC: Catholic Biblical Association, 1983), 87ff.

[37] For the view that knowledge of common traditions best explains the evidence outlined above, see Lona, *Clemensbrief*, 274; also 58–61.

[38] F. Prostmeier, *Der Barnabasbrief* (Göttingen: Vandenhoeck und Ruprecht, 1999), 111–34.

also feature. One could argue that the intellectual atmospherics of Barnabas comport more closely with those of Philo than is the case with 1 Clement.

Many of the similarities which scholars highlight relate to particular details. At 5.10 Barnabas notes that Jesus had to come in the flesh because otherwise people would have been unable to look at him, just as people are not able to look at the sun, "even though it is the work of his hands and will cease to exist." At a number of places Philo talks about the impossibility of looking at the rays of the divine sun (*Fug.* 165; *Abr.* 76; *Spec.* 1.40 and 275), often in the context of knowledge of God, and indeed can speak about the sun as one of God's works (*Deus* 78). In this latter reference, interestingly, both ideas found in Barn. 5.10 appear together.[39] In Barn. 12.5–7, the author uses the fact of Moses creating an image of a serpent (Num 21:4–8), as implicitly demanding a deeper interpretation, in this case a Christological one, in which Christ is presented as the serpent who saves in contrast to Eve, who brings death. Philo also addresses the question as to why a serpent has been made by Moses as well as distinguishing between this serpent and the one which tempted Eve (*Leg.* 2.78–81; *Agr.* 95–101), admittedly in a different setting and with different interpretative details. Barnabas (Barn. 13) and Philo are the first to combine in a single interpretation Gen 25:22–25 and Gen 48:13–19, though in very different ways.[40] Some small details in Barnabas' interpretation of the two goats on the day of Atonement are possibly echoed in Philo;[41] and similar observations can be made about the interpretation of the red heifer at chapter 8.[42] We only know of Philo and Barnabas who refer to the Ten Commandments as the ten words (Barn. 15.1; *Her.* 168–70). This occurs in Barnabas' discussion of the Sabbath (Barn. 15), where other elements of his interpretation find echoes in Philo.[43] Similar echoes are seen in the interpretation of Exod 33:1 and 3 from Barn. 6.8–19, involving the association of man with the earth,[44] and the theme of a second creation (in Philo seen in Platonic terms of the intelligible man and the sensible man and in Barnabas in terms of created man and of the baptized and then eschatologically saved man).[45] Also relevant is chapter 10 where Barnabas interprets the food laws allegorically, sharing with Philo both the principle that these laws can be understood in an ethical way, and some

---

[39] "We cannot look even upon the sun's flame untempered, or unmixed, for our sight will be ... blasted by the bright flashing of its rays ... though the sun is one of God's works in the past" (*Deus* 78). See also *Abr.* 76.
[40] Compare Barn. 13.2–6 and Philo, *Leg.* 3.88–93.
[41] The extra-biblical claim that the goats should be alike (ὅμοιος) (Barn. 7.10) is partially evidenced in Philo. So at *Her.* 161, Philo describes Moses as a eulogist of equality (ἰσότητος), and in the same context describes the two goats ritual of the Day of Atonement, implying their equality. J. P. Martín, "L'interpretazione allegorica nella lettura di Barnaba nel giudaismo alessandrino," *Studi Storico-religiosi* 6 (1982): 177–78.
[42] Barnabas shares some of the extra-biblical details found in Philo, including reference to the mixing of water and ashes, the reference to a vase (here the same word, ἀγγεῖον, is used), the sprinkling with hyssop of the ashes on the people (*Spec.* 1.262). See also 1.269 where Philo states that elsewhere he has engaged in a detailed allegorical interpretation of the ritual, though this interpretation is not preserved.
[43] The seventh day is the true beginning of the birth of the world, the true beginning of perfection (*Opif.* 89; *Mos.* 1.207, 2.210). See Barn. 15.5. Also see *Spec.* 2.211 and Philo's reference to an eighth day, which is the closing of the feast.
[44] See *Leg.* 2.59; *Migr.* 2.7; *Her.* 69; *Gig.* 60. Compare also Barn. 6.12–13 and *Opif.* 69 and *Leg.* 1.31.
[45] For the distinction between the creation of the ideal man and the sensible man, see *Opif.* 134–37; *Leg.* 1.31–2.53; *Plant.* 44; *Her.* 57 (see n. above); and Wis 10:1.

specific details, in this case Philo's comments on the allegorical interpretation of the chewing of the cud and splitting of the hoof.[46]

None of the passages discussed above provide decisive evidence of Barnabas' direct knowledge of Philo. What we find are small details in common rather than developed exegetical traditions, themes rather than shared vocabulary. In some instances, one could argue that Barnabas derived his own often specifically Christian interpretations from a reading of Philo, though often this would have involved a close knowledge of his source and a striking transformation of it (e.g. in the case of the allegorization of Exod 33 in Barn. 6).[47] In addition, rarely does Barnabas show any knowledge of the Philonic context; and in the ethical sections of his epistle he never reflects Philo's anthropology, even at a simple level. It is also significant that a number of these parallels are echoed in other Judeo-Greek writings, rabbinic sources as well as some Christian ones, raising the question of common traditions.[48] The idea that Barnabas emerges from a world thick with exegetical traditions that were similar to ones witnessed in Philo but not unique to him, is especially clear in chapter 10 where the parallels with the Letter of Aristeas, in terms both of the apologetic context of the interpretation as well as the individual details, appear closer[49] than those evidenced in Philo,[50] though even in the case of the former, the level of similarity hardly indicates that Barnabas had direct knowledge of this text. At best one can say that Barnabas betrays some knowledge of Judeo-Alexandrian traditions relating to the allegorical/apologetic interpretation of the Jewish food laws,[51] which have in his or others' hands become Christianized;[52] and that this may account for the other similarities with Philo.[53]

---

[46] See n. 49 below for further discussion.

[47] Philo distinguishes between the two creations in terms of the ideal and the sensible in contrast to Barnabas' Christianized interpretation in which the Platonic overtones of Philo's anthropology have been replaced by a strongly eschatological Christian vision of "new creation." Martín argues that the latter, with its reference to the last times being as the first, is parallel to Philo, *Opif.* 82, where in explaining why man was created last, Philo announces that God wanted the beginning and the end to be united, the beginning being heaven and the end man. But the relationship between the two is somewhat labored and what Barn. writes bears much closer similarity to biblical precedents.

[48] e.g. the parallels in Barn. 7 and 8, where rabbinic and early Christian parallels to the extra-biblical details are available. See J. Carleton Paget *The Epistle of Barnabas: Outlook and Background* (Tübingen: Mohr Siebeck, 1994), 136–42.

[49] For the developed apologetic context of both Barnabas and Aristeas compare Let. Aris. 169 with Barn. 10.11d. For more detailed parallels between Barnabas and Aristeas in terms of content, see Barn. 10.4 and 10c and Let. Aris. 145–48; Barn. 10.8 and Let. Aris. 144.2, 163.2f, 165–67; Barn. 10.11d and Let. Aris. 153f (here sharing in common the verb μελετᾶν).

[50] Barnabas and Philo share an interest in the allegorical interpretation of the prohibition not to eat pork (Barn. 10.3 and Philo, *Spec.* 4.101–2), birds of prey (Barn. 10.4; Philo, *Spec.* 4.116); and animals without split hooves and who don't chew the cud (Barn. 4.11; Philo, *Spec.* 4.106–8; *Post.* 148–50; and *Agr.* 132). The first two of these interpretations have little in common (for Barnabas the pig represents those who when they are well off forget the Lord, and when they are badly off acknowledge him, while for Philo the pig represents a dangerous luxury because its meat is so fine and fat). In the case of birds of prey, Barnabas concentrates on condemning those who lawlessly plunder and Philo upon those who attack others. Barnabas and Philo share the view that chewing the cud refers to rumination of a moral kind, although this is much more developed in Philo than in Barnabas. They also refer to the splitting of the hoof in the same context as chewing the cud, but in Barnabas the interpretation is eschatological, which is not the case in Philo. Again there are no striking verbal parallels, and little evidence that Barnabas has any knowledge of Philo's extended discussion of this subject in *Spec.* 4.100–131.

[51] The exclamation at 10.11, "See how well Moses legislated!," implies a Jewish origin.

[52] Martín, "L'interpretazione allegorica," 183, does not suggest that Barn. has direct knowledge of Philo.

[53] e.g. some of the material in Barn. 15 to do with the Sabbath. From Aristoboulos onwards, it is clear that Jewish Hellenistic authors speculated about the meaning of the Sabbath.

3.3 Theophilus of Antioch

Only one work of Theophilus of Antioch survives, his apology addressed to the pagan Autolycus, though Eusebius maintains that he wrote others.[54] Those scholars who have discussed the work have often sought to emphasize its Jewish characteristics, in part inspired by the clear parallels the work shows with an array of Jewish texts both rabbinic and Jewish-Hellenistic, and in part because of the only muted presence of specifically Christian concerns, understood as Christological concerns.[55]

In consideration of the first of these observations, Philo's work has loomed large. Some have played up parallels with rabbinic works, seeing Philonic influence as secondary.[56] Others have argued that, although Judeo-Hellenistic traditions are dominant, to posit a direct Philonic influence is not justified.[57] Others have argued for direct literary dependence.[58]

One is well placed to compare Philo with Theophilus. In what appears to be one of the earliest examples of extended Christian commentary, the latter engages in an interpretation of the creation story in Gen 1–3, a set of chapters of particular interest to Philo. Like Philo he terms the creation story, as this appears in Gen 1, the Hexaemeron (2.13);[59] and introduces it, again like Philo, fulsomely: "No man can adequately set forth the whole exegesis and plan of the Hexaemeron, even if he were to have ten thousand mouths and ten thousand tongues" (2.12). He goes on, like Philo, to note the comparative inadequacies of other pagan writers who have undertaken such a task, though here he mainly reflect Philo's tone, not his expression.[60] What follows constitutes both an account of the Hexaemeron and a set of interpretative observations, some of which are stimulated by difficulties arising from the text of Genesis prompting some to see evidence of a tradition of commentary known as "questions and answers," which Philo engages in both explicitly, in his so-called *Questions and Answers in Genesis and Exodus*, and implicitly in his more extended allegorical commentaries.[61] Some also see evidence of Philonic influence in Theophilus' statement about God at 3.9, which could be said to emerge from his exegesis of the creation story, and bears a close relationship to the so-called five "dogmata" of *Opif.* 170–72.[62]

---

[54] Eusebius, *Hist. eccl.* 4.24.1 mentions a work against Hermogenes and one against Marcion (in addition to three books addressed to Autolycus, described, interestingly, as "basic" (στοιχειώδη).

[55] N. Zeegers, "Les trois cultures de Théophile d'Antioche," in *Les apologistes chrétiens et la culture grecque*, 135–76, who argues strongly the Christian character of the text.

[56] R. M. Grant, "Theophilus of Antioch to Autloycus," *HTR* 40 (1947): 237–41; Zeegers, "Trois cultures".

[57] W. R. Schoedel, "Theophilus of Antioch: Jewish Christian?," *ICS* 18 (1993): 279–97. In broad terms Schoedel reflects the position of R. M. Grant, *Greek Apologists of the Second Century* (Philadelphia: Fortress Press, 1988), 157–59.

[58] Martín, "Teófilo," 176: "Teófilo pudo haber tenido en sus manos las obras de Filón."

[59] See Philo, *Leg.* 2.12; *Decal.* 100; also *Opif.* 13.

[60] Philo, *Opif.* 4–6. For of the verbal similarities between this section of the *Opif.* and *Autol.* 2.13, see Runia, *Philo*, 115–16, noting that these are "insufficiently exact to convince a hard-nosed sceptic."

[61] See 2.19 and the Greek ζήτημα ἐν ἀνθρώποις ἀνεύρετον. Schoedel, "Theophilus," 289–90, argues that the phrase conveys the sense of a perplexing question caused by a text (Gen 1:26) not being clear about the special mode of human creation, which is then solved by Gen 2:7. Note also that Theophilus and Philo both move in systematically from literal to allegorical interpretation (see esp. 2:14, 15, 16, and 17).

[62] Runia, *Philo*, 114–15, presents the evidence, noting the relative paucity of verbal parallels.

The parallels above imply a shared religious atmosphere. This is further reflected in some of the exegetical details of Theophilus' discussion of the Hexaemeron. Both comment on the fact that heaven is made first (2.13; *Opif.* 27), that the waters are divided into equal parts (2.13; *Her.* 136), that one part is bitter, or briny and the other sweet (*Her.* 136; *Somn.* 1.17–18). Both, in what appears a non-biblical detail, note that God created two heavens, one regarded by Theophilus as visible and the other as invisible (2.13; *Opif.* 36). Both note that the decision to create seeds and plants before the stars was aimed at preventing some from attributing creation to the heavenly bodies (2.15; *Opif.* 45–46). Both comment in broadly allegorical terms on the reference to the sun and moon (2.15; *Opif.* 56–57). Both refer to the three days preceding the fourth day as "*trias*" and associate it with divine powers (2.15; *Opif.* 50, 51; *Leg.* 1.3; *QG* 4.2, 4, 8).[63] Both comment on the attribution to more individuals than God of the creation of man in Gen 1:26, implying at different points that this could be an indication of God talking to his powers, described by Theophilus as Logos and wisdom (2.18; *Opif.* 72). Both associate the Logos of God with God's engagement with the waters and with the creation of light (2.13; *Opif.* 38).

Both address the issue of Adam's work in the garden of Eden and both answer it in terms of Adam keeping of God's commandments (2.24; *Leg.* 1.53–54, 1.88–89). Lying behind this is the question why someone should need to work in paradise (see *QG* 1.14). Both agree that Adam was created mortal and immortal (2.27; *Opif.* 134–35), and comment upon the fact that Eve is made from Adam, associating it with the unity of God, if by slightly different means (compare 2.28 with *QG* 1.15). Both address the question of why God asks Adam where he is, and give answers, if slightly different, which touch on God's mercy or concern with Adam. There are smaller details in common. At 2.24 Theophilus associates Eden with luxury (see *Leg.* 1.45; *Cher.* 125; *Post.* 32; *Plant.* 38), describes Adam as a child (2.25; see *Leg.* 1.94, 3.53, 3.64), the serpent as the originator of idolatry (2.28; *QG* 1.36), and likens Noah to Deucalion and rest (2.30; *Praem.* 23; *Spec.* 3.77).

This appears like a formidable list of parallels. But is it? First, we should note that a number of these parallels, along with some additional ones, can be found in rabbinic sources.[64] These may appear in documents later in date than Philo, and the parallels may be less frequent, but the fact that, though in a different language, they converge at points with Philonic material, may point to the existence of a pool of common traditions about Gen 1–3 from which Theophilus drew. It is likely that the creation story elicited comment from an early stage in Jewish history and that such comment was widely distributed. It may have been sufficiently frequent so as to have created a word like "hexaemeron" to describe its subject (Philo in his use of the term gives no sense that he is introducing something new).

---

[63] Martín, "Teófilo," 163–64.
[64] Zeegers, "Trois cultures," 140–57. See *Autol.* 2.10, where the apparent association of the Logos with "beginning" is paralleled in Gen. Rab. 1.1; *Autol.* 2.13 where the reference to the sky being created before the earth is paralleled in Gen. Rab. 7.1; *Autol.* 2.15 where the issue of the plants being created before the luminaries is also raised in Midrash Tadshe 1, p. 88. For further discussion, see Schoedel, "Theophilus of Antioch," 280–88.

Secondly, Theophilus, despite sharing some exegetical details with Philo, almost never betrays evidence of Philo's essentially Platonic worldview. This may, of course, arise from the fact that he rejects such a worldview, cherry picking from the Alexandrian helpful material (perhaps through knowledge of Philo's *De opificio mundi* with which he has most parallels). In this context we could highlight Theophilus' comments at 2.13 on the two heavens, one visible and one invisible. Here Martín has argued the author picks up a detail which is not explicitly mentioned in the LXX, but found in Philo. Theophilus accepts Philo's basic observation, which takes the firmament as the reference to one heaven (what he terms the visible heaven at *Opif.* 36), but fails, when referring to an invisible heaven, to hint at Philo's Platonic distinction, which would see the latter as a reference to the ideal and the former to the corporeal, heaven.[65] And yet a view that claims that Theophilus actively rejects such a reading will struggle to discern signs of intentional disagreement in 2.13. Similarly, in 2.18, Theophilus combines Gen 1:26 and its claim that man was made in the image of God with a reference to him being made by God's hand, a statement not found in Genesis, but perhaps hinted at in Gen 2:7.[66] Where Philo appears sharply to differentiate between these two ideas (the creation of man in Gen 1:26 is a reference to the creation of the ideal man; Gen 2:7 to the sensible man),[67] Theophilus combines the two,[68] ignoring the Philonic distinction, without indicating that he knows about it.[69] A similar note of difference without a hint at argument with a known source is found in 2.24, where in contradistinction to Philo (*QG* 1.12–13), Theophilus holds the rivers of paradise to be real. Related to this point about the failure to hint, even by accident or by rejection, at a Platonically dualist view of the hexaemeron, one should emphasize the fact that where Theophilus does engage in what could be termed allegorical exegesis this barely ever reflects the kinds of allegorical exegesis we find in Philo.[70]

Moreover, at places where there may be grounds for seeing similar exegetical traditions, there is little verbal similarity. For instance, at 2.27 Theophilus states that man was made neither mortal nor immortal, here possibly in response to a

---

[65] Schoedel, "Theophilus," 281, cites Theophilus' failure to note the distinction between the intelligible and sensible worlds. Martín, "Teófilo," 177, reiterates the absence in Theophilus of a Platonizing dualism. Such a judgment does not affect his thesis of Philonic influence, and is partially explained by the anachronistic distinction he draws between allegorical Alexandrian and non-allegorical Antiochene exegesis.

[66] See our discussion of 1 Clem. 33.4–5 above.

[67] See *Opif.* 134–35. After quoting Gen 2:7, he writes: "By this also he shows very clearly that there is a vast difference between the man thus formed and the man who came into existence earlier after the image of God."

[68] Martín, "Teófilo," 166.

[69] For further discusión, see J. P. Martín, "La antropología de Filón y la de Teófilo de Antioquia: sus lecturas de Genesis 2–5," *Salmanticensis* 36 (1989): 23–71. It is true that Philo speaks of the man made at Gen 2:7 warmly (see *Opif.* 148; *Virt.* 203), and can on occasion appear to blend the two creations (*Opif.* 69; see also 74). But the main emphasis of his discussion lies in distinguishing the two accounts of Gen 1:26 and Gen 2:7 as at *Opif.* 134. For the complexities associated with Philo's understanding of these two passages, see B. A. Pearson, "Philo and Gnosticism," *ANRW* 2.21.1 (Berlin: de Gruyter, 1984), 295–342, esp. 323–25.

[70] For Theophilus (2.15) the sun refers to God and the moon to man, with emphasis upon the perfection, power, intelligence, and immortality of God; and the mortality of man (the moon's waning characteristic) but also his ability to be reborn, here in relation to the future resurrection. In Philo, *Opif.* 56–57, the sun stands for sovereignty (God has assigned to it the sovereignty of the day) and the moon, to whom night has been assigned, for the multitude.

Marcionite criticism of the creation story.[71] Philo comes close to making the same claim at *Opif.* 134–35, and uses the same language as Theophilus for mortal and immortal (θνητὸν καὶ ἀθάνατον). But not only is the latter's assertion founded upon an exegesis of Gen 2:7 (a passage to which Theophilus may allude at 2.18, but in a very different context—see above), but there is no hint in the Theophilan context of any of the distinctive Philonic vocabulary, e.g. the claim that man is the borderland (μεθόριον) between mortal and immortal nature, and that he is mortal according to the body and immortal according to the mind.[72] And similar points could be made in relation to other passages cited. For instance, while it is clear that Philo and Theophilus share the same conviction about why, in the hexaemeron, a number of things come into existence before the luminaries, shared vocabulary is not present.

It is true that evidence of the preservation of Judeo-Alexandrian traditions in Antioch has not yet been forthcoming,[73] but that is no reason to dismiss the possibility of their existence.[74] Martín's alternative proposal that a library containing Judeo-Alexandrian works existed in the city is equally unevidenced.[75] As already stated, the difficulty in all of this lies in the fact that we are ignorant about a range of issues, which might enable us to make firmer judgments.

My final point follows on from what has just been said. Theophilus is not afraid to quote, though the sources of those quotations have been queried—was he, for instance, using some sort of pre-existing anthology?[76] He cites a number of pagan philosophers and poets, the author of the third Sibylline Oracle (2.36) and Josephus (3.23). If he had possessed a copy of a set of Philo's works, why does he not quote him as Clement quotes him some thirty years later? Some counter this by claiming that the citation of poets and historians was normal, but not that of exegetes, as evidenced by Philo.

What emerges is evidence of common material, but the claim that Theophilus had read Philo seems less clear. When shared traditions are cited to account for the similarities, appeal is certainly being made to something unevidenced, as Martín rightly asserts. But what we in fact know of Antioch, Christian, pagan or Jewish, of the mid- to late second century could be written on the back of a postage stamp.[77] Therein lie our difficulties.

---

[71] The threat of Marcion may lie behind much of what is written about the creation story in Genesis.

[72] In fact, the problem which concerns Theophilus, namely the difficulty associated with calling man solely mortal or solely immortal, is not one that appears to afflict Philo. His claims about the immortal and mortal nature of man arise out of exegetical engagement with Gen 2:7.

[73] Martín, "Teófilo," 176.

[74] J. Schwartz, "Quelques réflexions à propos de trois catastrophes," in *Les juifs au regard de l'histoire: Mélanges en l'honneur de Bernhard Blumenkranz*, ed. G. Dahan (Paris: Picard, 1985), 21–29, esp. 26–28, suggests that in the wake of the Trajanic revolt, Jews may well have fled to Antioch, producing such works as 4 Macc., the updated Sib. Or. 5, and the probably Jewish section of the *Pseudo-Clementine Homilies*, running from 4 to 6.

[75] Martín, "Teófilo," 176, though tentatively.

[76] Zeegers, "Trois cultures," 137.

[77] Martín, "Teófilo," 178.

3.4 Justin

In the debate about Philo's influence upon the burgeoning Christian community, Justin has loomed large.[78] This is partially because he is one of the most innovative writers of this period, partially because of the emphases of his work, which make use of Philo credible—an exegetically oriented apologist with a more than passing interest in philosophy. But Justin differs from Philo in his aims. He is not principally an exegete intent upon detailed, philosophically oriented exegesis of the Pentateuch, where Plato and others become aids to a deeper understanding of those texts. The partially extant works of Justin[79] constitute defenses of the Christian group, and in particular their scripturally based convictions about Jesus.

Runia suggests that if we assume that Numenius knew Philo, this might imply that copies of his work were circulating in Syria in the second century and so available to Justin when he was resident in Palestine;[80] and as has already been seen, some have argued that Philo's works would have been available to Justin in a library at Rome, a city which Philo had visited, and which had deeply influenced his own intellectual development.[81] All of this remains conjectural.

When scholars consider the relationship between Justin and Philo, a range of subjects have been discussed. For some more general themes have been important, such as creation or ideas about God but the evidence in this respect is weak, too generalized to carry any weight.[82] Others have suggested that exegetical method betrays some evidence of dependency; but again the evidence vouchsafed is not compelling—Philo was not the only Jewish interpreter of scripture to operate by a medley of rules.[83] Connected with the subject of scripture, Justin is the first Christian to present a version of the story found in the Letter of Aristeas of the translation of the Hebrew Bible into Greek, sharing with Philo the exclusive attribution of the decision to create the translation to Ptolemy Philadelphus (other accounts include Demetrius the librarian in the decision),[84] though without mentioning any of the other distinctive, and possibly helpful details, found in Philo's account.[85]

---

[78] See discussions in Goodenough, *Justin*, esp. 139–76; W. A. Shotwell, *The Biblical Exegesis of Justin Martyr* (London: SPCK, 1965), 93–115; L. W. Barnard *Justin Martyr: His Life and Thought* (Cambridge: Cambridge University Press, 1967), 81–83, 92–97; E. Osborn, *Justin Martyr* (Tübingen: Mohr Siebeck, 1973), 95–97; D. C. Trakatellis *The Pre-Existence of Christ in the Writings of Justin Martyr* (Missoula, MT: Scholars Press, 1976), 53–92; O. Skarsaune, *The Proof from Prophecy: A Study in Justin Martyr's Proof-Text Tradition: Text-Type, Provenance, Theological Profile* (Leiden: Brill, 1987), 409–24; Runia, *Philo*, 97–104; M. Niehoff, "Justin's *Timaeus* in Light of Philo's," *SPhiloA* 28 (2016): 375–92.
[79] See Eusebius, *Hist. eccl.* 4.18.1–10, for a list of these works.
[80] Runia, *Philo*, 97.
[81] Niehoff, "*Timaeus*."
[82] Niehoff, "*Timaeus*."
[83] When Justin characterizes Jewish interpretation, he presents it as regressively literalist (see *Dial.* 112–13). But one should assume that such a characterization was polemical and contrary to what Justin knew was the case.
[84] See Justin, *1 Apol.* 31.2–4; Philo, *Mos.* 2.28–33.
[85] See Niehoff, "Timaeus," 376. Most helpful to Justin would have been Philo's assertion, which is additional to anything in the Letter of Aristeas, that the individual translations of the seventy-two agreed exactly with each other, and that the rendition from Hebrew into Greek was perfect (*Mos.* 2.37–40—and so, rendering the LXX much more than a translation), not least because he knew that there were Jews who questioned the authority of

A subject which has attracted special attention is the Logos. Philo and Justin are respectively the first extant Jewish and Christian thinkers to speak at some length about the latter. Their reasons for doing so differ—some see Philo as utilizing the Logos as a means to overcome his developed view of the transcendence of God (*Decal.* 105).[86] For Justin the Logos is principally useful as a means of exploring the subject of Christ's identity and his relationship with God; and as a means of appropriating aspects of Greek culture for the Christians.[87] But whatever the motivation for their discussion, Philo and Justin agree on a number of the functions they attribute to the Logos, not least in creation (*Opif.* 24 and 139; *Spec.* 1.81; *Cher.* 36),[88] in their understanding of the identity of the Logos—as God's firstborn and the oldest of his creatures (*Leg.* 3.175; *Conf.* 147), and the names they give the Logos (*Conf.* 146; *Dial.* 61.2),[89] as well as their view of the Logos' relationship to human kind, as the reason in which all men partake (*Opif.* 139; *Deus* 134–35) (though in the case of Justin in which Christ participated most fully 2 *Apol.* 10 and 13). In this respect both have an understanding of the *logos spermatikos* (*Her.* 119; 2 *Apol.* 10), though this is more developed in Justin than Philo where it has an appropriative role in which Greek philosophical culture in particular becomes part of Christian history through identification of the Logos with Christ. Both also present the Logos as another or a second God (*QG* 2.62; *Leg.* 2.86), apparently, though this is disputed in the case of Philo, attributing a hypostatic quality to the Logos.[90] Some have seen this aspect as more emphatic in the case of Justin,[91] who spends a significant section of his *Dialogue* emphasizing the distinctive aspect of the Logos, conceived of as Christ, seeing this not simply in name but in number,[92] a point which comes out in his interpretation of a series of theophanies in the Bible.[93] In this context some have seen the reference in *Dial.* 128, which speaks of the Logos (and other named entities) as "indivisible and inseparable from the Father, just as they say that the light of the sun on earth is indivisible and inseparable from the sun in the heavens […], a power which he can choose to spring forth and return to himself … ," as a refutation of Philo's understanding of the Logos as absolutely a part of the divine identity (a form of modalism), though others see such a description as non-Philonic because they reject a modalist view of Philo's Logos.[94]

---

the LXX (see *Dial.* 68). Most of Justin's distinctive details (the attribution of the decision to translate to Herod the Great; the introduction of two embassies on the part of the Egyptian king; and the claim that it was the prophecies, not just the Pentateuch, which were translated, are Christian) cannot be attributed to Philo.

[86] See R. Williamson, *Jews in the Hellenistic World: Philo* (Cambridge: Cambridge University Press, 1989), 105–6; and D. T. Runia, *Philo of Alexandria and the* Timaeus *of Plato* (Leiden: Brill, 1986), 449–50.

[87] See Barnard, *Justin Martyr*, 87.

[88] Philo is clear that Logos is the *kosmos noetos*, that is, the ideal plan on which the universe is based (*Opif.* 19 and 36). This idea is not found in Justin.

[89] At *Conf.* 146 Philo refers to the Logos as the Son of God, first born, the ruler of the angels. "And many names are his, for he is called 'The Beginning,' and the name of God, and his word and the man after his image."

[90] See Williamson, *Philo*, 107–8.

[91] Barnard, *Justin Martyr*.

[92] See *Dial.* 56.11: "He is distinct from him who made all things, numerically (ἐν ἀριθμῷ, I mean, but not in will (ἐν γνώμῃ)."

[93] On these, see below.

[94] See Barnard, *Justin Martyr*, 89, though he rejects the idea that Justin is directly opposing Philo here. See also Skarsaune, *Proof from Prophecy*, 422–23, arguing that some of what is said in *Dial.* 128.2 comes close to statements

But however these differences are assessed, Philo provides the closest parallels to Justin on the Logos. What is lacking, however, is evidence of sufficiently distinctive conceptual or verbal parallels to make dependence likely. In the latter respect it is striking that Philo customarily refers to the Logos as πρωτόγονος, where Justin prefers πρωτότοκος,[95] never once using the former term to describe the Logos, a small but possibly telling detail.[96] Against this background, common traditions have been invoked to account for the similarities already cited.[97] Certainly it is difficult to read Philo's scattered discussions of the Logos without sensing it is a subject whose existence his audience assumes.[98]

In this context a series of Old Testament 'theophanic' passages to which Justin gives a Christological interpretation[99] are thought to reveal significant parallels to exegesis of the same passages in Philo.[100]

It is not possible here to discuss in detail the observations in support of this position. A few comments will suffice. First, Oskar Skarsaune's view that Justin's section on the theophanies only shows a "distant" relationship to what we read in Philo, "operative in general modes of argument rather than in concrete exegesis of texts," is broadly true. It is true that we almost never in this context witness similar combinations of texts,[101] or similar exegetical conclusions.[102] It is also the case that those who assume a direct knowledge on the part of Justin of Philo's work assume a detailed knowledge of the latter, which is not witnessed elsewhere.[103] Sometimes Philo's arguments are contradicted by Justin;[104] but it cannot be shown that Justin is consciously contradicting

---

in Philo but the idea of the *dunamis* being sent out from the Father and then drawn into him has no analogue in Philo. See most recently Hubbard, "Justin".

[95] See *Dial.* 62.4, 138.2

[96] For references to the Logos as πρωτόγονος, see *Agr.* 51; *Conf.* 63, 146; *Somn.* 1.215. Justin uses the term at *1 Apol.* 58.3, here describing Christ but not the Logos. Philo uses πρωτότοκος but it is never developed in relation to Logos (though see *Sacr.* 118 and 126). Goodenough's view (*Justin*, 147–55) that Justin's description of the Logos as πρωτότοκος was influenced by Philo seems unwarranted. It is more likely that Justin's source was Col 1:15 or Rom 8:29.

[97] Hubbard, "Justin," invokes the possibility of Justin's knowledge of common Jewish Hellenistic traditions here in the context of a discussion of the extent to which Justin betrays knowledge of Jewish sources in his *Dialogue*.

[98] "… part of a stream of tradition" (Chadwick, "Philo," 144), though he states that Philo's Logos is an "essential clue to the Christian development" (145).

[99] See especially *Dial.* 56–57 (Gen. 18 A); *Dial.* 58 (various texts from Gen 31–35 dealing with Jacob's dream); *Dial.* 5–60 (Exod 3:2–3, the burning bush).

[100] See especially Trakatellis, *Pre-Existence*, 53–92.

[101] For Justin a key to his interpretation of Gen 18 at *Dial.* 56 lies in Gen 19:24. The claim that such a combination occurs at Philo, *Somn.* 1.85 is not true. There Gen 19:24 is not the focus of Philo's exegesis and the Logos is not associated with the third man of Gen 18. See Skarsaune, *Proof from Prophecy*, 412.

[102] In the interpretation of Gen 18, Justin assumes that he is interpreting the text literally. Philo, at *Abr.* 107–41, assumes that at the literal level the reference is to three angels and it is only in the allegorical interpretation that he differentiates between the three in an account of the soul's vision of God, here assuming a vision of God and his two *dunameis*. Similarly, it is difficult to demonstrate that Philo is the source for Justin's elaborate interpretation of the vision of Jacob at Gen 28:11. For further allegorical interpretation of the passage, see Philo, *Sacr.* 59 and *Mut.* 15.

[103] Note Trakatellis, *Pre-Existence*, 73–80, where he seeks to show that Philo assumes, like Justin, that the vision of the burning bush in Exod 3 is one of the Logos, through a combination of passages (*Mos.* 1.65–70 with *Spec.* 1.81; *Conf.* 97 and *Somn.* 1.238). Here it is assumed that Justin knew Philo sufficiently well to make the combination and the deduction about the Logos. In fact, in Philo's interpretation of the Exodus passage, it seems clear that he thinks that God makes an appearance with the angel.

[104] Compare *Dial.* 58 with *Somn.* 1.68–74. The conclusions of Philo seem distinct from those of Justin.

Philo's views, though recently the claim has been made that Justin's striking failure to use the word 'Logos' in his interpretation of these theophanies in *Dialogue* (in contradistinction to what he does in *1 Apol.* 63), could be construed as arising out of opposition to Philo's own sustained Logos-orientated interpretation of the same passages, not least because Justin is strongly opposed Philo's understanding of the Logos in these passages.[105] Whatever might be the case, Philo witnesses to a discussion of a series of texts (Gen 18, 28–35; Exod 3.2–3) relating to theophanies in which the question of the relationship of God to the theophany is a subject of debate and where there are occasional coincidences between his own conclusions and those of Justin, some of which involve reference to the Logos, though Justin omits to mention the term.[106] While it is true that Justin's reading of these texts can be explained on the basis of his scriptural knowledge, the broad similarities with Philo show that Justin may have been drawing upon pre-existing discussion among Jews, discussion of which he shows some knowledge (see *Dial.* 59[107] and possibly 128,[108] for instance).[109] And yet the level of similarity between the two is not enough to support the idea that Justin knew Philo.[110]

Justin shares an interest in other Old Testament passages with Philo.[111] But again it is difficult to prove dependence. One thinks of Justin's discussion of Gen 1:26 and 3:22 at *Dial.* 62.1–3. Justin's citation is motivated by the binitarianism noted above. A similar combination of passages is found in Philo, *Conf.* 169–82. Like Justin, Philo accepts that "us" in both passages refers to other "powers" as he terms them, but his discussion is motivated by a desire to deal with a difficulty inherent in the reference to "us," and while exploring the nature of the powers, as in *Opif.* 72–75, he makes use of the reference to exculpate God of any responsibility for the sinful side of man's nature. Again the parallels with Justin are too general to be deemed significant.[112] Other parallels are also unconvincing.[113] Similarly striking is the absence of any evidence of Philonic allegorical exegesis of the Torah, even though Justin engages in such interpretation (see *Dial.* 40). Surely knowledge of Philo, allied to a one-sided opposition to literal readings of certain legal texts, would have been helpful to Justin?

---

[105] Hubbard, "Justin," citing the way in which Philo subordinates the vision of the Logos to the vision of God. Hubbard does not, however, argue that this is proof of Justin's knowledge of Philo.

[106] So Philo interprets that theophany at Pniel (Gen 32:22–31) in a similar way to Justin, assuming the angel to be the Logos, also called God's servant (see *Somn.* 1.129), a description of the Logos found in Justin (*Dial.* 57.3, 58.3) and in Philo (*Deus* 57; *Mut.* 87).

[107] *Dial.* 59: A Jew would say that both an angel and God appeared to Moses.

[108] See n. 93 above.

[109] "The best we can do is to say that it seems likely that Justin is responding to traditions like those attested to in Philo" (Hubbard, "Justin," 20).

[110] For the variety of ways in which the evidence could be interpreted, see Runia, *Philo*, 104.

[111] A list and discussion of these is found in Shotwell, *Justin*, 93–115.

[112] Justin refers in this context to a number of Jewish opinions on the subject, some associated with Jewish teachers (here God is seen as addressing himself, or talking to the elements), or a Jewish "hairesis," in which God is seen as addressing angels. None of these explanations comport with anything we find in Philo, even if Philo assumes that God is referring to powers of a lesser kind which engage in the creation of man. For relevant rabbinic and other passages, see P. Bobichon, *Dialogue avec Tryphon*, Vol. II: *Notes de la traduction, appendices, indices* (Fribourg: Academic Press, 2003), 948–52.

[113] Compare the interpretation of Gen 9:3 in *Dial.* 20.2 and *QG* 2.58. Philo anticipates Justin's interpretation of this line to mean that just as all herbs can be eaten, so can all meat, but rejects that interpretation on a number of grounds, ending up with an allegorical interpretation. None of what he says bears any relationship to Justin's discussion.

3.5 Conclusion

I have attempted to show that the matter of Christian usage of Philo before Clement of Alexandria cannot be resolved. It is, of course, reasonable to assume that Philo's works would have been widely known among Christians from an early stage. Insofar as we know, it is a Christian who first cites his work explicitly; and it contained much that was amenable to the growing community of Christ worshippers, particularly converts from the higher intellectual echelons of society. An early history of Christian reception is believable. But such a history cannot be demonstrated. What we have instead is evidence of Philo-like traditions, ranging from the exegetical to the broadly conceptual/theological (though, interestingly, not the straightforwardly apologetic),[114] but lacking sufficiently strong verbal parallels to lead to an assertion of direct dependence. The tendency in the face of such evidence has been to claim that Christians had access to a body of Judeo-Hellenistic traditions of which Philo was a representative, if a distinctive one, though some have appealed to direct engagement with pagan philosophy or scripture as a better explanation. The former thesis can appear vague in the face of our ignorance of Hellenistic Judaism outside of Philo and a few other authors, and especially of the Judeo-Greek tradition after Josephus. But such a tradition existed. We could imagine that Theophilus had access to some Philonic works, possibly *Opif.* and some of the *Questions and Answers* series, and he may have cherry-picked from these, managing not to copy Philo word for word, or use distinctive Philonic vocabulary, and introducing a different meaning into his source. But proving this is impossible. Contact between Jews and Christians may have been considerable in this period and distinctions between those communities may have been much less marked than a writer like Justin implies. In such circumstances, which could be indicated by Theophilus, exchange of varieties of material would have been frequent, if now untraceable.

This chapter, then, has its principal value in indicating continuities between early Christian writings and Jewish Hellenism rather than proving the literary dependence of the former on Philo.[115] Belief that this investigation would elucidate the means by which the Christian Clement happened upon the Philonic corpus has been shown to be empty, though many continue to assume a history of Christian transmission as the best explanation for Clement's knowledge of Philo. However, against this "agnostic" background, Clement's claim that Philo was a Pythagorean might imply that his "Christianization" began with Clement, rather than the latter reflecting a possibly lengthy pre-history.

---

[114] As far as I know, no one claims that second-century Christians knew *Prov.*, *Flacc.*, *Legat.*, etc.
[115] See Runia, *Philo*, 340: "But even if we were to conclude that no direct Philonic influence can be admitted, there still remain many examples of similarity of thought that demand explanation. It is important to realize that Philo has his *Sitz im Leben* in Hellenistic Judaism, which in its totality was much broader than Philo and even Alexandrian Judaism."

4
Clement of Alexandria

Annewies van den Hoek

The early Christian philosophers Clement and Origen were well acquainted with the works of their fellow Alexandrian writer Philo. Not only did they quote their Jewish predecessor by name, but they also used his words on numerous other occasions with little or no acknowledgment. The Christian authors benefited from Philo's biblical knowledge and his allegorical interpretations and followed in his philosophical tracks. Clement's link with Philo and other Jewish-Hellenistic or Jewish-Christian sources was primarily a literary one, and there is no evidence that he was in direct contact with an actual Jewish community. The few fragments of the works of predecessors who worked in the "Alexandrian tradition," such as of Basilides, Valentinus, and Heracleon, show that they too had a primarily Greek intellectual training, but their writings are too fragmentary to reveal a connection with Philo. These writers and others whose works have been lost or were never written, such as the legendary Pantaenus, may have functioned as a link between Philo and the later Christian Alexandrian tradition, but the nature and extent of this transmission remain speculative.[1]

Comparing two authors is always a difficult task, often because of the different nature of their subject matter and the pressing questions of their times. Unlike Clement, Philo by and large deals with the Pentateuch: the *Quaestiones* contain short explanations of verses from the books of Genesis and Exodus. In the Allegorical Commentary the author inches through parts of Genesis verse by verse with lengthy elaborations, and in the Exposition of the Law he handles his elucidations more thematically. It has been argued that the structure of these works may reflect an environment of instruction that would have taken place on various levels and was meant for different audiences, ranging from groups of informed insiders well exercised in biblical hermeneutics to a broader audience of people on the outside.[2] The Jewish community in Philo's days

---

[1] D. T. Runia, *Philo in Early Christian Literature: A Survey* (Assen: Van Gorcum, 1993); D. T. Runia, *Philo and the Church Fathers: A Collection of Papers*, VCSup 32 (Leiden: Brill, 1995); A. van den Hoek, *Clement of Alexandria and His Use of Philo in the Stromateis: An Early Christian Reshaping of a Jewish Model* (Leiden: Brill, 1988); A. van den Hoek, "How Alexandrian Was Clement of Alexandria? Reflections on Clement and His Alexandrian Background," *HeyJ* 31 (1990): 179–94; A. van den Hoek, "Origen and the Intellectual Heritage of Alexandria: Continuity or Disjunction?," in *Origeniana Quinta*, ed. R. J. Daly (Peeters: Leuven, 1992), 40–50; A. van den Hoek, "Techniques of Quotation in Clement of Alexandria: A View of Ancient Literary Techniques," *VC* 50 (1996): 223–43; A. van den Hoek, "The Catechetical School of Early Christian Alexandria and Its Philonic Heritage," *HTR* 90 (1997): 59–87. Since this contribution was written in 2018, it was impossible to take into consideration the recent publication of A. Le Boulluec, "Clément d'Alexandrie lecteur de Philon," in *Les études philoniennes: regards sur cinquante années de recherche (1967–2017)*, ed. S. Morlet and O. Munnich, SPhA 13 (Leiden: Brill, 2021), 422–40.

[2] J. R. Royse, "The Works of Philo," in *The Cambridge Companion to Philo*, ed. A. Kamesar (Cambridge: Cambridge University Press, 2009), 32–64.

was relatively large and autonomous with an affinity for Greek or Hellenistic culture. After the relative tranquility of the previous period of Ptolemaic rule, however, the Roman colonization of Egypt had brought periods of serious disruption for the community, with ethnic tensions between Greeks and Jews and anti-Jewish riots. At one point, Philo was called away from his customary intellectual activities to head a mission to the imperial court in Rome in the hope of righting the wrongs done to the Jews in Alexandria.[3]

Unlike Philo and Origen, Clement, who flourished a hundred and fifty years after Philo's death, was not a native of Alexandria. Before his arrival there, he had traveled throughout the Eastern Mediterranean on an intellectual quest for mentors, but the only teacher whom he mentions by name is Pantaenus (*Strom.* 1.11.2). According to Eusebius, Pantaenus headed a school of sacred learning in Alexandria, and Clement was his successor (*Hist. eccl.* 5.10, 6.6, 6.13–14). Clement left Alexandria in 202/203, perhaps to avoid persecutions, and he may have gone to Palestine (as Pierre Nautin argues) or to Cappadocia (as tradition has it) (*Hist. eccl.* 6.14.8).[4] The length of his time in Alexandria is not precisely known, but Clement wrote a substantial part of his works there: the *Protrepticus*, the *Paedagogus*, and most of the *Stromateis*. André Méhat devised a chronology of Clement's life based on information from his works; internal cross references helped to establish a chronological order, all of which is tentative: *Protrepticus* (c.195); *Paedagogus* (c.197); *Stromateis* 1 (c.198); *Stromateis* 2–5 (199–201); *Stromateis* 6–7 (203); the last parts of the *Stromateis* were presumably written after Clement's departure from Alexandria.[5] The *Protrepticus* is an exhortation to non-Christians to convert to Christianity, which Clement characterizes as the only true philosophy. The work is apologetic, denouncing Greek religion and mythology, and arguing that the Jewish scriptures are older (and thus more venerable) than the philosophy of Plato. The *Paedagogus* is a tripartite work in which Christians (recently or soon to be baptized) are introduced to various theological and ethical questions. A first book provides a theoretical perspective while two others focus on practical matters of daily life: eating, drinking, dress codes, hairstyles, and so on. The *Stromateis*, intended for an educated audience, contains a series of theological treatises and is filled with quotations from both Greek literature and Jewish and Christian traditions. The books are loosely composed, exploring the relationships between Christian philosophy and Greek learning as well as between faith and knowledge. Some deal with hermeneutical problems and the use of symbolic language, while others discuss moral issues connected with marriage and martyrdom. All-pervading is the idea that the faithful should pursue perfection and live a restrained lifestyle.[6]

---

[3] See Philo's "historical" treatises *In Flaccum* and its sequel *Legatio ad Gaium*; and E. M. Smallwood, *Philonis Alexandrini Legatio ad Gaium: Edited with an Introduction, Translation, and Commentary* (Leiden: Brill, 1961); P. W. van der Horst, *Philo's Flaccus: The First Pogrom: Introduction, Translation, and Commentary*, PACS 2 (Leiden: Brill, 2003).

[4] P. Nautin, *Lettres et écrivains chrétiens des IIe et IIIe siècles* (Paris: Cerf, 1961), 18, 101.

[5] A. Méhat, *Étude sur les "Stromates" de Clément d'Alexandrie* (Paris: Seuil, 1966), 54.

[6] Major editions of Clement's works by Stählin-Früchtel-Treu: GCS *Clemens Alexandrinus* I–IV, ²1970, ³1972, ⁴1985, ²1980 (index); by various editors in the French series Sources Chrétiennes: SC 30 (1951), 38 (1954), 278–79 (1981), 428 (1997), 446 (1999), 463 (2001).

Clement shared with his Jewish predecessor great intellectual prowess and a natural aptitude for *paideia*. He indicated himself that a division existed between beginning and more advanced students, just as there was later for Origen, who put the beginners in the hands of a "teaching assistant" and kept the advanced students for himself.[7] The allegories that Clement took over from Philo relate to stories of the Pentateuch, such as Hagar and Sarah or the life of Moses. In addition, Clement's treatment of anthropomorphic expressions of God, knowledge and wisdom, ascent and contemplation and his allegorizing of biblical scenes in terms of virtuous life often run parallel to Philo's handling of similar themes. Clement, however, reworks the material in various ways and for new purposes.

Modern scholarship has, at times, been selective and unbalanced. Some scholars have concluded that Philo and Clement were related primarily because of their speculation about the Logos, while others maintained that the two could be compared in any other aspect *except* for their treatment of the Logos.[8] To avoid such contradictory interpretations and assess Philo's influence on Clement more precisely, the present author attempted to define the actual points of comparison by making an inventory of possible derived passages. In addition, the significance of this influence was addressed; did references from one to the other author merely function as rhetorical devices, or did they reach farther into the core of the recipient's thinking? The context from which the passages originated was also of significance for understanding the relationship, being almost as important as the references themselves. Decades of (mostly) German scholarship helped with the inventory (see n. 6 above), but often their net was cumulatively cast too wide, with too many variables, particularly when common sources or general philosophical ideas were involved.

4.1 Methods and Techniques

As indicated above, a first step was made to construct an annotated database of Philonic passages in Clement's *Stromateis* that was both comprehensive and verifiable, a kind of *catalogue raisoné*.[9] An as yet unpublished study using the same methodology examines earlier works of Clement: the *Protrepticus* and *Paedagogus*.[10] With a large corpus of writing like that of Philo, these inventories will undoubtedly remain incomplete, and it is inevitable that new discoveries lie ahead through specialized and detailed studies or through chance finds. In addition, internet tools such as the *TLG* are facilitating research considerably.

For analysis of the inventories, categories were devised to provide a system that was not too complex and offered a way to classify and tabulate the relationships between

---

[7] For Clement, see *Strom.* 1.2.2, 1.9.1, 1.13.2; for Origen, see Eusebius, *Hist. eccl.* 6.15.1.
[8] See van den Hoek, *Clement of Alexandria*, 8.
[9] Van den Hoek, *Clement of Alexandria*, 19–22.
[10] A. van den Hoek, "Clement of Alexandria and His Use of Philo in the *Protrepticus* and *Paedagogue*," SPhiloA 36 (2024): forthcoming.

the two authors, a classification that ranged from literal to less literal. For the tabulation, four alphabetic indicators were chosen: A stands for literal, B less literal, C perhaps a common source, and D no relationship—or expressed in terms of dependency: A is certain, B probable, C not provable, and D no dependence at all. It should be noted that Clement often quotes his sources in a distinct pattern that appears not only in borrowings from Philo but also in biblical or other material, such as the *First Letter of Clement to the Corinthians*, quoted in the fourth book of the *Stromateis* (4.105–19). In such cases the borrowings stay in the sequence in which they occur in their original source. A clear example of this technique of sequential borrowing can be observed in *Strom.* 2.78–100 where Clement quotes extensively from Philo's *De virtutibus* and in which he gives a kind of "Reader's Digest" version of his source. In some sequences, a peculiar phenomenon occurs. Clement did not always start from the earliest point within the source he was using; he would begin with a reminiscence and then leap back to the beginning of his source and restart with quotations in sequence, selecting a few lines from each column until he had run through the whole scroll. The practice could be explained in a visual way; the author first cited from memory and then looked for the specific text. Leafing through the manuscript, or rather, unrolling the scroll, he might have become more and more interested in it and read it through completely. This method can be observed on multiple occasions. In one case the process seemed to have been reversed; instead of rolling the scroll forward, from beginning to end, Clement rolled it backwards![11] It is quite possible that while reading through a manuscript initially he would have taken notes or would have had them taken for use in his final text.

The sequences also tend to have some inner rationale; they often start out with relatively literal quotations and subsequently decline to a less literal and more abbreviated format. Without exception, all borrowings are heavily abbreviated and condensed, which again indicates the use of notes. In addition to Philo, Clement tends to draw on other authors as well, such as Clement of Rome, Barnabas, and Hermas, for their quotations from the LXX. His technique is to focus not only on a biblical passage but also to include phrases of the author he is consulting as a kind of wrapping material, so that some of their words remain attached to the biblical quotation. This is also how the source can be recognized; the shreds of alien wrapping supplied by Philo, Clement of Rome, Hermas, or Barnabas make it clear that the LXX was not consulted directly.[12] Sometimes, however, when a quotation within a quotation occurs, Clement extends the biblical component from his own memory; the biblical passage becomes longer than it had been in his intermediary source.

When one compares a truncated chunk of borrowing to the text of Clement's source, as can be done with the treatises of Philo or the *Letter of Clement to the Corinthians*, it is often striking how abruptly the material is presented. Abbreviations, discontinuities, and modifications can give Clement's sentences a strange twist or an illogical turn.

---

[11] Clement, *Strom.* 2.5.3–2.6.3 compared to Philo, *Post.* 5–18; van den Hoek, *Clement of Alexandria*, 150–51.
[12] For Philo, see van den Hoek, *Clement of Alexandria*, 152. For Clement of Rome, see van den Hoek, *Clément d'Alexandrie, Les Stromates, Stromates IV: Introduction, texte critique et notes*, trans. C. Mondésert, SC 463 (Paris: Cerf, 2001), 230–31 n. 1.

Repeatedly, confusion and disorder are created; words are altered in strange ways, and sentences are chopped into cryptic fragments. The development of Clement's thought at times would be incomprehensible if the original text was not at hand.

Despite his cut-and-paste technique, illogical insertions, and abrupt transitions, Clement is also capable of clever and ingenious inventions. At times, he subtly turns the words of his source to serve his own purposes. Thus, material is transformed by conversion and rearrangement. An impressive ability to vary and juggle is persistently manifest. Clement makes use of another technique: that of addressing himself to his source. He sets up an implied dialogue that makes it clear that he questions his model and uses it critically. This dialogue may be created by the addition of a conjunction or an adverb that turns the borrowed material into a hypothesis rather than an assertion. Clement may also frame quotations in interrogative sentences. All these additions, have, of course, a considerable effect on the meaning and intention of the borrowed words.

Another distinctive technique is the process of accumulation. This process, which is characteristic of Clement's working method in general, occurs particularly in his quotations. Accumulation is often a product of his associative way of thinking; one word, as it were, evokes another without the support of a logical connection; various layers of imaginative thought are piled on each other. The technique is especially common in the construction of allegories. Schematically described, Clement departs from a biblical starting point; he introduces a first layer of allegories, derived from one source, and then follows with more interpretations taken from other sources or that he invents himself. He usually closes with a distinctly Christian allegory. At other times the development of a theme and not an allegory is involved. He seems to be working toward a biblical text, which he cites at the end, and he chooses his quotations from Greek authors in the light of the biblical text.

4.2 Philo's Words in Clement's Works

4.2.1 *Protrepticus* and *Paedagogus*

In the *Protrepticus* nine passages could be identified as derived from Philo: three with certainty and six with probability.[13] The *Paedagogus* reveals seven passages, five in the first, two in the second, and none in the third book–only one is a clear quotation (A), the others are probable references (B).[14] It is notable that most parallels occur in the first book of the *Paedagogus* but taper off afterwards with none in the third book. Of these sixteen passages in total, thirteen were connected to biblical texts (81 per cent).

---

[13] In this overview, only the most significant passages are listed, deserving A or B: *Protr.* 5.1–2, 22.3, 25.1, 67.2, 69.1–2, 93.1–2, 94.3, 109.2, 111.1. For the *Protrepticus*, see further J. C. M. van Winden, "Quotations from Philo in Clement of Alexandria's *Protrepticus*," *VC* 32 (1978): 313–18; A. Dinan, "Another Citation of Philo in Clement of Alexandria's *Protrepticus* (10, 93, 1–2)," *VC* 64 (2010): 435–44.

[14] Clement, *Paed.* 1.5.1–2, 21.3–4, 57.1–4, 71.1–2, 77.2; *Paed.* 2.75.1, 92.1.

The reason for seeing Philonic dependency in Clement's use of a biblical text alone was sometimes determined by the fact that Clement was the first and only author of his time to quote this text, which was also used by Philo; if there were additional indicators, such as common variants with the text of the LXX or common interpretations, the argument in favor of dependency would be reinforced. In general, Clement quoted the biblical passages and surrounding material from Philo for a variety of reasons, comparable to the way he operated in the later *Stromateis*; the borrowings range from allegorical interpretations and etymologies to discussions about ethical behavior, goodness and justice, repentance, and salvation, to knowledge of the truth and the designation or the perception of God.

Clement's borrowings in these early works tend to be short and relatively sporadic; the extensive or sustained sequences that later occur in the *Stromateis* are missing, but they are sometimes anticipated, mostly as snippets of phrases cited from memory. The material comes from well-known etymologies connected with names of patriarchs and matriarchs, such as Jacob/Israel and Rebecca. There are also allegorical interpretations, such as the serpent from the Genesis story interpreted not only as evil but also as desire or passion. Although the conjunction between "serpent" (ὄφις) and "desire" (ἡδονή) is a true and frequent Philonic alignment, it is rare in Clement, who shows the combination in just one passage, *Protr.* 111.1, and more generally in *Strom.* 4.100.3. Philo also can speak about a "serpent-like desire" (*Leg.* 2.105: ὀφιώδης ἡδονή) or its contrast "the serpent-fighting judgment" (*Leg.* 3.61: τὴν ὀφιομάχον οὖν γνώμην). Words like "serpent-like desire" did not find much following until centuries later.[15]

As mentioned above, most of the borrowings in the early works (81 per cent) are connected to biblical texts, though some of them are rather indirect. An example is the designation of the personal God as "the one who truly exists" (ὁ ὄντως ὤν, cf. Exod 3:14), which is also explained by Clement in the more neutral terms of the Platonic tradition as "that which is" or "the divine" (τὸ ὄν, τὸ θεῖον). The combination of these elements has a Philonic flavor though it is not always possible to indicate exactly where the correspondence lies. An interesting example is the relationship of *Paed.* 1.71.1–2 to Philo's *Leg.* 2.3:[16] in his passage, Clement discusses the goodness and justice of God and touches on divine transcendence. He includes biblical testimony from the Gospel of John (17:21–23) about God's "oneness," which amplifies for him the idea that "God is one and beyond the one, and above the monad itself" (ἓν δὲ ὁ θεὸς καὶ ἐπέκεινα τοῦ ἑνὸς καὶ ὑπὲρ αὐτὴν μονάδα). Clement observes that the pronoun "you" in the Johannine text[17] "indicates God, the one who alone truly exists, who was and is and

---

[15] For ὀφιώδης ἡδονή, see also *Leg.* 2.84, 2.88, 3.61, 3.66. Pseudo-Athanasius, *Homilia de passione et cruce domini* (PG 28:233 l. 41). The adjective ὀφιομάχος or ὀφιομάχης also appears in Lev 11:22 (LXX) and in Origen, *Sel. Gen.* (PG 12:97 l. 13).

[16] Cf. also *Contempl.* 2; *Praem.* 40; *QE* 2, 68. On these and similar texts, see D. T. Runia, "The Rehabilitation of the Jackdaw: Philo of Alexandria and Ancient Philosophy," in *Greek and Roman Philosophy 100 BC–200 AD*, ed. R. Sorabji and R. W. Sharples, Bulletin of the Institute of Classical Studies Supplement 95 (London: University of London, 2007), 483–500, esp. 495–500.

[17] John 17:21: "… that they may all be one, as *you*, father, in me and I in you …" (ἵνα πάντες ἓν ὦσιν, καθὼς σύ, πάτερ, ἐν ἐμοὶ κἀγὼ ἐν σοί …).

will be" (τὸν ὄντως μόνον ὄντα, ὃς ἦν καὶ ἔστιν καὶ ἔσται, δείκνυσιν θεόν). The point of comparison here is not "the one who alone truly exists" and its extension,[18] but the expression of divine transcendence: "God is one and beyond the one, and above the monad itself." John Dillon notes that Philo for whom the supreme principle is equal to the personal God of Judaism is "not always content to refer to God as the one but on occasion goes further, indulging in flights of negative theology."[19] It is reasonable to assume that Clement is influenced by Philo in a general way, although the exact reference is not easily available. In such a case one can speak of a Philonic flavor.

4.2.2 *Stromateis*

For a statistical analysis, the more expansive *Stromateis* have the advantage of the larger numbers. Four extensive sequences and an equal number of short sequences can be found.[20] The main sequences deal with the allegory of Hagar and Sarah, the story of Moses, the law and the virtues, and the temple and the high priest. As in Clement's earlier works, the contexts of the passages in which the Philonic substratum appears in sequence are not uniform. In the Hagar and Sarah story, in which Hagar allegorically represents preliminary studies and Sarah philosophy, Clement argues against contemporaries who view philosophy as useless or even dangerous. The context of the story of Moses is also apologetic; Clement maintains that Hebrew wisdom is older than Greek philosophy, and thus the figure of Moses is more venerable than Plato, a well-known apologetic theme. Moses is the exemplar of the perfect man, not as the Hebrew lawgiver as he was for Philo, but identified in a Christological way with the only-begotten son. It is worth noting that Clement uses Philo's words but within the framework of the Exodus story, as if the literary style of Philo was preferable and more pleasing to his Greek ears. In the third sequence, Clement cuts and pastes phrases from Philo's *De virtutibus* into his text to illustrate the role of the virtues in the spiritual life of the believer. The selection of the Philonic prescriptions based on biblical texts may have functioned in part to oppose adherents of the beliefs of Marcion. The last sequence, on the temple, vestments, and the high priest, involves symbolic interpretations for which the Exodus passage (Exod 26–28) forms the background. Philo appears to be driven by a strong cosmological impulse in his interpretations. Though not ignoring the cosmological aspects, Clement redirects the discussion toward the creative power of the Logos, which he views simultaneously as the redeeming power of Christ.

---

[18] For a discussion of the tenses (past, present, future) in this context, see Van den Hoek, *Clement of Alexandria*, 127.

[19] J. Dillon, *The Middle Platonists: A Study of Platonism 80 B.C. to A.D. 220* (London: Duckworth, 1977), 155–56. Dillon cautions, however, not to "treat an essentially rhetorical flourish as if it were a strictly philosophical statement." In a different context, David Runia calls attention to this passage (*Paed.* 1.71.2) in Clement and writes that "the possibility has to be considered that, when Clement calls Philo 'the Pythagorean', he is specifically thinking of this penchant for arithmologizing exegesis, *and also of a connection with a theology of the 'One God'*" ("Why Does Clement of Alexandria Call Philo 'The Pythagorean'?," *VC* 49 [1995]: 1–22, esp. 10, italics added).

[20] Extensive sequences: *Strom.* 1.28–32, 1.150–82, 2.78–100, 5.32–40. Short sequences: *Strom.* 2.5–6, 2.46–52, 5.67–68, 5.71–74.

In the short sequences, Clement inserted various biblical markers provided by Philo that all relate to the concept of God: knowledge of God, orientation toward God in gnosis, matters of anthropomorphic language of God, and questions about the locality of God.[21] In addition to these large and small blocks of Philonic material, there is an extensive list of isolated references covering a wide variety of topics. These isolated borrowings are comparable to the references in Clement's earlier works: etymologies and simple allegories based on biblical texts, various ethical elaborations, the concept of God in relation to humans, and biblical notions connected to Platonic themes. In his earlier works Clement seems to use this material when he is just treading water or embellishing. He continued along similar lines in the *Stromateis* but much more extensively and elaborately. The works of Philo that Clement draws on in the *Stromateis* are primarily those used in his earlier works,[22] but literal quotations, such as from *De plantatione* and *De agricultura* in *Protr.* 5.1–2 and *Paed.* 1.5.1–2 respectively, are not replicated in the *Stromateis*. Conversely, no references to the *Quaestiones in Genesim* occur in his earlier works. In terms of subject matter, themes connected with the Bible represent 74 per cent of the borrowings in the *Stromateis* and 81 per cent in the *Protrepticus* and *Paedagogus*—which shows essentially the same emphasis on biblical background; the slightly higher percentage in the earlier works may be influenced by the statistical law of small numbers or data points.

This formal method of cataloguing is meant to put all potential Philonic material in Clement's works into perspective, both to illustrate the context of the relationship and the ways in which it functions. The method can be used as a roadmap for further exploration of major subjects that have long been discussed in the literature, such as the Alexandrians' thinking about the principles of knowledge, about ethical behavior—control of the passions and the road to virtue, about the creation of the world, about God and the role of the Logos, about the transcendence of God and the contemplation of the highest divinity. In the past, scholarly discourse often elevated such subjects for comparative study in a thematic way but without considering the context in which they occurred.[23]

From the statistics, it can be concluded that the linking of philosophical concepts with biblical passages was Philo's greatest influence on Clement. In addition, Philo became Clement's guide for reading and exploiting texts of the Pentateuch that were not widely known at his time, although Philo only was a stepping stone in this process. Clement expanded the Philonic inclusions cumulatively with references to other texts, which often ended with a passage from the New Testament. Since Clement was well schooled in Greek literature and philosophy, he did not necessarily need Philo for exploiting Homer, Plato, and the vast number of other Greek authors that he quotes throughout his works.[24] Clement used Philo in a creative way, sometimes sloppily but never slavishly or without purpose, often employing him for apologetical or polemical

---

[21] See van den Hoek, *Clement of Alexandria*, 148–76.
[22] Philo, *Opif.*; *Leg.*; *Cher.*; *Post.*; *Agr.*; *Plant.*; *Migr.*; *Mut.*; *Somn.*; *Mos.*; *Spec.*; *Virt.*
[23] For a survey of previous studies, see van den Hoek, *Clement of Alexandria*, 5–19.
[24] This point is emphasized by Runia, *Philo in Early Christian Literature*, 155.

means. He bent Philo's cosmological and theocentric thought into a more anthropological direction, by including the incarnate Logos and incorporating the history of salvation. He equally moved Philo's view of the law in different directions; for Philo, the law and its prescriptions were directly connected to the implementation of virtuous life, but this was less so for Clement. For him the law led to Christ as the fulfillment of the law, while virtuous life meant following Christ. It should be noted that Clement in his adaptations often allegorized the prescriptions of the law, while Philo let the prescriptions literally stand as they were without the need of allegory.

4.3 Philo as Predecessor

Clement's working methods and the strings of literal quotations make it clear that Clement had direct access to Philo's works. It is therefore surprising that Clement only rarely mentions Philo by name, four times in all (*Strom.* 1.31.1, 1.72.4, 1.151.2, 2.100.3). In these four citations, Clement twice labels him as the "Pythagorean." David Runia has convincingly argued that the epithet indicates that Clement viewed Philo in close affinity with Pythagoreanism, which generally had a strong connection with Platonism in imperial times.[25] Various explanations have been advanced for Clement's unwillingness to acknowledge his debt to Philo. Eric Osborn sees it in terms of a duel with the Marcionites; Clement found it prudent to downplay his Jewish sources to avoid losing adherents to a group well known for its hostile attitude towards the teachings of Moses.[26] David Runia approaches the problem from a different angle. Philo may not have been mentioned explicitly because Clement saw himself in the same theological tradition. There are, indeed, other authors that Clement does credit rarely. Tatian is mentioned only a few times, and not always where one would expect it; his name is, for example, left out in one of the extensive borrowings in the first book of the *Stromateis*.[27] It has been suggested that Tatian was one of Clement's teachers before he came to Alexandria. Something similar may have happened to the other teacher, Pantaenus, of whom we know very little. Pantaenus' name is mentioned only once by Clement: namely, in his *Eclogae Propheticae* (56.2; cf. frag. 48). In the *Stromateis* Clement professes to be greatly indebted to him, but he does not refer to Pantaenus by name but in metaphoric terms only as the "true Sicilian bee" (1.11.2: Σικελικὴ τῷ ὄντι ἦν μέλιττα); on other occasions, he brings up the authority of an "elder" (πρεσβύτερος), which may refer to Pantaenus as well. Eusebius informs us that Clement mentions his teacher by name in his *Hypotyposes* and that he refers to Pantaenus' interpretations of scripture. Unfortunately, these works are mostly lost so that Eusebius' remarks cannot be verified (*Hist. eccl.* 5.11.2). Even if we include the *Hypotyposes*, the name of

---

[25] Runia, "Why Does Clement of Alexandria Call Philo." See more recently J. Otto, *Philo of Alexandria and the Construction of Jewishness in Early Christian Writings*, Oxford Early Christian Studies (Oxford: Oxford University Press, 2018), and the review by D. T. Runia in *VC* 74 (2020): 230–33.
[26] E. Osborn, "Philo and Clement," *Prudentia* 19 (1987): 35–49, esp. 35.
[27] Left out in *Strom.* 1.74.2–75.1, but mentioned in *Strom.* 1.101–2, 3.81–82, 3.92; *Ecl.* 38.

Pantaenus comes up very rarely. Denise Buell noted the special rhetorical function that omitting his teachers' names could have had for Clement. Not the individual identities of the teachers, but their roles as mediators between the apostles and Clement's own time would have been important. To put the names of his teachers in the foreground would have overemphasized "their importance as individuals," a charge that Clement makes against the followers of Marcion, Basilides, and Valentinus.[28] Logically, then, omitting Philo's name may seem to place him in the ranks of Clement's direct mentors.

In giving scant recognition to Philo, Clement stands in the good company of Origen who acknowledges Philo only three times and is even less forthcoming in his indebtedness to Clement.[29] Origen does not mention Clement by name, despite Eusebius' claim that "Clement, who succeeded Pantaenus, was head of the catechetical instruction at Alexandria up to such a time that Origen was also one of his students" (*Hist. eccl.* 5.10, 6.6, 6.13–14). Occasionally, however, Origen does refer to predecessors, and at least on four occasions it is very likely that he had Clement in mind (*Comm. Matt.* 12.31, 14.2; *Comm. Jo.* 2.25; *Comm. Rom.* 1.1, and above n. 29).

The works of Philo seem to have been a fixed presence in the libraries of both Clement and Origen. May one presume that Philo's works were already standard assets in Alexandrian libraries of previous decades? Unfortunately, this remains an open question. Origen saw to it that this bibliographic tradition continued to spread, for when he moved to Caesarea taking his books and scrolls with him, his collection included Philo's works. His library was to become the basis of that of Pamphilus and Eusebius, and some of the extant medieval manuscripts of Philo were copies of texts transmitted through the Caesarean library.[30]

It is known that the first documented Christian library was in Jerusalem, founded by Clement's pupil, Alexander (Eusebius, *Hist. eccl.* 6.20).[31] There is no explicit evidence of a Christian library in Alexandria at that time, but since Alexander studied there before going to Jerusalem, it seems plausible that he found his model in that city. As Eusebius reports, Origen had a private collection of books, some of which he sold because he could not or did not want to keep up with Greek literature (and he even expresses pleasure at the financial benefits he derived from the sale) (*Hist. eccl.* 6.3.9). His patron Ambrose provided Origen with scribes to produce his manuscripts. Whether others such as Clement had their own libraries or depended upon those of a patron or

---

[28] D. K. Buell, *Making Christians: Clement of Alexandria and the Rhetoric of Legitimacy* (Princeton: Princeton University Press, 1999), 83–89.

[29] Origen identifies Philo three times by name (*Cels.* 4.51, 6.21; *Comm. Matt.* 15.3) and mentions him as a predecessor on numerous other occasions; see Runia, *Philo in Early Christian Literature*, 160–62; Runia, *Philo and the Church Fathers*, 120–21; A. van den Hoek, "Philo and Origen: A Descriptive Catalogue of Their Relationship," *SPhiloA* 12 (2000): 44–121. In a letter preserved in Eusebius (*Hist. eccl.* 6.19.13), Origen calls Pantaenus a predecessor. Origen does not mention Clement by name but alludes to him as a predecessor at least four times: *Comm. Matt.* 12.31, 14.2; *Comm. Jo.* 2.25; *Comm. Rom.* 1.1. Compare also the remarks of Alexander in a letter to Origen, again preserved in Eusebius (*Hist. eccl.* 6.14.8), in which Alexander mentions the friendship that was extended to both Origen and himself by their predecessors Pantaenus and Clement.

[30] For a description of how Philo's writings survived, see Runia, *Philo in Early Christian Literature*, 16–31.

[31] G. Pasquali, "Biblioteca," in *Enciclopedia Italiana di scienze, lettere ed arti* 6 (1938): 942–47; H. Y. Gamble, *Books and Readers in the Early Church* (New Haven: Yale University Press, 1995), 154.

upon a communal collection is a tantalizing question that remains unanswered for lack of evidence.

The preservation of books is pivotal in the discussion of Philo and the Christian tradition in Alexandria. The books that Clement wrote in Alexandria show that he had access to a majority of the Philonic treatises. In the last three books of the *Stromateis* and the other works written after leaving the city, however, the number of citations from Philo drops off considerably; only a few literal quotations from the *Quaestiones in Genesim* remain. It thus seems likely that other libraries were less well furnished and that the presence of books influenced authors' abilities to cite, no matter how highly developed their memory was. Unfortunately, one cannot answer the question of how the Philonic corpus and other Jewish texts ended up in Christian libraries. In the absence of hard information, one can only speculate about the way in which Philo's manuscripts were transmitted in the later first and second centuries. One among many possibilities is that some Hellenized Jewish groups who studied the scriptures and Jewish-Greek writing in general could have "converted" to Christianity, while keeping their "ancestral" scrolls. Another scenario could be that, during or after the suppression of the Jewish revolt, Christians (among them Jews and non-Jews) might have appropriated or rescued (depending on the perspective) existing book collections. Unfortunately, both Judaism and Christianity of this period in Alexandria are shrouded in obscurity.

The Philonic corpus owes its preservation to the Christian tradition of Alexandria; its first appearance is in the works of Clement and its extension occurs via Origen in Caesarea. The link with Philo was no longer with a living Jewish tradition but with a literary heritage. The many works of Philo may not have come down to us were it not for the Christian Alexandrian tradition.

5
Origen of Alexandria

Michael B. Cover

Et quomodo justum erit quando quid in Evangelio tale reperitur, ad allegorias et novas intelligentias confugere: quando vero in Veteri Instrumento, statim accusare, et nullam explanationem, quamvis probabilis sit, recipere?[1]

5.1 *Ad Fontem*: Reassessing the Place of Philo in Origen's Exegesis and Thought

The rehabilitation of Origen as a speculative theologian and a "man of the church" stands out as one of the watershed accomplishments of scholarship on early Christianity in the twentieth century.[2] A similar *ressourcement* cannot be spoken of with regard to Origen's Jewish predecessor, Philo of Alexandria. Although copied, studied, transmitted, and *received* by Chalcedonian and non-Chalcedonian Christians,[3] and even depicted in the catenae as an honorary bishop,[4] Philo remains for many Origen scholars a borderland figure—neither sufficiently Jewish nor sufficiently Christian to be adopted into either's genealogy. He is, as the Renaissance Jewish scholar Azariah de' Rossi famously called him, "the man who fell between the stools."[5]

The aim of this chapter is to offer a new assessment of Philo's influence on Origen, particularly Origen's biblical exegesis. I will do so, first, by revisiting David Runia's

---

[1] Origen, *Hom. Luke* 16 (PL 26.254): "And how will it be just, whenever such a thing is discovered in the Gospel, to take refuge in allegories and new interpretations, but, whenever something similar is discovered in the Old Testament, to reproach it at once and to allow no explanation, however plausible it might be?" (author's translation).

[2] Origen, *Hom. Luke* 16 (PL 26.254): "Ego vero quia opto esse ecclesiasticus ... aequalem et in veteri et in nova Lege quaero rationem" (PL 26.254–55), "But I hope to be a man of the church .... I ask for an equal accounting for both the Old Law and the New"; trans. J. T. Lienhard, ed., *Origen: Homilies on Luke*, FC 94 (Washington, DC: Catholic University of America Press, 1996), 67–68. See H. de Lubac, "Origen: Man of the Church," *History and Spirit: The Understanding of Scripture According to Origen*, trans. A. Englund Nash (San Francisco: Ignatius, 2007 [1950]), 51–102. For Origen's rehabilitation, see A. Fürst, *Origenes: Grieche und Christ in römischer Zeit*, SAC 9 (Stuttgart: Hiersemann, 2017), 2.

[3] On Philo's Armenian reception, see A. Mancini Lombardi and P. Pontani, eds, *Studies on the Ancient Armenian Version of Philo's Works*, SPhA 6 (Leiden: Brill, 2011).

[4] G. E. Sterling, "The Place of Philo of Alexandria in the Study of Christian Origins," in *Philo und das Neue Testament*, ed. R. Deines and K.-W. Niebuhr (Tübingen: Mohr Siebeck, 2004), 21–52, esp. 22.

[5] Azariah de' Rossi, *The Light of the Eyes*, trans. J. Weinberg (New Haven: Yale University Press, 2001 [1573–75]), 159.

1993 study on this topic.⁶ I then offer a critical taxonomy of scholarship that touches on Philo's influence on Origen since 1993. Finally, I will offer a new portrait of Philo's influence on Origen as an exegete, suggesting that Philo's concatenation of secondary biblical lemmata provided Origen with a model of homiletic and commentary composition that remains too little explored. Case studies drawn from Origen's mature Caesarean works, including a preliminary analytical index of the Philonic references in Origen's newly discovered *Homilies on the Psalms* in Codex Monacensis Graecus 314 and Origen's transmission of a previously unknown Philonic fragment (perhaps stemming from *QE* 1), are presented in support of this argument.

5.2 *When* Did Origen Engage the Works of Philo?

Before turning to Runia's essay, it is necessary to address the questions of how and *when* Origen engaged the works of Philo. Few would question that Origen's first contact with the *corpus Philonicum* happened in Alexandria. Eusebius' extensive knowledge of the Philonic corpus has furthermore led scholars to conclude that Origen brought a copy of Philo's writings with him to Caesarea.⁷ Thus, Origen encountered and engaged Philo's writings early, and deemed them important enough to transport with him to Palestine. Although one might get the impression from these data that Philo's influence on Origen is primarily felt in his early Alexandrian works and that after his move to Palestine Origen's attention to Jewish writings turned to the exegetical labors of his living rabbinic neighbors, in fact, the truth is more complex. The story of Origen's engagement with the synagogue of Caesarea appears also to be a story of Origen's reengagement with the writings of Philo.⁸

In a long-neglected essay, Dominique Barthélemy argued that Origen's exchange with the Jews of Caesarea involved a heated debate over Philo and the Septuagint.⁹ Drawing on the work of Peter Katz,¹⁰ Barthélemy demonstrated that a number of Philo's biblical citations, especially in the Caesarean copies of the *Allegorical Commentary*, have been modified to conform to the recensional version of the Jewish translator Aquila. Barthélemy furthermore suggested on the basis of the theological

---

⁶ D. T. Runia, "Origen," in *Philo in Early Christian Literature: A Survey* (Assen: Van Gorcum, 1993), 157–83. For a more recent introductory survey, see J. M. Rogers, "Origen's Use of Philo Judaeus," in *The Oxford Handbook of Origen*, ed. R. Heine and K. J. Torjesen (Oxford: Oxford University Press, 2022), 83–99.

⁷ Eusebius, *Hist. eccl.* 2.18.1. See G. E. Sterling, "The School of Sacred Laws: The Social Setting of Philo's Treatises," *VC* 53 (1999): 148–64, esp. 160–63.

⁸ On the larger questions of Origen's relationship to Judaism, see Fürst, *Origenes*, 45–55; J. Otto, *Philo of Alexandria and the Construction of Jewishness in Early Christian Writings*, OECS (Oxford: Oxford University Press, 2018).

⁹ D. Barthélemy, "Est-ce Hoshaya Rabba qui censura le 'Commentaire Allégorique?' A partir des retouches faites aux citations bibliques, étude sur la tradition textuelle du commentaire allégorique de Philon," in *Philon d' Alexandrie: Lyon 11–15 septembre 1966* (Paris: Éditions du Centre National de la Recherche Scientifique, 1967), 45–78. See also M. Niehoff, "Origen's *Commentary on Genesis* as a Key to *Genesis Rabbah*," in *Genesis Rabbah in Text and Context*, ed. S. K. Gribetz et al. (Tübingen: Mohr Siebeck, 2016), 129–53.

¹⁰ P. Katz, *Philo's Bible: The Aberrant Text of Bible Quotations in Some Philonic Writings and Its Place in the Textual History of the Greek Bible* (Cambridge: Cambridge University Press, 1950).

Tendenz of a number of these changes that the scribe was Jewish and most likely a member of the circle of Rabbi Hoshaya.[11] The presence of a Hebrew-speaking scribe in Origen's library would have been essential for his work on the *Hexapla*.[12] Thus, Barthélemy proposes the scenario of a two-way cultural exchange, wherein Origen introduced the rabbis to Philo and his Jewish assistants introduced him to the rabbis and Aquila.[13]

Barthélemy prepared the way for a comparison of the emended and non-emended sections of the Allegorical Commentary, but did not undertake this project in his lifetime.[14] Such a comparison remains a desideratum. The broader thesis of Origen's renewed dialectical interest in Philo's Allegorical Commentary and the *Quaestiones* during his Caesarean period nonetheless comports well with the evidence of Origen's own writings; that evidence is presented in the third part of this chapter.

5.3 Philo's Influence on Origen: The Last Quarter Century

5.3.1 Revisiting Runia's Spaces of Philonic Reception

David Runia's 1993 chapter on Origen, which Justin Rogers has called "a landmark moment in the study of the reception history of Philo," provides a natural *point d'appui* for surveying advances in the field.[15] Runia's study does not merely list influential monographs, but offers a map of the grand narratives that still determine how Origen scholars today view Philo's importance. Runia's grand narrators include: Harry Wolfson, Robert Grant, Richard P. C. Hanson, Jean Daniélou, Henri Crouzel, and Henri de Lubac.[16] Relying on the schematization of Ulrich Berner, Runia suggests that among these scholars, "a fundamental divide exists between two interpretations of Origen's achievement."[17] Wolfson, Grant, and Hanson represent the "systematic group," which sees Origen primarily as a systematic philosopher and attributes great influence to Philo. Daniélou, Crouzel, and de Lubac fall on the other side of Runia's divide as representatives of the "non-systematic" or "mystical group"; these authors tend to downplay Philo's influence. Runia concludes this section of his chapter by referring to the important studies by Andrew Louth and Colin MacCleod, which in certain ways split the difference between the two groups; and

---

[11] These include the replacement of the word λόγος with νόμος in passages related to the pre-existent principle and the respelling of Ἰησοῦς as Ἰωσοῦσα (Barthélemy, "Qui censura le Commentaire Allégorique," 62). See also W. Bacher, "The Church Father Origen and Rabbi Hoshaya," *JQR* 3 (1891): 357–60.
[12] Barthélemy, "Qui censura le Commentaire Allégorique," 67.
[13] Barthélemy, "Qui censura le Commentaire Allégorique," 67.
[14] See Barthélemy, "Qui censura le Commentaire Allégorique," 77.
[15] J. M. Rogers, "Origen's Use of Philo Judaeus."
[16] Runia, "Origen," 169.
[17] Runia, "Origen," 169. See U. Berner, *Origenes*, EdF 147 (Darmstadt: Wissenschaftliche Buchgesellschaft, 1981).

second, by suggesting that far better than the quest for a "Gesamtbild" of Origen's achievement is, as Berner (citing de Lubac) reminds us, "Origenes bei der Arbeit [zu] beobachten."[18]

While I will heed Runia's advice to "watch Origen at work" in the third part of this chapter, here I wish to return to the middle or mediating space between de Lubac and Hanson, which Runia notes but does not fully explore, and suggest a couple more figures that ought to be added.[19] First, Runia's decision to treat only twentieth-century scholars, while prudential given of the state of research in the early 1990s, need not limit reception-historical attention now. For example, Alfons Fürst has recently called attention to the *Origeniana* (1668) by Pierre-Daniel Huet as a grand narrator worthy of scholarly attention.[20] Often heralded as the first critical scholar of Origen, Huet's assessment of Origen's rationalism concurs with Louth's judgment that for Origen, Christ succumbs to the Word as the primary hermeneutical center.[21] In this way, Huet and Louth conspire to reinvigorate a systematic middle space of Origen's thought (and thereby, his debt to Philo as Platonizing thinker) without the invective excesses of Hanson.

Another figure who is saliently absent from the typologies of both Runia and Berner, but certainly belongs to on the map of post-war twentieth-century figures, is Hans Urs von Balthasar.[22] Although closely connected to Daniélou in certain genealogies, von Balthasar stands as another important independent representative of the "middle space" that privileges both philosophy and exegesis, system and mysticism, in Origen's thought.[23] In a recent article on von Balthasar's reading of Origen, Brian Daley notes that the Swiss theologian eschews the temptation to see Origen in exclusively intellectualist or mystical terms, but charts instead three distinct strata in his thought: (1) "the mythic, narrative stratum, which includes his more controversial speculations"; (2) "a more Platonic stratum, which presents the life of grace as a gradual ascent in the mind"; and (3) "an intensely affective and mystical stratum, focused on 'the passionate and tender love of the Word.'"[24] Daley goes on to assert that while "Balthasar concedes here to some of the excessively speculating tendencies in the Platonism of his time ... [he] denies that he is pantheistic or Gnostic in his relation to created realities."[25] The same might be said, mutatis mutandis, of Philo.

---

[18] Runia, "Origen," 170.
[19] See Runia "Origen," 169 n. 65; Berner (*Origenes*, 88–98) called these positions "vermittelnde Deutungen."
[20] A. Fürst, ed., *Origenes in Frankreich: Die Origeniana Pierre-Daniel Huets*, Adamantiana 10 (Münster: Aschendorff, 2017).
[21] A. Louth, *The Origins of the Christian Mystical Tradition: from Plato to Denys* (Oxford: Oxford University Press, 1981), 65–66.
[22] Von Balthasar does warrant one minor mention by Berner (*Origenes*, 60) alongside Daniélou.
[23] See H. Urs von Balthasar, *Origen: Spirit and Fire. A Thematic Anthology of His Writings*, trans. R. J. Daly, 2nd edn (Washington, DC: The Catholic University of America Press, 1984 [1952]); H. Urs von Balthasar, "Wendung nach Osten," *Stimmen der Zeit* 136 (1939): 32–46; and H. Urs von Balthasar, "Patristik, Scholastik und Wir," *Theologie der Zeit* 3 (1939): 65–104.
[24] B. E. Daley, "Balthasar's Reading of the Church Fathers," in *The Cambridge Companion to Hans Urs von Balthasar*, ed. E. T. Oakes (Cambridge: Cambridge University Press, 2004), 187–206, esp. 193–94.
[25] Daley, "Balthasar's Reading of the Church Fathers," 194.

5.3.2 Five Scholarly Approaches

While scholarship on Philo's influence on Origen published in the quarter century since Runia's chapter could still be mapped in terms of the three major spaces charted above, in what follows, I present a representative selection of studies under five major headings: (1) ignoring Philo; (2) including Philo; (3) imitating Philo; (4) cataloguing Philo; (5) othering Philo.[26]

Ignoring Philo. Several recent studies of Origen's exegesis and education best fit the description of "ignoring Philo" as an important influence. Notable in this category are the 2007 monograph of Elizabeth A. Dively Lauro and the 2012 monograph of Peter Martens.[27] (Other essays by Martens belong to approach three, "imitating Philo"; see below.) In works such as these, Philo figures insignificantly—if at all. Studies of this type implicitly follow the paradigm of Crouzel and de Lubac (or the "mystical group"), for whom, as Runia writes, "Origen's debt to Philo is not essential to his central concerns. It is limited to the general influence of a shared world-view.... Origen transforms these influences in a way that makes the Philonic starting point scarcely relevant."[28]

Including Philo. A second group of studies might best be described as "including Philo." Studies in this group are typically theme-based and adduce a Philonic text as one example among two or three witnesses to a common theological or exegetical tradition. Recent examples include the articles of John Cavadini, Fred Ledegang, Mark DelCogliano, Paul Decock, and Maria Barbàra.[29] Of the making of such inclusive articles there is no end and the analytical perspicuity will vary depending on the aims of the author. Some (e.g. Ledegang) do seemingly no more than recognize topical similarities; others (e.g. Cavadini) offer a critical lens, through which Origen's exegetical artistry can be weighed in counterbalance with the exegesis of Philo and Ambrose. That at least three articles in this category were published in 2017 suggests that this approach will continue to be taken, even as fuller integrations are longer in coming.

Imitating Philo. Whereas studies in the first two approaches fail to account sufficiently for Philo's role in Origen's thought, studies in this third category, which depict Origen as an imitator of Philo, run the opposite risk of overplaying his influence. It is quite clear that Origen read and thought with Philo and recommended that other do so

---

[26] These five types offer descriptions of the approaches exemplified by particular studies, but are not meant to characterize the approaches of their authors.

[27] E. A. D. Lauro, *The Soul and Spirit of Scripture within Origen's Exegesis*, The Bible in Ancient Christianity 3 (Leiden: Brill, 2005); P. W. Martens, *Origen and Scripture: The Contours of the Exegetical Life*, Oxford Early Christian Studies (Oxford: Oxford University Press, 2012).

[28] Runia, "Origen," 169.

[29] J. Cavadini, "Exegetical Transformation: The Sacrifice of Isaac in Philo, Origen, and Ambrose," in *In Dominico Eloquio: In Lordly Eloquence: Essays on Patristic Exegesis in Honor of Robert Louis Wilken*, ed. P. Blowers et al. (Grand Rapids: Eerdmans, 2002), 35–49; F. Ledegang, "The Interpretation of the Decalogue by Philo, Clement of Alexandria and Origen," in *Origeniana Nona: Origen and the Religious Practice of His Time: Papers of the 9th International Origen Congress, Pécs, Hungary, 29 August–2 September 2005* (Leuven: Peeters, 2009), 245–53; M. DelCogliano, "Phinehas the Zealot and the Cappadocians: Philo, Origen, and a Family Legacy of Anti-Eunomian Rhetoric," *Annali di Storia dell'Esegesi* 34 (2017): 107–23; P. B. Decock, "Migration as a Basic Image for the Life of Faith: The Letter to the Hebrews, Philo and Origen," *Neot* 51 (2017): 129–50; M. A. Barbàra, "L'esegesi patristica del 'Vino' del Cantico dei Cantici," *Aug* 57 (2017): 569–91.

as well. The testimonia show Origen's high esteem for Philo,[30] and suggest that Philo's writings shaped Origen's exegetical praxis and pedagogy.[31] Sometimes, however, such similarities have led to exaggerated accounts of Philo's influence on Origen.[32]

Exemplary of the best kind of scholarship in the "Origen imitating Philo" line is the work of Alfons Fürst. In his 2017 intellectual biography of Origen, Fürst notes that Philo and Origen share "a certain religious kinship in their intellectual-spiritual *habitus*."[33] In addition to listing a number of common themes in their work, Fürst claims (following the study of E. Früchtel) that Philo paved the way for Origen's construction of a biblical education and Christian culture.[34]

For Fürst, Origen's exegesis does not parrot the method of Philo as a singular model, but rather weaves together, in a hithertofore unknown combination, a threefold cord drawn from (1) the Christian tradition, especially Pantaenus and Clement; (2) Jewish exegesis, both rabbinic and Alexandrian; and (3) the philological and philosophical scholarship of Alexandrian scholastic tradition. While Philo occupies the place of primary importance among Origen's Jewish influences, these influences are relegated (according to Fürst) to a third tier, following both the Christian and Alexandrian philological/philosophical influences.[35] The result is an entirely new kind of exegesis. Similarly, Peter Martens, in a 2012 essay in *The Studia Philonica Annual*, documents Origen's "admiring, but also unconstrained and imaginative, use of Philo."[36]

Cataloguing Philo. A fourth way of charting Philo's influence on Origen in the last quarter century is that recommended by Runia and carried out by Annewies van den Hoek: cataloguing Philo.[37] The aim of this line of scholarship is to construct an overall picture of Philo's influence in the most objective way possible. The first step in this project was Runia's own index to non-Philonic authors in the Cohn-Wendland critical edition of Philo, which included Origen.[38] Van den Hoek's own study, published in 2000, supplemented Runia's index with a reciprocal index of Philonic testimonia drawn from GCS editions of Origen's works.[39] Van den Hoek tallied more than four hundred *loci* (414)

---

[30] For the testimonia, see L. Cohn and P. Wendland, eds, *Philonis Alexandrini opera quae supersunt*, 7 vols (Berlin: Reimer, 1896–1915), 1:lxxxxv–cxiii; Runia, "Origen." See also the new index in §5.3 below.

[31] So Runia, "Origen," 182.

[32] See, for example, I. L. E. Ramelli, "Philo as Origen's Declared Model: Allegorical and Historical Exegesis of Scripture," in *Studies in Christian-Jewish Relations* 7 (2012): 1–17.

[33] Fürst, *Origenes*, 55. See now as well the study of M. R. Niehoff, "Origen's Commentaries on the Old Testament," in *The Oxford Handbook to Origen*, ed. R. Heine (Oxford: Oxford University Press, 2022), 195–210 which traces important Philonic currents in Origen's exegesis.

[34] Fürst, *Origenes*, 109. E. Früchtel, "Philon und die Vorbereitung der christlichen Paideia und Seelenleitung," in *Frühchristentum und Kultur*, ed. F. R. Prostmeier (Freiburg: Herder, 2007), 19–33.

[35] A. Fürst, *Von Origenes und Hieronymus zu Augustinus: Studien zur antiken Theologiegeschichte* (Berlin: de Gruyter, 2011), 85; A. Fürst, *Origenes*, 54–55.

[36] P. Martens, "*On the Confusion of Tongues* and Origen's Allegory of the Dispersion of the Nations," *SPhiloA* 24 (2012): 107–27. See likewise the *Colloquium Origenianum Tertium Decimum*, Aug. 15–19, 2022, Münster, Germany, convened by A. Fürst, M.-O. Boulnois, S. Fernández, P. Martens, L. Perrone, and E. Prinzivalli on the theme "Origen and Philosophy: A Complex Relation," which contained in its call for papers an interest in "the Alexandrian Background of Origen's Christian Philosophy," including Philo.

[37] In addition to Runia, "Origen," see D. T. Runia, "Philo and Origen: A Preliminary Survey," in *Origeniana Quinta: Papers of the 5th International Origen Congress Boston College 14–18 August 1989*, ed. R. J. Daly, BETL 105 (Leuven: Leuven University Press; Peeters, 1992), 333–39.

[38] D. T. Runia, "An Index to Cohn-Wendland's Apparatus Testimoniorum," *SPhiloA* 4 (1992): 87–96.

[39] A. van den Hoek, "Philo and Origen: A Descriptive Catalogue of their Relationship," *SPhiloA* 12 (2000): 44–121; A. van den Hoek, "Assessing Philo's Influence in Christian Alexandria: the Case of Origen," in *Shem in the*

in Origen's corpus wherein some reference to Philo could be felt.[40] The study remains, as Justin Rogers has commented, the clear starting place for all future detailed research focused on Philo's influence on Origen.[41]

Othering Philo. The fifth and final approach, which occupies an increasingly important part of the map of Philonic reception studies, considers the way Origen uses Philo in his construction of Jews and Judaism. I have called this approach "othering Philo," but it might also indicate the way that Origen might use Philo as a vehicle to "other" contemporary rabbinic Jews in Caesarea. Scholars adopting this approach take the opposite tack from the "imitating Philo" group and focus on the way Origen's use of Philo participates in the process of Christian self-fashioning. Jennifer Otto's recent book, *Philo of Alexandria and the Construction of Jewishness in Early Christianity*, offers a good example.[42] This approach is important as a complement especially to the first three, because it reads the phenomenon of Philonic influence on Origen from the viewpoint of Judaism rather than Christianity, and indicates the importance of studying Origen's reception of Philo for comparative religion as well as for early Christian theology. I briefly offer a new analysis in this vein below, charting parallel *loci* in which Origen treats Philonic and rabbinic tradition with similar respect and dissent.

5.4 Absorbing Philo: Toward a Rearticulation of Philonic Influence

The foregoing five approaches adopted by scholars in the last quarter century each have strengths and weaknesses. While eschewing the probably quixotic quest for a *Gesamtbild* depicting this relationship, I wish to propose a sixth approach, which I hope combines the best of the foregoing five. I have called this "absorbing Philo."

To say that Origen absorbs Philo means that Philo is so fully taken in, appropriated, and improved (from Origen's Christian perspective) that his influence is both everywhere and nowhere felt. Harold Bloom, in his study of comparative poetics, *The Anxiety of Influence*, posits the possibility of such an "absolute absorption of the precursor" in describing Shakespeare's relationship to Christopher Marlowe.[43] In such contexts, the absorbing author exhibits next to no anxiety about the predecessor; conversely, the predecessor's influence may be nearly missed by a critic because he has, in a certain sense, become completely swallowed up, digested, and redeployed. While Origen does show slightly more anxiety about Philo than Shakespeare does of Marlowe,[44] of

---

Tents of Japheth: Essays on the Encounter of Judaism and Hellenism, ed. J. Kugel, JSJSup 74 (Leiden: Brill, 2002), 223–39.

[40] Van den Hoek, "Philo and Origen," 46–47, 116.

[41] Rogers, "Origen's Use of Philo."

[42] Otto, *Philo of Alexandria and the Construction of Jewishness*; J. Otto, "Origen's Criticism of Philo of Alexandria," *StPatr* 92 (2017): 121–30.

[43] H. Bloom, *The Anxiety of Influence: A Theory of Poetry*, 2nd edn (Oxford: Oxford University Press, 1997 [1973]), 11.

[44] For a nuanced study of Origen's self-fashioning, see L. Perrone, "Origen's 'Confessions': Recovering the Traces of a Self-Portrait," *StPatr* 56 (2011): 3–27.

all the early Christian authors, Origen is the one who most characteristically "does not speak of himself."[45] Although he may from time to time make mention of Philo, his anonymous pattern of reference bespeaks an atypical comfort in his own exegetical skin.

Positing Origen's near-complete absorption of Philo is to seek a middle path that articulates both the dependence and independence with which Origen's theology operates vis-à-vis his Philonic predecessor. To present such a portrait, I will first briefly outline several ways in which Origen does *not* follow Philo. I will then turn to a close examination of Origen's exegetical dependence of Philo—particularly Philo's use of secondary biblical lemmata to adorn and deepen his theological allegoresis.

5.4.1 Origen's Departure from Philonic Influence in the Sphere of Biblical Exegesis

It is sometimes claimed (as we saw above) that Origen's Platonizing allegoresis of the Old Testament is largely an imitation of Philo's Platonizing allegory of the soul. This contention is only half true, and here it is worth charting some important divergences. First, there is the question of which books are subjected to allegorical interpretation. Whereas Origen ranges widely across the Law, the Prophets, and especially the Writings (e.g. the Song of Songs) like the Amoraic rabbis, detecting the same song of the Logos throughout, Philo's allegorical attentions are focused almost exclusively on the books of Moses (as the extant Essene *pesharim* are almost exclusively focused on the prophets). Origen's canon is thus in an important fashion wider that Philo's.[46]

Second, as regards exegetical method, Origen liberally adopted not only patterns of Platonizing allegoresis and Stoic etymologizing, but also the text-critical methods of Alexandrian scholarship.[47] Philo was, as Maren Niehoff has argued, probably familiar with these techniques and vestiges of them show up in his commentaries.[48] But by comparison, Origen seems far more at home with the text-critical methods of Zenodotus and Aristarchus than Philo does.

A third point on which Origen parts ways with Philo exegetically relates to the senses of scripture. While one cannot deny a broad similarity between Philo's allegoresis and Origen's, both of which depend upon the Platonizing distinction between body and soul (see Philo, *Contempl.* 78), Origen's threefold division of the body, soul, and spirit of scripture (*Princ.* 4.2.4) stands at a clear remove from Philo's more rudimentary pattern. As Mark Edwards expresses the problem, "Origen's conceit will be intelligible

---

[45] H. Crouzel, *Origène* (Paris: Lethielleux, 1985), 46.

[46] The prophets and the writings do appear in the matrix of Philo's biblical constructions, but they occupy something of a second (albeit still inspired) tier within Philo's scriptural hierarchy. For important studies, see e.g. C. Bøhm, *Die Rezeption der Psalmen in den Qumranschriften, bei Philo von Alexandrien und im Corpus Paulinum*, WUNT 2.437 (Tübingen: Mohr Siebeck, 2017); N. G. Cohen, *Philo's Scriptures: Citations from the Prophets and Writings. Evidence for a Haftarah Cycle in Second Temple Judaism*, JSJSup 123 (Leiden: Brill, 2007).

[47] See B. Neuschäfer, *Origenes als Philologe*, Schweizerische Beiträge zur Altertumswissenschaft 18 (Basel: Friedrich Reinhardt, 1987).

[48] M. Niehoff, *Jewish Exegesis and Homeric Scholarship in Alexandria* (Cambridge: Cambridge University Press, 2011).

only to those who already subscribe to the threefold anthropology which he derives from Paul, and who therefore believe, as he does, that the Word who is present in every word of scripture has taken on body, soul and spirit in the world in order to deliver the higher elements from their bondage to the lower."[49] While some, such as Louth, might disagree with Edwards' Christocentric (rather than Logocentric) characterization of Origen's hermeneutics, the idea that his threefold sense depends on a Platonism which reads Paul as attentively as Philo seems to caution against any simple elision of Philo's and Origen's methods.[50]

A final New Testament stumbling block for the theory of Origen's primary dependence on Philo arises from the Epistle to the Hebrews. Even a cursory study of Origen's *Homilies on Leviticus* or *Commentary on Matthew* will reveal the role played by the eschatological structure of Hebrews in Origen's thought—particularly the differentiation between the shadow of the law and the good things to come (Heb 10:1).[51] In Philo's allegoresis, by contrast—especially in the Allegorical Commentary—the somatic-apocalyptic dimension of Origen's allegories is almost completely eclipsed by a personalist ethics and a (possibly) reincarnational eschatology.[52]

5.4.2 Origen's Absorption of Philonic Exegesis

While Origen's biblical exegesis clearly does not follow Philo in every respect, there remains a reciprocal danger of overplaying this difference as well. Every generation must "watch Origen at work"—and to do so requires "watching Philo at work," particularly in his most ambitious exegetical composition, the Allegorical Commentary.

One of the hallmark features of Philo's Allegorical Commentary is the adduction of secondary and tertiary biblical lemmata. Philo weaves these biblical texts into his commentaries to amplify or deepen the spiritual vision that he is developing in the main line of the commentary. This process of association, which we find *in nuce* in the *Anonymous Theaetetus Commentary* and, in another form, in the Amoraic homiletic and exegetical midrashim, I have elsewhere called Philo's "poetics of association."[53]

Origen paid careful attention to Philo's poetics of association and drew on this model far more than that of the earlier Homeric and Platonic commentaries in composing his exegetical works. To illustrate Philo's influence, I present here several cases studies, drawn from two later works of Origen: the *Commentary on Matthew* (245–49 CE) and

---

[49] M. Edwards, *Image, Word, and God in the Early Christian Centuries*, Ashgate Studies in Philosophy and Theology in Late Antiquity (Farnham: Ashgate, 2013), 102–3.
[50] So also M. Zimmermann, *Schriftsinn und Theologisches Verstehen: Die heutige hermeneutische Frage in Ausgang von Origenes*, Adamantiana 9 (Münster: Aschendorff, 2017), 97.
[51] For a catalogue of more than sixty citations of Heb 10:1 in the *corpus Origenianum*, see *Biblia Patristica: Index des Citations et Allusions Bibliques dans la Littérature Patristique*, 6 vols and supplement (Paris: Centre National de la Recherche Scientifique, 1991), 3:454–55.
[52] The point is debated. See D. T. Runia, "Is Philo Committed to the Doctrine of Reincarnation?," *SPhiloA* 31 (2019): 107–25; S. Yli-Karjanmaa, *Reincarnation in Philo of Alexandria*, SPhiloM 7 (Atlanta: Society of Biblical Literature, 2015).
[53] M. B. Cover, "Philo's Poetics of Association: The Exegetical Structure of *De cherubim*," *SPhiloA* 35 (2023): 177–99.

the newly discovered fragments of Origen's *Homilies on the Psalms* (after 245 CE).[54] Both works are the product of Origen's Caesarean period. The presence of Philonic influence on this advanced stage of his exegesis demonstrates that, far from being a faddish fascination of the young Origen, Philo remained an important interlocutor for Origen in Caesarea during his time of engagement with the circle of Rabbi Hoshaya, as Barthélemy and others have claimed.

5.4.2.1 Philo's Influence in Origen's Matthew Commentary

A good first port of call from which to observe Origen and Philo at work is *Comm. Matt.* 17.17. Here, commenting on Matt 22:2 (the parable of the wedding banquet), Origen takes up the apparent problem of "the kingdom of heaven" being likened to a "human king" (ὡμοιώθη ... ἀνθρώπῳ βασιλεῖ).[55] To help clear scripture of the charge of anthropopathism,[56] Origen adverts first to "one of our predecessors who composed some books called the allegories of the laws" (viz. Philo).[57] According to this predecessor, the scriptures are ambiguous with regard to God's presentation: sometimes, as in Deut 1:31, God's behavior is likened to that of a human being: "The Lord God nursed you, as a human being (ὡς εἴ τις ... ἄνθρωπος) would do in the case of his own son." In other cases such as Num 23:19, Origen's predecessor notes, one finds statements like "God is not to be put upon like a man (οὐχ ὡς ἄνθρωπος)" (NETS, adapted).

Origen acknowledges that his tandem use of Deut 1:31 and Num 23:19 derives from Philo's previous exegetical labors. Philo pairs Num 23:19 with a very similar text, Deut 8:5, on at least seven different occasions.[58] In one of these cases, Philo appears to blend Deut 8:5 and Deut 1:31 (*Somn.* 1.237). An analytical synopsis (see Table 5.1) of these *loci* presented alongside *Comm. Matt.* 17.17 and *Hom. Jer.* 18.6, in which Origen deploys the same secondary lemmata without anonymous attribution, will help clarify what Origen owes to Philo and what is his own.[59]

Several conclusions about Philo's influence on Origen´s exegesis can be drawn from Table 5.1. First, it is clear that Origen knows a Numbers-Deuteronomy cluster of secondary lemmata from a Philonic commentary. Philo himself opines in *QG* 1.55 that he has "often" used this double proof,[60] and Origen had likely encountered it in a variety of treatises.

---

[54] For these dates, see Fürst, *Origenes*, 27.

[55] The Amoraic king *meshalim* also use this idiom, which may have drawn Origen´s attention to it. See D. Stern, *Parables in Midrash: Narrative and Exegesis in Rabbinic Literature* (Cambridge, MA: Harvard University Press, 1991).

[56] It is the charge of having human emotions, rather than a human body, that concerns Origen in this locus. Thus, he looks more to Philo than to Aristobulus.

[57] For a recent analysis of Origen's use of the title "predecessor," see Otto, *Philo of Alexandria and the Construction of Jewishness*, 91–135, esp. 127–35.

[58] F. Petit, *Quaestiones in Genesim et in Exodum: Fragmenta Graeca*, Les oeuvres de Philon d'Alexandrie 33 (Paris: Cerf, 1978), 54: *QG* 1.55; 2.54; *Leg.* 4 (Harris, fr. 8.1); *Sacr.* 94 + 101; *Deus* 52–54, 69; and *Somn.* 1.237. Cf. Runia "Origen," 176 n. 105.

[59] Among the Philonic witnesses, I omit Harris fr. 8.1. The Numbers-Deuteronomy cluster is adduced in the context of a discussion of Deut 30:15, but this cannot be the primary lemma. Hence, the original exegetical structure is lost. I am grateful to Alfons Fürst for drawing my attention to *Hom. Jer.* 18.6 as a critical parallel to *Comm. Matt.* 17.17.

[60] Philo, *QG* 1.55: ὡς πολλάκις ἔφην.

86 THE RECEPTION OF PHILO OF ALEXANDRIA

Table 5.1 The Numbers-Deuteronomy Cluster in Philo and Origen[a]

	Philo						Origen	
	QG 1.55	QG 2.54	Sacr. 94/ 101	Deus 52–54	Deus 69	Somn. 1.237	Hom. Jer. 18.6	Comm. Matt. 17.17
1° Lemma	Gen 3:22	Gen 8:21	Gen 4:4	Gen 6:7	Gen 6:7	Gen 31:13	Jer 18:8	Matt 22:2
MOT	T	T[b]	T	T	T	T	T	L
2° Lemma	Num 23:19	Num 23:19	Num 23:19 (§94)	Num 23:19	Num 23:19	Num 23:19	Num 23:19	Deut 1:31
MOT	L	L	L	L	L	L	L	L
2° Lemma	Deut 8:5	Deut 8:5	Deut 1:31/8:5[c]	Deut 8:5	Deut 8:5	Deut 1:31/8:5	Deut 8:5	Num 23:19
MOT							L	
2° Lemma							Deut 1:31	

[a] MOT = "mode of transition"; T = "thematic association"; L = "lexical association." For these abbreviations, see D. T. Runia, "The Structure of Philo's Allegorical Treatises: A Review of Two Recent Studies and Some Additional Comments," VC 38 (1984): 209–56, at 241.

[b] Although the word ἄνθρωπος is in the primary lemma (Gen 8:21), it refers to human beings not to God. Thus, I consider the transition thematic.

[c] Colson (Philo 2:169) understands Philo to cite Deut 1:31, but the precise reference is ambiguous.

Second, and more remarkably, Origen has, in Comm. Matt. 17.17 and Hom. Jer. 18.6, lifted this Numbers-Deuteronomy cluster and transposed it to amplify new primary lemmata: Matt 22:2 and Jer 18:8, respectively. Two features of this transposition in Comm. Matt. 17.17 illustrate the creativity and freedom with which Origen redeploys the Philonic cluster. First, looking (in Table 5.1) at the "modes of transition" between primary and secondary lemmata, one notes that Philo usually introduces this Numbers-Deuteronomy cluster through a thematic rather than lexical association. Origen follows Philo's lead in Hom. Jer. 18.4, but in Comm. Matt. 17.17, his introduction of this secondary cluster hangs upon a lexical connection as well. Noticing the divine referent of ἄνθρωπος in Matt 22:2, Origen seizes the opportunity to clarify misperceptions by reading it together with two other ἄνθρωπος texts from the Pentateuch. Origen thus does not simply borrow from Philo here, as he does in Hom. Jer. 18.4, but imitates and extends Philo's exegetical praxis at a natural place in his commentary. Second, and theologically more interesting, Origen demonstrates his exegetical freedom to adapt this Philonic tradition by inverting its sequence. As Table 5.1 illustrates, Philo always presents the sequence Numbers-Deuteronomy ("not as a human," "as a human"). This sequence encodes—albeit in an inverted order—a Philonic understanding of human pedagogy and progress (hence Philo's affinity for Deut 8:5, in which the verb παιδεύσει appears, rather than Deut 1:31). In the first stage of divine pedagogy, God speaks "as a human" (Deut 8:5)—"man to man," so to speak, with emotion. In the second stage, those who have made progress in virtue, "becoming like God as far as is possible," come to recognize that "God is not as a human" (Num 23:19). In *Deus* 69, Philo will associate these two stages with respective pedagogical πάθη in the student, fear and love. Philo presents these "two principles" throughout his works according to their order in the hierarchy of truth and perfection (see *QG* 1.55), which is in accord with the protological focus of his theology. God's unlikeness comes first; his likeness to humanity comes second.

As witnessed by *Hom. Jer.* 18.4, Origen knows the traditional Philonic sequence of this catena (Numbers-Deuteronomy). His inversion of Philo's sequence and his foregrounding of the Deuteronomy text ("God is as a human") to the prior position in the catena in the *Commentary on Matthew* achieves several things. First, it sets Philo's two stages of pedagogy in a soteriological order that conforms to the eschatological rather than protological center of Origen's thought. It also has the function of emphasizing theanthropic "divine sympathy," a theme which Runia sees more prominently at play in Origen's thought than in Philo's on account of the doctrine of the incarnation.[61] Rather than beginning with the understanding of the perfect ("God is not as a human"), Origen wishes to emphasize in his discussion of the parables of Jesus that the divine pedagogy in the economy *begins* with the seemingly anthropopaschite Deity, even though properly speaking for Origen, only the heterodox would claim that "the father of Christ" has human emotions.[62]

Origen's shift of the explicit reference for the "God is as a human" text from Deut 8:5 to Deut 1:31 in the *Commentary on Matthew* may owe something to this shift in theological emphasis. Again, on the witness of *Hom. Jer.* 18.4, Origen clearly knows *both* Deuteronomy prooftexts. It is therapeutic tenderness of divine nursing (ἐτροποφόρησε: Deut 1:31), however, rather than divine legal pedagogy per se (παιδεύσει: Deut 8:5) that Origen wishes to foreground in this context (cf. Gal 3:24–25). One should perhaps not make too much of this shift, because the longest version of Philo's Deuteronomy reference (*Somn.* 1.237) presents a composite citation of Deut 1:31 and Deut 8:5:

> Deut 8:5 ὡς εἴ τις παιδεύσαι ἄνθρωπος τὸν υἱὸν αὐτοῦ, οὕτως κύριος ὁ θεός σου παιδεύσει σε.
>
> Deut 1:31 ὡς ἐτροφοφόρησέν σε κύριος ὁ θεός σου, ὡς εἴ τις τροφοφορήσει ἄνθρωπος τὸν υἱὸν αὐτοῦ.
>
> *Somn.* 1.237 <ὡς> παιδεύσει σε κύριος ὁ θεός, ὡς εἴ τις παιδεύσειεν ἄνθρωπος τὸν υἱὸν αὐτοῦ.

While Philo's citation draws his preferred language of divine pedagogy from Deut 8:5, the syntax of the verse is clearly that of Deut 1:31—the same verse that Origen quotes.[63]

---

[61] See Runia, "Origen," 176.
[62] Origen, *Comm. Matt.* 17.18: χρησόμεθα οὖν ταῖς ἄνθρωπον ὀνομαζούσαις παραβολαῖς τὸν θεὸν εἰς ἀπολογίαν τῶν ὅσον ἐπὶ ταῖς λέξεσιν ἀνθρωποπαθῆ φασκουσῶν εἶναι τὸν Χριστοῦ πατέρα. But cf. *Comm. Cant.* 6; *Hom. Ezech.* 6.6: "ipse pater non est impassibilis." I am grateful to John Sehorn for this reference.
[63] *Pace* van den Hoek, "Philo and Origen," 94–95, who suggests that Cohn and Wendland have mistakenly referenced Deut 1:31 in *Somn.* 1.237.

In Origen's "correction" of Philo's quotation of Deut 1:31, we may see Origen the textual critic as much as Origen the theologian at work.

5.4.2.2 Philo's Influence in Origen's Newly Discovered Homilies on the Psalms

Origen's attention to Philo's use of secondary lemmata not only influenced his commentaries during the late 240s, but also his homilies. This point can be illustrated by the new *Homilies on the Psalms* discovered in the Codex Monacensis Graecus 314 and edited by Lorenzo Perrone in 2015.[64] Because of limitations of space, below I offer (in Table 5.2) a first analysis of the *loci* in Perrone's index to Philo as a supplement to the index of van den Hoek;[65] and a translation of three (or possibly four) new anonymous references to Philo, which might be appended to the catalogues of Cohn-Wendland and Runia. This catalogue is not exhaustive, but will hopefully provide a good starting point for future research.

Further comment on two of these anonymous references will help shore up the position on Philo's influence on Origen maintained in this chapter. First, *Hom. Ps.* 75.1.6 demonstrates to an even more extensive degree than *Comm. Matt.* 17.17 Philo's influence on Origen's exegetical practice. Not only does Origen here take over a secondary lemma from Philo (Exod 15:21), he elides Philo's exegesis with his own new primary lemma by equating the noun ἀναβατής of Exod 15:21 with the verb ἐπιβαίνειν in his own primary lemma, Ps 75:7. Origen then adduces a new tertiary lemma, 4 Kgdms 2:12, which Philo does not use, to explicate the second, more positive term of Exod 15:21. Origen's "reformulation" of Philo's argument not only borrows and redeploys Philonic tradition and secondary lemmata,[66] but also imitates and continues Philo's exegetical practice, extending this lemmatic cluster to include a new verse.

If *Hom. Ps.* 75.1.6 like *Comm. Matt.* 17:17 demonstrates the depth of Origen's debt to Philo in his technical exegesis, *Hom. Ps.* 36.4.1 fills in this picture at the hermeneutical level while also registering Origen's departures from his Alexandrian Jewish predecessor. Here, one must tread with some caution since Perrone is not entirely confident in identifying Origen's interlocutor here as Philo, and does not include this passage among those he comments on in his 2015 article.[67] The thought expressed is nonetheless entirely Philonic, and in a recent note I argue that Origen here clearly refers to Philo, and that the most plausible provenance of the tradition here cited, given our limited data, is the *Quaestiones in Exodum*.[68] Origen mentions that he takes this exegesis as a point of departure (ἀφορμή) in his homiletic preparation. The echo here of Prov 9:9a (δίδου σοφῷ ἀφορμήν, καὶ σοφώτερος ἔσται) is not accidental. Philo provides Origen's ἀφορμή for investigating the meaning of Exod 3:3 and Origen wishes to praise his interpretation. However, there is room to become, as Proverbs says, "wiser"

---

[64] L. Peronne, ed., *Origenes XIII: Die neuen Psalmenhomilien: eine kritische Edition des Codex Monacensis Graecus 314*, GCS (Berlin: de Gruyter, 2015).
[65] Perrone, *Die neuen Psalmenhomilien*, 640–41.
[66] Perrone, "Doctrinal Traditions," 196.
[67] Perrone, "Doctrinal Traditions," 195–99.
[68] M. B. Cover, "A New Fragment of Philo's *Quaestiones in Exodum* in Origen's Newly Discovered *Homilies on the Psalms*? A Preliminary Note," *SPhiloA* 30 (2018): 15–29.

ORIGEN OF ALEXANDRIA   89

Table 5.2 Analytical Catalogue of Philonic References in Origen's New Psalms Homilies

Hom. Ps. 15.1.1 (*Perrone 73–75)	Somn. 1.244; cf. QE 2.17	A[a]

In interpreting the superscript to Psalm 15, στηλογραφία τῷ Δαυίδ, Origen raises the problem that "inscribing a pillar" might be understood to indicate idolatry and its ethical counterpart, a wicked life. To solve this problem, Origen adduces as a secondary lemma Deut 16:22, "you shall not make for yourself a pillar, which the Lord hates." The verse, says Origen, indicates that it is only certain kinds of pillars of which God disapproves—the pillars which reflect a vicious life. As a counterexample, Origen adduces as a tertiary lemma Gen 35:20, in which Jacob erects a pillar to the memory of Rachel. This, says Origen, provides an example of raising a pillar that the Lord loves, a virtuous life. Origen's adducing of Deut 16:22 as a secondary lemma relies on Philo, who in Somn. 1.244 uses the same verse as a secondary lemma to exonerate Jacob, who in his primary lemma is said to have anointed a pillar to God (Gen 31:13). It is remarkable that both Origen and Philo interweave Deut 16:22 with similar verses in the Jacob narrative.

Hom. Ps. 36.4.1 (Perrone 157–58)	e.g. Leg. 3.18	A/B

Translation
  I made a start (ἀφορμή; cf. Prov 9:9aα) in trying to understand this text [Exod 3:3] to the best of my ability by reading the discussion of the one who said (ὁ εἰπών), "What does the phrase 'therefore, I will cross over and see what this great vision is' (Exod 3:3) mean?" This man said (ἔλεγε) in his discussion of that text that "the great vision cannot be seen by one who is rooted amid terrestrial plants and animals and everyday objects; rather it is necessary for the mind to cross over and indeed transcend the perceptible bodies of the cosmos and come to be in a more stable position for the contemplation of noetic realities, so that it might be possible to comprehend the great vision." These (ταῦτα) are the things that that man said (ἔλεγε) on the *locus*. But we, wishing to praise a wise man and add something to him (cf. Prov 9:9aβ), see something like the following meaning in these verses: Every person who sets out on the road (ὁδεύοντες) toward virtue must first make progress, in the hope that he should [one day] reach [perfection in] virtue. In this regard, he is always "crossing over" (Exod 3:3), "pressing on toward those things which are ahead and forgetting those things which are behind" (Phil 3:13) . . . .

Origen is trying to determine the meaning of Moses's "great vision" in Exod 3:3, which functions as a secondary lemma to Ps 36:23a (τὰ διαβήματα ἀνθρώπου). He mentions that he took his "starting point" (ἀφορμή) from an anonymous exegete (ὁ εἰπών) who suggests that "crossing over to see the great sight" (Exod 3:3) does not mean physical crossing over and sensory seeing, but that the "mind" (νοῦς) must "move beyond" (διαβῆναι), and in fact "move above" (ὑπερβῆναι), the bodies of the cosmos to get a firm footing from which to "see the noetic world" (τῇ θεωρίᾳ τῶν νοητῶν). Perrone hesitantly cites Philo as the identity of this interpreter ("Philo?"), and cross-references "e.g. Leg. 3.18."[b] Origen is not referring to an extant text of Philo, nor do we have preserved an exegesis of Exod 3:3 anywhere in Philo's corpus. In a recent article, I suggest that Origen here records a lost fragment from the *Quaestiones in Exodum*. I will return to this question below.

Hom. Ps. 67.1.5 (Perrone 185)	Somn. 1.229	B/C

Perrone references Philo's discussion of the metaphysical difference an article makes in the phrases ὁ θεός and θεός. Perrone also rightly references the John Commentary, where Origen himself already makes a similar point. Philonic influence may be indirect.

Hom. Ps. 67.2.4 (Perrone 209)	Leg. 3.121	C

Origen refers to a theory of musical pitch that is also attested in Philo. Perrone notes that the theory is also related in Clement of Alexandria (*Strom.* I.13.57.5). Philonic influence may be indirect.

Hom. Ps. 73.1.5 (Perrone 246)	Leg. 3.80 et al.	B

Origen refers to the λόγος as an inner "helmsman" (κυβερνήτης) of the soul, which Perrone suggests echoes a number of passages in Philo, including Leg. 3.80, 3.118; Cher. 36; Sacr. 51; and Migr. 67. The likelihood of some form of dependence on Philo is heightened by Origen's use of another Philonic word, οἴαξ, "rudder," which occurs alongside κυβερνήτης in Somn. 2.201 and Praem. 51.

Hom. Ps. 73.3.8 (Perrone 265)	Her. 225	B

Origen invokes the λόγος τομεύς (the "logos as knife/splitter/divider") tradition, which is also found in Philo. Heb 4:12 contains a similar idea, but some form of Philonic influence is likely.

(continued)

Table 5.2 Continued

Hom. Ps. 74.(1).5 (Perrone 277–78)[c]	Deus 76–7	A

Translation
  One of my predecessors inquired (ἐζήτησε), "if [Ps 74:9 speaks] of 'mixed wine', how [does it also speak] of 'unmixed wine'? But if it speaks of unmixed wine, how does it also speak of mixed wine?" (*Deus* 76–77). But see if what is said is able to be understood in this way....

As is his wont elsewhere,[d] Origen refers to Philo anonymously by way of the formula "one of those before me..." (τις τῶν πρὸ ἐμοῦ). The predecessor asks how Ps 74:9a–c (Origen's primary biblical lemma in the homily) can speak of a cup of "unmixed wine" (οἶνος ἄκρατος) that is simultaneously "mixed wine" (κέρασμα). Philo cites Ps 74:9a–b as a secondary lemma and raises just this question in *Deus* 76–77 in a discussion of the priority of God's mercy to God's justice.

Hom. Ps. 75.1.6 (Perrone 288–89)[e]	Leg. 2.103–4[f]	A

Translation
  "At your rebuke, O God of Jacob, those mounted on horses became drowsy" (LXX Ps 75:7). Another one of my predecessors noticed (ἐτήρησε)—and well did he notice!—that "to mount a horse" and "to be a horseman" are not the same thing—that is, "to be a rider" and "to be a horseman" are not the same. For the Egyptian is not a "horseman" but a "rider", [as Moses says] "horse and rider he has thrown into the sea" (Exod 15:21; cf. Philo, *Leg.* 2.103–4). [The Egyptian] does not "mount" the horse with knowledge, therefore he will fall. But the one who with knowledge "has mounted" his body and governs its pleasures and leads the body where he wishes and with its reins controls its impulses, so that it may not be carried along by the biting incitements of the flesh—this kind of person is not a "rider" as the Egyptian but a "horseman" like Elijah: as it is said concerning Elijah, "a chariot of Israel and its horseman" (4 Kgdms 2:12).[g]

Origen refers to Philo anonymously as "another one before me" (ἕτερος πρὸ ἐμοῦ). In interpreting his primary biblical lemma, Ps 75:5, Origen indicates that this predecessor notes a difference between the phrases "to mount a horse" (ἐπιβαίνειν ἵππου), i.e. "to be a mounted rider" (ἀναβάτην εἶναι), and "to be a horseman" (ἱππέα εἶναι). That both Origen and Philo adduce Exod 15:21 as a secondary (or, in Philo's case, tertiary) lemma ensures that Philo's exegetical as well as theological influence is felt in this passage.

Hom. Ps. 76.1.5 (Perrone 320–21)[h]	Ebr. 41–55	A

Translation
  One of my predecessors blamed (ἐμέμψατο)—and well did he blame!—Jethro, when he said "now I know that the Lord is great beside all the gods" (Exod 18:11), because here he seemed to make a theological statement, confusing the Lord with idols—given that he does not know other "gods" than these (*Ebr.* 41–45).

Origen again refers to Philo anonymously as "one of those before us" (τις τῶν πρὸ ἡμῶν). In discussing Ps 76:14b, Origen addresses the possibility that the question "who is a god like our god?" might be read in a henotheistic manner. To argue against this interpretation, Origen mentions that his predecessor rightly censured Jethro, who in Exod 18:11 proclaimed the half-heartedly monotheistic confession: "the Lord is great alongside (παρά) all the gods." Philo adduces the same secondary lemma (with opprobrium for Jethro) in *Ebr.* 45.

Hom. Ps. 77.2.7 (Perrone 380)	Her. 148/Spec. 4.233	C

Perrone footnotes two passages from Philo which show similarities with Philo's discussions about the astronomical bodies. Explicit Philonic influence is difficult to determine.

Hom. Ps. 77.7.3 (Perrone 440)	Mos. 1.109	B

Perrone references Philo, who asks a similar exegetical question to that found in Wis 11:17–19 (cited by Origen). Elsewhere, Perrone suggests that Origen "apparently... is referring to Philo when he afterwards mentions the explanation proposed by 'others' for whom "the dog-fly, a 'shameless' insect, refers to the exceeding shamelessness of the Egyptians.'"[i]

Note: Of the eleven loci in this table, four anonymously reference Philo. In these cases, I offer a fresh translation before the commentary.

[a] I use the format "X.Y.Z" to indicate "The Yth Homily on Psalm X, section Z" in the Perrone edition. In this instance e.g. "the first homily on Psalm 15, section one." Perrone's page number, where relevant, is given in parentheses for ease of reference. A, B, and C ratings indicate my judgment of the likelihood of direct Philonic influence;

Table 5.2 Continued

this schema borrowed from van den Hoek, "Philo and Origen." *I have added, as the first entry in Table 5.2, a passage not noted by Perrone in which Philonic influence is probable.

[b] Perrone, *Die neuen Psalmenhomilien*, 157 n. 1.

[c] For further analysis of this passage, see L. Perrone, "Doctrinal Traditions and Cultural Heritage in the Newly Discovered Homilies of Origen on the Psalms (Codex Monacensis Graecus 314)," *Phasis* 18 (2015): 191–212, at 198.

[d] Perrone, *Die neuen Psalmenhomilien*, 19.

[e] For further analysis of this passage, see Perrone, "Doctrinal Traditons," 195–97.

[f] See also Philo, *Agr.* 67–83.

[g] The Perrone edition wrongly italicizes ὥσπερ, but it is not part of the citation.

[h] For further analysis of this passage, see Perrone, "Doctrinal Traditions," 197.

[i] Perrone, "Doctrinal Traditions," 199.

still and so Origen adds to the Philonic interpretation (προσθεῖναι αὐτῷ; see Prov 9:9a) the voice of Paul from Phil 3:13. It is not merely "passing over" from the perceptible to the imperceptible that is necessary; one must also make the therapeutic step of truly forgetting one's past wrongs and pressing on toward perfection in the grace of Christ. If Origen here parts ways with Philo, it is nonetheless on friendly terms, and with gratefulness for a good beginning.

Origen's treatment of Jewish wisdom in *Hom. Ps.* 36.4.1 recalls another, more autobiographical passage in *Hom. Jer.* 20.2–3. Here, Origen introduces the "Hebrew tradition" that he learned from the apostate son of a contemporary rabbi, who had become interested in Christianity.[69] He first explains his Jewish contemporary's understanding of Jer 20:7 and then, without entirely rejecting or accepting it, offers an interpretation of his own. It is especially interesting that Origen treats Philo and his apostate Jewish interlocutor as similarly intermediate figures. Just as Origen, alluding to Prov 9:9 in *Hom. Ps.* 36.4.1, speaks of adding wisdom to a wise man, so in *Hom. Jer.* 20.3, with a double allusion to Matthew's parable of the talents and Luke's parable of the minas, he suggests that he wishes not to bury this single talent (i.e. the "Hebrew tradition") in the ground or hide it in a cloth, but to allow it to gain interest through his own exegetical labors.

5.5 Conclusion

In a famous *testimonium*, Augustine of Hippo expresses reservation about Philo's allegorical exegesis because of its lack of Christological content. Turning to Philo's allegory of Noah's ark in *QG* 2.6 as an example, Augustine notes that while Philo may rightly suggest that ark represents the human body, his explanation fails because "without

---

[69] This may be the same Jewish interlocutor mentioned by Origen in *Letter to Africanus* 7 (see Origen, *Homilies on Jeremiah and 1 Kings 28*, trans. J. C. Smith, FOTC 97 [Washington, DC: Catholic University of America Press, 1998], 223, n. 23). I am grateful to Alfons Fürst for drawing my attention to this passage.

being able to find the door [of the ark] (*ostio non invento*; viz. Christ, John 10:8 [*ego sum ostium*]), he could not understand the symbol" (*Faust.* 12.39).

This present chapter has asked a related question about Origen's relationship to Philo, but employing a different metaphorics. The question is not whether Origen and Philo enter through the same *door*, but whether the two Alexandrian exegetes walk along a similar *road*? I have tried to carve out a middle space in answering this question. On the one hand, Origen attends to and imitates Philo's poetics of association. On the other hand, Origen's hermeneutical principles are not merely Logocentric, as Philo's, but also Christocentric. As Origen says in *Hom. Ps.* 76.1.5:

> "God, who is within the saint, is your road" (LXX Ps 76:14). Who is the road of God that leads to God, except him who says, "I am the road and the truth and the life. (John 14:6)

In sum, Origen and his Alexandrian predecessor walk together in forging a new scriptural praxis and biblical culture; a Logocentric hermeneutic is their common "road less travelled by." But insofar as Philo's Logos is not Jesus Christ, Origen feels compelled to part ways.[70]

---

[70] I am grateful to Alfons Fürst, David Runia, Folker Siegert, and John Sehorn for their comments on this chapter.

6
Gnosticism

M. David Litwa

On the topic of Philo and so-called "Gnostics," the whole playing field has changed from what it was a quarter century ago. First of all, "Gnosticism" as a typological and global category has been largely exploded, despite some efforts at recalibration.[1] The meaning of "Gnostics" has been narrowed to designate a discrete sociological entity, known to scholars as "Sethians" or the "Seed of Seth."[2] Although I disagree that Sethians have a special claim on the modern category of "Gnostic," it is still fruitful to employ this group—with its own distinctive scriptures and rituals—as a basis for comparison. With the focus directed on a distinct socio-historical group, it does not make much sense to inquire: "Was Philo a Sethian gnostic?"[3] He certainly did not think that the creator of the world was evil or that the cosmos was created as a result of a fall. On the other hand, scholars still reasonably posit that elements of Philo's thought prepared the way for Sethian conclusions (a God beyond knowing, creation by lower powers, and so on).

Based on these and other shared elements, Birger Pearson called Philo "pre-gnostic."[4] Nevertheless, since there is no teleology in reception history—only the movement of ideas along unpredictable, forking tracks—an idea is not helpfully designated "pre-gnostic" unless a Gnostic system or spirituality exists, and it remains unclear whether

---

[1] M. Williams, *Rethinking "Gnosticism": An Argument for Dismantling a Dubious Category* (Princeton: Princeton University Press, 1996); K. King, *What Is Gnosticism?* (Cambridge, MA: Belknap Press, 2003). For a recalibration, see e.g. A. D. DeConick, "Crafting Gnosis: Gnostic Spirituality in the Ancient New Age," in *Gnosticism, Platonism and the Late Ancient World: Essays in Honour of John D. Turner*, ed. Kevin Corrigan and Tuomas Rasimus; Nag Hammadi and Manichaean Studies 82 (Leiden: Brill, 2013), 287–305.

[2] H.-M. Schenke, "The Phenomenon and Significance of Gnostic Sethianism," in *The Rediscovery of Gnosticism*, ed. B. Layton, 2 vols (Leiden: Brill, 1981) 2.588–616; J. D. Turner, *Sethian Gnosticism and the Platonic Tradition* (Leuven: Peeters, 2001), 63–69; D. Brakke, *The Gnostics: Myth, Ritual, and Diversity in Early Christianity* (Cambridge, MA: Harvard University Press, 2010). See the critique of Brakke in G. S. Smith, *Guilt by Association: Heresy Catalogues in Early Christianity* (Oxford: Oxford University Press, 2014), esp. 131–71; M. D. Litwa, "Did 'The Gnostic Heresy' Influence Valentinus? An Investigation of Irenaeus *Against Heresies* 1.11.1 and 1.29," *VC* 78 (2024): 138–60.

[3] R. McL. Wilson, "Philo of Alexandria and Gnosticism," *Kairos* 14 (1972): 213–19, at 214; cf. R. McL. Wilson, "Philo and Gnosticism," *SPhiloA* 5 (1993): 84–92.

[4] B. Pearson, "Philo and Gnosticism," *ANRW* 21.1 (1984): 295–342, at 341. In his later essay, Pearson is more hesitant; B. Pearson, "Philo, Gnosis, and the New Testament," in *Gnosticism, Judaism and Egyptian Christianity* (Minneapolis: Fortress, 1990), 165–82 at 181. Pearson reports that Jonas made Philo a gnostic (based on *Gnosis und spätantiker Geist* [Göttingen: Vandenhoeck & Ruprecht, 1954], 2:38–43, 70–121), but Jonas' gnosticism requires a fallen god—a notion absent in Philo (McL. Wilson, "Philo and Gnosticism," 92). See also M. Simon, "Éléments gnostiques chez Philon," in *Le Origini dello gnosticismo* (Leiden: Brill, 1967), 359–76; R. D. Srigley, "Albert Camus on Philo and Gnosticism," *SPhiloA* 7 (1995): 103–6.

in Philo's day such was the case.[5] Most of the evidence for Sethian texts indicates that they derive from Christian authors writing between the second and fifth centuries CE. Thus, the Sethian reception of Philo is, to a significant extent, an important (and often neglected) aspect of his Christian reception.[6]

There were, I believe, Philonic ideas and exegetical traditions that Sethians later adapted. Although one cannot easily pinpoint definite instances of the Sethian use of Philo in terms of quotations and allusions, one can point to Philonic traditions with a strong resonance in Sethian sources. Thus when I speak of the gnostic "reception" of Philo, I speak of Sethian ideas and exegetical traditions that reflect a transformation of distinctively Philonic material.

The term "distinctively" is key here, since there are many notions shared by Philo and the Sethians that can be attributed to their larger philosophical (mainly Middle Platonic) milieu. For instance:

1. The radical transcendence of the supreme deity.[7]
2. A distinction between supreme deity and a range of intermediaries.[8]
3. A distinction between mind (νοῦς) and a lower soul (ψυχή).[9]
4. The creation of humanity's lower soul by lesser powers.[10]
5. The heavenly or divine origin of the higher mind (νοῦς).[11]
6. The view that the earthly body is a kind of prison.[12]
7. The release of the soul or νοῦς at death.[13]

All these doctrines Philo and the Sethians held in common due to their shared acceptance of Platonism. Instead of discussing these traditions, then, I focus only on those that Philo distinctly transmitted. The goal is not to make genetic links between Philonic and Sethian texts, but carefully to consider parallels that may indicate a Sethian transformation of Philonic thought. My discussion begins with theological titles and notions and proceeds to exegetical topoi and practices.[14]

---

[5] A. D. DeConick argues that gnostic *spirituality* emerged at the start of the first century CE; *The Gnostic New Age: How a Countercultural Spirituality Revolutionized Religion from Antiquity to Today* (New York: Columbia University Press, 2016), 19–76. Most scholars, however, concur that Gnostic (Sethian) movements began in the early second century.

[6] D. T. Runia briefly treated the Christian gnostic reception of Philo (in *Philo and Early Christian Literature: A Survey* [Minneapolis: Fortress, 1993], 123–26) but limited himself to Valentinus and Basilides (without touching Nag Hammadi literature). K. L. King offers an interesting political, ethical, and social comparison in "The Body and Society in Philo and the *Apocryphon of John*," in *The School of Moses: Studies in Philo and Hellenistic Religion in Memory of Horst R. Moehring*, ed. J. P. Kenney (Atlanta: Scholars Press, 1995), 82–97.

[7] Plato, *Resp.* 6.506e–509a; Alcinous, *Handbook* 10.1–4. Cf. Philo, *Somn.* 1.67.

[8] Plato, *Tim.* 40d; 41a–b; Alcinous, *Handbook* 15–17. Cf. Philo, *Plant.* 50; *QG* 1.54.

[9] Plato, *Tim.* 69d–e; Alcinous, *Handbook* 23–24. Cf. e.g. Philo, *Her.* 264.

[10] Plato, *Tim.* 41a–b; cf. Alcinous, *Handbook* 23. Cf. Philo, *Opif.* 74–75; *Fug* 68–70.

[11] Plato, *Tim.* 41d–e; Alcinous, *Handbook* 23.1. Cf. Philo, *Her.* 274 (ἀπ' οὐρανοῦ καταβὰς ὁ νοῦς).

[12] Plato, *Phaed.* 81e; *Crat.* 400c; Pseudo-Plato, *Ax.* 366a. Cf. Philo, *Leg.* 3.42.

[13] Plato, *Phaed.* 64c. Cf. Philo, *Mos.* 2.288.

[14] Philonic texts below are translated from L. Cohn and P. Wendland, *Philonis Alexandrini opera quae supersunt Editio maior* (Berlin: Reimer, 1896; repr., Berlin: de Gruyter, 1963). Gnostic texts are translated from *The Coptic Gnostic Library: A Complete Edition of the Nag Hammadi Codices*, J. M. Robinson, 5 vols (Leiden: Brill, 2000). Unless otherwise indicated, all references to *Ap. John* are from Nag Hammadi Codex II 1.

6.1 God as the Standing One

In the early second century, the Syrian Platonist Numenius referred to the primal God (ὁ πρῶτος θεός) as "Standing" (ἑστώς).[15] David Runia has shown that ὁ ἕστως or simply ἕστως was a distinctive title for God already in Philo.[16] Not taken into consideration, however, was Michael Williams' study examining the standing deity in Sethian literature.[17] In the *Three Steles of Seth* (NHC VII 5), for instance, Seth says to his heavenly father Adamas: "You have stood (ⲁⲕⲁϩⲉⲣⲁⲧⲕ̄), since you are unceasing .... You have stood (ⲁⲕⲁϩⲉⲣⲁⲧⲕ̄); you have stood preeminent (*or* were the first to stand, ⲁⲕⲣ̄ ϣⲟⲣⲡ̄ ⲛ̄ⲁϩⲉⲣⲁⲧⲉⲕ)" (119.4; 121.9–15). The Coptic expression ⲁⲕⲁϩⲉⲣⲁⲧⲕ̄ probably stands for the Greek ἕστηκας ("You have taken your stand").[18]

Despite the terminological overlap, however, there is a difference in application. Philo's Standing One is the supreme deity or Existent. Adamas is not himself the supreme God, but the highest manifestation of the divine mind akin to Philo's Logos. Perhaps, however, this variation is a difference of focus, since beings which reflect God's nature can participate in the stability of the Standing One. This point is made explicit in *Zostrianos* (NHC VIII 1), where the hero stands upon each successive aeon and beholds the realities that stabilize and angelify him.[19] Philo's paradigmatic hero Moses shares in the immutable repose of the Existent (based on Deut 5:31). Philo and Sethians agreed, at least, on the notion of participation: any person of virtue can share in the wondrous quiescence of the divine.

6.2 Theanthropy

There is a peculiarly Sethian conception of the divine which may be described by the term "theanthropy." Theanthropy is not deification (the idea that humans can participate in the divine), or incarnation (that a pre-existent divine figure became human at certain point[s] in time). Theanthropy is the idea of a pre-existent divine figure such as Adamas who is archetypically Human, the model for all humanity.[20]

---

[15] Eusebius, *Prep. ev.* 11.20. Cf. Corp. herm. 2.12, bodiless νοῦς containing all things is αὐτὸς ἐν ἑαυτῷ ἑστώς; Corp. herm. 10.14: "the One alone stands at rest (ἕστηκεν) and is not moved."

[16] D. T. Runia, "Witness or Participant? Philo and the Neoplatonic Tradition," in *The Neoplatonic Tradition: Jewish, Christian and Islamic Themes*, ed. A. J. Vanderjagt and D. Pätzold (Cologne: Dinter, 1991), 36–56, at 47–51. In his n. 41, Runia cites the more important passages with their biblical lemmata: *Cher.* 18–19 (Gen 18:22); *Post.* 19–30 (Gen 18:22; Deut 5:31); *Gig.* 48–49 (Num 14:44; Deut 5:31); *Conf.* 30–32 (Deut 5:31; Exod 7:15); *Somn.* 1.241 (Gen 31:13; Exod 17:6); *Somn.* 2.221–30 (Exod 17:6, 24:10; Gen 18:22; Deut 5:31, 5:5); *Deo* (Gen 18:22). See also D. Winston and J. Dillon, *Two Treatises of Philo of Alexandria: A Commentary on De Gigantibus and Quod Deus Sit Immutabilis* (Chico, CA: Scholars Press, 1983), 261–63.

[17] M. A. Williams, *The Immovable Race: A Gnostic Designation and the Theme of Stability in Late Antiquity* (Leiden: Brill, 1985).

[18] Williams, *Immovable*, 53–54.

[19] Williams, *Immovable*, 73–74. For the Standing One in *Allogenes* (NHC XI 3), *Ap. John* (NHC II,1), and *Gos. Eg.* (NHC III,2; IV,2), see Williams, *Immovable*, 52–57, 103–52. For Moses angelified, see M. D. Litwa, *Posthuman Transformation in Ancient Mediterranean Thought: Becoming Angels and Demons* (Cambridge: Cambridge University Press, 2020), 74–93.

[20] See further H.-M. Schenke, *Der Gott "Mensch" in der Gnosis* (Göttingen: Vandenhoeck & Ruprecht, 1962); M. D. Litwa "The God 'Human' and Human Gods: Models of Deification in Irenaeus and the *Apocryphon of*

Although theanthropy was partially inspired by Jewish exegeses of Gen 1:26 (humanity "as" or "in" God's image) and Ezek 1:26-28 (the glory of Yhwh appearing as a massive human on a chariot throne), it is not characterized by a physicalist understanding of the divine.[21] Instead, theanthropy, pursuing a Platonic line, assumes that what is archetypally Human is not material, but noetic. The noetic nature of the divine Human is often metaphorized as Light, a Light that can be shared by human beings.

Plato spoke of the human Form (ἀνθρώπου εἶδος), but not of theanthropy (*Parm.* 130c). Philo, on the other hand, manifested an implicit theanthropic understanding of the divine when he spoke of God at the level of Logos. In *De aeternitate mundi* 134, Philo identified the human made in God's image and likeness (Gen 1:26) with a Platonic Idea (ἰδέα τις).[22] The archetype for this ideal human is the "intelligible and incorporeal" Logos (*Opif.* 146, cf. *QG* 1.4; *Leg.* 3.96). The relationship implies that the Logos is the model for the human mind, which Philo called the "true human" (*Her.* 231) and even a god within (*Opif.* 69; cf. *Mos.* 1.27).[23]

Philo did not thematize the divine Logos as Human—with the exception of one treatise. In the *De confusione linguarum*, he named the Logos, "the iconic Human" (ὁ κατ' εἰκόνα ἄνθρωπος, *Conf.* 146-147), the "Human whose name is Dawn" (ἄνθρωπος ᾧ ὄνομα ἀνατολή, *Conf.* 62-63, based on Zech 6:12), and "God's Human" (ἄνθρωπον θεοῦ, *Conf.* 40-41, based on Gen 42:11).[24] Naturally, Philo's presentation of the divine Logos as Human was based on his interpretation of biblical passages. Only one of them, it seems, proved decisive for Sethians—Gen 1:26.

Thus it is not clear that Sethians had to travel through Philo to arrive at theanthropy. Still, it is tempting to think that Philo's various levels of Humanity—the archetypal Logos, the human as Idea, and the human as embodied νοῦς—are reflected in Sethian texts that distinguish between a Primal Human, a mid-ranking figure called (Ger-)Adamas,[25] and the enlightened earthly Adam. Sethians also shared the idea that the

---

John," *ZNW* 18 (2013): 70-94, at 73-77; D. A. Giulea, *Pre-Nicene Christology in Paschal Contexts: The Case of the Divine Noetic Anthropos* (Leiden: Brill, 2014), 23-83. See also J. Holzhausen, *Der Mythos vom Menschen im hellenistischen Ägypten: Eine Studie zum 'Poimandres' (= CH 1), zu Valentin und dem gnostischen Mythos* (Bodenheim: Athenäum Hain Hanstein, 1994), 102-29. T. Rasimus argues that theanthropology is more properly Ophite than Sethian; *Paradise Reconsidered in Gnostic Mythmaking: Rethinking Sethianism in Light of the Ophite Evidence* (Leiden: Brill, 2009), 283.

[21] A physicalist understanding may be implied by the vision of the Human on the throne in Ezekiel the Dramatist (*OTP* 2.811-12).

[22] Runia interprets the "human according to the image" not as an Idea, but an ideal human (D. T. Runia, *Philo of Alexandria On the Creation of the Cosmos According to Moses: Introduction, Translation and Commentary* [Leiden: Brill, 2001], 323), but τις in ἰδέα τις probably expresses no more than the indefinite article in English. Compare T. H. Tobin, *The Creation of Man: Philo and the History of Interpretation* (Washington, DC: Catholic Biblical Association, 1983), 126; Holzhausen, *Mythos*, 104-6.

[23] Cf. *Fug.* 68-72; *Det.* 22-23; *Plant.* 42; *QG* 1.94. The "single Mind" (ἕνα [νοῦν]) who governs the universe (ὁ μέγας ἡγεμών) who also serves as the archetype of the human mind (ὡς ἂν ἀρχέτυπον) is probably the Logos (*Opif.* 69). Cf. "the truly incorporeal Being," described as the model for humanity (*QG* 2.56). See further Tobin, *Creation*, 57-76; T. K. Heckel, *Der Innere Mensch: Die paulinische Verarbeitung eines platonischen Motivs* (Tübingen: Mohr Siebeck, 1993), 42-75.

[24] On the development of these traditions, see Tobin, *Creation*, 108-34.

[25] For instance, *Three Steles of Seth* (NHC VII 5 118.26).

true human within is the immortal mind (νοῦς). This mind is called the "Adamas" within all the "Adams" (*Norea* [NHC IX 2 28.30–29.1]).[26]

Again, theanthropy only applies at a distinct level of deity. For Philo, the primal form of divinity, whom he calls "the Existent" (ὁ ὤν) excludes humanity (*Deus* 53; *QG* 1.55, 2.54, 2.62).[27] That is why the model Human is a form of mediate deity called the Logos.[28] Sethians also advanced this structural idea. They generally posited that the primal deity (called the Invisible Spirit) exists beyond Humanity, whereas his initial emanation (called Barbelo) is the Primal Human with other manifestations of divine Humanity below her.[29]

6.3 Wisdom as God's Wife

Philo inherited a theological lore in which Wisdom acted, narratively speaking, as a character separate from God before and during creation (Prov 8; Sir 24).[30] In the Wisdom of Solomon (composed, perhaps, during Philo's lifetime), Wisdom enjoys a συμβίωσιν θεοῦ, "a common life with God" (8:3). David Winston translates συμβίωσιν as "intimacy," an intimacy that, in context, may imply a kind of marriage.[31]

Philo directly called God the "husband of Wisdom" (σοφίας ἀνήρ) who sows the seed of happiness for the mortal race (*Cher.* 49).[32] Through Wisdom, said Philo, "the universe came into being" (τὰ ὅλα ἦλθεν εἰς γένεσιν, *Fug.* 109).[33] She is thus "Mother of all realities" (μητέρα τῶν συμπάντων, *Leg.* 2.49), and Mother of the cosmos through intercourse (συνών) with God (*Ebr.* 30).[34] God and Wisdom together produce the Logos, who is symbolized by the high priest (*Fug.* 108–9; *Somn.* 2.242). Philo's thought observably shifts depending on the text he is interpreting.[35] In another treatise, Philo claimed that Rebecca's father Bathuel (= daughter of God) actually represented God's

---

[26] Naturally, the idea of the inner human is part of the Platonic tradition, as indicated by the *Excerpt from Plato's Republic* (588a–589b) in NHC VI 5.
[27] In fact, the supreme God is not like anything at all (οὐδὲν δὲ ὅμοιον θεῷ, *Leg.* 2.1). See further R. A. Baer, *Philo's Use of the Categories Male and Female* (Leiden: Brill, 1970), 19.
[28] For the distinction between primal and mediate deity, see M. D. Litwa, "The Deification of Moses in Philo of Alexandria," *SPhiloA* 26 (2014): 1–27, at 7–8.
[29] This development is clearest in the longer version of *Ap. John* (NHC II 1 5.7); cf. *Eugnostus* (NHC III 76.14–24). There is some indication that in the shorter version of *Ap. John*, the "first Human" (ⲡⲉϨⲟⲩⲉⲓⲧ ⲛ̄ⲣⲱⲙⲉ, BG 48.2–3) in whose image humans are made was originally the high God (the Invisible Spirit), not Barbelo. See further A. H. B. Logan, *Gnostic Truth and Christian Heresy* (London: T&T Clark, 1996), 176, 183–84.
[30] See further B. Lang, *Wisdom and the Book of Proverbs: An Israelite Goddess Redefined* (New York: Pilgrim Press, 1986), 111–46.
[31] "Solomon" expresses his desire to marry wisdom in Wis 8:2, and in Wis 8:9 formally conducts her to a shared life with him (πρὸς συμβίωσιν, cf. v. 16). A similar meaning of συμβίωσιν appears in Philo, *Contempl.* 68 (Therapeutae are eager to share a common life with Wisdom); cf. *Congr.* 5. See further B. J. L. Peerbolte, "The Wisdom of Solomon and the Gnostic Sophia," in *Wisdom of Egypt: Jewish, Early Christian and Gnostic Essays in Honour of Gerard P. Luttikhuizen*, ed. A. Hilhorst and G. H. van Kooten (Leiden: Brill, 2005), 97–114.
[32] His base text was Jeremiah 3:4 where God addresses "most peaceful Virtue," calling himself "the husband of your virginity."
[33] Cf. *Somn.* 2.221: Wisdom's stream is a fount of being.
[34] In *Ebr.* 30, Wisdom is called Knowledge (Ἐπιστήμη), but Knowledge is another name for Wisdom, as indicated by Philo's immediate citation of Prov 8:22–23—"God made me [Wisdom] the first of his works, and founded me before this aeon."
[35] Cf. *Her.* 53, where those truly alive have Wisdom as their mother.

Wisdom. Wisdom is God's "daughter" insofar as she comes from him. But since Bathuel is also a father, Wisdom is more properly called "father" (*Fug.* 50–52).

The *Secret Book of John* develops several of these lines of thought. The author portrays the Invisible Spirit as emanator, through self-reflection, of a prototypical Wisdom—the androgynous "mother-father" Barbelo.[36] The fact that the supreme God produces the Barbelo from his own self-reflection makes her his "daughter." The fact that she produces additional aeons by his sovereign consent places her in the role of "wife"—although sexual imagery is excluded. The Invisible Spirit and Barbelo produce an only Child called Christ, the child of light anointed with goodness (6.10–33). The better known Sethian Wisdom is a lower entity—a distant daughter of Barbelo—who becomes mother of the universe (ⲧⲥⲟⲫⲓⲁ ⲛ̄ⲡⲣⲱⲧⲟⲅⲉⲛⲉⲧⲓⲣⲁ ⲧⲙⲁⲁⲩ ⲙ̄ⲡⲧⲏⲣϥ).[37] She takes on this motherly role not by intercourse with God, but as a result of her experience of deficiency (sometimes as a result of her own actions, sometimes due to others).[38] These notions do not line up point by point with Philo, yet one can see developed here a similar cluster of ideas, though taken in a different direction.

One might argue that on the topic of Wisdom, Philo's language never goes beyond metaphor. Wisdom is not actually separate from God, whereas in Sethian sources, she seems to be a distinct person with multiple manifestations in the divine Fullness. Yet Sethian lore may also have been a kind of allegory in narrative form. In Sethian narrative, the dynamics of divine evolution are explained by separate characters whose ontological status is actually unclear. Philo, for his part, does not expand his metaphors into full-blown narratives. Nonetheless, his language is—despite his urging to the contrary—highly mythic and suggestive of genuine, often striking complexity within the Godhead.[39]

6.4 The Image of Abortion

The goddess Hera, according to ancient mythology, desiring to produce offspring apart from her husband Zeus, bore Hephaestus lame of foot (Hesiod, *Theogony* 924–29). According to another version of the tale, she bore Typhon, monster of chaos (*Homeric Hymn to Pythian Apollo* 300–26). Ancient medical science supported the idea that births without male seed typically ended in miscarriage.[40] Thus

---

[36] A Sethian author addresses the Barbelo: "You are Wisdom" (ⲛ̄ⲧⲟ ⲟⲩⲥⲟⲫⲓⲁ, *3 Steles* [NHC VII 5 123.16–17). The "mother-father" title appears e.g. in *Ap. John* 20.9.

[37] Although the idea of Wisdom as mother of the universe is basic to Sethian thought, this particular phrase is taken from *Wisdom of Jesus Christ* (NHC III 4 104.17–19). See further R. van den Broek, "Jewish and Platonic Speculations in Early Alexandrian Theology: Eugnostus, Philo, Valentinus, and Origen," in *The Roots of Egyptian Christianity*, ed. B. Pearson and J. E. Goehring (Philadelphia: Fortress, 1986), 190–203, at 198.

[38] Turner, *Sethian Gnosticism*, 98–99, 226.

[39] See further A. Kamesar, "Philo, the Presence of 'Paideutic' Myth in the Pentateuch, and the 'Principles' or *Kephalaia* of Mosaic Discourse," *SPhiloA* 10 (1998): 34–65.

[40] Galen, *On the Usefulness of the Parts of the Body* 14.7, trans. M. Tallmadge May, 2 vols (Ithaca: Cornell University Press, 1968), 2:633–34; the "inactive, unformed flesh" of the mole is thought to be produced by the human female alone, but Galen denies this. See further R. Smith, "Sex Education in the Gnostic Schools," in *Images of the Feminine in Gnosticism*, ed. K. King (Minneapolis: Fortress, 1988), 345–60, esp. 349–52.

Philo may have only adapted common knowledge when he said that most of the offspring of the (female) soul alone are miscarried and deformed (ἀμβλωθρίδια, ἠλιτόμηνα, *Migr.* 33).

Yet in another treatise Philo added a detail with a resonance in Sethian protology. In *Deus* 14, Philo interpreted the line in Hannah's Song—"she that has born many children has become weak" (1 Sam 2:5)—to mean that the soul bears myriads of children "while standing apart from [or in rebellion against] the One (τοῦ ἑνὸς ἀποστᾶσα)."

This separate, self-willed activity was variously narrativized in Sethian treatises. In the *Secret Book of John*, Wisdom "wanted to bring forth something like herself, without the consent of the Spirit ... without her partner and without his consideration" (NHC II 2 9.28–35).[41] Such is the origin of Wisdom's deformed offspring—Yaldabaoth, who in turn creates myriads of angels to worship him. In composing *Deus* 14, Philo was of course talking about the soul, not Wisdom. Nevertheless, his reflections could have sparked a narrative development, especially if the Sethian Wisdom figure(s) are selectively modeled on Eve.[42]

6.5 The Divine Image

The *Secret Book of John* says that the Primal Human manifested a shape (ⲧⲩⲡⲟⲥ, 14.23), and revealed an appearance (ⲉⲓⲛⲉ, 14.24), later called "image" (ϩⲓⲕⲱⲛ, 14.29) through a watery mirror. In response, the lower creators make the animate (or "soulish") Adam who was both in the image of the Human and according to their own likeness (since they are beings of soul, *Ap. John* 15.3). The creation of the material body comes later, after the animate Adam receives the intelligent spirit of God, the true image of the Human deity. The creators recognize that the spirit-endowed Adam is more intelligent than them, and so they thrust him into a material body. This body is called the "shadow of death," "cave," and "fetter of forgetfulness" (21.4–5, 10, 12). It is designed as a prison house of distractions that has no obvious relation to the divine Image.[43]

For his part, Philo called the body a "baneful corpse" (*Leg.* 1.108; cf. *Migr.* 2; *Somn.* 2.237), the soul's grave (*Deus* 150; *Migr.* 16), a foul prison (*Leg.* 3.42; *Ebr.* 101; *Migr.* 9), wicked by nature, a plotter against the soul (*Leg.* 3.71; cf. *Spec.* 3.1–6), and the "dwelling place of endless calamities" (*Conf.* 177). Such rhetoric is actually commonplace. The distinctive similarity here is the non-bodily nature of the divine image. After quoting Genesis 1:26, Philo observed:

---

[41] Similarly in *Nature of the Rulers* (NHC II 4) 94.5–7, "Wisdom, who is called Faith, wanted to create something by herself, without her partner."

[42] See further G. MacRae, "The Jewish Background of the Gnostic Sophia Myth," *NovT* 12 (1970): 86–101.

[43] In *Rethinking*, 127–30, Williams attempted to show that the *material* body formed by the rulers attained something of the divine likeness by virtue of its upright posture. But in the texts cited, the earthly human only stands upright after receiving the divine breath or spirit, which I take to be the decisive factor for determining divine likeness.

nothing earthborn better resembles God than the human being. But let no one suppose that the likeness is in the character of the body. For neither is God in human shape nor is the human body shaped like God. Rather, the image is spoken of the mind (νοῦς), the ruler of the soul. For the mind in each individual was imaged according to the singular [Mind], that [Mind] of the universe [namely, the Logos] as a model. (*Opif.* 69)[44]

6.6 Sharing the Divine

Philo agreed with Sethians that the human νοῦς is at least partially constituted by divine breath or spirit (πνεῦμα) breathed into the first human being (*Opif.* 135; *Spec.* 4.123).[45] He rooted this view in Gen 2:7 (God "breathed into his [the first human's] face breath [πνόη] of life"), where, in the majority of cases, he made no distinction between πνόη and divine πνεῦμα.[46] Sethian interpreters also thought of the breath breathed into Adam as divine spirit (*Ap. John* 19.25–26). The supreme deity is itself called the Invisible Spirit, but the spirit breathed into Adam is typically the spirit of Wisdom.[47]

For Philo, the medium of πνεῦμα is the Logos. All human beings have a reflection, fragment, or ray of the shining Logos within them (*Opif.* 146). Since the Logos is God— or God in relation to the world—Philo could say that God breathed into Adam, "a portion of his own deity" (τῆς ἰδίου θειότητος, *Det.* 86). Consequently, the human mind is "a fragment of that divine and blessed soul" (τῆς θείας καὶ εὐδαίμονος ψυχῆς ἐκείνης ἀπόσπασμα, *Det.* 90)—evidently referring to the Logos. And since the Logos is divine, the higher mind is "a divine fragment" (ἀπόσπασμα θεῖον, *Somn.* 1.34).[48]

Thus even if one agrees that Philo showed a preference for the model/copy metaphor (the human mind as divine imprint),[49] Philo still attested—and did not deprecate—a tradition in which humans obtain a mind partially constituted by divine πνεῦμα. If this πνεῦμα (which effectively becomes the higher mind) is not earthly matter, it is still an οὐσία in the sense of a basic substance that can be shared.[50] A shared substance implies some kind of constituent shared by both humans and the divine Logos.

---

[44] See further G. H. van Kooten, *Paul's Anthropology in Context: The Image of God, Assimilation to God, and Tripartite Man in Ancient Judaism, Ancient Philosophy and Early Christianity* (Tübingen: Mohr Siebeck, 2008), 57–62.

[45] See further Runia, *On the Creation*, 326–27.

[46] The exception being *Leg.* 1.42.

[47] For the intellect as the divine element in human beings, see F. L. R. Lanzillotta, "Devolution and Recollection, Deficiency and Perfection: Human Degradation and the Recovery of the Primal Condition according to some Early Christian Texts," in *Wisdom of Egypt*, 443–60, at 448–49.

[48] Cf. *QG* 1.50–51. At one point, Philo draws a distinction between the earthly mind (νοῦς γεωδής) and the divine spirit (*Leg.* 1.32). This divine spirit evidently becomes a higher νοῦς which is unmixed with body. Van Kooten explains: "the *pneuma* is greater than or equal to the *nous* ... because, in Philo's view, it is within the *nous* that the *pneuma* is received" (*Paul's Anthropology*, 279). I would say that the πνεῦμα becomes the higher νοῦς.

[49] D. T. Runia, "God and Man in Philo of Alexandria," *JTS* 39 (1988): 48–75, at 69. D. Winston, on the other hand, remarks that Philo shows "no particular preference for 'image' or 'copy' over 'portion' or 'fragment'" (*Logos and Mystical Theology in Philo of Alexandria* (Cincinnati: Hebrew Union College Press, 1985), 29; cf. Tobin, *Creation*, 90–92.

[50] Philo called πνεῦμα θεῖον in humanity an οὐσία in *Spec.* 4.123.

A divine substance shared with humans—variously metaphorized as a breath, spirit, or light—is a key theme in Sethian systems. In various Sethian retellings of the Genesis creation story, the divine light power of Wisdom is stolen by the creator, but breathed into Adam (*Ap. John* 19.10–20.28). The fact that what is inbreathed manifests as light indicates its noetic aspect. Philo acknowledged the luminous nature of the human mind (νοῦς) when he called it an ἀπαύγασμα ("radiance," *Spec.* 4.123; *Opif.* 146; also used of Wisdom in Wis 7:26). When Moses' mind is preparing to soar back to heaven, Philo described it as "extremely sun-like" (ἡλιοειδέστατον, *Mos.* 2.288).

In sum, for Philo and later Sethians, divinity (in the form of divine πνεῦμα) becomes "naturalized" into humanity as νοῦς. The essence (οὐσία) of the rational and noetic soul is divine spirit (πνεῦμα θεῖον, *Spec. Leg.* 4.123; cf. *Her.* 55). Thus the true, noetic human is divine by creation—which is to say by divine design. Yet this is hardly a cause for self-exaltation. For both Sethians and Philo, the divine intellect in humanity is not natural but natura*lized*. It is a gift of God, given at creation, yet for this reason no less constitutive of a humanity's true self.

6.7 Luxurious Eden

Philo understood "Eden" to mean "luxury" (τρύφη, *Somn.* 2.242; cf. *QG* 1.7). The Alexandrian staunchly opposed luxurious practices (*Somn.* 1.123, 2.48–63) and referred to pleasures as "jailers" (*Migr.* 9). Nevertheless, Philo welcomed the delights of God's wisdom. He could link wisdom with luxury because he interpreted paradise—and specifically the tree of life—to mean wisdom (*QG* 1.8, 2.6; cf. 1.56), which was productive of virtue (*Leg.* 1.45).

Sethians also understood Eden to mean luxury. Yet they consistently interpreted it, along with the tree of life itself, in a negative sense. "The rulers took Adam and put Adam in paradise. They said, 'Eat,' meaning, Do so in a leisurely manner. But in fact their pleasure is bitter … their pleasure is a trap" (*Ap. John* 21.18–21). The rewriting of the tradition is, in both cases, striking. For Philo, fallen humans wallow in luxury to strengthen vice, whereas the lower creators in *Ap. John* design luxury to deaden the understanding of a spiritually intelligent humanity.[51]

6.8 Adam's Sleep

Philo called Adam's sleep (or rather trance, ἔκστασις, Gen 2:21 LXX) "the stillness and quietude of his mind" (τὴν ἡσυχίαν καὶ ἠρεμίαν τοῦ νοῦ) (*Her.* 257). Elsewhere the trance signifies the mind's withdrawal from the senses (*QG* 1.24). In one case, it is good

---

[51] It should be noted, however, that Philo once interprets Adam's contact with the "double tree" in Eden (including the tree of life) as causing death (*Somn.* 2.70).

for the mind to withdraw from the senses, for in doing so it can behold intelligible realities (νοητά, *Migr.* 190–91).

Yet Philo also presented Adam's sleeping mind as something negative. The mind falls into a trance when it ceases to be engaged with noetic realities (*Leg.* 2.31). When the mind sleeps, sense-perception awakens (*Leg.* 2.24). Sense-perception can lead to the experience of pleasure which can activate the passions. Those whose minds are controlled by passions are in danger of (moral) death (*Leg.* 2.29). In this sense, the trance (ἔκστασις) God brings upon Adam in the garden is a negative change (τροπή)—a change which is even called the soul's destruction (ὄλεθρος δὲ ψυχῆς, *Leg.* 2.34).

The author of *Ap. John* interpreted Adam's trance as a veiling of his (noetic) perception (ἀναισθησία [NHC III 1 29.6–7]) inflicted by the creator. The supporting text is Isa 6:10: "I [God] shall make their minds sluggish, that they may neither understand nor discern." In the *Nature of the Rulers* (NHC II 4), Adam's trance represents ignorance (ⲧⲙⲛ̄ⲧⲁⲧⲥⲟⲟⲩⲛ, 89.8–9). In both cases, the trance is pejorative and destructive. Yet whereas Philo took pains to say that God kept "the destroyer" from laying waste the minds of his chosen (*Leg.* 2.34, citing Exod 12:23), Sethians tended to highlight the creator's hostility. The redeemed must awaken from the stupor inflicted, not by vice, but by the creator (*Ap. John* 31.5–6).

6.9 Eve as a Means of Knowledge

Philo symbolized Eve as a means of acquiring knowledge; she is sense-perception (αἴσθησις). The knowledge gained by sense-perception, however, is inferior and even dangerous. It is linked to passions (*Leg.* 2.5–8), which can in turn lead the mind (represented by Adam) astray (*Leg.* 2.49–50, 70; cf. *Spec.* 4.188; *Conf.* 126).

In Sethian portrayals of Eve, she also represents an epistemic faculty. Yet instead of being sense-perception, she becomes—or is said to contain—a higher knowledge ("enlightened Insight") that awakens the sleeping mind of Adam. When enlightened Insight appears in the form of Eve, Adam sobers up from his drunkenness and determines to leave his father (the creator) and his mother (matter) (*Ap. John* 23.12–13).[52] In the *Nature of the Rulers* (NHC II 4), "the woman of spirit" likewise comes to the sleeping (that is, ignorant) Adam and bids him "Rise!" When he sees her, he calls her "Mother," "Physician," crying out: "You have given me life!" (89.13–15, adapting Gen 3:20). Such interpretations stand in the tradition of psychological allegory represented by Philo. But the meaning of the tradition is transformed. For Philo, Adam is on the level of spirit (the noetic level), and Eve on the level of the lower soul (sense-perception, *Cher.* 57). The opposite situation occurs in the *Nature of the Rulers*. Eve, on the level of spirit, enlivens Adam who was formerly reduced to soul (89.10–11). The interpretive goals are also different: Eve as lower knowledge brings Adam down to earthly matters, whereas Eve as higher knowledge raises him to spiritual life. In

---

[52] Cf. *Apoc. Adam* (NHC V 5 64.8): "She [Eve] instructed me [Adam] in the gnosis of the eternal God."

the background is a fundamentally different valuation of Eve eating from the tree of knowledge. For Philo, Eve led Adam into sin; for Sethians, Eve introduced Adam to true knowledge.

6.10 Forsaking Womanhood

On several occasions, Philo used the metaphor of "forsaking womanly things" (τὰ γυναικεῖα, *Somn.* 2.185; *Cher.* 50), meaning to forsake materiality and passions and to adhere to intelligible and divine reality. His base text was Gen 18:11, where the matriarch Sarah ceases menstruation (τὰ γυναικεῖα). Philo allegorized: "The passions (τὰ πάθη)," he wrote, "are female by nature (θήλεα δὲ φύσει). Sarah fittingly abandoned them for the male traits of healthy emotions (εὐπαθειῶν)" (*Det.* 28).

In terms of his gender coding, Philo was unoriginal. He followed widespread cultural norms by symbolizing the female by what is "material, passive, corporeal and sense-perceptible," and the male by what "is active, rational, incorporeal, and more akin to mind and thought" (*QE* 1.8; cf. 2.49).[53] Yet Philo was distinctive in symbolizing moral and spiritual progress by a sex change from female to male.

The tradition of escaping femininity crops up in Sethian texts as well. The Sethian hero Zostrianos, for instance, escapes from "corporeal darkness, psychical chaos, and dark, lustful femininity (ⲧⲙⲛⲧⲥϩⲓⲙⲉ ⲛⲛ ⲉⲡⲓⲑⲩⲙⲓⲁ) (*Zost.* 1.10–13) before his ascent to heaven and final admonition: "Do not ... entrust yourselves to things inferior to you as if to superior things. Flee the madness and the fetter of femininity (ⲧⲙⲛⲧⲥϩⲓⲙⲉ), and choose for yourselves the salvation of masculinity (ⲡⲓⲟⲩϫⲁⲉⲓ ⲛⲧⲉ ⲧⲙⲛⲧϩⲟⲟⲩⲧ)" (131.3–8).[54]

As in Philo, femininity represents inferior passions and matter; whereas masculinity symbolizes spirit, stability, and imperishability. To become noetic or spiritual is coded as becoming male. It is a way of sharing in the reality of transcendent entities, including aeons and angels (who are male, and even "triple-male," *Zost.* 24.4).[55]

For both Sethians and Philo, the gender imagery is symbolic. They metaphorized salvation as masculine and even masculinize female heroes (such as Eve, Hannah, Sarah, and Mary). In doing so, they inevitably reflected patriarchal values and reinforced male-dominant gender norms.[56]

---

[53] Cf. Philo, *Deo* 3: "the female is passive matter, while the male is the creator of the world." Text edited by F. Siegert in *SPhiloA* 10 (1998): 1–33, at 5.

[54] Further texts are discussed by F. Wisse, "Flee Femininity: Antifemininity in Gnostic Texts and the Question of Social Milieu," in *Images of the Feminine*, 297–307, to which add: *Second Discourse of Great Seth* 65.18–31 (becoming female means bringing forth jealousy, division, wrath, and desire). See also S. Petersen, "*Zerstört die Werke der Weiblichkeit!" Maria Magdalena, Salome und andere Jüngerinnen Jesu in christlich-gnostischen Schriften* (Leiden: Brill, 1999), 318–21.

[55] Williams argues that maleness in gnostic texts is another way of expressing immovability (*Immovable*, 100–102).

[56] If the point of spirituality is to become noetic and bodiless (as seems to be the case for both Sethians and Philo), then it is pointless to become male in any literal sense. See further M. A. Williams, "Variety in Gnostic Perspectives on Gender," in *Images of the Feminine*, 2–22.

6.11 The Edenic Serpent

Around 400 BCE, the mythographer Herodorus of Heraclea represented the serpent in the garden of the Hesperides as "the variegated reasoning of bitter desire" (τὸν πολυποίκιλον τῆς πικρᾶς ἐπιθυμίας λογισμόν) (*FGH* 31 frag. 14). In Philonic allegory, the Edenic serpent became both desire (*QG* 1.47–48) and pleasure (ἡδονή) (*Opif.* 157; *Leg.* 2.73, 2.87, 2.105, 3.66, 3.68, 3.75–76; *QG* 1.31). A similar tradition was developed in Sethian sources—only one more specific about the type of pleasure involved. In the *Secret Book of John*, the serpent teaches about sexual desire (ⲥⲡⲟⲣⲁ ⲛ̄ⲉⲡⲓⲑⲩⲙⲓⲁ, NHC III 1 28.21]) or the vice of sexual desire (ⲟⲩ ⲕⲁⲕⲓⲁ ⲛ̄ⲥⲡⲟⲣⲁ ⲛ̄ⲉⲡⲓⲑⲩⲙⲉⲓⲁ, II, 1 22.12–15).[57]

For Philo, the desire and pleasure that the serpent represents is more general, although he believed that sexual pleasure was the most extreme and hazardous (*Leg.* 2.74). In his exposition of Genesis, he also noted that Adam and Eve's desire for unity "gave rise to bodily pleasure, which is the starting-point of wicked and law-breaking deeds." Such deeds in turn result in the loss of blessed immortality (*Opif.* 152). Both Philo and Sethian authors agreed that pleasure could kill the soul (*Leg.* 2.77; cf. *QG* 1.51).

Interestingly, although for Philo the snake represents pleasure, when it is seized and tamed, it becomes instruction (παιδεία) (*Leg.* 2.92, employing Exod 4:4). In a Sethian retelling of Genesis, the serpent is called "instructor" (ⲡⲣⲉϥⲧⲁⲙⲟ, *Nat. Rulers* II 4 90.6; cf. *Orig. World* [NHC II 5 120.3–4]), but only when inhabited by the female spiritual principle.

6.12 The Family of Seth

For Philo, spiritual identity could be expressed in ethnic terms. In antiquity, family (γένος) was a fluid category and was not determined solely by physical characteristics. Shared virtue, knowledge, and ritual could alter one's γένος even if the term still functioned rhetorically as a marker of "natural" identity.[58]

For Philo, the family of Seth was important because it continued the line of righteous Abel (Gen 4:25), who is allegorized as the God-loving principle (*Sacr.* 3). Anyone whose nobility is determined by the love of virtue could name Seth as their ancestor (*Post.* 43). Seth represented the seed of divinely implanted virtue (*Post.* 170, 173). The children of Seth are the people who control their passions. They will always exist upon earth, though in small numbers. In time, their fate will be that of the patriarch Enoch: God

---

[57] Both the serpent and the creator are connected with sexuality and desire (*Ap. John* 22.12–15; 24.26–29, in part based on Gen 1:28) such that Rasimus identifies them (*Paradise*, 75–76).

[58] See further Williams, *Immovable*, 158–85; L. H. Martin, "Genealogy and Sociology in the Apocalypse of Adam," in *Gnosticism & the Early Christian World in Honor of James M. Robinson*, ed. J. E. Goehring et al. (Sonoma: Polebridge, 1990), 25–36; D. K. Buell, *Why This New Race? Ethnic Reasoning in Early Christianity* (New York: Columbia University Press, 2008); C. Johnson Hodge, *If Sons Then Heirs: A Study of Kinship and Ethnicity in the Letters of Paul* (Oxford: Oxford University Press, 2007).

will transfer them from a corruptible to deathless families (γένη)—perhaps meaning angels—so that they will not be found among earthly peoples (*Post.* 43).[59]

The Sethians looked back to Seth as their spiritual ancestor.[60] They considered themselves to be a "kingless generation," an immovable—because immortal—minority living among the more populous peoples of Ham and Cain. In times of disaster, they believed, divine Providence shielded their ancestors by transferring them to a safe haven. During the time of the great Flood, for instance, Noah and other members of the immovable family were placed in a bright cloud (*Ap. John* 29.11–12). When the creator later attacked the city of Sodom, great clouds of light descended upon the Sethians. They were rescued by angels and taken above the powers of darkness to live like angels on high (*Revelation of Adam* [NCH V 5 75–76])—a distinctly Enochic destiny.

Heresiographers spurned Sethian (and Valentinian) Christians for supposedly genetic determinism.[61] Nevertheless, Sethians could think of filiation in the same metaphorical way as Philo. Given Sethian suspicions about sex, their biological relation to Seth was probably not in view. The children of Seth had to prove themselves by their knowledge and virtue. Logically, then, the Sethian family could be expanded by people performing the same moral and ritual activities as Seth, their spiritual ancestor.[62]

6.13 Exegetical Inversion

If a passage of scripture did not confirm one's spiritual and moral preconceptions, its meaning could be transformed. In some cases, the meaning could be remade to such an extent that it contradicted the prima facie meaning accepted by other readers. We can call this process "exegetical inversion"—and Philo was a master at it.

In Genesis 38, for instance, the patriarch Judah has sex with his daughter-in-law Tamar (an incestuous act by Mosaic standards), renting her body with a pledge. Philo was not willing to let so great a moral fault besmirch the reputation of the patriarch. He reinvented Judah as a man who made a pledge not for incestuous sex, but for piety (*Fug.* 150). This interpretive move was more than innocent allegorizing, since there is nothing in the text itself which would suggest that Judah was pious in this deed. It is hard to avoid the conclusion that Philo deliberately modified the meaning of the text in order to protect the character of the patriarch.

Philo also reformed the lives of other biblical characters. He presented Tamar as stainless and worthy of good report (*Virt.* 222). The priests Nadab and Abihu were

---

[59] See further R. Kraft, "Philo on Seth: Was Philo Aware of Traditions Which Exalted Seth and His Progeny?," in *Rediscovery of Gnosticism* 2:457–58.

[60] For the gnostic figure of Seth, see G. A. G. Stroumsa, *Another Seed: Studies in Gnostic Mythology* (Leiden: Brill, 1984), 73–80; B. Pearson, "The Figure of Seth in Gnostic Literature," in *Gnosticism, Judaism, and Egyptian Christianity* (Minneapolis: Fortress, 1990), 52–83.

[61] See further I. Dunderberg, *Gnostic Morality Revisited* (Tubingen: Mohr Siebeck, 2015), 137–48.

[62] Note the conversion of the sons of Ham and Japheth in *Apoc. Adam* (NHC V 5 73.13–74.26). See further Williams, *Immovable*, 158–85; *Rethinking*, 193–202; cf. S. Pétrement, *A Separate God: The Christian Origins of Gnosticism*, trans. C. Harrison (London: Darton, Longman and Todd, 1990), 181–213; W. Löhr "Gnostic Determinism Reconsidered," *VC* 46 (1992): 381–90.

devoured by fire for sacrificing incorrectly (Lev 10:1–2). Yet Philo made them into "holy principles" (ἱεροὺς λόγους) taken up by "an undying splendor, since in sincerity they cast aside sloth and delay, and consecrated their serious intent to piety" (*Somn.* 2.67). These are deliberate and fairly radical transformations of the text. Where biblical heroes appear morally ambiguous or tainted, Philo consistently made them models of unquestionable good.

This point is especially true when it comes to the Jewish deity. Philo spent enormous intellectual energy defending the Pentateuchal god from charges of ignorance, changeability, and jealousy (*QG* 1.15, 55, 93, based on Gen 2:16, 3:22, 6:6). Sethian Christians rewrote these very texts with the opposite aim: to make the creator seem unambiguously bad. They portrayed him as a lion-faced serpent who unwittingly breathed divine spirit into Adam. He consistently tried to steal back the spirit; and to do so was prepared to stupefy Adam, rape Eve, and drown humanity with a flood.

At the same time, it would be misleading to suppose that Philo proved faithful to the meaning of biblical texts while Sethian Christians perverted it. Sethians, although they did not share Philo's apologetic strategies, were, like him, attempting to solve perceived problems in the text. They were constrained by biblical texts, even if their practice of rewriting might seem more aggressive than Philo's own.[63] It is safe to say that both Sethians and Philo developed assertive intellectual stances that allowed them to adapt the meanings of biblical texts for their own intellectual ends.

6.14 Conclusion

This discussion of exegetical inversion indicates that—despite continuity in the use of exegetical traditions—Philo and the Sethians were, attitudinally speaking, worlds apart. Philo's imaginative adventures in scripture attempted to inspire piety which he considered to be queen of the virtues.[64] Sethians, on the other hand, fostered a "transgressive orientation."[65] Philo strove to be "the good son," the obedient follower of divine law. Sethians proved their divine sonship by rejecting the laws of the creator, ascending past angels and archangels to aeons on high.

What intervened between Philo and the Sethians to help generate this altered attitude is still a matter of debate. Scholars plausibly surmise that the Jewish uprisings that occurred between 66 and 135 CE had an acute effect on the attitude toward Judaism and the Jewish deity.[66] Widespread anti-Jewish sentiment grew during this time, in

---

[63] Philo was a master of biblical paraphrase, which often comes close to "rewritten Bible" (for which, see G. W. E. Nickelsburg, "The Bible Rewritten and Expanded," in *Jewish Writings of the Second Temple Period: Apocrypha, Pseudepigrapha, Qumran Sectarian Writings, Philo, Josephus*, ed. M. E. Stone [Philadelphia: Fortress, 1984], 89–156).

[64] G. E. Sterling, "The Queen of the Virtues: Piety in Philo of Alexandria," *SPhiloA* 18 (2006): 103–23.

[65] DeConick, *Gnostic New Age*, 270–91; A. D. DeConick, "The Countercultural Gnostic: Turning the World Upside Down and Inside Out," *Gnosis* 1 (2016): 7–35.

[66] See C. B. Smith, *No Longer Jews: The Search for Gnostic Origins* (Peabody: Hendrickson, 2004).

particular among Egyptians, who had a history of polemically retelling the stories of Jewish scripture.[67]

Perhaps the most obvious intervening development, however, was the rise of Christianity. During the late first and early second centuries, Christians were busily appropriating the meaning of Jewish scriptures while selectively distancing themselves from actual Jews in order to escape the stigma of seditiousness as well as the Jewish tax (*fiscus Iudaicus*).[68] Some Christians, such as the author of the *Epistle to Barnabas* (probably Alexandrian) began to express an animus against practicing Jewish customs. This animus was, I surmise, in some cases re-expressed as an animus against Jewish law, and in turn against the ultimate author of that law, the Jewish deity. This animus might have motivated some ancient Christians to find and accentuate passages wherein the biblical creator failed to measure up to what was considered divine (omnibenevolent) status. The creator's statements, actions, and character proved not only that he was not good, but positively evil—that is, jealous, hostile, and angry—in contrast to the God revealed in Jesus Christ.

Philo probably died just as distinctly Christian exegetical developments were beginning. Nevertheless, for *understanding* these developments, his work provides an important key. Probably better than any other, Philo shows how a first-century Jewish intellectual was attuned to the problems raised by scripture—problems that persisted long after his time.[69] For instance: why did the Jewish deity appear jealous (Gen 3:22)? Why did he forbid the fruit of knowledge to the first humans (Gen 2:17)? Why did he apparently change his mind about creating humanity (Gen 6:6)?

Philo did his best to answer the problems raised by scripture during his lifetime. Yet his answers apparently proved unsatisfying to a new generation of Christian intellectuals with different pre-judgments about the validity of Judaism, its laws, and its scriptures. In short, the problems raised by Philo show that it was possible for later Christian interpreters to conclude from biblical stories themselves that the Jewish creator was not good, and thus not the true God.[70]

---

[67] See Josephus, *C. Ap.* 1.73–105, 228–52, 304–11 with E. M. Smallwood, *The Jews under Roman Rule from Pompey to Diocletian* (Leiden: Brill, 1976), 293–466; P. Schäfer, *Judeophobia: Attitudes toward the Jews in the Ancient World* (Cambridge, MA: Harvard University Press, 1997), 15–33; J. M. G. Barclay, "Hostility to Jews as a Cultural Construct: Egyptian, Hellenistic, and Early Christian Paradigms," in *Josephus und das Neue Testament: Wechselseitige Wahrnehmungen*, ed. C. Böttrich and J. Herzer (Tübingen: Mohr Siebeck, 2007), 365–86; J. M. G. Barclay, "The Politics of Contempt. Judeans and Egyptians in Josephus' *Against Apion*," in *Pauline Churches and Diaspora Jews* (Tübingen: Mohr Siebeck, 2011), 277–300; B. Bar-Kochva, *The Image of the Jews in Greek Literature* (Berkeley: University of California Press, 2010), 206–52; D. Tripaldi, "From Philo to Areimanios: Jewish Traditions and Intellectual Profiles in First-Third Century Alexandria in the Light of the Apocryphon of John," in *Jews and Christians in Antiquity: A Regional Perspective*, ed. P. Lanfranchi and J. Verheyden (Leuven: Peeters, 2018), 101–20.

[68] M. A. Williams, "The Demonizing of the Demiurge: The Innovation of Gnostic Myth," in *Innovations in Religious Traditions*, ed. M. A. Williams, C. Cox, and M. S. Jaffe (Berlin: de Gruyter, 1992), 73–107; M. Heemstra, *Fiscus Iudaicus and the Parting of the Ways* (Tübingen: Mohr Siebeck, 2010); M. D. Litwa, *Early Christianity in Alexandria: From Its Beginnings to the Late Second Century* (Cambridge: Cambridge University Press, 2024), 55–88.

[69] The extreme allegorists Philo complains about (*Migr.* 89–93) probably still considered themselves to be Jews. They are not to be equated with Sethians who are, by and large, not allegorical, but literal interpreters of Jewish scripture. See further D. M. Hay, "References to Other Exegetes," in *Both Literal and Allegorical: Studies in Philo of Alexandria's Questions and Answers on Genesis and Exodus*, ed. D. M. Hay (Providence: Brown University Press, 1991), 81–97.

[70] During his own time, Philo knew that some "impious people" declare that God is "the cause of evils" (τὸν θεὸν αἴτιον κακῶν), evidently on the basis of "Moses" or the Pentateuch (*Det.* 122). See further M. David Litwa, *The Evil Creator: Origins of an Early Christian Idea* (New York: Oxford University Press, 2021).

Naturally Philo would have vigorously opposed any use of his ideas that supported a negative evaluation of the creator or of the religion of Moses. Yet Philo, like all authors, had no control over the afterlife of his works. The scattered seeds of his thought were in many cases transformed into new and hybrid species of plants. History, as always, proved unpredictable; and the great Alexandrian exegete could not have foreseen that his school of thought would become a seedbed for Sethian Christian speculation.

7
Ancient Platonic Philosophy

Gregory E. Sterling

It is well known that Eusebius of Caesarea helped to catalogue the writings of Philo for the Episcopal library in Caesarea. When he provided an account of Philo's works, the Christian historian offered an assessment of the author: "Philo became widely known as a most distinguished man not only among our own people but also among those who are keen about pagan education. He was a Hebrew by ancestral race but inferior to none of the distinguished persons in office in Alexandria." Eusebius explained the basis for this claim: "The extent and scope of his labor that he devoted to theological and ancestral learning is, in fact, evident to all. It is not necessary to speak about his abilities in philosophy or the liberal studies of pagan education since it is related that he surpassed all in his time in his zeal for the Platonic and Pythagorean schools of thought" (*Hist. eccl.* 2.4.2–3).[1] Philo's expertise in philosophy was recognized by others including Josephus who said that the Alexandrian was "a most distinguished man ... an expert in philosophy" (*A.J.* 18.259).

But does Eusebius' claim that Philo was highly regarded beyond the confines of Jewish and early Christian circles have any merit? There is no question about his influence on early Christians, especially on Alexandrian and Cappadocian thinkers.[2] The same cannot be said for his possible influence on pagan authors which has been discussed sparingly. The most notable exception to this judgment is Harry Austryn Wolfson, who argued that Philo was "a philosopher in the grand manner."[3] Wolfson thought that Philo created a philosophical construct that endured until Spinoza dismantled it. He argued that "without a group of official disciples his (Philo's) teachings became the most dominant influence in European philosophy for well-nigh seventeen centuries."[4] Wolfson sought to demonstrate this in a series of works—some not complete at his death—primarily on the basis of Philo's system of thought and some of his major concepts—although he addressed specific issues as well.[5] While Wolfson was incredibly learned and creative, there are fundamental problems with his view, especially

---

[1] All translations are my own. On the role of Jewish authors in Eusebius, see S. Inowlocki, *Eusebius and the Jewish Authors: His Citation Technique in an Apologetic Context*, AGJU 64 (Leiden: Brill, 2006), esp. 223–88 and 268–69 for the text cited; see also her Chapter 9 in this volume.

[2] The most important comprehensive survey is D. T. Runia, *Philo in Early Christian Literature: A Survey*, CRINT 3.3 (Assen: Van Gorcum, 1993).

[3] H. A. Wolfson, *Philo: Foundations of Religious Philosophy in Judaism, Christianity, and Islam*, 2 vols (Cambridge, MA: Harvard University Press, 1947), 1:114.

[4] Wolfson, *Philo*, 1:115.

[5] See H. A. Wolfson, *Religious Philosophy* (Cambridge, MA: Belknap Press of Harvard University Press, 1961), v.

his systematization of Philo's thought and unification of Christian, Jewish, and Islamic medieval philosophy which were hardly as uniform as he imagined.[6] Virtually no one has accepted Wolfson's grand thesis, although this does not mean that he was wrong on all counts.

There have been more moderate voices who have called for an analysis of Philo's possible influence on Hellenistic philosophy, especially in the persons of Roberto Radice[7] and Jose Pablo Martín.[8] Still others have considered specific examples of possible influence, but no one has attempted to offer a comprehensive survey. While it is beyond the scope of this contribution to offer a full study, I would like to offer some preliminary reflections on Philo and the Platonic tradition that I hope will stimulate further work.[9]

We will consider the possible influence of Philo on three authors. I have selected these three because Plutarch and Numenius represent Middle Platonism and Plotinus Neoplatonism. They also worked in areas where Philo's treatises circulated: Plutarch lived in Greece but visited both Rome and Egypt, Numenius was from Apamea (Syria), and Plotinus spent his career in Alexandria and Rome. There is evidence that Philo's works circulated in Egypt,[10] Syria,[11] and Rome.[12] We will explore one parallel or one text that has parallels between each author and Philo. I will mention some other major parallels at the end of the relevant section. We want to determine whether it is probable, possible, or improbable that Philo influenced the philosopher either directly or indirectly through an intermediate thinker.

7.1 Plutarch

Plutarch (c.45/47–120 CE) was born in Chaeronea, a small city in northwest Boetia about 50 miles east of Delphi, to a prominent family (*Sull.* 16.8; *Dem.* 19.2). He frequently and warmly refers to members of his family with whom he maintained close

---

[6] For a critique, see D. T. Runia, "History in the Grand Manner: The Achievement of H. A. Wolfson," *Philosophia Reformata* 49 (1984): 112–33, esp. 130.

[7] R. Radice, "Le judaïsme alexandrine et la philosophie grecque: influences probables et points de contact," in *Philon d'Alexandrie et le langage de la philosophie*, ed. C. Lévy, Monothéismes et Philosophie (Turnhout: Brepols, 1998), 483–92.

[8] J. P. Martín, "El platonismo medio y Filón geún un studio de David Runia," *Methexis* 5 (1992): 135–43, esp. 141–43.

[9] In preparation for this study I also worked through the parallels with Seneca, Alcinous, and Celsus. I hope to publish the full treatment of all six philosophers in the near future.

[10] The main line of transmission of Philo's works came via Origen who carried them along with other Jewish works from Alexandria to Caesarea. See Runia, *Philo in Early Christian Literature*, 16–22; and G. E. Sterling, "Philo of Alexandria," in *A Guide to Early Jewish Texts and Traditions in Christian Transmission*, ed. A. Kulik (Oxford: Oxford University Press, 2019), 299–316. Philo's works did not stop circulating in Egypt after Origen took his copies. For a discussion, see J. R. Royse, "The Oxyrhynchus Papyrus of Philo," *Bulletin of the American Society of Papyrologists* 17 (1980): 155–65.

[11] Heliodorus, *Aeth.* 9.9, cited Philo, *Mos.* 2.195. For an analysis, see G. E. Sterling, "Recherché or Representative? What Is the Relationship between Philo's Treatises and Greek-Speaking Judaism?," *SPhiloA* 11 (1999): 1–30, esp. 20–21.

[12] There are two relatively secure pieces of evidence for this. First, Josephus knew and used some of Philo's works (see G. E. Sterling, "'A Man of the Highest Repute': Did Josephus Know the Writings of Philo?," *SPhiloA* 25 [2013]: 101–13). Second, the Latin translation probably rests on texts that were from Rome (see Sterling, "Philo of Alexandria," 309–11).

relationships throughout his life. The family's wealth enabled Plutarch to travel to Athens as a young man where he studied with Ammonius, a Platonic philosopher from Egypt.[13] The main evidence we have for Ammonius consists of the speeches Plutarch attributes to him in *Table Talk* and the Pythian treatises *On the E at Delphi* and *On the Obsolescence of Oracles*.[14] After his studies, Plutarch returned to Boetia where he served as a priest of Apollo at Delphi (*Quaest. conv.* 700E)[15] and ran a private philosophical school at Chaeronea.[16] These commitments did not prevent him from long trips, including journeys to Alexandria (*Quaest. conv.* 678C) and Rome (*Dem.* 2.2–3), two of the places where Philo's works were in circulation.[17]

Plutarch was an incredibly learned man who wrote extensively. The Catalogue of Lamprias (third or fourth century CE) attributes 227 works to him.[18] We have seventy-eight works that modern scholars have dubbed the *Moralia* because of their ethical bent and fifty biographical works—one of the largest corpora that has come down to us from the ancient world.[19] It is also one of the richest sources for citations. Plutarch quoted well over five hundred different authors and sources, although some might have been drawn from existing collections.[20] Plutarch was aware of Jews and Judaism: he mentioned them at least eighteen times in his corpus, primarily in historical references but also in some important statements about God.[21] We do not know how he encountered Jews whether in Boeotia or on his trips to Alexandria and Rome or both. Did he know Philo?

Before we examine a specific parallel we should note that Plutarch embraced the view that a common wisdom existed among many ancient peoples.[22] The priest at Delphi wrote: "Ancient natural philosophy (ἡ παλαιὰ φυσιολογία) among both Greeks and barbarians, took the form of an account of nature hidden in mythology, veiled for the most part in riddles and hints," or alternatively, "of a theology such as is found in

---

[13] Plutarch, *E Delph.* 385A–B, 387F. Cf. also *Def. orac.* 431A. The last two references have generated extensive discussion. See also *Adul. amic.* 70E; *Them.* 32.5. Plutarch was there long enough to become a citizen. See *Quaest. conv.* 628A.

[14] On Ammonius, see J. Opsomer, "M. Annius Ammonius, a Philosophical Profile," in *The Origins of the Platonic System: Platonisms of the Early Empire and Their Philosophical Contexts*, ed. M. Bonazzi and J. Opsomer, Collections des études Classiques 23 (Leuven: Peeters, 2009), 123–86.

[15] He wrote several treatises about Delphi including *The E at Delphi*, *The Oracles at Delphi*, and *The Obsolescence of Oracles*.

[16] M. Baltes, "Plutarchus [2]," *Brill's New Pauly*, 11:416, provides a list of the names of his students.

[17] He tells us that he learned Latin, but not until he was older (*Dem.* 2.2–3).

[18] For a convenient list, see F. H. Sandbach, *Plutarch's Moralia XV*, LCL (Cambridge, MA: Harvard University Press, 1987), 3–29. Some of the works in the Catalogue are no longer extant, some extant works are not in the Catalogue, and some works in the Catalogue are pseudonymous.

[19] Eight works often considered pseudonymous include *Lib. ed., Reg. imp. apophth., Fat., Amat. narr., Vit. X orat., Plac. philos., Animae procr.*, and *Mus.*

[20] On the citations in Plutarch, see W. C. Helmbold and E. N. O'Neill, *Plutarch Quotations*, Philological Monographs 19 (London: American Philological Association, 1959).

[21] See M. Stern, *Greek and Latin Authors on Jews and Judasim*, 3 vols (Jerusalem: The Israel Academy of Sciences and Humanities, 1974–1984), nos. 255–72 (1:549–76). Hereafter *GLAJJ*.

[22] The most important treatment of this is G. Boys-Stones, *Post-Hellenistic Philosophy: A Study of Its Development from the Stoics to Origen* (Oxford: Oxford University Press, 2001), 99–122. For the Stoic view, see D. Dawson, *Allegorical Readers and Cultural Revision in Ancient Alexandria* (Berkeley: University of California Press, 1992), 24–38. On this view as it relates to Philo and Plutarch, see G. E. Sterling, "Platonizing Moses: Philo and Middle Platonism," *SPhiloA* 5 (1993): 96–111; and G. E. Sterling, "When East and West Meet: Eastern Religions and Western Philosophy in Philo of Alexandria and Plutarch of Chaeronea," *SPhiloA* 28 (2016): 137–50, esp. 146–50.

mystery ceremonies in which what is spoken is less clear to the masses than what is unsaid, and what is unsaid gives cause for more speculation than what is said."[23] Plutarch most famously incorporated this perspective in *On Isis and Osiris*[24] and in *Amatorius* (762A and 764A). In both treatises he linked Egyptian myths and Platonism.[25] Philo shared the same perspective, only he worked with Mosaic traditions. For example, he argued that the texts in which God commanded Moses to build a tabernacle according to the pattern that Moses saw on the mountain contained the concept of Platonic ideas.[26] For both authors ancient wisdom was embedded within the mythos or texts and could be uncovered through philosophy by means of allegoresis. The same perspective will reappear in Numenius and Plotinus.

The place where both Plutarch and Philo believed the greatest convergence took place was in the understanding of God.[27] In this they both reflect what we know as "philosophical monotheism."[28] The most important statement of Plutarch's theology for our purposes is the speech of Ammonius, Plutarch's teacher, in *The E at Delphi*.[29] The dialogue offers seven interpretations of the enigmatic epsilon at the shrine (*E Delph.* 384F; *Def. orac.* 426E). Each speaker offered a different interpretation (*E Delph.* 385D–386A); Ammonius spoke last. It is not clear whether Ammonius' speech reflects his views or Plutarch's;[30] we will refer to Ammonius in this section rather than Plutarch. In the speech Ammonius drew the Platonic contrast between becoming and being which we will use to organize the comparison.

Becoming. Ammonius argues that humans do not have being: "For us there is no real participation in being, but every mortal nature, which is in the middle of coming into existence and passing away, provides a dim and uncertain apparition and phantom of itself" (*E Delph.* 392A). One of the most powerful images Ammonius offered for this position was the development of a human: "Therefore what comes into existence never reaches being because generation never stops nor remains stationary." He illustrated

---

[23] Plutarch, frag. 157 (Eusebius, *Praep. ev.* 3.1.1). See also frag. 190.

[24] For specific statements within this treatise, see *Is. Os.* 377F–378A. Cf. also his comments in 374E–F.

[25] R. Hirsch-Luipold, "Der eine Gott bei Philon von Alexandrien und Plutarch," in *Gott und die Götter bei Plutarch: Götterbilder–Gottesbilder–Weltbilder*, ed. R. Hirsch-Luipold, RVV 54 (Berlin: de Gruyter, 2005), 141–68, esp. 147.

[26] Philo, *Mos.* 2.74. See also 2.76 (citing Exod 25:40); *QE* 2.52 (citing Exod 25:8), 82 (citing Exod 25:40), 90 (citing Exod 26:30). For a detailed treatment, see G. E. Sterling, "Ontology versus Eschatology: Tensions between Author and Community in Hebrews," *SPhiloA* 13 (2001): 190–211, esp. 199–202.

[27] The two most important essays that have examined the similarities are Hirsch-Luipold, "Der eine Gott bei Philon von Alexandrien und Plutarch," 141–68; and F. E. Brink, "Philo and Plutarch on the Nature of God," *SPhiloA* 26 (2014): 79–92.

[28] I will set aside the issue of pagan monotheism and focus strictly on the philosophical material. On pagan monotheism, see P. Athanassiadi and M. Frede, eds, *Pagan Monotheism in Late Antiquity* (Oxford: Clarendon, 1999); and S. Mitchell and P. Van Nuffelen, *One God: Pagan Monotheism in the Roman Empire* (Cambridge: Cambridge University Press, 2010).

[29] On this dialogue, see F. E. Brenk, "Plutarch's Middle-Platonic God: About to Enter (or Remake) the Academy," in *Gott und die Götter bei Plutarch*, 27–50; repr. in F. E. Brenk, *With Unperfumed Voice: Studies in Plutarch, in Greek Literature, Religion and Philosophy, and in the New Testament Background*, Postsdamer Altertumswissenschaftliche Beiträge 21 (Stuttgart: Steiner, 2007), 121–43.

[30] The most trenchant critique that Plutarch spoke through Ammonius here is Opsomer, "M. Annius Ammonius, a Philosophical Profile," 123–86, esp. 172–74. Brink, "Philo and Plutarch on the Nature of God," 89–92, shares this concern.

this by using the stages of life set out by Pseudo-Hippocrates:[31] "but (generation) which is always changing makes an embryo from a seed, then a baby, then a child, next a boy, a young man, then a man, a mature man, an old man, laying aside the first generations and ages with those that follow" (*E Delph.* 392C). He continued: "But we ludicrously fear one death, we who have already died so many deaths and are in the process of dying." He explained by referring to Heraclitus—just as he had earlier cited him[32]—who said that "the death of heat is the birth of steam and the death of steam is the birth of water" (*E Delph.* 392C, citing Heraclitus, frag. 76) and then applied this to a human: "the person in their prime passes away as the old man comes into existence; the young man passes away into the man in his prime, the child into the young man, and the infant into the child." He then summarized: "the person of yesterday has died for the person of today, the person of today dies for the person tomorrow; no one remains and it is impossible to be one, but we become many" (*E Delph.* 392D).

Philo has a similar treatment of the stages of life in *De Iosepho*. In this *bios* the Alexandrian alternated between retelling the biblical text and allegorical interpretations on the retellings. After summarizing the story of Gen 39:20–41:45 (§§80–124), the commentator opened his allegorical interpretation (§§125–47) by suggesting that the dream Joseph interpreted represented life which is itself illusory because of its transitory character. He explained that every mature person understands this: "This is he who was at one time a baby, afterward a child, then an adolescent, then a boy, then a young man, then a man, and last an old man." He asked: "But where are all these? Has not the baby given way to the child, and the child to the one entering adolescence, and the one entering adolescence to the boy, and the boy to youth, and youth to the man, and the man to the old man, and death follows old age." This led him to observe: "Perhaps in fact, as each of the ages yields its power to the one after it, it dies; nature teaching us silently not to fear the death over all since we have easily endured the former (deaths): the death of the baby, the death of the child, the death of the adolescent, the death of the boy, the death of the young man, the death of the man, none of which are still present when we are in old age" (*Ios.* 127–29).

The similarities between Philo and Plutarch are striking (on which see Table 7.1).

The categories they used when describing the death of one stage as the birth of another are listed in Table 7.2.

The two Platonists agree with two exceptions: Philo has a category in youth that Ammonius does not and Ammonius has a stage in maturity that Philo does not. When they relate the death of each age, Philo works through the ages progressively while Ammonius works regressively. The agreement in the specific stages is not surprising since they were both drawing from the Pseudo-Hippocratean scheme.

---

[31] On this text, see M. L. West, "The Cosmology of 'Hippocrates,' *De Hebdomadibus*," *CQ* 21 (1971): 365–88; J. Mansfeld, *The Pseudo-Hippocratean Tract Περὶ ἑβδομάδων, ch. 1–11 and Greek Philosophy*, Philosophical Texts and Studies 20 (Assen: Van Gorcum, 1971).

[32] Plutarch, *E Delph.* 392B, introduced the fluctuating status of humans by quoting the famous saying of Heraclitus: "it is not possible to enter the same river twice" (Heraclitus, frag. 91). Plutarch also cited it in *Sera* 559C.

Table 7.1 Comparison of the Ages of Man

Age	Pseudo-Hippocrates*	Philo	Plutarch
Embryo			ἔμβρυον
Baby	παιδίον	βρέφος	βρέφος
Child	παῖς	παῖς	παῖς
Entering Adolescence		ἔφηβος	
Boy	μειράκιον	μειράκιον	μειράκον
Young Man	νεηνίσκος	νεανίας	νεανίσκιον
Man	ἀνήρ	ἀνήρ	ἀνήρ
Mature Man	πρεσβύτης		πρεσβύτης
Old Man	γέρων	γέρων	γέρων

* Pseudo-Hippocrates, *De hebdomadibus* 5. I have used the text in West, "The Cosmology of 'Hippocrates,' *De Hebdomadibus*," 369.

There are, however, a couple of features that make us wonder whether this is a case of dependence on a common source or direct dependence. Philo is the first witness to the Pseudo-Hippocratean *On the Sevens* (*De hebdomadibus*) (*Opif.* 105; *Ios.* 127–29). While the date of the text is disputed, it should probably be associated with the Pythagorean movement in the second and first centuries BCE.[33] Since there is not an English translation of the text, I will provide one:

> So there are seven seasons in the nature of a man which we call ages: the infant, child, boy, young man, man, mature man, and old man. The infant is until seven years and the development of (adult) teeth; the child is until puberty in the two times seven years; the boy is until the beard in the three times seven years; the young man is until the growth of the full body in the four times seven years; the man is until the fiftieth year minus one in the seven times seven years; the mature man is until the fifty-sixth year in the eight times seven years; the old man is from this point on.[34]

The use of the scheme by Philo and Ammonius who were both from the same area simply confirms its widespread use.[35] There is, however, a second point that makes the common use more telling. Philo and Ammonius both associated Heraclitean flux with the succession of human ages.[36] The Pseudo-Hippocratean treatise only applied

---

[33] For a summary of the debate about the dating of the document, see D. T. Runia, *Philo of Alexandria, On the Creation of the Cosmos: Introduction, Translation and Commentary*, PACS 1 (Leiden: Brill, 2001), 280–81, who provides bibliography.
[34] The text is found in West, "The Cosmology of 'Hippocrates,' *De Hebdomadibus*," 369.
[35] It is worth noting that Philo knew other schemes, e.g. *QG* 4.152; *Her.* 294–99; *Congr.* 82; *Opif.* 103–5; and *Aet.* 58.
[36] Philo was fond of Heraclitus and cited him by name six times out of a total of twenty-seven citations from fourteen fragments. For a list, see G. E. Sterling, "'The Jewish Philosophy': Reading Moses via Hellenistic Philosophy According to Philo," in *Reading Philo: A Handbook to Philo of Alexandria*, ed. T. Seland (Grand Rapids: Eerdmans, 2014), 129–54, esp. 145–46.

hebdomads to each age with an occasional notice of a biological development.[37] Philo and Ammonius are not the only philosophers to associate transitions in life with the Heraclitean concept that death brings birth; Seneca made the same connection. However, the Stoic made it without referring to the stages of life apart from youth and old age (*Ep.* 58.22–23). While it is possible that Philo and Ammonius independently made the connection between Pseudo-Hippocrates and Heraclitus, it is more likely that either Philo and Ammonius drew from a common source or that Ammonius was influenced by Philo.

Table 7.2 Comparison of the Ages of Man

Age	Philo	Plutarch
Baby	βρέφος	νήπιον
Child	παῖς	παῖς
Entering Adolescence	παρήβος/ἔφηβος	
Boy	μειράκιον	
Young Man	νεανίας	νέος
Man	ἀνήρ	
Mature Man		ἀκμάζων
Old Man	γέρων	γέρων

Being. The other ontological category is being. Ammonius asked: "What then is being really?" He answered: "The eternal, ungenerated, and incorruptible, to which no length of time introduces change" (*E Delph.* 392E). And what is this? "But God exists—if it is necessary to declare this—and exists in no time but in eternity which is immoveable, timeless, and unchanging; there is nothing before nor later nor future nor past nor older nor younger" (*E Delph.* 393A). It is for this reason that we address God with the words "you are" (εἶ) or even, I swear, as some of the ancients said: 'you are one' (εἶ ἕν)" (*E Delph.* 393B). This led Ammonius to explain the "one": "For the Deity is not many like each of us ... but being must be one, just as the one must be being" (ἀλλ' ἕν εἶναι δεῖ τὸ ὄν, ὥσπερ ὂν τὸ ἕν) (*E Delph.* 393B). Ammonius then gave three names for God that helped to explain God's unicity: Apollo which means "not many" (α–privative and πολλά),[38] Ieius the "one and only" (εἷς καὶ μόνος), and Phoebus which he understood to be "pure and undefiled."[39]

This remarkable text has generated a great deal of discussion. We will focus only on whether statements in Philo could have served as a source for Ammonius. Philo considered the First Principle Being and made this point repeatedly. In a comment on a secondary lemmata in his commentary on Gen 4:14, Philo underscored the point that it was impossible to flee God by introducing Exod 33:7 (*Det.* 150–66, esp. 160–66). Moses set a tent up outside the camp, far from the encumbrances of the body in order to

---

[37] On the ways in which different authors cited and applied the series of seven in the treatise, see West, "The Cosmology of 'Hippocrates,' *De Hebdomadibus*," 376–77.
[38] Plutarch offers the same etymology several times, e.g. *E Delph.* 388F; *Is. Os.* 354F, 381F.
[39] Plutarch, *E Delph.* 393C. Cf. also 388F for the first and third names.

worship God: "he says that this tent is called the tent of testimony, very precisely, since the tent of the Being exists (ἡ τοῦ ὄντος ὑπάρχῃ) and is not merely named. For among the virtues, God's virtue is real, existing in being." He explained: "God alone exists in being (καὶ ὁ θεὸς μόνος ἐν τῷ εἶναι ὑφέστηκεν). For this reason he will necessarily say of him: 'I am Being (ἐγώ εἰμι ὁ ὤν)'" (Exod 3:14). Philo went on to contrast God/Being with everything else: "those things after him are not in the realm of being (οὐκ ὄντων κατὰ τὸ εἶναι) but are only thought to exist by opinion" (*Det.* 160). This is one of four places where Philo cited Exod 3:14 and offered an interpretation;[40] he alludes to it many times, primarily in references to God.[41] The point that we need to understand is that Philo drew a bright ontological line between God and all else. Yet, this is a line that almost any Platonist could have drawn based on Plato's *Timaeus* and its sharp distinction between being and becoming (*Tim.* 27D–28A).

What sets these two cases apart is that both conceived of God as a personal being. Philo certainly understood God in this way. But so did Ammonius who thought that εἶ ("you are") was an address. Perhaps the most interesting means of appreciating this is to note that the two routinely moved from the masculine to the neuter. Philo had a number of expressions for God that were inspired by Exod 3:14. Some of his favorite expressions are "Being" (ὁ ὤν),[42] "the God who is actually Being" (ὁ ὄντως ὢν θεός),[43] or "truly Being" (ὁ ὢν πρὸς ἀλήθειαν) (*Mut.* 11). However, without any embarrassment or apology he also moved from the masculine of the LXX to the neuter expression of Platonism (τὸ ὄν) and called God "Being" (τὸ ὄν),[44] "actual Being" (τὸ ὄντως ὄν),[45] and "true Being" (τὸ πρὸς ἀλήθειαν ὄν).[46]

Ammonius did the same: he began with "God" (ὁ θεός) and claimed that God was "one" (εἷς ὤν), before turning to the neuter (τὸ κατὰ τοῦτον ὄντως ὄν). Again, he called God "him" (αὐτόν) and addressed him as "you are" (εἶ) before explaining "you are one" (εἶ ἕν) and referring to God as "the Deity" (τὸ θεῖον), "the one" (τὸ ἕν), "Being" (τὸ ὄν ... τοῦ ὄντος). He made the shift one more time by beginning with a reference to God (τῷ θεῷ) and then to Apollo (Ἀπόλλων) before returning to "the one" (τὸ ἕν) (Plutarch, *E Delph.* 393A–C). Why this freedom of gender? In some ways it is easier to understand how Philo could move from the Jewish/personal masculine to the Platonic/impersonal neuter than it is to grasp how Ammonius could move from the Platonic neuter/impersonal to a personal masculine. It might be that Ammonius used the masculine in favor of the shrine to Apollo; however, this is still an unusual move for a Platonist. While there is no evidence that Ammonius knew Exod 3:14, he might have encountered a source that identified "Being" (τὸ ὄν) and "Being" (ὁ ὤν). His interpretation of the enigmatic E as εἶ ("you are") would certainly fit. But is there more?

---

[40] See below under Numenius (pp. 119–20).
[41] For details, see L. A. Montes-Peral, *Akataleptos Theos: Der unfassbare Gott*, ALGHJ 16 (Leiden: Brill, 1987), 48–74.
[42] 4× in Philo. Cf. also the genitive (τοῦ ὄντος) 8×.
[43] Philo, *Det.* 139. Cf. also the genitive (τοῦ ὄντως ὄντος) in *Her.* 70.
[44] 59× in Philo.
[45] 4× in Philo.
[46] 2× in Philo.

It is important to remember that both insisted that God was one. Philo was emphatic about monotheism. In the famous statement that summarized the principles he considered fundamental for understanding the Pentateuch at the conclusion of *De opificio mundi*, the second of his five principles was that "God is one" (θεὸς εἷς ἐστι) (*Opif.* 171).[47] While Philo's understanding of God was a Platonized God similar to but not identical with Eudorus' "supreme God" (ὁ ὑπεράνω θεός), he was emphatic that God was one.[48] Philo frequently spoke of God as "one" and even used the phrase "one and only." For example, Philo opened his explanation of the statement in Gen 2:18 that "it is not good for the man to be alone" by affirming that while it is not good for a human to be alone "it is good for the Alone to be Alone." He offered several explanations of what this might mean. The first was "God being One (εἷς ὢν ὁ θεός) is alone and one of a kind; there is nothing like God." The second was that God pre-existed the cosmos. The third and best was "God is Alone and One (ὁ θεὸς μόνος ἐστὶ καὶ ἕν)" (*Leg.* 2.1–2). Philo's statement here and elsewhere may have been inspired by Deut 6:4, but it is interesting that he never cited this famous text. Whether this influenced him or not, he affirmed that God was "one and only."[49]

As we have seen, Ammonius also used the intriguing expression "one and only" (εἷς καὶ μόνος) as an etymological explanation for Ieius (a name for Apollo), incorrectly understood to come from ἴα ("one").[50] Ammonius may have suggested that this was the supreme God, the transcendent God of Neopythagorean thought adopted by Middle Platonists. On the other hand, he may have only meant that this god is unique, without peer.[51] I do not want to suggest that Ammonius and Plutarch were monotheists in the same way that Philo was; they were not.[52] However, Ammonius has appropriated language that was used for the supreme Deity—however understood.

Where did Ammonius and Plutarch derive this language? There is no question that Philo of Alexandria provides the closest extant parallels to the views of Ammonius in this period. The linkage of the Pseudo-Hippocratean stages of life with Heraclitean flux is striking. Seneca also knew the connection but did not make it as fully (*Ep.* 58.22–23). How should we judge the evidence? There are two ways that we can answer the question of dependence. On the one hand, we should recognize that the concepts and language are not unique to Philo and Ammonius but are attested elsewhere. This led John Whittaker to suggest that Eudorus stood behind the theology of Ammonius.[53] On the other hand, the lack of evidence from Eudorus has led others to be less specific and to speak of an Alexandrian philosophical context.[54] Was Philo part of this?

---

[47] Cf. the later statement in the same text: "Fourth that the cosmos is also one, since the Creator who made it similar to himself in its uniqueness is one."
[48] On the transcendence of God above all see, for example, *Opif.* 100; *Praem.* 39–40; and *Contempl.* 2.
[49] 7× in Philo. Cf. also the texts where both terms are used but not in a fixed phrase (5× in Philo).
[50] Plutarch, *E Delph.* 393C. See F. Babit's note in the LCL ad loc.
[51] Opsomer, "M. Annius Ammoniius, a Philosophical Profile," 158–59.
[52] For a comparison, see Hirsch-Luipold, "Der eine Gott bei Philon von Alexandrien und Plutarch," 154 and Opsomer, "M. Annius Ammoniius, a Philosophical Profile," 159.
[53] Whittaker, "Ammonius on the Delphic E," 190–92.
[54] Opsomer, "M. Annius Ammoniius, a Philosophical Profile," 165–66; and Hirsch-Luipold, "Der eine Gott bei Philon von Alexandrien und Plutarch," 161–67. See also J. Dillon, "Plutarch and God: Theodicy and Cosmogony

He was certainly part of the Alexandrian philosophical scene. Did he contribute to it? We would have been able to answer this with more certainty if so much of the evidence had not perished. We can say that Philo is the earliest and closest witness to the views articulated by Ammonius.[55]

7.2 Numenius of Apamea

The next author we will examine is Numenius of Apamea.[56] Unfortunately, we know very little about Numenius.[57] He came from Apamea, a major city on the Orontes River. Founded by either Seleucus I or Antiochus I as a military center,[58] the city produced two noteworthy philosophers: the Stoic Posidonius (c.135–51 BCE) and the Middle Platonist Numenius (second century CE). Numenius may have spent some time in Rome since Johannes Lydus referred to him as "Numenius the Roman"[59] and his works were important for Plotinus and his school.[60]

We have sixty fragments of his works: twenty-nine belong to four identifiable works, but the remaining thirty-one are unplaceable—although we know that he wrote at least three more works.[61] The most striking feature about his works that is relevant for our purposes is his commitment to bridge east and west, perhaps an intellectual agenda that reflected his own existential situation. He wrote: "With respect to this it will be necessary, after having stated and interpreted the testimonies of Plato, to return to and unite them with the views of Pythagoras," a sentiment that may help us understand why Numenius is sometimes considered a Pythagorean. He continued: "then to summon the highly regarded nations, adducing their rites, teachings, and basic tenets as far as they concur with Plato—whatever the Brahmans, Jews, Magi, and Egyptians have to say."[62] It is worth pointing out that the amount of material devoted to the Jews in Numenius is greater than that of any other group, although this could easily be the result of the interests of Origen and Eusebius who transmitted a large portion of this material. Still, we need to remember that Numenius was openly interested in Jewish thought.[63]

We will explore one of Numenius' fragments where the overlap with Philo's thought is striking: "Again, just as there is rapport between a cultivator (γεωργός) and the

---

in the Thought of Plutarch," in *Traditions of Theology: Studies in Hellenistic Theology, Its Background and Aftermath*, ed. D. Frede and A. Laks, Philosophia Antiqua 89 (Leiden: Brill, 2001), 223–37, esp. 236.

[55] For other areas where there are similarities between Philo and Plutarch, see in particular M. Niehoff, ed., *Homer and the Bible in the Eyes of Ancient Interpreters*, Jerusalem Studies in Religion and Culture 16 (Leiden: Brill, 2012), 127–53.

[56] For a more extensive treatment, see G. E. Sterling, "The Theft of Philosophy: Philo of Alexandria and Numenius of Apamea," *SPhiloA* 27 (2015): 71–85.

[57] On Numenius, see M. Frede, "Numenius," *ANRW* 2.36.2 (1987): 1034–75. For a brief treatment, see M. Frede, "Numenius [6] of Apameia," *Brill's New Pauly* 9:896–98.

[58] Strabo 16.2.10 said that it was the site for the breeding of the military elephants.

[59] Johannes Lydus in Numenius, frag. 57.

[60] See the comments of Porphyry, *Vit. Plot.* 14, 17. Cf. also 3.

[61] The standard edition of Numenius is É. des Places, *Numenius of Apameia, Fragments: Text établi et traduit*, Collection des universités de France (Paris: Les belles lettres, 1973).

[62] Numenius, frag. 1a.

[63] For his comments on Jews, see *GLAJJ* nos. 363–69 (2:209–16).

planter (ὁ φυτεύων), the first God has the same rapport with the Demiurge. The Self-Existent (ὁ μέν γε ὤν) sows the seed of every soul into everything that participates in him. The Lawgiver plants, distributes, and transplants into each of us what has already been set down by the former."[64]

There are two aspects of this fragment that merit consideration. The juxtaposition of the cultivator and the planter reminds every Philonist of the first two treatises in the Noah cycle within the Allegorical Commentary: *De agricultura* and *De plantatione*. The juxtaposition of the two is due to the presence of the noun "cultivator" (γεωργός) and the verb "plant" (φυτεύω) in Gen 9:20 which Philo took up in the two treatises respectively. The juxtaposition of cultivator/planter in both authors is hardly a surprise since the concepts are related and the imagery is common.[65]

The more important issue is how they are used. In Numenius the first god is the Good and absolute, while the second god is the Demiurge. For Numenius, the First God has the same relationship with the Second God as a cultivator has with a planter.

Philo never juxtaposed God with the Logos as cultivator and planter; however, he assigned similar roles to God and the Logos. So, for example, in *De plantatione*, Philo presented God as "the great planter" (ὁ μέγας φυτουργός) who created the cosmos, the macrocosm (§§1–27), and humanity, the microcosm (§§28–72) and did so through the agency of the Logos: in the case of the cosmos, the Logos is the bond that holds the cosmos together, a description that echoes Plato's account of the World Soul (*Tim.* 34B and 36E);[66] in the case of humanity, the Logos is the Image of God in which humanity is created, i.e. in the image of the Image.[67] Philo liked this imagery and used it elsewhere as well.[68] The functions of the First God and the Demiurge in Numenius are paralleled by the functions of God and the Logos in Philo.

There is, however, a more important similarity. Numenius described the First God as "the Self-Existent" (ὁ μέν γε ὤν). The phrase is not without complications. E. R. Dodds correctly noted that it is difficult to relate the actions attributed to the First God and the Demiurge in Numenius to Plato's description of them in the *Timaeus*. Dodds went on to suggest that ὁ ὤν required a predicate and emended the text to "the First God" (ὁ μέν γε α' ὤν).[69] John Whittaker pointed out that ὁ ὤν is a well-known Septuagintalism

---

[64] Numenius, frag. 13 (Eusebius, *Praep. ev.* 11.18.13–14).

[65] Philo juxtaposed the two eight times. Four of these cite Gen 9:20: *Det.* 105; *Agr.* 1; *Plant.* 1, 140. Four are based on the relation of the concepts: *Leg.* 1.47–48, 80; *Sobr.* 36; *Spec.* 1.305. In one case Philo juxtaposed the cognate noun "agriculture" (γεωργία) and the verb "plant" (φυτεύω): *Agr.* 25.

[66] For details, see A. C. Geljon and D. T. Runia, *Philo of Alexandria, On Planting: Introduction, Translation, and Commentary*, PACS 5 (Leiden: Brill, 2019), 102–5, esp. 103.

[67] For a detailed analysis, see G. E. Sterling, "Different Traditions or Emphases: The Image of God in Philo's *De opificio mundi*," in *New Approaches to the Study of Biblical Interpretation in Judaism of the Second Temple Period and in Early Christianity: Proceedings of the Eleventh International Symposium of the Orion Center for the Study of the Dead Sea Scrolls and Related Literature, June 2007*, ed. G. Anderson, R. Clements, and D. Satran (Leiden: Brill, 2013), 41–56.

[68] e.g. *Leg.* 1.43–44, 48. Cf. also *Post.* 171, which is strikingly close to the first statement in Numenius: "But God sows in souls nothing unproductive" (σπείρει δ' ὁ θεὸς ἐν ψυχαῖς ἀτελὲς οὐδέν). The "nothing unproductive" refers to "seed" (σπέρμα) in the context.

[69] E. R. Dodds, "Numenius and Ammonius," *Entretiens sur l'Antiquité Classique*, Vol. 5: *Les sources des Plotin* (Genève: Fondation Hardt, 1957), 4–11, esp. 15–16.

based on Exod 3:14 and does not require a predicate.[70] The famous translation of the Hebrew "I will be what I will be" (אהיה אשר אהיה)[71] as "I am the Self-Existent" (ἐγώ εἰμι ὁ ὤν) in the LXX makes the phrase a substantive. Whittaker has the better case and has been followed by the majority of scholars. Most importantly, this is the only time that he used the masculine. In twenty-two other texts Eudorus used the neuter τὸ ὄν,[72] following Plato's *Timaeus* (27D) and the Platonic tradition. Why did he shift from the standard neuter to the masculine? The most reasonable explanation is that he was inspired by the LXX or a source that drew from the LXX. We should remember his interest in Judaism.[73]

This recognition makes it natural to look at Philo as a possible source. The use of ὁ ὤν invites us to reflect more carefully on Philo's treatment of Exod 3:14. Let's examine the most famous of the four places he explained it.[74] Commenting on Gen 17:1 in *De mutatione nominum* (1–15), Philo asked: "Why is it a wonder if the Being (τὸ ὄν) is incomprehensible to humans, when even the mind in each of us is unknown to us?" He emphasized this by noting that even the name of God is unknown: "It therefore follows that it is not possible to assign a proper name to the true Being (τῷ ὄντι πρὸς ἀλήθειαν)." This led to the famous exchange between God and Moses in Exodus 3: "Don't you see that he said to the prophet who was eager to know what he should answer to those who would ask about his name: 'I am Being (ἐγώ εἰμι ὁ ὤν).'" Philo explained: "This equals: 'I am by nature Being (ἴσον τῷ εἶναι πέφυκα), not to be called by name'" (*Mut.* 11). However, God made a concession: "so that the human race would not be completely without a title for the Best, God permitted them to use via license of language (καταχρῆσθαι)—as if it were a proper name (κύριον ὄνομα)—'Lord God' (κύριος ὁ θεός) of the three natures: teaching, perfection, and practice whose symbols are recorded as Abraham, Isaac, and Jacob" (*Mut.* 12). The reference to the three ancestors and the name "Lord" led Philo to introduce Exod 6:3 by *gezera shawa*: "'I appeared,' he says, 'to Abraham, Isaac, and Jacob as their God, but my name 'Lord' (τὸ ὄνομά μου κύριον) I did not disclose to them.'" Philo argued that the word order was incorrect and should have been: "'my proper name (ὄνομά μου τὸ κύριον) I did not disclose to them,' but the license of language (τὸ ἐν καταχρήσει) was given for the reasons stated." He noted: "It is so impossible to name the Self-Existent (τὸ ὄν) that not even the powers that serve him tell us a proper name (κύριον ὄνομα)" (*Mut.* 13–14). The most intriguing aspect of this treatment for our purposes is that Philo has moved from the masculine of Exod 3:14 to the neuter of Plato; it appears likely to me that

---

[70] J. Whittaker, "Moses Atticizing," *Phoenix* 21 (1967): 196–201 and J. Whittaker, "Ammonius on the Delphic E," *CQ* 19 (1969): 185–92, esp. 189.

[71] The meaning of the Hebrew is disputed.

[72] Numenius frags. 2.19, 2.23, 3.1, 3.8, 3.9, 4.7, 4.9, 4.12, 5.5, 5.6, 5.13–14, 5.18 (*bis*), 5.19, 5.25, 6.7, 6.8, 6.15, 7.2, 7.13, 7.14, 8.2.

[73] e.g. *Souda*, Νουμήνιος: "He is the one who accused the mind of Plato of having stolen the concept of God and the origins of the cosmos from Moses. For this reason he said: 'What is Plato but Moses speaking in Attic?.'"

[74] Philo, *Det.* 160; *Mut.* 11; *Somn.* 1.231; *Mos.* 1.75. For Philo's understanding of Exod 3:14, see E. Starobinski-Safran, "Exode 3, 14 dans l'œuvre de Philon d'Alexandrie," in *Dieu et l'être: exégèses d'Exode 3, 14 et de Coran 20, 11–24*, Centre d'études des religions du Livre 152 (Paris: Études Augustiniennes, 1978), 47–55; and C. den Hertog, *The Other Face of God: "I Am That I Am" Reconsidered*, Hebrew Bible Monographs 32 (Sheffield: Sheffield Phoenix Press, 2012), 155–65.

Numenius—just like Ammonius—did the reverse and moved from the neuter of Plato to the masculine of Exod 3:14. The discussion in Philo would explain why he did so.

This is by no means the only place where there are striking agreements between Philo and Numenius. They also share a common understanding of the stability of God (see below).[75] How do we evaluate this evidence? Numenius' use of Exod 3:14 was probably a result of his knowledge of Philo. This means that his description of the contrast between the cultivator and the planter may also have been. Numenius' interest in Judaism would certainly have made him open to reading Philo's works and the fragment we have examined suggests that he did just that. The area where Philo exercised some influence was in the understanding of God. While Numenius had his own understanding of God, he appears to have accepted Philo's interchange between the personal ὁ ὤν and impersonal τὸ ὄν expressions for the First God.

7.3 Plotinus

Unlike the other figures we have considered, we have an ancient biography for Plotinus, written by one of his students.[76] With a Roman name, Plotinus was born into a well-placed family in Egypt.[77] He apparently did not begin the study of philosophy until later in life when he went to Alexandria in search of a teacher. After trying several well-known figures, he found Ammonius with whom he remained for eleven years (Porphyry, *Vit. Plot.* 3). Like Socrates, Ammonius wrote nothing and in fact preferred to keep his teaching confidential. The result is that we know very little about him.[78] During the course of his studies, Plotinus became intrigued enough by eastern thought that he accompanied Gordian III (emperor from 238–44 CE) on his campaign against the Sasanians. When Gordian was killed—either in battle or more likely by his own troops—Plotinus barely escaped with his life (Porphyry, *Vit. Plot.* 3).

While the trip was a disaster, it indicates Plotinus' interest in Eastern traditions. Plotinus never made a statement about ancient wisdom like those of Plutarch and Numenius; still he argued that the Egyptian sages understood that the Ideas were real "whether by accurate scientific or innate knowledge" (*Enn.* 5.8.6). This is probably also why he readily accepted an invitation to attend a séance led by an Egyptian priest (Porphyry, *Vit. Plot.* 10). More importantly, it may be one reason why Plotinus found Numenius so interesting (see below, pp. 122 and 124).

---

[75] Numenius, frag. 15 (Eusebius, *Praep. ev.* 11.18.20–21). Cf. also frag. 4 and Philo, *Post.* 22–31. See below under Plotinus.

[76] Porphyry, *Vit. Plot.* The bibliography on Plotinus is enormous. For a brief treatment, see Pierre Hadot, "Plotinus," *Brill's New Pauly* 11:395–403. And for a more extensive treatment of Philo and Plotinus, see G. E. Sterling, "Did Ancient Philosophers Read Philo? Philo of Alexandria and Plotinus," in *Ancient Philosophy and Early Christianity: Studies in Honor of Johan C. Thom*, ed. G. R. Kotzé and P. R. Bosman (Leiden: Brill, 2022), 37–63.

[77] Eunapius, *Vit. Soph.* 6. The *Souda*, s.v. Πλωτῖνος, places his birth in Lycopolis.

[78] On Ammonius, see F. M. Schroeder, "Ammonius Saccas," *ANRW* 2.36.1 (1987): 493–536.

Plotinus did not return to Alexandria, but chose to settle in Rome where he lived a comfortable but full life:[79] educating well-to-do children, arbitrating disputes, and running a philosophical school (Porphyry, *Vit. Plot.* 9). Initially he followed the lead of his teacher Ammonius and did not write; however, after a decade he began to write for his students. His surroundings proved to be comfortable enough that Rome became home for the remainder of his life. Plotinus thus spent his philosophical career in the two largest cities of the Roman empire where we know the works of Philo circulated.

Porphyry indicates that once Plotinus began to write, he continued to do so until his death (*Vit. Plot.* 4–5). The treatises went through editions by Amelius and Eustochius before Porphyry edited and arranged all fifty-four into six series of nine, hence the *Enneads*. Porphyry arranged the series so that they move psychagogically from ethics to the One.[80]

Porphyry opened his *vita* of Plotinus by calling him "the philosopher of our age" (*Vit. Plot.* 1). Anyone who works through the *Enneads* understands why. On the one hand, Plotinus is indebted to the Platonic tradition and repeatedly refers to it and argues that his thought was in harmony with Plato.[81] Like other Platonists, he did not read Plato in isolation, but had commentaries on the master read in his school (*Vit. Plot.* 14). He was particularly fond of the works of Numenius and was even accused of plagiarizing them, a charge that Amelius took seriously enough that he wrote a rebuttal (*Vit. Plot.* 17). For those who know the philosophical tradition, it is possible to identify sources for a great deal of material in the *Enneads*.[82]

On the other hand, reading Plotinus does not feel like a recitation of the Platonic tradition, but a creative rethinking of it.[83] Those who came after Plato and the ancients were important but only as they helped Plotinus think through the master. For this reason he did not cite subsequent authors by name—at least not after Epicurus (*Enn.* 2.9.15)! We therefore should not expect to find a reference to Philo or an unattributed citation any more than we would a reference to or unattributed citation of Eudorus or Plutarch.

Did Plotinus ever betray any awareness of Philo's works? One of the most striking agreements between Plotinus and Philo is their common use of the motif of stability.[84] Plotinus used the trope of "standing" or stability extensively. He offered a relatively full discussion of στάσις where he contrasted stability (στάσις) and stillness (ἠρεμία): he associated the former with the intelligibles and the latter with the sense-perceptibles (*Enn.* 6.3.27). Plotinus suggested that stillness implies a cessation of motion, while stability is an alternative of motion. For this reason, Plotinus associated rest (στάσις) with

---

[79] Porphyry, *Vit. Plot.* 9, says that he lived in the house of Gemina.
[80] Porphyry, *Vit. Plot.* 20, for the work of Amelius; and 7, 18, 19, 24–26, for the work of Porphyry.
[81] Plotinus, *Enn.* 6.4.16. Cf. also 3.7.1; 3.7.7; and 5.1.8.
[82] On Plotinus' sources, see *Les sources de Plotin (Dix exposées par E. R. Dodds et al.)*, Entretiens sur l'Antiquité Classique 5 (Geneva: Fondation Hardt, 1960).
[83] See also J. M. Rist, *Plotinus: The Road to Reality* (Cambridge: Cambridge University Press, 1967), 185.
[84] The most important treatment of this is D. T. Runia, "Witness or Participant? Philo and the Neoplatonic Tradition," in *The Neoplatonic Tradition: Jewish, Christian and Islamic Themes*, ed. A. Vanderjagt and D. Pätzold, Dialectica Minora 3 (Cologne: Dinter, 1991), 36–56.

Nous and the intelligibles (*Enn.* 5.1.7; 6.8.17). He used the concept to illustrate the transcendent nature of the One: "For since the nature of the One is generative of all things, it is none of them." He explained: "Therefore it is not anything—neither quality nor quantity nor mind nor soul nor in motion (κινούμενον) nor again stable (ἑστώς), nor is it in place nor in time, but itself by itself singular in form, or rather without form." He suggested that it existed "before any form, before movement (κίνησις), before stability (στάσις). For these things relate to being (τὸ ὄν) which make it many." He then returned to motion: "Why then, if it is not in motion (κινούμενον), is it not stable (ἑστώς)? Because each of these things or both by necessity relate to being (τὸ ὄν). What is stable is stable by stability (τό τε ἑστὼς στάσει ἑστώς) and is not the same as stability (στάσις), so that it is incidental to it and will no longer remain simple" (*Enn.* 6.9.3). Intriguingly, Plotinus also applied stability to the individual who has an experience of the One (*Enn.* 6.9.11), those who ascend to the One share in the qualities of the One or what is near the One. Thus stability refers primarily to the Nous and can be a quality that a human who ascends to the One experiences.

At first glance this appears to be a relatively straightforward philosophical analysis. It could be an extension of Plato's first hypostasis. However, it is interesting that this motif is attested first in Philo who developed it extensively. Philo offered his perspective in a series of biblical texts: texts that refer to God's standing,[85] texts in which a wise person either stands beside God[86] or is invited to stand with God,[87] and occasionally texts that simply refer to standing or motion.[88] He understood standing as a reference to God's stability.

The most important discussions come in two catenae formed by the catchword ἵστημι. We will examine one of these.[89] Philo offered an interpretation of Pharaoh's dream in Gen 41:17–24 in *De somniis* 2.215–302. The first lemma that he interpreted was Pharaoh's statement that "I thought that I was standing" (ᾤμην ἑστάναι [Gen 41:17]). Philo began with a critique, noting that the initial statement of the self-lover who is "subject to movement, turning, and change" shows that he thought that he "stood" but failed to recognize that "it is the quality to God alone to be unwavering and stable and if someone is God's friend" (*Somn.* 2.219). This led Philo to introduce seven texts (and two subordinate texts) connected by the catchword ἵστημι to illustrate his point. The first (Exod 17:6) quotes God's statement that "I stood there" which Philo suggests means that God "stands and remains the same, being unchangeable" (ἑστὼς ἐν ὁμοίῳ καὶ μένων, ἄτρεπτος ὤν, *Somn.* 2.221), a reference he expanded with a nod at Deut 8:15. The second text in the catena is Exod 24:10 when Israel saw God standing (εἱστήκει ὁ θεός). Philo explained that Moses "indicates that God does not change through his standing or secure stance" (διὰ στάσεως καὶ ἱδρύσεως, *Somn.* 2.222). The third text (Gen 9:11) refers to the establishment (στήσω) of God's covenant (= the Logos) with

---

[85] Gen 9:11 (Philo, *Somn.* 2.223–24); Exod 17:6 (Philo, *Somn.* 1.241; 2.221); and Exod 24:10 (Philo, *Somn.* 2.222).
[86] Gen 18:22 (Philo, *Cher.* 18–19; *Post.* 27; *Somn.* 2.226–27; *Deo*); and Deut 5:5 (Philo, *Somn.* 2.228–30).
[87] Deut 5:31 (Philo, *Post.* 28; *Gig.* 49; *Conf.* 30; *Somn.* 2.227–28).
[88] Gen 41:7 (Philo, *Somn.* 2.219–20); Gen 46:4 (Philo, *Post.* 29–30); and Num 16:48 ([= 17:13 LXX] Philo, *Somn.* 2.234–36).
[89] The other is *Post.* 22–31.

Noah which Philo thinks signals the desire of people to avoid the storm and "to find shelter in the calm and very best anchorage of virtue" (*Somn.* 2.223–25). Philo then gave two examples (the fourth and fifth texts) of individuals who either stood near God (Abraham in Gen 18:22 [ἑστὼς ἐνώπιον τοῦ κυρίου], *Somn.* 2.226–27) or were invited to stand with him (Moses in Deut 5:31 [σὺ αὐτοῦ στῆθι μετ' ἐμοῦ]). The invitation to Moses established Moses' virtue and God's "immovability." The person who stands beside the one who does not change shares in that quality and becomes self-standing (τὸ αὐτοστατοῦν) (*Somn.* 2.227–28). This led Philo to the sixth text (Deut 5:5) in which Moses said: "I stood between the Lord and you" (κἀγὼ εἱστήκειν ἀνὰ μέσον κυρίου καὶ ὑμῶν), placing the sage between God and humans. Philo underscored this with a sidelong glance at Lev 16:17 (*Somn.* 2.229–33).[90] The middle ground brought Philo to his seventh and final text (Num 16:48 = 17:13 LXX) where Aaron who is not a sage but is progressing stood (ἔστη) between the dead and living (*Somn.* 2.234–36). The Jewish exegete concluded with a statement that brought together the essential components in the catena: "It is the case then that stability (στάσις) and secure stance and eternal permanence in an identical state in keeping with an immutable and unchanging character is a property first belonging to Being (τὸ ὄν), then to the Logos of Being whom he called the covenant, third to the wise, and fourth to the one making progress" (*Somn.* 2.237). Philo associated stability (στάσις) with God and those who are God's friends.

As we hinted above, this same theme appears in Numenius who used the participle (ἑστώς) and the finite verb (ἕστηκε) to refer to the stability of the First Principle. The most important text is Numenius' contrast between the First and Second Principles: "These are the lives, the one of the First, the other of the Second God. This is to say that the First God will be stable (ἑστώς), but the Second God, on the contrary, is in motion (κινούμενος). The First deals with the intelligibles, the Second with the intelligibles and the sense-perceptibles."[91] It is possible that Numenius has taken inspiration from Plato's *Sophist* where Plato considered understanding absolute being as "motionless and stable" (ἀκίνητον ἑστός) (*Soph.* 248E), but rejected the view in favor of both stability and motion (*Soph.* 249C–D). This suggests that Numenius likely found his Jewish predecessor's views attractive who also argued that the First Principle was "stable."[92] Plotinus, who knew the works of Numenius, probably knew the motif from Numenius but changed the metaphysical framework in which the motif was applied to fit his own system, i.e. Plotinus applied it to the Nous rather than to the One.

Did Plotinus know the works of Philo? It seems to me that this is a case where Philo influenced a philosopher (Numenius) who in turn influenced a subsequent philosopher (Plotinus). There are other examples of parallels between the two that need to be analyzed, e.g. the presence of an "intelligible cosmos" in both,[93] the combination of the

---

[90] There is no catchword in Lev 16:17, only a thematic link with Deut 5:5.
[91] Numenius, frag. 15 (= Eusebius, *Praep. ev.* 11.18.20–21). Cf. also frag. 4.
[92] Sterling, "The Theft of Philosophy," 83–84. See also the discussion of Runia, "Witness or Participant?," 47–51, who argues that Numenius was the source for Plotinus not Philo.
[93] Plotinus used it 26×; Philo used it 18×. On the history of this phrase, see D. T. Runia, "A Brief History of the Term *Kosmos Noétos* from Plato to Plotinus," in *Traditions of Platonism: Essays in Honour of John Dillon*, ed. J. J. Cleary (Aldershot: Ashgate, 1999), 151–72.

cosmological and epistemology roles of the Logos in both,[94] their apophatic stances,[95] and the place of mysticism in both.[96]

7.4 Conclusion

Did Philo influence Hellenistic philosophy? The abrupt dismissal of this question by some is belied by the evidence that we have considered.[97] But how do we assess the evidence that we have assembled? There is a fundamental methodological challenge that needs to be addressed. Philo is frequently the first witness to a number of important philosophical concepts. What should we make of this? It is evident that the majority of texts from Middle Platonists have been lost, leaving Philo as a major witness. Should we argue from silence, dismiss his creativity and originality, and assume that he reports standard views but does not generate his own?[98] This seems to me to be a rush to judgment. Would we apply the same criterion to other thinkers of the period such as Plutarch or Numenius? Why should we apply it to Philo?

I would prefer to offer criteria for weighing the possibility of Philo's originality and potential influence on subsequent thought. First, is the concept a major concept that Philo discusses repeatedly or is it a footnote in his thought? If it only occurs once or twice, we would need to argue that the specific treatise in which the concept is found was known by a later thinker. If it occurs in multiple treatises, the possibilities of encounter are greater. Second, concepts that are rooted in Philo's exegesis of the Pentateuch deserve careful attention. The best illustration of this is the use of Exod 3:14 in Philo and the echoes in Plutarch and Numenius. It is also the case that ἑστώς comes out of the biblical text. It is possible that Philo knew the concept and when reading texts like Gen 18:22 exclaimed *mirabile dictu*, there it is in the biblical text! However, the fact that he developed it straight from the biblical text suggests that he used biblical language to formulate a philosophical thought. Third, when there are a significant number of Middle Platonic texts that address the same or related concepts but do not develop the concept(s) in the same way or as extensively as Philo does, we should take

---

[94] e.g. Plotinus, *Enn.* 3.2-3 and Philo, *Opif.* 15-25.

[95] e.g. Plotinus, *Enn.* 5.3.13, 5.3.14, 5.6.6 and Philo, *Mut.* 7-15. The most important treatment of the issue of the name of God in Philo and Plotinus is R. Radice, "The 'Nameless Principle' from Philo to Plotinus: An Outline of Research," in *Italian Studies on Philo of Alexandria*, ed. F. Calabi, SPhAMA 1 (Boston: Brill, 2003), 167-82.

[96] For a summary of scholarship and analysis, see T. Alekniené. "L' 'extase mystique' dans la tradition platonicienne: Philon d'Alexandrie et Plotin," *SPhiloA* 22 (2010): 53-82; repr. T. Alekniené, *A l'approche du divin: Dialogues de Platon et tradition Platonicienne*, Vestigia 42 (Fribourg: Academic Press, 2016), 203-45 (the volume is a collection of her essays of which several are relevant, e.g. pp. 247-69 and 271-320); Adam Afterman, "From Philo to Plotinus: The Emergence of Mystical Union," *JR* 93 (2013): 177-96; and Adam Afterman, *"And They shall be one Flesh": On the Language of Mystical Union in Judaism*, Supplements to the Journal of Jewish Thought and Philosophy 26 (Leiden: Brill, 2016), esp. 25-48. I am not sure that Philo held a view of *unio mystica* as Plotinus did. On mysticism in Plotinus, see J. Bussnich, "Mystical Elements in the Thought of Plotinus," *ANRW* 2.36.7:5300-5330.

[97] Rist, *Plotinus: The Road to Reality*, 101. Cf. also A. D. Nock, *Conversion: The Old and the New in Religion from Alexander the Great to Augustine of Hippo* (Oxford: Oxford University Press, 1933), 78-80, esp. 79, had a similar judgment although Nock recognized the citation of *Mos.* 2.195 in Heliodorus (see below).

[98] e.g. M. Baltes, "Idee (Ideenlehre)," *RAC* 17:213-46, esp. 235-38. The citation is from 236.

note. Fourth, we need to take into account the possibility that Philo influenced one thinker who, in turn, influenced others. The most notable possibility in this instance is Numenius who knew Philo and whom Plotinus knew. There is a sense in which it does not matter whether Philo's influence was direct or indirect. Finally, we should consider whether there is one point of contact or multiple points of contact between the two thinkers. A single point is sufficient when the evidence is compelling. When it is not, multiple points of contact are more impressive. While we have only considered one text or case for each philosopher, I have indicated where there are other notable agreements for each and have taken those into account in my own judgments.

What can we conclude? It is probable that Ammonius (and Plutarch through Ammonius) knew Philo's thought. The strongest piece of evidence is the use of Exod 3:14. Similarly, Numenius probably knew Philo's works. Again, the use of Exod 3:14 is the strongest link. Plotinus knew the works of Numenius and had at least indirect exposure to Philo's thought through the Apamean. It is thus probable that he knew the thought of Philo indirectly and possible that he knew it directly.

Does this matter? I think it does. Philo's influence was not in a minor area, but in theology. While Plato and other Platonists were far more fundamental for Plutarch, Numenius, and Plotinus than Philo, we should not ignore the Jewish exegete. Philo did not alter the direction of the tradition, but offered formulations that had an impact on the concept of the First and Second Principles. These formulations and nuances made the Platonic tradition more attractive to Christians than it would have been without them. In short, Eusebius' statement that Philo was "widely known ... among those who are keen about pagan education" is clearly hyperbolic, but it is not wrong.

8
Rabbinic Judaism

Steven D. Fraade

When I was first invited to contribute an essay on the reception of Philo of Alexandria within rabbinic Judaism, I responded that I could do so in one sentence or less: We have no evidence that Philo (or his writing) was directly known, all the less received, by the early rabbinic sages.[1] Perhaps more could be inferred regarding Philo's familiarity with rabbinic forebears who were contemporaries with Philo, for example the Pharisees, but even that would require a lot of methodological contortion.[2] So, I reshaped the subject to be: Why should modern scholars of Philo care about early rabbinic literature and thought, and vice versa?

My argument will be that in several important regards, Philo provides the closest antecedents to the forms and rhetoric of early rabbinic literature, notwithstanding their linguistic, geographic, and ideational distance from one another. In fact, the two most innovative of early rabbinic (tannaitic) forms of teaching, midrash (scriptural commentary) and mishnah (legal taxonomy), find their closest analogues, mutatis mutandis, in some of Philo's tractates.

8.1 Scriptural Commentaries

As a form (among others) of scriptural interpretation, line-by-line (or word-by-word) interpretation of a base text, divided into successive lemmata, commentary has two Jewish antecedents to rabbinic midrash: the *pesharim* of the Dead Sea Scrolls and Philo's Allegorical Commentary, *Questions and Answers on Genesis and Exodus*, and less explicitly in the Exposition of the Law. As I have argued widely and repeatedly, this is no simple, superficial trait, but of fundamental rhetorical, performative, and social significance. As Heinrich von Staden says of an entirely different type of ancient

---

[1] It is my honor to dedicate this study to my friend and colleague Greg Sterling on the occasion of his "milestone" birthday.
[2] The classic in this regard is S. Belkin, *Philo and the Oral Law: The Philonic Interpretation of Biblical Law in Relation to the Palestinian Halakah* (Cambridge, MA: Harvard University Press, 1940). More recently, see N. G. Cohen, *Philo Judaeus: His Universe of Discourse*, BEATAJ (Frankfurt: Peter Lang, 1995); E. Birnbaum, *The Place of Judaism in Philo's Thought: Israel, Jews, and Proselytes*, BJS 290, SPhiloM 2 (Atlanta: Scholars Press, 1996); L. H. Feldman, *Philo's Portrayal of Moses in the Context of Ancient Judaism* (Notre Dame: University of Notre Dame Press, 2008); and D. Winston, "Philo and Rabbinic Literature," in *The Cambridge Companion to Philo*, ed. A. Kamesar (Cambridge: Cambridge University Press, 2009), 231–53. Comparative studies of specific motifs abound. For a critique of the endeavor to align Philo with the Rabbis specifically, see L. Doering, "Philon im Kontext des palästinischen Judentums," in *Abrahams Aufbruch: Philon von Alexandria, De migration Abrahami*, ed. M. R. Niehoff and R. Feldmeier, SAPERE 30 (Tübingen: Mohr Siebeck, 2017), 147–66.

commentary, "In the commentaries using full, complete lemmata, the formal arrangement of the two ancient texts—the original and the exegetical—has significant implications for the socio-scientific dynamics of the triangle author-commentator-reader."[3]

Moving beyond the outer commentary form, three fundamental characteristics of rabbinic midrash as commentary, both legal and narrative, are found in Philo, with important differences, but not in the continuous *pesharim* of the Dead Sea Scrolls:[4] (1) interpreting one verse with another, commonly from a different part of scripture;[5] (2) multiple interpretations of the same lemma;[6] (3) dialogical rhetoric (questions and answers).[7] These common traits are best viewed not as the result of any direct contact, but of a shared Greco-Roman cultural context.[8] Alternatively (or additionally), Christian interlocutors such as Origen, especially during his time in Caesarea, may have played an important role in mediating between Philo and the rabbis.[9] We shall examine a sample of Philo's commentary in relation to its rabbinic midrashic parallels, with these features in mind.

8.2 Topical Arrangements of Laws

As any reader of the Hebrew Bible, especially its legal sections, can attest, its laws are not arranged in a "reader friendly" manner that would allow easy access to a particular subject of law (e.g. Sabbath regulations), whether for the sake of knowledge or application. This leaves aside the seemingly contradictory expressions on subjects of law that are found in the different legal strata of the Hebrew Bible, and the Pentateuch in

---

[3] H. von Staden, "'A Woman Does Not Become Ambidextrous': Galen and the Culture of Scientific Commentary," in *The Classical Commentary: Histories, Practices, Theory*, ed. R. K. Gibson and C. Shuttleworth Kraus, Supplements to Mnemosyne 232 (Leiden: Brill, 2002), 109–39, here 127.

[4] For Philo's employment of "rewritten Scripture," see S. D. Fraade, "Between Rewritten Bible and Allegorical Commentary: Philo's Interpretation of the Burning Bush," in *Rewritten Bible after Fifty Years: Texts, Terms, or Techniques? A Last Dialogue with Geza Vermes*, ed. J. Zsengellér, JSJSup 166 (Leiden: Brill, 2014), 221–32.

[5] Cf. Ὅμηρον ἐξ Ὁμήρου σαφηνίζειν ("explaining Homer from Homer"), attributed to Aristarchus in Alexandria. For a classic study, see Christoph Schäublin, "Homerum ex Homero," *MH* 34.4 (1977): 221–27.

[6] S. D. Fraade, "Rabbinic Polysemy and Pluralism Revisited: Between Praxis and Thematization," *AJS Review* 31 (2007): 1–40; S. D. Fraade, "'A Heart of Many Chambers': The Theological Hermeneutics of Legal Multivocality," *HTR* (2015): 113–28.

[7] For a few of my previous publications on these comparisons, see S. D. Fraade, *From Tradition to Commentary: Torah and Its Interpretation in the Midrash Sifre to Deuteronomy* (Albany: State University of New York Press, 1991), 1–23; S. D. Fraade, "Looking for Legal Midrash at Qumran," in *Biblical Perspectives: Early Use and Interpretation of the Bible in Light of the Dead Sea Scrolls*, ed. M. E. Stone and E. G. Chazon (Leiden: Brill, 1998), 59–79; S. D. Fraade, "Rabbinic Midrash and Ancient Jewish Biblical Interpretation," in *The Cambridge Companion to the Talmud and Rabbinic Literature*, ed. C. E. Fonrobert and M. S. Jaffee (Cambridge: Cambridge University Press, 2007), 99–120; S. D. Fraade, "Early Rabbinic Midrash between Philo and Qumran," in *Strength to Strength: Essays in Appreciation of Shaye J. D. Cohen*, ed. M. L. Satlow (Providence: Brown Judaic Studies, 2018), 281–93.

[8] See, most recently and extensively, M. R. Niehoff, ed., *Homer and the Bible in the Eyes of Ancient Interpreters*, Jerusalem Studies in Religion and Culture 16 (Leiden: Brill, 2012); Y. Paz, *From Scribes to Scholars: Rabbinic Biblical Exegesis in Light of the Homeric Commentaries*, Culture, Religion, and Politics in the Greco-Roman World 6 (Tübingen: Mohr Siebeck, 2022).

[9] For Origen and Philo, see Chapter 5 by Michael Cover in this volume. For more on Origen's possible exegetical ties to contemporary rabbinic sages, see most recently M. R. Niehoff, "Colonizing and Decolonizing the Creation: A Dispute between Rabbi Hoshaya and Origen," in *Scriptures, Sacred Traditions, and Strategies of Religious Subversion: Studies in Discourse with the Work of Guy G. Stroumsa*, ed. M. Blidstein, S. Ruzer, and D. Stökl Ben Ezra, STAC 112 (Tübingen: Mohr Siebeck, 2018), 113–29, including 122 n. 37, for Philo's influence on Origen. See also below, n. 44.

particular, or the seeming gaps in the laws, emphasizing, through repetition, some aspects while omitting others entirely. Efforts at overcoming these seemingly scattered, contradictory, and gapping aspects of biblical law are evident in several ancient Jewish writings (e.g. Jubilees, the Temple Scroll, the Damascus Document, and Josephus).[10]

Note, in particular, the apologetic statement by Josephus, prior to his synthetic presentation of the laws of Deut 16–18, which he refers to as the Mosaic "constitution" (πολιτεία), and places in his narrative scheme just prior to Moses' swan song (Deut 32) and death (Deut 34):

> §196 But here I am fain first to describe this constitution, consonant as it was with the reputation of the virtue of Moses, and withal to enable my readers thereby to learn what was the nature of our laws from the first, and then to revert to the rest of the narrative. All is here written as he left it: nothing have we added for the sake of embellishment, nothing which has not been bequeathed by Moses.
>
> §197 Our one innovation has been to classify the several subjects; for he left what he wrote in a scattered condition, just as he received each several instruction from God. I have thought it necessary to make this preliminary observation, lest perchance any of my countrymen who read this work should reproach me at all for having gone astray.
>
> §198 Here then is the code of those laws of ours which touch our political constitution. As for those which he has left us in common concerning our mutual relations, these I have reserved for that treatise on "Customs and Causes," which God helping, it is our intention to compose after the present work. (*A.J.* 4.196–98 [Thackeray and Marcus, LCL])

Apparently, God did not help, since we do not have Josephus' projected "Customs and Causes," which we might reasonably assume would have been topically grouped and ordered. What I find most interesting and striking here is Josephus' expressed need to pre-empt (and thereby draw attention to) what he anticipates to be the criticisms of his "countrymen" for having tampered with/improved upon revelation as recorded by Moses (from direct divine dictation) by shaping the "scattered" (σποράδην) laws into a coherent "constitution." Josephus' pre-emptive strike presumes that his "countrymen" would have been in a position to compare and contrast the contents (if not the wording) of what was "bequeathed by Moses" with what was to be published by Josephus.[11]

---

[10] For my treatment of these writings in this regard, see S. D. Fraade, "The Temple Scroll as Rewritten Bible: When Genres Bend," in *Hā-'îsh Mōshe: Studies in Scriptural Interpretation in the Dead Seas and Related Literature: Studies in Honor of Moshe J. Bernstein*, ed. B. Y. Goldstein, M. Segal, and G. J. Brooke, STDJ 122 (Leiden: Brill, 2018), 136–54. For a comparison of the Mishnah to the Damascus Document of the Dead Sea Scrolls in legal (and narrative) terms, see S. D. Fraade, "Ancient Jewish Law and Narrative in Comparative Perspective: The Damascus Document and the Mishnah," *Diné Israel: Studies in Halakhah and Jewish Law* 24 (2007): 65*–99*.

[11] Compare Philo, *Mos.* 2.40, where he says that someone fluent in Hebrew (Chaldaean) and Greek would be unable to detect any differences between the Hebrew biblical original and its Greek translation (in the Septuagint).

The culmination (at least in antiquity) of these efforts might be identified as the topical arrangement of laws in the Mishnah (conventionally viewed as the editorial production of R. Judah the Patriarch, *c.*220 CE), comprising six topical "orders" divided into sixty-three tractates. I shall argue that its closest antecedent is to be found in the topical arrangement of laws in the *Special Laws* of Philo. However, before turning to Philo, and his justification for ordering the laws under topical rubrics, let us consider a similar effort, rabbinically attributed to Rabbi ʿAkiba (*c.*125 CE), who is credited with having laid the foundation and framework for the later Mishnah:

> In like manner Rabbi Judah the Prince used to list the excellences of the Sages:
> ... Rabbi ʿAkiba he called "A well-stocked storehouse." To what might Rabbi ʿAkiba be likened? To a laborer who took his basket and went forth. When he found wheat, he put some in the basket; when he found barley, he put that in; spelt, he put that in; lentils, he put them in. Upon returning home he sorted out the wheat by itself, the barley by itself, the beans by themselves, the lentils by themselves. This is how Rabbi ʿAkiba acted, and he arranged the whole Torah in rings.[12]

In other words, if Rabbi ʿAkiba wished to cook lentil soup, he could easily obtain lentils from his pantry, without having to forage in the field.

Against this background let us see how Philo, the Second Temple writer who goes the furthest in systematically organizing the dispersed laws of the Pentateuch, does so. According to him, the Decalogue represents ten "headings," under which to organize the miscellaneous laws drawn from throughout the Pentateuch, just as the specific laws of Exod 21–24 follow immediately upon the Decalogue of Exod 20:2–14. For Philo's topical plan, see *Decal.* 154–74. Philo implicitly locates the justification for his legal reorganization within the order of scripture itself, a claim never made (so far as I can tell) by the rabbis for the topical structure of the Mishnah.[13] However, Philo is unique in another regard. Upon completing his discussion of those laws that he has included under the rubric of the tenth commandment, Philo constructs a collection of laws bearing on "justice" (δικαιοσύνη), largely, but not exclusively, drawn from Deut 16:18–18:22 (the same scriptural section that Josephus organizes as the "Mosaic constitution"), which

---

[12] Fathers According to Rabbi Nathan A 18 (ed. Schechter, 67; trans. Goldin, 90).

[13] Two large topical groupings of laws in Jubilees (on Passover and on the Sabbath) may be situated, and thereby implicitly justified, according to the scriptural narrative. After narrating the story of the Exodus from Egypt, Jubilees gathers laws of Passover from a variety of biblical locations, adds some biblically unattested Passover rules, and presents them as a coherent unit (49:1–23), with the heading, "Remember the commandment which the Lord commanded you concerning the Passover ..." (49:1). This is followed by a similar grouping and expansion of Sabbath laws (50:1–13; cf. 2:25–33 in the context of narrating creation) on the narrative occasion of the Israelites' arrival at the Wilderness of Sin (Exod 16:1), one stop before Mt. Sinai (as is explicitly stated in Jub 50:1), again beginning with a heading, "And behold the commandment of the sabbaths I have written for you and all the judgements of its laws" (50:6). The Sabbath laws are placed here presumably because of the narrative account of the manna (Exod 16). Thus, as much as Jubilees distributes a variety of legal traditions across its narrative span, here it uses the scriptural narrative occasions of the first two instances of collective law-giving (instructions for the observance of the first Passover and the listing of Sabbath rules with respect to the gathering of the manna), to collect an assortment of laws which are otherwise scattered throughout scripture and to integrate them seamlessly with those that are not scriptural at all, with little if any explicit exegetical linking of the latter to the former.

he was unable previously to include. Philo explains this additional topical grouping of laws, outside of the organizing structure of the Decalogue thus:

> §133 Enough then of this. But we must not fail to know that, just as each of the ten separately has some particular laws akin to it having nothing in common with any other, there are some things common to all which fit in not with some particular number such as one or two but with all the ten Great Words.
>
> §134 These are the virtues of universal value. For each of the ten pronouncements separately and all in common incite and exhort us to wisdom and justice and godliness and the rest of the company of virtues, with good thoughts and intentions combining wholesome words, and with words actions of true worth, that so the soul with every part of its being attuned may be an instrument making harmonious music so that life becomes a melody and a concert in which there is no faulty note.
>
> §135 Of the queen of the virtues, piety or holiness, we have spoken earlier and also of wisdom and temperance. Our theme must now be she whose ways are close akin to them, that is justice. (*Spec.* 4.133–35 [Colson, LCL])

In effect, Philo argues that the laws of justice are so constitutive of the system of virtues (and laws) as a whole, that they cannot be assigned to any single rubric, but must constitute an overarching one of their own. This is the challenge of any taxonomy of law: some will fit easily within their assigned rubrics, even if requiring some pressure, whereas others will not. The mishnaic tractate Sanhedrin (originally joined to Makkot, which follows it), is comparable to Josephus' "Mosaic constitution," as to the Temple Scroll 51:11–66:7 (based on Deut 16:18–22). However, the tractate 'Abot, resting uncomfortably in the same order of "Damages," could be seen as akin to Philo's overarching division of laws of justice, but with a common thread of (scholastic) ethics. However, such a claim is never made explicitly by the rabbis, as is made by Philo for his regrouped laws of justice.

8.3 Philo and Early Rabbinic Midrash on Seeing and Hearing at Sinai

I would like to revisit a particular text of tannaitic narrative midrash, on which I have previously written, in relation to a strikingly similar exegesis in Philo, in order to better understand how we might think about their exegetical convergences.[14] Our entry point will be a midrashic set of comments to Exod 20:15 (18), cited here in its entirety: וְכָל־הָעָם רֹאִים אֶת־הַקּוֹלֹת וְאֶת־הַלַּפִּידִם וְאֵת קוֹל הַשֹּׁפָר וְאֶת־הָהָר עָשֵׁן וַיַּרְא הָעָם וַיָּנֻעוּ וַיַּעַמְדוּ מֵרָחֹק; the NJPS translates this as: "All the people witnessed the thunder and lightning,

---

[14] See S. D. Fraade, "Hearing and Seeing at Sinai: Interpretive Trajectories," in *The Significance of Sinai: Traditions about Sinai and Divine Revelation in Judaism and Christianity*, ed. G. J. Brooke, H. Najman, and L. T. Stuckenbruck, TBN 12 (Leiden: Brill, 2008), 247–68, from which much of what follows is drawn. Here, however, I will give more attention to Philo than I did previously.

the blare of the horn and the mountain smoking; and when the people saw [it], they fell back and stood at a distance." Note that a single verb of seeing, רֹאִים, here (as in the NRSV) translated as "witnessed," governs the thunder, the lightning, the blare of the horn, and the smoking mountain. Our earliest rabbinic commentary to this verse, comprising two opposing views, is stunningly deceptive in its brevity and seeming simplicity:

> "And all the people saw the thunder": They saw what was visible and heard what was audible—These are the words of R. Ishmael. R. ʿAkiba says: They saw and heard that which was visible. They saw[15] the fiery word/commandment coming out from the mouth of the Almighty as it was struck upon the tablets, as it is said, "The voice of the Lord hewed out flames of fire." (Ps 29:7)[16]

The biblical, textual barb that generates these two interpretations is the use of the verb ראה, to see, for that which is audible: thunder. In the present biblical context, the word for thunder (קול) is also that for "voice," in particular, the voice of God (as well as for the blare of the horn).[17] Thus, whereas we might have expected the text to say "they heard the thunder and saw the lightning," with different verbs for that which is audible and for that which is visible, a *single* verb of seeing is instead employed for *both*. The simplest solution, as expressed in many modern translations, is to understand the verb ראה here as denoting not just the physical sense of seeing, but its broader meaning of cognizance and comprehension, allowing it to govern both the thunder and the lightning (as well as the blare of the horn and the smoking mountain).[18] Thus, we may compare, as do ancient exegetes, this use of the verb ראה with that in Exod 20:19 (22): "You yourselves *saw* that I *spoke* to you from the very heavens" (אַתֶּם רְאִיתֶם כִּי מִן־הַשָּׁמַיִם דִּבַּרְתִּי עִמָּכֶם). Thus, returning to Exod 20:15 and our midrash, we may understand R. Ishmael's interpretation as one that fills out a presumed ellipsis in that verse, whereby seeing is shorthand for hearing and seeing, with the former applying to the audible thunder and the latter to the visible lightning.[19]

This elliptical presumption and its exegetical solution are much older than R. Ishmael (early second century CE), as evidenced in the version of this verse in the Samaritan Pentateuch (*c*.100 BCE), which both supplies the missing verb of hearing and

---

[15] Although ואין is the reading in the best manuscripts (Oxford and Munich), as well as the first printing, רואין and ראו are found in other witnesses, with the former preferred by the Academy of the Hebrew Language data base and the latter (from *Yal. Shimʿoni*) adopted by Lauterbach and Horovitz-Rabin in their editions.

[16] Mek. Baḥodesh 9 (ed. Horovitz-Rabin, 235; ed. Lauterbach, 2:266). The text as I have presented it follows mainly MS Oxford, according to the data base of the Academy of the Hebrew Language. For late parallels, see Pirqe R. El. 41 (Warsaw, 98a) and Midr. Samuel 9:4 (ed. Buber, 74), as well as below, n. 24.

[17] For קול as the divine voice, in the immediate context, see Exod 19:5, 19.19.

[18] For "seeing" as representing all five senses combined, see Ibn Ezra to Exod 5:21, 20:15; U. Cassuto, *A Commentary on the Book of Exodus*, trans. I. Abrahams (Jerusalem: Magnes, 1967), 252. The emphasis on the verb ראה also allows for a word play between "seeing" and "fearing" (ירא), which verbs in certain forms can be morphologically identical. Thus, וַיַּרְא הָעָם, "the people saw," in the latter half of our verse, has been understood to mean "the people feared," represented by ויראו in the Samaritan Pentateuch and by φοβηθέντες in the Septuagint. See the use of ירא twice in Exod 20:17 (20).

[19] Whether this was in fact the historical Rabbi Ishmael's understanding or one that was editorially attributed to him is immaterial to my argument.

reorders the verse accordingly: "The whole people heard the thunder and the blare of the horn, and saw the lightning and the smoking mountain" (וכל העם שמע את הקולות ואת קול השופר וראים את הלפידים ואת ההר עשן).[20] Quite plainly, what is auditory is heard and what is visual is seen. Similarly, Josephus, in his "retold" account of revelation (*A.J.* 3.81), in what is certainly an exegetical paraphrase of our verse states: "As for the Hebrews, the sight that they saw and the din that struck their ears sorely disquieted them" (τούς γε μὴν Ἑβραίους τά τε ὁρώμενα καὶ ὁ ταῖς ἀκοαῖς προσβάλλων ψόφος δεινῶς ἐτάραττεν).[21]

By contrast, Rabbi ʿAkiba's interpretation[22] applies both faculties of sight and hearing to what is visual, and by implication also to what is audible, refusing a simple division of labor between the two senses. To him, therefore, scripture's locution of the people having seen what is normally thought to be audible (thunderings/voices) is to be taken literally, we might say mantically, and not to be circumvented as an ellipsis in need of filling, precisely as is done by R. Ishmael, the Samaritan Pentateuch, Josephus, and most modern translators. Whether to strengthen or to extend this interpretation, he (or an editor) invokes, in truncated form, a tradition that is found in several other exegetical locations in the tannaitic midrashim: what issued from God's mouth at Sinai were not simply words as sounds, but hypostatized divine utterances in the form of flying flames, that burned themselves into the tablets of the Decalogue.[23] While the divine words/commandments at Sinai could be experienced as both sight and sound, in R. ʿAkiba's extended interpretation the *emphasis* (following the lemma understood

---

[20] A. Tal, *The Samaritan Pentateuch Edited According to MS 6 (C) of the Shekhem Synagogue*, Texts and Studies in the Hebrew Language and Related Subjects 8 (Tel Aviv: Chaim Rosenberg School for Jewish Studies, Tel Aviv University, 1994), 76. In this particular case, the Samaritan Pentateuch would appear to be an "improvement" to the MT (that is, to its antecedent), rather than an independent witness.

[21] Josephus (or his source) may be dependent on the Septuagint's rendering of וַיַּרְא ("[the people] saw") as φοβηθέντες ("feared"), or at least a similar understanding. See above, n. 18. The association of divine speech with fire at Mt. Sinai is also found in Deut 5:20–24, following the Deuteronomic Decalogue, but there it is clear that while the divine voice issues out of fire, the voice itself is to be heard and not seen. For a similar separation of senses, and valorization of hearing, see Deut 4:36. The book of Deuteronomy, in reworking the Covenant Code (as well as the Priestly document), like the Samaritan Pentateuch and Josephus, removes any confusion caused by the Book of Exodus' mixing of auditory and visual perceptions. Note especially Deut 4:12: "The Lord spoke to you out of the fire; you heard the sound of words but perceived no shape—nothing but a voice" (וַיְדַבֵּר ה' אֲלֵיכֶם מִתּוֹךְ הָאֵשׁ קוֹל דְּבָרִים אַתֶּם שֹׁמְעִים וּתְמוּנָה אֵינְכֶם רֹאִים זוּלָתִי קוֹל). Although this most likely means that you saw nothing, but only heard a voice (see Ibn Ezra ad loc.; cf. 4:15–19), it could be construed to mean that you saw nothing but a voice. This is precisely how Philo interprets the verse in *Migr.* 48, treated below. For further discussion of Deut 4's reworking of the Sinaitic narratives of Exodus (and their traces in Deut 5) so as to eliminate or downplay the ocular experience, see S. A. Geller, "Fiery Wisdom: Logos and Lexis in Deuteronomy 4," *Proof* 14 (1994): 103–39; M. Carasik, "To See a Sound: A Deuteronomic Rereading of Exodus 20:15," *Proof* 19 (1999): 257–76; both of which cite previous scholarship; as well as M. Weinfeld, *Deuteronomy and the Deuteronomic School* (Oxford: Clarendon, 1972), 198–208; M. Weinfeld, *The Anchor Bible: Deuteronomy 1–11, A New Translation with Introduction and Commentary* (New York: Doubleday, 1991), 204, 212–13.

[22] Whether this was in fact the historical Rabbi ʿAkiba's interpretation or one that was editorially attributed to him is immaterial to my argument.

[23] For a fuller version of this tradition, in which each word (דיבור/דבר), upon issuing from God's mouth, would encircle the whole camp of the Israelites, before being engraved on the tablets, see Sifre Deuteronomy 343 (ed. Finkelstein, 399), commenting on Deut 33:2, אֵשְׁדָּת, "lightning flashing," or "fiery law" (according to the Masoretic note, dividing the word into two). For fuller treatment, with references to other locations and permutations of this tradition, some of which are even more physical (and erotic), and in which the hypostasization is carried further, see Fraade, *From Tradition to Commentary*, 45, 207, nn. 91–92, 224 n. 198. For other texts, see H. Bietenhard, "Logos-Theologie im Rabbinat: Ein Beitrag zur Lehre vom Worte Gottes im rabbinischen Schrifttum," *ANRW* 2.19.2 (1979): 580–618.

literally) is on their having been *seen*. This understanding of Exod 20:15 is intertextually secured (or extended) with the citation of Ps 29:7, a Psalm generally associated with Sinai in rabbinic interpretation, wherein God's voice (קול) is associated with hewing flames: קול יי חוצב להבות אש. According to this tradition, prior to the divine voice being inscribed as writing, so as to be perpetually read and heard, it enjoys an iconic fiery presence in Israel's *sight*. Paraphrasing another tannaitic midrash, we might say that the experience of revelation is one of מראה דיבור, the appearance (viewing) of the divine utterance, rather than one of מראה פנים, the appearance of the divine "face."[24]

Much the same interpretation of Exod 20:15 (18) is found in the Mekilta of R. Shim'on bar Yoḥai (a leading student of R. 'Akiba's), but unattributed, and without being juxtaposed to R. Ishmael's paraphrastic interpretation:[25]

> "The thunder and the lightning" (20:15a): Normally it is impossible to see the thunder, but here "[all the people saw] the thunder and the lightning." Just as they saw the lightning, so too they saw the thunder. "And when the people saw" (20:15b): What did they see? They saw the great glory [of God]. R. Eliezer said: From whence [do we know] that an Israelite maidservant saw that which the greatest of prophets did not see?[26] Scripture says, "And when the people saw": What did they see? They saw the great glory [of God].[27]

Once again, consistent with the view of R. 'Akiba in the Mekilta of R. Ishmael, the visionary experience of Israel at Mt. Sinai was exceptional, in that all of the people saw what is normally only heard. However, here that interpretation of Exod 20:15 is not connected intertextually to the tradition of seeing the divine utterances as fire (via Ps 29:7), but to that of seeing the glory of God (via the latter half of Exod 20:15).[28]

---

[24] See Sifre Numbers 103 (ed. Horovitz, 101), interpreting Num 12:8 (on God's having communicated with Moses במראה ["visually"], instead of MT ומראה ["plainly"], the former also being evidenced in the Septuagint, the Samaritan Pentateuch, the Peshiṭta, and the *targumim*) in light of Exod 33:20: אתה. זה מראה דיבור. "במראה". "אוֹ' זה מראה דיבור. או אינו אלא מראה פנים. שנ' בו "ויאמר לא תוכל לראות את פני" 'In appearance': This is the appearance of the divine utterance. You say this is the appearance of the divine utterance. But perhaps it is none other than the appearance of [the divine] face. [This cannot be, since] Scripture teaches in this regard, 'But, He said, you cannot see My face, [for man may not see Me and live.]'" This is the text chosen by the Academy of the Hebrew Language for its data base, mainly following MS Vatican. However, מראה פנים here follows MS Oxford and Yal. Shim'oni, while Horovitz and other printed editions (beginning with that of Venice, 1526) have מראה שכינה, "the appearance of the divine indwelling," as does MS London. MS Vatican has מראה דיבור followed by מראה alone, presumably a scribal omission. MS Berlin has מראה [דיבור] followed by מראה אלהים, "the appearance of God." R. Hillel ad loc. explains: דהיינו שהיה רואה ומבין בדבורו של הב"ה בפי' לא כעין משל וחידה, "Meaning, that he [Moses] would see and understand the word of the Holy One, blessed be He, meaning, not in the manner of a parable and riddle." Note also the comment of Zayit Ra'anan to Yal. Shim'oni (r. 739) on מראה דיבור: שהיה רואה הקול ("for he [Moses] would see the voice").

[25] Mek. of R. Shim'on bar Yoḥai Exod 20:15 (ed. Epstein-Melamed, 154–55). For text and translation, see also Mek. of R. Shim'on bar Yoḥai, ed. and trans. W. D. Nelson (Philadelphia: Jewish Publication Society, 2006), 253. The following translation, while consulting Nelson's, is my own.

[26] A similar statement is made, also in the name of R. Eliezer, with regard to the Israelites' visionary experience at the Reed Sea: Mek. of R. Shim'on bar Yoḥai Exod 15:2 (ed. Epstein-Melamed, 78).

[27] In the Hebrew of Exod 20:15 (18), there is no direct object to the phrase וַיַּרְא הָעָם, "and the people saw," allowing for the present question and the possibility that the object of their seeing was not just the thunder, as indicated in the first half of the verse, but something else, that being the glory of God (for which, see Exod 24:17). For an alternative understanding of וַיַּרְא הָעָם, see above, n. 18.

[28] See previous note.

Just as we discovered antecedents to R. Ishmael's interpretation in the version of the Samaritan Pentateuch and the paraphrase of Josephus, we will examine antecedents to R. 'Akiba's understanding of the verse in the writings of Philo.[29] We shall see that R. 'Akiba's *mantic* reading of signification in the seemingly elliptical wording of Exod 20:15, finds intriguing analogues (but with differences) in Philo's *allegorical* reading of the same, as they both seek to fill out the scriptural verse so as make meaningful its seeming gaps. Both chart a very different exegetical course from the reading of the same verse by R. Ishmael, Josephus, and the Samaritan Pentateuch. In *Decal.* 32–49, Philo discusses various aspects of the divine voice at Sinai, contrasting it to the human voice, and repeatedly stressing that the former is seen rather than heard in the normal way of hearing. It warrants citing at length:

§32 The ten words or oracles, in reality laws or statutes, were delivered by the Father of All when the nation, men and women alike, were assembled together. Did He do so by His own utterance in the form of a voice? Surely not. May no such thought ever enter our minds, for God is not as a man in need of a mouth and tongue and windpipe.

§33 I should suppose that God wrought on this occasion a miracle of a truly holy kind by bidding an invisible sound to be created in the air more marvelous than all instruments and fitted with perfect harmonies, not soulless, nor yet composed of body and soul like a living creature, but a rational soul full of clearness and distinctness, which giving shape and tension to the air and changing it to flaming fire, sounded forth like the breath through a trumpet; an articulate voice so loud that it appeared to be equally audible to the farthest as to the nearest.

§34 For it is the nature of human voices, if carried to a great distance, to grow faint so that persons afar off have an indistinct impression which gradually fades away with each lengthening of the extension, since the organism which produces them also is subject to decay.

§35 But the new miraculous voice was set in action and kept in flame by the power of God, which breathed upon it and spread it abroad on every side and made it more illuminating in its ending than in its beginning by creating in the souls of each and all another kind of hearing far superior to the hearing of one's ears. For that is but a sluggish sense, inactive until aroused by the impact of the air. But the hearing of the mind possessed by God makes the first advance and goes out to meet the spoken words with the keenest rapidity....

§46 Then from the midst of the fire that streamed from heaven there sounded forth, to their utter amazement, a voice, for the flame became articulate speech in the

---

[29] On Philo's view of revelatory communication at Sinai, see D. Winston, "Two Types of Mosaic Prophecy According to Philo," in *Society of Biblical Literature 1988 Seminar Papers*, ed. D. J. Lull (Atlanta: Scholars Press, 1988), 448–52; D. Winston, *Logos and Mystical Theology in Philo of Alexandria*, The Gustave A. and Mamie W. Efroymson Memorial Lectures, 1984 (Cincinnati: Hebrew Union College Press, 1985); M. R. Niehoff, "What Is in a Name? Philo's Mystical Philosophy of Language," *JSQ* 2 (1995): 220–52.

language familiar to the audience. So clearly and distinctly were the words formed by it that they seemed to see rather than hear them.

§47 What I say is vouched for by the law in which it is written, "All the people saw the voice," a phrase fraught with much meaning, for it is the case that the voice of men is audible, but the voice of God truly visible. Why so? Because whatever God says is not words but deeds, which are judged by the eyes rather than the ears.

§48 Admirable too, and worthy of the Godhead, is the saying that the voice proceeded from the fire. For the oracles of God have been refined and assayed as gold is by fire. §49 And it conveys too, symbolically, some such meaning as this: since it is the nature of fire both to give light and to burn, those who resolve to be obedient to the divine utterances will live forever as in unclouded light with the laws themselves as stars illuminating their souls, while all who are rebellious will continue to be burnt; burnt to ashes, by their inward lusts, which like a flame will ravage the whole life of those in whom they dwell.[30]

A similar idea, but expressed more briefly, can be found in Philo's *De migratione Abrahami* 47–49:

§47 For what life is better than a contemplative life, or more appropriate to a rational being? For this reason, whereas the voice of mortal beings is judged by hearing, the sacred oracles intimate that the words of God are seen as light is seen; for we are told that "all the people saw the Voice" (Exod 20:18), not that they heard it; for what was happening was not an impact of air made by the organs of mouth and tongue, but virtue shining with intense brilliance, wholly resembling a fountain of reason, and this is also indicated elsewhere on this wise: "You have seen that I have spoken to you out of Heaven" (Exod 20:22), not "you heard," for the same cause as before.

§48 In one place the writer distinguishes things heard from things seen and hearing from sight, saying, "You heard a voice of words and saw no similitude but only a voice" (Deut 4:12), making a very subtle distinction, for the voice dividing itself into noun and verb and the parts of speech in general he naturally spoke of as "audible," for it comes to the test of hearing: but the voice or sound that was not that of verbs and nouns but of God, seen by the eye of the soul, he rightly represents as "visible."

§49 And after first saying "You saw no similitude" he adds "but only a Voice," evidently meaning the reader to supply in thought "which you did see." This shows that words spoken by God are interpreted by the power of sight residing in the soul,

---

[30] For text and translation (by F. H. Colson), see the LCL 7:20–31. Translation here is from LCL with minor modifications by the author. For fire, representing Torah, having the ability both to give light and heat as well as (especially its esoteric teachings) to burn, see Mek. of R. Ishmael Baḥodesh 4 (ed. Horovitz-Rabin, 215; ed. Lauterbach 2:220–21); Mek. of R. Shimʿon bar Yoḥai Exod 19:8 (ed. Epstein-Melamed, 143–44); Sifre Deuteronomy 343 (ed. Finkelstein, 399–400); m. ʾAbot 2:10; t. Ḥag. 2:5 (ed. Lieberman, 381); y. Ḥag. 2:1 (77a) (ed. Sussmann, col. 782); b. Ḥag. 13a–b; ʾAbot R. Nat. 28 (ed. Schechter, 86); as well as discussion in Fraade, *From Tradition to Commentary*, 46–49 (with notes). For the "voice" of revelation not diminishing with distance/time, compare Mek. of R. Ishmael Baḥodesh 3, 4 (ed. Horovitz-Rabin, 214, 216; ed. Lauterbach, 2:218, 223).

whereas those which are divided up among the various parts of speech appeal to hearing.[31]

Finally, Philo refers to the tradition of revelation having been seen rather than conventionally heard in *Mos.* 2.213 (Colson, LCL 6:554–55), where he speaks of "commands promulgated by God not through His prophet but by a voice which, strange paradox, was visible and aroused the eyes rather than the ears of the bystanders."

To begin with, we should note that the three characteristic features of early rabbinic midrash, mentioned previously, which are also present in Philo's scriptural interpretations are all present in these particular passages: the employment of rhetorical dialogue (question and answer), interpreting scripture with scripture, and the incorporation of multiple interpretations of the same scriptural lemma (see *Decal.* 49).

If R. ʿAkiba is *laconic* in his expression of the common tradition that the divine voice issued and was perceived at Sinai in visible fiery form, which only secondarily became audible, Philo is, as we have come to expect, oppositely *loquacious*. They both link this shared understanding of the visual perception of revelation to the words of Exod 20:15 (18), although employing different inter-texts in so doing (Ps 29:7 for R. ʿAkiba; Exod 20:19 [22] and Deut 4:12 for Philo). Whether they simply come to a common understanding of the same verse independently of one another, or whether they draw on a shared tradition of interpretation is impossible to know for certain. However, in the present case, I think that strong credence can be given to the latter assumption of a shared exegetical tradition, even though they are relating to the same scriptural words in different languages (Hebrew for R. ʿAkiba and Greek for Philo). Undoubtedly, the fact that the Septuagint renders קולות for "thunder" with τὴν φωνήν, the same Greek word used for the קול (blare) of the horn and the קול (voice) of God is critical to Philo's interpretation, as is the use of קולות for thunder to R. ʿAkiba's interpretation. However, it should be emphasized that R. ʿAkiba's interpretation in the Mekilta appears as part of an ongoing commentary to the book of Exodus, to which his is one of several comments to Exod 20:15 (18), whereas Philo's appears within thematic treatises, within which he cites Exod 20:15 (18) for support of his argument. Of course, that tells us nothing of how each of these interpretations first arose (that is, whether or not from exegetical contemplation of the verse in its scriptural context), but it does tell us something about how their respective interpretations are rhetorically presented for their respective audiences' consumption.

Nevertheless, there are several components of Philo's interpretation that are not expressed in R. ʿAkiba's interpretation and which are uniquely or at least characteristically Philonic, needing to be understood in terms of Philo's particular historical/cultural context and ideological/rhetorical program. To begin with, Philo repeatedly stresses that divine speech is unlike human speech, something for which there is rabbinic evidence as well (notwithstanding the dictum attributed to R. Ishmael

---

[31] For text and translation (by F. H. Colson), see the LCL 4:158–59.

that "The Torah speaks in human language" (דברה תורה כלשון בני אדם).[32] But more broadly, Philo repeatedly emphasizes the superiority of sight over hearing, or at least over normal physical hearing. This emphasis needs to be understood in relation to a broader Platonic deprecation of the physical senses (in comparison to the faculties of the intellect), among which, however, sight is elevated above hearing.[33] In this regard, Philo stresses that the divine "voice" at Sinai was miraculous (and paradoxical), unlike any other voice, in that in issuing from fire, it was more of light than of sound, or at least, a unique sort of sound that issued not from the physical processes that normally produce or receive sound, but from a divine effulgence. Thus, to the extent that revelation was heard at Sinai, it was the "hearing of the mind possessed by God," and not by the physical organ of the ear. Similarly, to the extent that the language of revelation is comprehensible to humans, it was not produced in the same way that human speech is normally produced and heard.[34] Finally, it should be stressed that Philo *uniquely* understands Deut 4:12, which is never rabbinically adduced in this connection,[35] to denote *two* types of voices/speech: the human/grammatical, which is (merely) heard, and the divine, which is "seen by the eye of the soul."[36]

We shall now consider one final passage from the Mekilta's commentary on the Book of Exodus' account of the revelation at Sinai, which will suggest that Philonic and the early rabbinic interpretation share other interpretive moves, notwithstanding their very different historical/cultural contexts and ideological/rhetorical programs. Coming to Exod 20:19 (22), which was cited by Philo in conjunction with his interpretation of Exod 20:15 (18), the Mek. of R. Ishmael Baḥodesh 9 comments:[37]

---

[32] For the earliest attestations of this dictum, see Sifre Numbers 112 (ed. Horovitz, 121); Sifra Qedoshim parashah 10:1 (ed. Weiss, 91b); in only the first of which is the saying attributed to R. Ishmael. The saying is much more frequently evidenced in the Babylonian Talmud (thirty-two times) and in the aggadic midrashim (thirty-eight times), in only some of which is it attributed to R. Ishmael. For the rabbinic differentiation of divine speech from human, the *locus classicus* is the interpretation of Ps 62:12 and Jer 23:29 in Sifre Numbers 102 (ed. Horovitz, 100); y. Ned. 3:2 (37d) (ed. Sussmann, col. 1025); b. Sanh. 34a; b. Šabb 88b. For the most recent discussion, see A. Yadin, *Scripture as Logos: Rabbi Ishmael and the Origins of Midrash* (Philadelphia: University of Pennsylvania Press, 2004), 69–79.

[33] See also Philo, *Sacr.* 78 (Colson and Whitaker, LCL 2:153): "But when, unforeseen and unhoped for, the sudden beam of self-inspired wisdom has shone upon us, when that wisdom has opened the closed eye of the soul and made us spectators rather than hearers of knowledge, and substituted in our minds sight, the swiftest of senses, for the slower sense of hearing, then it is idle any longer to exercise the ear with words." Similarly, *Contempl.* 10–13 (Colson, LCL 9:119): "... the most vital of senses, sight. And by this I do not mean the sight of the body but of the soul, the sight which alone gives a knowledge of truth and falsehood" (10). Compare Plutarch, *Is. Os.* 75 (381B) (Babbitt, LCL 5:172–75): "[The crocodile] is declared to be a living representation of God, since he is the only creature without a tongue; for the Divine Word has no need of a voice, and through noiseless ways advancing, guides by Justice all affairs of moral men" (adapting Euripides, *Troades* 887–88; cf. Plutarch, *Moralia* 1007C). For a broader treatment, both in Philo and more generally, see D. Chidester, *Word and Light: Seeing, Hearing, and Religious Discourse* (Urbana: University of Illinois Press, 1992).

[34] Compare above, n. 33.

[35] The closest is the early medieval Midr. Leqaḥ Ṭov ad loc. (ed. Buber, 14), which connects the verse to the tradition of the divine voice having encircled the Israelite camp at Sinai (see above, n. 24), but without any of the visual associations. Elsewhere, however, the verse is understood to *preclude* the seeing of God (or his voice), which is how the verse is usually understood: Pesiq. Rab Kah., supplement 7 (ed. Mandelbaum, 471); Tanḥ. Ha'azinu 4; Ibn Ezra ad loc. See above, n. 22.

[36] This text is important to Daniel Boyarin (*Border Lines: The Partition of Judaeo-Christianity* [Philadelphia: University of Pennsylvania Press, 2004], 114) in arguing for a Jewish "logos theology" that is both "pre- and pararabbinic." However, Boyarin fails to indicate its comparative and contrastive intersections with early rabbinic midrash.

[37] The text, as I have presented it, follows mainly MS Oxford, according to the data base of the Academy of the Hebrew Language. The text within square brackets is from MS Munich. Its absence from MS Oxford most

"You yourselves have seen [that I spoke to you from the heavens]": There is a difference between what a person sees and what others tell him. For regarding what others tell him he may have doubts in his mind [concerning its veracity]. Here, however, "You yourselves have seen." R. Nathan (c.200 CE) says: "You yourselves have seen": Why is it said? Since it says, "All the kings of the earth shall praise you, O Lord, for they have heard the words You spoke" (Ps 138:4). One might think that just as they heard, so too they saw. Therefore, Scripture says, "You yourselves have seen": The nations of the world have not seen.

This interpretation shares with Philo the view that seeing is superior to hearing, although here the comparison is between one's own seeing and hearing from others. Both Philo and the Mekilta employ Exod 20:19 (22) to valorize Israel's receiving of God's revelation at Sinai via sight rather than normal hearing. However, in Philo's use of the verse, to illustrate the superiority of seeing over hearing, it is not clear whether he intends a polemical argument: superiority over whose hearing? He may be saying that Israel's revelatory knowledge (and attainment of reason and virtue) is superior to that which is not based on visual (mystical?) experience, but merely on oral transmission, for example that of the non-Jewish philosophers. If that is his intent, he does not explicitly express it. Alternatively, Philo may simply be making a philosophical argument, buttressed by scriptural citations, that would have resonated well with an educated audience, whether Jewish or non-Jewish. However, by grounding his philosophical argument in Jewish scriptures, Philo may implicitly be claiming a privileged status for those scriptures as the ultimate source of philosophical wisdom.

The Mekilta's interpretive argument is two-fold, with both parts of the argument being grounded in the word אתם ("you"), which is not strictly required by Hebrew syntax, and therefore must bear particular meaning.[38] The opening anonymous interpretation stresses the superiority of first-hand seeing (ראיתם אתם) to second-hand hearing (אחרים משיחין), since the latter is potentially suspect. The second half of the argument, attributed to R. Natan, has a different emphasis, even though it is based in the same regard for אתם as being non-superfluous: "You yourselves (and no others) have seen...." This becomes manifest through the citation of the inter-text from Psalms, which might be understood (were it not for Exod 20:19 [22]) to be an expression of the *universal* receiving of divine revelation: all of the nations have "heard the words You spoke."[39] Having heard, perhaps they also saw. Our verse comes to assert that whatever the nations have heard, it is nothing compared to what Israel *alone* has seen. Israel

---

likely represents a scribal error of homoioteleuton. For critical printed editions, see Horovitz-Rabin, 238; Lauterbach, 275.

[38] Although Exod 20:15 (18) ("All the people saw...") says much the same thing, as midrashically understood it does not place the same emphasis on "you" in an exclusive sense.

[39] Other rabbinic texts stress either that the nations were offered the Torah before it was revealed to Israel, or that they overheard its revelation to Israel, or that the Torah is available to them. See Fraade, *From Tradition to Commentary*, 32–49; M. Hirshman, *Torah for the Entire World* (Tel Aviv: Hakibbutz Hameuchad, 1999) (Hebrew).

enjoys an *exclusive* revelatory intimacy with God, based on unmediated seeing that is not shared by the nations, however much they may claim to have heard God's words.

Although, once again, Philo and the Mekilta employ the same scriptural verse to affirm the superiority of seeing over hearing as modes of revelatory reception, and may be responding to the same scriptural barb ("You yourselves have seen [rather than heard] that ... I spoke with you"), they do so in very different rhetorical manners, suggesting that their exegetical programs thereby reflect their very different historical/cultural contexts and ideological/rhetorical programs. Neither should the exegetical similarities cause us to lose sight of the rhetorical and structural differences, nor should those differences cause us to lose sight of the exegetical similarities.

Before concluding with some broader assessment, I want to return to our Philonic passages to highlight two traditions, unrelated to the question of seeing, that are closely aligned with similar expressions in tannaitic midrashim. In *Decal.* 33, Philo says that the miraculous sound of revelation "sounded forth like the breath through a trumpet an articulate voice so loud that it appeared to be equally audible to the farthest as well as the nearest," in other words, that, unlike the physical sound of a normal instrument, it did not diminish with distance from its source. We find a similar idea in Mekilta of R. Ishmael Baḥodesh 3 (MS Oxford):

> "The voice of the horn was very loud" (Exod. 19:16): Ordinarily, the more the sound is prolonged, the weaker it becomes. But [here][40] the longer the sound is prolonged the stronger it becomes. And why was it softer at first? In order to accustom the ear according to its capacity for hearing.

Notwithstanding differences in form and content, the two passages share a tradition that the sounds of revelation, unlike normal sounds, did not diminish with distance from their source.[41]

My final example is from *Decal.* 49, where Philo states that "it is the nature of fire both to give light and to burn," the former quality affecting those who obey the commandments whereas the latter quality affecting those who are rebellious. This is very similar to an interpretation of Deut 33:2 in Sifre Deut. 343 (ed. Finkelstein, 399–400):

> "Lightning flashing at them from his right" (Deut. 33:2): Just as with fire, whoever gets [too] near to it is burned, while whoever gets [too] far from it is chilled, so it is with words of Torah: as long as a person labors with them, they [bring] life to him, but if he departs from them, they kill him.

Again, despite important structural and rhetorical differences between Philo and the midrash, they are remarkably similar as to content, stressing the double-edged

---

[40] Found in MS Munich.
[41] Compare *Decal.* 35.

nature of fire as a metaphor for Torah observance and study, whether pursued or abandoned.[42]

8.4 Conclusion

We have seen strong similarities between Philo's and the early Rabbis' use of dialogical commentary (*midrash*) and of arranging laws according to their topical rubrics (*mishnah*), notwithstanding differences between the two. Even more striking are the similarities between their scriptural interpretations of the visual aspects of revelation at Mt. Sinai. Nevertheless, I see no evidence in these many points of comparison that the rabbinic midrashists and mishnaists (often the same individuals), or their redactors, had any direct familiarity with the writings or teachings of Philo, nor that Philo had any direct exposure to proto-rabbinic (e.g. Pharisaic) works of scriptural interpretation. That is largely because the "parallels" are more profoundly of content than of exegetical terminology (even allowing for language difference) or strategic rhetoric. While to a large extent we can attribute the similarities of content to a shared scriptural text (even allowing language difference) and its exegetical exigencies, the number and complexity of the similar traditions of an interpretative nature that we have seen suggest something more than self-contained independent paths. The similarities, mutatis mutandis, are too profound and insufficiently superficial to attribute entirely to exegetical coincidence.

Rather, we need to seriously entertain the possibility of shared narrative interpretive traditions that circulated broadly in and between Palestine and Alexandria, and possibly beyond, which were not necessarily the creations of either Philo or the named Rabbis (e.g. R. 'Akiba) to whom they are attributed. How exactly these traditions circulated, for example between Alexandria and Palestine, is difficult to say. Presumably there were Jewish merchants who traveled between the two, especially the coastal ports (e.g. Caesarea), who, if they attended synagogues in both places, would have absorbed and possibly shared scriptural lessons and homilies, serving thereby as conduits for the broad circulation of such teachings. Similarly, we know that scholars traveled back and forth, both Jewish and early Christian (e.g. predecessors of Origen, Eusebius, and Jerome),[43] who would have been interested in Philo's teachings and spread them as they traveled and come into contact, whether directly or indirectly, with early and proto-rabbinic scholars.[44] Such a view of the trafficking in narrative scriptural interpretations

---

[42] For further discussion, including similar rabbinic expressions of the double-edged nature of fire as a metaphor for Torah, see my book, *From Tradition to Commentary*, 45–49.

[43] For Origen, see above, n. 9 and Michael Cover, Chapter 5 in this volume. He would have been too late to have influenced tannaitic interpretations of the first two centuries, upon which we focused our attention. For Eusebius and Jerome, see also in this volume Sabrina Inowlocki and Matthew Kraus, Chapters 9 and 14, respectively.

[44] See, of late, A. Tzvetkova-Glaser, *Pentateuchauslegung bei Origenes und den frühen Rabbinen* (Frankfurt: Peter Lang, 2010); E. Grypeou and H. Spurling, eds, *The Exegetical Encounter between Jews and Christians in Late Antiquity* (Leiden: Brill, 2009).

between Alexandria and Palestine would have to presume, at some point in the process, the participation of bilingual (Hebrew-Greek) tradents.[45]

However we imagine the indirect sharing of legal and narrative interpretive traditions between Philo and the early Rabbis, it is important to attend not only to these exegetical similarities, but as much (if not more) to the profoundly different ways those traditions are rhetorically incorporated into their respective literary settings, each in accord with its culturally specific ideological presuppositions and pedagogical purposes. Recognizing how much exegetical tradition they have in common can only highlight how *differently* and uniquely each body of interpretation gives particular cultural shape to that which they hold in common. Vive la différence!

---

[45] On Jewish multilingualism in antiquity, see my essays, "Language Mix and Multilingualism in Ancient Palestine: Literary and Inscriptional Evidence," *Jewish Studies* 48 (2012): 1*–40*, with a Hebrew version in *Leshonenu* 73 (2011): 273–307; "Before and After Babel: Linguistic Exceptionalism and Pluralism in Early Rabbinic Literature," *Diné Israel* 28 (2011): 31*–68*.

II
LATE ANTIQUITY

9
Eusebius

Sabrina Inowlocki

As the famous father of church history, Eusebius made a durable mark on the history of Christianity, both as a privileged source for the grand narrative of the origins of Christianity and as a goldmine from which to dig out nuggets of information as well as excerpts of texts otherwise lost or unknown (Greek, Christian, or Jewish). Paradoxically, in spite of his influence, the bishop's reputation as a writer, a historian and a theologian has nevertheless been tainted with suspicion and criticism since antiquity.[1] However, in the last decades, as an increasing number of studies have treated his works as discourses rather than as narratives to be taken at face value, he has gradually been rehabilitated as a significant author on his own right.[2] In many respects, Eusebius deserves this redemption, as his work undeniably constitutes an extremely rich and innovative intellectual project worthy of being studied on its own terms.

Nevertheless, I will argue in this chapter that doing justice to Eusebius' works and his innovative use of textual sources should not lead us to turn a blind eye to his manipulation of texts, as is still occasionally the case.[3] The citation process, which is central to Eusebius' method and approach, is already in itself a methodology of control over

---

[1] See all relevant bibliography in M. Verdoner, *Narrated Reality: The* Historia ecclesiastica *of Eusebius of Caesarea* (Frankfurt: Peter Lang, 2011), 31–34.

[2] Since the seminal works of R. M. Grant, *Eusebius as Church Historian* (Oxford: Clarendon, 1980) and T. D. Barnes, *Constantine and Eusebius* (Cambridge, MA: Harvard University Press, 1981), see e.g. J. Ulrich, *Euseb von Caesarea und die Juden: Studien zur Rolle der Juden in der Theologie des Eusebius von Caesarea* (Berlin: de Gruyter, 1999); M. J. Hollerich, *Eusebius of Caesarea's Exegesis in the Age of Constantine* (Oxford: Oxford University Press, 1999); A. Kofsky, *Eusebius of Caesarea against Paganism* (Leiden: Brill, 2000); A. J. Carriker, *The Library of Eusebius of Caesarea* (Leiden: Brill, 2003); A. P. Johnson, *Ethnicity and Argument in Eusebius'* Praeparatio Evangelica (Oxford: Oxford University Press, 2006); S. Inowlocki, *Eusebius and the Jewish Authors, His Citation Technique in an Apologetic Context* (Brill: Leiden, 2006); S. Morlet, *La Démonstration évangélique d'Eusèbe de Césarée* (Paris: Études Augustiniennes, 2009); M. Verdoner, *Narrated Reality*; S. Inowlocki and C. Zamagni, eds, *Reconsidering Eusebius: A Fresh Look at His Life, Work, and Thought* (Leiden: Brill, 2011); A. P. Johnson and J. Schott, eds, *Eusebius of Caesarea: Tradition and Innovation*, Hellenic Studies Series 60 (Cambridge, MA: Harvard University Press, 2013); J. Corke-Webster, *Eusebius and Empire: Constructing Church and Rome in the Ecclesiastical History* (Cambridge: Cambridge University Press, 2019); M. Hollerich, *Making Christian History: Eusebius of Caesarea and His Readers* (Berkeley: University of California Press, 2021); and the forthcoming monograph by D. J. DeVore, *Eusebius' Ecclesiastical History and Classical Culture: Philosophy, Empire, and the Formation of Christian Identity* (Cambridge: Cambridge University Press, forthcoming); and S. Inowlocki, "Les enjeux idéologiques de la réception des extraits philoniens sur la cause seconde dans la Préparation évangélique," *Eusèbe de Césarée et la philosophie: Christianisme et philosophie en Palestine au tournant du IVe s. de notre ère*, ed. S. Morlet (Turnhout: Brepols, forthcoming).

[3] e.g. J. Otto, rejecting the view that Eusebius misused and exploited Philo, concludes that his use of Philo should be understood through the lens of his hardships during the persecutions and the sincerity of his faith (*Philo of Alexandria and the Construction of Jewishness in Early Christian Writings* [Oxford: Oxford University Press, 2018], 136–95).

texts and authors, which involves a certain degree of manipulation.[4] This is especially relevant to the case of Philo, as he is mostly cited in the works by Eusebius that are most openly apologetical in scope: the *Praeparatio evangelica* (*Praep. ev.*) and the *Historia ecclesiastica* (*Hist. eccl.*).[5] I will focus on these texts because it is there that Eusebius most abundantly resorts to Philo, both explicitly and implicitly.[6]

Eusebius most likely inherited Philo's writings from Pamphilus, his master, who had himself collected all the works of Origen he could find.[7] It is assumed that the Philonic works he knew and used originated from Origen's library. There can be no doubt that he contributed somehow to the process of preservation and transmission of Philo's texts both through the importance he conferred on them in his own writings and through the care he must have given to the preservation of the manuscripts themselves, a task continued by Euzoius when he transferred them onto parchment somewhere between 376 and 379.[8]

Eusebius' use of Philo as a philosopher and an exegete was instrumental in helping him shape his Christian apologetic project and played a central role in his plan to comprehensively map Christian theological and cultural territory. In particular, Philo's citations contributed to the legitimization of Eusebius' reconstruction of Christian origins as well as his version of "orthodox" Christian doctrine.

In order to demonstrate the way in which Eusebius uses Philo, and submits him to his own rhetoric of triumphalism and supersessionism, I shall focus on two main points: Eusebius' representation of Philo and his use of Philo's excerpts (§9.1), and his faithfulness to Philo's text from a philological point of view (§9.2). I will not be able to delve into detail on each topic within the confines of this short chapter. Therefore, I will present the most exemplary cases and issues and send the reader to relevant studies when necessary. Throughout this chapter, I hope to demonstrate that Eusebius is both innovative and manipulative in his use of Philo. I will argue that he intentionally distorts and repurposes Philo's *persona* and texts in order to legitimate, defend, and promote Christianity. The result is a clear-cut case of literary appropriation.[9] This

---

[4] See Inowlocki, *Eusebius and the Jewish Authors*, and "Eusebius' Construction of a Christian Culture in an Apologetic Context: Reading the *Praeparatio evangelica* as a Library," in *Reconsidering Eusebius*, 199–223.

[5] On scholarly research about Eusebius and Philo, see the recent article by S. Morlet, "Les recherches sur Philon et Eusèbe de Césarée depuis 1967," in *Les études philoniennes: Regards sur cinquante ans de recherche (1967–2017)*, ed. S. Morlet and O. Munnich (Leiden: Brill, 2021), 441–72.

[6] For the complete references to Eusebius' citations of Philo, see D. T. Runia, *Philo in Early Christian Literature: A Survey* (Assen: Van Gorcum, 1993), 212–34; D. T. Runia, "Philo in the Patristic Tradition," in *Reading Philo: A Handbook to Philo of Alexandria*, ed. T. Seland (Grand Rapids: Eerdmans, 2014), 268–86, 278–79. See also A. P. Johnson, "Philonic Allusions in PE 7.7.8," *ClQ* 56 (2006): 239–48; M. Niehoff, "Eusebius as a Reader of Philo," *Adamantius* 21 (2015): 185–94; Otto, *Philo of Alexandria*, 136–95.

[7] See D. T. Runia, *Philo in Early Christian Literature*, 16–30; D. T. Runia, "Caesarea Maritima and the Survival of Hellenistic-Jewish Literature," in *Caesarea Maritima: A Retrospective after Two Millennia*, ed. A. Raban and K. G. Holum (Leiden: Brill, 1996), 476–95. A different opinion is suggested by Morlet: Pamphilus' and Eusebius' libraries could be distinct and it might be that Philo did not reach Eusebius through the Origen-Pamphilus channel (Morlet, "Les recherches sur Philon et Eusèbe," 461–69). On Pamphilus, see S. Inowlocki, "The Hand of the Slave and the Hand of the Martyr: Pamphilus of Caesarea, Autography, and the Rise of Textual Relics," *Journal of Late Antiquity* 16 (2023): 289–23.

[8] See Runia, *Philo in Early Christian Literature*, 16–24; cf. Jerome, *Vir. ill.* 113; and Carriker, *The Library of Eusebius*, 164–77.

[9] By literary appropriation I mean the literary practice by means of which an author uses (in the form of citations, reminiscences or other) the text of another author, distorting, transforming, and subjecting it to his own authority, as is the case with Eusebius. For more on this notion, see the article by A. Haimson Lushkov, "Citation, Spoliation, and Literary Appropriation in Livy's AUC," in *Rome, Empire of Plunder: The Dynamics of Cultural Appropriation*, ed. M. P. Loar et al. (Cambridge: Cambridge University Press, 2018), 30–46.

should be borne in mind by any reader interested in Philo's works and their reception. Moreover, this chapter also aims to recast Eusebius' appropriation of Philo in the framework of an evaluation of his views of Jews and Judaism.

9.1 Eusebius' Representation and Use of Philo

Eusebius' representation of Philo is generally studied in the context of his view of Jews and Judaism.[10] More specifically, his labelling of Philo as a "Hebrew" (Ἑβραῖος) (*Praep. ev.* 7.12.14, 7.17.4, 7.20.9; *Hist. eccl.* 2.4.2), a term which carries strong theological and historical connotations in his apologetic discourse, has raised a great deal of attention. Indeed, the term Ἑβραῖος should be understood in contradistinction to the term Ἰουδαῖος, as has often been noted.[11] In the *Praep. ev.*, where it is laid out most clearly, the distinction between Ἰουδαῖος and Ἑβραῖος is both a chronological and an ethnic one: "Jews" and "Hebrews" did not live during the same period, and their names originate from different ancestors (7.6.1–2, 7.8.20–21).[12] According to Eusebius' theory, whereas the "Hebrews" lived before Moses, the "Jews" began to "proliferate" from the time of Moses onward. Unlike the "Jews," the ancient "Hebrews" did not need the laws and codes of conduct dictated by Moses. They followed a free form of religion that conformed to nature. In Eusebius' sacred library, they become "icons of holiness" (*Praep. ev.* 7.7.4, 8.18) to be emulated, a metaphor clearly borrowed from Philo himself (*Abr.* 3–4).[13]

The "Jews," in contrast, came after the pious Hebrew patriarchs. They became a multitude and were subject to the negative influence of the Egyptians to the point that their lives became similar in every respect to those of the Egyptians (*Praep. ev.* 7.8.37). Moses was sent to them to put an end to this corruption. The Mosaic legislation was meant to last until Christ's proclamation (7.8.40). The post-Christ "Jews" were held responsible for the murder of Christ and in the *Hist. eccl.*, Josephus serves as the main witness for their destruction.

One would be mistaken, however, to assume that the label "Jew(ish)" is unequivocally negative in Eusebius. His picture of the "Jews" is largely ambivalent and varies

---

[10] Most central is the study by Ulrich, *Euseb von Caesarea und die Juden*, 88–99. I disagree with his lenient judgment regarding Eusebius' anti-Judaism, for reasons that are exposed in this article. As I argue in this paper, Eusebius' positive judgment of Philo can hardly be used as an argument supporting a positive judgment of the Jews on his part.

[11] For instance, A. S. Jacobs, *Remains of the Jews: The Holy Land and Christian Empire in Late Antiquity* (Stanford: Stanford University Press, 2004), 21–55; Inowlocki, *Eusebius and the Jewish Authors*, 105–38; Johnson, *Ethnicity and Argument*, 128–52; Ulrich, *Euseb von Caesarea und die Juden*, 88–110; E. Iricinschi, "Good Hebrew, Bad Hebrew: Christians as *Triton Genos* in Eusebius' Apologetic Writings," in *Reconsidering Eusebius*, 69–86; A. Gregerman, *Building on the Ruins of the Temple: Apologetics and Polemics in Early Christianity and Rabbinic Judaism*, Texts and Studies in Ancient Judaism 165 (Tübingen: Mohr Siebeck, 2016), 126–37; Otto, *Philo of Alexandria and the Construction of Jewishness*, 136–95.

[12] While the "Jews" come from the tribe of Juda, he argues, the "Hebrews" are named after their ancestor Heber. In an alternative explanation preferred by Eusebius, he claims that they derive their name from its symbolic meaning of "migrants."

[13] On the importance of this metaphor, see Johnson, "Philonic Allusions in *PE* 7.7.8" and Inowlocki, "Eusebius' Construction of a Christian Culture," 211; also Johnson, *Ethnicity and Argument*, 112.

according to the context and his apologetic needs.[14] On the one hand, he needs to create a disruption between the "Jews" and the "Hebrews" in order to re-locate the continuity between the "Hebrews" and the Christians instead.[15] On the other hand, the "Hebrew" connection to "Jews" and Judaism enables Eusebius to claim the scriptures through an unbroken line of transmission from the ancient Hebrews to the Christians. By defending Moses and his followers, he could also counter the attacks levelled at the Christians by the Greeks through their Jewish lineage. This makes the "Jews" a crucial part of the Christian heritage in Eusebius' discourse, at least in *Praep. ev.* 8–10. Thus, the categories "Jew/ish" and "Hebrew" allow for great fluidity in order to serve Eusebius' purposes. In this apologetic framework, it is not surprising to see that Philo can be exploited by Eusebius in both a "Hebrew" and a "Jewish" context.

9.1.1 Philo in the *Historia Ecclesiastica*

Let us turn first to the *Hist. eccl.* Redacted between 300 and 325,[16] it offers a collection of texts by authoritative ecclesiastical writers.[17] Eusebius takes great pains to cite some lengthy passages of authors to which he appends a bio-bibliography. Philo comes first in this bio-bibliographical gallery, enjoying a rather lengthy treatment in the second book of the *Hist. eccl.* (2.17–18). In fact, Eusebius provides biographical information on Philo on no less than three occasions: first, when he uses his material on Caligula, second, when he introduces his extensive citations of Philo's *De vita contemplativa*, and third, after the same citations, when he provides his lengthy notes on Philo's bibliography.

It is noteworthy that the *Hist. eccl.* reads not simply as a history of Christianity, but rather, as its title indicates, as a historical narrative of the origins and development of the ecclesiastical institutions, doctrines, literature and way of life of which Eusebius sees himself as the heir. Ἐκκλησιαστικός, in Eusebius' vocabulary, refers to the Christian intellectual elite with which he identifies.[18] Thus it is highly significant that Philo, a Jew, is included in a text that maps out the institutional and intellectual/scholarly Christian succession in which a certain kind of doctrinal authority (Christian "orthodoxy") is grounded.[19] Moreover, as one of Eusebius' purposes in the *Hist. eccl.* is clearly

---

[14] See Ulrich, *Euseb von Caesarea und die Juden*, 57–131, Inowlocki, *Eusebius and the Jewish Authors*, 105–38. Books 8 and 9 of the *Praep. ev.* are strikingly positive in their presentation of the "Jews," as we shall see.

[15] This view is much more prominent in the *Dem. ev.*

[16] See most recently the chronology in S. Morlet and L. Perrone, *Eusèbe de Césarée, Histoire ecclésiastique: Commentaire* (Paris: Cerf, 2012), 1:13 and M. Verdoner, *Narrated Reality*, 38.

[17] See L. Perrone, "Eusebius of Caesarea as a Christian Writer," in *Caesarea Maritima*, 515–30; and M. Alexandre, "L'approche des vies d'écrivains dans l'Histoire Ecclésiastique," in *Vies anciennes d'auteurs grecs: mythe et biographie*: actes de la table ronde (Université François Rabelais, June 15, 1994), ed. Ph. Brunet and M.-P. Noël (Tours: Université François Rabelais, 1998), 117–44.

[18] See also D. J. DeVore, *Greek Historiography, Roman Society, Christian Empire: The* Ecclesiastical History *of Eusebius of Caesarea* (PhD diss., unpublished, University of California Berkeley, 2013), 225.

[19] On successions and lineage in Eusebius and others, see A. Tropper, "Tractate Avot and Early Christian Succession Lists," in *The Ways that Never Parted: Jews and Christians in Late Antiquity and the Early Middle Ages*, ed. A. H. Becker and A. Yoshiko Reed (Tübingen: Mohr Siebeck, 2003), 159–88.

to de-legitimize the Jews' claim to be the elected people and present them as an object of divine punishment for their murder of Christ (see e.g. 1.1), the presence of extensive citations of Philo requires some clarifications.

9.1.1.1 Philo as Historical Witness of the Jewish Miseries under Gaius
Eusebius clearly insists on Philo's double background as both a "Hebrew" by ethnicity and as learned in Greek philosophy. His testimony helps him to substantiate Josephus' narrative of the miseries endured by the "Jews" in the time of Jesus,[20] thanks to quotations from his work about "what happened to the Jews under Gaius in five books" (*Hist. eccl.* 2.5.1). Eventually, the purpose of these quotations is to demonstrate that these miseries constitute divine retribution against the "Jews" for their murder of Christ. In this case, Philo's "Hebrew" identity conveniently serves as a means to distinguish him from the Jewish mob of Jesus' time.[21] As we shall see, the privileged relationship drawn by Eusebius between Philo and Christianity justifies the special Hebrew status which he ascribed to him.

Eusebius also makes sure to underline that Philo held a prominent role in Alexandria's society. Recalling the madness of Caligula and the failure of Philo's embassy in Rome, Eusebius surprisingly chooses to cite Josephus instead of Philo.[22] He then summarizes Philo's claims about Sejanus' responsibility in the new emperor Tiberius' hatred of the Jews. Philo's *Legatio* 346, however, is cited to recount Caligula's desecration of the synagogues of Alexandria and his project to transform the Temple into a personal sanctuary.[23] Eusebius refers to Philo's *De virtutibus* as a second work narrating many other calamities against the Jews under Caligula in Alexandria (*Hist. eccl.* 2.6.3). The Philonic material concerning the period of Caligula[24] is connected to Josephus' *Bellum Judaicum* (2.169–74). Philo's excerpts are thereby used in the same way as those of Josephus in order to demonstrate that the Jews' miseries were a divine punishment for their murder of Christ.[25]

Philo's narrative of the calamities undergone by the Jews is peppered with claims by Eusebius that Philo wrote much more on the miseries of the Jews than he excerpted (*Hist. eccl.* 2.5.6, 2.6.3). Eusebius also deliberately conflates Philo's narrative of the situation of the Jews in Alexandria and in Rome with Josephus' depiction of the events at

---

[20] Eusebius' use of Philo to narrate this period will be influential as can be seen e.g. from George the Syncellus and George Harmatalus, as noted by D. T. Runia, "Philo in Byzantium: An Exploration," *VC* 70 (2016): 259–81, esp. 271–72.
[21] However, later in the *Hist. eccl.*, this does not keep Eusebius from counting him as one of the many "Jewish" authors used by Clement of Alexandria in order to prove that the Jews are anterior to the Greeks (*Hist. eccl.* 6.13.7).
[22] *Hist. eccl.* 2.5.2–5 cf. Philo, *Legat.* 162–64 and Josephus, *A.J.* 18.257–60.
[23] Eusebius also deals with that episode in the *Dem. ev.* 8.2 but it is unclear which Philonic passage he is quoting. I supported the idea that he was intentionally tampering with Philo's *Legatio* in order to reinforce his own supersessionist claims. See S. Inowlocki, "The Reception of Philo's *Legatio ad Gaium* in Eusebius of Caesarea's Works," *SPhiloA* 16 (2004): 30–49.
[24] See also Eusebius' references to Philo's mention of Sejanus, the desecration of Alexandrian synagogues by Flaccus, the images of Gaius placed in the synagogues at *Chron.* 213–15.
[25] On this subject, see O. Irshai, "Jews and Judaism in Early Church Historiography: The Case of Eusebius of Caesarea (Preliminary Observations and Examples)," in *Jewish Life in Byzantium: Dialectics of Minority and Majority Cultures*, ed. R. Bonfil et al. (Leiden: Brill, 2011), 799–828.

Jerusalem. By doing so, he creates a more convincing picture of the disfavor into which the Jews had fallen both with the Romans and with divine providence itself.

Eusebius' use of Philo is most similar to his use of Josephus in this passage: he is turned into an eye-witness of the Jews' divine punishment for their murder of Christ.[26] Furthermore, in light of his cruel rebuttal by Gaius, which is mentioned both directly by Eusebius and in Josephus' citation, Philo now himself embodies the humiliation undergone by the "Jews" in the time of Christ's death. However, as I will argue below, this depiction of Philo will be inverted later in the *Hist. eccl.*

Although in this instance, both Philo's and Josephus' excerpts serve the same purpose, their roles are nevertheless different in the *Hist. eccl.* Compared to Josephus, Philo is the *Hebrew* witness par excellence of the *Hebrew* beginnings of Christianity: he has witnessed the lives of "the first heralds of the Gospel teaching and apostolic customs handed down from the beginning" (*Hist. eccl.* 2.17). In contrast, Josephus is the great *Jewish* witness of the miseries of the *Jews*: as is clear from his biographical notice, he is the "son of Matthias, a priest of Jerusalem who fought against the Romans in the early stages and was an unwilling witness of the later events" (*B. J.* 1.3 in *Hist. eccl.* 3.9). While Philo's status as a "Hebrew" and quasi-Christian author certainly stems both from his testimony on the Therapeutae, considered as Christians by Eusebius, and from his alleged encounter with Peter, Josephus' status remains that of a *Jewish* witness in spite of his citation of the *Testimonium Flavianum*. As A. Whealey has pointed out, Eusebius' use of this text was surprisingly modest from an apologetic and theological point of view.[27]

9.1.1.2 Philo as Witness for the Ecclesiastical Way of Life

Further in the second book of the *Hist. eccl.*, Eusebius goes back to Philo and devotes a lengthy account to his *De vita contemplativa*. As I have argued in a previous study, Eusebius' account is a piece of rhetoric aiming to claim the Therapeutae not as proto-Christians or proto-monks but as the first Christians in Alexandria.[28] Eusebius states that, according to tradition,[29] Philo had an encounter with Peter in Rome. This anecdote must have been scarcely believable, even at the time: he immediately adds that it

---

[26] On Eusebius' use of Josephus in the *Hist. eccl.*, see G. Hata, "The Abuse and Misuse of Josephus in Eusebius' Ecclesiastical History, Books 2 and 3," in *Studies in Josephus and the Varieties of Ancient Judaism*, ed. S. J. D. Cohen and J. J. Schwartz (Leiden: Brill, 2006), 91–102, and "Eusebius and Josephus: The Way Eusebius Misused and Abused Josephus," *Patristica: Proceedings of the Colloquia of the Japanese Society for Patristic Studies*, supp. 1 (2001): 49–66; R. M. Grant, "Eusebius, Josephus and the Fate of the Jews," *SBL Seminar Papers* 115.17 (1979): 69–86; R. Carrier, "Origen, Eusebius, and the Accidental Interpolation in Josephus' *Jewish Antiquities* 20.200," *JECS* 20 (2012): 489–514; and recently N. P. Legh Allen, *Christian Forgery in Jewish Antiquities: Josephus Interrupted* (Newcastle: Cambridge Scholars Publishing, 2020) (which I did not have the opportunity to read, unfortunately); K. H. Dahm, "Commotion, Rebellion, and War: Eusebius of Caesarea's Narrative of Jewish Revolts against Roman Rule in His Ecclesiastical History," *JECS* 29 (2021): 495–523.

[27] A. Whealey, "The *Testimonium Flavianum*," in *A Companion to Josephus*, ed. H. H. Chapman and Z. Rogers (Oxford: Wiley-Blackwell, 2016), 346.

[28] Since I have analyzed this account in depth elsewhere I will only re-visit certain aspects of this section of the *Hist. eccl.*; S. Inowlocki, "Eusebius of Caesarea's *interpretatio christiana* of Philo's *De vita contemplativa*," *HTR* 97 (2004): 305–28.

[29] It is unclear to which tradition Eusebius refers to. See Carriker's analysis of the expression λόγος (κατ)ἔχει: *The Library of Eusebius*, 63–68.

is "not unlikely" since the *Contempl.* contains the rules of the church such as they are still observed in his own time (*Hist. eccl.* 3.17.1). The whole passage demonstrates that the Therapeutae are the first Christians of Egypt, converted by Mark (2.16.1), and more specifically, that they constitute the first Christian ascetics living an ecclesiastical life in Egypt.[30] He goes as far as to claim that Philo describes the functions of deacon, and even of bishop (2.17.23). A comparison between Philo's *Contempl.* and Acts confirms in his eyes this identification,[31] even though he seems to have been aware of the resistance such claims would or did raise.

In the context of the *Hist. eccl.*, Philo's *Contempl.* becomes thereby foundational in terms of institution as well as in terms of philosophical and ascetic way of life (2.17.23). His Therapeutae now constitute the starting point of a chain of succession of philosophical Christians, including Pantaenus and Clement of Alexandria, which also connects them to the school of Origen, Pamphilus, and Eusebius himself.[32] Alexandria and Caesarea are now conveniently linked through the use of Philonic textual material fitting his own agenda.[33]

The language Eusebius uses to describe Philo's relationship to the Therapeutae clearly raises the question of Philo's relationship with Christianity.[34] Remarkably, Eusebius never goes so far as to state that Philo converted to Christianity. In fact, this is the tour de force that he achieves in the *Hist. eccl.*: he demonstrates Philo's recognition of and admiration for Christianity, but carefully refrains from crossing the line of claiming his conversion (2.17.2). By doing so, he positions Philo both as a favorable Hebrew eyewitness to the beginnings of Christianity in Egypt and as a founding figure of ecclesiastical Christianity—notably through the connection with Peter and Mark. This is a clear example of the difficult balancing act demanded by his handling of Philo: an attempt to simultaneously "out-Judaize" him and to preserve his Jewishness for apologetic purposes.[35] The label "Hebrew" applied both to Philo and the Therapeutae plays a major role in negotiating this paradox (*Hist. eccl.* 2.17.2).[36]

9.1.1.3 Philo as the First Ecclesiastical Author
At *Hist. eccl.* 2.18, Eusebius goes back to Philo for the third time, focusing on his work as an exegete and providing a full list of his writings. The bibliographical list is enshrined

---

[30] Eusebius insists on the term ἐκκλησιαστικός: *Hist. eccl.* 2.17.14 and 23.
[31] *Hist. eccl.* 2.17.6 = Acts 2:45 and 4:34–35.
[32] See on this subject L. Penland, "The History of the Caesarean Present: Eusebius and Narratives of Origen," in *Eusebius of Caesarea: Tradition and Innovations*, 148–68; "Eusebius Philosophus?," in *Reconsidering Eusebius*, 87–97.
[33] On the origins of Egyptian Christianity, see J. Mélèze Modrzejewski, *The Jews of Egypt: From Rameses II to Emperor Hadrian* (Princeton: Princeton University Press, 1997), 222–32; W. Bauer, *Orthodoxy and Heresy in Earliest Christianity*, ed. R. Kraft and G. Krodel (Philadelphia: Fortress, 1971), 44–49; H. Koester, *Introduction to the New Testament*, Vol. 1: *History and Literature of Early Christianity*, 2nd edn (Berlin: de Gruyter, 2000), 225–45; B. A. Pearson and J. E. Goehring, eds, *The Roots of Egyptian Christianity* (Philadelphia: Fortress, 1986), 97–102.
[34] Inowlocki, "Eusebius of Caesarea's *interpretatio christiana*," 319–22.
[35] Indeed, Eusebius needs him to remain a Jew in order to keep his credentials in terms of "Jewish"/"Hebrew" knowledge and as a privileged witness to the suffering of the Jews.
[36] Note that, according to Eusebius, the Therapeutae are of "Hebrew" origin, and therefore still "Judaize."

into a double description of Philo. The first one provides a laudatory portrayal of Philo as an exegete.

Strikingly, even as an interpreter of scriptures, Eusebius presents him in a Greek garb: "Eloquent," "vast in thoughts," he says, he wrote a "varied and multifarious comment on the sacred words" (ποικίλην καὶ πολύτροπον τῶν ἱερῶν λόγων πεποίηται τὴν ὑφήγησιν, *Hist. eccl.* 2.18.1). Using two adjectives that are reminiscent of the Greek hero Ulysses (2.18.1),[37] Eusebius marks the "multi-culturalism" of Philo's exegesis, in which Hebrew and Greek philosophies are intertwined. Indeed, Philo's presentation as a bi-cultural (Greek and Hebrew) savant, as in *Hist. eccl.* 2.6, clearly aims to enhance his prestige.

Following Philo, several Christian figures—including Origen and Pamphilus, no less—are praised by Eusebius for their expertise in Greek culture.[38] Philo is thus marked by Eusebius as ushering in a long tradition of Greek and Christian erudition that he will emphasize on many occasions.[39]

There would be much to say about the bibliography provided by Eusebius[40] but here I will restrict myself to note that it functions as a way of marking Philo as an authoritative exegete of the biblical text. Indeed, so far in the *Hist. eccl.*, Eusebius did not tackle this aspect of Philo's work. In the light of his bibliography, it becomes clear that most of his work deals with scripture.

Interestingly, at the end of Philo's bio-bibliography, Eusebius returns to Philo's stay in Rome under the reign of Claudius (during which he would have met with Peter) (*Hist. eccl.* 2.17.1). He claims "it is said" (λέγεται) that Philo read to the Roman senate his *De virtutibus* in which he described Gaius' impieties (2.18.8). According to Eusebius, he was admired to such an extent that his words were judged worthy of being placed in libraries. Whether historical or not, as Yun Lee Too points out, the inclusion of a work in libraries was a very important honor, tantamount to canonization if imperial libraries were involved.[41] This note indicates the importance of the status Eusebius wished to bestow on Philo.

No other source prior to Eusebius mentions this episode. In the context of Eusebius' *Hist. eccl.*, I would argue that it functions as a counter-story to Philo's disastrous embassy

---

[37] The adjectives ποικίλην καὶ πολύτροπον are characteristic of Homer's depiction of Ulysses. See P. Pucci, *Odysseus Polytropos: Intertextual Readings of the Odyssey and the Iliad* (Ithaca: Cornell University Press, 1993). Following Eusebius, Philo's style and language will be often commented upon in the Byzantine tradition as Runia's study shows ("Philo in Byzantium").

[38] Dorotheus in *Hist. eccl.* 7.32.2–4; Anatolius in *Hist. eccl.* 7.32.6; Stephen in *Hist. eccl.* 7.32.22; Pamphilus in *Mart. Pal.* 7.4–5, 11.1, 4.5–6, 5.2; Pierius and Melitius in *Hist. eccl.* 7.32.25–28; Heraclas in *Hist. eccl.* 6.15. Cf. Julius Africanus, Tatian, and Clement of Alexandria in *Praep. ev.* 10.9.26; Origen in *Praep. ev.* 6.10.50.

[39] See J. M. Rogers, "Origen in the Likeness of Philo: Eusebius of Caesarea's Portrait of the Model Scholar," *Studies in Jewish-Christian Relations* 12 (2017): 1–13. On the school of Caesarea, see Penland, "Eusebius Philosophus?"

[40] See e.g. M. Alexandre, "Du grec au latin: les titres des oeuvres de Philon d'Alexandrie," in *Titres et articulations du texte dans les oeuvres antiques: actes du colloque international de Chantilly 13–15 Décembre 1994*, ed. J.-Cl. Fredouille et al. (Paris: Études Augustiniennes, 1997), 255–86; Runia, *Philo in Early Christian Literature*, 19–21; Carriker, *The Library of Eusebius*, 164–77.

[41] We are not told precisely which libraries (imperial? public? private?). This is unlikely to be historical information. Did Eusebius confuse Philo with Josephus whose autobiography he cited also in the *Hist. eccl.* and which presented similar claims (3.9.2)? See Yun Lee Too, *The Idea of the Library in the Ancient World* (Oxford: Oxford University Press, 2010), 239–40.

to Gaius: while in the latter, he is being ridiculed, humiliated, his life being even endangered by Gaius, in the former, he is admired by the senate and his criticism of Gaius is celebrated to the point that his book is accepted in Roman libraries. Eusebius seems eager to provide a happy ending to Philo's disastrous embassy.

Ironically, immediately after this positive note, Eusebius mentions the expulsion of the Jews from Rome under Claudius (Suetonius, *Claud.* 25). It is no coincidence that he presents these two episodes back-to-back. It is in fact indicative of the status he seeks to attribute to Philo: Philo is clearly uprooted from the flock of his co-religionists and marked as an exception. Philo's presence then recedes from the *Hist. eccl.* to leave room for numerous quotations from Josephus on the miseries of the Jews under Pilate.

To sum up, Eusebius' careful presentation of Philo's bio-bibliography definitely turns him into no less than the first ecclesiastical writer of the *Hist. eccl.* By claiming that he was a benevolent eye-witness to the first Christian ecclesiastical community in Egypt and an acquaintance of Peter, he provides him with the credentials to become, if not Christian, at least a part of the most important lineage of the work: that of Alexandrian Christianity. Therefore, although Eusebius is careful never to erase Philo's Jewish identity, by recasting his *persona* in an entirely new Christian context, he successfully positions Philo—both as a source and as a character—in the Christian landscape as a starting-point alternative to the apostles, to a Christian lineage ultimately leading to himself.

9.1.2 Philo in the *Praeparatio Evangelica*: Intermediary and Ambassador

While Eusebius mainly uses Philo as a witness in the *Hist. eccl.*, in the *Praep. ev.*, where he also makes extensive use of his quotations, Philo is used as a crucial intermediary. On the one hand, he supplies a missing link between the ancient Hebrews and the Christians; on the other hand, he enables Eusebius to configure the relationship between Hebrew/Jewish theology and Greek philosophy (mainly Plato).

The *Praep. ev.*, like the *Hist. eccl.*, has been long considered solely as a reservoir of Greek fragments before being re-appraised over the last years as a work worthy of being studied on its own terms.[42] A major apologetic work, together with its "sister" the *Demonstratio evangelica*, it was redacted in parallel to the *Hist. eccl.* and published between 313 and 317.[43] While its explicit aim is to answer the pagan charges against the Christians, I would argue that, similarly to the *Hist. eccl.*, it functions as a projection of Eusebius' library, real or imagined.[44] In parallel, it provides a polemic and apologetic "history of religions" from the origins to the rise of Christianity.

---

[42] See e.g. Johnson, *Ethnicity and Argument*; Kofsky, *Eusebius of Caesarea against Paganism*; Morlet, *La Démonstration évangélique*; Inowlocki, *Eusebius and the Jewish Authors*.

[43] See the tentative chronology in S. Morlet and L. Perrone, *Eusèbe de Césarée, Histoire ecclésiastique: Commentaire* (Paris: Cerf, 2012), 1:13.

[44] See my "Eusebius' Construction of a Christian Culture," as well as S. Inowlocki, "What Caesarea Has to Do with Alexandria? The Christian Library between Myth and Reality," *Scripta Classica Israelica* 43 (2024): 1–19.

In the *Praep. ev.*, Philo is depicted as a crucial "Hebrew" interpreter of scriptures (7.12.14, 17.4, 20.9) whose testimony enables Eusebius to claim the antiquity of the Christian doctrines as well as their philosophical legitimacy. His role is clearly enounced in the following passage, a quotation on the "second cause":[45]

ἵνα δὲ μὴ σοφίζεσθαί με ταῦτα νομίσῃς, ἑρμηνέα σοι τῆς ἐν τῇ γραφῇ διανοίας Ἑβραῖον ἄνδρα παραστήσω, τὰ οἰκεῖα πατρόθεν ἀκριβοῦντα καὶ παρὰ διδασκάλων τὸ δόγμα μεμαθηκότα, εἰ δή σοι τοιοῦτος ὁ Φίλων. ἐπάκουσον οὖν καὶ τοῦδε, ὅπως τὰς θείας ἑρμηνεύει φωνάς·

Lest, however, you should suppose that these are my subtleties, I will offer you as interpreter of the meaning of the Scripture a man of Hebrew race, who received from his forefathers an accurate knowledge of the history of his country and learned the doctrine from his teachers; that is, if you accept Philo as such a man. Listen then to him, how he interprets the divine utterances. (*Praep. ev.* 7.12.14)[46]

Eusebius substitutes Philo' voice for his own in order to provide a (supposedly) more authoritative testimony. Here Philo's credentials as an interpreter are clearly outlined: his ethnicity combined to his genealogical and intellectual lineage once again enhance his authority both in terms of historical knowledge and doctrine (*Praep. ev.* 7.12.14).[47] Thus "Philo the Hebrew" becomes the guarantor of Eusebius' scriptural interpretations, which clearly aim to Christianize the biblical text. As a result, the λόγος as second cause can now be rooted in the authoritative writings of a "Hebrew" theologian.

Further on, Philo even becomes instrumental in blurring the lines between "Hebrew" and "Christian." When supposedly dealing with the "Hebrew" doctrine of matter, Philo is in fact the only "Hebrew" quoted by the side of the Christian theologians Dionysius of Alexandria, Origen, or "Maximus" (*Praep. ev.* 7.21.5).[48] Eusebius clearly traces this doctrine back to him, which goes on to show that, as in the *Hist. eccl.*, he accepts him as the starting point of a Christian succession conveying authoritative and "orthodox" doctrine.

---

[45] On Eusebius' use of the Philonic excerpts on the second God, see Inowlocki, "Les enjeux idéologiques de la réception des extraits philoniens sur la cause seconde dans la *Préparation évangélique*."

[46] Greek text from K. Mras, *Eusebius Werke, Band 8: Die Praeparatio evangelica*, GCS 43.1, 43.2 (Berlin: Akademie, 1954–56). Trans. E. Gifford, *Eusebii Pamphili Evangelicae Praeparationis* (Oxford: Oxford University Press, 1903).

[47] Cf. *Dem. ev.* 6.18 (291b) in which Josephus' "precise knowledge of the exoteric Jewish commentaries" (τὰς ἔξωθεν ἰουδαϊκὰς δευτερώσεις ἀπηκριβωκώς) guarantees the validity of Eusebius' interpretation of scripture.

[48] K. Mras assumed an author Maximus. However, some scholars have worried that a long passage of the *De resurrectione*, identical with a passage in the *Dialogue of Adamantius*, is quoted by Eusebius under the name of "Maximus." A number of solutions have been proposed, among others in T. Zahn, "Die Dialoge des 'Adamantius' mit den Gnostikern," *ZKG* 9 (1888): 193–239; T. D. Barnes, "Methodius, Maximus, and Valentinus," *JTS* 30 (1979): 47–55; I. Ramelli, "'Maximus' on Evil, Matter, and God: Arguments for the Identification of the Source of Eusebius, PE VII,22 with Maximus of Tyre," *Adamantius* 16 (2010): 230–55; and Carriker, *The Library of Eusebius*, 225–30. I am thankful to David Runia and Dawn Lavalle-Norman for providing complementary bibliography on this point.

Philo's "Hebrew-ness" is also strongly exploited in order to articulate Eusebius' views on the relationship between "Hebrew" (meaning, in fact, Christian) and Greek philosophy. When Eusebius addresses the doctrine of the second cause in *Praep. ev.* 11, he resorts again to Philo the "Hebrew", inserting his testimony into a chain of quotations from scriptures, Plato, Plotinus, Numenius, and Amelius (11.15–19). In these passages, Eusebius again insists on Philo's ability to clarify the meaning of scriptures.[49] His quotations clearly serve to establish a continuity between "Hebrew" (aka Christian) doctrines and that which Eusebius sees as the best of Greek philosophy, namely Plato (*Praep. ev.* 11.9.8).[50] This continuity is artificially created through Philo's testimony mainly for apologetic reasons; it enables Eusebius to present Christianity as the heir to an ancient, philosophically legitimate tradition that outshone Judaism and Greek philosophy; it justifies the Christian appropriation of the Hebrew scriptures and legitimizes the Christian preference for so-called barbarian texts over Greek philosophy. Yet, this supposed continuity results in fact from Philo's own influence on other Christian authors. For instance, in *Praep. ev.* 11.24, Eusebius uses one of Philo's citations on the ideas and the creation of an intelligible world in order to bridge Plato's thought on the subject with that of Clement of Alexandria (*Strom.* 5.93.4–94.5 in *Praep. ev.* 11.25). In fact, Clement had borrowed his own exegesis from Philo but Eusebius is obviously content to mention their agreement (*Praep. ev.* 11.24.12).[51]

Strikingly, in passages where he deals with Philo as an historical source, Eusebius makes it clear that he is related to the "Jews." As we have seen, in *Hist. eccl.* 2.5.4, he is represented as presiding over the "Jewish" embassy to Gaius. In *Praep. ev.* 8, in which he addresses the "Jews" and their πολιτεία, he stops labelling Philo a "Hebrew." Philo becomes a representative of the "wise men among the Jews" (8.12.20–22). Moreover, when citing the *Hypothetica*, he explains that this work was written by Philo in defense of the "Jews," against their accusers (8.6.1) thus acknowledging Philo's connection to the Jewish people. Eusebius also feels free to present Philo as the author of an apology for the "Jews."[52] In these passages, the genealogical continuity between "Hebrews" and "Jews" is restored: the "Jews" are the youths (τοὺς νέους) of the Hebrews, as well as their παῖδες and they are thought to be in agreement (σύμφωνα) with their ancestors (προπατόρων) (8.12.21, 14.72).

Unlike the *Hist. eccl.*, the *Praep. ev.* represents the "Jews" as the link between the "Hebrews" and the Christians. Hence, their history and theology are presented in a positive light. In this context, Philo can serve as their ambassador. It is noteworthy,

---

[49] Cf. *Praep. ev.* 11.14.10 ("Philo the Hebrew interprets more clearly the meaning of the doctrine"); 11.23.12 (Philo and Clement of Alexandria as "exegetes of the sacred laws," "clarify the meaning of Moses' writings"); 13.18.12 ("Philo, the expert in Hebrew matters, interprets these words [Deut 4:19], clarifying them extensively"). See Inowlocki, *Eusebius and the Jewish Authors*, 245–47.

[50] Cf. the famous word "either Plato philonizes or Philo platonizes" used by later authors such as Jerome; see Runia, *Philo in Early Christian Literature*, 313.

[51] See A. van den Hoek, *Clement of Alexandria and His Use of Philo in the* Stromateis: *An Early Christian Reshaping of a Jewish Model* (Leiden: Brill, 1988); Otto, *Construction of Jewishness*, 48–90.

[52] *Praep. ev.* 8.11.1–19 = Philo, *Pro Iudaeis Apologia* = Philo, *Hypothetica* (Colson LCL 9.436–43 [412–13]).

however, that in this context, even if Eusebius refrains from calling him a "Hebrew," he never explicitly labels him as being a "Jew" either.[53]

Even when explicitly presented as an apologist for the "Jews," Philo in fact serves as a spokesperson for the Christians. This can be seen, for instance, in the case of Philo's *Hypothetica*, which is cited abundantly in *Praep. ev.* 8.6–7. The apologetic and polemical material contained in this work (as well as in Josephus' *Contra Apionem*) could be conveniently appropriated by Eusebius in order to counter pagan attacks against Moses and the law (8.8). The real purpose was to defend not Judaism, but rather Christianity, which had inherited the criticism first addressed to the Jews against their lawgiver and their legislation. Any proper defense of Christianity needed to address the same attacks, as can be seen, for instance in Origen's *Contra Celsum*. Consequently, again, Philo's apologetic material is exploited by Eusebius seemingly in a defense of Judaism, but in reality, in a methodical project to defend and promote Christianity. The same strategy is used at *Praep. ev.* 8.14 where he uses Philo to defend the concept of divine providence.

Interestingly, while in the *Hist. eccl.* Eusebius extensively uses "Philo the Hebrew" in order to claim the Therapeutae as the first Egyptian Christians, in *Praep. ev.* 8, Philo's account of the Essenes is appropriated as a report on the "Jewish" way of life (8.11–12).[54] Philo is singled out as the most valuable witness of the Essenes, providing a testimony based on many "national records" (τῶν οἰκείων ὑπομνημάτων, 8.10.19).[55] This difference in ethnic treatment is certainly due to the fact that Porphyry had defined Josephus' Essenes as "Jews" in his *De abstinentia* 4.2.2. It would have been difficult for Eusebius to argue now that these were in fact Christians.[56]

It is worth noting that, while Philo's allegorical reading of scriptures is often seen as a central criterion for his inclusion in the Christian tradition, when Eusebius deals with the Jewish practice of allegory, he prefers to cite the *Letter of Aristeas* and Aristobulus (*Praep. ev.* 8.9 and 8.10). Perhaps these passages could more easily fit physically in Eusebius' text. Yet, throughout the *Praep. ev.*, Philo's allegorical exegesis is ignored by Eusebius. Tellingly, Philo does not appear (at least explicitly) as an exegete in the *Dem. ev.* either, where scriptures are openly and directly handled as a Christian matter. It is striking that a dimension of Philo's work that affected Christianity to such an important extent has been obfuscated by Eusebius the apologist.

To conclude, in the *Praep. ev.*, "Jewish" history and doctrines need to be defended as they were used by the Greeks in polemical attacks against Christianity. Philo's role in Eusebius is to answer these attacks, not as a Christian in disguise, but as an indispensable "Hebrew" auxiliary subservient to the Christian cause.

---

[53] Cf. D. T. Runia, "Philonic Nomenclature," *SPhiloA* 6 (1994): 6.

[54] Interestingly, Epiphanius will turn Philo's Essenes into Christian monastics: see Runia's discussion, *Philo in Early Christian Literature*, 228–29. See also S. Inowlocki, "From the Church to the Monastery: Philo's *Vita Contemplativa* in Late Ancient Christian Literature," in *Jerusalem Studies in Jewish Thought*, ed. M. Niehoff and S. Weisser (forthcoming) (Hebrew).

[55] Eusebius had certainly at least Josephus in mind. Porphyry is cited further.

[56] See Inowlocki, *Eusebius and the Jewish Authors*, 173–74.

9.2 Eusebius' Faithfulness in Citing Philo

As is well known, Eusebius made an extensive use of citations in the *Hist. eccl.* and the *Praep. ev.*[57] *Oratio recta, oratio obliqua*, paraphrase, and summary are all techniques he uses in his different works. In the *Hist. eccl.*, he creatively mingles these different techniques, while in the *Praep. ev.* he mainly uses *oratio recta*. On many occasions he explicitly claims to quote texts faithfully[58] and even provides precise lemmata.[59] Because he is our only source for numerous otherwise lost excerpts, the question of his faithfulness greatly matters to the philologists and the historians of philosophy. It is also crucial if we are to understand his methodology in appropriating his sources. In addition, this issue may shed light on the ideological stances taken in modern scholarship on Eusebius.

Eusebius is generally considered to be remarkably faithful in his citations.[60] As a result, in numerous instances where original manuscripts of patristic texts are of inferior quality, preference is given to the text quoted by Eusebius. This is the case, for instance, with Josephus' *Contra Apionem*[61] as well as the *Letter of Aristeas*[62] both quoted in the *Praep. ev.*

However, it should be noted that the manuscripts of the *Praep. ev.* in which these texts are quoted are in fact inferior. The most ancient of them only goes back to the thirteenth century,[63] and is considered inaccurate and replete with *lacunae*. Needless to say, the *Hist. eccl.* also raises numerous philological issues regarding citations, one of the most important cases in point being Eusebius' citation of the *Testimonium Flavianum* as well as other Josephan material.[64] Although most scholars agree on the

---

[57] See e.g. J. Freudenthal, *Hellenistische Studien* (Breslau: H. Skutsch, 1875), 1:3–16; P. Henry, *Recherches sur la Préparation Evangélique d'Eusèbe et l'édition perdue des Œuvres de Plotin publiée par Eustochius* (Paris: Bibliothèque de l'École des Hautes Études, Sciences religieuses, 1935), 11–26; M. E. Hardwick, *Josephus as a Historical Source in Patristic Literature through Eusebius*, BJS 128 (Atlanta: Scholars Press, 1989), 69; H. Schreckenberg, *Die Flavius-Josephus-Tradition im Antike und Mittelalter* (Leiden: Brill, 1972), 85; J. Coman, *Utilisation des Stromates de Clément par Eusèbe dans la Préparation Evangélique*, Überlieferungsgeschichtliche untersuchungen (Berlin: Akademie, 1981), 123; Inowlocki, *Eusebius and the Jewish Authors*, 85–90, 191ff.

[58] e.g. *Praep. ev.* 1.9.20, 1.10.49, 2.2.52, 3.7.2, 4.15.9, 5.1.11, 10.6.15, 11.18.26.

[59] For more on this, see J. R. Royse, "Philo's Division of his Works into Books," *SPhiloA* 13 (2001): 59–85; Carriker, *The Library of Eusebius*, 166–69; Inowlocki, *Eusebius and the Jewish Authors*, 178–85 and 190–223.

[60] R. M. Grant, for instance, sees Eusebius as the most faithful of the Christian citing authors of antiquity: "The Appeal to the Early Fathers," *JTS* 11 (1960): 13–24; des Places were extremely enthusiastic about Eusebius' transmission of Plato's *Laws* and *Epinomis* declaring that the manuscripts of the *Praep. ev.* outshone those of Plato (see his collected *Études platoniciennes 1929–1979*, Études préliminaires aux Religions orientales dans l'Empire romain 90 (Leiden: Brill, 1981), 249–58. And yet, interestingly, in the case of Plato, for instance, the French editor Favrelle praises Eusebius' faithfulness in citing while demonstrating how he did tamper with the Platonic text. See G. Favrelle, *Eusèbe de Césarée: Préparation évangélique*, Livre XI, SC 292 (Paris: Cerf, 1982), 315–16, 382ff. See Inowlocki, *Eusebius and the Jewish Authors*, 86ff.

[61] Th. Reinach and L. Blum, *Flavius Josèphe: Contre Apion* (Paris: Les belles lettres, 1930), xi.

[62] A. Pelletier, *La Lettre d'Aristée à Philocrate: introduction, texte critique, traduction et notes*, SC 89 (Paris: Cerf, 1962), 23.

[63] K. Mras, *Eusebius Werke*, XIII–LI.

[64] The bibliography is immense. See, among others, J. P. Meier, *A Marginal Jew: Rethinking the Historical Jesus*, Vol. 1: *The Roots of the Problem and the Person*, ABRL (Garden City, NY: Doubleday, 1991), 78–83; P. Winter, "Josephus on Jesus and James," in E. Schurer, *The History of the Jewish People in the Age of Jesus Christ*, rev. and ed. G. Vermes and F. Millar (Edinburgh: Clark, 1973), 428–41; J. Neville Birdsall, "The Continuing Enigma of Josephus' Testimony about Jesus," *BJRL* 67 (1985): 609–22; S. Pines, *An Arabic Version of the Testimonium Flavianum and its Implications* (Jerusalem: Israel Academy of Sciences and Humanities, 1971); S. Mason, *Josephus and the New Testament* (Peabody, MA: Hendrickson, 1992); G. Vermes, "The Jesus Notice of Josephus Re-examined," *JJS* 38 (1987): 1–10.

fact that Eusebius did not fabricate the whole passage,[65] several have cast some doubts on his innocence.[66]

My own study of the *Praep. ev.* and *Dem. ev.* has revealed that Eusebius most likely does not fabricate any text, but that, on several occasions, he feels free to make modifications in the text he quotes either by omission, addition, substitution, or even slight alteration.[67] These changes almost always have a polemical or apologetic purpose that fits his own objectives, which suggests that he is likely responsible for them, and did not reproduce an already interpolated text. Likewise, he may have omitted some material he finds embarrassing from a theological point of view.[68] He also occasionally harmonizes different citations from different authors in order to make his case stronger. Many such examples can be found in his citations of Philo. As this has already been analyzed elsewhere in detail,[69] I will not go back to each case, but rather limit myself to provide a few significant examples.

Although Eusebius' citations of Philo are generally reliable, a careful examination reveals that his manuscripts sometimes provide unfaithful readings. In the citations presented in the *Praep. ev.*, Cohn and Wendland have asserted that the texts of the *De agricultura*, *De plantatione*, and *De confusione linguarum* quoted in books 11 and 7 sometimes present corruptions of their own. According to them, Eusebius occasionally provides a deliberately corrupted text or a text copied carelessly.[70] But they never explain such cases fully. Many can be found throughout the *Praep. ev.*, in spite of Eusebius' claims of faithfulness to the text he quotes.

In the *Hist. eccl.*, Eusebius claims to cite Philo's *Contempl.* faithfully (συλλαβαῖς αὐταῖς), although he freely mixes *oratio recta*, *obliqua*, and summaries, perhaps for the sake of *variatio*.[71] In *Hist. eccl.* 2.17.19–20, where he cites *Contempl.* 78, Philo's τὰ οἰκεῖα has been changed to ἡ οἰκία, which could be caused by iotacism, while the words ἡ λογικὴ ψυχή have been omitted. However, given that the content of the passage is significantly modified as a result of these minor changes, one can wonder whether Eusebius did so for a specific purpose. A more careful examination of the text in the form adopted by Eusebius shows that the Philonic passage no longer addresses the rational soul's ability to contemplate beauty of thought in familiar objects, but rather the community's allegorical reading of scriptural words. Given Eusebius' Christianization of the Therapeutae, it can be safely assumed that he made these changes deliberately.

---

[65] e.g. J. Carleton Paget, "Some Observations on Josephus and Christianity," *JTS* 52 (2001): 577–78; Inowlocki, *Eusebius and the Jewish Authors*, 207–9; A. Whealey, "Josephus, Eusebius of Caesarea, and the Testimonium Flavianum," in *Josephus und das Neue Testament*, ed. C. Böttrich and J. Herzer (Tübingen: Mohr Siebeck, 2007), 73–116, and Whealey, "The Testimonium Flavianum," 352–54.

[66] Most recently K. Olson, "Eusebian Reading of the *Testimonium Flavianum*," in *Eusebius of Caesarea: Tradition and Innovations*, 169–202; K. Olson, "Eusebius and the *Testimonium Flavianum*," *CBQ* 61 (1999): 305–22.

[67] Inowlocki, *Eusebius and the Jewish Authors*, 190–220.

[68] See e.g. the deliberate deletion of the reference to the heavenly bodies as gods when citing from Philo at *Praep. ev.* 11.24.1–6 = *Opif.* 24–27.

[69] Inowlocki, *Eusebius and the Jewish Authors*, 190–222.

[70] L. Cohn and P. Wendland, *Philonis Alexandrini opera quae supersunt*, 8 vols (Berlin: Reimer, 1896–1930), 1:x–xi.

[71] For a detailed study of his handling of the text of *Contempl.*, see Inowlocki, "Eusebius of Caesarea's *interpretatio christiana*," 314–18.

In the *Praep. ev.*, Philo is abundantly quoted in order to demonstrate that the doctrine of the λόγος as second god was a "Hebrew" doctrine. This is notably the case in *Praep. ev.* 7.13.1–2. Although the expression "second god" (δεύτερος θεός) never appears in Philo's corpus as we have it, it does occur in one of Eusebius' Philonic quotations (*Praep. ev.* 7.13.1–2 = QG 2.62),[72] of which the original Greek text is lost.[73] This has led some prominent scholars to consider it a Christian interpolation.[74]

The fact that later in the *Praep. ev.*, another philological problem regarding the word λόγος appears again in a quotation of Philo may confirm this hypothesis. When Eusebius quotes *Plant.* 8–10 in *Praep. ev.* 7.13.4–6, on two occasions, all his manuscripts read λόγος while Philo's manuscripts' unanimous reading is νόμος. This change entails the presence in Philo's text of a doctrine of the λόγος with Christian overtones. Cohn and Wendland have followed Eusebius, accepting it as Philonic, while Goodenough and Daniélou saw it as a Christian interpolation.[75] Barthélemy, some thirty years after Goodenough, using distinctively anti-Jewish stereotypes, argued that the discrepancy should be attributed to an interpolation made by a Jew in some Philonic manuscripts.[76] However, this hypothesis should be rejected.[77]

It can hardly be determined whether Eusebius would have been responsible for this change in Philo's text. However, his treatment of Philonic citations in the *Praep. ev.* and the *Hist. eccl.* demonstrates that he did not shy away from occasionally tampering with the text. If Philo had been a witness to the first Christian communities in Egypt and even had an encounter with Peter in Rome, Eusebius may have deemed him able to have spoken of the Logos as a second god and binding force of the universe.[78] It may

---

[72] On this passage, see D. T. Runia, "Philo, *Quaestiones In Genesim* 2.62 and the Problem of Deutero-Theology," in *Armenian, Hittite and Indo-European Studies: A Commemoration Volume for Jos J. S. Weitenberg*, ed. U. Bläsing, Hebrew University Armenian Studies 15 (Leuven: Peeters, 2019), 259–69.

[73] See Inowlocki, *Eusebius and the Jewish Authors*, 195–96.

[74] e.g. M. Harl, *Philon d'Alexandrie, Quis rerum divinarum heres sit: introduction, traduction et notes*, Les Œuvres de Philon d'Alexandrie 15 (Paris: Cerf, 1966), 159, n. 2.

[75] E. R. Goodenough, *By Light, Light: The Mystic Gospel of Hellenistic Judaism* (Amsterdam: Philo Press, 1968), 56–57; J. Daniélou, *Théologie du judéo-christianisme* (Tournai: Desclée, 1958), 216–19, and most recently, A. C. Geljon and D. T. Runia, *Philo of Alexandria, On Planting: Introduction, Translation, and Commentary*, Philo of Alexandria Commentary Series 5 (Leiden: Brill 2019), 106–7.

[76] D. Barthélemy, "Est-ce Hoshaya Rabba qui censura le 'Commentaire allégorique'? À partir des retouches faites aux citations bibliques, étude sur la tradition textuelle du Commentaire allégorique de Philon," in *Philon d'Alexandrie, Lyon 11–15 Septembre 1966: colloques nationaux du Centre National de la Recherche Scientifique*, ed. R. Arnaldez et al. (Paris: Editions du Centre National de la Recherche Scientifique, 1967), 45–79. For a definitive assessment of Barthélemy's disturbingly anti-Jewish tone and misinformed argument, see O. Munnich, "Les retouches faites aux lemmes bibliques dans le Commentaire allégorique de Philon d'Alexandrie: bilan et proposition," in *Les études philoniennes*, 137–83, esp. 143–44.

[77] In my book *Eusebius and the Jewish Authors*, 197–200, I supported this hypothesis but I have since changed my mind about this. There is no philosophical argument strong enough to categorically reject the unanimous reading of Philo's manuscripts, which is also the *lectio difficilior*. Barthélemy's methodology is rather speculative as he assumes the existence of a Jewish "retoucheur" from numerous interpolations which he ascribes to the same hand, that of a Jew whom he then vilifies in strongly anti-Jewish terms: "un lettré juif très ignorant en littérature et en philosophie grecques, comme un homme simple ... comme un monothéiste vétilleux ... comme plus soucieux de défendre l'honneur d'Israël que de montrer de la sympathie aux goyim. Rien de tout cela ne surprend chez un rabbin palestinien du IIIè siècle" ("Est-ce Hoshaya Rabba," 71).

[78] Eusebius does describe the λόγος as δεσμὸς ἀρραγής at *Laus Constantini* 12.7.1. The expression δεσμοῖς ἀρρήκτοις is used in *Contra Hieroclem* p. 374 (C. L. Kayser, *Flavii Philostrati opera*, vol. 1 [Leipzig: Teubner, 1870; repr. Hildesheim: Olms, 1964]).

also be that a simple copying mistake has occurred here and that the debate has been overloaded with ideological stakes.[79]

Contrary to the general consensus regarding Eusebius' faithfulness as a citer of texts, this brief analysis indicates that although in Philo's case Eusebius never goes so far as to fabricate an entire passage, it is necessary to maintain caution when dealing with his citations. Eusebius' claims to faithfully cite other authors cannot be taken at face value.[80] Even if his handling of texts is in line with the textual approaches of his time, from a philological viewpoint, his citations cannot be uncritically approached.[81]

9.3 Conclusion

Eusebius' use of Philo and his writings is, without a doubt, innovative. He significantly contributed to Philo's long and fruitful reception in the Christian tradition by re-shaping his *persona* and his texts in a Christian fashion and by participating to the transmission of his texts at Caesarea.

It is worth noting that the weight of his use of Philo lies more in the new status he created for the Jewish philosopher than in the details of the texts he used. In most quotations, Eusebius does not spend much time analyzing what Philo wrote. His authority is what mattered: as a "Hebrew" heir to both the ancient Hebrew philosophers and masters, as an expert on both Greek philosophy and biblical matters, as an acquaintance of Peter and the supposedly Christian Therapeutae, Philo was turned into an invaluable defender of the Christian faith. He was the first writer presented at length in a lemma of the *Hist. eccl.* and his destiny was engraved for centuries to come in Eusebius' Christian historiographical monument.

However, Eusebius did not achieve this by grossly tampering with Philo's text or by plainly claiming that he was a Christian. On the contrary, his tour de force lies in the subtlety with which he adapts Philo's citations to his own needs and shapes Philo's *persona* throughout his *Hist. eccl.* and *Praep. ev.*, providing various depictions of the Jewish philosopher as a "Hebrew" interpreter, a defender of the Mosaic Law, an expert in Greek philosophy, or even an admirer of Mark's disciples. What remains constant, however, is Eusebius' willingness to locate Philo in a cultural, political and religious landscape where Christianity is the great winner.[82]

Therefore, if we owe much of the transmission of Philo's writings to Eusebius, our gratitude should not deter us from thinking lucidly about the literary appropriation to which he has subjected Philo. If Philo undeniably escapes the negative treatment Eusebius inflicted upon most Jews, he is nevertheless objectified to serve his apologetic

---

[79] This possibility has recently been raised by O. Munnich, "Les retouches faites aux lemmes bibliques dans le Commentaire allégorique de Philon d'Alexandrie: bilan et proposition," in *Les études philoniennes* 137–83, at 139.
[80] See Inowlocki, *Eusebius and the Jewish Authors*, 33–47.
[81] As noted also by Harl, *Quis rerum divinarum heres sit*, 158–59.
[82] J. Otto's remark that Philo, in spite of his philosophical enlightenment, remains a suffering Jew, and therefore, is for Eusebius a "tragic figure" (*Construction of Jewishness*, 193), is an extrapolation. It is true that Philo is a tragic figure in this context, but it is in our eyes, not in Eusebius'.

purposes. Eusebius ushers in not only a long Christian tradition of including Philo, but also a tradition that dispossessed Philo of his own truth. To the best of our knowledge, Philo knew nothing of Christianity. He was a Jewish Greek philosopher deeply involved in the cause of his community, a prolific allegorist who unknowingly paved the way for Christian theology by synthesizing Greek and biblical culture in an Alexandrian fashion. Eusebius turns him into an "ideal Jew," that is, into an ancillary Jew.[83]

Behind these "ideal Jews," whose lifestyle and writings could be usefully appropriated to serve the Christian cause, the multitude of real Jews—contemporary and past—is conveniently reduced to a shapeless mass of Ἰουδαῖοι.[84] These are the Jews who were Egyptianized and needed the Mosaic law (*Praep. ev.* 7.8.37–40; *Dem. ev.* 1.6.17a–19d), who resisted the translation of Moses' writings into Greek so the nations could not access the bits of Hebrew truth legated by Moses (*Praep. ev.* 8.1.7), who killed Christ and were dispossessed of their city and Temple as a result of their actions (e.g. *Hist. eccl.* 2.6), and finally, disappeared after their failed revolt under Bar Kochba (*Hist. eccl.* 4.6)[85]—at least according to Eusebius' writings. Therefore, Eusebius' abundant use of Philo of Alexandria as well as his occasionally positive description of the "Jewish" way of life should not obfuscate his contribution to the development Christian anti-Judaism.[86]

---

[83] See the somewhat similar conclusion of D. J. DeVore, who compares Philo's role in Eusebius to John the Baptist's role in Jesus' Church ("Eusebius' Un-Josephan History: Two Portraits of Philo of Alexandria and the Sources of Ecclesiastical Historiography," *StPatr* 66 [2013]: 161–79, at 173).

[84] I agree here with the analyses of Jacobs, *Remains of the Jews*, 35–36; and J. Schott, *Christianity, Empire, and the Making of Religion in Late Antiquity* (Philadelphia: University of Pennsylvania Press, 2008), 9–11.

[85] In the *Martyrs of Palestine* (27), however, they reappear as a contemporaneous paradoxical manifestation of the wicked idolatrous biblical Jews, opposed to the now pious Christian Egyptians.

[86] This project has received funding from the European Union's Horizon 2020 research and innovation program under the Marie Skłodowska-Curie grant agreement No. 101025412.

10
Didymus the Blind

Justin M. Rogers

Didymus "the Blind" (*c*.313–393 CE) was one the fourth century's most famous biblical exegetes.[1] Counting among his students Jerome, Rufinus, Palladius, and Evagrius Ponticus, Didymus operated a school of sacred learning that influenced both east and west. He entertained the famed monk Antony, and was himself an early hero of Egyptian monasticism. Didymus was also a champion of Nicene orthodoxy, and the Latin translation of his *De spiritu sancto* helped to elevate the Holy Spirit as a hypostasis on par with the Father and the Son. However, doctrinal associations with the controversial Origen cast a shadow on the reputation of Didymus later in his life, and eventually led to his condemnation at the Second Council of Constantinople in 553.[2] As a result, his exegetical works fell out of favor with Christian readers, and were known to early modern scholars only from excerpts in the catenae.[3]

In 1941, however, the British were clearing quarries about 10 miles south of Cairo for the storage of munitions when Egyptian workers uncovered a large cache of Christian papyri dating to the fifth or sixth centuries CE. Among the discovered codices were over two thousand pages of Didymus' biblical commentaries on Genesis, Job, Psalms, Ecclesiastes, and Zechariah. The commentaries follow a similar structure, with the literal or surface level of interpretation coming first, followed by a deeper analysis of the "anagogical" meaning.[4] In the *Commentarii in Psalmos* and *Commentarii in Ecclesiasten* Didymus occasionally stops to answer student questions, offering us a rare glimpse inside an early Christian classroom.[5] Most of the commentaries reflect an audience at an intermediate level of education.

These commentaries also illustrate the traditional nature of Didymus' exegesis. As we can observe in other late antique commentaries, Didymus self-consciously positions

---

[1] The sobriquet "the Blind" was apparently already applied to Didymus in his own lifetime, as witnessed by Jerome's epithet Didymus *videns* ("the seeing"). See the prologues to Jerome's translations of Origen's *Hom. Jer.* and *Hom. Ezek.*

[2] On the early history of the Origenist controversy, see E. Prinzivalli, *Magister Ecclesiae: il Dibattito su Origene fra III e IV Siecolo*, SEAug 82 (Rome: Institutum Patristicum Augustinianum, 2002).

[3] The monographs J. Leipoldt, *Didymus der Blinde*, TU 29 (Leipzig: Hinrichs, 1905); and G. Bardy, *Didyme l'Aveugle* (Paris: Beauchesne, 1910) remain valuable, although both were written, of course, without knowledge of the Tura papyri.

[4] On the term ἀναγωγή and its importance in the writings of Didymus, see W. A. Bienert, *"Allegoria" und "Anagoge" bei Didymos dem Blinden von Alexandrien*, PTS 13 (Berlin: de Gruyter, 1972).

[5] On the scholastic nature of the Psalms and Ecclesiates commentaries, see R. A. Layton, *Didymus the Blind and His Circle in Late-Antique Alexandria* (Urbana: University of Illinois Press, 2004), 13–35; B. Stefaniw, *Christian Reading: Language, Ethics, and the Order of Things* (Berkeley: University of California Press, 2019), 61–91.

himself within an exegetical tradition, rarely citing his sources by name, but utilizing a number of Jewish and Christian works.[6] The names of Clement and Origen, however, occur only once each.[7] This is remarkable in Origen's case, especially since scholars, both ancient and modern, have pointed out Didymus' considerable debt to the great Adamantius.[8] A strange and intriguing exception is the name of Philo. Although he uses Philo far more often than he names him, Philo's name occurs more frequently in the works of Didymus than any other non-biblical author.

Research into Didymus' use of Philo has progressed slowly, and many Didymus scholars continue to pay little attention to Philonic influence.[9] There are notable exceptions, however. Albert Henrichs surveyed Philo's influence on the patristic theme of secular education as a preparation for philosophy,[10] and Emilien Lamirande discussed Philonic influence on Didymus' exegesis of the account of human creation.[11] But the first attempt at a survey was David Runia's seminal *Philo in Early Christian Literature*.[12] Since that point Runia's student, Albert Geljon, has published a study of the Philonic elements in Didymus' exegesis of Cain and Abel,[13] and a survey of Didymus' use of Philo.[14] Building on the work of these scholars, I attempted the first comprehensive investigation of Didymus' use of Philo in 2017. I was able to uncover numerous direct references, as well as exegetical and thematic parallels. We shall endeavor to discuss the most salient of these in the following pages.

10.1 Direct References to Philo in the Tura Commentaries

Didymus was a prolific author. We have explicit testimony of more than thirty works, although we cannot know what percentage of his total literary output these represent.[15] Didymus engaged in apologetics and philosophy, but built his reputation on biblical

---

[6] On Didymus' sources, see J. M. Rogers, *Didymus the Blind and the Alexandrian Christian Reception of Philo*, SPhiloM 8 (Atlanta: SBL, 2017), 59–74.

[7] Clement (*Comm. Eccl.* 7.34); Origen (*fr. in 1 Cor 16:17–18*).

[8] Jerome refers to Didymus as "a most open defender of Origen" (*Origenis apertissimus propugnator*, *Ruf.* 1.6). For details, see G. D. Bayliss, *The Vision of Didymus the Blind: A Fourth-Century Virtue-Origenism* (Oxford: Oxford University Press, 2016), 20–23.

[9] B. Stefaniw's recent monograph on Didymus, for example, scarcely mentions Philo and never cites the work of Runia, Geljon, and myself (*Christian Reading*).

[10] A. Henrichs, "Philosophy, the Handmaiden of Theology," *GRBS* 9 (1968): 437–50.

[11] E. Lamirande, "Le masculin et le feminin dans la tradition alexandrine: le commentaire de Didyme l'Aveugle sur la 'Genèse,'" *Science et Esprit* 41 (1989): 137–65.

[12] D. T. Runia, *Philo in Early Christian Literature: A Survey*, CRINT 3.3 (Assen: Van Gorcum/Fortress, 1993), 197–204.

[13] A. C. Geljon "Philonic Elements in Didymus the Blind's Exegesis of the Story of Cain and Abel," *VC* 61 (2007): 282–312.

[14] A. C. Geljon, "Philo's Influence on Didymus the Blind," in *Philon d'Alexandrie: Un penseur à l'intersection des cultures Gréco-Romaine, Orientale, Juive et Chrétienne*, ed. Sabrina Inowlocki and Baudouin Decharneux (Monothéismes et Philosophie; Turnhout: Brepols, 2011), 357–72.

[15] Jerome remarks that to give an account of Didymus' works would be "a work in itself" (*Vir. ill.* 109.2). Consequently, the list he provides is imprecise. Jerome mentions commentaries on the entire corpus of biblical Psalms, Matthew, John, Isaiah (in eighteen books), Hosea (in three books), Zechariah (in five books), and Job. To these he adds three dogmatic works (*On Dogma*, *Against the Arians*, and *On the Holy Spirit*), and states that Didymus wrote many other books.

164   THE RECEPTION OF PHILO OF ALEXANDRIA

exegesis. Of the five extant commentaries from Tura, the name of Philo occurs in only two: the *Comm. Eccl.*, and, of course, the *Comm. Gen.* However, two obvious nods to Philo can be located in the *Comm. Zach.*, and it is here that we begin.

10.1.1 The *Commentary on Zechariah*

Didymus' five-volume *Comm. Zach.* was written at the request of Jerome.[16] The work survives virtually intact, with only about eight of over four hundred original pages missing. We know Origen himself wrote a commentary on Zechariah that was known to Jerome, but is now lost.[17] It is possible that Didymus had access to Origen's commentary, but his exegesis appears mostly original.[18] We should not expect Didymus to utilize Philo in a commentary on Zechariah. After all, Philo references the prophet only once, quoting from Zech 6:12, and attributing it to "one of Moses' disciples" (*Conf.* 62–63). But there are two references in the *Comm. Zach.* that certainly point to Philo.

In the first of these references, Didymus is discussing the phrase "the riders of horses shall be put to shame" (Zech 10:5 LXX) when he introduces Philo as "a certain sage of ancient times" who "distinguished horseman from rider, calling the latter worthless and the former commendable: the one who rides without skill, not holding the horse in check, is a mere rider [ἀναβάτης], as the aforementioned sage made clear, since it is only the one riding with equestrian skills who is rightfully referred to as a horseman [ἱππεύς]" (*Comm. Zach.* 3.273 [FC 111:240]).[19]

It is characteristic of Philo to antithesize biblical synonyms, and draw moral lessons from his antitheses.[20] And Philo indeed distinguishes the terms ἱππεύς and ἀναβάτης (e.g. *Leg.* 2.104; *Agr.* 67–76). There can be little doubt, then, that Didymus refers to Philo here. Philo's role as an ancient σοφός is particularly enlightening, as is his identification as "one of the ancients." Nowhere else in the writings of Didymus is Philo referenced in this fashion, and the only other author in the *Comm. Zach.* to be cited as "one of the ancients" is Aristotle.[21]

In a second passage discussing the phrase "a sword shall be on his arm and on his right eye" (Zech 11:17 LXX), Didymus makes the following comments: "This sword was given to Abraham under the form of an oracle in order to remove him 'from the land, from his kindred and his father's house,' by 'land' meaning the body with which he was clad, by 'kindred' those of identical pursuits and way of life, and by 'father's

---

[16] Or so Jerome claims (*Vir. ill.* 109.2).
[17] Jerome, *Comm. Zach.* praef.
[18] Megan Hale Williams assumes that Origen was the primary source for Jerome's exegesis of Zech in the earlier chapters, while Didymus becomes more prominent when the Origenian material runs out. Comparison with the Origenian material cited by Jerome and Didymus illustrates the discordance (Megan Hale Williams, *The Monk and the Book: Jerome and the Making of Christian Scholarship* [Chicago: University of Chicago Press, 2006], 196–97).
[19] Translations of *Comm. Zach.* are from R. C. Hill, *Didymus the Blind: Commentary on Zechariah*, FC 111 (Washington, DC: Catholic University of America Press, 2006).
[20] e.g. the distinction between a "farmer" (γεωργός) and "a worker" (ἐργάτης) of the ground (*Agr.* 1–25).
[21] *Comm. Zach.* 123.21, referencing Aristotle, *Eth. nic.* 5.4.7.

house' the word uttered [ὁ προφορικὸς λόγος] by the mind, in the commentary of one of the sages on the Mosaic teaching" (*Comm. Zach.* 4.167 [FC 111:283]).

Again, Philo is referred to as a σοφός who "offers interpretation of the Mosaic paideia" (περὶ τὴν μωσαϊκὴν παίδευσιν ἡρμήνευσεν). Although there is no specific passage in which Philo says exactly what we have here, *Migr.* 1–4 offers a similar allegorical interpretation of land, kindred, and father's house (Gen 12:1). But this passage says nothing of a sword. Didymus may also be thinking of *Cher.* 31, which explains how Abraham "took a copy of the flaming sword" [cf. Gen 22:6] in order "to cut out and burn up his mortal nature" so that his mind might rise up to God unencumbered. Didymus may not be thinking of a single Philonic passage, but the interpretation he passes along fits well within the Philonic thought world.

10.1.2 The *Commentary on Ecclesiastes*

The *Comm. Eccl.* is a series of live lecture transcripts that once covered the entire book of Ecclesiastes, but is now badly damaged. The commentary does not appear ready for "publication," and it seems to belong to an earlier period in Didymus' career. Consequently, sources are cited more often than in the *Comm. Zach.*, and indeed Philo is mentioned by name twice.

The first mention of Philo covers one of Philo's most familiar allegorical constructs, the Hagar-Sarah relationship. Commenting on "the wife whom you have loved all the days of your life" (Eccl 9:9), Didymus introduces as a secondary biblical lemma "the wife of your youth" (Prov 5:18). Insisting the "wife" in question is "true ethical virtue," Didymus suggests one must abide with "another man's wife" before engaging beloved virtue. Scandalous though the point seems, even at the allegorical level, Didymus cites Philo for proof: "In a similar way Philo showed that Hagar produces offspring before perfect virtue. For if one does not beget children by these (women) of inferior status, one cannot become the father of undefiled achievements and of the teachings of wisdom."[22]

Didymus then turns to Paul to clarify what Philo means, claiming, "The Apostle made the same point [as Philo] by using the terms 'letter' [γράμμα] and 'spirit' [πνεῦμα], and it is impossible to understand anagogical matters without first examining in detail the historical aspects" (*Comm. Eccl.* 276.22–24, trans. mine). As the passage indicates, Didymus accepts Philo's allegory of "encyclical" studies as preparatory for wisdom (virtue), and follows Philo in citing Sarah and Hagar as proof. But he clumsily transitions to the Pauline allegorical frame of reference, drawing an analogy to the historical and allegorical senses of scripture. The "letter" of the text must be established before advancing to the "spirit," just as Hagar (secular studies) must be engaged before advancing to Sarah (wisdom/virtue).[23] This move is based on an exegesis already

---

[22] *Comm. Eccl.* 276.20–22, trans. Runia, *Philo*, 199.
[23] As with Origen, the "lower levels" of exegesis are necessary and helpful to those weaker in faith (e.g. Origen, *Cels.* 4.71, 6.2; Didymus, *Comm. Gen.* 168.10–27).

worked out in the *Comm. Gen.* whereby Paul's allegory in Gal 4:22–31 is combined with Philo's allegorical understanding of Hagar and Sarah.[24] We shall return to this passage in a moment.

The second named reference to Philo in the *Comm. Eccl.* comes in a heavily lacunose text in which the name of Philo can be reasonably restored.[25] Didymus is focusing on the subversive line, "I have seen slaves on horses and rulers walking like slaves on the ground" (Eccl 10:7). He then turns to Philo, citing the treatise *De vita Mosis* by name, and quoting part of *Mos.* 2.2.[26] Philo says the only way cities can progress toward the better life is "either if kings become philosophers or philosophers kings." Didymus follows a near verbatim quotation with the words, "They were superior to the Gentiles as a 'royal priesthood' [Exod 19:6], and thus held the rule of kings, just as Abraham, about whom is said, 'You are a king from God among us' [Gen 23:6]" (*Comm. Eccl.* 300.18–19).

Didymus does not need Philo for the philosopher-king motif, since Philo himself borrows the doctrine from Plato (Plato, *Resp.* 473d).[27] Didymus cites the name of both author and treatise here because he wishes to reference the entirety of Philo's *De vita Mosis*. Indeed, the Philonic quotation can be reasonably understood as a summary of the treatise's contents. Moses rose from slave to king against all odds, just as Didymus' exegetical verse states. Philo's *De vita Mosis* is the portrait of a historic golden age in which piety reigned supreme, and thus could be idealized by Didymus. The popularity of the model can be observed in Gregory of Nyssa's own, Philo-inspired *De vita Moysis*.[28] If Didymus' comments were not interrupted by a student's question (marked by the mysterious term επερ), he would have continued to expound upon the Philonic theme.[29] Alas.

10.1.3 The *Commentary on Genesis*

One of the earliest of the Tura commentaries appears to be the *Comm. Gen.* This commentary follows more rigidly the dualistic structure of literal and allegorical levels of interpretation, and reflects a greater tendency to name sources.[30] Fortunately for us, a higher concentration of Philonic material occurs in the *Comm. Gen.*, which just so happens to cover approximately the same lemmatic material as Philo's own Allegorical

---

[24] See J. M. Rogers, "The Philonic and the Pauline: Hagar and Sarah in the Exegesis of Didymus the Blind," SPhiloA 26 (2014): 57–77.

[25] *Comm. Eccl.* 300.15. The text is lacunose before and after we have legible τῷ Μωσέως Βίῳ.

[26] The Greek reads [... Φίλων ἐν] τῷ Μωσέως βίῳ .... Although this Philonic work is curiously missing from the catalog of Eusebius (*Hist. eccl.* 2.18), Clement cites the work by exactly the same title as we have here (*Strom.* 1.153.2–3).

[27] See Runia, *Philo*, 200.

[28] See A. C. Geljon, *Philonic Exegesis in Gregory of Nyssa's De vita Moysis*, BJS 333, SPhiloM 5 (Providence: Brown Judaic Studies, 2002).

[29] *Comm. Eccl.* 300.20.

[30] Robert Hill observes that, in the entire *Comm. Zach.*, Didymus refers to sources only five times (*Didymus the Blind: Commentary on Zechariah*, 11). By contrast, the *Comm. Gen.* mentions over twenty sources by name. The *Comm. Ps.* and the *Comm. Eccl.* reflect a similar tendency to name sources.

Commentary.³¹ Hill sees a pervasive Philonic and Origenian influence in the *Comm. Gen.*: "The commentator is consistently indebted throughout the work to his mentors Origen and Philo, often incorporating their commentary verbatim."³² Origen, however, is never named in the work, while Philo is mentioned by name seven times in four passages, more often than any other single, non-biblical source. We shall now turn to these passages.

10.1.3.1 On Cain and Abel

Philo is mentioned three times in Didymus' comments on Cain and Abel. The first comes immediately after a quotation of the biblical lemma, "and she continued to bear Abel, brother of Cain" (Gen 4:2a): "Philo takes it to mean they were twins resulting from one conception" (*Comm. Gen.* 118.24–25 [FC 132:115]).³³ Didymus then offers another Jewish source, the "Book of the Covenant," to suggest the brothers were not twins, without himself weighing in on either interpretive option.³⁴ Philo certainly implies Cain and Abel were twins, although he does not say so explicitly in his extant works.³⁵ Didymus has read Philo thoroughly enough to draw the inference.

Second, Didymus refers to Philo's allegorical presentation of Cain and Abel as "types" of souls, stating, "While the student [ὁ φιλόκαλος] will know all that Philo said in treating this passage allegorically, I should nevertheless present it as far as I can" (*Comm. Gen.* 119.2–4 [FC 132:115]). Here Didymus uses Philo as a springboard to his own allegorical level of interpretation, acknowledging his debt, and apologizing to more advanced students for repeating what they already know from Philo.³⁶

Didymus goes on to sprinkle typical Philonic language throughout his allegorical interpretation, noting the soul's tendency to generate "evil offspring" before sobering up, and progressing through stages of virtue to arrive at perfection. Again, Didymus may be thinking principally of the opening paragraphs of Philo's *De sacrificiis*, but he expands his comments to cover the general scope of Philo's Stoic-inspired doctrine of progress and perfection. It is clear that Didymus summarizes a much larger and more complicated Philonic topic.³⁷

Third, Didymus continues to follow the structure of Philo's *De sacrificiis* in his presentation of Cain and Abel, this time referring to their occupations (*Sacr.* 11–12). He states, as does Philo, that Cain is honored in birth order, but Abel in

---

[31] Runia makes this observation, although it may be purely coincidental (*Philo*, 200).

[32] R. C. Hill, *Didymus the Blind: Commentary on Genesis*, FC 132 (Washington, DC: Catholic University of America Press, 2016), 5. Hill wonders whether the tendency to rely on Philo so heavily is a reflection of inexperience (Hill, *Didymus the Blind: Commentary on Genesis*, 11).

[33] Translations of *Comm. Gen.* are taken from Hill, *Didymus the Blind: Commentary on Genesis*.

[34] Didymus is the first Christian author to mention "the Book of the Covenant." For a discussion, see D. Lührmann, "Alttestamentliche Pseudepigraphen bei Didymos von Alexandrien," *ZAW* 104 (1992): 231–49.

[35] *QG* 1.78; *Sacr.* 1–4 (with the comments of Rogers, *Didymus the Blind*, 83–84).

[36] The term φιλόκαλος is found ten times in the Tura commentaries, and in each case, points students to approved sources for further study. Included in these references are scripture (e.g. *Comm. Gen.* 70.13), Didymus' other commentaries (e.g. *Comm. Zach.* 377.20), Josephus (*Comm. Zach.* 364.18), and Philo (twice: here and *Comm. Gen.* 139.12).

[37] Hill suggests the *Comm. Gen.* was authored primarily with "spiritual neophytes" in mind, at least in select passages (*Didymus the Blind: Commentary on Genesis*, 6).

occupation:[38] "Philo was right to say on this that those due to have responsibility for others and of themselves should be trained beforehand in shepherding" (*Comm. Gen.* 119.19–21 [FC 132:116]). The theme that shepherding is an appropriate preparation for leadership is common in Philo, and is a stock Greek theme.[39]

Then Didymus turns to his allegorical level of exegesis, stating that Abel is not shepherding sheep, but sense perceptions (αἰσθήσεις, *Comm. Gen.* 119.24), a quintessentially Philonic theme (*Sacr.* 49; *Post.* 98; *Agr.* 42; *Congr.* 96–97). He then switches metaphors, referring to the soul who installs reason as a charioteer and commander over the irascible and appetitive parts of the soul (*Leg.* 1.72–73, 3.128; *Sacr.* 45; *Migr.* 67). Turning back to Cain, Didymus remarks that he is not called a farmer (γεωργός), but a "worker of the ground" (ἐργαζόμενος τὴν γῆν).[40] The former, as Philo states, is a more honorable profession, and Cain merely feeds his soul by means of earthly goods.[41] There is no doubt that Didymus copies Philo's presentation of Cain and Abel, one of the most striking allegories in the Allegorical Commentary.[42]

10.1.3.2 On the Descendants of Cain

Didymus discusses the posterity of Cain, specifically the men mentioned in 4:18. After a brief literal interpretation, Didymus remarks, "If, on the other hand, you want to take this anagogically, you could begin the anagogy with a translation of the names and conduct it without undue detachment. Philo also treated of these matters, from which the students could on inspection draw due benefit" (*Comm. Gen.* 139.10–14 [FC 132:131]). It is possible that *Post.* 66–75 is in view here, if in fact Didymus had a specific passage in mind. More noteworthy is Didymus' willingness to refer readers to Philo in place of his own interpretation, and to recognize the key role etymology plays in Philo's allegorical method.

10.1.3.3 On Adam and Seth

As is the case in the previous passage, Didymus again drops the name of Philo in place of his own allegorical level of interpretation. He states, "If, however, you are fascinated by the number of years and the significance of names, Philo would supply a mystical meaning without detachment. So apply to him; it would prove helpful" (*Comm. Gen.* 147.15–18 [FC 132:138]). Didymus shows awareness of Philo's interest both in etymology and arithmology as a means of breaking open the ἀναγωγή.[43] Whether

---

[38] Philo actually abandons the point in *Sacr.* to take a lengthy excursus, and resumes with his interpretation in §45, making precisely the same point Didymus makes next in his exegesis. Perhaps, Philo, *QG* 1.59 offers a more succinct parallel.

[39] *Agr.* 41, 66; *Mos.* 1.60; Cf. *Ios.* 2, where Philo acknowledges "the race of poets" as recognizing the truth of the concept.

[40] The lengthiest presentation of the Philonic theme is *Agr.* 1–25.

[41] See A. C. Geljon "Philonic Elements," 282–312, esp. 294–99.

[42] Four Philonic treatises cover the life of Cain: *Cher.*, *Sacr.*, *Det.*, and *Post.*

[43] Didymus rarely by-passes opportunities to launch into etymological and arithmological interpretation, so *Comm. Gen.* 139.10–14 and 147.15–18 are somewhat unique; M. Simonetti, "Lettera e allegoria nell'esegesi veterotestamentaria di Didimo," *Vetera Christianorum* 20 (1983): 341–89, esp. 354–55.

Didymus had access to a Philonic text that actually treats Gen 5:1-2 in an etymological and arithmological fashion is impossible to know.[44] No single extant Philonic work or fragment covers the territory to which Didymus directs his readers.

10.1.3.4 On Sarah and Hagar

The interpretation of Sarah and Hagar is perhaps the single most important scriptural allegory Philo bequeaths to the Alexandrian Christian tradition. Adapting an existing Stoic allegory of Odysseus, Philo argues it was necessary for Abraham to mate first with Hagar (secular education) to prepare himself for Sarah (virtue). Clement and Origen borrow the interpretation, but Didymus is the first author on record to attempt a harmony between the allegories of Philo and Paul.[45] The two mentions of Philo's name occur in conjunction with Paul's.

After offering a literal interpretation borrowed from Philo, Didymus turns to the allegorical level: "In an anagogical sense ... it can be interpreted to mean that blessed Paul took the two women to be a type of the two Testaments. Philo also adopted this approach, though to a different effect, figuratively taking Sarai as perfect virtue and philosophy" (*Comm. Gen.* 235.25-30 [FC 132:210, modified]). Didymus then supports the Philonic allegory of Sarai as virtue and wisdom from biblical proof texts before resetting the interpretation. He writes, "While Sarai is interpreted as virtue that is perfect and spiritual, then, the Egyptian handmaid Hagar is said by Philo to betoken the preliminary exercises [προγυμνάσματα], and by Paul the shadow" (*Comm. Gen.* 236.5-9 [FC 132:210]). Didymus proceeds to harmonize the two interpretations, noting the "shadow" is encountered before the substance, and thus the surface meaning of the Old Testament text must be engaged before one reaches the spiritual, Christian level. The Hagar and Sarah allegories of Philo and Paul coalesce in Didymus to form a single interpretation on the subject of scriptural education.

10.1.4 Conclusion

Some general observations are now in order. First, Didymus, not surprisingly, depends on Philo most in the *Comm. Gen.* This is because two lemmatic commentary sets of Philo follow the Septuagintal text of Genesis, the Allegorical Commentary and the *Questions and Answers*. But we can observe an additional reason. Heavy reliance on sources, and especially on Philo, seems to be a mark of Didymus' earlier exegetical works. The two clear, yet anonymous, references to Philo in the *Comm. Zach.* seem to

---

[44] While we have discussions of the names of Adam and Seth and the 120 years Didymus mentions immediately before his reference to Philo (146.2-22), we do not have both in the same Philonic passage. Runia raises the intriguing possibility that Didymus had access to a lost portion of the Allegorical Commentary (*Philo*, 201). Perhaps this could be a reference to the lost Περὶ ἀριθμῶν.

[45] See Rogers, "The Philonic and the Pauline."

reflect a later practice, while the *Comm. Gen.* reflects an earlier habit of naming sources explicitly.[46]

Why does Didymus turn toward a more anonymous style? It is possible that he formalizes his own works as he becomes an increasingly famous figure, and thus conforms to the more familiar style of late antique commentaries in general. As for the name of Philo specifically, we might hypothesize that Philo had become "too hot to handle" in the late fourth century. Gregory of Nyssa, for example, shows that Philo was a tool in the bag of Arian theologians.[47] Didymus was a staunch anti-Arian, and might wish to conceal his debt to one of their favorites. Whatever the reason, Didymus continues to use Philo throughout his career, but increasingly scales back explicit references to his Alexandrian predecessor.

10.2 Exegetical Methodology and Thematic Borrowing

The nine mentions of Philo's name in the Tura commentaries indicate a pervasive Philonic influence on Didymus' theology and exegesis. This influence is felt not only at the micro-level but also at the macro-level. Exegetical methodologies and controlling themes borrowed from Philo reveal themselves throughout the Tura commentaries. Didymus patterns his enthusiasm for etymological and arithmological interpretation after Philo, although he depends on Philo's help more on the former. Moreover larger, controlling exegetical themes can be identified, such as the creation of the world, the names of God, and the doctrine of pre-passion.

10.2.1 Methodological Borrowings

10.2.1.1 Etymology
The patristic tradition assigns to Philo the authorship of an etymological handbook of Hebrew names, which Jerome claims to have revised.[48] It is doubtful that Philo could have authored such a work, and probably himself depends on handbooks.[49] Didymus does not seem to have relied heavily on handbooks, but instead depends on Origen and

---

[46] Precisely dating the Tura works is difficult. Layton broadly suggests the *Comm. Gen.* and *Comm. Job* are written in the 360s, with the *Comm. Ps.* and *Comm. Eccl.* following in the 370s, and the *Comm. Zach.*, written at the request of Jerome in 386, being completed shortly thereafter (*Didymus the Blind*, 6–7). Prinzivalli concurs with Layton's general scheme (*Magister Ecclesiae*, 26).

[47] See Runia, *Philo*, 244–49.

[48] Eusebius, *Hist. eccl.* 2.17; Jerome, *Nom. hebr.*, praef. Jerome reports Origen's attribution of the work to Philo, and claims it can be located "in all the libraries."

[49] Philo's knowledge of Hebrew has been defended occasionally on the basis of his frequent etymologies (e.g. T. Rajak, "Philo's Knowledge of Hebrew: The Meaning of the Etymologies," in *The Jewish-Greek Tradition in Antiquity and the Byzantine Empire*, ed. J. K. Aitken and J. Carleton Paget [Cambridge: Cambridge University Press, 2014], 173–87, but most have concluded he knew virtually no Hebrew (e.g. L. L. Grabbe, *Etymology in Early Jewish Interpretation*, BJS 115 [Atlanta: Scholars Press, 1988]).

Philo for his etymologies and allegorical applications.[50] Of some twenty-six names etymologized in the *Comm. Gen.*, twenty-one of these find parallels in the works of Origen and/or Philo.[51]

Twice Didymus recommends students turn to Philo for the meaning of Hebrew names, as we saw above (*Comm. Gen.* 139.10–14, 147.15–18). Just as importantly, in those texts Didymus highlights etymology as a means of breaking open the anagogical meaning. Like Philo, Didymus first cites the biblical Hebrew name in Greek transliteration, then gives its etymological meaning, and finally offers an allegorical application of the Hebrew etymology. So, etymology is not only a practical instrument for biblical exegesis, it is also an important structural tool for the commentator. It allows him to ground his allegorical interpretation directly within the wording of the biblical text. Etymology gives the impression that even seemingly meaningless terms contain deeper essential truths.

Two examples shall suffice to illustrate Didymus' dependence on Philo for Hebrew etymologies. First, Philo pays close attention to migrations in the biblical narrative.[52] Cain's exit "from the face of God" is remarkable, and thus the location to which Cain travels, Nod, must carry special significance (Gen 4:16). Philo indeed interprets Nod as one of several Hebrew terms indicating movement as opposed to rest. "Nod," Philo says, means "tossing" (σάλος), "a symbol of vice agitating the soul" (*Cher.* 12; cf. *Post.* 32). Didymus borrows this etymology, stating, "*Nod* means 'tossing' [σάλος], in fact; after all, where must the one who has forsaken the virtue of peace settle if not in 'tossing,' in the unstable and unsteady thing that vice is?" (*Comm. Gen.* 135.26–136.2 [FC 132:128]).

Didymus goes on, just as Philo, to contrast Adam's "banishment" (ἐκβάλλω, Gen 3:24) with Cain's "exit" (ἐξέρχομαι, Gen 4:16, *Post.* 10–11) to conclude that "instead of being settled or expelled, he [Cain] took a headlong course towards vice with an ardent desire" (*Comm. Gen.* 136.11–12 [FC 132:129]). This entire line of interpretation is Philonic, and there can be no doubt that Didymus depends on him here.

A second example may be regarded as a logical opposite of the first. Whereas Cain abandons the repose of the divine presence for a state of agitated wandering, Abram migrates away from bodily sensation toward a more secure form of knowledge.[53] Philo routinely etymologizes "Haran," the location from which Abram travels (Gen 12:4), as "holes" (*Migr.* 188; *Fug.* 45; *Somn.* 1.41; *Abr.* 72). He infers from this etymology that Abram abandons the bodily "holes" through which the senses perceive (and can be

---

[50] Didymus knew no Hebrew; B. Kramer and J. Kramer, "Les éléments linguistiques hébreux chez Didyme l'Aveugle," in Ἀλεξανδρῖνα: *Hellénisme, judaïsme, et christianisme à Alexandrie. Mélanges offerts au P. Claude Mondésert* (Paris: Cerf, 1987), 313–23.
[51] See Rogers, *Didymus the Blind*, 133–42.
[52] Two entire treatises in the Allegorical Commentary are devoted to migrations (*Post.* and *Migr.*), and, in a certain sense, the lives of Cain and Abraham are parallel migrations in opposite directions.
[53] Philo etymologizes "Canaan" negatively as "tossing" (σάλος), leaving the bizarre impression that Abram migrated toward an agitation of soul. Perhaps this is the reason Origen corrects the etymology of Canaan (actually, Χαναναία, but taken as Χαναάν by Didymus) to "prepared by humility" (ἡτοιμασμένη ταπεινώσει). See Origen, *Comm. Matt.* 11.16; and Didymus, *Comm. Gen.* 213.4.

tempted and misled) for a more reliable knowledge bestowed by God (*Migr.* 187–91; *Somn.* 1.41–60).

After formally marking a transition from the literal to the anagogical sense, Didymus says "Haran, then, means 'holes,' and as such is a symbol of the senses, since the places where the senses are located have holes, as it were" (*Comm. Gen.* 213.4–6 [FC 132:186, modified]). Didymus then states that God is really calling Abram to distance himself from the senses, just as Philo had done. Finally, Didymus admits that sense perception is a necessary evil, but the sage must tread carefully on the road to which they lead.[54] There can be no question that Didymus borrows these etymologies and their allegorical interpretations from Philo.

Although Origen is an important source for Didymus' biblical etymologies, Philo stands as the primary witness. First, Didymus explicitly credits Philo with biblical etymology. He does not merely borrow this accreditation from a predecessor, for Origen himself never names Philo in connection with an etymology, despite using some one hundred Philonic etymologies himself.[55] Second, Didymus on a number of occasions cites a Philonic etymology, which is immediately followed by a Philonic allegorical interpretation.[56] This proves Philo is not merely a linguistic resource, but an honoured predecessor in the tradition of etymological allegory.

10.2.1.2 Arithmology

Arithmology is another common instrument of allegory in the Philonic corpus. Twice Philo refers to a separate treatise he authored on numbers in the Bible (*Mos.* 2.115; *QG* 4.110). But this πραγματεία, as he calls it, has not survived. Numerical symbolism is popular in the early Alexandrian Christian tradition, but is not generally employed as an exegetical tool.[57] Even Origen does not seem interested in arithmology to the extent Philo was.[58] However, with Didymus, we find "one of the densest uses of numerological interpretation in any patristic author."[59] Didymus does not follow Philo as closely in his arithmology as he does in his etymology, for he is capable of producing his own interpretations. Nevertheless, as we saw above, Didymus explicitly credits Philo with providing the "mystical meaning" of biblical numbers (*Comm. Gen.* 147.15–18). So, it is difficult to know exactly when Didymus copies Philo, when he utilizes arithmological handbooks, and when he offers his own interpretations *de novo*. Nevertheless, there is at least one instance where a single Philonic text seems to be utilized.

---

[54] On sense perception as a necessary evil; cf. Philo, *Leg.* 1.103, 2.24, 3.67; *Sacr.* 106.
[55] See A. van den Hoek, "Philo and Origen: A Descriptive Catalogue of Their Relationship," *SPhiloA* 12 (2000): 44–121.
[56] See the chart in Rogers, *Didymus the Blind*, 140–41.
[57] Second-century arithmology is used more to highlight philosophical principles and celestial symbolism; see J. Kalvesmaki, *The Theology of Arithmetic: Number Symbolism in Platonism and Early Christianity*, Hellenic Studies 59 (Cambridge, MA: Center for Hellenic Studies, 2013).
[58] See Rogers, *Didymus the Blind*, 150–54.
[59] A. B. Nelson, "The Classroom of Didymus the Blind," (PhD diss., University of Michigan, 1995), 155.

Philo dedicates more space to the number seven than to any other number.[60] It is no surprise, then, to find Didymus following Philo's comments.[61] One passage in particular appears to have been borrowed from Philo's *De opificio mundi* 89–100 (*Comm. Gen.* 183.27–184.23). Commenting on the animals brought into the ark "seven by seven," Didymus launches the allegorical level of meaning by observing three mathematical peculiarities. First, "All the numbers in the decade generate or are generated by a factor of 2 or 3 except 7."[62] Second, "if you make a series of 7 numbers beginning with 1 and double them, you will get an even number that is a square ... and also a cube."[63] Third, "a series of 7 numbers starting from the monad and tripled amounts to 729, which is itself a square and a cube."[64]

The mathematics here are rather simple, and are original neither to Philo nor to Didymus.[65] However, five factors prove Didymus depends on Philo for his interpretation. First, he refers to the Sabbath rest in connection with the number (Philo, *Opif.* 89). Second, he uses the language of seven as a motherless "virgin."[66] Third, Didymus arranges numbers within the decade into three categories: (1) those that generate but are not generated; (2) those that are generated but do not generate; and (3) those that both generate and are generated.[67] Fourth, although Philo does not break down the mathematics as Didymus does, he cites as examples 64 and 729 (*Opif.* 91). Fifth, Didymus here resists the urge to cite a series of biblical proofs, as is his normal practice, in order to offer a purely mathematical one, more characteristic of Philo. Didymus could have gotten all of this language and information from other sources, but it is obvious that here he utilizes a single Philonic text to enlighten his students on the mathematical properties of the number seven.

For ancient Pythagorean arithmologists, the decade was sacred.[68] Philo appears to have a great respect for Pythagorean principles, and furnishes sound mathematical proofs along with biblical ones. Origen, by contrast, may allegorize a number by citing scripture exclusively, and without mentioning mathematical proofs. He can even arithmologize half numbers (*Comm. Rom.* 3.8.4)! Didymus is not as cavalier as Origen, but neither is he as soundly grounded in arithmology as Philo. He prefers biblical

---

[60] Philo's longest excursus on the number seven is *Opif.* 89–127 (see D. T. Runia, *On the Creation of the Cosmos According to Moses*, PACS 1 [Leiden: Brill, 2001], ad loc.). For general comments with a special focus on the number seven, see H. Moehring, "Arithmology as an Exegetical Tool in the Writings of Philo of Alexandria," in *The School of Moses: Studies in Philo and Hellenistic Religion in Memory of Horst R. Moehring*, ed. J. P. Kenney, BJS 304, SPhiloM 1 (Atlanta: Scholar's Press, 1995), 141–76.

[61] Didymus too devotes more attention to the number seven than to any other number, the Tura commentaries featuring over twenty separate discussions of the number (Rogers, *Didymus the Blind*, 163).

[62] These texts follow the translation of Hill, *Didymus the Blind: Commentary on Genesis*, 168–69.

[63] Didymus furnishes the proofs. The seven numbers are 1, 2, 4, 8, 16, 32, and 64. $8 \times 8 = 64$ and $4 \times 4 \times 4 = 64$.

[64] Didymus again furnishes the proofs. The seven numbers are 1, 3, 9, 27, 81, 243, and 729. $27 \times 27 = 729$ and $9 \times 9 \times 9 = 729$.

[65] Cf. Anatolius 35.14–21. The third-century compendium of Anatolius reflects a common arithmological tradition from which both Philo and Didymus draw.

[66] See *Opif.* 100 where Philo cites the Greek mythological background.

[67] Philo highlights these categories immediately after the mathematical discussion of squares and cubes that Didymus appears to quote (*Opif.* 99).

[68] Philo repeats this common sentiment (*Opif.* 47, 99; *Congr.* 90; *Decal.* 20–31).

proofs, but seems willing to cite arithmological lore when he has a trusted source, such as the Philonic corpus, on which to lean.

10.2.2 Thematic Borrowings

10.2.2.1 Creation

The creation of the cosmos holds a special interest for Didymus. Nearly one-third of the original *Comm. Gen.* is devoted to the explication of the creation narrative (Gen 1:1–2:3). Philo too devotes a great deal of attention to the creation account, despite the puzzling omission (or is it lost?) of an allegorical treatise on Gen 1.[69] Although this section of Didymus' work is fragmentary, we can routinely make out sections that reflect Philonic influence, especially following the *De opificio mundi*.

First, we note that Didymus does not read the days of Gen 1 as literal, twenty-four hour periods. Rather, because God "acts outside of time" and because the sun was not created until the fourth day (Gen 1:14–19), the number six must bear symbolic significance (*Comm. Gen.* 34.2-29; cf. Philo, *Opif.* 13). Didymus then offers an arithmological interpretation, just as Philo had done (*Leg.* 1.2-3). Six is a perfect number, "So God, who is responsible for a creation that is perfect, brought it into being in the first perfect number, definitely not for us to claim that six days passed as the sun followed its course six times, the sun not having existed for the first three days, but because the number six was adopted for the sake of reasonableness and harmony" (*Comm. Gen.* 34.24-29 [FC 132:44–45]).

Second, Didymus explains human hegemony over animals in terms reminiscent of Philo. After quoting Gen 1:26, Didymus is provoked toward a Philonic application of the term "beasts" (κτήνη) as "passions and movements of the soul" that must be guided by a charioteer (*Comm. Gen.* 70.15-12). This exact image is set forth in Philo's *De opificio mundi* (87–88). Didymus also informs us that rule of the beasts within the soul is a responsibility of being made in the image of God. The "human" of Gen 1:26-28 cannot indicate a physical body, since "God does not possess a human form" (*Comm. Gen.* 56.15-16).[70] At the allegorical level, the text challenges us to enthrone Reason (Logos for Philo and Christ for Didymus) as the leader of the soul. Although Didymus Christianizes Philo's meaning, he does not need to stretch it far, for Philo too explains the Logos as the image of God (*Opif.* 25, 31).

10.2.2.2 The Names of God

The biblical text of Genesis features an abrupt shift from the name God (*'elohim*) in 1:1–2:3 to Yahweh God (YHWH *'elohim*) in 2:4. Modern scholars have traditionally

---

[69] See the discussion in M. R. Niehoff, *Philo of Alexandria: An Intellectual Biography*, ABRL (New Haven: Yale University Press, 2018), 247–50. Didymus can be taken as evidence to indicate that, if such a treatise was ever authored, it had been lost by the fourth century CE.
[70] Runia takes this as a direct quotion from Philo's *Opif.* 69 ("L'exégèse philosophique et l'influence de la penseé philonienne dans la tradition patristique," in *Philon d'Alexandrie et le langage de la philosophie*, ed. C. Lévy, Monothéismes et Philosophie [Turnhout: Brepols, 1998], 327–48, esp. 336–42).

seen this strange feature as evidence of two sources, P and J, respectively. But ancient exegetes read the two names as evidence of divine attributes (the rabbis) or powers (Philo). Philo says: "From the divine Logos, as from a spring, two powers split off. The one is the creative power, in accordance with which the craftsman placed all things and ordered them, and this power is named 'God' [θεός]. The other is the kingly power, in accordance with which the creator rules what has come into being, and this power is called 'Lord' [κύριος]" (*QE* 2.68 [Marcus, LCL]). Didymus too adopts this useful philological approach, writing, "By the name God [θεός], the text means the creative aspect, but by the name Lord [κύριος] indicates a ruler and king" (*Comm. Gen.* 31.16–18).[71] Although Didymus does not cite Philo for this interpretation by name, there can be little doubt that it owes its origins to him, for the names of God are explained almost verbatim in Philonic fashion.

10.2.2.3 The Doctrine of Pre-passion
A final area of thematic influence falls within Philo's doctrine of virtue. Because the ethical summit of ὁμοίωσις θεῷ requires the total extirpation of the passions, commentators need to explain certain problematic scriptural statements.[72] Abraham, for example, experiences a passion in his grief over the death of Sarah, who supposedly represents perfection in virtue.[73] This does not mean Abraham fell from virtue; rather, that he receded within virtue. So, one option was to suggest there are two kinds of virtuous figures, ones who can fall and ones who cannot. The Stoics had already created this loophole.[74]

A second and more comfortable option was to posit pre-passion, or "anticipatory feeling" (προπάθεια), as a means to distance the sage from passion proper. Philo appears to be among the earliest witnesses to this doctrine, although not necessarily as an apologetic tool.[75] Philo cites Gen 4:26, and asks why Enosh is associated with hope. He answers, "'Enosh' is interpreted as 'man.' And this is now taken, not as a mixture, but as the logical part of the soul, the mind, to which hope is particularly fitting.... And hope is a certain anticipation of joy [προπάθεια τις τῆς χαρᾶς]; before joy there is an expectation of good" (*QG* 1.79 [Marcus, LCL]). This is the only clearly Philonic passage describing pre-passion, but it stands as an important one, as we shall see.

Alexandrian Christians found the doctrine of pre-passion especially useful since the New Testament seemingly attributes passions to Christ.[76] Origen uses the term more

---

[71] Cf. *Comm. Gen.* 91.13–22. Κύριος is associated with providence in *Comm. Ps.* 226.9–11.

[72] On the connection between ethical perfection and freedom from passion, see S. Lilla, *Clement of Alexandria: A Study in Christian Platonism and Gnosticism*, Oxford Theological Monographs (Oxford: Oxford University Press, 1971), 99–117.

[73] See *Abr.* 256–57 with the comments of S. Weisser, "Why Does Philo Criticize the Stoic Ideal of Apatheia in *On Abraham* 257? Philo and Consolatory Literature," *ClQ* 62 (2012): 242–59.

[74] Cf. Seneca, *Ep.* 75.9. The hard-line Stoic position that one cannot regress or fall from virtue is a vulnerable point which Plutarch attacks; see R. A. Wright, "Plutarch on Moral Progress," in *Passions and Moral Progress in Greco-Roman Thought*, ed. J. T. Fitzgerald, Routledge Monographs in Classical Studies (London: Routledge, 2008), 136–50.

[75] See M. Graver, "Philo of Alexandria and the Origins of the Stoic ΠΡΟΠΑΘΕΙΑΙ," in *Philo of Alexandria and Post-Aristotelian Philosophy*, ed. F. Alesse, Studies in Philo of Alexandria 5 (Leiden: Brill, 2008), 197–221.

[76] e.g. Matt 26:37, which uses the verb λυπέω with reference to Jesus.

as an apologetic device, and apparently then only reluctantly.[77] He is thus closer to the pure Stoic usage, utilizing pre-passion as an defensive tool.[78] Didymus expands the patristic application of the doctrine, however, using the term προπάθεια over forty times, often in a positive sense.[79] In general, his usage also seems to share more in common with Philo's positivity than with Origen's apologetics.

Didymus wishes to place pre-passion on the scale of what Bayliss terms "a psychological continuum."[80] For example, Didymus says, "Pre-passion alone acquits from any charge, it does not subject someone to a charge; but passion subjects one to a moderate charge; while disposition [διάθεσις] is evil-doing [κακία]; and much worse the action which is added to it" (*Comm. Ps.* 43.23–25).[81] Didymus recognizes the two Stoic compromises available: either one can regress and progress within the domain of virtue, or one can experience pre-passion, bringing no fault, and keeping one's virtue perfectly intact. Didymus simply combines the two options. One wonders whether Philo himself might have done the same. Although Philo gives us very little to go on, we can nevertheless observe that pre-passion for Philo is morally neutral, and even positive, as it is for Didymus. Didymus likely did not derive his position from Origen or from the Stoics, but from Philo.

10.3 Conclusion

In conclusion, there are certain fundamental differences between the works of Philo and Didymus. First, Philo writes for students much more advanced than those Didymus teaches. Often, what is implicit in Philo is spelled out in Didymus, and what is complicated in Philo is simplified in Didymus. This indicates the latter found Philo helpful enough to "dumb down" for his readers. Second, Philo is much more apt to labor on in an allegorical interpretation, taking him far afield from the scriptural lemma. Didymus generally sticks close to the text, rarely allowing a comment to drag on for more than a papyrus page. In at least one place Didymus utilizes a Philonic interpretation, skipping a long Philonic excursus, and resuming when Philo finally gets back to the text.[82] Third, Didymus reflects the influence of Origen in allowing scripture to be its own primary interpreter. Even where Didymus borrows material from Philo, he often cites proof texts from elsewhere in the biblical canon.

Despite the differences between the two thinkers and their works, remarkable similarities remain. First, both are exegetes of the biblical text first and foremost. Each of

---

[77] Origen feels compelled to remind readers that scripture sometimes uses terminology in a non-technical sense (e.g. *Sel.* ad Ps 4:5; *Comm. Matt.* ad Matt 26:37).
[78] See Rogers, *Didymus the Blind*, 179–80.
[79] In general, see R. A. Layton, "*Propatheia*: The Origins of the Passions in the Exegesis of Origen and Didymus," *VC* 54 (2000): 242–62; Bayliss, *The Vision of Didymus*, 201–20. Bayliss sees a much greater Philonic influence than Layton allows.
[80] Bayliss, *The Vision of Didymus*, 202.
[81] Translation from Bayliss, *The Vision of Didymus*, 208.
[82] Didymus simply moves from the material in *Sacr.* 11 to 45, ignoring §§12–44 (see above).

Didymus' citations of Philo fall into the category of biblical exegesis. Whether Didymus even knew about the apologetic and philosophical works of Philo is impossible to determine. Second, both are interested in using the Bible as a means of provoking spiritual growth. Progress and perfection are regular themes, and even serve to direct large blocks of exegesis, such as Philo's themes of flight and migration, or Didymus' use of the Psalms as a guidebook for spiritual ascent. Third, both are committed to the deeper, allegorical meaning of scripture as the primary instrument by which assimilation to God takes place.

The commentaries of Didymus reflect a thorough Philonic influence. Philo's name occurs only nine times in the five Tura commentaries, but his influence was much deeper than these examples reflect. Remarkably, Didymus follows Philo sequentially through at least two treatises, mingling his own exegetical comments with those of his Jewish master.[83] We can observe such an approach in his treatment of the Genesis account of creation, where Didymus follows large segments of *De opificio mundi*. We can observe the same in the Cain and Abel narrative, which follows the opening paragraphs of *De sacrificiis*, and does acknowledge the Philonic debt explicitly. Didymus thus shows a knowledge of the Allegorical Commentary, and the Exposition of the Law, although the only treatise mentioned by name is *De vita Mosis* (which is thought to belong to the latter work). The example of Didymus offers clear evidence that Philo's influence was alive and well in Alexandria over three centuries after his death.

---

[83] Didymus' exegetical use of Philo is similar to that of Clement, as A. van den Hoek has demonstrated. See *Clement of Alexandria and His Use of Philo in the Stromateis: An Early Christian Reshaping of a Jewish Model*, VCSup 3 (Leiden: Brill, 1988).

11
The Cappadocians

Albert C. Geljon

That the Cappadocian Fathers had read Philo and incorporated Philonic exegesis in their own writings has long been recognized. The way in which they dealt with Philo and their attitude towards Philonic thought is the subject of extensive scholarly investigation. Pioneering work was carried out by several French scholars in the middle of the twentieth century, with a focus on Gregory of Nyssa. Cardinal Jean Daniélou edited Gregory's *De vita Moysis* in the Sources Chrétiennes series, referring to Philo's writings at many places and showing that Gregory was well acquainted with them.[1] A few decades later I myself made a detailed examination of Philo's influence on Gregory's *De vita Moysis*.[2] In addition, Daniélou devoted an article to Philo's influence on Gregory.[3] He also wrote many articles on various aspects of Gregory's thought, in some of which Philonic parallels were pointed out.[4] Michel Aubineau noted similarities between Philo and Gregory's *De virginitate*, showing that Philo is one of Gregory's sources.[5] Research on Philo and Basil's *Homilies on the Hexaemeron* was done by Stanislas Giet, who argued that Basil, among others, uses Philo as a source.[6] In 1993 Runia presented an overview of the research on Philo and the Cappodicians in his study on Philo in early Christian literature, in which he gives a critical evaluation of the results of scholarship.[7] Philo's allegorical exegesis and its influence on Gregory of Nyssa is the focus of a lengthy article by Ilaria Ramelli published in 2008. She also discusses extensively Origen's role in the transmission of Philo's allegories to Gregory.[8] Finally, a very brief survey of Gregory of Nyssa's reading of Philo by Manuel Mira is found in *The Brill Dictionary of Gregory of Nyssa*. This survey is mainly based on the research of Daniélou.[9]

---

[1] J. Daniélou, *Grégoire de Nysse, La vie de Moïse*, SC 1 (Paris: Cerf, 1955, 1968²).

[2] A. C. Geljon, *Philonic Exegesis in Gregory of Nyssa's* De vita Moysis, SPhiloM 5 (Providence: Brown Judaic Studies, 2002).

[3] J. Daniélou, "Philo et Grégoire de Nysse," in *Philon d'Alexandrie: Lyon 11–15 Septembre 1966*, ed. R. Arnaldez, C. Mondésert, and J. Poilloux (Paris: CNRS, 1967), 333–45.

[4] J. Daniélou, "*Akolouthia* chez Grégoire de Nysse," *RevSR* 27 (1953): 219–49; J. Daniélou, "La notion de confins (*methorios*) chez Grégoire de Nysse," *RSR* 49 (1961): 161–87; see also his *L'être et le temps chez Grégoire de Nysse* (Leiden: Brill, 1970), 85–93, 117–32.

[5] M. Aubineau, *Grégoire de Nyssa, Traité de la Virginité*, SC 119 (Paris: Cerf, 1966), 105–16.

[6] S. Giet, *Basile de Césarée, Homélies sur l'Hexaéméron*, SC 26 (Paris: Cerf, 1968), 47–69.

[7] D. T. Runia, *Philo in Early Christian Literature: A Survey*, CRINT III 3 (Assen: Van Gorcum, 1993), 235–61.

[8] I. L. E. Ramelli, "Philosophical Allegoresis of Scripture in Philo and Its Legacy in Gregory of Nyssa," *SPhiloA* 20 (2008): 55–99.

[9] M. Mira, "Philo of Alexandria," in *The Brill Dictionary of Gregory of Nyssa*, ed. L. F. Mateo-Seco and G. Maspero, VCSup 99 (Leiden: Brill, 2010), 601–3.

In this article I will offer an overview of Philo's influence on all the three Cappadocians, based on the research of the last fifty years. Because it is of course not possible to give an exhaustive treatment of the subject, I shall focus on striking examples. Detailed examination and discussion of more examples can be found in the secondary literature which I cite.

11.1 Basil of Caesarea

Born in *c*.330 to a wealthy Christian family Basil started his education at the school of rhetoric in Caesarea in Cappadocia.[10] He continued his studies in Constantinople, where he attended lectures of the rhetorician Libanius, and finally in Athens, where he studied together with his friend Gregory of Nazianzus (349/350–355). On his return to Cappadocia he participated in the ascetic life of the monastic community of his mother and sister on their family estate in Annesa in Pontus. Together with Gregory of Nazianzus he composed the *Philocalia*, an anthology of Origen's writings, which is a clear indication of the great interest they had in the Alexandrian theologian. On the death of the bishop of Caesarea in 370, Basil became his successor. After nearly ten very active years in the role he sadly succumbed to a serious disease and died in 379.

Because of the thorough education he had received it may be expected that Basil was well acquainted with the philosophical and theological tradition, of which Philo had become a part. However, he mentions Philo by name only once, referring to an exegesis of the nature of manna.[11] In a letter, addressed to Amphilocius of Iconium, he writes: "Philo in explaining manna, as though he had been taught by a certain Jewish tradition, said that such was its quality that it changed according to the imagination of the eater" (*Ep.* 190.3 [Deferrari, LCL]).[12] The difficulty here is that such an interpretation is not found in the extant writings of Philo. James Royse suggested that Basil deploys a lost book of the *Quaestiones in Exodum*.[13] Adam Kamesar, however, argues that Basil's source is Wisdom 16:20–21, so that the reference can be explained on the basis that Basil regards Philo as the author of Wisdom. Because the Book of Wisdom was seen as deuterocanonical, Basil prefers to present Philo as having been taught by the oral Jewish tradition.[14] It is striking that Basil is obviously aware of Philo's Jewishness but refers to it in a neutral way and does not criticize it openly.

More Philonic influence can been seen in his interpretation of the creation account in Genesis, which he sets out in nine *Homilies on the Hexaemeron* expounding the six days of creation. In all likelihood Basil delivered the homilies in the last year of his

---

[10] For Basil's life, see P. J. Fedwick, "A Chronology of the Life and Works of Basil of Caesarea," in *Basil of Caesarea: Christian, Humanist, Ascetic. A Sixteen-Hundredth Anniversary Symposium*, ed. P. J. Fedwick, 2 vols (Toronto: Pontifical Institute of Mediaeval Studies, 1981), 1:3–20.
[11] Runia, *Philo in Early Christian Literature*, 236.
[12] The letter was written in 374 CE.
[13] J. Royse, "The Original Structure of Philo's *Quaestiones*," *SPhilo* 4 (1976–77): 41–78, esp. 58–59.
[14] A. Kamesar, "San Basilio, Filone, e la tradizione ebraici," *Henoch* 17 (1995): 129–40.

life, during the period of Lent in 378 in Caesarea.[15] In these homilies he gives a literal explanation of the creation account, explicitly denouncing allegorical exegesis (for instance in 2.5, 3.9, 9.1). He very often shows his great admiration for the creation and the wisdom of the creator and he underscores that the visible world is a means to know the invisible creator, quoting Rom 1:20 (1.6, 3.10).

There can be no doubt that in his homilies Basil often relies on the prior exegetical and philosophical tradition. In so doing, it is probable that he also used Philo's treatise on the creation account *De opificio mundi*. Stanislas Giet, the editor of the homilies in the Sources Chrétiennes series, recognizes Philo's *Opif.* as an important source together with others.[16] Following in Giet's footsteps Emmanuel Amand de Mendieta lists four direct sources which Basil employed: the Greek Bible; the *Commentary on Genesis* by Origen; a philosophical handbook; and Philo's *De opificio mundi*.[17]

To illustrate Basil's use of Philo as a source in this work we mention a few points of contact:[18]

1. At the beginning of the first homily Basil discusses Moses as author of the narrative, telling us that Moses was adopted by Pharaoh's daughter and had a royal education, in which he was taught by Egyptian wise men (1.1 [2.10–14]).[19] In his *De vita Moysis* Philo also relates Moses' royal education at some length, referring to Egyptian teachers as well (1.20–24). That Moses was instructed in the wisdom of the Egyptians was a tradition which is also reflected in Acts 7:20–22 and in Ezekiel Tragicus (*Exagoge* 37). Therefore we can assume that it was a Jewish-Hellenistic tradition which has been taken over by the Christian writers.[20] Basil continues the story of Moses by remarking that the young Moses hated the pomp of royalty and returned to the humbler state of his own people (1.1 [2.14–15]). The same idea is found in Philo: Moses regards his sharing in the good fortune of his adoptive family as false, and the circumstances of his natural parents as genuinely his own, although they were not known to him for some time (*Mos.* 1.32). After Moses had killed an Egyptian man, he fled to Midian (Exod 2:11–15), and Basil narrates that he led a contemplative life for forty years (1.1 [3.2–3]). That Moses had a philosophical life in the desert is also recorded by Philo (*Mos.* 1.48).

---

[15] As argued by E. Amand de Mendieta, "La préparation et la composition des neuf 'Homélies sur l'Hexaéméron' de Basile de Césarée," *StPatr* xvi, part ii, 1985: 349–67 (356–58). The date is a matter of dispute.

[16] Giet, *Basile de Césarée*, 47–69.

[17] Amand de Mendieta, "La préparation," 364–67. See also C. Köckert, *Christliche Kosmologie und kaiserzeitliche Philosophie*, STAC 36 (Tübingen 2009: Mohr Siebeck), 322–24.

[18] Based on the references in Giet, *Basile de Césarée*; and Runia, *Philo in Early Christian Literature*, 238.

[19] References are to pages and lines in E. Amand de Mendieta and S. Y. Rudberg, *Basilius von Caesarea. Homilien zum Hexaemeron* (Berlin: Akademie Verlag, 1997).

[20] See e.g. Clement, *Stromateis* 1.153.23; Gregory of Nyssa, *De vita Moysis* 1.17–18; in Basil, *De legendis gentilium libris* 3; *Enarratio in propheta Esaiam* 433C.

2. In 2.3 (25.12–13) Basil criticizes the view according to which God is an active power and matter has a passive nature, posing the question how they come into contact. He probably has Philo in mind, who describes God as active cause and matter as passive object. God, the mind of the universe, sets passive matter in motion and gives life to it (*Opif.* 8–9).[21]
3. Struck by the fact that in Gen 1:5 the first day is not called "first day," but "one day," Basil remarks that "one" has a kinship with eternity or is an image of eternity (2.8 [36.1–6]). This reminds us of Philo, who interprets the number "one" as referring to the intelligible world of ideas and so connects it with eternity as well (*Opif.* 15, 35). As a Christian exegete, however, Basil links "one day" with the day of the Lord, the day of the resurrection.
4. Basil frequently expresses his admiration (θαῦμα) for God as creator of the cosmos with all its marvels (1.7 [12.16–19]; 1.10 [18.7–11]) and in 4.1 (58.1) he calls God "the great juggler and artist" (ὁ μέγας θαυματοποιὸς καὶ τεχνίτης). Basil's language may be inspired by Philo, who in a discussion of creation gives God the rare epithet θαυματοποιός (*Plant.* 3).[22] Both Philo and Basil refer to God as τεχνίτης.[23] It appears also in Wis 13:1 and Heb 11:10. Philo's admiration for God is set in a polemical context directed to those who have more admiration for the cosmos than for God (*Opif.* 7). This theme is absent in Basil.

As we have seen, Basil freely includes Philonic exegesis into his own interpretation without mentioning him by name. By way of contrast, he also explicitly denounces Jewish thought, as we can see from the ninth homily. There he deals with the problem of the plurality in God's saying "Let us make man" (Gen 1:26) and refers to a Jew. The text runs as follows:

> Where, tell me, is the Jew, who in the previous sections, even though the light of the doctrine of God was shining forth as if through a window and a second person (of the Trinity) was being disclosed in a secret fashion but was not yet revealed in full clarity, continued to fight against the truth, asserting that God was conversing with himself? (9.6 [158.11–15])[24]

---

[21] D. T. Runia, *Philo of Alexandria, On the Creation of the Cosmos According to Moses: Introduction, Translation and Commentary*, PACS 1 (Leiden: Brill, 2001), 123.
[22] P. Petit, "Émerveillement, prière, et esprit chez saint Basile le Grand," *Collectanea Cisterciensia* 35 (1973): 81–107, 218–38, esp. 220. The applying of θαυματοποιός to God is also found in Athanasius, *De semente* (spurious) (PG 28.168b); Didymus, *De Trinitate* 27.1.
[23] Philo, *Leg.* 1.18, 1.31, 3.99; *Cher.* 32, 128; *Congr.* 105; *Plant.* 31 etc.; Basil 1.7 (12.13, 13.8), 2.2 (23.11), 3.5 (47.18), etc.
[24] Translations from D. T. Runia, "'Where, Tell Me, Is the Jew ...': Basil, Philo and Isidore of Pelusium," *VC* 46 (1992): 172–89, at 173–74.

Later on he points to the Jews, writing:

> that race hostile to the truth, the Jews, are pushed into a corner and affirm that there is a plurality of persons whom the word of God addresses. According to them it is to the angels that stand around him that he says, "let us make man." (159.13–16)

In earlier scholarship Basil's reference to the Jew is usually seen as referring to Philo.[25] However, in a detailed study of this passage and its background David Runia shows that Philo does not interpret the Genesis text as saying that God was conversing with himself.[26] According to Philo the plural form is used by God because God made use of helpers in creating human beings. These subordinate helpers created that part of human beings that is responsible for evil deeds (*Opif.* 73–75). Furthermore, Runia rightly observes that Basil sometimes speaks of the Jew, sometimes refers to the Jews in the plural. This is a strong indication that the Jew is a collective figure, who represents the opinions of Jewish interpreters of the text. The Jewish view is contrary to the Christian interpretation which assumes the presence of the Logos of the Trinity in the text. Philo is never explicitly criticized by Basil, which may be taken as indicating a positive attitude towards him.[27]

11.2 Gregory of Nyssa

It is widely recognized that Gregory of Nyssa was the most philosophically minded of the three Cappadocians.[28] He was born as the younger brother of Basil a few years later, around 335, and he was educated by Basil, to whom he often refers as "teacher." His sister Macrina also had a share in his Christian education. It is very likely that he also studied in Cappodician Caesarea, just as Basil had done. After his studies he began a career as a rhetorician, but in 371 he was appointed as bishop of the small town of Nyssa by his brother. A few years later he was deposed by the Arian emperor Valens, but he returned to his see in 378. He was a prominent participant in the council of Constantinople in 381, where the Nicene creed was confirmed. The date of his death is unknown, but in all likelihood he died not long after 394.

Gregory's writings show that he had a profound knowledge of classical literature and philosophy and had certainly read Homer, the tragedians, Plato, Aristotle, Plotinus, and others.[29] In addition he was also acquainted with the works of Philo, as appears in the first instance from the references in *Contra Eunomium*.[30]

---

[25] Giet, *Basile de Césarée*, 514 n. 3; Daniélou, "Philon et Grégoire de Nysse," 336.
[26] Runia, "Where, Tell Me," 173–80.
[27] But he does not go as far as, for example, Isidore of Pelusium, who argues that Philo anticipates the doctrine of the Trinity. See the chapter by Madalina Toca and Johan Leemans in this volume.
[28] For his life, see G. May, "Die Chronologie des Lebens und der Werke des Gregor von Nyssa," in *Écriture et culture philosophique dans la pensée de Grégoire de Nysse*, ed. M. Harl (Leiden: Brill, 1971), 51–67; A. M. Silvas, *Gregory of Nyssa: The Letters*, VCSup 83 (Leiden: Brill, 2007), 1–57.
[29] See Aubineau, *Grégoire de Nysse*, 41–49.
[30] Daniélou, "Philo et Grégoire de Nysse," 333–34; Runia, *Philo in Early Christian Literature*, 243–61.

11.2.1 *Contra Eunomium*

Just like his brother Basil, Gregory was involved in the conflict with Eunomius, the leader of the Neo-Arians, and at the beginning of the 380s he composed the voluminous treatise *Contra Eunomium*, in which he refutes Eunomius' doctrine.[31] In the third book of this work we find his only extant references to Philo by name.[32] These occur in Gregory's defense of Basil against an attack by Eunomius, writing as follows:

> In his own accustomed style Eunomius patches together the rags of verbal fragments cast off at crossroads, and once again poor old Isocrates is nibbled at for words and phrases to compile his case, and sometimes even the Hebrew Philo gets the same treatment, contributing fragments for him from his own works. (3.5.24)[33]

In this passage Gregory criticizes Eunomius' style, accusing him of copying words and phrases from other writers, for instance Isocrates and Philo. We should note that Gregory gives Philo the epithet ὁ Ἑβραῖος.

In the other passage where Philo is named, Gregory continues his negative attitude and accuses him of copying not only Philo's words but also his ideas:

> His (Eunomius') "supremest God," he says, "before such other things as are generated, controls his own power" (ὁ ἐξοχώτατος θεὸς πρὸ τῶν ἄλλων ὅσα γεννητὰ τῆς αὐτοῦ κρατεῖ δυνάμεως). The statement has been lifted word for word from Philo the Hebrew into his own book by our wordsmith, and whoever cares may detect Eunomius' plagiarism from the actual works of Philo. I have drawn attention to this at the present time, not so much to sneer at the poverty of the wordsmith's own words and thoughts, as intending to demonstrate the affinity between Eunomius' doctrines and the words of the Jews. For Philo's argument would not match his ideas word for word, if there were not some family likeness between his thought and Philo's. Thus we may find included in the Hebrew's text the words, "God, before such other things as are generated," and immediately after there is tacked on by the new Judaism, "controls his own power." How absurd this is will be clearly demonstrated if the statement is examined. (3.7.8–9)[34]

---

[31] S. G. Hall, "*Contra Eunomium libri I et II*," in *The Brill Dictionary*, 298–310. Critical edition: W. Jaeger, *Gregorii Nysseni Opera*, I–II (Leiden: Brill, 1960).

[32] Daniélou, "Philo et Grégoire de Nysse," 333–34; Runia, *Philo in Early Christian Literature*, 244–49; C. Moreschini, "Further Considerations on the Philosophical Background of *Contra Eunomium* III," in *Gregory of Nyssa, Contra Eunomium III: An English Translation and Supporting Studies*, ed. J. Leemans and M. Cassin, VCSup 124 (Leiden: Brill, 2014), 595–612, esp. 598–601; M. Cassin, "'Plumer Isocrate': usage polémique du vocabulaire comique chez Grégoire de Nysse," *REG* 121 (2008): 783–96, discusses the satirical vocabulary and imagery of the passage.

[33] Trans. by S. G. Hall in *Gregory of Nyssa, Contra Eunomium III*, 142.

[34] Trans. S. G. Hall in *Gregory of Nyssa, Contra Eunomium III*, 172–73.

184 THE RECEPTION OF PHILO OF ALEXANDRIA

Gregory here claims that Eunomius has taken from Philo the words "supremest God, before the other things that are generated controls his own power" but actually these words are not found in the existing writings of Philo. It is possible that Gregory had read them in a Philonic treatise now lost, but more likely he has in mind Philonic statements of a similar kind, for instance *Leg.* 3.4: πρὸ γὰρ παντὸς γενητοῦ ὁ θεός ἐστι. Similar expressions are found in *Leg.* 3.175 (ὁ λόγος τοῦ θεοῦ ... πρεσβύτατος ... τῶν ὅσα γέγονε) and *Migr.* 183 (πρὸ παντὸς τοῦ γενητοῦ [sc. ἐστιν ὁ θεός]). Furthermore, Gregory may have remembered that Philo frequently refers to God's δύναμις or δυνάμεις. It becomes clear from his text that he sees an affinity between Eunomius' thought and that of Philo, and associates him with the doctrine of the Jews.[35] The reference to Philo indicates that Gregory had read and studied Philo's writings. In other treatises Philo's influence can been detected as well.

11.2.2 *De virginitate*

The treatise *De virginitate* is regarded as the first work that Gregory wrote, probably before his installation as bishop in 371.[36] The work is an encomium of virginity and its aim is, according to Gregory himself, to inspire in the readers a desire for the virtuous life (*Virg.* pr. 1, GNO VIII/1, 247.1–2). In the introduction to the treatise the French editor Michel Aubineau discusses its sources, among whom he notes Philo.[37] He lists several parallels with his writings, some of which are just commonplaces, but he convincingly shows that there are motifs that clearly indicate Philo's influence. There are especially many parallels with *De vita contemplativa*, the treatise in which the Alexandrian exegete describes the communal life of the Therapeutae. Aubineau observes, among others, the following points of contact:[38]

1. An important notion in both Philo and Gregory is the theme of spiritual marriage. In *Contempl.* 88 Philo portrays the women of the community as being virgins and desiring no mortal offspring but immortal children, whose spiritual father is God (see also *Leg.* 3.180–81; *Cher.* 42, 43, 48). In the same way Gregory speaks of wisdom and justice as the offspring of a virgin and conceived by God (*Virg.* 14.3, GNO VIII/1, 308.11–17).
2. Part of the theme of spiritual marriage is the description of the Therapeutae as carried away by a heavenly love and possessed like corybants (*Contempl.* 11).

---

[35] M. R. Barnes argues that the similarity between Philo and Eunomius consists in seeing God's creative power or *dynamis* as separate form his nature and as having an independent existence: "Eunomius of Cyzicus and Gregory of Nyssa: two traditions of transcendent causality," *VC* 52 (1998): 59–87, esp. 71.
[36] L. F. Mateo-Seco "*De virginitate*," in *The Brill Dictionary*, 774–76. May, "Chronologie," 55–56, dates the work somewhere between 370 and 378. Critical edition: J. P. Cavarnos, *Gregorii Nysseni Opera*, VIII/1 (Leiden: Brill, 1952).
[37] Aubineau, *Grégoire de Nysse*, 105–16.
[38] See also Runia, *Philo in Early Christian Literature*, 249–51.

Gregory employs similar language to characterize the soul that loves God (*Virg.* 20.4, GNO VIII/8, 328.6–12).
3. Philonic influence may be seen in the discussion of Israel's crossing of the Red Sea. It is striking that Gregory does not offer the common Christian reading of the crossing as a symbol of baptism, but interprets it in a Philonic way as symbolizing the departure of the soul out of the body and the land of the senses (*Virg.* 4.6, GNO VIII/1, 273.25–274.11; Philo *Migr.* 77; *Spec.* 2.147). Gregory's depiction of Miriam, who was leading the female choir at the Red Sea, as the first to practice virginity may be borrowed from Philo (*Virg.* 19, GNO VIII/1, 323.1–16; Philo *Contempl.* 87; *Agr.* 80–81).
4. The expression "to live for the soul alone" (μόνῃ τῇ ψυχῇ ζῆν, *Virg.* 4.8, GNO VIII/1, 276.15–16) is borrowed from Philo, who uses it on a number of occasions (*Mos.* 1.29; *Her.* 82; *Contempl.* 90). Runia notes that the phrase μόνῃ τῇ ψυχῇ ζῆν is not found in Plato, Clement, Origen, Basil, or Gregory of Nazianzus.[39]

Evaluating Aubineau's overview of Philonic elements in *De virginitate*, Runia rightly concludes that the treatise is one of the stages on the road that connects Philo's mysterious community with later Christian monasticism.[40] There are, however, important differences between Philo's view on the ascetic life and the ideals of the Christian monks, for example in their attitude towards marriage and the ascetic life.[41]

11.2.3 *Apologia in Hexaemeron* and *De hominis opificio*

After Basil's death in 379 Gregory wrote two treatises that deal with the creation account as a sequel and supplement to Basil's *In Hexaemeron*.[42] In *Apologia in Hexaemeron* he discusses some points of Basil's exegesis on a more advanced level, answering questions posed by his brother Peter. Because Basil does not deal with the creation of human beings, Gregory discusses this subject separately in *De hominis opificio*. Just as Basil exploits some Philonic themes in his exegesis, so Gregory also borrows notions from Philo's interpretation without mentioning his name.[43] I will mention some striking examples.

---

[39] Runia, *Philo in Early Christian Literature*, 251 n. 73.
[40] Runia, *Philo in Early Christian Literature*, 251.
[41] A. Guillaumont, "Philon et les origines du monachisme," in *Philon d'Alexandrie*, 361–73, esp. 370–73.
[42] J. A. Gil-Tamayo, "*Apologia in Hexaemeron*," in *The Brill Dictionary*, 387–89; G. Maturi, "*De hominis opificio*," in *The Brill Dictionary*, 544–45. Critical edition of *Hex.*: H. R. Drobner, *Gregorii Nysseni Opera*, IV/1 (Leiden: Brill, 2009); for *Op. hom.* PG 44.124–256.
[43] For Philonic themes, see G. B. Ladner, "The Philosophical Anthropology of Saint Gregory of Nyssa," *DOP* 12 (1958): 59–94; Daniélou, "Philo et Grégoire de Nysse," 335; M. Alexandre, "La théorie de l'exégèse dans le *De hominis opificio* et l'*In Hexaemeron*," in *Écriture et culture philosophique dans la pensée de Grégoire de Nysse*, ed. M. Harl (Leiden: Brill, 1971), 87–110; Runia, *Philo in Early Christian Literature*, 252–56; Ramelli, "Philosophical Allegoresis," 90.

1. Gregory frequently underlines that a coherence and logical order is present in the creation account. In the beginning God created all things together and at once, but the description by Moses shows a logical order and necessary consequence. Gregory expresses this idea using the keywords ἀκολουθία, τάξις, and εἱρμός.[44] The notion of order plays also a part in the history of salvation; the process towards the goal of history and the resurrection takes place according to a logical consequence.[45] It is highly probable that Gregory has taken over the idea of order in the creation from Philo. Just like Gregory, the Alexandrian exegete states that God created all things simultaneously, but they also show an order. He describes order as a sequence and series of things that precede and follow (τάξις ἀκολουθία καὶ εἱρμός ἐστι προηγουμένων καὶ ἑπομένων, Opif. 28; cf. 65, 131). We find the same terms later used by Gregory. It is important to note that the role of logical sequence in the process leading towards salvation is absent in Philo.

2. In Op. hom., Gregory discusses the creation of human being. In his view a double creation is referred to in Genesis. One creation has been made in God's image, which is indicated by the words "God made humankind; according to divine image he made it." But the following words "male and female he made them" (Gen 1:27) refer to the creation in which there is a distinction between male and female. The words of the Apostle Paul "In Christ Jesus there is neither male nor female" (Gal 3:28) point to the creation according to the divine image. As a result of the double creation, human beings have a composite nature. They have a divine, rational, and intelligent part, in which there is no distinction between the sexes, and an irrational and bodily part, divided into male and female (181A–D). Gregory may have been inspired by the idea of a double creation as found in Philo. The Jewish exegete makes a distinction between the creation of the intelligible human being, which is described in Gen 1:27 and the earthly man made from clay from the earth, told in Gen 2:7 (Opif. 69–71, 134–35). It is clear that Gregory differs from Philo with regard to the biblical verses on which the distinction is based. Gregory sees the double creation related in Gen 1:27, whereas in Philo's exegesis Gen 1:27 refers to the creation of the intelligible human being, and the forming of the earthly man is described in Gen 2:7.

3. In Opif. 77–78 Philo poses the question why the human being was made as the last of all creatures and he answers that God is like the giver of a banquet who invites his guests when everything is ready. The same question and answer are given by Gregory, who pictures the same image of God as one who gives a banquet (Op. hom. 2, 132D–133B).

---

[44] For instance, Hex. GNO IV/1, 6.4–6, 14.11–12, 18.13–19.12, 23.13–24.3, 37.7–13, 72.7–10; Op. hom. 128B, 144C.

[45] An. et. res., GNO III/3, 78.1–6; Cant. 5, GNO VI, 144.19–145.6, 15, 458.12–459.1; Inscr. GNO V, 118.1–4.

11.2.4 *De vita Moysis*

In the final part of his life Gregory wrote the treatise that is usually referred to as *On the Life of Moses/De vita Moysis*, but in fact the title *On virtue or on Moses' Life* does more justice to the manuscript tradition.[46] Gregory's work is divided into two books. In book 1, entitled *historia*, he gives a sketch of Moses' life on the basis of the biblical account, while book 2 shows how Moses' life can be an example for a life according to virtue. As a result, allegorical exegesis is absent in book 1 but abundantly employed in book 2. The treatise is addressed to a Christian who has asked Gregory about the perfect life (*Vit. Moys.* 1.2). Philo, too, composed a treatise on Moses' life, which consists in two books as well, but shows a different approach. Philo presents Moses' life under four headings: Moses as philosopher-king, as lawgiver, high priest, and as prophet. In book 1 he discusses Moses as philosopher-king and in book 2 he describes the deeds that Moses did in the other three roles. In his presentation of Moses' life Philo reads the Bible in a literal way, except for some symbolical interpretations; elaborate allegorical exegesis is entirely absent. It is Philo's aim to make Moses' life better known, so *De vita Moysis* is directed to a broad audience. Despite differences between Philo's *Life of Moses* and Gregory's one in approach, aim and scope, there are similarities between the two works, as pointed out by several scholars.[47]

To begin with we find an anonymous reference to Philo in Gregory's cosmological interpretation of the priest's garments.[48] He refers to "one of his predecessors" who interprets the dark-blue of the robe as signifying air (2.191). Philo also sees the vestment of the high priest as a representation of the cosmos and he too explains the dark of the robe as a symbol of the air (2.122). Because this interpretation is not found in other discussions of the priest's garments, for instance in Josephus and Origen, it is very likely that Gregory here refers to Philo. It is interesting to see that Gregory doubts whether this interpretation is correct but he does not reject it. Another Philonic echo can be seen in Gregory's explanation of the four-cornered shape of the breast piece of the high priest as a sign of steadfastness in the good (Philo 2.128; Gregory 2.199).[49] Finally, the interpretation of the hardness of the nut of Aaron's staff as symbolizing the hardness of the virtuous life has also been taken over from Philo's *Mos.* (2.182; Gregory 2.185).

More influence of Philo's *Mos.* can be traced in the first book, where Gregory retells Moses' life, and in which he often uses the same or nearly the same phraseology as Philo in the same context.[50] These phrases do not occur in the scriptural narrative or

---

[46] M. Simonetti, "*De vita Moysis*," in *The Brill Dictionary*, 788–90. The critical edition is by H. Musurillo, *Gregorii Nysseni Opera*, VII/1 (Leiden: Brill, 1964).

[47] J. Daniélou, "Moïse: exemple et figure chez Grégoire de Nysse," *Cahiers Sioniens* 8 (1954): 267–82; Daniélou, "Philo et Grégoire de Nysse," 343–44; Daniélou, *Grégoire de Nysse*, 18–22; A. Malherbe and E. Ferguson, *Gregory of Nyssa: The Life of Moses* (New York: Paulist Press, 1978), 5–6; P. Merri, "La vita di Mosè di Filone Alessandrino e di Gregorio Nissene: note sull' uso dell' allegoria," *Annali della Facoltà di Lettere e Filosofia della Università di Perugia* 20 (1982): 31–53.

[48] Geljon, *Philonic Exegesis*, 138–40.

[49] A. Conway-Jones, *Gregory of Nyssa's Tabernacle Imagery in Its Jewish and Christian Contexts* (Oxford: Oxford University Press, 2014), 213–14.

[50] Geljon, *Philonic Exegesis*, 159–61.

in the relevant passages of the Christian writers. Examples are, for instance, the characterization of Moses' father-in-law (*Mos.* 1.59; *Vit. Moys.* 1.19), the description of the burning bush (*Mos.* 1.65; *Vit. Moys.* 1.20), and the story of the crossing of the Red Sea (*Mos.* 1.177; *Vit. Moys.* 1.31). Gregory's use of Philo's *De vita Moysis* is thus limited to phraseology, for the most part in book 1, and to a few symbolic interpretations.

It is important to note, however, that Gregory clearly exploits allegorical themes from other Philonic treatises.[51] The most important Philonic theme is the interpretation of Egypt and related persons and events. Gregory interprets Pharaoh as a lover of passions and Egypt as the land of the passions (*Vit. Moys.* 2.35). The exodus of the Israelites out of Egypt is the liberation of the soul from the passions (*Vit. Moys.* 2.26). Generally, Gregory borrows the entire complex of allegory of Egypt and the Egyptian king from Philo, who very often elaborates it (*Leg.* 3.12–13, 3.212; *Post.* 115; *Ebr.* 19, 208–9). It is striking that other Christian exegetes, for instance, Origen, do not give an allegorical reading of this theme in the way that Philo and Gregory do. A second theme that can be traced back to Philo, is education. Gregory's interpretation of Moses' basket as education consisting of several subjects, can be seen as a transposition of Philo's interpretation of Bezaleel's work, which consists of several disciplines as well (*Vit. Moys.* 2.7; *Somn.* 1.205). Just as Philo regards Hagar as a symbol of school education, Gregory interprets Pharaoh's daughter in the same manner (*Vit. Moys.* 2.12; *Leg.* 3.244–45). A third Philonic theme is related to the interpretation of the serpent. Discussing the story of the serpents that bite the Israelite people in the desert (Num 21:4–9), Gregory explains them as beastly desires. The people are healed by the brazen serpent made by Moses, which is a symbol of Jesus' cross (*Vit. Moys.* 2.276–277). It is likely that he follows Philo, who interprets the serpents as pleasures that bring death (*Leg.* 2.77–79). Gregory does not take over Philo's explanation of the brazen serpent as the principle of self-control, but prefers the common patristic tradition. In this way he brings in a Christian element in a Philonic allegory. The last theme that shows Philo's influence is the interpretation of the royal highway (Num 20:17, 21:22). Just as Philo, Gregory connects the biblical royal highway with the Aristotelian description of virtue as the mean between two extremes (*Vit. Moys.* 2.288–89; Philo, *Deus* 162–64). Gregory also takes over the way that Philo speaks metaphorically about the highway of virtue, which is placed opposite to the "no-road" of vice (*Vit. Moys.* 2.290; Philo, *Det.* 18; *Agr.* 101).

These allegorical themes are borrowed from writings that belong to the Allegorical Commentary, but recently Markéta Bendová has pointed to some similarities between Gregory's *De Vita Moysis* and Philo's *De Abrahamo*, a treatise the belongs to the Exposition of the Law.[52] First, in both writings there is a combination of retelling and allegorical reading of a biblical text. Secondly, in Philo's allegorical interpretation biblical figures are seen as types of soul. They represent different stages of the soul who moves towards the good, undergoing transformations. In the same way in Gregory's

---

[51] Geljon, *Philonic Exegesis*, 161–67.
[52] M. Bendova, "The Influence of Philo's *De Abrahamo* on Gregory of Nyssa's *De Vita Moysis*," *AUC Theologica* 8 (2018): 91–109.

thought the soul's progress involves repeated transformations. A difference is that for Gregory only Moses functions as a model for the soul, whereas for Philo several biblical figures are models for the several stages of the progress of the soul. The third similarity is the idea that the person who serves God for no other reason than him alone receives as reward friendship with God.

11.2.5 Exegetical and Philosophical Themes

Throughout his writings Gregory reveals a significant debt to Philo in his development of exegetical and philosophical themes. We shall now discuss some important themes which are all in one way or another connected to the notion of transcendence.

1. Both Philo and Gregory state emphatically that God is incomprehensible and invisible in his essence and both base this on Exod 20:21, in which it is said that Moses enters the darkness where God was. Both explain the darkness as referring to God's incomprehensibility and invisibility.[53] Origen offers the same exegesis of Exod 20:21, combining it with Ps 17:12: "God made darkness his secret place" (*Cels.* 6.17; *Comm. Io.* 2.172). Because Gregory makes the same combination of Exod 20:21 and Ps 17:12 we can assume that Origen is the intermediary between Philo and Gregory. Before Origen, Clement of Alexandria, following Philo, already interprets the darkness as indicating God's incomprehensibility and he quotes literally from Philo's exposition in *Post.* 14 (*Stromateis* 2.6.1). A further parallel between Philo and Gregory is that in their discussion on divine unknowability both involve Exod 33:12–32, where it is recorded that Moses asks God to manifest himself. God answers that Moses cannot see his face because a human being cannot see God's face and live (Exod 33:20). Moses will see God's back but not his face. Both Philo and Gregory interpret Moses' longing for God as the infinite quest of the soul for God (Philo, *Fug.* 165; *Spec.* 1.32–50; Gregory, *Vit. Moys.* 2.219–55).[54] Gregory urges that one should always rekindle the desire to see God (*Vit. Moys.* 2.239), and in the same way Philo remarks that Moses keeps his desire to see God aflame (*Spec.* 1.50). A noticeable difference is that Gregory makes it clear that the endless ascent of the soul is the consequence of God's infinity. Because God is without any limit, the ascent of the soul to God is also without

---

[53] Philo: *Post.* 14; *Mut.* 7; Gregory, e.g. *Cant.* GNO VI, 181.4–21, 322.11–323.9; *Inscr. Psal.* GNO V, 44.18–19; *Vit. Moys.* 2.163-64. See I. Gobry, "La ténèbre (γνόφος): l'héritage alexandrin de Saint Grégoire de Nysse," *Diotima: Revue de recherche philosophique* 19 (1991): 79–82; D. Carabine, "Gregory of Nyssa on the Incomprehensibility of God," in *The Relationship between Neoplatonism and Christianity*, ed. T. Finan and V. Twomey (Dublin: Four Courts Press, 1992), 79–99; Y. de Andia, *Henosis: L'union à Dieu chez Denys l'Aréopagite*, PhA 71 (Leiden: Brill, 1996), 334–40; Geljon, *Philonic Exegesis*, 128–34; Ramelli, "Philosophical Allegoresis," 88–89.

[54] A. Dihle, "Das Streben nach Vollkommenheit nach Philon und Gregor von Nyssa," in *Stimuli: Exegese und ihre Hermeneutik in Antike und Christentum: Festschrift für Ernst Dassmann*, JAC Ergänzungsband 23, ed. G. Schöllgen and C. Scholten (Münster: Aschendorffsche Verlagsbuchhandlung, 1996), 329–35, esp. 332–33; Geljon, *Philonic Exegesis*, 142–45; Ramelli, "Philosophical Allegoresis," 89–90.

end (*Vit. Moys.* 2.236–38). Both the Alexandrians Clement and Origen do discuss Exod 33:12–32 but not with reference to the endless ascent of the soul.

2. For Gregory God's incomprehensibility is rooted in his infinity, a concept which occupies an important place in his doctrine of God.[55] He is the first theologian to devote extensive discussion to the subject of God's infinity and to argue for it on a philosophical basis. For that reason Ekkehard Mühlenberg has claimed that Gregory was the "discoverer" of divine infinity.[56] His thesis has been criticized and it can be argued that in his presentation of divine infinity Gregory was able to link up with Philo.[57] It is true that Philo never explicitly calls God infinite, but in his writings there are certainly starting-points for the idea of divine infinity. The Jewish exegete describes God's blessings as uncircumscribed (ἀπερίγραφοι; *Opif.* 21; *Her.* 31), that is being without limits. In *Praem.* 85 he calls eternity uncircumscribed (ἀπερίγραφος) and without boundaries (ἀόριστος) and in one passage God himself is even called uncircumscribed (*Sacr.* 59). These references are indications that Philo is prepared to attribute infinity to God himself as well. Generally, Philo gives prominence to God's transcendence and within this context he states that God is enclosing, not enclosed (*Leg.* 1.44). God fills and encloses all other things, but he himself is enclosed by nothing else, since he is one and he himself is the whole. W. R. Schoedel has rightly argued that by underlining God's transcendence in this way Philo creates a context where the notion of divine infinity can easily emerge.[58]

3. In *Eun.* 2.85–105 Gregory interprets Abraham's migration from his country as the endless quest for the knowledge of God. God's nature is, however, incomprehensible and the ascent requires the mediation of faith. Gregory is here depending on both Philo and Origen. The allegory of Abraham's migration as the quest for God is rooted in Philo's *Migr.* The emphasis on Abraham's faith that was credited to him as righteousness reflects Origen's discussion in his *Commentary on Romans* (4.2–3). The distinction between God's essence, which is unknown, and his existence has its origins in both Philo and Origen (Gregory, *Eun.* 2.95–98; Philo, *Post.* 167–69; *Fug.* 161–65).[59]

4. Both in Philo and in Gregory the idea of the divine Logos occupies a prominent place but at the same time there is an essential difference between the two

---

[55] Gregory discusses the doctrine in, among others, *Eun.* 1.167–71, 359–69, 574, 2.236, 446–68, 3.1.103–7; *Cant* 5, GNO VI, 157.14–21. See further Th. Böhm, *Theoria Unendlichkeit Aufstieg: Philosophische Implikationen zu De Vita Moysis von Gregor von Nyssa*, VCSup 35 (Leiden: Brill, 1996), 107–231; L. Karfíková, "Infinity," in *The Brill Dictionary*, 423–26; O. Sferlea, "À propos de l'infinité divine dans le débat trinitaire du Contra Eunome III: le noyau de la réfutation est-il philosophique ou bien scripturarie?," in *Gregory of Nyssa, Contra Eunomium III*, 675–85.

[56] E. Mühlenberg, *Die Unendlichkeit Gottes bei Gregor von Nyssa: Gregors Kritik am Gottesbegriff der klassischen Metaphysik*, Forschungen zur Kirchen- und Dogmengeschichte 16 (Göttingen: Vandenhoeck & Ruprecht, 1966), 19, 26–28, 47, 50.

[57] A. C. Geljon, "Divine Infinity in Gregory of Nyssa and Philo of Alexandria," *VC* 59 (2005): 152–77.

[58] W. R. Schoedel, "Enclosing, Not Enclosed: The Early Christian Doctrine of God," in *Early Christian Literature and the Classical Intellectual Tradition*, ed. W. R. Schoedel and R. L. Wilken (Paris: Beauchesne, 1979), 75–86, esp. 75–76.

[59] Ramelli, "Allegorical Allegoresis," 83–84.

thinkers.[60] In general terms, in Philo the Logos may be regarded as that aspect of the transcendent God that is directed towards creation. Sometimes, however, the Logos becomes a separate hypostasis, which appears to exist outside God and stands on an intermediate level between God and creatures. In this perspective Philo calls the Logos God's first-born, the eldest of the angels and the archangel (*Conf.* 146), while God himself is presented as the source of the Logos (*Det.* 82; *Post.* 69), which would indicate that the Logos is subordinated to God. Although there is a similarity between the Logos in Philo and in the Christian tradition of Gregory, their conceptions of the Logos are very different. In Philo the Logos stands on a lower ontological level than God himself and is never called ὁ ὤν. In Gregory's view the Logos, who as God's Son is Christ, has to be placed on the same level of being as God the Father and so could be called ὁ ὤν, as appears from his interpretation of the appearance of God in the burning bush, where God makes himself known as ὁ ὤν (Exod 3).[61] In his interpretation the burning bush shows the mystery of the Lord's incarnation. He who is, appears in the bush (*Vit. Moys.* 2.20–23). Arguing in *Eun.* that Christ can be called an angel he states that in Exod 3 the name angel is used for him who is (*Eun.* 3.9.37). Gregory sees Philo's position presented in the doctrine of Eunomius and his followers, to whom he refers as the new Judaism (*Eun.* 3.7.9, the passage with a direct reference to Philo, see above, p. 183). In his view they refuse to attribute real being to the Son and so they deny his existence (*Eun.* 1.179). Gregory strongly defends the Nicene creed, which asserts the true godhead of God the Son.

5. A notion that is also common to both Philo and Gregory is the description of mystical experience as "sober drunkenness." This oxymoron (μέθη νηφάλιος) was if not invented by Philo[62] certainly promulgated by him and so passed via Origen (*Comm. Io.* 1.30.206) to Gregory. Gregory presents David, Paul, and Peter as examples of people who experienced sober drunkenness.[63]

6. Gregory characterizes human being as standing on the border line (μεθόριος) between the sensible and the intelligible worlds (*Cant.* 11, GNO VI, 333.13–15; *Beat.* 8, GNO VII/2, 164.16–17). This border does not represent a transition from one realm to the other, but rather it emphasizes the opposed character of both worlds. Being on the border line the human soul has the freedom to choose between good and evil and between the intelligible and the sensible world. Gregory is following Philo, who also describes the human being as standing on the border line between mortal and immortal nature. He is mortal in respect of the body, and immortal in respect of the

---

[60] M. Azkoul, *St. Gregory of Nyssa and the Tradition of the Fathers* (Lewiston: Mellen Press, 1995), 103–37; Geljon, *Philonic Exegesis*, 56–58; Ramelli, "Philosophical Allegoresis," 85–86.

[61] A. C. Geljon, "Philo of Alexandria and Gregory of Nyssa on Moses at the Burning Bush," in *The Revelation of the Name YHWH to Moses*, Themes in Biblical Narrative 9, ed. G. H. van Kooten (Leiden: Brill, 2006), 225–36.

[62] *Leg.* 1.84, 3.82; *Ebr.* 148; *Fug.* 32, 166; *Opif.* 71; *Mos.* 1.187; *Prob.* 13. The classical study is H. Lewy, *Sobria Ebrietas: Untersuchungen zur Geschichte der antiken Mystik* (Gießen: Töpelmann, 1929). According to Lewy the origin of the theme lies in Philo. It is, however, also found in an epigram on Cleopatra's ring (*Anthologia Palatina* 9.752), which is attributed to Asclepiades of Samos (c.300 BCE) by K. J. Gutzwiller, "Cleopatra's Ring," *GRBS* 36 (1995): 383–98.

[63] *Cant.* 10, GNO VI, 308–9; cf. *Cant.* 5, GNO VI, 156.18; 12, GNO VI, 362.12; *Ascens.* GNO IX, 324.18–20.

mind (*Opif.* 135). Gregory does not so much assert that human being belongs to two worlds, but rather that he has the freedom to lean towards one side or another side.[64]

11.3 Gregory of Nazianzus

Being of about the same age as Basil, Gregory was educated in Cappodocian Caesarea and later on studied in Caesarea in Palestine and in Alexandria.[65] In the last-named city he was able to acquaint himself with the Alexandrian theological tradition. After finishing his studies in Athens, where he became a friend of Basil, he was active as a presbyter in Cappadocia. He alternated his pastoral activities with long periods of contemplative solitude. From 379 until 381 he served as bishop in Constantinople, where he delivered his famous theological orations.

Because of the thorough education that he enjoyed and his studies in Alexandria, it may be assumed that he was at least to some extent familiar with Philo's treatises, although in contrast to the two other Cappadocians he never refers to Philo by name. There has rarely been any research on the relationship between Gregory and Philo with the exception of one lengthy study by Francesco Trisoglio.[66] In his research the Italian scholar focuses on *Oratio* 14, which is devoted to the theme of loving the poor.[67] First he draws up a sheer endless list of conceptual parallels between Gregory's speech and Philo's treatises, some of which are commonplaces.[68] As an example we can mention the parallels which use the imagery of the body as prison of the soul.[69] Gregory employs the verb συνζεύγνυμι to indicate the connection of the soul with the body (865A) and Philo, who also sketches this image, uses the same verb (*Post.* 60; *Her.* 92). Both writers also employ the verb συνδέω within this context (868A; *Leg.* 1.108, 3.72). Gregory regards the body as a kindly enemy and a treacherous friend (865B). In the same way Philo describes the body as wicked and plotting against the soul (*Leg.* 3.69). Gregory's picture of human beings as contained in a lowly body is reminiscent of Philo's description of the mind as contained in the body as in a vessel (869B; *Migr.* 193). Secondly, Trisoglio lists lexical parallels between the two authors, for example the expression δοῦναι τὰ πρεσβεῖα (860A; *Post.* 63) and the combination of ἄτακτον καὶ ἀνώμαλον (900C; *Opif.* 97).[70] On the basis of these similarities and external evidence (Gregory's education for instance) he concludes that Gregory had a profound acquaintance with Philo's writings.[71]

---

[64] Daniélou, "La notion de confins"; Runia, *Philo of Alexandria: On the Creation*, 329; Ramelli, "Philosophical Allegoresis," 95–96; B. S. Santos, "A natureza do homem como *fronteira* (*methórios*) em Fílon de Alexandria e Gregório de Nissa," *Revista de Filosofia Aurora* 24 (2012): 597–613.

[65] For his life, see B. E. Daley, *Gregory of Nazianzus*, The Early Church Fathers (London: Routledge, 2006), 1–26.

[66] F. Trisoglio, "Filone Alessandrino e l'esegesi Christina," *ANRW* 2.21.1, ed. W. Haase (Berlin: de Gruyter, 1984), 588–730.

[67] Since there is no modern edition of this oration we still have to use Migne PG 35.858–910.

[68] Trisoglio, "Filone Alessandrino," 600–79.

[69] Trisoglio, "Filone Alessandrino," 611, 613, 617, 620.

[70] Trisoglio, "Filone Alessandrino," 679–87.

[71] Trisoglio, "Filone Alessandrino," 694–96.

Trisoglio's research has been criticized by David Runia because he fails to demonstrate that Gregory actually alludes to any particular passage in Philo and the parallels are always general.[72] What is more, Trisoglio does not consider the relevant thematic or terminological tradition by which Gregory may be influenced. Trisoglio draws a parallel between Gregory's picture of lepers as ἄνθρωποι νεκροὶ καὶ ζῶντες (869A) and Philo's ζῶντες ἔνιοι τεθνήκασι καὶ τεθνηκότες (*Fug.* 55), but he does not refer to the Heraclitean provenance of this image. Runia concludes that it can be considered likely that Gregory studied Philo's writings, but that this study did not result in allusions to or adaptations of particular passages.

Another Italian scholar Claudio Moreschini agrees with Runia's criticism of Trisoglio's study, but he argues that Gregory has taken over some doctrines from Philo, for instance the notion of God's incomprehensibility and his simplicity.[73] He also argues that Gregory borrows the allegorical interpretation of the trees in paradise as Adam's thought from Philo (*Or.* 38.12; *Plant.* 36–37).[74]

11.4 Conclusion

After this brief presentation of Philo's influence on the Cappadocians we are in a position to make some concluding remarks. Of the three Cappadocian theologians Gregory of Nyssa employs Philo the most, but his attitude to Philo is ambiguous. On the one hand, he criticizes Philo's doctrine of the divine Logos, seeing a kinship between Philo's thought and the ideas of his adversary Eunomius, on the other hand, he takes over and reworks Philonic allegories without referring to him by name. In addition he develops a negative theology, in which God is seen as incomprehensible, unnameable, and infinite, an approach that has its starting points in the writings of the Jewish Alexandrian exegete. Gregory's brother Basil was also acquainted with Philo's writings—he names him once—and uses them among others as a source in his homilies on the creation account. It is highly probable that their mutual friend Gregory of Nazianzus was also familiar with Philo's writings, but there are no clear borrowings in his orations. The Cappadocians were able to incorporate Philonic exegesis and theological themes in their own interpretation without hesitation, but also without referring to his name. This shows that Philo's exegesis has become an integral part of the Christian exegetical tradition. But when the focus is on the Jew Philo and his Jewishness, their attitude is rather critical.

---

[72] Runia, *Philo in Early Christian Literature*, 241–43.
[73] C. Moreschini, *Filosofia e Letteratura in Gregorio di Nazianzio* (Milan: Vita e Pensiero, 1997), 38, 48; Moreschini, "Further Considerations," 600.
[74] C. Moreschini and P. Gallay, *Grégoire de Nazianze: Discours 38–41*, SC 358 (Paris: Cerf, 1990), 128 n. 1; Moreschini, "Further Considerations," 600–601.

12
Isidore of Pelusium

Madalina Toca and Johan Leemans

Isidore of Pelusium (c.360–440 CE) spent the first part of his life in the city of Pelusium, the capital of Augustamnica I, in the region of the Nile delta. For the longest part of his life he was a monk not too far away from the city and still in permanent contact with life in Pelusium through a lively correspondence (c.2,000 letters extant). His letters reveal a good knowledge of Philo of Alexandria, whom he quotes a few times and whose writings he alludes to even more frequently. In this chapter we will give a survey and analysis of all borrowings from and references to Philo in Isidore's letters. Much of the groundwork has already been done in two major articles by David Runia, who discusses in considerable detail the five letters in which the Philonic borrowings are unmistakable.[1] The borrowings brought to light by Ludwig Früchtel[2] in two articles of 1938 have not been studied in depth so far, and some more may be gleaned from editions and translations of (or secondary literature on) Isidore or Philo, as will be seen below. All those instances of Isidore's Philo-reception will be revisited.

Isidore's Philo-reception should be assessed within the wider framework of his *paideia*. His letter-corpus bears testimony to an extensive knowledge of non-Christian and Christian culture. Among the Christian authors he is familiar with are Clement of Alexandria, Origen, Basil of Caesarea, Gregory of Nazianzus, and, above all, John Chrysostom. His acquaintance with the classical authors seems to have been mainly indirect, through compendia and florilegia, with an obvious penchant for Demosthenes, but Plato and Xenophon are also present in his oeuvre. While an anti-Jewish bias shared with many Christian authors is not absent in his letters, he is well informed and not unsympathetic at all towards Judaism and its representatives. There is a notable presence of Flavius Josephus but more strongly of Philo of Alexandria. In short: Philo is but one of Isidore's authors of reference.[3]

---

[1] D. T. Runia's articles "Philo of Alexandria in Five Letters of Isidore of Pelusium" and "'Where, Tell Me, Is the Jew ... ?': Basil, Philo and Isidore of Pelusium" are both reprinted in his collected essays volume *Philo and the Church Fathers*, VCSup 32 (Leiden: Brill, 1995), 155–81, 126–43, and summarized in his *Philo in Early Christian Literature: A Survey* (Assen: Van Gorcum, 1993), 203–9.

[2] L. Früchtel, "Isidoros von Pelusion als Benützer des Clemens Alexandrinus und anderer Quellen," *Philologische Wochenschrift* 58 (1938): 61–64, and "Neue Quellennachweise zu Isidoros von Pelusion," *Philologische Wochenschrift* 58 (1938): 764–68. D. T. Runia mentions these parallels in *Philo in Early Christian Literature*, 205 n. 112.

[3] The most important point of reference for Isidore remains P. Évieux, *Isidore de Péluse*, ThH 99 (Paris: Beauchesne, 1995). For a good survey of Isidore's *paideia*, see U. Treu, "Isidor II (von Pelusium)," *RAC* 18 (1998): 982–1002; and L. Bayer, *Isidors von Pelusium klassische Bildung* (Paderborn: F. Schöningh, 1915).

The aim of this chapter is to offer a fresh synthetic overview on Isidore's Philo-reception. We will be mainly drawing on the above-mentioned earlier research by Früchtel and Runia, with two further parallels drawn from the Cohn-Wendland edition of Philo,[4] and will be also briefly referring to the use of Philo in the catenae-literature, especially to the instances where excerpts from Philo are intertwined with those from Isidore, as identified by F. Petit.[5] Except for Runia's work, none of these parallels had yet received any treatment.

As further secondary literature on the topic, a few more contributions by Runia should be mentioned. In a 2002 article, he discusses Philo's use by Didymus the Blind and Isidore of Pelusium, as a legacy of the Alexandrian tradition,[6] and still elsewhere he briefly refers to Isidore's appraisal of Philo's theology.[7] In his relatively recent article on Philo in Byzantium,[8] Runia describes his use of the *Thesaurus Linguae Graecae* for finding (traces of) Philo in the works of Byzantine authors from 500 up to 1500 CE, starting mainly from the named references to Philo, but not exclusively so. Since then the TLG has updated its features, and it currently supports the textual comparison of two works, highlighting similar strings of texts. The tool is called "parallel browsing."[9] However, there are also limitations to it. A first constraint has to do with the incomplete nature of the material added to the TLG database. Fortunately for Isidore of Pelusium, the third SC volume (SC 586: letters 1701–2000) has been taken up recently, which means that, as of April 2020, the entire corpus is incorporated in the TLG database. The situation is perhaps less clear for Philo's works, especially for the most problematic ones, or for those that only survive in fragments. A second deterrent is the fact that this comparison would not indicate loose paraphrases of Philo in Isidore's letters ("false negatives") and at the same time would generate a number of matches which do not point to Isidore's use of Philo ("false positives"). In fact, the majority of the results are false positives as the similarities consist in their shared usage of the same Old Testament passages, though in different contexts and with different interpretations. However, an important addition of the TLG database is the updating of its "proximity search" tool, which allows for "word forms," "*lemmata*" or "texts" searches in proximity, and of its *lemma* recognition. This tool is particularly helpful in verifying whether a particular sequence of *lemmata* is only used by a specific author, or shared by others as well, allowing for a better understanding of possible textual filiations. Overall, for this contribution, the TLG searches were useful methodologically for drawing attention

---

[4] L. Cohn, P. Wendland, and S. Reiter, eds, *Philonis Alexandrini opera quae supersunt* (Berlin: Georg Reimer, 1902), 4:98–99 and (Berlin: Georg Reimer, 1906), 5:282.

[5] F. Petit, *La Chaîne sur l'Exode*, Vol. IV: *fonds caténique ancien (Exode 15,22–40,32)*, Traditio Exegetica Graeca 11 (Leuven: Peeters, 2001), 124.

[6] D. T. Runia, "One of Us or One of Them? Christian Reception of Philo the Jew in Egypt," in *Shem in the Tents of Japheth: Essays on the Encounter of Judaism and Hellenism*, ed. J. L. Kugel, JSJSup 74 (Leiden: Brill, 2002), 203–22.

[7] D. T. Runia, "Philo of Alexandria," in *The First Christian Theologians: An Introduction to Theology in the Early Church*, ed. G. R. Evans (Malden, MA: Blackwell, 2004), 77–84.

[8] D. T. Runia, "Philo in Byzantium," *VC* 70 (2016): 259–81.

[9] Isidore is registered as "Isidorus Pelusiota {2741}" and Philo of Alexandria as "Philo Judaeus {0018}."

to the possibility of false positives (i.e. shared use of pre-existing material, biblical or gnomic), and for identifying new parallels between the two authors as well as parallels in other authors.

We will begin this chapter with a brief presentation of the five letters that contain clear, unambiguous references to Philo. As these have already been discussed in great detail by Runia,[10] this presentation will be rather concise and focus on the role the Philo-reference plays in the letter. The bulk of the chapter will then focus on the series of possible parallels between Isidore and Philo signaled by Früchtel and Cohn-Wendland, and we will be adding the intertwined usage of Philo and Isidore in the catenae-literature, all of which have remained so far unstudied.

12.1 Runia's "Five Letters": *Nominatim* References

Ep. 643 [2.143]: Addressed to a certain Paul, this long letter explains that the orthodox doctrine of the Trinity should steer a *via media* between divine oneness (as Judaism does) and divine threeness (as in Greek polytheism).[11] Isidore had in a previous letter already given his views on this matter to the same correspondent (*Ep.* 642 [2.142]) but, presumably honoring a request for a longer treatment of the matter, he now comes back to it at much greater length. Isidore seems to have two main goals. Firstly, he wants to demonstrate that the Old Testament contains numerous passages in which Judaism indicates an awareness of nuances in its strict monotheism. Many passages do indicate that next to the Father there are also other persons within the deity. Secondly, he brings Philo to the fore as an example thereof; in quite a few passages Philo, who is mentioned *nominatim* more than once, is used to demonstrate that within Judaism there is this awareness. In several instances Philo is "quoted" but it is difficult to find these passages in the Philonic œuvre as we have it today. In any case, this letter is an important testimony of the deep influence of Philo, considered a paradigmatic figure within Judaism, carrying authority. Crucially, Isidore is not only familiar with Philo but takes it for granted that his name and authority also carry weight with his correspondent.

Ep. 770 [2.270]: This is a letter to a bishop Apollonius, who consulted Isidore on several occasions with exegetical questions. In this letter Isidore deals with the meaning of the word μήποτε in Isa 6:10 and quoted in Matt 13:15. Isidore defends the hypothesis that it means "*perhaps* they see with eyes and hear with ears," rather than "*lest*," as this latter interpretation would entail God actually wishing for them to remain blind and

---

[10] See esp. Runia, "Five Letters," 159–79. The first four letters were previously mentioned in the Cohn-Wendland edition (L. Cohn, *Philonis Alexandrini Opera quae supersunt*, vol. 1 [Berlin: Georg Reimer, 1896], cvii–cviii), and all of them in the article of Früchtel, "Neue Quellennachweise zu Isidoros," 764–65. On *Ep.* 643, see also more recently S. Berkmüller, *Schriftauslegung und Bildgebrauch bei Isidor von Pelusium*, AKG 143 (Berlin: de Gruyter, 2020), 106.

[11] For every letter we will refer to Évieux's numbering first, followed by PG 78's numbers in square brackets (Évieux, *Isidore de Péluse*, 411–18). For letters 1–1213 we will use the PG 78 edition, while for letters 1214–2000 the SC 422, 454, and 586 editions.

deaf. He brings forward four arguments: (1) utterances of the crowd of Jews about the Savior in John 7:25–26; (2) "the men of wisdom (σοφοί), of which Philo is reputed to be one" use μήποτε with the meaning "perhaps"; (3) the divinely inspired θεόπνευστος Paul does the same (2 Tim 2:24–25); (4) Sir 19:13. Strikingly, but not surprisingly for a Christian author, Philo is "only" one of the σοφοί, whereas Paul is styled as divinely inspired. Yet, the reference to Philo as such is also surprising: among the larger group of σοφοί, Philo is singled out and the confidence with which Isidore confirms that Philo used μήποτε with the meaning "perhaps" (as he indeed does, e.g. in *Abr.* 171; *Mos.* 1.280; and perhaps in *Fug.* 94) reveals an intimate knowledge of the Philonic writings. Also, the concern not to give an interpretation to scripture that is unworthy of God is Philonic (e.g. *Det.* 13; *Deus* 52). In conclusion: though only mentioned briefly, the *nominatim* reference to Philo does indicate Isidore's knowledge of Philo's writings and thought, but the extent of it remains unclear.

Ep. 819 [3.19]: In this letter to Athanasius, a priest of the church of Pelusium, Isidore provides his correspondent with some arguments in a dispute he had with "a Jew" who was of the opinion that "the Lawgiver [Moses] spoke his words with no more than the literal meaning." This indicates a discussion on theological topics between Jews and Christians in late antique Egypt, which was no isolated event. Quite often, as was probably also the case here, these discussions focused on whether it was legitimate to read the Old Testament in a Christological way, an issue of central importance for Christians in the development of Trinitarian theology and Christology. Isidore strongly supports the legitimacy of an allegorical reading of the Old Testament in support of which he refers to the testimony of two Jewish authoritative voices, which should carry substantial weight with Athanasius' Jewish conversation partner: "Philo the master of speculative thought and Josephus the great historian." Isidore is brief about Philo, merely mentioning that he "turns almost the entire Old Testament into allegory." This is, given Philo's focus on the Pentateuch, a slight exaggeration. Josephus, though, is quoted verbatim, as the introductory formula "as he writes explicitly" already indicates. What follows is a quotation from *A.J.* 1.24 in which it is stated that Moses sometimes used enigmatic language, in other instances allegory and in still other instances, straightforward literal speech. In this letter, Josephus' testimony is played out at much greater length than Philo's and it carries more weight for the intended purpose. Nevertheless, it remains that Philo is indeed mentioned as an authoritative Jewish author and as a master of allegorical exegesis.

Ep. 881 [3.81]: This is a letter to Zosimus, priest in Pelusium and a member of the circle of bishop Eusebius that led the local ecclesiastical community in the worst possible way, including corruption, simony and abuse of power, according to Isidore's criticisms in his many letters to these church leaders.[12] "I am not surprised that you, who are uneducated in all other matters, have also displayed your ignorance in this case." Thus begins Isidore's letter and the tone is representative for much of his other correspondence with Zosimus and his fellows. In *Ep.* 881 Isidore explains that there are

---

[12] Évieux, *Isidore de Péluse*, 206–23.

not only evil passions (with which Zosimus is presumably already well acquainted!) but also good and humane passions, such as mercy, that bring about a change in behavior from the worse to the better. Testimonies of three of Isidore's most favorite authorities are brought forward for corroboration and exhortation to Zosimus to adjust his behavior: Demosthenes, "Flavius Josephus," and Philo. First, he refers to Philip of Macedonia's decision to hand over the Olynthian prisoners because he was moved— which led to a change of heart—and he inserts a brief quotation from Demosthenes (*Fals. leg.* 195). Next, Isidore refers to Josephus, "a man highly distinguished for his learning and rhetorical ability." When describing the revolutionaries at their peak during the siege of Jerusalem, he observed that when harshness is hardened in practice, the human person becomes less and less accessible for good and humane passions. Isidore is allegedly quoting here from Flavius Josephus, in whose *Bellum Judaicum* the episode is described. The actual quotation, however, does not occur in Josephus but comes from Philo's *De Iosepho* 82. Apparently, Isidore was betrayed by his memory here. His third and final witness is Philo, "reputed, on account of the sublimity of his language, to be either the disciple or teacher of Plato." The example adduced is that of Moses, and the change of heart he went through after having slandered, "filled with righteous anger," "some Egyptians." Isidore inserts here a quotation from Philo but in fact it is a composite quotation from memory of bits and pieces that can be found in *De vita Moysis*. Both this composite quotation and the unwitting quotation from Philo ascribed by Isidore to Flavius Josephus bear testimony to his knowledge of and high esteem for the Philonic heritage.

Ep. 1757 [4.176]: In this very brief letter to Eulogius, one of Isidore's correspondents with an interest in theological matters, he draws heavily on Philo's writings and thought. It is a kind of pastiche: there are no direct quotations nor is Philo's name mentioned, yet the Philonic imprint on thought and terminology is clear. The letter cursorily deals with some main elements from the Pentateuch as a legal code, the opening of salvation history, and as pointing towards the eschaton. Philonic traces can be detected in the following elements. Moses is styled as "the hierophant" (e.g. *Spec.* 1.41), who did not write history for entertainment but intended to draw up a legal code (*Mos.* 2.48). This code opens with the Creator and his creating activity, so that humanity would not mistakenly venerate elements of the cosmos (*Opif.* 7; *Spec.* 1.13–20). The code also mentions the rewards of the pious and the punishments of the sinners (*Mos.* 2.45–53; possibly also *Opif.* 1–12; *Abr.* 1–2; and *Praem.* 1–3). On this basis Moses started his legislative work, laying out the law for his people so that they may strive for piety and justice: the events from the past (the creation narratives) are an exhortation to that effect (e.g. *Mos.* 2.51).

12.2 Früchtel's Examples with Further Parallels

Früchtel's first article mentions three possible parallels under the "miscellaneous" (*sonstiges*) category (*Ep.* 609 [2.109]–*Somn.* 2.164–65, *Ep.* 1631 [5.302]–*Anim.* 100, *Ep.* 1647 [4.6]–*QG* 3.48), while all the rest are mentioned in the second. As we shall demonstrate, some of these proved to be direct citations of Philo's works, but more often they are loose paraphrases, references to a shared Hellenistic background or simply shared gnomic material.

For instance, the parallel between *Ep.* 609 [2.109] and *Somn.* 2.164–65 rests on the notion that the consumption of wine (οἶνος with Isidore) or intoxicating drink (μέθυσμα with Philo) affects people in different ways and leads to different reactions. Beyond this general idea, there is virtually no verbatim agreement between the two in Greek, and further parallels can be found elsewhere, e.g. Demosthenes, *Fragmenta* 13 frag. 27; *Sententiae Pythagoreorum* no. 193; and Stobaeus, *Florilegium* 2.33.12.[13] This is a fairly clear example of closeness in content, without textual contact, which makes direct usage of Philo improbable and difficult to prove. The fact that there are textual parallels between Isidore and a few fragments from gnomic literature, makes one wonder whether he might have used one of these instead, or might have relied on his memory, though with four *lemmata* in a similar form direct usage of these compendia is highly possible.

Among Früchtel's examples, there are several other cases where the parallels between Philo and Isidore gravitate around gnomic material or other similar topoi. *Ep.* 904 [3.104] and *Somn.* 2.147 and *QG* 2.60 present parallel material around a war metaphor: internal war is worse than external war (*Ep.* 904 [3.104]): "There is nothing more painful (ἀργαλεώτερον) than war among one's people (ἐμφυλίου πολέμου)," *Somn.* 2.147: "The civil war (ἐμφύλιον πόλεμον) … [is] the cruellest (ἀργαλεώτατον) of wars," and *QG* 2.60: "For family strife is even worse than that of strangers (ξένων / ἀλλοτρίων)." There is another Isidorian parallel, *Ep.* 1225 [5.10], "In our own being, the war is more painful than the civil war" (ἔνθα ὁ πόλεμος ἀργαλεώτερός ἐστι τοῦ ἐμφυλίου) and, according to a TLG search, there is no other place where the three terms ἐμφύλιος, πόλεμος, and ἀργαλέος are used in proximity, although the image of war among one's people is widely used (Plutarch, Dio Cassius, Flavius Josephus, Polybius, Appianus, Gregory of Nyssa). The fact that their uses of the same war metaphor do not coincide suggests that Isidore might draw on a shared background rather than directly depending on Philonic material.

Similarly, *Ep.* 960 [3.160] and *Mos.* 1.31 both refer to God finding a way where there is none (ἐν ἀπόροις πόρον εὑρεῖν). Früchtel signaled this as an instance of Isidore's use of Philo,[14] but this is not entirely plausible, since there is no verbatim equivalence between the two passages beyond this expression, and the biblical episodes referred to by the two authors are also different: Gen 12:11–19 in Isidore; Exod 14:10–14 in Philo.

---

[13] Isid., *Ep.* 2.109: Ἐπειδὴ γὰρ μόνων τῶν ὑγρῶν ἠθοποιὸν ὁ **οἶνός** ἐστι, **κίρναται τρόπον** τινὰ τοῖς **τρόποις** τῶν **χρωμένων**. Demost., *Fragmenta* 13 frag. 27: Ὥσπερ οἶνος κιρνᾶται τοῖς τῶν πινόντων **τρόποις**, οὕτω καὶ φιλία τοῖς τῶν **χρωμένων** ἤθεσιν. Stobaeus, *Flor.* 2.33.12: Ὥσπερ ὁ **οἶνος κιρνᾶται** τοῖς τῶν πινόντων **τρόποις**, οὕτω καὶ φιλία τοῖς τῶν **χρωμένων** ἤθεσι (= *Sententiae Pythag.* 193).

[14] Früchtel, "Neue Quellennachweise zu Isidoros," 765. He also mentions a possible link with Euripides' tragedy, probably referring to *Iphigenia Taurica* 895: "Who, either god or mortal or something unexpected, might accomplish a way that is no way (πόρον ἄπορον ἐξανύσας), and reveal a release from troubles for the only two children of the house of Atreus?," in *Euripides: The Complete Greek Drama*, ed. W. J. Oates and E. O'Neill, Jr, vol. 1. *Iphigenia in Tauris*, trans. R. Potter (New York: Random House, 1938), 1059ff.

Moreover, the idea appears elsewhere: for instance, John Chrysostom uses it in *In Genesim* 32.7 and 51.3,[15] also in connection with Abraham and Sarah's episode, which is in this sense a better parallel, and makes for a weak basis for arguing that Isidore used Philo. Isidore might have relied on his memory of Philo, on commonly known expressions (Mark 10:27), or he might have actually drawn on Chrysostom with whom he also shares the biblical theme he discusses.

The point of contact between *Ep.* 1156 [3.356] ("But envy brought forth war against the good deeds," **Φθόνος γὰρ ταῖς εὐπραγίαις** ἀντιστρατεύεσθαι πέφυκεν) and *Ios.* 5 ("envy, which is ever the enemy of high success … ," **Φθόνος ὁ ἀεὶ ταῖς μεγάλαις εὐπραγίαις** ἀντίπαλος) also proved to be a gnomic notion: envy is the enemy of welfare or good deeds, with parallels (closer to Philo) in Epiphanius, *Panarion* 3.416,[16] and Nilus of Ancyra, *Ep.* 1.257, possibly reminiscent of Pindar's *Pythian Odes* 7.14–15.[17] Since the evidence is scarce and there are numerous authors that use a combination of these words, this proposed parallel too remains a weak conjecture. While the formulations are quite close to one another and the meaning is clearly the same, the two authors use it in different exegetical contexts (Isidore in relation to Dan 6:3, Philo with regard to Gen 37:8–11).

Similarly, the proposed parallel between *Ep.* 1162 [3.362] ("just as a word without an action is incomplete, so is an action without a word," Ὥσπερ λόγος ἄπρακτος ἀτελής· οὕτως καὶ πρᾶξις ἄλογος) and *QE* 2.110 ("to speak without acting is ineffective, τὸ λέγειν ἄνευ τοῦ πράττειν ἀτελές)[18] revolves around the notion that action without word and word without action are equally ineffective, used in different contexts, and with other (perhaps more likely) patristic parallels. Früchtel rightly notes that Isidore repeatedly uses this comparison[19] and points out a possible parallel in Demosthenes, *Olynthiac* 2.12.[20] There is however a closer textual equivalence with Gregory of Nazianzus' *Funebris oratio in laudem Basilii* 43.3,[21] rendering quite unlikely that for *Ep.* 1162 [3.362] Isidore drew directly from Philo, as Gregory is a more suitable candidate. However, neither Isidore's

---

[15] PG 53: 303 and PG 54: 455. Other possible parallels: John Chrysostom, *Ad Stagirium* (PG 47: 438) and *De Sacerdotio* 1.4, 1.7 (SC 272: 86, and 98).

[16] "For this is the work of the devil, who envied our father Adam at the beginning and is the enemy of all men—as certain wise men have said, envy is always the opponent of great successes" (καὶ γὰρ τοῦτό ἐστι τὸ ἔργον αὐτοῦ, τοῦ φθονήσαντος ἀπ' ἀρχῆς τῷ πατρὶ ἡμῶν Ἀδὰμ καὶ πᾶσιν ἀνθρώποις ἐχθραίνοντος, ὡς καί που <ὑπό> τινων σοφῶν εἴρηται ὅτι φθόνος ἀεὶ ταῖς μεγάλαις εὐπραγίαις ἀντίπαλος). See F. Williams, *The Panarion of Epiphanius of Salamis, Books II and III: De Fide* (Leiden: Brill, 2013), 582.

[17] This possible parallel is mentioned by Williams, *The Panarion*, at 582: "I feel some rejoicing at a new success [ἐμποψία]; but I am grieved that envy is the requital for good works [φθόνον ἀμειβόμενον τὰ καλὰ ἔργα]."

[18] This fragment was first identified by Früchtel (1938) as coming from *QE* 2.110. Both Harris (1886) and Petit (1978) marked it as an "unidentified fragment." In *Fragments of Philo Judaeus* (Cambridge: Cambridge University Press, 1886), 108, J. R. Harris mentions that it stems from Codex Rupefucaldinus (= Berlin gr. 46), f. 30 and F. Petit, *Quaestiones in Genesim et in Exodum: Fragmenta graeca*, Les Oeuvres de Philon d'Alexandrie 33 (Paris: Cerf, 1978), 303, leaves it as an "unidentified fragment" (= *QE* frag. 27). See J. R. Royse, *The Spurious Texts of Philo of Alexandria* (Leiden: Brill, 1991), 36–37, 209, 222.

[19] Früchtel, "Neue Quellennachweise zu Isidoros," 766.

[20] In *Ep.* 1618 [4.85], Isidore directly quotes Demosthenes: μαρτυρεῖ καὶ Δημοσθένης λέγων ὡς 'Ἅπας μὲν λόγος, ἂν ἀπῇ τὰ ἔργα, μάταιόν τι φαίνεται καὶ κενόν.' With the exception of ἔργα where Demosthenes has πράγματα, the quotation is accurate. Isidore also quotes here from the letter to Titus: Θεὸν ὁμολογοῦσιν εἰδέναι, τοῖς δὲ ἔργοις ἀρνοῦνται.

[21] Gregory of Nazianzus, *Funebris oratio* 43.3: "For it is equally ineffective an action without a word, and a word without action" (καὶ γὰρ ὁμοίως ἀτελὲς ἄλογος πρᾶξις καὶ λόγος ἄπρακτος).

nor Gregory's fragments seem to directly reflect Philo's *QE* 2.110, and the idea they emphasize could equally be a topos given its more aphoristic nature.

Similar considerations can be put forth for the parallels suggested between *Ep.* 1450 [5.169] and *Mos.* 2.27 ("good things shine even if envy can briefly overshadow them"), *Ep.* 1647 [4.6] and *QG* 3.48 ("self-conceit is the eradication of improvement"), and *Ep.* 1809 [4.155] and *Spec.* 1.339 and *Mut.*17 ("learning late is better than ignorance").[22] In all cases it is not impossible that Isidore used Philo. Yet the fact that the shared material is limited, gnomic in nature, and used in different contexts for differing aims, with other parallels available as sometimes more likely sources for Isidore, makes them less safe as witnesses for Isidore's use of Philo since shared use of common sources or Isidore's use of different sources cannot be ruled out.

The remaining examples will be discussed in more detail since the usage of Philo is either very likely or certain.[23]

Isid., *Ep.* 1043 [3.243]:

The [word] 'woman' (γυνή) is connected with 'birth' (γονήν). She shall be called 'woman' (γυνή), that is to say 'begetter' (γονίμη), because she was taken from her man who wants to make [her] fertile (γόνιμον ποιεῖν).

Philo, *QG* 1.28:

And the woman is called the power of giving birth with fecundity, and truly so; either because after receiving the seed, she conceives and gives birth, or, as the prophet says, because she came from man .... (LCL trans.)

Isidore offers an interpretation on Gen 2:23 ("she shall be called woman, because she was taken out of man") as an exercise in etymology, linking the term "woman" (γυνή) to her role as a begetter (γονίμη): as a result of the man's union with a virgin (παρθένος), she becomes a woman (γυνή), and therefore able to beget (γονίμη). The relationship between the man and the woman is further described with an agricultural metaphor: the fertile soil is sown and impregnated by the seed. Isidore then adds several relational analogies ("father-children," "master-servant") in order to show that when one thinks of a "man," one immediately implies a "woman."

---

[22] *Ep.* 1809: "Learning late is better than staying ignorant" (κρεῖττον γὰρ ὀψιμαθεῖς ἢ ἀμαθεῖς εἶναι), Philo, *Spec.* 1.339: "... the contemplation of which creates a subtle intelligence and generates a great thirst for knowledge" (... ὧν ἡ θέα περιττὴν φρόνησιν ἐξειργάσατο καὶ πολὺν ἵμερον ἐπιστήμης ἐγέννησε), and *Mut.* 17: "The king has been manifested, king indeed from the first, but hitherto unrecognized by the soul, which so long unschooled has not remained in ignorance for ever" (ἐφάνη ὁ βασιλεύς, ἐξ ἀρχῆς μὲν ὤν, οὔπω δὲ τῇ ψυχῇ γνωριζόμενος, ἢ καὶ ὀψιμαθὴς μέν, οὐ μὴν εἰσάπαν ἀμαθὴς διετέλεσεν). There are several other parallels, closer to Isidore: Clitarchus, *Sententiae* 81; Sextus Empiricus, *Adversus mathematicos* 6.13; *Vita Aesopi* 109; Libanius, *Ep.* 1352.

[23] *Ep.* 715 [2.215] and *Spec.* 3.77–78 should be ruled out as a false positive, since the shared material is exclusively biblical (a quotation of Deut 22:27).

Although Philo's Greek fragment is lost, and what we rely on is a reconstruction from the Armenian, in his exegesis of Gen 2:23 he uses both the etymological association between "woman" (կին) and "the power of giving birth (զորութիւն ծնունելոյ)," and the fact that the begetting happens through the insemination of the seed (սերմն). For both of them the role of man as the inseminator is seen as a central one, while the woman is the receiver of the generational seed, through which she becomes a "begetter."[24] There are therefore three points of contact between Isidore and Philo's passages: the connection between γυνή and γεννάω, the function of the man's seed, and the fact that both of these points are put forward as exegetical interpretations on Gen 2:23.

Following Aucher's Armenian edition (1826, p. 20), Früchtel also signals the association between "woman" and "begetting" in Plato, *Cratylus* 414A.[25] However, the connection between the Gen 2:23 exegesis and the "etymological" interpretative key are common to Isidore and Philo only, which makes it a very likely case of borrowing.[26]

Isid., *Ep.* 1088 [3.288]:

For a shameless eye (ὄμμα ἀναιδές) and an elevated neck (αὐχὴν μετέωρος) and a continuous move of the eyebrows (ὀφρύων συνεχὴς κίνησις) and a pompous walk (βάδισμα σεσοβημένον) and not blushing at any shame (τὸ ἐπὶ μηδενὶ τῶν αἰσχρῶν ἐρυθριᾶν) is proof of a lewd soul (τεκμήριον ψυχῆς ἐστιν αἰσχίστης) which impresses on the body the invisible stamp of one's own passions (τοὺς ἀφανεῖς τῶν οἰκείων παθῶν χαρακτῆρας ἐντυπούσης τῷ σώματι).

Philo, *QG* 4.99:

But a shameless look (ἀναιδὲς βλέμμα) and an elevated neck (μετέωρος αὐχήν) and a continuous movement of the eyebrows (συνεχὴς κίνησις ὀφρύων) and a womanish walk (βάδισμα σεσοβημένον) and not blushing at, or being ashamed of, any evil at all (τὸ ἐπὶ μηδενὶ τῶν φαύλων ἐρυθριᾶν) is the sign of a lewd soul (σημεῖά ἐστι ψυχῆς αἰσχίστης), which clearly pictures and describes the forms of its invisible disgraces on its visible body (τοὺς ἀφανεῖς τῶν οἰκείων ὀνείδων τύπους ἐγγραφούσης τῷ φανερῷ σώματι).[27] (LCL trans.)

In *QG* 4.99, Philo explains why "[the scripture] uses a double expression" when referring to the virgin in Gen 24:16: "a virgin, whom no man had known." According to Philo, one expression would be in relation to her body and the other to her soul. He adds that the repetition is not at all "superfluous," but "necessary" because it strengthens both the "beauty of

---

[24] For Philo, see D. Sly, *Philo's Alexandria* (London: Routledge, 1996), 161, and W. Loader, *Philo, Josephus, and the Testaments on Sexuality* (Grand Rapids: Eerdmans, 2011), 28.
[25] "The word 'woman' (γυνή) seems to me to be much the same as 'birth' (γονή)" ('γυνὴ' δὲ γονή μοι φαίνεται βούλεσθαι εἶναι.)
[26] Gen 2:23 is also interpreted by Theophilus, *Ad Autolycum* 2.20, Chrysostom, *Hom. Gen.* 15, Epiphanius, *Panarion* 1.9.11, etc. though with no points of contact with Isidore of Pelusium.
[27] For the Greek text: Petit, *Quaestiones in Genesim et in Exodum*, 175–76.

form" and of the soul. Philo continues that just as the inner beauty is visible on the outside, a lustful soul leaves its imprint on the body as well. It is in this image of the disgraceful bodily appearance as a sign of a lustful soul that Philo's and Isidore's texts converge.

Isidore's letter addressed to two characters both named "Nilammon" is an admonishment against the impious behaviors of the addressees, without any allusion to the Genesis context. It is interesting to see how Isidore directly quotes Philo, extracting the quotation from its Philonic context, and integrating it in a completely different one.[28]

Isid., *Ep.* 979 [3.179]: "…a cultivated look (βλέμμα ἥμερον), and a restrained eyebrow (ὀφρὺς κατεσταλμένη), and not a pompous walk (βάδισμα μὴ σεσοβημένον), and a needful cloth (ἱμάτιον χρειῶδες) …." As Früchtel points out, βάδισμα σεσοβημένον ("a pompous walk") is also present in Isidore's *Ep.* 979 [3.179], albeit preceded by a negation, as is also βλέμμα common to both Philo, *QG* 4.99, and Isid., *Ep.* 979 [3.179].[29] This example offers a high degree of lexical congruence, which points to a very likely direct usage of Philo on Isidore's part.

Isid., *Ep.* 1631 [5.302]:

It would not be just for those who did not act equally, to be assigned equally. It is a proof of equality and justice (Οὐδὲ γὰρ δίκαιον τοῖς μὴ τὸ ἴσον πεποιηκόσι τὸ ἴσον ἀπονεμηθῆναι· ἰσότητός ἐστι καὶ δικαιοσύνης ἀπόδειξις).

Philo, *Anim.* 100:

To grant equality to those who are not equals is the height of injustice (Τὸ νέμειν ἴσα τοῖς ἀνίσοις τῆς μεγίστης ἐστὶν ἀδικίας; in Armenian: Հաւասարութեանն բաշխելովն տայլով, անհաւագոյն անիրաւութեանց է).[30]

The text of Philo's *De animalibus* has only survived in Armenian. However, the corresponding fragment preserved in Greek in Parisinus gr. 923, fol. 208,[31] albeit minimal, allows us to presuppose the textual relationship between the two. In *Ep.* 1631 [5.302], Isidore discusses in a theological context the concepts of equality and justice, in contrast with unevenness and injustice. To him, it is a sign of equity that those who do not act equally should not be rewarded in the same way. Finally, Isidore adds an eschatological nuance and mentions that if unevenness in the earthly realm is conceded according to one's efforts, in the world to come it is a manifestation of justice.

In a different context, influenced by Stoic and Platonic philosophy,[32] Philo pleads that it is only natural for beings who have no reason to belong in a different category

---

[28] Finally, Philo inserts the distinction between the corruptible and incorruptible beings, and between the undefiled and the defiled, which is again not present in Isidore's letter.
[29] The same passage as in *QG* 4.99 appears also in John of Damascus, *Sacra parallela* (PG 96: 284), but this is rather a witness to Philo.
[30] Terian, *De Animalibus*, 218.
[31] Terian, *De Animalibus*, 200 and 218.
[32] Terian, *De Animalibus*, 201, and also his dissertation *Philonis Alexandrini De Animalibus: The Armenian Text with an Introduction, Translation, and Commentary* (Chico, CA: Scholars Press, 1981), 206.

than the rational ones, since forcing the concept of equality to what is unequal is unjust, and also that ascribing self-restraint to non-rational beings is an offence to humans.

What both texts have in common is the idea that comparing unequal things or forcing equality to things unequal is an injustice. Yet it is difficult to prove Isidore's as coming from Philo, or from a different (Stoic?) source. Their viewpoints are different—theological and eschatological for Isidore, and philosophical for Philo—and though there is some textual overlap between the two (οὐδὲ δίκαιον, δικαιοσύνης–ἀδικίας; τὸ ἴσον, ἰσότητός–τοῖς ἀνίσοις, ἴσα; ἀπονεμηθῆναι–νέμειν), this fragment is fairly aphoristic in nature, which makes it easy to (mis)attribute to whomever necessary. Philo's fragment is quoted verbatim in John of Damascus' *Sacra parallela* (PG 96: 60 and 88), and it is not impossible that a previous collection similar to this anthology was actually used by Isidore as a source. In any case, as no further evidence is available, Philo remains a possible source for Isidore but beyond this, nothing can be proven.

Isid., *Ep.* 1723 [4.87]:

How can you equate the deprivation of money and deprivation of liberty (ποῦ γὰρ ἴσον χρημάτων στέρησις καὶ ἐλευθερίας), for which those sensible are willing to sacrifice not only their property but are ready to die (ὑπὲρ ἧς οὐ μόνον τὰς οὐσίας προΐεσθαι, ἀλλὰ καὶ ἀποθνῄσκειν οἱ νοῦν ἔχοντες ἐθέλουσιν)?

Philo, *Mos.* 1.141:

For what resemblance is there between forfeiture of money and deprivation of liberty (ποῦ γάρ ἐσθ' ὅμοιον ζημία χρημάτων καὶ στέρησις ἐλευθερίας), for which men of sense are willing to sacrifice not only their substance but their life? (ὑπὲρ ἧς οὐ μόνον προΐεσθαι τὰς οὐσίας οἱ νοῦν ἔχοντες ἀλλὰ καὶ ἀποθνῄσκειν ἐθέλουσιν ....) (LCL trans.)

Just like Philo in *Mos.* 1.140–42, in *Ep.* 1723 to a member of the Pelusian *curia*, Isidore offers a justification for the passage depicting the Israelites' "borrowing" goods from Egypt (Exod 3:22): on the one hand the Egyptians did not pay the Israelites for the time they served, contrary to what would be just, and on the other, the enslavement is a bigger injustice than their taking of goods. Thus, the Egyptians are not to be seen as victims, but as those who inflicted upon the Israelites the deprivation of property and of liberty. Philo also adds the notion that according to the laws of war the "appropriation" of the enemy's goods is justifiable; unjust, according to Philo, is the Egyptians' treatment of the Israelites as prisoners of war. On his part, Isidore quotes the Exodus text after his first explanation as an augmentation of his argument, while in the Philonic text a paraphrase is preferred. In short, it seems that we do have here not only textual but also exegetical agreements between the two authors. Moreover, there is no other author to use the same lexical forms. All in all, this example appears to be a decisive case of Isidore's dependency on Philo.

12.3 Cohn-Wendland Edition

Früchtel draws attention to two further parallels mentioned in the Cohn-Wendland edition,[33] though to our knowledge they have not yet received any discussion. Of this, one is a clear textual dependency of Isidore on Philo (*Ep.* 915 [3.115]–*Ios.* 176), the other a reference to content, without textual congruence (*Ep.* 1089 [3.289]–*Virt.* 59–60).

Isid., *Ep.* 915 [3.115]:

For if he had put up as a fence with the older one, who brought in the best judgement, perhaps he would have overthrown the plot. For he was younger than him (ἐκείνου μὲν γὰρ νεώτερος ἦν), being the second in terms of age, but older than the others (τῶν δ' ἄλλων πρεσβύτερος), and it was likely that the others who were fearing or were persuaded by the judgment of the eldest, might have put away the plot, and above all the fourth who was angry with the things that were done, and this very thing, having great weight (πολλὴν ῥοπήν) to not act for it.

Philo, *Ios.* 176:

But perhaps too he thought that that brother had the greatest responsibility for the wickedness, since he might be almost called the officer of the company.... For if he had ranged himself with the eldest when he counselled kindness and humanity, being, though younger than he, older than the others (νεώτερος μὲν ἐκείνου, τῶν δ' ἄλλων πρεσβύτερος ὤν), the wrongdoing might well have been stopped. For the two highest in position and honor would have been united in sentiment and purpose on the question, and this of itself would have had great weight (πολλὴν ῥοπήν) to turn the scale. (LCL trans.)

Philo's *Ios.* 175–76 is an interpretation of Gen 42:25 referring to the story of Joseph's brothers' search for grain in Egypt and his imprisonment of Simeon, the second eldest brother. Trying to offer an explanation as to why Simeon was the one taken hostage among the brothers, Philo hypothesizes the following: (1) Firstly, in a chiastic structure Simeon corresponds to Joseph—the former was the second born of all brothers, and the latter the youngest but one; thus "the second of a large number corresponds to the last but one, just as the first corresponds to the last." (2) Secondly, Philo attributes to Joseph the thought that Simeon had the greatest share of the guilt; thus, as the second-born son, he might have been the most prone to align himself to the eldest and guide their younger brothers towards nefarious acts.

In *Ep.* 915 to Eudaemon, Isidore interprets the same passage along the lines of Philo's second hypothesis (2), and even reproduces a few words (almost) in the same order as they appear in *Ios.* 176. He is of the same opinion that Simeon, "being, though younger

---

[33] See Cohn-Wendland 4:98–99, and 5:282.

than he [the first born], older than the others (νεώτερος μὲν ἐκείνου, τῶν δ' ἄλλων πρεσβύτερος ὤν)," might have plotted with the eldest, and negatively influenced the younger ones. The chiasm used by Philo in his first argument is not used by Isidore in his letter. In any case, as there are apparently no other witness to use the three *lemmata* in proximity in these grammatical forms (νεώτερος, ἐκείνου, πρεσβύτερος), this seems a fairly clear example of a verbatim (albeit limited) quotation from Philo.

Isid., *Ep.* 1089 [3.289]:

I admire the God-loving Moses in many things .... For having two sons born from himself (δύο υἱοὺς τεχθέντας παρ' αὐτοῦ) ... he did not appoint any of them as his successor to assume leadership, as it rather belongs to virtue than to family relations (ἀλλὰ τὸν ἀρετῇ μᾶλλον ἢ γένει προσήκοντα).... The privilege is owing not to family relations, but to virtue (χρεωστεῖται τὸ γέρας, οὐ γένει, ἀλλ' ἀρετῇ). Nor shall the son of the king (τὸν βασιλέως υἱόν), if unworthy (ἀνάξιος) of the matter, be inscribed for virtue, but the one who has the soul worthy of a king (βασιλικὴν ψυχήν) and who is able to hold the knowledge of virtue (τὴν τῆς ἀρχῆς ἐπιστήμην χωρῆσαι δυνάμενον).

Philo, *Virt.* 59–60:

(59) ... "My lord," someone would ask, "what are you saying? Have you not legitimate children (γνήσιοι παῖδες) or, if not them, nephews (ἀδελφιδοῖ)? ... (60) But if you have found even them to be unfit, preferring the nation above your closest and most familiar relations (τῶν συγγενεστάτων καὶ οἰκειοτάτων), you still have a blameless friend (φίλος ἄμεμπτος) who has given proof of complete virtue to you .... Why do you not think fit to approve of him, if the choice is a matter not of birth but of excellence of character? (τί δὴ τοῦτον, εἰ μὴ γένους ἀλλὰ καλοκἀγαθίας ἡ αἵρεσίς ἐστιν, οὐκ ἀξιοῖς δοκιμάζειν;)"[34]

These passages offer an interpretation of Moses' reckoning of his succession (Num 27:16–17), on which both Philo and Isidore concur: Moses did not look among his sons and nephews for a successor, as it did not seem fit. Philo's interpretation[35] in the form of an imaginary dialogue between Moses and an interlocutor is missing in Isidore, but they both offer a lengthy explanation on the fact that, in such important matters, the choice of a successor must be made on the basis of virtue, and not on family ties. In Isidore's letter, one explicitly reads his disapproval of handing over both the imperial and ecclesiastical dignities, whereas Philo does not tackle this matter.[36]

---

[34] Transl. from W. T. Wilson, *Philo of Alexandria, On Virtues: Introduction, Translation, and Commentary*, Philo of Alexandria Commentary Series 3 (Leiden: Brill, 2011), 56.

[35] For a commentary on Philo's *Virt.*, see Wilson, *On Virtues*, esp. 158–61.

[36] Philo's interest was to show that "in its fundamental character and priorities, the Jewish nation is based not on blood but on virtue" (see Wilson, *On Virtues*, 160), while Isidore and Origen (*Hom. Num.* XXII. 4) might have had in mind their own immediate contexts. For Origen, L. Doutreleau suggests as a possible allusion his tension with Bishop Demetrius (SC 461, 94), and it is also not impossible for Isidore's letter to echo his animosity towards Bishop Eusebius of Pelusium, or the priests in Zosimus' entourage.

The same passage from Num 27:16–17 is also dealt with by Origen, *Hom. Num.* XXII. 4 (SC 461, 92–95), and Theodoret, *Quaest. in Num. 47* (PG 80: 397). Origen shares with Philo the dialogue format between Moses and an imaginary interlocutor, and with Isidore the addition regarding the "rulers for the people" (*principes populo*) and the "rulers of the churches" (*principes ecclesiarum*), and perhaps the formulaic language with which they start the passage.[37] The exact relationship between the three authors and the possibility of Isidore being more dependent on Origen than on Philo are difficult to assess with more precision because, on the one hand, Origen's text is only extant in Latin, and on the other, because of the lack of lexical equivalence between Philo and Isidore. All in all, given their structural and thematic congruences, it is not unlikely that Isidore's interpretation is the result of a paraphrase from Philo, possibly with Origen's mediation.

12.4 F. Petit: Intertwined Usage in the Catenae

Finally, we will briefly draw attention to an interesting phenomenon where the receptions of the two authors are occasionally intertwined. On the one hand, a Philonic excerpt is attributed to Isidore in the *Catena in Exodum* (frag. 669 to Exod 23:4–5), yet it was shown to be a combination of Philo's QE 2.11 and 2.12.[38] According to F. Petit, who established its Philonic provenance, Procopius' *Commentary on the Octateuch* (CPG 7430), and John of Damascus' *Sacra parallela* offer some complements to this fragment, the latter correctly attributing it to Philo.[39]

On the other hand, the opposite case is also attested: on the penultimate folio of codex *Urb. gr. 125* (308v), a letter of Isidore is misattributed to Philo. James R. Royse follows Cohn in doubting its authenticity[40] and identifies this spurious fragment (frag. sp. 48) as Isidore of Pelusium's *Ep.* 47 [1.47].[41]

12.5 Conclusion

Besides the four examples analyzed by Runia where Philo is mentioned nominatim—*Epp.* 643 [2.143], 770 [2.270], 819 [3.19], and 881 [3.81]—for the rest of the parallels the degree to which one could establish a direct usage of Philo's works, a reference to a shared Hellenistic background, an exegetical interpretation derived from Philo, or on the contrary no verifiable usage at all, varies considerably.

---

[37] Origen, *Hom. Num.* XXII. 4: *Sed interim uideamus Moysi magnificentiam*; Isid., *Ep.* 1089 [3.289]: Ἐν πολλοῖς μὲν καὶ ἄλλοις ἄγαμαι τὸν θεοφιλῆ Μωσέα.
[38] F. Petit, *La Chaîne sur l'Exode*, 4:124.
[39] F. Petit, *La Chaîne sur l'Exode*, 4:124; Petit, *Quaestiones in Genesim et in Exodum*, 246–47; D. T. Runia, "Philo in Byzantium," 265.
[40] Cohn-Wendland, 1:lix: "sequitur fragmentum alibi, ut videtur, non traditum, quod an Philonis sit dubito."
[41] J. R. Royse, *The Spurious Texts of Philo of Alexandria*, 118.

The analysis has shown at least three other clear examples of a *very likely* direct use of Philo's works in Isidore's letters. The most decisive case (*Ep.* 1723 [4.87]–*Mos.* 1.141) involves not only a high verbal agreement between the two, with no apparent parallels in other authors, but also agreements in their biblical interpretation; the other two cases involve high verbal agreements (*Ep.* 1088 [3.288]–*QG* 4.99), or parallels in their etymological and exegetical interpretations (*Ep.* 1043 [3.243]–*QG* 1.28). To these a fourth example could be added (*Ep.* 915 [3.115]–*Ios.* 176), which shares both some verbal agreements and the exegetical context. In all cases, the borrowing happens without any acknowledgment.

At the opposite end, there are at least two examples where the possibility of Isidore's drawing on Philo is *very unlikely*: there is no verbal agreement between the texts compared (*Ep.* 609 [2.109]–*Somn.* 2.24 (164–65), *Ep.* 715 [2.215]–*Spec.* 3.76), beyond—in the case of the second example—their quoting of the same biblical verse. In fact, most of the results yielded by the TLG "parallel browsing" feature highlight especially false positives, where the point of contact between Isidore and Philo is only the quotation of the same biblical verse, without a shared biblical interpretation.

The rest of the examples are then distributed on the spectrum between the two poles. Most of these instances are aphoristic in nature, which makes them popular and easily adaptable to all sorts of contexts.[42] Some are also present in gnomic anthologies (e.g. Clitarchus, *Sententiae Pythagoreorum*: *Ep.* 1809 [4.155]–*Mut.* 17, *Spec.* 1.339), or in ancient Greek and Hellenistic writers (Demosthenes, Plutarch, Diogenes Laertius, etc.: *Ep.* 1647 [4.6]–*QG* 3.48), which makes it virtually impossible to prove whether the parallels are stemming directly from Philo, from these anthologies, or simply from a shared tradition. Thus, the possibility of a coincidental agreement between Isidore and Philo is as valid a scenario as is direct usage. However, one can still assume a *possible* dependency of Isidore on Philo on the basis of some (albeit limited) verbal agreement. Among the parallels with a gnomic character, the most *likely* instances of Philonic dependence are those for which the verbal agreement, though limited, is strengthened by the absence of further parallels in any other text (e.g. *Ep.* 1450 [5.169]–*Mos.* 2.27; *Ep.* 1631 [5.302]–*Anim.* 100).

Conversely, there are also a few examples that indicate an *unlikely* usage of Philo in Isidore, especially those where a better patristic parallel can be identified (*Ep.* 1162 [3.362]–*QE* 2.110, with a parallel in Nazianzus, *Funebris oratio* 43.3, and *Ep.* 960 [3.160]–*Mos.* 1.31 with a parallel in Chrysostom, *In Genesim* 32.7) as a more probable source, with no sufficient contextual clues to presuppose a mediated usage of Philo. In one case, however, where the patristic parallel (Origen, see *Ep.* 1089 [3.289]–*Virt.* 59–60) is closer to Philo than to Isidore, the possibility remains that Isidore used Philo directly, if at all.

---

[42] e.g. *Ep.* 1450 [5.169]–*Mos.* 2.27; 1809 [4.155]–*Mut.* 17; *Spec.* 1.339; 1647 [4.6]–*QG* 3.48; 1631 [5.302]–*Anim.* 100; 1156 [3.356]–*Ios.* 5, 904 [3.104]; 1225 [5.10]–*Somn.* 2.147; *QG* 2.60; 1162 [3.362]–*QE* 2.110; 960 [3.160]–*Mos.* 1.31.

If we were to further the discussion on the way in which Isidore uses Philo, one of the difficulties lies in the fact that even in cases where they both share the same *lemmata*, Isidore seems to repurpose the passage he might have borrowed from Philo and use it in a different context, without sharing its initial thematic content. Thus, it would be an adaptation of the quotation to a different exegetical or ethical context, in which case we can speak more of "traces" rather than "influence" of Philo in Isidore's letters.

A caveat of this assessment of Philo's reception in Isidore is the fact that a number of the parallels we are dealing with stem from passages which are not extant (or are extremely fragmentary) in Greek, but have only survived in Armenian translations. Thus, the basis for a comparison is far too scarce in Greek (sometimes two to five words), and at the same time difficult to assess with precision from its existing translations. Even so, the data discussed here seems to indicate beyond doubt that Isidore knew (at least to some extent) and used several Philonic works, in particular *QG*, *Mos.* (which he uses four times each), and *Ios.* (twice).

To conclude, in addition to the few instances where Philo is used nominatim as an authoritative figure (*Epp.* 643, 770, 819, 881), most possible parallels speak less of Isidore's use of Philo and more of the attachment of them both to the broader Hellenistic context. Along with the three exegetical examples highlighted by Runia (*Epp.* 770, 881, 1757), the remaining four discussed in this contribution most likely reflecting direct dependence suggest that Isidore's usage of Philo is primarily exegetical, and occasionally parenetic. Albeit limited to precious few certain instances, Isidore's exegetical usage of Philo shows the former to be receptive to the latter's literal, even more technical, e.g. etymological, interpretations, as well as to allegorical readings of scripture,[43] whereas parenetic examples show Isidore using Philo mostly for literary embellishment as he can adopt and adapt the latter's imagery in new contexts.[44]

---

[43] *Ep.* 1723 [4.87]–*Mos.* 1.141; *Ep.* 1043 [3.243]–*QG* 1.28; *Ep.* 915 [3.115]–*Ios.* 176.
[44] *Epp.* 1088 [3.288] and 979 [3.179]–*QG* 4.99.

13
Ambrose

Maria E. Doerfler

Ordinary men must learn beforehand what they are to teach, and receive from [God] what they are to pass on to others. In my case, not even this was allowed. I was snatched into the priesthood from a life spent at tribunals and amidst the paraphernalia of administrative office, and I began to teach you things I had not learnt myself. The result was that I started to teach before I had started to learn. With me, then, it is a matter of learning and teaching all at the same time, since no opportunity was given me to learn in advance.[1]

This frequently reiterated lament in the writings of Ambrose, the famed fourth-century bishop of Milan, bears the marks of both episcopal humility and rhetorical strategy.[2] A classic example of *captatio benevolentiae*, Ambrose's plaint nevertheless offers a fair summation of the early days of his ecclesiastical career. Born to a senatorial family in 340 CE in the Roman province of Gaul, the future bishop had prepared himself for imperial service, including the progression of administrative posts known as the *cursus honorum*.[3] Despite his Christian upbringing and his elder sister's commitment to consecrated virginity, however, Ambrose, like many of his contemporaries, had put off baptism, perhaps reasoning, as Eusebius depicts Constantine doing, that the imperial purple and baptismal white were incompatible with one another, and best worn sequentially.[4] When Ambrose was acclaimed as the city's bishop in 374 CE—a call that came, by his and his hagiographer's accounts, both to his surprise and against his own

---

[1] Ambrose, *De officiis* 1.1.3–4, in I. J. Davidson, *Ambrose, De Officiis: Edited with an Introduction, Translation, and Commentary*, 2 vols (Oxford: Oxford University Press, 2001), 1.119.

[2] See e.g. *Paen* 2.67 for a very similar motif. For a more in-depth discussion of Ambrose's rhetorical self-judgment at the time of his acclamation to the episcopacy, see also A. Lenox-Conyngham, "The Judgment of Ambrose the Bishop on Ambrose the Roman Governor," *StPatr* 17 (1982): 62–65.

[3] The twentieth and twenty-first centuries have produced a number of biographies of Ambrose, including E. Dassmann, *Ambrosius von Mailand: Leben und Werk* (Stuttgard: Kohlhammer, 2004); H. Savon, *Ambroise de Milan* (Paris: Desclée, 1997); D. H. Williams, *Ambrose of Milan and the End of the Nicene-Arian Conflicts* (New York: Oxford University Press, 1995); N. McLynn, *Ambrose of Milan: Church and Court in a Christian Capital* (Los Angeles: University of California Press, 1994); F. Homes Dudden, *The Life and Times of St. Ambrose* (Oxford: Clarendon Press, 1935).

[4] See Eusebius' presentation of the Emperor Constantine as, after his baptism, "[putting] on bright imperial clothes which shone like light, and [resting] on a pure white couch, being unwilling to touch a purple robe again" (*The Life of Constantine* 4.62.5; in A. Cameron and S. G. Hall, *Eusebius*, Life of Constantine: Introduction, Translation and Commentary, Clarendon Ancient History Series [Oxford: Clarendon Press, 1999], 178).

desires[5]—his path to ordination was hasty, and the newly minted ecclesial leader apparently faced his office less than optimally prepared. For the Christians of Milan, Ambrose's early days of episcopal service yielded a moderately wealthy, highly educated, and politically skilled bishop—not, however, an accomplished theologian or skillful homilist capable of navigating the contentious religious discourses of the late fourth-century Roman Empire.

In due course, Ambrose would remedy many of these shortcomings; by the time Augustine encountered him in the 380s CE, he already enjoyed a reputation as a captivating rhetor to whose sermons both converted and unconverted flocked.[6] The bishop's theological education proceeded, particularly during the early years of his episcopacy, by his study of—and, at times, extensive borrowing from[7]—the works of his Greek-speaking forebears: Origen, Didymus the Blind, and particularly Philo of Alexandria. Scholars have counted more than six hundred references to Philo's writings in Ambrose,[8] earning the bishop the nicknames "Philo Christianus"[9] or "Philo Latinus"[10]—in addition to other, less flattering monikers from some of his late ancient contemporaries.

Given scholars' early and thoroughgoing recognition of Ambrose's Philonic heritage,[11] the twentieth and twenty-first centuries have produced a considerable volume of studies on this topic. The interest Ambrose has received in scholarship over the past two decades has contributed both to the continued production of monographs, articles, and dissertations on his use of Philo, and to shaping the directions these studies have pursued. Students interested in a scholarly introduction to Ambrose's interaction with Philo can scarcely do better than to turn to David Runia's 1993 chapter on this topic in his magisterial study, *Philo in Early Christian Literature*.[12] My aim in this essay is not to reduplicate Runia's labors, but to build on them, particularly inasmuch as the

---

[5] See e.g. Paulinus of Milan, *Life of Ambrose* 3.6-9. On this topic cf., however, T. D. Barnes, "The Election of Ambrose of Milan," in *Episcopal Elections in Late Antiquity*, ed. J. Leemans, Arbeiten zur Kirchengeschichte 119 (Berlin: de Gruyter, 2011), 39-60.

[6] See e.g. Augustine's depiction of Ambrose as eloquent rhetorician and divinely inspired preacher in *Confessions* 5.13.23-24.

[7] For a discussion of Ambrose's "plagiarism," see below (n. 19).

[8] Enzo Lucchesi has counted 601 instances of Ambrose's use of Philo in his writings; 490 of these appear in the bishop's various treatises, with *De Cain et Abel*, *De Noe*, and *De Abrahamo* II accounting together for more than three-quarters of that number, as well as an additional 111 instances in Ambrose's letters (*L'usage de Philon dans l'oevre exégétique de Saint Ambroise* [Leiden: Brill, 1977], 127-28).

[9] J.-B. Aucher, *Philonis Judaei Paralipomena Armena* (Venice: L. Lazarus, 1826), v.

[10] See e.g. L. Cohn and P. Wendland, eds, *Philonis Alexandrini Opera quae supersunt* (Berlin: Reimer, 1896), 1:lxii ("Maxime omnium scriptorum ecclesiasticorum Philonem usurpavit Ambrosius episcopus Mediolanensis, quem in scriptis quibusdam quasi latinum Philonem esse dixeris"). The other side of the commemorative coin may be the fact that in Byzantine catenae of his works, Philo is frequently "Philo the Bishop" (Φίλωνος ἐπισκόπου). See J. R. Royse, *The Spurious Texts of Philo of Alexandria: A Study of Textual Transmission and Corruption with Indexes to the Major Collections of Greek Fragments* (Leiden: Brill, 1991), 14-15. For a concise discussion of Philo's "afterlife" in Christian transmission, see also D. T. Runia, *Philo in Early Christian Literature: A Survey* (Minneapolis: Fortress Press, 1993), 3-33.

[11] For an overview of the recognition of Philo's importance to Ambrose, see H. Savon, *Saint Ambroise devant l'exégèse de Philon le Juif* (Paris: Études Augustiniennes, 1977), 9-12. See also, more concisely and drawing on Savon's survey, V. Nikiprowetzky, "Saint Ambroise et Philon," *REG* 94 (1981): 193-99.

[12] Runia, *Philo in Early Christian Literature*, 291-311.

work of the intervening twenty-five years has borne out some of the trends noted by Runia, while introducing new trajectories of engagement and revealing further opportunities for scholarship.

To this end, this chapter begins with an introduction to the primary source evidence for Ambrose's use of Philo, before turning to a brief discussion of what are still the two most influential monographs on the relationship between Philo and Ambrose: Hervé Savon's two-volume study *Saint Ambroise devant l'exégèse de Philon le Juif*, and Enzo Lucchesi's *L'usage de Philon dans l'œuvre exégétique de Saint Ambroise: une 'Quellenforschung' relative aux Commentaires d'Ambroise sur la Genèse*.[13] These studies address two key scholarly trajectories, one primarily interested in what Ambrose's witness to Philo's writings can tell readers about their textual tradition (Lucchesi); the other concerned with how Ambrose's engagement with Philo reflects Ambrose's own theological and philosophical agenda (Savon). The final section of this essay, in turn, examines additional scholarly trends at the intersection of Ambrosian and Philonic scholarship, including an ongoing interest in Ambrose's and Philo's respective *exegetical strategies*—a vast topic, which persistently accommodates new and fruitful approaches; the use of Philo in Ambrose's *epistolary corpus*; and, finally, the two authors' respective *constructions of gender*.

13.1 Ambrose and Philo: An Introduction

Ambrose only mentions Philo's name once in the entirety of his extant oeuvre—and that to criticize his Alexandrian source. The latter, Ambrose writes in his interpretation of God's placing Adam in Eden, "limited his interpretation of this Scriptural passage to its moral aspect, because he, being a Jew, did not understand its spiritual meaning."[14] This remark strikes modern readers as scant recognition and harsh judgment for a writer whose interpretations and insights proliferate in Ambrose's literary remains.[15] Scholars have at times suggested that this reticence on Ambrose's part may reflect his discomfort with revealing his dependence on a Jewish source.[16] Yet Ambrose was no more forthcoming with the Christian authors on whom he depended, even where those Christian sources enjoyed impeccable theological pedigree, suggesting a broader authorial strategy.[17]

---

[13] See above respectively at nn. 11 and 8.

[14] *Philon autem, quoniam spiritalia Iudaico non capiebat affectu, intra moralia se teniut* ... (Ambrose, *De paradiso* 4.25 [CSEL 32/I.281, ed. Schenkl]).

[15] Lucchesi counts fifty-two borrowings from Philo in the *De paradiso* alone (*L'usage de Philon*, 127); in a similar fashion, Savon develops an incisive analysis of Ambrose's exegetical program on the basis of his brief juxtaposition of Philo's "moralia" and the "spiritalia" of the Christian exegetes in this passage (*Saint Ambroise*, 55–81).

[16] See e.g. F. C. Conybeare, *Philo about the Contemplative Life* (Oxford: Clarendon Press 1895), 329.

[17] Such is the case, for example, with regard to Ambrose's extensive (and unacknowledged) use of Basil of Caesarea as a source for his *Hexameron*. For a discussion of Ambrose's use of Basil and other sources, including Philo, in his *Hexameron*, see inter alia J. C. M. van Winden, "In the Beginning: Some Observations on the Patristic Interpretation of Genesis 1,1," *VC* 17 (1963): 105–21; J. Pépin, *Théologie cosmique et théologie chrétienne*

As Neil McLynn has argued, "Ambrose's credentials were based ultimately upon his knowledge of Greek. His fluency in the language has been questioned, but there were few to test him in late fourth-century Italy."[18] Faced with a position of precarious authority, Ambrose, in other words, made use of the skills and resources at his disposal to build both his theological education and his reputation. That is not to say that the bishop's late ancient counterparts necessarily approved of what today would certainly pass for plagiarism: Jerome, Ambrose's equally educated contemporary, for example, with characteristic harshness compared Ambrose to a crow who sought to enhance his own, lackluster feathers with those of other birds.[19]

How extensive, then, was Ambrose's debt to Philo, and how did he come upon the latter's writings in the first place? The answer to the second question is, by necessity, only tentative. Scholars have suggested that the person to introduce the newly minted bishop to his Alexandrian source was Simplicianus, presbyter at Milan and Ambrose's "father in grace," as Augustine calls him.[20] Simplicianus had spent time in Rome, perhaps during the tenure of Ambrose's episcopal successor, the "Arian" Auxentius. While there, he had made the acquaintance of the famous rhetorician Marius Victorinus, and likely had been exposed to parts of Philo's literary corpus as well, later conveying his discoveries to his episcopal protegé.[21]

Too much of Simplicianus's history and with it the history of Ambrose's Philonic formation are obscure to us. What is clear, however, is that Ambrose, once introduced to Philo, made use of the latter early and often. Ambrose's literary engagement with Philo may be divided into three categories: his so-called "Philonic treatises," a moniker bestowed upon them by Savon; his epistolary corpus, wherein many of his exegetically focused letters bear a Philonic cast; and the remainder of Ambrose's oeuvre, in which Philo plays a considerably more sporadic role. We will address these in turn.

(Ambroise, Exam. I. 1, 1–4) (Paris: Presses Universitaires de France, 1964); R. von Henke, *Basilius und Ambrosius über das Sechstagewerk: Eine vergleichende Studie*, Chrêsis VII (Basel: Schwabe, 2000).

[18] McLynn, *Ambrose of Milan*, 56.

[19] Jerome had anathematized Ambrose's alleged plagiarism of Didymus the Blind's treatise on the Holy Spirit in the bishop's *De Spiritu Sancto*, and may have leveled a similar charge against Ambrose in the introduction to his translation of Origen's *Homilies on Luke*. In both texts, Jerome thus caricatures his unnamed opponent as a crow, who, lacking in his own plumage, resorted to nabbing that of other birds (Rufinus, *Apol*. 2.26 [CCL 20:101]). For an argument that Jerome attacks Ambrose's inept exegesis rather than his plagiarism, see e.g. N. Adkin, "Jerome on Ambrose: The Preface to the Translation of Origen's Homilies on Luke," *Revue Benedictine* 107 (1997): 5–14. The question of whether "plagiarism" and other modern notion of violations of authorial rights are appropriately applied to late ancient texts exceeds the scope of this essay, but has generated considerable scholarship in recent years. See e.g. B. D. Ehrman, *Forgery and Counterforgery: The Use of Literary Deceit in Early Christian Polemics* (Oxford: Oxford University Press, 2013), esp. 52–55.

[20] Augustine, *Confessions* 8.2.3 (*perrexi ergo ad Simplicianum, patrem in accipienda gratia tunc episcopi Ambrosii et quam vere ut patrem diligebat*).

[21] This theory has been pressed particularly by Lucchesi, for whom Ambrose, as discussed below, represents a unique witness to a Roman trajectory of Philonic manuscripts. The latter had been, according to Lucchesi, drawing on Eusebius's *Ecclesiastical History*, deposited in Rome's library, discovered there by Simplicianus, and made their way to Ambrose through him (*L'usage de Philon*, 19–20).

13.1.1 Philo in Ambrose's "Philonic" Treatises

Hervé Savon has designated among Ambrose's works five "traités philoniens": treatises in which Philo serves not merely as an occasional interlocutor for Ambrose but furnishes, as Savon put it, "a canvas for the entire work."[22] These treatises bear similarities with one another that go beyond their dependence on Philo, most notably the fact that they all deal with the allegorical interpretation of the Pentateuch. Four of them, each addressing the early chapters of Genesis, are moreover attributable to Ambrose's early years as a bishop—the very era during which Ambrose claimed to have been engaged in teaching and learning simultaneously. These include:

1. *De paradiso*. Published perhaps in 377 CE,[23] this work represents Ambrose's effort to explain "the facts about Paradise, its place, and its nature to those who are desirous of this knowledge."[24] The treatise provides an exposition, largely allegorical in nature, of Gen 2:8–3:19, drawing on Philo's *QG* 1.8–47 and *Leg.* 1.12–2.18.
2. *De Cain et Abel*. This treatise reflects a continuation of *De paradiso*, composed likely in the same year. Ambrose here offers an allegorical interpretation of Gen 4, incorporating an almost verbatim Latin translation of Philo's *QG* 1.64–77.
3. *De Noe et Arca*. Composed during a time of anxiety, perhaps in 378 CE,[25] this treatise reflects an allegorical exposition of Noah, one of Ambrose's prototypical "just men," and the events of Gen 6–10, drawing on *QG* 1.87–2.82.
4. *De Abrahamo* II. The first of Ambrose's catechetical treatises on the Israelite patriarchs, *De Abrahamo* falls into two parts, the earlier of which presents the events of Gen 12:27–25:10 *ad litteram*, using Abraham as a moral exemplar for Ambrose's audience. Part II, by contrast, relies extensively on Philo's *QG* 3, as well as likely now-lost parts of the second and third books of the *QG*,[26] to provide a second, allegorical pass over Gen 12:27–18:16.

A fifth and final work needs to be added to these: Ambrose's *De fuga saeculi*, dating from the early 390s CE, nearly fifteen years after the composition of Ambrose's other "Philonic treatises." *De fuga* was with good likelihood presented originally as a sermon, as both the treatise's opening and doxology suggest. Like its predecessors, Ambrose here engages in allegorical interpretation of Genesis: the stories of Jacob, Moses, and other heroes of the Hebrew scriptures (and, on occasion, of the New Testament) are

---

[22] "un canevas à tout l'opuscule" (Savon, *Saint Ambroise*, 14).
[23] Dudden, *Life and Times of St. Ambrose*, 680.
[24] *Quidnam sit paradisus et ubi qualisve sit investigare et explanare cupientibus* (Ambrose, *De Paradiso* 1.1; CSEL 32.1.265, ed. Schenkl).
[25] So Dudden, *Life and Times of St. Ambrose*, 681. Cf., however, Schenkl's and Kellner's alternative—and considerably later—proposals (Schenkl, *CSEL* 32.ix; J. B. Kellner, *Der heilige Ambrosius, Bischof von Mailand, als Erklärer des alten Testaments: Ein Beitrag zur Geschichte der biblischen Exegese* [Regensburg: Manz, 1893], 95ff.).
[26] For further discussion of this topic, see below (p. 219).

made to illustrate the need for Christians to withdraw from the world. To this end, Ambrose incorporates large sections of Philo's nearly eponymous treatise *De fuga et inventione*.[27]

Despite its "Philonic" identity, Ambrose's engagement with Philo in this work differs considerably from his earlier efforts, as Savon has argued.[28] Even in the intervening years, however, Philo rarely seems to have been far from Ambrose's consideration: the bishop's epistolary corpus attests to Ambrose's consistent reading of Philo and his continued incorporation of the latter's works into his own.

13.1.2 Philo in Ambrose's Epistolary Corpus

Ambrose's collected letters are second only to aforementioned treatises in the scope and consistency with which the bishop made use of Philo's writings. Over a dozen of Ambrose's letters bear clear marks of Philo's influence, extending not only to the content of Philo's exegesis, but frequently to the analytical progression and order in which Ambrose addresses the interpretive questions presented. Savon has divided the Philonically infused portions of Ambrose's epistolary corpus rather loosely into four general categories: four letters addressing problems from Exodus and Leviticus; two concerning challenges from his work on the *Hexameron*; two others providing biblical foundation for a philosophical *dictum*; while in others Ambrose makes use of Philo to solve a theological challenge or matters of pastoral counsel.[29]

Table 13.1 below addresses the main topics of these letters, Ambrose's most important borrowings, as well as the Philonic passages in question.[30] Long neglected in both Ambrosian and Philonic scholarship, these writings, both individually and as a corpus, have in recent years generated a measure of scholarly attention.[31] Their potential nevertheless remains far from exhausted—as is the case for instances of Ambrose's use of Philo in the remainder of his works.

---

[27] The latter proved a fruitful intertext for Ambrose: it also appears in his *Eps.* 3, 4, 10, and 55. For an analysis of the correspondences between *De fuga et inventione* and *De fuga saeculi* in parallel columns, see M. Ihm, "Philo und Ambrosius," *Neue Jahrbücher für Philologie und Paedagogik* (1890): 282–88.

[28] Savon, *Saint Ambroise*, 329–76.

[29] Savon's taxonomy is certainly not the only imaginable one, nor in all instances the most intuitive, inasmuch as it separates, for example, Ambrose's three letters dealing with *Hexameron* from one another. Paul M. C. Elliott has recently proposed another taxonomy, dividing Ambrose's Philonic epistolary corpus into "Exegetical letters" (*Eps.* 1, 2, 3, 4, 14, 28, 29, 31, 34, 44, 48, and 55) and "Philosophical/hortatory letters" (*Eps.* 6, 7, 10, 36) ("Ambrose of Milan and His Use of Philo of Alexandria in His Letters on the *Hexameron*" [PhD diss., Hebrew Union College, 2018], 32).

[30] For a juxtaposition of the relevant sections from most (but not all) of these letters with their Philonic source in parallel columns, see W. Wilbrand, *S. Ambrosius quos auctores quaeque exemplaria in epistulis componendis secutus sit* (Münster; Aschendorff, 1909), 1–20.

[31] A discussion of some of the most interesting examples of this scholarship appears below (pp. 223–24).

Table 13.1 Philonic Borrowings in the Epistles of Ambrose

Number Z-F/PL[a]	Bibl. Text	Phil. Text	Topic
1 / 7	Exod 30:12–16	*Her.* 141–43, 186–92	Interpretation of the shekel, the manna, and the Passover.
2 / 65	Exod 24:5–6	*Her.* 183–85	Interpretation of the blood on the altar.
3 / 67	Lev 10:16–20	*Fug.* 157–60	Why did Moses listen to Aaron?
4 / 27	Exod 8:26	*Fug.* 4–24, 44	Sacrifice of the abominations of Egypt to the Lord.
6 / 28	n/a	*Prob.* 2–8, 43	Exhortation on the life of the priest.
7 / 37	1 Cor 7:23	*Prob.* 17–117	Liberty in Christ; explanation of the philosophical dictum "*quia omnis sapiens liber, omnis autem insipiens serviat.*"
10 / 38	n/a	*Fug.* 16	Continuation of Ep. 7: Wealth of the good man.
14 / 33	Deut 21:16	*Sacr.* 19–20, 118	Meaning of the law concerning the two wives; repetition of themes from *De Cain et Abel*.
28 / 50	Num 22–24	*Mos.* 1.264–304	Can God lie? (Including a paraphrase of Philo concerning Balaam.)
29 / 43	Gen 1–2	*Opif.* 69–86, 147	Why was humanity created only after the animals?
31 / 44	Gen 1	*Opif.* 8–13, 100–26	Six days of creation; mystical meaning of the numbers seven and eight.
34 / 45	Gen 2–3	*Opif.* 139–71	The nature of paradise and its allegorical significance.
36 / 2	n/a	*De Jos.* 40–48, 123, 126, 144	Exhortation to a new bishop.
44 / 68	Deut 28:23	*Praem.* 132	What is the meaning of "your heaven shall be brass, and your earth iron"?
48 / 66	Exod 32:2–7	*Ebr.* 69–71	Moses' instruction to have every man kill his neighbor.
55 / 8	Gen 22:7	*Fug.* 132–37, 143, 168–71	Is scripture written according to the rules of art?

[a] These numbers reflect, respectively, the CSEL edition of the letters by Otto Faller and Michaela Zelzer (CSEL 82/1–2) ("Z-F") and in the Patrologia Latina 16.849–1286 ("PL").

13.1.3 Philo in Ambrose's Other Writings

Philonic references appear sporadically throughout the rest of Ambrose's corpus. One instance that has garnered considerable scholarly attention involves the *Hexameron*, already mentioned on several occasions above. The latter draws predominately on the eponymous homilies by Ambrose's elder contemporary, Basil of Caesarea. Yet when Ambrose arrived at a discussion of the human body, he evidently found Basil's exposition unsatisfactory.[32] Ambrose thus leads the reader through a discussion of individual body parts, reaching in due course the "channel of refuse" (*ductus reliquiarum*)—that is to say, the anus.[33] Perhaps recollecting his extensive use of Philo's reading of Noah's ark as the human body in his *De Noe et Arca*,[34] Ambrose here, too, provides the Philonic interpretation alongside other readings: the path through which the body expels refuse is thus akin to the ark's side-door, mentioned in Gen 6:17, which the Creator fittingly removed as far as possible from the human countenance.

Another example of Philo's pervasive if ephemeral influence arises in Ambrose's sermon "Against the Arians." Ambrose therein refers to Christ "as a giant, because he is one in a double, composite nature, and shares both in divinity and in humanity."[35] The striking visual of the two-natured giant resonates with Philo's metaphorical interpretation of the Nephilim of Gen 6:1–4. The latter, according to Philo were originally "sons of heaven." When they in due course fell, they became "sons of the earth," such that "the two become one flesh."[36]

This transition is a devolution for Philo, but becomes a celebration of Christ's joint humanity and divinity in Ambrose. Yet whether Ambrose was himself responsible for the image's transformation, or whether he encountered it thus already in the work of intermediaries like Origen remains unclear.[37] The same uncertainty afflicts many

---

[32] For the sources of the *Hexameron*, see W. Gossel, *Quibus ex fontibus Ambrosius in describendo corpore humano hauserit (Ambros. Exaem. VI. 54–74)* (PhD diss., Leipzig, 1908); M. Klein, *Meletemata Ambrosiana: mythologica de Hippolyto doxographica de Exameri fontibus* (Königsberg: Lankeit, 1927); J. Pépin, *Théologie cosmique et théologie chrétienne*, 45–48; J. Pépin, "Exégèse de *In principio* et théorie des principes dans l'*Exameron* (I 4,12-16)," in *Ambrosius Episcopus: Atti del Congresso internazionale di studi ambrosiani di Milano 1974*, ed. G. Lazzati, Studia Patristica Mediolanensia 6 (Milan: Vita et Pensiero, 1976), 1.427–82; Henke, *Basilius und Ambrosius über das Sechstagewerk*, 17–23. For an incipient bibliography concerning additional recent publications on the relationship between Ambrose and Basil in their respective hexameral homilies, as well as the other literary influences on Ambrose's work, including Philo, see above n. 19.

[33] *Hexameron* 6.9.72 (CSEL 32.1.259, ed. Schenkl). Augustine, by contrast, famously rejects and ridicules this detail of Philo's—and Ambrose's—exegesis (*Quaestiones et solutiones in Genesim* 2.6).

[34] Ambrose, *De Noe et Arca* 8.24 (CSEL 32.1.428, ed. Schenkl).

[35] Ambrose, *Contra sermonem Arianorum* 8.6 (PL 42.689); compare also the fifth strophe of Ambrose's Christmas hymn, *Veni, redemptor gentium: Procedate thalamo suo / pudoris aula regia / geminae gigas substantiae* ("twin-substanced giant") / *alacris ut currat viam*. The full text of the hymn appears in A. S. Walpole, *Early Latin Hymns* (Cambridge: Cambridge University Press, 1922), 50–57. For later trajectories of this metaphor, see J. de Ghellinck, "Note sur l'expression 'Geminae Gigas substantiae,'" *RSR* 5 (1914): 416–21.

[36] Cf. Philo, *Gig.* 65 (with reference to Gen 2:24).

[37] For a discussion of Ambrose's deployment and possible reception of this image, see B. E. Daley, "The Giant's Twin Substances: Ambrose and the Christology of Augustine's *Contra sermonem Arianorum*," in *Augustine: Presbyter Factus Sum*, ed. J. T. Lienhard et al. (New York: Peter Lang, 1993), 477–95. See also J. W. Smith, *Christian Grace and Pagan Virtue: The Theological Foundation of Ambrose's Ethics* (Oxford: Oxford University Press, 2011), 167.

of the references and particular etymological explanations in Ambrose's remaining oeuvre: while they may bear the "scent" of Philo's influence, connections between the bishop's writings and his study of his Alexandrian source remain a matter of guesswork.

On the basis of these considerable witnesses to Ambrose's use of Philo, scholars from the sixteenth century onward have studied the literary relationship between the two writers. The subsequent section provides a snapshot of these scholarly developments, including their climax in the twentieth century: the publication of Hervé Savon's and Enzo Lucchesi's monographs.

13.2 Savon, Lucchesi, and Their Successors

The history of scholarship concerning Ambrose's engagement with Philo has been, almost from its very beginning, one of polarization between scholars focused on Ambrose as *transmitter* and those who treated Ambrose as *transformer* of Philo's oeuvre.

Quite shortly after the first recognition of Philo as a source for Ambrose's writings in 1566, Thomas Mangey thus used Ambrose to establish Philo's text.[38] In a similar vein, Hans Lewy, nearly two centuries later, made use of Ambrose's *De Abraham* II.1–48 to recover what he deemed a missing section in Philo's *QG*: a lacuna between books 2 and 3 of *QG*, and the concomitant absence of any discussion of Gen 12–15:6 from Philo's work.[39] The amenability of Ambrose's writings to this kind of "*Quellenforschung*," however, frequently carried with it judgments concerning Ambrose's skill and creativity as a theologian. The nineteenth-century philologist Karl Schenkl accordingly suggested that Ambrose, at least in his "Philonic" treatises, imitated Philo slavishly, changing only wording and language while retaining intact Philo's ideas and topics.[40] By contrast, Schenkl's contemporary Theodor Förster argued for Ambrose's intellectual independence from his model; from Philo, Förster claimed, Ambrose had learned only the methods of allegorical exegesis—the ideas transmitted by those methods, however, were distinctly Ambrose's own.[41]

Roughly a century after Förster's and Schenkl's initial exchange, a similar tension between Ambrose as faithful witness to Philo and Ambrose as creative developer of his source appeared in the work of Savon and Lucchesi. Lucchesi's focus in his monograph is thus trained primarily on Philo and what Ambrose's work may be able to tell scholars about the Alexandrian's original corpus.[42] In Lucchesi's assessment, the answer to the latter question is: "quite a lot." That is particularly the case when it comes to Ambrose's works in which the bishop uses Philo consistently, that is to say: his *De Cain et Abel*,

---

[38] T. Mangey, *Philonis Judaei opera quae reperiri potuerunt omnia*, 2 vols (London: G. Boyer, 1742).
[39] H. Lewy, *Neue Philontexte in der Überarbeitung des Ambrosius, mit einem Anhang: neu gefundene griechische Philonfragmente. Sonderausgabe aus den Sitzungsberichten der Preussischen Akademie der Wissenschaften, Phil.-Hist. Klasse*, vol. IV (Berlin: Verlag der Akademie der Wissenschaften, 1932).
[40] K. Schenkl, *Sancti Ambrosii Opera: Pars Prima qua continentur libri Hexameron, De paradiso, De Cain et Abel, De Noe, De Abraham, De Isaac, De bono mortis*, CSEL 32.1 (Vienna: P. Tempsky, 1866), passim.
[41] T. Förster, *Ambrosius, Bischof von Mailand: Eine Darstellung seines Lebens und Wirkens* (Halle: Eugen Strien, 1884), 102–12.
[42] See above at n. 8.

De Noe et Arca, and *De Abraham* II. In these, Lucchesi argues, Ambrose provides a superior witness to Philo's writings, including aspects thereof that are not or are no longer extant in current manuscripts.

By comparing passages from *Sacr.* with Ambrose's Latin rendering thereof, Lucchesi thus identifies a couple of instances where Ambrose differs from the treatise's two manuscript traditions as well as the so-called Coptos papyrus.[43] These instances suggest to Lucchesi that Ambrose was drawing on another, independent (and now lost) set of Philonic manuscripts, making his witness particularly valuable for students of Philo.[44] If, Lucchesi argues, the Armenian version of *QG* differs substantially from the extant Greek manuscripts, and may have reached the West independently of the Alexandrian/Origenist transmission, might the same not be true for Ambrose's source?

Lucchesi presses a number of far-reaching arguments on the basis of Ambrose's potential witness to Philo, including, inter alia, a Christian rearrangement of *QG* in the extant manuscripts, and, building upon Lewy's work, the existence of an entire volume—now lost—between books 2 and 3 of *QG*. By contrast, in texts where Ambrose does not follow Philo in as straightforward a fashion as in aforementioned treatises, Lucchesi posits the existence of an intermediary source, most likely Origen, to account for Ambrose's deviation from Philo. This model obviously allows for little creativity on Ambrose's part: his function as author has been reduced to that of translator and transmitter of his sources.

The very year Lucchesi's monograph appeared also saw the publication of Savon's *Saint Ambroise devant l'exégèse de Philon le Juif*. Despite similarities in their areas of inquiry, Savon's approach differs considerably from Lucchesi's in focus, methodology, and conclusions. Where Lucchesi's interest rests with establishing Philo's text through Ambrose, Savon instead examines Ambrose's engagement with Philo for clues concerning the former's intellectual and theological development. To this end, Savon not only compares individual passages from Ambrose's "Philonic" treatises with their source, but focuses on the structure and literary denouement of Ambrose's writings: even instances where the bishop seems to simply appropriate Philo's reasoning at times appear as striking editorial subversions in light of Ambrose's unfolding argument. To do so, Savon examines in depth a handful of selected passages, including Ambrose's defense against Apelles,[45] selections from *De Abraham* II concerning the immortality of the soul and the "fifth substance" in Philo,[46] the four rivers of paradise in *De paradiso*,[47] and the origins of vice and virtue in *De Cain*.[48]

---

[43] For a discussion of the transmission of Philo's corpus, see J. R. Royse, "The Works of Philo," in *The Cambridge Companion to Philo*, ed. A. Kamesar (Cambridge: Cambridge University Press, 2009), 62–64 and Chapter 16 in this volume.

[44] Lucchesi's conclusions have been critiqued by, inter alios, his own *Doktorvater*, D. Barthélemy (*Études d'histoire du texte de l'Ancient Testament*, Orbis Biblicus et Orientalis 21 [Göttingen: Editions Universitaires Fribourg, 1978], 391); and Yves-Marie Duval, who noted that a project of Lucchesi's scope required a scholar's thoroughgoing familiarity with both Ambrose and Philo, and concluded that "il me semble que l'auteur ne connait peut-être pas suffisamment Ambroise et tous les problèmes qu'il pose" (review of E. Lucchesi, *L'usage de Philon dans l'œuvre exégétique de saint Ambroise*, *Latomus* 38 [1979]: 728–29, at 729).

[45] Savon, *Saint Ambroise*, 32–42.
[46] Savon, *Saint Ambroise*, 185–95.
[47] Savon, *Saint Ambroise*, 215–41.
[48] Savon, *Saint Ambroise*, 243–325.

In this vein, Savon builds a case for Ambrose's development as a reader and adaptor of Philo across four steps, beginning with Ambrose's choice of Philo as a privileged interlocutor, and ally in defending scripture against the attacks of "rationalists" and Marcionites.[49] Yet while Ambrose evidently found Philo's allegorical approach congenial to his aims and inclinations, Ambrose's allegory differs from Philo's: while the latter remains on the moral level of biblical interpretation, Christians, Ambrose argues, can rise to the heights of mystical interpretation.[50] Ambrose's critical stance towards Philo becomes apparent in Parts II and III of Savon's volume. Part II examines, in turn, Ambrose's censorship of Philo where the latter's writings struck Ambrose as potentially troubling: in his philosophical leanings;[51] his Judaism;[52] and, related thereto, his amenability to use by Ambrose's "Arian" contemporaries.[53] Part III, by contrast, explores Ambrose's Christianization of Philonic themes. These developments culminate in Ambrose's development of a coherent vision—a shift, as David Runia aptly puts it, from an ontological view of the universe to a soteriological one.[54] Part IV of Savon's work accordingly presents a mature Ambrose at the height of his interpretive powers, having successfully integrated Philonic themes into a new theological vision for his fourth-century Christian audience.[55]

An illustrative example of Lucchesi and Savon's different approaches emerges from their respective engagement with Ambrose's *De fuga saeculi*, arguably the latest of his "Philonic treatises." While Ambrose makes use of his source extensively—on two occasions even in the block-text format that characterizes many of his earlier works—*De fuga* does not resemble its Philonic counterpart in topos and literary structure in the ways in which, for example, Ambrose's *De Noe* reflects *QG*. Both Savon and Lucchesi recognize the special status of *De fuga* among Ambrose's works, while nevertheless drawing very different conclusions from that shared judgment. Lucchesi accordingly discerns in the treatise a diversion from Ambrose's exegetical *habitus*, leading him to question whether Ambrose actually knew the Philo of *Fug.*, or knew him only by way of other exegetes beholden to Philo.[56] Indeed, Lucchesi concludes the latter in this as in other instances in Ambrose's corpus where Philo appears in a less systematic fashion than in earlier works: in these cases, Ambrose encountered and re-presented not Philo himself but an intermediary.[57] Where, in other words, Ambrose's use of Philo does not lend itself to treating the bishop as a reliable transmitter of his source, Lucchesi posits the existence of another, hypothetical text to serve as Ambrose's model.

This approach, while consistent with Lucchesi's commitment to Ambrose's *modus operandi* as transmitter, does not, however, account for the possibility of

---

[49] Savon, *Saint Ambroise*, 25–54.
[50] Savon, *Saint Ambroise*, 55–81.
[51] Savon, *Saint Ambroise*, 89–96.
[52] Savon, *Saint Ambroise*, 96–118.
[53] Savon, *Saint Ambroise*, 118–39.
[54] For this characterization, see Runia, *Philo in Early Christian Literature*, 306.
[55] Savon, *Saint Ambroise*, 329–76.
[56] Lucchesi, *L'usage de Philon*, 52.
[57] Lucchesi, *L'usage de Philon*, 53–88.

Ambrose's creative engagement with Philo. Savon, whose Ambrose appears with equal consistency as a transformer of his sources, naturally posits a different solution: *De fuga*, in Savon's assessment, is thus both the most mature of Ambrose's Philonic writings and the exemplar par excellence of his gift for bricolage. By interweaving Philo with New Testament texts, and Middle Platonic with Neoplatonic writers, particularly Plotinus, Ambrose thus crafts a treatise whose primary thrust intersects with but ultimately transcends any of his sources. The work, in short, reflects the "*jeu subtil*" with which Savon characteristically credits Ambrose: the bishop emerges as a theological master-craftsman, for whom Philo's writings, like those of Ambrose's other sources, are merely so many spolia to be incorporated into a new edifice.[58]

Considered with the benefit of forty years' hindsight, the most sober assessment of Ambrose's engagement with Philo may lie somewhere between Savon's and Lucchesi's proposals. Savon's portrayal of Ambrose thus has been rightly challenged for its apologetic thrust, as well as for minimizing Ambrose's dependence on Origen.[59] By contrast, Lucchesi's tendency to draw sweeping conclusions from narrow if tantalizing glimpses is frequently more thought-provoking than conclusively satisfying. The monographs of both scholars nevertheless continue to serve as archetypes of two trajectories of scholarship on Ambrose and Philo: the study of their intersection for insights concerning Ambrose, and, conversely, those intersections' potential to yield information about writers and thinkers *other than* Ambrose. While Lucchesi illuminates the most obvious non-Ambrosian focal point, namely Philo, other scholars have focused their attentions on those to whom Ambrose may have mediated Philo. Chief among these is Augustine, Ambrose's most famous baptizand.[60] Still other scholars, by contrast, have treated Philo himself—and, by extension, Ambrose—as a channel of transmission, for example by examining the philosophical character of the materials Ambrose received from Philo.[61]

In the same vein, Savon's focus on Ambrose as creative recipient and active transformer of Philo's patrimony has continued to thrive; aspects of it indeed underlie many of the most fruitful scholarly explorations of the relationship between Philo and Ambrose at the turn from the twentieth to the twenty-first century. The following, final section of this chapter will identify three such trajectories that distinguish themselves both in terms of the results they have already produced, and in the promise they hold for future scholarship.

---

[58] Savon, *Saint Ambroise*, 366.
[59] C. Aziza, Review of H. Savon, *Saint Ambroise devant l'exégèse de Philon le Juif*, *Latomus* 39.1 (1980): 241–42.
[60] See further Ilaria Ramelli, Chapter 15 in this volume; also e.g. B. Altaner, "Augustinus und Philo von Alexandrien: eine quellenkritische Untersuchung," *ZKTh* 65 (1941): 81–90; P. Courcelle, "Saint Augustin a-t-il lu Philon d'Alexandrie?," *REA* 63 (1961): 78–85; P. Courcelle, *Les Confessions de Saint Augustin dans la tradition littéraire: antécédents et postérité* (Paris: Études Augustiniennes, 1963), 49–58.
[61] See e.g. P. Garnsey, "The Middle Stoics and Slavery: Hellenistic Constructs," in *Hellenistic Constructs: Essays in Culture, History and Historiography*, ed. P. Cartledge, P. Garnsey, and E. S. Gruen (Berkeley: University of California Press, 1997), 159–74; J. Pépin, *Théologie cosmique et théologie chrétienne*, esp. 251–74, 527–32.

13.3 Future Trajectories in the Study of Ambrose's Use of Philo

If Savon's and Lucchesi's monographs constitute a highpoint in the history of scholarly engagement with Ambrose's use of Philo, and have set the agenda for much later work on this subject, the intervening decades have similarly opened new pathways for academic inquiry. To systematize these is to risk doing injustice to important and excellent individual contributions. Three trajectories of scholarship nevertheless emerge, including that of Philo as Ambrose's exegetical interlocutor; the writers' respective approaches to gender and sexuality; and the role of Philo in Ambrose's epistolary corpus.

13.3.1 Philo as Ambrose's Exegetical Interlocutor

By far the most intensive and consistent level of interest in Ambrose's reception of Philo has been directed at the two authors' respective approaches to biblical exegesis. At times, this interest has taken the form of a mere side-by-side comparison of particular sources, frequently with an eye to one of the two research trajectories already discussed above. Others have gone beyond collation and deployed the latter to investigate theological, socio-cultural, or even scientific aspects of their sources' contexts. The latter include, for example, studies on the influence of Philo's Logos-centric understanding of life and death on later Christian authors[62] and examinations of the presence of Philo in Ambrose's catechetical preaching.[63] In a similar vein, Raffaella Passarella's recent essay illuminates the uses of medical terminology and changing understandings of physiology in Philo's and Ambrose's writings.[64] In *De Noe*, for example, Ambrose draws extensively, at times verbatim, on Philo's *QG*, a fact apparent only in light of the text's transmission in an eighth or ninth century Armenian manuscript.[65]

Both Ambrose and Philo interpret Noah's ark allegorically as the human body, an exploration of the digestive processes. Passarella traces both the influence of classical sources, particularly Galen and Cicero, upon later authors' understanding of the processes of digestion and the terminology used and importance assigned to different parts of the digestive apparatus. From this careful study emerges a fascinating picture of conceptual developments and their lexical manifestation in the centuries between Philo's and Ambrose's work, as reflected in the latter's careful manipulation of terms and themes even in his most faithfully Philonic works.

---

[62] D. Zeller, "Philons spiritualisierende Eschatologie und ihre Nachwirkung bei den Kirchenvätern," in *Vom Jenseits: Jüdisches Denken in der europäischen Geistesgeschichte*, ed. E. Goodman-Thau (Berlin: de Gruyter, 1997), 19–35.

[63] M. L. Colish, *Ambrose's Patriarchs: Ethics for the Common Man* (Notre Dame: University of Notre Dame Press, 2005).

[64] R. Passarella, "Medicina in allegoria: Ambrogio, Filone e l'arca di Noè," in *Tra IV e V secolo: Studi sulla cultura latina tardoantica*, ed. I. Gualandri, Quaderni di Acme 50 (Milan: Cisalpino, 2002), 113–39.

[65] For a recent and excellent discussion of the parallels between the two texts, see J. Paramelle, *Philon d'Alexandrie: Questions sur la Genèse II 1–7: texte grec, version arménienne, parallèles latins*, Cahiers d'Orientalisme 3 (Geneva: Patrick Cramer 1984).

These examples merely illustrate the scope and diversity of recent publications elucidating Philo's impact on Ambrose's exegetical practices.[66] Such publications include studies concerning Cain and Abel, including their presentation as archetypes of rational and vital powers;[67] the figures of Isaac[68] and Aaron, including the latter's priestly robe;[69] and Ambrose's work in *De paradiso* more broadly.[70] One genre among Ambrose's works nevertheless merits particular attention for both its exegetical footprint and Philonic pedigree: the bishop's epistolary corpus.

13.3.2 Philo in Ambrose's Letters

Writing in 1993, David Runia expressed understandable disappointment that the "extended usage of Philo in Ambrose's letters has received virtually no attention" in scholarship.[71] In the intervening years, both the letters themselves and Ambrose's deployment of Philo therein have attracted greater, if still sporadic consideration. Aspects of this analysis have remained focused on the discovery of textual parallels, the groundwork for which was laid already in 1909 by Wilhelm Wilbrand.[72] More recent studies of Ambrose's letters have, however, turned to questions of Ambrose's understanding and deployment of Philo, and how such findings might speak to their respective social and philosophical contexts.

On the one hand, this scholarship appears to be carried out in a largely atomizing fashion—one letter at a time. Hervé Savon and Adam Kamesar, for example, have each considered Ambrose's use of Philo in, respectively, *Eps.* 1 and 55. By the same token, however, each example of Ambrose's epistolary oeuvre is put to use to broader methodological ends, by illustrating an aspect of Ambrose's greater interpretive program.

Savon's analysis of *Ep.* 1 thus illuminates not only Ambrose's extensive modification of Philo's writings, but attends to the pressing question of why, considering the bishop's evident dissatisfaction with much of Philo's interpretation, Ambrose turned

---

[66] For considerations of Ambrose's exegetical technique more broadly, see e.g. L. F. Pizzolato, *La dottrina esegetica di sant'Ambrogio*, Studia Patristica Mediolanensia 9 (Milan: Vita e Pensiero, 1978). For Ambrose as part of an exegetical tradition rather than *sui generis* in his encounter with Philo, see also W. Seibel, *Fleisch und Geist beim heiligen Ambrosius*, Münchner Theologische Studien 11/14 (Munich: Zink, 1958).

[67] See e.g. H. Dijkhuis, *Käins kinderen: over Kaïn en de oorsprong van het kwaad* (Amsterdam: Boom, 1999); V. Messana, "Caino ed Abele come εἴδη archetipali dell città terrena secondo Agostino ed Ambrogio," *Sileno* 4 (1976): 269–302, esp. 273–76; H. Savon, "Saint Ambroise critique de Philon dans le *De Cain et Abel*," *StPatr* 13.2 (1975): 273–79.

[68] See e.g. J. C. Cavadini, "Exegetical Transformations: The Sacrifice of Isaac in Philo, Origen, and Ambrose," in *In Dominico Eloqui: In Lordly Eloquence: Essays on Patristic Exegesis in Honor of Robert Louis Wilken*, ed. P. M. Blowers et al. (Grand Rapids: Eerdmans, 2002), 35–49; J. Daniélou, "La typologie d'Isaac dans le Christianisme primitif," *Bib* 28 (1974): 363–93, esp. 376–80.

[69] See e.g. R. Gryson, "Les Lévites, figure du sacerdoce véritable, selon Saint Ambroise," *ETL* 56 (1980): 89–112; R. Gryson, "Le vêtement d'Aaron interprété par saint Ambroise," *Muséon* 92 (1979): 273–80.

[70] See e.g. W. K. Bietz, *Paradiesesvorstellungen bei Ambrosius und seinen Vorgängern* (PhD diss., Giessen, 1974); A. R. Sodano, "Ambrogio e Filone: leggendo il *De paradiso*," *Annali della Facoltà di Lettere e Filosofia, Università di Macerata* 8 (1975): 65–82.

[71] Runia, *Philo in Early Christian Literature*, 294.

[72] W. Wilbrand, *S. Ambrosius quos auctores quaeque exemplaria in epistulis componendis secutus sit* (PhD diss., Münster, 1909), 1–29.

to the Alexandrian source in the first place. The bishop's rhetorical training, Savon argues, thus presents the practice of mimesis as *agon*, the struggle between the exemplar and its successful instantiation and adaptation by the writer or speaker intent on its imitation.[73] Far from a rejection of Philo, Ambrose's vigorous engagement with his work reflects his commitment to his source. In a similar vein, Kamesar's analysis of *Ep.* 55 draws out not only the nature of Ambrose's (mis-)reading of Philo, but connects his approach to his source material to wider interpretive trends in Ambrose's corpus.[74] Ambrose's Christologically and textually informed understanding of the divine word and his role as heir to later Platonic developments, Kamesar suggests, thus both contribute to his misapprehension of Philo's meaning and to Ambrose's paradoxically faithful deployment thereof.

The impact of these conclusions notwithstanding, a more holistic consideration of Ambrose's use of Philo in his broader epistolary program still remains a *desideratum*. Paul M. C. Elliott's recent monograph, *Creation and Literary Re-Creation: Ambrose's Use of Philo in the Hexameral Letters*, has begun to address this lacuna by providing a closer examination of Ambrose's three "hexameral letters": *Eps.* 29, 31, and 34.[75] Elliott's careful analysis of Ambrose's deployment of Philo in each of these is helpful in its own right; his overview of Philo's role in Ambrose's letters more generally, while secondary to Elliott's aims, nevertheless supplements sporadic earlier attempts at such a survey in an insightful fashion. Taken together, these works both provide clear evidence of the fruitfulness of this aspect of Philonic/Ambrosian scholarship, and illustrate the desirability of additional work on Ambrose's epistolary corpus and its witness to and development of Philo.

13.3.3 Ambrose and Philo on Gender and Sexuality

A third avenue that has received tentative attention in scholarship and remains open for further consideration is the connection between Philo's and Ambrose's understanding of gender, and particularly Ambrose's construction of virginity. This topic commends itself to scholars for several reasons: first, and perhaps most prominently, the early years of Ambrose's episcopacy were not only those of his most intensive engagement with Philo, but also the bishop's most fruitful foray into writing to and about female virginity. Alongside the sermon collections that would in due course become *De paradiso*, *De Cain et Abel*, and *De Neo et Arca*, Ambrose thus authored three books *De virginibus* and a treatise addressed to widows—all while he was "not yet a priest for even three years, without personal experience or knowledge."[76] Ambrose's work here

---

[73] H. Savon, "Remploi et transformation de thèmes philoniens dans la première lettre d'Ambroise à Just," in *"Chartae caritatis": Études de patristique et d'Antiquité tardive offertes à Yves-Marie Duval*, ed. B. Gain, G. Nauroy, and P. Jay (Paris: Institut d'études augustiniennes, 2004), 83–95, at 95.
[74] A. Kamesar, "Ambrose, Philo, and the Presence of Art in the Bible," *JECS* 9 (2001): 73–103.
[75] P. M. C. Elliott, *Creation and Literary Re-Creation: Ambrose's Use of Philo in the Hexameral Letters* (Piscataway, NJ: Gorgias Press, 2019).
[76] Ambrose, *Virg* 2.6.39 (*Tutte le opere di Sant'Ambrogio: Verginità e vedovanza*, ed. F. Gori, Biblioteca Ambrosiana 14.1 [Rome: Biblioteca Ambrosiana, 1989]).

bears traces of some of his Christian forebears, including Cyprian and Athanasius,[77] and yet the influence of Philo on Ambrose's conceptions of gender remains equally pressing. Already Luigi Franco Pizzolato's suggestion that Ambrose adopts Philo's view of woman's relative inferiority vis-à-vis man, but allows for a dramatic reassessment of this relationship in light of the eschatological transformation of humanity, points to a potential treasure-trove for further scholarly consideration.[78]

Recent scholarship on gender and virginity in late antiquity in general, and in particular with an eye to Ambrose's iterations thereof, may lend texture to some earlier proposals concerning Philo's role in Ambrose's thought on the relationship between men, women, and Christ. There is, for example as of yet no parallel to Colish's work on Ambrose's formation of the laity and his concomitant use of Philo in his catechetical sermons for the bishop's writings to virgins and ascetics more generally.[79] In the same vein, Ambrose's apparent and extensive appropriation of Philo's exegesis provides starting points for considering the transformation the latter's interpretation of women biblical characters enjoyed at the bishop's hands. An initial foray into studying these trajectories appeared in a recent monograph by John L. Thompson in the context of a longitudinal study of patristic and Reformation-era exegetes reading of women in the so-called "texts of terror."[80] In a similar vein, Maria Ludovica Arduini has demonstrated the trajectories of gendered identification for mind (*nous-mens*) with Adam and sense-perception (*aisthesis-sensus*) with Eve from its pre-Christian origins through Ambrose and into the work of the eleventh-century exegete Rupert of Deutz.[81]

It is not surprising that Philo figures significantly in these conversations; nor do the figures discussed exhaust either Philo's exegesis of biblical women or Ambrose's engagement with his readings. As the recognition of Philo's impact on Ambrose continues to expand beyond the polarity of Ambrose as Philo's transmitter or transformer, and move into considering the bearing these transmissions and transformations had upon Ambrose's socio-historical context and exegetical progeny, they also promise to generate new horizons of scholarly inquiry.

13.4 Conclusion

The beginning of the twenty-first century has proved to be an era of continuing fruitfulness for the study of Ambrose's use of and witness to Philo. Over the past half-century,

---

[77] L.-T. Lefort, "Athanase, Ambroise et Chenoute 'sur la virginité,'" *Muséon* 48 (1935): 55–73; Y.-M. Duval, "L'originalité du *De virginibus* dans le mouvement ascétique occidental: Ambroise, Cyprien, Athanase," in *Ambroise de Milan: XVIe centenaire de son élection épiscopale*, ed. T.-M. Duval (Paris: Études augustiniennes, 1974), 15–66.

[78] L. F. Pizzolato, "La coppia umana in S. Ambrogio," in *Etica sessuale nel Cristianesimo delle origini*, ed. R. Catalamessa, Studia Patristica Mediolanensia 5 (Milan: Vita e Pensiero, 1976), 180–211.

[79] Colish, *Ambrose's Patriarchs*. But see the references to Philo in A. B. Laughton, *Virginity Discourse and Ascetic Politics in the Writings of Ambrose of Milan* (PhD diss., Duke University, 2010), passim.

[80] J. L. Thompson, *Writing the Wrongs: Women of the Old Testament among Biblical Commentators from Philo through the Reformation* (Oxford: Oxford University Press, 2001), esp. 34–36, 118–21, 191–98.

[81] M. L. Arduini, "Il tema 'vir' e 'mulier' nell'esegesi patristica e medievale di *Eccli.*, XLII,14: a proposito di una interpretazione di Ruperto di Deutz," *Aev* 54 (1980): 315–30, esp. 324–30.

the balance of scholarship has shifted from efforts at "Quellenforschung" and the concomitant emphasis on Ambrose as Philo's faithful transmitter, to the focus on what Ambrose's understanding of his Alexandrian forebear can tell contemporary readers about the bishop's theological formation and his social and intellectual location. The scholarship of preceding decades, including contributions by Ernst Dassmann, Enzo Lucchesi, David Runia, and Hervé Savon, continues to bear fruit in more recent academic forays—not least of all since a number of the scholars in question remain active participants in these conversations.

Building on this foundation, the methodological shifts of recent decades have empowered new and valuable scholarly approaches. Yet despite the salutary appearance of new topoi in the study of Ambrose and Philo and forays into long-desired areas of scholarship, much remains to be done. This is the case not only for Ambrose's "Philonic" treatises, but particularly for other areas of Ambrose's oeuvre. The latter promise to provide glimpses at Philo's influence on Ambrose's role as theologian, philosopher, homilist, and ecclesiastical leader, even in literary genres that have traditionally attracted scant attention, like Ambrose's letters and hymns. The conjunction of a rich history of scholarship and scope for new scholarly ventures suggest that Ambrose will continue to figure prominently in studies of Philo's reception for decades to come.

14
Jerome

Matthew A. Kraus

Also handed down is ... another pseudepigraphal text entitled the Wisdom of Solomon ... [which] is nowhere to be found among the Hebrews. Rather its very style exudes Greek eloquence. And several ancient writers attribute this treatise to the Jew Philo. Therefore, just as the Church then reads the books of Judith, Tobit, and Maccabees, but does not accept them as canonical Scriptures, it also should read these two volumes [Ben Sira and Wisdom of Solomon] for the edification of the people, not for the purpose of establishing the authority of ecclesiastical dogmas. (*Praef. In libros Salomonis*, dated to 398 CE)[1]

Previous reception studies have concentrated on identifying specific references to Philo's writings in Jerome's works, usually taking the lengthy notice about Philo in Jerome's catalogue of authors in *De viris illustribus* 11.1–7 as a starting point.[2] Despite the extensive list of Philonic treatises in this passage, these studies have demonstrated a scarcity of specific references drawn from these treatises throughout Jerome's writings. There has been little attempt, however, to explain the discrepancy between extensive familiarity with the titles of the Philonic corpus and the apparent disinterest in their contents.[3] The passage from the preface to the Latin translation of the Books of Solomon offers a more productive orientation. For Jerome's reference to Philo as the possible author of the Wisdom of Solomon encapsulates his reception of Philo: the learned Jewish Greek philosopher primarily serves rhetorical and instructive, not doctrinal, purposes. While he remains noncommittal about Philonic authorship of the Wisdom of Solomon, he refers to its possibility in order to advance his claim that the

---

[1] Author's translation; text from PL 28.1242–1243. See also A. Canellis, ed., *Jérôme, Préfaces aux livres de la Bible*, SC 592 (Paris: Cerf, 2017). Basil, *Ep.* 190.3 also alludes to Philonic authorship of the Wisdom of Solomon; A. Kamesar, "San Basilio, Filone, e la tradizione ebraica," *Henoch* 17 (1995): 129–40.

[2] P. P. Courcelle, *Late Latin Writers and Their Greek Sources* (Cambridge, MA: Harvard University Press, 1969), 81–83; H. Savon, "Saint Ambroise et Saint Jérôme, lecteurs de Philon," *ANRW* 2.21 (1984): 731–59; D. T. Runia, *Philo in Early Christian Literature: A Survey*, CRINT 3 (Assen: Van Gorcum; Minneapolis: Fortress Press, 1993), 312–30; H. Newman, "Jerome and the Jews" (PhD diss., Hebrew University of Jerusalem, 1997) (Hebrew).

[3] It has been recognized that Jerome essentially copies Eusebius' notice on Philo in *Hist. eccl.* 2.18 and also had access to the library at Caesarea Maritima which would explain his dilettantish knowledge of Philo. See D. T. Runia, "Caesarea Maritima and the Survival of Hellenistic-Jewish Literature," in *Caesarea Maritima: A Retrospective after Two Millenia*, ed. A. Raban and K. G. Holum, Documenta et Monumenta Orientis Antiqui 21 (Leiden: Brill, 1996), 482–84.

work has educational value, not ecclesiastical authority.[4] The notice indicates Jerome's awareness of Philo's reputation, but it does not imply deep familiarity with the content of his writings. It further suggests that Philo's writings could be a source of edification, not Church teaching. Therefore, in addition to considering specific references to the Philonic corpus in Jerome, this essay addresses the reception of Philo's persona and shows how Jerome employs the image of Philo more than his words.

14.1 The Persona of Philo in the Writings of Jerome

It is not surprising that the relatively lengthy notice about Philo in *De viris illustribus* 11.1–7, raises different expectations about Philo's reception:

> Philo the Jew, Alexandrian by birth, and of priestly descent, is placed by us among the ecclesiastical writers because he wrote a book about the first church of the evangelist Mark at Alexandria and gives us praise, recording Christians living not only there but also in many other provinces as well and describing their dwellings as monasteries (lit. "single dwellings").[5]

The passage continues with details about their monastic life such as sharing wealth and devotion to singing, prayer, learning, and chastity followed by references to his embassies to Rome, his friendship with Peter, and admiration of him by early Christians. He then follows with a list of Philo's works: "On the Confusion of Tongues" (*Conf.*), "On Nature and Discovery" (*Fug.*), "On That Which We Sensibly Seek and Reject" (*Sobr.*), "On Learning" (*Congr.*), "On the Heir of Divine Things," "On the Division of Equals and Opposites" (a second title to *Her.*), "On the Three Virtues" (*Virt.*), "Why Are the Names of Certain Ones Changed in Scriptures" (*Mut.*), "On Pacts" (lost), "On the Life of the Wise Man" (*Migr* and *Abr.*), "On the Giants" (*Gig.*), "Why Dreams Are Sent by God" (*Somn.*), "Questions and Answers on Exodus" (*QE*), "On the Tabernacle and Ten Commandments" (*Spec.* 1 = On the Tabernacle; *Spec.* 2 = On the Decalogue), "On Victims and Promises or Curses" (*Spec.* and *Praem.*), "On Providence" (*Prov.*), "On the Jews" (*Hypoth.*), "On the Conduct of Life" (*Ios.*), "On Alexander" (*Anim.*), "How Speechless Creatures Might Have Their Own Reason" (also *Anim.*), "How Every Fool Is a Slave" (lost), "On the Life of the Suppliants" (*Contempl.*), "On Agriculture" (*Agr.*), and "On Drunkenness" (*Ebr.*).[6] Clearly dependent on Eusebius' *Ecclesiastical History* for the list of works,

---

[4] Runia, *Philo*, 319.

[5] Text in A. Ceresa-Gastaldo, *Gerolamo, Gli uomini illustri*, Biblioteca patristica 12 (Florence: Nardini 1988), 96–99, translation adapted from Runia, *Philo*, 313. See also C. Barthold, ed., *Hieronymus: De Viris Illustribus, Berühmte Männer* (Mülheim: Carthusianus, 2010).

[6] These titles are culled from Eusebius' *Ecclesiastical History* and include mistakes or shortened versions of titles. See Ceresa-Gastaldo, *Gerolamo*, 258; Barthold, *Hieoronymus*, 284–87. Abbreviations of modern version of titles included in parentheses.

Jerome's own hand is also detectable.[7] Besides the focus on information relevant to early Christian history, Jerome also emphasizes testimonies about monasticism, a topic directly relevant to his own interests.[8] It is nonetheless strange that he does not mention Philo's allegorical method, a point emphasized by Eusebius. For example, every book listed by Eusebius in *Hist. eccl.* 2.18 is also here except "The Allegories of the Sacred Laws" and "Problems and Solutions in Genesis and in Exodus."[9] He is much more interested in Philo as an historical source rather than for doctrinal or even exegetical authority.[10] This is all the more surprising because he is fully aware of the Alexandrian's philosophical reputation as he concludes: "Concerning this man it is commonly said among the Greeks—either Plato follows Philo or Philo Plato—so great is the similarity in doctrines and style."[11]

We can also detect this peculiar relationship with Philo in Jerome's atypical use of this author. Jerome often employs classical, rabbinic, and Christian sources.[12] In contrast to his use of Philo, he regularly cites these sources by name with direct, identifiable quotations. We can even identify many of the "hidden" references to classical, Christian, and Jewish authors, including Josephus.[13] Normally, his sources can be divided into three categories:

1. Classical, Jewish, and Christian authorities whom he cites often and at length, either by name, such as Cicero, Porphyry, Josephus, Baranina, and Origen or generically ("pagan literature," "divine texts," "the Jews say," or "many of ours").[14]
2. Christian authorities whom he draws on at length without citation such as Didymus and Origen.
3. Brief references to a classical, Jewish, or Christian source for a nice turn of phrase or to mention a relevant work.

Philo, however, receives frequent and high praise from Jerome, but the actual influence of Philo on his writings is almost inversely proportional to the character and number of specific references to this "most learned man of the Jews." Because of Philo's relatively lengthy notice in *De viris illustribus*, we would expect a pervasive Philonic presence in Jerome's works, but instead we encounter admiration without representation.[15]

---

[7] Courcelle, *Late Latin Writers*, 83; C. Borgeais, "La personnalité de Jérôme dans son *de Viris Illustribus*," in *Jérôme entre l'occident et l'orient*, ed. Y.-M. Duval (Paris: Études augustiniennes, 1988), 283–93.

[8] A. Fürst, *Hieronymus: Askese und Wissenschaft in der Spätantike* (Freiburg: Herder, 2003).

[9] Later, Eusebius offers a separate notice of the five books of "Problems and Solutions" on Exodus, just as Jerome refers to five books on Exodus.

[10] Courcelle, *Late Latin Writers*, 83.

[11] Trans. Runia, *Philo*, 4, 313.

[12] H. Hagendahl, *Latin Fathers and the Classics: A Study on the Apologists, Jerome and Other Christian Writers*, Studia Graeca et Latina Gothoburgensia (Göteborg: Almqvist & Wiksell, 1958); Courcelle, *Late Latin Writers*; Newman, "Jerome and the Jews."

[13] Newman, "Jerome and the Jews," 203.

[14] On pagan citations, see Courcelle, *Late Latin Writers*; and Hagendahl, *Latin Fathers*. On Jewish interlocutors see, Newman, "Jerome and the Jews," 70–129. A study of Jerome's citation technique for Christian authors remains a desideratum.

[15] That Jerome most likely did not possess the Philonic titles mentioned in *Vir. ill.* (Runia, "Caesarea," 484) explains the dearth of direct quotations from Philo, but not the admiration and rhetorical function of mentioning his name.

A brief overview of the additional references to Philo confirms this. Altogether, Jerome makes nineteen explicit references, which have been listed by Runia.[16] They fall into several categories:

1. History (translation of Eusebius, *Chron.* 203, 213, 204, 214 [four references in total], *Vir. ill.* 11.1–7, 13.2).
2. Asceticism (*Ep.* 22.35.8; *Vir. ill.* 11.1–7; *Jov.* 2.14).
3. Realia (*Ep.* 29.7.1; *Praef. Iob*; *Comm. Dan.* 1.1.4a).
4. Philonic writings (*Chron.* 203, 213; *Praef. Nom. hebr.*; *Vir. ill.* 11.4–7; *Praef. In Libros Salomonis*).
5. Christians (*Vir. ill.* 8.4, 11.1–3).
6. Exempla (*Ep.* 70.3.3).
7. Philosophy (*Comm. Am.* 3.6; *Pelag.* 3.6).
8. Etymology (*Comm. Am.* 2.9).
9. Allegory (*Comm. Am.* 2.9; *Comm. Ezech.* 4.16.10b).

In these references, he cites Philo alone twelve times; four times with Josephus; and three times with Josephus and others. It should be noted too that, with the exception of the passages from the commentaries on Amos (2.9) and Ezekiel, as well as the repeated references to the seven ages of life (*Comm. Am.* 3.6; *Pelag.* 3.6), the majority of these cite Philo more as an historical source, or out of antiquarian interest, than as an exegete. His philosophical interpretations barely interest Jerome.

Although previous studies analyzing Jerome's relationship to Philo have noted the paucity of Philonic influences, they have not explained why Jerome consistently expresses his admiration and knowledge of Philo. Rather, Courcelle, Savon, Runia, and Newman have primarily focused on whether he had direct familiarity with Philo.[17] For example, Courcelle argues that just because Jerome copies the notice in *De viris illustribus* from Eusebius (*Hist. eccl.* 2.4.2. and 2.17.1ff.), this does not mean that he did not encounter Philo's work directly (contra Sychowski).[18] Runia astutely notes that Jerome, first among the Latin fathers, represents Philo as similar to Plato because of the "form and content" of his writings, but he too concentrates on whether Jerome had direct knowledge of Philo's writings.[19] He agrees with Courcelle that the dependence of the notice in *De viris illustribus* on Eusebius does not mean complete ignorance of Philo's writings. For example, his references to Philo's writing on the Essenes cannot be dependent on Eusebius who describes them as proto-Christian. Moreover, Courcelle notes that most of Jovinian derives from Porphyry's *De abstinentia*, so the reference to

---

[16] D. T. Runia, "References to Philo from Josephus up to 1000 AD," in *Philo and the Church Fathers: A Collection of Papers*, VCSup (Leiden: Brill, 1995), 228–39.

[17] Courcelle, *Late Latin Writers*, 81–83; H. Savon, "Saint Ambroise et Saint Jérôme, lecteurs de Philon," *ANRW* 2.21 (1984): 731–59; Runia, *Philo*; Newman, "Jerome and the Jews."

[18] Courcelle, *Late Latin Writers*, 82. Cf. S. von Sychowski, *Hieronymus als Litterarhistoriker: Eine quellenkritische Untersuchung der Schrift des H. Hieronyms "De viris illustribus"*, Kirchengeschichtliche Studien 2.2 (Münster: Heinrich Schöninch, 1894), 69–70, 95–97.

[19] Runia, *Philo*, 314.

the Essenes represents a Hieronymian insertion directly from Philo.[20] References not found in Eusebius, such as to Pentecost at *Ep.* 22 and the seven ages in *Comm. Am.* 3.6 and *Pelag.* suggest independent reading of Philo.[21] Mention of Hebrew as Chaldean (*Comm. Dan.*), awareness of the LXX origin stories (*Qu. hebr. Gen.*, praef.; *Prol. Pent.*), and Philo's comparison of the hyacinth on the high priest's robe to air (*Comm. Ezech.* 16:10) all further suggest direct familiarity with his writing.[22] This last example is problematic because in the parallels (*Mos.* 2.118; *Spec.* 1.85; *QE* 2.117), Philo situates air in the sublunary realm while Jerome claims that for Philo, hyacinth/air signifies the heavenly realm. Jerome intentionally or unintentionally misrepresents Philo to support his conclusion that the passage as a whole refers to holy beings approaching the heavenly realm.[23] For Runia, then, Philo is primarily a tool for Jerome's historical more than exegetical and theological interests.[24] He represents a contemporary of early Christians, a link in the "scriptural tradition" of biblical exegetes, and a source of Judaica.[25] Nevertheless, according to Runia, Jerome lacks a "*critical* historical sense" that makes him more amenable to the notion of Philo encountering early Christians.[26]

Even though the specific references to Philo have been listed and discussed elsewhere, it is useful to consider some of these from a different perspective. Instead of resolving whether Jerome indeed directly drew from Philo, it is worthwhile to examine why he attributes these references to Philo. This requires attention to the context of the passages. For example, Jerome writes in *Epistula* 22.35.8 (384 CE): "The Essenes also follow these rules, as we learn from Philo, Plato's imitator, and from Josephus, the Greek Livy, in the second book of his *Jewish Captivity*" (2.8 [Wright, LCL]). He is probably referring here to *Quod omnis probus liber sit* 75–87.[27] The remark appears in Jerome's most famous ascetic letter, on virginity, at the end of a discussion about cenobites. In another letter of the same year, *Epistula* 29.7.1 (384 CE), the reference reflects his familiarity with Philo's writings: "However, because we have exceeded the brevity of a letter ... and because Josephus and Philo, the most learned men of the Jews, and many of us Christians, have extensively covered this topic [the dress of the priest], you will hear me, as they say, in front of a live audience." Philo discusses the priestly

---

[20] Courcelle, *Late Latin Writers*, 82.

[21] Runia, *Philo*, 315.

[22] Runia, *Philo*, 316. Although he does not mention him by name, *Comm. Ezech.* 8:7 on Ezek 27:7 is also probably based on Philo because it is similar to the passage here. "Linen (*byssus*) refers to the earth because it comes from the earth, and hyacinth represents the air, purple represents the sea, from which it is made, with twice-dipped red. All of these colors are woven in the clothing of the high priest which I have often mentioned because they symbolize the four elements, earth, fire, air and water from which all things exist."

[23] According to Runia (*Philo*, 316), the Philonic parallels do not refer to linen as symbolizing earth, unlike in *Comm. Ezech.* 8:7 where Jerome refers to all four elements (earth, fire, air, water). Therefore, he suggests that while Philo, *Congr.* 117 is possible, Jerome more likely draws on Josephus, *A.J.* 3.185; *B.J.* 5.213.

[24] D. T. Runia, "Philo and the Early Christian Fathers," in *The Cambridge Companion to Philo*, ed. A. Kamesar (Cambridge: Cambridge University Press, 2009), 210–30.

[25] Runia, *Philo*, 316.

[26] Runia, *Philo*, 316, following R. Hagendahl and J. H. Waszink, "Hieronymus," *RAC* 15 (1989): 117–39, at 135: "wie ihm ... historisches Denken völlig fremd ist." The mere fact that Jerome prefers the Aristean version of the LXX's origin to the more miraculous one of Philo and later writers indicates that Hagendahl and Waszink exaggerate Jerome's lack of historical acumen.

[27] Courcelle, *Late Latin Writers*, 82, who also suggests the preface to *De vita contemplativa* as a source.

vestments primarily in *Spec.* 1.83–99 and *Mos.* 2.109–35.[28] I will examine below how Jerome appropriates Philo when discussing the symbolic meaning of the priests' garments in *Epistula* 64.

The mention in the preface of *De nominibus hebraicis* (388 CE) exemplifies how Jerome exploits Philo's authority regardless of whether he directly utilized the Alexandrian:

> Philo, the most learned man of the Jews, also according to the testimony of Origen, is confirmed to have published a book of Hebrew names and to have organized their etymologies alphabetically. Since this work is commonly available among the Greeks, and fills the libraries of the world, it was my goal to translate it into Latin. However, I found the manuscripts so contradictory and the order so confused, that I determined it was better to be silent than to produce something that deserved condemnation.

Therefore, Jerome decides to cull through scriptures from the beginning and systematically arrange the Hebrew names by biblical book in alphabetical order. He further adds in the preface that he has reserved some information for other works, such as his *Quaestionum hebraicarum liber in Genesim*. He describes this as a new kind of treatise that will be preferable to the belching and vomit of the Jews and concludes by praising Origen who produced a work on Hebrew names that expanded Philo, "so that what Philo, as a Jew, had omitted, he would supply as a Christian." Despite his frequent use of etymologies, there is no evidence that Philo wrote such a work.[29] Therefore, we more likely have a case here of Jerome indirectly following Philo through Origen. Philo appears here primarily for rhetorical reasons to buttress Jerome's claim that his work improves on the Jewish original in two ways. First, he addresses the problems in the manuscript tradition and, second, his references to Origen make it clear that he too will be providing Christian improvement to the Jewish original. This is similar to his justification for translating the Bible from the Hebrew. The Latin versions of the LXX were also in disarray and he, as a Christian, could translate from the Hebrew more accurately than the fabled seventy Jewish scholars who predated Jesus by a few centuries.[30]

He also cites Philo as an authority, among others, in *Epistula* 70.3.3 (397 CE). "What am I to say about Philo, whom critics call another or Jewish Plato." Jerome justifies the use of pagan sources by citing biblical figures such as Moses and Paul, and various

---

[28] J. Laporte, "The High Priest in Philo of Alexandria," *SPhiloA* 3 (1991): 71–82; R. Hayward, "St. Jerome and the Meaning of the High-Priestly Vestments," in *Hebrew Study from Ezra to Ben-Yehuda*, ed. W. Horbury (Edinburgh: T & T Clark, 1999), 90–105; A. Canellis, "La Lettre 64 de Saint Jérôme et le symbolisme des couleurs," *VC* 72 (2018): 235–54.

[29] L. L. Grabbe, *Etymology in Early Jewish Interpretation: The Hebrew Names in Philo* (Atlanta: Scholars Press, 1988).

[30] A. Kamesar, *Jerome, Greek Scholarship, and the Hebrew Bible: A Study of the Quaestiones Hebraicae in Genesim*, Oxford Classical Monographs (Oxford: Clarendon Press, 1993), 64–69. Jerome probably also has Philo in mind when he refers to some author (*nescio quis… auctor*) of the preposterous story (*mendacium*) of the translators miraculously composing the same translation despite being in separate cells (*Prol. Pent.*). After all, he shows familiarity with *Mos.* 2.26–44 (*Comm. Dan.* 1.1.4a) and 2.109–35 (*Epp.* 29.7.1, 64; *Comm. Ezech.* 4.16.10b). He then continues with an explicit endorsement of Aristaeus and Josephus' realistic version. It is likely that he does not mention Philo by name to avoid diminishing Philo's reputation.

Christian authors as well as Josephus who exploited their pagan erudition to promote biblical teachings with parallels from the gentile philosophers and poets already considered authoritative by pagans. Philo thus represents a Jew, with impressive Jewish and pagan learning, that he exploits to defend his people, not pollute his tradition.

Another mention of Philo appears in a lengthy comment on Amos 6:2–6 in a discussion appropriate to the Jewish philosopher: "For nothing is more fleeting than the world and the things of the world. We lose these while we cling to them and through infancy, childhood, youth, and the vigorous, middle-aged, and mature times of life as well as the final years of old age, into which seven sections Philo divided human life; we change and rush and ignorantly reach the limits of death." Philo refers to the seven ages of life in *De opificio mundi* 103–5. After a historical reading of the text, Jerome turns to the LXX for "the cloudy sky of allegory." The verses deal with the disposition of the mind which controls whether one succumbs to evil. He follows the Septuagint reading of Amos 6:5, as "you who make noise at the sound of musical instruments; they think of them as if abiding, not fleeting." Then he cites Epicurus, Vergil, and Horace who testify to fleeting aspects of this world. This is a rare instance where he draws on Philo for a philosophical trope relevant to his exegesis. It makes sense to draw on Philo when he repeats the trope that it is wise to consider the best from all places: "If we wished to treat with our mind, and to discuss the philosophy of all the nations, Egypt, India, and Persia, we would find that their borders are narrower than the borders of holy Scriptures."

In addition to explicit citations, there are instances where Jerome attributes to anonymous individuals etymological interpretations that might depend on Philo:

1. *Qu. hebr. Gen.* 17:15 (388 CE): "Those people are mistaken who think that the name Sara was written first with one R and that another R was afterwards added to it; and because among the Greeks the R represents the number 100, they surmise many absurd things about her name. At any rate, in whatever way they maintain that her name was altered, it ought not to have a Greek but a Hebrew explanation, since the name itself is Hebrew .... Now this is the reason why her name was changed in this way: formerly she was called 'my ruler', the mother of a household of one house only; thereafter she was called 'ruler' absolutely, that is *archousa*."[31]

2. *Ep.* 78.3.2 (399 CE): "Some interpret Ramesse as 'stormy shaking' or 'the bitterness and shaking of the moth', but we prefer the more accurate translation 'thundering of joy'. The people, wishing to depart into the desert, gathered at this city which is on the furthest borders of Egypt. They did it for this reason: abandoning the disturbances of the world, they began to separate themselves from their old faults and the moth of their sins which previously was gnawing at them. And they

---

[31] Trans. R. Hayward, *Saint Jerome's Hebrew Questions on Genesis*, Oxford Early Christian Studies (Oxford: Clarendon Press, 1995). Although rejecting the Greek tradition, according to Hayward, *Saint Jerome's Hebrew Questions*, 165, he could be drawing on Philo for the etymology (*Cher.* 5, 7, 41; *Mut.* 77; *QG* 3.53; *Abr.* 99; *Congr.* 2). The claim that Sarah's name changed by doubling the R is erroneous.

turned all that bitterness into sweetness all for the purpose of hearing the voice of God thundering on Mt. Sinai."

"Some" could refer to Philo, *Somn.* 1.77 where he states that "Ramses ... means ... moth-shock" (Whitaker, LCL).[32] It is more likely, however, that Jerome follows Origen here in a homily on the book of Numbers, where he mentions a similar etymology, *commotio tineae* "shaking of the moth," which clearly translates Philo and relates the moth-imagery to the progress of the soul.[33] Therefore, it is more likely that Jerome follows Origen here.

14.2 Philonic Influences in the Translation and Exegesis of Scripture

Another underexplored area of Philonic influence lies in Jerome's translation of scripture which can reflect Jewish traditions. While recent studies have identified numerous interpretive renditions based on exegetical traditions, it is difficult to identify uniquely Philonic influence. In the case of Exod 5:1, Jerome renders $w^e yahogu$, "celebrate a festival," as "sacrifice" (*sacrificio*). We can identify the influence of the parallel passage in Philo, *Mos.* 1.87 which has the Greek cognate verb for sacrifice (ἱερουργέω).[34] Origen and rabbinic tradition also could be sources here.[35] The lack of a uniquely Philonic parallel is typical in the Vulgate, and so we can only concede that the direct use of Philo is unlikely and that it is more likely that Jerome did not draw on him at all or he relied on Philo to confirm his translation.[36]

The few references to Philo may result from Jerome's historical orientation. Moreover, since he acknowledges Philo's philosophical credentials, but he himself focuses on translating and commenting on the biblical text, mentions of Philo are expected to be rare.[37] Nevertheless, since he does include allegorical interpretations, he may draw on Philo, like Ambrose, but not mention him by name as this would not be in Jerome's

---

[32] According to Philo, the storage city of Ramses symbolizes perception which disturbs the soul as if it were being eaten by a moth.

[33] Origen, *Hom. Num.* 27.9: "Now the first starting place was from Ramesse; and whether the soul starts out from this world and comes to the future age or is converted from the errors of life to the way of virtue and knowledge, it starts out from Ramesse. For in our language Ramesse means 'confused agitation' (*commotio turbida*) or 'agitation of the worm' (*commotio tineae*). By this it is made clear that everything in this world is set in agitation and disorder, and also in corruption; for this what the worm means. The soul should not remain in them, but should set out and come to Sochoth" (translated from the Latin of Rufinus by R. Greer, *Origen: An Exhortation to Martyrdom, Prayer and Selected Works*, Classics of Western Spirituality [Mahwah, NJ: Paulist Press, 1979]).

[34] M. A. Kraus, *Jewish, Christian, and Classical Exegetical Traditions in Jerome's Translation of the Book of Exodus: Translation Technique and the Vulgate*, VCSup (Leiden: Brill, 2017), 145–47. Josephus (*A.J.* 2.269) and the Talmud (b. Hag. 10b) also understand the term as "sacrifice" but lack the linguistic parallel.

[35] Origen, *Hom. Num.* 20.5 and b. Avodah Zarah 17b.

[36] Similar examples include Exod 2:3/*Mos.* 1.10–12 (Kraus, *Jewish*, 143); Exod 26:1/*Mos.* 2.97; QE 2.62 (Kraus, *Jewish*, 160); Deut 4:17/*Spec.* 1.16ff.; 1.18ff.; 3.189 (S. Weigert, *Hebraica Veritas: Übersetzungsprinzipien und Quellen der Deuteronomiumübersetzung des Hieronymus*, BWANT [Stuttgart: Kohlhammer, 2016], 162–67); Deut 16:21–22/*Leg.* 1.51 (Weigert, *Hebraica Veritas*, 229); Deut 20:20/*Spec.* 4.227; *Virt.* 154 (Weigert, *Hebraica Veritas*, 191–92); Deut 34:6/*Mos.* 2.291 (Weigert, *Hebraica Veritas*, 211–12).

[37] Runia, *Philo*, 316–17.

interest.[38] This opens the door to the possibility of unattributed allegorical readings drawn from the Philonic corpus. Runia closes this door by taking over the explanation put forward in Savon's study of the *Letter to Fabiola* (*Ep.* 64).[39] While the passage about the parts of the sacrifice belonging to the priest is similar to Philo, *Spec.* 1.145–47, Savon argues that literal exegesis parallels rabbinic material and the allegorical reading with its Philonic features derives from Origen. Runia also concurs with Savon's claim that Jerome would read a variety of authors and then compose his writings through a secretary. This results in a haphazard mixture of his ideas and cited, uncited, or incorrectly cited references from others. Runia takes a balanced view that Jerome may draw on Philo whether he claims to or not, and may not draw on Philo, even if he does claim him as a source. Newman concurs with Runia, that Jerome refers to Philo specifically in numerous places and knew some of his work directly, not just through others.[40] However, it is hard to tell if he appropriated a specific interpretation from a Jewish teacher, Philo, or a source influenced by Philo.[41] Newman does, however, go further in acknowledging some possible additional uses of Philo without citing him by name in *Qu. hebr. Gen.* and *Comm. Os.* 3.2–3.[42] He further notes that Jerome never brings Philonic tradition in the name of Jews or Hebrews except in *Epistula* 64.18.[43] Philo or Josephus may have influenced Jerome's observation that gifts to the priests are from the profane, not holy parts of the animal in *Ep.* 64.2.[44] Josephus reads Deuteronomy 18:3 (*A.J.* 4.74) as referring to slaughter at home while Philo refers to slaughter (not on an altar) used for food (*Spec.* 1.147).[45] Newman does qualify Savon's reading of *Epistula* 64 by acknowledging some Philonic influence despite the preponderant reliance on Josephus. After all, Jerome mentions Philo and Josephus' writings about the clothes of the high priest (*Ep.* 29.7) and characterizes his description of the clothing as presented in the Jewish custom (*Ep.* 64.9). He also refers to the allegorical teaching of the Hebrews (*Ep.* 64.18) where the term "Hebrews" most likely refers to Josephus and Philo (*Spec.* 1.82–97).[46] It is striking that the one time he has Philo in mind when referring to the traditions of the Jews or Hebrews, he does not mention Philo by name.

While Jerome may have directly utilized Origen rather than Philo for his etymological works, he follows Philo in utilizing the onomastic genre.[47] Such generic influence may also account for Jerome's decision to title his work *Quaestionum hebraicarum*

---

[38] Runia, *Philo*, 317.
[39] Runia, *Philo*, 317–19; cf. Savon, "Saint Ambroise," 752–55.
[40] Newman, "Jerome and the Jews," 79.
[41] See Kamesar, *Jerome, Greek Scholarship*, 112–17; Hayward, *Saint Jerome's Hebrew Questions*, 164–65.
[42] Following Hayward, *Saint Jerome's Hebrew Questions*, 18; M. Rahmer, *Die Hebräischen Traditionen in den Werken des Hieronymus: Die Commentarii zu den XII Kleinen Propheten* (Berlin: M. Poppelauer, 1902), 2:17–18. The passage from Hosea could parallel m. Sotah 2.1 as well as *Spec* 3.57 as both draw the parallel the Sotah's beastly action and her offering of barley flour, the food of beasts. Newman, "Jerome and the Jews," 183 n. 261 also considers *Ep.* 64.5 a Philonic reference, but agrees that *Ep.* 78.3 is taken from Origen's *Hom. Num.* which he uses extensively in the letter.
[43] Newman, "Jerome and the Jews," 79.
[44] Newman, "Jerome and the Jews," 183 n. 260.
[45] Newman, "Jerome and the Jews," 183.
[46] The reference to seventy-two bells and pomegranates in *Ep.* 64.14 could be a Jewish tradition found in Vay. Rab. 21.7; b. Zevahim 88b (Newman, "Jerome and the Jews," 183 n. 261).
[47] Newman, "Jerome and the Jews," 82.

liber in Genesim thereby labeling it as *Quaestiones* literature. The title was not inevitable, since the work mixes genres by including traditional *quaestiones*, implied *quaestiones*, and elements of commentary similar to the *Quaestiones* of Philo and Theodoret as well as material more closely aligned with the *excerpta*/scholia genre.[48] While he may have preferred to include *Quaestiones* in the title to highlight the significance of the "questions" in the work and align himself with similar Antiochene works,[49] he also, as in the case of the *De nominibus hebraicis*, situates himself in a tradition that can be traced back to Philo. For he was aware that Philo composed *Quaestiones*. He does not mention Philo by name, however, most likely because he portrays the *Qu. hebr. Gen.* as a new work. This, however, does not prevent him from drawing on Philo in the work itself. This can include agreeing or taking issue with a Philonic interpretation. For example, in 25:8, *Qu. hebr. Gen.* has:

> And what we have set out as *in a good old age, an old man and full*, in the Greek codices is put as full of days. Although this appears to state the meaning, in that he died full of light and of the works of the day, it none the less makes for greater *anagōgē* [spiritual meaning] if *full* is put simply on its own.[50]

In *QG* 4.152 Philo similarly comments on the redundancy of the Bible: "Moreover, I am greatly puzzled by the addition ... 'full of days' ... for the Father does not allow the life of the virtuous man to be empty ... in any place for evil (to enter) his mind ..." and attributes it to a tropological reference to virtue (Marcus, LCL). While Hayward correctly identifies the parallel to Philo, he does not note that Jerome rejects the LXX reading "full of days" on which Philo bases his interpretation.[51] One can sense here how Jerome uses Philo critically: he deploys the anagogical interpretation to justify the superiority of the Hebrew text to the Greek versions.[52]

Jerome does not always follow Philo in the *Qu. hebr. Gen.* There is a difference, however, between Jerome's rejection of Philo's fanciful explanation for Seth by deriving it from "drink" not "place" (*Qu. hebr. Gen.* 4.25), and his critique of the etymologies for "man seeing God" for Israel and "son of days" for Benjamin in *Qu. hebr. Gen.* 32:28–29 and 35:18. Both etymologies appear in Philo.[53] Hayward claims that Jerome is rejecting Philo here, but as has been noted, Kamesar shows that he does not specifically reject Philo per se but takes issue with his methodology: Philo's etymologies for the *De nominibus hebraicis* fail to rely on the Hebrew.[54] In the index to his translation and

---

[48] Kamesar, *Jerome, Greek Scholarship*, 92–95. The "composite make-up" of the *Qu. hebr. Gen.* is probably modeled on Origen's *excerpta*, but the fact that he includes *Quaestiones* in the title rather than *excerpta* or *commentarioli* "takes on special significance" (Kamesar, *Jerome, Greek Scholarship*, 95).

[49] Kamesar, *Jerome, Greek Scholarship*, 95.

[50] Trans. Hayward, *Saint Jerome's Hebrew Questions*, 60.

[51] Hayward, *Saint Jerome's Hebrew Questions*, 191.

[52] The Vulgate at Gen 25:8 has *plenus dierum* "full of days." The proper Latin expression would be *plenus annis* "full of years" which Philo explicitly rejects: "For (Scripture) says that the virtuous man is full not of years but of days" (*QG* 4.152, Marcus, LCL). The failure to use the proper Latin expression is especially noticeable because he renders *zaken* with the idiomatic *provectae aetatis* "of advanced age."

[53] "Israel" (*Legat.* 4; *Leg.* 2.34) and "Benjamin" (*Somn.* 2.36).

[54] Hayward, *Saint Jerome's Hebrew Questions*, 18–19; Kamesar, *Jerome, Greek Scholarship*, 91–93, 112–21.

commentary on *Qu. hebr. Gen.*, Hayward makes over eighty references to Philo. Despite his claim that Jerome follows Philo occasionally, such as at 25:8 and 26:12,[55] a closer examination of these references indicates that the majority of them simply contain similar readings that also appear in the Greek versions or in other authors. In the remaining citations, Philo offers an alternative that Jerome specifically rejects, or Jerome simply offers a reading at odds with what we find in Philo. This is why Kamesar's focus on method makes more sense. Jerome is not engaging with specific Philonic readings by themselves, but rejects the Greek-based method for the Hebrew, which will naturally lead to differences in interpretation.[56] It is also noteworthy that many of the references to Philo in *Qu. hebr. Gen.* claimed by Hayward relate to etymologies. Since Philo himself often comments on etymologies, we would expect numerous parallels in anyone utilizing etymological lists of names and places.

There is one place, however, where we do find Philonic influence in Jerome, namely in *Epistula* 64 (396 CE), contrary to Savon's claims. The letter includes a lengthy description of the high priest's garments and their literal and allegorical meaning. While properly identifying Josephus as a primary source, he missed several Philonic references which have been noticed by Robert Hayward and Aline Canellis.[57] The letter consists of various discussions about the Levitical priest with a large section devoted to a literal and allegorical description of the vestments of the priests. Because he refers to Philo and Josephus' writing on the vestments of the high priest in other letters whereas in this letter he only refers specifically to Josephus, Savon reasonably assumes that Josephus was his only source. However, he refers to Hebrew interpretation three times, first in 64.9.2 and then in 64.18.1 and 64.19.1 The first passage introduces the discussion of the priestly vestments as follows: "before I examine their mystical meaning, according to the Jewish manner, I will explain simply what is written so that after you see the priest clothed and all his adornment revealed before your eyes, then we can examine the reasons for each of these things" (trans. mine). While one could understand "the Jewish manner" as referring to the literal interpretation of scriptures ("what is written") and the "mystical understanding" as representing the Christian interpretation, it could also refer to his entire approach, namely "the Jewish manner" entails explaining the literal meaning followed by the allegorical meaning. This is precisely what Josephus himself does in the *Jewish Antiquities*. Moreover, when he introduces the allegorical reading in 64.18, he alludes again to Jewish learning: "let us speak first of what we have learned from the Hebrews, and then afterwards we will lift the veil to its spiritual meaning according to our custom" (trans. mine). The Jewish allegorical reading follows. One could claim, with Savon, that by "Hebrews," Jerome is only referring to Josephus here. In my view, however, he is drawing on both Josephus and Philo.[58] For instance, the cosmic symbolism of the four colors referring to the four elements,

---

[55] Hayward, *Saint Jerome's Hebrew Questions*, 18.
[56] Kamesar's thorough study of the *Hebrew Questions on Genesis* thus never claims that Jerome follows or engages with Philo, but merely notes the many parallels between the authors.
[57] Hayward, "St. Jerome and the Meaning"; Canellis, "Lettre 64 de Saint Jérôme."
[58] Hayward, "St. Jerome and the Meaning," 94–102; Canellis, "Lettre 64 de Saint Jérôme," 248–54.

linen (earth), purple (sea), hyacinth (air), and red (fire and ether) appears in both authors. Since Josephus begins his allegorical explanation with these connections and given Jerome's preference for him, we might attribute the source to Josephus alone despite the Philonic parallel.[59] Nevertheless, there are several points where Jerome agrees with Philo against Josephus. For Josephus, the tunic of the high priest signifies the earth with its linen and the firmament with its hyacinth color, while for Philo and Jerome the hyacinth represents air.[60] Jerome also includes differing Philonic and Josephan readings: the pomegranates and bells indicate lightning (Josephus) or the harmoniousness of earth and water and all the elements (Philo), and the two stones of the ephod indicate the sun and moon (Josephus) or the two hemispheres (Philo).[61] Finally, Jerome includes the Philonic rationales for the symbolism. The four elements indicate that the high priest prays on behalf of the universe, not just Israel; earth and air on the tunic represent how we are raised from earthly to heavenly things.[62] In his discussion of the gold plate with the name of God for the turban of the high priest, not only does Jerome follow Philo (*Mos.* 2.131) in claiming that it signifies "that all things below are governed according to God's will" (64.18.8) unlike Josephus, he then continues with his own view (*ego puto*, "I myself think") that the same idea is figured in other names and the four cherubim from Ezekiel 1.[63] He would not emphasize his own view if he had not been recently drawing on other sources. Thus, he transitions to the Christian reading by concluding in reference to the previous allegorical discussion: "We have touched upon the Hebrew explanation," promising to discuss the "infinite forest of meanings" at another time.

What follows is a discussion of Christian meanings. These could derive from Origen, but also Philo.[64] For example, the four rows of stones on the breastplate represent the four virtues—*prudentia, fortitudo, iustitia,* and *temperantia*—that can be combined in twelve different ways and/or could represent the four Gospels. A letter/spirit distinction and discussion of the pants seems close to Origen's homily on Leviticus.[65] It is certain that Jerome incorporates elements of Origen's *Hom. Lev.* 6 in his allegorical reading of

---

[59] *A.J.* 3.183. Josephus is describing the veil of the temple here immediately before he explains the symbolism of the high priest's tunic. Jerome probably misreads Josephus here. Cf. Philo, *Mos.* 2.88; *QE* 2.85.

[60] Hayward, "St. Jerome and the Meaning," 99 (Josephus, *A.J.* 3.184; Philo, *Mos.* 2.118).

[61] Hayward, "St. Jerome and the Meaning," 99; Josephus, *A.J.* 3.184–85; Philo, *Mos.* 2.119: "The bells represent the harmonious alliance of these two [earth and water] since life cannot be produced by earth without water or by water without the substance of earth, but only by the union and combination of both" (Colson, LCL). Jerome similarly notes that "they represent the earth and water and the harmony of all the elements with each other and how all things are thus connected to each other, so that all things all things are contained each individual thing" (trans. mine). At *Mos.* 2.24.122, Philo indicates that the two stones may refer to the sun and moon or the two hemispheres. For Josephus (*A.J.* 3.163), the breastplate signifies an oracle, for Philo and Jerome, it represents the place of reason (*Mos.* 2.112, 2.125, 2.128; *Spec.* 1.86–88; *QE* 2.110–16; Jerome, *Ep.* 64.18.6–8). See Hayward, "St. Jerome and the Meaning," 93.

[62] Hayward, "St. Jerome and the Meaning," 98. Canellis claims that Jerome synthesizes the interpretations of Philo and Josephus ("Lettre 64 de Saint Jérôme," 249).

[63] See Hayward, "St. Jerome and the Meaning," 102–3 and Canellis, "Lettre 64 de Saint Jérôme," 249, who also note Jerome's independent use of sources.

[64] Canellis, "Lettre 64 de Saint Jérôme," 248–54.

[65] Origen touches upon the allegorical meaning of the priestly vestments briefly in *Hom. Exod.* 9, but there is little similarity to Jerome. For example, Origen (*Hom. Exod.* 9.4) notes that the bejeweled ephod refers to divine, not human works and the four rows of stones on the breastplate represent the four Gospels, a reading recognized, but not strongly endorsed by Jerome. It should also be noted that Origen focuses on the Tabernacle.

the priestly garb. This includes structural, textual and conceptual parallels. For instance, when he begins to discuss the Christian allegory near the end of the letter starting at 64.19, like Origen, he focuses on the description of the priestly vestments in Leviticus 8 rather than Exodus 28, the basis of Jerome's literal and allegorical Jewish readings. In addition, both authors conclude with a specific explanation of why the undergarments of the priest are mentioned in Exodus, but not in Leviticus (Jerome, *Ep.* 64.21.3; Origen, *Hom. Lev.* 6.6). We also find verbal parallels: explaining why Moses washed Aaron before giving him his clothes, Jerome notes that "what Moses washes, is a representation of the law" (*Ep.* 64.19.2), while Origen states: "how can Moses wash you? ... We have often said that Moses symbolizes the law in Holy Scriptures" (*Hom. Lev.* 6.2). They both allude to the connection between the clothes of the high priest and Adam.[66] They share conceptual frameworks such as the need to combine words and deeds and how the breastplate symbolizes that knowledge precedes teaching (Jerome, *Ep.* 64.20.4; Origen, *Hom. Lev.* 6.4.). Nevertheless, he does not follow Origen slavishly. For example, he argues that baptism cleanses while Origen argues that the law cleanses. Likewise, while both admire the order of the vestments' description, for Origen, the breastplate (*logium/rationale*) is made after the ephod, because wisdom comes after deeds (6.4). For Jerome (20.3), works are on the shoulder, reason on the breast and priests consume the breast and the breastplate has both the open (the stones on the front of the breastplate) and the hidden (teaching and truth).[67] The twelve stones on the outside of the breastplate in four rows, represent the four virtues of prudence (*prudentia*), courage (*fortitudo*), justice (*iustitia*), and moderation (*temperantia*).[68] Mixed together, they produce the number twelve.[69] To be sure, there are several discussions in the letter that do not appear in Origen's homily.[70] What is striking here is that Jerome agrees with Philo against Origen.[71] According to Philo (*QE* 2.112), in addition to representing seasons, months and the zodiac, the stones

---

[66] Jerome, *Ep.* 64.19.3: "Prepared for the clothing of Christ we take off our skin tunics [*tunicas pellicias*]" of death; Origen, *Hom. Lev.* 6.2: "For the sinner had to be clothed in such skin tunics, which are characterized by mortality .... If you are washed and purified, Moses will cloth you in the clothing of incorruption." Similarly, Jerome, *Ep.* 64.20.5–6 and Origen, *Hom. Lev.* 6.4 explain the rationale in light of Hosea 10:12 to prove that the order of the breastplate's description make sense. Gregory of Nyssa, *Vit. Moys.* 2.191, 201 also alludes to Adam's clothing, which represent vices and mortality that must be discarded.

[67] Cf. Gregory of Nyssa, *Vit. Moys.* 2.200: "because the arms represent deeds and the heart symbolizes contemplation, the straps connecting the ornaments to the arms exhort us to unite philosophical practice with philosophical thinking." See A. Conway-Jones, *Gregory of Nyssa's Tabernacle Imagery in Its Jewish and Christian Contexts*, Oxford Early Christian Studies (Oxford: Oxford University Press, 2014), 209.

[68] Or the four Gospels. On the connection between the four virtues and Ezekiel 1, see Hayward, "St. Jerome and the Meaning," 103.

[69] It is not clear how four virtues mixed together make twelve. Perhaps he is referring to the twelve possible ways of pairing the four virtues, if the order of the pairing is taken into consideration.

[70] Conversely, there are numerous topics touched upon by Origen that Jerome does not include: the two tunics of the priests do not contradict the prohibition of two tunics in Luke 3:11 (6.3); why there are two girdings (6.4); the difference between minor and high priests, and why Aaron and Moses are always in the Tent of Meeting (6.6).

[71] Clement of Alexandria and Gregory of Nyssa also show Philonic influence, but in ways different from Jerome. See chapters in this volume by Annewies van den Hoek and Albert Geljon. Elsewhere, Geljon identifies the interpretation of the robe's blue color as representing air (*Mos.* 2.191) a point made by Philo (*Mos.* 2.122), but Gregory does not include the cosmological reading and for him air is adjectival not teleological. One's fleshly garments must be exchanged for airy ones to carry us on high. Gregory himself, although probably drawing on Philo, does not endorse the connection between the color blue and air (*Philonic Exegesis in Gregory of Nyssa's De Vita Moysis*, BJS 333, SPhiloM 5 [Providence: Brown Judaic Studies, 2002], 138–40). A. Conway-Jones, *Gregory of Nyssa's Tabernacle Imagery*, 213–14, notes additional parallels between Gregory and Philo (the twelve stones represent the virtues of the patriarchs and the square shape of the breastplate gems points to steadfastness). Beyond

also represent the four virtues of knowledge, moderation, courage, and justice.[72] Since "each of the four virtues consists of an element of three things," Philo also generates the number twelve from the four virtues.[73] In addition, it is Philo who notes that "the reason in it is twofold, one residing in thought, and the other uttered and revealed" (*QE* 2.116) which Jerome essentially translates: "the *rationale* is twofold, open and hidden" (*Ep.* 64.20.3).[74] Jerome thus draws on Philo directly, not through Origen, when presenting the Christian allegory of the priestly garments. Since he has finished discussing the Jewish interpretation, it would not be appropriate to explicitly cite Philo here, but that does not prevent him from appropriating Philo's interpretation for tropological exegesis in accord with his Christian reading of the text. His dependence on Philo and others here is "selective and creative" in order to remove "the untidiness of his sources" and show how the symbolism of the priestly garments "progresses in carefully determined order from lower to higher."[75]

Jerome does not mention Philo simply to name-drop or because he haphazardly recalls snippets from his broad reading prior to writing. Rather, the name of Philo and his characterization as a learned, eloquent, Jewish philosopher lends authority to his own writings, but not for Church doctrine. The fact that Jerome names Philo allots him an authoritative role in his self-fashioning. Recently, Cain, Williams, and others have called attention to Jerome's self-representation.[76] After his expulsion from Rome and the demise of his patron Damasus, Jerome sought to establish his authority through other means. He did this by representing himself as the promoter of asceticism and as a biblical scholar.[77] This can account for the peculiar appearances of Philo. Namely, Philo represents an authoritative witness to Christian asceticism. Moreover, Jerome cannot

---

an undeveloped reference to the cosmological symbolism of the garments, Clement of Alexandria (*Strom.* 5.32–40) draws very little from Philo in his primarily Christological interpretation of the priestly vestments (Conway, 211–12). See A. van den Hoek, *Clement of Alexandria and His Use of Philo in the Stromateis: An Early Christian Reshaping of a Jewish Model* (Leiden: Brill, 1988).

[72] Knowledge probably means prudence (φρόνησις) here because Philo is referring to four cardinal virtues common in Platonic and Stoic thought according to R. Marcus (LCL).

[73] Philo elaborates on this point: "(there is) knowledge and the thing known and knowing, just as (there is) moderation and the thing moderated and moderating" (Marcus, LCL).

[74] The translation of breastplate as *rationale*/λόγιον provides the connection to *ratio*/λόγος "reason." Philo, based on the LXX, refers to the Urim as δήλωσις and σαφήνεια which corresponds to the "uttered and revealed" form of the λόγος and calls the Thumim ἀλήθεια that represents the truth "residing in thought" or λόγος ἐνδιάθετος "reflexion" (*QE* 2.116, Marcus, LCL, p. 166, nn. k–n; p. 167 n. a). In Jerome's terms, "open" correlates with the uttered and revealed *logos* and hidden with the reason "residing in thought." See also *Leg.* 3.132, 3.140; *Mos.* 2.113, 2.128–29; and *Spec.* 4.69.

[75] Hayward, "St. Jerome and the Meaning," 104–5. Hayward also suggests that Jerome draws on Philo to highlight the military and athletic character of the priestly clothing to connect the priest to Roman imperial ideology (96, 105).

[76] M. H. Williams, *The Monk and the Book: Jerome and the Making of Christian Scholarship* (Chicago: University of Chicago Press, 2006); M. H. Williams, "Lessons from Jerome's Jewish Teachers: Exegesis and Cultural Interaction in Late Antique Palestine," in *Jewish Biblical Interpretation and Cultural Exchange: Comparative Exegesis in Context*, ed. N. B. Dohrmann and D. Stern (Philadelphia: University of Pennsylvania Press, 2008), 66–86; A. Cain, *The Letters of Jerome: Asceticism, Biblical Exegesis, and the Construction of Christian Authority in Late Antiquity*, Oxford Early Christian Studies (Oxford: Oxford University Press, 2009); J. van 't Westeinde, "Teach and Transform: Education and (Re)Constructing Identity in Jerome's Letters," StPatr 74 (2016): 223–37. See also A. Fürst, "Aktuelle Tendenzen der Hieronymus-Forschung: Impressionen von einer Tagung über Hieronymus in Cardiff," *Adamantius* 13 (2007): 144–51; and the essays by Rousseau, Rebenich, Cain, Fürst, and Raspanti in A. Cain and J. Lössl, eds, *Jerome of Stridon: His Life, Writings, and Legacy* (Surrey: Ashgate, 2009).

[77] Cain, *Letters of Jerome*; Williams, *The Monk and the Book*; Williams, "Lessons from Jerome's Jewish Teachers."

claim expertise in Jewish traditions without at least mentioning Philo. However, because of Jerome's philological and historical bent, there is little in Philo's actual writings relevant to his work except of course, his most Hebraic writings on etymologies. In the case of etymologies, Jerome presents himself as the Christian Hebrew scholar correcting the Greek-based scholarship of his Jewish predecessor.

14.3 Conclusion

Numerous factors, then, account for Jerome's lack of direct interest in Philo's writings: his focus on the Hebrew text, his emphasis on *historia* rather than allegory, his commentary primarily on prophetic texts, and his view of Jews as the source of the literal, historical, and Hebraic readings. All of these make the content of Philo's writings of little interest or relevance to Jerome. But Philo as a figure represents a powerful analogue and contrast to Jerome.[78] Both write about asceticism, both composed similarly titled works, and both engaged in biblical exegesis. Philo, however, relied on the Greek Bible translated prior to the birth of Jesus, while Jerome works directly with the Hebrew from a Christian orientation. A Jewish champion of asceticism dedicated to biblical studies during the lifetime of Jesus contrasts nicely with a Christian champion of asceticism whose post-Christ understanding of Jewish and Hebrew traditions and language establish him as a voice of ecclesiastical authority in late antiquity.

---

[78] On the construction of Jewish scholars in Jerome and other Christian writers, see A. S. Jacobs, *Remains of the Jews: The Holy Land and Christian Empire in Late Antiquity*, Divinations (Stanford: Stanford University Press, 2004).

15
Augustine

Ilaria L. E. Ramelli

Augustine is very important in the reception of Philo because, historically, he is "the last Church Father in the West to have any direct contact with Philonic thought before the collapse of the Roman Empire," as David Runia observed in a seminal work for the reception of Philo in patristic authors, although he himself adds: "I suspect that there still remains much to be discovered."[1] This is true of Philo's influence on Augustine and its modalities.

Augustine mentions Philo only once, in 398 CE in *Contra Faustum Manichaeum*, analyzed below. I shall show that this, however, is not the only instance of Philo's influence on Augustine and shall investigate how Augustine gained access to Philonic material, probably both directly (likely in translation and possibly in Greek) and indirectly (through several potential channels). I note that *Contra Faustum* is among Augustine's anti-Manichaean works, in which he was most influenced by Origen's thought.[2] Indeed, one major issue in the reception of Philo in Augustine, I suspect, concerns Origen's potential mediation of Philo's ideas and themes, or simply emphasis on certain topics, together with Ambrose's mediation. Henry Chadwick observed: "There is direct influence from the Greek theologian [Origen] upon the making of his [Augustine's] own mind at certain important points."[3] Investigation in this sense has now been offered, but further research is needed.[4] Augustine's reception of Philo appears to have taken place both directly through some reading and indirectly through Ambrose and the Milanese circle and also, as is emerging from recent and ongoing research, through Origen. Here, the issues of language and transmission are crucial, especially given Augustine's rudimentary knowledge of Greek; already at school he "hated Greek" (*Conf.* 1.13).[5] For this reason he exhorted Jerome to translate Origen into Latin: "translate the works of those who have expounded our scriptures in Greek so wonderfully. So, you can enable us to

---

[1] D. T. Runia, *Philo in Early Christian Literature: A Survey* (Assen: van Gorcum, 1993), 320–30, at 330. Italian edition: *Filone di Alessandria nella prima letteratura cristiana*, trans. R. Radice, with my collaboration (Milan: Vita e Pensiero, 1999); D. T. Runia, "Philo and the Early Christian Fathers," in *The Cambridge Companion to Philo*, ed. A. Kamesar (Cambridge: Cambridge University Press, 2009), 210–30, esp. 224–25; D. T. Runia, "Philo Alexandrinus," *Augustinus-Lexicon* 4 (Schwabe: Basel, 2016), 716–19.

[2] Argument in I. Ramelli, "Origen in Augustine: A Paradoxical Reception," *Numen* 60 (2013): 280–307. On Augustine's anti-Manichaean works, see B. van Egmond, *Augustine's Early Thought on the Redemptive Function of Divine Judgement* (Oxford: Oxford University Press, 2018), from the *Dialogues of Cassiciacum* (ch. 2) to the *Confessions* (ch. 5); see below n. 21.

[3] H. Chadwick, "Christian Platonism in Origen and Augustine," in *Origeniana Tertia*, ed. R. Hanson and H. Crouzel (Rome: Ateneo, 1985), 217–30, at 218.

[4] See already Ramelli, "Origen in Augustine."

[5] Acknowledged also by Runia, *Philo*, 320: "unlike Ambrose, [Augustine] was not fluent in the Greek language."

have those remarkable commentators, and especially one, whose name you mention in your works with unusual pleasure," that is, Origen.[6] The fact that Augustine does so in his very first letter to Jerome indicates a particular urgency in this matter.

Augustine embraced much of Origen's philosophical theology, from ontology to eschatology, while paradoxically convinced that he did not know Origen's thought.[7] The most surprising point in Augustine's initial adhesion to Origen's ideas regards the doctrine of *apokatastasis*—a doctrine also found in Philo, who inspired patristic theories of *apokatastasis*, but with important differences[8]—which he later recanted in *Retract.* 1.7.6. The early Augustine drew from Origen many other elements of contact concerning philosophical arguments and biblical exegesis and used Origen's (anti-Gnostic and anti-Marcionite) thought to defend Christian "orthodoxy" against Manichaean ideas, whereas, after he was informed about Origen's ideas by Orosius and Jerome, he began to condemn it, especially in *Civ.* 21.17 and 23 and *Haer.* 43. Here he shows that he was actually misinformed about it; for instance, he believed Origen to have advocated an infinite succession of aeons. Augustine's anti-Pelagian polemic modified his view of Origen's thought.[9] Another notable factor was Augustine's ignorance of the semantic distinction between αἰώνιος and ἀΐδιος, which got lost in Latin translations of both with *aeternus*, but was clear to Origen—and also to Philo.[10]

Before addressing the ways and sources through which Augustine came to know Philo's ideas, it will be important first to examine the way that he became acquainted with Origen's true ideas when he did adhere to them, probably without being aware of their authorship, as well as the later development, when he criticized aspects of Origen's thought.[11] Augustine's first writings, instead, reveal Origenian arguments, and Philo's influence: it is then necessary to determine whether at that time Augustine was aware that those arguments were Origen's and how he came into contact with Philo's ideas. Augustine's Platonic formation was based on Plotinus and Porphyry (translated), Ambrose and Victorinus; there seem to be traces of Augustine's direct reading of Origen's Christian Platonism (translated) around 400, especially regarding the doctrine of justification.[12] In *Enarrat. 2 in Ps.* 31, completed in the summer of 401, Augustine

---

[6] Augustine, Letter 28.2 = Letter 56 of Jerome. It is Augustine's first letter to Jerome, from 394 CE but delivered in 402.

[7] As argued in Ramelli, "Origen in Augustine."

[8] As I argue in "Philo's Doctrine of *Apokatastasis*: Philosophical Sources, Exegetical Strategies, and Patristic Aftermath," *SPhiloA* 26 (2014): 29–55; on a comparison between Philo's and Paul's doctrine of *apokatastasis* and their respective eschatologies: "Philo and Paul on Soteriology and Eschatology," lecture at the Seminar, *Philo and Early Christianity*, SNTS Annual Meeting, Athens, August 7–10, 2018, *Eirene* 57 (2021) 317–52.

[9] On these works, see e.g. D. Keech, *The Anti-Pelagian Christology of Augustine of Hippo, 396–430* (Oxford: Oxford University Press, 2012).

[10] I. Ramelli and D. Konstan, *Terms for Eternity: Αἰώνιος and ἀΐδιος in Classical and Christian Authors* (Piscataway: Gorgias, 2007; new editions 2011; 2013); I. Ramelli, "Time and Eternity," in *The Routledge Handbook to Early Christian Philosophy*, ed. M. Edwards (London: Routledge, 2021), 41–54. On Philo: H. Keizer, *Life, Time, Eternity: A Study of AIΩN in Greek Literature and Philosophy and Philo* (PhD diss., Amsterdam, 1999).

[11] In Ramelli, "Origen in Augustine."

[12] According to P. Courcelle, *Les lettres grecques en Occident* (Paris: Boccard, 1948), 185–87, Augustine knew Origen's eschatology from the controversy between Jerome and Rufinus in 397 and by consulting Orosius in 414. About ten years later he read the translation of Origen's *Homilies on Genesis* and probably Περὶ ἀρχῶν.

indicates that he had read Origen's *Commentary on Romans*, in the Latin translation by Rufinus, and adapted from it ideas about justification.

15.1 Origen between Philo and Augustine

Augustine narrates his conversion in *Acad.* 2.2.5, *Beat.* 1.4, and the *Confessions*. In the first passage, Augustine refers to *libri pleni*, perhaps Platonic Christian books,[13] but these may have included Origen's homilies on Canticles in Jerome's translation—completed in Rome in 383, and available in Milan in 386—as well as perhaps passages from the relevant commentary. Augustine thus read Origen in Latin, like some ("pagan") "Platonic books."[14] Moreover, Ambrose knew Origen well and used his exegesis of Canticles and other works in his homilies *De bono mortis* and *De Isaac vel anima*, which Augustine probably knew before his conversion. Indeed, Ambrose and the Milanese circle could have transmitted much of Origen's thought, and (mostly via him) Philo's, to Augustine. In *Ord.* 1.11.31, written in November 386, Augustine says that he read to Monica some books of earlier Christian authors—likely Origen *in primis*. From *Ord.* 1.11.32; 1.8.24, and *Acad.* 2.2.5, it transpires that Augustine shared Origen's ideas. The account of Augustine's reading of Rom 13:13–14 (*Conf.* 8.12.29) appears to be inspired by Origen's *Comm. Cant.* 2.4.28–30 on Abraham at Mamre (Gen 18).

It remains uncertain whether, when he initially shared many ideas with Origen, Augustine was aware that these were Origen's, or whether he absorbed them through Ambrose (acquainted with Philo as well),[15] the Milanese circle, partial translations and collections, and the like, some of which did not even identify Origen as the author. Through these, in addition to direct reading, he may have become acquainted with Philo and his attention may have been drawn to Philo or certain Philonic topics. Augustine does not mention his encounter with Origen's works in *Confessions* and fails to identify the *libri pleni*, probably to elude charges of Origenism. In the same years, such a concern induced Jerome to disavow Origen publicly, as Augustine knew. The controversy over Origen arose in 393, after the composition of Augustine's *De moribus*—a pivotal text with regard to his dependence on Origen. Augustine depends on Origen in many ways also in his anti-Manichaean *De Genesi contra Manichaeos*.[16] Origen's Homilies on Genesis had not yet been translated by Rufinus, but other channels are possible, such

---

[13] So G. Heidl, *Origen's Influence on the Young Augustine* (Piscataway, NJ: Gorgias, 2003), 7–18.
[14] Primarily Plotinus translated by Victorinus (*Conf.* 7.9.13: *quodsam Platonicorum libros ex graeca lingua in latinam versos*; 7.20.26: *lectis Platonicorum illis libris*).
[15] See Maria Doerfler, Chapter 13 in this volume.
[16] See J. Pépin, "Saint Augustin et le symbolisme néoplatonicien de la vêture," in *Augustinus Magister* (Paris: Études Augustiniennes, 1954), 1:293–306; R. Teske, "Origen and St. Augustine's First Commentaries on Genesis," in *Origeniana V* (Leuven: Peeters, 1992), 179–85, who hypothesized that Augustine was acquainted with Origen since 385 and supposed a mediation by Ambrose and the Milanese circle; further Ramelli, "Origen in Augustine." Likewise F. van Fleteren, "Principles of Augustine's Hermeneutics," in *Augustine: Biblical Exegete*, ed. F. van Fleteren (Frankfurt: Lang, 2001), 2–4; M.-A. Vannier, "Origène et Augustin, interprètes de la création," in *Origeniana VI*, 724, points to Ambrose, Jerome, and Basil; all were acquainted with Philo.

as Ambrose's homilies on the Hexaëmeron and on Paradise, Hilary's treatises on the Psalms, and Gregory of Elvira's treatise on the creation of humanity, or an oral mediation by Theodorus or Simplicianus. Augustine might have read a Latin compilation of Origenian interpretations of Genesis.[17]

Particularly in *De moribus ecclesiae catholicae* and *De moribus Manichaeorum*, Augustine availed himself of Origen's arguments, especially concerning ontology, protology, theodicy, eschatology, and *apokatastasis*, dependence on God's goodness, and the relation between providence and free will, as has been argued with precise parallels to Origen's texts, especially to Περὶ ἀρχῶν.[18] Partial versions and/or compilations of this work seem to have circulated even before Rufinus' translation (last years of the fourth century). It is precisely Augustine's anti-Manichaean polemic at that time, which includes his only nominal reference to Philo, that led him to emphasize the notion of God as the Good and of evil as deprived of ontological status (in opposition to the Manichaean tenet of Good and Evil as equally powerful). Augustine used against the Manichaeans the arguments constructed by Origen against the Gnostics.[19] *De incarnatione Verbi ad Ianuarium* was ascribed to Augustine, but it was in fact a collection of texts from Περὶ ἀρχῶν. Augustine adopted, among much else, Origen's idea that rational creatures can pass between the angelic, the human, and the demonic state.[20] Augustine's use of images from Canticles in *Conf.* 9.2.3 shows his familiarity with Origen's exegesis. In Aurelius' library in Carthage Augustine found some *commentarioli in Matthaeum*, likely a translation of exegetical passages from Origen, whose interpretation of the Lord's Prayer was taken up by Augustine in his commentary on the Sermon of the Mount, which he had commenced in 393/4. To this phase belongs Augustine's explicit allusion to Philo. Only later, due to the Origenistic controversy and his anti-Pelagian polemics, did Augustine reject Origen's positions. Paradoxically, meanwhile he believed he had learnt Origen's theories, although what was described to him by Orosius and others as Origen's thought was a misinterpretation. But earlier, precisely when Augustine believed that he did not know Origen's thought, he did know and use it, probably thanks to Ambrose, the Milanese circle, partial translations, compilations, and perhaps even anonymous manuscripts containing translations of Origen's works without indicating him as the author. That such manuscripts circulated is proved not only by the aforementioned *commentarioli* and *De incarnatione*, but also by Pamphilus,

---

[17] Heidl, *Influence*, 77–104. On Hilary's relation to Origen: I. Image, *The Human Condition in Hilary of Poitiers: The Will and Original Sin between Origen and Augustine* (Oxford: Oxford University Press, 2018); J. Sidaway, *The Human Factor: 'Deification' as Transformation in the Theology of Hilary of Poitiers* (Louvain: Peeters, 2016).

[18] See Ramelli, "Origen in Augustine."

[19] In addition to what I observed in "Origen in Augustine," Augustine's critique of Manichaean mythology (analyzed by T. Furher, "Augustine's Moulding of the Manichaean Idea of God in the *Confessiones*," *VC* 67 [2013]: 531–47) reproduces Origen's critique of "Gnostic" mythology.

[20] Not only in *De moribus*, but also in *Lib.* 3.217 and *Serm.* 45.10, where he consistently shared with Origen the idea of the resurrected body as spiritual, angelic, luminous, and ethereal, as well as the interpretation of the "skin tunics." B. Altaner, "Augustinus und Philo von Alexandrien: eine quellenkritische Untersuchung," *ZKT* 65 (1941): 81–90, reprinted in *Kleine patristische Schriften*, TU 83 (Berlin: Akademie, 1967), 181–93 thought that Augustine, *Gen. Man.* 2.21.32 reproduces Origen, *Hom. Lev.* 6.2. See A. Parvan, "Genesis 1–3: Augustine and Origen," *VC* 66 (2012): 56–92.

who attests that already around 300 CE manuscripts containing works by Origen circulated in anonymous form (*Apol.* 12). This can partially explain Augustine's knowledge of Philo as well, which was both direct and indirect.

15.2 Augustine's Reception of Philo: Direct, Mediated, or Both?

Therefore, if Origen's influence on Augustine in his anti-Manichaean phase was significant, when Augustine's philosophical theology was closest to that of Origen, it seems not accidental that the only explicit mention of Philo in Augustine's oeuvre comes from a work belonging precisely to his anti-Manichaean polemics. This appears to point to Origen's mediation or influence in Augustine's reception of Philo. Augustine probably read the beginning of Philo's *Quaestiones in Genesim*, as we shall see, and it is likely that Origen prompted him to read it, drawing Augustine's attention to this and other Philonic topics and eliciting Augustine's emphasis on them. This kind of influence parallels other kinds of Origen's influence on Augustine relating to Philo's ideas and method. A systematic reassessment of Origen's presence in Augustine—which in turn profits of recent, continuing investigation into Augustine and Manichaeism[21]—is indeed needed, and many clues suggest that Origen conveyed a number of Philonic themes to Augustine.

A parallel issue—although it does not present any linguistic problems—has been pointed out in the case of Gregory of Nyssa, another allegorical-cum-philosophical interpreter of scripture similar to Philo and Origen, who, even in his theoretical constructions and strongest philosophical arguments, always seeks scriptural support; Origen tends to expressly refer to Philo as a predecessor precisely in points that are crucial to his scriptural allegorical method.[22] Indeed, Philo's influence on Gregory is strong not only for biblical allegoresis in general—which Gregory inherited from Origen—but also for details of exegesis and thought, for each of which it is important to consider that they may be mediated by Origen as well (just as, for example, Philo's influence on Didymus is).[23] Philo's influence on Gregory's allegorical exegesis and philosophical thought often took place, again, through Origen. This is an interesting parallel to Augustine's knowledge of Philo qua mediated by Origen.

Augustine names Philo, as already mentioned, in *Contra Faustum Manichaeum*, which is among his anti-Manichaean works: these were most heavily influenced by Origen's ideas, including even his doctrine of *apokatastasis*.[24] In the context of

---

[21] Esp. Jason BeDuhn and Johannes van Oort; e.g. by the former: *Augustine's Manichaean Dilemma*, 2 vols, Divinations (Philadelphia: University of Pennsylvania, 2010–13); by the latter: "Augustin und der Manichäismus," *ZRGG* 46 (1994): 126–42; "The Young Augustine's Knowledge of Manichaeism," *VC* 62 (2008): 441–66, and many other publications.

[22] Argument in I. Ramelli, "Philosophical Allegoresis of Scripture in Philo and Its Legacy in Gregory of Nyssa," *SPhiloA* 20 (2008): 55–99. See also Albert C. Geljon, Chapter 11 in this volume.

[23] Runia, *Philo*, 200–203; R. Layton, *Didymus the Blind and His Circle in Late Antique Alexandria* (Urbana: University of Illinois, 2004), 144–51; A. Geljon, "Philonic Elements in Didymus the Blind's Exegesis of the Story of Cain and Abel," *VC* 61 (2007): 282–312.

[24] This doctrine is examined in I. Ramelli, *The Christian Doctrine of Apokatastasis: A Critical Assessment from the New Testament to Eriugena* (Leiden: Brill, 2013); for Augustine, Ramelli, "Origen in Augustine."

his crucial discussion of Philo, Augustine opposes the Manichaean claim that in the Old Testament there were no references to Christ and the Church—the same as the Marcionite (and "Gnostic") claim that Origen frequently refuted. Augustine, like Origen, replies with many typological and allegorical readings that connect the Old Testament with the New. It should be noted that Philo, Origen, and (at least the anti-Manichaean) Augustine were all allegorists, and both Origen and Augustine relied on Paul for the justification of their allegoresis.[25]

Augustine then criticizes the Jews who—like the Manichaeans—did not recognize that the Hebrew Bible contained prefigurations of Christ: an example is Philo's exegesis of the Ark. Augustine describes Philo as "a man of exceedingly great learning [*liberaliter eruditissimus*], belonging to the group of the Jews whose style the Greeks do not hesitate to match with that of Plato" (*Faust.* 12.39). Augustine refers here to the saying, ἢ Πλάτων φιλωνίζει, ἢ Φίλων πλατωνίζει, "either Philo imitates Plato or Plato Philo," quoted by Jerome in his portrait of Philo[26] in *Vir. ill.* 11.[27] In Jerome's gallery, known to Augustine, Philo is the only non-Christian, together with Josephus, who probably wrote the *Testimonium Flavianum* on Jesus and a passage on James "the brother of Jesus who was called Christ."[28] Jerome also included a "pagan," Seneca, but one who had criticized traditional pagan cults, and therefore was called by Tertullian *saepe noster*, and was believed to have exchanged letters with Paul.[29] Philo is included in Jerome's gallery because he supposedly described the first Alexandrian Christians: like Eusebius, Jerome assimilates the Therapeutae depicted by Philo to the Christian monks (*monachi*) of his day, and to the original ("communalist") Jesus-followers in Jerusalem.[30] For his account of Philo, Jerome depends on Eusebius, although his acquaintance with Philo's works must have been direct.[31]

Augustine was aware of the portrait of Philo in Jerome and knew Jerome's detail that Philo was *de genere sacerdotum*—a piece of information that is absent in all previous known sources but possibly historically accurate.[32] Jerome had access to the Caesarea

---

[25] I. Ramelli, "The Philosophical Stance of Allegory in Stoicism and Its Reception in Platonism, 'Pagan' and Christian," *International Journal of the Classical Tradition* 18.3 (2011): 335–71; I. Ramelli "The Reception of Paul in Origen: Allegoresis of Scripture, *Apokatastasis*, and Women's Ministry," in *The Pauline Mind*, ed. S. Porter and D. Yoon (New York: Routledge, 2024); I. Ramelli, "The Relevance of Greco-Roman Literary Themes for New Testament Interpretation," in *The Cambridge Handbook of Historical Biblical Exegesis*, ed. S. E. Porter and D. J. Fuller (Cambridge: Cambridge University Press, forthcoming).

[26] Jerome also mentions Philo about fifteen times. See here Matthew Kraus, Chapter 14 in this volume and A. Canellis, "La Lettre 64 de Saint Jérôme," *VC* 72 (2018): 235–54.

[27] Analyzed in I. Ramelli, "The Birth of the Rome-Alexandria Connection: The Early Sources on Mark and Philo, and the Petrine Tradition," *SPhiloA* 23 (2011): 69–95, where I also note similarities with the portrait of Origen; there are also in Eusebius similar portraits of Philo and Origen. My analysis is taken up by J. Rogers, "Origen in the Likeness of Philo: Eusebius's Portrait," *Studies in Christian-Jewish Relations* 12.1 (2017): 1–13, esp. 1, 8, 10.

[28] The partial authenticity of the *Testimonium* is argued by I. Ramelli, "Osservazioni circa il *Testimonium Flavianum*," *Sileno* 24 (1998): 219–35.

[29] I. Ramelli, "A Pseudepigraphon inside a Pseudepigraphon? The Seneca-Paul Correspondence and the Letters Added Afterwards," *JSP* 23 (2014): 259–89; I. Ramelli, "Seneca the Younger," in *The Blackwell Encyclopedia of Ancient History*, ed. A. Erskine (Oxford: Wiley-Blackwell, 2013), 11:6145–48; updated version 2021.

[30] See I. Ramelli, *Social Justice and the Legitimacy of Slavery: The Role of Philosophical Asceticism from Ancient Judaism to Late Antiquity* (Oxford: Oxford University Press, 2016), ch. 1.

[31] Rightly so Runia, *Philo*, 313–18.

[32] So D. Schwarz, "Philo's Priestly Descent," in *Nourished with Peace*, ed. F. Greenspahn, E. Hilgert, and B. Mack (Chico, CA: Scholars, 1984), 155–71.

library, where, in 376–79 CE, Bishop Euzoius had Philo's rolls transferred to parchment codices. By explaining that Philo described the first Christians in Alexandria as a result of his friendship with Peter, Jerome also strengthens the Rome-Alexandria connection, apparently first drawn by Clement.[33] This is further emphasized in *Vir. ill.* 8, which repeats that the ascetics described by Philo were the first Christians in Alexandria converted by Mark; Philo portrayed them as Jews because the first Alexandrian Christians were "Judaizing."[34] Jerome's account, after listing Philo's works, thus ends by reporting, for the first time, the widespread Greek saying, ἢ Πλάτων φιλωνίζει, ἢ Φίλων πλατωνίζει. Philo is a Platonic Jew for Jerome, Origen a Platonic Christian. The two Alexandrian Platonizing thinkers and exegetes epitomize Judaism and Christianity respectively: Philo, *disertissimus Iudaeorum* (*Vir. ill.* 8), and Origen, who had an *immortale ingenium* (*Vir. ill.* 54) and was a "teacher of the churches second only to the apostles" (*Comm. Ezech.* pr.). Not accidentally, with the *Liber interpretationis Hebraicorum nominum*, presented as a continuation of a work of Origen's, Jerome posits a chain of transmission from Philo to Origen, down to himself. Philo's Platonism was still highlighted by Theodore Metochites (†1332), who described Philo as "a αἱρεσιώτης of Plato's philosophy," i.e. a member of the Platonic school of philosophy (αἵρεσις).[35]

Augustine in his only explicit mention of Philo assimilates Philo and Plato only stylistically, while Jerome assimilated them in both style and content. Augustine is quick to state that Philo "did not believe in Christ" and therefore did not interpret the Old Testament in reference to Christ, as Origen was also aware, as much as he claimed him as a model for his allegoresis of scripture.[36] Thus, Augustine—who was no less interested in the interpretation of scripture than Philo was—in *Faust.* 12.39 shows how a Christian exegesis of Noah's ark as the body of Christ surpasses that of Philo (*QG* 2.1–7), since it explains the opening on the side of the ark as the piercing of Christ's side on the cross: "Philo, wishing to interpret the ark of the flood as constructed in accordance with the structure of the human body, dealt with all its aspects piece by piece. When he also *considered in a most subtle fashion the meaning of the dimensions involved, all aspects matched his interpretation exactly*."[37] It seems noteworthy to me that the dimensions of the ark were discussed at length by Origen, certainly in his *Homilies on Genesis* (2.5), where he refers the interpretation of the ark's dimensions to *prudentibus viris et Hebraicarum traditionis gnaris* (2.2), and very likely at more length in the lost *Commentary on Genesis*, where he may well have referred to Philo's interpretation.

---

[33] As I argued in Ramelli, "The Birth of the Rome-Alexandria Connection." On Philo and Rome, see also M. Niehoff, *Philo of Alexandria: An Intellectual Biography* (New Haven: Yale University Press, 2018).

[34] Jerome surely also remembered Origen's criticism of the "Judaizing" Christians of his day. The description of Mark ("was so learned [*tanta doctrina*] and lived in such continence [*vitae continentia*]") is the same as in Philo's and Origen's portrait (see above n. 27). Jerome felt the need to explain how Philo "seems" to be writing about Jews.

[35] Σημειώσεις γνωμικαί 16. See D. T. Runia, "Philo in Byzantium: An Exploration," *VC* 70 (2016): 259–81.

[36] See P. Fredriksen, *Augustine and the Jews* (New York: Doubleday, 2008).

[37] Trans. Runia with adaptations.

Augustine then comes to a criticism of Philo qua non-Christian:

> But when the exegesis came to the opening made in the side of the ark, every conjecture of human ingenuity failed. Something had to be said, however, and so that opening was interpreted in terms of the lower parts of the body, through which urine and excrement are released. This is what he dared to believe, declare, and write. It is not surprising that he did not discover the meaning of the opening and so went astray in this way. But if he had converted to Christ, with the veil removed, he would have discovered the sacraments of the Church flowing from that man's side.

An interpretation referring to excreta, albeit in relation to the bottom of the Ark and not its opening, was found in Origen's *Hom. Gen.* 2.1, as well as the Christological exegesis of the ark (2.3–5). It is this latter interpretation which Augustine takes over.

Augustine then, like Origen, does not believe that Philo was a Christian. It is clear that he was a Jew and did not believe in Christ. But "the appeal to a Jewish exegete has a certain strategic value,"[38] against the Manichaeans, who rejected the Jewish origins of Christianity. The same, I add, was true in the case of Origen, who referred to Philo strategically, including against the Manichaeans, exclusively in passages that were crucial for his exegesis.[39]

Besides ontology, protology, eschatology, *apokatastasis*, and biblical exegesis of the creation narrative onwards, there are many other areas, and even minute details, that mark Philo's influence on Augustine. Among the "broader areas of Augustine's thought where his reading of Philo has exerted its influence,"[40] Runia suggests the idea of the heavenly city[41] and the doctrine of God. These are certainly promising areas, and worth exploring. I have investigated the topic of the knowledge of God, mediated by Origen,[42] but there is more. In my view, not only in theology, but in many other cases as well, Philo's influence will have passed, through Origen. A systematic reassessment of Origen's influence on Augustine, in these respects too, is fruitful for the investigation of Philo's influence on Augustine.

15.3 The Reception of Philo in Greek and Latin

As already briefly stated,[43] Augustine may have read an early passage of Philo's *Quaestiones in Genesim* 2.1–7, in which Philo's exegesis of the ark is offered; this had already been taken up by Clement (*Strom.* 6.11.86–87). I surmised that Origen induced him to read it, given Origen's own interest in the interpretation of the creation story in

---

[38] Runia, *Philo*, 323.
[39] As I demonstrated in Ramelli, "Philosophical Allegoresis"; I. Ramelli, "Philo as Origen's Declared Model: Allegorical and Historical Exegesis of Scripture," *Studies in Christian-Jewish Relations* 7 (2012): 1–17.
[40] Runia, *Philo*, 324–25.
[41] On the city in Philo, see D. T. Runia, "The Idea and the Reality of the City in the Thought of Philo of Alexandria," *JHI* 61 (2000): 361–79.
[42] I. Ramelli, "Philo as One of the Main Inspirers of Early Christian Hermeneutics and Apophatic Theology," *Adamantius* 24 (2018): 276–92.
[43] Above after n. 21.

the light of both Plato and Philo. Athenagoras and Bardaisan, shortly before Origen, also interpreted the Genesis creation account in the light of Plato and Bardaisan's knowledge of Philo is a question worth exploring.[44]

Pierre Courcelle pointed to Ambrose's *De Noe* as Augustine's source;[45] Berthold Altaner argued that Augustine had read Philo in a Latin translation.[46] *Quaestiones in Genesim* survives in an Armenian translation. The Latin translation that is extant is of book 4.154–245, originally book 6,[47] not of books 1–2, although the latter might well have existed and been used by Augustine. The original Greek text of these *Quaestiones* on the Ark was discovered in an Athos manuscript in 1984 and published by Jean Paramelle.[48] Comparing the Greek fragments with the Old Latin translation of *QG* and the Latin texts of *Contra Faustum* and *De Noe*, Paramelle argued that Augustine relied on both Philo, translated into Latin, and Ambrose's *De Noe*.

Augustine knew Ambrose's *De Noe et arca*, which offers a paraphrase of Philo *QG* 2.1–7. Ambrose, who cites Philo explicitly only once (*Par.* 4.25) but seems to have been influenced by him on more than six hundred occasions,[49] read *Quaestiones in Genesim* in Greek,[50] while Augustine could not do so (or could do so very poorly). But Augustine heard and read Ambrose, who reported exactly Philo's allegorical exegesis of the ark as body. *De Noe* is indeed highly relevant to our investigation, as it relies extensively on *QG* 1.87–2.82 to substantiate Ambrose's own exegesis of the Noah story. Ambrose's interpretation of Gen 6:14–16 in *De Noe* 8.24 takes over Philo's exegesis, including that of the ark door, accepting—unlike Augustine—Philo's allegoresis of it as a passageway for excrement, which God positioned behind, so that humans might not see the relevant shameful action (Philo in *QG* 2.6 cited the δημιουργός—a Platonic term from the *Timaeus*—as the one responsible for choosing the back position for the anus, so that humans could avoid seeing a shameful act). Ambrose explicitly links Philo's exegesis to 1 Cor 12:22–23, on the weaker parts of the body as indispensable.[51] Adducing other

---

[44] I. Ramelli, *Bardaiṣan of Edessa: A Reassessment of the Evidence and a New Interpretation* (Piscataway, NJ: Gorgias, 2009; Berlin: de Gruyter, 2019); I. Ramelli, "Bardaisan of Edessa, Origen, and Imperial Philosophy: A Middle Platonic Context?," *Aram* 30 (2018): 1–26; I. Ramelli, "Plato's *Timaeus* in Athenagoras, Bardaisan and Origen," in *Plato's Timaeus and Its Reception*, ed. M. Boeri (forthcoming).

[45] P. Courcelle, "Saint Augustin a-t-il lu Philon d'Alexandrie?," *REA* 63 (1961): 78–85; P. Courcelle, *Late Latin Writers and Their Greek Sources* (Cambridge, MA: Harvard University Press, 1969), 197.

[46] B. Altaner, "Augustinus und Philo."

[47] F. Petit, *L'ancienne version latine des Questions sur la Genèse de Philon d'Alexandrie*, 2 vols (Berlin: Akademie Verlag, 1973). Armenian: F. Petit, *Quaestiones et solutiones in Genesim: e versione armeniaca* (Paris: Cerf, 1979–84); C. Mercier and F. Petit, *Quaestiones et solutiones in Genesim I et II–III, IV, V, VI e versione armeniaca: complément de l'ancienne version latine*, Les oeuvres de Philon d'Alexandrie 34B (Paris: Cerf, 1984) with the Latin text of *Quaestiones* which are lacking in the Armenian text. Greek fragments: F. Petit, *Philon d'Alexandrie, Quaestiones in Genesim et in Exodum: Fragmenta Graeca* (Paris: Cerf, 1978).

[48] J. Paramelle, E. Lucchesi, and J. Sesiano, *Philon d'Alexandrie: Questions sur la Genèse II, 1–7: text grec, version arménienne, parallèles latins* (Geneva: Cramer, 1984), 102–27. Ch. 3 of the Introduction is all devoted to the Latin parallels from Ambrose, *De Noe*, and the question whether Augustine read Philo in Latin or Greek. The synoptic edition lists the Armenian, Greek, French, and the Latin from Ambrose.

[49] E. Lucchesi, *L'usage de Philon dans l'oeuvre exégétique de Saint Ambroise* (Leiden: Brill, 1977). On the reception of Philo in Ambrose, see Maria Doerfler, Chapter 13 in this volume.

[50] Lucchesi, *L'usage*, 127–28; Ramelli, *Origen the Philosophical Theologian* (Berlin: DeGruyter, 2024), 451–94 on Origen-Ambrose-Augustine.

[51] "At vero apostolus quae videntur inquit membra corporis infirmiora esse necessaria sunt, uno ac simplici verbo descriptiones philosophiae supergressus, et quae putamus ignobiliora esse membra corporis, his honorem abundantiorem circumdamus, et quae inhonesta sunt nostra honestatem abundantiorem habent" (*De Noe* 8.24).

texts, Runia suggests that Augustine read the beginning of Philo's *QG* in the Old Latin translation, and maybe something of his *De opificio*, either in a Latin translation or in Greek, although he knew very little Greek.[52]

A similar problem occurs in the possible derivation of an expression by Augustine, *caelum caeli*, from the Philonic phrase οὐρανὸς οὐρανοῦ. Jean Pépin finds the literary evidence insufficient to assert dependence.[53] He assumes that Augustine's lack of Greek precludes his reading of the original, but does not rule out the possibility that Augustine may have encountered Philo's works in a Latin translation no longer extant. This, I note, can also be the case in other instances of Augustine's dependence on Philo, including *QG* 2.6.

Augustine knew Origen's creation account, although probably not (or not so well) in the Greek commentary on Genesis, or his Greek homilies, but in Latin versions, adaptations, and elaborations. Indeed, Origen seems to have transmitted a great deal to Augustine about the exegesis of the creation story.[54] Work is ongoing, although it would be good to find the original Greek text of his great above-mentioned Commentary on Genesis, of which only fragments are preserved.[55] This may have been an important channel in the transmission of Philo (especially his exegesis of Genesis) to Augustine. Gerd van Riel admits that Augustine "under the influence of Origen became aware of many specific Platonic doctrines that were useful in articulating Christian theology" and produces briefly the example of the doctrine of formless matter, which was supported by Philo (*Her.* 134, 140 on the divine ordering of formless matter through the Logos) and made its way into Augustine's exegesis of Gen 1:1–2 in *Conf.* 12.[56] Origen and the *Dialogue of Adamantius*—translated by Rufinus and possibly known to Augustine—paid much attention to it.[57] In *Conf.* 1–3 and *Gen. litt.* Augustine's exegesis of Gen 1–3 is heavily indebted to Philo, as Pépin, Solignac, and Runia have indicated.[58]

Here, again, the role of Origen must be investigated. It seems to me that Origen at least drew Augustine's attention to some Philonic themes, either depending on them,

---

[52] Runia, *Philo*, 326.

[53] J. Pépin, "Recherches sur le sens et les origines de l'espression *caelum caeli* dans le livre XII des *Confessions* de S. Augustin," *Archivum Latinitatis Medii Aevi* 23 (1953): 185–274.

[54] On Philo and Origen on creation, see D. T. Runia, "Cosmos, Logos, and Nomos: The Alexandrian Jewish and Christian Appropriation of the Genesis Creation Account," in *Cosmologie et cosmogonie dans la littérature antique*, ed. P. Derron (Vadoeuvres-Genève: Hardt, 2015), 179–209. On Augustine's linguistically mediated reception of Plato's *Timaeus*, see C. Hoenig, *Plato's Timaeus and the Latin Tradition* (Cambridge: Cambridge University Press, 2018), 215–79.

[55] K. Metzler, *Die Kommentierung des Buches Genesis* (Berlin: de Gruyter, 2010); K. Metzler, *Prokop von Gaza: Eclogarum in libros historicos Veteris Testamenti epitome*, Vol. 1: *Der Genesiskommentar*, GCS NF 22 (Berlin: de Gruyter, 2015).

[56] G. van Riel, "Augustine's Plato," in *Brill's Companion to the Reception of Plato in Antiquity*, ed. H. Tarrant et al. (Leiden: Brill, 2018), 448–69 at 464; on formless matter in Augustine and its sources van Riel, "Augustine's Exegesis of 'Heaven and Earth' in *Conf.* XII: Finding Truth amidst Philosophers, Heretics and Exegetes," *Quaestio* 7 (2007): 191–228.

[57] On the problem of formless matter, its sources, and its developments in Origen and patristic philosophy, see I. Ramelli, "The *Dialogue of Adamantius*: A Document of Origen's Thought? Part One," *StPatr* 52 (2012): 71–98; "Part Two," *StPatr* 56.4 (2013): 227–73; "Matter in the *Dialogue of Adamantius*: Origen's Heritage and Hylomorphism," in *Platonism and Christianity in Late Ancient Cosmology: God, Soul, Matter*, ed. J. Zachhuber and A. Schiavoni (Leiden: Brill, 2022), 74–124. This dialogue includes many ideas of Origen.

[58] Runia, *Philo*, 325–26.

or polemicizing with them. For instance, the text in *Gen. litt.* 6.22.33 is striking, since Augustine criticizes the doctrine of the death of the soul and attributes it to *quidam*. These may well include Philo, who supported it,[59] and it was specifically Origen who argued more than once against the substantial death of the soul, admitting only of moral death, sometimes with a polemical target that may have well included Philo.[60] This point was also taken over by Augustine in *De moribus*, in which, as I argued, he was using Origen's monistic arguments to contrast Manichaean dualism.

In Augustine's reception of Philo's double creation theory, I find again affinities with Origen, which may induce us to suspect that Augustine modified Philo in light of Origen's thought. As Runia notes,[61] Augustine divides into two Philo's noetic cosmos in the divine Logos: Augustine in a later commentary on Genesis (*Gen. litt.* 4–5) posits the *omnium creaturarum rationes* that existed in the Logos from eternity, and the independent existence of these *rationes-logoi* as *creaturae* (among which there is the human being in God's image). I observe that this distinction was clearly established precisely by Origen (e.g. *Princ.* 1.4.5, 1.2.2) and was of paramount importance for his doctrine of creation.[62] Augustine likely absorbed Philo's through Origen's mediation. In this connection, as noted by H. A. Wolfson, the point of departure of Philo's philosophy is the theory of the Ideas.[63] Philo's influence on Augustine on this score, too, was probably mediated by Origen, who applied the theory of Ideas/Forms (far from criticizing it) to his Logos Christology and doctrine of creation in his version of the Logos-Wisdom containing all Ideas/Forms/*logoi* of creatures.[64]

Moreover, not only did Philo's exegesis of Exod 3:14 influence Origen to the point of having him maintain the equation between God and Being—although Origen, mindful of Plato, also posited God as superior to Being and Nous—but Philo's interpretation of Exod 3:14–15 clearly impacted Augustine also. Runia has observed that Augustine's references to Exod 3:14–15 distinguish the two verses, v. 14 on God's name (*ego sum qui sum*) and v. 15 on the relation between God and the patriarchs (*dominus deus patrum vestrorum, Deus Abraham, Deus Isaac, et Deus Jacob*), even calling the respective names *nomen incommutabilitatis* (or *nomen substantiae*) and *nomen misericordiae* (*Serm.* 7.7, 2.5), the God of Being and the God of the Patriarchs, and that such a distinction seems to come from Philo.[65] For Augustine, "I am Who I Am" (*qui est*) refers to God's unchangeability,

---

[59] E.g. *Leg.* 1.105–7; *QG* 1.16.

[60] I pointed this out in I. Ramelli, "Spiritual Weakness, Illness, and Death in 1 Cor 11:30," *JBL* 130 (2011): 145–63; further Ramelli, "Philo's Doctrine."

[61] Runia, *Philo*, 326.

[62] On a comparison between Clement and Origen in this respect, both well acquainted with Philo, see I. Ramelli, "The Logos/Nous One-Many between 'Pagan' and Christian Platonism," *StPatr* 102 (2021): 11–44.

[63] H. A. Wolfson, *Philo: Foundations of Religious Philosophy in Judaism, Christianity, and Islam* (Cambridge, MA: Harvard University Press, 1948), 200.

[64] Discussion in "The Logos/Nous One-Many". Against the hypothesis that Origen criticized the theory of Ideas in *Princ.* 2.3.6, arguments in G. Boys-Stones, "Time, Creation, and the Mind of God," *OSAPh* 40 (2011): 319–37, at 334; I. Ramelli, "Alexander of Aphrodisias: A Source of Origen's Philosophy?" *Philosophie antique* 14 (2014): 237–90, at 274–76.

[65] Philo, *Mut.* 11–14; *Abr.* 51; *Mos.* 1.75–76; Augustine, *Enarrat. Ps.* 101.2.10, 121.5, 134.6; *Serm.* 2.5, 7.7. D. T. Runia, "Philo of Alexandria and the Beginnings of Christian Thought," *SPhiloA* 7 (1995): 143–60, esp. 145–47, 158–59; Runia, *Philo*, 329.

while "God of Abraham, Isaac, and Jacob" refers to God's mercy towards humanity. In this case "it is impossible to indicate" how Augustine could have come into contact with Philo's exegesis.[66] Was Augustine reading Philo's texts? If so, in Greek or in Latin? Or was he relying on an intermediate source? We can only make conjectures. Once again, I suspect, Augustine might have learnt Origen's interpretation of the names of God. In *Comm. Rom.* 4.5.171–83, Origen quotes Exod 3:14, *ego sum qui sum*, to extrapolate the equation that God is Being and immutable (as in Philo), *Deus solus est … et una est illa Dei substantia quae semper est*, and to argue that God called "those who are," i.e. the Patriarchs, named in v. 15, Abraham, Isaac, and Jacob, the ones who participate in the One Who Is (*qui sunt, id est qui participationem habent eius qui est, Abraham et Isaac et Iacob*).

Philo's ethics—especially, again, in *Quaestiones in Genesim*—also impacted Augustine. Sarah Byers, in particular, has shown that Augustine theorized "preliminary good emotions" (προευπάθειαι), probably under the influence of Philo.[67] Augustine's description of the joy of Sarah, indeed, suggests that he read (in Latin) Philo's *QG* 3–4.[68] Indeed, as noted, he also seems to have read *QG* 1–2. The whole treatment of *pathē, eupatheiai*, and *propatheiai* was prominent in Origen, who may have at least drawn Augustine's attention to these issues and their treatments in Philo.[69]

Among many ethical aspects, both Augustine's famous notion of the City of God—which has also metaphysical and eschatological implications in his thought—and an etymology related to it seem to have some roots in Philo. Augustine borrowed from Philo (*Somn.* 2.250), likely indirectly, the etymology of Jerusalem as "Vision of Peace" (ὅρασις εἰρήνης), which was found in *onomastica* and known to Clement, Origen, and thence Eusebius and Didymus, as well as Jerome, who offers the Latin translation *visio pacis* in *Liber interpretationis Hebraicorum nominum*.[70] Augustine likewise uses *visio pacis* in *Enarrat. Ps.* 9.12. Here, too, Philo's derivation is mediated: Augustine took it from Jerome, a Greek *onomasticon*, or Origen. Johannes van Oort pointed out that Philo took over Stoic ideas such as the cosmos as megalopolis, and opposed the visible and invisible world, identifying the latter with a city (*Opif.* 18).[71] In *Gig.* 60 the *politeia* of this world is opposed to that of the Ideas; in *Somn.* 2.250, Jerusalem is styled by Philo "the City of God." Of course, in Augustine, Manichaeistic dualism also helped shape his theory of two cities.[72] Augustine's theory of the two cities, of God and of men, seems

---

[66] Runia, *Philo*, 329; D. Hedley and D. J. Tolan, eds., *Participation in the Divine: A Philosophical History, From Antiquity to the Modern Era*, Cambridge Studies in Religion and Platonism (Cambridge: Cambridge University Press, 2024).

[67] S. Byers, *Perception, Sensibility, and Moral Motivation in Augustine: A Stoic-Platonic Synthesis* (Cambridge: Cambridge University Press, 2013), esp. ch. 4.

[68] W. Helleman-Elgersma, "Augustine and Philo of Alexandria's Sarah as a Wisdom Figure," *StPatr* 18 (2013): 105–15 is also of relevance, tracing common elements in Augustine's and Philo's exegesis, but without any attempt to clarify whether Augustine was reading Philo directly in this case or not, and through what channels.

[69] On the influence of Stoic taxonomy of passions on Philo's psychology, see also L. Kerns, "Soul and Passions in Philo of Alexandria," *StPatr* 11 (2013): 141–54; also D. Konstan and I. Ramelli, "The Use of ΧΑΡΑ in the New Testament and Its Background in Hellenistic Moral Philosophy," *Exemplaria Classica* 14 (2010): 185–204.

[70] Clement, *Strom.* 1.5.29.4; Origen, *Hom. Jer.* 13.2 (ὅρασις εἰρήνης); Eusebius, *Dem. ev.* 6.24.7; Didymus, *Comm. Zach.* 1.48; E. Scully, "Jerusalem's Lost Etymology," *VC* 70 (2016): 1–30, esp. 9–10.

[71] J. van Oort, *Jerusalem and Babylon: A Study into Augustine's City of God and the Sources of the Doctrine of the Two Cities* (Leiden: Brill, 1991), 250–51.

[72] So Van Oort, "Augustine's Knowledge," 442.

to go back to Philo's own use of oppositions in his allegorical reading of *Genesis*.[73] Especially the antithesis between love of oneself as the driving force of the earthly city opposed to the love of God as the gist of the heavenly city (*Civ.* 14.28)[74] seems to reflect the opposition posited by Philo between Cain's way of thinking inspired by love for oneself (φίλαυτον δόγμα) and Abel's way of thinking inspired by the love of God (φιλόθεον δόγμα). Augustine opposes God vs human being, good vs evil, life vs death, heaven vs earth, grace vs nature, love of God to the point of the nullification of oneself (*amor Dei usque ad contemptum sui*) vs love of oneself to the point of the nullification of God (*amor sui usque ad contemptum Dei*), Abel-Seth vs Cain, Sarah vs Hagar, and Israel vs Ishmael—the last two cases, I note, mediated by Paul's discourse in Gal 4:24, a text later taken by Origen as the justification of biblical allegoresis.[75] Thus, Philo even seems to lie behind Augustine's most characteristic theory, which owes so much to Stoic elaborations.

15.4 Conclusion

This chapter has investigated Augustine's reception of Philonic themes and the extent to which Augustine actually read Philo, with attention to direct and indirect channels he had at his disposal for learning Philo's ideas. For the former the chapter has discussed whether Augustine read Philo and in which language, Greek or Latin, especially in the case of the only named mention and discussion of Philo in Augustine. From the latter indirect viewpoint, it emerges that the transmission of Philo's ideas to Augustine was most probably mediated by Augustine's knowledge of Origen, together with Ambrose. I have suggested that Origen's influence on Augustine already in his anti-Manichaean phase was significant, and highlighted that this also appears to be the phase in which Augustine's philosophical theology was closest to Origen's. It is not accidental that the only explicit mention of Philo in Augustine's oeuvre comes from a work belonging exactly to his anti-Manichaean phase: *Contra Faustum Manichaeum*. Augustine most probably read the beginning of Philo's *Quaestiones in Genesim*, and it is probable that Origen prompted him to read it—as he and Ambrose likely facilitated Augustine's knowledge of Philo in other respects as well. Indeed, a systematic reassessment of Origen's presence in Augustine is important. Numerous clues suggest that Origen conveyed to Augustine many Philonic themes, as well as emphasis and attention to specific issues. Several examples have been offered, also with new arguments, including the main theme of the City of God, ethical issues, and the exegesis of the

---

[73] J. P. Martín, "Philo and Augustine: *De Civitate Dei* XIV 28 and XV: Preliminary Observations," *SPhiloA* 3 (1991): 283–94. Martín and J. Van Oort both point to Philo as a source behind Augustine's conception of the two cities, although the former emphasizes Philo's influence as a biblical exegete, while the latter understands Philo's influence to derive from his mediation of Platonic philosophy. See Van Oort, *Jerusalem and Babylon*.

[74] For its Gospel foundations, see I. Ramelli, "Simon Son of John, Do You Love Me? Some Reflections on John 21:15," *NovT* 50 (2008): 332–50.

[75] See Ramelli, "The Relevance."

names of God in Exod 3:4–15. Augustine relies on the *Quaestiones in Genesim*, as well as on Philo's allegorical works, mostly through indirect transmission. More broadly, it has been asked to what extent Philo's thought influenced Augustine, also taking into account the issue of language and what role Origen and Ambrose played in mediating Philo's concepts to Augustine.

III
THE MIDDLE AGES

16
The Greek and Latin Manuscript Traditions

James R. Royse

Before the advent of printing, the works of Philo were extensively copied, excerpted, and quoted almost exclusively within the Christian tradition. As a consequence, we find Philonic texts in a wide variety of places, mostly in Greek, but also within the early medieval translations into Latin and Armenian. Because of this extensive use, it is hardly possible to catalog all the places where his words may be present. Rather, what is attempted here is to present an overview of the manuscript materials that are of value for the establishment of the text of Philo. Naturally, many MSS are of very minor importance, containing perhaps only an inferior recension of a few extracts from Philo, while others are valuable witnesses to many of his complete works. Sometimes the materials cited have received inadequate attention, while other MSS are well known. In any case, it is hoped that the present classification will provide insight into the process by which the works of Philo have been preserved.

The study of the manuscript tradition of Philo is intertwined with the study of the fate of his individual works, and with the classification of these works into various larger structures. These structures have themselves had quite different textual histories, and there are quite a few Philonic works that have, as far as we can tell, disappeared completely.[1] Moreover, the "works" of Philo as found in the MSS often differ from what we now think of as his works (as found in the Loeb edition, for example, and in other translations into modern languages), and do not necessarily conform to Philo's original division of his works (at least insofar as that original division seems to be discernible).[2] For example, *Leg.* 1 and *Leg.* 2 are transmitted as separate books, but are really just two parts of one original book (as the Armenian tradition confirms).[3] Likewise, *Gig.* and *Deus* were originally one book, as is generally agreed.[4] And probably *Sobr.* and *Conf.*

---

[1] The most important studies that provide authoritative discussions of the classification of Philo's works are: L. Massebieau, "Le classement des oeuvres de Philon," *Bibliothèque de l'École des Hautes Études, Section des Sciences religieuses*, 1 (1889): 1–91 (separately published: Paris: Ernest Leroux, 1889); L. Cohn, "Einteilung und Chronologie der Schriften Philos," *Phil. Supplementband* 7 (1899): 387–436 (separately published Leipzig: Dieterich, 1899); E. Schürer, *Geschichte des jüdischen Volkes im Zeitalter Jesu Christi* 3 (4th edn; Leipzig: Hinrichs, 1909), 634–95 ("Philo der jüdische Philosoph, I. Philos Schriften"); and most recently J. Morris, in *SHJP* 3:809–70 ("The Jewish Philosopher Philo, I. Life and Works").

[2] See T. Mangey, ed., *Philonis Judaei opera quae reperiri potuerunt omnia* (London: William Bowyer, 1742), 1:357 n. *: "librarii passim pro lubitu, nec semper ad mentem Autoris, Philonis opuscula dispoduerunt & distinxerunt" (the scribes here and there arrange and distinguish the works of Philo as they wish, not always according to the mind of the author).

[3] See J. R. Royse, "The Text of Philo's *Legum Allegoriae*," *SPhiloA* 12 (2000): 1–28, here 2.

[4] PCW 2:xxi–xxii.

were originally one book.[5] Similarly, in the MSS *Mos.* 2 is divided, so that there are *Mos.* 2 (= *Mos.* 2.1–65) and *Mos.* 3 (= *Mos.* 2.66–292). Here Cohn restored the original division into two books, as indeed Philo states at *Virt.* 52.[6] Also, the various sections of *Virt.* and *Spec.* 1–4 are often transmitted independently; Cohn basically reconstructed the original order of these books.[7] Furthermore, many books have suffered losses: *Somn.* 2 and *Legat.* break off at the end, and *Contempl.* is perhaps only half or less of whatever original book it derives from. Similarly, the extracts from the *Hypothetica* (as found in Eusebius; see below, pp. 270–71) are portions of a larger original book.[8] And at many places there seem to be lacunae in the transmission. The earliest known example is at *Sacr.* 8, where Pap (see below, pp. 263–65) leaves four lines blank, presumably as being blank or unreadable in its exemplar; this gap remains, although unmarked, in all the other MSS as well.[9]

16.1 Resources

The fundamental resource for the study of the manuscript tradition of Philo is the prolegomena of the six volumes of the critical edition by Cohn and Wendland (1896–1915). While the material found there is no longer up to date and is much less complete than it was at the time of publication, it still provides a masterly overview of the main lines of the MSS that are the basis for the text of the works that are preserved completely (more or less) in Greek.[10] Cohn and Wendland and Reiter (for the second part of volume 6) personally examined most of the MSS that were then known, classified them into various families and groups, and cited the more important ones in their apparatus criticus with, as it seems, a very high level of accuracy. Most of these MSS are to be found in the libraries of Western Europe. Already Mangey examined, or had examinations made of, MSS in Oxford and Paris and elsewhere. As part of a planned edition that was to supersede Mangey's edition, Grossmann commissioned a young Tischendorf and others to find and collate Philo MSS in Paris, Florence, Venice, the

---

[5] *Sobr.* covers Gen 9:24–27, and *Conf.* covers Gen 11:1–9. *Sobr.* is unusually short, so Cohn argued that *Sobr.* and *Conf.* were one book, which was then divided. See Cohn, "Einteilung," 399–400. Moreover, as Cohn notes, an excerpt in the *Sacra parallela* from *Conf.* 167 is said to come from *Sobr.*; see PCW 2:261 n. This seems more likely than the suggestion of Massebieau ("Le classement," 25) that Gen 9:28–10:32 were covered in a lost final portion of *Sobr.* and a lost beginning portion of *Conf.* Philo may have completely omitted discussion of Gen 10. And, judging from QG, Philo would not have had much to say about Gen 9:28–29. Cf. Schürer, *Geschichte* 3:656; Morris, "Philo," 837.

[6] PCW 4:xxx; at *Virt.* 52 CG² read "three books," evidently influenced by the usual division.

[7] See e.g. J. R. Royse, "The Text of Philo's *De virtutibus*," SPhiloA 18 (2006): 73–101, here 75–81. Note that Mangey edits the first three sections of *Virt.* (2:375–407), then *Praem.* (2:408–37), and then the last section (*de nobilitate*) of *Virt.* (2:437–44). See Cohn's comment at PCW 5:xxviii.

[8] Colson, PLCL 9: 407–11; Morris, "Philo," 866–68.

[9] PCW 1:205 apparatus. The lacuna is at p. 67, col. B, ll. 2–5 of the papyrus. UF omit text on either side of the lacuna in order to avoid a (seemingly) nonsensical text, but the other MSS simply present a continuous text.

[10] PCW presents the material as thirty-eight books. However, as noted earlier, three books have been divided in transmission, so these thirty-eight correspond to only thirty-five of Philo's books. Moreover, *De vita contemplativa* is only a small portion of a book, and other books have lacunae of varying lengths.

Vatican, and Naples. Cohn and Wendland made a more systematic search, and were even able to borrow a MS from St. Petersburg.[11]

An important addition to the material found in PCW was made in 1938 by Goodhart and Goodenough, who took as part of their task of providing a comprehensive bibliography of Philo studies (i.e. G-G) the study of the MSS that were relevant to the text of Philo.[12] They present the results of their research in this area at the beginning of their bibliography, and list 353 items.[13] This list builds upon the work of PCW, but cites scores of MSS that are not mentioned in PCW, including MSS of the Armenian translation and MSS that contain collations of Philo MSS (items 279–88) or modern writings about Philo (items 377–86). There is much information of interest and value in what they present. Unfortunately, however, the work of Goodhart and Goodenough suffers from some fundamental flaws, which pervade their work on the MSS. They had no first-hand knowledge of the MSS that they cite (except for items 300 and 321a, which were owned by Goodhart), and indeed they had no particular expertise in the field of manuscript studies. At every turn, as a result, one finds errors of many sorts. For example, in their desire (itself reasonable enough) to be thorough, they include items 235–39, which cite Philo of Carpasia, not Philo of Alexandria.[14] Moreover, they organize the MSS used in PCW simply by the capital letters used to designate the witnesses. Thus, under "Family E" they place both the MS Oxoniensis Coll. Lincolniensis gr. 34 (item 76), called "E" in PCW 4 and 5, and the MSS of the epitome *De mundo* (items 77–79), called "E" in PCW 2 and 6, which has nothing to do with the Oxford MS. Similarly, under "Family D" (items 50–75) Goodhart and Goodenough place the MSS of the *Sacra parallela*, denoted in PCW as "D" (for "Damascenus") with superscripts, including there various other MSS of florilegia, while other MSS of the *Sacra parallela* and other florilegia appear under their "Greek Manuscripts, D" (items 143–50).

Thus, while Goodhart and Goodenough provide much useful information, for which every student of Philo must be grateful,[15] all too often their presentation bears little relationship to the data, and moreover what they report is often superficial or even based on misinterpretation of their sources, betraying over and over again their evident lack of first-hand knowledge of the manuscript materials.[16]

---

[11] PCW 1:xvi: it was twice sent to Berlin, where Wendland collated it.
[12] See the article "Bibliographies on Philo" elsewhere in this volume.
[13] i.e. items 35 through 386, plus 321a. There are some discrepancies; see e.g. n. 125 below.
[14] See G-G, 169, and J. R. Royse, *The Spurious Texts of Philo of Alexandria: A Study of Textual Transmission and Corruption with Indexes to the Major Collections of Greek Fragments*, ALGHJ 22 (Leiden: Brill, 1991), 113–14. These are citations in a catena on the Song of Songs.
[15] One significant contribution of their work is that it provides a convenient index (via shelfmarks) to the MSS that are covered, thus providing in effect (through the references at each MS) an index to the discussions in PCW. Otherwise, what PCW says about a specific MS can be discovered only by examining the prefaces to all six volumes.
[16] Naturally, reliance on indirect knowledge is the well-known bane of the bibliographer. For printed materials Goodhart and Goodenough were in contrast almost always able to examine the works to which they refer, and in that area their comments are (almost always) thorough and reliable.

Less comprehensive but nevertheless of great importance is the study of MSS that Françoise Petit has made as part of her editions of the Latin version of the original book 6 of *QG*,[17] and of the Greek fragments of the *Quaestiones*.[18] Of special note is her research into the Greek *catenae* on the Octateuch, a primary source of the fragments of Philo. But one will find in her prolegomena to the latter edition an authoritative survey of many other sources.

The crucial tools for investigating MSS are the catalogs of the various libraries. Finally, a more recent resource that should be mentioned is the "pinakes" that is found at the Web site of the Institut de recherche et d'histoire des textes in Paris.[19] Among the many activities of the IRHT is providing a catalog of the catalogs of Greek MSS.[20] And the information gleaned from the catalogs is available online. Here one can search the database in various ways, including by author, to find, for example, all the MSS that contain works by "Philo Judaeus," as well as all the MSS that contain other sources of interest, such as "catena on the Octateuch," "Maximus," etc. The information cited usually derives from the catalogs, although it is often supplemented by more recent literature. It is an invaluable resource.

As part of my own research into the manuscript tradition of Philo, I have compiled for my own use a listing of the relevant MSS, and the present article draws upon that listing and the notes of my own examination of many of them (some three hundred so far). It is far from complete, but nevertheless permits me to supplement and to correct earlier sources. The reports below on the number of MSS of the various sorts rely on that listing; they should be viewed as provisional, but will give the reader at least an approximate idea of the resources available. Naturally, since Philo wrote in Greek and there is extensive evidence in Greek for his writings, the Greek MSS will occupy most of our attention. However, at the end we will also consider the tradition found in an early Latin translation. The more important evidence that is provided by the Armenian tradition is considered elsewhere.[21]

16.2 The Direct Tradition

We may begin by dividing the witnesses to Philo's text into the direct tradition (MSS that contain [at least more or less] complete works of Philo) and the indirect tradition (MSS of non-Philonic works in which Philo is quoted). The indirect tradition is relatively more important for the remains of Philo's Greek that are not included

---

[17] *L'ancienne version latine des Questions sur la Genèse de Philon d'Alexandrie*, Vol. 1: *Édition critique*; Vol. 2: *Commentaire*, TU 113–14 (Berlin: Akademie-Verlag, 1973).

[18] *Quaestiones in Genesim et in Exodum: fragmenta graeca*, PAPM 33 (Paris: Cerf, 1978).

[19] See //http:www.pinakes.org.

[20] Originally compiled by Marcel Richard, the list was continued by J.-M. Olivier, *Répertoire des bibliothèques et des catalogues de manuscrits grecs de Marcel Richard* (3rd edn; Turnhout: Brepols, 1995), to which there is now a two-volume supplement, J.-M. Olivier, *Supplément au répertoire des bibliothèques et des catalogues de manuscrits grecs* (Turnhout: Brepols, 2018).

[21] See the article "Armenian Christianity" by Olga Vardazaryan elsewhere in this volume.

in PCW, i.e. the Greek fragments, although PCW regularly cite a wide variety of indirect sources.

The earliest history of the transmission of the works of Philo is a matter of informed speculation. What seems to be the common view nowadays is that somehow these works found their way into the Catechetical School of Alexandria, where they were available to Clement and Origen. When Origen went to Caesarea in 233, he took copies of those MSS (or perhaps the MSS themselves) with him. And there they were used by Eusebius.[22] Now, Cohn argued that the archetype of the entire extant manuscript tradition of Philo's works went back to the fourth- or even third-century papyrus MSS that were found in the library at Caesarea.[23] These papyrus books were then transferred to parchment codices under the direction of Acacius and Euzoius, as we read in Jerome and also in a superscription now found in Vindobonensis theol. gr. 29 (see further below, pp. 267–68).[24] And one can see that our extant works are, almost always, found among the works listed by Eusebius (*Hist. eccl.* 2.18), which are presumably those to be found in the Caesarean library.[25] But we may wonder about the fate of Philo's writings in the three centuries leading up to their transfer.

Note, though, that the fact that two third-century codices of Philo's works were found in Egypt makes less likely that the archetype of all of our MSS derives from Caesarea. Cohn did not know of the Oxyrhynchus Papyrus, of course, and he probably underestimated the age of the Coptos Papyrus. Scheil had, implausibly, dated it to the sixth century, and Cohn thought that it might be earlier. But he would still have been able to think of it as deriving from the fourth-century codices compiled by Acacius and Euzoius. If our datings are correct, though, this would be impossible. Both these early papyri must derive from MSS of Philo before the establishment of the library in Caesarea. But they could well have been based on the MSS as they were found, say, in the time of Origen. In any case, the process of dissemination started by the third century.

16.2.1 The Papyrus Codices

The four papyrus codices are vastly different in contents, scope, and importance. The first is a third-century codex that contains two works of Philo, *Quis heres* and *De*

---

[22] See D. T. Runia, "Witness or Participant? Philo and the Neoplatonist Tradition," in his *Philo and the Church Fathers: A Collection of Papers* (Leiden: Brill, 1995), 190–95, and *Philo in Early Christian Literature: A Survey*, CRINT 3.3 (Assen and Minneapolis: Van Gorcum and Fortress, 1993), 16–31. It is usually left open in such discussions whether Philo's autographs (written one book per scroll) or subsequent copies were involved, since we have no information one way or the other. But I once speculated that perhaps the autographs were involved ("The Text of Philo's *Legum allegoriae*," 2 n. 6). On the early history of transmission, see the brief surveys in "The Text of Philo's *Legum allegoriae*," 1–2, and "The Text of Philo's *De virtutibus*," 73–74.

[23] PCW 1:iii–iv.
[24] PCW 1:iii.
[25] On some problems in this list, see n. 62 below.

sacrificiis, and is generally known as the Coptos Papyrus (from its alleged place of discovery),[26] and called "Pap" by Cohn and Wendland:

Parisinus suppl. gr. 1120/1.[27]

Generally dated to the third century,[28] this codex consists of forty-four folios (paginated as pp. 1–88), along with the original leather cover, and a final folio that is pasted to the inside back cover and numbered as p. 89. The text is in two columns. This papyrus was discovered in 1889, and was published by Vincent Scheil.[29] That edition was then used by Cohn and Wendland for their critical edition of *De sacrificiis* (in PCW 1) and *Quis heres* (in PCW 3). Their analysis showed the general excellence of the text.[30] In *De sacrificiis* Pap stands in a very close relationship to UF, but often agrees with the other MSS against UF, and in yet other cases alone preserves the true reading.[31] Indeed, Cohn declares: "papyrus integritate et praestantia scripturae non modo codices UF sed omnes codices Philonis longe superat."[32] In *Quis heres* (which UF do not contain), Pap often agrees with N (which belongs to the UF family), often agrees with G against the other MSS, and often has the true reading alone.[33] The superiority of Pap is confirmed by studying the readings of Pap throughout the critical apparatus to the two books. Although Pap does have its own errors, it is systematically the best witness.

Regrettably, however, Scheil's edition is far from adequate by today's standards (or even by the standards of his time).[34] Moreover, Scheil often misreads or misinterprets the surviving text. Cohn and Wendland did not themselves examine the codex,[35] but were sufficiently puzzled by what they found in Scheil's edition that they asked the papyrologist Carl Kalbfleisch to examine a few dozen places.[36] Indeed, Wendland was able to correct Scheil's edition at one place by looking at the plate of p. 2 that was

---

[26] But see the doubts expressed about this attribution by B. Nongbri, *God's Library: The Archaeology of the Earliest Christian Manuscripts* (New Haven: Yale University Press, 2018), 260–63.

[27] A small portion of the Gospel of Luke was found inserted within the codex, and is known as New Testament 𝔓⁴; it is cataloged as suppl. gr. 1120/2. Nongbri's ch. 7 (*God's Library*, 247–68) is devoted to 𝔓⁴, and has many valuable comments on Pap itself.

[28] A survey of the various datings is offered by T. C. Skeat, "The Oldest Manuscript of the Four Gospels?," *NTS* 43 (1997), 26 (see also 29 n. 19[–20]), who says that since the dating by Hunt (in 1912), "a third century date has been generally accepted." Scheil, the editor, assigned the codex to the sixth century, but already Cohn thought that it might be earlier (PCW 1:xlii).

[29] "Deux traités de Philon. Traités réédités d'après un papyrus du VIᵉ siècle environ," *Mémoires publiés par les membres de la Mission archéologique française au Caire* 9, fasc. 2 (1893), vii, 151–215.

[30] See also Colson and Whitaker (PLCL 2:93, 4:282–83) as well as M. Harl, ed., *Quis rerum divinarum heres sit* (PAPM 15, 1966), 154–55.

[31] PCW 1:xliv–xlvi, xlvi–xlvii, and xlvii–xlviii, respectively.

[32] PCW 1:xlvii: "The papyrus is far superior in its purity and excellence of writing not only to the codices UF but to all codices of Philo." Note that here and also in their apparatus, Cohn and Wendland do not consider Pap to be a "codex." This can lead to some confusion in the citations.

[33] PCW 4: iii, iv–v, and v–vii, respectively.

[34] See the comments by Cohn, PCW 1:xxx.

[35] I have always found this to be a bit puzzling. Certainly one or the other was in Paris often enough to examine other MSS there, and they could have easily (it seems) looked at the Coptos Papyrus. Apparently papyri were considered so different from later MSS that Pap could properly be examined only by a papyrologist.

[36] See the report on *Quis heres* at PCW 3:ix–xi, and note the corrections to the apparatus of *De sacrificiis* found at PCW 3:xxx n. 1.

published in the edition (see his note at *Her.* 14). But a more systematic examination of the papyrus reveals many more inaccuracies in Scheil's edition. The result is that the text of Pap is even better than Cohn and Wendland believed.

Although most of the folios have suffered significant damage, the bulk of the text survives, having been protected by the cover, which is still more or less intact and stored separately from the forty-four folios, each of which is under glass. Indeed, this is the oldest book for which the original cover has survived.[37] Here we are able to read two books of Philo as they existed a millennium before the other MSS of these books, and thus to understand the sorts of changes that occurred over the centuries. One fundamental observation is that the altered readings frequently depart from the readings that might be expected given Philo's reliance on the LXX.[38] In this matter of Philo's quotations from the Bible, as in so many other features, the Coptos Papyrus is the outstanding MS of Philo, and fully deserves to be placed first in our survey.[39]

The other three papyrus codices survive to a much smaller extent. The Oxyrhynchus Papyrus provides brief portions of six known works (*Leg.* 1; *Leg.* 2; *Sacr.*; *Det.*; *Post.*; *Ebr.*) as well as a few fragmentary folios of at least one otherwise unknown work of Philo, and also enough material that we can reconstruct what books were originally present.[40] This is a third-century codex, the remains of which have been published in six places:

P.Oxy. 9.1173.
P.Oxy. 11.1356.
P.Oxy. 18.2158.
P.Oxy. 82.5291.
PSI 11.1207.
P.Haun. 8.

It is an unusually large codex; page number 289 is extant, and it seems that *Quod deterius* would have extended to p. 373. It is in any case certain that the larger fragments that have not been identified (*P.Oxy.* 1356, f. 4, f. 10; *P.Haun.* f. 1) do not come from any of Philo's surviving works, and there are also three smaller fragments (*P.Oxy.* 1356, Fr. 1; *P.Oxy.* 2158, Fr. 1 and Fr. 2) that have not been placed. Thus, this codex originally contained at least one and perhaps several otherwise lost works of Philo. The reconstruction referred to above takes the original contents to have been: *Sacr.*; *Leg.* 1; *Leg.* 2; the lost *De pietate*; the lost *De ebrietate* 1; *Ebr.* (identified as *De ebrietate* 2); *Post.*; and *Det.*

It is interesting that the Coptos Papyrus and the Oxyrhynchus Papyrus both contained *De sacrificiis*, and one can usefully compare these two third-century witnesses to

---

[37] See C. Roberts, *Buried Books in Antiquity: Habent Sua Fata Libelli* (London: The Library Association, 1963), 11–14 on the papyrus generally, and especially 14: "It is beyond reasonable doubt the earliest bound book extant."
[38] On Philo's use of the LXX, see J. R. Royse, "Philo," in *Textual History of the Bible*, Vol. 1: *The Hebrew Bible*, part 1C: *Writings*, ed. A. Lange and E. Tov (Leiden: Brill, 2016), 741–46.
[39] See J. R. Royse, "The Biblical Quotations in the Coptos Papyrus of Philo," *SPhiloA* 28 (2016): 49–76. I am in the process of producing a new edition of this MS.
[40] See J. R. Royse, "The Oxyrhynchus Papyrus of Philo," *BASP* 17 (1980): 155–65.

that book. One place where their testimony is instructive is *Sacr.* 32. At p. 63 col. B l. 10 of Pap, Scheil reports ακροχολος, for which Cohn reports no variation. But in fact Pap reads ακραχολος, as does the Oxyrhynchus Papyrus (*P.Oxy.* 1173, f. 9r, l. 9). And the spelling with ακρα- is also found at *Ebr.* 223 in GU and printed by Wendland, whereas ακρο- is found in FH.[41] At *Somn.* 2.192 Wendland prints ακρο- on the authority of A, the sole MS there. But ακρα- is the correct form (see LSJ s.v., note), and the support from the two papyri at *Sacr.* 32 shows, I believe, that it was Philo's spelling. Thus, GU are correct at *Ebr.* 223, and ακρα- should be edited also at *Somn.* 2.192 against the slender MS evidence.[42] Even though this is a minor matter of orthography, one sees how the later MSS have corrupted what Philo wrote. And similar corruptions have certainly occurred throughout all the other works where we do not have any such early evidence.

There are two further papyri of Philo, each of which preserves only a portion of one folio. The Berlin papyrus consists of the remains of one folio of *Quod Deus*: *P.Berol.* P 21342. This is a sixth- to seventh-century codex, containing *Deus* 151, 154–55.[43] And the Vienna papyrus contains the remains of one folio of *De virtutibus*. This is a fifth-century codex, containing *Virt.* 64–65, 69–70. The remains have been published in three places:

P.Vindob. G 21649.
P.Vindob. G 30531.
P.Vindob. G 60584.[44]

16.2.2 The Medieval Codices

We turn now to the much later MSS, which provide the greater part of the evidence for Philo's writings. I have counted sixty-three MSS here, which range from MSS that contain many of the works of Philo that survive in Greek to MSS that contain only one such work. PCW rests upon Cohn's and Wendland's (and Reiter's) thorough investigation into many of these, and its apparatus provides a report of their readings. Full descriptions and analyses can be found in the prolegomena to the volumes of PCW; here only some of the more important witnesses will be briefly mentioned.

Among the oldest MSS (that is, apart from the papyri) are:

Seldenianus supra 12 (Oxford, X cent.; S in PCW). *Spec.* 3.37–end; *Spec.* 4; *Virt.* Its text is very valuable, and it also confirms the order of the sections of *Virt.*, which are usually transmitted separately.

---

[41] Another portion of the Oxyrhynchus Papyrus, edited as PSI 11.1207 f. 1v, l. 3, contains *Ebr.* 223, but breaks off at α[κρ....

[42] I called attention to this evidence in "New and Neglected Readings from *De sacrificiis* and Other Works of Philo," a presentation to the Philo of Alexandria Seminar at the annual meeting of the Society of Biblical Literature in Denver, November 19, 2018.

[43] The text was identified by R. Daniel and was edited by W. Brashear, "Literary and Sub-Literary Papyri from Berlin," *Proceedings of the 20th International Congress of Papyrologists*, Copenhagen, August 23–29, 1992, ed. A. Bülow-Jacobsen (Copenhagen: University of Copenhagen Press, 1994), 284–94, at 290–91.

[44] See F. Morelli, "Philo Vindobonensis restitutus. No c'è due senza tre: P. Vindob. G 30531 + 60584 + 21649," *ZPE* 173 (2010): 167–74, who brings together all three fragments.

Vaticanus gr. 316 (Vatican City, IX–X cent.; R in PCW 5). This is a palimpsest, which contains remains of *Migr.*; *Ios.*; *Mos.* 1; *Mos.* 2.71–end; *Decal. Spec.* 1; *Spec.* 2.1–95. Unfortunately Cohn discovered this MS only after the publication of PCW 4, and so could use it only for PCW 5, where it proves to be a very valuable witness.[45] This is one of two palimpsests of Philo's works; the other is Atheniensis EBE 880.

Further important MSS are the following:[46]

Atheniensis EBE 880 (Athens, X–XI cent.; not in PCW). This is another palimpsest, containing *Det.*; *Post.*; *Gig.*; *Deus*; *Ebr.*; *Sobr.*; *Conf.*; *Virt.* C; *Virt.* D; *Sacr.*; *Agr.*; *Somn.* 1; and perhaps other works.[47]

Monacensis Cod. graec. 459 (Munich, XIII cent.; A in PCW). Philonic corpus. Used by Mangey. This also contains scholia of significance.[48]

Marcianus Gr. Z. 41 (= 366) (Venice, early XIV cent.; B in PCW 1 and 3). Philonic corpus.

Marcianus Gr. Z. 42 (= 382) (Venice, XII. cent.; B in PCW 4 and 5). *Mos.* 1; *Mos.* 2B; *Mos.* 2A; *Virt.* A; *Ios.*; *Abr.*

Vindobonensis theol. gr. 29 (Vienna; early XI cent.; V in PCW).[49]

This MS contains only *Opif.* 1–91 on ff. 147r–154v (as well as some non-Philonic material). The MS is remarkable for containing at f. 146v a table of works of Philo, listing: *Opif.*; *QG* 1, 2, 3, 4, 5, 6; *QE* 2 5; *Post.*; *Decal.*; *Spec.* 3, 4.[50] The scribe leaves the rest of the folio blank after *De opificio mundi* breaks off, indicating that the exemplar itself was mutilated. The table thus describes the contents of an archetype. Cohn argues that the *Quaestiones* would hardly be copied after the sixth century, because of the extensive excerpting in the catenae and florilegia, and thus this archetype was probably no later than the sixth century. In fact, after this table occurs a cruciform subscription, which refers to Euzoius, bishop of Caesarea in the mid-fourth century, saying: Εὐζόιος ἐπίσκοπος ἐν σωματίοις ἀνενεώσατο. This is interpreted by Cohn as meaning that Euzoius had the works of Philo transferred from papyrus to parchment, and that the archetype of Vindobonensis theol. gr. 29 was one of these parchment copies. This view

---

[45] See Cohn, "Ein Philo-Palimpsest (Vaticanus gr. 316)," SPAW (1905), 36–52, where he notes its special importance for the text of *Spec.* 1. See further G. Mercati, "Appunti dal palinsesto Vaticano di Filone," *RB*, n.s. 12 (1915): 540–55; and J. R. Royse, "The Text of Philo's *De Decalogo* in Vaticanus gr. 316," *SPhiloA* 27 (2015): 133–42.

[46] I have marked several of these as simply containing a "Philonic corpus," i.e. an extensive set of Philonic works. Details can be found in the descriptions in PCW, as well as in G-G.

[47] See P. J. Alexander, "A Neglected Palimpsest of Philo Judaeus: Preliminary Remarks *editorum in usum*," in *Studia Codicologica*, ed. K. Treu, TU 124 (Berlin: Akademie-Verlag, 1977), 1–14. The text of the MS agrees closely with that of UF and contains some new readings of interest (Alexander, 10–11). Also, apart from fragments it is only the second MS (thus joining U) found to contain *De posteritate Caini*.

[48] PCW 1:vi–vii; D. T. Runia, "Philo in Byzantium," *VC* 70 (2016): 259–81, here 262 and 279 n. 88; see also Runia, Chapter 20 in this volume.

[49] See the full discussion at PCW 1:xxxv–xxxvii.

[50] On this listing, see J. R. Royse, "The Original Structure of Philo's *Quaestiones*," *SPhilo* 4 (1976–77): 41–78, here 54; photograph in Runia, *Philo in Early Christian Literature*, facing pp. 20 and 21.

is confirmed by the fact that the citations made by Eusebius, who lived in Caesarea, from *De opificio mundi* agree closely with the text found in this descendant, and Cohn judges this MS to be the best of the codices (except Pap) considered in PCW 1, and to preserve the text closest to the archetype.[51]

> Parisinus gr. 433 (Paris, XVI cent.; L in PCW). Philonic corpus. Used by Turnebus (his L) and Mangey.

An important family is represented by U and F.

> Vaticanus gr. 381 (Vatican, XIV cent.; U in PCW). Philonic corpus.

This MS was the only one known to Cohn and Wendland that contained *De posteritate Caini* (which is now known to survive, at least in part, also in Atheniensis EBE 880.)

> Laurentianus Pluteus 85.10 (Florence, XV cent.; F in PCW). Philonic corpus.

The MS originally contained many of Philo's works, and around 1550 Jacobus Diassorinus filled some lacunae and also added further works, all apparently taken from Turnèbe's printed edition.

> Laurentianus Pluteus 10.20 (Florence, early XIII cent.; M in PCW). Used by Mangey. Philonic corpus.

> Vaticanus Palatinus gr. 248 (Vatican, XIV cent.; G in PCW). Used by Mangey. Philonic corpus.

> Marcianus Gr. Z. 40 (= 365) (Venice, XIV cent.; H in PCW). Philonic corpus.

> Parisinus gr. 435 (Paris, XI cent.; C in PCW). Used by Turnèbe and Mangey.[52] Philonic corpus.

> Vaticanus gr. 379 (Vatican, XIV cent.; not cited in PCW). Philonic corpus.

This MS almost always agrees with F, and is thus not cited in PCW.[53] However, besides containing many other Philonic books, this MS includes a brief portion of *Her.* (which was overlooked by Cohn),[54] as well as on its final pages the longest continuous portion of the *Quaestiones* in Greek, namely *QE* 2.62–68.[55]

---

[51] See further Runia, *Philo in Early Christian Literature*, 21–22. At the end of PCW 1 is a plate of the MS.
[52] See Mangey, *Opera* 1:xviii: "videtur egregiae notae Codex" (it seems to be a codex of excellent quality).
[53] PCW 1:xxv–xxvii.
[54] See J. R. Royse, "The Text of Philo's *Quis rerum divinarum heres* 167–173 in Vaticanus 379," in *Theokratia* 3 (Leiden: Brill, 1979), 217–23, where the text is collated and found to agree closely with the Coptos Papyrus.
[55] See J. R. Royse, "Philo of Alexandria, *Quaestiones in Exodum* 2.62–68: Critical Edition," *SPhiloA* 24 (2012): 1–72. Further details on the history of the editions of this portion may be found there. I may add that the first notices

Athous Vatopediou Monasterii 659 (Mt. Athos, Vatopediou Monastery, XIV cent.; not in PCW).

Ff. 58r–145v comprise an exegetical compilation on the Pentateuch, in which are found, on ff. 68r–71r, extensive excerpts from *QG* 2.1–7 (sections 1, 2, 3, and 6 are virtually complete; the others have some lacunae) as well as other excerpts from Philo.[56]

These last two MSS are remarkable for preserving extensive portions of *QG* and *QE*. Indeed, Vaticanus gr. 379 is our best evidence for what a MS of the *Quaestiones* would have looked like.

Besides the MSS that contain one or more works, there are also MSS that contain collections of excerpts from Philo's writings. I here distinguish (as do Cohn and Wendland) collections from Philo and the usual florilegia and catenae that contain excerpts from many writers, among whom is Philo. The latter will be considered as part of the indirect tradition. But looking only at the collections from Philo, we find some distinct groupings. One such collection is what is usually called the *De mundo*, sometimes viewed as a separate work of Philo,[57] sometimes viewed as a spurious work, but perhaps best viewed as a collection of excerpts from various Philonic works.[58] Two other important collections that are cited throughout PCW are R and N.

Parisinus gr. 1630 (Paris, XIV cent.; R in PCW 1 and 2, Par. in PCW 5).

The exemplar of this MS had a valuable text, apparently related to UF.

Neapolitanus II C 32 (Naples, XV cent.; N in PCW).

The text is closely related to F, and in *Her.* often agrees alone with the Coptos Papyrus. Among other collections we may note the following:

Vindobonensis hist. gr. 67 (Vienna, XII cent., Vind. in PCW). Contains a wide range of excerpts.

Vindobonensis theol. gr. 64 (Vienna, late XIV cent.; not in PCW). This contains excerpts from *Mos.* 1.140–42, 1.44–47; *QG* 4.198, 4.200 (c), 4.202 (a); *Contempl.* 78.[59]

Finally, in a few MSS there is a florilegium of twenty-five brief texts from Philo with the title: ἐκ τοῦ Φίλωνος τοῦ Ἑβραίου περὶ οὗ εἴρηται· ἢ Φίλων πλατωνίζει ἢ Πλάτων

---

of this extract from *QE* are found in the collations that exist in Londiniensis add. 6448 (done for Mangey) and Parisinus suppl. gr. 867.

[56] J. Paramelle, with the collaboration of E. Lucchesi, *Philon d'Alexandrie: Questions sur la Genèse II 1–7*, with an arithmological interpretation by J. Sesiano, Cahiers d'Orientalisme 3 (Geneva: Patrick Cramer, 1984). See my review, J. R. Royse, *SPhiloA* 1 (1989): 134–44.

[57] And so printed by Mangey, *Opera* 2:601–24.

[58] See Royse, *Spurious Texts*, 144; Morris, "Philo," 868–69; Runia, "Byzantium," 344, in this volume.

[59] The standard catalog, H. Hunger and O. Kresten, *Katalog der griechischen Handschriften der Österreichischen Nationalbibliothek. Teil 3/1. Codices Theologici 1–100* (Vienna: Verlag Brüder Hollinek, 1976), 118 and 120, correctly identifies five of these, but for *Mos.* 1.44–47 states (120): "nicht Philon von Alexandreia!"

φιλωνίζει (i.e. "From Philo the Hebrew concerning whom it is said: either Philo platonizes or Plato philonizes").[60]

16.3 The Indirect Tradition

Besides the MSS that transmit the works of Philo, there are many early sources that cite Philo and that are valuable witnesses to the text of his works. The individual MSS of these sources are often cited in the literature on Philo.

16.3.1 Eusebius

Eusebius (c.260–339 CE) provides a very early witness to the works of Philo.[61] His list (*Hist. eccl.* 2.18.1–8) of Philo's works, usually thought to be based on the holdings of the ecclesiastical library at Caesarea, is a crucial piece of evidence of the extent of the Philonic corpus.[62] And in his *Praep. ev.* Eusebius makes extensive citations from Philo's works.[63] These include substantial extracts from the *Hypothetica* (or *Apologia Iud.*), a work that is otherwise completely unknown. Also, Eusebius quotes about a quarter of *Prov.* 2, which is otherwise known only from the Armenian version (except for a few citations from florilegia). He quotes almost all of *QG* 2.62 (omitting the final sentence), which again is otherwise known only from the Armenian. And he has several citations from works of Philo that have survived in Greek; for those he provides an important witness, which is often preferred by Cohn and Wendland to the Philo MSS themselves.[64] For example, at *Plant.* 8 and 10, Wendland edits λόγος and λόγου, respectively, as found in Eusebius alone, whereas the Philo MSS have νόμος and νόμου.[65]

The overall accuracy of Eusebius' quotations of earlier writers is generally judged to be very high.[66] The citations from Philo in particular can be judged by a comparison with the Philo MSS and with the Armenian version, and Eusebius is seen to be, in general, very faithful to the texts that were lying before him. Of course, we do not have Eusebius' actual citations; what we have are later MSS that have descended from

---

[60] PCW 1:lxix, lxxxxiv, 2:xiv, 3:xv, 4:xxii, 5:xvii, 6:xxxix.
[61] See the overview in Runia, *Philo in Early Christian Literature*, 17–20, 212–34.
[62] This list presents its own set of problems, as Runia (*Philo in Early Christian Literature*, 19–20) observes. Eusebius fails to include *Mos.* 1–2, *Aet.*, and even *Opif.* (from which he quotes), and he evidently knew of only one book *De providentia*, which must have been our book 2, from which he quotes extensively. On the omission of *Mos.* 1–2 from the list, see further A. Carriker, *The Library of Eusebius of Caesarea*, VCSup 67 (Leiden: Brill, 2003), 173–74, as cited by Runia, review of Metzler, *Exoduskommentar*, SPhiloA 33 (2021): 331–35, here 334.
[63] Runia, *Philo in Early Christian Literature*, 223.
[64] See the discussions in the various prolegomena to PCW.
[65] See Royse, "The Text of Philo's *Legum Allegoriae*," 20–21, on the relation of these changes to the "aberrant text" in Philo. For further examples where the editors prefer readings of Eusebius, see PCW 2:x–xi. (At *Prob.* 3 and 49 Cohn edits νόμον and νόμος, respectively, on the authority of MS M alone, where the other MSS have λόγον and λόγος; see PCW 6:vi.)
[66] PCW 1:lxi: Eusebius "multa et satis ampla excerpta e variis Philonis libris ad verbum transcripta servavit" (preserved many and rather extensive excerpts copied literally from various books of Philo). See also e.g. S. Inowlocki, *Eusebius and the Jewish Authors: His Citation Technique in an Apologetic Context*, AJEC 64 (Leiden: Brill, 2006), 220–22.

Eusebius' original work. Fortunately, the testimony from these MSS is presented with a high degree of accuracy in the critical edition of *Praep. ev.* by Karl Mras (GCS). For the Philonic material the relevant MSS are the following five:[67]

Bononiensis 3643 (Bologna, XIII cent.; O in Mras).
Neapolitanus II AA 16 (Naples, XV cent.; N in Mras).
Parisinus gr. 465 (Paris, XIII cent.; B in Mras).
Parisinus gr. 467 (Paris, XVI cent.; D in Mras, cited only supplementarily).
Marcianus Gr. Z. 341 (= 735) (Venice, XV cent.; I in Mras).

And there are substantial differences among those MSS. In particular, for the citations from *Prov.* 2 the MS I is often seen to agree with the Armenian where the other MSS have corruptions.

Besides Eusebius' quotations from various works of Philo in *Praep. ev.*, in his *Hist. eccl.* Eusebius quotes seven extracts from *De vita contemplativa* in the course of his discussion of the Therapeutae, whom he took to be a group of early Christians (*Hist. eccl.* 2.16.2–18.8). These Eusebian extracts are systematically cited in the apparatus to *Contempl.* in PCW 6, although not the individual MSS of Eusebius.[68] But these seven extracts had a more extended life. At some point they began to be copied independently of the works of Eusebius, and in fact often appear toward the end of MSS of Ps-Dionysius Areopagita.[69] Cohn cites five such MSS, and I have noted twenty-four more. While it is intriguing that these citations from Philo made their way into these MSS, their textual value seems to be minimal.[70] (These extracts are also found in the Latin translation; see below, pp. 277–79.)

16.3.2 Procopius

A source that is closely related to the catenae on the Octateuch (see below, pp. 273–74) is known as the *Epitome*, which is ascribed to Procopius of Gaza (*c.*465/470–526/530 CE). The precise relation between this *Epitome* and the catenae is not entirely clear.[71] The *Epitome*, like the catenae, consists of quotations from early Church writers as well as Philo, although, unlike the catenae, these quotations are not explicitly ascribed to their sources. Harris first noted that Procopius uses Philo extensively,[72] then Wendland

---

[67] See the extensive discussion by K. Mras, *Eusebius* 8.1 (GCS; Berlin: Akademie-Verlag, 1954), xiii–li.
[68] For the MSS of *Hist. eccl.*, see E. Schwartz, *Eusebius* 2.3 (GCS; Leipzig: Hinrichs, 1969), xvii–ccxlviii.
[69] PCW 6:ii–iii.
[70] Cohn states (PCW 6:iii): "singulorum codicum varias lectiones, cum nihil valeant, non adnotavi" (I have not noted the variant readings of the individual codices, since they have no value).
[71] Petit, *Quaestiones*, 18–19; K. Metzler, ed., *Prokop von Gaza: Eclogarum in libros historicos Veteris Testamenti epitome*, Vol. 1: *Der Genesiskommentar*, GCS NF 22 (Berlin: de Gruyter, 2015), xx–xxv. See the review of the latter by Runia, *SPhiloA* 29 (2017): 260–64.
[72] J. R. Harris, ed., *Fragments of Philo Judaeus* (Cambridge: Cambridge University Press, 1886), 5: "The commentary of Procopius on the Pentateuch is full of passages and abridgements from Philo."

made a more thorough investigation of the Philonic material to be found there, which consists of numerous quotations from the *Quaestiones*, several quotations from *Mos.* 1–2, and one citation from *Ios.*[73] PCW regularly refers to the quotations from the works that were edited by them.[74] Finally, Petit systematically cites the most important MSS of Procopius in her edition of the Greek fragments of the *Quaestiones*.[75] Unfortunately, since the quotations are not assigned to their authors, the identification of them is not straightforward. Rather, one must compare the text of Procopius with the text of Philo, either in Greek or in the Armenian version, and find correspondences. For the *Quaestiones* the task is simplified by the fact that both Procopius and Philo follow the order of the biblical text. Moreover, Procopius often does not make precise quotations, but rather paraphrases.[76]

Recently Karin Metzler has edited both the *Epitome* of Genesis and the *Epitome* of Exodus, and has described the MSS in detail.[77] There are about two dozen MSS of Procopius. For the *Quaestiones* Petit relies on a MS in Munich, which is missing eight folios; for those folios Petit cites two other MSS. These MSS are:

Monacensis Cod. graec. 358 (Munich, XI cent.).
Athous Koutloumousiou Monasterii 10 (Mt. Athos, XI cent.).
Leidensis BPG 50, a copy of Monacensis Cod. graec. 358 (Leiden, XVI–XVII cent.).

16.3.3 Ps-Eustathius

A neglected witness to Philo's text is a *Commentary on the Hexaemeron*, which is incorrectly ascribed to Eustathius. Among many other earlier authors, the unknown writer, Ps-Eustathius, quotes once from *Aet.*, three times from *Ebr.*, thirteen times from *Anim.*, and, most surprisingly of all, six times from *Prov.* 1, which was unknown even to Eusebius. Here again, as with Procopius, we have the utilization of material without any explicit mention of the source, and so only a comparison with the original works allows us to determine what the sources were. Fortunately, this was done in great detail by Friedrich Zoepfl.[78] For Philo this involves the comparison with the Greek works as well as with the Armenian version. Here indeed a study of the MSS of Ps-Eustathius is crucial, since there is only one edition, by Allatius in 1629, which was then reprinted in PG 18. An examination of the MSS shows the inadequacy of Allatius' edition. Moreover,

---

[73] P. Wendland, *Neu entdeckte Fragmente Philos: Nebst einer Untersuchung über die ursprüngliche Gestalt der Schrift De sacrificiis Abelis et Caini* (Berlin: Georg Reimer, 1891), 29–105.
[74] PCW 4:xxvii–xxviii.
[75] Petit, *Quaestiones*, 18–20.
[76] Petit, *Quaestiones*, 19; Metzler, *Genesiskommentar*, lxxxix–xc.
[77] Metzler, *Genesiskommentar*, xxxix–lxxxviii. K. Metzler has subsequently edited the *Epitome* of Exodus: *Prokop von Gaza: Eclogarum in libros historicos Veteris Testamenti epitome*, Vol. 2: *Der Exoduskommentar*, GCS NF 27 (Berlin: de Gruyter, 2020). See Runia, Review of Metzler, *Exoduskommentar*.
[78] *Der Kommentar des Pseudo-Eustathius zum Hexaëmeron*, ATA 10 (Münster: Aschendorff, 1927). See 41–43 for the citations from Philo. Max Wellmann had earlier noted that Ps-Eustathius used Philo.

Zoepfl knew the Armenian version of Philo only through Aucher's translation into Latin. Naturally, a critical comparison requires the use of the MSS of Ps-Eustathius (of which there are about two dozen) and the Armenian version itself of *Anim.* and *Prov.* 1 (and indeed ultimately the Armenian MSS of those books). Such a comparison reveals that Ps-Eustathius often preserves material more or less verbatim from Philo. It also reveals that Ps-Eustathius at other times simply paraphrases what he found in Philo. But in any case, we have here an important new source of Philo's Greek.[79]

A vast source of Philonic material is provided by various collections of texts that drew upon many other writers as well. These collections are usually classified as catenae and florilegia.

16.3.4 Catenae

A catena MS is a MS of one or more books of the Bible (i.e. books of the LXX or the NT), in which are cited, usually in the margins to the biblical text, various passages meant to explain or illuminate the biblical text.[80] These catenae draw upon various Church writers, but also upon Philo and Josephus, whose works were transmitted within the Christian tradition. In principle, a text from any work of Philo might be found in a catena on any biblical book. But in fact the citations tend to be grouped in a way that was convenient for the compiler. As a result, one particularly convenient procedure was to follow along in works of Philo (and others) that followed the biblical text in a straightforward manner. And thus we find passages from Philo's *QG* and *QE* cited extensively in the catenae on Genesis and Exodus, respectively, which also include a few quotations from the works that have been preserved in Greek.[81] There are, as well, extensive citations from Philo in some catenae on the Psalms, the catena by Nicetas on Luke, and the catena by Nicetas on Hebrews. The catenae MSS fall into various families.

The catenae on Genesis and Exodus have been utilized in Philonic studies starting with Mangey. But they have been cited most systematically by Petit in her edition of the Greek fragments of the *Quaestiones*. Her sources include the following catenae on the Octateuch (of which there are some sixty MSS), where she divides them into two groups, the first being much superior to the second.[82] First group:

> Petropolitanus gr. 124 (St. Petersburg, XIII cent.).
> Sinaiticus gr. 2 (Mt. Sinai, XII cent.).
> Basileensis A.N.III.13 (Basel, X cent.).
> Mosquensis Bibl. Synodalis gr. 385 (Moscow, X cent.).

---

[79] For further information and a listing of the MSS, see J. R. Royse, "Fragments of Philo of Alexandria Preserved in Pseudo-Eustathius," *SPhiloA* 30 (2018): 1–14.
[80] See Royse, *Spurious Texts*, 14–25.
[81] PCW 3:xv, 4:xxii–xxiv, 5:xv.
[82] *Quaestiones*, 17–18.

Second group:

Vaticanus Palatinus gr. 203 (Vatican, XI cent.)
Parisinus gr. 128 (Paris, XII cent.; cited in PCW—this was already used by Mangey).[83]
Hierosolymitanus Sancti Sepulcri 3 (Jerusalem, XII–XIII cent.).

One finds less systematic use of Philo in other catenae. A prolific compiler of catenae was Nicetas of Heracleia, whose dates are uncertain, but who flourished in the latter part of the eleventh century.[84] Of special interest is his catena on Luke, whose chief representative is: Vaticanus gr. 1611 (Vatican, 1116–17 CE). Philo is cited seven times.[85] The citations are from QE 1.19,[86] as well as from *Decal.*,[87] and *Spec.* 2–4.[88] Moreover, there is one spurious fragment.[89]

To Nicetas is also attributed a catena on Hebrews, which survives in a few MSS. The MS that is usually cited is: Parisinus gr. 238 (Paris, XIII cent.).[90] This contains two texts ascribed to Philo: one seems to come from the section of QG that discusses Gen 14:20 (which is missing in the Armenian),[91] and the other is from QG 1.62.[92]

16.3.5 Florilegia

The florilegia are collections of texts that are ordered according to various topics, such as love, greed, friendship, God, and sin.[93] There are such collections of Greek philosophical topics, such as the famous work of Stobaeus, which itself draws upon earlier collections. Within the Christian tradition, the ultimate source seems to be what is known as the *Sacra parallela*, commonly attributed to John of Damascus.[94] This work, which has not been preserved in its original state, was organized into three books, with texts drawn from the Bible (again the LXX and the NT), early Christian writers, and Philo and Josephus. The Philonic texts are drawn from his existing works in Greek,

---

[83] *Opera* 2:675–80.
[84] J. Sickenberger, *Die Lukaskatene des Niketas von Herakleia*, TU NS 7.4 (Leipzig: Hinrichs, 1902), 28–29; Christos Th. Krikones [Χρῖστος Θ. Κρικώνης], Συναγωγὴ Πατέρων εἰς τὸ κατὰ Λουκᾶν Εὐαγγέλιον ὑπὸ Νικήτα Ἡρακλείας (κατὰ τὸν κώδικα Ἰβήρων 371), Βυζάντινα Κείμενα καὶ Μελέται 9 (Thessaloniki: Κέντρον Βυζαντινῶν Ἐρευνῶν, 1973), 17.
[85] Sickenberger, *Lukaskatene*, 83; Krikones, Συναγωγὴ Πατέρων, 65.
[86] Petit, *Quaestiones*, 236–37.
[87] PCW 4:xxiv.
[88] PCW 5:xvi–xvii.
[89] Royse, *Spurious Texts*, 133.
[90] Edited by John A. Cramer, *Catenae Graecorum patrum in Novum Testamentum* 7 (Oxford: Oxford University Press, 1843 [repr. Hildesheim: Olms, 1967]), 279–598. Editors of Philo have used only Cramer's edition.
[91] See Royse, "Original Structure," 49 and n. 64.
[92] See Petit, *Quaestiones*, 29, as well as the texts at 227–28 and 59–60, respectively. These texts are found in the MS at ff. 335v–336r and f. 371r, respectively.
[93] See Royse, *Spurious Texts*, 26–58. The standard survey of the Greek florilegia, including detailed references to the MS evidence, is M. Richard, "Florilèges grecs," *DSpir* 4 (Paris: Beauchesne, 1964), 475–512.
[94] Found at PG 95:1040–1588 and 96:9–442 (from Vaticanus gr. 1236), and PG 96:441–544 (from Berolinensis Phillippicus 1450, i.e. codex Rupefucaldinus).

from *QG*, *QE*, *Prov.*, and *Anim.*, and (as it seems) from lost portions of the known works (such as the *Quaestiones*), since there are dozens of texts ascribed to Philo (and often specifically to the *Quaestiones*) that cannot be located within what remains of Philo.[95] A clear example of the use of an unknown work was provided by Ludwig Früchtel, who made the fascinating discovery that a text found in the Oxyrhynchus Papyrus of a work that is otherwise unknown overlaps with a fragment found in the *Sacra parallela*.[96] Of the various recensions of the *Sacra parallela* I count about fifty MSS. PCW systematically cite several of these, and often follow their evidence against the direct evidence.[97] Their evidence is even more important for the fragments, where they often supply the only surviving Greek.[98] The MSS cited by PCW and by Petit are:

Coislinianus 276 (Paris, X cent.; D^C in PCW).

Hierosolymitanus Sancti Sepulcri 15 (Jerusalem, XI cent; D^H in PCW).[99]

Vaticanus gr. 1553 (Vatican, X cent.; D^K in PCW).

Laurentianus Pluteus 8.22 (Florence, XIV cent.; D^L in PCW).[100]

Marcianus Gr. Z. 138 (= 596) (Venice, X cent.; D^M in PCW).

Marcianus Gr. III 4 (= 1076) (Venice, XVI cent.; D^N in PCW).[101]

Parisinus gr. 923 (Paris, IX cent.; D^P in PCW). Apart from its text this MS is famous for its illuminations.

Berolinensis Phillippicus 1450 (Berlin, XII cent.; D^R in PCW), known as Codex Rupefucaldinus.

Vaticanus gr. 1236 (Vatican, XV cent.; D^V in PCW).

Thessalonicensis Blateon 9 (Mt. Athos, X cent.; not in PCW).

Atheniensis Metochion Sancti Sepulcri 274 (Athens, XIV cent.; not in PCW).

---

[95] For the texts ascribed to the *Quaestiones* but that are not found in the Armenian or Latin version, see Petit, *Quaestiones*, 214–28 (#17, though, is not ascribed to *QG*), 279–306. But see Petit's warnings that the ascription to *QG* or *QE*, or even to Philo, may be mistaken. Note further that her *QG* unidentified #7 in fact comes from *QG* 3.3, and her *QE* unidentified #27 in fact comes from *QE* 2.110; see J. R. Royse, "Further Greek Fragments of Philo's *Quaestiones*," in F. E. Greenspahn, E. Hilgert, and B. L. Mack, eds, *Nourished with Peace: Studies in Hellenistic Judaism in Memory of Samuel Sandmel* (Chico: Scholars Press, 1984), 143–53, here 150 and 151–52.

[96] "Zum Oxyrhynchos-Papyrus des Philon (Ox.-Pap. XI 1356)," *PhWoch* 58 (1938): 1437–39. *P.Oxy.* 1356, f. 10v, containing an unknown text, overlaps a small Philo fragment found in the *Sacra parallela* (as edited by H. Lewy, "Neue Philontexte in der Überarbeitung des Ambrosius. Mit einem Anhang: Neu gefundene griechische Philonfragmente," SPAW, Philosophisch-historische Klasse, 4 [1932], 82–83, no. 27). See on this agreement Royse, "The Text of Philo's *De virtutibus*," 87–91, with a correction at J. R. Royse, "The Text of Philo's *De Abrahamo*," *SPhiloA* 20 (2008): 151–65, here 151 n. 2.

[97] PCW 1:lxiii–lxvii, where eight MSS are cited.

[98] Petit, *Quaestiones*, 23–24.

[99] Added to their list at PCW 2:xii.

[100] This MS contains the remains of three different florilegia; see the overview in J. R. Royse, "The Text of Stobaeus: The Manuscripts and Wachsmuth's Edition," in *Aëtiana IV: Papers of the Melbourne Colloquium on Ancient Doxography*, ed. J. Mansfeld and D. T. Runia, PhA 148 (Leiden: Brill, 2018), 156–73, here 159–62.

[101] Cohn cites this as "Venetus append. graec. class. III,4. 88,3, olim Nanianus 228." It is clear that Cohn is referring to what is now known as "Gr. III 4," since that MS in fact was "Nanianus CCXXVIII," as the catalog informs us. But the "88,3" is puzzling, and I inquired about this at the Biblioteca Marciana in 2016. It turns out that "88,3" is Cohn's rendering of "LXXXVIII, 3," which is an old signature of the Marciana, designating the location of MSS by bookcase and shelf. On the inside front cover of the MS, at the top, one still reads: "LXXXVIII. | 3." Nevertheless, it seems that that old number would not have been used in Cohn's time. But Wendland uses the latter shelfmark at

There are yet further florilegia that build upon the *Sacra parallela* by adding citations from secular writers. Among the more important of these for Philo studies are the *Loci communes* attributed to Maximus,[102] the *Melissa* attributed to Antonius,[103] and the *Sententiae* attributed to John Georgides.[104] An interesting florilegium, which had a much less extensive history, is the Corpus Parisinum, found in two MSS.[105] Here the various texts are grouped by author.

Parisinus gr. 1168 (Paris, XIV cent.; Flor. Par. in PCW).

Digbeianus 6 (Oxford, XIV cent.; not cited in PCW).

A further late florilegium is found in a few MSS, among which are:[106]

Baroccianus 143 (Oxford, XII cent.). Texts from this MS were already edited by Mangey.[107]

Monacensis Cod. graec. 429 (Munich, 1346 CE).

Scholars of Philo beginning with Mangey have drawn upon various MSS of these florilegia. And the various classes are systematically cited in PCW and by Petit.[108] Even for those works of Philo that have good manuscript attestation, these citations are of value, since their text derives from MSS that belong to a different textual tradition. And for the various works that have been lost in Greek (*QG*, *QE*, *Prov.*, and *Anim.*) the citations in the catenae and the florilegia are often the only Greek evidence that we have. One should keep in mind, however, that errors often occur in the ascriptions found in these sources, especially in the later florilegia. Thus, an ascription to Philo is by no means a guarantee that the text involved in fact comes from Philo. Indeed, many texts have been mistakenly assigned to Philo on the basis of such ascriptions.[109]

---

his *Neu entdeckte Fragmente Philos*, 19. So presumably Cohn was simply repeating what Wendland had reported to him.

[102] Found at PG 91:721–1018. S. Ihm, *Ps.-Maximus Confessor: Erste kritische Edition einer Redaktion des sacroprofanen Florilegiums Loci communes nebst einer vollständigen Kollation einer zweiten Redaktion und weiterem Material*, Palingenesia 73 (Stuttgart: Steiner, 2001), xxx–lxiv, describes many of the MSS, and analyzes their interrelationships (lxxv–xcix). Some one hundred MSS are known.

[103] Found in PG 136:719–1018. It is cited regularly in PCW; see 1:lxviii, 2:xiv, 6:xlvi–vii. There are some forty-five MSS.

[104] Found at PG 117:1057–1164. See P. Odorico, *Il prato e l'ape*, Wiener Byzantinistische Studien 17 (Vienna: Austrian Academy of Sciences, 1986). About a dozen MSS are known.

[105] D. M. Searby, *The Corpus Parisinum: A Critical Edition of the Greek Text with Commentary and English Translation*, 2 vols (Lewiston, NY: The Edwin Mellen Press, 2007). Searby cites both the Paris and Oxford MSS; see 1:186–90 and 2:512–19 for the texts from Philo.

[106] PCW 1:xcviii.

[107] *Opera* 2:674.

[108] *Quaestiones*, 25–27.

[109] See Royse, *Spurious Texts*, generally, on this problem, as well as J. R. Royse, "Three More Spurious Fragments of Philo," *SPhiloA* 17 (2005): 95–98. For a list of unidentified texts that are ascribed to Philo, see J. R. Royse, "Reverse Indexes to Philonic Texts in the Printed Florilegia and Collections of Fragments," *SPhiloA* 5 (1993): 156–79, here 174–79 (§4).

16.4 The Latin Tradition

The early Latin translation of Philo's works probably dates from the late fourth century.[110] This version includes the pseudo-Philonic *Antiquitates*, and an early printed edition even included Jerome's *De nominibus Hebraicis* and a later Latin translation of the epitome *De mundo*.[111] Moreover, the early Latin version must have included other Philonic books, for, as Petit observes, the phrase "hic in prioribus translatis libris" (here in the preceding translated books) occurs in a gloss at *QG* 4.195.9*, l. 21, and apparently Ambrose and Augustine used a Latin version of the *Quaestiones* that was more extensive than what is now preserved, even though its exact contents cannot be determined.[112] In particular, though, it seems that the version included Philo's lost *De numeris* (Περὶ ἀριθμῶν), since, as Petit observes, some glosses to the version appear to preserve extracts from that book.[113]

The genuine texts found in the version include what was the original *QG* 6,[114] namely (following the current system based on the Armenian) *QG* 4.154–245 with twelve additional sections between *QG* 4.195 and 196.[115] Those twelve sections are not preserved in Armenian, probably due to the loss of a folio or two either in the Greek exemplar used by the Armenian translators or in an early copy of the Armenian version itself. The material is clearly Philonic, and in fact three Greek fragments can be located within those twelve additional sections.[116] This work has been critically edited by Petit with extensive notes and commentary.

The other genuine portion of Philo preserved in the Latin version is *Contempl.* 1–41, which breaks off in the middle of a sentence; this text was edited by Cohn.[117] This mutilated version must have originally extended to the end of that book, i.e. the end as now found in the Greek and Armenian traditions. Of course, the entirety of *De vita contemplativa* is only a portion of some more extensive work.

Unfortunately, though, the Latin version is not well done.[118] Moreover, it does not have the literal nature of the Armenian version, and thus the reconstruction of Philo's original Greek terms is much less certain.

The *editio princeps* of the Latin version was published by Augustus Iustinianus in 1520.[119] In this edition the final lines of *QG* 4.245 are missing, as is the beginning of *De*

---

[110] PCW 1:li–lii; Petit, *L'ancienne version latine* 1:13 (see 1:8–13 generally on dating). See further "Philo in the Medieval West" elsewhere in this volume.

[111] PCW 1:l–li.

[112] PCW 1:lii; Petit, *L'ancienne version latine*, 1:7.

[113] See Petit, *L'ancienne version latine*, 2:89 (on 4.195.9* l. 20). Earlier comments to a similar effect were made by Wendland, *Neu entdeckte Fragmente Philos*, 85 n. 2; and F. C. Conybeare, *Philo about the Contemplative Life* (Oxford: Clarendon Press, 1895), 145.

[114] On the identification of this material as the original *QG* 6, see Royse, "Original Structure," 51–52.

[115] See Petit, *L'ancienne version latine*, 1:4; these additional sections are cited as *QG* 4.195.1*, etc. Petit has restored a second question after the usual no. 8*, called no. 8**; see *L'ancienne version latine*, 1:4 n. 3, and 1:70.

[116] Petit, *Quaestiones*, 199–201.

[117] PCW 6:xviii–xxix.

[118] Petit calls it "très mauvaise" (*L'ancienne version latine* 1:13).

[119] *Philonis Iudaei centum et duae quaestiones et totidem responsiones morales super Genesim* (Paris: 1520).

vita contemplativa, and the two works are simply run together, so that we read: "… nullas accipiendo personas. Illud pro colore …."[120] We thus have "nullas accipiendo personas" from near the end of *QG* 4.245 (Petit 245 l. 14), followed by "Illud pro colore" of *Contempl.* 2 (PCW 6:xix l. 14). Except for the Freiburg fragments, this is the arrangement that we find in all extant MSS, apart from some minor variation.[121] It is thus evident that in their ancestor there was the loss of one folio, on which occurred the end of *QG* 4.245 and then the beginning of *De vita contemplativa*.[122]

However, in 1527 Johann Sichard (Sichardus) published an edition that was based on a MS of Lorsch, which is now lost, except for a few fragments found at Freiburg.[123] In this edition we have the ending of *QG* 4.245, followed by the beginning of *De vita contemplativa*.[124] This edition is then the source for the texts as printed by Petit and Cohn, respectively.

The version is found in sixteen MSS, many of which are preserved in German libraries.[125]

Friburgensis, Fragm. 63 (Freiburg im Breisgau, early VII cent.; Sichard's Lorsch MS, L in Cohn and Petit).

We have here only portions of two folios of what is by far the oldest extant MS of the Latin version. Earlier it was at Lorsch, and Sichard described it as a twin of a MS at Fulda, which is now at Kassel. The MSS at the Monastery of St. Nazarius in Lorsch have experienced considerable vicissitudes, and have now been completely dispersed.[126] This MS was considered lost, and was known only though the citations by Sichard.[127] But in 1983 these existing fragments were discovered at Freiburg, and were edited by Petit.[128] They contain portions of *QG* 4.235–36, 237–38, 244–45, and 245. This last piece in fact contains the remains of a few lines at the end of *QG* 4.245 that are missing in all the other MSS, and were previously known only through the transcription by Sichard, which was not quite accurate. Petit judges two of the new readings to be authentic.

---

[120] The text is foliated; this is on f. 10.
[121] F has "personam," and for "pro colore" the MSS have "colere."
[122] PCW 6:xiv; Petit, *L'ancienne version latine* 1:31.
[123] *Philonis Iudaei Alexandrini, Quaestionum et solutionum in Genesin, De Essaeis, De nominibus Hebraicis, De mundo* (Basel: 1527).
[124] *Philonis Iudaei Alexandrini, Quaestionum et solutionum in Genesin, De Essaeis, De nominibus Hebraicis, De mundo* (Basel: 1527), pp. 82–83, and then p. 84.
[125] See Cohn, PCW 6:xv–xvii; Petit, *L'ancienne version latine* 1:30–47, for a description of fifteen of the MSS (including the Lorsch MS). To their list may be added Bryn Mawr Gordan MS 69, once owned by Goodhart, which however I have not seen. Further, Cohn (PCW 6:xvii) cites Urbinas lat. 61, but Petit (*L'ancienne version latine* 1:30 n. 1), says that "61" is the old number, and that the current shelfmark is Urbinas lat. 73, as she has at 1:37. Let me report that I received this MS at the Vatican in 2015 as Urbinas lat. 61. G-G cites the MS twice, as both 61 (G-G #318, taken from Cohn) and 73 (G-G #323, taken from Conybeare).
[126] See the summary by Petit, *L'ancienne version latine* 1:30 n. 3.
[127] Cohn, PCW 1:li, 6:xiii, xv; G-G #298; Petit, *L'ancienne version latine*, 1:30–31.
[128] "Le fragment 63 de la Bibliothèque de l'Université de Fribourg-en-Brisgau," *CM* 9 (1983): 164–72. The facts concerning the discovery of these fragments are presented by V. Sack, "Fundbericht zu Fragment 63 der Universitätsbibliothek Freiburg i. Br," *CM* 9 (1983): 173–74.

Petit cites four MSS in the apparatus to her edition (published before the discovery of the Freiburg fragments):

Casselanus theol. 4 num. 3 (Kassel, XI cent.; F in Cohn and Petit) This was earlier at Fulda, and was used by Sichard.

Gordanus 16 (location?, XI cent.; A in Cohn and Petit). Formerly Admontensis 359, then owned by Goodhart.

Budapestiensis Musei Nationalis Hungarici lat. medii aevi 23 (Budapest, XII cent.; B in Cohn and Petit).

Berolinensis lat. quart. 703 (Berlin, latter XV cent.; G in Petit).

16.4.1 Eusebian Extracts from *De vita contemplativa* in Latin

Of a different provenance is the Latin translation of the seven Eusebian extracts from *Contempl.* (as discussed above, pp. 270–71).[129] Like the Greek extracts these have been transmitted within the tradition of Ps-Dionysius Areopagita, attaching themselves to MSS of his works in Latin.[130] These extracts are found in about a dozen MSS. But they appear to have been unknown to, or at least ignored by, Cohn in PCW 6. Their textual value would be very minimal.

16.5 Conclusion

Besides the varied nature of the witnesses to the text of Philo, there is also the varying attestation of his works. Some works have only very narrowly survived. For example, *De somniis* 2 is found only in A and two citations in florilegia.[131] On the other hand, *De vita Mosis* appears in dozens of MSS.[132] Of other works we have only a few fragments. For example, Harris prints a few texts that are ascribed to the fourth book of the *Legum allegoriae*.[133] And the unknown work or works that are very fragmentarily found in the Oxyrhynchus Papyrus are not attested elsewhere. Extensive portions of Philo's corpus

---

[129] See further A. Treiger, Chapter 19 in this volume.
[130] These extracts have been printed and studied by R. Forrai, "The Interpreter of the Popes: The Translation Project of Anastasius Bibliothecarius" (PhD diss., Central European University, Budapest, 2008); see the discussion, including (incomplete) lists of both Latin (141, table 3) and Greek (142, table 4) MSS that contain the extracts, at 137–47, and the Latin fragments themselves at 202–4.
[131] PCW 3:xx.
[132] G. E. Sterling counts thirty-nine; see "Philo of Alexandria's Life of Moses: An Introduction to the Exposition of the Law," *SPhiloA* 30 (2018): 31–45, here 35.
[133] Harris, *Fragments*, 6–8. However, one of these is known to be spurious; see Royse, *Spurious Texts*, 192.

survive only in the Armenian version, while a few sections survive only in the Latin version. Much of the extant Greek text of *De providentia* 2 is known only because Eusebius chose to make extensive quotations from it (which we can then compare with the Armenian version), while we owe what we have of the *Hypothetica* to Eusebius alone. And there are some works that, as far as we can tell, have not survived at all.[134]

Naturally, these variations reflect the differing interests of later authors and translators and scribes, but are no doubt often due simply to chance. As with ancient literature in general, we are continually confronted with frustrating losses in our sources. But much survives, and so we must be grateful to all those who produced the MSS on which our knowledge of the works of Philo depends.

---

[134] All these issues are discussed in the works cited above in n. 1. See also the convenient overview in D. T. Runia, "Confronting the Augean Stables: Royse's *Fragmenta Spuria Philonica*," SPhiloA 4 (1992): 78–86, here 78–79. It is possible that we have some remnants of the lost works among the many brief Greek fragments that are assigned simply to "Philo" in later florilegia.

17
Medieval Jewish Philosophy and Mysticism

Elke Morlok and Ze'ev Strauss

In one of the premier achievements of the *Wissenschaft des Judentums*, Solomon Judah Loeb Rapoport's encyclopedia of rabbinic literature *'Erekh Milin*, we find the following statement in his entry on Alexandria:

> The wondrous fact is that our master ha-RaMBaM, may his memory be blessed—who had never read Philo's books, for he did not know Greek—matched him exactly in all the matters of the Torah. Like Philo, he thought that human perfection is predicated upon the attainment of more and more negations of the attributes of the creator's essence. In this manner, both of them have an identical philosophical interpretation of the biblical *'eheyeh 'ašer 'eheyeh* [Exod 3:14] …. There, you will find that Philo's statements are identical in every respect to those of Maimonides's *Guide* (1:63). The author of *The Light of the Eyes* has already drawn attention to this great similarity. And this also applies to his [Philo's] rendering of numerous stories from the Torah and names into allegories and moral instructions.[1]

This cited passage showcases the striking parallels between Philo and celebrated medieval Jewish philosophers, which many of the pioneers of the academic study of Judaism began to notice and draw attention to. Rapoport's condensed comparison between Philo and the most renowned Jewish philosopher of the Middle Ages, Maimonides, covers a wide array of pivotal theological themes, such as negative theology, human perfection, the metaphysical meaning of God's names, and moral allegories of biblical narratives.[2] During the nineteenth century, it became increasingly common to view medieval Jewish thought through a Philonic lens. It is hardly surprising, given this background, that Salomon Munk, for example, designated Yiṣḥaq 'Arama—whose biblical commentaries gravitated towards philosophical-allegorical readings of the Pentateuch—as "a second Philo."[3] Within the context of Philo's impact on the Jewish *Gedankenwelt*, Kabbalah secures an even more prominent role.

---

[1] S. L. Rapoport, "Alexandria," in *Sefer 'erekh milin*, ed. S. L. Rapoport (Prague: Moshe ha-Levi Landau, 1852), 100 (our translation). For an elaboration on this passage, see Z. Strauss, "Solomon Judah Rapoport's Maskilic Revival of Philo of Alexandria: Rabbi Yedidya ha-Alexandri, a Pioneer of Jewish Philosophy," *SPhiloA* 31 (2019): 201–26.
[2] See e.g. S. Weisse, *Philo von Alexandrien und Moses Maimonides: Ein vergleichender Versuch* (Dessau: Herzogl. Hof-Buchdruckerei, 1884), 23–26.
[3] S. Munk, *Philosophie und philosophische Schriftsteller der Juden: Eine historische Skizze*, trans. B. Beer (Leipzig: Heinrich Hunger, 1852), 85.

A vast number of Jewish and Christian thinkers from the Renaissance up to the Enlightenment regarded Philo's allegorical treatises as one of the chief sources of kabbalistic thought patterns.

In this chapter, we intend to outline the reception of the Philonic worldview within medieval Jewish Neoplatonism and mysticism. The present examination will consist of three essential steps. The first part will focus on Harry A. Wolfson's overly optimistic view of Philo's influence on medieval Jewish thought. Alternative and more cautious ways of speaking of Philo's impact on medieval Jewish thought will be offered in the second part, this time primarily by discussing the intermediary role of midrash literature as a vehicle for the Hebrew-language dissemination of the Philonic body of thought. The third part will turn to notions of language, creation, and their diverse intersections found in sources of medieval Jewish mysticism, which bear strong conceptual resemblance to pronouncedly Philonic ideas. To this end, the study will limit itself to three representative examples from medieval Jewish mystical thought, in chronological order. The investigation will begin with Solomon ibn Gabirol's (1020/21–1058?) Neoplatonic doctrine of creation in both his *Fons vitae* and his poem *The Kingly Crown*, and it will highlight the parallels with Philo's Judeo-Platonic cosmology. The analysis will then proceed to kabbalistic thinkers and texts, which were shaped by the Gabirolian and Neoplatonic worldviews and are often aligned with Philo's philosophy: both Joseph ben Abraham Gikatilla (1248–c.1305) and the *Zohar* will be brought to the fore in order to reveal their use of distinct Philonic concepts. Our goal is by no means to present an exhaustive overview of the reception history of Philo in medieval Jewish thought; instead, our account will confine itself to a brief analysis of a few representative mystical Neoplatonist writings which are often associated in the literature with the Philonic worldview and to showing in what manner one may credibly speak in this respect of Philo's "medieval reception."

17.1 Wolfson's *Pan-Philonismus*: Philo as the Founder of Medieval Philosophy

From the outset of his monumental work on Philo's thought, *Philo: Foundations of Religious Philosophy in Judaism, Christianity, and Islam*, Wolfson expresses his surprisingly high opinion of the Alexandrian's impact on the history of philosophy:[4] "The purpose of this book has been to delineate and depict the philosophy of Philo as it shaped itself in his own mind and in its own setting and to indicate briefly how in its main features it was the most dominant force in the history of philosophy down to the seventeenth century."[5] Wolfson expounds this viewpoint at the end of the book's

---

[4] Jens Halfwassen coined the term *Pan-Philonismus*, with its clear negative undertone, to denote this.
[5] H. A. Wolfson, *Philo: Foundations of Religious Philosophy in Judaism, Christianity and Islam*, 2 vols (3rd rev. edn; Cambridge, MA: Harvard University Press, 1962), 1:vii.

second chapter, "Handmaid of Scripture." After presenting Philo as the great systematic innovator, he writes:

> If the answer given by us is correct, then Philo will emerge from our study as a philosopher in the grand manner, not a mere dabbler in philosophy. He did have the power of intellect to be able to reject the theories of other philosophers and to strike out a new and hitherto unknown path for himself.... Like any great and original philosopher in the history of philosophy, Philo's own philosophy was a reaction against that of his predecessors and contemporaries and, in that sense, like any philosopher in history if not properly studied, he may be called an eclectic.[6]

From the closing paragraph of chapter 5, "Creation and Structure of the World," emerges the same *Philonbild* of a person whose historical significance can hardly be overestimated. As a philosopher, Philo introduced "five new elements to his general statement ... that the creation of the world is a cardinal principle of scriptural religion": (1) the indestructibility of the world; (2) arguments against both the Aristotelian precept regarding the world's uncreatedness and (3) the Stoic teaching of the recurring emergence and destruction of the worlds; (4) the theory of *creatio ex hylis*;[7] and (5) whether God is capable of having willed and created a world that is different from the present one.[8] Wolfson's account of the post-Philonic Christian, Muslim, and Jewish doctrines of creation views them as revolving around the essential conceptual groundwork already laid down by Philo, either affirming it or negating it.[9] The scarcity of the medieval Jewish sources Wolfson adduces—in this context, he only mentions Maimonides's *Guide of the Perplexed* and Judah Halevi's *The Kuzari*—stands out in light of his far-reaching thesis.

Wolfson's presupposition regarding Philo's direct influence on such Jewish thinkers of the Middle Ages takes its cue from Hartwig Hirschfeld's hypothesis regarding a Genizah fragment presented as the introductory words of a work titled *Muqaddimah* written by "the Alexandrian,"[10] which is actually a loose and condensed translation of *Decal.* 2–17.[11] As David Winston remarks, the fragmentary text seems to be taken from the *Book of Light* by the Karaite author Jacob Qirquisani.[12] Both Philo and the Judeo-Arabic fragment not only pose the same question as to why Moses declared the laws in the desert and not in a city, but also provide precisely the same answer, claiming that the cities are idolatrous and sinful places.[13] The striking parallels can be discerned by placing both texts side by side:

---

[6] Wolfson, *Philo*, 1:114.
[7] For a further in-depth analysis, see A. Altmann, "A Note on the Rabbinic Doctrine of Creation," *JJS* 7 (1956): 195–96.
[8] Wolfson, *Philo*, 1:322–23.
[9] Wolfson, *Philo*, 1:323.
[10] As Winston already notes with recourse to Leopold Cohn, "Philo's treatise *On the Decalogue* could be considered a prologue to his Special Laws" (D. Winston, "Philo's *Nachleben* in Judaism," *SPhiloA* 6 (1994): 107).
[11] H. Hirschfeld, "The Arabic Portion of the Cairo Genizah at Cambridge (Seventh Article)," *JQR* 16 (1904): 65 (English translation by Hirschfeld).
[12] Winston, "*Nachleben*," 106.
[13] PLCL 7:7 (*Decal.* 2).

To the question why he promulgated his laws in the depths of the desert instead of in cities we may answer in the first place that most cities are full of countless evils, both acts of impiety towards God and wrongdoing between man and man.[14]	Chapter I. Prolegomena of the Alexandrian. He says: Why did the Creator give the Ten Commandments to the children of Israel, as well as the rest of the Torah in the desert, and why did this not take place in a town? The answer is that this was done on account of the idolatrous practices which took place in the cities. God considered his Torah too exalted to be revealed in a place where such things were carried on, and gave it in the desert which was free from them, and on a sanctified mountain.[15]

Following Hirschfeld, Wolfson infers that it is "well established that there existed a condensed Arabic version of Philo's *De Decalogo* before the time of Hallevi."[16] Based on this premise, Wolfson goes on to entertain the possibility of a direct literary link between Philo's account of the Sinaitic revelation as outlined in *Decal.* and Halevi's *The Kuzari* and Maimonides's *Guide of the Perplexed*.[17]

Wolfson's daring thesis is stated in even more unequivocal terms in the preface of his collection of essays titled *Religious Philosophy*, in which he characterizes Philo as nothing less than the ultimate founder of medieval philosophy.[18] The key significance of Philo's impact on medieval Jewish philosophy in Wolfson's apologetic account is pinpointed by David T. Runia:

> It should be clear by now how absolutely vital Wolfson's interpretation of Philo's role is for the success of the whole enterprise. If Philo is left out of account, the influence of Jewish philosophy—no matter how great it is thought to be—cannot be said to have begun before the activity of Saadia and Isaac Israeli in the early tenth century, for before then both Rabbinic and Talmudic thought had had no impact on the philosophical tradition whatsoever.[19]

---

[14] PLCL 7:7 (*Decal.* 2).

[15] Genizah fragment, "Portion," 65–66; trans. H. Hirschfeld.

[16] H. A. Wolfson, "Hallevi and Maimonides on Prophecy (Continued)," *JQR* 33 (1942): 68. See E. Parker and A. Treiger, "Philo's Odyssey into the Medieval Jewish World: Neglected Evidence from Arab Christian Literature," *Dionysius* 30 (2012): 120–21, 127–30.

[17] Wolfson, "Prophecy," 66–70. It is noteworthy that this is not the only example of Philonic passages translated into Arabic in the Middle Ages. As Parker and Treiger have revealed in their seminal article, there were also several sections from *Contempl.* (§§21–22, 25, 28–29, 34–35, 68, 78) within medieval Christian tradition translated into Arabic ("Odyssey," 142–45). See also Chapter 19 in this volume.

[18] H. A. Wolfson, *Religious Philosophy: A Group of Essays* (Cambridge, MA: Harvard University Press, 1961), first page of preface (no pagination). Cf. D. T. Runia, "History of Philosophy in the Grand Manner: The Achievement of H. A. Wolfson," in *Exegesis and Philosophy: Studies on Philo of Alexandria*, ed. D. T. Runia (Aldershot: Variorum, 1990), 114–15.

[19] Runia, "History of Philosophy," 121. Cf. W. Z. Harvey, "Hebraism and Western Philosophy in Harry Austryn Wolfson's Theory of History" [Hebrew], *Daat* 4 (1980): 103–9.

Wolfson's "Judaeocentric hypothesis," as Runia terms it,[20] seems to be actually rooted in an impetus that is not uncommon in the *Wissenschaft des Judentums*. A similar outlook is, for example, already expressed in *Die Sinne* by David Kaufmann, a great authority of his time in the field of medieval Jewish philosophy. Within the context of Philo's allegorical reading of the five kings (Gen 14:9) as the five senses in *Abr.* 236, he voices a similar hypothesis: "At this juncture, I can express this merely as a suggestion that I presuppose a *historical link, through Christian mediation*, between the exegesis of Philo in question and its revival among Jews of the Middle Ages."[21] In the final analysis, Runia maintains that Wolfson's ambitious thesis goes far too far in affirming that "Philonic thought 'dominates' medieval philosophy."[22] He explains this by saying that Wolfson not only underestimates "the contribution of patristic philosophy," but that he also overlooks "significant differences between Philo and later thinkers."[23] He correctly concludes his critique with the following assertion: "Wolfson's 'Philonic tradition' has an attractive simplicity, but the reality it attempts to portray is more complex."[24]

17.2 Philo's Doctrine of Creation, Midrashic Literature, and Medieval Jewish Thought

Our examination tends, in light of Wolfson's hyperbolic *Pan-Philonismus*,[25] towards a more moderate assessment of the Alexandrian's role in intellectual history.[26] The question of how—if at all—one can speak of a reception of Philonic ideas within medieval Jewish thought still remains unresolved. That midrashic thought—most notably in the context of interpretations of the biblical account of creation—was in some places shaped by Philo's body of thought, at times through the mediation of the early church fathers,[27] appears to be a viable possibility. Medieval Jewish thinkers with a strong Neoplatonic predilection were particularly drawn to the speculative outlook on godly creation provided by many of the Palestinian haggadic midrashim. Wolfson attempts to emphasize that Philo and midrashic literature both resort to common ancient Palestinian traditions[28] and that the Alexandrian did not exert any influence on rabbinic writings. "Nowhere in the Talmudic literature, however," he maintains, "is there any evidence that the knowledge of Philo [is] reflected in it."[29] He goes on to state that "in the entire Greek vocabulary that is embodied in the Midrash, Mishnah, and Talmud there is not a

---

[20] Runia, "History of Philosophy," 121.
[21] D. Kaufmann, *Die Sinne: Beiträge zur Geschichte der Physiologie und Psychologie im Mittelalter aus hebräischen und arabischen Quellen* (Leipzig: F. A. Brockhaus, 1884), 18 n. 44a.
[22] Runia, "History of Philosophy," 126.
[23] Runia, "History of Philosophy," 126. For a more detailed discussion on Wolfson's interpretation of Philo and the immediate debates it sparked, see René Bloch's newly published study, "Bringing Philo Home: Responses to Harry A. Wolfson's *Philo* (1947) in the Aftermath of World War II," *HTR* 116 (2023): 466–89.
[24] Runia, "History of Philosophy," 127.
[25] Wolfson, *Philo*, 1:vii.
[26] See Runia's suggestion to rectify the Wolfsonian stance in "History of Philosophy," 127: "The philosophical movement which the pioneering work of Philo initiated lasted until …."
[27] For a monographic and learned treatment of the subject, see D. T. Runia, *Philo in Early Christian Literature: A Survey*, CRINT 3 (Assen: Van Gorcum, 1993).
[28] Wolfson, *Philo*, 1:90–93.
[29] Wolfson, *Philo*, 1:92.

single technical philosophic term."³⁰ Wolfson merely adds a footnote in which he refers to secondary literature "on rabbinic passages which are supposed to be dependent upon Philo."³¹ The following footnotes, 32–34, in which he rules out any possibility of direct dependence of rabbinic literature on Philonic or Greek philosophical notions, make his position clear.³² While Wolfson does seem correct in underlining the fact that Philo must have had knowledge of ancient Palestinian traditions,³³ he again overemphasizes this point, being too willing to overlook textual evidence that indicates the contrary.

A representative example of Wolfson's unwillingness to concede any distinct Philonic impact on the midrashic corpus can be found in his depiction of Philo's parable of the creation of the world as the establishment of a μεγαλόπολις (*Opif.* 17–20, 24). While acknowledging that this metaphorical explanation "sounds like the parables of the rabbis,"³⁴ he points out *en passant* in a footnote that a similar parable is found in the beginning of *Genesis Rabbah*. In his portrayal of the Philonic parable, he actually attempts to accentuate the conceptual and terminological differences between Philo's parable and the midrash, insofar as he presupposes Philo's intentional avoidance of terms used in *Gen. Rab.* 1:1 such as διφθέρα or πίναξ:³⁵ "Philo is careful not to mention that the architect makes a diagram of his plan, for that would destroy the purpose of his parable."³⁶ In his seminal article on Philo's parable, "*Polis* and *Megalopolis*: Philo and the Founding of Alexandria," Runia convincingly uncovers the "indications in Philo's text that in composing his image he is actually thinking of the foundation of his own city, Alexandria, by Alexander the Great in the year 331 B.C."³⁷ In so doing, Runia substantially reinforces the idea that this Platonic image originated from Alexandria and at the same time makes the likelihood of it having roots in ancient Palestinian traditions seem rather implausible.

When one examines the depiction in *Gen. Rab.* 1:1, which is attributed to Rabbi Hoshaya, a prominent first generation Caesarean amora, one cannot simply gloss over its striking resemblance to Philo's parable in the beginning of *De opificio mundi*. In the first volume of his monumental *Die Agada der palästinensischen Amoräer*, Wilhelm Bacher points out that Hoshaya's image of God creating the world through the mimetic, demiurgic act of gazing at the Torah as an intelligible *Weltentwurf* (כך היה הקב"ה מביט בתורה ובורא העולם ["In the same way, the Holy One, Blessed-be-He, looked into the Torah and created the world"])³⁸ "strikingly overlaps with Philo's

---

³⁰ Wolfson, *Philo*, 1:91–92.
³¹ Wolfson, *Philo*, 1:91–92 n. 31.
³² Wolfson, *Philo*, 1:92, nn. 32–34.
³³ B. J. Bamberger provides objective arguments for this hypothesis: "Philo and the Aggadah," *HUCA* 48 (1977): 153–85.
³⁴ Wolfson, *Philo*, 1:242.
³⁵ See further M. R. Niehoff, "*Creatio ex Nihilo* Theology in *Genesis Rabbah* in Light of Christian Exegesis," *HTR* 99 (2006): 60–61.
³⁶ Wolfson, *Philo*, 1:243. Cf. Winston, who with reference to Ephraim E. Urbach argues along similar lines: Winston, "*Nachleben*," 105.
³⁷ Published in D. T. Runia, "*Polis* and *Megalopolis*: Philo and the Founding of Alexandria," *Mnemosyne* 42 (1989): 398. For his arguments, see 400–406.
³⁸ H. Albeck and J. Theodor, eds, *Midrash Bereshit Rabba: Critical Edition with Notes and Commentary* (Jerusalem: Wahrmann Books, 1965), 2. The English translation is taken from Niehoff with slight modifications, "*Creatio*," 60.

thought."[39] Bacher, in his "The Church Father, Origen, and Rabbi Hoshaya," appears to go so far as to regard the Hebrew as a direct rendition of the Greek ἀποβλέπων εἰς τὸ παράδειγμα (*Opif.* 18), an intelligible act of creation that Philo also attributes—like the midrash—to God (*Opif.* 19).[40] Bacher is the first researcher to put forward the argument that Rabbi Hoshaya's Philonic image was transmitted to him in Caesarea by none other than Origen, "the most important champion of that philosopher's allegorical tendency."[41] Turning our attention to current Philo studies, one notices that this thesis is accepted by well-known experts. Runia, for example, makes the following claim with full conviction in his article "Caesarea Maritima and the Survival of Hellenistic-Jewish Literature":

> [The second indication that Philo and Aristobulus were part of Origen's library is that] there is the well-known passage at the beginning of *Genesis Rabbah*, in which Rabbi Hoshaya uses the image of a king and an architect in order to illustrate how God consulted the Torah in the creation of the universe. I am convinced that the image is taken over from Philo's commentary on the creation account in *De opificio mundi*, and is meant to correct his Logos doctrine. The rabbi resided in Caesarea, and was on friendly terms with Origen. Surely it was through this relationship that he was acquainted with Philo's works. It is the only place in rabbinic literature, as far as I know, where it is possible to detect a reaction to Philo's views, albeit under the cover of anonymity.[42]

Reading through the rest of *Genesis Rabbah*, one notices that the metaphor of the king or ruler and his palace,[43] applied respectively to God and the world's premeditated rational structure, runs like a common thread throughout this entire ancient midrashic compilation. In *Gen. Rab.* 9:3/12:12, for instance, we encounter a similar image, in which God—compared to a king needing two separate glances to look at the different stories of a palace—takes in both realms simultaneously, the upper and lower, with a single glance. It is important to observe that *Genesis Rabbah* was not only an important source for later haggadic midrashic compilations—such as *Tanḥuma*—but also a notable reference point for medieval Jewish thinkers.[44]

---

[39] W. Bacher, *Die Agada der palästinensischen Amoräer*, vol. 1 (Strasbourg: Trübner, 1892), 107 n. 2.

[40] W. Bacher, "The Church Father, Origen, and Rabbi Hoshaya," *JQR* 3 (1891): 359. Niehoff concedes such parallels with more caution, as she also enumerates differences between Philo's parable and the midrashic image. As she astutely observes, "Philo's parable is far more detailed" in comparison to the more general portrayal found in *Gen. Rab.* Furthermore, the relationship between the king and architect differs in both accounts. What is more, the scriptural foundation Hoshaya grounds his parable in (Prov 8:30) diverges from Philo's way of presenting his parable: see Niehoff, "*Creatio*," 61.

[41] Bacher, "Origen," 359. See also 360. Niehoff alludes to this fact as well; cf. Niehoff, "*Creatio*," 61–62.

[42] D. T. Runia "Caesarea Maritima and the Survival of Hellenistic-Jewish Literature," in *Caesarea Maritima: A Retrospective after Two Millennia*, ed. A. Raban and K. G. Holum (Leiden: Brill, 1996), 493.

[43] See Philo's *Leg.* 3.99, in which he speaks of God's planned cosmos in terms of a μεγίστη οἰκία.

[44] For further examination of this theme, see J. Elbaum, "*Yalqut Shimʿoni* and the Medieval Midrashic Anthology," in *The Anthology in Jewish Literature*, ed. D. Stern (New York: Oxford University Press, 2004), 159–75.

17.3 Solomon ibn Gabirol's Metaphysics of the *Verbum* and Dunash ibn Tamim's Allegorical Exegete Named "the Alexandrian"

We will now turn to the most influential Jewish philosopher of the Middle Ages, Solomon ibn Gabirol—known for his crucial impact on High Scholasticism—whose Neoplatonic work *Fons vitae* contains various components that stand out in their resemblance to Philonic concepts. It was above all the Gabirolian hypostasis operating as God's mediator in creation[45]—generally designated as Will (*voluntas*), but also referred to as Wisdom (*sapientia*) and Word (*verbum*)—that prompted researchers to draw attention to the parallels it exhibits to Philo's Logos theology. One finds, for example, the following overview of this scholarly tendency in Elliot R. Wolfson's article "Philo and the Medieval Jewish Mysticism": "A number of scholars have also noted the indirect influence of Philo on medieval Jewish philosophers. For example, Poznański, building on the work of Wittman, suggested that Solomon ibn Gabirol's notion of the will (*voluntas*), which on occasion is characterized in terms that are associated with the divine speech (*verbum*), may reflect the Philonic doctrine of the Logos."[46]

> The Gabirolian hypostasis of the Will is represented as noetic light and universal intellect containing the totality of forms, which emanated from God's knowledge. In section 43 of *Fons vitae*'s chapter 5, Ibn Gabirol even accounts for the creation of the world through universal form in its expression as Word.[47]

Such a portrayal, along with numerous others present in *Fons vitae*—regardless of their resemblance to Philonic ideas—still do not seem to point to any distinct Philonic influence.

A cursory observation of Ibn Gabirol's *Fons vitae* suffices to identify its extensive dependence on medieval Jewish and Muslim Neoplatonism and its methodological avoidance of mentioning any particular Jewish notion.[48] In fact, the only philosophical source on which he explicitly draws is Plato, and he seems to have had a particular predilection for the *Timaeus*.[49] An effective method of revealing some of the traditional Jewish sources underlying Ibn Gabirol's Neoplatonic thought is to examine his Hebrew poem *The Kingly Crown*, which he probably wrote around the time of *Fons*

---

[45] See e.g. Avencebrolis (Ibn Gabirol), *Fons vitae, ex arabico in latinum translatus ab Johanne Hispano et Dominico Gundissalino*, ed. C. Baeumker and G. von Hertling, Beiträge zur Geschichte der Philosophie des Mittelalters, Texte und Untersuchungen 1.2, 2nd edn (Münster: Aschendorff, 1995), 1:2, 1:7, 2:13 (henceforth *Fons vitae*). For the English translation of Ibn Gabirol's *Fons vitae*, this article uses Ibn Gabirol, *The Font of Life (Fons vitae)*, trans. J. A. Laumakis (Milwaukee: Marquette University Press, 2014) (henceforth *The Font of Life*).

[46] E. R. Wolfson, "Traces of Philonic Doctrine in Medieval Jewish Mysticism: A Preliminary Note," *SPhiloA* 8 (1996): 101 (emphasis in original). Cf. O. Fraisse, "Einleitung," in Ibn Gabirol, *Fons vitae. Lebensquelle: Kapitel I und II*, ed. O. Fraisse, Herders Bibliothek der Philosophie des Mittelalters 21 (Freiburg: Herder, 2009), 34.

[47] *Font of Life*, 259–60 (*Fons vitae*, 5:43). Cf. *Fons vitae*, 5:35.

[48] See J. Schlanger, *The Philosophy of Solomon Ibn Gabirol* (Jerusalem: Magnes Press, 1980), 51–96.

[49] *Fons vitae*, 4:8, 4:20, 5:17.

vitae's composition and which exhibits the chief tenets of his Neoplatonic outlook,[50] but does so by drawing on ancient Jewish thought. For example, in the ninth section of this poem devoted to the primordial wisdom as God's mediator of creation, he presses into service ideas and terminology from *Gen. Rab.* 1:1: "You are wise, / ... as though you were wisdom's tutor [וְהַחָכְמָה הָיְתָה אֶצְלְךָ אָמוֹן]. / You are wise, / and your wisdom gave rise to an endless desire/ in the world as within an artist or worker [שָׂמֵתּוֹ כְּפוֹעֵל וְאָמָן]— / to bring out the stream of existence from Nothing, / ... giving it shape without tools [וּפוֹעֵל הַכֹּל בְּלִי כְלִי]."[51] His employment of these haggadic-midrashic concepts could suggest that he considered them to resonate well with metaphysical precepts relating to creation in Plato's *Timaeus*.[52]

Ibn Gabirol's dependency on ideas found in *Genesis Rabbah* is by no means limited to his poetic works. In *Fons vitae*, we can also detect, for instance, a metaphysical reformulation of a renowned haggadic interpretation provided by Šemu'el bar Naḥman that explains God's creation of light as Him wrapping Himself in a white garment (*Gen. Rab.* 3:4). In *Fons vitae*'s chapter 3, section 45, we read: "Because the lower substances are clothed in the light from the higher of them, and everything is clothed by the light of the sublime and holy first maker, as was already shown when we spoke about the flowing of some substances from others."[53] Primarily alluding to Philo's *Somn.* 1.75, in which "the Logos is identified with the light which was created in the beginning" and "God himself ... is the archetype of all light,"[54] Alexander Altmann postulates that bar Naḥman's "description of God putting on a garment of light is modelled on the Philo passage we have quoted."[55] Against this background, we may argue that Ibn Gabirol's depiction here, through the mediation of *Genesis Rabbah*, is at its core Philonic. In sum: the task of conclusively isolating distinct Philonic thought patterns in Gabirolian philosophy is quite hard, if not impossible. At most, one may posit a *philonische Färbung* in Ibn Gabirol's convoluted system.

Within the context of Ibn Gabirol's Jewish sources, we only mentioned *Genesis Rabbah*. But another ancient Jewish source, and one upon which he drew to a greater extent, is the enigmatic writing *Sefer Yeṣirah*. This writing, in particular its early medieval commentaries, is also relevant to our topic. As David Neumark already hinted, a reference to Philo appears in the Judeo-Arabic *Yeṣirah* commentary attributed to Isaac Israeli's (c.832–c.932) pupil Dunash ibn Tamim (c.890–c.956).[56] In this commentary— which, according to Tzvi Langermann, "was widely circulated, both in the original

---

[50] For further analysis, see A. Altmann, "He'arot ' al ha-neo-'aplaṭoniyut šel šelomo 'ibn-gabirol," in *Faces of Judaism: Selected Essays*, ed. A. Shapira (Tel Aviv: Am Oved Publishers, 1983), 91–97; S. Pessin, *Ibn Gabirol's Theology of Desire: Matter and Method in Jewish Medieval Neoplatonism* (Cambridge: Cambridge University Press, 2013), 53–90, 119–24, 131–33, 140–48, 165–69.

[51] Ibn Gabirol, *Selected Poems of Solomon Ibn Gabirol*, trans. P. Cole, Lockert Library of Poetry in Translation (Princeton: Princeton University Press, 2001), 149.

[52] For the connection between *Gen. Rab.* 1:1 and the *Timaeus* (29a), see Altmann, "Note," 195.

[53] *The Font of Life*, 170. Cf. *Fons vitae*, 5:42 (*The Font of Life*, 259). In Ibn Gabirol's poem "He Dwells Forever," we find an almost explicit allusion to this Amoraic depiction (*Poems*, 126).

[54] Altmann, "Note," 198 (emphasis in original).

[55] Altmann, "Note," 202.

[56] D. Neumark, *Geschichte der jüdischen Philosophie des Mittelalters nach Problemen dargestellt*, 3 vols (Berlin: Georg Reimer, 1907), 1:133 n. 2.

290   THE RECEPTION OF PHILO OF ALEXANDRIA

Arabic and in Hebrew translations"[57]—we encounter the following perplexing passing remark:

| ומי שרוצה לעמוד על ביאור זה יקרא ספרנו אשר חברנוהו בזה והוא מחובר ומסודר בסדר בראשית מן התורה ברמז לא יתכן לפרשם אלא לראוים להם והם מעטים בלתי נמצאים. ושמעתי ש"א [= שאחד] ששמו אליסכנדרי פירש מבראשית עד ויכולו בה' מאות עלה ואע"פ שלא ראינו פירושו כבר ראינו מהשגתו הענין. | And those who wish to understand this elucidation can read our book, which we wrote on this theme and which is written and structured according to the order of the biblical Genesis in the way of allegory. It is impossible to comprehend it except for the ones who are worthy, and they are the practically non-existent few. And I heard that one man, whose name is the Alexandrian, wrote five hundred pages of interpretation from *berʾešit* [Gen 1:1] up to *wa-yakhūllu* [Gen 2:1]. And even though we have not seen his commentary, we understood the subject matter from his reflection.[58] |

Without delving into the theme of the Karaite reception of Philo in the Middle Ages, four points regarding this cursory remark by Ibn Tamim warrant our attention: (1) Provided that this passage is an authentic part of the *Yeṣirah* commentary and that "the Alexandrian" is a reference to Philo,[59] it would seem to indicate that knowledge of Philonic allegories was not uncommon, even if it was to a limited extent and not first-hand, in the circles of Isaac ben Israeli and even those of Sa'adia Ga'on.[60] Alexander Altmann, for example, when discussing Sa'adia Ga'on's (882/92–942) commentary on *Sefer Yeṣirah*, speaks of an "amalgamation of Λόγος and Ἄνθρωπος dat[ing] back to the early Hellenistic period,"[61] an amalgamation that he believes is specifically found in Philo's theory of the Logos.[62] To this, Altmann adds that "Saadya's *Kābōd nibrā* out of

---

[57] Y. T. Langermann, "Dunash ibn Tamim," in *The Biographical Encyclopedia of Astronomers*, ed. T. Hockey et al. (New York: Springer, 2007), 315.

[58] M. Grossberg, trans., *Sefer Yetzirah Ascribed to the Patriarch Abraham with Commentary by Dunash Ben Tamim* (London: E. Z. Rabbinoyiṭsh, 1902), 28–29.

[59] This can only be assumed with reservation. For this reason, e.g. Neumark (*Geschichte*, 133) alludes to another manuscript, in which the statement in question is not cited in the name of Ibn Tamim ("vgl. übrigens L.B. d. Or. [*Literaturblatt des Orients*] 1845 S. 140, wo diese Stelle etwas anders lautet, und, wenn ich mich recht erinnere, gar nicht im Namen Abusahals zitiert wird"). Cf. "*ha-ʿatakot mi-perush R' yaʿaqov ben nissim Z"L le-sefer yeṣirah*," in A. ben Ascher, *Kontres hamassoreth*, ed. L. Dukes (Tübingen: Ludwig Friedrich Fues, 1846), 80; G. Vajda, *Le commentaire sur le "Livre de la Création" de Dūnaš ben Tāmīm de Kairouan (Xe siècle)*, rev. and ed. P. B. Fenton, Collection de la Revue des Études Juives (Leuven: Peeters, 2002), 58, 220.

[60] A. Altmann, "Saadya's Theory of Revelation: Its Origin and Background," in *Saadya Studies: In Commemoration of the One Thousandth Anniversary of the Death of R. Saadya Gaon*, ed. E. I. J. Rosenthal (Manchester: Manchester University Press, 1943), 23.

[61] Altmann, "Revelation," 23.

[62] Altmann, "Note," 198.

which the *dibbur niḇrā* speaks is likewise an amalgamation of the two elements *Logos* and *Anthropos.*"[63] (2) Ibn Tamim acknowledges the fact that he is acquainted with key positions of Philo's allegorical reading of the biblical account of creation. (3) He has knowledge of one of Philo's voluminous works, which covers the opening chapter of Genesis. As Neumark suggests, he might be referring to *Opif.*[64] Neumark also raised the possibility that the high page count of 500 refers to the entire Philonic corpus, in which *Opif.* is merely the opening treatise. (4) The context of this mention indicates that he sees a deep affinity between Philo's *Schöpfungsspekulation* and *Sefer Yeṣirah*, as well as his own allegorical work on Genesis. This seems to imply that the author was fascinated with Philo's mystical ideas regarding godly creation.

17.4 Philonic Perspectives in the Major Treatises of Medieval Kabbalah

These Philonic notions were further developed within medieval kabbalistic traditions as presented in Gikatilla's *Ginnat 'Egoz* (Garden of the Nut) and *Shaʿare 'Orah* (Gates of Light) as well as the magnum opus of Jewish mysticism, the *Sefer ha-Zohar* (Book of Splendor).[65] To substantiate this claim, we will discuss relevant passages of these treatises whose concepts reveal some resemblance to Philonic thought patterns relating to creation.[66] As indicated above, Elliot Wolfson has hinted at similarities between the Philonic Logos and Metatron or angels on the divine throne in anthropomorphic form in Jewish mysticism.[67] In *Sefer ha-'Orah* (Book of Light),[68] Jacob ben Jacob ha-Cohen interprets Gen 1:3 as pertaining to Metatron as God's utterance (*'amirah*) to Moses, which he in turn understands as the thought of the intellect. According to Jacob ha-Cohen, Moses can unite with Metatron in this unique vision of speech, which bears a strong phenomenological resemblance to the view of Philo's Logos theology and

---

[63] Altmann, "Revelation," 23. For an overview of Saʿadia Gaʾon's possible familiarity with Philonic thought, see Y. T. Langermann, "On the Beginnings of Hebrew Scientific Literature and on Studying History through 'Maqbiloṯ' (Parallels)," *Aleph* 2 (2002): 182; Parker and Treiger, "Odyssey," 120–21, 123, 127, 129.

[64] Neumark, *Geschichte*, 133 n. 2.

[65] On Gikatilla, see E. Morlok, *Rabbi Joseph Gikatilla's Hermeneutics* (Tübingen: Mohr Siebeck, 2011); on the *Zohar*, see B. Huss, *The Zohar: Reception and Impact* (Oxford: Littman Library of Jewish Civilization, 2016); G. Scholem, *Die Geheimnisse der Schöpfung. Ein Kapitel aus dem kabbalistischen Buche Sohar* (Frankfurt: Suhrkamp, 2018); D. Matt, ed., *The Zohar. Pritzker Edition*, 12 vols (Stanford: Stanford University Press, 2003–17).

[66] We are aware that further proof of interaction between the two literary corpora will have to be given and that we are relying here on phenomenological similarities. However, as a link between *Sefer Yeṣirah* and Philo was already established by Dunash ibn Tamim, we deem it plausible that further links between Philo and medieval kabbalistic conceptions can be established, as *Sefer Yeṣirah* is one of the basic sources for the further development of medieval mystical thought. On Philo and *Sefer Yeṣirah*, see Y. Liebes, *Ars Poetica in Sefer Yetsira* [Hebrew] (Tel Aviv: Schocken, 2000); Y. Liebes, "The Work of the Chariot and the Work of Creation as Mystical Teachings in Philo of Alexandria," in *Scriptural Exegesis: The Shapes of Culture and the Religious Imagination. Essays in Honour of Michael Fishbane*, ed. D. A. Green and L. S. Lieber (Oxford: Oxford University Press, 2009), 105–20.

[67] Wolfson, "Traces," 105–6; E. R. Wolfson, *Through a Speculum That Shines: Vision and Imagination in Medieval Jewish Mysticism* (Princeton: Princeton University Press, 1997), 255–63; cf. also E. R. Goodenough, *By Light, Light: The Mystic Gospel of Hellenistic Judaism* (New Haven: Yale University Press, 1935), 366.

[68] MS Jerusalem, Schocken Library 14, fol. 60a; Wolfson, "Traces," 105.

his description of the revelation at Mt Sinai (see below, pp. 293–94). Moreover, Elliot Wolfson has also made a similar inference regarding God's unknowability, his negative conception in Philo, or/and a possible Gnostic Valentinian source.[69]

Moshe Idel has examined the intrinsic link between God's creative power in speech and his revelation in an angelic being called either Metatron or "son," while drawing attention to the presence of a similar connection in Philo's doctrine of the Logos, also with respect to its feminine aspect.[70] The divine representative, the angel, in Exod 23:20–24 is depicted as the "firstborn son," the divine word, the beginning, the high priest, or the most important divine name as a theophoric mediator, e.g. in Philo's *Conf.* 145–47.[71] Idel summarizes "if we put together Philo's views on the Logos as son of God, name, image, and seal found in disparate discussions in his writings, it would be possible to see the Alexandrian thinker as one of the major sources for the theories reflected in the Jewish-Christian, Gnostic and neo-Platonic sources."[72] Idel discusses sonship as described in *Conf.* 145–48 while proposing that the text distinguishes between three types:[73] (1) the Logos in relation to God, (2) humans described as Sons of God, and (3) the Sons of Man themselves; namely, the Sons of the Logos. He proposes an exchange of qualities between the Greek concepts of the agent intellect on the one hand and the Jewish theories of sonship and angelology on the other (especially in the ecstatic branch of Jewish mysticism). A synthesis of a conceptual framework and particular language creates a theoretical pattern that echoes basic concepts on a more abstract and esoteric level, and their exoteric expressions, both in written form and in the revelations, are echoed in linguistic and imaginary forms in medieval mysticism.[74] Therefore, if Christian theories about sonship depend on Philo, certain elements in

---

[69] E. R. Wolfson, "Inscribed in the Book of the Living: *Gospel of Truth* and Jewish Christology," *JSJ* 38 (2007): 234–71, esp. 250. Wolfson refers to Irenaeus, *Against Heresies*, 1.20.1–2, who reports a story transmitted by the Marcosians, in which Jesus is a child learning his letters. His teacher asks him to pronounce "Alpha," he replies by saying the letter, but when the teacher asks him to say "Beta" (or bet), he responds, "Do thou first tell me what Alpha is, and then I will tell thee what Beta is." Irenaeus adds: "This they expound as meaning that He alone knew the Unknown, which He revealed under its type Alpha." The nexus between the unknown and the letter *alef* is a well-attested motif in medieval kabbalistic sources, an idea that is exegetically grounded in the fact that the consonants of the term *alef* can be rearranged to spell *pele* (mystery/wonder). D. T. Runia, "Naming and Knowing: Themes in Philonic Theology with Special Reference to *De mutatione nominum*," in *Knowledge of God in the Graeco-Roman World*, ed. R. B. van den Broek (Leiden: Brill, 1988), 69–91, esp. 76–78; R. Radice, "The 'Nameless Principle' from Philo to Plotinus: An Outline of Research," in *Italian Studies on Philo of Alexandria*, ed. F. Calabri (Leiden: Brill, 2003), 167–82, esp. 178–81.

[70] M. Idel, *Ben: Sonship and Jewish Mysticism* (New York: Continuum, 2007), index, s.v. Philo; M. Idel, *The Privileged Divine Feminine in Kabbalah* (Berlin: de Gruyter, 2019), 17.

[71] Idel, *Ben*, 23, 25, 26, 29, 31; Idel adduces a passage from *Conf.* 146–47 (PLCL 4:89–91): "But if there be any as yet unfit to be called a Son of God, let him press to take his place under God's First-born, the Word, who holds the eldership among the angels, their ruler as it were. And many names are his, for he is called, 'the Beginning,' and the Name of God, and His Word, and the Man after His image, and 'he that sees,' that is Israel.... For if we have not yet become fit to be thought sons of God yet we may be sons of his invisible image, the most holy Word. For the Word is the eldest-born image of God." Idel stresses the theophanic vector and the double sonship, when *anthropos* is designated as the firstborn and the eldest son, a hypostatic and incorporeal entity, or as the Logos/seal (*sphragis*) similar to Philo himself (cf. M. R. Niehoff, *Philo on Jewish Identity and Culture* [Tübingen: Mohr Siebeck, 2001], 203–5). On language as a seal in Philo, see M. R. Niehoff, "What Is in a Name? Philo's Mystical Philosophy of Language," *JQR* 2 (1995): 243–59; on sealing the six dimensions in *Sefer Yeṣirah* by letter combination, see Liebes, *Ars Poetica*, 177–89. In other mystical treatises, the son is identified as Metatron or the angel of the face or the Great Angel who plays a pivotal messianic function (Idel, *Ben*, 211).

[72] Idel, *Ben*, 31.

[73] Idel, *Ben*, 34–35.

[74] Idel, *Ben*, 314–15.

late antique Judaism might have served as springboards for some forms of theological speculation that were later imposed on the biblical texts, transforming them into prooftexts for a novel elaborated theology.[75]

If we try to avoid reading Logos theology as specific to Christianity, with Philo as a sort of "Christian *avant la lettre*,"[76] we can conceptualize it as a common element in the Jewish and Jewish-Christian imagination.[77] The Logos as the "first-begotten son of the uncreated Father"[78] is intimately connected to both light and word in Philo (*Migr.* 47–48), as the sacred oracles imitate the words of God, which are seen in the same way as light is seen. In his interpretation of Exod 20:18 the voice of God is seen by the eye of the soul, and Moses rightly introduces it as "visible."[79] In Philo's vacillation on the point of ambiguity between the separate existence of the Logos as God's son and its total incorporation within the Godhead, Moses is conceptualized as the intellectual son of the divine who is able to "see the voice," a concept which is extended to the entire nation's ability to comprehend Hebrew, the material of creation within Jewish mysticism. According to one of the Fragment-Targums,[80] God declared to Moses in Exod 3:14, "I am the *Memra*." Thus, the Logos is that which is revealed to Moses, simultaneously providing him with support and redeeming the Israelites. This speculative explanation supplies a point of origin for the term *Memra* as deriving from Gen 1:3, with the divine "I am" as a name of the *Memra* itself.[81]

We can read Philo's *Decal.* 35–36 and 45–49 in a similar way:

> But the new miraculous voice was set in action and kept in flame by the power of God which ... made it more illuminating in its ending than in its beginning by creating in the souls of each and all another kind of hearing far superior to the hearing of the ears.... [T]he hearing of the mind possessed by God makes the first advance and goes out to meet the spoken words with the keenest rapidity....
>
> Then from the midst of the fire that streamed from heaven there sounded forth ... a voice, for the flame became articulate speech in the language familiar to the audience, and so clearly and distinctly were the words formed by it that they seemed to see rather than hear them. What I say is vouched for by the law in which it is written, "All the

---

[75] Idel, *Ben*, 635; cf. also G. G. Stroumsa, "Christ's Laughter: Docetic Origins Reconsidered," *JECS* 12 (2004): 288.

[76] J. E. Bruns, "Philo Christianus: The Debris of a Legend," *HTR* 66 (1973): 141–45; cf. also Runia, "Survey," 52–54.

[77] D. Boyarin, "The Gospel of the *Memra*: Jewish Binitarianism and the Prologue to John," *HTR* 94 (2001): 243–84, esp. 248.

[78] Cf. Winston, *Logos*, 16.

[79] Niehoff, "What Is in a Name?," 226, demonstrates how Philo idealizes language, conceptualizing the ideal language as having pre-existed with God himself, thus entirely pertaining to the realm of the eternal, unchanging, most real, and most true. It is likely that the enormous importance that Philo attributes to language and its active function as part of the deity is inspired by his natural assumptions about God's speech-acts throughout the biblical writings. The idea then appears to have been conceptualized in Platonic terms of ideal forms. Cf. Boyarin, "*Memra*," 251–52, and 257 n. 53; D. Abrams, "The Boundaries of Divine Ontology: The Inclusion and Exclusion of Metatron in the Godhead," *HTR* 87 (1994): 291–321, esp. 292, 316–21; and Wolfson, "Prophecy," 69.

[80] M. L. Klein, ed. and trans., *The Fragment-Targums of the Pentateuch According to Their Extant Sources*, 2 vols (Rome: Biblical Institute Press, 1980), 2:47.

[81] Boyarin, "*Memra*," 259. According to M. J. Edwards ("Justin's Logos and the Word of God," *JECS* 3 [1995]: 262), the Logos theology of both John and Justin Martyr represents an old Jewish pattern of religious thought, from which rabbinism later departed.

people saw the voice" [Exod 19:18] ..., for it is the case that ... the voice of God is truly visible. Why so? Because whatever God says is not words but deeds .... Admirable too, and worthy of the Godhead, is the saying that the voice proceeded from the fire, for the oracles of God have been refined ... as gold is by fire.... [I]t is the nature of fire both to give light and to burn, those who resolve to be obedient to the divine utterances will live forever ....[82]

Philo interprets the revelation of the Torah and the seeing of the divine voice (Exod 19:18) at Mount Sinai as having metaphorically occurred from amidst a fire. God's voice is incorporated in his visible deeds and has at the same time a purifying function.[83] The terms and nature of such a divine revelation to God's son Moses, representing the entire nation, reminds one of the flame of impenetrable darkness (*boṣina di qardinuta*) in the description of the creational process in *Zohar* 1:15a. Also in this context, the complex and ambiguous theme of divine unity and the incorporation of the divine speech into the supernal ontology while simultaneously generating a "separate space" is metaphorically portrayed as the origin of the emanational flow from within the Godhead, prior to all creation, which finally substantiates itself in the ten sefirot, the divine *logoi* of Gen 1:1.[84]

Zohar 1:15a reads these first verses of the Hebrew Bible as follows:

"In the beginning" (Gen 1:1). At the head of potency of the King, he engraved engravings in luster on high. A spark of impenetrable darkness flashed within the concealed of the concealed, from the head of Infinity (*En Sof*)—a cluster of vapor forming in formlessness, thrust in a ring, not white, not black, not red, not green, no color at all. As a cord surveyed, it yielded radiant colors. Deep within the spark gushed a flow, splaying colors below, concealed within the concealed of the mystery of *En Sof*. It split and did not split its aura, was not known at all, until under the impact of splitting, a single, concealed, supernal point shone. Beyond that point, nothing is known, so it is called ראשית, Beginning, first command of all.[85]

The first command,[86] *ber'ešit*, is identified with a point of light emanating from a dark flame, concealing the innermost mystery of the divine being. At its critical point of transition, the ambivalence between concealment and revelation, between nonexistence and existence, is expressed in the "absolute metaphor" of the dark flame,[87]

---

[82] PLCL 7:23, 29–30; cf. also *Conf.* 32, 22–23 and *Aet.* 33–34, 86–87, 92.

[83] On Philo's interpretation of the godly voice during the Sinaitic revelation, see Y. Amir, "Die Zehn Gebote bei Philon von Alexandrien," in *Die hellenistische Gestalt des Judentums bei Philon von Alexandrien*, ed. Y. Amir (Neukirchen-Vluyn: Neukirchener Verlag, 1983), 131–63.

[84] One should keep in mind that from the earliest readings on, the first two letters of the Hebrew Bible were read as *bar* (son) in the Aramaic translation of the Pentateuch known as *Targum Neofiti*. For the zoharic reading of these first consonants, see Liebes, *Ars Poetica*, 147–48.

[85] We follow the translation of Matt, *Zohar*, 1:107–9.

[86] Cf. *m. 'Abot* 5:1. Only nine explicit commands are found in Gen 1, but the decade is completed by counting *ber'ešit* as the first.

[87] Gerold Necker suggests Hans Blumenberg's metaphorology as an exegetical tool for analyzing kabbalistic texts, as an alternative to Scholem's symbolism. One of the main examples for absolute metaphor can be found in

similar to "seeing the voice" at Sinai. In accordance with *Sefer Yeṣirah*, creation is conceived as the pre-existential formation of language in an emanational overflow associated with the transfer from beyond color to color. Like the view that the divine may only be described by means of negation and negative attributes, the "dark" or "very hard" flame includes the idea of a light that is too bright to be perceived.[88] "Within the concealed of the concealed" refers to the first sefira, *Keter* (crown), as pre-existing with the *En Sof*. The initial act of divine autogenesis or self-revelation is identified with the deity's female powers, according to another passage found in *Zohar* 3:48b.[89] This passage is an interpretation of the "Lamp/Spark of Darkness" from *ber'ešit* and refers to its secret potential, which was so effective that it penetrated most of the following kabbalistic views. The spark becomes the divine tool of God's light,[90] having been transformed into a straight line after the divine self-limitation, famously known by the name of *ṣimṣum*.

However, we should consider not only the visible, but also the acoustic aspect of these lines. Finally, the creation process culminates in the first "command," the first language, the first word, the first Logos, the son of *En Sof*. The material manifestation of the deity is to be found in the first word of the Bible, whose commands are revealed to Moses at Sinai by a "voice," which may be seen by the enlightened soul as in Philo's description of the Decalogue.[91] Although we are dealing here with common and widespread semantic fields of late antiquity such as light, sound, darkness, and so on, we might discern a certain resemblance in the usage of paradoxical images in order to approach divine secrets and their revelation to humans.

Accepting the widespread hypothesis that Jewish mysticism reintegrated ancient patterns marginalized by rabbinic literature,[92] we can discern comparable phenomenological, hermeneutical, and theological patterns in these two passages. The overflow of lights reaches its climax in a voice that manifested in creational and revelatory deeds.

The kabbalists could penetrate these secrets of the pre-existing divine aura[93] by stripping away the linguistic garments of the divine ontology via mystical exegesis, as demonstrated in both literary strata of the work of Gikatilla. In the magnum opus

---

bozina di qardinuta; see G. Necker, "Hans Blumenberg's Metaphorology and the Historical Perspective of Mystical Terminology," *JSQ* 22 (2015): 184–203, esp. 194–98 on the flame as an absolute metaphor.

[88] See the comments of Matt, *Zohar*, 1:107–08; G. Scholem, *Sefer ha-Zohar shel Gershom Shalom*, 6 vols (Jerusalem: Magnes Press, 1992), 1:66–67; Necker, "Metaphorology," 195.

[89] Matt, *Zohar*, 7:304.

[90] Already in Sa'adia's commentary on *Sefer Yeṣirah*, the divine glory is identified with the Shekhina, which is according to *Sefer Yeṣirah* the "Spirit of God," referred to as "second and subtle air" or "light," comparable to Philo's designation of the divine glory as Logos. Cf. Wolfson, "Prophecy," 56.

[91] We are reminded of Ibn Gabirol's "pronunciation of the word" in *Fons vitae*, 5:43, mentioned in the quote above.

[92] M. Idel, "Rabbinism versus Kabbalism: On G. Scholem's Phenomenology of Judaism," *Modern Judaism* 11 (1991): 281–96.

[93] Gershom Scholem suggested that this concept might be derived from Ibn Gabirol: see G. Scholem, "'Iqbotaw shel Gebirol be-Qabbalah," in *Me'assef Sofere 'Ereṣ Yisra'el*, ed. Aaron Kabak (Tel Aviv: Keren ha-Tarbut, 1940), 167–68; G. Scholem, *Origins of the Kabbalah*, ed. R. J. Z. Werblowsky, trans. A. Arkush (Princeton: Princeton University Press, 1987), 331–47. A comparison with *Sefer Yeṣirah* 2:6 and Gabirol's *Keter Malkhut* 9:97–101 is especially interesting for our topic; cf. Matt, *Zohar*, 1:108 f n. 11.

of his first creative period, *Ginnat 'Egoz* (Garden of the Nut), the inner energy of the divine language, Hebrew, is activated via linguistic techniques derived from his teacher Abraham Abulafia (1240–c.1291/92).[94] The biblical text is deconstructed into its very atoms and rearranged according to a new, prophetic narrative.[95] The divine creational energetic impulse is set free via the kabbalist's linguistic-exegetical techniques and his ability to recreate language anew,[96] in the sense of the true *merkaba* perceived as letter-combination.[97] In his early writings, the inner connection between the semantic part of the word and its numerical value supplies the code for the proper understanding of the text, thus revealing the basic truth of reality in language as static. As we read in *Ginnat 'Egoz* (41) for example: "With regard to the existent Name, which never changes, YHWH is His Name: This is the unique Name to call His blessed true being. And just as He the blessed never changes, so His Name never changes, as it is said: 'For I am YHWH, I have not changed'" (Mal 3:6).[98] All motion is maintained by the motion of the vocal sounds, moving not only language but the entire universe. According to the third part of *Ginnat 'Egoz*, the *binyyan* (building) designates not only the semantic construct, but also the creational construct of the universe.[99] Adela Yarbro Collins has already shown possible points of contact between Judaism and the Pythagorean tradition in Philo[100] and apocalyptic Jewish literature,[101] especially in *1 Enoch* and the *Testament of Abraham*.

To return to language, Yehuda Liebes states that Philo distinguishes between a lower type of language for the masses, which describes the created world, and the higher type of language, concerning the eternal God, which Moses preserved as an oral teaching for the elite. In both concepts, sound and voice are preserved for the revelation of the divine being. In his conception of speech being superior to writing, Philo follows Plato's *Phaedrus* (274–75).[102] His teaching of esotericism is an interesting mixture of

---

[94] M. Idel, *Language, Torah and Hermeneutics in Abraham Abulafia* (Albany: SUNY Press; 1989).

[95] Morlok, *Gikatilla*, 172–208; H. Lachter, "Kabbalah, Philosophy, and the Jewish-Christian Debate: Reconsidering the Early Works of Joseph Gikatilla," *JJTP* 16 (2008): 1–58.

[96] These techniques are indicated in the title of the book, *ginnat*, which is used as an acronym for *gematria* (numerical value), *notarikon* (acronym), and *temurah* (letter combination). For Pythagorean number theory as a pattern for Gikatilla's hermeneutics, see Morlok, *Gikatilla*, 72, 77–82.

[97] See also Gikatilla's *Sha'ar ha-Niqqud*, 34b and 37b–38a; Morlok, *Gikatilla*, 47–53, 84–87. In contrast to the twenty-two letters of the Hebrew alphabet, which are corporeal and revealed in their pronunciation, the letters of the Tetragrammaton are hidden, albeit being the secret source of all vocal and cosmic motion. A person who is initiated into the secret interpretation of the *merkabah* (lit. combination) may understand the inner secrets of hidden worlds and heavens, as he is able to enter the "inner *pardes*," the knowledge of the vocalization points. He will envision the primordial glory of the creator within his creation. See also Liebes, "Work of the Chariot."

[98] Morlok, *Gikatilla*, 50. Cf. also Halevi's description of the prophetic moment as the Holy Spirit enwrapping "the prophet at the time when uttering his prophecy" (*Kuzari*, 4:15); Wolfson, "Prophecy," 58.

[99] Morlok, *Gikatilla*, 87.

[100] She regards Philo as "a Neo-Pythagorean with considerable justification"; see A. Yarbro Collins, "Numerical Symbolism in Jewish and Early Christian Apocalyptic Literature," in *Religion (Hellenistisches Judentum in Römischer Zeit: Philon und Josephus)*, ed. W. Haase, ANRW II 21.2 (Berlin: de Gruyter, 1984), 1256. D. T. Runia, "Why Does Clement of Alexandria Call Philo 'the Pythagorean'?," *VC* 49 (1995): 1–22. Cf. esp. Philo's *Opif.* 100; *Leg.* 1.15; *QG* 1.17, 1.99, 3.16, 3.49; *Prob.* 2; *Aet.* 12, where he explicitly mentions such traditions.

[101] Collins, "Numerical Symbolism," 1253–56.

[102] See Plato, *Works* [Hebrew], trans. Y. G. Liebes, 4 vols (Jerusalem: Schocken, 1960), 3:418–19, cf. also 3:331. Cf. M. B. Cover, "The Sun and the Chariot: The *Republic* and the *Phaedrus* as Sources for Rival Platonic Paradigms of Psychic Vision in Philo's Biblical Commentaries," *SPhiloA* 26 (2014): 151–67.

Greek and Jewish conceptions.[103] Gikatilla (and the *Zohar*) teach esoteric knowledge in a similar way. In *Ginnat 'Egoz*, letter-combination leads to the true *merkabah*, and its secrets via sounds (cf. *Decal.* above).[104] In both treatises, the keys to such exegetical endeavors are only transmitted from teacher to students orally, never to be fully revealed in writing.[105] Another parallel between Gikatilla and Philo is the metaphor of weaving to describe the creational process. In *Sha'are 'Orah*, 1:48, the biblical text is established as a woven tapestry of divine names in a hierarchical order, resembling the ontological pyramid.[106] Words are presented as archetypal signs, a universal subtext in a metonymic chain through which all legible things can be deciphered. All ten sefirot depend on the Tetragrammaton as well as numerous cognomina referring to angelic powers. These cognomina "organize" other linguistic elements in the biblical text which refer to mundane affairs. This linguistic pyramid assumes a certain transformation of the fewer and higher elements into lower ones. This is encapsulated in the metaphor of the lower elements being the "garment" of the higher. Divine creation is again interpreted as divine speech; the kabbalist may penetrate the divine secrets by re-weaving the names within the sefirotic matrix. The creation of the universe through weaving, similar to the creation myth in Plato's *Timaeus* (41b–c: the weaving of the mortal with the immortal)[107] is also found in Philo.[108] In *Somn.* 1.203–8,[109] Philo refers to the cosmos as a "variegated piece of embroidery," and he associates both the philosophers and the human artist with the craft of weaving, depicting the "weave" of the Logos methodically,[110] particularly in his interpretation of the *Timaeus*.

In the fifth gate of *Sha'are 'Orah* (1:195–96), Gikatilla portrays how the mystical exegete has to remove the text's garments in order to reach its inner root, the Tetragrammaton, and unite with the divine.[111] The removal of the garments equivalent to the recollection of the original status of the letters and sounds[112] resulting in nakedness, might be compared to the Philonic idea of forgetting the material world, through

---

[103] Liebes, "Work of the Chariot," 116; G. G. Stroumsa, "*Paradosis*: Esoteric Traditions in Early Christianity," in *Hidden Wisdom: Esoteric Traditions and the Roots of Christian Mysticism*, ed. G. G. Stroumsa, 2nd rev. edn (Leiden: Brill, 2005), 27–45, esp. 32–33.

[104] Morlok, *Gikatilla*, index, s.v. Chariot/*Merkavah*.

[105] On oral transmission in kabbalistic traditions following *m. 'Abot* 1:1, see Morlok, *Gikatilla*, 40, 183, 200; M. Idel, "On Transmission in Jewish Culture," in *Transmitting Jewish Traditions: Orality, Textuality, and Cultural Diffusion*, ed. Y. Elman and I. Gershoni (New Haven: Yale University Press, 2000), 138–65.

[106] Morlok, *Gikatilla*, 193–94.

[107] Cf. also Proclus, *On Plato Cratylus*, trans. B. Duvick (Ithaca: Cornell University Press, 2007), 30, on the etymological connection between Circe and Core and the etymological basis for Circe in κερκίζειν (to separate a web with a shuttle [κερκίς]); cf. Duvick's notes on pages 127–28 nn. 125–26.

[108] G. E. Sterling, "*Creatio Temporalis, Aeterna, vel Continua*? An Analysis of the Thought of Philo of Alexandria," *SPhiloA* 4 (1992): 15–41; D. Winston, "Theodicy and the Creation of Man in Philo of Alexandria," in *Hellenica et Judaica: Hommage à Valentin Nikiprowetzky*, ed. A. Caquot, M. Hadas-Lebel, and J. Riaud (Leuven: Peeters, 1986), 110; Winston, "Philo's Theory of Eternal Creation: *De Prov.* 1.6–9," *PAAJR* 46–47 (1980): 593–606, esp. 600 on weaving. The most elaborate study is D. T. Runia, *Philo of Alexandria and the Timaeus of Plato* (Leiden: Brill, 1986). On weaving the divine body, see N. P. Constas, "Weaving the Body of God: Proclus of Constantinople, the Theokotos, and the Loom of the Flesh," *JECS* 3 (1995): 169–94.

[109] PLCL 5:405–9.

[110] Cf. *Sacr.* 82–85. Cf. also J. Whitman, "Present Perspective: Antiquity to the Late Middle Ages," in *Interpretation and Allegory*, ed. J. Whitman (Leiden: Brill, 2003), 54 n. 73.

[111] Morlok, *Gikatilla*, 113–23.

[112] Morlok, *Gikatilla*, 207.

continuous meditation on the deity (*Leg.* 2.55–56; *Ebr.* 85), which might perhaps also be alluded to in the passage from *Decal.* above. Both in Philonic and kabbalistic texts, the final aim of such an elevated spiritual state might be described as noble (ethical) conduct in the presence of the divine.[113] The mystic's voice and the divine voice secure a central role in this process of revelation, which is analogous to the meditative prayer/exegesis of the initiated, who have to utter the Hebrew terms and transform both them and themselves into vessels for the divine overflow in order to explain the divine revelation to their respective communities.[114]

17.5 Conclusion

When writing an article on the reception of Philo during the Jewish Middle Ages, one is often confronted with bewilderment, from which the question emerges: Is there such a thing? The present chapter has attempted to put forward the claim that yes, there is such a thing, and this thing requires acknowledgment and further analysis. With that said, our study does not advance this stance without a substantial caveat, maintaining at the same time that Philo's impact should not be overemphasized, or extended to domains where the resemblance to Philo appears rather to originate from a similar exegetical method applied to scripture. We might assume that concepts of the Logos and creational theology in particular made their way in via complex networks such as midrashic thought, commentaries on *Sefer Yeṣirah*, and Neoplatonic and Pythagorean writers who were familiar with Jewish, Greek, and/or Arabic treatises on the topics mentioned. Of pivotal importance is the transition between language in written and oral form, as exemplified by Philo and kabbalistic authors, for example Gikatilla and the composers of the *Zohar*. It is difficult to reach a verdict as to whether those writers had access to Philonic compositions or whether there were other channels of transmission. Despite these negative answers, we are able to discern various similarities between Philonic and medieval writings. These similarities need to be elaborated upon in future research. Drawing on the formulation offered by Runia regarding Philo's overall impact on the intellectual world, we may say that the philosophical movement initiated by Philo's pioneering work also helped to shape some important aspects of medieval Jewish thought.

To sum up, it seems almost impossible to spot traces of a direct influence from Philo's writings on medieval philosophical and mystical literature. However, when taking a closer phenomenological look at hermeneutical and exegetical patterns and theological terminology, one may discern certain parallels between those literary corpora.

---

[113] E. R. Wolfson, "Heading the Law beyond the Law: Transgendering Alterity and the Hypernomian Perimeter of the Ethical," *EJJS* 14 (2020): 215–63.

[114] At this point, the kabbalists take over the role of Moses at Sinai and function as the "sons" of the divine, who explain the "sound" to the people. In an elitist manner, the concept of revelation of Maimonides is preserved by the kabbalists (Wolfson, "Prophecy," 75). Cf. also J. Garb, "Powers of Language in Kabbalah: Comparative Reflections," in *The Poetics of Grammar and the Metaphysics of Sound and Sign*, ed. S. La Porta and D. D. Shulman (Leiden: Brill, 2007), 233–69. On the resemblance between Philo's "articulate voice" in *Decal.* 33 and Halevi's concept of prophecy, see Wolfson, "Prophecy", 67–70, and n. 19 above on an Arabic version of *Decal.* As Gikatilla knew Arabic, it is quite conceivable that he consulted this version. On Gikatilla and Arabic, see Morlok, *Gikatilla*, 160.

18
Armenian Christianity

Olga Vardazaryan

This overview of the reception of Philo's legacy in medieval Armenian literature does not pretend to be comprehensive. Not only does the scope of present scholarship make it impossible but there is also the problem of sources. Many texts of medieval Armenian authors have no critical editions, and some are still unpublished.[1] Some texts have not been sufficiently studied, especially with respect to revealing allusions, parallels, or latent citations. Unfortunately, scholars working with medieval Armenian texts do not yet have an instrument with some of the capacities and functions of the TLG, so a systematic collation of texts has been done only rarely and manually.[2] On the other hand, Armenian medieval savants who study Philo's or Pseudo-Philo's Armenian versions are mostly interested not in their content, but in the specific language of these texts. The "Hellenizing" or "Hellenophile" translators[3] in fact created a new stylistic system, a basis for the scholarly sociolect; they translated texts, including but not limited to Philo, with varying degrees of literalism that served for later authors as a source of *inventio verborum*. The use of such a virtual lexicon (and some grammatical Grecisms) is a witness to their acquaintance with the Armenian corpus of Philo's and Pseudo-Philo's works,[4] which in some respects is a fact of reception. But in each particular case one has to decide if the presence of a specific word from the translation in an original Armenian writing reveals ideological influence of the CPhA or is simply a technical, essentially rhetorical procedure that has nothing to do with the content of Philo's text. Such cases are numerous;[5] with the exception of several important examples, dealt with

---

[1] The series *Matenagirkʻ hayocʻ* (*Armenian Classical Authors*, henceforth ACIA) takes as its goal the comprehensive critical publication of all original Armenian writings, starting with the early fifth century (when the Armenian alphabet was created). To this point, twenty-two large volumes have been published, reaching the twelfth century. Up to 2010, the volumes of the series were issued in Lebanon (Antilias), published by the Armenian Catholicosate of Cilicia, since 2011 in Erevan, by the Matenadaran, Mashtots Institute of Ancient Manuscripts, in both cases without specifying a publishing house. In references to this edition we indicate the volume, page(s), and number(s) of section(s), e.g. ACIA, vol. 5, 1050:65–67. Armenian names and terms are given in the Library of Congress Romanization Table transcription, except where the names of books and articles are cited whose authors followed other conventions.

[2] See e.g. the painstaking research of G. Muradyan, *Grecisms in Ancient Armenian*, Hebrew University Armenian Studies 13 (Leuven: Peeters, 2012), and many other works of the same author.

[3] The latest review on the issue of Armenian "Hellenizing" translations with a detailed bibliography can be found in G. Muradyan, "The Hellenizing School," in *Armenian Philology in the Modern Era: From Manuscript to Digital Text*, ed. V. Calzolari and M. E. Stone, HdO Section 8 Uralic & Central Asian Studies 23.1 (Leiden: Brill, 2014), 321–48.

[4] Henceforth CPhA—Corpus Philoneum Armeniacum.

[5] See A. Terian, "The Hellenizing School, Its Time, Place, and Scope of Activities Reconsidered," in *East of Byzantium: Syria and Armenia in the Formative Period*, ed. N. G. Garsoïan, T. F. Mathews, and R. W. Thomson (Washington, DC: Dumbarton Oaks, 1980), 182–83; G. Muradyan, "Le style hellénisant des *Progymnasmata* arméniens dans le contexte d'autres écrits originaux," in *Actes du Sixième Colloque international de Linguistique arménienne*, ed. A. Donabédian and A. Ouzounian = *Slovo* 26–27 (1999): 83–94.

below, we are not going to discuss them. Finally, we confine ourselves to the influence of the existing CPhA on medieval Armenian literature; the question of the possible acquaintance of Armenian medieval scholars with other works of Philo, not translated or not extant in Armenian versions, has not been studied at all, so the question is not here taken up. We also do not examine the facts of the indirect reception, i.e. the acquaintance with Philonic topics via Greek authors bearing any influence by Philo and translated into Armenian. This aspect too remains to be studied.

18.1 The Armenian Philonic Corpus

The "Armenian Philo" contains:

1. The translations without or mostly without extant Greek originals: *Prov.* 1–2, *Anim.*,[6] *QG* 1–4, *QE* 1–2, and a fragment *Deo*, as well as two Pseudo-Philonic sermons *De Sampsone* and *De Jona* (a full homily and a fragment of another sermon with the same title).[7] The chapter on the Decad, which is always inserted between *Spec.* 3.1–7 and *Decal.* in CPhA manuscripts,[8] may be a fragment of Philo's non-preserved treatise "On Numbers."[9]
2. The translations with extant Greek originals: *Contempl., Abr., Leg.* 1–2, *Decal., Spec.* 1.79–81 (Arm. title *On the Priests*), 1.131–61 (Arm. *On the Twelve Gems*), 1.285–345 (Arm. *On the Altar Supplies*), *Spec.* 3.1–7, *Spec.* 3.8–64 (Arm. *On That You Shall Not Commit Adultery*).[10]

Were these texts chosen randomly "for tutorial purposes," as N. Akinean and after him H. Levi, A. Terian, and others believed,[11] or did they come down to us in such a composition as a result of natural losses or artificial selection, or, from the very beginning, did the compilers of the corpus invest in it some kind of structuring idea? Today it is impossible to say. At any rate, in the view of the Armenian scholiast of the twelfth–thirteenth centuries the entire corpus "treats of the virtues and chastity" and

---

[6] Both published in Philonis Judaei, *Sermones Tres Hactenus Inediti, I. et II. De Providentia, et III. De Animalibus, ex Armena versione antiquissima ab ipso originali textu Graeco ad verbum stricte exequuta, nunc primum in latine fideliter translata per P. Jo. Baptistam Aucher Ancyranum, monachum Armenum et doctorem Mchitaristam* (Venice: Typis Coenobii PP. Armenorum in insula S. Lazari, 1822) = Philo, 1822.

[7] Published in *Philonis Judaei Paralipomena Armena libri videlicet quatuor in Genesin. Libri duo in Exodum. Sermo unus de Sampsone. Alter de Jona, tertius de tribus angelis Abraamo apparentibus, Opera Hactenus Inedita ex Armena versione antiquissima ab ipso originali textu Graeco ad verbum stricte exequuta saeculo v. nunc primum in Latinum fideliter translata per P. Jo. Baptistam Aucher.* Venice: Typis coenobii Armenorum in insula S. Lazari, 1826 = Philo, 1826.

[8] All three texts are united in manuscripts under the general title "On the Ten Commandments." Published in *Philo the Hebrew's Sermons Which Have Reached Us* (in Armenian), ed. G. Zarbhanalean (Venice: Mekhitharian Press, 1892) = Philo, 1892.

[9] Perhaps a fragment of Philo's "De numeris," see A. Terian, "A Philonic Fragment on the Decad," in *Nourished with Peace: Studies in Hellenistic Judaism in Memory of Samuel Sandmel*, ed. Frederick E. Greenspahn, Earle Hilgert, and Burton L. Mack, Scholars Press Homage Series 9 (Chico, CA: Scholars Press, 1984), 173–82.

[10] Published in Philo, 1892.

[11] Terian, "The Hellenizing School," 183.

ARMENIAN CHRISTIANITY 301

is divided into seven sections or steps ("writings"), designed to lead the reader to "spiritual proficiency":[12]

1. "Providence": *Prov.* 1–2 + *Anim.*
2. "Genesis": *QG* 1–3.
3. "Patriarchs or Contemplatives": *Abr.*
4. "Allegories": *Leg.* 1–2.
5. "[And God] appeared [before Abraham]": *QG* 4.
6. "Exodus": *QE* 1–2 + *Spec.* 1.79–81, 131–61, 285–345; *Spec.* 3.1–7 + *Decal.* + *Spec.* 3.8–64; *Samp.* + *Jona* + *Deo.*
7. "Contemplative": *Contempl.*[13]

18.2 Time and Place of Translation

There is no direct information on where, when, and why the CPhA was translated into Armenian. The earliest manuscript (with the Armenian version of *Prov.* and *Anim.*) is dated to 1223,[14] but the traces of the knowledge of the CPhA lead to the earliest works of Armenian literature.

Usually, the date of emergence of the CPhA was associated with the appearance of the Armenian Hellenizing translations in general. It is believed that Philo was one of the first, if not the first author, to be translated with the preservation of the Greek syntax and tracing of words' morphology. Yakob Manandean, who elaborated the theory of a "Hellenophile School" and divided its activities into three sequential periods, dated its first period to the first half of the sixth century.[15] Abraham Terian does not accept this periodization and is of the opinion, following N. Akinean's view,[16] that the school

---

[12] Hypothesis B, 53. The texts of the hypotheses to CPhA are published in O. Vardazaryan, "The 'Causes' to the Writings by Philo: Texts and Studies," *Proceedings of the "V. Brusov" Erevan State University of Linguistics, Social Studies* 3 (2005): 185–233 (in Armenian).

[13] Hypothesis A, 25–27, indicates that another order is possible: items 1, 3, 4, and then 2 + 5, with the obvious intention of reading QG as a single book. Nevertheless, in further presentation, characterizing separately each of the seven units of the corpus, the author of this "cause" adheres to the first scheme. Anonymous B and David Kobairetsi adhere to the same order in the presentation of units, although when listing the mentioned "writings" they can sometimes change their places. As for the "Cause to Philo," here the first "writing" is described before the seventh—perhaps due to some mechanical damage to the text (cf. M. E. Shirinian, "Philo and the Book of Causes by Grigor Abasean," in *Studies on the Ancient Armenian Version of Philo's Works*, ed. Sara Mancini Lombardi and Paola Pontani, Studies in Philo of Alexandria 6 [Leiden: Brill, 2011], 175, n. 74; and G. E. Sterling, "Philo of Alexandria," in *A Guide to Early Jewish Texts and Traditions in Christian Transmission*, ed. A. Kulik et al. [Oxford: Oxford University Press, 2019], 313).

[14] MS M 2101. A fragment of *QG* (Philo, 1826, 109–13, with lacunae) has been preserved on parchment endleaves (probably eleventh–twelfth century) in MS M 6353 (fifteenth century). Other early fragments are unknown. For the abbreviation of the collections of Armenian manuscripts, see https://sites.uclouvain.be/aiea/wp-content/uploads/2021/07/10_List-of-acronyms.pdf.

[15] *The Hellenizing School and the Periods of its Development* (Vienna: Mekhitharists' Press, 1928), 202, 208 (in Armenian).

[16] First formulated in N. Akinean, "Hellenists' School (572–603)," *Handēs Amsōreay (Monthly Magazine), Zeitschrift für Armenische Philologie* 5–6 (1932), 284–92 (in Armenian). This theory is followed by most Western scholars: H. Lewy, *The Pseudo-Philonic De Jona*, Vol. I: *The Armenian Text with a Critical Introduction*, Studies

was active between 570 and 730 in Constantinople within the context of the Byzantine schools.[17] Another date of the translations is advocated by Manuk Abeghyan,[18] Gevorg Jahukyan,[19] and Sen Arevshatyan; the last author places the first period of Hellenizing translations between the 450s and the early 480s.[20] On the basis of several neologisms created in Philo's version and used by Lazar Pʻarpetsʻi in the late fifth century, Gohar Muradyan states the dating to the second half of the same century is more probable.[21]

The localization of the Armenian translation school in Constantinople as suggested by Abraham Terian and other scholars raises many questions. First, there is no evidence of it either in Armenian or in external sources; second, the contacts of Armenians with the Greek intellectual tradition, accepted by Greek Christendom, could take place not only in the capital of the empire, but also in many other places, and much earlier than the sixth century; for example, in the cities of Armenia Minor, in Cappadocian Caesarea, in Antioch, and, in particular, in Jerusalem, with which the Armenian Church has been strongly associated, and in the Holy Land in general.[22] At any rate, this is a topic for a separate study. The only thing that can be assumed with great caution is that the translator of Philo came from the northeastern regions of Greater Armenia, since the later Armenian scholiasts of the twelfth–thirteenth centuries recognize "Albanian" glosses in the text—unquestionably Armenian words characteristic of the dialects of the Armenian principalities of Artsakh and Utik (and possibly of the language of some Armenian communities on the left bank of the Kura River).[23]

18.3 Quotations by Early Authors

The first list of the medieval Armenian authors familiar with Philo was composed by the first editor of Armenian Philo, Yovhannēs Mkrtichʻ Awgerean (Latin name Johannes Baptista Aucher).[24] No other general survey of the reception of the CPhA in Armenian

---

and Documents 7 (London: Christophers, 1936), 9; F. Siegert, "Der Armenische Philo. Textbestand. Editionen. Forschungsgeschichte," *ZKG* 100.3 (1989): 353–69; D. T. Runia, "Philo in Byzantium: An Exploration," *VC* 70 (2016): 266.

[17] A. Terian, "The Hellenizing School," 183; A. Terian, *Philonis Alexandrini De Animalibus: The Armenian Text with an Introduction, Translation and Commentary*, Studies in Hellenistic Judaism, Supplement to Studia Philonica 1 (Chico: Scholars Press, 1981), 7; A. Terian, "Armenian Philonic Corpus," in *A Guide to Early Jewish Texts and Traditions in Christian Transmission*, 318.

[18] *History of Old Armenian Literature*, Vol. 1: *Collected Writings* 3 (Erevan: Academy of Science of ArmSSR, 1968), 118–19, 647–52 (in Armenian).

[19] *Grammatical and Orthographical Works in Ancient and Medieval Armenia* (Erevan: Erevan State University, 1954), 52–53 (in Armenian).

[20] *The Formation of the Philosophical Science in Ancient Armenia (V–VI cc.)*, 2nd edn (Erevan: National Academy of Sciences, 2016), 166–87 (in Russian).

[21] "On the Date of Two Sources of Movsēs Khorenatsʻi," *Historico-Philological Journal of the Armenian Academy* 4 (1990): 94–104 (in Armenian).

[22] Y. Tchekhanovets, *The Caucasian Archaeology of the Holy Land: Armenian, Georgian and Albanian Communities between the Fourth and Eleventh Centuries CE*, HdO 1.123 (Leiden: Brill, 2018), esp. 19, 25–32.

[23] *Aghvank* is an Armenian designation for the Caucasian Albania. See also O. Vardazaryan, "An Application of the Dionysian *Ars* in Armenian Medieval Scholiography," *REArm* 39 (2020): 82.

[24] Philo, 1822, Praefatio, III–VI.

literature exists, but many studies have appeared touching upon the influence of this or that unit of the corpus on particular Armenian texts. Our main goal is to collect and systematize those attestations.

Philo's influence can be seen in the works of the first Armenian historians, traditionally dated to the fifth century, Eghishē,[25] Lazar P'arpets'i, and Movsēs Khorenats'i. The date of Lazar P'arpets'i's *History of Armenia* and his letter to his patron Vahan Mamikonean has never been disputed; it is late fifth to early sixth century. He used words not characteristic of Classical Armenian (eighteen in total); these are neologisms calqued from Greek by the Armenian translator of Philo, which he knew partly immediately from the CPhA, partly through the mediation of the half-translated collection of rhetorical exercises, the *Book of Chreia*.[26] This is a quite reliable terminus ante quem, at least for the translation of *Leg.*, *Abr.*, *Decal.*, *QG*, *QE*, *Anim.*, and the Pseudo-Philonic *De Sampsone*. But probably this dating could be moved back several decades.

The point is that Eghishē's work *On Vardan and the Armenian War* dedicated to the rebellion of the Armenians against the Persian authorities, as a response to the forced conversion of Christians into Mazdeism in the days of Yazdegerd II, is traditionally dated shortly after this event which took place in 451. The author presents himself as an immediate participant and witness, whereas Lazar P'arpets'i in his *History* recounting the same period has probably used this work, although for unknown reasons he is silent about its author.[27] Eghishē's text is rich in Philonic reminiscences; some were pointed out already by Aucher.[28] Later scholars showed many other parallels, also in Eghishē's theological works.[29] But these are not direct quotations, so it is not clear whether Eghishē used the ready-made Armenian version of the CPhA, or read Philo in Greek.[30]

The *History of Armenia* by Movsēs Khorenats'i is unfortunately not a very reliable instrument for dating Philo's translations, since his traditional date, the 470s, is still debated by scholars who have moved him to the fifth, eighth, or ninth centuries.[31] Just like Eghishē, Movsēs Khorenats'i is abundant in citing Philo without mentioning him by name:[32] they both weave Philonic phrases or whole passages they like into their

---

[25] There are several variants of transcription of the name. I prefer this, but Elisaeus and Elishe is also possible.
[26] G. Muradyan, "On the Date of Two Sources of Movsēs Khorenats'i," 102–4.
[27] Robert Thomson, who summarized the previous views, was sure that he could not have lived earlier than the sixth century; see Elishe, *History of Vardan and the Armenian War*, translation and commentary by R. W. Thomson (Cambridge, MA: Harvard University Press, 1982), 29.
[28] Philo, 1822, Praefatio, IV–V.
[29] B. Kiwleserean, *Eghishē, a Critical Study* (Vienna: Mkitarists' Press, 1909), 151–65; L. Khachikyan, *Commentary on Genesis by Eghishē*, ed. L. Ter-Petrosyan (Erewan: Zvart'nots', 1992), 124–36; H. Keoseyan, "Some Sources of the Sermons by *Eghishē*," *Historical-Philological Journal* 4 (1988): 108–12; G. Uluhogean, "'Guidance for Hermits' by Eghishē and Its Interrelations with Surrounding Culture (Endeavor of Interpretation)," in *Armenia and Christian Orient* (Erewan: "Gitutiun" Publishing House of NAS RA, 2000), 341–46.
[30] Eghishē, *History of Vardanides*, trans. into Modern Armenian by E. Ter-Minasyan (Erewan: Armenian State Press, 1946), Introduction, 25–26.
[31] The views of earlier researchers are surveyed by R. W. Thomson: Moses Khorenatsi, *History of the Armenians*, new rev. edn of the 1978 Harvard University Press edition, translation and commentary on literary sources by R. W. Thomson (Ann Arbor: Caravan Books, 2006).
[32] Philo's influence on Movsēs Khorenats'i was presented in detail by R. W. Thomson (see previous note).

own historical narrative, sometimes not even caring about their original meaning in the Philo text.

Mambrē the Lector (Vertsanogh) has no reliable dating (traditionally from the mid- to the end of the fifth century, "critically" to 576–77);[33] according to a legend, he was the younger brother of Movsēs Khorenats'i. He is credited with five homilies, a philosophical *Questions and Answers* (a fictitious dialogue with David the Invincible), and a single fragment of the *Commentary on Grammar* by Dionysius Thrax. An unmarked quotation in his *Sermon on the Resurrection of Lazarus* certainly refers not to the Greek text of *Contempl.* 45, but to its Armenian version, since they diverge from each another:[34] "Had they been put to sleep by mandrakes, or were they benumbed from unmixed wine?"[35]

Contempl. 45 in Armenian[36]	*Contempl.* 45 in Greek
After drinking unmixed wine, they doze off, get wet (?) <and> benumbed like from a mandrake.	Others again of the drinking companions, who seem to be more moderate, burp out after drinking of undiluted wine, as if it were mandrake.

The first Armenian author who directly mentions Philo by name is Anania Shirakats'i (seventh century),[37] the great man of erudition who worked in the fields of mathematics, cosmology, geography, and the calendar. According to Anania while discussing the substance of heaven, some ecclesiastical authors agree with "exoterics," while others, following Philo, believe that heaven is "a mind, and not something material"[38] (cf. *Leg.* 1.1 = Philo, 1892, 105). Obviously, he perceived Philo not as a church author, but also not as a representative of the "external" pagan tradition. The context does not allow one to determine whether Philo, in Anania's view, belonged to the circle of "inner" authors, or to certain "neutrals," since the reference is not commented on in any way.

Anania refers to Philo again in his treatise "On the Heavenly Bodies." Rejecting the superstition which ascribes to sorcerers the ability to bring the stars and the moon down from heaven (for it is not given to humans to bring down to earth what God has established), he pursues the example of Abraham, who, having gained experience in astronomy, came himself to realize the fallacy of human notions, to the idea of the perishability of luminaries and to the reverence of God who moves them. "Philo tells us about this (cf. *QG* 3.1 and *Abr.* 69–71), and what he said is true, because if you examine, you will see that Holy Scripture also means this."[39]

---

[33] Terian, "The Hellenizing School," 178.
[34] Cf. Terian, "The Hellenizing School," 177.
[35] *ACIA*, vol. 1, 1097:48.
[36] Philo, 1892, 18.
[37] Terian, "The Hellenizing School," 177.
[38] "On the Heaven," in *ACIA*, vol. 4, 715:59–60.
[39] "On the Heaven," *ACIA*, vol. 4, 725:48.

Finally, Anania refers to Philo (*QE* 1.9) to confirm that the calculation of the days for the celebration of Passover among the Jews was based on the lunar calendar, and the commandment to keep the Passover lamb until the fourteenth day refers to the full moon in the lunar month.[40]

From that moment on, the number of direct references to Philo by Armenian authors begins to increase continuously.

Step'anos Siwnets'i (late seventh to mid-eighth century), a well-known author and religious figure, refers to the beginning of *QG* 1.12 in his commentary on Genesis,[41] namely to Philo's account of the rivers Tigris and Euphrates. They are said to flow from the Armenian mountains, but the Garden of Eden and the sources of the other two rivers of Paradise are not mentioned—so one can think that Eden is located somewhere else, and the four rivers are fed by a large underground stream, which exits in different places. Step'anos characterizes such an interpretation according to 2 Cor 3:6 as "Jewish adherence to the letter" and says "to examine the power of the scripture." It is curious, however, that he also takes over the allegorical interpretation according to the "life-giving spirit" (the common source in Eden is the power of divine wisdom, the four rivers flowing from Eden are the four virtues) again from Philo, without mentioning him by name.[42]

The absence of a name in this context is remarkable, because, as it turns out in the "Brief Interpretation of the Four Evangelists" by the same Step'anos, Philo is not an unquestionable authority for his audience: "And Philo the Hebrew, *if you accept this man*, in his interpretation of the Mosaic scripture said that the 'darkness over the abyss' is outside of the whole world; look, it means that the wicked of the world are being expelled from the whole world, and not only from the paradise of the Lord."[43] The oddity of this reference (Philo has nothing of the kind) may be explained perhaps as a specific transformation of Philo's exegesis of the tree of the knowledge of good and evil, which is actually located in the Garden of Eden, but potentially *outside it* (*Leg.* 1.56–62).

The treatise *Lord Yovhannēs the Lector's Preliminary Summary of the History of These Words*, attributed to Catholicos Yovhannēs III Odznets'i (Catholicos in 717–28),[44] contains an apology for the Armenian annual cycle of biblical readings, which is adopted by the Armenian Church.[45] This is probably one of the many introductions to

---

[40] "What Anania the Calculator Said about the Passover of the Lord," *AClA*, vol. 4, 677.

[41] Two fragments from MS M4794 published in the *AClA*, vol. 6, 105–13, are ascribed to Step'anos by the editor Y. K'eoseyean. In his recent publication of three sections (1, 2.1, and 2.2) of the same work (2.1 coincides with K'eoseyean's second fragment, pp. 107–13), Michael Stone agrees with him that it is indeed an old commentary, but he is skeptical about its attribution to Step'anos; see *The Genesis Commentary by Step'anos of Siwnik' (Dub.)*, edition, translation, and comments by M. E. Stone, with additional annotations by Sh. Efrati, CSCO 695 = Scriptores armeniaci 32 (Leuven: Peeters, 2021), 6–8. Stone has pointed to parallels between this text with QG: "the name Ishmael which is 'hearing of God'" (p. 42, *QG* 4.32), also some exegeses in p. 48, *QG* 4.2, 10; p. 50, *QG* 4.27; p. 52, *QG* 3.43, 127; p. 54, *QG* 3.47; p. 84, *QG* 4.42, 51; p. 92, *QG* 4.86; p. 100, *QG* 4.154.

[42] The fragment from MS M4794 is published in *AClA*, vol. 6, 105–6.

[43] *AClA*, vol. 6, 214:16.

[44] *AClA*, vol. 7, 156–57.

[45] Y. K'eoseyean, "Yovhan Odznets'i and His <Literary> Heritage," *AClA*, vol. 7, 17 n. 12. The assumption that this text could serve as a preface to the *Armenian Book of Canons* by the same Yovhannēs seems less probable (cf. A. Yakobean, "The Newly Discovered [Preamble to the] Festal Calendar: *Lord Yovhannēs the Lector's*

the Armenian *Typicon*, the Jerusalem origin of which, indeed, is confirmed by modern research.[46] According to Yovhannēs, the Armenian ecclesiastical usage goes back to the ancient community of Jerusalem, which was established by James, the brother of the Lord. Philo's name is included among a number of "historians," on whom the author relied in his judgments. Later, in the "cause" of the thirteenth century, this motif will be elaborated: it is Philo's sermon on the Therapeutae that would prove to be evidence of the Christian community of James and its ecclesiastical institutions.[47] It is possible that the passage of Yovhannēs is the earliest vestige of such an interpretation of Philo's treatise in Armenian literature.[48]

Philo had a notable influence on the Armenian historian T'ovmas Artsruni (ninth–tenth centuries), author of *The History of the House of Artsruni*.[49] In his attitude to the philosopher, he shares the enthusiasm of Eusebius and does not avoid direct references to Philo. He inserts Philo's exegeses, mostly borrowed from *QG* ("the serpent is the worst animal," "the serpent is a symbol of voluptuousness," a number of etymologies, etc.) mainly into the introductory part of the book, where he traces the history of the Artsruni royal family back to the time of the biblical Patriarchs. It is perhaps particularly noteworthy how T'ovmas, without mentioning the author, transforms the original Philonic interpretation of the "cultivation" of the Garden of Eden (Gen 2:15; *QG* 1.14) in terms of the development of religious virtues,[50] and also attributes to Philo the apocryphal story of Shem who carried Adam's bones to Noah's ark.[51]

A small catena to the book of Genesis contains abridged and paraphrased excerpts from *QG* in the oldest Armenian paper manuscript M2679, 981 AD (213v–231v). The catena is called *From some [things] said by Philo*,[52] although his name (unlike other sources—Ephraim, Severian, John Chrysostom, etc.) is not mentioned in the text itself. The scribe and compiler of the manuscript, the priest David, could be considered as the author of the catena.

In the tenth–eleventh centuries Philo is referred to by Timotheos Vardapet, the compiler of the *Brief Preface to the Genesis*. The text of this commentary exists in several

---

Preliminary Summary of the History of These Words," Handēs Amsōreay, Zeitschrift für Armenische Philologie (Vienna: Mechitarist Order, 2006) (in Armenian), 91–99.

[46] A. Renoux, *Le codex arménien Jérusalem 121*, Vol. I: *Introduction aux origins de la Liturgie Hiérosolymitaine: lumières Nouvelles*, Patrologia Orientalis 35 (Brepols: Turnhout, 1969); Vol. II: *Édition compare du texte et de deux autres manuscrits. Introduction, textes, traduction et notes*, Patrologia Orientalis 36 (Brepols: Turnhout, 1971); Vol. III: *Le Lectionnaire de Jérusalem en Arménie: Le Čašoc'*. Vol. I: *Introduction et liste des manuscrits*, Patrologia Orientalis 44 (Brepols: Turnhout, 1989).

[47] "Beginning and Cause of the Lections, saying by Yakob," in O. Vardazaryan, *Philo the Alexandrian in Perception of Armenian Middle Ages* (Erewan: "Lusabats'" Publishing House, 2006), 177–79. This Yakob must be Yakob Klayets'i (Catholicos 1268–86).

[48] For more details, see O. Vardazaryan, "The 'Armenian Philo': A Remnant of an Unknown Tradition," in *Studies on the Ancient Armenian Version of Philo's Works*, ed. Sara Mancini Lombardi and Paola Pontani, Studies in Philo of Alexandria 6 (Leiden: Brill, 2011), 195–98.

[49] For a detailed list of allusions, reminiscences, and direct quotations, see Thomas Artsruni, *History of the House of the Artsrunik*, translation and commentary by R. W. Thomson (Detroit: Wayne State University Press, 1985).

[50] *ACIA*, vol. 11, 1:57.40.

[51] *ACIA*, vol. 11, 1:63.103.

[52] *ACIA*, vol. 10, 921–51, esp. 922–24, 926–32.

versions, some of which have not yet been published. At the end of the version contained in the M1981 manuscript, the Philonic passages *QG* 1.1–3 and 12–13 are used.[53]

The author Tiran or Tiranun, who lived around the same time, refers to Philo's *QG* 1.32[54] in his commentary on certain biblical passages, *Answers to the Questions of the Kings of Aghvank*.[55]

A curious reference to Philo is found in the corpus of letters of Grigor Magistros (c.990–1058), an Armenian and Byzantine military leader, diplomat, poet, translator, a man of universal knowledge, including an excellent command of Greek; he was fond of learned Greek literature and even imitated it. The dogmatic "Letter to Emir Abrehim,"[56] an unknown Muslim ruler whose mother was an Armenian from a noble family, and who was interested in questions of the Christian faith, contains a discourse already familiar to us (see Shirakats'i), about Abraham, who has ascended from astronomy to the knowledge of God, as well as the following passage:[57] "For Moses said: 'Whoso sheddeth man's blood, by man shall his blood be shed: for in the image of God made he man (Gen 9:6).' Look, why he did not say 'made in my image' but 'in the image of God'? This you will learn from Philo (for he is a Jew and not a Christian), how he speaks of the Word of God."

It is noteworthy that Magistros simply refers his addressee to the text of Philo, which was evidently publicly available in the Armenian scholarly community of that time, and is even sure that Abrehim will easily find the right place (*QG* 2.62), in which Philo speaks of the Logos as "the second God." Even more interesting is that the structure of this reference is very similar to the one used by Isidore of Pelusium to the same text of Philo, in a letter to a certain Paul (*Ep.* 2.143 [= *Ep.* 643 Évieux], 3–20): Philo, although a zealous Jew, cannot resist the power of truth contained in the Old Testament, and is forced to admit that the corresponding biblical verse refers to the Logos as the "second god," that is, the second person of the Trinity.[58] It is possible of course that Magistros, by virtue of his erudition, was familiar with the letters of Isidore and took over his method of argumentation, although in a completely different historical context.

The scholar and ecclesiastical figure of the end of the tenth to the early eleventh centuries, Yovhannēs Taronets'i Kozeṙn, in the preamble of his commentary on the book of Genesis tries to find at least some link between Philo and Paul:[59] "And so, when Christ entered the city of Hierapolis, founded by Moses, the idols that stood on the city wall collapsed and scattered. And the ambassadors who came there from India, and *the disciples of Philo* at that moment were there, and went to Athens and told <about this>. And they [i.e. the Athenians] admired and wondered who this God is, who is stronger

---

[53] *AClA*, vol. 10, 919–20.
[54] *AClA*, vol. 10, 961.37.
[55] See n. 23 above.
[56] Letter 9(70), "To Emir Abrehim On the Faith by Grigor son of Vasak," *AClA*, vol. 16, 213:14.
[57] *AClA*, vol. 16, 226:7.
[58] See for details D. T. Runia, "Philo in Five Letters of Isidore of Pelusium," in D. T. Runia, *Philo and the Church Fathers. A Collection of Papers*, VCSup 32 (Leiden: Brill, 1995), 126–43, 159, 161, 164.
[59] See O. Vardazaryan, "The 'Armenian Philo': A Remnant of an Unknown Tradition," 198–99.

than all idols. And so they set up an altar to the 'unknown god,' saying that if he does not do good, then 'at least' he will avert trouble (cf. Acts 17:13)."[60]

Pōghos Tarōnats'i († 1123) in a polemical letter tries to justify the use of unleavened bread in the Eucharist of the Armenian Church, also connecting Philo with Paul: "Paul's disciple Philo says in the commentary on *Exodus*: 'eat unleavened bread for seven days'. Why didn't he prescribe leavened [bread]? He said that it symbolizes the bubbling of those puffed-up and arrogant" (cf. QE 1.15).[61]

18.4 Monastic Schools where Philo's Works Were Copied, Studied, and Commented

The majority of the manuscripts containing the whole CPhA or a part of it are dated to the thirteenth–fourteenth centuries. Of twenty-five complete manuscripts seven were copied comparatively late, in the seventeenth to nineteenth centuries; five are copies of known protographs of the thirteenth and fourteenth centuries.[62] Even if one takes into consideration inevitable losses, such figures bear witness to the fact that Philo's works were not as popular as, for example, the writings of the Cappadocian fathers or John Chrysostom; Philo's readership was much more restricted. Who were these readers?

Wherever names are preserved in the colophons, these are renowned doctors of the Church, the *vardapets*: the monks whose duty was the interpretation of the Bible (which also supposed the study both of patristic and "external" books), the instruction of clerics and especially of the future *vardapets* themselves, as well as legislatory and judicial functions within the framework of canonical law.[63] To this list of the undoubted readers of the CPhA—the commissioners and scribes of the manuscripts—we have to add those who wrote various kinds of commentaries on it. These too are *vardapets*, the doctors of the church; the mainly paraphrastic scholia written by them, introductions to the scholia (the so-called "causes," i.e. hypotheses), as well as the glossaries collected from the scholia—all this is the product of explanatory readings of authors included in school canon; such readings were intended to guide the disciples of particular monastic schools.

---

[60] ACIA, vol. 16, 37–38.
[61] ACIA, vol. 17, 450; a similar passage is on pp. 584–85.
[62] See the detailed survey of manuscripts containing the CPhA in Terian, *Philonis Alexandrini De Animalibus*, 14–25; the same list, with some precisions, is found in Philo, *Alexander vel de ratione quam habere etiam bruta animalia (De animalibus) e versione armeniaca, Introduction, traduction et notes par A. Terian*, PAPM 36 (Paris: Cerf, 1988), 29–36. See also O. Vardazaryan, "Colophons on the Manuscript Tradition of 'Armenian Philo," in *Levon Khachikian 9. Proceedings of the International Conference dedicated to the 90th Anniversary of the Founder-director of the Matenadaran (October 9–11, 2008)* (Erevan: Nayiri, 2010) (in Armenian), 261–72.
[63] On the institution of *vardapets* and history of monastic schools in Armenia, see L. Melikset-Bek, *Armenian Vardapets of the Northern Regions and Their Identity* (Holy Etchmiadzin: Publishing House of Mother See of Holy Etchmiadzin, 2016); G. Amadouni, "Le role historique des Hiéromoines arméniens," OCA 153 (1958): 279–306, esp. 295–96; S. La Porta, "Monasticism and the Construction of the Armenian Intellectual Tradition," in *Monasticism in Eastern Europe and the Former Soviet Republics*, ed. I. A. Murzaku (London and New York: Routledge, 2015), 339–42.

So we may extend the audience of the CPhA to the school in which this or that *vardapet* taught, or even to a sequential series of these schools. The scholarchs-*vardapets* usually were succeeded by their closest disciples; even if a school founded in this or that monastery by force of circumstances changed its location, the memory of the succession was preserved. Such "school genealogies" are attested in many manuscripts.[64] Sometimes they go back to remote, even legendary antiquity, but of interest to us is the part of them that is well documented and is immediately related to the Philonic tradition.

The Narek school was located in the monastery of Narek near the southern shore of Lake Van. It was founded and flourished in the tenth century. The school produced three prominent authors: Khosrov Andzewats'i (c.902–64), Anania Narekats'i († late tenth century), and Khosrov's son, Anania's disciple, the renowned poet Grigor Narekats'i (951–1003), declared Doctor of the Church in 2015.

In *An Explanation of Numbers* (formerly ascribed to Anania Shirakats'i),[65] Anania interpreted the number symbolism in the Bible, extensively quoting Philo, both with and without references.[66] Three more references to Philo are found in a large work by the same author—*The Root of Faith: Ananias the Armenian Vardapet, The resolution of the dispute with the dyophysites, which confessed inconsistently with the right faith, introducing duality into a single nature, that is, God the Word and the man Jesus Christ* (finished in 983 or 987).[67] The first reference is a paraphrased quotation on the perfection of the triad (*QG* 4.30), included in the discourse on the Trinity; the second is made in a narration about a serpent-seducer—in fact, in a variation of the Philo allegory "serpent = pleasure" (*QG* 1.48); finally, in the chapter "To the castrated," in the expression "those who of their own accord change the image of nature's creation, *defile something that should not be defiled*," Ananias uses a phrase from *QG* 4.99.

Grigor Narekats'i is author of the famous monumental poem *Book of Lamentations*. The influence of the CPhA on the poem still needs study,[68] but according to Abraham Terian, some Philonic exegeses, especially those concerning the divine Logos, probably served as "archetypes" (we would say: "constructive elements") for images in Grigor's other poetic works.[69]

---

[64] N. Akinean, "Die theologische Schule von Bitlis," *Handes Amsorya, Zeitschrift für Armenische Philologie* (Vienna: Mechitarist Order, 1951), 3–7 (in Armenian), cols 173–83: §2 "The order of *vardapets*" (cols 178–81).
[65] *ACIA*, vol. 10, 440–55.
[66] e.g. *ACIA*, vol. 10, 440:6 = *Leg.* 1.3; 454:180 = *QG* 4.23.
[67] Parts of this work have been preserved in the treatise of the author of the eleventh century, Anania Sanahnets'i, "Objections to the dyophysites" (Hr. Tamrazyan, Anania Narekats'i's Dogmatic Treatise "The Root of Faith," *ACIA*, vol. 10, 456).
[68] In his recent translation of the poem, Abraham Terian has not pointed to such influence; see his *From the Depths of the Heart: Annotated Translation of the Prayers of St. Gregory of Narek* (Collegeville, MN: Liturgical Press Academic, 2021).
[69] A. Terian, "Philonic Precursors of Certain Images in St. Gregory of Narek," *Bulletin of Matenadaran* 26 (2018): 14–29 (in Armenian); A. Terian, "Armenian Philonic Corpus," 322–26. For the text, see A. Terian, *The Festal Works of St. Gregory of Narek: Annotated Translation of the Odes, Litanies, and Encomia* (Collegeville, MN: Liturgical Press, 2016).

18.4.1 Monasteries Haghpat and Sanahin

Anania Sanahnets'i or Haghpatets'i (†1070s) penned several sermons and commentaries, including the *Commentary on the Gospel of Matthew*, of which only the bipartite introduction and commentary on the first seven chapters of this Gospel have been preserved. The second part of the introduction, the preamble to the commentary proper begins with a paraphrase of *Prov.* 1.6–7 (= Philo, 1822, 4–5) as a substantiation of divine providence in relation to the economy of the Logos:

> The greatest of philosophers Philo accepted [the idea] of the incomprehensible wisdom of God's plan not only by his own mind, but also by other ancient teachers who were full of the Spirit. They said that God did not start the world in the past, during the creation of the world, but He is always making it most beautiful. For, they said, the Godhead ought not to be ever inactive, because this is something of idleness and passivity. But they said that God as a Creator made everything without beginning, always thinking to adorn it .... For God's will does not occur to anything afterwards, since His will is always with Him; His natural movements never run short, and He will always make knowingly. And for sensible beings, they said, he laid the foundation so that the sensible world should serve as a pointer to the intelligible world, for this [sensible] world should serve as a kind of image, for about [this world] they say that it is the sense-perceptible pointer of God's intelligible [world]. From which it is clear that everything can be seen without beginning in the preliminary knowledge that God has .... Therefore, in the preliminary knowledge of God, everything is revealed in types and classes (*lit.* orderings), and even more so—the sacrament of the economy of the Word.[70]

In the *Sermon on John the Baptist* he writes:[71]

> [Near Mount Sinai] the Word took shape in the form of fire; first it was seen to the eyes as flame, then it was heard to the ears, as Philo says: "The words of God are not speech, but a visible object." (cf. *Decal.* 47)

Yovhannēs Sarkawag[72] (1045–1129), a prominent *vardapet*, mathematician and specialist in calendar, theologian and poet, the scholarch of the school of Ani, then of Haghpat monastery, read Philo with his students, but, according to later evidence,[73] just for the sake of the numerological passages contained in Philo's texts. From these

---

[70] *ACIA*, vol. 17:108–12.
[71] *ACIA*, vol. 17: 233.
[72] *Sarkawag* in Armenian means "deacon."
[73] *The Declamation on the Blessed Man of God, Sarkawag, His Life and Death, and on the Other Saints of the Same Epoch*, in A. G. Abrahamyan, *The Works by Yovhannēs the Philosopher* (Erevan: Erevan State University Press, 1956), 121.

readings little has survived: tables of odd/even and polygonal numbers, and cubes, compiled by Yovhannēs as a commentary on the fragment about numbers in the preamble to the *Decal.* and *QG* 2.5.[74] An attempt to attribute several scholia to Sarkawag[75] is most likely unfounded,[76] but it is possible that in these texts debris of his works could have been preserved.

His disciples were Sargis Kund (twelfth century) and Samuēl Anetsʻi (1105–85). The latter repeats the passage from Eusebius of Caesarea's *Chronicle* concerning the year 35: "James, the brother of our Lord Jesus Christ accepted from the Apostles the ordination as the bishop of the residents of Jerusalem. Philo Alexandrinus was acknowledged as a learned man."[77]

Sargis Kund knows about Philo from Eusebius of Caesarea's *Church History* (Eusebius, *Hist. eccl.* 2.5). Arguing that perfect persons do not grumble when they are hated and oppressed, he adds: "As Philo said about Gaius, king of Rome: 'With words he oppressed us and he hates us, but our God will eventually be reconciled with us.'"[78]

David Kʻobayretsʻi (*c.*1150–after 1207), graduate and *vardapet* of the same Haghpat, wrote one of the *hypotheses* (lit. "causes") on the CPhA.

Something should be said about the "Book of Causes" by Grigor Abasyan (*c.*1180–*c.*1240). "Causes," i.e. hypotheses dedicated to works of different authors can be found separately in codices of variegated content, but from around the thirteenth century onward, Armenian doctors began to collect them in anthologies. The most famous collection of such prefaces might have been compiled by Grigor Abasyan, abbot of Sanahin monastery, then hieromonk of Makaravank since 1237 at least.[79] The collection came in two copies—early (M1879, thirteenth century) and very late and indirect (V47, nineteenth century; copied from an unpreserved copy of 1725, an eventual apograph of the M1879). Apart from these two copies, no other collection of "causes" contains any mention of Grigor Abasyan.[80]

The title of the collection, "*The Book of Causes of Lengthy and Subtle Writings Taken from the Holy Fathers and Teachers (Vardapets) and brought together through the efforts of the great Head of Rabbunis, Grigor son of Abas*," was added to the vignette of the

---

[74] G. B. Petrosyan, *Mathematics in Armenia in Ancient and Middle Ages* (Erevan, Erevan State University Press, 1959), 150–55 (in Armenian); Abrahamyan, *The Works by Yovhannēs the Philosopher*, 148–57 (in Armenian); J. Einatean, "Yovhannēs Sarkawag's Treatise On Polygonal Numbers," *Bulletin of Matenadaran* 23 (2016): 260–90 (in Armenian).

[75] G. Grigoryan, "The Armenian Commentaries to Philo's Works," *Bulletin of Matenadaran* 5 (1960): 95–110.

[76] Pʻ. Antʻapyan, "On the Text of the 'Scholia to the Philo's Seven Writings' by Yovhannēs Sarkawag," *Historical-Philological Journal* 1 (1983): 177–90.

[77] Samuel Anetsʻi and Continuators, *The Chronicle from Adam to 1776*, critical text, study, and commentary by K. Matevosyan (Erevan: Nayiri, 2014), 118; cf. Eusebii Pamphili Caesariensis episcopi, *Chronicon bipartitum, nunc primum ex armeniaco textu in latinum conversum, adnotationibus auctum, graecis fragmentis exornatum*, opera P. Jo. Baptistae Aucher Ancyrani, pars II (Venice: typis coenobii armenorum in insula S. Lazari, 1818), 266–67: "Jerosolymitarum I. Episcopus ab Apostolis ordinationem suscipit, Jacobus Frater Domini nostri Jesu Christi. Philo Alexandrinus vir eruditissimus agnoscebatur."

[78] Sargis Kund, *Commentary on the Catholic Epistles (Attributed to Athanasios of Alexandria)*, ed. Y. Kʻeoseyean and G. Tēr-Vardanean, Commentaries on the New Testament 17 (Vagharshapat: Holy See of Edjmiadzin, 2003), 205.

[79] M. E. Shirinyan and G. Khachatryan, "Book of Causes," *Ashtanak: Armenological Periodical* 4 (2011): 24.

[80] J3325, attributed by the scholars to the same group (Shirinyan and Khachatryan, "Book of Causes," 19), actually contains the usual collection of "causes" that does not have any signs of special dependence on M1879.

first page of the codex M1879, by the hand of the influential cleric and poet Khachʻatur Kecharetsʼi (c.1260–1331), whose name and sporadic notes are found throughout the manuscript. These circumstances, as well as the presence of texts most likely created after Grigor's death,[81] make us cautious about assigning Grigor as the compiler of the collection, and even more so about thinking that he could be the author of any articles included in it. The complex of "Philonic" hypotheses contained in the "Book of Causes" (Anonymous B, the "summary cause" of David Kobayretsi and the hypothesis for *Prov.* compiled by Mkhitʻar Gosh), in this very combination, are also found in other, less-known collections of "causes" that have nothing to do with Grigor Abasyan; collation of the texts shows that M1879 and its copy do not contain the best text (this is especially true of Mkhitʻar Gosh's "cause").[82]

18.4.2 Succession of Nor Getik

Mkhitʻar Gosh (1130–1213), one of the most authoritative vardapets of his era, an active church and political figure, known primarily as the compiler of the *Lawcode*, was a head of the school in the monastery of Getik and founder of the monastery and the school of Nor (New) Getik. He is the author of the "cause" to *Prov.* and the most probable author of the earliest scholia to *Prov., Anim., Spec.* 1.285–345 ["On the Altar Supplies"], *Samp., Decal., Jona, Deo* in MS M1672 (thirteenth century).[83]

Acquaintance with Philo is also reflected in Mkhitar's own works. In the preamble to his *Lawcode*, which had a serious impact on the formation of Armenian, and not only Armenian, legal culture, he relies on *Abr.* 5–6 in discussing the "natural" or "unwritten" law.[84] In the numerological passage at the end of the same preamble, treating, in particular, the number six,[85] he follows *QG* 3.38, 49, and other similar places. While composing the "Parables" or "Fables" he also used some motives drawn from Philo: for example, he constructs a dispute of wheat and gold (Parable 168), obviously under the influence of *Prov.* 2.18.[86] Finally, in his "Concise Commentary on Jeremiah," on Jer 9:24, Mkhitʻar remarks: "Herodotus[87] and Philo bear witness to circumcision of Egyptians,"[88] meaning *QG* 3.47 (male and female circumcision versus only male in scripture).[89]

---

[81] E.g. the "cause" of Yakob Klayeci (see above, n. 47).
[82] Cf. M. E. Shirinian, "Philo and the *Book of Causes* by Grigor Abasean," in *Studies on the Ancient Armenian Version of Philo's Works*, ed. Sara Mancini Lombardi and Paola Pontani, Studies in Philo of Alexandria 6 (Leiden: Brill, 2011), 155–89.
[83] Published by O. Vardazaryan, ed., "The 'Cause' and Scholion of Mkhitʻar Gosh," *ACIA*, vol. 20, 435–39 (introduction), 440–50 (text).
[84] *The Lawcode [Datastanagirkʻ] of Mxitʻar Goš*, translated with commentary and indices by R. W. Thomson, Dutch Studies in Armenian Language and Literature (Amsterdam and Atlanta, GA: Rodopi, 2000), 6:69.
[85] Thomson, *The Lawcode*, 74.
[86] For more details, see O. Vardazaryan, "The Parables of Mkhitʻar Gosh," *ACIA*, vol. 20, 15–41, esp. 35–36.
[87] Herodotus, *Hist.* 2.36–37, 104, but the Armenian source for this is unknown, since there is no evidence of Herodotus translated into Armenian.
[88] *ACIA*, vol. 19, 199.
[89] Cf. *The Genesis Commentary by Stepʻanos of Siwnikʻ* (Dub.), 54.

Vanakan Vardapet (1181–1251) was a disciple of Mkhit'ar Gosh, in the school of the monasteries Nor Getik, and founder of the monastery and the school of Khoranashat. Philo's influence on him has not yet been studied, but it is important not only in view of his position in the school genealogy, but also because one of the scholia on CPhA, the *Introduction to Philo*,[90] is stylistically close to Vanakan's unpublished *Questions and Answers*.

The scribe of the earliest manuscript containing the Armenian version of Philo (*Prov.* and *Anim.*), MS M2101 (dated to 1223), is Vanakan's disciple Step'anos Akht'amarts'i.

Vanakan's disciples were Vardan Arewelts'i (c.1198–1271) and Kirakos Gandzakets'i (c.1200–71). Vardapet Aṛak'el from the monastery Aṛak'elots' (of Apostles) in the province Kayen (northeastern part of historical Armenia, Artsakh), the commissioner of MS M5254 (1280), was probably another disciple of Vanakan.[91] Among other important texts, this miscellany contains one of the "causes" to the CPhA (Anonymous A).

Kirakos Gandzakets'i, speaking about Vanakan's doctrine of the Trinity, writes: "'Pay attention, the first prophet Moses says, be careful' (Deut 8:11). Philonios [sic!] too instructs: 'Learn according to the triad which in your body is soul, mind and word.'"[92] Probably this is an inaccurate reminiscence of Philo's *QG* 3.5 (the rational part of the soul is divided into mind and the uttered word).

Vardan Arewelts'i was a disciple of Mkhit'ar Gosh in Nor Getik, later continuing his education in the school of Vanakan Vardapet in the Khoranashat monastery. From 1235 to 1253 (with interruptions) he was the head of his own school in Kayen and the founder of many other schools in the same region. As a very active clerical and political figure, he had close connections with Hetum I's royal court of Cilicia and with Catholicos Constantine I Bardzrberdts'i, as well as with northern schools and *vardapets*. He was an extremely productive and erudite author, most of whose literary legacy has not yet been published. The manuscripts of his *Commentary on the Pentateuch* contain about twenty citations from Philo; his collection of homilies with biblical topics, which he composed for King Hetum II (*Zhghlank—Miscellany*)[93] contains some reminiscences of the CPhA. He could mention Philo simply as "the Hebrew," whereas Vardan usually does not avoid directly naming Philo as his source. This means that his readers did not need any explanation as to who "the Hebrew" was, just like in ancient Greece nobody had to explain that "the Poet" is Homer:

> The Hebrew says that God has two main potencies: one is creative, the other is royal. With the creative one He made all, and with the royal He takes care (cf. *Abr.* 121). With their help He said: "We will make." But we know well, [these are] the Son and the Holy Spirit (M2544, fol. 104v).

---

[90] O. Vardazaryan, "The Armenian Scholia to the Works of Philo of Alexandria," *Historical-Theological Journal* 185.1 (2005): 203–4.
[91] T. Minasyan, "Aṛak'el Vardapet (Arkhimandrite) and the Scriptorium of Deghdzut," *Bulletin of Matenadaran* 29 (2020): 298–308.
[92] Kirakos Gandzakets'i, *History of Armenia*, ed. K. Melik'-Ohanjanyan (Erevan: Academy of Science of ArmSSR, 1961), 339.
[93] We know this text from MS M 2544 (fourteenth century), 277 fols.

There are some other applications of Philo's exegeses in Vardan's *Miscellany*:

> And what did he say: there was not a man to till [the ground]. He had not yet started to till, but a spring went up from the earth and watered all the face of the earth. And how could one spring water all the face of the earth, not only because of the abundance of the soil, but of the unevenness of mountains and planes? Philo has said that the nature of waters is one; and he calls one spring all [the waters?] that water [lit. give drink to] the world (fol. 108r; cf. *QG* 1.3).

> Pheison is a sign of prudence, Geon of courage, Tigris of chastity, Euphrates of justice (112v; cf. *Leg.* 1.63; *QG* 1.12).

> And having placed the man in paradise, he says [that he did this] for two reasons, to dress it and to keep it. Dressing is digging pits, watering, and keeping is to guard it from beasts' (cf. *QG* 1.14).

In his sermons Vardan also resorts to Philo's interpretations, e.g. of the decad in *QG* 4.92 (Sermon "On the Decalogue")[94] or to *Abr.* 271, while reasoning on infantile adults ("On Solomon [Song 8:1–6]").[95]

Probably, to Vardan Arewelts'i also belongs the commentary to David the Invincible's "Encomium on the Theoleptic Holy Cross," in which Philo's thesis about the two virtues of trees—having many branches and fruitfulness (*QG* 1.9)—is included in the passage about the divine virtue of the Holy Cross.[96]

The *Explanation of Feasts* (Tōnapatchaṛ) is a collection of interpretations of the feasts of the Armenian liturgical calendar, the pericopes read on their occasions, and the circumstances of the creation of various texts. Written on the basis of the *Commentary on the Lectionary* by Grigoris Arsharuni (seventh to eighth century), it was repeatedly revised and supplemented until the thirteenth century, and has come down to us in a fairly large number of manuscripts. Only twelve units of one of its recensions, in which Vardan Arewelts'i took part, have been published so far.[97] Here we meet already familiar scenarios: the departure of the community founded by James the Righteous to Egypt ("And there, completing their lives with good deeds, they died; Philo tells about their lives; and the monks of Thebais descend from them")[98] and another endeavor to establish connection between Philo's disciples and the Athenian unknown god.[99] The textual borrowing in this part of the collection is restricted to only one instance: "Sages called Euphrates 'mother of fruits' ... while the philosopher Philo

---

[94] Vardan Arewelts'i, *Sermons & Panegyrics*, ed. Hakob Kyoseyan (Erevan: Erevan State University Publishing House, 2000), 41.
[95] Vardan Arewelts'i, *Sermons & Panegyrics*, 116.
[96] A. Melkonyan, "Newly Found Commentary on David the Invincible's *Barjrac'uc'ēk'* by Vardan Arewelts'i," *Bulletin of Matenadaran* 22 (2015): 390–401, esp. 397.
[97] A. Ohanjanyan, ed., *Collection Tōnapatchaṛ*, vol. 1 (Vagharshapat: Holy See of Edjmiadzin, 2016).
[98] Ohanjanyan, *Tōnapatchaṛ*, 277 (cf. *Lord Yovhannēs the Lector's Preliminary Summary of the History of These Words*).
[99] Ohanjanyan, *Tōnapatchaṛ*, 142 (cf. *Yovhannēs Taronets'i Kozeṛn*).

calls it a symbol of justice, which is the harmonizer of the other parts of virtue" (cf. *Leg.* 1.72; *QG* 1.12–13).[100]

Vardan Arewelts'i's disciple Yovhannēs Erznkats'i Pluz (c.1230–93) in his compilative commentary on the Dionysian *Art of Grammar* has an allusion to *QG* 1.14 and *Leg.* 1.43–47):[101]

> Paradise, in which he [Adam] was placed, was founded in such a way as to bring double benefits: both as the seat of the body, and as the eternal [existence] of the soul. Physically, he was happy to plant saplings and seedlings [lit. "create trunks and roots"] of lush herbs, evergreen shoots and ever-blooming flowers, but incorporeally to acquire two forms of the soul: solitude in thoughts for reflection on mental wisdom and the fruition of parts of the soul in virtuous deeds.

A. Tamrazyan[102] notes the influence of Philo on Yovhannēs Erznkats'i sermons, but this matter requires a more detailed philological analysis.

A scholion, *Introduction to Philo*, is a product of this school. Its earliest version is in MS J1288 (dated to 1273), copied in the monastery [Nor] Getik; the commissioner of the manuscript was Mkhit'ar, the disciple of Yovasap', who was Vanakan Vardapet's disciple.

Mkhit'ar Ayrivanets'i (1230/35–1297/1300), the scholarch of the Ayrivank' monastery, composed in 1283 the huge miscellany M1500, which contains inter alia the whole CPhA. He is not a member of any succession, but he had friendly relations with Vanakan and his disciples, especially with Vardan Arewelts'i on the one hand, and with the Gladzor university on the other.[103]

18.4.3 Succession of Gladzor

Vardan Arewelts'i's disciple Nersēs Mshets'i († 1284) was the founder of the Gladzor University and the one who commissioned MSS M3932 (1275) and M3935 (thirteenth century).

Nersēs Mshets'i's disciple, Esayi Nchets'i (1255/60–1338) was the second scholarch of Gladzor and the commissioner of MS M5239 (1274); after the death of Nersēs Mshets'i in 1284, he copied a corpus of scholia in the first part of MS M437. Another corpus of scholia was inserted into the same manuscript by the hand of Sargis, a disciple of Esayi, also after his teacher's death in 1337/8. MS V1221 (1314) containing a group of scholia to CPhA was written and illuminated during Esayi's life by the

---

[100] Ohanjanyan, *Tōnapatchaṛ*, 112.
[101] Yovhannēs Erznkats'i, *Compilative Commentary on Grammar*, ed. L. Khach'erean (Los Angeles: Alco Printing Company, 1983), 88.
[102] A. Tamrazyan, "The Reinterpretation of the Theory of Human Constitution in the Armenian Medieval Exegetic Tradition," in *Essays and Studies*, ed. A. Tamrazyan (Erevan: Nayiri, 2013).
[103] E. Harut'yunyan, *Mxit'ar Ayrivanets'i: Life and Works* (Erevan: Academy of Science of Armenian SSR, 1985), 30, 36–37.

graduates of Gladzor Mkhitʻar Erznkatsʻi and Tʻoros Taronatsʻi. Probably the same Mkhitʻar Erznkatsʻi (in the scribal notes he pejoratively called himself Mukhik) copied the Old Testament part of the collection of "causes" in MS M1981 (fifteenth century); the collection starts with already familiar commentary on the book of Genesis by the tenth-century author Timotʻeos (fols 176r–183r).[104]

Found in two manuscripts[105] (M 1247/thirteenth century and M631/fourteenth century), the prefigurative *paschal* catena on Exodus 12 possibly was created in the same environment.[106] The commentary to each lemma begins with Philo's passage from *QE* I (in literal form or in paraphrase), as an interpretation according to the Old Testament.[107]

Other Gladzor University graduates were:

Yovhannēs Erznkatsʻi-Tsotsoretsʻi, the founder of the school in Tsortsor (c.1270–1338?). He commissioned MS M2104 (dated 1318), probably the oldest part of V1334 (fourteenth century), the collections of scholia in M59 (thirteenth to fourteenth century) and M598 (1303), containing the scholion *Introduction to Philo*.

Kirakos Erznkatsʻi (1270–1356), the scholarch of the school in Erznka from 1315, and his nephew Yovhannēs Erznkatsʻi are the commissioners of the CPhA in MSS M2100 (1325) and M2102 (1342).

Yovhannēs Orotnetsʻi (1315–86) was the disciple of Esayi Nchetsʻi. He transferred the Gladzor school to the Hermon monastery, then to Orotnavankʻ in the Siwnikʻ province; in 1373 he founded the Tatʻew monastery, and in 1379 he moved with his disciples to the Erznka (Ernjak) province. He composed an exposition (*hawakʻumn*—lit. *Sylloge*) of *Prov.* (it is unclear whether he is the author of the epitomized scholion, or whether his own scholion was abridged by one of his disciples).[108]

The renowned disciple of Yovhannēs Orotnetsʻi was Geworg Erznkatsʻi (c.1350–1416), the abbot of the Avag monastery in Erznka, where the earliest known copy of the *Sylloge* was made: MS M1701 (1412).

Philo's impact on Grigor Tatevatsʻi (1346–1409), another famous student of Yovhannēs Orotnetsʻi, has yet to be studied.

---

[104] With another recension of the same commentary, as collation has proven, begins the Grigor Abasean's "Book of Causes" in M1879, there anonymous. In both manuscripts it is followed by an anonymous commentary on Exodus, very similar in style, which also contains references to Philo. Probably it is also compiled by Timotheos.

[105] The same text may also be included in the manuscript V499, which was not available to me.

[106] See L. Khachikian, "Gladzor University and Its Students' Graduation Theses," in L. Khachikian, *Works* (Erevan: Nayiri, 2012), 1:302–26.

[107] O. Vardazaryan and deacon Th. Eranyan, "An Anonymous Commentary on Exodus 12," *Etchmiadzin* 9 (2010): 86–112 (in Armenian).

[108] For the text and a study of it, see O. Vardazaryan, "Yovhan Orotnetsʻi's *Sylloge of the Exposition on Philo the Sage's* De providentia," *Bulletin of Matenadaran* 17 (2006): 213–59.

18.4.4 Philo in the Armenian Kingdom of Cilicia

Surprisingly, the manuscript tradition of the CPhA in the Armenian kingdom of Cilicia (1080–1375) is not rich. Only three codices are preserved: the famous V1040, copied in 1296 by the scribe Vasil for the learned king Hetum II; J333, copied in 1298 probably from the protograph of the royal codex in the monastery of Mount Armen not far from the Lambron citadel; M2057 (1328), a copy of the CPhA donated to *vardapet* Yakob Krakac'i in honor of his appointment as tutor of the royal heir. Philo seems not have enjoyed special attention in Cilicia. With the exception of the archbishop of Tarsus, Nersēs Lambronats'i, who had read enough of Philo and applied his exegeses, no other Cilician author seems to display serious interest in Philo's works.

Nersēs Shnorhali (June 4, 1102–August 13, 1173), eminent cleric and prolific author, theologian, poet and Catholicos of all Armenians from 1166, wrote in an epistle to his brother: "The trees of paradise without falsehood are material and evergreen plants, and as Philo says, 'paradise' literally is a dense place, abounding with very venerable friuts, but as to the sense, they symbolically point to something else"[109] (cf. QG 1.6, commenting on Gen 2:8: "'Paradise' literally needs no explanation, for it is a dense place, abounding with all sorts of trees, but symbolically it is wisdom, divine and human knowledge, also of their causes").

Sargis Shnorhali, a twelfth-century author writes: "In this case we have many examples of virtue among birds and quadrupeds, as the turtle-dove is chaste, and the stork is just, for he feeds his father in his old age, and the cock is watchful"[110] (cf. *Anim.* 61: "Among the birds the stork exhibits supreme justice by feeding its parents in return").

Nersēs Lambronats'i (1153–98), the archbishop of Tarsus, an exceptionally prolific author and translator, reveals Philo's strong influence in the *Commentary on Psalms*,[111] unfortunately still unpublished.

Notably, in his other work, *Commentary on Proverbs*, Nersēs reports the only negative opinion about Philo in the Armenian Church. He claims that church exegetes (literally "testers," "checkers") do not approve the use of Philo's research on giants (Prov 21:16),[112] since it is mingled with many "Jewish legends."[113] Meanwhile, the only, very brief and restrained passage in the CPhA, which interprets the theme of angels' intercourse with human daughters and the emergence of a generation of giants (QG 1.92)

---

[109] "Epistula I. Domini Gregorii Armeniorum Catholici epistola ab ejus fratre Nersete Episcopo …," in *Sancti Nersetis Clajensis Armeniorum Catholici Opera, nunc primum ex Armenio in Latinum conversa notisque illustrate studio et labore D. Josephi Cappelletti, presbyteri Veneti*, Vol. I: *Sancti Nersetis Clajensis Armeniorum Catholici Epistolae* (Venice: Typis PP. Mechitaristarum in insula S. Lazari, 1833), 25–79, here 54–55.

[110] Sargis Shnorhali, *Commentary on the Catholic Epistles* (Constantinople: Abraham Terzean's Publishing House, 1828), 415.

[111] A. Tamrazyan, "Reinterpretation of the Theory of Human Constitution in the Armenian Medieval Exegetic Tradition," in A. Tamrazyan, *Essays and Studies* (Erevan: Nayiri, 2013).

[112] The Armenian text represents the exact translation of the Septuagint: "A man that wanders out of the way of righteousness shall rest in the congregation of giants."

[113] *Nerses von Lampron, Erklärung der Sprichwörter Salomos*, ed. and trans. Maximilian von Sachsen, 3 vols (Leipzig: O. Harrassowitz, 1919–26) (non vidi). Nerses is cited by Aucher in Philo, 1822, p. v, in a note.

has been adapted so much that it would probably make sense to talk about *Armenian* legends, as the giants here are "the creatures and likenesses of Hayk."[114] What Nersēs might have in mind is not entirely clear, but it seems that he probably did not mean the actual text of Philo in his Armenian translation, but a much more elaborate plot such as that set forth, for example, in the apocryphal "Book of Enoch"[115] or, more likely, in the "Testament of Reuben" from the "Testament of the Twelve Patriarchs."[116] That such apocryphal stories really could have been circulating under the name of Philo is also confirmed by the fact that Philo's Enoch, as it is represented in the hypothesis (Anonymous B, 58), "was looking with great zeal for the place from which Adam came out of paradise,"[117] although there is nothing of the kind in the texts of the Alexandrian himself. But in the Book of Enoch, the latter actually ascends to the place where he is shown the Garden of Eden and the Tree of Knowledge, because of which the progenitors were banished from Eden.[118] Probably, the apocryphal story about the remains of Adam, also attributed to Philo in the "History" of Towma Artsruni, testifies to the same practice.

Movsēs Erznkats'i (c.1250–1323), a disciple of the Cilician *vardapet* Geworg Skevrats'i and Yovhannēs Erznkats'i Pluz, while revising the *Commentary on the Breviary* by Khosrov Andzewats'i,[119] adds the following reference to Philo (*Abr.* 121 = Philo, 1892, 65): "Blessed are You, Lord our God. When he [David?] says 'Lord' and 'God', he proclaims the name of the ruling and creating, for 'Lord' is a royal name, denoting domination and a fair trial …. 'God' is the name of creating, which reveals, according to the philosopher, [His] providence …."

18.4.5 The Decline of Armenian Philonic Tradition

The decrease in the number of manuscripts indicates that in the fifteenth and sixteenth centuries interest in Philo gradually faded. From this period only a fragment is extant in the NOJ 186 (sixteenth century), also two copies of the *Sylloge* in M1701 (1412), and in M1931 (fifteenth century), as well a collection of short paraphrastic scholia in M2059 (1599).

Simēon Jughaets'i (fl. c.1537–67?), in his manual on logic, in the chapter "No soul is a body," opposing the thesis that the elements, being a body, have a creative ability, writes:

---

[114] The legendary progenitor of Armenians.

[115] See *1 En.* 6–16, in R. H. Charles, ed., *The Apocrypha and Pseudepigrapha of the Old Testament* (Oxford: Clarendon, 1913), 191–99.

[116] *A Museum of the Armenian Ancient and New Literature*, Vol. 1: *Non-canonical Books of the Old Testament* (Venice, Mekhitarists Press, 1896) (in Armenian), 33–34.

[117] O. Vardazaryan, "The 'Causes' to the Writings by Philo," 204.

[118] *1 En.* 32, *The Apocrypha and Pseudepigrapha of the Old Testament*, 207, compare also the development of this topic in "Words of Adam to Seth" (*A Museum*, 1:331–32) and in the "Testament of Seth" (320–21).

[119] Khosrov Bishop of Andzewk', *Commentary on the Breviary*, ed. Mowsēs, erudite vardapet (Ortaköy: Poghos Arapean Apuchekhts'i & Sons Publishing House, 1840), 98–99.

It should be said that the elements are not the creative principles of the subjects, but the material ones, for the matter of every natural body is mixed out of the four elements; but the design is from the soul, for, as Proclus and Gregory, and all contemplators of nature, believed, the body, by its own nature, is prone to division and dispersion, and to endless crushing, and therefore needs something that can prolong, match, fasten and carry it—something that we call soul. But here it is necessary to extend the speech a little, in order to answer the objection: some said that there is no providence [that is, the ability to care and set goals—O.V.] in beings. Philo and Gregory[120] answered them with the greatest boldness, but since their writings are at your hand, what has been said, apparently is enough.[121]

The author is clearly referring to the argumentation in the very beginning of *Prov.* (*Prov.* 1.2–3): the one who reasons about the non-existence of providence does so as a subject of providence (i.e. according to Siměon, as an "essence" in which providence is "contained," or to which it is "inherent"). As far as I know, this is the only passage in the Armenian tradition where Philo's philosophical thought is applied to the discussion of a philosophical problem proper. It is noteworthy that Siměon is still sure that his audience is well-read in Philo and capable of comprehending immediately what he is talking about.

Another text indicates that acquaintance with Philo in the school environment was still quite common at that time: *The Testament and Interpretation of the Passions of our Lord Jesus Christ, Set forth by James the Apostle, the Lord's Brother.* This tale, containing the name of James only in the title, was constructed from the Acts of the Apostles and various apocrypha, apparently by one of the later Armenian compilators. It tells about the events that followed the crucifixion, resurrection, and ascension of Jesus Christ: about the despair of the Sanhedrin, about the efforts of the Jerusalem priests to hide what had happened, about the execution of Pilate, even about the appeal of Tiberius to the Armenian (sic!) King Abgar[122] with a request to punish the Jews, and so forth. In this motley mixture, curious passages are also found related to the "three men of Galilee": Philo the priest, Addai the teacher, and Haggai the Levite, who came to Jerusalem and reported that they saw Jesus resurrected and sitting on a cloudy mountain surrounded by eleven disciples.[123] Here we are undoubtedly dealing with a secondary literary fiction, since in the three Galileans of the "Testament" it is easy to recognize the reflection of another triad from the *Gospel of Nicodemus*: the priest

---

[120] Siměon confused Gregory of Nyssa with Nemesius of Emesa; see K. Mosikyan, "Nemesius of Emessa's *On the Nature of Man* in Medieval Armenian Literature," *Bulletin of Matenadaran* 26 (2018): 177–206 (in Armenian), here, 200.

[121] Siměon Jughaets'i, *Book of Logic* (Constantinople: Yovhannēs and Poghos Press, 1794), 169–70.

[122] King Abgar V of Osroene (who according to the legend had correspondence with Jesus Christ) in Armenian historiographic tradition, starting with Movsēs Khorenats'i (*History* 2.26), is regarded as an Armenian king, and his capital Edessa as part of Armenia.

[123] *This Little Book tells, Firstly, about the Coming of Jesus to Jerusalem, Secondly, about the Torments that He Endured before Judge Pilate and the High Priests Anna and Kaifa. Said by the blessed James, the brother of the Lord* (Constantinople: Astuatsatur Kostandnupolsets'i's Press, 1703), 85–87, 111–12. The text, like many late secondary apocryphal compilations, has never been examined.

Phinehas, the teacher Addai and the Levite Haggai, who testified about the departed, brought out of hell by Christ.[124] Such a substitution would hardly have been possible, if the name of Philo had not received a fairly wide distribution in the Armenian school milieu—even, probably, wider than we can learn from written sources; it is also noteworthy that this substitution is made in the text ascribed to "James the Righteous": the compilers of the tale seem to be familiar with the version of the school legend that connected these two characters in a single plot.[125]

In the seventeenth century some restoration of the tradition is observed; besides the manuscripts containing the CPhA—M2103 (seventeenth century), M2056 (1646), ITU 114 (1668)—scholia were extensively copied: M1053 (1648), M1919, M2379, M3276, J1096 (1633), J3305 (1656–71). It is noteworthy that codex M1480 (1617), containing a collection of scholia, was intended as a donation to Barsegh Baghishets'i,[126] the scholarch of the monastery Amrdolu of Baghesh (Bitlis), which inherited the traditions of the Tat'ew and Erznka schools.[127] The late owner of the collection of scholia M59 (thirteenth century), Kirakos of Astapat, was also a monk in Amrdolu.

In the eighteenth century, the living tradition of reading and commenting on the CPhA came to an end, giving way to pure academic interest, mostly connected with the preparation of the texts for publication. Manuscripts of the CPhA were searched for, and one of the customers, Isaac Bishop of the district Gegham, especially notes the rarity of the copy he ordered for the library of the Holy See of Etchmiadzin.[128] At the end of the eighteenth century, the Venetian congregation of the Mekhitarists started the work of the publication of the Armenian Philo.[129]

18.5 Conclusion

The medieval Armenian learned tradition related to Philo is absolutely unprecedented: the Armenian Philonic Corpus which was translated at the dawn of Armenian literature, did not collect dust in monasteries, but was read and reread, retold, learned by heart, was interpreted and served as a source of learned language and knowledge of various topics; in brief, "a great, wise and admirable Philo"[130] was appreciated and honored in medieval Armenia, as probably nowhere else in the Christian world.

---

[124] "Evangelium Nicodemi sive Gesta Pilati," in *Evangelia apocrypha*, ed. C. Tischendorf (Leipzig: Avenarius et Mendelssohn, 1853), 242–43, 258, 260, 350–52, 363–64, 396.

[125] See above, "*Lord Yovhannēs the Lector's Preliminary Summary of the History of These Words*" and n. 47, as well as "*Explanation of Feasts*" and n. 98.

[126] N. Akinean, *The School of Baghesh [Bitlis] 1500–1704: A Contribution to the History of Armenian Church and Literature* (Vienna: Mkhitarists' Press, 1952), 70–87 (in Armenian).

[127] Akinean, *The School of Baghesh*, 1–11.

[128] M2595 (1786–87), fol. 280v. For more details of this manuscript, see O. Vardazaryan, "The Armenian Scholia to the Works by Philo of Alexandria," 186–88.

[129] See O. Vardazaryan, "Colophons on the Manuscript Tradition of 'Armenian Philo,'" 266–72; A. Sirinian, "'Armenian Philo': A Survey of the Literature," in *Studies on the Ancient Armenian Version of Philo's Works*, 10–16.

[130] Hypothesis B, 1 (p. 198).

CPhA was in demand in various areas: first of all, of course, in exegesis, but occasionally in dogmatics also. Unexpectedly, it had a stimulating effect on mathematics in Armenia and some impact on legislation. Curiously, Philo does not seem to have interested the Armenian reader as a philosopher. But here one should not rush to judgment: it is quite possible that the philosophical topics were discussed and assimilated in the process of classroom readings. A detailed study of scholia can bring us closer to understanding the true state of affairs in this area.

In school folklore, Philo appears as the historian of the first Christian community; but in his audience's view he also turns out to be a source of apocryphal legends that were in circulation in church and near-church circles. None of the authors listed here is trying to present Philo as a Christian. This scenario probably also belongs to the oral tradition, recorded by the scholiasts only by chance.[131]

Of course, this research needs to be continued: new texts and, perhaps, new approaches will shed more light on the fate of Philo's legacy in medieval Armenia.[132]

---

[131] O. Vardazaryan, "The 'Armenian Philo': A Remnant of an Unknown Tradition," 194–95.
[132] I consider it my pleasant duty to express my deepest gratitude to my colleague Gohar Muradyan for her constant support in writing this article. Without exaggeration, I can say that without her participation, I would hardly have been able to complete this work.

19

Christian Arabic Literature

Alexander Treiger

Christian Arabic reception of Philo of Alexandria has received scant scholarly attention.[1] Thus, Georg Graf's *Geschichte der christlichen arabischen Literatur*—the magisterial five-volume analytical catalog of Christian Arabic literature, written in the 1940s and 1950s—mentions no translations of Philo into Arabic and provides only two cursory references to Philo.[2] Scholarly literature subsequent to Graf is, likewise, virtually silent on Christian Arabic transmission of Philo's works. Nonetheless, as will be shown below, at least one Christian Arabic Philonic translation, albeit of a fragmentary nature, exists: seven passages from Philo's *De vita contemplativa* are preserved in an "appendix" to the eleventh-century Arabic translation of the Dionysian corpus. Moreover, additional references to, and quotations from, Philo appear in medieval Christian Arabic sources. Some pseudo-Philonic material is attested as well. The present article will survey all the hitherto discovered evidence for Christian Arabic transmission of Philo (including Pseudo-Philonic material).

19.1 Philonic Passages in the Appendix to the Arabic Translation of the Dionysian Corpus

While working on the Arabic translation of the Dionysian corpus (the version prepared by the Chalcedonian Orthodox scribe ʿĪsā ibn Isḥāq al-Ḥimṣī, better known as Ibn Saḥqūn, in Damascus in 1009),[3] the present writer was fortunate to discover seven

---

[1] The only exception is E. Parker and A. Treiger, "Philo's Odyssey into the Medieval Jewish World: Neglected Evidence from Arab Christian Literature," *Dionysius* 30 (2012): 117–46. The survey below offers a revised and augmented version of the Christian Arabic section of that article (originally penned by the present writer). I extend my sincere gratitude to the late Wayne J. Hankey, a long-time editor of *Dionysius*, and to Emily Parker for their kind permission to revise and re-publish this material. A full list of references to Philo in Arabic (and also Syriac) literature has now been published: D. T. Runia, Y. Arzhanov, and A. Treiger, "References to Philo of Alexandria in Greek, Latin, Syriac and Arabic Literature up to 1500 C.E.," *SPhiloA* 35 (2023): 231–59.

[2] The first reference (G. Graf, *Geschichte der christlichen arabischen Literatur*, 5 vols [Vatican: Biblioteca Apostolica Vaticana, 1944–53], 1:266 n. 1) is spurious, for it is based on a questionable reading of the Arabic translation (from Coptic) of Severus of Nastarawah's *Homily on the Life of St. Mark*; cf. J.-J.-L. Bargès, *Homélie sur St Marc, apôtre et évangéliste par Anba Sévère, évêque de Nestéraweh* (Paris: Ernest Leroux, 1877), 170–3; Arabic section, 39. The second reference (Graf, *Geschichte*, 1:486) is a Pseudo-Philonic citation in a collection of pagan philosophers' testimonies to the Trinity, incorporated in the eleventh-century Nestorian encyclopedia *Kitāb al-Majdal*. See discussion below.

[3] On this translation, see A. Treiger, "New Evidence on the Arabic Versions of the *Corpus Dionysiacum*," *Le Muséon* 118 (2005): 219–40; A. Treiger, "The Arabic Version of Pseudo-Dionysius the Areopagite's *Mystical Theology*, Chapter 1," *Le Muséon* 120 (2007): 365–93; C. Bonmariage and S. Moureau, "Corpus Dionysiacum Arabicum: Étude, édition critique et traduction des *Noms Divins* IV, §1–9," *Le Muséon* 124 (2011): 181–227 and

Philonic passages—all of them from the *De vita contemplativa*—preserved in an "appendix" to the Arabic Dionysius.[4] This appendix includes three texts, all of which were derived at second hand from Eusebius' *Ecclesiastical History*: Polycrates of Ephesus' *Epistle to Victor* (CPG 1338; Eusebius, *Hist. eccl.* 3.31), Clement of Alexandria's *Can a Rich Man Be Saved* (CPG 1379; Eusebius, *Hist. eccl.* 3.23),[5] and the Philonic passages under discussion (Eusebius, *Hist. eccl.* 2.17). Two short but intriguing notes (on which more below) follow the three texts.

It is virtually certain that this Arabic appendix has the same origin as the Arabic Dionysius: namely, that it was translated from Greek into Arabic by Ibn Saḥqūn in Damascus in 1009, as part of the Dionysian corpus. In fact, there are multiple Greek manuscripts of the Dionysian corpus (all of them with scholia produced in the sixth century by John of Scythopolis) that contain this appendix. The Greek manuscript from which Ibn Saḥqūn was working obviously belonged to this type; hence, for the sake of completeness, after translating the Dionysian corpus into Arabic, Ibn Saḥqūn translated the appendix as well.[6]

The most comprehensive study of this appendix—in the original Greek and in the ninth-century Latin translation by Anastasius Bibliothecarius—is by the Hungarian scholar Réka Forrai.[7] Forrai indicates that she was unable to find any Greek manuscripts of the Dionysian corpus that contain the appendix but do *not* include John of Scythopolis' scholia. This suggests that the appendix may be part of the scholia.[8] Moreover, she makes the important point that two of the three texts cited in the appendix are also mentioned in the scholia: Philo's *De vita contemplativa* is mentioned in John of Scythopolis' scholion on Dionysius' *Epistle 1*;[9] Clement of Alexandria's *Can a Rich Man Be Saved* is referenced in a scholion on *Epistle 10*;[10] Polycrates' letter is

---

419–59. On Ibn Saḥqūn, see also S. Noble, "A Byzantine Bureaucrat and Arabic Philosopher: Ibrāhīm ibn Yuḥannā al-Anṭākī and His Translation of *On the Divine Names* 4.18–35," in *Caught in Translation: Studies on Versions of Late Antique Christian Literature*, ed. M. Toca and D. Batovici (Leiden: Brill, 2020), 276–312, at 271; A. Treiger, "Section VI: Arabic [Translations of Byzantine Literature]," in *The Oxford Handbook of Byzantine Literature*, ed. S. Papaioannou (Oxford: Oxford University Press, 2021), 642–62, at 644 and 654.

[4] At the end of MS Sinai ar. 268. MS Sinai ar. 314 must have also included this appendix, but, unfortunately, the concluding section of this manuscript is lost.

[5] These Arabic fragments of Polycrates of Ephesus and Clement of Alexandria are, likewise, not mentioned by Graf.

[6] Strangely, however, Ibn Saḥqūn's Arabic translation of the Dionysian corpus does *not* include John of Scythopolis' prologue and scholia. However, it does include (for the *Ecclesiastical Hierarchy*, the *Divine Names*, and the *Mystical Theology* alone) the anonymous hexameter epigrams found in some Greek manuscripts of the Dionysian corpus (see Treiger, "Arabic Version," 367).

[7] R. Forrai, "The Notes of Anastasius on Eriugena's Translation of the *Corpus Dionysiacum*," *Journal of Medieval Latin* 18 (2008): 74–100, here 91–100; cf. Forrai's PhD diss., "The Interpreter of the Popes: The Translation Project of Anastasius Bibliothecarius" (Central European University, Budapest, 2008), 137–47. See also P. M. Barnard, ed., *Clement of Alexandria, Quis Dives Salvetur* (Cambridge: Cambridge University Press, 1897), xxiii–xxv.

[8] Forrai, "Notes of Anastasius," 99. Unfortunately, the latest edition of John of Scythopolis' scholia on Dionysius' *Divine Names*—B. R. Suchla, ed., *Ioannis Scythopolitani Prologus et Scholia in Dionysii Areopagitae Librum De Divinis Nominibus cum additamentis interpretum aliorum*, Corpus Dionysiacum IV/1 (Berlin: de Gruyter, 2011)—does not seem to mention the appendix.

[9] P. Rorem and J. C. Lamoreaux, *John of Scythopolis and the Dionysian Corpus: Annotating the Areopagite* (Oxford: Clarendon Press, 1998), 263.

[10] Rorem and Lamoreaux, *John of Scythopolis*, 250.

not mentioned in John of Scythopolis' scholia, but is relevant to Dionysius' *Epistle 10*, insofar as it mentions the death of St. John the Theologian, who is the addressee of this epistle.[11] Finally, the concluding note of the appendix has parallels to John of Scythopolis' famous *Prologue* to the scholia.[12] In view of all this, Forrai suggests that this appendix was added "to the Greek text at a very early stage, probably even by John of Scythopolis himself."[13] This conclusion is further strengthened by the fact—also duly noted by Forrai—that both John of Scythopolis and the appendix derive their knowledge of Philo's *De vita contemplativa* exclusively from Eusebius. In his scholion on Dionysius' *Epistle 1*, already mentioned above, John of Scythopolis mentions that Philo discusses the "Therapeutae" at the *end* of the *De vita contemplativa*. Yet, it is only in Eusebius' quotations from Philo that this discussion occurs at the end; hence, the conclusion seems unavoidable that John of Scythopolis did not know Philo's treatise directly, but relied exclusively on Eusebius; it would therefore stand to reason that it was John of Scythopolis too who appended those same Philonic quotations from Eusebius at the end of his scholia.[14]

Thus what we have in MS Sinai ar. 268 is a Christian Arabic translation of John of Scythopolis' still unpublished appendix, which includes fragments of Polycrates of Ephesus, Clement of Alexandria, and Philo—all derived at second hand from Eusebius' *Ecclesiastical History*. The appendix also includes two notes—likely penned by John of Scythopolis himself—dealing, respectively, with the background of Philo's Therapeutae (what kind of Jews—or Christians—they were) and with various church authorities' references to Dionysius.

What follows is an annotated English translation (from Arabic) of the last section of the appendix that includes the Philonic passages and the two notes. As one can see, Ibn Saḥqūn's version is, unfortunately, rather crude and frequently distorts the sense of the original; moreover, it does not always make good sense in Arabic and is therefore extremely difficult to translate into English. An attempt has been made to make the translation as intelligible as possible, while remaining faithful to Ibn Saḥqūn's Arabic (even as it frequently fails to accurately reflect the Greek); significant discrepancies between the Arabic and the underlying Greek and other peculiarities of the Arabic translation are discussed in footnotes. The numbering of the Philonic passages and of the two notes is my own.[15]

1. By Philo (Fīlūs), on the believers among the Christian faithful from the people of circumcision who were in Egypt, and also on the monks, from the treatise he wrote on the visible and observable world and on supplication [due] therein.[16]

---

[11] Forrai, "Notes of Anastasius," 91–3.
[12] Forrai, "Notes of Anastasius," 98–9.
[13] Forrai, "Notes of Anastasius," 100.
[14] Forrai, "Notes of Anastasius," 92; cf. Rorem and Lamoreaux, *John of Scythopolis*, 58 and 250.
[15] For the Arabic text and the parallel Greek text of Eusebius, *Hist. eccl.* 2.17, see Parker and Treiger, "Philo's Odyssey," 142–46.
[16] A mistranslation of Περὶ βίου θεωρητικοῦ ἢ ἱκετῶν.

The emergence and coming-to-be of the universe is multidirectional, for it is necessary for it to partake of the perfect good. In Greece, upon all those who are summoned (?), and in the vicinity of the borders of the barbarians, and especially around Alexandria, among these excellent [men] there were those who would bring cure in every direction, just as they were healers[17] in their own town, living in their own abode, homeland, and country and preserving those who [dwelled] in the vicinity of the lake known as "Mary" [i.e. lake Mareotis]—namely those who are weaker and so would find an opportunity in the [good] preservation of the air and its healthy composition.

Eusebius, *Hist. eccl.* 2.17.7–8 = Philo, *Contempl.* 21–22

2. By [Philo], from the [same] treatise.
In every private [space] there is a certain pure[18] dwelling, called "source of purity"[19] and "monastery"[20] in which solitaries [engage] in mysteries of the pure world. The necessities of the body, all of them, cannot be separated (?) from one another, even if they are indispensable for others. But in those [men], in virtue of their knowledge of the laws and of the wondrous sayings of the prophets, praises [for the divine] grow and are perfected, in piety and purity.

Eusebius, *Hist. eccl.* 2.17.9 = Philo, *Contempl.* 25

3. By [Philo], from the [same] treatise.
The duration of stay does not extend until evening, because for all of them (?)[21] this becomes asceticism and eremitic life,[22] I mean, for those who philosophize in their own town out of love for wisdom and so employ symbols and indications which they think are translation[s] of the concealed nature. In virtue of pure thought and careful consideration, these [symbols]—[transmitted] from ancient men who were not the leaders of [any one] sect among these[23]—become clear to masters of consideration. They have left behind the youths [whose] vision is drawn together, namely those people of syllogism who used the first symbols and imitated the state of the previous sect.

Eusebius, *Hist. eccl.* 2.17.10–11 = Philo, *Contempl.* 28–29

4. By [Philo], from the [same] treatise.
So much so that they do not only contemplate this but also produce songs of praise and hymns to God in complete and perfect metres and melodies [based] on exceedingly pure numbers, so that they necessarily rejoice.

Eusebius, *Hist. eccl.* 2.17.13 = Philo, *Contempl.* 29

---

[17] *āsiyan* ~ Gr. θεραπευταί.
[18] This is Ibn Saḥqūn's usual way of rendering ἱερός or σεμνός, both meaning "sacred."
[19] *ma'din al-ṭuhr* ~ Gr. σεμνεῖον.
[20] *dayr* ~ Gr. μοναστήριον.
[21] The text is partially effaced, and the reading is conjectural.
[22] Reading *nuskan wa-siyāḥatan*. Both terms translate the Greek term ἄσκησις.
[23] The sense is unclear, and the translation bears little similarity to the underlying Greek.

5. By [Philo], from the [same] treatise.
[Certain] people have well-founded self-control, and so they proceed toward it with [their] soul for the sake of other causes, having made the virtues to be their food or drink. There is no one among them who does not come forth before the setting of the sun and is not revealed as being worthy of the light that delivers the body from darkness by necessity. For this reason, day and night is a short day for them, and ... (?)[24] it happens that it is only after three days that they remember food, because their love for wisdom gives them knowledge that keeps their mind away from food. In virtue of this [knowledge], they become firm. They are people who rejoice in this manner and get their nourishment from wisdom. They are nourished by temperance, self-sufficiency, and renunciation of the body, for [wisdom] has given them teachings that keep them satisfied for a long period of time. Even after six days they barely taste food, though they do eat of necessity.

Eusebius, *Hist. eccl.* 2.17.16–17 = Philo, *Contempl.* 34–35

6. By [Philo], from the [same] treatise.
Here there are [also] curing women, aged virgins who have remained[25] in purity, but not because of necessity—as is the case of the [female] sacristans among the pagans. They preserve their souls, especially in virtue of knowledge that they have voluntarily acquired in [their] struggle and love for wisdom. They are concerned with [their] livelihood and hasten toward it, being cognizant of the passions surrounding the body. Yet at the same time they are ready to face death, for the likeness of a soul loving and adoring God has already been born within them.

Eusebius, *Hist. eccl.* 2.17.19 = Philo, *Contempl.* 68

7. By [Philo], from the [same] treatise.
As far as indications of the pure books are concerned, these [too] become clear to them and do not escape their understanding. [This happens] through intellectual symbols, for every [religious] legislation is likely to become the source of life for these men. The body has certain definite, visible ranks, while the soul [exists] in virtue of the utterances set forth and produced for it by the hidden, invisible intellect, differently and separately. [The soul's] characteristic feature is to contemplate, as one observes [an image] in the mirror. Its appellations possess wondrous matters in the noetic [realm], which get revealed to the extent of its contemplation.

Eusebius, *Hist. eccl.* 2.17.20 = Philo, *Contempl.* 78

Note No. 1
Eusebius the all-loving[26] has mentioned this. Philo is saying these things regarding the impure Jews, but some say, regarding the Nazarene Jews, while others [say] he

---
[24] One word is unclear.
[25] The word is partially effaced, and the reading is conjectural.
[26] Here and below, a mistranslation of Eusebius' sobriquet ὁ Παμφίλου ("the [disciple and friend] of Pamphilus").

[is speaking] about those from the people of circumcision who believe in Christ, yet formally keep the Law of Moses, while still others [claim he is speaking] about the perfect Christians, who belong to the group living a life of monastic seclusion and are publicly known as the "healers" [i.e. Therapeutae]. It is not only Eusebius the all-loving and Philo the Jew, but also the blessed Dionysius, the judge,[27] the disciple of the apostle Paul and the bishop of Athens, who in his treatise on the universal ecclesiastical hierarchy [speaks about] the monk[s] donning the monastic habit and calls [them] curer[s] and healer[s] [i.e. Therapeutae].[28]

Note No. 2
The evangelist Luke mentions this blessed Dionysius, the judge, in the Acts of the Apostles, i.e. in the *Praxeis*,[29] as also Dionysius the bishop of Corinth, an ancient and blessed man of many fruits,[30] says in his epistle to the congregation of the Athenians,[31] and Eusebius the all-loving does in his *Ecclesiastical Narration and History*.[32]

19.2 References to, and Quotations from, Philo in Christian Arabic Sources

19.2.1 References to Philo

Other than Ibn Saḥqūn's translation discussed above, there are some references to Philo in Christian Arabic literature. In their works written in Arabic, at least three Christian historians—Agapius of Manbij (d. 942), al-Makīn ibn al-ʿAmīd (d. 1273),

---

[27] Here and below, "judge" (*qāḍī*) translates "Areopagite."
[28] Dionysius the Areopagite, *Ecclesiastical Hierarchy*, VI.1.3, 532D–533A; G. Heil and A. M. Ritter, eds, *Corpus Dionysiacum II*, 2nd edn (Berlin: de Gruyter, 2012), 116. The Greek text of Note No. 1 is unpublished and inaccessible to me, but cf. Anastasius Bibliothecarius' Latin translation (cited in Forrai, "Notes of Anastasius," 93): "Meminit horum et Iosebius Pamphili. Quidam autem dicunt haec Philonem de sociis iudeis dicere, alii de nazareis iudeis, alii ex circumcisione fidelibus et credentibus in Christum et custodientibus legem Moisi, alii de perfectis christianis. Talis autem erant aeresis monachicam viventes vitam therapeyte merito nominati sunt. Non solum autem Iosebius Pamphili sed et Philo Iudaeus sed et beatus Dionysius Ariopagita discipulus sancti Pauli Apostoli sanctus Athenarum episcopus in eo qui est de ecclesiastica ierarchia monachos ait antique et therapeytas nominat."
[29] The Greek name of the Book of Acts, often used in Arabic as well. The reference is to Acts 17:34.
[30] The translator Ibn Saḥqūn mistranslated the personal name Polycarp as an epithet ("of many fruits") applied to the previously mentioned Dionysius of Corinth.
[31] In the original Greek, this is possibly a reference to Polycarp's *Epistle to the Philippians* (CPG 1040); Polycarp's *Epistle to the Athenians* is unknown. This Polycarp may be the intended addressee of Dionysius the Areopagite's *Epistle 7*. Interestingly, Migne's PG edition and some Greek manuscripts of the scholia on the Dionysian corpus include this clause on Dionysius of Corinth and Polycarp as part of John of Scythopolis' prologue—see Suchla, *Ioannis Scythopolitani Prologus et Scholia*, 103 (apparatus); Rorem and Lamoreaux, *John of Scythopolis*, 145–6 n. 6.
[32] The Greek text of Note No. 2 is cited in Forrai, "Notes of Anastasius," 98, based on two Venetian manuscripts: "τοῦ δὲ μακαρίου Διονυσίου τοῦ Ἀρεοπαγίτου μέμνηται Λουκᾶς ὁ εὐαγγελιστὴς ἐν ταῖς πράξεσι τῶν ἀποστόλων καὶ Διονύσιος ἐπίσκοπος Κορίνθου ἀνὴρ ἀρχαῖος καὶ ὁ μακάριος Πολύκαρπος ἐν τῇ πρὸς τὴν ἐκκλησίαν Ἀθηνῶν ἐπιστολῇ καὶ Εὐσέβιος ὁ Παμφίλου ἐν τῇ ἐκκλησιαστικῇ ἱστορίᾳ." In the Arabic translation we have a case of hendiadys: two synonymous words are used to translate the Greek ἱστορία.

328   THE RECEPTION OF PHILO OF ALEXANDRIA

and Bar Hebraeus (d. 1286)—refer to Philo's embassy to Gaius. Agapius' report (largely based on Eusebius, *Hist. eccl.* 2.18) is as follows:

> In the first year of [Gaius Caligula's] reign [i.e. 38 CE], Flaccus, king of Egypt, made an expedition and subjugated [the Jews] for seven years, filling their sanctuaries with statues and offerings to idols. They, in turn, sent ambassadors to Gaius to inform him of this. One of them was the Hebrew philosopher Philo, the author of many treatises about the calamities that befell the Jews in his time. He ridiculed King Gaius, blaming him for his ignorance and for the fact that he had made himself out to be a god. He praised [true] worshippers found in Egypt.[33] He wrote a commentary on the first book of the Torah and mentioned that when [Noah][34] woke up his [nakedness] had been covered. He wrote five treatises on the legal regulations, five on the Exodus of the Sons of Israel, and four on the matters mentioned in the Law [of Moses]. His treatises were read in the assemblies of the Romans during the reign of [Claudius].[35] The [Romans] praised them highly and deposited them in the imperial libraries in Rome.[36]

Agapius' report is cited verbatim by al-Makīn ibn al-ʿAmīd; however, in his account, Philo's name got corrupted and reads as "Nikon" or "Niphon."[37] It is evident that, unlike Agapius, al-Makīn no longer knew who Philo was.

Bar Hebraeus' report of the same incident is much shorter. It mentions Philo (alongside Josephus) as a "wise ambassador" sent to the emperor Gaius, but does not refer to any of Philo's books:

> Gaius Caesar reigned four years. In the first year of his reign he appointed Herod Agrippa as a governor over the Jews for the period of seven years. In that same year, Pontius Pilate killed himself. Flaccus was sent as a judge to Jerusalem. He filled the Jewish sanctuaries with statues, and so they sent two wise ambassadors—the Hebrews Philo and Josephus—to the emperor, because they were deeply concerned[38] about the official's actions.[39]

---

[33] An apparent reference to the Therapeutae.
[34] The text is corrupt here. The reference is to Philo's *De sobrietate*.
[35] The text is corrupt here. The only plausible reading is "Claudius," as in the parallel passage in Eusebius.
[36] L. Cheikho, ed., *Agapius Episcopus Mabbugensis, Historia Universalis*, CSCO ser. III, t. 5 (Beirut: E typographeo catholico, 1912), 245–46; A. Vasiliev, ed. and trans., *Kitāb al-ʿunvān, Histoire universelle, écrite par Agapius (Mahboub) de Menbidj*, Seconde partie (I), Patrologia Orientalis 7.4 (Paris: Firmin-Didot, 1911) [26–7]/482–83.
[37] MS Paris, BnF ar. 294, fol. 182r–v; MS Vat. ar. 168, fol. 134r. This part of al-Makīn's chronicle is still unedited (Martino Diez is preparing a critical edition).
[38] For this difficult word (Ar. *yataḍawwarūna*), see R. Payne Smith, *Thesaurus Syriacus*, 2 vols (Oxford: Clarendon Press, 1879–1901), vol. 2, col. 1525; R. Dozy, *Supplément aux dictionnaires arabes*, 2 vols (Leiden: Brill, 1881), 2:15a.
[39] Bar Hebraeus, *Tārīkh mukhtaṣar al-duwal*, ed. A. Ṣāliḥānī (Beirut: al-Maṭbaʿa al-kāthūlīkiyya, 1890), 114–15. For the parallel text in Bar Hebraeus' *Chronography*, written in Syriac, see P. Bedjan, ed., *Gregorii Barhebraei Chronicon Syriacum* (Paris, 1890), 48; English translation: E. A. W. Budge, trans., *The Chronography of Abû'l Faraj, the Son of Aaron, the Hebrew Physician, Commonly Known as Bar Hebraeus*, 2 vols (Oxford: Oxford University Press, 1932), 1:49.

Philo's embassy is also mentioned in the Arabic translation of the Latin historian Orosius' (d. c.420) *Historiae adversus paganos*:

> The Jews at that time were being afflicted with murder and plunder, and some of them sought refuge in Alexandria, with one of its kings named Philo, who was highborn and noble. They sent him as a legate to Gaius Caesar to intercede on their behalf. Though Gaius Caligula was harsh toward all men, he was especially so toward the Jews, and so he did not heed to his request, and Philo returned in utmost disgrace. [The emperor] ordered that all the [Jewish] sanctuaries and places of sanctification be defiled, and that all of them be filled with images of the idols. He also decreed that he himself be worshiped there, out of a tyrannical desire for deification.[40]

19.2.2 Quotations from Philo

As far as citations from Philo go, the most important place to look for them is Christian Arabic florilegia.[41] One example will suffice here. The eleventh-century Christian Arabic theologian and prolific translator of patristic literature from Greek into Arabic, ʿAbdallāh ibn al-Faḍl from Antioch, translated into Arabic Pseudo-Maximus the Confessor's florilegium *Loci communes*.[42] This florilegium belongs to the genre of the so-called sacro-profane florilegia, in that each chapter cites first the sacred authorities (the Holy Scripture and the church fathers) and then sayings of, or attributed to, ancient Greek authors, including Thales, Pythagoras, Solon, Euripides, Socrates, Plato, Aristotle, Isocrates, Demosthenes, Diogenes, Epicurus, Menander, and many others. There, we find some twenty-odd quotations from Philo's works—all of them duly

---

[40] ʿAbd al-Raḥmān Badawī, ed., *Ūrūsiyūs, Tārīkh al-ʿālam: al-tarjama al-ʿarabiyya al-qadīma* (Beirut: al-Muʾassasa al-ʿarabiyya li-l-dirāsāt wa-l-nashr, 1982), Book VII.5, 424; M. Penelas, ed., *Kitāb Hurūšiyūš: Traducción árabe de las* Historiae adversus paganos *de Orosio* (Madrid: Consejo superior de investigaciones científicas, 2001), Book VII.5, §40, 341–42. For an English translation of the corresponding Latin text, see Paulus Orosius, *The Seven Books of History against the Pagans*, trans. R. J. Deferrari (Washington, DC: Catholic University of America, 1964), Book VII.5, 293.

[41] Arabic translations of Greek patristic works that cite Philo would be another obvious place to consider. However, it does not seem that any of these works (conveniently listed in D. T. Runia, *Philo in Early Christian Literature: A Survey* [Minneapolis: Fortress Press, 1993], 348–56; reprinted with corrections in D. T. Runia, "References to Philo from Josephus up to 1000 AD," *SPhiloA* 6 [1994]: 111–21) were translated into Arabic. However, further research in this area is needed.

[42] On ʿAbdallāh ibn al-Faḍl, see A. M. Roberts, *Reason and Revelation in Byzantine Antioch: The Christian Translation Program of Abdallah ibn al-Fadl* (Oakland: University of California Press, 2020). On ʿAbdallāh ibn al-Faḍl's still unpublished Arabic translation of *Loci communes*, see A. Treiger, "Greek into Arabic in Byzantine Antioch: ʿAbdallāh ibn al-Faḍl's *Book of the Garden* (*Kitāb ar-Rawḍa*)," in *Ambassadors, Artists, Theologians: Byzantine Relations with the Near East from the Ninth to the Thirteenth Centuries*, ed. Z. Chitwood and J. Pahlitzsch (Mainz: Verlag des Römisch-Germanischen Zentralmuseums, 2019), 227–38. For the Greek original of the *Loci communes*, see S. Ihm, ed., *Ps.-Maximus Confessor, Erste kritische Edition des sacro-profanen Florilegiums* Loci communes (Stuttgart: Franz Steiner Verlag, 2001). On the Philonic material in the *Loci communes*, see also J. R. Royse, *The Spurious Texts of Philo of Alexandria: A Study of Textual Transmission and Corruption with Indexes to the Major Collections of Greek Fragments* (Leiden: Brill, 1991), 28–31 and Index, 250, s.v. "(Pseudo-)Maximus Confessor" (I am grateful to David T. Runia for this reference).

translated into Arabic by ʿAbdallāh ibn al-Faḍl.[43] For instance, in the Arabic version of chapter 17 ("On Education") we read:

> Philo said: It is unavoidable that an inexperienced horse rider should fall down over cliffs and precipices, just as when he is endowed with experience he is saved from these matters.
> He said also: It is difficult to be educated in great [things] before small [things].[44]

The first maxim is taken from the *Legum allegoriae* (1.73), where it appears in the context of Philo's discussion of the fourth river flowing out of Eden, Euphrates (Gen 2:14), symbolically understood as the fourth (in Philo's arrangement) cardinal virtue: justice.[45] The second maxim is adapted from Philo's *De vita Moysis* (1.62), where Philo explains why it was necessary for Moses to train himself first in herding sheep for his father-in-law as a preparation to becoming a perfect king.

19.2.3 Pseudo-Philonic Material

In addition to these authentic quotations, some "Pseudo-Philonic" citations appear in the so-called pagan testimonia collections, where mostly spurious quotations from pagan authors (Plato, Aristotle, Plutarch, Hermes Trismegistus, and others) are adduced in support of the Christian doctrines of the Trinity and the Incarnation. Here are two typical examples:

> Philo said: You can see those people exaggerating or limiting the number of virtues and ranks; as for me, I say that the one, great, and exalted God is three[fold].[46]
> Philo said: The Son of God shall come, having become incarnate and made Himself similar to the mortals of the earth.[47]

It is unfortunate that this interesting genre of Christian Arabic literature has not been studied (though there are some studies of similar collections in Greek and Syriac), and so it is impossible at present to know the provenance of these pseudo-Philonic quotations.[48]

---

[43] See chs 1, 2, 6, 7, 8, 12, 13, 17, 18, 21, 26, 27, 32, 39, 40, 41, 45, 60, 62, 66, 68, and 70 of the Arabic translation. Interestingly, Philo is grouped together with the church fathers, rather than the pagan Greek authors.
[44] MS Vat. ar. 111, fol. 117v; cf. Ihm, *Ps.-Maximus Confessor*, 402–3.
[45] On this maxim (sometimes misattributed to Justin Martyr), see Royse, *Spurious Texts*, 40–41 and 41 n. 65.
[46] Cited in the eleventh-century Nestorian encyclopedia *Kitāb al-Majdal*, *bāb* 2, *faṣl* 3 (MS Paris, BnF ar. 190, fol. 68v; Graf, *Geschichte*, 1:468 refers to the parallel manuscript Vat. ar. 108, fols 53r–54r).
[47] Cited in ʿAbdallāh ibn al-Faḍl's *Book of Benefit*, ch. 33 (MS Beirut, Bibliothèque Orientale 541, fol. 41v) and in Gerasimos' *An Exhaustive Compilation on the Healing Doctrine* (MS Beirut, Bibliothèque Orientale 548, fol. 128v).
[48] For an overview, see Graf, *Geschichte*, 1:483–6. On related Syriac material, see S. Brock, "A Syriac Collection of Prophecies of the Pagan Philosophers," in S. Brock, *Studies in Syriac Christianity* (Ashgate: Variorum, 1992), essay VII; Y. Arzhanov, *Syriac Sayings of Greek Philosophers: A Study in Syriac Gnomologia with Edition and Translation*, CSCO 669 / Subsidia 138 (Louvain: Peeters, 2019).

Finally, an eighteenth-century Christian Arabic manuscript from the Sbath Collection, now at the Vatican (MS Vat. Sbath 343, fols 15v–21v), contains a peculiar text about "the special properties (*khāṣṣiyyāt*) of the Psalms, according to the teacher and philosopher Philo the Jew (*Bīlūn al-yahūdī*)." The text "shows the effects produced by each of the 150 psalms on the sick and on those afflicted by evil spirits."[49] For example, "the first psalm is an admonition to the intelligent person; it is to be written and read to vanquish the enemy at the hour of Mars"; "the fourth psalm is on account of someone who is in distress and sorrow; he should read it three times daily, facing the sun while fasting, and the Creator will deliver him from his pain and strengthen him by His grace"; "the forty-first psalm is to be written on silver or lead; then, when someone is stung by a snake or a scorpion, he should wipe it off with honey and drink it—this is beneficial and well-tested"; "the one-hundred-and-twentieth psalm is to be read by a priest nine times over a woman with a flow of blood at the hour of Saturn, and the Creator will heal her and deliver her." Obviously, this treatise has no identifiable connection to the historical Philo, and is influenced rather by popular astrology, folk medicine, and magic.

19.3 Conclusion

This survey has presented all the hitherto discovered evidence for translations of, and references to, Philo in Christian Arabic literature. It demonstrates that an actual Philonic text—the *De vita contemplativa*—exists in Arabic, albeit in a fragmentary form (derived from Eusebius via, presumably, John of Scythopolis). In addition, Philonic quotations appear quite frequently in Christian Arabic florilegia (such as ʿAbdallāh ibn al-Faḍl's translation of the Greek "sacro-profane" florilegium *Loci communes*). Pseudo-Philonic materials, such as the spurious quotations in Christian Arabic collections of "pagan testimonia" and the Vatican text on the special properties of the Psalms, exist as well. There is thus strong evidence of Arabic transmission of Philonic thought—as well as disparate ideas falsely attributed to Philo—as part of the heritage of Arabophone Christianity in the Middle East.[50]

This evidence has something important to teach us about the avenues of access to Philonic thought available in the Middle East. As in late antiquity, so also in the early Islamic period, it was the Christians who were the custodians of Philo's legacy—and, no

---

[49] P. Sbath, *Bibliothèque de manuscrits Paul Sbath: Catalogue* (Cairo: H. Friedrich et Co., 1928), 1:151; cf. J. Nasrallah, *Histoire du mouvement littéraire dans l'église melchite du Ve au XXe siècle*, vol. IV/1 (Louvain: Peeters and Paris: Chez l'auteur, 1979), 242.

[50] Though the Arabic Dionysius—with its Philonic appendix—was used by a variety of Arabic-writing Christian theologians, particularly in Egypt (e.g. by the thirteenth-century Copto-Arabic authors al-Muʾtaman ibn al-ʿAssāl and Ibn Kātib Qayṣar), we have, so far, no direct evidence of Jews or Muslims reading this text. Nevertheless, as pointed out by Krisztina Szilágyi, there is a considerable amount of Christian Arabic material in the Cairo Genizah (see K. Szilágyi, "Christian Books in Jewish Libraries: Fragments of Christian Arabic Writings from the Cairo Genizah," *Ginzei Qedem* 2 [2006]: 107*–62*). This a clear sign that Arabophone Jews were reading Christian Arabic works, and it is certainly possible that some Jewish authors (and perhaps Muslim authors too) might have had access to this Philonic translation.

less importantly, of the vast body of patristic thought directly or indirectly inspired by Philo. After the Muslim conquest of the Middle East in the seventh century, it is, consequently, the Middle Eastern Christian communities who were in the best position to provide access to this Philonic legacy.

Arabic-speaking Christians (often bilingual, trilingual, or even multilingual—with access to sources in Greek, Syriac, and Coptic, and sometimes Armenian and Georgian) are an important "bridge community" that connected the worlds of late antiquity and early Islam. Any research into possible influences of ancient and late antique sources on medieval Arabic thought should therefore *begin* with a careful survey of what is available in Christian Arabic. Still insufficiently explored and for the most part (an estimated 90 per cent) unpublished, Christian literature in Arabic holds the promise of solving long-standing mysteries of intellectual history. This is particularly true of the virtually unstudied Christian Arabic translations of many hundreds of Greek patristic works: by the Cappadocian fathers, Evagrius, John Chrysostom, Dionysius the Areopagite, Maximus the Confessor, John of Damascus, and many others. These translations were produced in such important translation centers as the monastery of Mār Sābā in Palestine (in the eighth to tenth centuries) and in Antioch during the period of Byzantine reconquest of northern Syria (969–1084).[51] Once this vast body of material is carefully investigated and assessed, there is a real chance of discovering additional references to—and perhaps even translations of—Philo unknown today.

---

[51] On these translations, see Roberts, *Reason and Revelation in Byzantine Antioch*; B. Roggema and A. Treiger, eds, *Patristic Literature in Arabic Translations* (Leiden: Brill, 2020); A. Treiger, "Christian Graeco-Arabica: Prolegomena to a History of the Arabic Translations of the Greek Church Fathers," *Intellectual History of the Islamicate World* 3 (2015): 188–227; A. Treiger, *The Church Fathers in Arabic Translations* (Leiden: Brill, 2025).

20
Byzantium

David T. Runia

If a synoptic view is taken of the reception of Philo of Alexandria during the almost twenty centuries after his death, there can be little doubt that the period that has been least studied is the millennium between 500 and 1500, the Byzantine period in the east and the medieval period in the west.[1] The period before 500, which we might call the patristic era, is now being researched in more and more detail.[2] For the centuries following the invention of printing in the west there still remains much to be done, esp. especially for the period from the sixteenth to the eighteenth centuries. But for the Byzantine and medieval periods there is virtually nothing.[3]

The present article surveys the fate of Philo's writings and thought in the Byzantine period. There is so far no single study that gives an adequate overview of what happened to the Philonic heritage during this time. The article's purpose is to discover (1) who read Philo and wrote about him; (2) what part of his legacy did they utilize; (3) what were their motives in referring to him; and (4) what was their attitude towards him as a thinker, particularly as a Jewish author in an overwhelmingly Christian context. Byzantium in our title refers to the imperial capital, the undisputed center of scholarly activity during this period, but it is also meant more broadly. Two aspects of the theme will not be included, the legacy of Byzantine manuscripts of Philo's works and the account of the Armenian translation of Philo made in Byzantium in the sixth century. These topics are the subject of separate chapters in the present volume.[4]

Before proceeding a brief word should be devoted to methodology. As in my previous work on Philo in early Christian literature, my starting-point has been named references to Philo, supplemented with whatever other material I was able to find. In so doing I have made extensive use of the resources provided by that wonderful

---

[1] This article is a revised and shortened version of the article "Philo in Byzantium: An Exploration," *VC* 70 (2016): 259–81, which in turn was based on a paper originally presented at a conference on "Philo's Readers: Affinities, Reception, Transmission and Influence" held at Yale University on 30 March–2 April 2014. Full references to editions of Byzantine authors cited in this article can be obtained from the Thesaurus Linguae Graecae.

[2] See the chapters in the first two sections of the present volume.

[3] There are only some very brief remarks in D. T. Runia, *Philo in Early Christian Literature*, CRINT 3.3 (Assen: Van Gorcum, 1993), 271, 332. The article by S. B. Bowman, "Philo," in *The Oxford Dictionary of Byzantium*, ed. A. P. Kazdhan (New York: Oxford University Press, 1991), 3:1655, is useful but very brief. For Philo in the Latin medieval west, see Chapter 21 in this volume. For a full list of references to Philo up to 1500 CE see now: D. T. Runia, Y. Arzhanov, and A. Treiger, "References to Philo of Alexandria in Greek, Latin, Syriac and Arabic Literature up to 1500 CE," *SPhiloA* 35 (2023): 231–59.

[4] See "The Greek and Latin Manuscript Traditions" by James R. Royse and "Armenian Christianity" by Olga Vardazaryan in the present volume.

instrument of classical scholarship, the Thesaurus Linguae Graecae. It is a most fortunate development that a considerable proportion of Byzantine writings up to the fall of Constantinople have been taken up in the database.[5] The limitations of this approach are evident. Learned allusions to Philonic texts that do not carry his name will be missed unless they have been spotted by scholars. Nevertheless I am convinced that this method will allow a convincing picture of the reception of Philo's writings and thought to be outlined. This will be valuable for further research on the subject.[6]

20.1 The Early Byzantine Period

We first turn to the beginnings of the Byzantine era, that period of the later Roman Empire when in the east the seat of power and learning begins to center more and more on the imperial capital Byzantium. A good person to start with is John Lydus (c.490–565). A civil servant in the imperial bureaucracy for more than forty years, John also prided himself on his learning and scholarship. His earliest work still extant is entitled *On the Months*, a history of calendars and feasts, in which he demonstrates impressive erudition in historical and antiquarian matters. This work makes extensive use of Philonic material, most of which has gone unnoticed by its editors.[7] Philo himself is mentioned by name in one passage only, in which he is discussing the ten different Sibyls in the ancient world. Of these the first (and most famous) was known as the Chaldean and Persian Sibyl, but also as the Hebrew Sibyl. Lydus appeals to Philo's account of the life of Moses to demonstrate that the Hebrews were also known as Chaldeans,[8] thereby justifying the identification. We note that he simply refers to Philo as the author of the life of Moses, without drawing attention to the fact that he is Jewish.

Earlier in the work John discusses the various aspects of the calendar involving days, weeks and months and this gives him numerous opportunities to dwell on the features of numbers. In his 1931 study of Philo's arithmology Karl Staehle identified no less than thirty-eight passages which show strong resemblance and some cases are verbally identical to Philonic texts in the *Quaestiones* and the Exposition of the Law. Most of these focus on the numbers one to eight, but there are also passages on the numbers 12, 13, and 30.[9] The relationship of these passages to Philo is not fully clear. In a detailed examination of those related to *De opificio mundi* I concluded that it was more likely that he used Philo than they both used a common source. It is even possible that he had access

---

[5] Of course, many unpublished works, esp. florilegia and exegetical writings, have so far not been included. So, for example, most of the writings of Nicetas Serrenus (see below at n. 53) are absent.

[6] For the full list of named references to Philo up to 1500 CE see D. T. Runia, Y. Arzhanov, and A. Treiger, "References to Philo of Alexandria." It replaces the list up to 1000 CE published in Runia, *Philo in Early Christian Literature* and updated in D. T. Runia, *Philo and the Church Fathers* (Leiden: Brill, 1995), 228–39.

[7] Only the two passages where Philo is explicitly named are identified; see R. Wuensch, *Ioannis Laurentii Lydi liber de mensibus* (Leipzig: Teubner, 1898), 103; A. C. Bandy, *On the Months (De mensibus): Three Works of Ioannes Lydus 1* (Lewiston: Mellon Press, 2013), 233.

[8] *Mens.* 4.47 103.16–104.1 Wuensch; 4.52 176.13–21 Bandy. This is a peculiarity of *Mos.* and a few other treatises, mainly in the Exposition of the Law; see C.-K. Wong, "Philo's Use of Chaldaioi," *SPhiloA* 4 (1992): 1–14.

[9] K. Staehle, *Die Zahlenmystik bei Philon von Alexandreia* (Leipzig: Teubner, 1931), 18–64.

to Philo's lost book on numbers, the Περὶ ἀριθμῶν.[10] Two other extracts from Philo have been identified, both from the first book of *De somniis*.[11] The one describes the nature and appearance of the moon; the other, which includes a quote from Euripides, compares human affairs to movement up and down a ladder. Philo uses the motif in his interpretation of Jacob's ladder. John is not interested in this exegetical aspect, but uses it in order to illustrate the workings of chance. In both cases Philo's words are written out almost verbatim without any indication that the passage was taken from elsewhere.

In his use of Philo as a source for history and for arithmology John follows in the footsteps of Alexandrian church fathers such as Clement and Didymus. The texts from *De somniis* are interesting because they concern what we might call scientific and popular-philosophical themes. Though he mentions that Moses' writings were translated into Greek under Ptolemy,[12] he does not use Philo for theological or exegetical purposes.

A little earlier than John two other authors made extensive and very different use of Philo's works for purposes of understanding the first two books of the Bible. An unknown author, very likely making use of the resources of the Episcopal Library of Caesarea, initiated a new kind of exegetical work called the catena, listing large numbers of extracts from the works of the church fathers in the order of the biblical text which they comment on. In his *Catenae on Genesis and Exodus* he included numerous quotes from Philo's *Quaestiones* (and also a few from the *De vita Moysis*).[13] Philo is named as the author, quite often and rather strikingly as "Philo the bishop." The date for the work is estimated to be the turn of the sixth century.[14] This material was also utilized by Procopius of Gaza (465–538) in his commentary on *Genesis*, part of his larger work, the commentary on the *Octateuch*.[15] Some time later Philo's works were even more extensively exploited in the so-called *Sacra parallela* attributed to John of Damascus (675–750). This highly influential work is more theological than exegetical, drawing

---

[10] D. T. Runia, *Philo on the Creation of the Cosmos According to Moses* (Leiden: Brill, 2001), 303–4. The book may still have been available at this time, because an extract from it appears to have been translated by the Armenian translators; see A. Terian, "A Philonic Fragment on the Decad," in *Nourished with Peace: Studies in Hellenistic Judaism in Memory of Samuel Sandmel*, ed. F. E. Greenspahn, E. Hilgert and B. L. Mack (Chico, CA: Scholars Press: 1984), 173–82; reprinted in A. Terian, *Opera Selecta Teriana: A Scholarly Retrospective* (New Rochelle, NY: St Nersess Armenian Seminary, 2008), 289–300.

[11] *Mens*. 3.12 54.12–17 Wuensch, 102.21–24 Bandy (*Somn*. 1.145); *Mens*. 4.7 72.21–73.10 Wuensch, 128.22–30 Bandy (*Somn*. 1.153–55). L. Cohn and P. Wendland, *Philonis Alexandrini opera quae supersunt* (Berlin: Georg Reimer, 1896–1915), ad locc. (henceforth C–W) overlooked the former text but not the latter.

[12] *Mens*. 4.47 103.25 Wuensch, 176.20 Bandy.

[13] For an overview of the surviving *Catena in Genesim*, with a grounded hypothesis on its anonymous source, see F. Petit, "La chaîne grecque sur la Genèse, miroir de l'exégèse ancienne," in *Stimuli: Exegese und ihre Hermeneutik in Antike und Christentum*, ed. G. Schöllgen and C. Scholten (Münster: Achendorff, 1996), 243–53. Both this work and the *Catena in Exodum* have been edited by her in seven volumes: *La Chaîne sur la Genèse*, 4 vols (Louvain: Peeters, 1992–96); *La Chaîne sur l'Exode*, 3 vols (Louvain: Peeters, 1999–2001). On Philo's presence in these works, see J. R. Royse, *The Spurious Texts of Philo of Alexandria* (Leiden: Brill 1991), 14–25; D. T. Runia, "Philonica in the *Catena in Genesim*," SPhiloA 11 (1999): 113–20.

[14] According to Petit *La Chaîne sur la Genèse* 1.xv the terminus post quem is the second half of the fifth century.

[15] The *Genesis* commentary has very recently been edited and translated into German by K. Metzler, *Prokop von Gaza Eclogarum in libros historicos Veteris Testamenti epitome*, Vol. 1: *Der Genesiskommentar*, GCS N.F. 22 (Berlin: de Gruyter, 2015); *Prokop von Gaza Der Genesiskommentar. Aus den "Eclogarum in libros historicos Veteris Testamenti epitome" übersetzt und mit Anmerkungen versehen*, GCS N.F. 23 (Berlin: de Gruyter, 2016). Metzler argues that both the catenist and Procopius made use of material originally bequeathed to the Library of Caesarea by Origen. In so doing Procopius (but not the catenist) has suppressed all named references to Philo. The evidence provided by these two sources was already included in F. Petit, *Quaestiones in Genesim et in Exodum: fragmenta graeca*, OPA 33 (Paris: CERF, 1978).

on all of Philo's expository writings and including many extracts from the Allegorical Commentary.[16] Much research remains to be done on the use of Philo in these three sources. For centuries they have been mined for evidence of lost writings of Philo and for further information on the textual transmission of the corpus Philonicum. But no analysis has ever been carried out on *how* Philo's writings were used in these massive compilations.

Quite different and rather unfortunate is the reference to Philo found in Anastasius (*c*.610 to *c*.700), the abbot of St. Catherine's monastery in the Sinai. In his chief work the *Hodēgos* (*Guidebook*), Anastasius demonstrates his obsession with orthodoxy and the fight against heresy. This is the context for his references to Philo. He cites the "most skilled of exegetes Ammonius of Alexandria" who wrote a book against Julian of Halicarnassus.[17] The argument is typically convoluted. "The detestable Philo (ὁ μιαρὸς Φίλων)" has great difficulty as a Jew accepting Christ's divine nature, given all the human sufferings he undergoes, but at least he does not deny his human nature.[18] This can thus be taken as a back-handed compliment. Anastasius takes over the negative reference to Philo, which is unprecedented in the entire Byzantine tradition.[19] Much more positive is the reference to Philo in an exegetical work on the Hexameron attributed to Anastasius.[20] On two occasions, when discussing the events in paradise the author mentions "Philo the philosopher" in a list of "exegetes of the churches" which includes names such as Papias, Irenaeus, Pantaenus, and Clement.[21] Here Philo reverts to his customary role as "honorary Church Father."

20.2 The Ninth- and Tenth-Century Renaissance

We make a jump now to the ninth century, skipping two and a half centuries which the distinguished French scholar Paul Lemerle has called the "dark ages" of the Byzantine era.[22] This century is dominated by the amazingly learned and industrious scholar and man of the church, Photius (*c*.810–*c*.893). In his great work, the *Bibliotheca*, written at a relatively young age when he was not yet Patriarch, he records the vast number of books he had read. Three brief chapters are devoted to Philo (cod. 103–5),[23] forming

---

[16] On this work, see Petit, *Quaestiones*, 21–22; Royse, *Spurious Texts*, 26–28.
[17] Active in the first half of the sixth century; see M. Geerard, *Clavis Patrum Graecorum*, 5 vols (Turnhout: Brepols, 1974–87), 3:350.
[18] *Viae dux* 13.10.1–96 (CCG 8.251).
[19] See the discussion in Runia, *Philo in Early Christian Literature*, 210–11. But many unanswered questions remain, particularly the account the text gives of the dispute between Philo and "the apostolic disciple Mnason" mentioned in Acts 21:16.
[20] *Hex.* 7b3.251, 5.469 in the edition of C. A. Kuehn and J. D. Baggarly, *Anastasius of Sinai Hexaemeron* (Rome: Pontificio Istituto Orientale, 2007). The editors are inclined to the view that the work is by Anastasius, but they recognize that there is some lingering uncertainty (p. xxiii).
[21] *In Hexaemeron*, Book 7b.3.3.251 p. 469 Kuehn–Baggarly. Note that the second list is taken over and slightly modified by Michael Glycas, the twelfth-century Byzantine historian, in his *Quaestiones in sacram scripturam* 11, 145.19 Eustratiades. The context is the same exegetical theme of paradise.
[22] P. Lemerle, *Le premier humanisme Byzantin: notes et remarques sur enseignement et culture à Byzance des origines au Xe siècle* (Paris: Presses Universitaires de France, 1971), 74.
[23] Text and translation in R. Henry, *Photius Bibliothèque*, 8 vols (Paris: Les belles lettres, 1959–77), 2:71–2.

part of a cluster mainly devoted to Alexandrian writers and including Clement (cod. 103–11).

We are told that he has read six works of Philo, grouped in three sets of two treatises: first the *Legum allegoriae* and the *De Iosepho*, called by its alternative title Περὶ βίου πολιτικοῦ; next the lives of those among the Jews living the theoretical and practical life, i.e. *De vita contemplativa* and *Quod omnis probus sit*;[24] finally the two historical treatises, *In Flaccum* and *Legatio ad Gaium* (perhaps relying on his memory, he gives them different names).[25] In these last-named works, he notes, Philo shows more than elsewhere the "rhetorical force and the beauty of his language" (or one might translate "style"). A very brief critique of his thought follows: "He goes astray in many areas, assuming (the existence of) ideas and writing down other things foreign to Jewish philosophy."[26] After indicating exactly when Philo lived, Photius then mentions his many and varied treatises. These, he writes, "contain ethical subjects and commentaries on the Old Testament, which for the most part strain hard to convert the text to allegory. From here, I think, the entire method of allegorical interpretation of scripture has been able to penetrate into the Church." The final section gives details of Philo's interactions with the early Church, details which have been passed down from earlier biographical notices. Photius ends with a flourish by praising the power of Philo's style and quoting the famous proverb "Either Plato philonizes or Philo platonizes."[27]

In his fine analysis of these chapters, the Belgian scholar Jacques Schamp pointed out that the last five of the six works that Photius says he has read occur in the same sequence in the previously mentioned early thirteenth-century manuscript which contains most of Philo's treatises, the Laurentianus plutei X, 20 (M in C–W's apparatus).[28] Maybe this is a clue to an earlier manuscript that the Byzantine scholar used for his reading. He seems a little vague in his descriptions, so he may be relying on his memory.[29] Of particular interest are the two points of criticism that he raises. The first concerns the ideas, doubtless with reference to Philo's Platonism. There are plenty of references to the ideas in *Legum allegoriae* books 1 and 2 starting on the very first page, so Photius may be remembering those. But perhaps his criticism has a wider scope. Here it may be legitimate to adduce the more explicit criticism that he makes of Clement of Alexandria, the first Christian to exploit Philo's works, of whom he writes: "In some of these statements he appears to speak rightly (ὀρθῶς), but in others he strays completely into the realm of impious and mythic doctrines. He puts forward the view that matter stands outside time and that there are ideas which are introduced on the basis

---

[24] The work meant here must be *Prob.*, not the missing "prequel" to *Contempl.* which was most likely lost at a much earlier date.

[25] One name that he gives, Φλάκκος ψεγόμενος, is given as an alternative in the MS Vaticano-Palatinus gr. 248 (G in C–W; no. 83 in H. L. Goodhart and E. R. Goodenough, "Manuscripts of Philo," in *The Politics of Philo Judaeus: Practice and Theory*, ed. E. R. Goodenough [New Haven: Yale University Press, 1938], 146).

[26] My translation is based on W. T. Treadgold, *The Nature of the Bibliotheca of Photius* (Washington, DC: Dumbarton Oaks Center, 1980), 84 n. 6.

[27] On this proverb, first attested in Jerome but certainly older, see Runia, *Philo in Early Christian Literature*, 313.

[28] J. Schamp, *Photios historien des lettres: la Bibliothèque et ses notices biographiques* (Paris: Les belles lettres, 1987), 460. This manuscript is No. 100 in Goodhart–Goodenough, "Manuscripts of Philo," 149.

[29] As suggested by Treadgold, *Bibliotheca of Photius*, 84.

338   THE RECEPTION OF PHILO OF ALEXANDRIA

of certain expressions (in scripture)."[30] What Photius accuses Clement of here is precisely what the latter learned from Philo, and it may also play a role in the background of his criticism of Philo himself. In his formulation Photius implies that the doctrine of the ideas is foreign to Judaism (which it is of course, certainly to the Judaism of his own time), as well as other doctrines. Despite his rapprochement with Christianity, Philo is thus judged as a Jewish thinker. The other criticism is more subtle. Photius refers to the method of allegorical interpretation that is so central in Philo's work, and essential to the *Legum allegoriae* which he read. The two terms ἐκβιαζόμενα (strain hard) and εἰσρυῆναι (penetrate) have a slightly negative connotation, but this should not be exaggerated. As Ashwin-Siejkowski has shown,[31] Photius inclined to the more literal approach of the Antiochene school, but did retain some appreciation for the Alexandrian allegory provided it was not done to excess.

Second only to Photius as a humanist and man of letters was his pupil Arethas of Patras (c.860–c.940). Though appointed archbishop of Caesarea in Cappodocia, he spent much of his time in the capital. He is particularly famous for his library of Platonic manuscripts, which still survive and form the basis of our modern texts of Plato and numerous other authors including Justin Martyr and Clement of Alexandria.[32] Would this library have contained a codex of Philonic works? The answer is very likely no. The only reference to or use of Philo that I could find is in his *Commentary on the Apocalypse of John*, a revised and expanded version of an earlier work by his sixth-century predecessor in Caesarea, Andrew. In commenting on the seven churches in Asia (Rev 1:4), he explains more fully than Andrew the power of the hebdomad in perishable creation and includes a reference to Philo when he adds "in which it is not thought superfluous to be in harmony with that most contemplative Jewish man Philo, in his book on the philosophy according to Moses."[33] This is an obvious reference to the *De opificio mundi* and its excessively long section on the hebdomad, which no reader is ever likely to forget. Arethas will have been such a reader, but he makes no use of its specific doctrines in the work and nowhere else refers to Philo.

A touchstone of Byzantine learning at the end of the first millennium is the *Souda*, the splendid alphabetically ordered encyclopedia consisting of more than 30,000 lemmata. Philo appears in eight entries, most of which are quite substantial.[34] There is in fact more material than can be dealt with adequately in the present context, so I will be selective and just mention a number of highlights.

The main entry on Philo himself (Φ 448) follows the tradition that goes back to Eusebius and Jerome. The emphasis falls on Philo's learning, style, and literary productivity. Unlike in Photius, a substantial list of his works is presented and there are no

---

[30] *Bibl.* 109 2.80.1–4 (my translation). For an alternative (in my view less convincing) translation, see P. Ashwin-Siejkowski, *Clement of Alexandria on Trial: The Evidence of "Heresy" from Photius' Bibliotheca*, VCSup (Leiden: Brill, 2010), 23.
[31] Ashwin-Siejkowski, *Clement of Alexandria*, 12–14.
[32] See detailed account of his library in Lemerle, *Le premier humanisme*, 205–41.
[33] *Comm. in Apoc.* at PG 106.504; cf. Andreas, *Comm. in Apol.* 1.1 Schmidt on Rev 1:4, where there is no reference to Philo.
[34] Texts in A. Adler, ed., *Suidae Lexicon*, 5 vols (Leipzig: Teubner, 1928–38).

critical comments. It is emphasised at the end of the notice that the value of his treatises lies in their usefulness (ὠφέλεια). Much less detail is given on Philo's life and links with early Christianity than in Photius.

Material from Philo is used to illustrate the meaning of two key philosophical concepts, δύναμις (power, Δ 1573) and θεός (God, Θ 178).[35] The latter excerpt is all the more interesting because it is taken from a letter of Isidore of Pelusium in which he compliments Philo the Jew on perceiving important aspects of the Christian mystery of the Trinity.[36] These excerpts show how the far-reaching integration of Philo into the patristic tradition has extended into the Byzantine era. The lemma on βίος (life, Β 294) starts off with the words ἐκ τῶν Φίλωνος (from the works of Philo) followed by the opening phrase "the Church of Christ prescribes two lives and ways of living." The excerpt is in fact from Eusebius.[37] Is this just a mistake, or does the encyclopediast really think that Philo might have written this? But for the lemmata on Josephus (I 503) and the Therapeutae (Θ 228) the reader is left in no doubt that Philo is a Jewish author. Indeed, in the latter lemma the content of *De vita contemplativa* is summarized, but no mention is made of a possible Christian connection.[38]

Many of the entries in the encyclopedia are lexical, explaining distinctive words or phrases. There is only one such entry for Philo, but it is particularly interesting. It concerns the participle ἀγαλματοφορούμενος (A 136), derived from the verb ἀγαλματοφορέω, "carry as an image." It is the most distinctive of the so-called *verba Philonica*, used by Philo no less than seventeen times and imitated by patristic authors such as Origen, Eusebius, Didymus the Blind, and John Chrystostom.[39] The same entry is found attributed to Philo in five other Byzantine lexica, including the one composed by Photius himself.[40] This of course shows the compilatory and derivative nature of Byzantine lexicography and is not necessarily based on attentive study of Philo's writings. We return to the subject of Philo's language and style later in this article.

The historical information on Philo found in Photius and the *Souda* is also found in various forms in the many histories and chronicles produced during the Byzantine period. The earliest Byzantine historian to mention him is George the Syncellus (died after 810), who in his account of world history up to 284 CE cites

---

[35] *Souda* s.v. The former lemma is fascinating because its first half is a brief excerpt from the well-known text about the two powers at *QE* 1.23 (of which no other Greek excerpts survive), but I have not been able to trace the provenance of the second half.

[36] On this text, see D. T. Runia, "Philo of Alexandria in Five Letters of Isidore of Pelusium," in *Heirs of the Septuagint. Philo, Hellenistic Judaism and Early Christianity: Festschrift for Earle Hilgert* [= SPhiloA 3 (1991)], ed. D. T. Runia, D. M. Hay, and D. Winston (Atlanta: Scholars Press, 1991), 295–319, esp. 299–306; reprinted in Runia, *Philo and the Church Fathers*, 155–81.

[37] *Suppl. min. ad quaest. ad Marinum* PG 22.1008; cf. *Dem. ev.* 1.8.1–4 (longer version of same text).

[38] Note also that the text of summary is derived from Eusebius' account in *Hist. eccl.* 2.16–17 rather than directly from Philo's text.

[39] On such words and the particular case of this term, see further D. T. Runia, "Verba Philonica, Ἀγαλματοφορεῖν, and the Authenticity of the *De Resurrectione* attributed to Athenagoras," *VC* 46 (1992): 313–27; reprinted in Runia, *Philo and the Church Fathers*, 102–16.

[40] Eudemus rhetor Περὶ λέξεων ῥητορικῶν folio 2b Niese (read οὕτως Φίλων for οὐ φίλων); Pseudo-Zonaras *Lexicon* A p. 35.4 Tittmann; Photius *Lexicon* A 91 Theodoridis; Anonymus lexicographus Συναγωγὴ λέξεων κτλ A 68 Cunningham; Lexica Seguieriana *Coll. verb. util.* A p. 7.3 Bachmann. Note that many references in lexica to "Philo" are in fact to a work on etymologies by Herennius Philo, who lived about half a century after Philo of Alexandria.

Philo three times on events during the reign of Gaius.[41] Much more interesting is the *Chronicle* of George Harmatalus written two generations later. When describing the reign of Gaius he first says that "Philo and Josephus the Hebrew sages were prominent (ἐγνωρίζοντο)," using a common formula from the chronographic tradition.[42] Philo is regarded as a trustworthy witness for the apostolic age, particularly through his description of the Therapeutae who, following Eusebius, he connects with the evangelist Mark.[43] Remarkably Philo is also mentioned in George's account of the Arian controversy, when—just like the *Souda*—he cites Isidore's famous letter on the Trinity.[44] The references to the Therapeutae and Isidore's letter are taken over by George Cedrenus in the late eleventh century.[45] After the three Georges there are in the period from the twelfth to the fourteenth century five further chronographers and historians who mention Philo, but do little more than repeat earlier material.[46]

20.3 From the Eleventh Century Onwards

Returning to the golden age of Byzantine humanism, we encounter a century later the extraordinarily impressive figure of Michael Psellus (1018–c.1082). As the greatest polymath of his time, and perhaps of the entire Byzantine era, we would expect him to be acquainted with Philo. Yet in the numerous works that survive he only mentions our author by name twice.

In the collection of his minor orations there is a very long piece entitled *Encomium of the Monk John Kroustoulas Reading in the (Church of the) Holy Shrine*.[47] In it Psellus records how he happened to enter the church and was astounded by the crowd of people who had assembled to hear this gifted preacher. Psellus' oration is an extravagant piece of epideictic rhetoric, in which he takes every opportunity to display his very considerable erudition and linguistic skill. It is crammed with literary and philosophical allusions. Fairly early on Philo is named out of the blue as part of a digression on the malleability of the intellect. Psellus tells us that Philo names this faculty in allegorical terms (τροπικῶς) "spring," and he then continues with a number of themes from the interpretation of Gen 2:6–7 in *Legum allegoriae* Book 1 (the same book read

---

[41] *Ecloga chronographica* 399.5, 402.14, 19 Mosshammer. The claim at 232.18 that Philo refers to Olympiads is mistaken, unless George had access to works we no longer possess.

[42] *Chronicon* 324.17 de Boor.

[43] *Chonicon* 328.2, 332.5, 334.7, 339.11.

[44] *Chronicon* 526.18, 527.21, 529.19; on Isidore's letter, see above at n. 36.

[45] *Compendium historiarum* 351.10, 353.9, 507.18, 508.15, 510.13 Bekker.

[46] They are John Zonaras (twelfth century), Michael Glycas (twelfth century), Joel Chronographus (thirteenth century), Nicephorus Callistus Xanthopulus (thirteenth–fourteenth century) and Ephraem Aeniensis (fourteenth century). Note also that the canonist Michael Blastares (d. 1346) refers to the "more eloquent Hebrews" Philo and Josephus in relation to the date of Easter (*Coll. alph.* Pi 7.60 Potles-Rhalles), following the much earlier *Chronicon Paschale* (c.650).

[47] The text has been edited twice, by P. Gautier, "Eloge inédit du lecteur Jean Kroustoulas par Michel Psellos," *Rivista di studi bizantini e neoellenici* 17–19 (1980–82): 119–47; and as no. 37 in A. R. Littlewood, *Michaelis Pselli Oratoria Minora* (Leipzig: Teubner, 1985), 137–51.

by Photius).⁴⁸ The entire passage occupies no more than four lines. But nearing the end of his account Psellus mentions the preacher's humility and this leads him to cite the story of Alexander's boast recorded by Philo in *De cherubim*. Remarkably he then devotes an entire paragraph to quotes from the Allegorical Commentary—excellently identified by the editor Littlewood⁴⁹—which together form an exhortation to the good and virtuous life. There is no hint whatsoever in the text that they are derived from Philo. No doubt Psellus here follows the ancient practice (also found in Clement),⁵⁰ in which a single mention of a name in a work is meant to place the learned reader on the alert. It again reminds us that many allusions to Philo's writings may still be hidden in Byzantine works waiting for scholarly identification.

The date of the oration is not known, but we may deduce that prior to its composition Psellus had read and memorized substantial sections of Philo's Allegorical Commentary.⁵¹ Remarkably he makes no reference to Philo elsewhere (unless there are allusions yet to be discovered), with just one exception, namely in a sarcastic poem directed at a monk who had a ridiculously over-inflated opinion of his literary and philosophical talents. First there is list of great philosophers, including Plato and Aristotle, who have been defeated by this man, followed by the names of two great rhetors, Demosthenes and Hermogenes. Compared with you, he then adds, "the works of Philo and Josephus are nonsense" (λῆρος).⁵² It is gratifying to see Philo's name in such a context. But it does remain surprising that Psellus in his vast *œuvre* does not allude to him more often.

A younger contemporary of Psellus was Niketas of Serres (c.1050–c.1120), who held the post of *didaskalos* at Hagia Sophia before becoming Metropolitan of Herakleia Pontike. His best-known work is the *Catena on the Gospel of Luke*, compiled in Constantinople.⁵³ Seven excerpts from Philo are part of a collection of more than 3,300 texts drawn from more than sixty patristic and Byzantine authors (Josephus is cited once). One passage is taken from the *Quaestiones in Exodum*,⁵⁴ one from *De sobrietate*, the remainder from *De decalogo* and *De specialibus legibus*, including a very long

---

⁴⁸ *Orat. min.* 37.134–37 Littlewood. Of the four elements of this text the first and last are derived from *Leg.* 1.28 and 1.31–42 respectively. The phrase οὐράνιον φύτον taken from Plato *Tim.* 90a is cited at *Det.* 85 and *Plant.* 17 and Psellus may have remembered it from there. The phrase οἰκήτορα τοῦ παραδείσου is not found in the extant corpus Philonicum. See also the annotated translation by S. Papaioannou, "Encomium for the Monk Ioannes Kroustoulas Who Read Aloud at the Holy Soros," in *Michael Psellos on Literature and Art: A Byzantine Perspective on Aesthetics*, ed. C. Barber and S. Papaioannou (Notre Dame: Notre Dame University Press, 2017), 218–44.
⁴⁹ Littlewood, *Michaelis Pselli*, 150–51 (allusions at *Orat. min.* 37.427–47).
⁵⁰ See esp. the reference to Philo at *Str.* 2.100.3, which provides the "hint" for the large-scale use of Philo in 2.78–100. The same practice may be followed by Lydus, who in the *De mensibus* uses Philo often, but refers to him only once.
⁵¹ The passages alluded to are: *Cher.* 63; *Sacr.* 35, 40; *Post.* 145; *Leg.* 1.102; *Gig.* 60; *Post.* 174; *Agr.* 24. To judge by the two passages taken together Psellus must have read the Allegorical Commentary at least up to *Agr.* (I correct my statement in "Philo in Byzantium: An Exploration" [see n. 1 above], 273 n. 64).
⁵² *Pselli poemata* 68.29–37 Westerink.
⁵³ Edited by C. T. Krikones, Συναγωγὴ πατέρων εἰς τὸ κατὰ Λοῦκαν εὐαγγέλιον ὑπὸ Νικήτα Ἡρακλείας (Thessalonike: Kentron Byzantinôn Ereunôn, 1973). But the details of his usage are better presented by Wendland in C–W 2.xv–xvi. On the MSS, see also Goodhart–Goodenough, 'Manuscripts of Philo,' 240–48.
⁵⁴ This does not necessarily mean that Niketas had access to the original Greek text (now lost), since he could have taken it over from an existing source. But this text is cited nowhere else; cf. Petit, *Quaestiones*, 236. As was noted above in n. 35, there is a passage in the *Souda* from the same work.

passage on the Jewish feasts in order to illustrate the mention of the feast of unleavened bread in Luke 22:1. It appears that Niketas used a codex of the highest quality and his excerpts have proved most valuable for the constitution of the Philonic text.[55] In his activity as catenist and use of Philo the Byzantine theologian follows in the footsteps of the early sixth-century catenist on Genesis and Exodus, but now for the purpose of understanding a book from the New Testament.

There are a number of other prominent authors in the twelfth century who make reference to Philo. Basil of Ohrid, Metropolitan of Ohrid (d. 1169), in his debate with Anselm of Havelberg defends the value of Greek education and tells his opponent to listen to Philo who first "fertilized" (σπερμογονεῖ) with Hagar and then in his old age with Sarah, referring to the well-known allegory in *De congressu*.[56] His successor, the celebrated Homeric commentator Eustathius (c.1115–69), twice refers to Philo's phrase ὁ γεγωνὸς λόγος when commenting on *Il*. 12.337 and *Od*. 5.400.[57] In addition, in an allusion recently identified by Karin Metzler, in the *De emendanda vita monachica* he allusively calls Philo "the sweet Hebrew rhetor" who recounts the monastic life of the Essenes.[58] Almost a century later the remarkably learned emperor of Nicaea, Theodore II Lascaris (1221–58), in his letters twice makes erudite allusions to Philo, calling him "the Platonizing Philo and in this respect divine" and noting his reversal of the genders of female and male in relation to virtue and mind (cf. *Abr*. 101–2).[59]

The final port of call on our long journey is the fourteenth century, which follows on the massive disruptions of the thirteenth. The Byzantine Empire still continues, but would appear to be in terminal decline. Yet it is only now that we encounter an entire critical essay on Philo's writings and thought. Written by the eminent scholar and statesman Theodore Metochites (1270–1332), it has been recently edited and translated by the Swedish scholar Karin Hult.[60] Metochites describes his essays as *Semeioseis gnomikai*—a difficult title which Hult translates as *Sententious Notes*. They are brief memoranda, we read, written by one who lives "in the dregs of time," when everything has been examined and said, and it is only possible to review what others have achieved.[61] The chapter on Philo is number 16 in the series and follows essays on Plato, Aristotle, and Josephus.

---

[55] See Wendland in C–W 2.xv–xvi; Cohn in C–W 4.xxiv, 5.xvi–xvii.
[56] *Dialogi Anselmi Havelbergensis episcopi* 1 37.4 Schmidt.
[57] *Commentarii ad Homeri Iliadem* 3.405.24 Van der Valk, *Commentarii ad Homeri Odysseam* 1.223.9 Stallbaum; Philo uses the phrase at *Cher*. 9, *Deus* 83, *Migr*. 169 with reference to the λόγος προφορικός, as Eustathius notes.
[58] 195.13 Metzler: ἀλλ' εἰ χρὴ οὕτω φάναι, κατὰ τοὺς περιᾳδομένους Ἐσσαιούς, οὓς ὁ γλυκὺς Ἑβραῖος ῥήτωρ καθιστορεῖ, οἷς μᾶλλον ἀφομοιώσεται τὸ κοινοβιακὸν μοναχικόν. See further K. Metzler, *Eustathios von Thessalonike und das Mönchtum: Untersuchungen und Kommentar zur Schrift* De emendanda vita monachica, Corpus fontium historiae Byzantinae 45 (Berlin: de Gruyter, 2006), 592.
[59] *Epistulae* 94.17 Festa; see also *Ep*. 121.51; Κοσμικὴ δήλωσις 26.11 Festa. Similarly, the allusion of Gregory Antiochus (second half of the twelfth century) to the phrase ψηλαφητὸν σκότος which he "learnt from the all-wise Philo" reveals close reading of Philo's allegorical treatises (cf. *Somn*. 1.114).
[60] *Semeioseis gnomikai*, ch. 16 Περὶ Φίλωνος; see K. Hult, *Theodore Metochites on Ancient Authors and Philosophy: Semeioseis gnomikai 1–26 & 71*, Studia Graeca et Latina Gothoburgensia 65 (Goteburg: Acta Universitatis Gothoburgensis, 2002), 150–57. Philo is also mentioned in ch. 17: Ὅτι πάντες ὅσοι ἐν Αἰγύπτῳ ἐπαιδεύθησαν τραχύτερον τῷ λέγειν χρῶνται, see Hult *Theodore Metochites*, 158–65.
[61] *Sem. gnom.* 1.

Metochites starts off by citing and criticizing the well-known proverb which compares Philo and Plato. Though elegantly phrased, it is a patent exaggeration. Philo is a man of great wisdom, but he cannot be compared to Plato. In fact Philo is a follower (αἱρεσιώτης) of Plato's philosophy. He is focused on theological doctrine,[62] ethics, and mathematics, and follows Plato in not despising natural philosophy but showing less interest in it. Philo writes well, but as befits a man dedicated to the pursuit of wisdom, it is not his main aim. He was not at all involved in politics even though there was plenty of opportunity to do so (this is a surprising misconception on Metochites' part).[63] Having made a thorough study of his own tradition, he devoted his labor to the sacred writings of Moses and attributed the whole of wisdom to them, whether through a literal reading or the techniques of allegory.[64]

The final part of the essay is devoted to a full discussion of Philo's language and style, which I can summarize only in very brief terms. His style is portrayed as lofty in thoughts, rhythms, and composition. At the same time, it is simple and unmannered,[65] as befits a philosopher, but not without solemnity and dignity. The beauty of Philo's language consists not in figures or in the convoluted flow of his statements, but rather in the clarity and innovations of his words. But it can also be somewhat harsh, the result of Philo's nature and his Alexandrian background.[66]

Metochites' fascinating critique builds on earlier briefer remarks by Josephus, Eusebius and Photius, and is deserving of a much fuller analysis than it has received so far.[67] He anticipates the results of modern research not only by stressing Philo's Platonism, but also in his emphasis on the central role of exegesis in his work. It is striking that, even though he recognizes the doctrinal nature of Philo's thought, he praises rather than criticizes it, and unlike Photius does not disapprove of the elaborations of his allegories. The nuances and subtleties of his critique are directed above all at Philo's language and style.

Metochites was not alone among late Byzantine authors in showing interest in Philo's style and language. An almost exact contemporary was the learned monk and physician Joseph Rhakendytes ("Rag-wearer," c.1260–c.1330). In his *Synopsis of the Art of Rhetoric* he mentions Philo in the chapter on language (or style, λέξις). Language is divided into the plain and the elaborate and it is not difficult to predict where Philo is placed: "As examples of elaborate language," he writes, "you can take among the ancients Philo, Synesius, and Philostratus."[68] We should note that this

---

[62] The term here is δογματικός, 150.20. Hult's translation "interested in metaphysics" is not convincing.

[63] Perhaps caused by the contrast with Josephus. But he must have known about the embassy from Eusebius and works such as the *Souda*, if not from the treatises *Flacc.* and *Legat.*

[64] I would prefer to translate οἰκεία σοφία at 154.30 with "his native (i.e. Jewish) wisdom" rather than "his own wisdom."

[65] As Hult rightly notes, ἀφροντίστως (156.22) is the proper attitude towards style for a philosopher, since it is not his primary concern.

[66] See his essay 17 (title above in n. 60); the idea that stylistic harshness is due to an Egyptian (i.e. Alexandrian) background would appear to be Theodore's own theory.

[67] In addition to the very brief notes of Hult, see also the remarks of T. H. Billings, *The Platonism of Philo Judaeus* (Chicago: University of Chicago Press, 1919), 3.

[68] *Synopsis artis rhetoricae* 4 526.14 Walz.

judgment disagrees with that of Theodore (but the context differs). Some decades later Thomas Magistros (c.1275–c.1348), who spent his entire career in Thessalonike, produced an extensive work entitled *Selection of Attic Names and Words*, in which he demonstrates his knowledge of and love for ancient Greek writers. Philo is mentioned twice, for his use of the words ἐξαπιναίως and ξενία, both times in the company of the great Athenian historian Thucydides.[69] Another lexicographer who studied his language and cites him four times is Andrew Lopadiotes (active early fourteenth century).[70] Clearly at this stage in the long history of Byzantine philological scholarship, Philo was regarded as part of the classical canon. Observations on his use of language and particular words show that his works continued to be studied with interest and attention to detail.[71]

A final rather mysterious document still needs to be mentioned.[72] In six Philonic manuscripts (one now lost) we find a treatise with the title Περὶ κόσμου (*On the Cosmos*) attributed to our author. Remarkably it was in fact the very first treatise to be printed under his name in 1497.[73] It may legitimately be called "Philonic," because virtually its entire contents were penned by the Alexandrian. Yet it was not he who put it together. It is in fact a compendium of passages taken from his works. The first part consists of a cento of extracts from the sequence of allegorical treatises *De gigantibus* to *De confusione linguarum*.[74] The second part amounts to an epitome of extended passages from *De aeternitate mundi*. Both the manuscript evidence and detailed analysis of how all the excerpts are put together point to a late Byzantine compiler, most likely active in the century or so preceding the fall of Constantinople in 1453, who—surprisingly for his time—was greatly interested in theological and philosophical ideas in Philo's writings, particularly as related to the creation, nature, and structure of the cosmos. It would be fascinating to know who this person was,[75] but he remains wholly concealed behind the façade of his excerpts, not even beginning the treatise with an introductory statement.

---

[69] *Ecloge*, Epsilon 150.9, Xi 252.11 Ritschl. The remarks are based on sound observation. Philo uses the former word thirty times, more than anyone else except the historians Cassius Dio and Procopius.

[70] *Lexicon Vindobonense* A 195 (ἀνάγωγον), E 294 (εὐδαιμονίζω), Υ 43 (ὑπογραφαί), 44 (ὑφ' ἕνα καιρόν) Nauck. Note also the collector of sayings Arsenius Apostolius (second half of the fifteenth century) who quotes various passages from Philo's works: *Apophthegmata* 1.38h, 3.29b, 3.60i, 5.24b, 6.48k, 7.59k, 8.77a, 11.17d von Leutsch. The references in 5.24b and 11.17 are mistaken: cf. Stob. *Anth.* 4.7.24, 4.22d.105, where the sayings are attributed to the ancient sage Chilon; the reference to the wife of Philo in 8.77a is not likely to relate to our Philo (derived from Stob. 4.23.54).

[71] A late example is the Byzantine theologian John Eugenicus (c.1394–c.1455) who in his *Memorandum adhortatorium ad Theodorum Porphyrogenitum* includes a quotation from *Her*. 15 on how the harmonious melody of noetic music can only be apprehended by the noetic musician (i.e. the mind), "as the wise Philo truly states"; see 71.33 Lampros.

[72] For what follows, see D. T. Runia, "The Late-Byzantine Philonic Treatise *De Mundo*: Analysis of Its Method and Contents," in *Ancient Texts, Papyri, and Manuscripts: Studies in Honor of James R. Royse*, ed. A. T. Farnes, S. D. Mackie, and D. T. Runia, NTTSD 64 (Leiden: Brill, 2022), 303–28.

[73] See ch. 22, p. 367.

[74] With the single exception of the passage *Virt*. 212–16 from the Exposition of the Law.

[75] It is not likely that he is to be identified with the anonymous scholiast or Gennadius Scolarius to be discussed in the final paragraph below.

20.4 Conclusion

It is time to draw some conclusions. Let these be five in number:

1. Throughout the millennium of the Byzantine era Philo was regarded with respect and sometimes admiration as a thinker and a writer. It is no exaggeration to say that he was part of two canons, (a) the patristic canon for theology and biblical interpretation, and (b) the canon of ancient authors for style and language. But it must be concluded that overall his direct impact was modest. Although his works continued to be copied, it cannot be said that he was often or extensively used or cited (an exception must be made for the catenae and florilegia in the sixth to eighth centuries). This is not to say that the influence of his thought was negligible. As Photius recognized, in terms of method Philo can be regarded as the origin of a whole stream of patristic exegesis. Mostly, however, this influence was indirect, via later authors, and not, it would seem, directly through extensive reading and study of his writings.
2. Philo is almost invariably recognized as a Jewish author, but with one notable exception this is not a source of criticism, let alone slander.[76] A fine example is his prominence in the article on God in the *Souda*, where Isidore of Pelusium's positive judgment on his quasi-Trinitarian theology is taken over (he is not called "the Jew" here, but this occurs on a number of occasions elsewhere in the encyclopedia).
3. During the period we have studied, Philo's writings and thought are put to a variety of uses. There are references to theological, philosophical, and arithmological themes. His expertise as an exegete who frequently resorts to allegory is well known, but not used as much as we might expect. He is exploited as a source for Jewish practices at the time of the New Testament and the beginnings of Christianity. It is standard practice for historians and chronographers to mention him as a near-contemporary of Jesus.
4. It is a surprise, however, to discover that the Byzantines were greatly interested in Philo from a literary point of view, viewing him as a worthy practitioner of Greek style and language. His writings were read from this perspective, judgments and comparisons were made, rare words and striking phrases were noted and alluded

---

[76] The exception is the obscure Ammonius of Alexandria cited by Anastasius; see above n. 18. We should note also Gennadius Scholarius, who cites Philo as a witness to the disasters that befell the Jews (taken from Eusebius) in a late work entitled *Refutatio erroris Judaeorum* (3.273.3 Petit-Sidérides-Jugie); cf. also *De prophetiis principalibus Jesu Christi* 3.314.32 Petit-Sidérides-Jugie. On the writings of this fifteenth-century churchman, see M.-H. Blanchet, *Georges-Gennadios Scholarios (vers 1400–vers 1472): un intellectuel orthodoxe face à la disparition de l'empire byzantin*, Archives de l'Orient chrétien 20 (Paris: Institut Français d'Études Byzantines, 2008), 478–87, and also further below n. 79.

to. This is an area in which we moderns are less sensitive than the ancients and there are things that we can learn from them.

5. In the period we have explored there are two valuable critiques of Philo, by Photius in the ninth century and Theodore Metochites in the thirteenth. Though making a number of interesting remarks, they are not as penetrating as one might expect. The most interesting case of a doctrinal critique is found in the important thirteenth-century manuscript Monacensis Graecus gr. 459. In the margin of this manuscript a later reader makes various comments, attacking Philo's doctrines of matter, the pre-existence of souls and the rationality of the heavenly bodies.[77] In his description Cohn indicated that the handwriting pointed to the fifteenth century.[78] There are linguistic and thematic indications that the reader might have been Gennadius Scolarius, Patriarch of Constantinople in the decades after its fall in 1453.[79] Gennadius was both anti-Jewish[80] and anti-Platonist, so it would be hardly surprising if he was critical of Philo. His views would thus anticipate the first dogmatic critique of Philo by a Christian in early modern times, the Jesuit theologian Petavius.[81] But by that time the world of Byzantium that we have explored in this article belonged to the past.

---

[77] Text at C-W 1.vi–vii.
[78] C-W 1.vi.
[79] This was pointed out to me by Sami Yli-Karjanmaa (Helsinki). It is striking that Gennadius uses the expression προΰπαρξις ψυχῶν found in the scholion no less than six times in various works, notably in his *Quaestiones theologicae de praedestinatione divina et de anima* (2.1.12, 2.1b.3, 2.2.3, 2.2.14). There are autographs of Gennadius in existence in Moscow, but on examination of a digital copy James Royse concluded that the handwriting is most likely not the same as that of the scholiast of the Munich manuscript.
[80] See above n. 76 and text thereto.
[81] Dionysius Petavius, *Theologica dogmata* (Paris 1644), II 7; cf. Billings, *Platonism*, 4. See now Giovanni Benedetto, Chapter 25 in this volume.

21

The Latin West from 500 to 1500 CE

David T. Runia and Frans van Liere

The middle of the first millennium of our era marks a turning point in the history of the Greco-Roman civilization around the Mediterranean Sea. A political and administrative separation had taken place between the eastern and western parts of the Empire. Communication had become more difficult and less frequent. In the west the last emperor of Rome had been deposed and new forms of political organization were being developed, accompanied by much disruption of civil and cultural institutions. It would be nearly a thousand years before the full legacy of antiquity was again available to scholars and the reading public.

The aim of this chapter is to present an account of the knowledge of and interest in Philo's writings and thought in the Latin west in the period from 500 to 1500 CE. Remarkably such an account has never been attempted hitherto. Wilpert provided a useful overview in an article that takes Nicholas of Cusa as its starting point.[1] Runia in his study on Philo in early Christian literature devoted a few pages to the subject and drew up a list of all references to Philo up to 1000 CE.[2] But a full overview up to the end of the medieval period has so far been lacking. The availability of modern databases makes it a straightforward task to locate named references to authors in the broad expanse of medieval literature in Latin.[3] Given the paucity of knowledge of Philo and his writings, this method of focusing on named references will give us the evidence that we need.[4]

The chapter will commence with a section on the transmission of knowledge about Philo and his writings in the west from the sixth century onwards up to the fifteenth century, when the twin developments of the rediscovery of Greek literature and the invention of printing ushered in a new era of classical and patristic studies. Thereafter, the main themes of medieval knowledge of and interest in Philo will be pursued in

---

[1] P. Wilpert, "Philon bei Nikolaus von Kues," in *Antike und Orient im Mittelalter: Vorträge der Kölner Mediaevistentagungen 1956–1959*, ed. P. Wilpert, Miscellanea mediaevalia 1 (Berlin: de Gruyter 1962), 69–79.

[2] D. T. Runia, *Philo in Early Christian Literature: A Survey*, CRINT III 3 (Assen: Van Gorcum 1993), 26, 330–32, 354–56; updated in D. T. Runia, *Philo and the Church Fathers: A Collection of Papers*, VCSup 32 (Leiden: Brill, 1995), 228–39. A fuller list of references up to 1500 CE has now been published: D. T. Runia, Y. Arzhanov, and A. Treiger, "References to Philo of Alexandria in Greek, Latin, Syriac and Arabic Literature up to 1500 CE," SPhiloA 35 (2023): 231–59.

[3] In particular the Latin Library of Texts (A and B) and the Monumenta Germaniae Historica published by Brepols, together with the Patrologia Latina Database published by Chadwick-Healey. It is not possible within the confines of this chapter to give full bibliographical details of the texts cited. These can be easily found in the databases or via the internet.

[4] The incidence of anonymous references and allusions to Philonic texts will be much less than in a context in which there is ready and extensive access to his writings.

a number of separate sections. We will be focussing on specific discussion of Philo, not the influence of more general themes, such as the use of allegorical interpretation, which by then had passed into the mainstream of patristic thought. Towards the end of the chapter we will pay special attention to his standing as a philosopher and a theologian, and also to his status as a Jew in an era when there was much hostility to the Jewish religion and its adherents.

21.1 The Transmission of Knowledge about Philo and His Writings in the Latin West

The linguistic divide between the Greek-speaking east and the Latin-speaking west, while certainly never absolute in the first centuries of our era, did mean that Philo's original writings never circulated to a great extent in the west. Eusebius tells us that after his involvement in the embassy to the emperor his writings were so admired that they were deposited in libraries in Rome (*Hist. eccl.* 2.18.8). But there is no trace of any knowledge of Philo in Latin literature until the late fourth century,[5] when we find references in the church fathers Ambrose, Jerome, and Augustine, and also in the commentary on Plato's *Timaeus* of Calcidius. Of these, Ambrose and Jerome (who spent much time in the east) certainly had access to some of Philo's works in Greek. In the case of Augustine, whose Greek was limited, this is less certain. It may be assumed that Philo's original writings in Greek were not available in the west after the early fifth century. How then was knowledge of his life, writings and thought transmitted in the west in the next thousand years?

A first point that can be made is that from the sixth century onwards until the time of Charlemagne and beyond, it was the Christian church, and in particular the monastic institutions associated with it, that were chiefly responsible for preserving and transmitting knowledge of classical and patristic writings in Latin.[6] Against this background the sources of knowledge of Philo's life, writings, and thought can be confined to the following four groupings:

1. References to Philo were widely disseminated through the works of the above-mentioned Latin church fathers. Of these Ambrose used Philo the most. It is estimated that he borrowed or was dependent on Philo on at least six hundred occasions. But he only refers to Philo by name once, and later readers, not having access to most of Philo's writings, would not have been aware of this large-scale debt.[7] Augustine knew Philo less well. He too only refers to him once in a well-known text on the allegorical interpretation of Noah's ark. Other usage is similarly well concealed.[8] The church father who provided by far the most information was

---

[5] But see below n. 44.
[6] L. D. Reynolds and N. G. Wilson, *Scribes and Scholars: A Guide to the Transmission of Greek & Latin Literature*, 4th edn (Oxford: Clarendon Press, 2013), 80–87.
[7] See Maria Doerfler, Chapter 13 in this volume.
[8] See Ilaria L. E. Ramelli, Chapter 15 in this volume.

Jerome.[9] His widely known biographical work *De viris illustribus* contains a brief account of Philo (ch. 11), explaining why he should be placed among the ecclesiastical writers and giving a list of his writings (based on Eusebius).[10] Elsewhere he conveys important information about Philo's connection to the Old Testament and its interpretation, including the information that according to some he is the author of the book Wisdom of Solomon included in the Latin Bible. But for details of Philo's life and literary production there was another source available in Latin that is more copious in its details than what Jerome supplies: Eusebius.

2. In Book 2 of his *Ecclesiastical History* Eusebius gives the longest account that we have on Philo's life and writings (2.16–18). Its main purpose was to identify Philo's Therapeutae as Christians and the earliest members of the Alexandrian church. The information on Philo is meant to corroborate this interpretation. Eusebius' seminal work not only strongly influenced Jerome, but was also translated into Latin by the presbyter Rufinus of Aquileia. Copies of the translation, amplified with further historical material up to the year 395, were widely available in the Latin west.[11] Like Jerome, later readers uncritically accepted Eusebius' identification. It heightened Philo's prestige if he could serve as a witness to the origins of two such important features of the Christian world, monasticism and the church of Alexandria. In an earlier chapter (2.4.2–6.4) Eusebius had also given quite an extensive account of Philo's ambassadorial mission to Gaius in 39 CE, a fact that he also included in his *Chronicle*, which Jerome later translated.[12] All this information turned Philo into a significant historical figure who lived at the time of the events recorded in the New Testament. It earned him a mention in the *Historia adversus paganos* of Augustine's protegé, Orosius (7.5.6–7).

3. In the period from 550 to 750, three authors who were to exert much influence in the medieval world refer to Philo, namely Cassiodorus, Isidore of Seville, and the Venerable Bede. The information that they provide is dependent on Jerome or goes back to Greek church historians. Cassiodorus (485–c.580), in his *Institutiones*, a manual of sacred and profane literature for scholars, states that according to Jerome the book of Wisdom was not written by Solomon, but "by a certain highly learned Jew Philo."[13] Another reference to Philo is found in Cassiodorus' *Historia ecclesiastica tripartita*. It is a translation of the account of the origins of Egyptian monasticism in Sozomen's *Church History*. Philo here is a called a Pythagorean, not a Jew.[14] Two generations later in Spain, Isidore of Seville (c.570–636) in his *Etymologiae* also refers to Wisdom in a discussion of the books in the biblical canon. This book is not found among the Hebrews, he

---

[9] See Matthew Kraus, Chapter 14 in this volume.
[10] Jerome, *De viris illustribus* 11, PL 23, 621C.
[11] Eusebius Pamphili, *Eusebius Werke*, Vol. 2: *Kirchengeschichte*, ed. E. Schwartz, T. Mommsen, F. Winkelmann, GCS, N.F. 6.1–3 (Berlin: Akademie Verlag, 1999 [first edn 1903–9]).
[12] Eusebius Pamphili, *Eusebius Werke*, Vol. 7: *Die Chronik des Hieronymus*, ed. R. Helm, GCS 47 (Berlin: Akademie Verlag, 1956), 178–80.
[13] Cassiodorus, *Inst.* 1.5.5, p. 24.19 Mynors: *a Philone doctissimo quodam Iudaeo*.
[14] *Historia Ecclestiastica Tripartita* 1.11.8–10, pp. 35.51–36.71 Jacob–Hanslik.

writes, copying out a sentence from Jerome's introduction to the work,[15] and for this reason even its title has the "scent of Greek eloquence." He adds: "They say that it is the work of Philo the Jew, and moreover that it obtains its name because it plainly gives expression to the advent of Christ and his passion."[16] No indication is given, however, as to how these references to Christ occur. We will return to this question below.[17]

The English biblical scholar and historian Bede (c.672–735), in the prologue of his exposition of the Gospel of Mark, recounts how Philo, "the most learned of the Jews," was a witness of the first beginnings of the church in Alexandria, whose members were still observing Jewish customs and living communally as the apostle Luke relates of the Jerusalem community. He then adds further details about Philo's interaction with the apostles after Christ's death, and also the information that he supplies on the on the date of the Jewish Passover, which was essential for the calculation of the date of Easter. For the most part Bede is indebted to Jerome's biographical notice in the *De viris illustribus*. The final detail about the Easter date is not in Jerome, however, but taken directly from Rufinus' translation of Eusebius' *Historia Ecclesiastica*. It is also mentioned in his chronographical work *De temporum ratione*.[18] A century later, the Benedictine monk Hrabanus Maurus (780–856) would incorporate Bede's text in his own computational treatise, *De computo*.[19] This recycling of information taken from patristic authors is typical of the period. Seldom, if ever, does new information about Philo emerge. But there is an important exception to this process which we still need to discuss. Fortunately, it adds a great deal of interest to our subject.

4. In none of sources mentioned so far do we come across original texts of Philo, with the exception of some quotes in Eusebius, translated by Rufinus. But two of his writings *were* preserved, albeit in a mutilated form, during the medieval period. They were located in a slender volume called the *Liber Philonis*. Its survival is a fascinating story.

There exist fifteen manuscripts of the *Liber*, not all of them with the volume's complete contents. They are mainly derived from monastic institutions in Germany and Austria. Most of the manuscripts contained four works: Jerome's brief biography of Philo, *De viris illustribus* 11; the Latin translation of the *Liber antiquitatum biblicarum* (*LAB*) falsely attributed to Philo; and Latin translations of Book 6[20] of the *Quaestiones*

---

[15] Jerome *Praefatio in libros Salomonis*, PL 28.1308A; SC 592, p. 430 Canellis.
[16] *Etymologiae* 6.2.30: *Liber Sapientiae apud Hebraeos nusquam est, unde et ipse titulus Graecam magis eloquentiam redolet. hunc Iudaei Philonis esse adfirmant, qui proinde Sapientiae nominatur, quia in eo Christi adventus, qui est sapientia Patris, et passio eius evidenter exprimitur.*
[17] See below n. 53 and text thereto.
[18] Bede, *In Marci evangelium expositio*, Prol., CCSL 120, p. 431 Hurst; *De temporum ratione* 30, PL 90, 430A; CCL 123, p. 375.78 Jones.
[19] Hrabanus, *De computo*, 53, PL 107, 697AB; CCCM 44, p. 264.32 Stevens.
[20] Usually, QG is regarded as having four books, but in fact the ancient division was into six books, as the pinax of the Viennese codex Theol.gr. 29 shows; see see Runia, *Philo and the Church Fathers*, 21. The Latin translation

et solutiones in Genesim and of *De vita contemplativa* 1–41 under the title *Liber de statu Essaeorum, id est Monachorum, qui temporibus Agrippae regis monasteria sibi fecerunt*. The translation of the two Philonic works is by the same translator.[21] It is a poor translation, with many solecisms and strange neologisms. The former work has been edited by F. Petit, who demonstrates that it was most likely used by Ambrose and Augustine, and so can be dated to the last quarter of the fourth century.[22]

The *Liber Philonis* is mentioned in the book inventory of the library of the Abbey of St. Riquier, dated to 831.[23] This has led Petit to suggest that it was donated to the monastery by its founder at or after its foundation in 790. Angilbert may have acquired it during one of his three journeys to Italy.[24] B. Bischoff thinks it more likely that the manuscript belonged to the library of Charlemagne and that a copy reached St. Riquier from there.[25] In 1983 a discovery was made which strengthens the latter theory. Fragments of a lost Philo codex, recycled as a book covering made in 1554, were found in the library of Freiburg im Breisgau.[26] It is almost certain that these fragments belonged to the lost codex of Lorsch used by Sichardus in his edition of the *Quaestiones* published in 1527.[27] The uncial text would seem to indicate that it goes back to an Italian manuscript dated to the first half of the seventh century.[28] It is very likely that the monastery of Fulda also had a copy of this text, which, as we shall see, Hrabanus used in his commentary on Chronicles.[29] A manuscript of the *Liber Philonis* today in Kassel shares certain characteristics with the text that Hrabanus cited, and it is likely that both were copied from this lost Fulda codex.[30] Most surviving manuscripts, however, date from the eleventh century onwards, and they all appear to derive from copies located in Benedictine monasteries confined to a limited area of Bavaria and Austria.[31] About half a dozen manuscripts date from the fourteenth and fifteenth centuries, mostly of

---

starts at *QG* 4.154, which is most likely the beginning of the original book 6. The translation contains eleven sections with additional scholia not preserved in the Armenian translation. See further J. R. Royse, "The Works of Philo," in *The Cambridge Companion to Philo*, ed. A. Kamesar (Cambridge: Cambridge University Press 2009), 32–64, at 36.

[21] But *LAB* has been translated by a different person; see B. Löfstedt, "Zu den lateinischen Übersetzungen von (Ps.) Philons Schriften," *Eranos* 89 (1991): 101–6, at 101.

[22] F. Petit, *L'ancienne version latine des Questions sur la Genèse de Philon d'Alexandrie, volume I édition critique*, TU 113 (Berlin: Akademie-Verlag 1973), 12–13. For the text of the other incomplete treatise see Cohn-Wendland 6.xviii–xxix.

[23] Hariulf, *Chronique de l'Abbaye de Saint-Riquier (Ve Siècle-1104)*, ed. F. Lot (Paris: Picard, 1894), 93; and G. Becker, *Catalogi bibliothecarum antiqui* (Bonn: Max. Cohen, 1895), no. 194 on p. 28.

[24] Petit, *L'ancienne version*, 14.

[25] B. Bischoff and V. Brown, "Additions to *Codices Latini Antiquiores*," *Medieval Studies* 47 (1985): 317–66, no. 1825, at 327.

[26] On this discovery, see F. Petit, "Le fragment 63 de la Bibliothèque de l'Université de Fribourg-en-Brisgau," *Codices Manuscripti* 9 (1983): 164–72; Bischoff and Brown, "Additions," 327. The fragments can be viewed in the Bibliotheca Laureshamensis digital on the Freiburg i. Br. Universitätsbibliothek website.

[27] J. Sichardus, ed., *Philonis Iudaei Alexandrini, libri antiquitatum. Quaestionum et solutionum in Genesim. De Essaeis. De nominibus Hebraicis. De mundo, Gvlielmo Bvdaeo interprete* (Basileae: Adamus Petrus, 1527).

[28] For the dating see the report in Petit, "Le fragment 63," 164.

[29] Hrabanus Maurus, *In Paralipomenon*, PL 109, col. 284C, 287C.

[30] B. Schaller, "Zur Überlieferungsgeschichte des ps.-Philonischen 'Liber Antiquitatum Biblicarum' im Mittelalter," *JSJ* 10 (1979): 64–73, at 71.

[31] For an overview of the fifteen MSS see Petit, *L'ancienne version latine*, 30–39; D. J. Harrington, *Pseudo-Philon, Les Antiquités Bibliques*, SC 229 (Paris: Cerf, 1976), 16–19.

German provenance, including codex Kues 16, which was used and cited by Nicholas of Cusa (1401–66).[32]

We may conclude that, on the basis of these textual sources, the transmission of knowledge about Philo in the High and Late Middle Ages (750–1500) was quite limited. It was dependent for the most part on patristic sources, mainly Jerome and Eusebius via Rufinus, supplemented with information from the *Liber Philonis*. But the material provided by the latter was scanty because of that collection's restricted circulation. In the remainder of this chapter we shall give a description and analysis of the extent of the medieval knowledge about Philo based on these sources.

21.2 Philo and the Exposition of Scripture

Unlike in the Greek tradition, medieval Latin authors did not describe Philo in general terms as a commentator on scripture. However, certain exegetical traditions on the book of Genesis attributed to Philo kept surfacing in medieval Bible commentaries. Almost invariably, they derive from the *Liber antiquitatum biblicarum*, the first (Pseudo-Philonic) work in the *Liber Philonis*. The earliest author to cite this work is Hrabanus, but here already there is confusion about the name of the source. According to Hrabanus' commentary on *Chronicles*, Philo records in his *Quaestiones super Genesim* that from the sons of Noah, while he was still alive, 914,000 people were born, excluding women and children.[33] However, Hrabanus is drawing on *LAB* 5.8, not the *Quaestiones* in the *Liber Philonis*, which only deal with Gen 25:20 to 28:9. Possibly the titles were mixed up or unclearly labeled in the copy he used, or he himself may have been confused. The Hrabanus citation was subsequently incorporated into the *Glossa ordinaria* on Chronicles[34] and the *Historia scholastica* of Peter Comestor (*c*.1100–1179) on Genesis,[35] with some variations in the number of Noah's progeny (which Comestor reports as 24,100). Later chroniclers, such as Helinand of Froidmont (*c*.1150–*c*.1229) and Ximenes de Rada (d. 1247), using the Glossa or the *Historia scholastica* as their source, incorporated the quotation verbatim.[36] Another early user of *LAB* is Remigius of Auxerre (*c*.841–908), who notes that Philo says that tower builders are confused in two ways, through incomprehension of language and through ignorance (from *LAB* 7.5).[37] Both Hrabanus and Rupert of Deutz (*c*.1075–1129)[38] also report the tradition that

---

[32] See Wilpert, "Philon bei Nikolaus von Kues."

[33] See above n. 29.

[34] *Bibliorum Sacrorum Glossa Ordinaria* on 1 Par. 1:19 (https://gloss-e.irht.cnrs.fr/php/editions_chapitre.php?id=liber&numLivre=16&chapitre=16_1, viewed April 8, 2019).

[35] Peter Comestor, *Historia scholastica* 39, PL 198, 1088D; CCCM 191, p. 75, l. 45 Sylwan.

[36] Rodericus Ximenii de Rada, *Breuiarium historie catholice* 1.25, CCCM 72A, 50, ll. 38–40 Valverde, on which see E. Smits, "A Contribution to the History of Pseudo-Philo's 'Liber Antiquitatum Biblicarum' in the Middle Ages," *JSJ* 23 (1992): 197–216.

[37] *Expositio super Genesim* CCCM 136, l. 2351 Van Name Edwards.

[38] Rupert of Deutz, *De Trinitate et operibus eius* 11, PL 167, 500B; CCCM 21, p. 496, l. 407, Haacke, and his *Commentary on Job*, prologue, PL 168, 961. The inclusion of this particular quotation in the latter work could be

Dinah, Jacob's daughter, was the wife of Job, derived from *LAB* 8.8. While it is possible that Rupert had independent access to a copy of the *Liber Philonis*, Schaller points out that this one fragment seems the limit of Rupert's access to pseudo-Philo; it is very likely, therefore, that his information was derived from Hrabanus.[39] Another reference to the *LAB* is found in the work of Albertus Magnus, who in his *Commentary on the Sentences* cites the tradition that at the time of Abraham, very few people worshipped God (cf. *LAB* ch. 6); while this could refer to the Hrabanus tradition, Albertus refers to the *LAB* as "Philo's Pentateuch."[40] It would thus appear that very little use was made of the genuine Philonic work *Quaestiones in Genesim*. One notable exception, however, is Cusanus, who in his *Apologia doctae ignorantiae* twice quotes from this work. First he cites question 51 on the exegesis of Jacob's well (Gen 26:32) in order to point out that the soul only knows one thing, namely that it knows nothing as certain. A little later, he notes that according to Philo Moses calls "angels" those beings which the Greeks call "demons."[41] In addition, in the same work he cites Philo to point out that all animals possess reason; however, indicating that his source is Jerome's biographical work.[42]

An interesting text is found in the letter collection of the scholar and bishop John of Salisbury (c.1115–80). His *Ep.* 209 offers an introduction to the canonical books of scripture and their authors, building on the work of Isidorus, Hrabanus Maurus, and Cassiodorus. The latter authors generally maintain that these books were written by the men that are mentioned in their titles. John noted that Philo expresses a different opinion on this in the work entitled *Quare quorundam in scripturis mutata sint nomina*, as listed by Jerome. Without stating the exact content of Philo's dissent (but one may assume that the controversy was about the end of Deuteronomy, which according to some was written by Moses himself in the spirit of prophecy, but according to others by Joshua or Ezra), John goes on to state that Gamaliel (meaning the Talmud), and "common report among the Jews who know the correct literal interpretation of the Law, agree with Philo's opinion." It is a rare case where a title of a Philonic treatise is taken from Jerome, and we should certainly not take it to mean that John had access to this work.[43]

---

construed as an argument for Rupert's authorship of this work, which has been questioned. Also, Rupert, *De victoria verbi Dei* 3:5, PL 169: 1273D, and *De meditatione mortis* 2.3, PL 170, col. 381.7 on Dinah as Job's wife. For the Hrabanus citation, see n. 29.

[39] Schaller, "Überlieferungsgeschichte," 68.

[40] "... ut narrat Philo in suo Pentateucho," *Commentarii in quartum librum Sententiarum* 33A art. 7, p. 299A42 Borgnet.

[41] *Apol.* 4, p. 3.6–20 Klibansky (from *QG* 4.9*, one of the eleven quaestiones preserved in the Latin translation but missing in the Armenian and confirmed by a Greek florilegium fragment; see R. Marcus, "Old Latin Additions," in *Philo Supplement*, LCL (Cambridge, MA: Harvard University Press, 1953), 2:273; *Apol.* 10, p. 8.9–11 (from *QG* 4.188).

[42] *Apol.* 21, pp. 14.27–15.2 Klibansky; Jerome, *De vir. ill.* 11.

[43] John of Salisbury, *Epistulae* 209, pp. 326–27 Millor–Butler–Brooke. On the tradition that the Talmud was authored by the Jewish sage Gamaliel, see F. van Liere, "Twelfth-Century Christian Scholars and the Attribution of the Talmud," *Medieval Perspectives* 17.2 (2002): 93–104.

21.3 Philo and the Authorship of the Wisdom of Solomon

As we have already seen, there was a strong tradition dating back to the late ancient period that Philo was not only an authority on the interpretation of scripture, but also the author of a deutero-canonical work, the Wisdom of Solomon. This assertion was backed by the testimony of Jerome, Cassiodorus and Isidore of Seville.[44] From Hrabanus in the ninth century to Cusanus in the fifteenth, nearly twenty authors mention Philo as the author of this book. These include some of the most distinguished writers of the period, such as Hugh of St. Victor (c.1096–1141), John of Salisbury, Henry of Ghent (c.1217–93), Bonaventura (1217/18–1274), Roger Bacon (c.1219–c.1292), Thomas Aquinas (1224/25–1274) and Cusanus.[45] Most authors also state that Philo is a Jew. Hugh, Philip of Harvengt (c.1100–1183) and Bonaventura all take over Jerome's words that his style "breathes the scent of Greek eloquence."[46] Bonaventura in his *Commentary on the Book of Wisdom* tries to reconcile the tradition of Philo's authorship with the title of the book, "Wisdom of Solomon." He does so in proper Aristotelian fashion. The book has a triple efficient cause. The first is God, who inspired the book, the second is Solomon, who wrote the book, while the proximate (and third) cause is Philo, the "wisest of the Jews," who lived in the time of the apostles and compiled Solomon's sayings into its present form.[47] Later, citing Jerome again, he adds that Philo, though a Jew, was highly skilled in the Greek language. Philip of Harvengt twice calls Philo *sapiens*, a covert reference to this authorship. Bonaventura takes this a step further, describing him as *sapientissimus* ("very wise"), and Cusanus uses this superlative no less than four times.[48] It is worth noting that the idea that Philo was the author of the work is by no means unreasonable. Many scholars have observed similarities between its thought and that of Philo, leading them to postulate an Alexandrian origin.[49] One eminent scholar has even suggested that it was written at the time of the troubles that plagued the Jewish community during the reign of Gaius, which led to Philo's participation in the embassy to the emperor.[50]

---

[44] See above text at nn. 13 and 16. Jerome does not mention the purported authorship in his biographical notice on Philo at *De vir. ill.* 11, but it is noted in his Preface to the book; see above n. 15. The attribution may go back to the second century if the evidence of the *Canon Muratorius* and Tregelles' emendation are accepted; see Runia, *Philo in Early Christian Literature*, 276. It is confined to the Latin tradition.

[45] Hrabanus, *Commentarius in Ecclesiaticum libri tres prologus* PL 109, p. 671.30; Hugh of St. Victor, *Didascalion de studio legendi* 4, pp. 73.28, 82.21 Buttimer; John of Salisbury, *Epistulae* 209, p. 330.33 Millor–Butler–Brooke; Henry of Ghent, *Lectura ordinaria super Sacram Scripturam*, p. 23.56 Macken; Bonaventura, *Commentarius in librum Sapientiae* 6–7, *Opera omnia*, 6:108; Roger Bacon, *Opus maius* (pars VII *Moralis philosophia*), 1:217.19 Massa; Thomas Aquinas, *In Dionysii De divinis nominibus* 4.9.360, p. 136.98 Marietti; Nicolaus Cusanus, *Apol.* 4, p. 3.6 Klibansky; *Coniectura de ultimis diebus* 14, p. 98.6 Wilpert. For a full list see the updated "References to Philo from Josephus up to 1500 CE," above n. 2.

[46] Hugh, see n. 45; Philip, *Responsio de damnatione Salomonis* PL 203, p. 629.44; Bonaventura, see n. 45.

[47] Bonaventura, *Commentarius in librum Sapientiae* 6–7, *Opera omnia*, 6:108–9.

[48] As noted by Wilpert, "Philon bei Nikolaus von Kues," 69 n. 1.

[49] See e.g. C. Larcher, *Études sur le Livre de la Sagesse*, Études bibliques (Paris: Gabalda, 1969); M. R. Niehoff, "Die 'Sapientia Salomonis' und Philon—Vertreter derselben alexandrinisch-jüdischen Religionspartei?," in *Sapientia Salomonis (Weisheit Salomos), eingeleitet, übersetzt und mit interpretierenden Essays versehen*, ed. K.-W. Niebuhr, SAPERE 27 (Tübingen: Mohr Siebeck, 2015), 257–71.

[50] D. Winston, *The Wisdom of Solomon*, AB 43 (New York: Doubleday, 1979), 59–63.

Various authors claim to be citing Philo when they quote from Wisdom. Examples of such citations can be found in the works of Philip of Harvengt, John of Salisbury, Vincent of Beauvais (c.1190–1264) and Thomas of St. Victor (c.1200–1246).[51] In his *Exposition on the Heptateuch*, Andrew of St. Victor (c.1110–75),[52] states that some authors "of considerable authority," relying on the testimony of the apocryphal book Wisdom, attempt to assert that God created all things all at once (*semel*). This view might be justified, he says, by the interpretation that God created "all things at the same time in formless matter" (*simul Deus omnia creauit in informi materia*), but that afterwards he carried out various creative acts in six days. But these scholars have been misled, he continues, by incorrect translation and the authority of the book. It might be the view of Philo, the author of that work, but it is certainly not the view of Moses, the author of Genesis. The puzzle is where Andrew thinks these scholars found this view in Wisdom. The editors regard the words *creauit in informi materia* as a quotation of Wisdom 11:17, which reads *creauit ex materia inuisa*. Nowhere in the work does its author say that all things were created "at once" or "at the same time." It is just possible that Andrew was conflating the statement in Wisdom with Ecclesiasticus 18:1 that "God who lives in eternity created all things at the same time (*creauit omnia simul*)."

But we should now return to one of the late ancient sources which refers to Philo as author of Wisdom. As noted above,[53] Isidore of Seville observes that the book "obtains its name because it plainly gives expression to the advent of Christ and his passion." None of the texts cited above allude to this observation or explain what it might refer to. The mention of the coming of Christ is very general, but the reference to his passion would appear to be more specific. It must have been known to medieval authors, as we know from evidence that is not textual but from the world of art. In the chapter house of the Cathedral of Le Puy in the Auvergne, about 150 km southwest of Lyon, there is an early medieval fresco (c.1200) in which the depiction of the crucifixion is flanked by the images of four prophets, Isaiah, Jeremiah, Hosea, and—remarkably—Philo (see Fig. 21.1).[54] Each prophet is holding a scroll containing the text of a prophecy. In Philo's case it is a cento of texts from Wisdom (2:10, 2:20, 2:16) (see Fig. 21.2). Further light is shed on this depiction by a collection of small gilded reliquary busts in the Cathedral of Münster, Westphalia in Germany. Formerly located on the high altar, they are now to be seen in the Treasury of the Cathedral.[55] There are fourteen of them, representing the

---

[51] Philip, *De silentio* 12, PL 203, pp. 966.11, and 16, p. 971.39 on silence, citing Wisdom 1:11, 18:15; John, *Metalogicon* 4, p. 41.30 Hall–Keats-Rohan: faith as the foundation of truth, citing 3:9; Vincent, *De morali principis institutione* 11.36 Schneider: on the ruler should rule his people with wisdom, citing 9:11–12; Thomas of St. Victor, *Explanatio in libros Dionysii de divinis nominibus* 4, p. 235.1365 Lawell: on Pseudo-Dionyius' name of love, citing 8:2; same text also cited by Thomas Aquinas, see above n. 45.
[52] *Expositio super Heptateuchum*, 738–51, CCCM 53, p. 27 Lohr-Berndt.
[53] See above n. 16 and text thereto.
[54] The fresco is mentioned in the article on Philo in *DBSup* 7:1289, and by D. Winston, *Logos and Mystical Theology in Philo of Alexandria* (Cincinnati: Hebrew Union College Press, 1985), 10.
[55] On these busts, see G. Schimanowski, "Philo als Prophet, Philo als Christ, Philo als Bischof," *Grenzgänge. Menschen und Schicksale zwischen jüdischer, christlicher und deutscher Identität: Festschrift für Diethard Aschoff*, ed. F. Siegert, Münsteraner Judaistische Studien 11 (Münster: LIT Verlag, 2002), 36–49. The other prophets in Le Puy are all represented (Jeremiah twice), as well as Daniel, David, Joel, Zachariah, Jacob, Amos, Nahum, and Zephaniah; further details in P. Pieper and W. Rösch, *Der Domschatz zu Münster* (Münster: Aschendorf, 1981); U. Grote, *Der Schatz von Münster* (Münster: Aschendorff, 2019), 112–16 (both with illustrations). The busts are dated to c.1390/1400.

Fig. 21.1 Medieval fresco in the chapter house of the Cathedral of Le Puy, France. It depicts the four prophets Isaiah, Jeremiah, Hosea, and Philo. Image Holly Hayes / EdstockPhoto.

Fig. 21.2 Close up of the depiction of Philo (written Filo) holding a scroll with the prophetic text drawn from Wisdom of Solomon 2:10, 2:20, and 2:16. The text reads: *dixerunt inpii opprimamus virum iustum / iniuste. morte turpissima condemnemus / eum. tamquam nugaces estimati sumus ab illo* (The ungodly said let us oppress a just man injustly. Let us condemn him to a most disgraceful death. As worthless people we have been regarded by him). Image Holly Hayes / EdstockPhoto.

Old Testament prophets and each bearing a scroll with their name and a text. Here—remarkably again—there are two copies of Philo's bust, each carrying the text *Philo morte turpissima condempnemus illum* (Wis 2:20), the central text in the Le Puy fresco (see Figs 21.3–4). From these two artistic representations we may deduce that the

Fig. 21.3 Gilded silver bust of Philo the Prophet in the treasury of the Cathedral of Münster, Germany. The scroll contains the text of Wisdom 2:20, *mortem turpissima contempnemus illum* (let us condemn him to a most disgraceful death). Image courtesy of Stephan Kube, Greven, Germany.

Fig. 21.4 Second gilded silver bust of Philo the Prophet in the treasury of the Cathedral of Münster, Germany holding the same text. The cap he is wearing may indicate his Jewish status. This bust features a rock crystal containing the relics of the saints Walpurga and Vincent. Image courtesy of Stephan Kube, Greven, Germany.

speech of the wicked in Wis 2:1–20, and in particular some of its comments on what they will do to the righteous person was taken to be a prophecy of the death of Christ.[56] The evidence of Isidore suggests that this interpretation goes back to the late ancient world. It must have been known to medieval scholars, though we are not aware of any textual evidence for it.

21.4 Philo as a Historical Figure and as a Historian of the Early Church and Monasticism

The third area in which Philo left a modest footprint in the medieval period was his role as a historical figure who lived at the time of Jesus and the apostles and as a historian of the early church and the beginnings of monasticism. Here too medieval authors were dependent on the information that they received from the late ancient world, in particular Jerome's biographical notice and Eusebius' *Church History* via the translation of Rufinus.

One early writer to mention Philo in a historical context was the British monk Gildas the Wise (*c*.500–570). In his polemical account of the post-Roman history of Britain, he recounts that the Britons, after suffering greatly at the hands of their enemies the Saxons and the Scots, rose up against them, "trusting not in man but in God according to the saying of Philo, 'where human assistance ceases, divine assistance must come to the rescue,'" literally citing Philo's saying as it is recorded in Rufinus' translation of Eusebius.[57] It may be surmised that it came to the author's mind because he had just described the failure of three embassies that the Britons had sent to Rome on their own behalf.

After Gildas and Bede,[58] the first medieval historian or chronicler who devotes space to Philo is Freculf, bishop of Lisieux in Normandy from 825 until his death in 852. A chapter of his *Histories* is entitled "On Philo who during the time of Gaius adorned the church with his praises and the extent of the evils which the Jews suffered under the same ruler as punishment for the crucifixion."[59] Basing his account on Eusebius (with some additions from Jerome), he describes Philo as a most distinguished writer who was considered foremost in his knowledge not only of our philosophy (i.e. scripture) but also of the philosophy of the Greeks, adding that in his study of the Platonic and Pythagorean teachings he surpassed all his contemporaries.

---

[56] The passages in Wis 2:1–20 and 5:1–13 are based on the suffering servant motif of Isaiah 53; see Winston, *The Wisdom of Solomon*, 120. Interestingly Otto of Freising (*c*.1114–58), *Chron*. 3.12, p. 148.11 Hofmeister, notes that Philo as author writes in the manner not of prophets but of historiographers, citing the texts Wis 2:10, 2:13, and 2:20, two of the three texts on the Le Puy fresco.

[57] *De excidio et conquestu Britanniae*, p. 36.8 Mommsen; cf. Rufinus, *Eus. hist. eccl.* 2.5.5, p. 119.5 Mommsen: "quia necesse est adesse divinum, ubi humanum cessat auxilium." This is ultimately based, it seems, on *Legat*. 196. Both the Philonic and the Eusebian texts differ quite markedly from Rufinus' gnomic formulation.

[58] On Bede see above n. 18 and text thereto.

[59] *Historiarum libri XII*, Part 1, 2.11; texts on Philo at pp. 457.7–458.42, 460.71 Allen.

A brief account of Philo's voyage to Rome and his encounter with the emperor follows, including the statement about divine assistance for the Jews cited earlier by Gildas.[60] Then, citing Jerome, he states that Philo returned to Rome a second time and developed a friendship with the apostle Peter, "for which reason he adorned the church of his [Peter's] disciple Marcus in Alexandria with his praises." He adds that Philo "wrote a book on their life and practices, in which he records that not only in Alexandria but also in many other regions there are both men and women of this sect and he calls their dwellings 'monasteries.'" He then cites a whole section from Jerome, describing the Alexandrian church as being "such as the monks now imitate" and similar to the church at Jerusalem recorded by Luke in Acts. Finally, he couples Philo's evidence with that of Josephus in order to describe how "the divine vengeance condemned the Jews" on account of the crime that they committed against the Saviour. Contemporary with Freculf, the Benedictine monk and scholar Walafrid Strabo (c.808–49), in the chapter on canonical hours in his treatise on ecclesiastical usages, cites Philo as a "witness that the early church in Alexandria among many other excellent practices sang hymns before dawn."[61]

After Freculf and Walafrid, the legend of Philo Christianus and the information that he provides on the history of the beginings of the Christian church is repeated time and time again in chronicles and histories produced by writers such as Haymo of Halberstadt (d. 853), Ado of Vienne (d. 874), Herman of Reichenau (1013–54), Bernold of Constance (c.1054–1100), Ordericus Vitalis (1075–c.1142), Honorius Augustodonensis (1080–1154), and others.[62] Other authors, following the example of Bede, mention Philo in connection with the life of the evangelist Mark. These include Peter Damian (c.988–c.1073) in one of his sermons, Rupert, abbot of Deutz (c.1075–1129) in his *Dialogue on the Truly Apostolic Life*, and Jacob of Varazze (c.1230–98) in his *Legenda aurea* on the lives of the saints.[63]

As we have already seen, both Jerome and in his wake Freculf emphasize the connection between Philo's description of the community of the incipient Alexandrian church and the Christian monastic tradition. Centuries later Conrad, abbot of Eberbach (c.1140–1221), in his account of the beginnings of the Cisterician order, first mentions the early Christians in Jerusalem and Antioch and then continues:[64] "Philo, the most learned of the Jews, in the book that he gave the title 'On the contemplative life' also wrote at length about their most fervent zeal for the Lord. It is obvious that the

---

[60] See above at n. 57. The same *bon mot* is also recorded by Sedulius Scotus (d. c.870) in *Collectaneum miscellaneum* 15.10–11 Simpson. Sedulius, who spent time in Lisieux, is no doubt dependent on Freculf. It is also cited by Berthold of Zwiefalten (c.1089–1169) in the context of the building of a monastery: *Liber de constructione monasterii Zwivildensis* 32, p. 113.29 Abel.

[61] *De exordiis et incrementis quarundam in observationibus ecclesiasticis rerum* 26, p. 505.9 Boretius-Krause. This is based on Eus., *Hist. eccl.* 2.17.22 in Rufinus' translation, and ultimately goes back to *Contempl.* 83–89.

[62] See further the list in the updated "References to Philo from Josephus up to 1500 CE," above n. 2.

[63] Peter, *Sermones* 15.42–59 Lucchesi; Rupert, *Dialogus quae sit vita vere apostolica* 4.3, p. 285.46–55 Arduini (this work has also been attributed to Honorius Augustodonensis); Jacob, *Legenda aurea* 59, p. 265.35 Graesse.

[64] Conrad, *Exordium Magnum Cisterciense siue Narratio de initio Cisterciensis Ordinis* dist. 1, 2.29–32 Griesser.

name, life and institution of monastic communities derives from these people." There are two points of interest here. From Conrad's text it is not clear why he claims that monasticism owes its name to these early accounts. But the association becomes clear when we recall that both Jerome and Freculf pick up on a small but fascinating detail in Eusebius' account, namely that Philo describes the Therapeutae as spending time in a small room in their houses which he calls a μοναστήριον, *monasterium* in Latin. This usage, the first ever recorded in extant literature, is at the origin of the later term for monastic communities.[65] Peter Damian also refers to it, as does, as we shall see, Abelard.[66] Secondly, Conrad refers to the title of Philo's treatise as *De vita theorica*. This was probably not derived from Jerome, who in his biography gives the Greek title, but from Eusebius via Rufinus.[67] Remarkably we have found no evidence that any medieval author made use of the actual text of this work which formed part of the *Liber Philonis*.[68]

Perhaps the most interesting reference to Philo's contemplatives in the Middle Ages is found in one of the letters of Peter Abelard (1079–1142) to Heloise. Writing in her role as Abbess, Heloise had asked her mentor and former lover about the origin of the religious life of nuns. In reply he gives a lengthy account of how women ministered to Jesus and played important roles in the early church.[69] He then cites passages from Eusebius (giving chapter and verse) and also from the *Tripartite History*, in which the role of the women is given special prominence:[70]

> Along with the men I have mentioned, there are also women, most of them elderly virgins who maintain their chastity not out of some necessity but out of devotion. They consecrate themselves body and soul to the pursuit of wisdom and think it unworthy to give over to lust the vessel which had been prepared to receive that wisdom, or to bring forth mortal children when their relations ought to be the sacred and immortal intercourse with God's word, which leaves no offspring subject to the corruption of death.

Abelard's letter is the only medieval text which draws attention to the striking presence of women devotees in the community that Philo describes. This is no doubt the result of the unique circumstance of his relationship to Heloise.[71]

---

[65] Philo, *Contempl.* 25, 30; Eusebius, *Hist. eccl.* 2.17.9; *Rufini Eusebii translatio* (at *Hist. eccl.* 2.17.9). The term is also used in the title of the Latin translation of *Contempl.*; see above text at n. 21.

[66] Peter Damian, see above n. 62; Abelard, see below n. 68. Interestingly Abelard speaks of the *vita monasteriorum Aegypti*, i.e. he transfers the term from Philo's text to current usage. This is perhaps already hinted at when Jerome writes (*De vir. ill.* 11) *habitacula eorum dicens monasteria*, cited by Frechulf and Peter Damian.

[67] Stephanus de Borbone (c.1190–1261) at *Tractatus de diuersis materiis praedicabilibus* 3.5.1, p. 183.122 Berlioz, in citing the Philo material in Eusebius as an example of the value of fasting for the spiritual life, gives a different title *De speculativa vita*, which of course amounts to the same.

[68] See above text at n. 21. Note that the translation only goes as far as *Contempl.* 41.

[69] Peter Abelard, *Ep. VII*, PL 178.234B–235A.

[70] *Hist. eccl.* 2.17.19 via Rufinus: translation by W. Levitan, *Abelard and Heloise: The Letters and Other Writings* (Indianapolis: Hackett, 2007), 138. On the reference in the *Historia Tripartita* see above text at n. 14. Further references to Philo's account in *Theologia christiana* 2.9.162 Mews and *Theologia 'Scholarium'* 2.153 Buytaert-Mews (texts almost identical); Preface to Second Book of *Hymnarius Paraclitensis*, J. M. Ziolkowski, *Letters of Peter Abelard, Beyond the Personal* (Washington, DC: Catholic University of America Press, 2008), 47; and without mentioning Philo in *Ep. ad Hel.* 8, PL 178, p. 274D.

[71] A. de Vogüé, "Échos de Philon dans la Vie de Saint Sulpice de Bourges et dans la Règle d'Abélard pour le Paraclet," *Analecta Bollandiana* 103 (1985): 359–65, briefly discusses these texts and also notes how in the much

21.5 Philo as a Jew and as a Theologian

For the medievals, Philo's chief distinguishing characteristic was that he was a Jew. All the late ancient sources on which they were dependent for their knowledge—Jerome, Eusebius via Rufinus, Cassidorus, Isidore—emphasized this strongly. When cited or referred to, Philo is often introduced in a neutral fashion as *Philo Iudaeus*, e.g. by Hugh of St. Victor, Abelard and Bonaventura.[72] Very often, however, this was expanded with a more elaborate description involving a superlative, whether *doctissimus* (Hrabanus, Cusanus), *disertissimus* (Bede, Peter Damian, Conrad of Eberbach, Jacob of Varazze), *insignissimus scriptorum* (Freculf), etc.[73] Often so, because of his purported authorship of Wisdom he too is called *sapiens* or *sapientissimus*.[74] From these epithets it is clear that Philo as a Jew was regarded positively. Abelard notes that Philo's evidence on the early church is all the more credible because he is a Jew (and not a Christian witness).[75] The exception to this emphasis on Philo as a Jew appears to occur when he is cited in an exegetical context. Then generally he cited without further introduction, for example by Hrabanus and John of Salisbury.[76] The implication is that Philo is part of the tradition of exposition of scripture and needs no further introduction.[77]

One exceptional text deserves separate mention. In an early example of the *Contra Iudaeos* literature, Amulo, bishop of Lyon from 841 to 852 and an exact contemporary of Freculf, writes a letter in which he issues a warning to his fellow-ecclesiastics regarding the danger that the Jews presented to Christian society.[78] It contains a strong attack on Josephus and Philo:[79]

> And since our discussion concerns the false and blind doctors of the Jews ..., we think we should also warn regarding the books of Josephus and Philo (who, though learned men, nevertheless were impious Jews), since there are some among us who admire them too much and enjoy them even more than the divine scriptures, that they should not be regarded as worthy of being followed too much. Since these men are foreign to the truth, they are not without error. When extensively relating and expounding the

---

earlier (ninth-century?) anonymous *Vita Sulpicii* 38, Philo's account in Eusebius has influenced the description of the "innumerable clerics and monks" of which the saint had become the father. The passage, he notes, is a "veritable cento of Rufinus" (p. 361).

[72] See above nn. 45 and 68.
[73] See above nn. 45 (Hrabanus, Cusanus), 18 (Bede), 62 (Damian, Jacob), 63 (Conrad), 59 (Freculf).
[74] See above nn. 47–48 and text thereto.
[75] See above n. 68.
[76] See above nn. and 45.
[77] This continues a practice from the ancient reception of Philo; see D. T. Runia, "One of Us or One of Them? Christian Reception of Philo the Jew in Egypt," in *Shem in the Tents of Japheth*, ed. J. L. Kugel, JSJSup 74 (Leiden: Brill, 2002), 203–22, at 221.
[78] On the context of the letter, we follow the reading of Bat-Sheva Albert, "Adversus Iudaeos in the Carolingian Empire," in O. Limor and G. G. Stroumsa, eds, Contra Iudaeos: *Ancient and Medieval Polemics between Christians and Jews* (Tübingen: Mohr Siebeck, 1996), 119–42, at 140.
[79] Amolo von Lyon, *Liber de Perfidia Judaeorum*, ed. Cornelia Herbers-Rauhut, Monumenta Germaniae Historica, Quellen zur Geistesgeschichte des Mittelalters 29 (Wiesbaden: Harrassowitz, 2017), 44.

divine histories, they include much of their own that is false and superfluous, and they distort and weaken the sound meaning of the words of God in accordance with their treacherous opinion.

For this reason, Amulo goes on to say, the church fathers only used their material when it was in agreement with the scriptures and relating what they themselves had experienced, in fact amounting to very little. He then cites the famous passage from Augustine's *Contra Faustum*, in which he attacks Philo's allegorical interpretation of Noah's ark, and concludes with very strong language, calling the two writers "pseudo-Christians, not learned men but deceivers, whose words against Christ contain so much blasphemy that the ears of the faithful should not endure them." The polemics here would appear to be inspired by the political context. Amulo, like his predecessor Agobard, seems to have been particularly concerned about the perceived influence of Jews at the court of his sovereign, Louis the Pious.[80] The inclusion of the reference to Philo may indicate increased awareness because of the circulation of the *Liber Philonis* by this time, but Amulo himself does not appear to be acquainted with its contents.[81]

In general, however, both Philo and Josephus, despite their Jewish identities, or perhaps even because of it, were used as evidence for God's anger toward and vengeance upon the Jews in the destruction of Jerusalem and the subsequent exile of the Jewish people. Already Eusebius cites details from the *Legatio ad Gaium* in order to demonstrate "the divine vengeance that struck the Jews because of their crimes against Christ."[82] Freculf in his *Chronicle* refers to this *ultio divina*, citing Philo and Josephus as his witnesses.[83] A more direct connection between Philo and the disasters of the Jews is found in the notorious anti-Jewish treatise of the French cleric and diplomat Peter of Blois (c.1130–1205), *De perfidia Judaeorum*.[84] Using the same logic as Abelard, but in an explicitly hostile tone, he writes that the faith of the early Christians was "confirmed indubitably and in unison not only by the oracles of the prophets but also by both Jews and Gentiles, enemies of Christ, in their ancient accounts." He then adds, basing his account on the same evidence in Eusebius: "At this time Philo, a most distinguished writer not only in Latin but also in Greek philosophy, was especially prominent. This person quite openly relates how serious and terrible the divine vengeance was which the Jews sustained in return for the crimes committed against Christ." Thus, like his contemporary Josephus, Philo the Jew is cited here with approval for the purpose of reinforcing a harsh anti-Jewish message.[85]

What then about the learning and expertise in philosophy that was so strongly emphasized by the late ancient sources? It is mentioned, as we have just seen, by

---

[80] Herbers-Rauhut, *Amolo von Lyon*, p. xxii.
[81] On this text in the Carolingian period, see above at n. 23.
[82] *Hist. eccl.* 2.5.6 via Rufinus's translation.
[83] See above n. 59.
[84] Ch. 24, PL 207, 852B.
[85] On Josephus, see also F. van Liere, "Josephus at Saint Victor. A First Edition of Andrew of Saint Victor's *Principatum Israelitice Gentis*," *Journal of Medieval Latin* 26 (2016): 1–29.

Peter of Blois, but such references are not as frequent as we might expect. Much earlier, the same information about his knowledge of Greek philosophy is given by Freculf when introducing Philo.[86] Abelard states when quoting from the *Historia tripartita* that Philo is a Pythagorean.[87] Three writers of *Chronicles* make reference to the *bon mot* in Jerome's biographical notice that, "either Plato Philonizes or Philo Platonizes":[88] Otto of Freising,[89] Sicard of Cremona (c.1155–1215), and Thomas Ebendorfer (1388–1464), but in each case they do little more than write out Jerome's words.[90] Two other writers briefly make reference to Philo's role as a philosopher. Conrad of Mure (c.1210–81) in his learned lexicon *Fabularius* writes under the heading Philo: "This is the proper name of a great philosopher; see further under *philosophus*." Philo's name is then found a few pages later under a long list of philosophers. He also rather oddly cited for a *bon mot* on women: "What is the most beautiful dowry of a married woman? a chaste life."[91] The other text is part of a poem by the obscure poet Ricardus (no later than thirteenth century) entitled *Passio sanctae Catharinae*.[92] At the beginning of the third book he says he spurns the errors of the gentiles, "nam neque Phylonis laudo neque dogma Platonis" (nor do I praise either the doctrine of Philo or of Plato). This may just possibly be another reference to the Jerome's famous saying, but it is certainly not meant in a positive spirit.

As for the substance of Philo's thought, medieval writers do not record Philo as a theologian who had significant views on theology or scripture. The only occasion that we have found when a writer refers to what might be called a Philonic doctrine is right at the end of our period, when Cusanus, drawing on the *Liber Philonis*, says that according to Philo, Moses regards demons as angels.[93] The reason for this neglect, if we can call it such, is evident. Because of the limited and one-sided transmission of Philo's writings they did not have access to the main features of his thought. If it had been available—for example his views on the Logos or the divine powers or the creation of humanity—they would surely have been interested.

21.6 Conclusion

During the period from Bede to the death of Cusanus in 1464 Philo had a very modest presence in the medieval world. He was known as a Jew and a philosopher, as an exegete with information on the book Genesis, as the author of an apocryphal work of

---

[86] *Historiarum libri XII*, Part 1, 2.11, p. 457.7 Allen; see above at nn. 59–60.
[87] See above text at nn. 68–69 and on the *Historia* text at n. 14.
[88] *De vir. ill.* 11; on this proverb see Runia, *Philo in Early Christian Literature*, 4.
[89] For his dates see above n. 56.
[90] Otto, *Chron.* 3.12, p. 148.17 Hofmeister; Sicardus, *Chron.* p. 101.3 Holder Egger; Thomas Ebendorfer, *Chronica regum Romanorum*, Book 2, p. 112.8 Zimmerman.
[91] *Fabularius*, Lexicon P, pp. 440.573, 443.636, 448.749 van de Loo.
[92] Ricardus quidam, *Passio sanctae Catharinae*, Book 3.14, CCCM 119, p. 192 Orbán.
[93] See above n. 41 and text thereto.

scripture and as such a prophet on Christ's passion, and as a historian of the beginnings of the Christian church. There is no originality in their appropriation of this knowledge. Time and time again the same themes recur, often copied verbatim from earlier sources, whether patristic or medieval. Philo's thought, for which he is now best known, was wholly obscured during the Latin Middle Ages for the simple reason that there was no access to it. When all of a sudden we encounter a text of the Italian humanist Antonio Bonfini (1434–1502) in which he quotes, probably in his own translation, the words of *De opificio mundi* 24: "as Philo says, the intelligible world is nothing else than the *verbum* of God in the act of creation," we recognize that we have entered a different world.[94] At about the same time in Rome the Umbrian humanist Lilio Tifernas (c.1417–86) was undertaking the massive task of translating Philo's Greek writings, now available, into Latin.[95] Philo's long period of obscurity in the west was coming to an end.[96]

---

[94] *Symposion de virginitate et pudicita coniugali* 3.54, p. 123.25 Nyomda.
[95] On Lilius' unpublished translation of Philo now kept in the Vatican library (Vat.lat. 181), see U. Jaitner-Hahner, *Humanismus im Umbrien und Rom. Lilius Tifernas, Kanzler und Gelehrter des Quattrocento*, Saecula Spiritalia 25 (Baden-Baden: Valentin Koerner, 1993), 332–404. Bonfini's translation of *Opif*. 24 differs from that of Lilius.
[96] See Joanna Weinberg, Chapter 23 in this volume.

IV

THE RENAISSANCE AND EARLY MODERN PERIOD

22
Early Printed Editions of Philo's Writings

David T. Runia, Gregory E. Sterling, and Michael B. Cover

The introduction of movable type printing in the west by Johannes Gutenberg and others following in his wake in the second half of the fifteenth century brought about a revolution in the distribution of ancient texts.[1] There was a flurry of *editiones principes* of Latin authors from 1465 onwards. But, partly due to technical difficulties in printing Greek type, it took much longer for Greek authors to be published with the new technology.[2] A breakthrough occurred when Aldus Manutius (1449–1515) established a printing house dedicated to the publication of Greek texts in Venice. From 1494 to 1515 the Aldine press issued a remarkable number of Greek texts.[3]

It was Aldus who was responsible for printing the first piece of Philonic text in the original Greek, but it is an unusual case. When publishing the first edition of the complete works of Aristotle in 1495–98, Aldus decided to include the work Περὶ κόσμου which has been transmitted under Aristotle's name (though it is now regarded by most scholars as pseudonymous).[4] He then, it would seem, thought it would be a good idea to attach to that work another short treatise bearing the same name ascribed to Philo.[5] This work is not an authentic work of Philo but presents a selection of his texts on theology and cosmology stitched together by a late Byzantine compiler.[6] It is published

---

[1] The specialist scholar to whom this chapter was assigned was unable to complete the task. The present chapter attempts to set out the main themes of this important topic. The authors wish to thank Joanna Weinberg, Giovanni Benedetto, and James Royse for their valuable comments on a draft version. In 2018 a conference was organized by Frédéric Gabriel and Smaranda Marcelescu in Lyon, France, on the reception of Philo in Europe in the sixteenth to eighteenth century. The papers of this conference, when published, will shed much light on the subject of this chapter. In this chapter there will be frequent reference to the invaluable bibliographical work of H. L. Goodhart and E. R. Goodenough, "A General Bibliography of Philo," in *The Politics of Philo Judaeus: Practice and Theory*, ed. E. R. Goodenough (New Haven: Yale University Press, 1938), henceforth abbreviated G-G. On this bibliography see further §35.4. Scans of the majority of the books discussed in this chapter are available online, notably in Google Books and on Archive.org. In the chapter there will be some variation in the use of Latinized and vernacular names of scholars as befits the context, but the names of places of publication will always be modern and Anglicized.

[2] Useful lists of Latin and Greek *editiones principes* are given by J. E. Sandys, *A History of Classical Scholarship*, 3 vols (Cambridge: Cambridge University Press, 1903–8), 2:103–5. Philo is not included in the list of Greek authors (he is wholly ignored in this classic study).

[3] M. Sicherl, *Griechische Erstausgaben des Aldus Manutius: Druckvorlagen, Stellenwert, kultureller Hintergrund*, Studien zur Geschichte und Kultur des Altertums 1.10 (Paderborn: Ferdinand Schöningh, 1997), has provided analyses of all Manutius' first editions of Greek texts. N. G. Wilson has collected all of the prefaces to these editions in *Aldus Manutius: The Greek Classics*, ed. and trans. N. G. Wilson, The Tatti Renaissance Library 70 (Cambridge, MA: Harvard University Press, 2016).

[4] *Aristotelis opera*, 5 vols (Venice: Aldus Manutius, 1495–98), vol. 2, fols 215–25.

[5] *Aristotelis opera*, vol. 2, fols 226–36 (= G-G 387).

[6] On this work, see now D. T. Runia, "The Late-Byzantine Philonic Treatise *De Mundo*: Analysis of Its Method and Contents," in *Ancient Texts, Papyri, and Manuscripts: Studies in Honor of James R. Royse*, ed. A. T. Farnes, S. D. Mackie, and D. T. Runia, NTTSD 64 (Leiden: Brill, 2022), 303–28.

under the heading Φίλωνος Περὶ κόσμου.[7] In his dedicatory epistle Aldus says it is the work of "Philo Judaeus, a man of the highest learning," and quotes the famous proverb linking together Philo and Plato.[8] It was a very modest start.

The next two publications of Philonica again do not print his original text, but they make available to a broader public Latin translations of his writings which date back to the ancient world. They are drawn from the so-called *Liber Philonis*, a slender collection of Latin texts associated with Philo which is first recorded in the early ninth century in northern France, and later circulated mainly in southern Germany and Austria.[9] In 1520, one of the works it contains, the ancient Latin translation of book 6 of the *Quaestiones in Genesin* (= QG 4.154–245), was separately published in a folio pamphlet of twenty-two pages in Paris by the Dominican scholar Agostino Giustiniani (1470–1536).[10] Its elegant title page depicts an action shot of work in a printer's workshop (see Fig. 22.1). This publication anticipates by seven years the first edition of the complete *Liber Philonis* by the German humanist Johannes Sichardus (1499–1552).[11] Published in Basel, it contains five texts: *Liber antiquitatum (biblicarum)* of Pseudo-Philo; the 102 *quaestiones* already published by Justinianus;[12] the fragment entitled *De Essaeis*, a Latin version of *De vita contemplativa* 1–41 by the same translator; the pseudonymous *De nominibus Hebraicis* translated by Jerome; and the Philonic cento *De mundo* in a Latin translation by the celebrated French humanist Guillaume Budé (1468–1540).

These three volumes (or parts thereof) are the result of the efforts to print the writings of Philo up to the middle of the sixteenth century. It took quite some time before the complete works of the two major ancient Jewish authors writing in Greek became available in print (the *editio princeps* of Josephus was published first published in 1544).[13] Until then scholars who wished to study these writings had no alternative but to consult manuscripts that were available to them scattered in libraries throughout Europe. In New College at Oxford there is a large manuscript containing thirty-eight of Philo's treatises (or parts of them). The first half was written by Arsenius Apostolius, bishop of Monemvasia (c.1468–1538), the second half by a scribe in Padua and dated to December 23,

---

[7] A photograph of the first page of the Aldine text is found in G–G opposite p. 186.
[8] *Aristotelis opera*, preface, 2:2. On the proverb see below n. 20, and also Chapters 14 (at n. 11), 20 (at n. 27), or 21 (at n. 88) in this volume.
[9] On this, see further §21.1.4 in this volume.
[10] Augustinus Justinianus, ed., *Philonis Judaei Centum et duae Quaestiones, et totidem responsiones morales super Genesim* (Paris: Prelum Ascensianum, 1520) = G-G 444.
[11] Johannes Sichardus, *Philonis Iudaei Alexandrini, Libri antiquitatum. Quaestionum et solutionum in Genesin. De Essaeis. De nominibus Hebraicis. De mundo* (Basel: Adamus Petrus, 1527) = G-G 445. Sichardus did not print Jerome's life of Philo, which was also contained in the *Liber Philonis*, while the last two works are additional. A reduced volume containing only the *Quaestiones* was published in Basel by Henricus Petrus in 1538 (= G-G 446), and subsequently by the same publisher a folio version as part of a larger compilation in 1550 (see G-G 448, lacking *De mundo*).
[12] Oddly the *quaestiones* printed in Sichard's text are not numbered, unlike in Justinianus.
[13] A Latin translation already appeared as Flavius Josephus, *De antiquitate Judaica. De bello Judaico* (Augsburg: Johann Schüssler, 1470). The *editio princeps* in Greek was by A. P. Arlenius and S. Gelenius, eds, *Flavii Josephi opera* (Basel: H. Frobenium, 1544). On the unpublished Latin translation of Philo's Greek writings by Lilio Tifernas in the 1470s, see §21.5 in this volume.

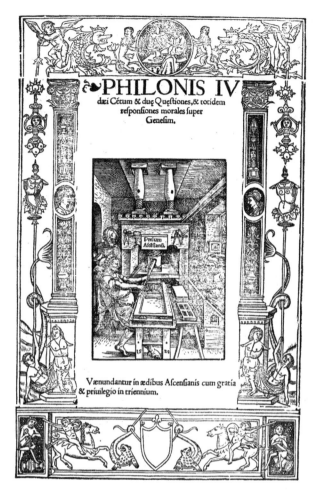

Fig. 22.1 Title page of the earliest publication of a Philonic treatise, albeit in an ancient Latin translation, by Augustus Justinianus, Paris: Prelum Ascensianum, 1520. Beinecke Rare Book and Manuscript Library, Yale University. Image by David T. Runia.

1533.[14] This is what scholars were still doing, nearly eighty years after the appearance of Gutenberg's Bible. But this situation would soon undergo a dramatic change for the better.

22.1 Adrianus Turnebus

The change took place not in Italy, where the ground-breaking work of the Aldine Press had taken place, but in Paris. It was the work of Adrianus Turnebus or Adrien

---

[14] Oxoniensis Collegii Novi 143 (= G-G 95). On this MS, see L. Cohn, *Philonis Alexandrini opera quae supersunt* (Berlin: Georgius Reimerus, 1896), 1:xix; J. R. Royse, "Philo of Alexandria at New College," *New College Notes* 13.4 (2020): 1–9.

Turnèbe.[15] Born on 5 February 1512, in Les Andelys, Normandy, Turnebus left home at an early age to study with Jacques Touissant at the *Collège du Justice*. Touissant was an eminent Hellenist and later the initial holder of the chair in Greek in the *Collège des lecteurs royaux* (today the *Collège de France*). Turnebus so excelled in the classical languages that at his funeral, his lifelong friend and fellow classicist Léger du Chesne said: "Turnebus knew Greek so well that he seemed to have been born in Athens and Latin so well that he appeared to have devoted his time to Latin and nothing else."[16]

Following the completion of his doctorate in 1532, Turnebus held relatively minor academic posts at four different institutions in Paris. His life changed when Touissant died and he was offered his mentor's position as *lecteur royal* at the *Collège des lecteurs royaux*. He accepted and remained at the institution for the duration of his life (1547–65). The prestige and the circumstances of this position enabled Turnebus to begin publishing—at least we do not know of any publications prior to this post. His industry and skill attracted attention at the royal court and led to his appointment as the royal printer for Greek (*Imprimeur du Roy pour le grec*, 1551–55), after Robert Estienne had been forced to flee Paris for Geneva when he ran afoul of the Sorbonne. Turnebus used his faculty and royal appointments—one of only two individuals who were both professors and printers during this period—to great advantage. From 1547 to 1565, he published at least sixty-one works which were supplemented by twenty-two posthumous works.[17] These included twenty-four editions embracing the works of twenty-two Greek and twelve Latin authors. Among these was the *editio princeps* of Philo of Alexandria, published in 1552, a year after Turnebus had become the royal printer for Greek in 1551.[18]

Turnebus, following the modus operandi of humanists since the fifteenth century, understood that his task was to put the texts of ancient authors into the hands of his contemporaries as efficiently as scholarship would permit rather than to spend years searching extensively for manuscripts or working painstakingly through the evidence. This is clear from the record: he issued eight editions in 1552, seven in 1553, two in 1554, three in 1555, two in 1556, one in 1558, and another posthumously in 1577. In the case of Philo, he had three manuscripts at his disposal from the Royal Library at Fontainebleau: Parisinus graecus 433, 434, and 435. The three are separately listed in the manuscript analysis that Cohn and Wendland developed for their *editio maior*

---

[15] On Turnebus, see J. Lewis, *Adrien Turnèbe (1512–1565): A Humanist Observed*, Travaux d'Humanisme et Renaissance 320 (Geneva: Libraire Droz S.A., 1998); and N. Constantinidou, "Constructions of Hellenism through Printing and Editorial Choices: The Case of Adrien de Turnèbe. Royal Lecturer and Printer in Greek (1512–1565)," *International Journal of the Classical Tradition* 25 (2018): 262–84. For a fuller account of Turnebus' edition and its contribution to Philonic Studies, see the article in the procedings of the Lyon conference (see above n. 1) by G. E. Sterling, "Adrianus Turnebus and the *Editio Princeps* of Philo (1552)" (forthcoming).

[16] Léger du Chesne, *Oratio funebris*, in Adrien Turnèbe, *Viri clariss. Adriani Turnebi ... Opera, nunc primum ex bibliotheca amplissimi viri: Stephani Adriani f. Turnebi ... in unum collecta, emendata, aucta et tributa in tomos III ... Additi sunt singulis tomis singuli indices rerum et verborum locupletissimi*, 3 vols (Strasbourg: Lazare Zetzneri, 1600), 3:100.

[17] The counts are based on the list in Lewis, *Adrien Turnèbe*, 334–37.

[18] Φίλωνος Ἰουδαίου εἰς τὰ τοῦ Μωσέως κοσμοποιητικά, ἱστορικά, νομοθετικά. Τοῦ αὐτοῦ μονόβιβλα. *Philonis Judaei in libros Mosis De mundi opificio, historicos, De legibus. Eiusdem libri singulares. Ex bibliotheca regia* (Paris: A. Turnèbe, 1552).

(1896–1915): Parisinus graecus 433 is designated as MS L, 434 belongs to family H, and 435 is given the siglum C. The manuscripts differ in contents and order: 433 has twenty-nine of Philo's treatises, 434 contains twenty-two, and 435 has eight—some only partially. Turnebus used 433 or L as the base for his edition and made corrections as he went.

The folio size edition is handsome. The title on its opening page states in Greek and Latin not only the name of Philo, but also the structure of the *corpus Philonicum* as Turnebus understood it (see below, p. 372), the source of the manuscripts, the mark of the royal printer (a serpent and a vine coiled around an upright lance), and a dedication to King Henry II (see Fig. 22.2)

The preface is composed in Greek in an elevated style that demonstrates Turnebus' control of the language. Dedicated to Charles, the cardinal of Lorraine, for supporting humanism against its critics, Turnebus explains why he elected to edit and publish Philo's works: "We admired this book selected from the Royal Library for its accuracy

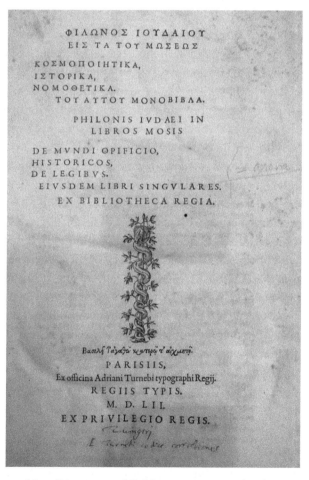

Fig. 22.2 Title page of the *editio princeps* of Philo's treatises preserved in the original Greek, published by Adrian Turnèbe, Royal Printer of Greek, Paris 1552. Beinecke Rare Book and Manuscript Library, Yale University. Image by Gregory E. Sterling.

and clarity (in expounding) the sacred discourses and for the philosophy in it." He explained what he meant: "For Philo was either the first or the most significant of all who saw that there was a certain common connection among all the liberal disciplines and who perceived—not as some think that theology and philosophy are separated from one another by a great frontier—but rather that they were related or even sisters." The statement echoes Philo's allegorical explanation of Sarah (philosophy as the servant of wisdom) and Hagar (the preliminary studies as the servant of philosophy),[19] but also more importantly indicates that Turnebus, like Charles, was interested in arguing for harmony between humanism and the sacred. The specific form of philosophy that Turnebus recognized in Philo was Platonism: "He makes use of the Platonic intellectual frameworks in such a straightforward and perceptive way that it has become a proverb that either Plato philonizes or Philo platonizes."[20]

In keeping with medieval practices, Turnebus included *testimonia*: the entry from the *Souda* and two citations from Eusebius' account of Philo in the *Historia ecclesiastica*.[21] Interestingly, he did not include any of Josephus' statements, although the Jewish historian's works by this time were available both in Latin and in Greek.[22]

For the edition proper, Turnebus faced the daunting task of introducing some sense of order into the manuscript tradition. In his preface, Turnebus candidly wrote: "we have found a great deal of confusion in the order of his works." The French humanist used three principles to bring order out of the chaos of the manuscripts. First, he applied Philo's description of the three-part structure of the Exposition of the Law in *De praemiis* 1–3 to the corpus as a whole. This is clear from the agreement between Philo's statement and the title page: the three parts of the Philonic corpus are the cosmological (κοσμοποιητικά), the historical (ἱστορικά), and the legislative (νομοθετικά). Second, he attempted—although not with entire success—to follow the sequence of the biblical narrative. He was explicit about this principle in his preface: "We have arranged them in the way that we think they were originally set out by the author who followed—we suppose—the words and stories about Moses sequentially as in a series." Third, he realized that these two principles did not address every work in the corpus and drew from Eusebius' statement that "there are some single volume works of his (μονόβιβλα)."[23]

What should we make of Turnebus' arrangement? It is important to note that the three manuscripts at Turnebus' disposal did not contain the full corpus: they were missing *Leg.* 2, *Post., Mut., Somn.* 2 from the Allegorical Commentary, large sections of *Virt., Spec.* 2 and 4 from the Exposition of the Law, and other material. For example, he did not include the *Hypothetica*, although it would have been available via editions of Eusebius' *Praeparatio evangelica*.

---

[19] Philo, *Congr.* 79.
[20] On the aphorism, see Jerome, *Vir. ill.* 11 (PCW 1:ciii); Isidore of Pelusium, *Ep.* 3.81 (PCW 1:cviii); Photius, *Biblioth. Cod.* 105 (PCW 1:cx); Suidas, s.v. Φίλων (PCW 1:cx); Theodorus Meochita, *Miscell.* 16 (PCW 1:cxi–cxiii). Cf. also Numenius, frag. 8, "What is Plato but Moses speaking in Greek?" and Augustine, *Faust.* 12.39 (PCW 1:cv), who notes that the Greeks compare Philo's eloquence to Plato's.
[21] Eusebius, *Hist. eccl.* 2.4.1–6 and 2.17.1–18.8.
[22] See above n. 13.
[23] Eusebius, *Hist. eccl.* 2.18.6.

Even with a smaller corpus than what we have today, the order was difficult and Turnebus' struggle is evident. In nine instances, the table of contents provides a different arrangement than the sequence of the printed texts although the pagination in the table of contents is correct. Turnebus apparently first set the type for the texts and then set the type for the table of contents. In preparing the table of contents, he came to different conclusions about the order. He thus kept the pagination that was already set, but altered the sequence in the table of contents to reflect his later understanding (clearly computers offer advantages today!).

As was noted above, Turnebus attempted to follow the sequence of the biblical text but he was not completely consistent; for example, he inexplicably put *Gig.* and *Deus*, which deal with Gen 6:1–4 and 6:4–12 respectively, after *Ebr.* and *Sobr.*, which cover Gen 9:21 and 9:24–27 respectively. Quite understandably he found the sequence of material in *Spec.* and *Virt.* to be particularly vexing. It was not until the *editio maior* of Cohn and Wendland that this puzzle was solved. Finally, Turnebus did not recognize the three major commentary series in the corpus that are widely accepted by contemporary scholars. The result is that he situated treatises that belong to the Exposition of the Law among the treatises of the Allegorical Commentary. So, he (mis)placed *Opif.*, the first work in the Exposition of the Law, as the first of the works in the cosmological treatises which come primarily from the Allegorical Commentary—a position that it has held ever since with the exception of the modern German and Hebrew translations.[24] Similarly, he placed *Abr.*, *Ios.*, and *Mos.* in their biblical sequence and did not grasp the introductory character of *Mos.*[25] While it is easy to note the limits of Turnebus' arrangement from the viewpoint of the twenty-first century and nearly a half of a millennium of scholarship, his arrangement has the advantages of following the internal clues provided by Philo and the external sequence of the biblical text that Philo followed in his different commentaries.

Although Turnebus worked quickly, he proceeded with care and skill. This is clear from his use of quotation marks and his emendations. The French scholar noted each time the Alexandrian Jewish commentator cited the biblical—and non-biblical—text by placing quotation marks in the left margin. While one can quibble about some of the decisions—he did not distinguish between a citation and a paraphrase or allusion—the quotation marks are still worth consulting. His mastery of Greek led Turnebus to offer emendations more readily than many of us would be comfortable with today. He followed Lorenzo Valla's principle of *emendatio ope ingenii* when he saw difficulties in the text. He wrote: "even if it is full of peril and risk to trust in one's own conjecture when handling authors, nevertheless in many circumstances only conjectures work

---

[24] On the place of *Opif.* in the Exposition of the Law, see A. Terian, "Back to Creation: The Beginning of Philo's Third Commentary," *SPhiloA* 9 (1997): 19–36; and D. T. Runia, *Philo of Alexandria On the Creation of the Cosmos According to Moses: Introduction, Translation and Commentary*, PACS 1 (Leiden: Brill, 2001), 1–4.

[25] On the placement of *Mos.*, see G. E. Sterling, "Philo of Alexandria's *Life of Moses*: An Introduction to the Exposition of the Law," *SPhiloA* 30 (2018): 31–45.

well."[26] His control of Greek was so good that Cohn and Wendland tend to accept his suggestions—74 per cent of them in *Plant*.[27]

Turnebus was a brilliant scholar and a major figure in classical scholarship in sixteenth-century Paris. His most famous student, Joseph Scaliger, called his teacher "the greatest and most learned man"[28]—high praise from one of the century's greatest classicists. His edition of Philo has had a significant impact. His immediate successors built on it and developed what Leopold Cohn called the *textus vulgatus*. We are fortunate that the *fons* of the tradition began with such a scholar.

22.2 Early Latin Translations

It did not take long before the treatises in Turnebus' edition, now that their Greek text was available, were translated in their entirety into Latin. This was the achievement of the Czech classical scholar Sigismundus Gelenius (1497–1554). The last thirty years of his life he lived in Basel, where he worked as a lector in the famous publishing house of Froben, assisting with the editing of texts and the translation of many editions of Greek texts into Latin. The translation of Philo's writings was his final work, published in Basel just before his death in early 1554.[29] That four reprints were made in different formats within the seven years of its first appearance is an indication of its popularity and wide diffusion.[30]

Remarkably, Gelenius nowhere indicates the source of the text that he is translating. In a dedicatory epistle he places Philo in his historical context and recommends his writings, even if they have not seen the light of the gospel, but no mention is made of Turnebus' edition and its manuscript basis. The order of the treatises in the table of contents is almost the same as in Turnebus, but the division into groups of writings is not taken over, the treatises simply being numbered from 1 to 43. One area in which Gelenius appears to have made a lasting contribution is in the creation of Latin titles for Philo's treatises, twenty-four of them in the table of contents displaying the titles still in use to the present day.[31]

---

[26] A. Turnebus, *Adversariorum, tomus primus duodecim libros continens cum indice copiosissimo*, 2 vols (Paris: Gabriel Ruoni, 1564–65), 1:5.

[27] Based on J. R. Royse, "The Text of Philo's *De plantatione*," SPhiloA 29 (2017): 139–58, additional note by D. T. Runia at 158.

[28] J. A. Scaliger, *Scaligerana* (Cologne, 1695), 145.

[29] Sigismundus Gelenius, *Philonis Iudaei, scriptoris eloquentissimi, ac philosophi summi, lucubrationes omnes quotquot haveri potuerunt, nunc primum Latinae ex Graecis factae* (Basel: Nicolaus Episcopius, 1554) = G-G 451. The publisher Nicolaus Episcopius had a close connection with the house of Froben. On Gelenius, see A. Ammann, *Josephus Frobenianus Editions- und Rezeptionsgeschichte des Flavius Josephus im Basler Humanismus* (Basel: Schwabe Verlag, 2020).

[30] Lyon: Theobaldus Paganus, 1555; Basel: Nicolaus Episcopius, 1558, 2 vols; Basel: Nicholaus Episcopius, 1561; Lyon: Nicolaus Petronillus; and also Haeredes Seb. Gryphi/Antonius Vincentius, 1561, 2 vols (see G-G 451). The last-named edition also included the translations of Johannes Christophorson and Joannes Vaeuraeus, on which see below n. 35.

[31] As noted by M. Alexandre, "Du grec au latin: les titres des œuvres de Philon d'Alexandrie," in *Titres et articulations du texte dans les œuvres antiques: actes du Colloque International de Chantilly, 13–15 décembre 1994*, ed. J.-C. Fredouille et al. (Paris: Institut d'Études Augustiniennes, 1997), 255–86 at 279. Gelenius included Jerome's catalog in *Vir. ill.* 11 among the Testimonia at the beginning of the volume, but his own titles mostly differ from what is found there.

One year earlier than Gelenius, the English divine John Christopherson (c.1519–58) published a much smaller volume of Latin translations in which he adopts a quite different approach to the text.[32] Educated in classics and theology at Cambridge, he remained faithful to the Catholic church and rose to prominence during the reign of Queen Mary, whose chaplain and confessor he became, as well as Master of Trinity College from 1553 until just before his death in 1558. The volume contains translations of *De opificio mundi*, *De decalogo*, and two sections of *De specialibus legibus* 4 which appear as separate treatises in the manuscripts. As the book's title indicates, Christopherson is aware that he is the first to publish a Latin translation of Philo's writings. On the title page he also announces that the work contains a list of nearly four hundred errata in Greek in the four treatises as recently published in Paris (i.e. by Turnebus, who here too is nowhere named), which he claims to have identified through the collation of manuscripts. The list is published in two columns at the end of the volume. The manuscripts referred to were most likely those which he consulted on a visit to the Marciana Library in Venice, mentioned in the long letter to his College which precedes the main text. The very first example in the list appears to confirm this: In the third line of *Opif.*, he says Turnebus' reading ἐξετύφωσαν (deceived) should be replaced by ἐξετύφλωσαν (blinded), which is the reading of the two Venetian MSS 40 and 41, but not taken over by Cohn in his two editions.[33]

In his letter Christopherson explains what he believes the modus operandi of the translator should be, defending himself against those who might notice that his Latin version deviates from the Greek text:[34]

> In translating as well as in editing ancient writers my principle is, and has always been, not to add anything of my own, nor to invent anything, but, when I discharge the duty of the translator, to express truthfully the author's meaning, and when I work as a corrector, to compare carefully printed copies with the manuscripts.

Clearly, he is of the view that at this stage in the publication of classical texts, the translator has an obligation to look at the manuscript evidence for the text and emend the printed version where necessary. It should be noted that his translation also contains brief scholarly marginalia, such as the reference to Peripatetic doctrine at *Opif.* 7 and Eusebius' citation of the same text, and also the identification of biblical texts cited by Philo, which are printed in small caps. This is the first time that a printed text of Philo receives any form of annotation or commentary.

---

[32] *Libri quatuor. I. De mundi fabricatione, quae est à Moyse descripta. II. De decem praeceptis, quae capita legum sunt. III. De magistratu seu principe deligendo. IV. De officio Iudicis, iam primum de graeco in latinum conuersi* (Antwerp: Joannes Verwithaghen 1553) = G-G 450.

[33] Full details in the app. crit. of L. Cohn, *Philonis Alexandrini libellus de opificio mundi* (Breslau: Wilhelm Koebner, 1889), and the *editio maior* of Cohn-Wendland.

[34] Christopherson, *Libri quatuor*, p. b2r: translation in A. W. Taylor, "Humanist Philology and Reformation Controversy: John Christopherson's Latin Translations of Philo Judaeus and Eusebius of Caesarea," in *Tudor Translation*, ed. F. Schurink (Basingstoke: Palgrave Macmillan, 2011), 79–100, at 83. This fine article illuminates the method and theological context of Christopherson's translation work.

In the early years after the appearance of Turnebus' edition other Latin translations of limited scope were published by Joannes Vœurœus, Turnebus himself, and Laurence Humphrey.[35] It would, however, be the translations of Gelenius which would command the field, but not before they had been supplemented by other translations of treatises which were as yet missing in Turnebus' edition.

In these years after the publications by Turnebus and Gelenius, a beginning was made in the task of translating Philo's writings into the vernacular languages. In 1563, a few years after his two editions, Humphrey also published an English translation of *De nobilitate* as part of a larger work on the subject of nobility.[36] It is the first printed text of Philo in English.[37] In Italy, too, a few treatises were translated into Italian. The scholar and priest Pietro Francesco Zini (c.1500–c.1580), Canon of S. Stefano in Verona published both a Latin and an Italian version of *De Iosepho*.[38] In the title of the translation the biblical patriarch is called the "vero e perfetto gentiluomo." But the only extended translation of Philo's writings into a modern language during the sixteenth century was the work of the lawyer and scholar Pierre Bellier, published in 1575. In this quarto volume he offers translations of a broad selection of Philonic treatises.[39] As explained in the notice to the reader, he includes only two allegorical works (*Leg.* 1, *Plant.*), because these writings are more suited to theologians and philosophers than the general reader who does not belong to those professions. He thus includes various parts of the Exposition of the Law, the biography of Moses, and all of the apologetic and historical works printed in Turnebus' text. Very usefully he adds marginalia summarizing the contents and making occasional comments. Of further interest is his statement that, on a visit to the Vatican Library during the papacy of Pius V (1566–72), he found some writings missing in the Greek edition, including *Mut.* and *Leg.* 2,[40] adding that he also

---

[35] Ioannes Vaeuraeus, ed., *Philonis Iudaei de divinis decem oraculis, quae summa sunt legum capita, Liber Iohanne Vaeuraeo interprete* (Paris: Carolus Stephanus, 1554) = G-G 453; Adrianus Turnebus, *Philonis Iudaei de vita Mosis, lib. III* (Paris: Adrianus Turnebus, 1554) = G-G 452. Humphrey's two works contained both Greek text and Latin translation of *De iudice* (= *Spec.* 4.55–78) and *De nobilitate* (= *Virt.* 187–227) respectively: Laurentius Humphrey, *Interpretatio linguarum, seu de ratione convertendi et explicandi autores tam sacros quàm prophanos, libri tres* (Basel: Hieronymus Frobenius and Nicolaus Episcopius, 1559) = G-G 392; *Optimates, sive de nobilitate. Adiunctus est propter utilitatem et affinitatem argumenti, Philo Iudaeus De nobilitate* (Basel: Ioannes Oporinus, 1560) = G-G 394. They were provoked by a dispute with Christopherson; see Taylor, "Humanist Philology," 85–86.

[36] L. Humphrey, *The Nobles, or of Nobilitye. The original nature, dutyes, right, and Christian Institucion thereof three bookes. Fyrste eloquentlye written in Latine by Lawrence Humphrey... late englished. Whereto, for the readers commoditieye, and matters affinitye, is coupled the small treatyse of Philo, a Iewe. By the same Author out of the Greeke Latined, nowe also Englished* (London: Thomas Marshe, 1563) = G-G 466.

[37] A photo of the first page of the "small treatise" is reproduced in G-G, opposite p. 202.

[38] *Iosephi patriarchae vita a Philone Hebraeo graecè composita; et a Petro Francisco Zino Canonico Veronensi in latinum conuersa: In qua optimi viri civilis forma describitur* (Venice: Christophorus Zanetus, 1574) = G-G 455; *Il ritratto del vero e perfetto gentiluomo espresso da Filone Ebreo nella vita di Giuseppe Patriarca, e fatto volgare da Piet. Franc. Zino* (Venice: Giolito, 1574) = G-G 503; *Exempla tria insignia naturae, legis, et gratiae, cùm in vita Iosephi patriarchae, & magni Mosis à Philone Hebraeo; tum à D. Gregorio Nyssae Pontifice, in forma perfecti hominis Christiani ad Olympium Monachum; eleganter expressa* (Venice: Bologninus Zalterius, 1575) = G-G 455 (combined with the biographies of Moses by Philo and Gregory of Nyssa). For the translations of *Mos.* by Giulio Ballino (Venice 1560) and of *Opif.* by M. Agostino Ferentelli (1570 and reprints), see G-G 501–2. On early translations of Philo into Italian, see the article by F. Calabi in the forthcoming Lyon volume (above n. 1).

[39] *Les oeuvres de Philon Iuif, autheur tres-eloquent, et philosophe tres-graue. Contenans l'interpretation de plusieurs diuins & sacrez mysteres, & l'instruction d'un chacun en toutes bonnes & sainctes moeurs. Mises de grec en françois, par Pierre Bellier* (Paris: Nicolas Chesneau, also Michel Sonnius, 1575) = G-G 481.

[40] These were indeed unpublished and were soon to be published by Hoeschel, on whom see the following section. But the others he mentions are already present in Turnebus' edition (some with alternative titles) or are spurious.

found some errors in the Greek text he used. Bellier's work was reprinted on a number of occasions and in 1612 an enlarged edition was published which contained three new treatises translated by Fédéric Morel.[41] This incomplete collection of French translations was not superseded until the Lyon translation project of 1962–92.

22.3 David Hoeschel

In the meantime, further Philonic treatises (including those consulted by Bellier in the Vatican Library) continued to surface. Far and away the most significant "second editor" and publisher of Philo's works of the late sixteenth and early seventeenth century was the Lutheran Augsburg humanist, David Hoeschel (1556–1617).[42] Born four years after the publication of Turnebus' edition, Hoeschel studied at the Santa Anna Gymnasium in Augsburg under renowned humanist Hieronymus Wolf and went on to university studies at Leipzig (1577) and Wittenberg (1579). As a *magister artium liberalium*, he returned to Augsburg in 1581 to serve as teacher at his *alma mater*, where he would eventually (from 1593) become rector as well as head of the Augsburg Stadtbibliothek. From this station, Hoeschel maintained correspondences with some of the most celebrated Protestant and Catholic humanists of his generation (including Isaac Casaubon, Joseph Scaliger, and Justus Lipsius), stayed on friendly terms with the Jesuits in his home city, and published the fruits of his scholarly labors. Tolerant and learned, Hoeschel was the model of the early modern humanist in the republic of letters.[43]

The year 1587 was a particularly significant one for Hoeschel, as it saw the appearance of two scholarly editions: a selection of Greek sermons by the Cappadocian fathers and John Chrysostom, together with a fragment of Cyril of Alexandria,[44] as well as his most important contribution to Philonic scholarship, *Philonis Iudaei opuscula tria*.[45]

Unlike Turnebus, who worked principally from the manuscripts available to him in the library at Fontainebleu, Hoeschel had at his disposal the great Codex monacensis graecus 459—a thirteenth-century manuscript in two hands (G-G 35; PCW 1:iv). Apart from a handful of Byzantine marginalia, Hoeschel found the manuscript elegant,

---

[41] *Les œuvres de Philon Iuif... Reueuës, corrigées & augmentées de trois liures, traduits sur l'original Grec, Par Fed. Morel* (Paris: David Gilles, 1612) = G-G 482. On Morel, see further below at nn. 47 and 50.

[42] For a fuller account of Hoeschel's contribution to Philonic Studies, see the article in the proceedings of the Lyon conference (see above n. 1) by M. B. Cover, "Paris and Augsburg Revisited: David Hoeschel, Bürgerhumanimus, and the Interconfessional Completion of Turnèbe's Philo" (forthcoming).

[43] This biographical summary draws especially on the entry of L. Lenk, "Höschel, David," in *Neue Deutsche Biographie* 9 (Berlin: Dunker and Humboldt, 1972), 368–69. See further C. Scott Dixon, "Urban Order and Religious Coexistence in the German Imperial City: Augsburg and Donauwörth, 1548–1608," *Central European History* 40.1 (2007): 1–33, esp. 24–31.

[44] David Hoeschel, Ὁμιλίαι θεοφόρων τινῶν πατέρων: *Homiliae quaedam sacrae, Basilii M., Gregorii Nysseni, Nazianzeni, Ioan. Chrysostomi, Cyri Germani; in praecipuas anni ferias: cum fragmento Cyrilli Alexandrini* (Augsburg: Manger, 1587).

[45] David Hoeschel, *Philonis Iudaei opuscula tria: 1, Quare quorundam in sacris literis mutata sint nomina; 2, De formatione Euae ex Adami latere; & de utriusque lapsu; 3, Somniorum Iosephi, Pharonis, picernaeque ac pistoris, allegorica expositio: Graeca nunc primum edita, studio & opera Davidis Hoeschelii A. M. eiusdemque Notatiunculis alicubi illustrata* (Frankfurt: Joannes Wechelus, 1587) = G-G 397.

legible, and useful for text-critical work. He also discovered, to his great delight, three previously unpublished Philonic treatises: *De mutatione nominum*, the second book of the *Legum allegoriae*, and the second book of *De somniis*.

Hoeschel's *Opuscula tria* offered first editions of all three treatises in the above sequence, following their ordering in Codex monacensis gr. 459. This has the effect of placing *De mutatione nominum*—an entirely new treatise—first, followed by missing books from treatises already partially published by Turnebus. The published text contains numerous emendations by Hoeschel, sometimes written in the margins (marked with an asterisk) and sometimes simply included in the main text without attribution. The margins of Hoeschel's edition are also punctuated with biblical references and quotation marks—an early attempt to tally Philo's biblical lemmata. Intriguingly, the preparation for these labors—both the text-critical work and the mapping of scriptural references—can be found in Hoeschel's own hand in the margins of the Codex monacensis gr. 459 itself.[46] The reader also finds in the *Opuscula tria* an occasional summary of the content of a portion of the treatise by Hoeschel (in either Greek or Latin), although these are sporadic.

Hoeschel introduced his edition with a preface, dedicated to the twin mayors or "duumviri" of Augsburg: Anton Christoph Rechlinger, an outspoken Roman Catholic, who had been *Stadtpfleger* since the 1570s; and Johannes Welser, a member of the famous patrician banking family, some of whom had become Lutherans. Hoeschel's dedication of his preface to these two men would appear to be an irenic move, aimed at improving Protestant-Catholic relations and restoring peace in the biconfessional city. Although written in Latin, Hoeschel peppers his preface with Greek words and phrases, drawn principally from Plato, Homer, and Philo, to paint a portrait of *Philo Hebraeus*—a clever doctor of souls, who "spices" the cup of scriptural truth with the sweetness of Greek philosophy, for the sake of healing the theological patient.

In addition to the text and introduction, Hoeschel also appended an extensive set of "notes" ("notationes"), or as he will call them in the preface, "notatiunculae." He thus became the first early modern author to provide a "commentary" on a Greek text of Philo. The *notatiunculae* comment on a number of features in the text. Sometimes, he offers a parallel from the Philonic corpus itself, using the page numbers of the Turnebus edition for reference. Other times, he adduces a similar thought from an early Christian text—especially those authors published in his 1587 collection of the fathers. At still other points, a relevant classical background is mentioned. In thus offering context, "parallel exegesis," and *Nachleben*—as well as biblical lemmata in the margins of the edition—Hoeschel covers many of the same categories as a modern commentary (such

---

[46] For a detailed study of Hoeschel's marginal notes and emendations in *Codex monacensis graecus* 459 and their relationship to the presentation of the text in the *Opuscula tria*, see M. B. Cover, "Of Dreams and Editions: Emendations, Conjectures, and Marginal Summaries in David Hoeschel's Copy of *De somniis* 2," in Farnes, Mackie, and Runia, *Ancient Texts*, 243–68.

as in the PACS series) would, but of course he does so in the manner of a sixteenth-century scholar. He did not, however, provide a Latin translation of the new works. This was done for *De mutatione nominum* six years later by the Parisian printer and humanist Frédéric Morel (1552–1630).[47]

In 1614, three years before his death, at the end of a long and illustrious career, Hoeschel returned to Philonic scholarship and published *Philo Judaeus De Septenario*, this time with his own press, *Ad insigne pinus*.[48] The volume contained three new Philonic "first editions" ("nunc primum edita"): *Spec.* 2.39–214a and two short Greek excerpts from the philosophical treatise, *De providentia* 2 (PLCL §§2–7, 39–41), both of which are found in Eusebius (*Praep. ev.* 8.14). All three texts were missing from the Turnebus edition (1552) and the 1613 Geneva edition of the *textus vulgatus*. Hoeschel was thus again supplementing Turnebus—especially the notoriously lacunose and disjointed *De specialibus legibus*, the contours of which were not to become fully clear until centuries later.[49] In this case too in the same year a Latin translation of the section from *De specialibus legibus* was published in Paris by Morel. It also contains a portrait of Philo as a Jew, taken from the collection of famous lives by the French priest and explorer André Thevet (1516–90), accompanied by an elegaic couplet in Greek by Morel himself (see Fig. 22.3).[50]

De Septenario was dedicated to Philipp Hainhofer, the Augsburg banker, artisan, and diplomat, who is best remembered for his production of curiosity cabinets. Hoeschel makes no reference in the prologue to the *De providentia* fragments, but chooses to focus his remarks on the mystical depth and allegorical significance of the number seven. The texts are presented in much the same fashion as *Opuscula tria* with text critical variants in the margins, but without *notatiunculae*. In their place, Hoeschel has appended pertinent texts on the hebdomad by Nicetas of Heraclea, Hippocrates,[51] and Gregory Nazianzen. Although text-critical in origin, *De Septenario* retains a thematic center. Hoeschel's publishing life was thus bookended by editions of Philo, which were to become one of the most enduring legacies of his scholarly career.

---

[47] *Philonis Judaei liber singularis, quare quorundam in scripturis sacris mutata sint nomina. Ex interpretatione Federici Morelli* (Paris: apud F. Morellum, 1593) = G-G 456.

[48] David Hoeschel, *Philo Judaeus De Septenario: Eiusdem fragmenta II. e libro de Providentia: omnia e codicibus nunc primum edita* (Augsburg: Ad insigne pinus, 1614) = G-G 399.

[49] Additional textual material from *Spec.* 2 was not published until 1818 by Cardinal Angelo Mai, *Philonis Iudaei de cophini festo et de colendis parentibus, cum brevi scripto de Iona* (Milan: Regiis Typis, 1818) = G-G 412.

[50] *Philonis Iudaei, de septenario, liber singularis. In hoc, praeter mystici huius numeri arcana pleraque, feriarum etiam maximè solennium ceremoniae in lege olim obseruatae accuratè exponuntur. Federicvs Morellvs Professorum Regiorum Decanus, nunc primum latine vertit notísque illustrauit* (Paris: apud F. Morellum Architypographum Regium, 1614) = G-G 459; on the previous translation see above n. 47. The portrait is taken over from A. Thevet, *Vrais pourtraits et vies des hommes illustres* (Paris: Vesve Kervert et Guillaume Chaudière, 1584), fol. 84–85 (missing in G-G). On this portrait, see J. Weinberg, "Pagan, Church Father or Rabbi: The Debate over Philo of Alexandria in Early Modern Europe," forthcoming in the proceedings of the conference *Medieval Afterlife of Hellenistic Judaism* held in Bern in 2023 (Bern, Schwabe Verlag). The Hebrew letters on Philo's cap and robe are meant to indicate Philo's Jewishness, but are devoid of any significant meaning. (We are indebted to Joanna Weinberg for this information on Thevet's portrait.)

[51] On the seven ages of man as reported at Philo, *Opif.* 105.

Fig. 22.3 Engraving of Philo accompanied by a Greek poem, by Frédéric Morel in his Latin translation of a Philonic treatise, Paris 1614. (Here is Philo, glory of the Hebrews, image of Plato, / For whom the good was dear (*philon*), the not-good was not dear.)

22.4 Four Editions of the *Textus Vulgatus* of Philo's Works

In the century following the major contributions of Turnebus and Hoeschel, four large folio volumes containing bi-lingual texts of Philo's complete works in Greek saw the light of day. Because they made no attempt to improve on the text that the earlier scholars had produced, Leopold Cohn described them as containing the *textus vulgatus* of Philo,[52] a term which we readily take over. For the textual history of the Philonic text they are of no value, but the historian must recognize that they supplied knowledge of Philo's writings to the scholarly public for almost 130 years.

The first of these editions was published in Geneva in 1613 by the bookseller Pierre de la Rovière.[53] It is the first extended bi-lingual edition of Philo's works, presenting the

---

[52] Cohn, *Philonis Alexandrini*, "Prolegomena," lxxiii–lxxiv.

[53] Φίλωνος Ἰουδαίου ἐξηγητικὰ συγγράμματα. *Philonis Iudaei opera exegetica in libros Mosis, de mundi opificio, historicos, & legales, quae partim ab Adriano Tvrnebo Professore et Typographico regio, è Christianissimi Regis Bibliotheca, et partim à Davide Hoeschelio ex Augustana edita & illustrata sunt. Accessère extra superiorum ordinem eiusdem Philonis sex opuscula quorum alia sunt* ἐπιδεικτικά, *alia* διδασκαλικά, *alia denique historica res quae Iudaeis auctoris aeuo contigère describentia, Nunc Graecè & Latinè in lucem emissa ex accuratissima Sigismvndi*

text in parallel columns. The title is still based on that of Turnebus, including his triple division of Philo's writings, but is expanded with the statement that the text is taken from the editions of Turnebus and Hoeschel, together with a note explaining the fourth category of treatises in Turnebus' title (these become the μονόβιβλα in the table of contents), followed by the acknowledgment that the Latin version is the work of Gelenius. An unsigned learned preface places Philo in his context, praises his erudition, and describes at some length his reception by the church fathers, instructing his readers that they should bear in mind that they are reading a Jewish philosopher and not an orthodox theologian. The author ends by explaining the source of his texts and adding the interesting comment that "more and better results will be achieved by those who have access to the copious supply of manuscripts which lie hidden in diverse libraries" and that he would be happy for the present publication to be superseded if that were to happen.[54] But in the meantime he hopes the reader will enjoy the fruits of his labor. After the customary five ancient testimonia and the table of contents, the treatises—fifty in number[55]—are then printed with virtually no further assistance for the reader,[56] except a copious index in three columns at the conclusion of the volume.

A generation later in 1640, a new edition of the *textus vulgatus* saw the light of day, adorned with a spectacular title page displaying a copper-plate engraving of a triple-masted royal ship (see Fig. 22.4).[57] This was the trademark of its publishers, an association of Parisian booksellers called the "La compagnie du grande navire," established in 1585 for the purpose of publishing the works of church fathers, among whom Philo was presumably reckoned as belonging *honoris causa*.[58] The first thing to be noticed is that the title has been streamlined. Instead of referring to the division of Philo's exegetical works introduced by Turnebus, it simply describes its contents as *Omnia quae extant opera*, no doubt because of the extra contents to be mentioned below. After a less informative dedicatory epistle compared with the preface of its predecessor, followed by a table of contents now in two columns, the volume for the most part presents exactly the same text and translation, though the typeface has been reset, with fewer lines on each page resulting in a different pagination. Towards the end of the volume, however, additional material is furnished. The extra textual material published by Hoeschel in 1614 is added, together with the Latin translation published by Morel in

---

Gelenii interpretatione cum rerum indice locupletissimo (Coloniae Allobrogum (Geneva): Petrus de la Rouiere, 1613) = G-G 398.

[54] He adds that Hoeschel had once promised to do this, referring to the final words of his dedicatory letter in the 1587 volume, on which see above text following n. 46.

[55] It must be borne in mind that some of these are now regarded as parts of larger treatises, i.e. of *Spec.* 1–4 and *Virt.*

[56] Except that the marginalia in Hoeschel's volume are retained and a very few are added elsewhere.

[57] Φίλωνος Ἰουδαίου Συγγράμματα. *Philonis Iudaei, omnia quae extant opera. Ex accuratissima Sigismundi Gelenii, & aliorum interpretatione, Partim ab Adriano Turnebo, Professore Regio, è Christianissimi Regis Bibliotheca, partim à Davide Hoeschelio ex Augustana, edita & illustrata. Huic nouissimae editioni accessere Variae lectiones & elegantissimus eiusdem Philonis, de septenario libellus, & de providentia Dei fragmenta, Cum rerum indice locupletissimo* (Paris: [Compagne du grand navire], 1640) = G-G 402.

[58] On the association and its trademark, see further J. Biron, "La *Sacra Bibliotheca Sanctorum Patrum* (1589) de Marguerin de La Bigne et la Compagnie de la Grand-Navire," in *Le Livre médiéval et humaniste dans les Collections de l'UQAM*, ed. B. Dunn-Lardeau and J. Biron (Quebec: Figura, 2006), 127–44.

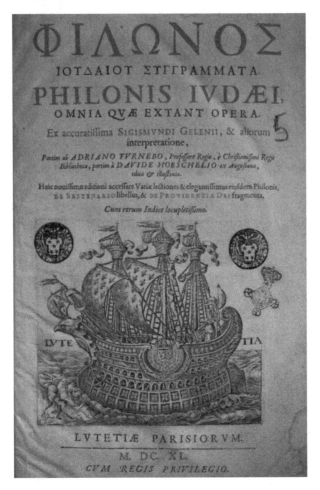

Fig. 22.4 Title page of *Omnia quae extant opera* of Philo Judaeus, published by the Compagnie du grand navire, Paris, 1640.

the same year.[59] Then usefully the list of variant readings published by Turnebus at the end of his *editio princeps* is reprinted with adjusted page references, followed by those of Hoeschel's 1587 volume. Thereafter the *Notationes* of Hoeschel's two volumes are included, as are some pages of *Notae* by the Ciceronian scholar Rolandus Petreius on the text of Philo's *De iudice*.[60] The same index as in the 1613 volume but now in two columns concludes the edition. It thus represents only a modest advance over its predecessor.

Half a century later in 1691, a new version, amounting to little more than a reprint of the 1640 volume, was published in Frankfurt on the Oder, then located in the

---

[59] On these two works see above at nn. 48 and 50. The quite extensive marginalia of the two works are taken over.
[60] Taken over from his volume *Epistolae duae, una: Q. Ciceronis ad M. Tullium, de petitione consulatus. Altera ... His accesserunt ... Rolandi Petreii notae ad quoddam Προλεγόμενον Philonis, de officio judicis* (Paris: Andreas Wechelus, 1564), fols 52–59 (= G-G 395).

powerful state of Prussia.[61] Apart from the dedicatory letter to Frederick III, the elector of Brandenburg and duke of Prussia[62]—which notes that the publication is happening at a time of war and says very little about Philo except to make a pointed contrast between the present Princeps and the Princeps the author had to face—the contents are identical to the 1640 volume. Remarkably, however, the Greek text was reset in a new improved font, with care taken to ensure that every page begins and ends at the same place as its predecessor.[63] This edition will have assisted in increasing the distribution of Philo's works, but little else.

The fourth and last edition of the *textus vulgatus* of Philo's *Opera omnia* in Greek is a curious case, but not without interest and importance for the development of knowledge about him and his writings.[64] This volume is for the most part identical to the previous one, for the very good reason that it is the same printing, except that it has a new title page, and it contains an insert of fourteen pages, printed on superior paper and separately paginated, placed after the table of contents and before the opening treatise.

The first four pages of the insert are a newly written preface addressed to the reader by the German theologian and educator, Christian Schöttgen (1687–1751), who had recently been appointed Rector of the Gymnasium of the Holy Cross in Dresden. This is where the preface was written, and it is dated the sixth day of Epiphany 1729. In its opening paragraph Schöttgen explains what happened:[65]

We give you Philo, benevolent reader, not new, but new-ancient, or, if you prefer, clothed in new attire. It is almost forty years ago that this edition was prepared and perhaps most people were convinced that it has long been sold out. But not long ago the publisher came across a number of copies, which he announces he is putting up for sale at his firm, something which he has judged to be advantageous both to himself and to the learned. So when the task of introducing the volume was conferred on me, I intended to gather together what could be said about Philo and his life and writings. But I changed my mind when, consulting the *Bibliotheca Graeca* of the most eminent

---

[61] Φίλωνος Ἰουδαίου Συγγράμματα. *Philonis Iudaei, omnia quae extant opera. Ex accuratissima Sigismundi Gelenii, & aliorum interpretatione, Partim ab Adriano Turnebo, Professore Regio, è Christianissimi Regis Bibliotheca, partim à Davide Hoeschelio ex Augustana, edita & illustrata. Huic nouissimae editioni accessere Variae lectiones & elegantissimus eiusdem Philonis, de septenario libellus, & de providentia Dei fragmenta, Cum rerum indice locupletissimo* (Frankfurt on the Oder, 1691) = G-G 402a. According to the title pages we have seen there are at least two different versions of this edition, the one published by Jeremiah Schrey & J. G. Conradi, the other by Jeremiah Schrey and the heirs of Heinrich Joh. Meyer (the copy owned by Goodhart and now in the Beinecke Library at Yale University). The two title pages have identical wording but display different engravings.

[62] He became King Frederick I of Prussia in 1701, after the publication of this edition.

[63] Presumably the plates of the earlier volume were unavailable or too worn to use. It should be noted that the index is placed straight after the table of contents, and not at the end of the book as in the previous two editions.

[64] Φίλωνος Ἰουδαίου Συγγράμματα. *Philonis Iudaei, omnia quae extant opera. Ex accuratissima Sigismundi Gelenii, & aliorum interpretatione, Partim ab Adriano Turnebo, Professore Regio, è Christianissimi Regis Bibliotheca, partim à Davide Hoeschelio ex Augustana, edita & illustrata. Huic nouissimae editioni accessere Variae lectiones & elegantissimus eiusdem Philonis, de septenario libellus, & de providentia dei fragmenta, cum rerum indice locupletissimo. Accedunt noviter Notitia Vitae et Operum Philonis, ex viri celeberrimi Joannis Alberti Fabricii Bibliotheca Graeca et Praefatio Christiani Schoettgenii* (Frankfurt on the Oder: Jeremiah Schrey & J. G. Conradi, 1729) (not in G-G). See further the article of D. T. Runia in the proceedings of the Lyon conference (see above n. 1): "When the Old and the New Overlap: The 1729 Edition of Philo's *Opera omnia*" (forthcoming).

[65] Translation by D. T. Runia.

384   THE RECEPTION OF PHILO OF ALEXANDRIA

man Joannes Albertus Fabricius, I saw that almost everything had been dealt with by him. So when I compared all that I had gathered together with that work, I did not want to burden the world of letters with it, but I only selected a few matters which had not been noted by Fabricius and added them to his commentary on Philo by way of annotations.

The additions to which he refers are explained on the title page, replacing the engraving in the earlier edition. The date is also removed, without a new one being added.

For the first time, therefore, an edition of Philo's works is graced with a detailed introduction with an overview of his life and writings. It was the work of the celebrated classical scholar Johann Albertus Fabricius (1668–1734), Professor at the Akademische Gymnasium in Hamburg. Among his many writings was the remarkable *Bibliotheca Graeca* in fourteen volumes. The extract on Philo is taken from the fourth volume published in 1717.[66] In writing this section, Fabricius was returning to a subject which he had treated in his youthful Leipzig dissertation on Philo's Platonism.[67] The presentation covers four subjects: Philo's life; an extensive survey of his writings, including those falsely attributed to him;[68] a list of editions and translations hitherto produced; and, finally, an incredibly learned list of thirty-eight other ancient bearers of the name Philo. It is very much a mixed bag of information, with many pertinent observations, including that Philo's writings deserved to be better edited and interpreted than had happened so far, and that the order of his writings could be improved. He rightly notes, for example, that book 2 of the *Legum allegoriae* was first edited by Hoeschel, but that in the Genevan and Parisian editions it is wrongly called book 3 and separated at a far distance from the other two books.[69]

The prefatory comments of Schöttgen take a very different approach. Writing as a theologian and biblical scholar, he focuses on three topics. The first is Philo's Platonism. His language and doctrines are certainly influenced by Plato, as well as by other ancient philosophers, but ultimately he wishes to be none other than a Jew, i.e. adopting the corrupted custom (*depravata consuetudo*) of the Jews, who delight in using allegorical and mystical interpretations of the scriptures in opposition to the divine Word (§6). Secondly, it is evident from his writings that he had no knowledge of Hebrew (§8). Thirdly, he polemicizes against Philo's allegorical method of reading scripture, taken over by Origen and obscuring the divine Word for many centuries. This work of the devil persisted "until humanistic studies were reformed through the agency of the

---

[66] J. A. Fabricius, *Bibliotheca Graeca*, 14 vols (Hamburg: Liebezeit & Felginer, 1714–28 [1717]), 4:104–22 (not in G-G); in the revised edition by G. C. Harles (Hamburg: Carolus Ernestus Bohn, 1790–1812), vol. 4 (1795), 721–50 = G-G 566.

[67] J. A. Fabricius, *Exercitatio de Platonismo Philonis Judaei* (Leipzig: Andreas Zeidler, 1693); reprinted in J. A. Fabricius, *Opusculorum historico-critico-literariorum sulloge quae sparsim viderant lucem* (Hamburg: Vidua Felgineria, 1734), 147–60 = G-G 916. On the scholarly importance of this work, see D. T. Runia, *Philo of Alexandria and the Timaeus of Plato*, PhA 44 (Leiden: Brill, 1986), 28.

[68] It should be noted, however, that this account is primarily bibliographical and says little about the content of the treatises.

[69] Fabricius, "De Philone Judaeo," (see n. 64), II.2, p. 6.

divine Luther" (§10). Schöttgen writes as a Lutheran theologian and controversialist, which does not mean that his views do not contain some interesting insights.[70]

This volume, which may not have had a wide distribution, is the first attempt to publish a full edition of Philo's works that includes some orientation in Philo's life and writings. It may be argued that, like the Roman deity Janus, it has a double face, looking backwards and forwards.[71] It looks back because it reproduces the same text that goes back almost two centuries to the *editio princeps* of Turnebus and the Latin translation of Gelenius, and the very little that was added to them by Hoeschel soon afterwards. The introductory remarks of Schöttgen also reflect the primarily theological bias of the early modern reception of Philo. It looks forward, however, through the inclusion of the inserted material from Fabricius' great reference work, to the opening up of scholarship on Philo which was to take place in the centuries to follow.

22.5 Conclusion

The efflorescence of printed texts of ancient authors in the sixteenth and seventeenth centuries allowed Philo's works to be collected together in large volumes and distributed much more widely than before. But this process was slow to get underway. The *editio princeps* of Philo's Greek writings was published later than many significant classical and patristic authors. Turnebus followed the editing methods current in his time, using a single manuscript as his base and applying his considerable philological skills to improve the text. His folio volume contained the majority of Philo's Greek writings. It was supplemented by the two much smaller volumes of Hoeschel. After this, textual work stagnated for more nearly a century and a half. Looking back from a modern perspective, it is noteworthy how little assistance was offered to the readers of these large folio editions when consulting them and using them to gain an understanding of their contents.[72] One thinks, for example, of the biblical citations underlying the exegetical treatises and the classical quotations and allusions that are scattered throughout Philo's works. While some effort in identifying and labeling these was undertaken by Turnebus and Hoeschel, it was finally with Mangey's edition that they came to be marked in notes and marginalia. The English scholar also began the process of critically examining other manuscript evidence for the text. The publication of his great work in 1742 thus brought an end to the period of scholarship surveyed in this chapter.[73]

---

[70] For example, his conviction that Philo's terminology is Greek, but that its meaning is influenced by Hebrew connotations unknown to Plato, Socrates, and Demosthenes, anticipates the thesis on Philo's language by N. Cohen, *Philo Judaeus: His Universe of Discourse* (Frankfurt: Peter Lang, 1995).

[71] As Runia argues in the paper cited above in n. 64.

[72] As Giovanni Benedetto points out to us, these editions were prepared for scholars working in the *Res publica litterarum*, for whom exclusivity was the ideal.

[73] On Mangey and the context of his edition, see Chapter 25 in this volume.

23
The Jewish Rediscovery of Philo in Early Modern Europe

Joanna Weinberg

Medieval Jews knew of an authoritative Jewish writer named Philo the Jew of Alexandria—this is attested in a twelfth-century fragment attributed to Yerahmeel ben Solomon of southern Italy.[1] As early as the tenth century, Karaite writers appear to have had some kind of access to Philo's writings.[2] Yet it was only in the late Renaissance that Philo and his writings emerged from the nebulous medieval undergrowth to be given explicit (and passionate) scrutiny by scholarly Jews. These readers of Philo, an intellectual elite, had acquired proficiency in a wide range of subjects which, strictly speaking, lay outside the conventional rabbinic curriculum. They knew about the latest products on the market and were in a position to read Philo in Latin translation, as well as imbibe contemporary discussions about the Second Temple period, and in particular, Hellenistic Jewish culture.[3] Their unprecedented fascination with Philo may therefore be understood partly as awareness of and reaction to the fraught discussions among Christians of various denominations about the identity of Philo and the interpretation of his writings.

It was in the fifteenth century that Italian humanists turned their attention to Philo. The Umbrian scholar Lilio Tifernate made every effort to acquire the Greeks manuscripts. In the 1470s and 1480s, on commission of Pope Nicholas V, he produced

---

[1] For a fuller discussion of this topic see my chapter in the forthcoming volume *Philon d'Alexandrie dans l'Europe moderne: réceptions d'un corpus judéo-hellénistique (xvie-xviiie s.)*, ed. F. Gabriel and S. Marculescu. A revised version of this paper will be published in German in *The Medieval Afterlife of Hellenistic Judaism: Reception and Reinvention in Western Europe*, ed. C. Bay, A. Ellis, J. Mania, S. Moscone, and L. Tröger (Basel: Schwabe, 2024).

[2] This fragment (Bodleian, MS Heb. D.11) was first published by A. Neubauer, *Catalogue of the Hebrew Manuscripts in the Bodleian Library*, ed. A. Neubauer and A. E. Cowley (Oxford: Clarendon Press, 1906), 2:211–12. It is Heb. D11 fol. 125 with the heading Book of Herod. It was reprinted by D. Flusser, *The Josippon [Josephus Gorionides]*, (in Hebrew) (Jerusalem: Bialik, 1978), 1:434–5. The reference to Philo, "the Alexandrine" in the Karaite work of Yaqub al Qirqisani was already noted by Harkavy and then discussed in all subsequent scholarship on Karaism. See B. Chiesa, "Yaqub al Qirqisani come fonte storiografica," in *Yaqub al Qirqisani on Jewish Sects and Christianity*, ed. B. Chiesa and W. Lockwood (Frankfurt: Peter Lang, 1984). For a critical overview of these discussions, see D. T. Runia, *Philo in Early Christian Literature: A Survey* (Assen: Van Gorcum; Minneapolis: Fortress, 1993), 15–16. See also Elke Morlok and Ze'ev Strauss, Chapter 17 in this volume. In the epilogue to this chapter, I will indicate how Philo re-emerged among Karaites in the seventeenth and eighteenth centuries.

[3] For a recent discussion of this phenomenon, see A. Grafton, "Christian Hebraism and the Rediscovery of Hellenistic Judaism," in *Jewish Culture in Early Modern Europe: Essays in Honor of David B. Ruderman*, ed. R. J. Cohen, N. B. Dohrmann, A. Shear, and E. Reiner (Pittsburgh: University of Pittsburgh Press, and Cincinnati: Hebrew Union College Press, 2014), 169–80. On Joseph Scaliger's important contributions to the topic, see A. Grafton, *Joseph Scaliger: A Study in the History of Classical Scholarship* (Oxford: Oxford University Press, 1993), 2:415–18; and A. Grafton, "Joseph Scaliger et l'histoire du Judaïsme Hellénistique," in *La république des letters et l'histoire du Judaïsme antique XVIe–XVIIe siècles*, ed. C. Grell and F. Laplanche (Paris: Presses de l'Université de Paris-Sorbonne, 1992), 51–63. See also L. Canfora, *Ellenismo* (Bari: Laterza, 1987), 86–88.

various Latin translations of Philo's works with commentary.[4] Over the course of the sixteenth century Philo's writings were much in demand and became available in the original Greek, and in Latin and some of his works were translated into the vernacular (French, Italian, and English). Spurious texts attributed to Philo also dominated the market-place. A best-seller was the notorious forgery *Breviarium de temporibus* minted by the Dominican monk Annius of Viterbo and published with his other masterly counterfeit antiquities in Rome in 1498.[5] In 1527, the genuine and spurious became even more contaminated in Johannes Sichardus' (Sichardt) volume of Philonic collectanea.[6] Philo the Jew was clearly held to be an authoritative author whose works deserved to be brought to the public eye.

It was difficult to publish any work of Philo without referring to the patristic *testimonia*. Philo's status appeared to be assured by his Christian admirers and his philosophical disquisitions engaged the attention of various humanists who were attracted to the Pythagorean and Platonic features of his discourses. The printers could be sure that there would be a receptive public for their Philonic products.[7] Their clientele included a small coterie of Jewish scholars living in sixteenth-century Italy.[8] By means of their investigations the name of Philo became reintroduced to the Hebrew speaking public and the "Judaeus" part of the name became a matter of serious consideration.[9]

Three Jewish scholars—David Provenzali (b. 1506?), Azariah de' Rossi (c.1511–c.1577), and Judah Moscato (c.1533–90)—all born or resident in the Lombard town of Mantua, read Philo in Latin translation, and began to ponder whether the Hellenistic Jew had any connections with their own rabbinic legacy.[10] According to de' Rossi,

---

[4] See C. L. Stinger, *Humanism and the Church Fathers: Ambrogio Traversari, 1386–1439 and Christian Antiquity in the Italian Renaissance* (Albany: SUNY Press, 1977), 144–45; and U. Jaitner-Hahner, *Humanismus in Umbrien und Rom: Lilius Tifernas, Kanzler und Gelehrter des Quattrocento*, 2 vols (Baden-Baden: Koerner, 1993). Lilius' translations were never published.

[5] Annius' forged Philo, a complete chronology of all four monarchies of Persia, Babylon, Greece, and Rome, is a somewhat bizarre product given that Philo was not reputed as a historian or chronologer. Nevertheless, many sixteenth-century scholars including Azariah de' Rossi (on whom see below, pp. 388–93) were beguiled; in fact, de' Rossi translated the entire text into Hebrew in ch. 32 of his *Light of the Eyes*.

[6] Johannes Sichardus (1499–1552) printed in Basel (1527) the *Book of Biblical Antiquities* falsely attributed to Philo, the genuine *Quaestiones et Solutiones in Genesin*, *De Essaeis* (a fabricated title corresponding to part of *De vita contemplative*), the attributed works *De nominibus Hebraicis* and *De mundo*. This trio of books had been available in Latin translation from the early Middle Ages. See Cohn, PCW I, L–LII.

[7] The works of Philo (and Josephus) were not read exclusively by theologians or philosophers, but were of interest to all manner of scholars in the sixteenth century, including naturalists such as Melchior Guilandinus and Ulisse Aldrovandi. See A. Berns, *The Bible and Natural Philosophy in Renaissance Italy* (Cambridge: Cambridge University Press, 2019), 90–92.

[8] On the cultural world of these figures, see *Cultural Intermediaries: Jewish Intellectuals in Early Modern Italy*, ed. D. B. Ruderman and G. Veltri (Philadelphia: University of Pennsylvania Press, 2004).

[9] It is interesting to note how sixteenth-century authors refer to Philo: Augustino Ferentilli titles his Italian translation of *De opificio mundi*: *La creatione del mondo descritta da Filone Hebreo* (Venice: Gabriel Giolito di Ferrarii, 1572) but does not mention the "Hebreo" aspect of Philo in his preface to the translation. On Philonic nomenclature, see D. T. Runia, *Philo and the Church Fathers: A Collections of Papers* (Leiden: Brill, 1993), 25–53. Runia states that the epithet "Alexandrian" is rarely used of Philo (p. 49). It is therefore significant that de' Rossi stresses Philo's Alexandrian identity (see below, pp. 388–93).

[10] These are singled out here because we have considerable written evidence about their use of Philo. Another distinguished Mantuan, and colleague of the scholars discussed in this chapter, Abraham Portaleone (1542–1612), author of the *Shiltei ha-Gibborim* (*Shields of the Mighty*), an antiquarian treatise on all aspects of the Temple ritual, also cited Philo in ch. 35, 31b. See G. Miletto, *Glauben und Wissen im Zeitalter der Reformation* (Berlin and New York: de Gruyter, 2004), 178–79. Another contemporary, Abraham Menahem ben Jacob ha-Kohen Rapa, who was involved in the controversy over de' Rossi's *Light of the Eyes* also made reference to "Philon the Jew" in

David Provenzali was the first Jew "to promulgate his name among our people by means of his learned studies."[11] We know little about this innovator. He served as rabbi in Mantua, Ferrara, and Casale Monferrato and is reputed for his initiative undertaken with his son Abraham—which was never implemented—to found a Jewish high school in Mantua in 1564. The school's curriculum has been described as a kind of counterpart to the Jesuits' "Ratio studiorum," developed in the 1580s—where equal attention was given to the teaching of the humanities and the inculcation of moral and religious mores.[12] One of the express aims of the Jewish educational establishment was to enable young Jewish men, wishing to become physicians, to avoid the dangers of Christian institutions. The curriculum thus included not only traditional studies in written and oral Torah, as well as Hebrew grammar and rhetoric, but also Latin, to ensure that pupils possessed the linguistic ability to study essential works of logic, philosophy, and medicine. Clearly, both David and Abraham Provenzali and other members of this illustrious family were proficient in all these areas; and evidently, as will become clear, they came to appreciate the writings of Philo Judaeus as somehow belonging to their own Jewish past.[13]

23.1 Azariah de' Rossi

Though David Provenzali may have been the first Jewish promoter of Philo, it was Azariah de' Rossi who effectively introduced Philo to Jewish readers when he penned a critique of Yedidyah the Alexandrian in four chapters (3–6) of his pioneering historiographical masterpiece, the *Light of the Eyes* (Mantua, 1573–75).[14] This work contained learned chapters on the chronological and historical problems that beset the scholarly study of the Second Temple period which had either been totally neglected by his

---

his commentary on the Pentateuch, *Minhah belulah* (Verona, 1594), and in one case cited *De Abrahamo* (17r). Thanks to Nachi Weinstein for drawing my attention to these passages.

[11] De' Rossi made this assertion at the end of his response to Moses Provenzali's critique of his *Light of the Eyes* (see D. Cassel's edition of *Me'or Einayim* [Vilna: Yosef Reuven Rom, 1866], 506).
[12] On Provenzali, see G. Miletto, "The Teaching Program of David ben Abraham and His Son Abraham Provenzali in Its Historical-Cultural Context," in *Cultural Intermediaries: Jewish Intellectuals in Early Modern Italy*, 127–48. Writing in 1612, Abraham Portaleone refers to his teacher David Provenzali "of blessed memory" as the "best preacher in Italy" (*Shiltei ha-Gibborim* [Mantua, 1612], 185v).
[13] Azariah de' Rossi refers to Abraham, David, and Judah Provenzali in various passages of the *Light of the Eyes*, and on several occasions refers to their assessment of Philo. Their brother Moses wrote a critique (Hassagah) of de' Rossi's *Light of the Eyes* which was published in the second printing of the work.
[14] The first scholar to discuss de' Rossi's discussion of Philo was R. Marcus, "A 16th Century Hebrew Critique of Philo: Azariah dei Rossi's *Meor Eynayim*, Pt. I, cc. 3–6)," *HUCA* 21 (1948): 29–71. For an analysis of de' Rossi's critique set in its historical context, see J. Weinberg, "The Quest for Philo in Sixteenth-Century Jewish Historiography," in *Jewish History: Essays in Honour of Chimen Abramsky*, ed. A. Rapoport-Albert and S. J. Zipperstein (London: Peter Halban, 1988), 163–88. See also C. Touati, "Judaïsme talmudique et rabbinique: la découverte par le judaïsme de la Renaissance de Flavius Josèphe et de Philon le Juif," *Annuaire École Pratique des Hautes Études*, Ve. section: *Sciences Religieuses* 97 (1988–89): 214–17; G. Veltri, "The Humanist Sense of History and the Jewish Idea of Tradition: Azaria de' Rossi's Critique of Philo Alexandrinus," *JSQ* 2.4 (1995): 372–93. For discussion of Philo and rabbinic thought, see D. Winston, "Philo and Rabbinic Literature," in *The Cambridge Companion to Philo*, ed. A. Kamesar (Cambridge: Cambridge University Press, 2009), 231–53.

predecessors or else inadequately treated.[15] In discussing such subjects as the origins of the Septuagint, Philo of Alexandria, Jewish chronology, geography, and the antiquity of the Hebrew language, de' Rossi brought to bear a vast erudition. Knowledge of classical, patristic, medieval, and Renaissance literature was combined with a masterly expertise in traditional Jewish sources. With these tools, de' Rossi was able to demonstrate the relevance of Jewish sources for certain areas of research which had been mainly the preserve of Christian scholars. On the other hand, de' Rossi also scrutinized and investigated the problems and contradictions found in the rabbinic texts and endeavoured to resolve them by means of what he regarded as "reliable authorities." Though conscious of treading on rabbinic toes de' Rossi set out to correct and emend traditional calculations and proffer precise historical information. Crucial to his enquiries into the Jewish past were the testimonies of three Hellenistic authors: (Pseudo-)Aristeas, Philo, and Josephus, all of whom supplied first-hand evidence of matters related to the Second Temple. In the second section of the work, de' Rossi produced an annotated Hebrew translation of the *Letter of Aristeas* now entitled "Splendour of the Elders." The translation served as the basis for his pioneering study on the origins of the Septuagint.[16] In addition, throughout the book, de' Rossi translated extracts from the writings of Josephus and Philo.[17]

Of these three writers, it was only Philo who required special handling:[18]

> I have turned to him, even calling on him by name, because his works contain invaluable information for my purposes which are unobtainable from other such sources. He had a preeminent position among our people slightly prior to the destruction of the Second Temple and he witnessed and recorded many things which ought to be publicized. The truth of the matter is that however much I suspect the integrity of this man as regards God and the holy people, I cannot pass an immediate and absolute verdict on him.

De' Rossi was aware that his position on Philo was different from that of David Provenzali and his brothers whose views he graciously reported in the course of his own discussion.[19] Though he adopted the Hebraized form of the name, "Yedidyah," which they had coined, he divested it of any Jewishness by attaching to it the toponymical designation "the Alexandrian."

De' Rossi, like his contemporaries, read Philo in Sigismund Gelenius' Latin translation printed in Lyon in 1555.[20] The prefatory *testimonia* from Eusebius, Augustine,

---

[15] All references will be to J. Weinberg, *The Light of the Eyes of Azariah de' Rossi: An English Translation with Introduction and Notes* (New Haven: Yale University Press, 2001).

[16] See J. Weinberg, "Azariah de' Rossi and Septuagint Traditions," *Italia* 5.1–2 (1985): 7–35.

[17] e.g. for his antiquarian section on the priestly vestments (chs 46–50) he translated from *Mos.* 2.109–16 and *Spec.* 1.83–98.

[18] *Light of the Eyes*, ch. 3, 101.

[19] See *Light of the Eyes*, ch. 5, 131 n. 27, where he accepts David Provenzali's interpretation of one passage; ch. 6, 158, where he acknowledges that his contemporaries had some justification in defending Philo; ch. 9, 189–90, about Philo's knowledge of Hebrew and Aramaic where he refuses to retract his view.

[20] Gelenius' translation was first published in Basel in 1554. From de' Rossi's reference to page numbers it is clear that he was using the two-volume Lyons edition, *Philonis Iudaei, scriptoris eloquentissimi, ac philosophi*

Jerome, and the entry in the *Souda* lexicon as given by the sixteenth-century encyclopedist Raphael Maffei Volaterranus could leave no doubt about the high regard in which Philo was held by Christians. Whether reporting Philo's encounter with apostles in Rome during his embassy to the emperor Caligula, or his inadvertent account of monastic life (in *De vita contemplativa*), these biographies mentioned Philo's Jewish origins for the most part only in passing. Clearly, then, de' Rossi was fully aware of Philo's status in Christian tradition. Moreover, these short descriptions of the life and writings of Philo were not de' Rossi's sole source of information. On display throughout his book is an impressive knowledge of early Christian writings, and for the purpose of his study of Philo, in particular, Eusebius.[21] So in attempting to probe the nature of Philo's Jewish identity de' Rossi was responding both to the positive adoption of the Alexandrian Jew on the part of his Jewish colleagues, and to the various Christian attitudes towards Philo, including their appreciation of the "profane" writer's exegetical Platonism.[22]

The quest to establish the religious identity of Philo had to be grounded in historical evidence. Thus de' Rossi devoted the first chapter of his critique to an excursus on the Jewish sects that flourished in Second Temple times. In assembling the relevant materials from Josephus, the New Testament, Philo, and early Christian writers, de' Rossi trod the same path as contemporary theologians and chronologers who used this evidence in order to comprehend the contours of the early Christian Church and often to prove the authenticity of their own confessional allegiance.[23] What was new in de' Rossi's account was the inclusion of the Boethusians, a sect mentioned only in rabbinic writings, and usually associated with the Sadducees. On somewhat flimsy evidence he ended this first chapter with the provisional conclusion that the Boethusians held views on the soul and reward and punishment in the afterlife that demonstrated affinity with the Essenes.[24]

In the following chapters de' Rossi then proceeded to probe Philo's credentials in a series of mini-investigations into certain facets of Philo's theology, biblical interpretation, knowledge, or ignorance of Hebrew and Aramaic, and adherence to or

---

summi, lucubrationes omnes quotquot haberi potuerunt (Lyons: apud Ioannem Franciscun de Gabiano, 1555). On Gelenius, an outstanding textual scholar born in Prague, but who spent most of his life in Basel working in Froben's printing press, see P. Petitmengin, "Gelenius (Sigismundus) (1497–1554)," in *Centuriæ latinæ II. Cent une figures humanistes de la Renaissance aux Lumières*, ed. C. Nativel (Geneva: Droz, 2006), 337–51; and A. Ammann, *Josephus Frobenianus: Editions- und Rezeptionsgeschichte des Flavius Josephus im Basler Humanismus* (Basel and Berlin: Schwabe, 2020).

[21] See e.g. his statement about earthquakes: "Yedidyah the Alexandrian tackles the problem well in the first book of *De decalogo* which is no longer extant, but which is cited by the early Christian Eusebius of Caesarea, in the eighth book of the *Praeparatio*" (*Light of the Eyes*, p. 19).

[22] This was Adrien Turnèbe's designation for Philo in the preface to his Latin translation of *De vita Mosis Philonis Iudaei de vita Mosis lib. III Adriano Turnebe interprete* (Paris: A. Turnèbe, 1554): "... ut et homines pii documentum vitae exemplumque haberent, et in profano scriptore recognoscerent, quae in sacris libris legerunt, multorumque locorum perobscuruorum explicationem addiscerent." In the Greek preface to the *editio princeps* of Philo, however, Turnèbe alludes to Philo's Hellenizing and Judaizing modes of exegesis.

[23] See Weinberg, "Philo in Sixteenth-Century Jewish Historiography," 167; and A. Grafton and J. Weinberg, *"I Have Always Loved the Holy Tongue": Isaac Casaubon, the Jews, and a Forgotten Chapter in Renaissance Scholarship* (Cambridge, MA: Harvard University Press, 2011), 187–90.

[24] *Light of the Eyes*, ch. 3, 109–10.

disregard of rabbinic legal interpretation. These chapters combine approval and condemnation. Thus, in chapter 4, on the basis of carefully selected passages, de' Rossi asserted: "Generally speaking, as one passes from gate to gate of his forty-three works (and they are readily accessible from the indices which give lists of subject-matter) you will come to the realization that as regards the divine, the exaltation of our perfect Torah, the panegyrics of Moses the chosen of God, and the blessedness which awaits all who keep the commandments, he speaks as a man of exalted station who may be called by the name of Israel."[25] Thrown into the examination was a comparison between the *Book of Biblical Antiquities (Liber antiquitatum biblicarum)* and certain rabbinic Aggadot. Although de' Rossi knew that the authenticity of this work had been questioned, he was attracted to its narrative which contained so many traditions that were paralleled in rabbinic texts.[26]

Nevertheless, all the positive assessments get thrown to the wind in the following chapter. Philo is found wanting on four counts: use of the Septuagint and ignorance of Hebrew and Aramaic; belief in primordial matter; unacceptable allegorization of scripture; unawareness of traditional interpretation of biblical precepts. Of these charges, the last one is:[27]

> weighty enough to sink him like lead into bottomless waters. It is as follows: Reading from beginning to end of his works you will not come across any indication that he took upon himself the Oral Tradition alongside the Written Torah. As the primary example, you should take his work *On the Special Laws*. You will notice that whenever our sages of blessed memory have in accordance with their traditional reading slightly deviated from the plain sense of the verse in order to elicit a particular law, his interpretation follows Scripture to the letter, and his translation retains the structure of the verse without alteration. He does this with the expression *eye for an eye* (Exod 21:24) which the sages of blessed memory traditionally interpret as signifying monetary compensation.

Such outspoken condemnation was not the last word on the judgement of Philo. Rather, in the final chapter of his critique, with a remarkable sleight of hand, de' Rossi offered the reader various reasons for Philo's lapses: political reasons had dictated Philo's use of the Septuagint; the concept of "creatio ex nihilo" could be detected in his writings; Philo had admitted that the allegorization of biblical precepts did not permit nullification of the actual observance of the precepts.

But this defense had a sting to it. The final pages of the critique were devoted to a lengthy collation of Philo's statements about the nature of the soul and angels.[28] According to de' Rossi, the concepts represented in these texts did not evince Pharisaic

---

[25] *Light of the Eyes*, ch. 4, 120.
[26] See Weinberg, "Philo in Sixteenth-Century Jewish Historiography," 173–74.
[27] *Light of the Eyes*, ch. 5, 140–41.
[28] *Gig.* 6–15; *Plant.* 14; *Conf.* 174–75; *Som.* 1.138–46. These passages are contrasted with a selection of rabbinic references to the heavens, spirits, and angels.

or Sadducean convictions. Close scrutiny of Josephus' statements on the Essenes revealed that Philo espoused Essene beliefs.[29] As regards the literal interpretation of biblical precepts such as "eye for an eye," Philo's views coincided with those of the Boethusians.[30]

Thus, after an extensive apparently objective scrutiny of Philo's Jewish or rather Pharisaic credentials, de' Rossi arrived back at the hypothesis raised from the very outset that Philo was a sectarian of the Essene or Boethusian variety. He thus concluded:[31]

> In view of all that has been written in this chapter, I say to the Jewish people that I cannot pass an unconditional verdict on this Yedidyah or Philo, to use his Greek name, or indeed any other name or surname he has been given. I cannot absolutely absolve or convict him. I shall call him neither Rav nor sage,[32] heretic nor sceptic. My only name for him shall be Yedidyah the Alexandrian.

According to de' Rossi, therefore, Philo was neither a proto-Christian, nor a Pharisee or Sadducee, but rather a sectarian of the Essene variety. Sitting on the fence de' Rossi managed to salvage Philo's Jewish identity by dubbing him a Jew of "unorthodox" beliefs. It is clear, however, that his study of Philo was not simply a tussle of war over one influential individual from first-century Alexandria. Rather, his critique of Philo as well as his chapters on the origins of the Septuagint adumbrate some of the fashionable debates regarding Greek Jews, use of the Greek language in the so-called Hellenistic era, and the nature of Hellenistic Judaism that scholars of the calibre of Joseph Scaliger, Daniel Heinsius, and Claude Saumaise (Salmasius) were to spearhead during the next decades.[33]

As noted above, de' Rossi was only too fully aware that his assessment of Philo was not shared by his contemporaries, and in particular, by David Provenzali. Only recently has a section of David Provenzali's response to de' Rossi come to light.[34] Nevertheless, what is extant gives us some idea about Provenzali's method of countering de' Rossi, or simply developing his argument. He called his work a "Magen Yedidyah, a shield of Philo, for the Lord has chosen him; alternatively, David's defense—a golden ornament, nose-ring, and necklace." In the *Shield*, Provenzali was

---

[29] Josephus, *B.J.* 2.154–58; *A.J.* 18.18–23.
[30] *Spec.* 3.195. De' Rossi refers to the scholion to *Megillat Ta'anit* 4 where the Boethusians are reproached for interpreting this and similar precepts literally.
[31] *Light of the Eyes*, 159.
[32] This is an allusion to Babylonian Talmud, Baba Metsia 85b–86a about Samuel Yarhinaa who, despite healing Rabbi Judah ha-Nasi was not ordained as "Rav," but retained the title "sage."
[33] For a classic discussion of the historical questions related to Hellenism, see A. Momigliano, "Prologue in Germany," in A. Momigliano, *Nono contributo alla storia degli studi classici e del mondo antico*, ed. Riccardo di Donato (Rome: Edizioni di storia e letteratura, 1992), 543–62.
[34] Budapest, Hungarian Academy of Sciences, MS A 490 (65). Only two of the four parts are extant. I am grateful to Abraham David who informed me of the existence of this precious manuscript. I will be discussing this manuscript in greater depth in the essay indicated in n. 1.

set on a mission: to undermine de' Rossi's unjustified verdict on "a righteous and perfect man, a worker of righteousness who spoke truth, the sage, perfect in every respect, Rabbi Yedidyah the Alexandrian Jew of priestly stock." The wording betrays all. Not only does Provenzali insist on Philo's rabbinic qualifications, but here and elsewhere in the tract draws attention to Philo's priestly descent, thus echoing Jerome's statement in his *De viris illustribus*. The sacerdotal title conferred authenticity on Philo's genuine Jewish lineage. It is indeed telling that de' Rossi never referred to Philo as a priest or of priestly stock.

Provenzali's critique of de' Rossi is complex and also sometimes totally justified. Provenzali took him to task for what he regarded as a rather impressionistic reading of the sources.[35] For example, de' Rossi did not distinguish between the Essenes and Therapeutae.[36] The Boethusians mentioned only in the rabbinic texts, according to Provenzali, were hardly soul-mates of the Essenes, but rather of the Sadducees with whom they shared some basic sectarian views. For the benefit of the reader who could not read Latin and who would be led astray by de' Rossi, Provenzali proffered long translations in Hebrew of the relevant passages from Josephus and Philo.

Time and time again Provenzali ushered forth arguments, somewhat casuistically, to prove Philo's knowledge of Hebrew; he even went as far as to say that when Philo referred to Chaldean he really meant Hebrew.[37] Philo's allegorical and figurative reflections on Hebrew words were not supposed to convey literal meanings. Like the rabbinic midrashim, Philo consciously and deliberately constructed theologically inspiring discourses.

For David Provenzali, then, Philo's rabbinically Jewish identity was an issue of fundamental importance. His critique is couched in assertive, even dogmatic terms; he never really betrays the reason for his passionate defense of Philo. In contrast to Provenzali, and also implicitly responding to Christian adoption of Philo, de' Rossi stressed Philo's anomalous status in relation to rabbinic Judaism and desisted from reclaiming Philo with open arms. Yet, ultimately, de' Rossi did make some concessions and indicated that he would accept some, but not all of Provenzali's criticisms. "Philo should be honoured as a holy man of God and respected by us all."[38]

---

[35] Yet in his revision of his book, *Light of the Eyes*, p. 107, de' Rossi seems to be responding to Provenzali's criticism when he writes: "According to Philo, these Essenes who were assigned the name 'the holy ones', as was said, devoted themselves to the active life. He spoke about them in chapter thirty-six [i.e. *That Every Good Man Is Free*]. But from what he says at the beginning of chapter thirty-seven [i.e. *On the Contemplative Life*], it seems that those devoted to the contemplative life were called healers, i.e. healers of the soul [Therapeutae]. In any case, there is no reason to assume that they did not belong to the Essene sects, for Josephus and Eusebius apply that which is said about the one group to the other."

[36] For an overview on the issue of the identity of the Therapeutae, see F. Calabi, *God's Acting, Man's Acting* (Leiden: Brill, 2008), 173–81.

[37] It is quite likely that this view is intended to counter de' Rossi's allegation that Philo often confused the two languages.

[38] This is clear from his Response (Teshuvah) to Moses Provenzali's Hasagah (Critique) of the chronological and calendrical part of his work which was inserted into the third printing of the *Me'or Einayim*, Mantua, 1575 (ed. D. Cassel, Vilna: Yosef Reuven Rom, 1866), 506.

23.2 Judah Moscato

Friend of both de' Rossi and Provenzali, Judah Moscato was yet another scholar who read Gelenius' Latin Philo with great assiduity. Moscato came to Mantua from Osimo in the Marche in about 1570 and remained there until his death in 1590.[39] An important rabbinic figure in the Mantuan community and its representative, Moscato possessed a wide-ranging knowledge of Jewish and non-Jewish literature. His highly stylized and rhetorical mode of composition is evident in the two major works he wrote: a collection of sermons entitled *Nefutsot Yehudah* [*The Dispersions of Judah*] (Venice, 1589) and an extensive commentary, *Qol Yehudah*, on Judah Halevi's twelfth-century defense of Judaism, the *Kuzari*. It was published with the text posthumously in 1594—it constituted the third printing of the Hebrew translation of Halevi's Judeo-Arabic classic work. Moscato's commentary remained the basic guide to the *Kuzari* for centuries to come.[40] Both the sermons and the commentary are permeated with references to a wide range of philosophical, kabbalistic, and rabbinic sources, providing a kind of synthesis of classical, medieval, and contemporary ideas. Moscato demonstrated a particular penchant for the *Timaeus* as well as a tendency to promote *Prisca Theologia* notions as used in the work of Pico della Mirandola and Marsilio Ficino whose works he cited.

Moscato had read de' Rossi' work—indeed he had been embroiled in the controversy which erupted during and after the publication of the *Me'or Einayim*. An implicit reaction to de' Rossi by Moscato is discernible in his appellation for Philo.[41] For on several occasions Moscato, like Provenzali, calls Philo "Rabbi Yedidyah the sage who is called Filone." This designation, as we have seen in the case of Provenzali, not only suggested that Moscato did not agree with de' Rossi's cautious approach to Philo, but that he regarded him as one of the rabbis of old.

Philo appears several times in both the commentary and the sermons.[42] In all cases Philo is cited with approval and usually his ideas are claimed to demonstrate congruity with a long line of Jewish authorities including the Talmudic rabbis and medieval

---

[39] Moscato (c.1532–90) came to Mantua as an exile from Osimo in the Marche. He became embroiled in a controversy over the conversion of Abramo Barocco and was arrested and put in jail where an attempt to no avail was made to convert him to Christianity. See Gianfranco Miletto, "Judah Moscato: Biographical Data and Writings," in *Rabbi Judah Moscato and the Jewish Intellectual World of Mantua in the 16th–17th Centuries*, ed. G. Veltri and G. Miletto (Leiden: Brill, 2012), 1–13.

[40] For an analysis of one of his sermons and discussion of his cultural and particularly kabbalistic context, see M. Idel, "Judah Moscato: A Late Renaissance Jewish Preacher," in *Preachers of the Italian Ghetto*, ed. D. Ruderman (Berkeley: University of California Press, 1992), 41–66. For a discussion of the humanist context of his commentary on the Kuzari, the *Qol Yehudah*, see A. Shear, *The Kuzari and the Shaping of Jewish Identity 1167–1900* (Cambridge: Cambridge University Press, 2008), 135–39; on his homiletics, see I. Bettan, *Studies in Jewish Preaching: Middle Ages* (Cincinnati: Hebrew Union College Press, 1939), ch. 5; on rhetoric, see A. Altmann, "Ars Rhetorica as Reflected in Some Jewish Figures of the Italian Renaissance," in *Jewish Thought in the Sixteenth Century*, ed. B. D. Cooperman (Cambridge, MA: Harvard University Press, 1983), 1–22; and for his use of Kabbalah, see M. Idel, "On Kabbalah in R Judah Moscato's Qol Yehuda," in *Rabbi Judah Moscato*, 57–77.

[41] In *Qol Yehuda* (Venice: Giovanni di Gara, 1594) 3, 65, Moscato refers explicitly to de' Rossi twice. In the second passage like Provenzali he disputes de' Rossi's description of the Boethusians.

[42] Moscato cites Philo four times in the *Qol Yehudah* and eleven times in the *Nefutsot Yehudah*. See my forthcoming paper (n. 1) for a detailed discussion of Moscato's method of citing Philo.

authorities, in particular, the thirteenth-century exegete Nahmanides (Moses ben Nahman). What is particularly striking is the extent to which Moscato had absorbed Philo's allegorical method and applied it to his own interpretations. This becomes evident in the sermon for Pentecost which is devoted to the question, often debated in rabbinic writings, whether action or study takes priority in the religious life.[43] The exegetical matter at stake was the story of Dinah and the behavior of her brothers Simeon and Levi; in Moscato's words, symbols respectively of the speculative and practical intellect. Moscato admitted that his exegetical approach had been stimulated by Philo's discourse to which he had added his own contribution and from which he had also deviated somewhat. Though he often referred to title of work and page numbers in Gelenius' edition in this case he simply acknowledged his debt to Philo. The relevant passage from *De mutatione nominum* (194–200) does indeed demonstrate the extent to which Philo's approach to the story of Genesis 34 informed Moscato's own interpretive stance including his play on the etymological significance of the name of Dinah (judgment).[44]

Moscato employed Philo amidst a host of other authorities. It is clear, however, that Rabbi Yedidyah was, in certain respects, a kind of model for Moscato—Philo's allegorical notions suited his own form of kabbalistic and philosophical discourse. Without entering into the questions of Jewish identity that had agitated both de' Rossi and Provenzali, Moscato simply welcomed Philo into his own particular syncretistic universe.

23.3 Simone Luzzatto

The debate over Philo did not completely disappear, but rather appeared in a somewhat different form in a pioneering apologetic tract written by Simone (Simhah) Luzzatto (1583?–1663), an erudite rabbi who served the community of Venice.[45] In his *Discorso circa il stato de gl'Hebrei. Et in particular dimonanti nell'inclita Città di Venetia* of 1638, ostensibly written to avert the threatened expulsion of the Jews from Venice, Luzzatto set out to demonstrate how the Jews were part and parcel of the Republic's social, economic, and political fabric. The objective of the second half of this remarkable treatise was to combat traditional forms of anti-Jewish polemic, particularly of the Tacitean variety, and to show up Jews and Judaism in a positive light both in terms of their history and religious ideals that were also universal ones.[46]

---

[43] *Nefutsot Yehudah* (Venice: Giovanni d Gara, 1589), Sermon 18, 87r.

[44] Having attributed Simeon with the symbol of speculative intellect in its capacity "to hear" the divine word and Levi with the practical intellect that brings about right action, Moscato describes Dinah as the one that brings judgment by actualizing the hylic intellect. Philo refers to Simeon and Levi as "blending the two natures ... uniting hearing with action." He calls Dinah "incorruptible judgement, the justice which is the assessor of God."

[45] On Luzzatto, see G. Veltri and A. Lissa, *Discourse on the State of the Jews* (Berlin: de Gruyter, 2019).

[46] Tacitus was regarded as an important political thinker in seventeenth-century Italy. Luzzatto's decision to refute Tacitus' attacks on Judaism (*Histories* 5.2–13) is typical of his subversive rhetoric that aimed at undermining negative portrayals of Judaism that might have been conveyed to avid readers of Tacitus.

Philo was one of the Jewish writers of antiquity that served Luzzatto's purpose well. Indeed, he cited the "golden sayings" of "the very eloquent Philo" on seven occasions.[47] Like his Jewish predecessors, Luzzatto read Philo in Gelenius' translation. Though Luzzatto also approved of the historian Josephus, he clearly felt particular affinity for Philo who seems to have represented for him an authentic and fundamental strand of his Jewish legacy.

In section (consideratione) sixteen of the *Discorso* Luzzatto presented a taxonomy of Jewish sages. The three classes consisted of rabbis and Talmudists, theologian/philosophers (*teologi filosofanti*), and Kabbalists and teachers of the arcane. Luzzatto placed Philo among the philosophers, "those who combined human reason with the authority of the divine word and managed to expound scripture with harmonious concord." Philo possessed not only an extraordinary erudition in Greek but also an incomparable ability to comprehend the human and divine in his generally allegorical exposition of scripture. Having referred to Origen as an emulator of Philo, Luzzatto then pronounced:[48]

> It is not credible that he [Philo] completely eschewed the literal and historical sense of Scripture. But he behaved in such a way as to attract and mollify the souls of the Greeks to whom he directed his endeavours. That is why he preferred to use the Septuagint even though it deviated from the Hebrew text in certain respects. His purpose was to accommodate himself to the mind-set of the Greeks. His works have been translated from Greek into Latin, but have not yet been rendered in Hebrew. Had he put his mind to educating the Jews rather than converting the Greeks, he might have reaped greater fruit from his labours—he would have brought honour on the nation and gained greater appreciation from them than from the Greeks; for his own people would have been more receptive to apprehending his doctrine.[49]

Luzzatto seems to be suggesting that Philo's works contained fundamental doctrines that somehow got overlooked because of his overtly allegorizing method of interpreting scripture and use of the Septuagint. Had he used Hebrew and communicated his ideas to his fellow Jews—argued Luzzatto—unmitigated success would have been assured.

In this somewhat obscure passage we get a glimpse of the inner-Jewish debate over Philo. Luzzatto had distilled these discussions into one short paragraph. "Our Philo" was a Jew whose erudition in Greek and insistence on addressing Greeks had prevented generations of Jewish readers from benefitting from his pearls and exposition of scripture.[50] The implicit criticism of Philo for this abandonment of his own people does recall de' Rossi's strictures, as Aescoly noted many years ago:

---

[47] Simone Luzzatto, *Discorso* (Venice: Gioanne Calleoni, 1638), 48r, 51v, 63r–v, 78r, 79r, 82r–v.
[48] *Discorso*, 78r.
[49] For a different interpretation of the passage, see B. Septimus, "Biblical Religion and Political Rationality in Simone Luzzatto, Maimonides and Spinoza," in *Jewish Thought in the Seventeenth-Century*, ed. B. Septimus and I. Twersky (Cambridge, MA: Harvard University Press, 1987), 399–443, esp. 419–20.
[50] In the preface to *Philonis Iudaei opuscula tria* (Augsburg: Joannes Wechelus, 1587), David Hoeschel seemed to appraise Philo in similar terms. He argued that he he did not render the literal meaning of holy scripture, but

Thus it was that when I pondered over the anomalous nature of such a person, I considered that he was certainly raised at the feet of many of the great gentile sages and philosophers that lived in his Greek city of Alexandria in Egypt. And while he cultivated those vineyards, he neglected his own precious vineyard which would have enabled him to gain the joy of drawing the holy waters from the fountains of salvation.[51]

Unlike de' Rossi, however, Luzzatto's criticism seems to imply that Philo was fully able to handle the Hebrew text and that his ideas were fully consonant with Jewish tradition. In this respect, he was putting forward a view in agreement with Provenzali who insisted against de' Rossi that Philo was perfectly proficient in Hebrew. Altogether, one could argue that Luzzatto belonged more to Moscato's and Provenzali's camp than to de' Rossi's. Philo's prominence in this notable apologetic monograph would indicate that Luzzatto had followed in the footsteps of his illustrious Jewish predecessors and continued the trend for the rehabilitation of Philo the Jew.

23.4 Epilogue: Philo among the Karaites

Philo did not remain within the confines of Italy. In northern and eastern Europe long before Josef Flesch set out to present Philo's "wondrous" works in Hebrew for a Jewish readership, efforts were made to reclaim the Greek Jew.[52] Indeed, the debate that had energized the Jewish scholars of sixteenth-century Italy reappeared on many occasions and sometimes with similar vehemence among the Karaites of the Crimea and Lithuania throughout the seventeenth and early eighteenth centuries. It would appear that Philo represented a strand of Judaism that was appealing to those who felt pushed to the margins of Jewish society: his philosophical and non-rabbinic culture of ancient lineage and his "expulsion" from the canon of Jewish literature set him apart in a state not unlike that of the Karaites in relation to the Rabbanites.

Interest in Philo is already attested in a letter written by the Karaite Zerah ben Nathan of Troki (1567–1657/8) addressed to the distinguished scholar and printer Menasseh ben Israel in Amsterdam.[53] Zerah informed Menasseh that his teacher Joseph Delmedigo had translated some of Philo's works into Hebrew, but they had allegedly been stolen. Saddened by this pitiable loss Zerah had asked Delmedigo to supply indices of the Philonic corpus.[54]

---

rather, used allegory in a Greek manner, so that his doctrines might seem not to deviate from their philosophy. Thanks to Michael Cover for suggesting the similarity between the two writers.

[51] *Light of the Eyes*, ch. 5, 134. The connection was discerned by A. Aescoly in the notes to the Hebrew translation of the *Discorso* (Jerusalem: Mosad Bialik, 1950), 170 n. 85.
[52] On Flesch, see Z. Strauss, "Solomon Judah Rapoport's Maskilic Revival of Philo of Alexandria: Rabbi Yedidya ha-Alexandri as a Pioneer of Jewish Philosophy," *SPhiloA* 31 (2019): 201–26.
[53] J. Mann, *Texts and Studies in Jewish Literature* (Philadelphia: Hebrew Press of the Jewish Publication Society of America for the Author, 1935), 2:730–31 and transcription with notes, 1225–28.
[54] A. Neubauer, *Aus der Petersburger Bibliothek. Beiträge und Documente zur Geschichte des Karäerthums und der karäischen Literatur* (Leipzig: O. Leiner, 1866), 75. Delmedigo himself (see *Mikhav ahuz* to Zerah) stated that he had translated some of the works of R. Yedidyah the Alexandrian who wrote many books in Greek: "and

The Karaites derived their knowledge of Philo principally from two sources: Azariah de' Rossi's *Light of the Eyes* and Christian writings or informants. As Golda Akhiezer has demonstrated, Karaite libraries were not depositaries of Karaite productions alone; rather, from the sixteenth-century onwards Karaites in Ottoman Istanbul or in Crimea and Lithuania had access to and were avidly reading a wide range of rabbinic and medieval Jewish traditional sources and on occasion also Christian literature.[55] The need to legitimize their status propelled early modern Karaites to trace their lineage to Second Temple times and to reverse Rabbanite accounts of the history of the schism. In the process of showing their authentic credentials certain Karaite scholars turned to Philo. In a copybook entitled *Beit Abraham*, Abraham ben Josiah (1636–88), one of the few Lithuanian Karaites who knew Latin, quoted an extract from Jerome's entry on Philo in *De viris illustribus* listing Philo's works, which he claimed to have transcribed from a book entitled *Theatrum mundi*.[56] He contrasted this list with that of de' Rossi's count of forty-three books. On another page, following de' Rossi's lead, he also translated the titles of the works into Hebrew.[57]

Particularly striking is the use of Philo in the work of Solomon Yedidyah ben Aaron of Troki.[58] Solomon had contacts with Christians, in particular Johannes Uppendorf, rector of the gymnasium of Riga from 1678–98, who had invited Solomon to visit Riga in order to discuss Karaite beliefs. Solomon's work *Appiryon asa lo* written in 1696, a work that reflects these discussions, contains a long disquisition on Philo who is summoned as a witness against the Rabbanites.[59] Once again, de' Rossi provided the author with the starting-point for his arguments.[60] Solomon read de' Rossi's four-chapter critique of Philo with great care, and selected the material relevant for his polemic. The Talmudists had failed to mention him and accord him respect unlike the gentile sages who called him Philonius [sic]. De' Rossi's attack on Philo for his rejection of Oral Torah was misplaced. "He lived in the time of the Second Temple when there were thousands of householders in Alexandria. Had there been a tradition in their time they would have punished him and banished him like other sectarians of theirs." Inevitably, the question of Philo's exegetical approach is raised. According to Solomon, Philo's

---

I thought of binding these 'beloved' ones into one volume. Then I would publish them as 'signs and wonders' for the wisdom of the House of Israel. But they were stolen from me and I have not yet been able to come across them again."

[55] G. Akhiezr, *Historical Consciousness, Haskalah, and Nationalism among the Karaites of Eastern Europe* (Leiden: Brill, 2018).

[56] *Beit Abraham*, Institute of Oriental Studies, St Petersburg, MS B263, 15b–16a. I am grateful to Daniel Lasker who helped me access the manuscript. On Abraham ben Josiah, a son of Joseph Delmedigo's student, see Akhiezer, *Historical Consciousness*, 90–99.

[57] *Beit Abraham*, 17a. This author was examining all manner of works. He also quoted the emblem book of Antoine de Bourgogne, *Lapis lydius sive vanitas per veritatem falsi* (Antwerp, 1639).

[58] See Akhiezer, *Historical Consciousness*, 129–37.

[59] There are two versions of the work: the short version published first by A. Neubauer in *Aus der Petersburger Bibliothek*; and the long version printed in Ramla: Mekhon "Tif'eret Yosef" le-ḥeker ha-Yahadut ha-Ḳarait, 2 vols (2000).

[60] *Appiryon asa lo*, Ramla, 2:369–70. Part of this passage is also discussed by Akhiezer, *Historical Consciousness*, 135. This passage will be discussed at greater length in the article mentioned in n. 1.

commentaries are his defense because unlike the Rabbanites' Mishnayot he espoused the literal meaning of the verses.

Solomon produces here novel arguments to bolster his anti-Rabbanite polemic.[61] De' Rossi's ambivalent attitudes towards Philo are swept away and in a somewhat anachronistic fashion Solomon claims Philo as one of his own: in antiquity he had not been dubbed a sectarian. Philo's credentials are fully endorsed by reason of his literal commentaries on Torah. At first sight, such an assertion seems counter-intuitive. However, it should be remembered that in chapter 5 de' Rossi had censured Philo for his literal interpretation of some of the legal injunctions (e.g. Deut 25:11–12). Solomon clearly reversed de' Rossi's verdict and regarded Philo as a kindred spirit.

It would appear that Philo and his writings spontaneously generated questions of identity. Though the debates continued, many thought it was desirable to claim to be "a distant descendant of Philo, the Jew from Alexandria."[62]

---

[61] See Akhiezer, *Historical Consciousness*, 135.
[62] The phrasing is from Momigliano, "Prologue in Germany," 550.

24

Post-Tridentine Catholic Thought

Eric J. DeMeuse

The sixteenth century witnessed a renaissance in Philonic studies rivaled only by developments from the nineteenth century onward.[1] The extensive bibliography of Goodhart and Goodenough, as well as the chapter on early Printed editions (ch. 22) above, attest to the proliferation of "editions" and translations of Philo's works during this period.[2] One reason for this renewed interest in "Philo Judaeus," as he was called by Christian writers of the period, was the rise of Renaissance humanism. In 1520, the Italian Dominican and biblical humanist Agosto Giustiniani (1470–1536) published the first sixteenth-century Latin edition of Philo,[3] and other humanists from across the continent quickly followed suit. The motivations for their work were manifold. Many, like the French Hellenist Guillaume Budé (1468–1540), were intrigued by Philo's connection to Greek philosophy.[4] Fellow Frenchman Adrien Turnèbe (1512–65), likewise fascinated with Philo's interweaving of "Jewish revelation and Greek philosophy,"[5] was also interested in Philo's depiction of the virtuous life.[6] Giustiniani struck a similarly Erasmian chord when he assured Louise of Savoy that Philo's *QG* "has nothing of disguise or vanity, and by simple words and without any rhetorical apparatus, can move the hearts of men," adding that she ought to ask her priest to explain Philo's "moral responses."[7] These new editions did little to alter the exalted status Philo

---

[1] D. T. Runia writes that after 1500 printed editions of Philo "begin to see the light of day and the contours of the modern study of his writings and thought gradually start to emerge." See "Philo in Byzantium," *VC* 70 (2016): 260; see also David Runia, Chapter 20 in this volume. See, in the nineteenth century, H. L. Goodhart and E. R. Goodenough, "A General Bibliography of Philo Judaeus," in E. R. Goodenough, *The Politics of Philo Judaeus: Practice and Theory, with a General Bibliography of Philo* (New Haven: Yale University Press, 1938) (hereafter G-G), 191 (§413); 194–95 (§431); 197–98 (§§440–41).

[2] For a listing of these editions, see G-G 187–201 (§§388–97). "Editions" here meaning anything from individual treatises or pseudo-works to selective collections or florilegium. On translations into vernacular languages, see the following. French: 1542 (Lyons; G-G §480) and 1575 (Paris; G-G §481); Italian: 1548, 1560, 1570, and 1574 (all Venice; G-G §§500–503); and English: 1563 (London; G-G §466). The first German translation listed in G-G §487 is a 1778 rendering of *De vita Mosis*.

[3] Philo Judaeus, *Philonis Judaei Centum et duae quaestiones, et totidem responsiones morales super Genesim*, ed. and trans. Agosto Giustiniani (Paris: 1520). This edition was in fact the republication of an ancient Latin translation.

[4] Budé, following Aldus Manutius, coupled the *De mundo* attributed to Philo (see G-G 145) with Aristotle's *De mundo*. Budé is not persuaded that the work was actually written by Philo, and notes that the author, "whoever he was," seems to follow the philosophy of the Greeks more closely than that of the Hebrews. *Aristotelis philosophi nobilissimi de mundo libellus* (Paris: Ascensianis, 1526).

[5] J. Lewis, *Adrien Turnebe, 1512–1565: A Humanist Observed* (Geneva: Librairie Droz S.A., 1998), 168.

[6] See the introductory letter in *Philonis Iudaei de vita Mosis, lib. III, Adr. Turnebo interprete* (Paris: Turnebus, 1554).

[7] "Accipe itaque centum & duas in librum Geneseos quaestiones & argutissimas, nec minus morales responsiones, quas ubi tibi explicari iusseris sive publicis in concionibus, sive privatim, a sacerdotibus illis, qui animae tuae curam gerunt.... Est siquidem farrago haec tota solida, firma, constans, dulcis, spiritalis, & amoena,

enjoyed among Christians from the time of the church fathers. With some notable exceptions, Thomas Billings's nearly hundred-year-old claim still generally holds true, that "up to the middle of the sixteenth century Philo was almost universally venerated by the Christian Church."[8]

Yet just as the Aristotelian revival of the thirteenth century suffered condemnation by the Parisian Bishop Tempier in 1277, the Philonic renaissance of the sixteenth was not without its critics. Some detractors can be gleaned from the pages of Philo's defenders, though such opponents often go unnamed and their arguments unnuanced.[9] There is, however, at least one instance of direct censure from ecclesiastical authorities. In 1582, ecclesiastical censors in Rome issued ninety condemnations against the *De republica Hebraeorum* of Italian humanist Carlo Sigonio, with thirteen of those condemnations specifically directed at Sigonio's use of Philo.[10] These thirteen vary in rationale, some lacking any reason—Censure 66 merely reads, "On page 331, he cites Josephus and Philo."[11] The majority accuse Sigonio of violating the decrees of the Council of Trent. Censure 4 reads:

> Various errors are stirred up if you do not grasp or interpret precisely the truths of the Scriptures exactly as the holy Council of Trent commands concerning the Vulgate Edition (session 4), where it enumerates all the books which should be considered approved under the penalty of anathema. But there neither Philo nor Josephus are enumerated, both of whom the life-giving Spirit of God does not enlighten.[12]

The fourth session of Trent (April 8, 1546) listed the canonical books, approved the Vulgate Edition of scripture, and forbade any interpretation of the scriptures contrary

---

nil habens aut fuci, aut vanitatis, & que verbis simplicibus, & sine aliquo rhetorico apparatu, possit movere corda hominum as psequenda [sic] omni studio caelestia & divina." Giustiniani, *Philonis Judaei,* dedicatory letter (all translations, unless otherwise noted, are my own).

[8] T. H. Billings, *The Platonism of Philo Judaeus* (Chicago: University of Chicago Press, 1919), 4. J. Weinberg adopts Billings's chronology in her article "The Quest for Philo in Sixteenth-Century Jewish Historiography," in *Jewish History: Essays in Honor of Chimen Abramsky,* ed. A. Rapoport-Albert and S. J. Zipperstein (London: Peter Halban, 1988), 163. The "almost" here is important, especially given Augustine's famous criticism of Philo in the *Contra Faustum*. On this see §24.3 below.

[9] See e.g. the French Franciscan André Thevet's life of Philo in *Pourtraits et vies des hommes illustres* (Paris: Kervert et Chaudiere, 1584), fols 84–85, discussed further below, p. 403–04.

[10] W. McCuaig, "The Tridentine Ruling on the Vulgate and Ecclesiastical Censorship in the 1580s," *Renaissance and Reformation* 18.3 (1994): 43. McCuaig notes that Sigonio's works were never put on the index of forbidden books.

[11] "Pag. 331. Citat Josephum, & Philonem." The censures against Carlo Sigonio, as well as Sigonio's replies, are compiled by Filippo Argelati in volume six of the former's *Opera omnia* (Milan: 1737). McCuaig considers the censures as listed by Argelati "very defective." By McCuaig's description, however, the defect seems more one of omission in certain places than of distortion. Further, if McCuaig's critical edit of two of the censures reveals anything about the whole, then the bulk of the changes are accidental/grammatical rather than substantial. See McCuaig, "The Tridentine Ruling," 51–53. McCuaig does consider Argelati's edition of Sigonio's replies to be "fairly sound" and in any event the only text we have of them.

[12] "Primum varii errores excitantur, si Scripturae vera ad unguem non accipias, aut interpreteris, prout sacrum Concil. Trident. jubet de vulgata Editione sess. 4. ubi enumerat omnes libros, qui habendi sunt pro approbatis, sub anathematis poena. Ibi verò neque Philon, neque Josephus recensentur, quos non Spiritus Dei vivificus illustravit; sed occidens littera, & velamen eorum cordibus impositum, tenebris involvit," *Opera omnia,* vol. 6, col. 1186. Related censures are as follows: Censure 33 (col. 1208); Censure 48 (col. 1217); Censure 54 (col. 1220); Censure 67 (col. 1226); Censure 85 (col. 1234).

to that sense held by Holy Mother Church and "contrary to the unanimous teaching of the Fathers."[13] This last point the censors also flung at Sigonio when they suggested that he should consult the opinions of the holy doctors, not those of Philo.[14]

Despite certain arguments that these censors represent "the authentic voice of the Counter Reformation" and the dominant attitude well into the seventeenth century,[15] I think such a claim distorts the effect of post-Tridentine censorship on renaissance culture and, with it, on the study and use of Philo.[16] This chapter will demonstrate that Philo retained his exalted status among Catholics throughout the latter half of the sixteenth century (§24.1), and that defense of Philo even became a central feature of the Catholic defense of monastic vows (§24.2). This survey does not suggest that Philo's works went uncriticized by Catholic exegetes (§24.3). These criticisms, however, appear less an effort to avoid the stigma of a now unacceptable character, and more a genuine disagreement on interpretive points. And given the fact that church fathers were often criticized in the same breath, Philo could hardly have fallen far from grace. In short, it is Sigonio's response to his censors that sums up the general opinion of Philo after Trent: "We grant that there are bad things mixed with good (*mala bonis permixta*) in the works of Philo and Josephus .... But with respect to Philo, I would be excessive if I wished to bring forward each and every person who not only celebrated him, but even followed him ...."[17]

24.1 The Philo Renaissance Continues

A year after the closing of the Council of Trent in 1563, Roland Petrei sent his commentary on Philo's *De specialibus legibus* (Spec. 4c; G-G §395), coupled with letters between Quintus and Marcus Cicero, to a Parisian press, dedicating the work to

---

[13] *Canons and Decrees of the Council of Trent*, trans. Rev. H. J. Schroeder, O.P. (St. Louis: Herder, 1941), 17–19. Contrary to popular belief, the Council did not disallow other versions of the scriptures; see J. W. O'Malley, *Trent: What Happened at the Council* (Cambridge, MA: Belknap Press, 2013), 96.

[14] Censure 10: "Atque ideo hic, qui rempublicam Hebraeorum informat, ex sacra scriptura et sanctis doctoribus decreta et instituta petere debebat, non a Josepho, Philone, etc....''; edited text in McCuaig, "The Tridentine Ruling," 52. Related censures are as follows: Censure 1 (*Opera omnia*, vol. 6, col. 1177); Censure 32 (col. 1207); Censure 46 (col. 1217); Censure 47 (col. 1217); Censure 77 (col. 1231).

[15] McCuaig, "The Tridentine Ruling," 51.

[16] McCuaig's governing thesis is that "there was a fundamental conflict between the culture of the Italian Renaissance, which had vanished by the end of the century, and the culture of the Counter Reformation" (43). While some scholars have begun to chip away at this assessment in the decades following McCuaig's article; see e.g. R. G. Hobbs, "Reading the Old Testament after Trent: Cardinal Robert Bellarmine and his Italian Predecessors on Psalm Four," *Reformation & Renaissance Review* 12 (2010): 207; and R. A. Markys, *Saint Cicero and the Jesuits: The Influence of the Liberal Arts on the Adoption of Moral Probabilism* (Burlington, VT: Ashgate, 2008), his overriding presumption regarding the disconnect between humanism and Tridentine Catholicism remains dominant. See e.g. A. Prosperi, "Religion," in *The Cambridge Companion to the Italian Renaissance*, ed. M. Wyatt (Cambridge: Cambridge University Press, 2014), 277.

[17] "Damus itaque in Philonis & Josephi operibus esse mala bonis permixta .... Quod vero Philonem respicit, nimius essem, si vellem singulos producere, qui ipsum non celebrarunt modo, verum etiam sequuti sunt ...." Sigonio adds, "& num tota Reipublicae Hebraicae moles exinde labatur & concidat, quod Sigonius ad operis sui structuram duobus Hebraeorum praestantissimis viris utatur aliquando." *Opera omnia*, vol. 6, cols 1179–80, *In censuram 1. Responsio*.

Cardinal Odo Castilioneus.[18] Fédéric Morel published his own Latin translation of Philo's *De mutatione nominum* in Paris a few decades later,[19] and in 1575 the first French edition of *Les oeuvres de Philon Iuif* appeared.[20] In the dedication of this work, translator Pierre Bellier praises the "*grand et divin Philon*," adding to the common proverb "Either Plato philonizes or Philo platonizes" that, "As for me, it seems that just as the body is more excellent than the shadow which follows it, so also Philo is more excellent than Plato, because the former mounts the heights of divinity and there enters in, but the latter only approaches it, having drawn the greatest part of his divine opinions from the ancestors and precursors of Philo in a voyage that he made into Egypt."[21] Bellier conjectures that Plato imbibed his wisdom from the Mosaic font—the stock of Philo—and thus it is Plato who philonizes, not the other way around.[22] Here Bellier goes beyond even Jerome, who famously called Philo *Platonici sermonis imitator*.[23]

Following the example of St. Jerome, some scholars included Philo in their "lives of illustrious men," a popular genre during the Renaissance and into early modernity. The French ecclesiastic André Thevet's *Pourtraits et vies des hommes illustres* presents a telling depiction of Philo.[24] Perhaps best known among Philonists for its famous and enigmatic image of the Hellenistic Jew, Thevet's *Lives* hit the press in 1584. In the four pages dedicated to Philo, Thevet praises him as one who "has surpassed all the other philosophers, both ancient and modern," and has no difficulty "placing him in the ranks of the Ecclesiastical Doctors," since Jerome—never one to favor the Jews—placed him there.[25] But not all agree with Thevet:

> And when I hear anyone scoffing at our Philo (*nostre Philon*), I cannot resist laughing at their daydreams, and on the other hand condemning their malign and perverse nature, for they want to bring dishonor on Philo … [and] they want to make him a pagan because of the proverb which has made the comparison between him and Plato, that

---

[18] Roland Petrei, ed., *Epistolae duae, una: Q. Ciceronis ad M. Tullium: De petitione consulatus … His accesserunt eiusdem Petreii notae quoddam Προλεγόμενον Philonis, de officio iudicis* (Paris: Andream Wechelum, 1564).

[19] Fédéric Morel, trans., *Philonis Judaei liber singularis, quare quorundam in scripturis sacris mutata sint nomina. Ex interpretatione F. Morelli* (Paris: F. Morellum, 1593).

[20] Pierre Bellier, trans., *Les Oeuvres de Philon Iuif, autheur tres-eloquent, et philosophe tres-grave* (Paris: Nicolas Chesnau, 1575). According to Didot, Bellier "consecra tous ses loisirs à la traduction de Philon." *Nouvelle biographie générale* (Paris: Firmin Didot Frères, 1866), vol. 5, col. 264.

[21] "Ou Platon philonize, our Philon platonize … Celà se dit communément: mais quant à moi, il me semble que, d'autant que le corps est plus excellent que l'ombre qui le suit, d'autant aussi est Philon plus excellent que Platon: car celui là monte iusques au comble de la divinité, & y donne dedans, mais cetui ne fait qu'en approcher, aiant puisé la plus grande partie de ses divines sentences des ancestres & devanciers de Philon au voiage qu'il fit en Egipte," Bellier, *Les Oeuvres de Philon Iuif*, epistre.

[22] Sigismund Gelen adopts a similar line of argumentation in his 1555 Latin translation of Philo's works. See Weinberg, "The Quest for Philo," 169.

[23] Jerome, *Epistola* 22.35, in *PL* 22:421, ed. J. P. Migne (Paris: Garnier, 1845).

[24] Formerly a Franciscan, Thevet obtained secularization in 1559. See F. Obermeier, "Thevet, André, OFM, später säkularisiert," in *Biographisch-Bibliographisches Kirchenlexikon* (2003), vol. 22, cols 1348-58 (bbkl.de).

[25] "… il a surpassé tous les autres Philosophes tant anciens que modernes …. De ma part, ie ne feroie point de difficulté de le mettre au rang des Docteurs Ecclesiastiques, puis que ie voy que ce grand & admirable docteur de l'Eglise sainct Hierosme a bien daigné l'y colloquer, qui n'estoit point souspeçonné de favoriser aux Iuifs." André Thevet, *Pourtraits et vies des hommes illustres* (Paris: Kervert et Chaudiere, 1584), ch. 39, fols 84–85.

Philo platonizes, or that Plato philonizes. There they have drawn a consequence that Philo is contrary to the Christian religion, because he platonizes.[26]

Thevet responds emphatically that Philo does not oppose Christianity with his platonizing: "But would this be the reason," he writes, "to relegate Philo to the pagans, because he platonized? Very few people who have affection for Christianity could agree with this: otherwise, St. Augustine would be banished from the company of Christians, he who was so devoted to this divine philosopher."[27] For Thevet, Philo remains among the revered writers in ecclesiastical history.

Though not as prolific as those in France, the Venice presses also contributed to continuing the Philo renaissance after Trent with canon Petro Francisco Zino's Latin editions of Philo's *De Iosepho* and *De vita Mosis* in 1574 and 1575 respectively,[28] and with the first Italian translations of the *De opificio mundi* (1570) and *De Iosepho* (1574).[29] Only one work attributed to Philo was published in Rome—the *Liber antiquitatum biblicarum* in 1599—though this work was attributed by many at that time, as it is today, to "Pseudo-Philo."[30] Nevertheless, toward the turn of the century Rome gave rise to a crucial defender of Philo, the Italian Jesuit Robert Bellarmine.

Bellarmine, of course, was himself an ecclesiastical censor, a role he played most infamously in the Galileo affair. But Bellarmine did not interpret the decrees of Trent like Sigonio's censors—R. Gerald Hobbs even cites Sigonio's censors as "rivals [to Bellarmine's] understanding of Trent."[31] Bellarmine's use of Philo further supports Hobbs' thesis. In volume 1 of Bellarmine's famous *De Controversiis christianae fidei*, he critiques those who "falsely attribute too much purity to the Hebrew source" of the scriptures. Yet he still defends that source, despite its alloys, and refutes those who suppose that the Hebrew scriptures were corrupted by the malice of the Jews (*malitia Judaeorum*).[32] Bellarmine praises the "incredible devotion of the Jews towards the

---

[26] "Et quand i'entends railler aucuns de nostre Philon, ie ne puis me contenir de me rire de leurs resveries, & d'autre part condamner leur maligne & perverse nature, pour ce qu'ilz veullent tirer au des-honneur de Philon .... Ces contreroolleurs le veulent faire Payen, à cause du proverbe, qui a esté faict sur la comparaison de luy & de Platon, que Philon platonise, ou que Platon philonise: de là ilz tiré une consequence que Philon estoit contraire à la religion Chrestienne, puis qu'il platonisoit." Thevet, *Pourtraits et vies*, 85.
[27] "... seroit-ce la raison de releguer Philon au Paganisme, pae ce qu'il a platonisé? Bien peu de gens trouvera-on qui estás affectionnez à la Chrestienté, puissent l'accorder: autrement faudroit que sainct Augustin fust banny de la compaignie des Chrestiens, lequel a tellement esté addonné à ce divin Philosophe." Thevet, *Pourtraits et vies*, 85.
[28] Petro Francisco Zino, ed., *Iosephi patriarchae vita a Philone Hebraeo graecè composita* (Venice: Christophorus Zanetus, 1574); Petro Francisco Zino, *Example tria insignia naturae, legis, et gratiae, cùm in vita Iosephi patriarchae, & magni Mosis à Philone Hebraeo ...* (Venice: Bologninus Zalterius, 1575).
[29] M. Agostino Ferentilli, *Discorso universale di M. Agostino Ferentilli ... Aggiuntavi La Creatione del Mondo, descritta da Filone Hebreo* (Venice: Gabriel Giolito di Ferrarii, 1570); Petro Francisco Zino, *Il ritratto del vero e perfetto gentiluomo espresso da Filone Ebreo nella vita di Giuseppe Patriarca* (Venice: Giolito, 1574).
[30] *Historia Antiqua* (Bibliopolio Commeliniano, 1599). For a modern treatment of this work, see H. Jacobson, *A Commentary on Pseudo-Philo's* Liber antiquitatem biblicarum, *with Latin Text and English Translation*, 2 vols (Leiden and New York: Brill, 1996).
[31] Hobbs, "Reading the Old Testament after Trent," 232. Hobbs notes that "the understanding of Bellarmine would prevail in the long run."
[32] Robert Bellarmine, S.J., *Disputationum Roberti Bellarmini Politiani, S.J., S.R.E. Cardinalis, De controversiis christianae fidei adversus hujus temporis haereticos*, 4 vols (Ingolstadt: Adam Sartori, 1601). The first edition appeared between 1581 and 1593 in Ingolstadt. English translations from volume 1 of this work will be taken from K. Baker, S.J., trans., *Controversies of the Christian Faith* (Ramsey, NJ: Keep the Faith, 2016).

sacred books" by invoking Philo's claim that the Jews did not change a letter of the law in over two thousand years, and that "any Jew would rather die a hundred times than allow the law to be changed in any way."[33] He further mines Philo along with the church fathers to defend the Septuagint, a twofold (literal and spiritual) interpretation of the scriptures, monarchy as the best form of governance, and the spiritual authority of the papacy.[34] The use of Philo to buttress these latter arguments seems to be somewhat widespread at the time, as Bellarmine's Spanish confrere Francisco Suárez also cites Philo's *De monarchia* (beginning at §3 of his *Spec.* 1) alongside Justin, Athanasius, Jerome, and Cyprian.[35]

Bellarmine cites Philo other times, but the most informative appears in the cardinal's *De scriptoribus ecclesiasticis*. In a genre akin to that employed by Jerome and Thevet, Bellarmine chronicles writers of the Church "who flourished to the praise of ecclesiastical wisdom ... from Moses as the first writer of the Church up to our age."[36] In addition to praising Philo's allegorical readings,[37] Bellarmine devotes an entire entry to *Philo Hebraeus*, "a man most learned by everyone's consensus." He lauds Philo for revering the Alexandrian Christians—something we will explore below—and for being a first (*primus*) expositor of the Old Testament.[38] Philo is thus praised for the precise reason Signonio's censors rebuke him: for his exegetical acumen, which Bellarmine elsewhere describes as "subtilissime."[39]

Bellarmine was no anomaly among Italian scholars in his high opinion of Philo. Fellow Jesuit and papal envoy, Antonio Possevino, writes that the works of Philo "excel in style, eloquence, gravity, piety, and truth."[40] And the Dominican Sixtus of Sienna, in his *Bibliotheca sancta* (first published in 1566), affirms Philo as one to whom "all of the Christian fathers extend their praises" and who admirably and most clearly (*praeclarissime*) exposits the literal, moral, and allegorical senses of the

---

[33] Bellarmine, *Controversies*, 107. Bellarmine invokes Philo here via Eusebius' *Praep. ev.* 8.2 [Baker's translation mistakenly reads 3.2, see *De Controversiis*, vol. 1, col. 88, C]. In 8.2, however, Eusebius quotes the *Letter of Aristeas*, which does not explicitly state that the language has been preserved without change. Bellarmine likely meant to cite the nearby *Praep. ev.* 8.6. There, Eusebius quotes Philo's *Hypoth.* 6.9: "... they held it all to come from God and after the lapse of many years, how many I cannot say exactly, but at any rate for more than two thousand, they have not changed a single word of what he wrote but would even endure to die a thousand deaths sooner than accept anything contrary to the laws and customs which he had ordained" (trans. F. H. Colson, LCL [Cambridge, MA: Harvard University Press, 1941], 420–21). Bellarmine misreads Philo's "a thousand" as "a hundred" (*centies*).

[34] Bellarmine, *Controversies*, 117ff., 184, 618, 833. Bellarmine explicitly references *Mos.* 2 re: the LXX, and *De victimis* (*Spec.* 1.33ff.) re: the papacy, gleaning from the latter passage that in the Old Testament, "the high priest was greater than the king."

[35] Francisco Suárez, S.J., *Opera omnia*, ed. M. André and C. Berton (Paris: Ludovicus Vivès, 1856–78), vol. 12, *De fide theologica*, disp. 9, sec. 6, no. 8.

[36] "... sapientiae Ecclesiasticae laude floruerunt." Robert Bellarmine, *De scriptoribus ecclesiasticis*, vol. 1 (Lyons: Horatius Cardon, 1613), preface. Cited in C. Bultmann, "Historical-Critical Inquiry," in *The Hebrew Bible: A Critical Companion*, ed. J. Barton (Princeton: Princeton University Press, 2016), 433 (translation adjusted).

[37] Bultmann, "Historical-Critical Inquiry," 434. Regarding the moral sense of Moses, Bellarmine writes: "... Philo Hebraeus, qui has allegorias subtilissimè explanavit." Bellarmine, *De scriptoribus*, 2.

[38] "Philo Hebraeus, vir omnium consensu doctissimus .... Et praeterea iure numeratur inter Scriptores Ecclesiasticos Testamenti veteris, quoniam scripturas divinas Testamenti veteris primus exposuit." Bellarmine, *De scriptoribus*, 19.

[39] Bellarmine, *De scriptoribus*, 2.

[40] "Praeterea, quae legitima Philonis opera extant ... quippe stylo, eloquentia, gravitate, pietate, veritate praestant"; Antonio Possevino, *Bibliotheca selecta de ratione studiorum* (Cologne: Joannes Gymnicus, 1607 [1st edn 1593]), book 16, sec. 4, ch. 1, E.

divine scriptures, excelling in the latter.[41] Sixtus goes on to devote five more columns to enumerating and describing Philo's "many and most noble volumes on the Old Testament."[42] Notably, Sigonio invokes Sixtus for support in his response to the censors.

Though this summary is brief and focuses only on select yet significant figures of the post-Tridentine age, it suffices to show the esteemed reputation of Philo among leading scholars and even ecclesiastical authorities of the period. Indeed, the chorus *Philo Iudaeus, vir disertissimus* resounded from the exegesis of Spanish Jesuit Alfonso Salmerón to the historiography of Italian cardinal Cesare Baronio.[43] During this period, Philo even became a crucial component of the Catholic defense of monastic vows. Following the testimony of Eusebius, scholars such as Baronio and the Mainz Jesuit Nicholas Serarius argued that Philo's Therapeutae proved an ancient instantiation of Christian monasticism, and in this regard they readily employed Philo as a credible historiographical source *against* the Protestants. Philo thus became a crucial figure not only for classical historiography and exegesis, but also for early modern identity, though not at the expense of critical inquiry.

24.2 Philo against the Reformers

Martin Luther's famous *De votis monasticis* of 1521 sparked numerous defenses of monastic vows by Catholic controversialists,[44] and already in 1530, Leuven theologian Jacob Latomus called Philo's Therapeutae to the Catholic defense.[45] It was Eusebius who first conflated Philo's Therapeutae, described in the *De vita contemplativa*, with early Christian ascetics, deeming them some of the "first heralds" of the gospel in Alexandria.[46] According to Jean Riaud, this attribution was adopted by all the ecclesiastical writers of the first centuries and continued as the dominant opinion well into

---

[41] "Philo Iudaeus .... Fuit praeterea ultrà quàm dici queat, admirabilis in divinis Scripturis exponendis, quas triplici sensu iuxta LXX editionem praeclarissimè explicavit, literali scilicet, morali, & praecipue allegorico, in quo quidem expositionis genere ita excelluit" (Sixtus of Sienna, *Bibliotheca sancta* [Lyons: Sumptibus, 1593], book 4, p. 289). Sixtus of Sienna was raised Jewish and instructed in Rabbinic studies before he converted against the wishes of his parents, see J. W. Montgomery, "Sixtus of Sienna and Roman Catholic Biblical Scholarship in the Reformation Period," *Archiv für Reformationgeschichte* 54 (1963): 220–21. It is unclear that this upbringing had any impact on his reception of Philo, since as David Winston notes, one searches the Rabbinic writings in vain for an explicit reference to Philo ("Philo and Rabbinic Literature," in *The Cambridge Companion to Philo*, ed. A. Kamesar [Cambridge: Cambridge University Press, 2009], 231), and Azariah de' Rossi did not draw the attention of the Italian Jewish community to Philo until after the death of Sixtus (1569).

[42] "Scripsit autem in vetus Testamentum plurima & nobilissima volumina." Sixtus of Sienna, *Bibliotheca sancta*, bk. 4, p. 290.

[43] Salmerón frequently uses this phrase in his *Comentarii in evangelicam historiam, & in Acta Apostolorum, in duodecim tomos distributi* (Madrid: Ludovico Sanchez, 1598), 1:49, 59, 78, 156, etc. See also Cesare Baronio, *Annales Ecclesiastici* (Rome: Typographia Vaticana, 1588), 1:19, D.

[44] Martin Luther, *D. Martin Luthers Werke: Kritische Gesamtausgabe* (Weimar: Hermann Boehlau, 1883–1983), 8:564–669; *Luther's Works*, American edn, ed. J. Pelikan and H. T. Lehman (St. Louis: Concordia Publishing House, 1955–67), 44:243–400.

[45] Jacob Latomus, *Libellus de fide et operibus, et de votis atque institutis monasticis* (Antwerp, 1530), as noted in J. Machielsen, "Sacrificing Josephus to Save Philo: Cesare Baronio and the Jewish Origins of Christian Monasticism," *IJCT* 23.3 (2016): 240.

[46] Eusebius, *Hist. eccl.* 2.17, LCL 153, trans. K. Lake (Cambridge, MA: Harvard University Press, 1926), 156–57.

the sixteenth.⁴⁷ Yet another strand of thought intermingled with that of Eusebius. In the fourth century, a Latin translation of Philo's work circulated under the title *Liber de statu Essaeorum, id est Monachorum, qui temporibus Agrippae regis monasteria sibi fecerunt*, thus adding the Jewish sect of the Essenes into the mix, though not to the exclusion of Eusebius' theory.⁴⁸ A 1550 edition of part of *De vita contemplativa* was published under the same title.⁴⁹ During the course of the late sixteenth century, these two strands would, with the help of Josephus, be parsed in the throes of reformation controversy. Nevertheless, Philo was not simply commandeered for pro-papal polemics. Philo is certainly used to defend the antiquity of monastic practice; of this there is no doubt. Yet Josephus' account of the Jewish Essenes prompts various responses among Catholic scholars, who consequently engage in a real historiographical effort and one not wholly dictated by confessional interests.

Lutheran Matthias Flacius Illyricus and his fellow Centuriators of Magdeburg first challenged the traditional position of Eusebius.⁵⁰ In their *Ecclesiastica historia* (originally published in 1559), the Centuriators note Eusebius' claim that Mark preached the gospel in Alexandria, yet "What Eusebius recalls from Philo concerning the Christians around Alexandria, it is more probable that he refers to the Essenes, the celebrated sect of the Jews, for the Christians did not yet have such practices."⁵¹ The Centuriators maintain that the group described in Philo's *De vita contemplativa* is the Essenes, and since Josephus points to the existence of the Essenes before the time of Christ, they could not have been Christians.⁵²

The Catholic response came swiftly but not uniformly. Cesare Baronio offers the most famous treatment in his 1588 *Annales ecclesiastici*, a direct response to the Centuriators' own *Historia*.⁵³ Jan Machielsen has recently outlined Baronio's complex analysis of the Therapeutae, a word which Baronio does not use to describe the group. Rather, Baronio begins with the presumption that the group described in Philo's *De vita contemplativa* is not wholly distinct from the Essenes. Now he must try to prove that they were Christians. Faced with the attacks of the "novatores," as he calls his opponents, Baronio embarks on two strands of argument. First, he develops an argument from silence: the Essenes could not have existed before Christ, since nowhere in the

---

⁴⁷ J. Riaud, "Les Thérapeutes d'Alexandrie dans la tradition et dans la recherche critique jusqu'aux découvertes de Qumran," in *Aufstieg und Niedergang der Römischen Welt* (Berlin: de Gruyter, 1987), 20.2:1212.
⁴⁸ D. T. Runia, *Philo and the Church Fathers: A Collection of Papers* (Leiden: Brill, 1995), 32.
⁴⁹ See G-G, 199 (§448).
⁵⁰ Riaud, "Les Thérapeutes," 1215.
⁵¹ "Scribit Eusebius lib. 2, cap. 16, Marcum primium in Aegyptum missum, ibique Evangelicam historiam a se compositam tradidisse, primumque ecclesias Alexandriae constituisse …. Quod autem Eusebius ex Philone commemorat de Christianis circa Alexandriam, id magis verisimile est de Essenia, Iudæorum celebri secta, referri. nondum enim Christiani talia exercitia habuerunt." *Ecclesiastica historia* (Basel: Joannes Oporinus, 1562), vol. 1, col. 18, nos. 10–44.
⁵² *Ecclesiastica historia*, vol. 1, col. 236, nos. 1–12. Jewish scholar Azariah de' Rossi (1511–78) adopts a similar line of argumentation against the Catholic appropriation of Philo, arguing contra Eusebius that "there is no reason to assume that [the Therapeutae] did not belong to the Essene sects," *The Light of the Eyes*, trans. J. Weinberg (New Haven: Yale University Press, 2001), 107.
⁵³ See G. A. Guazzelli, "Cesare Baronio and the Roman Catholic Vision of the Early Church," in *Sacred History: Uses of the Christian Past in the Renaissance World*, ed. K. Van Liere et al. (Oxford: Oxford University Press, 2012), 52–71.

scriptures or even among pagan authors are the Essenes mentioned. Second, however, the testimony of Josephus concerning the existence of this sect before Christ must be reckoned with, and here Baronio concedes ground. He grants that even if the Essenes existed before Christ, they remain distinct from the group which Philo describes in *De vita contemplativa*. For Baronio, according to Machielsen, "Philo's Essenes had converted to Christianity but preserved those parts of their way of life which their new faith did not contradict."[54]

Francisco Suárez simplifies and strengthens Baronio's analysis by eliminating the first argument from silence and focusing on the second. In his *De statu religionis*, Suárez writes:

> Although it is probable that Philo speaks of Essene Christians, since he discusses those who began to profess a new way of perfection at that time, Josephus, however, seems to speak of Jews, for he shows them to be more ancient among the Jews, and he distinguishes them from the Pharisees and Sadducees, and he refers to certain teachings of theirs which are not consonant with the Christian religion.... Therefore, it is likely for the Essenes to have existed both before and after Christ, and many among them to have converted to the faith through the preaching of Mark in Alexandria, and to have preserved and perfected their moral way of living concerning the good itself in Christianity, and thus indeed Philo speaks the truth about the Christians, yet not to the exclusion of the more ancient Essenes.[55]

Suárez here emphasizes and deepens the distinction between the two ancient groups.[56] Like Baronio, he esteems the Essenes, though he does not deem them true religious (*non veri religiosi*), and he considers Philo's Therapeutae to be Christian converts and monks (*monachos*). Other Catholic authors offer a variety of perspectives. Antonio Possevino facilely remarks: "Let the prudent reader join together Josephus with Philo, and he will discover that each one writes about the life of the same people. Indeed I remove only a few things that Josephus interweaves into his book from Jewish superstition."[57] Bellarmine maintains that Philo writes of Alexandrian Christians and not about a sect of the Jews,[58] yet concerning Josephus he thinks both opinions probable: that

---

[54] Machielsen, "Sacrificing Josephus to Save Philo," 241–43.

[55] "At vero quanquam de Philone probabile sit loqui de Essenis Christianis, quia tractat de illis, qui novam perfectionis viam eo tempore profiteri coeperant, Josephus autem de Judaeis videtur loqui, nam antiquiores inter Judaeos illos esse significat, et a Pharisaeis et Sadducaeis illos distinguit, et quaedam eorum dogmata refert, quae cum Christiana religione non consonant.... Verisimile ergo est et ante et post Christum fuisse, et multos ex illis ad fidem conversos per Marci praedicationem Alexandriae, moralem vivendi modum de se bonum in Christianismo retinuisse et perfecisse, et ideo verum quidem esse Philonem de Christianis loqui, non tamen excludere antiquiores Essenos." *Opera omnia*, vol. 15, bk 3, ch. 1, no. 13.

[56] On this question Suárez also engages the ancient authorities of Porphyry, Epiphanius, Pliny, and others.

[57] "Conserat prudens Lector Iosephum cum Philone, & utrumque eorumdem vitam scribere comperiet. Pauca quidem excipio, quae Iosephus ex Iudaica superstitione in suo libro interservit." *Bibliotheca selecta*, bk 5, ch. 56, C. Possevino adds that the name "Essenes" finds its root in the name "Iesu."

[58] "Philo scripsit librum insignem laudibus eorum Christianorum, qui sub Marco Evangelista in Aegypto vivebant; quem librum scriptum de laude Christianorum, non de secta aliqua Judaica, ut putant Centuriatores Cent. 1, lib. 2, cap. 3, col. 18, testatur"; Bellarmine, *De controversiis*, Vol. 2: *De notis Ecclesiae*, bk 4, ch. 16, B; also "Philo scribit de primis illis Monachis, in lib. de vita contemplativa supplicum"; Bellarmine, *De controversiis*, Vol. 2: *De monachis*, bk 2, ch. 39, A.

Josephus and Philo speak of different groups and that both speak about Christians.[59] Thevet is even more ambivalent. He notes that some think Philo speaks of Christian monasteries, and others that Philo speaks of Essene conventicles. "What makes me enter into greater doubt," he writes, "is that Jean Tritheme writes that Philo the Jew offered great welcome to the disciples of St. Mark. To be able to draw from that that they were religious or Essenes, it is not at all clear to me." All that is evident, Thevet continues, is the affection and ardor with which Philo was moved for those who embrace the evangelical truth.[60]

By and large, however, almost all Catholic thinkers of the sixteenth century deemed Philo's Therapeutae to be the first manifestation of Christian monasticism.[61] Yet what Machielsen and the testimonies offered here reveal is that engagement with other ancient texts provoked nuance and disagreement on how this group came about and in what their relation to Judaism consisted. Between the facile conflation of the Essenes and Therapeutae in the Centuriators of Magdeburg, and the equally facile conflation of the Essenes, Therapeutae, and Christians in Possevino, there is a spectrum of opinions regarding Philo's *De vita contemplativa*. Further, Baronio, Bellarmine, Suárez, and others drove a wedge between the Essenes and the Therapeutae which had an enduring effect on scholarship,[62] as even today, though most deem the Therapeutae Jewish, many like Joan E. Taylor consider them a distinct community from that of the Essenes.[63] Thus, while Philo's Therapeutae certainly played a role in early modern confessional identity, this appropriation should not be deemed a violent misuse of Philo, but an attempt by post-Tridentine scholars to interweave ancient historiography and the weighty testimony of the fathers with that of Philo to give an account of that still mysterious sect on the banks of Lake Mareotis.

24.3 Philo and the Scriptures: *Mala Bonis Permixta*

The testimony of the fathers, of course, could not always be harmonized with that of Philo. The first censure against Sigonio notes that even if Philo was liberally educated and rivaled Plato in Greek eloquence, he did not have Christ, the end and focus of

---

[59] Bellarmine, *De controversiis*, vol. 2, bk 2, ch. 5, cited in Machielsen, "Sacrificing Josephus to Save Philo," 241.
[60] "Ce qui me faict entrer en plus grande doubte est que Iean Tritheme escrit, que Philon Iuif faisoit grand accueil aux disciples de sainct Marc de pouvoir de là tirer que ce fussent religieux ou Esseens, ie n'y vois aucune apparence. Seulement de cela me semble qu'on doit recueillir certain tesmoignage de l'affection & ardeur de zele, dont Philon estoit poussé à l'endrouct de ceux, qui embrassoient la verité Evangelique." *Pourtraits et vies des hommes illustres*, ch. 39, fol. 85.
[61] While this position was dominant among Catholics and largely rejected by Protestants, there were exceptions. See e.g. Huguenot Joseph Scaliger's criticism of those Protestants who conflated the Therapeutae and Christian monks, in A. Grafton, *Joseph Scaliger: A Study in the History of Classical Scholarship* (Oxford: Clarendon Press, 1993), 2:300–301.
[62] Machielsen remarks that "Not even Scaliger was quite able to put them together again"; "Sacrificing Josephus to Save Philo," 245. Grafton writes that Scaliger "showed from Philo's own works that the religious community that the Alexandrian Jew Philo described was Jewish, like that of the Essenes described by Josephus"; *Joseph Scaliger*, 2:299.
[63] J. E. Taylor, *Jewish Women Philosophers of First-Century Alexandria: Philo's "Therapeutae" Reconsidered* (Oxford: Oxford University Press, 2003), 12

all scripture.[64] The censor proceeds to cite Augustine's *Contra Faustum*, wherein the Doctor of Grace famously criticizes Philo's interpretation of the door of Noah's ark as the lower parts of the body (*inferior corporis partes*), an interpretation arising from Philo's ignorance of Christ.[65] While many in the sixteenth century, like Sixtus of Sienna, praised Philo's exegetical acumen, others took issue with various interpretations made by the Hellenistic Jew. Yet, as will be shown, those exegetes who do disagree with Philo seem to be haunted neither by the censors nor even by Augustine.

Spanish exegete Benedict Pererius, S.J., provides a representative example of such critics. In his commentary on Genesis, published in Rome in the 1590s, Philo appears as an authoritative source, whose opinions are frequently listed alongside the church fathers, and Pererius has no problem calling him one of the "most learned of the Jews." But this does not prevent Pererius from taking issue with certain exegetical moves.[66] His strongest critique comes while discussing the creation of man. Regarding the words *Faciamus hominem*, Pererius writes:

> Philo, in his book *De opificio mundi*, affirms that "man," whose creation is described by these words, is not to be understood as sensible man, i.e., what we are, but as intelligible man, i.e., the idea and exemplar of man.... In which Philo certainly wanted to follow Plato's doctrine of Ideas; but he applies it to this place not only falsely, but even ignorantly, foolishly, and absurdly.[67]

Here Pererius displays his most vicious rhetoric toward Philo. But it is the exception, not the rule, as elsewhere his disagreements with Philo rarely approach these extremes.

In fact, Pererius often criticizes church fathers in the same breath as Philo. Earlier in his commentary, for example, Pererius thinks Philo's reason for God commencing the creation of animals on the fifth day—namely, that animate creatures differ from inanimate creatures in possessing five senses—is frivolous (*verum frivola est ratio*), since certain animals only have one sense, that of touch, and other, more perfect animals have interior as well as exterior senses.[68] However, Pererius also refutes Augustine, who

---

[64] "Philo Judaeus tametsi liberaliter eruditus, eloquio graeco cum Platone certaverit, quae tamen interpretatus est, non ad Christum intelligendum, qui legis est finis, & totius Scripturae scopus retulit; in illum enim non crediderat..."; *Opera omnia*, vol. 6, col. 1177.

[65] "Nec mirum, si ostio non invento, sic aberraret à foribus; quod si ad Christum transisset, ablato velamine, Sacramenta Ecclesiae à Christi latere manentia invenisset"; *Opera omnia*, vol. 6, col. 1177. The text of Augustine reads: "Non mirum, si ostio non invento sic erravit. Quod si ad Christum transisset, ablato velamine, Sacramenta Ecclesiae manantia ex latere hominis illius invenisset." Augustine, *Contra Faustum* 12.39, in *PL* 42:275, ed. J. P. Migne (Paris: Garnier, 1865).

[66] "duo Iudaeorum doctissimi Philo & Iosephus"; Benedict Pererius, S.J., *Commentarii et disputationes in Genesim* (Ingolstadt: David Sartorius, 1590), 1:121.

[67] "Philo in lib. De Mundi opificio affirmat, hominem, cuius creatio his verbis describitur, non esse intelligendum hominem sensibilem, scilicet quales nos sumus; sed intelligibilem, hoc est, ideam & exemplar hominis.... In quo voluit quidem Philo Platonis doctrinam de Ideis sequi; verum quod ad hunc locum pertinet, non falso tantum, sed etiam inscienter, inepte & absurde." Pererius, *Commentarii*, 1:469.

[68] "Philo tradit, propterea quinto die coepisse creationem animalium, quod animal sit animal propter sensum; quinque autem esse sensus, qui numerus congruit cum die quinto quo creari animalia coeperunt. Verum frivola est ratio: nam nec animal ut sit animal opus habet quinque sensibus, sed solo tactu, quo uno cum praedita sint quaedam animalia, ceteris sensibus carent; & praeter quinque sensus externos, sunt alii sensus interiores in perfectis animalibus"; Pererius, *Commentarii*, 1:180–81. For Philo's position, see *Opif.* 20.

argued that God only created the fish causally and potentially on the fifth day. This Pererius deems hardly in accord with the narrative Moses offers.[69] Relatedly, Pererius also takes issue with Philo's stance that "six days" does not refer to an interval of time, but to the perfection of the world, since six is a perfect number.[70] He again couples Philo with Augustine, the latter arguing that the world was created at one point in time (*puncto temporis*). Pererius refutes both in favor of an understanding of creation little by little over six days (*paulatim et particulatim per sex dies*).[71] And though he exhibits significantly more reserve when dealing with Augustine, he still speaks rather strongly here: "the contrary opinion to that of Augustine, indeed I judge not only more probable, but even of certain and indubitable truth."[72] Thus in both instances, Philo is neither pitted against Augustine nor is he necessarily dethroned from his esteemed status among the ecclesiastical writers. Pererius recognizes the authority that Philo carries in the Christian tradition and deems it necessary to explain his opinions, even if in certain places he ultimately and strongly disagrees with them.

Plenty of exegetes, however, found much more to praise in Philo than did Pererius. As already mentioned, Sixtus of Sienna lauds Philo's threefold exegesis, and especially his allegories, and Alfonso Salmerón holds the Alexandrian in high esteem. In the seventeenth century, Spanish Jesuit Benito Fernandez frequently invokes the testimony of Philo in his Genesis commentary, often inserting lengthy quotations from Philo[73] and noting in the majority of places that Philo "speaks well" (*bene loquitur*) or "rightly" (*recte*) or "eloquently" (*eloquenter*) or "acutely" (*subtiliter*).[74] Philo's widespread use can be witnessed later in that century in the commentaries of exegetes like Cornelius Jansen and the Franciscan François Carrière.[75]

Taken together, these scholars saw in Philo's works what Sigonio saw, *mala bonis permixta*, bad things mixed with good things. Exegetes like Pererius found plenty to criticize in Philo, calling into doubt Billings' claim that it is not until 1644 and the work of French Jesuit Denys Petau that "we first find any objection raised to Philo's theological opinions."[76] Yet the overriding emphasis must be placed on the "good things,"

---

[69] "S. Augustinus lib. 3, de Genesi ad literam cap. 4, existimat hoc die quinto non esse creatos pisces actu, sed tantummodo causaliter & potentialiter .... Verum hoc minime concordat cum narratione Mosis"; Pererius, *Commentarii*, 1:181.

[70] "Cum igitur Moses ait, Deum sex diebus absoluisse mundi fabricam, non est id, auctore Philone, ad intervalla sex dierum referendum, sed intelligendum est illo dierum numero significari mundi perfectionem quae per numeri senarii perfectionem designatur..."; Pererius, *Commentarii*, 1:230. See Philo, *Leg*. 1.2.

[71] This literal reading is not unique to Pererius or even to Catholics at that time. Lutheran scholastic Johann Gerhard also rejects Philo's and Augustine's interpretations on the six days of creation in favor of fidelity to the letter, yet his rhetoric toward Philo is less heated than that of Pererius. See *On Creation and Angels*, in *Theological Commonplaces VIII*, trans. R. J. Dinda, ed. B. T. G. Mayes (St. Louis: Concordia, 2013), §21.

[72] "Verumtamen contrariam Augustino sententiam, equidem non modo probabiliorem iudico, sed etiam certae ac indubitatae veritatis censeo"; Pererius, *Commentarii*, 1:231.

[73] See inter alia vol. 3, cols 305, 429, 653, 693, 1179, etc. He does this approvingly, and often merely adds a parenthetical "*scribit/adiungit/ait Philo*"; Benito Fernandez, S.J., *Commentaria atque observationes morales in Genesim*, 3 vols (Lyons: Horatius Cardon, 1618–27).

[74] See inter alia vol. 1, cols 661, 797, 1018, 1254; vol. 3, col. 846.

[75] See Cornelius Jansen, *Pentateuchus sive commentarius in quinque libros Moysis* (Louvain: Jacob Zegerius, 1641); and François Carrière, *Commentarius in universam scripturam* (Lyons: Horatius Boissat & Georgius Remeus, 1663).

[76] Billings, *The Platonism of Philo Judaeus*, 4. Regarding Billings' larger focus precisely on the "Platonism" of Philo, Pererius appears an especially noteworthy counter to Billings' thought that thinkers before Petau were "compelled by the tradition to regard Philo as a great, original thinker whose thoughts were in some sense

as exegetes continued to praise Philo's rhetorical eloquence and exegetical judgment, wrestling with him as they did with the church fathers.[77]

24.4 Conclusion

Through this brief survey of the Catholic reception of Philo after the Council of Trent, I have demonstrated the esteem which not only humanists but even ecclesiastical authorities like Bellarmine and Possevino held for Philo. This esteem did not render Philo immune to criticism anymore than similar (and even greater) reverence immunized the church fathers, but it does show that the revival of Philonic scholarship begun in the early part of the sixteenth century suffered little noticeable lag after the Council of Trent.

This overall positive reception of Philo among Catholics must be seen within the broader currents of sixteenth-century Philonic reception. The Therapeutae controversy poignantly highlights the ways in which Catholic and Protestant uses of Philo were deeply intertwined and polemically—though not necessarily ahistorically—informed. Joanna Weinberg has shown how this Christian controversy even effected the Jewish scholar Azariah de' Rossi's (1511–78) appropriation of Philo.[78] But the Therapeutae controversy is only one frame of this complex and interwoven plot. The new editions and translations of Philo produced before and after the Council of Trent reached wide audiences, including de' Rossi. And Philo remained an exegetical source not only for Catholics but for Protestant theologians as well who often, like Pererius, listed the Alexandrian's opinions among those of the church fathers.[79] Much work remains to be done to disentangle these various trajectories and to discern the ways that they have affected our reception of Philo today.

One thing is certain from my small contribution to this effort: the identity of Philo remained as elusive in the sixteenth century as it is today. André Thevet's phrase—*nostre Philon*—proves as instructive as it is deceptive. On the one hand, it nicely sums up the opinion of most post-Tridentine Catholic thinkers, who claimed Philo as an ecclesiastical source whose authority most closely resembled that of a church father. Yet, on the other hand, Philo was not quite a church father or an

---

authoritative," as the passages I cite above indicate that one of the areas the Pererius took issue with Philo was in his Platonizing of the biblical text.

[77] As the case of Pererius exemplifies, church fathers were also subject to reserved criticism during this period. On specific instances of this see my "Spanish Jesuits and 'the Greeks': Reception and Perception of the Eastern Church in Luis de Molina, Francisco Suárez, and Gabriel Vásquez," *JTS* 69.1 (2018): 133–69.

[78] Weinberg, "The Quest for Philo," 166.

[79] Lutheran scholastic Johann Gerhard (1582–1637), for example, would frequently invoke Philo as an authority to be reckoned with in his *Theological Commonplaces*, positively utilizing Philo's exegesis on the burning bush in *Mos.* 1.67 and praising Philo's beautiful exposition of man as a microcosm of creation in *Opif.* See J. Gerhard, *On the Church*, in *Theological Commonplaces XXV*, trans. R. J. Dinda, ed. B. T. G. Mayes (St. Louis: Concordia, 2010), §27; and J. Gerhard, *On Creation and Angels*, in *Theological Commonplaces XXV*, §34.

ecclesiastical doctor—as the title *Iudaeus* suggests—and his widespread use across confessions and religions suggests that Catholic thinkers could hardly claim him as "ours." Rather, Philo proved both familiar and foreign to *all* groups involved, such that none could definitively make such a claim. Consequently, the sixteenth-century Philonic revival further complicated Philo's enduring legacy for ensuing generations of scholars.[80]

---

[80] A version of this chapter first appeared as "*Nostre Philon*: Philo after Trent," *SPhiloA* 29 (2017): 87–109. This chapter has been adapted with the kind permission of the Society of Biblical Literature Press.

25
Thomas Mangey and Philonic Scholarship from the Sixteenth to Eighteenth Centuries

Giovanni Benedetto

On July 6, 1725, Richard Bentley, who had already for a quarter of a century been Master of Trinity College, Cambridge, and since 1717 was also Regius Professor of Divinity, presided over the creation of seven Doctors of Divinity, an academic ceremony that is known to us thanks to Bentley's address, "the only one of his Commencement-speeches that is published,"[1] namely in the Terence edition of 1726.[2] The *oratiuncula* appears immediately after the famous *De metris Terentianis* ΣΚΕΔΙΑΣΜΑ, an "introduction that foreshadowed the modern study of archaic Latin metre."[3] Among the seven new doctors was Thomas Mangey (1683/4–1755), graduate of St. John's, Cambridge, of which he was later to become a fellow for some time.[4] Much of Mangey's production is apologetic, anti-deistic, and anti-Socinian,[5] but the work with which his name will forever be linked is the two-volume edition of *Philonis Judaei Opera quae reperiri potuerunt*, published in London in 1742. On the title page Mangey presents himself as *Canonicus Dunelmensis*, canon of Durham.[6]

Mangey's was the first edition of Philo to be produced by an English scholar after more than two centuries, that is, since the publication in 1553 of *De opificio mundi* and three other treatises in a Latin translation by John Christopherson (†1558). This humanist and Roman Catholic clergyman was at that time living in Leuven (the volume appeared in Antwerp),[7] where he had taken refuge to escape the reign of Edward

---

I thank my wife Heleen Keizer for greatly helping me with the English version of my text.

[1] J. H. Monk, *The Life of Richard Bentley, D. D.*, 2 vols (London: J. G. & F. Rivington, 1833; repr., Osnabrück: Biblio, 1969), 2:228.

[2] *Richardi Bentleii cum septem in Theologia Doctores crearet, Oratiuncula; Cantabrigiae in comitiis habita, Julii VI, MDCCXXV*: I quote from the 2nd edn of R. Bentley, ed., *P. Terentii Afri Comoediae. Recensuit, notasque suas et Gabrielis Faerni addidit Richardus Bentleius. Editio altera denuo recensita, ac Indice amplissimo ... aucta* (Amsterdam: R. & J. Wetstein & G. Smith, 1727); the pages of the long introductory section are not numbered.

[3] S. Grebe, "Bentley, Richard (1662–1742)," in *The Dictionary of British Classicists*, ed. R. B. Todd, 3 vols (Bristol: Thoemmes Continuum, 2004), 1:69.

[4] For the history of the College, see E. Miller, *Portrait of a College: A History of the College of Saint John the Evangelist in Cambridge* (Cambridge: Cambridge University Press, 1961).

[5] F. Deconinck-Brossard, "Mangey, Thomas," *Oxford Dictionary of National Biography* 36: 412–13. A collection of sermons, held also before the House of Commons and at the Royal Chapel of Whitehall, was published in T. Mangey, *Eight Sermons Preach'd on Several Occasions. By Thomas Mangey, D.D. Rector of St. Mildred's, Breadstreet, and Prebendary of Durham* (London: W. Innys, 1725).

[6] Mangey is absent from the three volumes of Todd, *Dictionary of British Classicists*.

[7] J. Christopherson, *Philonis Judaei scriptoris eloquentissimi gravissimique libri quatuor, quorum primus est, De mundi fabricatione, quae est a Moyse descripta, secundus, De decem praeceptis, quae capita legum sunt, tertius, De magistratu seu principe deligendo, quartus, De officio Iudicis, iam primum de Graeco in Latinum conversi: Ioanne Christophorsono Anglo, interprete* (Antwerp: Ioannes Vervvithaghen, 1553).

VI.[8] In the introductory epistle, addressed to Trinity College, of which he was a fellow, Christopherson claims to have been able to consult four manuscripts of Philo's works in Venice,[9] from which he must have drawn useful readings in order to correct "almost four hundred" errors (*errata fere quadringenta*) present in the luxurious Philonic *editio princeps* of the Greek text alone, edited by Adrianus Turnebus and published in Paris in the previous year (1552).[10] An appendix to Christopherson's volume brings together the readings correcting Turnebus: it is preceded by an introductory page, where the English scholar claims to have gathered them in order to explain "why not infrequently in our translation we came to disagree with him." When Mangey at the end of the *Praefatio* to the first volume of his edition enumerates the manuscripts he had been able to use,[11] he cites among them four manuscripts found in England, including a *Cantabrigiensis* from Trinity College, and assumes that this was the manuscript from which Christopherson actually drew the readings used to emend Turnebus' text.[12]

Two and a half centuries after Christopherson, Mangey's edition is spoken of, in the *editio nova* of volume IV of Fabricius' *Bibliotheca Graeca*, enlarged and updated by G. C. Harles (1795), as follows:

> Philo has lain there for a long time indeed, because apart from Turnebus, Hoeschel and Christopherson the others contributed next to nothing to healing his textual wounds, still less to a valid interpretation of his discourse. Strongly desired therefore was the new edition that Mangey had promised for so long.[13]

The reference, besides to the now forgotten Christopherson, is to the *editio princeps* of Turnebus of 1552, as well as to two editions produced by the Bavarian (but with Lutheran sympathies) David Hoeschel (1556–1617), a scholar known above all as the

---

[8] See, in the *Oxford Dictionary of National Biography*, J. Wright, "Christopherson, John," a short article published online, May 26, 2005 (https://doi.org/10.1093/ref:odnb/5373, no page nos.). With the accession to the throne of Mary Tudor in the same year (1553) and the subsequent Roman Catholic reaction, Christopherson returned to England and became Master of Trinity College (Cambridge). In 1557 he was consecrated bishop of Chichester, "playing a major role in enforcing the Marian regime's heresy legislation," but was arrested in November 1558, a few days after the advent of the new Queen Elizabeth. He died about a month later under arrest. His merits "in reviving the study of Greek at Cambridge" (Wright, end of article) were many but there is no mention of him even in Sandys' *History of Classical Scholarship*.

[9] Christopherson, *Philonis Judaei scriptoris eloquentissimi gravissimique libri quatuor*, p. a3v.

[10] A. Turnebus, ed., *Philonis Iudaei in libros Mosis de mundi opificio, historicos, de legibus. Eiusdem libri singulares. Ex Bibliotheca Regia* (Paris: Adrianus Turnebus, 1552). A description of the edition is given in J. Lewis, *Adrien Turnèbe (1512–1565): A Humanist Observed* (Geneva: Librairie Droz, 1998), 167–69.

[11] See also L. Cohn, ed., *Philonis Alexandrini opera quae supersunt* (Berlin: typis Georgii Reimeri, 1896), 1:lxxv–lxxvii.

[12] "Praefatio," in T. Mangey, ed., *Philonis Judaei Opera quae reperiri potuerunt omnia*, 2 vols (London: Gulielmi Bowyer, 1742), 1:xix; but see J. A. Fabricius and G. C. Harles, "De Philone Iudaeo," in *Ioannis Alberti Fabricii Bibliotheca Graeca sive notitia scriptorum veterum Graecorum ... editio nova variorum curis emendatior atque auctior curante Gottlieb Christophoro Harles* (Hamburg: apud Carolum Ernestum Bohn, 1795), 4:745 regarding the codices Marciani. After examining the codex Cantabrigiensis, L. Cohn ("Prolegomena" in *Philonis Alexandrini libellus de opificio mundi*, ed. L. Cohn [Wroclaw: G. Koebner, 1889; repr., Hildesheim: Georg Olms, 1967], xxxii), believed that the readings accepted by Mangey were largely conjectures of Christopherson, "and mostly bad ones" ("et plerasque pravas").

[13] Fabricius and Harles, "De Philone Iudaeo," 748, my translation (Fabricius vol. IV originally appeared in 1717). On Fabricius' chapter as "the first scholarly account of Philo's life and writings," see D. T. Runia, *Philo in Early Christian Literature: A Survey* (Assen: Van Gorcum; Minneapolis: Fortress, 1993), 31.

first editor of the Greek text of the *Bibliotheca* of Photius (1601).[14] Before and after that edition, Hoeschel published in 1587 and then in 1614 four new Philonic treatises as well as fragments from *De providentia*.[15] The subsequent complete editions of Philo published in the seventeenth and early eighteenth centuries are from the textual point of view "wholly dependent on Turnebus and Hoeschel: they have contributed nothing new."[16]

Before thanking the classical philologists and his compatriots Jeremiah Markland (1693–1776) and John Taylor (1703–66)[17] for the help given him in establishing the text as well as in improving the translation,[18] Mangey mentions having received from the Swedish scholar Eric Benzelius the younger (formerly librarian of the University of Uppsala, later bishop of Gothenburg and then of Linköping, and who had just in 1742 been designated archbishop of Uppsala and primate of Sweden) an edition of Philo extensively annotated with *variae lectiones* of manuscript origin ("ex Codd. Augustano & Seldeniano") and with conjectures. Mangey used these annotations only partially, having heard that the Swedish clergyman was planning to publish a new Philo edition; Benzelius, however, did not realize his plan, as he died shortly thereafter in September 1743.[19]

It is precisely by recalling Benzelius' unrealized edition that one of the leading German philologists and theologians of the eighteenth century, J. A. Ernesti (1707–81), opens his extensive review of Mangey's edition in the most important European periodical dedicated to book reviews, the *Acta Eruditorum Lipsiensia*.[20] Ernesti, then *Professor litterarum humaniorum* at the University of Leipzig and concerned with the application of the philological method to the interpretation of the New Testament,[21]

---

[14] On Photius' *Bibliotheca*, see L. Canfora, *Il Fozio ritrovato: Juan de Mariana e André Schott* (Bari: Edizioni Dedalo, 2001); and G. Carlucci, *I Prolegomena di André Schott alla Biblioteca di Fozio* (Bari: Edizioni Dedalo, 2012).

[15] Cohn, *Philonis Alexandrini opera quae supersunt*, lxxii–lxxiii.

[16] Thus the judgment of Cohn, *Philonis Alexandrini opera quae supersunt*, lxxiii–lxxiv, with reference to the Geneva edition of 1613 which includes Gelenius' translation, to the Parisian edn of 1640, and to two Frankfurt editions of 1691 and 1729 which faithfully reproduce the 1640 edn. More on the 1729 edn below, at n. 61.

[17] On Markland and Taylor, see C. Collard, "Markland, Jeremiah (1693–1776)," in Todd, *Dictionary of British Classicists*, 2:629–30, and P. Harding, "Taylor, John (1704–66)," in Todd, *Dictionary of British Classicists*, 3:951–52, respectively; Markland's and Taylor's profiles are present in the chapter "Greek Scholarship, 1700–1780" of the ever-useful M. L. Clarke, *Greek Studies in England 1700–1830* (Cambridge: Cambridge University Press, 1945; repr., Amsterdam: Hakkert, 1986), where Mangey again is not mentioned.

[18] Mangey, *Philonis Judaei Opera quae reperiri potuerunt omnia*, 1:xix. Markland's conjectures also appear in the appendix at the end of the second volume of the edition, *Praetermissa et corrigenda in Philonis Judaei Operum Tomo Secundo, una cum Variarum Lectionum et Conjecturarum Novarum Spicilegio*; about Markland's contribution to the textual criticism of Philo, see J. R. Royse, "Jeremiah Markland's Contribution to the Textual Criticism of Philo," *SPhiloA* 16 (2004): 50–60. The Latin version printed by Mangey remains that of S. Gelenius in *Philonis Iudaei, scriptoris eloquentissimi, ac philosophi summi, lucubrationes omnes quotquot haberi potuerunt, nunc primum Latinae ex Graecis factae* (Basel: apud Nicolaum Episcopium iuniorem, 1554), variously amended because it was considered often imprecise.

[19] As noted by Fabricius and Harles, "De Philone Iudaeo," 728 n. p, which also mentions relations with Mangey; cf. the entry dedicated to Benzelius in *Svenskt biografiskt lexikon* 3 (1922), available at https://sok.riksarkivet.se/sbl/Presentation.aspx?id=18503. Benzelius' extensive correspondence with scholars from all over Europe is attested in A. Erikson, ed., *Letters to Erik Benzelius the Younger from Learned Foreigners*, 2 vols (Göteborg: Kungl. Vetenskaps- och Vitterhets-Samhället, 1980); and A. Erikson and Nylander E. Nilsson, eds, *Erik Benzelius' Letters to His Learned Friends* (Göteborg: Kungl. Vetenskaps- och Vitterhets-Samhället, 1983).

[20] *Nova Acta Eruditorum* 1745, 385; the review occupies pp. 385–402. For the attribution of the review (anonymous as is usual), see Fabricius and Harles, "De Philone Iudaeo," 749.

[21] As recalled in the recent study by M. Nuß, "Ernesti, Johann August," in *Geschichte der Altertumswissenschaften: Biographisches Lexikon*, ed. P. Kuhlmann and H. Schneider (Stuttgart: Metzler, 2012),

first reviews the presentation of Philo's life and works given in Mangey's *Praefatio*. Various points are summarized and underlined: Philo's Judaism and his lifelong faithfulness to the Mosaic religion; his belonging "no doubt" (*haud dubie*) to the current of the Pharisees, to which his tendency toward allegorism is also to be related;[22] his Platonism, rich in eclectic elements as was customary at the time; Philo's λόγος doctrine, especially in relation to the Gospel of John; and the fact that Philo would not have known Hebrew.[23] The reviewer then considers the structure of the edition, first of all noting the presence of until then unpublished treatises, i.e. *De posteritate Caini* and parts of *De specialibus legibus*—respectively from a Vatican codex[24] and a Seldenian at the Bodleian Library in Oxford[25]—as well as the greatly increased number of fragments, taken both from manuscripts and from other authors (in particular Eusebius and John of Damascus).[26] Ernesti then focuses on the order chosen by Mangey in the publication of the treatises, "clearly different from the vulgate," and surveys the list of codices used by the English editor.

The remaining part of the review is occupied by a harsh critique of a large number of emendations inserted by Mangey into the text: he is accused of often being too daring, in line with the British conjectural tradition (*Britannico more*).[27] Worth noting is Ernesti's reproach of Mangey for not having given adequate account of the readings of the manuscripts he used.[28] This critique is particularly interesting from a historical

---

372–74, regarding in particular his *Institutio interpretis Novi Testamenti* (1761). On Ernesti as a transitional figure with respect to a full historical consideration of the New Testament, see W. G. Kümmel, *Il Nuovo Testamento: Storia dell'indagine scientifica sul problema neotestamentario*, trans. V. Benassi (Bologna: EDB, 2010), 78–80.

[22] Ernesti, review of Mangey, 387, referring to a Jewish practice of allegorizing "long before Philo," by Aristobulus and others. On Aristobulus, Philo, and the Jewish tradition of allegorical interpretation in Alexandria, see E. Matusova, "Allegorical Interpretation of the Pentateuch in Alexandria: Inscribing Aristobulus and Philo in a Wider Literary Context," *SPhiloA* 22 (2010): 1–51.

[23] Mangey accepts the opinion of Scaliger and P. D. Huet that Philo did not know Hebrew. It is interesting to note that Fabricius proves to be much less certain in this regard, also in connection with the weight to be given to imprecise Hebrew etymologies in Philo's writings. See now on this theme T. Rajak, "Philo's Knowledge of Hebrew: The Meaning of the Etymologies," in *The Jewish-Greek Tradition in Antiquity and the Byzantine Empire*, ed. J. K. Aitken and J. C. Paget (Cambridge: Cambridge University Press, 2014), 173–87.

[24] The transcript of which was sent to Mangey from Rome "cum ejusdem Codicis collatione"; cf. Mangey, *Philonis Judaei Opera quae reperiri potuerunt omnia*, 1:xvii.

[25] Cf. Mangey, *Philonis Judaei Opera quae reperiri potuerunt omnia*, 2:335 n.*. The Latin translation is by Benzelius, whose actual role in the discovery of this section coming from the Seldenian codex deserves to be further investigated, since he had the opportunity to consult manuscripts in the Bodleian Library during a stay in England when he was young, discovering, for example, unpublished homilies by John Chrysostom; cf. *Supplementa homiliarum Joannis Chrysostomi archiepiscopi Constantinopolitani. Ex codd. Mss. Bibliothecae Bodlejanae eruit, latine vertit et notis illustravit Ericus Benzelius*, Uppsala 1708 (which also contains two parts already published in 1702 and 1705). In the original edition of Fabricius' *Bibliotheca Graeca*, Benzelius was indicated as the next publisher and perhaps implicitly as the discoverer of *De specialibus legibus* book IV ("integrum vero ex MS. codice Seldeniano descripsit, et edendum in se recepit Praestantissimus Benzelius," thus J. A. Fabricius, "De Philone Judaeo," in *Bibliothecae Graecae liber IV* (Hamburg: apud Christianum Liebezeit, 1717), 111; and Fabricius and Harles, "De Philone Iudaeo," 734.

[26] Cf. Cohn, *Philonis Alexandrini opera quae supersunt*, lxxv. The *Philonis Judaei fragmenta* are collected in Mangey, *Philonis Judaei Opera quae reperiri potuerunt omnia*, 2:625–80. It was intended to include a collection of fragments in the editio maior of Cohn-Wendland, but this did not happen.

[27] Ernesti, review of Mangey, 393; see also pp. 396–97: "infinite conjectures," few worthwhile, and even with grammatical errors. Ernesti particularly accuses Mangey of having bent in too many cases the interpretation of the text to his own conjectures where there was no reason for emendation at all ("ubi nulla emendandi causa erat").

[28] Ernesti, review of Mangey, 394: "we very much desire an account of each variant observed in the manuscripts"; "since quite a long time scholars in this field have rightly instituted that they should take care to faithfully

point of view, in relation namely to the gradual emergence of the concept of *apparatus criticus*, and will be confirmed by Cohn, the subsequent critical editor of Philo's oeuvre.[29]

25.1 Mangey and the Christian Use of Philo

Mangey's edition of *Philonis Judaei Opera* opens with a dedicatory epistle addressed to the then archbishop of Canterbury, John Potter (1673/74–1747), himself a scholar of Greek and patristics, still known for his *Archaeologia Graeca*,[30] his edition of Lycophron's *Alexandra* (1697; 1702), as well as his edition of the works of Clement of Alexandria (1715).[31] This edition of Clement by Potter is singularly important in the history of Philo exegesis since the English scholar for the first time clearly recognized that "Clement had made extensive use of Philo's writings and that it was necessary to identify such usage for the proper understanding of the text."[32] It is no coincidence, then, that it is to the editor of Clement in particular that Mangey dedicates his work, for which indeed Potter appears to have been a source of inspiration and support.[33]

Whereas only the last three pages of Mangey's preface are dedicated to proper philological aspects (the novelties of the edition, the manuscripts used, and the contributions received from other scholars),[34] most of the twenty pages are occupied by two specific interpretative issues. The first of these is the character and extent of Philo's allegorism. The second and more important theme is Philo's doctrine περὶ λόγου, first of all in its relation to the New Testament, in particular to the Gospel of John,[35] but also

---

produce each *varia lectio*." Several of these critical remarks are present also in Fabricius and Harles, "De Philone Iudaeo," 748.

[29] Cf. Cohn, *Philonis Alexandrini opera quae supersunt*, lxxv–lxxvii. For a view of the textual practice of Cohn, "in the context of his times, a careful and fairly conservative editor" but in various cases too much inclined to altering the text, see D. T. Runia, "Introduction," in *Philo of Alexandria: On the Creation of the Cosmos according to Moses* (Leiden: Brill, 2001), 40, and J. R. Royse, "The Cohn-Wendland Critical Edition of Philo of Alexandria," *SPhiloA* 33 (2021): 197–207.

[30] J. Potter, *Archaeologia Graeca, sive veterum Graecorum, praecipue vero Atheniensium, ritus civiles, religiosi, militares et domestici, fusius explicati per Joannem Potterum* (Lugduni Batavorum: Excudit Petrus Vander Aa, 1702), reworking and amplification of a previous English edition.

[31] J. Potter, *Clementis Alexandrini Opera quae extant, recognita et illustrata per Joannem Potterum, episcopum Oxoniensem* (Oxford: E Theatro Sheldoniano, 1715).

[32] Runia, *Philo in Early Christian Literature*, 136. For Clement's relations with Philo, I refer to the observations of D. T. Runia, "Philo and the Early Christian Fathers," in *The Cambridge Companion to Philo*, ed. A. Kamesar (Cambridge: Cambridge University Press, 2009), 211–14; D. T. Runia, "Philon von Alexandria," *RAC* 27 (2016): 612–13.

[33] Mangey, *Philonis Judaei Opera quae reperiri potuerunt omnia*, 1:ix: "when I was failing, you gave me courage, when stuck and uncertain, counsel" ("Tu labanti animos, haerenti et incerto consilia porrexisti").

[34] For a volume dedicated to the paratexts in the printed editions of the Greek and Latin classics (fifteenth–eighteenth centuries), see G. Abbamonte, M. Laureys, and L. Miletti, eds, *I paratesti nelle edizioni a stampa dei classici greci e latini (XV–XVIII sec.)* (Pisa: Edizioni ETS, 2020).

[35] Brief and useful general observations in R. Radice, "La 'ricezione' di Filone nella cultura cristiana dei primi quattro secoli: aspetti storici e metodologici di questo tema nell'opera di D. T. Runia *Filone di Alessandria e la prima letteratura cristiana*," in *Filone di Alessandria nella prima letteratura cristiana: uno studio d'assieme* by D. T. Runia, trans. R. Radice (Milan: Vita e Pensiero, 1999), vii–viii, in relation to the Italian translation of Runia, *Philo in Early Christian Literature*; cf. also Runia, "Philon von Alexandria," 611. For a reconsideration of the delicate theme, without references to its great fortune in the *Res publica litterarum*, see e.g. H. W. Attridge, "Philo and John: Two Riffs on One Logos," *SPhiloA* 17 (2005): 103–17; for a larger inquiry with much recent bibliography,

as a subject of apologetic controversy against contemporary anti-Trinitarians, either Christian or Jewish ("contra odiernos tum Judaeos tum Unitarios").[36] From the start Mangey expresses the view that Philo's λόγος doctrine represents Jewish thought.[37] The subject of the Philonic λόγος alone occupies more than a third of the preface.

Such extensive attention to theological themes, with contemporary application, is not present in any of the prefaces to the previous complete editions of Philo, from Turnebus' *editio princeps* (completely in Greek, including introduction and notes),[38] to the editions of 1613 and 1640, and to their reprints made between the end of the seventeenth and early eighteenth centuries.[39] On the other hand, however, this attention perfectly corresponds to the "Christian use of Philo"[40] common since the sixteenth century in both Catholic and Protestant contexts. In the course of the seventeenth century, theological attention became increasingly widespread throughout the *Res publica litterarum* in a large number of dissertations and treatises (most of them not specifically dedicated to the study of Philo) that are marked by the religious wars and the fracture of Western Christianity. To these characteristics of seventeenth-century Philonic exegesis is added in Mangey's case his personal involvement (certainly not without the support of the dedicatee Archbishop Potter) in the theological controversies of eighteenth-century England. The Dissenters had long since been joined by other strong opponents of the orthodox currents of the Church of England, with a radicalization evident since the 1690s, years which:

> were marked by an intense agitation about the Trinity, culminating in the great Trinitarian Controversy of the turn of the century. In the larger sense the Trinitarian

---

H. W. Attridge, "Training Eyes to See Rightly: Educational Principles in Philo and the Fourth Gospel," *SPhiloA* 32 (2020): 41–54.

[36] Mangey, *Philonis Judaei Opera quae reperiri potuerunt omnia*, 1:ix. On the resumption of the Trinitarian controversies after the Glorious Revolution and their political significance, see B. S. Sirota, "The Trinitarian Crisis in Church and State: Religious Controversy and the Making of the Postrevolutionary Church of England, 1687–1702," *Journal of British Studies* 52 (2013): 26–54; on the "new outburst of Patristic studies" in England at the end of the seventeenth century with an apologetic purpose, both Trinitarian and anti-Trinitarian, see now D. Lucci, "Ante-Nicene Authority and the Trinity in Seventeenth-Century England," *Intellectual History Review* 28 (2018): 101–24.

[37] The doctrine "has flown forth from the books of the Hebrews" ("ex Hebraeorum libris effluxisse"): Mangey, *Philonis Judaei Opera quae reperiri potuerunt omnia*, 1:ix; a little further on it is stated that Philo is a reliable witness for the Logos conception of the Jews before the birth of Christ. A specific attack on the positions of Mangey was mounted a few years later by I. B. Carpzov, *Dissertatio inauguralis critico theologica de λόγῳ Philonis non Iohanneo adversus Thomam Mangey Anglum* (Helmstadt: Paul. Dieteric. Schnorr, 1749); on the dispute, see Fabricius and Harles, "De Philone Iudaeo," 724 n. h.

[38] Turnebus (cf. above, at n. 10) in the dedicatory epistle to the cardinal of Lorraine, in Greek, exalts the reconciliation of theology and philosophy in the work of Philo, which clearly demonstrates how "in the overall assimilation of pagan thought into Christianity, Philo's works assume great importance for Renaissance writers"; Lewis, *Adrien Turnèbe*, 169.

[39] A succinct mention of theological issues (related to whether or not Philo is a Platonist) is made by Schoettgen in the preface to the 1729 vulgate edition, for which see below at n. 61.

[40] Cf. E. J. Demeuse, "*Nostre Philon*: Philo after Trent," *SPhiloA* 29 (2017): 87–109, so far the only specific contribution of a certain breadth on the history of post-Renaissance Philonic exegesis. M. Jones, "Philo Judaeus and Hugo Grotius's Modern Natural Law," *JHI* 74 (2013): 339–59, has shown that "Philo is Grotius's first source for his definition of natural law"; particularly interesting is the involvement of the seventeenth-century English scholar John Selden in the debates on natural law, since Selden was the owner of one of the oldest existing Philo manuscripts, the Seldenianus 12, now in the Bodleian Library (cf. D. T. Runia et al., "Philo of Alexandria: An Annotated Bibliography 2013," *SPhiloA* 28 (2016): 407).

Controversy was a symptom of the disturbing effect on traditional Christianity of accumulated pressures from all the rational tendencies of a rational age. The prominence of Trinitarian disputes at the end of the century can thus be viewed as pointing to the end of one phase of the English Enlightenment and the beginning of a new one.[41]

Not only in England but generally in Protestant Europe between the end of the seventeenth and middle of the eighteenth centuries, Philo's role in the context of the Trinitarian controversies was significant. It is now appropriate to examine how Mangey reflects the scholarly debates of that same period on the philosophical, and in particular the Platonist, views of Philo.[42]

25.2 Johann Albert Fabricius

For a discussion of Philo's "Platonism," Mangey[43] refers to the "short and excellent booklet" presented in Leipzig in 1693 by the 25-year-old Johann Albert Fabricius (1668–1736)[44] and traditionally considered a turning point in Philo studies.[45] Right from the frontispiece Fabricius announces that he is opposing a thesis by Johannes Jonsius (1624–59), a typical seventeenth-century German polymath whose very learned *De scriptoribus historiae philosophicae libri IV* (1659)[46] can be considered one of the first modern "histories" of ancient philosophy. A second and expanded edition of Jonsius' work was produced by J. C. Dorn in 1716, including a highly interesting bio-bibliographic appendix ranging from the Western and Byzantine Middle Ages to the outbreak of the *Querelle des Anciens et des Modernes* at the end of the seventeenth century.[47]

---

[41] Thus M. I. J. Griffin, Jr, *Latitudinarianism in the Seventeenth-Century Church of England*, ann. R. H. Popkin, ed. Lila Freedman (Leiden: Brill, 1992), 105.

[42] For an account of many recent works treating the history of the exegesis of several Greek and Latin authors between the sixteenth and eighteenth centuries, see O. Montepaone, *Auctorem producere. L'Apocolocyntosis nelle edizioni a stampa dall'Umanesimo sino alla rifondazione scientifica di inizio Ottocento* (Milan: Ledizioni, 2021), 10–15.

[43] Mangey, *Philonis Judaei Opera quae reperiri potuerunt omnia*, 1:viii.

[44] J. A. Fabricius, *Exercitatio de platonismo Philonis Judaei Viro doctissimo Johanni Jonsio opposita, Et indultu Amplissimae Facultatis Philosophicae pro loco Dissertationis argumentum proponenda a M. Joh. Alberto Fabricio* (Leipzig: Zeidler, 1693), reprinted with other similar academic dissertations of his hand in J. A. Fabricius, *Opusculorum historico-critico-literariorum sylloge quae sparsim viderant lucem nunc recensita denuo et partim aucta* (Hamburg: Sumptibus viduae Felgineriae, 1738), 147–60. Profile and bibliography on Fabricius in R. Häfner, "Fabricius, Johann Albert," in Kuhlmann and Schneider, *Geschichte der Altertumswissenschaften*, 383–85.

[45] Cf. T. H. Billings, *The Platonism of Philo Judaeus* (PhD diss., University of Chicago, 1919), 6, in the opening chapter, "A Survey of the History of Philonic Interpretation," where also worthy of note, in the footsteps of Fabricius-Harles, is the role attributed to Philo in the Trinitarian controversies of the seventeenth and eighteenth centuries; see also D. T. Runia, *Philo of Alexandria and the Timaeus of Plato* (Leiden: Brill, 1986), 28. For Platonic reception in Philo, see S. Yli-Karjanmaa, "Philo of Alexandria," in *Brill's Companion to the Reception of Plato in Antiquity*, ed. H. Tarrant, F. Renaud, D. Baltzly, and D. A. Layne (Leiden: Brill, 2018), 116–29.

[46] J. Jonsius, *De scriptoribus historiae philosophicae libri IV* (Frankfurt: Götzius, 1659). A positive judgment of the work is given by C. Bursian, *Geschichte der classischen Philologie in Deutschland von den Anfängen bis zur Gegenwart*, 2 vols (Munich: Oldenbourg, 1883), 1:314–15, who places it on the same level as its model, the much better known *De historicis Graecis* by J. G. Vossius.

[47] J. C. Dorn, *Ioannis Ionsii Holsati de scriptoribus historiae philosophicae libri IV. Nunc denuo recogniti atque ad praesentem aetatem usque perducti cura Io. Christophori Dornii cum praefatione Burcardi Gotthelfii Struvii*

Touching on Philo in his chronologically arranged review,[48] Jonsius starts from the passage in the *Ecclesiastical History* where "Eusebius tells us that Philo is recorded as having exceeded his contemporaries in his zeal for the philosophical discipline of Plato and Pythagoras."[49] Jonsius intends to demonstrate however that in what we have of Philo there is no trace of Platonic influence (*superstites libri Philonis nomine Platonicum genium non spirant*) and that the definition by Josephus of Philo as "not ignorant of philosophy" (φιλοσοφίας οὐκ ἄπειρος)[50] should be taken to refer not to Greek philosophy, but to the three main Jewish *sectae* (Essenes, Sadducees, Pharisees) discussed by Josephus and to Jewish religion and thought in general.

In his reply, Fabricius first cites the relevant passages of Jonsius, noting right away that the position of his predecessor is contrary to the ancient tradition.[51] Fabricius admits that among Jewish authors writing in Greek, and likewise among Christians, φιλοσοφία is sometimes used to indicate their own religion, and that from Josephus' description as such ("not ignorant of philosophy") one cannot per se deduce a reference to Platonic philosophy; that this reference exists can, however, be affirmed on the basis of the consensus of the ancient tradition and on the basis of Philo's extant writings themselves.[52] The most influential and original part of Fabricius' discussion is undoubtedly where he identifies—albeit in a rather general way[53]—Platonic doctrines in Philo. In so doing he does not completely deny but tends to play down the idea that Plato depended on biblical sources,[54] a view put forward from Numenius onwards and well attested among the fathers of the church,[55] which had enjoyed a renewed fortune thanks to the "biblical comparativism" so dear to the seventeenth century, particularly in the Protestant world.[56] Fabricius likewise explicitly avoids dwelling at length on the

---

(Jena: apud viduam Meyerianam, 1716). At the end of the volume, a very clear, brief account of the beginning of the epochal *Querelle* is given with reference to Charles, p. 227.

[48] Jonsius, *De scriptoribus historiae philosophicae*, 225 (*liber* III *caput* IV).

[49] D. T. Runia, "Why Does Clement of Alexandria Call Philo 'the Pythagorean'?," in *Philo and the Church Fathers: A Collection of Papers* (Leiden: Brill, 1995), 56; more recently Runia, "Philo and the Early Christian Fathers," 219–21. The passage (*Hist. eccl.* ii 4, 2) can be read among the "Testimonia de Philone eiusque scriptis" in Cohn, *Philonis Alexandrini opera quae supersunt*, lxxxxviii; with Italian translation in R. Radice and D. T. Runia, "Appendice: Testimonia de Philone da Giuseppe Flavio al 1000 d.C.," in *Filone di Alessandria nella prima letteratura cristiana*, 380–81.

[50] Josephus, *A.J.* 18.8.1: first *testimonium* on Philo in Cohn, *Philonis Alexandrini opera quae supersunt*, lxxxxv.

[51] Fabricius, *Opusculorum historico-critico-literariorum sylloge*, 150. I quote from the reprint, in which the pages are numbered.

[52] Fabricius, *Opusculorum historico-critico-literariorum sylloge*, 153.

[53] As critically observed by W. Völker, *Fortschritt und Vollendung bei Philo von Alexandrien: Eine Studie zur Geschichte der Frömmigkeit* (Leipzig: J. C. Hinrich, 1938), 31.

[54] Fabricius, *Opusculorum historico-critico-literariorum sylloge*, 153: Plato probably accepted something from the Jews (*quaedam accepisse*—Fabricius cites for this position Clemens of Alexandria and Numenius); that he accepted much or all can be stated only by whom is equally ignorant about Plato and about ancient philosophy and about Jewish religion.

[55] Cf. Runia, *Philo in Early Christian Literature*, 11ff.; about Numenius, see now G. E. Sterling, "The Theft of Philosophy: Philo of Alexandria and Numenius of Apamea," *SPhiloA* 27 (2015): 71–85 and ch. 2 above.

[56] An example of "comparative exegesis" between classical and biblical texts in Germany in the first half of the eighteenth century is the academic dissertation of J. H. Withof translated and annotated in G. Benedetto, ed., *J. H. Withof. Callimaco e i Telchini* (Palermo: Sellerio Editore, 1995).

theme of the Philonic λόγος,[57] at the center of many Trinitarian disputes of his time and of the previous century, and prefers to point out in Philo undisputed parallels with the *Timaeus* as well as with the Platonic doctrine of the soul,[58] thus refuting the assertions of Jonsius that Philo's writings "do not breathe a Platonic spirit" and that Philo was versed only in Jewish, and not also in Platonic wisdom.

It should be noted that there is a particular scholar of whom Fabricius makes extensive use, citing him for an entire page,[59] namely the French Jesuit Dionysius Petavius (1583–1652), one of the great Roman Catholic apologists of the century but also editor of Synesius and of Epiphanius. Petavius at the beginning of the third volume of his imposing series *De theologicis dogmatibus*, had recognized in Philo's doctrine of the angels Platonic as well as Jewish elements ("a true Platonist and an equally true Pharisee").[60] Thus we have here yet another example of the continuous overlap in the seventeenth century between Philonic exegesis and theological reflection, both Roman Catholic and Protestant—an overlap still alive and well in the philological discussions of the subsequent century.

That any trace of Platonism might be attributed to Philo will still be vehemently denied in the last edition preceding that of Mangey, namely, the Frankfurt vulgate edition of 1729,[61] in which Fabricius' *Exercitatio* is not even mentioned.[62] The editor, C. Schoettgen, deserves mention by reason of his conviction that Philo wrote "in the Hellenistic, that is, Judeo-Greek language in which the words are Greek, but the meanings and phrases are translated from Hebrew, a way of speaking that Plato, Socrates and Demosthenes would not understand."[63] The rejection of Philo's "Platonism" tends here to coincide with the affirmation of his non-"Greekness," following the same interpretative line of Jonsius (and note that Schoettgen likewise rejects any suggestion of Stoic elements in Philo).

---

[57] Fabricius, *Opusculorum historico-critico-literariorum sylloge*, 155.

[58] On Philonic quotations from Plato, "usually cited simply by name, if at all," and for the few places where Philo does actually quote the *Timaeus*, see J. R. Royse, "Philo's Division of his Works into Books," SPhiloA 13 (2001): 75.

[59] Fabricius, *Exercitatio de Platonismo Philonis Judaei*, c. X.

[60] I quote from D. Petavius, *Opus de theologicis dogmatibus, auctius in hac nova editione. Tomus tertius. In quo de Angelis, de Mundi opificio, de Pelagianis ac Semipelagianis, deque Tridentini Concilii interpretatione, et S. Augustini doctrina disseritur* (Antwerp: G. Gallet, 1700), 2. Petavius' work is reported (in a Venetian edn of 1745) in H. L. Goodhart and E. R. Goodenough, "A General Bibliography of Philo Judaeus," in *The Politics of Philo Judaeus: Practice and Theory*, ed. E. R. Goodenough (New Haven: Yale University Press, 1938; repr., Hildesheim: Georg Olms, 1967), 215; cf. also Runia, *Philo in Early Christian Literature*, 31.

[61] C. Schoettgen, "Praefatio ad Lectorem," in *Philonis Judaei omnia quae extant Opera ex accuratissima Sigismundi Gelenii, et aliorum interpretatione, partim ab Adriano Turnebo, partim a Davide Hoeschelio, ex Augustana, edita et illustrata [...]. Accedunt noviter Notitia vitae et operum Philonis, ex viri celeberrimi Joannis Alberti Fabricii Bibliotheca Graeca, et Praefatio Christiani Schoettgenii* (Frankfurt: Jeremiam Schrey and J. G. Conradi, 1729): "the last edition of the Philonic vulgate" (Runia, *Philo in Early Christian Literature*, 31 n. 163).

[62] The 1729 edn on the other hand reprints on pp. 5–14 the whole of Fabricius' "De Philone Judaeo," i.e. ch. IV of his *Bibliothecae Graecae liber IV* (1717).

[63] "lingua Hellenistica, h.e. Judaeo-Graeca, in qua voces quidem sunt Graecae, significationes autem et phrases ex lingua Hebraica conversae, quale loquendi genus Plato, Socrates et Demosthenes non intelligerent." In Schoettgen's opinion, Philo's *lingua Hellenistica* is to be compared with the Yiddish spoken by German Jews, "a corrupted German, defaced by Hebraisms" ("perinde atque hodie Judaei Germanica lingua utuntur, sed corrupta, et Hebraismis deturpata"). Worthy of study would be Philo's role in the famous and acrimonious debate between D. Heinsius and Salmasius on the meaning of *lingua Hellenistica*, cf. R. Pfeiffer, *History of Classical Scholarship from 1300 to 1850* (Oxford: Oxford University Press, 1976), 123.

While with respect to Philo's Platonism Mangey substantially does no more than refer to the booklet of Fabricius, he dwells at greater length on the influence that other Greek philosophical currents exerted on Philo's thought: first of all, Pythagoreanism, already noted by various Christian authors starting with Clement of Alexandria and Eusebius, and then especially Stoicism, the presence of which, according to Mangey, is manifest in Philo more than in any other ancient writer. In fact, Mangey believes that the best definition for Philo is that of eclectic.[64] Fabricius, too, in the conclusion of his *Exercitatio de Platonismo Philonis Judaei* had highlighted the eclectic substance of Philonic thought, recalling with favor the opinion that Philo sometimes seems a Stoic ("Philonem aliquando Stoicissare"), for which is cited both the great Justus Lipsius and the English theologian and antiquarian H. Dodwell, and by evoking Eusebius' report of Philo as a follower not only of Plato, but also of Pythagoras.[65] Given the keen attention paid in recent research to the interplay of Platonism and Stoicism in the work of Philo,[66] it will be useful now to turn to some moments of the discussions conducted within the seventeenth and eighteenth-century *Res publica litterarum* about forms and limits of Stoicism (and Platonism) in Philo.

25.3 Justus Lipsius and Henry Dodwell

The scholar whom Fabricius seems to consider the first to express the view that Philo "stoicized" is Justus Lipsius, and the work of Lipsius that Fabricius is referring to is the *Manuductio ad Stoicam philosophiam*, one of the influential treatises at the origin of the revival of Stoicism, and therefore of the movement of Neo-Stoicism, in the tormented Europe of the sixteenth and seventeenth centuries. The treatise appeared in 1604, in the final phase of Lipsius' relatively short but very industrious life (he will die in March 1606 at fifty-eight years of age). While presenting itself as a tool for the interpretation mainly of Seneca,[67] the *Manuductio* is actually a detailed and annotated collection of ancient *testimonia* on Stoicism and can be considered the first modern exposition of Stoic doctrine and its later reception.[68] Discussing the success of Stoicism among great figures of antiquity as well as among Christians, Lipsius includes Philo in his list, remarking to have noted "much in which he Stoicizes, even if the general opinion has

---

[64] "Among the Eclectics" ("in Eclecticorum partibus"): Mangey, *Philonis Judaei Opera quae reperiri potuerunt omnia*, 1:ix.

[65] Fabricius, *Exercitatio de Platonismo Philonis Judaei*, c. XV. For the Eusebius passage, see above at n. 49.

[66] D. T. Runia, "From Stoicism to Platonism: The Difficult Case of Philo of Alexandria's De Providentia I," in *From Stoicism to Platonism: The Development of Philosophy, 100 BCE–100 CE*, ed. T. Engberg-Pedersen (Cambridge: Cambridge University Press, 2017), 159–78; see M. R. Niehoff, "Philo's Role as a Platonist in Alexandria," *Études platoniciennes* 7 (2010): 35–62, on "Philo as a Platonist in Stoic garb" (12) particularly in the last phase of his career, through "an innovative synthesis of Platonic transcendentalism and Stoic immanentism" (15). M. R. Niehoff, *Philo of Alexandria. An Intellectual Biography* (New Haven and London: Yale University Press, 2018), identifies strongly transcendent Platonist positions as characteristic of the young Philo.

[67] Lipsius in 1605 published the works of Seneca. The *Manuductio* "closely reflects Lipsius' reading of Seneca"; M. Morford, *Stoics and Neostoics: Rubens and the Circle of Lipsius* (Princeton: Princeton University Press, 1991), 27.

[68] See the extensive and up-to-date entry of J. Papy, "Justus Lipsius," *The Stanford Encyclopedia of Philosophy* (Spring 2019 Edition), online version <https://plato.stanford.edu/archives/spr2019/entries/justus-lipsius/>.

him Platonizing."[69] After mentioning the fortune of Stoicism in antiquity and its spread among the ruling classes of the Roman Empire, culminating in the philosopher and emperor Marcus Aurelius, Lipsius dedicates the final part of the chapter to Christian authors, and in particular to the goodwill towards Stoicism shown by Clement of Alexandria and Jerome (to the latter we owe the well-known dictum that the Stoics "concord with our doctrine on most points").[70] The conclusion of the chapter touches on Lipsius' own time, revealing the personal aspect of his interest in Stoic doctrine. The Flemish scholar quickly but clearly lets the readers understand that he returned to the Christian (and Roman Catholic) faith *through Stoicism*, and he unexpectedly evokes the figure of Charles Borromeo (1538–84), archbishop of Milan for over twenty years and decisive protagonist of the initial phase of the Counter-Reformation, who for his spiritual benefit used to frequently read Epictetus.[71] It is therefore not by chance that Lipsius mentions Philo's *Stoicissare* in a context that immediately leads to the fortune of Stoicism in Rome and among Christians. Moreover, as we have seen, Lipsius insists not only on the compatibility of Stoic with Christian thought, but also on the preparatory value of Stoic wisdom and practice with respect to Christian *pietas*, even in the present, as shown by a model of saintliness such as Charles Borromeo was already considered in his lifetime.

A close connection with current theological interests can also be found in the second author cited by Fabricius as an advocate of Philo's "Stoicism,"[72] namely, the Englishman Henry Dodwell (1641–1711). Unlike Mangey (and unlike Christopherson, one of the last English Roman Catholic bishops in the sixteenth century), Dodwell did not take holy orders, but was nevertheless heavily involved as a layman and as a scholar in the political-religious as well as specifically ecclesiastical events of his time. Born in Ireland to parents of English origin, he fled to England as a child to escape the Irish revolt of the 1640s; years later he returned to the island to study at Trinity College, Dublin, subsequently also obtaining a fellowship which he declined precisely because of his unwillingness to enter the clerical state. From the early 1680s he regularly frequented Oxford, continuing his philological and above all patristic studies, in accordance with the Oxonian environment and its traditional belief in a "close relationship between the church of primitive Christianity and the Anglican episcopal church."[73] Having become

---

[69] Lipsius, *Manuductio ad Stoicam philosophiam*, I, Dissertatio XVII: "plura ... notavi, in quibus Stoicissat: etsi Platonissare eum communis fama tulit." I quote from *Iusti Lipsii Opera* (Lyon: apud Horatium Cardon, 1613), 1:762.

[70] Careful examination in A. Capone, "*Stoici, qui nostro dogmati in plerisque concordant*: Gerolamo e lo stoicismo," *Adamantius* 24 (2018): 435–50.

[71] *Iusti Lipsii Opera*, 1:763. Lipsius was for many years engaged in correspondence with Federico Borromeo (1564–1631), who like his great cousin became cardinal archbishop of Milan, and was founder of the Ambrosiana Library; cf. R. Ferro, *Federico Borromeo ed Ericio Puteano: Cultura e letteratura a Milano agli inizi del Seicento* (Milan: Biblioteca Ambrosiana; Rome: Bulzoni, 2007).

[72] A generic mention (which depends on Fabricius and Harles, "De Philone Iudaeo") of the polemics in the seventeenth and eighteenth centuries around Philo's Platonism or Stoicism is found in the introductory chapter of Völker, *Fortschritt und Vollendung bei Philo von Alexandrien*, 31–32, otherwise almost entirely concentrated on the nineteenth and twentieth centuries. G. D. Farandos, *Kosmos und Logos nach Philon von Alexandria* (Amsterdam: Rodopi, 1976), has nothing substantial on Philo research before the nineteenth century. Dodwell does not appear in Goodhart and Goodenough, "A General Bibliography of Philo Judaeus."

[73] T. Harmsen, "Dodwell, Henry," in *Oxford Dictionary of National Biography*, published online (https://doi.org/10.1093/ref:odnb/7763).

known through his editions and treatises (for example, the very erudite *Dissertationes Cyprianicae* of 1682), in April 1688 Dodwell was nominated Camden Professor of History at the University of Oxford. He published his most important lectures as *Praelectiones academicae in schola historices Camdeniana* (1692),[74] focusing in particular on the *Historia Augusta* but also on intricate epigraphic and chronological issues.[75] However, the start of Dodwell's commitment as Camden Professor coincided with a decisive event in British history, the Glorious Revolution, with the fall of James II as a result of the triumphal advance of William of Orange (November 1688–January 1689). Faced with the requirement to swear allegiance to the new sovereigns, William and Mary, but faithful to his beliefs as a High Church Tory and to the legitimacy of James II as king of England, Dodwell refused and thus became a nonjuror (even one of the leading exponents of the movement until his return to the Church of England shortly before his death).[76] The consequence was that in November 1691 he lost his Professorship.[77]

Dodwell had just in 1689 published a volume of over five hundred pages entitled *Dissertationes in Irenaeum*, a collection of six dissertations on the life and works of the author of *Adversus haereses*. As an appendix he added a fragment (found in codex Baroccianus 142 of the Bodleian Library) of Philip of Side (active in the first half of the fifth century)[78] containing a list of the heads of the catechetical school of Alexandria.[79] Commenting on Philip of Side's statement that Pantaenus was a "Pythagorean philosopher" (φιλόσοφος Πυθαγόρειος), Dodwell notes that Eusebius instead calls him a Stoic. He deduces that in the late second century the two definitions were

---

[74] In Harmsen, "Dodwell, Henry," the title is wrongly quoted as *Praelectiones academicae in schola* rhetorices *Camdeniana*.

[75] Reference to Dodwell in J. E. Sandys, *A History of Classical Scholarship*, Vol. II: *From the Revival of Learning to the End of the Eighteenth Century (in Italy, France, England, and the Netherlands)* (Cambridge: Cambridge University Press, 1908), 357, where he is noted as "best known for his chronological works" (so also in J. E. Sandys, *A Short History of Classical Scholarship from the Sixth Century B.C. to the Present Day* [Cambridge: Cambridge University Press, 1915], 251); mentioned with regard to his chronological studies also in Clarke, *Greek Studies in England 1700–1830*, 110 n. 3.

[76] Cf. C. D. A. Leighton, "The Religion of the Non-Jurors and the Early British Enlightenment: A Study of Henry Dodwell," *History of European Ideas* 28 (2002): 247–62; see L. Lehnus, "Callimaco redivivo tra Thomas Stanley e Richard Bentley," *Eikasmos* 2 (1991): 285–309, now in L. Lehnus, *Incontri con la filologia del passato* (Milan: Dedalo, 2012), 47–80, for an example of the importance of the events involving the nonjurors in English classical studies during the seventeenth and eighteenth centuries.

[77] See the well-informed entry on Dodwell in J. P. Bernard, T. Birch, and J. Lockman, eds, *A General Dictionary, Historical and Critical* (London: J. Bettenham, 1736), 4:616. Important for the nonjurors was "what they called the 'church point'—the unacceptability of the State's removal of those bishops who declined to violate their oaths to the dethroned king"; cf. C. D. A. Leighton, "Ancienneté among the Non-Jurors: A Study of Henry Dodwell," *History of European Ideas* 31 (2005): 1–16.

[78] For what remains of his Χριστιανικὴ Ἱστορία, see K. Heyden, "Die *Christliche Geschichte* des Philippos von Side. Mit einem kommentierten Katalog der Fragmente," in *Julius Africanus und die christliche Weltchronik. Julius Africanus und die christliche Weltchronistik*, ed. M. Wallraff (Berlin: de Gruyter, 2006), 210–43. Dodwell understands that the fragment does not preserve the original text of Philip of Side, but is the result of a much later reworking, perhaps by the Byzantine author Nicephorus Callistus.

[79] Editor princeps is H. Dodwell, *Dissertationes in Irenaeum. Auctore Henrico Dodwello A.M. Histories in Academia Oxoniensi Praelectore Cambdeniano. Accedit fragmentum Philippi Sidetae, hactenus ineditum, De Catechistarum Alexandrinorum Successione, cum notis* (Oxford: E Theatro Sheldoniano, 1689), 488 (short commentary now in Heyden, "Die *Christliche Geschichte* des Philippos von Side," 214–15). On the next page Dodwell provides the Latin translation of the fragment; the *Notae* occupy pp. 490–514. The last section of the volume, confirming Dodwell's chronological interests, is a *Synopsis* in chronological order of the historical facts mentioned in the volume, with references to chapter and section.

interchangeable, as seen also in the case of Philo, defined as "Pythagorean" by Clement of Alexandria,[80] but according to Dodwell to be considered Stoic.[81] Dodwell's reference to Philo in the context of a discussion on the origins of the Alexandrian catechetical school and its philosophical inspiration is particularly fascinating in light of the decisive role that recent research has attributed to that school, under the leadership of Pantaenus, for the very preservation of Philo's writings.[82] Fabricius in speaking about Philo's *Stoicissare* makes explicit reference to Dodwell's comment *ad fragmentum Philippi Sidetae*, but the English scholar himself in that comment refers to another of his own writings ("alibi probavimus").[83] The identification of this work allows us to further contextualize Dodwell's statement about Philo's Stoicism, linking it to philosophical and religious controversies in seventeenth-century England.

In 1672, Dodwell published in Dublin the posthumous work *De obstinatione*, of his late tutor and friend John Stearne (1624–69).[84] The treatise, dedicated to the *obstinatio bona*, or perseverance, is of explicit Neo-Stoic inspiration; in the opening of the *praefatio* Stearne (who was briefly the first lecturer in Hebrew at Trinity College Dublin), after quoting Marcus Aurelius, immediately mentions a passage in which Philo praises the Stoic precept of "living in accordance with nature."[85] As a quasi-introduction to Stearne's short treatise, Dodwell opens the edition with almost three hundred pages of *Prolegomena Apologetica*,[86] demonstrating the necessity of a recourse to philosophy, and especially to the Stoics, in theological discussions. In this way Dodwell intends to defend theological reasoning *adversus modernos Socinianos*, that is, against the anti-Trinitarians, who will be the target (seventy years later) also of Mangey's preface, as we have seen.[87] With the purpose of demonstrating that Stoic philosophy is necessary for Christian philosophy, Dodwell points out that Stoicism was well accepted among Jews and Christians in Alexandria during the imperial age. In this context he quotes Philo for having consciously tried to render Stoic doctrines compatible with Mosaic tradition, and immediately afterwards mentions the philo-Stoicism of the three major exponents of the Christian school of Alexandria, Pantaenus, Clement, and Origen, who likewise endeavored to adapt the Stoic dogmas to the Christian scriptures.[88] It turns out, therefore, that almost twenty years before his notes *ad fragmentum Philippi Sidetae*, published in 1689, Dodwell (recalling perhaps the Dublin teaching of the

---

[80] On the question, see Runia, "Why Does Clement of Alexandria Call Philo 'the Pythagorean'?"; J. Otto, "Philo, Judaeus? A Re-evaluation of Why Clement Calls Philo 'the Pythagorean,'" *SPhiloA* 25 (2013): 115–38.

[81] Dodwell, *Dissertationes in Irenaeum*, 507.

[82] Runia, *Philo in Early Christian Literature*, 135; Runia, "Philo and the Early Christian Fathers," 213. On Pantaenus, see in particular A. Le Boulluec, "Aux origines, encore, de l' 'école' d'Alexandrie," *Adamantius* 5 (1999): 8–36; Runia, "Philon von Alexandria," 612.

[83] Fabricius, *Exercitatio de Platonismo Philonis Judaei*, c. XV; Dodwell, *Dissertationes in Irenaeum*, 507, with n. 25: "Proleg. Apol. ad Dom. Stearn de Obstinatione."

[84] D. Coakley, "Stearne [Sterne], John," *Oxford Dictionary of National Biography* published online (https://doi-org/10.1093/ref:odnb/26410). Of manifest Stoic inspiration is also J. Stearne, *Aphorismi de Foelicitate* (Dublin: Typis Johannis Crooke, Typographi Regii, 1664), with a maxim by Epictetus cited on the title page.

[85] Philo of Alexandria, *De Migratione Abrahami*, 28.

[86] H. Dodwell, "Prolegomena Apologetica," in J. Stearne, *De obstinatione. Opus posthumum, pietatem Christiano-Stoicam, scholastico more, suadens* (Dublin: Benjamin Tooke, Typographus Regius, 1672), 1–282.

[87] See above at n. 36.

[88] Dodwell, "Prolegomena Apologetica," 143.

Stoic and Hebraist Stearne) already in some way connected Philo's "Stoicism" to that of the *Patres* of the Alexandrian catechetical school. Noteworthy moreover in the *Prolegomena Apologetica* is Dodwell's frequent reference to Lipsius, thus confirming the decisive importance of the father of modern Neo-Stoicism also for the study of the reception of Stoicism in the ancient world.

25.4 Conclusion

In 1898, two years after the appearance of the first volume of his *Philonis Alexandrini opera quae supersunt*, L. Cohn (1856–1915) published an extensive review of É. Herriot's *Philon le Juif*.[89] At the beginning Cohn traces in two pages a historical panorama of the philological and editorial reception of Philo from the Italian humanism of the fifteenth century onwards. He notes that after the partial Philo editions of Hoeschel of 1587 and 1614, containing four previously unpublished treatises, "philological work for a long time was almost completely at a standstill," and that in the seventeenth and eighteenth centuries, apart from J. A. Fabricius, "one can hardly name a philologist who seriously dealt with Philo." Just as it was in the Middle Ages, Cohn continues, Philo returned to being the domain of theologians, "who in numerous commentaries and monographs wanted to shed light above all on the relationship between Philo and the New Testament, in reality heaping only errors upon errors." However, the first critical edition of the Philonic corpus also came from a theologian: "with Thomas Mangey's edition begins a new era of the text of Philo" ("mit Thomas Mangeys Ausgabe beginnt eine neue Epoche des Philotextes"). Though complaining, just as in the *Prolegomena* to his own edition, about Mangey's lack of accuracy in the use of collations, Cohn on the whole judges here his only predecessor in more positive terms than he did two years earlier, also with regard to his conjectures and emendations of the text.

In conclusion, the aim of the present contribution has been to show, through a selection of examples, how much of seventeenth- and early eighteenth-century exegesis has converged in Mangey's *Praefatio* to his Philo edition, and above all to what extent knowledge of the interpretation of Philo in those centuries is required to fully understand Mangey's positions. For a true evaluation of the meaning, importance, and limits of the works produced by the philological, antiquarian, and theological erudition of the *Res publica litterarum* it is necessary to overcome (or rather, to relativize) the philology/theology dichotomy reflected so clearly in Cohn's judgment and, from F. A. Wolf onwards, underlying the very conception of *Altertumswissenschaft*. Especially in the case of an author like Philo of Alexandria, for such a long time characterized as *Philo Christianus* in the history of his textual and interpretative tradition,[90] one easily observes how many studies of theological inspiration, sometimes paradoxically, represent

---

[89] L. Cohn, "Philo von Alexandria," *NJKA* 1 (1898): 514–40, review of É. Herriot, *Philon le Juif. Essai sur l'école juive d'Alexandrie* (Paris: Hachette, 1898). The quotations in English are my own translations from the German, p. 515.

[90] Runia, *Philo in Early Christian Literature*, 3–33; Runia, "Philon von Alexandria."

real steps forward in the interpretation and understanding of his work. An illustration is the seventeenth- and eighteenth-century debate around Philo's Platonism and/or Stoicism discussed above (pp. 421–24),[91] a debate revealing close, even when implicit, links with contemporary philosophical and theological disputes, above all in the Anglican world.

---

[91] It would be useful to retrace and illuminate the seventeenth- and eighteenth-century debate around Philo's eclecticism in detail, starting of course from the survey in Fabricius and Harles, "De Philone Iudaeo," 723–24 n. h), on which are based the lines drawn by Billings, *The Platonism of Philo Judaeus*, 5–7. See now also G. E. Sterling, "The First Critical Edition of Philo: Thomas Mangey and the 1742 Edition," *SPhiloA* 33 (2021): 133–59.

26

German Philosophy, 1650–1850

Dirk Westerkamp

Philo of Alexandria is a crucial figure both for the study and the writing of philosophical historiography in the seventeenth, eighteenth, and nineteenth centuries. Within "German" philosophy (in the following simply meaning academic philosophy at universities in territories where German dialects were spoken since the late seventeenth century), Philo of Alexandria was discovered within the context of early Enlightenment philosophy.[1] His thought played an important role in the development of eighteenth-century historiographical holism (Horn, Heumann, Brucker). Since his writings seemed to belong neither to *philosophia hebraeorum* nor to *philosophia graecanica* nor to a *philosophia barbarorum*, they were, at first, considered a puzzling monolith within the history of philosophy (Jonsius, Budde, Buhle).

Thus, seventeenth- and eighteenth-century historiographical holism established general, albeit controversial historiographical classification systems within which the *philosophia judaeorum* played a crucial yet much-debated role between the traditions.[2] Most of the time, its (late) antique, medieval, and mystical strands are included *as* excluded. Philo's thought is marked by a double "in between" or *metaxy*. Historically as well as systematically, Philo's thought was perceived as caught between different stools: Plato and the church fathers, Rabbinic Judaism and Johannine Logos, early Kabbalah (which, in eighteenth-century historiography, was believed to first emerge during the second century CE) and Hellenistic syncretism.

Within the context of German Idealism, Philo was regarded as the central figure in the attempt to relate reason and revelation, substance- and subject-philosophy (Hegel, Schelling).[3] Eventually, the Jewish Hegelians took Philo's thought as a blueprint of their own struggle to conceptualize Jewish thought within an idealist framework (Krochmal, Hirsch, Formstecher).

---

[1] Cf. D. Westerkamp, "The Philonic Distinction: German Enlightenment Historiography of Jewish Thought," *History and Theory* 47 (2008): 533–59.
[2] Cf. A. Lerousseau, *Le judaïsme dans la philosophie allemande 1770–1850* (Paris: Presses Universitaires de France, 2001).
[3] Cf. D. Westerkamp, "Platon in Moses. Hegels Kritik der Substanzmetaphysik und die *philosophia hebraeorum*," in *Hegel-Jahrbuch 2005* (Berlin: Akademie, 2005), 106–13.

26.1 Philo and Historiographical Holism: Taxonomical Challenges

Whereas Thomas Stanley's *History of Philosophy* (1655) did not discuss Jewish philosophers at all,[4] Georg Horn's *Historia philosophiae* (1655) seems to be the first seventeenth-century historiography to introduce a *philosophia judaeorum* or *philosophia ebraeorum*[5] into its outline of the evolution of philosophical thought. Horn (1620–70) argues that one can speak of a *philosophical* Jewish thinking no earlier than the first centuries BCE, when the influence of Hellenism penetrated the Jewish realm and "Greek philosophy was spread also in Judea."[6] It is this context within which Philo's writings were situated. As early as in Horn's *Historia philosophiae*, the topos emerges of Philo as the only "true" ancient Jewish *philosopher*. "True" refers to his philosophy also in the sense of "opposed to the 'false philosophy' of the Talmud and of rabbinic Judaism."[7] This cliché formed the influential eighteenth-century topos according to which Philo's "true" Platonic philosophy and the "false philosophy" of the Talmud are two different sides of the same coin. The confluence of both strands is, according to Christoph August Heumann (1681–1764), the reason for the "pseudo-philosophy" ("unächte Philosophie") of Jewish thought, especially of Talmud and Kabbalah, which are believed to have both emerged with the *Mishnah*, the *Sefer Yetzira*, and the *Zohar* in the second century CE.

Yet, this negative account of Jewish thought was not predominant. Robert Fludd's *Philosophia Moysaica* (1638), Henry More's *Conjectura Cabbalistica* (1653), and Ralph Cudworth's *The True Intellectual System of the Universe* (1678) contained very sympathetic accounts of "Hebrew wisdom." Fludd maintained that "moysaic philosophy" should not be measured by the yardstick of Greek *sophia* but vice versa.[8] Within this context, Philo's thought marks the transition point between the Hebrew wisdom of *philosophia hebraeorum* and a Greek- and Platonic-influenced "Judaica Philosophia"[9] beginning with Aristobulus and Philo.

Against this backdrop, eighteenth-century historiography came to divide preChristian thought into a *philosophia graecanica* and a *philosophia extra-graecanica*, the latter being again subdivided into a *philosophia hebraeorum* and a *philosophia barbarorum*.[10] On a systematic level, philosophy was divided into an inductive *philosophia empirica* (following the *lumen revelationis*) and a deductive *philosophia scientifica* (following the *lumen rationis*).

---

[4] T. Stanley, *The History of Philosophy* (London: Humphrey Moseley and Thomas Dring, 1655); Latin translation: *Historia philosophiae* (Leipzig: Thomas Fritsch, 1711).
[5] G. Horn, *Historia philosophica* (Lyon: apud Johannem Elsevirium, 1655), 126.
[6] Horn, *Historia philosophica*, 227.
[7] *Historia philosophica*, §23, 88.
[8] R. Fludd, *Philosophia Moysaica* (Gouda: Petrus Rammazenius, 1638), fol. 6r.
[9] H. More, *Conjectura Cabbalistica*, in *Henrici Mori Scriptorum Philosophicorum* (London: J. Martyne and G. Kettilby, 1679), 552.
[10] Ch. A. Heumann, *Acta philosophorum* (Halle: Rengerische Buchhandlung, 1715), 1:472.

Clearly, Philo's nimbus as a "true" philosopher drew on his aura as a Platonic "Moses Alexandrinus," inspired by the "Moses Atticus": Plato. This view, however, was not shared by all. Since at least Johann Franz Budde's claim that Philo could not be counted among the Platonists,[11] the Platonic currents in Philo's thought were scrutinized with a hermeneutic of suspicion. We find an echo of this suspicion in Johann Jacob Brucker's (1696–1770) endeavor to write the first "complete history of Jewish Philosophy."[12] The fourth volume of his *Kurtze Fragen aus der philosophischen Historie* (1734) discusses the "philosophy of the Patriarchs" as well as Philo's thought. But it lets "Jewish Philosophy" "according to a Greek method"[13] begin not with Philo but with Saadia Gaon, i.e. in the ninth century CE. Ultimately, the lores of Jewish philosophy were not "brought into a formal shape before Saec. XII [i.e. the twelfth century]."[14]

This, however, seems at odds with Brucker's conclusion that "Philo adopted the entire system of Plato *idealisticum, Mosi supponati* and explained the creation of the world according to this [method]."[15] The contradiction is mitigated by the fact that Brucker assumes he has found, not in Philo's Pythagoreanism but in his purported materialism, a decisively anti-Platonic strand of thought: "According to Philo's concept the world was not created by GOD insofar as his goodness required it but insofar as the powers of matter allowed him to create."[16] The positive aspect of Brucker's rejection of Philo's Platonism seems to be that he instead stresses the originality of Philonic thought, which was able "to derive the Studium Allegoriae from Judaism"[17] alone.

This, again, seemed to have led—according to a number of eighteenth-century historians of philosophy—to an ambivalent dynamic of thought: In the wake of Philo, his *studium allegoriae* divided Jewish thought into a *philosophia hebraeorum aperta* and a *philosophia hebraeorum mystica*, the latter of which emerged, as these historians claim, with the *Sefer Yetzira* in the second century CE after Philo. The bad reputation of Kabbalah and Jewish mysticism in the eighteenth-century historiography of philosophy appears to have further obscured the reception of Philo for a long time. Brucker and others, however, invented at least a specific line of interpretation that was, for better or worse, predominant for the next two centuries: Philo's thought was and is the first real synthesis of reason and revelation—be it a flawed agglomeration or a successful combination of biblical exegesis and philosophical reasoning.

Against the backdrop of these distinctions, it is plain to see why Philo's philosophy had been accorded an epoch-making historical place within this outline. His Middle Platonism bridges the gap between *philosophia graecanica* and *philosophia hebraeorum*; in creating a *philosophia judaeorum* which entails not only the

---

[11] J. F. Budde, *Introductio ad historiam philosophia ebraeorum* (Halle: Orphanotrophium Glavcha-Halensis, 1702), 101.
[12] J. J. Brucker, *Kurtze Fragen aus der philosophischen Historie*, 9 vols (Ulm: Daniel Bartholomai und Sohn, 1734), 4:2.
[13] Brucker, *Kurtze Fragen*, 4:b3.
[14] Brucker, *Kurtze Fragen*, 4:511.
[15] Brucker, *Kurtze Fragen*, 4:357.
[16] Brucker, *Kurtze Fragen*, 4:358.
[17] Brucker, *Kurtze Fragen*, 4:354.

philosophical interpretation of scripture but includes an approach that takes the Tanak to contain in itself a specific philosophy in an allegorical garb, Philo tries to reconcile reason and revelation, or in Hegel's words: Philo's philosophy presents "Plato in Moses."[18] Within this context of the Enlightenment historiographical discourse, the place of Philo's philosophy remained to be discussed controversially.

26.2 δεύτερος θεός? Philo's Binitarianism

Following the mainstream of eighteenth-century historiography while at the same time going against the grain,[19] Harry Austryn Wolfson went so far as taking Philo as the first and most influential turning point in the history of philosophy in general: "What is new in Philo?" he famously asked in concluding his seminal two-volume work on *Philo* (1929). Wolfson's answer: "Everything." And what is principally new after Philo up to early modernity? "Nothing." It is with Spinoza's philosophy that the Philonic synthesis of philosophy and scripture is denounced.[20] Wolfson detects four radically new philosophical conceptions in Philo: his principles "radically change its [i.e. Greek philosophy's] theory of knowledge, by introducing to it a new source of knowledge; they radically change its metaphysics, by introducing a new conception into the nature and causality of God, who is the main subject of metaphysics; they radically change its physics, by introducing a new conception into the working of its laws; they radically change its ethics, by introducing a new source of morality."[21]

What was so "new" or "revolutionary" in Philo, according to Wolfson, is obviously Philo's synthesis of "Plato and Moses," especially in his conception of Logos theology, forming an implicit heretical binitarianism. The term Jewish "binitarianism,"[22] used by Daniel Boyarin,[23] names a specific tenet of rabbinic theology in the first centuries BCE and CE. Within its tenet of thinking, special emphasis is given to the theological discussions and disputes over the interpretation of God's creative word. As Alan Segal, Darrell Hannah,[24] and Daniel Boyarin have pointed out, the rabbinic and para-rabbinic Memra-theology, already appearing in the Aramaic translations of the Hebrew Bible, conceive of God's Word (*memrah*) as a hybrid power: as a separate force belonging to God while at the same time producing something that is utterly distinct and remote from him. Within "first-century Judaism," which not only absorbed Middle

---

[18] Hegel, *Vorlesungen über die Philosophie der Religion*, Sämtliche Werke, ed. H. Glockner (Stuttgart: Fromann-Holzboog, 1927–39), 15:19.
[19] See D. T. Runia, "History of Philosophy in the Grand Manner: The Achievement of H. A. Wolfson," *Philosophia Reformata* 49 (1984): 112–33.
[20] See H. A. Wolfson, *Philo: Foundations of Religious Philosophy in Judaism, Christianity, and Islam*, 2nd edn (Cambridge, MA: Harvard University Press, 1948), 2:456.
[21] Wolfson, *Philo*, 2:456.
[22] See B. G. Bucur, "'Early Christian Binitarianism': From Religious Phenomenon to Polemical Insult to Scholarly Concept," *Modern Theology* 27.1 (2011): 102–20.
[23] See D. Boyarin, *Border Lines: The Partition of Judeo-Christianity* (Philadelphia: University of Pennsylvania Press, 2004).
[24] See D. D. Hannah, *Michael and Christ: Michael Traditions and Angel Christology in Early Christianity* (Tübingen: Mohr Siebeck, 1999), 80.

Platonic elements but produced its own variant of Middle Platonism, this necessarily led to the question as to whether there might be "two powers in heaven."[25] Although this lore of the "two powers in heaven" was quickly suspected as heretical by the rabbinic authorities,[26] they could not explain away that the concept of a divine power of speech-act has to take into account the specific dialectics of a divine word being "separate from but [at the same time] *homoousios* with God."[27] Boyarin concludes that "The Gospel of John ... when taken together with Philo and with the Targum, provides further important evidence for Logos theology, used here as a general term for various closely related binitarian theologies, as the religious Koine of Jews in Palestine and the Diaspora."[28]

From this one could infer that within the many religious trends in late antiquity, Logos theology (in its manifold confessional variations) provided an intermediate figure serving as a missing link between a creative and absolute power and that which is created by his productive word. One could argue that it was as religiously revolutionary as it was philosophically necessary to establish a Logos theology within which the creative word was not simply a power to prevent the absolute from coming into direct contact with matter but within which this word materializes itself and irreducibly delivers this creative power to the world and matter.

According to seventeenth- and eighteenth-century historiography, Philo's Logos theology seems to stand exactly at the crossroads of this development. Philo clearly distinguishes a divine Logos from the human *nous* in order to harmonize his terminology with that of the Septuagintal use of Logos.[29] Within his Middle Platonic system, Philo locates the Platonic ideas, the *kosmos noētos*, which the world consists of, exactly *in* the divine Logos: "even so the universe [κόσμος] that consisted of ideas would have no other location [τόπος] than the Divine Reason [τὸν θεῖον λόγον], which was the author of this ordered frame" (*Opif.* 20). In stark contrast to that which it creates, the divine Logos is "incorruptible" (ἄφθαρτος) (*Conf.* 41) and "eternal" (ἀίδιος) (*Plant.* 18). At the same time, however, the Logos rests *in* the world. That is the background of Philo's decisive step of *personalizing* the Logos. He terms the Logos "high priest," symbolizing that the immaterial Logos of the intelligible world is nevertheless also the immanent Logos of the physical world. Obviously, Philo needs a remarkable semantic extension of the notion "logos" in order to display the Logos as an instrument of world-making (*Leg.* 3.96), as a means to reign over the world (*Agr.* 51), and as a medium of revelation (*Legat.* 99).

Already eighteenth-century historians such as Budde, Brucker, and Buhle came to think that while all these metaphors or allegories might still be in accordance with some heretical trends in first-century rabbinic theology, Philo's radical interpretation of the

---

[25] See A. F. Segal, *Two Powers in Heaven: Early Rabbinic Reports about Christianity and Gnosticism* (Leiden: Brill, 1977).
[26] D. Boyarin, "The Gospel of the Memra: Jewish Binitarianism and the Prologue to John," *HTR* 94 (2001): 243–84, here 254.
[27] Boyarin, "The Gospel of the Memra," 259.
[28] Boyarin, "The Gospel of the Memra," 260.
[29] See Wolfson, *Philo*, 2:253.

Logos as God's "daughter" or "son" poses the question of whether he overstretches his metaphorical semantics. *Sophia* is Philo's Greek term for the Jewish Law, *halakha* (הלכה); and since God is the father of the *sophia*, she can be termed his "daughter" (*Fug.* 50–52). What is more complex, though, is that Philo seems to found the Jewish Law in the world on a cosmic law which he personifies in an ideal and archetypal human being which he terms a "copy of the divine image [μίμημα θείας εἰκόνος]" (*Opif.* 25) or even the first-born "son" (υἱός) (*Agr.* 51; *Deus* 298).

Boyarin thus asks if Philo might already be on the "way to Damascus"[30] and how his Logos theology can be related to the Johannine Logos. This is precisely the question seventeenth- and eighteenth-century historians of philosophy posed. Thus, given the contemporary Memra theology in (para-)rabbinic first-century Judaism, it seems apt to suppose that Philo wrote for an educated Hellenistic Jewish audience for which Logos theology was a "virtual commonplace."[31] This audience could not have been shocked by a lore which postulates the Logos as an essential yet separate part of God; it could have been shocked only by a theology that postulates the Logos as a personified "second god" (δεύτερος θεός) (*QG* 2.62).

In sum, Philo's philosophy, namely his Logos theology, seems to blur clear-cut distinctions that seventeenth-, eighteenth-, and nineteenth-century philosophical historiography had invented. Among these distinctions are the difference between *philosophia graecanica* and *extra-graecanica*, between *philosophia barbarorum* and *philosophia hebraeorum*, and between *philosophia christiana* and *philosophia judaeorum*. The idea of its taxonomy is central to the rather quiet but deeply influential scientific revolution that takes place in seventeenth- and eighteenth-century European scholarship: the invention of a continuous philosophical tradition from antiquity to early modernity. Historiographical holism aimed at nothing less than establishing a universal historical order of philosophical traditions and at construing (or reconstructing) an unbroken chain of *philosophia perennis*. In search of philosophical ideas, arguments, and connections, all the older narratives, myths, and texts of eastern and western traditions are sieved, evaluated, and canonized. This is the context within which Philo's writings were re-evaluated.

26.3 Philo's *Philosophia Judaeorum*: Six Historiographical Topoi

The Philonic synthesis of scripture and Platonic philosophy with its productive yet provocative and highly ambiguous Logos theology caught the attention of seventeenth- and eighteenth-century philosophers and historians of philosophy. It led to a number of legends, commonplaces, and topoi, all of which were relevant to the further reception of Philo. Among these topoi are the following:

---

[30] Boyarin, *Border Lines*, 114.
[31] Boyarin, *Border Lines*, 249.

1. *First Jewish philosopher*: Philo and Aristobulus (of the latter we have only a smattering of first-hand testimonies)[32] are the first Jewish thinkers deserving the name "philosopher." This is generally considered to be due to the fact that Philo's philosophy had to be studied in the framework of Platonism. Already at this point, however, the historiographical disputes start: whereas Budde, Brucker, and others argue that the Philonic synthesis proves the "corruption"[33] of the *philosophia graecanica* by Jewish philosophy, others claim that the "Jewish concepts of religion" are "ennobled by the spirit of Greek philosophy."[34] Both conclusions (one seemingly negative, the other seemingly positive), however, rest on the very same negative premise—that Jewish religion is "trübe" (*turbid* or *gloomy*)—with two possible consequences: it either depraved Greek thought or had to be ennobled by it.

The assumption of Philo being the first Jew who was a "real" philosopher did not go undisputed, though. Budde and others took Moses and the patriarchs as genuine Hebrew philosophers in a broad sense so that Philo's philosophy would be but a different strand of *philosophia hebraeorum*. To the present day, however, the prevailing interpretation is that of Philo as the first Jewish philosopher.

2. *Plato Alexandrinus* and *Moses Atticus*: The Platonist subtext of Philo's philosophy of the *kosmos noētos* was taken as proof of its philosophical relevance by a number of seventeenth- and eighteenth-century historians of philosophy. In their interpretation, Jonsen and others refer to the patristic "encomium": ἢ Φίλων πλατωνίζει, ἢ Πλάτων φιλωνίζει: "either Philo platonizes or Plato philonizes."[35] Here, a specific twist comes into eighteenth-century interpretation of Philo. The first half-sentence is as clear as the second half-sentence seems puzzling. Why should Plato be "philonizing"? This is to be explained by the fact that in eighteenth-century "orientalism," the oriental and Hebrew wisdom is seen not only as a distorted and gloomy wisdom of the past but also as the first and purest wisdom ever. This is the notorious *ex oriente lux* topos.[36] Friedrich Ast, who coined the term "orientalism" in his 1807 *Grundriss der Geschichte der Philosophie*, emphasizes that "the Greek world, just like the Christian world, is an offspring [*Sprösslinge*] of the oriental wisdom [*Bildung*]."[37]

Within this Enlightenment historiography, we find the idea that *in nuce* all wisdom is already there from the beginning; the history of thought is simply unfolding this primordial *Bildung*. Part of the oriental wisdom is the Hebrew wisdom. From this, as Justin Martyr and Clement of Alexandria speculated,[38] Greek philosophy was informed by oriental wisdom, with the result that Platonism is prefigured in biblical

---

[32] For the extant *testimonia*, see C. R. Holladay, ed., *Fragments from Hellenistic Jewish Authors*, Vol. III: *Aristobulus* (Atlanta: Scholars Press, 1995).
[33] Budde, *Introductio ad Historiam Philosophiae Ebraeorum*, §18, 54.
[34] E. Reinhold, *Lehrbuch der Geschichte der Philosophie* (Jena: Friedrich Mauke, 1839), §157, 255.
[35] J. Jonsius, *De Scriptoribus Historiae Philosophicae Libri IV*, 2nd edn (Jena: apud Viduam Meyerianam, 1716), III.4:14.
[36] See H. Zedelmaier, *Der Anfang der Geschichte: Studien zur Ursprungsdebatte im 18. Jahrhundert* (Hamburg: Felix Meiner, 2003).
[37] F. Ast, *Grundriss der Geschichte der Philosophie* (Landshut: Joseph Thomann, 1807), 17.
[38] Justin Martyr, *1 Apol.* 59; Clement of Alexandria, *Strom.* 6.7.57, 2–3. See G. G. Stroumsa, *Barbarian Philosophy: The Religious Revolution of Early Christianity* (Tübingen: Mohr Siebeck, 1999), 57–84.

thought. From this it is inferred that the philosophy of the Bible not only predates Plato's thought but also influenced it. Plato is a "Moses Atticus" just as Philo is a "Plato Alexandrinus" whose thinking is already prevalent in the oriental wisdom which influenced Plato. Astonishingly enough, quite a number of eighteenth-century philosophers subscribe to this rather dubious patristic interpretation of Philo.

3. *Philo's synthesis of Torah and (Platonic) Philosophy as a paradigm of philosophia perennis*: Just as two hundred years later in Harry Austryn Wolfson, the Enlightenment historiography of philosophy detects a new *Gestalt* of philosophy from Philo's works. The reconciliation of scripture and philosophy, of reason and revelation, seems to be a "role model" for later attempts at harmonizing religion and philosophy. Here, Philo's Platonic nobilitization of Jewish religion corrects—as the Kantian Wilhelm Gottlieb Tennemann (1761–1819) puts it—the "oriental imagination"[39] of Judaism. Tennemann argues that this, however, could have alienating consequences for both sides. While Philo "secretly introduces Platonic ideas into the Hebrew wisdom," he at the same time contaminates the "Platonic system with oriental philosophems."[40] Dietrich Tiedemann (1748–1803), in contrast, is very positive: Philo succeeded in grounding the religious truths of fact in philosophical truths of reason ("zuletzt auf Vernunftgründe").[41] Eighteenth-century camps of philosophy are obviously divided, but the Philonic synthesis of *philosophia orientali* and *philosophia graecanica* remains a philosophical challenge—for better or worse.

4. *Philo Christianus*: Much of seventeenth- and eighteenth-century historiography is occupied with the *Philo Christianus* legend, which is mainly due to Philo's Logos philosophy. Unsurprisingly, the fact that Philo was a contemporary of Jesus sparked the imagination of seventeenth- and eighteenth-century philosophers, theologians, and historians. Surprisingly, we find little speculation as to whether Philo and Jesus met, but it is speculated that Philo met the other "radical"[42] Judeo-Christian theologian in Rome: Paul. Since Philo was part of a Jewish delegation that spoke to Emperor Caligula around 40 CE, this is at least historically possible. More interest was shown, however, to the parallels in Logos philosophy, especially Philo's binitarianism. Already the Cambridge Neoplatonist Henry More insisted that Philo's concept of the Logos clearly prefigures the personalization of Christ as a *theanthrōpos*. The same theological parallels led Brucker to his speculation "as to whether John, the evangelist, must have read Philo's writings, borrowed the word λόγος from him, and brought Philo's incorrect thoughts in a good and orthodox order?"[43]

In the context of eighteenth-century historiography's distinction of four religio-philosophical trends in first-century Judaism (the Pharisees, the Sadducees, the

---

[39] Tennemann, *Grundriß der Geschichte der Philosophie* (Leipzig: Johann Ambrosius Barth, 1829), §73, 53.
[40] Tennemann, *Grundriß der Geschichte der Philosophie*, §197, 204.
[41] D. Tiedemann, *Geist der spekulativen Philosophie* (Marburg: in der Neuen Akademischen Buchhandlung, 1793), 3:138.
[42] See D. Boyarin, *A Radical Jew. Paul and the Politics of Identity* (Berkeley: University of California Press, 1994).
[43] Brucker, *Kurtze Fragen*, 4:509.

Essenes, and the Therapeutae), Philo is taken to be one of the Therapeutae whereas Jesus is regarded as an Essene.[44] There are speculations, however, that Philo could have belonged to an Essene sect of Proto-Christians.[45]

5. *Philo's rationalism as a floodgate*: Within eighteenth-century historiography, Jewish mysticism and rabbinic scholasticism belong to the most criticized trends in the history of human thinking. Philo's allegorical-hermeneutical Platonism is seen not only as a precursor of Christian philosophy but also as a kind of dam or floodgate against mystic and Kabbalist trends of Philo's own tradition. This is seen to be proved by the fact that since Philo's writings remained without influence on the *philosophia hebraorum*, in the course of the second-century CE rabbinic dogmatism and Jewish mysticism grew strong (again) and seemed to prevent any serious philosophical enterprise within Judaism. Philo's philosophy marks a demarcation line within the Jewish tradition and divides it into *philosophia aperta* and *philosophia mystica*. The very early dating of the *Sefer Yetzira* (second century) and the *Zohar* (which is dated as early as the third century CE)[46] fit into this picture: as soon as the Philonic floodgates opened, mysticism poured into the *philosophia hebraorum*. This brings us to the last topos.

6. *Philo's double exile*: Philo's philosophy had little impact on later Jewish philosophy. Neither Saadia nor Maimonides nor Crescas seem to have read Philo. From this, Budde, Heumann, Brucker, and others infer that the extinguished "candle" of "posttalmudic" oriental philosophy had to be lit again by Arab and Judeo-Arabic philosophy in the ninth century.[47] The fact that Philo's philosophy had been forgotten by his own tradition thus forms the topos of a double exile. Not only is Philo's pseudo- or proto-Christianity exiled from the "real" *philosophia christiana* (which he influenced heavily), he is in fact also exiled by his very own people who "discarded" him—or in Manuel Joël's expression from the end of the nineteenth century: they see him primarily as the "church father of the Church Fathers."[48]

In sum: within seventeenth- and eighteenth-century historiography of philosophy, Philo's philosophy was taken to be (1) the dividing line between *philosophia orientalis* and *philosophia judaeorum*; and (2) the dividing line between the *philosophia hebraorum* of the patriarchs and rabbinic theology and a Hellenic strand of *philosophia judaeorum*. It was also taken to be (3) the missing link between the *philosophia judaeorum* and the *philosophia christiana* of the church fathers by providing a (not always sound but fruitful) first genuinely philosophical synthesis of scripture and philosophy, revelation and reason.

---

[44] See Buhle, *Geschichte der neueren Philosophie*, 9 vols (Göttingen: Johann Friedrich Röwer, 1796–1805), 1:620.
[45] See Heumann, *Acta philosophorum*, 3:503–29.
[46] See Brucker, *Kurtze Fragen*, 4:400.
[47] Budde, *Introductio ad Historiam Philosophiae Ebraeorum*, §30, 114: "Cum vero in media ista nocte apud Arabes nova lux philosophiae bonarumque artium oriretur, Iudaei quoque sibi non defuerunt, sed certatim ad studia literarum tractanda sese accinxerunt."
[48] M. Joël, *Beiträge zur Geschichte der Philosophie* (Breslau: H. Skutsch, 1876), 2:31.

26.4 The Philonic Distinction: German Idealism (Hegel, Schelling)

26.4.1 Hegel

Compared with the historiographies of his time, Hegel introduces a different approach to Philo's philosophy in his late 1820s *Lectures on the History of Philosophy*. Instead of simply discarding the former principles of eighteenth-century historiography and its order of discourse, Hegel maintains that he discovered the very foundation of all the different hermeneutic principles in the systematic "discovery of the conceptions of the Absolute."[49] This pattern guides Hegel's account of Jewish philosophy. He, then, first and foremost examines the Jewish conception of the Absolute. The Jewish God, he argues, belonged "only to Abraham and to his seed"; he was an "exclusive One,"[50] that is, he is pure *identity*: "Before him all other Gods are false."[51] To this, Hegel objects that "the distinction between true and false is quite abstract since it forgets to acknowledge that a ray of light even shines into the false Gods."[52]

According to Jan Assmann, the "Mosaic distinction"[53] created the cycle of the "counter-religion" in western history, in which one religion's belief system is "truth" while all others are false. Hegel, by contrast, says: "However erroneous a religion may be, it possesses truth, although in a mutilated phase [sic]."[54] For him, this is the key to the understanding of the history of philosophy as well. Whereas the historiography of the Enlightenment argued on the basis of a "Mosaic distinction," where some philosophical traditions are false (and therefore excluded) and others are true (and hence included), Hegel calls for an inclusive pattern. He emphasizes that no step in the intellectual development of human knowledge should be regarded as superfluous or simply wrong. Instead, it contains some of the truth while other truths are still waiting to be discovered.

With this alethic realism in mind, Hegel attributes a second intellectual advancement to Jewish philosophy and religion: Judaism discovered the subjectivity of the One substance. Jewish thought was not the only one to introduce the idea of the One. But whereas the Platonic and Neoplatonic *to hen* is impersonal and beyond human knowledge, Jewish thought invented a personal One: "It is precisely this subjectivity that constitutes this progress as compared with Persian religion: the Persian power of light is an impersonal unity, that which is One, while the Jewish God is personal, he who is

---

[49] G. W. F. Hegel, *Encyklopädie der philosophischen Wissenschaften, Gesammelte Werke*, ed. W. Bonsiepen and H.-C. Lucas (Hamburg: Meiner, 1992), 9:11.
[50] Hegel, *The Philosophy of History*, trans. T. Knox (Chicago: Encyclopedia Britannica, 1952), 246.
[51] Hegel, *The Philosophy of History*, 246.
[52] Hegel, *The Philosophy of History*, 246.
[53] See J. Assmann, "The Mosaic Distinction: Israel, Egypt, and the Invention of Paganism," *Representations* 56 (1996): 48–67; see also Assmann, *Moses the Egyptian. The Memory of Egypt in Western Monotheism* (Cambridge, MA: Harvard University Press, 1998).
[54] Hegel, *The Philosophy of History*, 246.

One."⁵⁵ This formula—"Der Fortschritt gegen die persische Lichtreligion ist eben diese Subjektivität: Die persische Lichtmacht ist nur Eines, der jüdische Gott ist Einer"⁵⁶—is obviously difficult to translate into English, as the English definite article has no grammatical gender and cannot mark the difference between "that which is" and "he who is" One. With his formulation, however, Hegel obviously refers to the Greek conception of *to hen*. In the *Parmenides*, Plato states that the One is an absolute identity we cannot name, or define, or know, or grasp (*Parm.* 142a). Naming, defining, etc. a priori mean to apply difference to something which is above all difference.

To a certain extent, this also holds true of the notion of the Jewish God who is unnameable, undefinable, unknowable. But unlike the neuter Greek *hen*, the Jewish One is a personal God (and the Hebrew language has no neuter gender), so that the subjectivity of personalization, as Hegel termed it, can be traced back to the very roots of the Greek language (used by the Jewish philosophers Aristobulus and Philo) and is the move from *to hen* to *ho heis*. Philo and Numenius also speak of *to on* and *ho ōn*. If this progress from the impersonal *to hen* to the subjective *ho heis* is an achievement of Jewish thought, how would the Jewish philosophers then solve the implicit logical problem, namely the question of how the transcendent One who, as Plato said, is "beyond being" (*epekeina tēs ousias*) can be related to the world of being? How can this transcendent identity produce difference (the world) without becoming different in itself? Hegel's argument against the Neoplatonists (who held an emanation theory) is that it cannot. A *principle of difference* had to be introduced into the world of thought (since it was already there in the "real" world). And this (principle of) difference, Hegel claims, is the Logos: the creating and acting word of God that becomes another person. With regard to Assmann's "Mosaic distinction" between true and false religion we might term this principle the "Philonic distinction" relating to an identity of identity (self) and difference (other) within the monotheistic conception of god.

Hegel makes quite a remarkable claim here. He gives the *philosophia hebraeorum* the credit for introducing the concept of a self-identical absolute One while at the same time giving the *philosophia judaeorum* the credit for introducing an identity-distinguishing Logos into the realm of monotheism. Philo's Logos-philosophy implemented a difference, an inner dualism into monotheism itself. This implies further that even before the Christian Logos came, the *philosophia judaeorum* had formulated the philosophical principle of the second period in the history of philosophy:

> Thus, ... in Philo the ὄν [being] is the first, the inconceivable, the uncommunicative, unnameable, ἀμέθεκτος God; likewise with a number of Neoplatonists. The second is the Logos, especially the νοῦς, the self-revealing, self-emerging God, the ὅρασις θεοῦ [the form/vision of God], the σοφία, λόγος, then the archetype of humanity, this man

---

⁵⁵ Hegel, "The Lectures of 1831 (Excerpts)," in *Lectures on the Philosophy of Religion*, ed. P. C. Hodgson (Berkeley: University of California Press, 1987), 2:721–60, at 739.
⁵⁶ Hegel, "Religionsphilosophie (1831)," in *Vorlesungen über die Philosophie der Religion*, ed. W. Jaeschke (Hamburg: Meiner, 1985), 1:611–48, at 625.

who is the impress of the heavenly and eternal revelation of the hidden Godhead—
φρόνησις, Chokma.⁵⁷

Hegel lays stress on the fact that Philo—even before Jesus, let alone Christian philosophy, had made their appearance—termed the Logos the "Son of God"⁵⁸ and introduced a conception of difference, the "Philonic distinction," into the concept of the absolute as identity. Only with this move could Philo bridge the gap between the concept of God as the absolute One (a concept Hegel terms as "abstract" or "deficient" [*mangelhaft*])⁵⁹ and God as a living God.

In this respect, Hegel anticipated some of the questions discussed in current research. Maren Niehoff⁶⁰ and Daniel Boyarin have shown how Logos theology had been an important current in pre-Christian Jewish thinking. Boyarin has also emphasized that Philo's philosophy perceived the Logos (or *memra* in Aramaic) as a substance of its own, whence a binitarian structure would have been attributed to the Jewish God. Boyarin, then, attacks those scholars who believe that Philo used the word Logos (or *memra*) as just another name for the transcendent God himself:

> It seems not to have occurred to any who hold this view that it is fundamentally incoherent and self-contradictory. Surely, this position collapses logically upon itself, for if the Memra is just a name that simply enables avoiding asserting that God himself has created, appeared, supported, saved, and thus preserves his absolute transcendence, then who, after all, did the actual creating, appearing, supporting, saving? Either God himself, in which case one has hardly "protected" him from contact with the material world, or there is some other divine entity, in which case the Memra is not just a name.⁶¹

Boyarin makes the same point that Hegel made. With his "binitarianism," Philo introduced the concept of another Logos as a second person, created by the father (i.e. identical with him) but at the same time independent from (and thus nonidentical with) him. According to Hegel's implicit argument, it was not Christian but Jewish philosophy that made the difference in late antique thinking. Philo is, as Hegel says, "Plato in Moses,"⁶² i.e. he combines both worlds: *philosophia graecanica* and *philosophia hebraeorum*.

While Hegel gives much attention to Philo's philosophy, he depicts medieval Jewish thought as a "noteworthy" but by and large obsolete trend. This is not primarily due to a lack of medieval erudition, but to a theoretical argument about the principle: Hegel refuses to see any major progress with regard to the development of a new "Prinzip"

---

⁵⁷ Hegel, *Lectures on the Philosophy of Religion*, 3:84.
⁵⁸ Hegel, *Vorlesungen über die Geschichte der Philosophie* (Berlin: Duncker and Humblot, 1835; repr. Stuttgart: Fromann-Holzboog 1959), 15:22.
⁵⁹ Hegel, *Vorlesungen über die Geschichte der Philosophie*, 23.
⁶⁰ M. Niehoff, "What Is in a Name? Philo's Mystical Philosophy of Language," *JSQ* 2 (1995): 220–52.
⁶¹ Boyarin, "The Gospel of the Memra," 253.
⁶² Hegel, *Vorlesungen über die Philosophie der Religion*, Sämtliche Werke XV, 19.

(which would have been the principle of the identity of difference, the "Philonic distinction"). This is why he claims that the medieval Jewish thinkers all in all remained on the epistemic level of Philo and the fathers of the church. As Hegel repeatedly parallels the Jewish thinkers with the fathers, we notice that he is not intending to link the development of thought primarily to a certain form of religion but to the unfolding of a triadic set of principles of which the "Philonic distinction" is the second. Within this process the abstract substance (God as the identical *substratum* of endless attributes) became a concrete subject (God as a self-revealing mind that produces and reproduces itself through the attributes).

26.4.2 Schelling

Schelling's reception of Philo has to be situated within the late conceptions of his "philosophy of revelation." Here, Philo's thought plays a crucial role in the conception of the different "potencies" of the theogonic dynamics which Schelling believes he has found as a fundamental pattern in humanity's (intellectual) history. The threefold dialectic method by which he construes all known mythologies and the revelations of the Old and New Testament as a theogonic process in which the Absolute reproduces itself through an absolute self-contraction leads to number of religious-philosophical distinctions. In his Munich lectures on the *Philosophy of Revelation* (1831/32), he describes his method as follows: the theogonic process should be made detectable "from the nature of the principles that are effective in this process and that are demonstrable in the historically developing mythologies of the different nations. Of these mythologies one can show that they are the moments of the same proceeding development."[63]

Schelling thus construes a number of triadic yet "successive potencies"[64] by which the *real* aspect and the opposing *ideal* aspect translate into a third aspect which encompasses all previous ones. Within the theogonic super-triad—polytheism, theism, monotheism—Schelling's historiographical architecture of the earlier theogonic process includes Philo's writings. They are, he argues, to be taken as witnesses of the lore of Christ's pre-existence in all of the theogonic stages. Whereas Greek mythology is the synthesis of Egyptian and Indian mythology, Schelling construes Christianity as a synthesis of Judaism and gnosticism. For this Christocentric account, he is interested in Philo's conception of the "Urvernunft"— Schelling's specific translation of Philo's semantics of Logos. Schelling insists that the Philonic use of Logos has no predecessor in "Alexandrian philosophy" and he ponders, "how could John [the evangelist] assume that his readers were familiar with Philo's writings ... which were not very

---

[63] F. W. J. Schelling, *Urfassung der Philosophie der Offenbarung*, ed. W. E. Ehrhardt (Hamburg: Meiner 1992), 239 (Lecture 34).
[64] Schelling, *Philosophie der Offenbarung 1841/42*, ed. M. Frank (Frankfurt am Main: Suhrkamp 1993), 270 (Lecture 25).

widespread … ?"[65] For Schelling, Philo's conception of the Logos is crucial with regard to the understanding of what he calls the "second potency" of the theogonic process of revelation: the "demiurgic personality"[66] of the Absolute which is personified in the Logos: "For Philo, the λόγος was the divine intellect, stepping between God and the world, so that he could exempt God as much as possible from contact with the world. Philo, however, never speaks of the λόγος in absolute terms, instead he calls him ὁ θεῖος λόγος or θεοῦ λόγος, but this expression was not at all used in Alexandrian philosophy."[67] The *novum* of Philo's Logos semantics, however, could also be derived from the Old Testament, Schelling insists. From this use, not from Philo, John gained his Logos-conception: "The Hebraic word *davar*, דבר, equates to the Greek λόγος which [in the Prologue to John] designates the subject and the object."[68]

From his exegesis of the epistles of Peter and Paul as well as the Gospel of John, Schelling then gains a threefold structure of monotheistic principles. First, there is the Petrine distinction of ground, order, and reality, which is the principle of the Roman church;[69] second, the Pauline distinction of freedom, sedition, and secession, which constitutes the principle of Protestantism;[70] third, the Johannine principle which will constitute the ecumenical church yet to come.

The second theogonic aspect with regard to which Schelling has to refer to Philo's writings is the question as to whether the Mosaic laws were communicated through angels, "as the New Testament states … or directly by God. Philo makes a big effort to prove this."[71] It seems Schelling's overall purpose is to distinguish the Middle Platonic Jewish from the gnostic conception of the "demiurgic personality" and both from its Christian interpretation. This is due to his systematic idea that the history of world religions and philosophies has to be interpreted as humanity's coming-to-its-self-consciousness. This process, he claims, was shaped by the mythological and religious narratives it had to undergo.

In sum: among the German idealists, Hegel and Schelling were interested in the Philonic distinction (and conception) of reason and revelation, theogonic person and demiurgic personality, substance and subject of the Absolute. Hegel reads Philo as one of the founders of an interpretation of the wandering spirit of the Absolute in that he created an early, pregnant, albeit flawed synthesis of philosophy and scripture *as well as* a Philonic distinction between the Absolute and the personified absolute Word different from him—all culminating in the distinction between God and Logos, substance and subject, principle and person within the One in itself.

---

[65] Schelling, *Urfassung der Philosophie der Offenbarung*, 462 (Lecture 56).
[66] Schelling, *Philosophie der Offenbarung 1841/42*, 271 (Lecture 26).
[67] Schelling, *Philosophie der Offenbarung 1841/42*, 271.
[68] Schelling, *Urfassung der Philosophie der Offenbarung*, 469 (Lecture 57). Schelling's thesis seems echoed in Boyarin's interpretation that the prologue to John can be interpreted as a kind of midrashic commentary to Gen 1:1; cf. Boyarin, *Border Lines*, 128–47.
[69] Schelling, *Urfassung der Philosophie der Offenbarung*, 692 (Lecture 82).
[70] Schelling, *Urfassung der Philosophie der Offenbarung*, 709 (Lecture 83).
[71] Schelling, *Urfassung der Philosophie der Offenbarung*, 665 (Lecture 79).

26.5 Philo and Jewish Hegelianism (Hirsch, Krochmal, Formstecher, Hess)

Historically almost parallel to the emergence of the *Wissenschaft des Judentums*,[72] a certain (anti-)Hegelian current of Jewish philosophy arose between 1830 and 1850—a strand of thinking which could be termed "Jewish Hegelianism,"[73] alluding to Emil Fackenheim's characterization of Samuel Hirsch.[74] The Jewish Hegelians—by no means a coherent group—did not simply seek to refute Hegel's apparently negative view of Jewish thought. They made, quite to the contrary, a daring attempt at reconciling the Jewish history of philosophy with the logotectonic construction of history provided by Hegel's history of philosophy as well as his philosophy of history.

From a systematic stance, such a Hegelian-anti-Hegelian reformulation of the history of philosophy would have to demonstrate (1) that Jewish philosophy is not the obsolete *philosophia hebraeorum* whose history was portrayed by the eighteenth-century historians of philosophy in an all too one-dimensional way, but that it has historical continuity to it as well as a philosophical potential as yet inexhausted; and (2) that this is so precisely *because* Jewish philosophy took part in the general shift from substance to subject metaphysics, as Hegelians would term it. It was indeed these two points that the Jewish Hegelians—Nachman Krochmal (1785–1840), Samuel Hirsch (1815–89), Salomon Formstecher (1808–89), and Moses Hess (1812–75)—sought to substantiate.

Krochmal sets out, in his *More Nevuhke ha-Zman* (1840/51), the *Guide of the Perplexed of the Modern Age*, to argue against Hegel that Jewish thought, in contrast to other religious or mystico-philosophical manifestations of "oriental" thought, has never disappeared. Judaism still exists, as does Jewish philosophy, which not only has a vivid, philosophically productive past and present to offer but also has a relevant future ahead of it. This move against Hegel is based explicitly on Hegel's logical terminology of the *Science of Logic*.[75] Krochmal's reception of Philo has to be situated within this context.[76] Whereas Philo's philosophical reasoning seems to be often rather "poor"[77] and his biblical exegesis "inept," Krochmal sees in Philo, or *Yedidya*, as he calls him, an important wise man (*maskil*) and decisive 'platonizer' of the rabbinic lore: "We have to take into account that in his [Philo's] mind, Platonism was the predominant issue and the extant legends of the Jewish theologians are, more or less, to be taken as allegories of

---

[72] Cf. Görge K. Hasselhoff, Chapter 29 in this volume.
[73] For a detailed analysis, cf. D. Westerkamp, *Die philonische Unterscheidung: Aufklärung, Orientalismus und die Konstruktion der Philosophie* (Munich: Fink, 2009), 145–90.
[74] Cf. E. Fackenheim, "Samuel Hirsch and Hegel," in Fackenheim, *Jewish Philosophers and Jewish Philosophy*, ed. M. L. Morgan (Bloomington: Indiana University Press, 1996), 21–40.
[75] N. Krochmal, *More Nevuchim ha-Zman*, ed. Leopold Zunz (Lemberg, 1851), ch. 16; German translation: *Führer der Verwirrten der Zeit*, trans. and ed. A. Lehnhardt, 2 vols (Hamburg: Meiner 2012), 2:659–82. See J. M. Harris, *Nachman Krochmal: Guiding the Perplexed of the Modern Age* (New York and London: New York University Press, 1991).
[76] Cf. R. Goetschel, "Philon et le Judaïsme hellénistique au miroir de Nachman Krochmal," in *Hellenica et Judaica. Hommage à V. Nikiprowetzky*, ed. A Caquot et al. (Leuven and Paris: Peeters, 1986), 371–83.
[77] N. Krochmal, *The Writings of Nachman Krochmal*, ed. S. Rawidowicz, 2nd ed. (Waltham, MA: Ararat, 1971), 175 (in Hebrew).

the Platonic ideas."[78] For Krochmal, Philo's method of allegorical interpretation is to be honored as the only way to avoid the *aporiai* of the exegetical materialism to which the literal interpretation of the Tanak leads as well as the *aporiai* of the exegetical idealism to which the interpretation of those who think that the "facts of revelation" are just "empty vessels of human ideas"[79] leads.

An adherent of Krochmal, "disciple of Spinoza," and left-wing Hegelian, Moses Hess also followed closely the trail of Hegel's philosophy of history but amalgamated it with a Judeo-political messianism in his *The Holy History of Mankind* (1837). In rather orthodox Hegelian terminology, he observes that the "schism of mankind" persisting since the days of the destruction of the Second Temple could only be redeemed by a new Jerusalem and a universalistic, inclusive "religion of truth" which were to become the foundation of a future union of nations.[80] It is interesting to see, however, that Philo of Alexandria does not seem to play any role in this historical process and is absent in Hess' main writings.

This is different in Samuel Hirsch's seminal *Die Religionsphilosophie der Juden* (1842), perhaps the only "classic" of Jewish Hegelianism. Here, Hirsch depicts the future as a time when a universalistic, "absolute religiousness" will reign and confessional differences lose their importance. In order to allow this to happen, however, the spiritual and systematic differences have to be brought to light; they have to be *cleared* in the double sense of the word (clarified and erased). In his construction, Hirsch distinguishes the "passive religiosity" of paganism from the "active religiosity" of both Judaism and Christianity, the latter being "extensive" and the former being "intensive." The reconciliation of both, provided by the "absolute religiousness" (a Hegelian term), will in the end reconcile "Israel with the world."[81] Further than Krochmal and Hess, and in an endeavor to underpin Krochmal's findings, Hirsch argues that the tendency to subjectivize the Absolute—a tendency reserved by Hegel for the philosophy of a Christian heritage—is no less alive in Jewish philosophy. Hegel's achievement in the *Science of Logic*, i.e. the explication of the Absolute as absolute subjectivity, has been anticipated according to Hirsch in the "absolute philosophy" of the Jews. To dismiss the habitual association of Jewish thought with substance metaphysics, Hirsch takes several steps. One of them is to rehabilitate Philo's subject-philosophy of the Logos. Philo's thought, however, seems to be both a blessing and a curse since the critics of Judaism (such as Hegel, Schelling, and others) seem to paint their picture of Judaism primarily from Philo's writings, while in reality his thinking informs but the margins of Jewish tradition.

The benefit of Philo's thought for the work of historical and spiritual reconciliation Hirsch hopes for is implied in the contiguity of his Logos theology to that of John. It

---

[78] Krochmal, *Führer der Verwirrten der Zeit*, 1:426.
[79] Krochmal, *Führer der Verwirrten der Zeit*, 1:427.
[80] M. Hess, *Die heilige Geschichte der Menschheit: Von einem Jünger Spinoza's* (Stuttgart: Hallbergische Verlagshandlung, 1837), 339–42.
[81] S. Hirsch, *Die Religionsphilosophie der Juden oder das Prinzip der jüdischen Religionsanschauung und sein Verhältnis zum Heidenthum, Christenthum und zur absoluten Philosophie* (Leipzig: H. Hunger, 1841), §79, 879.

is, according to Hirsch, Pauline theology that laid grounds for the partition of Judeo-Christianity into Judaism and Christianity. Paul, not John, "sets Christianity in strict opposition to Judaism" insofar as he "transfers Christianity from the real into a transcendent world."[82]

Hirsch unambiguously subscribes to Hegel's condemnation of pure substance metaphysics as a method of "simple negativity."[83] In a second step he proceeds undauntedly to define Jewish philosophy as the interpretation of an Absolute which is not substance but also not only a subject, but rather trinitarian as well. The explosiveness of his statement is by no means defused by the touch of irony with which he presents it: "The Hegelians think what a shame it must be for the Jews not to have a trinitarian God. But—Gentlemen!— the Jewish God is trinitarian in the Hegelian sense. And this is so because we believe in him as in a living God. We do not believe in him as in an Indian Brahma, or a Persian Zeruane Akrene, or an Egyptian Reith, nor even do we believe in him as we would in a Greek *fatum*."[84] Hirsch thus keeps faithfully to the successive stages in Hegel's construction of religious history: China, India, Buddhism, the Persian religion of light, Egypt, and Greece. But, like Krochmal, he detaches the Jewish religion from "oriental" thinking and shows it to be a historical as well as transhistorical "moment" (as Hegel would put it), i.e. a factor existing in each and every epoch in the development of the absolute spirit or mind. The same goes for Jewish philosophy which, to the Jewish Hegelians, is no longer the *philosophia hebraeorum* of old to be subsumed under the *philosophia extra-graecanica* and banished to the prehistory of philosophy, but on the contrary is the *only* thinking which in *all three* periods—the period of substance (identity of God), the period of the Logos (difference), and the period of the spirit or mind (identity of identity and difference)—was able to vitally contribute to the definition of the Absolute.

Similar to Hirsch's "absolute religiousness," Salomon Formstecher in his *Die Religion des Geistes* seeks to carve out the primordial distinctions of paganism, Judaism, and Christianity. His argument is dependent on Hegel insofar as he tries to prove that Judaism is the true and real "religion of spirit [*Geist*]" and that Philo, though introducing the first philosophically sound concept of divine subjectivity (and thus at one with Hegel's construction), nevertheless has a deficient notion of subjectivity, i.e. an "objective" one. This is due to its Platonic materialism (an echo of Brucker's thesis). With Plato's "ethical God" embedded in its foundation, Philo's writings present but "a pagan theory in a Jewish garb."[85] Accordingly, Philo's "theosophy" is charged by Formstecher for being an "unorganized syncretism" which he, as a reform rabbi,[86] finds typical for "the lack of character of an epoch which broke with its ancient form but did not create a new, modern one, yet."[87]

---

[82] Hirsch, *Die Religionsphilosophie der Juden*, §69, 750.
[83] Hirsch, *Die Religionsphilosophie der Juden*, §72, 821.
[84] Hirsch, *Die Religionsphilosophie der Juden*, §72, 796.
[85] S. Formstecher, *Die Religion des Geistes: Eine wissenschaftliche Darstellung des Judenthums nach seinem Charakter, Entwicklungsgange und Berufe in der Menschheit* (Frankfurt am Main: J. C. Hermann, 1841), ch. XII, 280.
[86] Cf. B. Kratz-Ritter, *Salomon Formstecher: Ein deutscher Reformrabbiner* (Hildesheim: Olms, 1991).
[87] Formstecher, *Die Religion des Geistes*, ch. XII, 280.

In Formstecher's view, Philo's Memra theology is the symbol of syncretism between a pagan-Platonic conception of the Absolute and Jewish midrash. It pays tribute to the pagan need of visibility of the Absolute but only insofar as this Absolute reveals himself in a sensual, yet not visible medium: language. As a specific power (*dynamis*), Philo's God:

> is the organic synthesis between the hidden, unrecognizable God and the material world, so that he can be determined as a visible God. This *dynamis*, flowing into God, is his creating word (λόγος, ממרה) which, in his function as God's messenger ..., forms the material world into wisdom (σοφία). In this sense, Dynamis, Logos, Angelos, and Sophia determine one and the same being according to its relations.[88]

According to Formstecher's interpretation, the decisive step of Judaism could not be made already by the Philonic distinction and the "subjectivization" of the Logos. The Philonic distinction may be the *agens* but not the *telos* of Jewish tradition. Its mission, Formstecher argues, consists in the removal of all oriental and pagan elements in monotheism;[89] or in positive terms, in the spiritualization and liberalization of humanity. "The very essence of Judaism is: the realization of the ideal of the good; its character is: maintaining the opposition against paganism."[90] This can't be achieved through Philonic syncretism, but at least the "Philonic Distinction" leaves the choice either (1) to accept it, or (2) to fall behind it, or (3) to overcome it. According to Formstecher, Christianity made the first, Islam the second, and Judaism the third decision.[91]

As seems clear, then, Philo's Logos theology and the "Philonic Distinction" played a decisive role in this attempt at overcoming a historical formation marked by a Christocentric historiography. Logos theology, the Enlightenment, orientalism, and Jewish emancipation together constituted the context of Jewish Hegelianism and its reformulation of a *philosophia judaeorum*. The Jewish Hegelians' situation was far more precarious than that of the secular Young or "left wing" Hegelians, and there can be little wonder that it proceeded from and produced conflicting motives. On the one hand they rehabilitated their own descent from "Jewish philosophy" in order to wrench it away from the negative judgment pronounced by the Enlightenment historiographies and Hegel's history of philosophy, and to be able to appropriate it for themselves. On the other hand, they remained closely tied to Hegel's construction of a philosophy and religion of the absolute spirit or mind because, as Samuel Hirsch put it in 1841, "the left camp of Hegelian philosophy," by criticizing Christianity, threatened Judaism as well.[92]

The Jewish Hegelians protested against Hegel's derogation of the (post-)Philonic Jewish philosophy but not against his principle-theoretical construction of epochs. Furthermore, they saw a common origin in the rabbinic, Philonic, and Johannine

---

[88] Formstecher, *Die Religion des Geistes*, ch. XII, 281.
[89] Formstecher, *Die Religion des Geistes*, ch. XIII, 449.
[90] Formstecher, *Die Religion des Geistes*, ch. XIII, 449.
[91] Cf. Formstecher, *Die Religion des Geistes*, ch. XIII, 407.
[92] Hirsch, *Die Religionsphilosophie der Juden*, §62, 623

"doctrine of the logos"[93] and deferred the bifurcation of confessional paths to a relatively late date. Thus, in the first two "post-Christian" centuries, a "binitarian" Logos theology developed whose Hellenistic, Jewish rabbinic, and Christian components could not be separated but by force; and it was only with the emergence of a rabbinic and a patristic orthodoxy that the subsequent developments of thought and belief gradually parted ways.

In sum, two arguments that are central to but only implicit in the texts of the Jewish Hegelians Krochmal, Hess, Hirsch, and Formstecher can be made explicit: (1) Hegel's principle-theoretical construction of the history of philosophy and religion supports the creation of a Jewish philosophical tradition in its own right because the principle Hegel postulates for the second epoch—the presence of the divine Logos as identical with and at the same time different from the absolute—is not peculiar to Christianity but can be seen instead as an innovation introduced by Jewish theologians and philosophers around the beginning of the Common Era. (2) This step enables the *philosophia judaeorum* to be detached from the context of a purely "oriental" thinking and be acknowledged as a lively tradition of modernity as well. The Jewish Hegelians seem to have fully accepted the implicit consequence of Hegel's account, namely that the "Philonic distinction" becomes the watershed between "oriental" and "non-oriental" thinking. On the basis of the argument that the categories of difference, spirit or mind, and subject(ivity) are not extraneous to Jewish thought; Judaism—in the words of Salomon Formstecher—can be reconstructed as an absolute "religion of spirit"[94] and thereby lay claim to a title denied to it by Hegel, who bestowed it exclusively on Christianity.

26.6 Outlook: Philo in German strands of *Religionskritik* (Feuerbach, Bauer, Strauss)

The general critique of religion (which in its criticism of Christianity, according to the Jewish Hegelian Samuel Hirsch, threatened Judaism as well) is the latest historical context within which the reception of Philo in German philosophy between 1650 and 1850 can be placed. In Ludwig Feuerbach's *The Essence of Christianity* (1841), chapters 8–9 on "the secret of the Logos" and the "world-creating principle in God" have a distinct Philonic subtext. Feuerbach's assumption that "the second person, as it is the self-revealing, uttering, itself expressing God (*Deus se dicit*) is the world-creating principle in God"[95] draws on Philo's expression of the *dynamis kosmopoiētikē* in *Opif.* 21. For Feuerbach, this Judeo-Christian idea of the world-creating language of God on which humans depend simply mirrors one of the most fatal religious ideas, since it precludes language from conversation and communication between human beings and instead

---

[93] Hirsch, *Die Religionsphilosophie der Juden*, §68, 706.
[94] Formstecher, *Die Religion des Geistes*, ch. IX, 99.
[95] L. Feuerbach, *Das Wesen des Christentums*, ch. 8, in *Gesammelte Werke*, ed. W. Schuffenhauer (Berlin: Akademie, 1967), 1:162.

projects or transposes *their* creating powers onto an abstract anonymous deity. The linguistic powers of the supernatural Logos of this deity usurps the universal structure of conversation as an interpersonal relation between a real 'You' and a real 'Me'. Against this theological interpretation of the Logos, the *Religionskritik*, critique of religion, has to restore the *anthropological* interpretation of human conversation.

Referring to Philo's and Paul's expression of the Logos as "an image of the father," Feuerbach interprets the principle of the Logos as an abstract "image of reason" which, as a mere simulacrum, becomes a spiritual illusion that substitutes reality. For him, this is the—literally—"non-sensical"[96] essence of all religion. Hence, reason can never be an "image" but only a product of communication between real persons or the result of conversation of humanity (as the *Gattung*) with itself. Philosophically, Feuerbach's critique of Logos theology and its "secret of the Logos" demands a "reversion" of the theological conception of language and imagination to an anthropological one. Hermeneutically, Feuerbach is immersed in a theological and philological discussion carried out by Jewish Hegelians as well as the *Wissenschaft des Judentums* and the "Tübinger Schule" of theology: the debate on the filiations between Jewish and Christian interpretations of Logos theology with regard to the question of the emergence of Christianity or the "Urchristentum."

This crucial nexus is extensively discussed by Bruno Bauer, David Friedrich Strauss, and the "Tübinger Schule" in terms of a historical-critical hermeneutics of the Bible. Against Strauss, Bauer asserts the descent of Christian thought and theology from Jewish Alexandrian philosophy and hermeneutics and calls Philo the "very father of Christianity."[97] To this view those Jewish theologians and philosophers, like Salomon Formstecher and Salomon Ludwig Steinheim, for whom the integration of Philo into the camp of Judaism seemed to be much too difficult and uncomfortable, could not help but subscribe. Perhaps Steinheim borrowed his expression that Philo "is the true father of the *Logos-Lehre* and, with it, of the very first Christian church (*der urchristlichen Kirche*)"[98] from Bruno Bauer.

For Jewish Hegelians, some critical Christian theologians, and the Young Hegelian critics of religion alike, it seems clear that in Philo's writings Jewish rabbinic, (Middle) Platonic, Stoic, and gnostic currents of thinking are amalgamated into a complex, puzzling, even murky synthesis which already contains all the (proto-)Christian conceptions which formed "Urchristentum." In his eulogy for Bruno Bauer, Friedrich Engels summarizes with consent: "One sees only the keystone is yet missing and the whole of Christianity is already present in its basic outlines: The incorporation of the Logos becoming flesh in a specific human being and his expiatory sacrifice on the cross in order to redeem sinful mankind."[99]

---

[96] Feuerbach, *Grundsätze der Philosophie der Zukunft* (1843), in *Gesammelte Werke*, 9:301.
[97] Cf. B. Bauer, *Kritik der evangelischen Geschichte der Synoptiker*, 2 vols (Leipzig: Otto Wigand, 1841).
[98] S. L. Steinheim, *Die Offenbarung nach dem Lehrbegriffe der Synagoge*, 4 vols (Frankfurt and Altona: Siegmund Schmerber, et al., 1835–65), 4:178.
[99] F. Engels, "Bruno Bauer und das Urchristentum" (1882), in *Marx Engels Werke* (Berlin: Dietz, 1962), 19:297–305; 300.

26.7 Conclusion

Within German philosophy between 1650 and 1850, Philo of Alexandria figured as the first Jewish philosopher. Early Enlightenment philosophical historiography discovered his thought as a leading model for the reconciliation of reason and revelation, of philosophy and scripture. Since his writings seemed to belong neither to the *philosophia hebraeorum* nor to the *philosophia barbarorum*, they were considered a puzzling monolith within the history of philosophy. Both historically and systematically, Philo's thought was perceived by German Philosophy as caught between different stools: Plato and the church fathers, Rabbinic Judaism and Johannine Logos, early Kabbalah and Hellenistic syncretism. In Philo's writings, eighteenth- and nineteenth-century German philosophy—particularly Hegel, Schelling, and the Jewish Hegelians—found a philosophical Pandora's box. They were more than willing to open it.

V

FROM THE EIGHTEENTH TO THE TWENTIETH CENTURIES

27
The Rise of New Testament Criticism

David Lincicum

Among the corpora of ancient texts that have survived from the period of Jewish and Christian origins, Philo's oeuvre is only rivaled by Josephus for breadth and variation. Given the erudition of those who have sought to make sense of the New Testament, it is only natural that Philo should take a position of honor among the possible comparanda invoked to illuminate the New Testament. The task of this chapter is not to investigate the question of whether the authors of the New Testament had direct knowledge of Philo's writings, or reflect indirectly the influence of his thought,[1] but rather to investigate the patterns of engagement with Philo by New Testament scholars over the past several centuries. There can be no question of doing justice to the full complexity of Philo's reception in this sprawling tradition. This essay will focus on the development of New Testament scholarship from the mid-eighteenth century to the mid-twentieth century, particularly in German, English, and to a lesser extent in French, and will draw on illustrative examples that together indicate shifting questions posed to Philo in service of the interpretation of the New Testament and the closely related project of constructing Christian origins.

In accord with the broad historicization of European thought, theologians and scholars increasingly attempted to achieve a historical view of the New Testament's circumstances of origin. To do so, they looked to Philo, among other ancient figures, to construct the *Umwelt* of the early Christian movement. The comparative enterprise born from this historicist impulse still dominates large portions of New Testament scholarship today.[2] Philo is looked to as a product of the encounter of Judaism (often viewed in orientalizing terms) and Hellenistic philosophy, who provided a sort of *praeparatio evangelica* in anticipating the universalizing impulses of Pauline literature, the Platonizing impulses of Hebrews, and the philosophical synthesis of the Johannine literature and subsequent Alexandrian Christian theologians. At the same time, the history of scholarship attests a flurry of disagreement about Philo's proper role in the study of the New Testament: is he our best exponent of the type of Greek-speaking Judaism that gave rise to the Christian movement's first flourishing, or rather a syncretistic thinker whose scriptural exegesis is marred by Platonic intrusions and so can only serve as a foil to the literature collected in the New Testament?

---

[1] See T. Seland's essay in this volume.

[2] This is not to claim that New Testament scholarship has an absolute beginning in the eighteenth century, since the roots of contemporary philological approaches go back to at least the Renaissance; see J. H. Bentley, *Humanists and Holy Writ: New Testament Scholarship in the Renaissance* (Princeton: Princeton University Press, 1983).

27.1 The Comparative Turn in the Study of the New Testament

Even before the eighteenth century, in the learned days of the Republic of Letters, erudite scholars—"the last Europeans who could plausibly claim that they were masters of their entire civilization"[3]—amassed extensive selections from ancient classical texts and set them alongside the New Testament. The so-called *Observationes* literature attempted to shed light on obscure or difficult turns of phrase or historical phenomena by adducing parallels from ancient literature.[4] In this quest for understanding, Philo became an important source. For example, in the learned *Annotationes in Novum Testamentum* by the versatile Dutch jurist Hugo Grotius (1583–1645), Philo is often invoked to illustrate a lexical usage or shed light on a historical question. In commenting on Matt 4:23, Grotius poses the question whether *proseuche* and synagogue refer to the same thing, and resolves his question by adducing Philo's usage in *Legat.* 156 to demonstrate their equivalence.[5] Or again, Philo is invoked in elucidating John 1:1–3, as a mediator of the Platonic concept of the *logos* to the Fourth Gospel.[6]

A series of treatises throughout the eighteenth century took up the comparative project and sought to marshal Philo's texts in order to facilitate comparative understanding of the New Testament. For example, in 1728 Johannes Albert, then a minister still a dozen years away from his Leiden professoriate, assembled a list of several dozen parallels between New Testament texts and Philonic *loci*, presenting them with brief comment in canonical order from Matt 6:34 to Rev 19:9.[7] In greater detail, the German classical philologist C. F. Loesner worked selectively but sequentially from Matt 1:1 through Rev 22:18 in over five hundred pages, supplying parallels with brief commentary.[8]

This comparative work came to a notable expression in two works in the mid-eighteenth century. In 1750, Johann Benedict Carpzov IV published, in 664 pages of closely argued text, his *Sacrae exercitiationes in S. Pauli Epistolam ad Hebraeos ex Philone Alexandrino*.[9] After an initial discussion of various Philonic problems, Carpzov, who sees himself carrying on the work of the *Sacra parallela* tradition, proceeds sequentially through Hebrews from 1:1 to 13:13, adducing parallels and comparanda along the way, often at the level of grammatical or lexical similarity. On the basis of this work, Carl Siegfried called the Helmstedt philologist the "leading Philonist of

---

[3] A. Grafton, *Worlds Made by Words: Scholarship and Community in the Modern West* (Cambridge, MA: Harvard University Press, 2009), 9.

[4] See esp. L. M. White and J. T. Fitzgerald, "Quod est comparandum: The Problem of Parallels," in *Early Christianity and Classical Culture: Comparative Studies in Honor of Abraham J. Malherbe*, ed. J. T. Fitzgerald, T. H. Olbricht, and L. M. White, NovTSup 110 (Leiden: Brill, 2003), 13–39.

[5] H. Grotius, *Annotationes in Novum Testamentum*, 9 vols (Groningen: W. Zuideman, 1826–34), 1:79–80.

[6] Grotius, *Annotationes in Novum Testamentum*, 4:8.

[7] J. Albert, "Annotationum philologicarum in Novum Testamentum ex Philone Judaeo collectarum specimen," in *Museum Historico-Philologico-Theologicum* 1.1 (Bremen: H. Jaeger, 1728), 104–26.

[8] C. F. Loesner, *Observationes ad Novum Testamentum e Philone Alexandrino* (Leipzig: A. F. Boehmium, 1777); cf. A. F. Kühnius, *Spicilegium Christophori Friderici Loesneri observationum ad Novum Testamentum e Philone Alexandrino* (Pforten: E. C. Benek, 1785).

[9] Helmstadt: Weygand, 1750.

his day."[10] A year later saw the appearance of the first volume of the Swiss theologian Johann Jakob Wettstein's *Novum Testamentum Graecum*, which furnished numerous parallels to illustrate the language and ideas of the New Testament.[11] In Wettstein's *Index auctorum veterum*, Mangey's edition of Philo appears not under *Judaeorum*, but under *Graecorum & Latinior. Philosophorum*. Many of these parallels seem to function, once again, at the more narrowly lexical or semantic level. As Wettstein says in his appended treatise, *De interpretatione*, "We learn the meaning of words and phrases chiefly from other passages of the same writer, then from other sacred writers, and from the translation of the seventy, and also from writers who lived about the same time or place."[12] Wettstein's comparative project outlived the usefulness of his edition of the New Testament, and found renewed expression in the late twentieth century in the "Neuer Wettstein" project.[13]

In 1831, the Marburg Reformed theologian Wilhelm Scheffer published a Latin treatise on the use of Philo in New Testament interpretation.[14] In it, he surveys the state of Judaism in the first century, including Philo in particular, attends to some specific exegetical cases, and canvasses different "uses" for Philo to shed light on the New Testament: *usus historicus*, *usus grammaticus*, *usus dogmaticus* (comparing Philo's concepts of, for example, φῶς or πνεῦμα), and *usus elocutorius* (scriptural interpretation). In the end, he suggests that there is an analogy between Philo and the New Testament according to τὸ γράμμα but not τὸ πνεῦμα.[15] Notable is the attempt to press beyond the mere assembling of parallels and the attempt to conceptualize different types of comparative projects.

In the converse side of the comparative project, Philo could also be used as a foil for the first Christians. For example, the German Rationalist theologian Johann August Ernesti, in a section of his famous treatise on biblical interpretation devoted to the "error of the Jewish expositors," speaks against the propriety of allegory. The German editor of the fifth edition, Christoph Friedrich von Ammon, suggests in a footnote that, "we find Paul after Philo, openly supporting the allegorical interpretation in Gal. iv.24," while the British translator of the work, Charles Terrot, adds his own note following this: "That Scripture may be properly interpreted, in a sense which we are well assured was never in the writer's mind, and that it has thus been interpreted by St. Paul *after Philo*, are fancies too revolting to common sense, and too directly opposed to all reverence for the word of God, to be readily received among us."[16] The debate within the pages of a single volume indicates varying levels of anxiety in seeing Philo as a close

---

[10] C. Siegfried, "Carpzov, Johann Benedict," *Allgemeine Deutsche Biographie* 4 (1876): 22–23.
[11] J. Wettstein, *Novum Testamentum Graecum*, 2 vols (Amsterdam: Ex Officina Dommeriana, 1751–52).
[12] *Novum Testamentum Graecum*, 2:878.
[13] G. Strecker, "Das Göttinger Project 'Neuer Wettstein,'" *ZNW* 83 (1992): 245–52; P. W. van der Horst, "Johann Jakob Wettstein nach 300 Jahren: Erbe und Anfang," *TZ* 49 (1993): 267–80; G. Strecker and U. Schnelle, eds, *Neuer Wettstein: Texte zum Neuen Testament aus Griechentum und Hellenismus* (Berlin: de Gruyter, 1996–).
[14] W. Scheffer, *Quaestionum Philonianarum*, part. 2: *De usu Philonis in interpretatione Novi Testamenti* (Marburg: Chr. Garthe, 1831).
[15] Scheffer, *De usu Philonis*, 55.
[16] J. A. Ernesti, *Principles of Biblical Interpretation*, 2 vols, trans. C. H. Terrot (Edinburgh: T&T Clark, 1832 [orig. 1792]), 1:22–24, italics original. Terrot adds, "Hebraisms to be interpreted by the aid of such authors as Philo and Josephus" (1:114–15).

comparandum of the early Christian literature. The blithe anti-Judaism of Philo's Christian interpreters often leads them to cast him as belonging to an erroneous background, as a foil against which early Christian truth stands out more clearly.

These works were produced under the spell, or at times the suspicion, of the comparative method that marked the early modern and Enlightenment periods.[17] But in certain ways, they establish the basic tasks that still occupy philological research today. In that sense, what Roy Gibson argues for classical Latin poetry is equally true for the New Testament: "Parallels are used, among other things, to support a reading in a text, to help construe the text, establish register, identify allusions/intertexts, and build a context for interpretation. In effect, parallel texts frequently constitute the bulk of the system within which the commented text is to be read."[18] Philo becomes an important part of the "system" in which the New Testament makes sense. The type of phenomenon Philo is adduced to explain varies; it may be "semantic, syntactic, connotative, conceptual, contextual—or simply one of similarity of content."[19] But in this period Philo is established as a central comparandum, whether as a foil or a point of similarity, for making sense of the New Testament.

27.2 Philo as Context and Source for the New Testament

In addition to Philo's importance as a point of comparison for linguistic parallels, Philo has been persistently associated with discrete parts of the New Testament. Certain features of the letters of Paul, the letter to the Hebrews, and the Gospel of John ensured that a healthy industry of analysis of the putative influence of Philo on the authors of the New Testament would remain busy for years to come.[20]

C. D. Yonge, the English classicist who also produced translations of Cicero, Diogenes Laertius, Athenaeus, and others, gave voice to this sentiment in the preface to the second edition of his translation of Philo's works, with a particular focus on the apostle Paul: "For the Christian reader these treatises have a peculiar interest from the ample materials which many of them furnish for the illustration of St. Paul's Epistles;

---

[17] See J. Z. Smith, *Drudgery Divine: On the Comparison of Early Christianities and the Religions of Late Antiquity* (Chicago: University of Chicago Press, 1990), esp. 1–53; J. Z. Smith, "In Comparison a Magic Dwells," in *A Magic Still Dwells: Comparative Religion in the Postmodern Age*, ed. K. C. Patton and B. C. Ray (Berkeley: University of California Press, 2000), 23–44, cf. 237–41; J. Z. Smith, "Adde Parvum Parvo Magnus Acervus Erit," *History of Religions* 11 (1971): 67–90.

[18] R. Gibson, "'Cf. e.g.': A Typology of 'Parallels' and the Function of Commentaries on Latin Poetry," in *The Classical Commentary: Histories, Practices, Theory*, ed. R. Gibson and C. Shuttleworth Kraus, Mnemosyne Supplements 232 (Leiden: Brill, 2002), 331–57, here 331.

[19] Gibson, "Typology of 'Parallels,'" 333.

[20] Note the bibliography of older titles on the theme assembled at G-G, 290–97. See also the excellent surveys in D. T. Runia, *Philo in Early Christian Literature: A Survey*, CRINT III/3 (Assen: Van Gorcum; Minneapolis: Fortress, 1993), 63–86; G. E. Sterling, "The Place of Philo of Alexandria in the Study of Christian Origins," in *Philo und das Neue Testament: Wechselseitige Wahrnehmungen. I. Internationales Symposium zum Corpus Judaeo-Hellenisticum 1.–4. Mai 2003, Eisenach/Jena*, ed. R. Deines and K.-W. Niebuhr, WUNT 172 (Tübingen: Mohr Siebeck, 2004), 21–52; F. Siegert, "Philo and the New Testament," in *The Cambridge Companion to Philo*, ed. A. Kamesar (Cambridge: Cambridge University Press, 2009), 175–209; P. J. Bekken, "Philo's Relevance for the Study of the New Testament," in *Reading Philo: A Handbook to Philo of Alexandria*, ed. T. Seland (Grand Rapids: Eerdmans, 2014), 226–67.

materials so copious and so valuable that an eminent divine of the present day has pronounced an opinion … that all the other ancient commentators on the Scriptures put together have not left works of greater value for that most important object."[21] Some readers of the Pauline corpus argued for direct dependence on Philo,[22] while most viewed any possible relationship as indirect or simply as due to both authors being representatives of Greek-speaking Judaism. Paul's exegesis has been a particular point of comparison with Philo.[23]

In a long "dissertation" in his commentary on the Pauline epistles, Benjamin Jowett, the Oxford divine and classicist, treated "St Paul and Philo."[24] He entertains the possibility that Philo might have met "our Lord" and that he could have done so on one of his pilgrimages to the Temple.[25] Paul, however, did not have direct contact with Philo, and Jowett suggests that the similarities between Philo on the one hand, and Paul and John on the other, are due to "the circumstances of their living in a common atmosphere and using a common language," where there was a "wide diffusion of the Alexandrian modes of thought."[26] Jowett is relatively dismissive of Philo. The Alexandrian is, in his estimation, "absolutely devoid of any historical sense of truth,"[27] he "adapts the words of Scripture to his own moral ideas,"[28] he entirely disregards the context of a passage of Scripture when he cites it,[29] he uses stock equivalences in his allegorical interpretation,[30] is ignorant of Hebrew,[31] "perpetually raises unmeaning questions, which he disposes of by still more unmeaning answers,"[32] and shows an extravagant interest in number symbolism.[33] At the same time, Philo supplies an important witness to a *logos* theology and a system of intermediaries, and one can point to a number of parallels between Philo and the New Testament, such as the invisibility of God, the role of angels in the giving of the law, the centrality of the Word,[34] the concept of creation, elements of his anthropology, and other such ideas.[35] Jowett rejects direct influence from Philo on Paul or other authors of the New Testament, but argues that Philo attests the form of

---

[21] C. D. Yonge, *The Works of Philo Judaeus, the Contemporary of Josephus, Translated from the Greek*, 2nd edn (London: George Bell & Sons, 1890), 1:vi; this paragraph is not in the 1st edn. Who the "eminent divine" might be is unclear.

[22] E.g. J. R. Harris, "The Influence of Philo upon the New Testament," *ExpT* 37 (1926): 565–66, argues that 2 Tim 3:4 might be considered a reference derived from Philo; S. C. Mott, "Greek Ethics and Christian Conversion: The Philonic Background of Titus II 10–14 and III 3–7," *NovT* 20.1 (1978): 22–48.

[23] H. Vollmer, *Die alttestamentlichen Citate bei Paulus* (Freiburg i.B. and Leipzig: Mohr Siebeck, 1895), 84–98 ("Das litterarische Verhältnis des Paulus zu Philo"); C. Siegfried, *Philo von Alexandria als Ausleger des alten Testaments an sich selbst und nach seinem geschichtlichen Einfluess betrachtet* (Jena: Hermann Dufft, 1875), 304–10; C. Toussaint, *L'Hellénisme et L'Apôtre Paul* (Paris: Ê. Nourry, 1921), 220–25.

[24] B. Jowett, *The Epistles of St. Paul to the Thessalonians, Galatians, Romans; with Critical Notes and Dissertations*, 2nd edn (London: J. Murray, 1859), 1:448–514. On Jowett, see P. Hinchliff and J. Prest, "Jowett, Benjamin (1817–1893)," *Oxford Dictionary of National Biography* (https://doi.org/10.1093/ref:odnb/15143).

[25] B. Jowett, *Epistles of St. Paul*, 454.
[26] B. Jowett, *Epistles of St. Paul*, 454 and 502.
[27] B. Jowett, *Epistles of St. Paul*, 459.
[28] B. Jowett, *Epistles of St. Paul*, 459.
[29] B. Jowett, *Epistles of St. Paul*, 460.
[30] B. Jowett, *Epistles of St. Paul*, 460.
[31] B. Jowett, *Epistles of St. Paul*, 460.
[32] B. Jowett, *Epistles of St. Paul*, 460.
[33] B. Jowett, *Epistles of St. Paul*, 461.
[34] B. Jowett, *Epistles of St. Paul*, 489.
[35] B. Jowett, *Epistles of St. Paul*, 495; cf. also 500.

Judaism that gave birth to the Christian movement: "Alexandrianism was not the seed of the great tree which was to cover the earth, but the soil in which it grew up."[36]

Other scholars have drawn much more contrast between Paul and Philo, particularly on the basis of a sharp division between Hellenistic and Palestinian Judaism. This dichotomy was perpetuated by scholars like Albert Schweitzer. The German-Alsatian scholar and polymath interestingly grants Paul's knowledge of Hellenistic Jewish thought,[37] but argues that Paul's letters show no influence of it: "Its problems, its speculations regarding the Logos, Spirit, and Wisdom, its ethics, do not interest him; he makes no use of its theories. On the other hand he is concerned with eschatology and with the person of the Messiah, which for it seem to have no existence."[38]

Hebrews' use of a teasingly similar set of terms (for example, ὑπόδειγμα, σκιά, ἀντίτυπος, εἰκών, πρᾶγμα, ἀληθινός), themes, and exegetical traditions signaled some possible relation to the Philonic corpus, and the question of Philonic influence on Hebrews was debated from the time of Grotius and Carpzov onward. The Göttingen biblical scholar J. D. Michaelis, who held that the letter was initially written in Hebrew and only subsequently translated into Greek, was emphatic that Hebrews was composed independently of Philonic influence: "for the opinion, that the author had ever read Philo, there is no ground whatsoever: since their mode of arguing on the same subject, and on the same passages of the Old Testament, is totally different."[39] In the mid-twentieth century, the Dominican Ceslas Spicq took advantage of the lack of a firm geographical location associated with the letter and famously contended that the author of Hebrews had met Philo, listened to him appreciatively, and drew directly on his work in the composition of the homily/letter,[40] on the one hand, while Ronald Williamson sought painstakingly to refute a view of such direct influence, on the other, calling attention particularly to the eschatological horizon of Hebrews that is largely lacking in Philo.[41]

One of the most striking points of possible confluence between Philo's writings and the New Testament is to be found in the Fourth Gospel's *logos* Christology. As is well known, Philo indulges in reflection on the nature and the roles of God's *logos*.[42] Already in the seventeenth century, the Remonstrant theologian Jean Le Clerc offered a paraphrase of the prologue to the Fourth Gospel, which began, "In the beginning was REASON, and that REASON was with GOD, and GOD was that

---

[36] B. Jowett, *Epistles of St. Paul*, 513.

[37] A. Schweitzer, *Paul and His Interpreters: A Critical History*, trans. W. Montgomery (London: Adam & Charles Black, 1912), 91: "the most probable assumption is that he was acquainted with the whole of the earlier and later Hellenistic literature. Whether this can be more or less clearly proven by certain real or supposed parallels does not really matter.... The important point is that he does not use the ideas which are here offered to him."

[38] Schweitzer, *Paul and His Interpreters*, 92.

[39] J. D. Michaelis, *Introduction to the New Testament*, trans. Herbert Marsh, 4th edn (London: Rivington, 1823), 4:244.

[40] C. Spicq, *L'épître aux Hébreux* (Paris: Gabalda, 1952–53), 1:39–91.

[41] R. Williamson, *Philo and the Epistle to the Hebrews*, ALGHJ 4 (Leiden: Brill, 1970); cf. K. L. Schenck, "Philo and the Epistle to the Hebrews: Ronald Williamson's Study after Third Years," SPhiloA 14 (2002): 112–35. L. D. Hurst's survey of possible backgrounds to Hebrews is still useful: *The Epistle to the Hebrews: Its Background of Thought*, SNTSMS 65 (Cambridge: Cambridge University Press, 1990).

[42] e.g. D. Winston, *Logos and Mystical Theology in Philo of Alexandria* (Cincinnati: Hebrew Union College Press, 1985).

REASON."[43] Le Clerc justified this translation by pointing to the influence of Philonic thought on John: "It is certain that all his [i.e. Philo's] Writings were published a long while before ever St. *John* wrote; and his eloquence is such, that he was justly had in admiration by all who lived in his time, and is still read by learned Men with great delight."[44] Le Clerc suggests that Philo was known and appreciated by early Christians because, among other things, he esteemed God as Father and described divine reason in terms that anticipate Christian doctrine, although where Philo makes the *logos* inferior to God, John asserts its fully divine status.[45]

A long series of treatises analyzing the relationship of the Philonic and Johannine concepts of the *logos* followed, together with investigations of other connections between the authors.[46] Analyses range from those who see the author of the Fourth Gospel as standing directly under Philonic inspiration to those who note their broad similarities without proposing channels of direct influence. For T. H. Green, the British idealist and student of Benjamin Jowett who was also tasked with lecturing on the New Testament, "The λόγος of the Fourth Gospel, as identified with the Person of Jesus, is of course infinitely different from the λόγος of Philo." The nature of that difference consists in the fact "that the relation between God and the Word, according to Philo, is not so much one of distinct persons in one substance, as that between substance and essence; in other words between unknown substance and cognizable qualities."[47] Others cashed out the nature of that relationship in varying ways. Alfred Loisy, remembered chiefly as a driving impulse in the Catholic modernist movement, suggests, in a section of his influential commentary on the Fourth Gospel detailing Philo's relationship to the evangelist, "Philo the Jew could never have reconciled the deification of Jesus with his own philosophy. But the idea of a Word subsisting in God, a mediator of creation, living synthesis and revelation of all truth, is nothing less than purely Alexandrian and Philonic."[48] Similarly, James Moffatt, the Glaswegian New Testament scholar, noting the commonalities between Philo and John, argued that "the most noticeable channel for this Alexandrian influence on the Fourth gospel ... is Philonism," and that the author of the Fourth Gospel had been "trained in the Philonic spirit."[49] Even if Moffatt also noted the differences between the two, he says that they "only bring out the latter's familiarity with the Philonic methods and materials which he uses for higher ends."

---

[43] J. Le Clerc, *A Supplement to Dr. Hammond's Paraphrase and Annotations on the New Testament* (London: Sam. Buckley, 1699), 157; cf. 157–86.

[44] Le Clerc, *Supplement*, 167 (italics original).

[45] Le Clerc, *Supplement*, 174.

[46] e.g. H. C. Ballenstedt, *Philo und Johannes oder fortgesetzte Anwendung des Philo zur Interpretation der Johannes Schriften, mit besonderer Hinsicht auf die Frage: ob Johannes der Verfasser der ihm zugeschriebenen Schriften seyn könne* (Göttingen: Heinrich Dieterich, 1812), esp. 11–45; F. Deletzsch [sic; read Delitzsch], "The Logos in John and Philo," *American Presbyterian and Theological Review* 2 (1864): 506–15; J. Réville, *La doctrine du Logos dans le quatrieme évangile et dans les oeuvres de Philon* (Paris: G. Fischbacher, 1881); W. E. Ball, "St. John and Philo Judaeus," *Contemporary Review* 73 (1898): 219–34.

[47] T. H. Green, "Lectures on the Fourth Gospel," in *Unpublished Manuscripts in British Idealism: Political Philosophy, Theology and Social Thought*, ed. C. Tyler (London: Thoemmes, 2005), 1:135–88, here 136–37 [orig. c.1877].

[48] A. Loisy, *Le Quatrième Évangile* (Paris: Alphonse Picard et Fils, 1903), 120; cf. 120–22.

[49] J. Moffatt, *An Introduction to the Literature of the New Testament* (Edinburgh: T&T Clark, 1911), 523 and 525 respectively.

More moderately, C. H. Dodd contends that the Fourth Gospel "presupposes a range of ideas having a remarkable resemblance to those of Hellenistic Judaism as represented by Philo," even if "the treatment of those ideas is indeed strikingly different."[50]

These works on Paul, Hebrews, and John are merely illustrative examples of the widespread urge to find parallels that might explain or at least illuminate the rise of the early Christian movement and its particular constellation of beliefs and practices.

27.3 From Analogy to Genealogy

In the late eighteenth and early nineteenth centuries, historicist impulses led increasingly to the project of reconstructing Christian origins, in addition to exegetical investigations of the text as such.[51] Philo is deployed more and more as a source for historical information about the state of pre-Christian Judaism, sometimes offering an anticipation of the putatively universalist impulses of the early Christian movement. In that sense, we see a noticeable shift from studies that consider Philo an important analogy to the New Testament, in matters linguistic or otherwise, to those that think of Philo as in some sense a genealogical predecessor of the early Christian movement that produced the New Testament.[52]

For the Berlin church historian August Neander, a Christian convert from Judaism, Philo stands as the prime example of Alexandrian Judaism and its deep interest in reconciling philosophical and scriptural thought through allegory. Ultimately, however, this philosophically inspired attempt at grasping the ultimate meaning of scripture falls short: within the Old Testament, Neander argues, "dwells a spirit enveloped under a form still more limited and more limiting than elsewhere, struggling towards a future revelation and development, whereby it was destined to be freed from this confinement"—i.e. struggling toward Christian revelation—but because Philo and his compatriots lacked this spirit, they were willing to succumb to "a foreign spirit ... borrowed from the Platonic philosophy."[53] Neander found in Alexandrian Jewish theology two basic elements: a "*mystico-rationalist* element, sprung from the influence of the Platonic philosophy on the Jewish theism; and a *supranaturalist* element, derived from the Jewish national spirit and education."[54] Depending on how these two factors

---

[50] C. H. Dodd, *The Interpretation of the Fourth Gospel* (Cambridge: Cambridge University Press, 1953), 73; cf. 54–73.

[51] S. Alkier, *Urchristentum: Zur Geschichte und Theologie einer exegetischen Disziplin*, BHT 83 (Tübingen: Mohr Siebeck, 1993); M. C. Legaspi, *The Death of Scripture and the Rise of Biblical Studies*, OSHT (Oxford: Oxford University Press, 2010); on the historicist turn more broadly, note also F. C. Beiser, *The German Historicist Tradition* (Oxford: Oxford University Press, 2011); G. Scholtz, "The Notion of Historicism and 19th Century Theology," in *Biblical Studies and the Shifting of Paradigms, 1850–1914*, ed. H. G. Reventlow and W. Farmer, JSOTSup 192 (Sheffield: Sheffield Academic Press, 1995), 149–67.

[52] To use J. Z. Smith's terms, we might refer to this as a shift from morphological to evolutionary models of comparison ("In Comparison a Magic Dwells," 27–28).

[53] A. Neander, *General History of the Christian Religion and Church*, trans. J. Torrey, 13th American edn (Boston: Houghton, Mifflin and Company, 1871 [German orig. 1825]), 1:54; on Neander's view of theological progress in history, see J. Bennett, "August Neander and the Religion of History in the Nineteenth-Century 'Priesthood of Letters,'" *Historical Journal* 63.3 (2020): 633–59.

[54] *General History*, 1:64, emphasis original.

combined, they might lead to one of two results: "either to secure a point of union for Christianity, or to call forth an opposition to it."[55] So Philo functions as a source of possible views preparatory for the Christian message, but must be handled with some caution.

A few years later, in 1829, in the midst of the work that would result in his *Philo und die judisch-alexandrinische Theosophie*, August Friedrich Gfrörer wrote to the great Tübingen theologian, Ferdinand Christian Baur, "There is no dogma in the New Testament, no proposition of Christian morality that does not find its parallel or explanation here! Love, faith, hope, detachment, from the flesh and the world are also the first virtues of these Alexandrians."[56] Gfrörer's work served as the preparation for his own *Kritische Geschichte des Urchristenthums*, and Leopold Cohn would later look back and suggest that Gfrörer was "less concerned in interpreting Philo himself out of his writings than in explaining the origin of Christianity from Philo."[57]

For his part, Baur invoked Philo as a prime instance of the synthesis of Jewish and Hellenistic ideals that prepared the way for the emergence of early Christianity.[58] Baur saw Philo and the Alexandrian tradition as putting aside "the limits of the old Jewish particularism," particularly through the allegorical interpretation of scripture that enabled a reconciliation of philosophical and scriptural ideas. As a result, for Baur, Alexandrian Judaism and its teachings:

> took on a greatly modified and generally freer and more spiritual shape. New ideas were introduced that came from a worldview completely different than that of Judaism; and in particular the Old Testament concept of God was raised far above all those elements that belonged merely to the limited sphere of Jewish theocracy. The profound influence that the Alexandrian philosophy of religion—in its highest and most elaborate form as it appears in the writings of Philo—later exercised on Christian theology is the clearest proof that the mode of thought on which it was based had great affinity with the spirit of Christianity.[59]

Baur's own idealistic philosophical inclinations clearly influence his evaluation, but he is not alone in understanding Philo as a significant predecessor to the early Christian movement. Baur's student, David Friedrich Strauss, accorded Philo a brief but structurally significant place in his notorious *Das Leben Jesu kritisch bearbeitet*. He viewed Philo as a notable precursor to the mythical style of interpretation Strauss found in the

---

[55] *General History*, 1:65.
[56] A. F. Gfrörer to F. C. Baur, 30 December 1829, in C. Hester, ed., *Ferdinand Christian Baur. Die frühen Briefe (1814–1835)*, Contubernium 38 (Sigmaringen: Jan Thorbecke, 1993), 79; Gfrörer's work was published as *Philo und die judisch-alexandrinische Theosophie*, 2 vols (Stuttgart: E. Schweizerbart's Verlagsbuchhandlung, 1831).
[57] L. Cohn, "The Latest Researches on Philo of Alexandria," *JQR* 5 (1892): 24–50, here 25.
[58] Note that Baur's son-in-law, Eduard Zeller, would go on to treat Philo's philosophical ideas at length: Cf. E. Zeller, *Die Philosophie der Griechen in ihrer geschichtlichen Entwicklung*, 3rd edn (Leipzig: L. F. Fues, 1881), 3:2.338–418.
[59] F. C. Baur, *Christianity and the Christian Church in the First Three Centuries*, ed. P. C. Hodgson; trans. R. F. Brown and P. C. Hodgson (Eugene, OR: Cascade, 2019), 19; cf. F. C. Baur, *History of Christian Dogma*, trans. R. F. Brown and P. C. Hodgson (Oxford: Oxford University Press, 2014), 59.

Gospels: "Many had prepared the way, but it was Philo who first fully developed the doctrine of both a common and a deeper sense of the Holy Scriptures."[60] Ernest Renan, in his best-selling *Vie de Jésus*, deemed Philo "truly the elder brother of Jesus."[61] Bruno Bauer, a radical Hegelian, went farther than both of them and declared Philo the true father of Christianity.[62]

The interpretation of Philonic thought as a *praeparatio evangelica* continued throughout the nineteenth century. In his own work on the historical Jesus, the mediating theologian Karl Theodor Keim urged that "A history of Jesus cannot pass over the man who, on account of the age in which he lived, and the great similarity and contrasts between him and Jesus, challenges comparison with the latter, even though it can be shown that the course of life of Jesus did not in any way come into contact with that of Philo."[63] Philo is "a man of fusion and reconciliation."[64] Keim, however, is not uncritical of Philo, and deems him "a forerunner of Jesus, though he did not know him, and was far from rising to his level."[65] But Philo "scattered seed in Judaism, the noblest grains of which bore fruit in Christianity,"[66] particularly in Paul, John, and the later Alexandrian church. Likewise, Otto Pfleiderer, Baur's last disciple, argued that Philo does not approach the theology of John, since he cannot conceive of an incarnation, but "Philo was a preparation for Christianity, in that he demanded of the Hellenistic Judaism of the Dispersion the spirit of individualistic, inward-turned piety and a universally broadened morality; therewith he blazed the way for an ethical-spiritual religion, based on monotheism, but freed from the limitations of Judaism."[67]

The great historians of early Judaism and Christianity continued to frame Philo with reference to the New Testament and early Christianity, well into the twentieth century. Emil Schürer, writing in an influential handbook that is still used today in revised form, argued that Philo's "strongest and most enduring influence was ... exercised, in a direction which still lay outside Philo's horizon, upon the development of Christian dogma. The New Testament already shows unmistakeable traces of Philonean wisdom."[68] In Adolf von Harnack's epochal treatment of *The Mission and Expansion of Christianity*, Philo appears, together with Josephus, as a flagship example of the tendency to depict Judaism as a philosophical religion, a direct anticipation of early Christian universalism and a factor that contributed significantly to the success of the early Christian mission.[69] F. J. Foakes Jackson and Kirsopp Lake, in their significant work on the Acts of

---

[60] D. F. Strauss, *The Life of Jesus Critically Examined*, trans. Maryann Evans [= George Eliot] (London: Chapman Brothers, 1846; repr. Philadelphia: Fortress, 1972), §3 (p. 41).
[61] E. Renan, *The Life of Jesus* (n.p.: Burt, 1863), 29.
[62] B. Bauer, *Philo, Strauss und Renan und das Urchristenthum* (Berlin: Gustav Hempel, 1874).
[63] K. T. Keim, *The History of Jesus of Nazara*, trans. A. Ransom, 2nd edn (London: Williams and Norgate, 1876), 1:280; cf. 276–96.
[64] Keim, *History of Jesus of Nazara*, 282.
[65] Keim, *History of Jesus of Nazara*, 296.
[66] Keim, *History of Jesus of Nazara*, 296.
[67] O. Pfleiderer, *Christian Origins*, trans. D. A. Huebsch (New York: B. W. Huebsch, 1906), 54–55.
[68] E. Schürer, *A History of the Jewish People in the Time of Jesus Christ*, 2nd edn, trans. J. Macpherson, S. Taylor, and P. Christie (Edinburgh: T&T Clark, 1898–1910), 2:3.381.
[69] A. von Harnack, *The Mission and Expansion of Christianity in the First Three Centuries*, trans. James Moffatt (London: Williams & Norgate, 1908), 1:11–12; cf. S. J. D. Cohen, "Adolf Harnack's 'The Mission and Expansion

the Apostles, describe Philo as "though in no sense Christian," nevertheless "the parent of much Christian terminology and even theology."[70] And Rudolf Bultmann calls attention to the significance of Philo as a central representative of Hellenistic Judaism, important for the evidence he supplies for the use of allegory and for the conception of the world as a cosmos with an attendant natural theology, although Bultmann laments his lack of a sense for the historical and any robust eschatology.[71]

27.4 The *Religionsgeschichtliche Schule* and Twentieth-Century Developments

Beyond the use of Philo in constructing the world that gave birth to the Christian movement, the twentieth century also sees the rise of what one might call "deep comparison," that is, the attempt to understand Philo on his own terms before bringing his thought into the project of making sense of the New Testament.

H. A. A. Kennedy complained in the early twentieth century about the attempt to find parallel ideas in Philo and the New Testament: "Such a task has frequently been attempted in one form or other, and it is doubtful whether it has led to important results. So much depends on the contexts of the passages singled out and the background against which they stand. And these are features of the situation which have usually been ignored."[72] In mid-century, Samuel Sandmel offered his famous warning against "parallelomania," which he defined as "that extravagance among scholars which first overdoes the supposed similarity in passages and then proceeds to describe source and derivation as if implying literary connection flowing in an inevitable or predetermined direction."[73] As though in answer to such worries, the century witnessed the emergence of some large-scale attempts to marshal comparative evidence from Philo's works as a means of helping to understand the New Testament. The *Religionsgeschichtliche Schule* gave impetus to deep study of ancient sources in quest of a historical account of the religious factors that shaped the early Christian world.

Largely spurred by that movement, the Corpus Hellenisticum Novi Testamenti project began, in the second decade of the twentieth century, by dividing four basic spheres of research among various contributors. Lexical, grammatical, and stylistic matters would be treated by Adolf Deissmann; the Septuagint by Hans Lietzmann; Philo, Josephus, and the literature of Hellenistic Judaism by Hans Windisch; and Hellenistic

---

of Judaism': Christianity Succeeds Where Judaism Fails," in *The Future of Early Christianity: Essays in Honor of Helmut Koester*, ed. B. A. Pearson (Minneapolis: Fortress, 1991), 163–69.

[70] F. J. Foakes Jackson and Kirsopp Lake, *The Beginnings of Christianity, Part I: The Acts of the Apostles* (London: Macmillan and Co., 1920), 1:154.

[71] R. Bultmann, *Primitive Christianity in Its Contemporary Setting*, trans. R. H. Fuller (London and New York: Thames and Hudson, 1956), 94–100.

[72] H. A. A. Kennedy, *Philo's Contribution to Religion* (London: Hodder and Stoughton, 1919), 23.

[73] S. Sandmel, "Parallelomania," *JBL* 81.1 (1962): 1–13, here 1. Note that Sandmel explicitly includes Philo and the New Testament in his purview: "Wilfred Knox's cautious listing of passages in Philo which have some echoes in Paul seems sounder to me than Gerald Friedlander's view that Paul had necessarily read Philo" (8).

and classical authors by Ernst von Dobschütz.[74] The German project soon attracted British (F. C. Burkitt and F. H. Colson) and Scandinavian (A. Fridrichsen) collaborators, but after the death of Windisch and others, the project was divided and the Corpus Judaeo-Hellenisticum Novi Testamenti came to Halle under G. Delling's leadership. Together with Windisch and Delling, H. Hegermann and N. Walter among others made contributions to Philonic research, seeking to illuminate the New Testament and early Christianity on the basis of deep investigations of Philo's corpus, rather than selective raids in search of parallels.[75] Linked with the Corpus Hellenisticum is the "Neuer Wettstein" project, mentioned above, that has published, as of this writing, five volumes since its beginning in 1996, all of which prominently feature selections from Philo in parallel to New Testament *loci*.

At the same time, Philo sometimes fell between two stools in the study of the context of the New Testament world. H. L. Strack and P. Billerbeck's *Kommentar zum Neuen Testament aus Talmud und Midrasch* focused, as its title suggests, on Jewish literature preserved in Hebrew and Aramaic. We also find a turn toward Aramaic and Hebrew tradition in the wake of the Second World War and the discovery of the Dead Sea Scrolls, reflected in the work of scholars like Joachim Jeremias, Matthew Black, W. D. Davies, E. P. Sanders, and Martin Hengel.[76] At times Philo seems to be a victim of the divide between Greco-Roman and Jewish "backgrounds" to the New Testament, seen by some as too Hellenized to offer a pure Jewish background to the writings of a Galilean sect. The work of scholars like Hengel deconstructed such a sharp division between Jewish and Greco-Roman contexts by stressing that Israel had been Hellenized since at least the third century BCE,[77] even if the dichotomy persisted in perplexing ways.

The *Religionsgeschichtliches Textbuch zum Neuen Testament* assembled by Klaus Berger and Carsten Colpe, then expanded into a larger English edition by Eugene Boring, includes some 626 and 976 texts respectively, and does contain selections from Philo.[78] 112 out of 976 texts in the English translation are Philonic, with parallels adduced from across Philo's corpus, but most frequently from *Allegorical Interpretation* (8), *Life of Moses* (20), *Special Laws* (13), and *On Dreams* (10).

---

[74] See C. F. Georg Heinrici, "Instruktionstext für Mitarbeiter am Corpus Hellenisticum Novi Testamenti" [orig. 1915], in *Frühjudentum und Neues Testament im Horizont Biblischer Theologie. Mit einem Anhang zum Corpus Judaeo-Hellenisticum Novi Testamenti*, ed. W. Kraus and K.-W. Niebuhr, WUNT 162 (Tübingen: Mohr Siebeck, 2003), 303; see the other essays on pp. 303–82 for an instructive history of this project.

[75] See e.g. G. Delling, "Zum Corpus Hellenisticum Novi Testamenti," *ZNW* 54 (1963): 1–15; G. Delling, *Studien zum Neuen Testament und zum hellenistischen Judentum. Gesammelte Aufsätze, 1950–1968* (Göttingen: Vandenhoeck & Ruprecht, 1970); H. Hegermann, *Die Vorstellung von Schöpfungsmittler im hellenistischen Judentum und Urchristentum*, TU 82 (Berlin: Akademie, 1961).

[76] See the survey in W. Baird, "Historical Backgrounds: Judaism," in his *History of New Testament Research*, Vol. 3: *From C. H. Dodd to Hans Dieter Betz* (Minneapolis: Fortress, 2013), 279–335, and note, for example, the comments of E. P. Sanders in *Paul and Palestinian Judaism* (Philadelphia: Fortress, 1977), 553–54.

[77] For the neglect of Philo, see e.g. P. Borgen, "Response Concerning the Jewish Sources," *NTS* 23 (1976): 67–75; G. E. Sterling, "'Philo Has Not Been Used Half Enough': The Significance of Philo of Alexandria for the Study of the New Testament," *PRSt* 30.3 (2003): 251–69; cf. Sterling, "The Place of Philo of Alexandria"; and M. Niehoff, "Abraham in the Greek East: Faith, Circumcision, and Covenant in Philo's Allegorical Commentary and Paul's Letter to the Galatians," *SPhiloA* 32 (2020): 227–48, here 227–28, n. 2.

[78] K. Berger and C. Colpe, *Religionsgeschichtliches Textbuch zum Neuen Testament* (Göttingen: Vandenhoeck & Ruprecht, 1987); M. E. Boring, K. Berger, and C. Colpe, *Hellenistic Commentary to the New Testament* (Nashville: Abingdon, 1995).

27.5 Conclusion

In his retrospective account of the *Studia Philonica Annual*, Gregory Sterling indicates that the largest disciplinary group represented in contributors to that journal is comprised of New Testament scholars.[79] The cross-pollination of interest is also noticeable in the fact that the monograph series that serve the professional guild of New Testament scholars (WUNT, BZNW, NovTSup, etc.) are replete with volumes and essays devoted to Philo, evidence of the close intertwining of Philonic and New Testament scholarship today.

Given the fractured nature of the field, it is difficult to characterize New Testament scholarship as a whole without running the risk of distortion. But surely it is uncontroversial to suggest that, in academic circles, the New Testament is most often studied in a comparative vein.[80] The comparative project is one that has deep roots in the early modern period, and inevitably involves one in the search for points of similarity and difference. As Smith notes, "Comparison requires the postulation of difference as the grounds of its being interesting (rather than tautological) and a methodical manipulation of difference, a playing across the 'gap' in the service of some useful end."[81] In the period from the eighteenth to the mid-twentieth century, we find students of the New Testament engaged in that negotiation of difference when it comes to Philo and other Hellenistic Jewish authors. Some want to minimize difference to suggest that, for example, the *auctor ad Hebraeos* or the author of the Fourth Gospel were effectively Christianized Philonists (to adapt the famous proverb first attested in Jerome: ἢ Ἰωάννης φιλωνίζει ἢ Φίλων ἰωαννίζει?). Others argue for a stark difference between Philo and the authors of the New Testament, still others for some mediating position between these extremes.

The seventeenth- and eighteenth-century *Observationes* literature demonstrated both industry and erudition in assembling linguistic and grammatical parallels to Philo. Subsequent work probed these collections more searchingly, attempting to ascertain not simply common ideas but points of possible dependence. Given the relative paucity of extant Hellenistic Jewish literature, Philo's corpus obtains a position of chief importance, while at the same time that very paucity reminds us that the vast majority of what was written by Jews in Greek in the first century has been irretrievably lost, and with it our hopes of drawing firmer connections or tracing with a steadier hand the paths that led from Alexandria to a Paul or a John in Corinth, Ephesus, or Rome.

We also witness a historiographical struggle toward appreciating Philo on his own terms, and not simply viewing him through a lens that is teleologically focused on the

---

[79] G. E. Sterling, "The *Studia Philonica, The Studia Philonica Annual*, and the Study of Philo of Alexandria (1972–2017)," in *Les études philoniennes: regards sur cinquante ans de recherche (1967–2017)*, ed. S. Morlet and O. Munnich, SPA 13 (Leiden: Brill, 2021), 37–81, esp. 50, 58, 59, 68.

[80] For sophisticated reflections on this, see J. M. G. Barclay and B. G. White, eds, *The New Testament in Comparison: Validity, Method and Purpose in Comparing Traditions*, LNTS 600 (London: Bloomsbury, 2020).

[81] Smith, "In Comparison a Magic Dwells," 40.

early Christian movement. The tendency to negatively contrast Philo with the authors of the New Testament is regularly encountered, and readers who approach him with the biases of Christian exceptionalism fault him for any number of perceived shortcomings, whether in his attachment to Platonizing exegesis or his lack of eschatology. Nevertheless, over time, and particularly with the rise of "deep comparison" in the twentieth century, Philo has been appreciated increasingly on his own terms, and only then held alongside the New Testament in an attempt at mutual understanding, without the value-laden judgments of some earlier generations.

Many of the shifts in scholarly approaches this essay has chronicled could be generalized to refer to New Testament scholarship as a whole. Unsurprisingly, Philo finds himself at the hands of the developing methodological sensibilities of professional biblical scholarship, but this also means that to study Philo's reception in New Testament scholarship is to attend, *in nuce*, to broader disciplinary shifts. Although this essay has not attempted to chart Philo's fate past the mid-twentieth century or so, with only a couple of minor exceptions, it is clear that the relationship between Philonic and New Testament scholarship is, if anything, even more intertwined today than in the past, and one can look forward to further mutually enriching exchanges in the years ahead.

28
The Jewish Enlightenment (*Haskalah*)

Ze'ev Strauss

Among scholars of the Jewish Enlightenment, there is a commonly accepted position that the Jewish enlighteners—unlike their Christian counterparts—considered the medieval Jewish philosophers, whose rationalistic reading of scripture shaped and legitimized their own progressive account of Judaism, to be their historical precursors.[1] However, although this picture is for the most part accurate, it is flawed and incomplete. It largely overlooks an important phenomenon within the Haskalah: the rapidly growing fascination with Alexandrian Jewish thought and tradition, as primarily manifested in the historical writings and allegorical exegesis of the ancient and tremendously influential thinker Philo of Alexandria.[2] From the 1780s onward, Philo's philosophical understanding of the Jewish faith began to feature prominently in the works of several of the greatest proponents of the Jewish Enlightenment in both Western and Eastern Europe. A vast number of these maskilic references to Philo cannot be understood merely in their narrower scientific sense, but must also be seen in their deeper apologetic and spiritual sense: the *Aufklärer* viewed Philo in their own maskilic image, as their earliest forerunner, who, in the first century of the Common Era, laid out an enlightened philosophical image of Judaism that aided them in their construal of medieval Jewish philosophy as being rooted in pre-Christian and pre-Islamic traditions of antiquity.[3]

The present chapter seeks to demonstrate this thesis by adducing Hebrew works of the eighteenth and nineteenth centuries written by two Jewish enlighteners of the first rank: Moses Mendelssohn (1729–86) and Solomon J. L. Rapoport (1790–1867). I want to argue that Mendelssohn's and Rapoport's treatments of Philo together constitute one of the two most significant landmarks within the Hebrew revival of Philo's body of thought in the Jewish Enlightenment. To substantiate this assertion, I will put forth the

---

[1] See e.g. A. Funkenstein, *Perceptions of Jewish History* (Berkeley: University of California Press, 1993), 243–47; S. Feiner, *Haskalah and History: The Emergence of a Modern Jewish Historical Consciousness* (Oxford: Littman Library of Jewish Civilization, 2001), 24–25, 50–51, 86, 112, 132, 217; R. Mahler, *A History of Modern Jewry: 1780–1815* (New York: Schocken Books 1971), 559.

[2] For a more general historical outline of this maskilic trend, see Y. Cohen's innovative doctoral thesis "The Reception of Classical World in Modern Hebrew Culture: From the Late Eighteenth-Century to the Early Twentieth-Centuries" (in Hebrew) (PhD diss., Ben-Gurion University of the Negev, Beersheba, 2018), 32–177.

[3] For a detailed examination of Philo's reception history in the *Wissenschaft des Judentums*, see M. R. Niehoff, "Alexandrian Judaism in Nineteenth Century *Wissenschaft des Judentums*: Between Christianity and Modernization," in *Jüdische Geschichte in hellenistisch-römischer Zeit. Wege der Forschung: Vom alten zum neuen Schürer*, ed. A. Oppenheimer, Schriften des Historischen Kollegs 44 (Munich: Oldenbourg, 1999), 9–28; D. R. Sills, "Re-Inventing the Past: Philo and the Historiography of Jewish Identity" (PhD diss., University of California, Santa Barbara, 1984); and Görge Hasselhoff, Chapter 29 in this volume.

following claims: (1) That Philo marks an important source of Mendelssohn's understanding of scripture and Judaism. (2) That it was above all Mendelssohn's Pentateuch edition (*Netivot ha-Šalom*)—and not Azariah de' Rossi's *Light of the Eyes*[4]—that was the preliminary source that led to the rediscovery and legitimation of Philo's ancient Hellenistic Judaism among important exponents of the Jewish Enlightenment and the *Wissenschaft des Judentums*. (3) That Rapoport, Naḥman Krochmal's (1785–1840) like-minded pupil and a great promoter of the *Wissenschaft des Judentums*, may be considered the most crucial figure disseminating Philo's body of thought within the Eastern European Haskalah. This chapter's aim is to be achieved in two essential stages. The first will focus on Mendelssohn's edition of the Pentateuch, *Netivot ha-Šalom* ("The Paths of Peace"; 1780–83), whose introduction and commentary draw in significant parts on Philo's *De vita Moysis*. The second will turn to two aspects regarding Rapoport's role in Philo's reception, both of which are generally overlooked in research: first, Rapoport's understanding of himself as Philo's chief defender against the past attacks of Azaria de' Rossi; and second, Rapoport's role as a driving force behind Josef Flesch's (1781–1839) Hebrew translations of and commentaries on Philo's works, which were published in 1838.

28.1 Mendelssohn's *Bi'ur* and Yedidyah ha-Alexandri's *Ḥayyei Mošeh*

There is hardly any Haskalah work whose sweeping intellectual and cultural impact is comparable to Mendelssohn's Pentateuch edition, which included a German translation and a Hebrew commentary (henceforth the *Bi'ur*).[5] Perez Sandler goes so far as to state that this composite work of the Berlin Haskalah, which had been canonical among European Jewry for approximately a hundred years, had an effect on modern Jewish tradition that was on par with the Luther Bible's impact on German society.[6] The *Bi'ur* advanced a substantial shift in the emphasis on traditional Jewish texts, bringing the Hebrew Bible to the fore while relegating rabbinic literature to a secondary role.[7] At the same time, other non-canonical Jewish sources were elevated to the status of legitimate works that would provide an improved understanding of Jewish history and scripture.

---

[4] For De' Rossi's treatment of Philo, see G. Veltri, "The Humanist Sense of History and the Jewish Idea of Tradition: Azaria de' Rossi's Critique of Philo Alexandrinus," *JSQ* 2 (1995): 372–93; J. Weinberg, "The Quest for Philo in Sixteenth-Century Jewish Historiography," in *Jewish History: Essays in Honour of Chimen Abramsky*, ed. A. Rapoport-Albert and S. J. Zipperstein (London: Halban, 1988), 163–87; N. G. Cohen, "Philo Judaeus and the Torah True Library," *Tradition: A Journal of Orthodox Jewish Thought* 41 (2008): 31–48, esp. 34–39; R. Marcus, "A Sixteenth Century Hebrew Critique of Philo (Azariah dei Rossi's 'Meor Eynayim,' Pt. I, cc. 3–6)," *HUCA* 21 (1948): 29–71; D. T. Runia, *Philo in Early Christian Literature: A Survey*, CRINT 3.3 (Assen: Van Gorcum, 1993), 32–33. See also ch. 23.1 above in this volume.

[5] Moses Mendelsohn, *Gesammelte Schriften. Jubiläumsausgabe* (henceforth JubA), Vol. 15.1: *Sefer Netivot ha-Šalom*, ed. I. Elbogen et al. (Bad Cannstatt: Frommann-Holzboog, 1983), 19–55.

[6] P. Sandler, *Mendelssohn's Edition of the Pentateuch* (in Hebrew) (Jerusalem: R. Mass, 1940), 71; cf. also 119–20.

[7] E. Breuer, *The Limits of Enlightenment: Jews, Germans, and the Eighteenth-Century Study of Scripture* (Cambridge, MA: Harvard University Press, 1996), 182–229.

Such a source is Philo's *De vita Moysis*, which Mendelssohn possessed[8] in Christian G. Heyne's German translation[9] and draws upon in three important instances in his *Bi'ur*: (1) In his masterful introduction to the *Bi'ur*, *'Or Li-Netivah* ("A Light for the Path"), he refers to *Mos.* 2.26–40 within the context of the Greek translation of the Hebrew Bible. (2) In his analysis of the colored wool known as *argaman* in Exod 25:4, he adduces *Mos.* 1.84–88. (3) He presents Philo's interpretation of the biblical poem, the Song of the Well (found in Num 21:18), in *Mos.* 1.256–57.

Mendelssohn's initial reference to Philo is in the section of his *'Or Li-Netivah* entitled "Regarding Translations," where he depicts the various Bible translations in the course of Jewish history as a necessity for the respective Jewish communities living in the diaspora. In so doing, he seeks to adduce a historical justification for his own ambitious translation project,[10] and specifically to show that "Yedidyah the Alexandrian known as Philo also related that event in the same way as the abovementioned Aristeas."[11] A large portion of this section is dedicated to testimonials related to the production of the Septuagint. The key source on which Mendelssohn predicates his discussion is the pseudepigraphic *Letter of Aristeas*. Surprisingly, Mendelssohn argues for the historical validity of this apologetic writing's portrayal of the genesis of the Greek Bible translation, while quarreling with "the view of recent writers" claiming that this document is "fabricated, falsified, and embellished."[12] To this end, Mendelssohn adduces Philo's testimony in *Mos.* 2.26–40, which in his view attests to the historical truthfulness of the *Letter of Aristeas*'s account regarding the emergence of the Septuagint: "It appears that one cannot refute the testimony of ancient [writers] in this matter, particularly the testimony of Philo who was a resident of Alexandria itself—the very city in which that translation was done—some three hundred years after those elders."[13] As Breuer and Sorkin rightfully note, Mendelssohn's designation of Philo as "Yedidyah" points to the substantial impact of Azariah de' Rossi's *Light of the Eyes*,[14] whose second part, *Hadrat Zeqenim*, offers a Hebrew translation of the *Letter of Aristeas* and is one of the pivotal sources of Mendelssohn's *Bi'ur*.[15] Comparing Mendelssohn's specific reference to Philo at this juncture with different parts of the eighth and ninth chapters of Azariah de' Rossi's *'Imrei Binah* ("Words of Understanding"), the third part of *Light of the Eyes*, exposes his heavy dependency on this Renaissance text:

---

[8] H. Meyer, *Verzeichniß der auserlesenen Büchersammlung des seeligen Herrn Moses Mendelssohn* (Berlin: 1786), 34 (no. 275).

[9] Philo, *Philo vom Leben Moses, das ist: von der Gottesgelahrtheit und dem prophetischen Geiste*, trans. C. G. Heyne (anonymized) (Dresden: Waltherische Buchhandlung, 1778).

[10] Mendelssohn, JubA 15.1:31–40.

[11] Moses Mendelssohn, *Moses Mendelssohn's Hebrew Writings*, trans. E. Breuer; introduced and annotated by E. Breuer and D. Sorkin; Yale Judaica Series 33 (New Haven: Yale University Press, 2018), 283.

[12] Mendelssohn [Breuer and Sorkin], *Hebrew*, 283. For the Hebrew original, see JubA 15.1:36.

[13] Mendelssohn, *Hebrew*, 283. For the Hebrew original, see JubA 15.1:36.

[14] In this chapter, I use the following editions in Hebrew and English: Azariah de' Rossi, *Me'or 'Einayim* (Mantua, 1573; repr. Vienna: Anton Edlen von Schmid, 1829); Azariah de' Rossi, *The Light of the Eyes*, trans. J. Weinberg (New Haven: Yale University Press, 2001).

[15] Breuer and Sorkin, *Hebrew*, 281 n. 38, 283 n. 46.

[...] וְאֵיךְ הוּא יְדִידְיָה בְּבֵאוּר קְצָת שֵׁמוֹת אָמַר הוֹרָאָתָם כָּךְ וְכָךְ בִּלְשׁוֹן כַּשְׂדִּי, בְּאוֹפֶן כִּי מִמֶּנּוּ נִקַּח <u>עֵדוּת</u> בְּרוּרָה שֶׁהַזְּקֵנִים מִן הָאֲרַמִּי בִּלְבַד הֶעְתִּיקוּ.

Yedidyah also gives the etymologies of some names, commenting on their meaning in Chaldean. We can take this as clear proof that the elders only translated from the Aramaic text. (De' Rossi, *Me'or*, 82 [*Light*, 189]; my emphasis)

וּבִפְרָט <u>עֵדוּת</u> יְדִיד' שֶׁהָיָה <u>מִתּוֹשָׁבֵי אֲלֶכְּסַנְדְּרִיאָה עַצְמָהּ</u>, הָעִיר אֲשֶׁר בָּהּ <u>נַעֲשָׂה מְלֶאכֶת הַהַעְתָּקָה הַהִיא</u>, <u>אַחֲרֵי הַזְּקֵנִים הָהֵם כְּשָׁלֹשׁ מֵאוֹת שָׁנָה</u>.

וְהַיּוֹתֵר זָר אֶצְלִי כִּי עָבַרְתִּי בְּכָל מ"ג סִפְרֵי יְדִידְיָה הָאֲלֶכְּסַנְדְּרִי הַנִּדְפָּסִים יַחַד וְהוּא הָיָה טֶרֶם חֻרְבַּן שֵׁנִי <u>מִתּוֹשָׁבֵי אֲלֶכְּסַנְדְּרִיאָה עִיר הַהַעְתָּקָה</u> עַצְמָהּ כְּמוֹ שֶׁזָּכַרְנוּ בַּפֶּרֶק הַקּוֹדֵם.

Particularly the testimony of Philo who was a resident of Alexandria itself—the very city in which that translation was done—some three hundred years after those elders. (Mendelssohn, JubA 15.1:36; my emphasis)[16]

What struck me as the strangest aspect of the whole matter emerged from my perusal of all forty-three works of Yedidyah the Alexandrian which were published in Alexandria, the city in which the translation was executed, as we indicated in the previous chapter.
(De' Rossi, *Me'or*, 74 [*Light*, 172]; my emphasis)

כִּי מִן <u>הַשִּׁבְעִי'</u> לִידִידְיָה נִמְשְׁכוּ קָרוֹב <u>לִשְׁלֹשׁ מֵאוֹת שָׁנָה</u>.[...]

Almost three hundred years elapsed between the lifetime of the Seventy and that of Yedidyah (De' Rossi, *Me'or*, 78 [*Light*, 179]; my emphasis)

This reference implies that Mendelssohn, closely following De' Rossi's treatment of the Septuagint in *'Imrei Binah*, considered Philo and his writings to be a legitimate source of information relating to Jewish history. Mendelssohn does not single out any particular passage from *Mos.* 2.26–40—even though he seems to have had first-hand knowledge of this section—but mentions Philo through the mediation of De' Rossi's analysis of this source. By no means does this fact undermine the conjecture that

---

[16] For the English translation, see Mendelssohn, *Hebrew*, 283.

Mendelssohn was familiar with Philo's body of thought. Quite the opposite seems to be the case: in light of Mendelssohn's constructive approach to 'Imrei Binah's treatment of Yedidyah ha-Alexandri, it becomes evident that he encountered numerous valuable aspects and facts pertaining to Philonic ideas. As a whole, these references indicate that Mendelssohn held Philo in high esteem, inasmuch as he refers to him in the introduction to *Netivot ha-Šalom*.

One might think that a cursory allusion to Philo in conjunction with the colored wool named *'argaman*, part of the Israelites' heave offering (Exod 25:4), neither constitutes a significant reference in the *Bi'ur* nor points to the importance of *Mos.* as a source thereof. However, this is a false assumption. Perez Sandler's monographic discussion of the *Bi'ur* has already highlighted the important role played by the study of colors mentioned in the Bible in Mendelssohn's commentary, while specifically referring to his thorough examination of the color *'argaman*.[17] Nor does the fact that Mendelssohn refers to Philo in this regard go unnoticed.[18] Mendelssohn's explanation reads as follows:

> *We-'argaman*, red-colored wool; Maimonides (Chap. 8 in the 13th *Halakha* to the *Vessels of the Sanctuary*) and Abraham Ibn Ezra wrote that it is red; in 2 Chr 2:6, it is designated as *'argon*, and it is also called the same in Aramaic and Arabic. And Abraham Ben David wrote: "to me, *'argaman* is woven of two or three sorts of colors, which is why it is called *'argaman*." It is also stated in a few sources in the *Zohar* that *'argaman* is formed of an array of colors, and it is referred to at times as being predominantly green, and at times as being predominantly red …. And the present position of the German translator [viz. Mendelssohn], [who claims] that it is the color of purple, does not constitute any divergence of opinion, for purple is comprised of multiple colors and it is primarily red and green, like light blue or more specifically the sapphire-blue color. And in this manner, Josephus in his *Antiquities of the Jews*, as well as the sage Philo [*ha-ḥakham filo*] in his book *The Life of Moses*, wrote that it is purple.[19]

Four points require our attention here:

1. Mendelssohn, who translates "purpurrote Wolle" in Exod 25:4, draws on Philo's designation of *'argaman*—following the LXX—as πορφύρα (*Mos.* 2.87), which he perceives to be a multicolored wool formed of red and green. The section that Mendelssohn has in mind here is *Mos.* 2.84–88. In *Mos.* 2.88, Philo assigns purple the symbolic meaning of the element of water, one of God's four building blocks in his creation of the physical cosmos: "But, in choosing the materials for the woven work, he selected as the best out of a vast number possible four, as equal

---

[17] Sandler, *Pentateuch*, 83.
[18] Sandler, *Pentateuch*, 83.
[19] JubA 16:240 (my translation).

in number to the elements—earth, water, air, fire—out of which the world was made, and with a definite relation to those elements;... purple from the water."[20]

2. Mendelssohn emphasizes the congruence of opinions between Philo and the Kabbalah, as well as medieval Jewish thought.

3. Mendelssohn's introduction of Philo as a Ḥakham should not be passed over as a customary designation. Accounting for the fact that De' Rossi's *Light of the Eyes* constitutes one of the *Bi'ur*'s most authoritative sources,[21] an unambiguous reference to Philo as a sage could be understood as having a provocative edge. This becomes more apparent if one recalls De' Rossi's famous and conclusive verdict passed in 'Imrei Binah's chapter 6: "I shall call him neither Rav nor sage, heretic nor sceptic. My only name for him shall be Yedidyah the Alexandrian."[22]

4. Mendelssohn's approach to the investigation of colors in the Hebrew Bible with reference to Hellenistic Jewish sources such as Philo and Josephus was not unusual among Christian commentaries written prior to the *Bi'ur*. This might suggest that there was an underlying Christian source for Mendelssohn's specific references here. If we also consult, for example, volume 1 of Romanus Teller's *Die Heilige Schrift des Alten und Neuen Testaments*, a running commentary formed from a wide array of English Bible commentators,[23] we encounter a similar reference to Philo and Josephus.[24]

Surely, Mendelssohn's most significant reference to Philo is in conjunction with biblical poetry, specifically in his explanation of the Song of the Well in Num 21:17–18.[25] The poem's importance stems from the innovative thematic focal point of Mendelssohn's *Bi'ur*, which brings to the fore the aesthetic and poetic elements of the Pentateuch. This is not merely a subjective assessment of the *Bi'ur*'s approach, but rather a fact that is acknowledged by Mendelssohn himself.[26] Turning to the *Bi'ur*'s elucidation of Num 21:18, one comes across the following reference to *Mos.* 1.255–57:

"Well, which the rulers dug," Moses and Aaron, *bim-ḥoqeq*..., and its meaning is the legislator, and the rod in the hand of the legislator is the legislative rod. It is a symbol of grandeur and honor. With it, the elders dug the well. This is an [exaggerated] poetic saying regarding the well, which they [viz. the rulers] excavated without toil and

---

[20] PLCL 6:493. See also *Congr.* 117.

[21] See G. Veltri, "Von Faszination und Irrtum des Humanismus: Jüdisches Denken in der italienischen Renaissance," in *An der Schwelle zur Moderne: Juden in der Renaissance*, ed. G. Veltri and A. Winkelmann (Leiden: Brill, 2003), 6.

[22] De' Rossi, *Light*, 159.

[23] For further discussion of Romanus Teller within the context of the *Bi'ur*, see Breuer, *Limits*, 93–94.

[24] Romanus Teller, *Die Heilige Schrift des Alten und Neuen Testaments* (Leipzig: Bernhard Christoph Breitkopf, 1749), 1.751. These references seem to be a common ground of eighteenth-century Christian commentators. See e.g. Johann Lund, *Die alten Jüdischen Heiligthümer, Gottesdienste und Gewohnheiten, in gründlicher Beschreibung, des ganzen Levitischen* (Hamburg: Johann Wolfgang Fickweiler, 1722), 13–14; and Johann J. Scheuchzer, *Kupfer-Bibel* (Augsburg: Christian Ulrich Wagner, 1731), 2.274.

[25] For an earlier version of this interpretation, see my article: Z. Strauss, "Jüdische Pädagogik, hebräische Dichtkunst und jüdisch-hellenistische Religionsästhetik in Mendelssohns *Bi'ur*," *Trumah* 25 (2022): 166–72.

[26] Mendelssohn, *Hebrew*, 351 (with slight modifications). For further analysis, see Y. Sela, "The Voice of the Psalmist: On the Performative Role of Psalms in Moses Mendelssohn's *Jerusalem*," in *Psalms in/on Jerusalem*, ed. I. Pardes and O. Münz-Manor (Berlin: de Gruyter, 2019), 114–15.

burden, in a miraculous manner. See Yedidyah, called Philo, who wrote in his *De vita Moysis* that the kings of this land and its inhabitants spent vast sums in order to dig this well. Its interior was laid with [precious] gems and was an extraordinarily splendid and valuable construction, which points to the wealth [and] honor of these kings. One may claim about this, according to this poetic saying, that the "well, which the rulers dug," [was] excavated by the generous men of the nation, "with a legislative rod."[27]

The following aspects of this commentary need to be addressed:

1. Even though a portion of the *Bi'ur*'s Numbers commentary was probably composed by Aaron Z. Jaroslav,[28] this specific explanation bears Mendelssohn's marked imprint. This was noted by Sandler, who—with reference to the passage in question—argues that the authorship of the aesthetic commentaries should be traced back to Mendelssohn.[29] Alongside the fact that this is a typical Mendelssohnian characterization of biblical Hebrew poetry as being predicated on parallelism,[30] the formulation used in his reference to Philo's *Mos.* is identical to the one found in his commentary on Exod 25:4.

2. The specific section from book 1 of *Mos.* on which Mendelssohn draws is §§255–57, in which Philo understands—based on the Septuagint[31]—the well-digging rulers (ἄρχοντες) in LXX Num 21:18a to be kings: "For, as they were told, it had been dug by the hands of no common men, but of kings, whose ambition was not only to find the water but so to build the well that the wealth lavished upon it should show the royal character of the work and the sovereignty and lofty spirit of the builders."[32] Philo ascribes great importance to the Song of the Well, actually prioritizing it over the Song of the Sea. While for Philo, allegorically speaking the Song of the Sea merely depicts the soul's overcoming of passions, the Song of the Well symbolizes a higher spiritual rank; namely, the soul's attainment of heavenly wisdom.[33] With this passage, Mendelssohn appears to want to emphasize the following points: (1) that the construction of the well was not undertaken by simple people, but by kings; (2) that the Israelite rulers lavished resources on the building activity; and (3) that its implementation involved great expense and strenuous labor, but was not the result of any miraculous deed. According to this

---

[27] JubA 18:176–77 (my translation).
[28] Breuer and Sorkin in Mendelssohn, *Hebrew*, 229 n. 32. In the *Bi'ur*'s introduction, Mendelssohn stated that he was the author of the Numbers commentary (JubA 15.1:41–42). See also A. Altmann, *Moses Mendelssohn: A Biographical Study* (Tuscaloosa: University of Alabama Press, 1973), 359–60, 417; Gottlieb in Mendelssohn, *Writings on Judaism, Christianity & the Bible*, ed. M. Gottlieb; trans. E. Sacks, C. Bowman, and A. Arkush; Brandeis Library of Modern Jewish Thought (Waltham, MA: Brandeis University Press, 2011), 185; Sandler, *Edition*, 98, 145–49.
[29] Sandler, *Edition*, 152.
[30] See Sandler, *Edition*, 152. For further analysis, see Breuer and Sorkin in Mendelssohn, *Hebrew*, 230.
[31] Philo, *Philo of Alexandria: Writings*, ed. S. Daniel-Nataf et al., 6 vols (Jerusalem: Bialik Institute and the Israel Academy of Sciences and Humanities, 1986–2012), 1:259 n. 235.
[32] PLCL 6:409 (*Mos.* 1.256).
[33] For this aspect of Philo's exegesis, see *Ebr.* 111–13; *Somn.* 2.269–71; *Post.* 151–53. See also A. C. Geljon and D. T. Runia, *Philo of Alexandria, On Planting: Introduction, Translation, and Commentary*, PACS 5 (Leiden: Brill, 2019), 175, 177.

interpretation, one may construe the Hebrew *bim-ḥoqeq be-mišʿanotam* to mean the great expenditures and efforts of the rulers. Moreover, (4) the well was made into a work of splendor; (5) there was a symmetrical relationship between the royal builders and their sublime work; and (6) by claiming that this poem shares the same concise parallel structure as the Song of the Sea and thereby elicits sublime sentiments within the listener's soul,[34] Mendelssohn seems to want to align this aesthetic objective with Philo's content-related depiction of the well as a work of utter splendor.

3. A large portion of Mendelssohn's explanation appears to be modeled on Romanus Teller's commentary on Num 21:18. This can be demonstrated by comparing both texts:

und bedienten sich dabey keiner andern Werkzeuge, als ihrer Stäbe i); sie hatten aber mit denselben die Erde kaum berührt, als das Wasser *wunderbarer Weise* sehr häufig herauslief k). [...] i) Der Herr le Clerc siehet diesen Umstand als *eine poetische Erdichtung* an, durch welche man zu erkennen geben will, wie *leicht das Werk von statten gieng*	ובו כרו הנדיבים את הבאר, והיא <u>מליצה שירית</u> על הבאר שהעלו <u>בלי עמל ויגיעה</u>, על <u>דרך פלא</u>
and they employed no other instruments than their rods i); with them, they barely touched the earth, as very frequently the water miraculously overflowed k).... i) The honorable le Clerc understands this situation as a poetic fiction, which seeks to signify how effortlessly the construction work proceeded. (Teller, *Schrift*, 534 [my translation; my emphasis])	With it, the elders dug the well. This is an [exaggerated] poetic saying regarding the well, which they [viz. the rulers] excavated without toil and burden, in a miraculous manner. (Mendelssohn, JubA 18:176–77 [my translation; my emphasis])

This dependency is exemplified by three points: (1) Mendelssohn's unusual wording for the Song of the Well as a *meliṣah širit* is merely a translation of Teller's "poetische Erdichtung," which he in turn borrowed from Jean Leclerc's *Genesis sive Mosis prophetæ*[35] or from William Wall's *Critical Notes on the Old Testament*.[36] Also, Teller's

---

[34] See D. Krochmalnik, "Das Andachtshaus der Vernunft. Zur sakralen Poesie und Musik bei Moses Mendelssohn," *Mendelssohn-Studien* 11 (1999): 26–29, 35–37; G. Schorch, *Moses Mendelssohns Sprachpolitik*, Studia Judaica 67 (Berlin: de Gruyter, 2012), 96–140.

[35] Jean Leclerc, *Genesis sive Mosis prophetæ* (Amsterdam: Henric Schelte, 1710), 417.

[36] William Wall, *Critical Notes on the Old Testament* (London: C. David, 1734), 1:110.

attached explanation that the poetic hyperbole conveys the excavation's effortlessness aligns seamlessly with Mendelssohn's presentation. According to Mendelssohn, the aim of the poetical *meliṣah* was to accentuate the ease with which the building work was realized. (2) Likewise, Mendelssohn's assertion regarding the miraculous manner of the well's effortless construction appears to be derived from Teller's "wunderbarer Weise." (3) Moreover, Teller even specifically refers to Philo's *Mos.* 1.255–57 through the mediation of Augustin Calmet's *Commentaire litteral sur tous les livres de l'Ancien et du Nouveau Testament*.[37] On encountering this reference, Mendelssohn probably turned to his German translation of *De vita Moysis*, where Philo expounds on the Song of the Well, and inserted §256 into his commentary. Through Philo, Mendelssohn seeks to flesh out an opposed interpretation; that is, that the building work was not a miraculous deed, but required much effort on the rulers' part. On the whole, Mendelssohn's dependence on Teller's commentary, without explicitly mentioning him, tends to reinforce a hypothesis already made by Sandler: "Mendelssohn was acquainted with the Christian exegesis, and there are reasons to assume that he was somewhat influenced by it, even though he attempted to conceal it from his Hebrew readers. This influence is especially manifest in his aesthetic interpretation—one of the aims he pursues throughout the entire 'Bi'ur.'"[38]

If one seeks to ascertain Mendelssohn's overall attitude towards Philo's body of thought and its view of Judaism, an effective way of doing so is to consult his commissioned German translation of Menasseh ben Israel's (1604–57) *Vindiciae Judaeorum*, which was published in 1782. As revealed by Mendelssohn's preface to this writing— whose translation into German was mainly undertaken by Marcus Herz[39]—it was still relevant to Prussian society in light of the dire civil state of its Jewry at the end of the eighteenth century.[40] As Altmann points out, in this edition, Mendelssohn attempted to demonstrate Judaism's tolerance by drawing (among others) on Philo, through the mediation of Menasseh's *Vindication of the Jews*.[41] In four thematic sections of *Vindiciae Judaeorum*, passages from *Legatio ad Gaium* (§§156–57, 279–80, 294–98, 306, 311–18) and *De specialibus legibus* 1 (§§53, 97, 168–69) are adduced for the purpose of evincing Judaism's universal, tolerant essence.

Mendelssohn was well aware of Philo's prominent role in this treatise, a fact that is exemplified by the text's first footnote, which relates to Menasseh's claim that the concept of *minim* in *Birkat ha-Minim* refers not to Christians, but rather to Jewish transgressors against the law:

> If, in this passage, we should understand by "empire of arrogance" a specific empire in the world, then the only possible thing that could be meant is the reign of the Roman

---

[37] Teller, *Schrift*, 534 n. i.
[38] Sandler, *Edition*, 19 (my translation). See C. Schulte, *Von Moses bis Moses … : Der jüdische Mendelssohn* (Hannover: Wehrhahn, 2020), 106.
[39] See Altmann, *Biographical*, 463–64; Gottlieb in Mendelssohn, *Writings on Judaism*, 39.
[40] Mendelssohn, *Hebrew Writings*, 43. See S. Rauschenbach, *Judentum für Christen. Vermittlung und Selbstbehauptung Menasse ben Israels in den gelehrten Debatten des 17. Jahrhunderts*, Frühe Neuzeit 164 (Berlin: de Gruyter, 2012), 229.
[41] Altmann, *Biographical*, 491.

Empire, under whose oppression the Jews of those days lived and during which this prayer was introduced. How can this, however, be reconciled with the assertion of our rabbi [i.e. Menasseh], which demonstrates this from passages of Josephus and Philo; namely, that the Jews carried out sacrifices and prayers for the well-being of the Roman emperor and kingdom? Indeed, according to the dictum of the rabbis, sin, but not the sinner, should be altogether anathematized.[42]

It would have been quite baffling if Mendelssohn had not broadly endorsed Manasseh's universalistic depiction of Judaism. By drawing on this German edition, whose title page names Mendelssohn as its translator, we can ascertain that he essentially affirmed Philo's ancient account of Judaism as a rational and tolerant worldview.

28.2 Rapoport as the Modern *Magen Yedidyahuh*

A further prominent figure of the Haskalah and one of the central intellectuals of the *Wissenschaft des Judentums*, who will now take center stage in this chapter, was Rapoport. It might come as a surprise that he is arguably the most significant Jewish thinker in the context of the Eastern European rediscovery of Philo. When one thinks of this rediscovery, the person who first comes to mind is usually not Rapoport himself, but his famous teacher, Naḥman Krochmal, known as the "Galician Mendelssohn," with whom Rapoport had an intimate intellectual relationship that persisted over three decades. Krochmal dedicated the best part of chapter 12 (*Ḥidot minni qedem*) of his *Guide of the Perplexed of the Modern Age* to Philo's thought and its intersections with rabbinic literature. Krochmal viewed Philo as a paragon of the ancient tannaitic mindset, which highlights the indispensability of the actual observance of the Jewish commandments alongside the theoretical contemplation that was prevalent among the detached Ḥasidim of his days. In his idealized maskilic image of Philo, Krochmal appears to appraise him through the lens of the Mendelssohnian concept of the ceremonial law as "the bond which was to connect action with contemplation, life with theory."[43] His simultaneously rabbinic and Mendelssohnian image of Philo also has a clear polemical thrust. Through it, he levels a maskilic critique against the Eastern European Ḥasidim of his days, whom he accuses of having deviated from Judaism's golden path—which stresses the concrete observance of the commandments—due to their excessive mysticism and *Schwärmerei*.[44]

If one analyzes the writings of Rapoport, Krochmal's *Meisterschüler* and a celebrated Eastern European member of the *Wissenschaft des Judentums*, one may be surprised

---

[42] JubA 8:48 (my translation). A very similar assertion can be found in *Jerusalem*: see JubA 8:190.
[43] Cf. F. Lachower, "Nigleh we-nistar be-mišnato šel ranaq," in *'Al gevul ha-yašan ve-hahadaš: Massot sifrutiyot* (Jerusalem: Bialik Institute, 1951), 262.
[44] Naḥman Krochmal, *Moreh nevokhei ha-zeman*, ed. Yehoyada Amir (Jerusalem: Carmel Publishing House, 2010), 7–9. For further elaboration, see R. Goetschel, "Philon et le judaïsme hellénistique au miroir de Nachman Krochmal," in *Hellenica et Judaica*, ed. A. Caquot et al. (Leuven: Peeters, 1986), 377–79; S. Rawidowicz, "Qeliṭat

THE JEWISH ENLIGHTENMENT (HASKALAH)   477

to discover that he, too, accords Philo a very significant role in his historiographical depiction of Judaism. His entry on Alexandria in his encyclopedia of rabbinic literature ʿErekh Milin showcases the fact that he even perceived himself as Philo's defender against the critique that De' Rossi leveled against his Hellenistic works, which deliberately disregarded the ancient rabbinic sages:

> Despite Philo's statements in certain passages, from which it appears to follow that he was very well aware of the presence of sages in the land of Israel who transmitted matters relating to religion and Torah to their pupils, he was not acquainted with most of these accepted subject matters passed down [orally] due to his remoteness of place and *a fortiori* from the original [Hebrew] language. Only due to this fact did a few elements make their way into his books which are irreconcilable with the orally transmitted Torah. He was, for heaven's sake, [however,] by no means part of the sect of the Sadducees, who merely believe in the literal sense of Scripture, although they heard the sayings of the great teachers. With respect to this matter, he was like an infant captured by remoteness [*tinoq šenišbah ba-merḥaqqim*], and for that reason he was not familiar with the language and etiquettes of his homeland and with all those things which were observed there and had been customary for a long time. And observe that this state was not only common in Egypt, but also in other lands outside of Israel. And we know that in several places in Babylon, the [Jewish] people did not know of the provisions relating to meat in milk [cf. *b. Ḥul.* 110a] [...]. Notwithstanding all these things, the shortcomings that *Light of the Eyes*'s author (in Chap. 5) attributed to Yedidyah or Philo the Alexandrian because his books did not follow the path of the Israeli sages in the Holy Land will be eliminated. These [deficiencies] merely resulted from a misapprehension and a lack of knowledge, not because he did not listen to the [learned] teachers; for this was the grave sin of the Sadducees in the land of Israel. And even if he had heard that the [learned] teachers in the land of Israel did not interpret the biblical text according to its literal sense, but rather according to their traditions, he would still not have known that they elevated such [oral] traditions to a guiding principle. Rather, he thought their sayings to be mere homilies. In this manner, we have gained this great sage and righteous man in every way, for he has done much for the people of Israel. He went to Rome to repeal the decrees [issued against the Jews], as is known from his own accounts, since this man is one of our close relatives, one of our saviors, and he that will remain shall be for our God. And he bestows honor on our Jewish brothers, who pride themselves on him in the eyes of the other nations.[45]

RaNaQ we-hašpaʿato," in *Hebrew Studies in Jewish Thought*, ed. B. C. I. Ravid (Jerusalem: Rubin Mass, 1971), 2:263; A. Lehnardt, "Einleitung," in *Führer der Verwirrten der Zeit*, ed. and trans. A. Lehnardt (Hamburg: Meiner, 2012), 1:xliv–l. For Krochmal's general apprehension of Philo, see Z. Strauss, "Yedidyah Ha-Alexandri and the Crisis of the Modern Jewish Age: Philo of Alexandria as an Exemplary Ḥasid in Naḥman Krochmal's Thought," *Religions* 12.6: 377 (2021): 1–27. https://doi.org/10.3390/rel12060377.

[45] Salomon L. Rapoport, "Alexandria," in *Sefer ʿErekh Milin* (Prague: Moshe ha-Levi Landau, 1852), 100–101 (my translation).

Rapoport wishes to refute De' Rossi's chief and concluding critique in *'Imrei Binah*'s chapter 5, which he calls a "fundamental shortcoming": "This last charge is weighty enough to sink him like lead into bottomless waters. It is as follows: reading from beginning to end of his works you will not come across any indication that he took upon himself the Oral Tradition alongside the Written Torah."[46] Rapoport approaches Philo's *Stillschweigen* on the oral halakhic traditions of the Pharisees by claiming that because he lived in Alexandria, which was a great distance away, he was unaware of the emergence of new authoritative oral traditions in Palestine. To illustrate Philo's utter blamelessness, he applies a rabbinic term to him, with a substantial modification: the Alexandrian is not even a *tinoq šenišbah bein ha-nokhrim/ha-goyim*—that is, an infant captured by Gentiles and brought up in accordance with their customs—but rather a *tinoq šenišbah ba-merḥaqqim*, an infant captured by the remoteness of place. In so doing, Rapoport also attempts to counter De' Rossi's association of Philo with the heretical Jewish Saducean and Boethusian sects, which consciously opposed the oral tradition of the rabbis.[47]

To understand the significant role that Rapoport's apologetics of Philo plays within *'Erekh Milin* as a whole, one need not look far. Surprisingly, it is in his entry on *'Etrog* (citron) that he lays out similar claims regarding Philo, while referring to himself as his defender against De' Rossi's harsh charges:

> It appears that in Alexandria in those days, they were not at all acquainted with all the matters that were spoken in the houses of learning regarding the existence of the oral Torah, even in light of the fact that this was a point of contention precisely during his lifetime [...]. With common sense, he claimed [this] [viz. Zacharias Frankel]: I was particularly pleased regarding this matter, for it also reinforces the words that we spoke (entry for "Alexandria," §5) for the sake of justifying Philo against those things which the rabbinic author of *Light of the Eyes* alleged because he [viz. Philo] seems to go against the oral tradition. This was only the case because in his time, numerous sayings of the oral Torah were exclusively taught in the houses of learning in the land of Israel and were not propagated in the rest of the lands. And he did not know and was not guilty, and he can only be attributed with an inadvertent sin, which is [why] God will forgive him. And that which he did know, he observed well and fixed with the nails of his common sense.[48]

Rapoport's employment of Zacharias Frankel's renowned work *Ueber den Einfluss der palästinischen Exegese auf die alexandrinische Hermeneutik* lays the groundwork for his allusion to Philo. It is through this book that Rapoport points to overlapping elements between Philo and the oral tradition. The specific point of reference is the ambiguous formulation in Lev 23:15, *mi-maḥarat ha-šabbat* ("the day after the sabbath"), as the time designated for the elevation of the *'Omer*, as well as the commencement of

---

[46] De' Rossi, *Light*, 140–41.
[47] De' Rossi, *Light*, 144–45.
[48] Rapoport, "'Etrog," in *'Erekh Milin*, 257 (my translation).

its counting. Rapoport alludes to the fact that Philo's allegorical reading of this biblical verse in *Spec.* 2.162 conforms to the Pharisaic understanding thereof—and counters the Sadducean one—inasmuch as he considers this time designation to mark the second day of Passover.[49] On this point, Rapoport clearly follows Frankel's depiction of the congruence between Philo and the Halakha: "Also in the Halakha [as in Philo], the second day of the festival is often designated as *yom hanef*; namely *ha-ʿOmer*, the swinging day (of the *ʿOmer*)."[50]

Rapoport's view of Philo's agreement with the Pharisaic sect is by no means an accidental stance limited to this specific section of *ʿErekh Milin*. A footnote in his seminal article about the *paytan* Eleʿazar Qalir aptly demonstrates this fact, and is quite revealing in this respect:

> I have already proven in my book *ʿErekh Milim*, with clear evidence against the author of *Meʾor ʿEinayim* (Chap. 3), that the Essene sect, which is mentioned in the books of Philo the Jew and Josephus, is not [the same as] the Boethusians mentioned in the *šišah sedarim*, since it is not remarked anywhere in Philo's or Josephus's writings that the Essenes deny the oral Torah in the explicit manner that this is said about the Sadducees. In his work *Quod omnis probus liber sit*, Philo wrote that all of their customs in each matter, which could exclusively be transmitted by means of godly enthusiasm, were passed down to them from their forefathers. Similarly, in his work *De vita contemplativa*, Philo wrote that they [viz. the Essenes] have many ancient books entailing numerous sublime subject matters, into which they delve and in which they immerse themselves. It is possible that those books were testaments of *Maʿaśeh Berešit* and *Maʿaśeh Merkavah*; see below. For this reason, I thought it obvious that this sect is part of the sect of the Pharisees, differentiating merely in people who are fiercer in their piety and their more ascetic life. They are [in accordance with] most of the wise Ḥasidim of antiquity found in the *Mišnayot*. The vast number of *Mišnayot* in chapter 6 of [m.] *ʾAbot* are based on them, and Philo therefore wrote in the abovementioned work about the [ascetic] grief-filled lives of these people, who eat nothing but a slice of bread with salt and drink a small quantity of water [m. *ʾAbot* 6:4].... I also thought it to be right that the Essenes be denoted as "the vatikin [who] would conclude the recitation of *šema* with sunrise" in *šišah sedarim* (*b. Ber.* 9b), and there they were also called the "holy community of Jerusalem." Various passages in Josephus and Philo reveal the Essenes' conformity to their prayer [rituals].[51]

In this passage, Rapoport not only dissociates Philo from the Sadducees, but simultaneously strives to classify him as a member of the Essene sect, which did not—as Deʾ

---

[49] Rapoport, "'Etrog," in *ʿErekh Milin*, 256.
[50] Zacharias Frankel, *Ueber den Einfluss der palästinischen Exegese auf die alexandrinische Hermeneutik* (Leipzig: Joh. Ambr. Barth, 1851), 136 n. d.
[51] Solomon L. Rapoport, "Zeman we-maqom R' elʿazar ha-qalir, we-ʿinyanei piyyutav we-piyyutei zulato, u-qeṣat ʿinyanei ha-tefilot," *Bikurei ha-ʿIttim* 10 (1830): 118.

Rossi argues—purposely disdain the concept of an oral tradition[52] and was actually a Pharisaic faction that put significant emphasis on ascetic and theoretical aspects of Judaism. He goes on to identify Philo and the Essenes/Therapeutae with the ancient Ḥasidim depicted in tannaitic literature and in the mishnaic tractate ʾAbot in particular. He also offers the suggestion that Philo and his Essene sect should be considered the source of the original Kabbalistic teachings of Maʿaśeh Berešit and Maʿaśeh Merkavah. The position he advanced might appear, prima facie, to originate with Abraham Zacuto's historical account of the Jewish nation in Sefer Yuḥasin, in which he maintains that the Essenes are the Ḥasidim.[53]

Rapoport's defense of Philo must also be understood in light of his famous and long-lasting quarrel with Samuel D. Luzzatto (1800–1865), as part of which he defends his most admired intellectual heroes, Maimonides and Abraham Ibn Ezra.[54] While Luzzatto insisted on "filtering out" the Hellenistic outlook that gained a strong foothold in the medieval Sephardic tradition—which he described as *Attizismus*[55]—Rapoport recognized that Hellenistic elements were already employed in tannaitic thought and were altogether quite beneficial for the development and fortification of the Jewish faith. One section from a letter that Rapoport wrote to Luzzatto, in which he attempts to rebut Luzzatto's charges against Maimonides and Ibn Ezra, outlines the essential aspects underlying his inclusive viewpoint regarding Hellenistic trends and influences:

> And you, blessed by God, are wasting your time and powers now in order to expose deficiencies and shortcomings in RʿABAʿ and RaMBaM, may their memory be blessed, and to increase the [diverging] branches between *Judaismus* and *Attizismus*. In fact, the former [*Judaismus*] not only adopted several [non-exclusive features] from the latter [*Attizismus*], but also numerous things from a wide array of other nation's [creative] spirits, with which we have confounded ourselves. Then why do you not mention Babylonism, Persianism, Arabism, Galicianism, and Germanism? For our rabbis, may their memory be a blessing, had a predilection for *Yefet* over all other nations, since they demanded of him that he should "dwell in the tents of Šem" [Gen 9:27].[56]

In light of such passages, it stands to reason that Rapoport's stance regarding these two great medieval Jewish thinkers is linked to his affirmative attitude towards Philo and his Hellenized Judaism. Hence, it hardly comes as a surprise that Philo is also mentioned in one of Rapoport's letters to Luzzatto, which brings speculative notions from

---

[52] Deʾ Rossi, *Light*, 102.

[53] Abraham Zacuto, *Sefer Yuḥasin* (Amsterdam: Shlomo ben Yosef Proops, 1717), 104.

[54] For further explanation, see I. E. Barzilay, *Shlomo Yehudah Rapoport (Shir) (1790–1867) and His Contemporaries: Some Aspects of Jewish Scholarship of the Nineteenth Century* (Tel Aviv: Massada Press, 1969), 103.

[55] For further analysis, see Barzilay, *Rapoport*, 102; O. Balsam-Geld, "Atticism, Judaism, and Luzzatto's Relationship to Philosophy and Philosophers," *Daat: A Journal of Jewish Philosophy & Kabbala* 84 (2017): 262–69; Y. Shavit, *Athens in Jerusalem, Classical Antiquity and Hellenism in the Making of the Modern Secular Jew* (Oxford: Littman Library of Jewish Civilization, 1997), 100–103, 157–70, 210–11, 240.

[56] Solomon L. Rapoport, *S. L. Rapoport's hebräische Briefe an S. D. Luzzatto (1833–1860)*, ed. E. Gräber (Przemysl: gr. Kat. Domkapitels, 1885), 2:115 (also see 107–8).

Sefer Yeṣirah to the fore. In this letter, he argues that the representation of language and the act of speech at the beginning of this mystical work, by which the divine creation is called into being, align well with Philo's Hellenistic concept of the two phases of the Logos, the λόγος ἐνδιάθετος and the λόγος προφορικός.[57] Returning to Rapoport's encyclopedic entry on Alexandria, in which Philo takes center stage, he calls attention to the remarkable fact that "Maimonides matched ... [Philo] exactly in all matters of the Torah,"[58] presenting the Alexandrian as Maimonides' ancient *Vordenker* while pointing to Maimonides' similar doctrine of negative theology, as well as his allegorical-moral reading of scripture.[59]

It is crucial to note that Rapoport's self-portrayal as Philo's great defender against De' Rossi's criticism appears to correspond to a recurring motif that is actually present in *Light of the Eyes*. In *'Imrei Binah*, one often encounters allusions to the Mantuan Provenzali brothers, who, in the words of David Winston, "championed the cause of Philo"[60] and therefore grappled with De' Rossi's critique of him in various points.[61] One specific footnote in *'Imrei Binah*'s chapter 5, in which De' Rossi names one of the Provenzali brothers, David, as "the defender of Yedidyah" (*magen yedidyahu*), is of special interest to our analysis: "Rabbi David Provenzali, may his shield and redeemer protect him, the defender of Yedidyah, reproved me for jumping to such an interpretation, and happily I accepted his reproof."[62] This seems to prompt the inference that Rapoport's self-portrayal as Philo's defender against De' Rossi, at least to a certain extent, took its cue from this depiction and its overall recurring role in *Light of the Eyes*. Bearing in mind Leopold Zunz's highly favorable description of Rapoport—whom he regarded as a "founder of critical [inquiry] within the science of Judaism"—as "the Azaria de' Rossi of our century,"[63] it should be stressed that Philo's status within Jewish tradition actually represented a grave point of disagreement between the two, a dispute in which the Galician was not willing to make the slightest of concessions.

Rapoport's central role within the context of the Eastern European rediscovery of Philo's thought also stems from the fact that he appears to have functioned as an important link between Krochmal's approach to Philo in terms of his Jewishness and other maskilic circles. This is best exemplified by Josef Flesch, the founding figure of the Moravian Haskalah,[64] whose ambitious life goal was to translate Philo's entire

---

[57] Rapoport, *Briefe*, 100.

[58] Rapoport, "Alexandria," 99 (my translation).

[59] Rapoport, "Alexandria," 99. For further analysis of this section, see Z. Strauss, "Solomon Judah Rapoport's Maskilic Revival of Philo of Alexandria: Rabbi Yedidya Ha-Alexandri, a Pioneer of Jewish Philosophy," *SPhiloA* 31 (2019): 213–18.

[60] D. Winston, "Philo and the Hellenistic Jewish Encounter," *SPhiloA* 7 (1995): 138.

[61] See G. Veltri, *Gegenwart der Tradition. Studien zur jüdischen Literatur und Kulturgeschichte* (Leiden: Brill, 2002), 294; I. Tishby, "Rabbi Moses Cordovero as He Appears in the Treatise of Rabbi Mordekhai Dato" (in Hebrew), *Sefunot: Studies and Texts on the History of the Jewish Community in Safed* 7 (1963): 127–28; Joanna Weinberg, Chapter 23 in this volume.

[62] De' Rossi, *Light*, 131 n. 27.

[63] Leopold Zunz, *Die Monatstage des Kalenderjahres, ein Andenken an Hingeschiedene* (Berlin: M. Poppelauer, 1872), 57.

[64] M. Miller, *Rabbis and Revolution: The Jews of Moravia in the Age of Emancipation* (Stanford: Stanford University Press, 2011), 89.

corpus into Hebrew and to include a detailed commentary. As Flesch's 1838 collection of translations of Philo's works, *Ḥayyei Mošeh*, reveals, he regarded Rapoport, from whom he sought advice and recognition for his unconventional intellectual venture, as the highest source of intellectual authority and inspiration: in the book's preface, he frames the entire book as an attempt to meet Rapoport's standards.[65] Rapoport's role within his great intellectual undertaking did not merely consist of words of encouragement, but involved active participation. Aside from giving Flesch concrete ideas for this book, Rapoport offered to provide him with a biographical essay on Philo which he could then use as an introduction to the translations proper.[66] From Flesch's account, we also learn that Rapoport regarded the Alexandrian as a thinker who was relevant to the Jewish people of his day, inasmuch as he was able to induce them to be more pious.

28.3 Conclusion

The findings of this study shed light on a phenomenon of the Haskalah which has received next to no acknowledgment in the field: the rediscovery of Philo by important Jewish enlighteners. It uncovers a surprising fact that one perhaps would not have anticipated: that it was above all Mendelssohn and Rapoport—thinkers who are hardly associated with Philonic thought—who were decisive for his rehabilitation. This chapter has examined the maskilic trend of modeling their carefully developed reassessment of Judaism on Hellenistic sources such as Philo, which provided them with a solid historical and conceptual basis for the reformulation of their faith in universal and rational terms. Its particular focus on the Hebrew maskilic revival of Philo is therefore by no means an accident. The aspect of the Hebrew language is also relevant, since it enabled these thinkers to (re)construct an image of Philo as a classical Jewish sage of Second Temple Judaism, as *Yedidyah ha-Alexandri*.

With regard to the seminal and inclusive approach to Philo taken by several of the maskilim—an approach that sought to harmonize his Hellenized Judaism, which advances the secular παιδεία alongside Jewish education[67] with rabbinic and medieval Sephardic traditions—these scholars appear to have at least rudimentarily grasped what Daniel Boyarin elucidates in his *Border Lines* about Philo's Jewish Logos theology: "This point [viz. that Philo's notion of the Logos was 'present among Semitic-speaking Jews, as well'] is important because it further disturbs the dichotomies that

---

[65] J. Flesch in Philo of Alexandria, *Ḥayyei Mošeh*, trans. J. Flesch (Prague: Moshe ha-Levi Landau, 1838), first and second pages of preface (no pagination).

[66] A biography in German (in Hebrew letters) of Philo was published in 1821: see anonymous, *Bikurei ha-'Ittim* 2 (1821): 22–23. Moshe Pelli assumes that its author was the journal's editor Salomon J. Cohen: see Pelli, "Bikurei Ha'itim" the "First Fruits" of Haskalah: An Annotated Index to "Bikurei Ha'itim," the Hebrew Journal of the Haskalah in Galicia (1820–1831) (in Hebrew) (Jerusalem: Magnes Press, 2005), 285.

[67] See G. E. Sterling, "The School of Moses in Alexandria: An Attempt to Reconstruct the School of Philo," in *Second Temple Jewish Paideia in Context*, ed. Jason M. Zurawski and Gabriele Bocaccini (Berlin: de Gruyter, 2017), 141–66.

have been promulgated between Hellenistic Judaism and rabbinic (by which is usually meant 'authentic', 'really real') Judaism."[68] Through their rediscovery of Philo's rich body of thought, the maskilim sought to reproduce a new universalistic image of the Jewish faith and its traditions, harkening back to Philo's ancient allegorical readings of scripture. In so doing, they dared to break the conventional mold, which constructed a distorted dichotomy between Hellenistic and Jewish wisdom in particular. The Jewish enlighteners recognized that in excluding Philo's view of Judaism, they would thus not only need to exclude various elements of tannaitic, amoraic, and Sephardic thought, but also crucial features of their own progressive maskilic account of the Jewish faith.

---

[68] D. Boyarin, *Border Lines: The Partition of Judaeo-Christianity* (Pennsylvania: University of Pennsylvania Press, 2004), 116.

29
The *Wissenschaft des Judentums*

Görge K. Hasselhoff

In the beginning of the nineteenth century a group of young Jewish scholars, among them Leopold Zunz, Immanuel Wolf, and Heinrich Heine, formulated a program to establish scholarly research on Judaism from a Jewish perspective.[1] Roughly thirty years later their efforts bore fruits when in Breslau the first modern Jewish seminary that aimed at training "modern" rabbis and teachers, i.e. educated like the Christian scholars, was founded.[2] The seminary's first director gathered some established and several young Jewish scholars who became the pioneers of a Jewish academic elite that laid the foundation of modern globally connected Jewish studies. Thus it soon became the first center for the study of the *Wissenschaft des Judentums* ("the science of Judaism"). From the very beginning the history of that Breslau *Jüdisch-Theologisches Seminar* (Jewish Theological Seminary = JTS) was connected with the study of Philo.[3] Three major exponents of the first generation of teachers (Zacharias Frankel, Heinrich Graetz, Manuel Joel) paved the way for the study of the Alexandrian exegete and philosopher in the second half of the nineteenth century. In the second and third generations, teachers and (former) students added to the enterprise which finally resulted in the critical edition by Leopold Cohn (and Paul Wendland), which is still the standard edition of Philo's Greek writings.

29.1 The First Generation

29.1.1 Zacharias Frankel

The foundation of the Breslau JTS in 1854 was accompanied by the publication of a scholarly program which contained an article by Z. Frankel and a historical sketch

---

[1] See Immanuel Wolf, "Ueber den Begriff einer Wissenschaft des Judenthums," *Zeitschrift für die Wissenschaft des Judenthums* 1 (1823): 1–24; G. K. Hasselhoff, "Idee und Leitgedanken des Bandes," in *Die Entdeckung des Christentums in der Wissenschaft des Judentums*, ed. G. K. Hasselhoff, Studia Judaica 54 (Berlin: de Gruyter, 2010), 3–16, at 3–13.

[2] On that seminary see G. K. Hasselhoff, "'Ueber den wissenschaftlichen Einfluss des Judenthums auf die nichtjüdische Welt' (M. Joel)—Zu einem Forschungsprogramm des Breslauer Jüdisch-Theologischen Seminars," *Kalonymos* 22.3 (2019): 4–8; for the status of rabbis in the nineteenth century, see C. Wilke, "*Den Talmud und den Kant*". *Rabbinerausbildung an der Schwelle zur Moderne*, Netiva 4 (Hildesheim et al.: Olms, 2003).

[3] M. R. Niehoff, "Alexandrian Judaism in 19th Century *Wissenschaft des Judentums*: Between Christianity and Modernization," in *Jüdische Geschichte in hellenistisch-römischer Zeit. Wege der Forschung: Vom alten zum neuen Schürer*, ed. A. Oppenheimer and E. Müller-Luckner, Schriften des Historischen Kollegs. Kolloquien 44 (Munich: Oldenbourg, 1999), 9–28, gives a different delimitation: She opens the debate with Isaac Marcus Jost

of the foundation of the seminary.[4] Frankel, who had been rabbi in Dresden and now served as the director of the seminary, contributed a summary of his research on the Septuagint in a forty-two-page study.[5] He opens that article with the thesis that during the Persian period of the exile, Judaism began to undertake the "investigation of Scripture" (*Schriftforschung*, 2) although a better term would be "exploration of Scripture" (*Schrifterforschung*, 2). He distinguishes between two types of such an exegesis, Palestinian and Alexandrian. Palestinian exegesis adheres strictly to the sense of the Hebrew meaning and differs from Alexandrian exegesis in not including any kind of metaphysical speculation (3). The next twenty pages or so are dedicated to the different approaches of the Palestinian exegetes starting with the *soferim* and ending with the rabbinic schools of the Talmudic age. Their intention is clear: the *halakhah* seeks for the law and the *hagada* for the religious feeling (*Gemüth*, 23). The Alexandrian investigation of scripture has to be characterized in contrast to these schools. It is "represented by Philo" (23) who based his exegesis on the Septuagint. As a translation, it is located in the "area of hermeneutics" (24). Among Philo's predecessors are exegetes such as Aristobulus but Frankel doubts that the church fathers transmitted his exegesis faithfully (24). Only with Philo can the real investigation of scripture be detected. Only Philo follows clear rules of interpretation, although he unfortunately was not able to read Hebrew (25–26). Nonetheless Philo does point to the noble house of the deity, namely the "prepared soul" (26). The soul's preparation consists of the Greek virtues and sciences, in Philo's case the Neoplatonic philosophy which leads him to a "reconciliation of belief and speculation (*Aussöhnung des Glaubens und der Spekulation*)" (27). But he errs in that he puts belief and science on the same level (27). Moreover, he does not read metaphysics via scripture but the other way around; he subordinates scripture to philosophical speculation when he more than once claimed that a philosophical idea is not his but that of Moses (28). From that methodology the Alexandrian exegetes developed their method of allegorical interpretation with the "wisdom of virtue as highest goal" (29). Wisdom and virtue are thereby understood as synonyms. From such a standpoint law could only be understood allegorically. But allegory leads to an "investigation of scripture through inspiration" (30). The relation between God and creation is determined by the Logos that represents the world of ideas in a Platonic sense but sometimes can be understood as a second deity (31). Despite his criticism of that kind of exegesis, Frankel summarizes some principles of the Alexandrian or Philonic investigation of scripture with a mixture of criticism and admiration. First, scripture does not say a word too much. If it does so, it requires investigation as to why an expression is doubled or whether there is a superfluous word (33–34). Second, a word might have

---

and ends with Moritz Friedländer; she differentiates between a "Setting the Stage in the early 1820s" and two phases of "Scholarship on Alexandrian Judaism" in the "1840s–1850s" and "from 1865 onwards". In this chapter I will limit my research on those scholars who in one way or other were affiliated to the JTS.

[4] Cf. *Programm zur Eröffnung des jüdisch-theologischen Seminars zu Breslau "Fraenkel'sche Stiftung" den 16. Ab 5614 / 10. August 1854* (Breslau: Korn, 1854).

[5] Z. Frankel, "Über palästinische und alexandrinische Schriftforschung," in *Programm zur Eröffnung*, 1–42 (references to this article are inserted in brackets in the main text); already in his monograph *Ueber den Einfluss der*

multiple senses (34–35). Third, an expression needs an explanation either because of its unusualness or because it is imprecise or because of its etymology (35–36). Fourth, a play on words generates numerous explanations (36–37). Fifth, several numbers in scripture are explained allegorically (37). Sixth, proper names, especially if they are Hebrew loanwords, are the basis of speculation and sometimes wild etymologies (37–39). Finally, seventh, sometimes an allegorical explanation is needed "because literal explanation does not make sense" (39; cf. 39–41). In short, the result of Alexandrian exegesis is: "Scripture was lost in fog, the historical basis is undermined, biblical persons are only images, and the law lost its binding strength" (41), and worse: "with that mysterious contemplation the specifically Jewish element got lost" (42).

Although Frankel's judgment of Philo is mostly negative, he laid the foundation for an engagement with the Alexandrian philosopher in his newly founded seminary.[6] He was not the only teacher of the first generation to do so.

29.1.2 Heinrich Graetz

In the several editions of the third volume of his *History of the Jewish People*, H. Graetz made use of Philo as a historian.[7] From edition to edition the number of references to him grew. Starting with the first edition from 1856, in the tenth chapter Philo is introduced as "the main representative" of those members of the Jewish community who had received a Greek education, and as "the Jewish Platonist" who described the messiah as a superhuman angelic person.[8] The whole passage is accompanied by a long "note" (note 10) in which Graetz argues that the work on the Therapeutae (*De vita contemplativa*) is wrongly ascribed to Philo because it is unbelievable that the Therapeutae could be Jewish (518–22). In the same section he even refers to Frankel's above-mentioned article (520). In the next chapter (ch. 11) Graetz summarizes Philo's report on Flaccus and his delegation to Rome (270–82). In this passage Philo is called "the Jewish philosopher" (275, 277) who was so important that he deserved to be treated in more detail (277–79).[9] His main philosophical aim was "to reconcile contemporary

---

palästinischen Exegese auf die alexandrinische Hermeneutik (Leipzig: Barth, 1851), we find some references to Philo. On Frankel, see also Niehoff, "Alexandrian Judaism in 19th Century *Wissenschaft des Judentums*," 14–16; A. Brämer, *Rabbiner Zacharias Frankel. Wissenschaft des Judentums und conservative Reform im 19. Jahrhundert*, Netiva 3 (Hildesheim et al.: Olms, 2000), 159, mentions only the later article on Philo (see next note).

[6] See also his later article Z. Frankel, "Zur Ethik des jüdisch-alexandrinischen Philosophen Philo," *MGWJ* 16 (1867): 241–52, 281–97, in which he mainly repeated his position in a more concentrated form.

[7] Even before Graetz was appointed to the seminary he devoted a number of lines to Philo as an aggadic-philosophical writer; see H. Grätz [!], "Die Construction der jüdischen Geschichte. Eine Skizze," *Zeitschrift für die religiösen Interessen des Judenthums* 3 (1846): 81–97, 121–32, 361–81, 413–21, at 369–72. M. Pyka, *Jüdische Identität bei Heinrich Graetz*, Jüdische Religion, Geschichte und Kultur 5 (Göttingen: Vandenhoeck & Ruprecht, 2009), limits himself to this article. See also Niehoff, "Alexandrian Judaism in 19th Century *Wissenschaft des Judentums*," 17–20, who concentrates on this early essay and the first edition of the *Geschichte*.

[8] H. Graetz, *Geschichte der Juden von dem Tode Juda Makkabi's bis zum Untergang des jüdischen Staates* (Leipzig: Leopold Schnauß, 1856), 259 with a reference to *De exsecrationibus* M. II. 435 (= C-W 5.374 [n. 165]). Further references to Graetz are inserted in brackets in the main line.

[9] On the last page his name is even inserted into the header line.

philosophy with Judaism," or to be more precise: "to demonstrate that Judaism was the true infallible philosophy" (280). The whole passage ends with Graetz's judgment that Philo was a "historian (*Geschichtsschreiber*)" (281). This evaluation is furthered by another long note in the appendix in which Graetz scrutinizes Philo's *Legatio ad Gaium* (546–53).[10] In chapter 13 again a longer passage on Philo is inserted (315–31). It opens with a rejection of a thesis by Wilhelm Martin Leberecht de Wette who, drawing on a long tradition that stretches at least back to Jerome, possibly to the Muratorian fragment, called Philo the author of the *Book of Wisdom* (315).[11] It continues with a general characterization of the Greek allegorists (similar to Frankel's, but more detailed; 315–18), which results in a detailed study of Philo's exegesis (318–31).[12] Here, Philo is called "the greatest spirit generated by the Alexandrian Jews" (318). Although Philo has to be counted among the allegorists, he nonetheless is important because he emphasizes the "ongoing validity" of the Mosaic Law (320). But his philosophical standpoint reduced his importance for Jews and Judaism, and he lost touch with "the truth of Judaism" (325). Graetz's description of Philo's philosophical system follows Eduard Zeller's *History of Greek Philosophy* (325 n. 3).[13] Graetz ends his characterization of Philo with two harsh statements: "The Philonic system is defective and unsatisfactory (*mangelhaft und unbefriedigend*)," (331) and: Philo became the "progenitor of a mystical *Weltanschauung* [worldview]" (331).[14]

The major change in the second edition from 1863 is the insertion of a new chapter on Christianity (as ch. 11).[15] Nonetheless all references to Philo remain the same. In the third edition dated to 1878 again the main line of argument concerning Philo remains the same.[16] Nonetheless we find several additions. Apart from minor supplements in the footnotes, changes concern the adjective "Judaic (*judäisch*)" instead of "Jewish (*jüdisch*)" (Philo now is "a Judaic philosopher," 357), but also points of argument. In the discussion of the *Book of Wisdom* the rejection of De Wette is left out and with it the idea that Philo might have been its author (406). The next passages on the allegorists and on Philo are reworked (mainly stylistically)[17] and footnotes are added on Philo's attitude toward the philosophical interpretation of the Bible (407 n. 1, 408 n. 1) as well as a reference to Carl Siegfried's major publication *Philo of Alexandria as Exegete of the*

---

[10] Already in chapter 8 under the sub-heading "Jews in Rome," some references to Philo are inserted in a similar manner (*Geschichte der Juden*, 170–72).

[11] A further reference to Philo in connection with the Bible can be found in "Note 2" on the Septuagint, *Geschichte der Juden*, 478.

[12] Again the header for pages 319–29 bears "Philo" as a title.

[13] Graetz seems to refer to E. Zeller, *Die Philosophie der Griechen. Eine Untersuchung über Charakter, Gang und Hauptmomente ihrer Entwicklung, Dritter Theil: Die nacharistotelische Philosophie, Zweite Hälfte* (Tübingen: Ludwig Friedrich Fues, 1852).

[14] On Graetz's ambivalent attitude towards the Jewish mystical tradition, see G. Y. Kohler, "Heinrich Graetz and the Kabbalah," *Kabbalah. Journal for the Study of Jewish Mystical Texts* 40 (2017): 107–30.

[15] H. Graetz, *Geschichte der Juden von dem Tode Juda Makkabi's bis zum Untergang des jüdischen Staates*, Zweite verbesserte und stark vermehrte Auflage (Leipzig: Oskar Leiner, 1863).

[16] H. Graetz, *Geschichte der Judäer von dem Tode Juda Makkabi's bis zum Untergange des jüdischen Staates*, Dritte verbesserte und stark vermehrte Auflage (Leipzig: Oskar Leiner, 1878). The subsequent references in the text are to this 3rd edn.

[17] Only in the final judgment is Philo's system no longer "unsatisfactory," but "inconsistent (*schwankend*)"; *Geschichte der Judäer*, 422.

Old Testament (407 n. 2).[18] The whole passage on Philo in chapter 13 is extended with more detail on his apologetic writings and actions (423–25; cf. 428). Further changes concerning Philo can be found within the supplementary notes: The discussion of the Therapeutae and Philo is reduced to a minimum, but still Graetz holds that Philo did not write *De vita contemplativa* (658). "Note 24" is replaced by a new one with the title "Philo and his writings" (678–83). Graetz introduces Philo's writings and states that all writings with a dedication are forged (680). In this context the treatises *Quod omnis probus liber* and *De vita contemplativa*, which in the earlier editions were discussed in note 10, are placed among the falsely attributed writings. Also, the historical writings *Legatio* and *In Flaccum* are discussed as being both written by Philo and falsely attributed: Their content goes back to one original Philonic writing but because of many verbal repetitions they seem to be the product of a later redactor.[19] In the last edition that Graetz himself issued, namely the fourth edition, which is extended especially in the notes in the appendix, we find no significant changes with regard to Philo except the new number 25 for the note on the Alexandrian philosopher.[20]

29.1.3 Manuel Joel

A third teacher of the first generation of the Breslau seminary also dedicated his attention to Philo, namely the teacher of classics and of philosophy of religion, Menachem Secharja (called Manuel) Joel.[21] In 1863–64 he published two articles on Philo. The first article was published in the *Monatsschrift für Geschichte und Wissenschaft des Judenthums*[22] in 1863 and was dedicated to the Philonic philosophical system in its relation to other contemporary philosophical trends.[23] In this article Joel first states that enough was written on Philo's system (especially by Zeller), but also on Philo's exegesis (by Z. Frankel in the article mentioned above). Therefore, he now wants to write on the relation to contemporary philosophical systems, especially the Stoa. In Joel's opinion Philo had some affinity to the Stoa, but there were also some hindrances. With the help of the Platonic theory of ideas and the Pythagorean mystical understanding of numbers he tried to reconcile the Stoa with Judaism.[24] The main problem

---

[18] See C. Siegfried, *Philo von Alexandria als Ausleger des Alten Testaments an sich selbst und nach seinem geschichtlichen Einfluss betrachtet. Nebst Untersuchungen über die Graecitaet Philo's* (Jena: Dufft, 1875).

[19] Cf. Siegfried, *Philo von Alexandria*, 681.

[20] H. Graetz, *Geschichte der Judäer von dem Tode Juda Makkabi's bis zum Untergange des jüdischen Staates*, Vierte verbesserte und stark vermehrte Auflage (Leipzig: Oskar Leiner, 1888) (two parts). For this survey I leave out the 5th edn which was edited by M. Brann in 1905 because it did not contain changes by Graetz. Brann himself inserts Leopold Cohn's findings into the long note on Philo.

[21] On Joel, see G. K. Hasselhoff, "Philosophie und Rabbinat: Manuel Joel," in *Religion und Rationalität*, ed. G. K. Hasselhoff and Michael Meyer-Blanck, Studien des Bonner Zentrums für Religion und Gesellschaft 4 (Würzburg: Ergon, 2008), 285–313; G. K. Hasselhoff, "Manuel Joel and the Neo-Maimonidean Discovery of Kant," in *The Cultures of Maimonideanism: New Approaches to the History of Jewish Thought*, ed. J. T. Robinson, Supplements to the Journal of Jewish Thought and Philosophy 9 (Leiden, Boston: Brill, 2009), 289–307; A. Rybińska, *Manuel Joël (1826–1890). Biografia kulturowa wrocławskiego rabina z kręgu* Wissenschaft des Judentums (Lublin: Wydawnictwo Uniwersytetu Marii Curie-Skłodowskiej, 2020).

[22] Although Z. Frankel had started to edit that journal in 1851 the *MGWJ* was the main journal of the JTS. It was one of the few Jewish journals that was not read only by a Jewish audience.

[23] M. Joel, "Ueber einige geschichtliche Beziehungen des Philonischen Systems," *MGWJ* 12 (1863): 19–31.

[24] Cf. Joel, "Ueber einige geschichtliche Beziehungen des Philonischen Systems," 21–22.

of the Stoa was the materialistic and pantheistic background of its metaphysics.[25] Joel then goes on to show similarities between Stoic philosophy and different aspects of the Philonic philosophy. He concludes his short article with the summarizing words "that Philonism ... is nothing but an adjustment (*Ausgleichung*) of Stoicism with Scripture, an adjustment that led Philo far beyond Stoicism and through the combination with other elements to his own standpoint."[26]

In a second article which was a republication of two papers read in Breslau, Joel elaborated on Philo and his philosophical system. The first part of this article is a description of the Hellenistic world and the allegorical method, while the second part deals with Philo and his philosophy itself.[27] Joel opens this second part with the programmatic statement "that Philo was a philosophical author" (41). Although himself a philosopher and historian of philosophy, Joel does not mean that as positively as it may sound. For him the philosopher not only produced truths but also—albeit intelligent—errors (42). Nonetheless Joel goes on to answer three major questions, namely what Philo wrote, what he taught in his writings and whom he influenced. Concerning Philo's writings, Joel limits himself to the remark that some of his writings were lost whereas others were falsely attributed to him. In them a philosophical system, but also a "boundlessness of allegorical explanations" (44) can be found. Concerning his second question, Joel points to what was "the new, the original" (45) written by Philo. To ascertain the distinctive nature of Philo's thought Joel introduces contemporaneous philosophical ideas, of which pantheism was the most intriguing. But pantheism in its "one-sided and erroneous" pagan Greek version was opposed by Philo who judged it "with his spirit, nourished and strengthened by Jewish doctrine" (48).[28] Philo's answer was that God was "separated from all that is personal and living" (51). For contact with that God humankind needed a special power, which was the Logos (52). Joel mentions his criticism of that concept, but he does not elaborate on it. As a third answer, Joel briefly points to Philo's reception within Christianity and Islam. The concept of the Trinity was borrowed from Philo which made him "the church father of the Church Fathers" (54). Also, the concept of Neoplatonism was shaped by him. Interestingly enough, no Jews were directly influenced by Philo. In fact, "in the centuries to come Philo was ignored by the Jews" (55). Nonetheless, Joel concludes, Philo's influence was "more enduring (*nachhaltiger*) than a superficial look" might have suggested (57).

After these two articles Joel was almost silent about Philo for the next twenty years. In the two volumes of his *Blicke in die Religionsgeschichte*[29] we find a handful of references to Philo. Yet it is no longer a presentation of the "unknown" Alexandrian, but

---

[25] Cf. Joel, "Ueber einige geschichtliche Beziehungen des Philonischen Systems," 22.
[26] Joel, "Ueber einige geschichtliche Beziehungen des Philonischen Systems," 31.
[27] M. Joel, "Ueber Philo, den hervorragendsten Vertreter der jüdisch-alexandrinischen Geistesrichtung," *Jahrbuch für Israeliten* 5624 (1863–64), N.F. 10 (Vienna: H. Engel & Sohn, 1864), 24–57. References to this article are inserted in brackets in the main text.
[28] Only with Spinoza was a compelling pantheistic model introduced that influenced, among others, Lessing, Goethe, Schleiermacher, and even Hegel (cf. Joel, "Ueber Philo, den hervorragendsten Vertreter der jüdisch-alexandrinischen Geistesrichtung," 50).
[29] M. Joel, *Blicke in die Religionsgeschichte zu Anfang des zweiten christlichen Jahrhunderts*, 2 vols (Breslau: Schottlaender, 1880–83).

rather some scattered references to him in connection with an ongoing argument about the religious history of the first two centuries CE. In one case Philo serves as a proof that there were antinomian tendencies within Judaism of his time.[30] In another case Joel corrects Eduard Zeller by showing that Philo's theory of prophecy was actually a copy of Plato's understanding of mantic prophecy.[31] In two instances Joel refers to Philo and Josephus as representatives of their time.[32] In another place he compares (Pseudo-?) Aristobulus with Philo.[33]

With these three examples of Frankel, Graetz, and Joel we see three different approaches to Philo that were typical of the methods of the Breslau JTS: Frankel emphasizes the "correct" Jewish approach to the Bible as is laid down in rabbinic exegesis. Philo's allegorical and Greek approach is deficient and rather "non-Jewish." Graetz on the other hand places Philo, whom he seems to dislike, within the ancient Jewish world. As such Philo deserves a full description. In addition, he serves as a source of ancient Jewish history. Joel appears as a kind of middle path between both colleagues. His main focus is on Philo as the protagonist of the Greek-speaking Judaism of his time. As a historian of philosophy, he is conscious of Philo's impact on later trends of the history of ideas, but as he does also with other philosophers, he requires the reader to follow these traces.

The fourth important teacher of the first generation was Jacob Bernays. During his time at the seminary he only wrote one small philological piece on Philo in which he suggests that the Pseudo-Philonic treatise *De incorruptibilitate mundi* was printed in the wrong order. To correct this he suggests a different order of the pages. The short study was not published in one of the Jewish journals but in the *Monatsberichte der Königlich Preußischen Akademie der Wissenschaften zu Berlin*.[34] The other two publications on Philo came out only a long time after Bernays had left the Breslau seminary in 1866.[35]

29.2 The Second and Third Generations

In the second generation of teachers and students of the seminary (after c.1870) there are quite a number of treatments of Philo, whether doctoral theses written by

---

[30] Cf. Joel, *Blicke in die Religionsgeschichte*, 1:29 with n. 1.
[31] Cf. Joel, *Blicke in die Religionsgeschichte*, 39–40. In another case (p. 88) Joel simply refers to Zeller's interpretation.
[32] Cf. Joel, *Blicke in die Religionsgeschichte*, 2:51, 69 (the latter shows similarities to Graetz's treatment of the figure of Sejanus according to Philo's *Legatio*).
[33] Cf. Joel, *Blicke in die Religionsgeschichte*, 177.
[34] [Jacob] Bernays, "Über die Herstellung des Zusammenhanges in der unter Philo's Namen gehenden Schrift περὶ ἀφθαρσίας κόσμου durch Blätterversetzung," *Monatsberichte der Königlich Preußischen Akademie der Wissenschaften zu Berlin* 1863 (Berlin: Verlag der Königlichen Akademie der Wissenschaften, 1864), 34–40. While significant and influential for a time, Bernays' view that the treatise was inauthentic has been mostly rejected; see e.g. D. T. Runia, "Philo's De Aeternitate Mundi: The Problem of Its Interpretation," *VC* 35.2 (1981): 105–51.
[35] See J. Bollack, *Jacob Bernays. Un homme entre deux mondes* (Villeneuve d'Ascq [Nord]: Presses universitaires du Septentrion, 1998), 108: in 1876 Bernays published a German translation of the treatise mentioned above and a further article in the *Monatsberichte*.

students or articles.[36] From the teachers of the seminary we have to mention Jacob Freudenthal, although he did not write anything dedicated to Philo directly. But in 1869 he published a public lecture on the reception history of Hellenistic philosophy, including Philo.[37] In this paper Freudenthal gives a helpful survey of 1,800 years of mainly Christian readings of Philo. But more important is that Freudenthal dedicated a number of courses taught at the seminary to Philo and selected writings.[38] At least one of his students, Leopold Treitel, in the preface of his doctoral thesis explicitly thanked him for that.

29.2.1 Leopold Treitel

Perhaps the most dedicated approach of the seminary's second generation to Philo was made by Leopold Treitel[39] who was the brother-in-law of the director of the JTS, Marcus Brann.[40] He was still a student of the JTS when he submitted a thesis written (or translated into?)[41] Latin to the Breslau Friedrich Wilhelms-Universität in 1871.[42] In the preface the only person he thanks is Jacob Freudenthal.[43] The following twenty-eight pages are dedicated to questions concerning the use of koine Greek in Philo's works.[44] Thus, the thesis is purely philological.

Two years later—Treitel was still a student at the seminary—he published a short article in the first volume of Rahmer's *Das Jüdische Literaturblatt*.[45] Without any references Treitel gave a survey of the feast days known to Philo and how the Alexandrian philosopher understood them. Thirty (!) years later Treitel—by that time rabbi in Laupheim, Baden—extended that short article and gave numerous references to Philo's works as well as to works by Philo scholars who had written since he left Breslau.[46] Nevertheless for Treitel the result of scrutinizing Philo's works remains: "This is the main feature that interweaves Philonic exegesis and religious philosophy: mysticism side by side

---

[36] According to Niehoff, "Alexandrian Judaism in 19th Century *Wissenschaft des Judentums*," 22, this is part of an institutionalization of the study of Philo. I would add that we find two trends that I will try to show in the following pages: On the one hand, we find more specialized studies on Philo, and on the other hand Philo became an undisputed part of Jewish identity.

[37] See [Jacob] Freudenthal, "Zur Geschichte der Anschauungen über die jüdisch-hellenistische Religionsphilosophie," *MGWJ* 18 (1869): 399–421.

[38] M. Brann, *Geschichte des jüdisch-theologischen Seminars (Fraenkel'sche Stiftung) in Breslau. Festschrift zum fünfzigjährigen Jubiläum der Anstalt* (Breslau: Schatzky, 1904), xxvi–xxviii: e.g. 1873: Philo and Josephus and their position in Hellenistic literature; 1878; 1884; 1885: Explanation of Philo's *De opificio mundi*.

[39] The only recent treatment of his writings can be found in K. Nele Jansen, *Die Rabbiner im Deutschen Reich 1871–1945*, 2 parts, Biographisches Handbuch der Rabbiner 2 (Munich: K. G. Saur, 2009), 610–12.

[40] On Brann, see recently B. Kalinowska-Wójcik, "Jüdische Geschichtsforschung im Schlesien des 19. und frühen 20. Jahrhunderts: Jacob Caro (1835–1904), Markus Brann (1849–1920) und Ezechiel Zivier (1868–1925)," in *Gelehrte—Schulen—Netzwerke. Geschichtsforscher in Schlesien im langen 19. Jahrhundert*, ed. J. Bahlcke and R. Gehrke, Neue Forschungen zur schlesischen Geschichte 28 (Vienna: Böhlau 2020), 331–66.

[41] Quite a number of theses had been translated for that purpose, among them Hermann Cohen's PhD thesis.

[42] Leopold Treitel, *De Philonis Judaei Sermone* (Breslau: Jungfer, 1870).

[43] Treitel, *De Philonis Judaei Sermone*, 1.

[44] Treitel, *De Philonis Judaei Sermone*, 2–29. On p. 30 we find a short CV.

[45] L. Treitel, "Die Bedeutung der jüdischen Feste nach Philo," *Das Jüdische Literaturblatt* 1 (1872): 74–75, 82–83.

[46] L. Treitel, "Der Nomos, insonderheit Sabbat und Feste, in philonischer Beleuchtung, an der Hand von Philo's Schrift De Septenario," *MGWJ* 47 (1903): 214–31, 317–21, 399–417, 490–514.

with rational, sober understanding, in parts of a profound world of thought."[47] In 1904, Treitel published an article in the *Theologische Studien und Kritiken*, an old and established Protestant journal, on Philo's place in religious and cultural history.[48] In the first part of this article Treitel gives a survey of studies on Philo within roughly the last fifty years, in both Jewish (Frankel) and Christian authors (among others Carl Siegfried and Adolf Harnack).[49] He then turns to Jewish feasts in Philo's interpretation.[50] This part of the article contains ideas of the 1903 article in abbreviated form. The summary stresses Philo's importance for the Greek and Roman world, especially Christianity, because in Philo Jewish particularism was extended to a cultural and religious universalism.[51]

Between 1909 and 1912 Treitel published several further works on Philo. The most important seems to be his translation of *De decalogo* in the first volume of the German translations of Philo's works edited by Leopold Cohn.[52] In the same year, 1909, his article "Agada bei Philo" appeared in the *Monatsschrift*.[53] This article starts with a lament for the fact that within Judaism the aggadah seems to have been mistreated. Treitel then asks what aggadah is. In discussion with Zunz, for whom aggadah includes all genres in the rabbinic writings that were not halakhah,[54] Treitel defines aggadah as "ethics and belief within Judaism."[55] Within Philo's works one had to differentiate between allegorical interpretation and aggadic midrash. The latter concerns the "real world."[56] The rest of the article scrutinizes Philo's *Quaestiones in Genesim* and *De vita Mosis* in discussion with Carl Siegfried. Here, Treitel states, for example, that the moral law of the Torah is natural law.[57] In another case Treitel asserts the proximity of Philo's aggadic approach to the Palestinian midrashim.[58] Two years later a further article appeared in the *Monatsschrift*, now dedicated to the question of allegorical interpretation.[59] Again, Treitel asserts the nearness of Midrash and Philo.[60] Nonetheless, one must differentiate between Alexandrian allegory, which points to "an esoteric and more or less mystical world," and Palestinian aggadah, which remains "in the world of the real things."[61] Despite his criticism of the allegorical method, concluding his article Treitel states that within allegorical interpretation some "homiletic gold nuggets" might be found.[62] In 1912, we find Treitel among the contributors to the *Judaica-Festschrift* for Hermann

---

[47] Treitel, "Der Nomos, insonderheit Sabbat und Feste," 514.
[48] L. Treitel, "Die religions- und kulturgeschichtliche Stellung Philos," *Theologische Studien und Kritiken* 77 (1904): 380–401.
[49] Cf. Treitel, "Die religions- und kulturgeschichtliche Stellung Philos," 380–83.
[50] Cf. Treitel, "Die religions- und kulturgeschichtliche Stellung Philos," 383–400.
[51] Cf. Treitel, "Die religions- und kulturgeschichtliche Stellung Philos," 400.
[52] In the edition mentioned below, 1:369–409.
[53] L. Treitel, "Agada bei Philo," *MGWJ* 53 (1909): 28–45, 159–73, 286–91.
[54] See [Leopold] Zunz, *Zur Geschichte und Literatur*, vol. 1 (Berlin: Veit und Comp., 1845).
[55] Treitel, "Agada bei Philo," 34
[56] Treitel, "Agada bei Philo," 35.
[57] Cf. Treitel, "Agada bei Philo," 36, 42.
[58] Cf. e.g. "Agada bei Philo," 39–40, 168, 287.
[59] L. Treitel, "Ursprung, Begriff und Umfang der allegorischen Schrifterklärung," *MGWJ* 55 (1911): 543–54. In light of the length of the article, it seems to have been a paper read to an audience.
[60] See Treitel, "Ursprung, Begriff und Umfang der allegorischen Schrifterklärung," 546, 550.
[61] Treitel, "Ursprung, Begriff und Umfang der allegorischen Schrifterklärung," 551.
[62] Treitel, "Ursprung, Begriff und Umfang der allegorischen Schrifterklärung," 554.

Cohen.[63] In his short article, Treitel concentrates on the "middle beings (*Mittelwesen*)" or divine powers, namely the angels. He states that these Philonic teachings were without an echo in the Palestinian Jewish world in Mishnaic or Talmudic times.[64] In 1915, Marcus Brann edited a volume of Treitel's essays under the title *Philonische Studien*, containing all the articles mentioned above.[65] Treitel's main merit seems to be that he emphasized the similarities but also the differences between Philo's theological methods (allegory, aggadah) and the Aramaic traditions in Palestine that resulted in the Midrashic and Talmudic literature.

29.2.2 Bernhard Loebel Ritter

In 1879 Bernhard Loebel Ritter submitted a thirty-two-page thesis to Halle University with which he obtained a doctoral degree.[66] In the same year a full-length study under the same title, *Philo und die Halacha. Eine vergleichende Studie unter steter Berücksichtigung des Josephus*, appeared at the J. C. Hinrichsche Buchhandlung, now comprising XII and 139 pages.[67] Although this study is too detailed to be summarized here, it deserves to be mentioned. The introduction of the book opens with a comparison and survey of "Egypt and Palestine" (3–9) and a sketch of "Philo and the Law"; in some points Philo diverges from the Palestinian halakhah (9–17). This short introduction is followed by five main chapters and forty subchapters in which Ritter scrutinizes 129 biblical passages containing legal precepts both in Philo and the halakhic writings from the Mishnah to Maimonides. It opens with a chapter on criminal law. First, he gives an interpretation of the *ius talionis* (18–21), followed by an overview of capital crimes (21–55) and non-capital crimes (56–67). A second chapter is dedicated to marriage laws (68–93), a third chapter to laws of succession (94–97). The fourth main chapter treats constitutional law (98–106) and finally the fifth chapter deals with ceremonial laws (107–26). In a sixth chapter Ritter adds reflections on single laws (127–32). To these chapters some additional longer notes are added (133–37).

---

[63] L. Treitel, "Die alexandrinische Lehre von den Mittelwesen oder göttlichen Kräften, insbesondere bei Philo, geprüft auf die Frage, ob und welchen Einfluß sie auf das Mutterland Palästina gehabt. Beitrag zur Geschichte der jüdischen Religionsphilosophie," in *Judaica: Festschrift zu Hermann Cohens siebzigstem Geburtstage* (Berlin: Bruno Cassirer, 1912), 177–84.

[64] See Treitel, "Die alexandrinische Lehre von den Mittelwesen oder göttlichen Kräften," 180.

[65] L. Treitel, *Philonische Studien*, ed. M. Brann (Breslau: Marcus, 1915). In 1923 a further book by Treitel appeared: Ludwig [!] Treitel, *Gesamte Theologie und Philosophie Philo's von Alexandria* (Berlin: Schwetschke, 1923). In a review by H. Leisegang (*Theologische Literaturzeitung* 48 [1923]: col. 199–201) it reads: "It seems that its author has lost touch with contemporary scholarship." Leisegang then lists numerous errors within Treitel's monograph. J. Jeremias argues similarly in his review (*Theologisches Literaturblatt* 44 [1923]: cols 264–5).

[66] B. Ritter, *Philo und die Halacha. Eine vergleichende Studie unter steter Berücksichtigung des Josephus* (s.l. [Leipzig]: Hundertstund & Pries, 1879) [*non vidi*].—It is quite likely that Ritter submitted only the first chapters as a thesis to the university (cf. the note to the printer in the longer version, see next note).

[67] B. Ritter, *Philo und die Halacha. Eine vergleichende Studie unter steter Berücksichtigung des Josephus* (Leipzig: Hinrichs, 1879). On p. 140 we find a reference to the printing press: "Druck von Hundertstund & Pries." References to this book are inserted in brackets.

In Ritter's study Philo is treated as a part of an observant Judaism. In his writings the Alexandrian interpretation of the law is preserved. In some cases, the legal tradition seems to have been identical with the (later) rabbinic law, in other places Philo helps to understand the development of certain legal traditions. Therefore, he deserves to be read.

29.2.3 Max Freudenthal

A different standpoint is taken by Max Freudenthal, who in 1891 produced a philosophical thesis on Philo's epistemology. Still a student in Breslau, his dissertation was first refused by the University of Tübingen in 1890 before it was accepted by the University of Greifswald in 1891.[68] It appeared in print as the first issue of volume 13 of the respected philological series *Berliner Studien*.[69] It consists of three parts of different length. In the introduction Freudenthal defines his field of research by delimiting his approach from the theological approaches which concentrate on Philo's allegorism. He states that, despite the acknowledgment of Philo's "pure notion of God," there was little research into his philosophical teachings (3). In the first main part he then characterizes Philo's epistemology, which he regards as mainly ethical (7–24). Since Philo's philosophy is primarily theosophical, "as a consequence it leads to teleology, determinism and occasionalism" (15). In the second main part, Freudenthal treats Philo's "cognitive psychology (*Erkenntnispsychologie*)" (24–75). That part is in itself divided into three chapters. The first chapter deals with the sources of cognition, namely *nous* and *aisthesis*, that he divides into the creation out of the world of ideas and the parts of the soul (24–42). The second chapter deals with the process of cognition, i.e. the physiology of sensation as well as sense perception and imagination (42–63). The third chapter is dedicated to the value of cognition, i.e. error, delusion, the basis of such teaching and its highest goal (63–75). In the conclusion Freudenthal repeats that Philo's interest was ethics and theosophy; everything else was subordinated to it. His system was not closed and finished. Therefore, he could add to it eclectically from the Stoa as well as from Plato and Aristotle. This eclecticism made Philo "despite of his dependency an independent thinker" (77).

29.2.4 Hermann Cohen and Others

Although Hermann Cohen studied at the Breslau Seminary for only a short time in 1857 when he was a very young man, he was strongly influenced by M. Joel as a teacher and Jacob Guttmann as a fellow student. Cohen is a good example of a thinker for

---

[68] Cf. Jansen, *Die Rabbiner im Deutschen Reich 1871–1945*, 200–203, at 201. Max Freudenthal was not directly related to Jacob Freudenthal.

[69] M. Freudenthal, *Die Erkenntnislehre Philos von Alexandria*, Berliner Studien für classische Philologie und Archäologie 13.1 (Berlin: Calvary, 1891). References to this work are inserted in brackets in the main text.

whom Philo is part of a Jewish tradition and for whom he needs no further justification to quote.

As an example, one might consider the festschrift *Judaica* that was dedicated to the Marburg philosopher on the occasion of his seventieth birthday: Among the forty-three contributions, there are four articles on Philo—that is more than on any other single person belonging to the Jewish tradition.[70] The topics dealt with range from "Philo's theory of the oath" by J. (Isaak) Heinemann,[71] to Treitel's above-mentioned article on angels, to two detailed studies on Philo's theory of the Logos by Leopold Cohn[72] and on Philo's influence on the development of Alexandrian Judaism by Jacob Horowitz.[73] That broad range of topics mirrors the few references to Philo in Cohen's oeuvre. There are no references to the Alexandrian philosopher in the works on Kant and in his "System of Philosophy," except for Cohen's ethics.[74] In his writings on *The Notion of Religion* and in the *Religion of Reason out of the Sources of Judaism* there are isolated references to Philo that identify him as one of the figures of Jewish history. First, Philo is identified as the ancient Jewish philosopher who tried to unify Plato's idealistic philosophy and Moses' revelation. For Philo, philosophy was thus part of religion.[75] Second, Philo's definition and interpretation of the Logos paved the way for Christian theology: "In the Logos the will, the divine will, becomes the intellect."[76] Third, Philo reformulates the Platonist idea of the notion of humankind as the unity of humankind: For him, "man becomes the idea of mankind. Thus, he first he formulates the homogeneous man as idea."[77]

Among the students who wrote on Philo and were more closely linked to the Breslau JTS we find Benjamin Rippner, Meyer Dienstfertig, and Salomon Tiktin. In 1872, Rippner wrote a long and detailed review of Max Heinze's book on the Logos in Greek philosophy.[78] One of Rippner's points is how the immaterialist God could create the material world with the Logos. Dienstfertig submitted a thirty-three-page PhD thesis to Erlangen University in which he scrutinized the ideas and definitions of "prophetology" in Jewish religious-philosophical writings of the first century CE. For him, Philo initiates a Jewish mysticism.[79] Tiktin submitted a fifty-nine-page PhD thesis to Bern University. His main interested was in Philo's understanding of virtues and

---

[70] See *Judaica: Festschrift zu Hermann Cohens siebzigstem Geburtstage*.
[71] J. Heinemann, "Philos Lehre vom Eid," in *Judaica*, 109–18.
[72] L. Cohn, "Zur Lehre vom Logos bei Philo," in *Judaica*, 303–31.
[73] J. Horowitz, "Entwicklung des alexandrinischen Judentums unter dem Einflusse Philos," in *Judaica*, 535–67.
[74] See H. Cohen, *Ethik des reinen Willens* (Berlin: Bruno Cassirer, 1904), 106 (on Logos and intellect), 200 (on the idea of humankind), 318 (on the Logos).
[75] See H. Cohen, *Der Begriff der Religion im System der Philosophie* (Gießen: Töpelmann, 1915), 7–8, 13.
[76] H. Cohen, *Ethik des reinen Willens*, 2nd rev. edn (Berlin: Bruno Cassirer, 1907), 111; cf. 335.
[77] Cohen, *Ethik des reinen Willens*, 210–11. Similar ideas can be found in Cohen's minor writings and also in his last book *Religion der Vernunft aus den Quellen des Judentums*, 2nd rev. edn (Frankfurt am Main: Kauffmann, 1929), 56 (Logos), 124 (on the Logos and on the idea of mankind), 279 (idea of mankind and pioneer of Christianity).
[78] See M. Heinze, *Die Lehre vom Logos in der griechischen Philosophie* (Oldenburg: Schmidt, 1872); and N. N. [Benjamin Rippner], "Ueber die Ursprünge des Philonischen Logos", *MGWJ* 21 (1872): 289–305.
[79] See M. Dienstfertig, *Die Prophetologie in der Religionsphilosophie des ersten nachchristlichen Jahrhunderts, unter besonderer Beachtung der Verschiedenheit in den Auffassungen des Philon von Alexandrien und des Flavius Josephus*, PhD diss., Erlangen (Breslau: Schatzky, 1892); on him, see Niehoff, "Alexandrian Judaism in 19th Century *Wissenschaft des Judentums*," 25.

duties. For him, Philo combined the Cynic idea of bliss as the highest form of virtue, philosophical ascetics, and the Stoic principal of human life in accordance with nature. The combination of these philosophical principles laid the foundation for Philo's reading of biblical ethics.[80]

29.3 The Critical Edition and the German Translation

Scholarly work on Philo received a new basis when Leopold Cohn and Paul Wendland produced their critical edition of Philo's works.[81] Although the editors were neither students nor teachers at the Breslau JTS, there is a connection between the edition and the institution. In 1888 Wendland, who was a Protestant school teacher (and later a professor), and Cohn, who was a classical philologist and librarian,[82] both participated in a competition of the Charlottenstiftung of the Prussian Academy of Sciences with an edition of Philo's *De opificio mundi*.[83] They both won prizes and afterwards decided to join forces for an edition of Philo's works.[84] Thus, the critical edition itself is a good example of a scholarly interreligious Christian-Jewish joint venture. From 1896 onwards, the *Opera* appeared with the Reimer publishing house (today part of de Gruyter). By 1915, by which time both had died, the six volumes of Greek text had been published. Wendland took responsibility for volumes II and III (1897–98) whereas Cohn edited volumes I (1896), IV (1902), and V (1906) alone, and volume VI (1915) together with Siegfried Reiter who took responsibility for the editions of *In Flaccum* and the *Legatio*.[85] From 1926 to 1930 the edition was completed by two index volumes that were provided by Johannes Leisegang. All volumes of the edition contain the critical Greek text. It is preceded by a Latin introduction that contains all necessary information required for a philological edition, paginated with Roman numerals. The publication itself was not a publication of the seminary; nonetheless it found a continuation within the JTS.

Cohn, who was member of the "Gesellschaft zur Förderung der Wissenschaft des Judentums" and of the Breslau "Verein für jüdische Geschichte und Literatur," took up a suggestion of the St. Petersburg Orientalist Daniil Avraamovich Chwolson to translate the Philonic oeuvre into German.[86] Chwolson himself donated money for

---

[80] See S. Tiktin, *Die Lehre von den Tugenden und Pflichten bei Philo von Alexandrien* (Breslau: Schatzky, 1895); on him, see Niehoff, "Alexandrian Judaism in 19th Century *Wissenschaft des Judentums*," 25.
[81] On this edition see J. R. Royse, "The Cohn-Wendland Critical Edition of Philo of Alexandria," *SPhiloA* 33 (2021): 197–207.
[82] See J.[acob] Guttmann, *Trauerrede an der Bahre des Professor Dr. Leopold Cohn, Oberbibliothekar an der Königlichen Universitätsbibliothek zu Breslau am 21. November 1915* (Breslau: Verein für jüdische Geschichte und Literatur zu Breslau, s.a. [1915]); Julius Guttmann, "Nekrolog," *Jahresbericht der Schlesischen Gesellschaft für vaterländische Cultur* 93 (1915), Nekrologe, 1:7–10, at 8.
[83] See L. Cohn, ed., *Philonis Alexandrini Libellus de opificio mundi*, Breslauer Philologische Abhandlungen (Breslau: Koebner, 1889), 4.4:[iii*]. In that same preface Cohn thanks Jacob Freudenthal.
[84] L. Cohn and P. Wendland, eds, *Philonis Alexandrini Opera Quae Supersunt* (Berlin: Reimer, 1896-1915) (for vols I–VI); (Berlin: de Gruyter, 1926–30) (for vol. VII.1–2).
[85] See, *Philonis Alexandrini Opera*, 6:xxxviii.
[86] See L. Cohn, ed., *Die Werke Philos von Alexandria in deutscher Übersetzung* (Breslau: M. & H. Marcus, 1909–29) (vols 1–5); (Breslau: Stefan Münz, 1938) (vol. 6); (Berlin: de Gruyter, 1964) (vol. 7). According to the title page of vol. 1 the translation was planned as the first volume in several parts of a series of German translations of different writings from Jewish-Hellenistic literature.

this enterprise.[87] Together with the rabbi Jacob Guttmann and the director of the JTS, M. Brann, Cohn took responsibility for the German translation of Philo's works.[88] Each treatise received a separate introduction by the translator that was followed by a close, rather literal translation. The translations themselves are accompanied by footnotes containing a limited number of annotations and textual corrections. Volume 1 is augmented by an introduction by Cohn;[89] volume 7 received a kind of afterword with an explanation of Philonic terms.[90] Cohn himself edited the first two volumes of the translation. In addition, his name was printed on the title page of the third volume that appeared in 1919. After Cohn's death, Isaak Heinemann became engaged in the translation of the Philonic corpus (vols 4–6; vols 5–6 together with Maximilian Adler); the endeavor was completed after the Shoah by Willy Theiler. Despite Chwolson's starting grant, it seems to have been a real problem to finance the publication of the subsequent volumes.[91]

The translations in the several volumes were provided by Jewish and Christian scholars alike. Cohn proofread all translations of the first two volumes and half of those of the third volume. Isaak Heinemann and Maximilian Adler did this work for the next volumes including volume 6. Finally, Willy Theiler read and corrected the translations of volume 7. The translators of volume 1 were Leopold Cohn and his brother Joseph Cohn who at that time was rabbi in Eschwege, Hessia, Benno Badt who was teacher in Breslau and a donor to the JTS, and the above-mentioned Leopold Treitel. The translations of the second volume were provided by Leopold Cohn and Isaak Heinemann. For volume 3 they were accompanied by the Christian philosopher Hans Leisegang. The translators of the fourth volume were Heinemann and Leisegang; here we witness a mistake: One treatise was translated independently by both Leisegang and the protestant minister Georg Helbig. Heinemann included Leisegang's translation and wrote a long apology to Helbig in the preface.[92] The translations of volume 5 were provided by the new co-editor Maximilian Adler, a Czech (and Jewish) philologist, Edmund Stein who studied philology and history and lived in Warsaw, Arthur Bernhard Posner who at that time was a rabbi in Kiel, and again by Joseph Cohn. For the sixth volume the editors mention only some of the translators, namely Hans Lewy who at that time was lecturer in philology at the Hebrew University in Jerusalem and the Swiss philologist Willy Theiler who at that time taught in Königsberg. The other translators are not mentioned; it is likely that Hans Leisegang was among them.[93] The original translations

---

[87] See Cohn, ed., *Die Werke Philos von Alexandria in deutscher Übersetzung*, 1:iii.

[88] Guttmann and Brann seem to have functioned as a "board." In the preface to vol. 4, Heinemann informs the reader that after their deaths their successors were Julius Guttmann and Hermann Vogelstein, again two scholars and rabbis connected with the Breslau JTS.

[89] See Cohn, "Einleitung," in *Die Werke Philos von Alexandria in deutscher Übersetzung*, 1:1–22.

[90] See Willy Theiler, "Sachweiser zu Philo," in *Die Werke Philos von Alexandria in deutscher Übersetzung*, 7:386–411.

[91] See the remarks in the prefaces to further volumes: 4:iv: "ins Ungeheuerliche wachsenden Druckkosten"; 5:v: "Geldschwierigkeiten"; 6:v: "materielle Schwierigkeiten."

[92] See 4:iv.

[93] See also D. R. Schwartz, "Philonic Anonyms of the Roman and Nazi Periods: Two Suggestions," *SPhiloA* 1 (1989): 63–73, at 70–72 gives good reasons to think that *Somn.* was translated by Leisegang and *Fug.* by Max Pohlenz.

for volume 7 seem to have been lost.[94] Except for the last editor, Willy Theiler, none of the translators was involved before.[95] Thus the translation was closely connected to the Breslau JTS. Due to financial problems the publication was delayed and finally interrupted by the politics of the Third Reich. Leopold Cohn, without whom neither the edition nor the translation would have been the same, was also among the authors who were to write the *Grundriss einer Gesamtwissenschaft des Judentums*, an introduction to the Hellenistic-Jewish literature that never appeared.[96]

29.4 Conclusion

Within the span of the eighty-four years that the Breslau JTS existed we see all stages of nineteenth-century scholarship on Philo. Starting with Frankel's skepticism of the value of studying the Alexandrian exegete, Philo soon became an ancient Jewish source of the history of the Jewish people (Graetz). M. Joel paved the way for Jewish philosophical research on him and Jacob Freudenthal introduced Philo into the seminary's curriculum. In the second and third generation of the seminary, philosophers, halakhists, and philologists discovered several totally different aspects of his oeuvre. With the critical edition and its translation, we find that, in the end, Philo was a respected and, at times, admired part of the *Wissenschaft des Judentums*.

---

[94] Adler and Heinemann in their preface to vol. 6 (p. v) sound as if the volume was nearly print-ready: "Der Druck des Schlußbandes ... ist bereits in Angriff genommen." In vol. 7, Theiler writes that he received the translations only in 1963–64.

[95] The translators were Karl Bormann, Cologne; Ludwig Früchtel, Gunzenhausen; Karl-Heinz Gerschmann, Giessen; and Friedrich Wilhelm Kohnke, Giessen.

[96] See D. Adelmann, *"Reinige dein Denken": Über den jüdischen Hintergrund der Philosophie von Hermann Cohen. Aus dem Nachlass herausgegeben, ergänzt und mit einem einleitenden Vorwort versehen von G. K. Hasselhoff* (Würzburg: Königshausen & Neumann, 2010), 162–68.

30
Modern Literature from the Nineteenth to the Twenty-First Century

David T. Runia

With his life straddling the last century preceding and the first century of our common era, Philo of Alexandria lived at a crucial juncture of human history. He experienced the reigns of the first four Roman emperors and had an audience in Rome with one of them. He was an exact contemporary of Jesus of Nazareth and it is not impossible that he heard of the events in Jerusalem that were to have such a profound impact on subsequent history. Most of his life was spent in Alexandria, the great metropolis on the eastern seaboard of the Mediterranean Sea, which also experienced turbulent times during those same years.

It is hardly surprising, therefore, that Philo makes an appearance in a number of literary works with a focus, whether direct or indirect, on that seminal period. In this chapter I shall discuss ten such works, predominantly in the area of historical fiction.[1] They will be divided into four groupings, and for each of them I shall examine how Philo appears in them, the manner in which he is portrayed, and whether there are any connections to the scholarly study of his legacy. The only condition I have set for inclusion in this set of literary works is that Philo's occurrence should have some substance (there will be one exception to this rule). I also wish to emphasize that the term "literary" is used in an inclusive sense, with no normative connotations. Our set of works range from high literature to what can be regarded as popular fiction.

There has hitherto been almost no research done on this subject, with the exception of one article. In 1991 Alan Mendelson wrote a piece entitled "Two Glimpses of Philo in Modern English Literature: Works by Charles Kingsley and Francis Warner."[2] My debt to this piece of pioneering research in what follows will be apparent. It will be noted that I cast my net a little wider than Mendelson did, not confining my works studied to those in the English language. I was able to compile my list with the aid of the modern technique of "crowd-sourcing." I sent emails to as many Philo scholars as I could, requesting them to send information on literary works involving Philo which

---

[1] My investigations are limited to works in prose.
[2] In *Heirs of the Septuagint. Philo, Hellenistic Judaism and Early Christianity: Festschrift for Earle Hilgert*, ed. D. T. Runia, D. M. Hay, and D. Winston, BJS 230 [= *SPhiloA* 3 (1991)] (Atlanta: Scholars Press, 1991), 328–43.

they happened to know about. I thank my colleagues for their generous response to this call, which yielded diverse works completely unknown to me. But I have not the slightest doubt that there are others that have escaped my net, including some in less well-distributed languages.

30.1 Two Classic Historical Novels

The first of our literary works, and only one to be written in the nineteenth century, has already been studied by Alan Mendelson. Its title is *Hypatia, or Old Foes with a New Face*, written by the prominent Victorian clergyman, historian, and social reformer, Charles Kingsley (1819–75).[3] The novel is set in the fifth century and has as its protagonist the famed Alexandrian female philosopher Hypatia, who was murdered by the supporters of the Christian bishop of the city, Cyril. Philo had thus been dead for almost four centuries, but even though his name only occurs in three chapters of the work, his spirit can be said, in Mendelson's words, "to hover over the entire book."[4] This is because a central character, the young Alexandrian Jew, Raphael Aben-Ezra, studies his treatises and to some degree identifies with his philosophy. Philo is first mentioned in a disturbing conversation between Raphael and the Prefect of the City, Orestes. The latter has received a letter from Cyril that the Jews are plotting to murder all the Christians. Raphael is quite unconcerned, revealing his world-weary indifference. He advises Orestes that it is best to remain ignorant of the true situation, ignorance being "the root and marrow of all philosophy." The philosopher will say: "we did not make the world, and are not responsible for it.—This is the sum and substance of all wisdom, and the epitome of all that has been said and written thereon from Philo the Jew to Hypatia the Gentile."[5] Some chapters later he is lying in bed reading "a manuscript of Philo," whom, he facetiously tells his mother, is even stupider than the Cabbala. But now he is told that Cyril's mob is attacking the Jews, which at last rouses him to action.[6]

The key chapter for Philo's presence in the novel is found much later, when another of Hypatia's pupils, the "Squire-Bishop" Synesius, enters center stage. As events in Alexandria move inexorably to their horrible climax, Raphael pays the bishop a visit. But whom should he encounter other than the venerable bishop of Hippo, Augustine, who preaches a sermon on the "grand old Hebrew psalms" of his nation. At first it seemed that he "was treating David as ill as Hypatia used to treat Homer—worse even than old Philo did, when in the home life of the old patriarchs, and in the mighty acts of Moses and Joshua, he could find nothing but spiritual allegories wherewith to paper the private experiences of the secluded theosophist." But as the sermon proceeds, he

---

[3] London: John W. Parker and Son, 1853, in two volumes. I quote the single volume edition of Thomas Nelson and Sons (London, 1903), citing chapter and page. For a more detailed treatment, see Mendelson, "Two Glimpses," 329–38. The somewhat enigmatic subtitle is meant to indicate, as emphasized in the author's preface, that the historical novel is relevant to contemporary concerns.
[4] Mendelson, "Two Glimpses," 330.
[5] Kingsley, *Hypatia*, ch. 2, "The Dying World," 26–27.
[6] Kingsley, *Hypatia*, ch. 6, "The New Diogenes," 85–87.

witnesses how Augustine moves from these "overstrained interpretations" to the assertion of a living, present God. It was all strange to Raphael "in its utter unlikeness to any teaching Platonist or Hebrew, which he had ever heard before ...."[7]

The apologetic intent of this Victorian Christian novel is by now coming through loud and clear. Philo's role, though limited, is not without interest. He represents a form of philosophical Judaism that is seen as more attractive than that of the Rabbis or the Kabbalah.[8] By studying it, Raphael receives a preparation for the Christian message, to which he becomes more and more sympathetic, though not in the form that Cyril represents it. Kingsley cleverly exploits the image of Philo as a forerunner of Christianity, to which he will have been introduced during his theological training in London and Cambridge.[9] Raphael is not a historical figure, as are Hypatia, Synesius, Augustine, and others whom Kingsley mentions. There were no usable philosophical Jews left in the fifth century. Philo is thus resurrected as a substitute, a Jew versed in philosophy and potentially open to a new religious message. But it is a one-sided portrait. He is an allegorist and an ivory-tower dweller, not a man of action like the admirable Synesius.

The second classic English historical novel in which Philo appears could not be more different than the first. Some eighty years later the gifted writer Robert Graves (1895–1985), facing financial difficulties, resolved to write a book that would be a commercial success. The result was the novel *I, Claudius* (1934), followed by the sequel *Claudius the God* (1935).[10] The future emperor Claudius is portrayed as a stammering, physically disabled apparent fool, who conceals his keen intelligence and thus manages to survive the poisonous intrigues of the first half-century of the Julio-Claudian imperial dynasty, so becoming a capable and effective though flawed ruler. The novel achieved great popularity, which was only increased when it formed the basis of a BBC television series in the 1970s.[11] The first book tells the story up to Claudius' ascension to the throne and includes a description of his perilous situation during the reign of Gaius Caligula. Philo, too, briefly participated in the events of Gaius' reign, but there is no mention of him in this book. Graves does, in the preface to the second book, mention him as among "the Classical writers" from whom he borrowed in composing the account.[12]

It is in the second novel that Philo makes his appearance. A key character is Herod Agrippa, who is also prominent in Philo's historical treatises.[13] In order to introduce him, Graves goes back in time and, in telling the story of the last king of Judaea, exploits the connections between Philo's family (especially his brother Alexander the Alabarch) and the imperial house. Philo is introduced as a "distinguished Jew with a reputation as the best philosopher in Egypt"[14] and a brief account is given of the events of 38 CE in

---

[7] Kingsley, *Hypatia*, ch. 21 "The Squire-Bishop," 325–27.
[8] Mendelson rightly points out the unacceptable negative image of Judaism that Kingsley, child of his time, portrays in his novel; see "Two Glimpses," 333–36. It also affects the portrayal of Raphael Aben-Ezra himself.
[9] On Kingsley's theological training, see Mendelson, "Two Glimpses," 329 n. 5.
[10] London: Arthur Barker, 1934 and 1935. I cite the single volume edition (Manchester: Carcaret, 1998). References are to chapter and page number in this edition.
[11] See below n. 17.
[12] Graves, *Claudius the God*, author's note, 341.
[13] *Flacc.* 25–39; *Legat.* 261–333.
[14] Graves, *Claudius the God*, ch. 4, 382.

Alexandria, Palestine, Syria, and Rome. However, in the account of the interview with Gaius in Rome he follows Josephus rather than Philo himself, adding the detail that at the end of the interview, in making his pronouncement that Gaius would now have God as his opponent, Philo speaks to his fellow-ambassadors in Hebrew so that none of the courtiers could understand him (this is implausible because Philo knew little or no Hebrew).[15] His other substantial role in the novel is fiction rather than fact. Herod becomes obsessed with stories about the Messiah who is to be born to the Jews (and later becomes convinced that he himself is the Messiah). In a letter to Claudius[16] he gives explanations regarding this figure that Philo has supplied, including that he must be a Jew belonging to the line of David and will be born in the village of Bethlehem.[17] Herod then goes on to describe the life of Joshua ben Joseph (i.e. Jesus) and the early Jesus movement. We see how Graves, like subsequent novelists,[18] cannot resist the temptation to give a place to the life and death of Jesus in their fictional accounts. For that purpose Philo can be handily invoked as a historical figure who had a knowledge of the contents of scripture. That there is virtually no messianism in Philo's writings and that he never makes references to prophecies such as that of the prophet Micah is of course quite beside the point.

30.2 Four Recent Historical Novels

During the past two decades or so there has been a spate of historical novels in which Philo plays a role. As we will see, this role differs greatly from case to case. I shall discuss them in order of publication. It will not be possible to go into too much detail, both as to plot and as to the way Philo is presented. Generally speaking, to a greater extent even than in *I, Claudius*, there is more fiction than there is fact.

We begin with the novel *La fortune d'Alexandrie* published in 1996 by the prolific French novelist Gerald Messadié (1931–2018).[19] In the same year it was crowned with the Prix Relay for a "roman d'évasion" (escapist novel). On the cover we see a depiction of its protagonist, the hetaira Delia, looking down on the city with the Pharos lighthouse in the distance. Early in the novel she meets Philo at a banquet, making quite clear what she thinks of him, "a small man without joy."[20] Not long thereafter Philo engages in a conversation with Hero the engineer, the latter representing a materialist

---

[15] Graves, *Claudius the God*, ch. 4, 383. This version is based on Josephus, *A.J.* 18.260.
[16] Graves, *Claudius the God*, ch. 21, 576–79.
[17] This feature of the novel recurs in the television series. According to the film synopsis of the series, located at Movie Mirrors Index, www.san.beck.org, episode 12 "A God in Colchester" (viewed October 10, 2018), the Syrian governor Marsus Vibius "gives Claudius more information about the Messiah and explains that he is a king who is to redeem Israel of all its sins. Their greatest living scholar Philo wrote that he must be descended from King David and be born in Bethlehem." The episode can be seen on disc 4 scene 10 of the DVD version of the series.
[18] See below section 3 of this chapter.
[19] Paris: JC Lattès, 1996. In 2012 the publisher Jean-Claude Lattès himself published a biography of Herod Agrippa, *Le dernier roi des Juifs* (Paris: NiL éditions), in which Philo is often mentioned.
[20] Messadié, *La fortune d'Alexandrie*, 24.

view of the world, in contrast to the spiritualist Philo.[21] The Jew is presented as both a banker and a philosopher.[22] It would not be expected that he will have much to do with the mystery of Delia's disappearance, but in fact he gets very involved. An essential part of the plot is assigned to the group of the Therapeutae, who are not Philo's devotees of God and the law, but rather the heretical group of Hemerobaptists, connected to the Essenes and the zealot (!) Jesus.[23] Throughout the novel, though Philo's involvement is important for the unfolding of the plot, he is generally presented in unflattering terms. And this is appropriate, since the novel itself is quite anti-Philonic in tenor and in much of its substance. Its heroine is a woman of pleasure, who scoffs at the notion of divine justice in Philo's presence.[24] On the final page we read that Philo has left for Rome to plead the case of the Jewish community, while Delia achieves happiness as she holds a banquet surrounded by men, including Hero.[25]

The next novel is also French. Entitled *L'Assassin et le Prophète*, it is the work of Guillaume Prévost (born 1964) and was published in 2002.[26] This is the only one of our literary works in which Philo is indisputably the protagonist. Not as a philosopher or a scholar, however, but as an adventurous sleuth. The cover describes its contents in aptly lurid terms: "Des somptueuses cérémonies du Temple aux infâmes geôles de la légion romains, un thriller biblique au cœur d'une Palestine brûlante et tourmentée." The book is indeed action-packed. Set in 6 CE, it starts with Philo as a young man making a journey to Jerusalem to worship in the Temple. The first murder is of the Pharisee Jephtha. It emerges that in the mouth of his corpse a tefillin is found containing a parchment with a prophecy, the first clue of the unfolding drama.[27] At this time Philo also meets Jephtha's daughter Bethsabée, beautiful but cruelly disabled after falling from a roof when a child. As the thriller progresses we read more about Philo. Visiting the synagogue of the Alexandrians in Jerusalem, he meets up with Abydelios, the old rabbi who for twenty-five years was in charge of the Grand Synagogue of Alexandria, where he was Philo's teacher. Philo tells him that the past two years he has been following the lessons of Arius Didymus. The rabbi's response is that he should distrust all these pagans, but Philo argues that their thought often seems inspired by the same principles as in the Bible.[28] Later he discusses with Bethsabée the necessity of obeying the prescriptions of the Law.[29] Next Philo also pays a visit to Qumran, where a further murder takes place. Inevitably, the prophecy has to do with the coming of the Messiah. No less inevitably, it would seem, Philo

---

[21] Messadié, *La fortune d'Alexandrie*, 39–43. Hero of Alexandria is a historical figure, though most likely born a generation after Philo. Some of his treatises survive.

[22] Messadié, *La fortune d'Alexandrie*, 103.

[23] Messadié, *La fortune d'Alexandrie*, 115, 147, 194. On this sect, indeed very likely connected with the Essenes, see L. H. Schiffman and J. C. VanderKam, eds, *Encyclopedia of the Dead Sea Scrolls*, 2 vols (Oxford: Oxford University Press, 2000), 1:352–53.

[24] Messadié, *La fortune d'Alexandrie*, 323.

[25] Messadié, *La fortune d'Alexandrie*, 422.

[26] Published in Paris by NiL éditions. The publisher is Nicole Lattès, wife of Jean-Claude Lattès, on whom see above n. 19.

[27] Prévost, *L'Assassin et le Prophète*, 66.

[28] Prévost, *L'Assassin et le Prophète*, 82–83.

[29] Prévost, *L'Assassin et le Prophète*, 140–41.

meets up with the young 12-year-old Jesus, and their adventures together form the climax of the thriller.[30] There is more of the historical Philo in this novel than in the previous one. Noteworthy, however, is that the author, no doubt giving preference to the rules of his genre rather than what he might have read in his research, takes no notice of Philo's reputation as a misogynist. We read that he is unmarried, devoted only to philosophy. But he had known a woman, an Egyptian widow who was not Jewish and so would never have been acceptable to his father.[31] And then on the final page but one of the novel, he invites Bethsabée to come with him when he returns to Egypt, and it seems that more is going to happen than just a kiss....[32]

The next novel caused somewhat of a sensation when it was published by the American writer Anne Rice (born 1941) in 2005. Entitled *Christ the Lord: Out of Egypt* and the first volume of a planned trilogy,[33] it ambitiously tells the story of the boy Jesus, aged from 7 to 12, in the first person, as he gradually awakens to who he is. Rice had previously achieved bestseller success with her *Vampire Chronicles* and numerous other works (her books have sold more than 100 million copies). As she describes in a lengthy Author's Note at the end of the novel, she experienced a strict Roman Catholic childhood but left the church behind at the age of 18.[34] After the death of her husband in 2001 she renewed her interest in Christianity and gave expression to this renewal through her work as a writer. In the note she emphasizes the thoroughness of her research and acknowledges the influence of the scholars Paula Fredriksen and N. T. Wright.[35] Philo's presence in the novel is limited but persistent. We very soon encounter his name. Jesus and his family are living in the Street of the Carpenters in Alexandria. His father Joseph has worked all day on a job at Philo's house. Jesus soon tells the reader that his teacher has taken him to visit Philo, a rich man and a scholar. Philo is impressed with his learning, teaches him Greek, and takes him to the Great Synagogue. When Joseph decides to return to Palestine, Philo visits him and asks whether he can keep Jesus and send him back to Joseph as an educated young man, but the request is refused. The family leaves the city and that is the end of Philo's direct involvement in the story.[36] But his name continues to be mentioned, for example when Jesus' uncle Cleopas gives the old Rabbi of Nazareth the gift of two small scrolls, each containing a treatise of Philo.[37] Rice is using the time-honoured techniques of the historical novel. Well-known figures are brought into interaction with each other, regardless of historical probabilities. But she has to make some interesting chronological moves in order to make her plot work

---

[30] This explains the dating of the novel. In a postscript Prévost cites Luke 1:41–50 describing Jesus' visit to the Temple.

[31] Prévost, *L'Assassin et le Prophète*, 146–47. For a balanced view on Philo's "misogyny," see D. Winston, "Philo and the Rabbis on Sex and the Body," *Poetics Today* 19 (1998): 41–62.

[32] Prévost, *L'Assassin et le Prophète*, 372.

[33] New York: Alfred A. Knopf. The sequel, *Christ the Lord: The Road to Cana* was published in 2008. The final volume has not been published.

[34] Rice, *Out of Egypt*, 303–22, at 306–7.

[35] Fredriksen's study, *Jesus of Nazareth, King of the Jews* (New York: Alfred A. Knopf, 1999), regularly refers to Philo.

[36] Rice, *Out of Egypt*, 4, 14, 17–19.

[37] Rice, *Out of Egypt*, 176.

the way she wants. Jesus and his family return to Jerusalem just in time to experience the uproar following the death of King Herod in 4 BCE. This means that Jesus' birth will have taken place in 11 BCE, and that, when he and Philo interact in Alexandria, if we accept the usual chronology of Philo's life, the latter could not have been much older than a teenager. Such improbable calibrations are hard to avoid, even in novels which—as the author claims—are well researched, because suitable historical figures are few and far between, and one has to make use of them when they are available.[38]

The fourth novel appeared in 2010, written by the prominent New York financier, historian, and journalist Daniel M. Friedenberg (1923–2011) and published in the year before his death.[39] It tells the story in novelistic fashion of its eponymous hero, Philo's nephew Tiberius Julius Alexander.[40] Naturally "Uncle Philo" plays a prominent role, particularly in the first half of the story up to Tiberius' definitive break with Judaism. The author had a passionate interest in Judaica, including Jewish history.[41] The novel accordingly includes a wealth of fascinating historical details, as well as intriguing flights of fancy. For example, we read that Philo was killed at the age of 65, when he was "struck down and killed by a horse and carriage on the Canopus Way in Alexandria while absentmindedly walking to the Great Library."[42] Here too our author cannot resist including the Therapeutae and the early "Yeshua movement" in his narrative.[43] An innovation of the novel, compared to the others that we have discussed so far, is that it includes a frame narrative that bridges past and present. Most of the book consists of a first-hand autobiographical account of its protagonist preserved on a damaged scroll found in a niche of St Catherine's monastery in the Sinai. The aging classical scholar Professor Freemont, a Jew by birth but like Tiberius alienated from his ancestral religion, is invited to decipher and translate it. The book is good fun and does not take itself at all seriously (unusually it does not have an author's note describing the sources used). Nevertheless, it seems a little worrisome that the work is a complete blend of fact and fiction, even to the extent that Professor Freemont is described as the translator of Philo's works in the Loeb Classical Library![44] The protagonist's account of and reflections on his life are written in a racy twentieth-century style that would be quite

---

[38] One may compare another very recent novel by best-selling author Sue Monk Kidd, *The Book of Longings* (Random House 2020). It features the wife of Jesus, Ana, who after his death joins the community of the Therapeutae and becomes their leader. In addition, another even more recent American historical novel in which Philo plays a prominent role is *The Lighthouse*, the first of a projected series of novels entitled *The Cyrenian* by K. Ciholas (Austin: Atmosphere Press, 2022). The main figure is Simon of Cyrene and most of the action is set in Alexandria and Rome. Philo is introduced as "one of the most influential men in the Roman empire" (154) and portrayed as a philosopher and writer (155, 169). The final part of the plot centres on the events of 38 CE. I am grateful to Piet van der Horst for drawing this novel to my attention.

[39] D. M. Friedenberg, *Tiberius Julius Alexander: A Historical Novel* (Amherst, NY: Prometheus Books, 2010).

[40] He is a character in Philo's dialogues, *De providentia* II and *De animalibus* (also sometimes titled *Alexander*). Recent studies discussing his relationship to Philo are S. Etienne, "Réflexion sur l'apostasie de Tibérius Julius Alexander," *SPhiloA* 12 (2000): 122–42; G. Schimanowski, "Die jüdische Integration in die Oberschicht Alexandriens und die angebliche Apostasie des Tiberius Julius Alexander," in *Jewish Identity in the Greco-Roman World*, ed. J. Frey, D. R. Schwartz, and S. Gripentrog, AJEC 71 (Leiden: Brill, 2007), 111–35.

[41] See the obituary published in the *New York Times* on September 18, 2011; available on legacy.com (viewed October 18, 2018).

[42] Friedenberg, *Tiberius*, 154.

[43] Friedenberg, *Tiberius*, 38–41, 73 (in a letter to Uncle Philo!).

[44] Friedenberg, *Tiberius*, 7.

506   THE RECEPTION OF PHILO OF ALEXANDRIA

at home in a contemporary work of pulp fiction. It is all a bit confusing, and as far as removed from Philo's own quasi-historical narratives as can be imagined.[45]

30.3 More Scholarly Attempts at Fiction

Having surveyed the above more or less extravagant fictional accounts, the question might now be asked: is it possible to include Philo in fiction with a historical basis that is more responsibly treated from a scholarly point of view?

As an example of such an approach we might cite the novel *The Shadow of the Galilean* by the German New Testament scholar Gerd Theissen (born 1943), first published in German in 1986 and translated into English in the following year.[46] As the title indicates, the novel is about Jesus and what can be known about him, even from an ancient, almost contemporary perspective. The story is set in the time just after Jesus' death, when Pilate is still governor of Judea. It is told in the first person by Andreas, a devout Jewish merchant from the town of Sepphoris, whom Pilate blackmails into acting as a spy in order to gather information about the incipient Jesus movement. The reader is of course above all interested in what the novel tells about that movement's founder. Andreas never meets Jesus, but only encounters his shadow, analogous to the way the modern reader meets Jesus through the gospels (even if they are much further removed in time than Andreas' fictional report).

Theissen's book, however, is not just set in the past. In a foreword, after every one of its chapters, and as an epilogue, the author engages in a correspondence with a Dr Kratzinger, allowing him to discuss the historical and methodological challenges which the novel poses. This can be seen as a more scholarly version of the frame narrative that we encountered in Friedenberg's novel. For example, in writing to him Theissen defends his decision to shift the chronology of the historical wilderness ascetic Bannus by about twenty-five years in order to suit his tale, claiming that "scholars often act in this anachronistic way."[47] The novel has an appendix on "The most important sources on Jesus and his time," which includes a paragraph on Philo.[48] Its text is even accompanied by twenty-three pages of notes replete with references to and discussions on those sources. Regrettably from our viewpoint Philo is, I believe, referred to by name only once in the work as "our philosopher Philo" when the author most interestingly paraphrases a text from *QG* 4.138 on Esau (Gen 27:3–4) in order to show "how Jesus transformed the theme of the father and the two sons into a new story" (i.e. the parable of the Prodigal son).[49] Elsewhere Philo provides information on Pilate, and the "extreme allegorists" of *Migr.* 89–93 form the basis of a conversation that Andreas

---

[45] These are mentioned rather didactically in the autobiographical account on p. 79.
[46] G. Theissen, *The Shadow of the Galilean: The Quest of the Historical Jesus in Narrative Form* (SCM Press: London, 1987). The 2001 reprint has a brief Preface by another New Testament scholar, J. D. G. Dunn.
[47] Theissen, *The Shadow*, 22.
[48] Theissen, *The Shadow*, 216.
[49] Theissen, *The Shadow*, 149–50.

has with "a Jew from Alexandria."[50] These covert references are explained in the notes, but could be picked up by a well-informed reader. A more responsible fictional account of events in Philo's lifetime could hardly be imagined.[51] The style too of the account, as read through the English translation, is sober and informative. It must be conceded to James Dunn that Andreas comes across as "rather modern," but he rightly adds that this was "probably inevitable."[52]

The only Philonist, to my knowledge, who has made an attempt to give a fictionalized account of Philo's epoch is the Finnish scholar Karl-Gustav Sandelin (born 1940). In a recent contribution to a Festschrift he engaged in what he called "an exercise in historical fiction."[53] It consists of a letter written by Eudaemon, the fictional younger brother of Tiberius Julius Alexander, to the historian Josephus. It recounts the events of his life and particularly his interaction with the early Christians, including the apostle Paul whom he meets in Corinth.[54] Eudaemon begins the letter with the words "Call me Isaac."[55] This odd move is explained two pages later: his father gave him the aspirational (Greek) name Eudaemon because his uncle Philo had seen this biblical figure as "a representative of the happy category of human beings who are spiritually taught by God without human mediation." Wisely he adds that he himself doubts whether he has been given such happiness. The views of "uncle Philo" are a *Leitmotif* of the piece, repeatedly invoked in order to shed light where appropriate on the Jewish world of life and thought described in the letter. In fact, for the Philonist, the effect is like reading a "roman à clef," with various titbits recalling Philonic texts (not explained—there are no footnotes) or even modern scholarship. For example, when we read Eudaemon saying "but I have often wondered whether the Therapeutae were just a fantasy in my uncle's head," the Philonist will immediately think of the attempt by Sandelin's fellow-Scandinavian Troels Engberg-Pedersen, to argue this case.[56] So although much of the account has to be pure imaginative reconstruction, many details are not only accurate, but also insightful from a scholarly point of view. But of course, it is just a short piece which is meant as a *jeu d'esprit*. It might serve as the basis for a historical novel with Philo's Alexandria at its core, but it would have to be considerably expanded and would be a challenge for the literary skills of its author.

---

[50] Theissen, *The Shadow*, 167.

[51] As David Lincicum points out to me, Theissen also refers to Philo almost twenty times in his *The Historical Jesus: A Comprehensive Guide* (co-authored with A. Merz; London: SCM Press, 1998, first published in German in 1996), which could be seen as the more strictly academic treatment of the ground he covers in his novel.

[52] Dunn, "Preface" (see above n. 46), xiii.

[53] K.-G. Sandelin, "The Letter of Eudaemon: An Exercise in Historical Fiction," in *Voces Clamantium in Deserto, Essays in Honor of Kari Syreeni*, ed. S.-O. Back and M. Kankaanniemi, Studier i exegetik och judaistik utgivna av Teologiska fakulteten vid Åbo Akademi 11 (Åbo: Åbo Akademi, 2012), 281–92. Syreeni is Sandelin's successor in the chair of New Testament exegetics at Åbo Akademi University.

[54] Paul is the other focal point of Sandelin's research. Philo and Paul already came together in his dissertation; K.-G. Sandelin, *Die Auseinandersetzung mit der Weisheit in 1. Korinther 15* (Åbo: Åbo Akademi, 1976).

[55] The author is here alluding to and inverting the opening line of Herman Melville's *Moby Dick* (I owe this observation to David Lincicum).

[56] Sandelin, "The Letter," 282. See T. Engberg-Pedersen, "Philo's *De vita contemplativa* as a Philosopher's Dream," *JSJ* 30 (1999): 40–64.

30.4 A Key Character in an Ancient "Market-Place of Ideas"

In the introduction to this chapter I mentioned Francis Warner, who wrote the historical play *Light Shadows* already discussed at some length nearly three decades ago by Alan Mendelson.[57] As a play it deviates from the works studied so far and I will not discuss it in detail. But I do want to point out one of its features which is important for our subject. Warner's play is set during the time of Nero's reign when the apostles Peter and Paul are put to death. As Mendelson notes, Philo is the only character who does not fit chronologically, even if he is presented as very elderly. The others are the Stoic Seneca, the poet Lucan, the Jewish historian Josephus, the Epicurean Petronius, Nero's wife Poppaea, the soldier Tigellinus, the emperor Nero himself, Paul, the evangelist Luke, and lastly, one of Paul's followers Thecla. Various members of this group of characters allow the dramatist to present an exciting interplay, or indeed clash, of ideas. Philo, described in the list of *dramatis personae* as "philosopher; an Alexandrian Jew," needs to participate in order to represent a form of Judaism with which Greek philosophers can interact and against which early Christian thinkers can react, a Judaism with philosophical elements, but also strongly loyal to its traditions of observance.[58] For this kind of interplay of ideas the genre of the play is ideal. Titbits of the historical background can be brought in, and Warner does this with considerable wit. But the method of dramatic interaction in brief scenes (there are thirteen of them) allows the characters to be divorced from anything like a realistic historical setting. The question can be asked whether it possible for a historical novel to achieve something like the same effect?

Looking back at the novels discussed so far, most of them make some reference to Philo's standing as a philosopher (and sometimes as a loyal Jew). But none of these can be remotely described as a "novel of ideas," with the partial exception of Kingsley's novel, which certainly works with ideas, but because it is set in a very different world of late ancient Alexandria, Philo's role in it is necessarily limited. Very recently, however, a work has appeared that very deliberately presents an interplay of ideas in the form of a quasi-historical, heavily didactic narrative, and in it Philo is accorded a climactic place.

The book is the work of the distinguished and prolific Dutch Jewish psychiatrist, Herman van Praag (born 1929). Its title, *Deference to Doubt: A Young Man's Quest for Religious Identity in First Century Judea*, gives a good indication of its contents and main theme.[59] It tells the story of Amos, a young Judean from a modest background (his father is a silversmith), who goes in search of his identity as a Jew. The date is about 25 CE (like in other books we have discussed, there is some creative chronology). Amos introduces himself as a "searcher and a doubter" who attempts to discover who

---

[57] Mendelson, "Two Glimpses," 343.
[58] Mendelson describes him as representing an "old style of monotheism—monotheism under the Jewish dispensation" (p. 338). It is legitimate to speak of "early Christian thinkers" because Warner writes the play from an overt Christian perspective, as befitting its first performance in Canterbury cathedral.
[59] Urim publications: Jerusalem, 2020; translation of the original Dutch version entitled *Slecht zicht: een hommage aan de twijfel* (*Dimmed View: A Homage to Doubt*) (Eindhoven: Damon, 2017). On the author, see the biographical notice https://en.wikipedia.org/wiki/Herman_van_Praag (viewed July 13, 2022).

he wishes to be. But this is immediately translated into Jewish terms: "I was born of a Jewish mother shortly after the death of King Herod and circumcised on my eighth day. I live in Jerusalem. Formally speaking, then, I am a Jew. But that's the 'outside.' What's the 'inside' of a Jew like? What should he think, believe and do to be an authentic Jew?"[60]

Encouraged by his father, Amos boldly undertakes visits to seven different personalities, each representing different kinds of contemporary Judaism. They are Jaacov the Pharisee; Judah the Priest; David the Zealot; Eli, member of the Qumran community; Jochanan (John), known as "the Baptist"; Joshua (Jesus) of Nazareth; and finally Philo of Alexandria, also known as Philo Judaeus. On each occasion he knocks at the door and subjects his interlocutors to a barrage of questions. The topics are often general, such as the nature and activity of "the Lord,"[61] the existence of free will, questions relating to soul, body, and the afterlife, and so on, but they can also be more specifically directed towards the thought of a particular thinker. His questions and his arguments are penetrating, often provocative. Time and time again he manages to expose doubts that these men have regarding their convictions or to show that their beliefs are difficult to defend. These results strengthen his view that the best way forward is to be a searcher and a doubter. His interaction with Jesus is particularly interesting in this regard. Jesus is sensitively portrayed as a man who is swept along by his radical ideas, but then has severe doubts when others believe him to be the Messiah.[62] Amos is even able to converse with Jesus during his crucifixion, the single most fantastical feature of the book.

Philo is the last thinker that Amos visits and their conversation takes up almost sixty pages of the book.[63] Van Praag has made a concerted effort to present key features of his thought that can shed light on the question of Jewish identity. These include his views on God and how he can be known, the process of creation, the role of the Logos (Van Praag presents it as an "executive intermediary," or in the form of Wisdom as "God's creative hand"),[64] the intelligible world, the fate of the soul, the evaluation of the body, the role of the passions and emotions, attitudes towards Hellenization and acculturation, the presentation of Moses as the perfect man, and the role of the interpreter. In each case Amos challenges him with counter-arguments and makes him defend his ideas. Philo is at first frustrated by these challenges, but at their parting he tells him: "I have never met someone who addressed me with such bravura but with whom I was unable to get really angry. I've come to see you almost as a rebellious son."[65] Amos confesses to his father at the end of the book that the encounter that impressed him the most was the one he had with to Philo, whom he describes as "an intellectual heavyweight with a tremendous exegetic capacity and empathy for his fellow man."[66] Nevertheless he found

---

[60] Van Praag, *Deference to Doubt*, 25.
[61] But in the Dutch original consistently "de Eeuwige" (the eternal), following Jewish practice. Van Praag seldom uses the word "God."
[62] Van Praag, *Deference to Doubt*, 153–99.
[63] Van Praag, *Deference to Doubt*, 201–62.
[64] Van Praag, *Deference to Doubt*, 218–19.
[65] Van Praag, *Deference to Doubt*, 262.
[66] Van Praag, *Deference to Doubt*, 270.

Philo's dependence on Greek ideas unacceptable and could not agree with many of his scriptural interpretations, despite their ingenuity.

Van Praag's book differs from the works of historical fiction that we have examined so far. It is an unashamedly didactic presentation of an "idea market" in its ancient setting.[67] It is not so much a novel as a long sequence of dialogues linked together with brief interludes of activity consisting mainly of travel. Its main weakness, apart from the fact that its repetitive format becomes somewhat tedious to read, lies very much on the surface. The young man Amos is scarcely a credible figure. As the author playfully admits,[68] he is a mouthpiece for his own views which are those of a modern liberal Jewish thinker approaching the end of his life. Frequently Amos' interlocutors learn more from him than he from them. The emphasis on doubt and the notion of a quest that will never reach definitive answers is plainly inspired by modernity (if not post-modernity). Setting this aside, however, the book can still be regarded as an entertaining and instructive exercise in the comparison of religious and philosophical ideas. The Philonist will certainly appreciate how Amos' conversation with the Master highlights aspects of his thought that raise questions from a modern perspective. The author might have done more with certain sceptical tendencies in Philo's thought, which moderate the picture of a rather dogmatic thinker and are closer to his own ideal. But it is fair to say that Van Praag's presentation is not sufficiently fine-tuned to include such subtleties.

30.5 Conclusion

It has been both amusing and instructive to analyze Philo's presence in ten works of modern literature. He is without doubt a distinctive presence. His location in the metropolis of Alexandria and his double persona as a philosopher and a devout Jew make him an attractive figure to include in works of historical fiction. For the most part he has to remain a minor figure. Not enough is known about him and his context to allow him to be more, unless the historical imagination is given free rein, as occurs in the French thriller of Guillaume Prévost.[69] Philo is useful as a historical figure precisely because he lived in an era of such crucial importance, both from a political and a religious perspective. Some of our authors place him in the political context of the Julio-Claudian emperors and the struggles of the Jews in Alexandria and Palestine during that period. Many make an obligatory reference to the Therapeutae, from which it is a natural jump to the Essenes and Qumran. All of them without exception connect Philo in one way or another with the life of Jesus and/or the origins of the Christian religion. It is this last move, of course, which is the most questionable from an historical point of view. But it is worth recalling that it stands in a long tradition that goes all the way back to antiquity

---

[67] For the image, see Van Praag, *Deference to Doubt*, 273. Note that the book has a justificatory preface and its chapters are divided into sections outlining the topics discussed (also listed in the table of contents).
[68] Van Praag, *Deference to Doubt*, 18: "He speaks in his own right, but in his views I often recognize my own. Not surprisingly. After all, I begot him myself."
[69] See above section 2 of this chapter.

and the various legends of Philo's interaction—never admittedly with Jesus, but with the apostle Peter and the early Christians of Alexandria.[70]

Many of the authors we have studied let us know, via prefaces, footnotes, and postscripts, that they have conscientiously studied the sources. Mostly these are historical rather than philosophical and exegetical. Predictably, in the world of fiction history carries greater weight than ideas. The exception is when ideas become the focus, as in the last works of our survey. Then the facts or fictions of history recede and make way for an interplay of ideas. Despite their artificiality, these works are perhaps the most interesting from the viewpoint of Philonic scholarship.

In all the works surveyed above there has been almost no room for fictional treatment of Philo scholars. Only in the narrative frame of Friedenberg's novel about Tiberius Julius Alexander did we meet the outrageous Professor Freemont, who in no way could be taken seriously. But there is one remarkable short story in which such a figure does make an appearance. It is "The safe deposit," first published by the celebrated Yiddish writer Isaac Bashevis Singer (1903–1991) in 1979, the year after he was awarded the Nobel Prize for Literature.[71] It tells the story of a dramatic day in the life of Professor Uri Zalkind. A Polish Jew, he escaped from Europe before World War II and had taught philosophy in New York for almost thirty years. Now an aging widower and living in Florida, he resolves to fly to New York to see his publisher and check up on a safe deposit in a New York bank which contains the jewels of his late wife Lotte. He could not have chosen a worse day. There is a blizzard in the city. Blinded by the snow and suffering from a dangerous urological condition, he stumbles from one disaster to the next. In trying to locate the bank, he loses his briefcase and all seems lost. But kindness prevails. A helpful guard assists him in opening the safe deposit, and soon thereafter the briefcase is returned by an honest and good-hearted older lady from Lodz called Esther. She takes him home, where during the night he collapses. He finds himself waking up in hospital and feeling "a rest that he had never known before," a state of mind that "was both astoundingly simple and beyond anything language could convey. He was granted the revelation he yearned for—the freedom to look into the innermost secret of being." "If I could only convey the truth to those who suffer and doubt!," he exclaims.[72] Esther enters his room, and the story comes to an end.

Philo and his philosophy appear at crucial moments of the account. The manuscript that he is taking to New York is *Philo Judaeus and the Cabala*.[73] When he collapses onto a bench at the bank, he is ready for death, recalling that for Philo death "redeems the soul from the prison of the flesh, from the vagaries of the senses." Singer adds that "although Zalkind had read everything that Philo wrote, he could never conclude from his writings whether matter was created by God or always existed—a primeval chaos,

---

[70] On these traditions, see the account in D. T. Runia, *Philo in Early Christian Literature: A Survey*, CRINT III.3 (Assen: Van Gorcum, 1993), 3–31.
[71] *The New Yorker*, April 16, 1979, 36–42; reprinted in *Old Love* (New York: Farrar, Strauss, Giroux, 1979), 183–98.
[72] Singer, *Old Love*, 198.
[73] Singer, *Old Love*, 184.

the negative principle of the Godhead."[74] In fact "he found contradictions in Philo's philosophy and puzzles that no mind could solve as long as it was chained in the errors of corporality."[75] When gazing at his wife's jewels he reflects on his past life. "Even though," we read, "he had doubts about Philo's philosophy and was sometimes inclined toward Spinoza's pantheism or David Hume's skepticism, he had accepted Philo's disdain for the deceptions of flesh and blood."[76] Drifting into sleep, he dreams that he is in a temple and a tall man with a white beard emerges, carrying a scroll written in Hebrew. "Peace be unto you, Philo Judaeus, my father and master," he says. "Peace unto you, my disciple Uri, son of Yedidyah," is the reply. "Rabbi, I want to know the truth!" "Here in the Book of Genesis is the source of all truth," Philo answers.[77] Uri recalls that Philo was not well versed in the Holy Tongue. What a lie, he exclaims. Other philosophers and rabbis appear, but then the dream degenerates into sensuality. When in Esther's apartment he starts conversing with her, she talks about her experiences in Russia during the war and says, "What we went through in all those years only God the merciful knows." The professor is inclined to tell her that, "even though God was omniscient, the well of goodness, one could not ascribe any attribute to Him. He did not provide for mankind directly but through Wisdom, called Logos by the Greeks." But, we read, "there was no use discussing metaphysics with this woman."[78]

In the space of a few pages our eminent author has given us an astonishingly well-informed portrait of a Philo scholar steeped in the time-honored way of reading him as a philosopher in the great metaphysical tradition. The comment on whether matter was created by God recalls Wolfson's great work,[79] and one wonders whether Singer may have studied it (though the idea that Philo's thought had contradictions was anathema to the great Philonist). Especially intriguing is the fact that in the dream Philo addresses Dr Zalkind as Uri, son of Yedidyah. Yedidyah was the name given to Philo by Azariah de' Rossi,[80] his first early modern Jewish reader, and it is still used in Hebrew scholarship.

But Philo's Platonic metaphysics also has a function in the unfolding of the plot. Dr Zalkind's Philonic disdain for the deceptions of flesh and blood, and, more generally speaking, his other-worldly Philonic philosophy have not brought him the truth and happiness that he sought. In his New York escapade they in fact turn out to be downright dangerous and nearly fatal. As for the final revelation, it is indeed not made explicit. But we may be sure of two things. It is anti-metaphysical and this-worldly, and it is brought about by the kindness and love shown to him by the woman who befriended

---

[74] This remark might seem a non sequitur, but the intent seems to be that the status of matter affects the evaluation of corporality.
[75] Singer, *Old Love*, 188.
[76] Singer, *Old Love*, 191.
[77] Singer, *Old Love*, 191.
[78] Singer, *Old Love*, 196.
[79] H. A. Wolfson, *Philo: Foundations of Religious Philosophy in Judaism, Christianity and Islam*, 2 vols, 4th edn (Cambridge, MA: Harvard University Press, 1968), 1:300–310. Earlier Singer had also written a story "The Spinoza of Market Street," anthologized in a collection with the same title (New York: Farrar, Strauss, Giroux, 1961), 3–24. Famously Wolfson regarded Philo and Spinoza as the two key figures in the history of post-classical western philosophy.
[80] J. Weinberg, *Azariah de' Rossi, The Light of the Eyes* (New Haven: Yale University Press, 2001), 101.

him. Hence its inclusion in a collection of stories about the love of the old and the middle-aged.[81] So we end this survey of Philo in modern literature with a motif that is far removed from the thought of the ancient Jewish master. This is hardly surprising. His philosophical views are not so attractive to modern sensibilities. But Philonists too will find "The safe deposit" a delight to read.

---

[81] See the "Author's Note" in Singer, *Old Love*, vii: "Literature has neglected the old and their emotions.... The only hope of mankind is love in its various forms and manifestations—the source of them all being love of life, which ... increases and ripens with the years."

VI
CONTEMPORARY PERSPECTIVES

31

Contemporary Receptions and Future Prospects among Classicists

Courtney J. P. Friesen

"Philo has no natural home in any particular discipline."[1] This stands as both a challenge and an opportunity for Philonic studies at a moment when academic fields become ever more specialized even amid increasing demands for interdisciplinary scholarship. Philo's distinctive positioning between Hellenism and Judaism render his corpus an especially productive site for the transgression of conventional disciplinary boundaries. To the extent, however, that the various academic areas concerned with the ancient world remain distinct, our reconstructions will be fractured and incomplete, and a dichotomous view of cultural and religious history—of Greeks, Romans, Jews, and Christians—will persist.

This chapter concerns classics and Philonic studies, arguing that a robust integration can yield mutually productive and fruitful results. The first section pursues a broad view of avenues whereby scholars might situate Philo in relationship to the classical canon, as an author of Greek prose under the Roman Empire. The remaining three sections thematize specific areas as illustrative of potential disciplinary rapprochements: literary education, or *paideia*; Greek identity and Roman imperial politics; and theater and performance.

31.1 Philo and the Canon: Between Classical and Post-Classical

Scholars of Philo have long been aware of his close proximity to the canon of classical Greek literature in language, style, and content.[2] In his review of F. H. Colson's ninth volume of Philo in the Loeb Classical Library, A. D. Nock remarked, "as a whole, the Greek of Philo is no less worthy of attention than Plutarch's and no less characteristic of the early Empire."[3] He adds, however, that for scholars such as

---

[1] M. Niehoff, review of M. Hadas-Lebel, *Philo of Alexandria: A Thinker in the Jewish Diaspora*, BMCR 2013.04.13. See also D. T. Runia, "Why Philo of Alexandria Is an Important Writer and Thinker," in *Philon d'Alexandrie: un penseur à l'intersection des cultures gréco-romaine, orientale, juive et chrétienne*, ed. S. Inowlocki and B. Decharneux, Monothéismes et philosophie (Turnhout: Brepols, 2011), 13–33.

[2] Translations of all texts are mine throughout. Texts of Philo are from the edition of Cohn and Wendland.

[3] A. D. Nock, "Philo and Hellenistic Philosophy," *Essays on Religion and the Ancient World*, ed. Z. Stewart, 2 vols (Oxford: Clarendon Press, 1972), 2:559–65, at 559. On Philo's distinctive Greek vocabulary, see also J. Leopold, "Philo's Vocabulary and Word Choice," in *Two Treatises of Philo of Alexandria: A Commentary on De Gigantibus*

himself, interested in Hellenistic philosophy, "Philo matters primarily as a source and not as a man."[4] But it is not merely that Philo wrote in sophisticated Atticizing Greek and made use of no-longer-extant philosophical sources; he exhibits intimate knowledge of the process of encyclical education which would have been conducted in *gymnasia* throughout the Hellenistic world (see e.g. *Congr.* 74–80).[5] Indeed, throughout his corpus, Philo's broad engagement with classical literature is displayed in quotations and allusions, not only in his well-known debt to Plato, but also Greek poets, above all Homer, and, to lesser degrees, Hesiod, Aeschylus, and Euripides, among others.[6] Nevertheless, perhaps in part due to the exigencies of disciplinary divisions, the academic fields of classical and Philonic studies have remained under-integrated, focused, as they are, on their respective corpora and methodologies.

Shifts in the dynamics of academic fields are underway, however. On the side of Philo scholars, evidence of progress can be seen through a comparison of three standard reference works on Philo: *ANRW* 2.21.1 and *The Cambridge Companion to Philo*—published in 1984 and 2009, respectively—have no entries devoted to Philo and the classics, whereas Torrey Seland's handbook *Reading Philo* does include a contribution, "Philo and Classical Education."[7]

---

and *Quod Deus Sit Immutabilis*, ed. D. Winston and J. Dillon, BJS 25 (Chico, CA: Scholars Press, 1983), 137–40; D. T. Runia, "Verba Philonica, ΑΓΑΛΜΑΤΟΦΟΡΕΙΝ, and the Authenticity of the *De Resurrectione* Attributed to Athenagoras," *VC* 46 (1992): 313–27.

[4] Nock, "Philo," 559.

[5] See esp. M. Alexandre, "La culture profane chez Philon," in *Philon d' Alexandre*, ed. R. Arnaldez, C. Mondésert, and J. Pouilloux (Paris: Cerf, 1967), 105–29; A. Mendelson, *Secular Education in Philo of Alexandria*, HUCM 7 (Cincinnati: Hebrew Union College Press, 1982), 25–46; J. J. Collins, *Jewish Wisdom in the Hellenistic Age* (Louisville: Westminster John Knox, 1997), 148–53. The view of Harry Wolfson that Philo must have been educated in a synagogue, due especially to the religious entailments of the *gymnasion* has been largely abandoned; *Philo: Foundations of Religious Philosophy in Judaism, Christianity, and Islam*, 2 vols, rev. edn (Cambridge, MA: Harvard University Press, 1968), 1:78–81.

[6] To be sure, this is not a new discovery; but scholarly attention to Philo's engagement with classical literature has increased markedly in recent times. With attention to poetry and mythology, see e.g. P. Boyancé, "Études Philoniennes," *REG* 76 (1963): 64–110; Alexandre, "La culture profane chez Philon," 109–12; F. Siegert, "Griechische Mythen im hellenistischen Judentum," in *Griechische Mythologie und frühes Christentum*, ed. R. von Haehling (Darmstadt: Wissenschaftliche Buchgesellschaft, 2005), 132–52, esp. 145–47; E. Koskenniemi, "Philo and Classical Drama," in *Ancient Israel, Judaism, and Christianity in Contemporary Perspective: Essays in Memory of Karl-Johan Illman*, ed. J. Neusner et al., Studies in Judaism (Lanham, MD: University Press of America, 2006), 137–51; E. Koskenniemi, "Philo and Greek Poets," *JSJ* 41 (2013): 301–22; R. Bloch, *Moses und der Mythos: Die Auseinandersetzung mit der griechischen Mythologie bei jüdischen-hellenistischen Autoren*, JSJSup 145 (Leiden: Brill, 2011), 173–89; K. Berthelot, "Philon d'Alexandrie, lecteur d'Homère: quelques éléments de réflexion," in *Prolongements et renouvellements de la tradition classique*, ed. A. Balansard, G. Dorival, and M. Loubet (Aix-en-Provence: Publications de l'Université Provence, 2011), 145–57; K. Berthelot, "Philo and the Allegorical Interpretation of Homer in the Platonic Tradition (with an Emphasis on Porphyry's *De antro nympharum*)," in *Homer and the Bible in the Eyes of Ancient Interpreters*, ed. M. R. Niehoff, Jerusalem Studies in Religion and Culture 16 (Leiden: Brill, 2012), 155–74; P. Nieto Hernández, "Philo and Greek Poetry," *SPhiloA* 26 (2014): 135–49; C. J. P. Friesen, "Dying Like a Woman: Euripides' Polyxena as Exemplum between Philo and Clement of Alexandria," *GRBS* 56 (2016): 623–45, esp. 630–39; C. J. P. Friesen, "Hannah's 'Hard Day' and Hesiod's 'Two Roads': Poetic Wisdom in Philo's *De ebrietate*," *JSJ* 46 (2015): 44–64; G. Roskam, "Nutritious Milk from Hagar's School: Philo's Reception of Homer," *SPhiloA* 29 (2017): 1–32; Erkki Koskenniemi, *Greek Writers and Philosophers in Philo and Josephus: A Study of Their Secular Education and Educational Ideals*, SPhA 9 (Leiden: Brill, 2019), 21–151.

[7] A. Kamesar, ed., *The Cambridge Companion to Philo* (Cambridge: Cambridge University Press, 2009); E. Koskenniemi, "Philo and Classical Education," in *Reading Philo: A Handbook to Philo of Alexandria*, ed. T. Seland (Grand Rapids: Eerdmans, 2014), 102–28.

In the field of classics, developments in the study of Greek literature in the Roman period hold promise for interdisciplinary integration. For example, the cultural movement of the mid-first through mid-third centuries falling under the rubric of the "Second Sophistic," long disparaged as derivative and degenerate, has, in recent decades, become the focus of vigorous and productive research, with growing appreciation for the literary merits of its authors. The distinctive configurations of Roman politics and Greek ethnic identities have made this period a touchstone for re-evaluating the disciplinary contours of the field of classics more broadly. Nevertheless, for various reasons, Philo has remained largely excluded from the standard historical and literary accounts. In the first place, the ancient biographer, Philostratus, who first coined the label δευτέρα σοφιστική (in contrast to ἀρχαία σοφιστική), situated its origins during the reign of Nero in connection with Nicetes of Smyrna, several years after Philo's death (though the fourth-century BCE Aeschines was its ancient founder; *Vit. soph.* 481, 511). Moreover, the sophists were professional orators and teachers of rhetoric and, by profession, Philo does not fit within this category. Early groundbreaking work on the Second Sophistic, consequently, had little to say about the Alexandrian. Glen Bowersock's landmark 1969 monograph *Greek Sophists in the Roman Empire* focused especially on figures who appear in Philostratus' account. For Bowersock, a sophist is defined as "a virtuoso rhetor with a big public reputation," and he thus concentrates his study on the public careers of leading orators.[8] Although Bowersock attends primarily to the second century, he recognizes this periodization as potentially arbitrary: "The Second (or New) Sophistic is a culmination, not a sudden burst or fad. This is true of the sophists' style as much as it is of their role in Roman history."[9]

Several major studies of the Second Sophistic have followed in the wake of Bowersock, focusing on an array of historical and cultural connections.[10] Only one, however, gives Philo serious attention: Graham Anderson's 1993 *The Second Sophistic*.[11] His chapter on "The Sophist and His Gods" includes a discussion of Judaism and Christianity, wherein he offers several brief but insightful observations regarding Philo. In leading a Jewish delegation to Rome, Philo "was already playing the traditional sophistic role

---

[8] G. W. Bowersock, *Greek Sophists in the Roman Empire* (Oxford: Clarendon, 1969), at 13. He nevertheless highlights broader cultural and literary interactions including Galen the physician (59–75), and "Other Literary Men," such as Dio of Prusa, Appian, Dio Cassius, Plutarch, and Lucian (110–17).

[9] Bowersock, *Greek Sophists*, 9.

[10] Standard treatments of the Second Sophistic include B. P. Reardon, *Courants littéraires grecs des IIe et IIIe siècles après J.-C.* (Paris: Les belles lettres, 1971); G. Anderson, *The Second Sophistic: A Cultural Phenomenon in the Roman Empire* (London: Routledge, 1993); S. Swain, *Hellenism and Empire: Language, Classicism, and Power in the Greek World AD 50–250* (Oxford: Clarendon, 1996); T. Schmitz, *Bildung und Macht: Zur sozialen und politischen Funktion der zweiten Sophistik in der griechischen Welt der Kaiserzeit*, Zetemata 97 (Munich: Beck, 1997); T. Whitmarsh, *Greek Literature and the Roman Empire: The Politics of Imitation* (Oxford: Oxford University Press, 2001).

[11] Anderson, *The Second Sophistic*, 203–5. Although Philo is rarely considered in relation to the Second Sophistic, other Jewish authors have been: on Josephus, see M. Gleason, "Mutilated Messengers: Body Language in Josephus," in *Being Greek under Rome: Cultural Identity, the Second Sophistic and the Development of Empire*, ed. S. Goldhill (Cambridge: Cambridge University Press, 2001), 50–85; and on the rabbis, see S. Schwartz, "The Rabbi in Aphrodite's Bath: Palestinian Society and Jewish Identity in the High Roman Empire," in *Being Greek under Rome*, 335–61; cf. S. Goldhill, "What Is Local Identity? The Politics of Cultural Mapping," in *Local Knowledge and Microidentities in the Imperial Greek World*, ed. T. Whitmarsh, Greek Culture in the Roman World (Cambridge: Cambridge University Press, 2010), 46–68, esp. 55–56.

of ambassador to the Emperor Gaius before Philostratus proclaimed the second beginning of the Second Sophistic with Nicetes." Moreover, he adds that "Philo's later account of the embassy is certainly not lacking in sophistic panache."[12]

The most far-reaching effort to situate Philo within the Second Sophistic, first published four years after Anderson's monograph, is by the New Testament scholar, Bruce Winter. In *Philo and Paul among the Sophists*, he argues that in Alexandria the sophistic movement was already under way much earlier than Philostratus' account suggests.[13] Surveying Philo's direct references to sophists, he demonstrates that, while often critical, they are not uniformly pejorative. Moreover, building on Anderson, Winter establishes the extent to which Philo's writings exhibit substantial rhetorical abilities.[14] His book has opened up promising interdisciplinary possibilities; of particular significance, the 2002 revised edition includes a foreword by Glen Bowersock, who writes, "Winter has succeeded in documenting, for the first time, the sophistic movement of the mid-first century [.... He] has uncovered the foundations of the Second Sophistic."[15] Such an evaluation by Bowersock, the pioneering scholar in the area of the Second Sophistic, establishes Philo as a compelling point of contact in future research.

Working independently of Winter, classicist Tim Whitmarsh, in his 2013 *Beyond the Second Sophistic*, issued an incisive call for expanding research beyond conventional boundaries to include especially Hellenistic Judaism. Whitmarsh's agenda is radical: to reevaluate "ideas about what counts as Greek literature."[16] The period of the so-called Second Sophistic—but for his purposes, "postclassical" Greek literature is the preferable label—is particularly useful in this endeavor, not least because the genres so strongly definitive of "the classics" were very much in flux as authors and orators experimented with them and challenged their cultural value. His study "does more than simply expand the canon. My aim is to do away entirely with the idea of the culturally central, the paradigmatic, to dispense with hierarchies of cultural value." This process involves moving beyond the authors with which classical scholars have traditionally concerned themselves and exploring "lateral engagement with other peoples' cultures, poetics and imaginative literature, the continuity with Hellenistic Greek culture." Historical accounts focusing only on authors such as Plutarch, Dio Chrysostom, and Aelius Aristides as paradigmatic risk producing a "picture of seamless panhellenism" which "is, ultimately, a scholarly fiction, resting on a circular process of exclusion of evidence to the contrary." As a corrective, Whitmarsh advocates "thinking more pluralistically," and it is precisely here that Jewish writers can provide an impetus for problematizing the Hellenocentrism that underlies many conventional studies of this time

---

[12] Anderson, *The Second Sophistic*, 203. He notes also regarding *De Iosepho* "sophistic techniques of amplification" and a "likely reminiscence of Thucydides" (at 204).

[13] B. W. Winter, *Philo and Paul among the Sophists: Alexandrian and Corinthian Responses to a Julio-Claudian Movement*, 2nd edn (Grand Rapids: Eerdmans, 2002) (orig. 1997).

[14] Philo's engagement with classical rhetoric is taken up further below, pp. 522–23.

[15] Bowersock adds, "A new edition of his authoritative work comes just at the right time. Rhetoric and its practitioners in the Roman Empire have lately attracted a new generation of innovative scholars for whom Winter's book will be indispensable" (in Winter, *Philo and Paul*, at ix).

[16] T. Whitmarsh, *Beyond the Second Sophistic: Adventures in Greek Postclassicism* (Berkeley: University of California Press, 2013), 2.

period.[17] Within this context, he raises the possibility of a "Jewish Sophistic," proposing that "Hellenistic Judaism thus offers a much better expression of what many critics seek in the Greek Second Sophistic, namely a coherent articulation of subaltern resistance through literature."[18]

The scholarly trajectory envisioned by Whitmarsh finds expression now in the 2017 *Oxford Handbook to the Second Sophistic*. In their programmatic introduction, William Johnson and Daniel Richter emphasize the "considerable fogginess" surrounding both the periodization of the Second Sophistic and the literary figures who belong within it. Consequently, their approach is "unusually broad-reaching …. Both in its scope and in its pluralism of voices the *Handbook* represents a somewhat new approach to the Second Sophistic, one that attempts to integrate Greek literature of the Roman period into the wider world of early imperial Greek, Latin, Jewish, and Christian cultural production."[19] Whitmarsh's contribution to the volume reiterates his earlier challenge to the artificiality of the conventional boundaries around the Second Sophistic, noting that there is no decisive shift in the year 50 CE that sets it off culturally. Indeed, centrally defining characteristics of the Second Sophistic—"rhetoric, archaism, Greek identity, and literariness"—are already evident in Hellenistic Alexandria, and he again cites Judaism as a leading demonstration.[20] Moreover, the *Handbook* includes an entire chapter devoted to "Jewish Literature" by Erich Gruen with Philo placed at the head of his survey. Philo "stands out as the most prominent and conspicuous instance of the Jewish intelligentsia steeped in Greek learning," and "comfortable, quite unselfconsciously so, in the culture of the Hellenes." This was not without tension, however. Indeed, throughout his corpus, "Philo's blend of Hellenism and Judaism was less a smooth process than a tense negotiation."[21]

While Gruen falls short of establishing what in particular about the Second Sophistic may be productively compared with Philo, Maren Niehoff's 2018 *Philo of Alexandria: An Intellectual Biography* places this on a stronger footing.[22] As a first of its kind, this volume (as suggested by the subtitle) sets out a biography of Philo taking as a point of departure his embassy to Rome, the most secure among otherwise very sparse historical data. Niehoff emphasizes the political influence of Rome as a force shaping Greek intellectual life and cultural identity, and demonstrates the pervasive extent to which Philo's later treatises engage in distinctively Roman religious and intellectual concerns. Within this context, Philo can be productively read alongside Greek authors who flourished during the Second Sophistic, such as Plutarch, Dio Chrysostom, and

---

[17] Whitmarsh, *Beyond the Second Sophistic*, at 4 and 6.

[18] Whitmarsh, *Beyond the Second Sophistic*, 213. He does not discuss Philo, focusing rather on Ezekiel's tragedy, the *Exagoge* (215–27), and the epic poets Theodotus and Philo (239–47). Compared with his earlier important work this represents a significant departure and expansion.

[19] W. A. Johnson and D. S. Richter, "Periodicity and Scope," in *The Oxford Handbook to the Second Sophistic*, ed. D. S. Richter and W. A. Johnson (Oxford: Oxford University Press, 2017), 3–10, at 3–4 and 7.

[20] Whitmarsh, "Greece: Hellenistic and Early Imperial Continuities," in *Oxford Handbook*, 11–24, at 5, 18–19.

[21] E. S. Gruen, "Jewish Literature and the Second Sophistic," in *Oxford Handbook*, 639–54, esp. 640–42, at 641 and 642. Philo is followed in Gruen's treatment by 4 Maccabees, Pseudo-Phocylides, and *Joseph and Aseneth*.

[22] It is striking that, in a handbook article on Judaism and the Second Sophistic, Gruen omits any consideration of Winter, who more than any other scholar established Philo's relationship with it.

Lucian. As she states, "[i]t is time now for a comprehensive analysis of Philo in light of the Second Sophistic." Moreover, "[c]omparisons between Philo and the authors of the Second Sophistic are fruitful because he anticipates many of their concerns and shows the beginning of important developments in the Roman Empire that have considerable implications for early Christianity and subsequent Western civilization."[23]

In sum, the respective fields of Philonic and classical studies are poised for fresh and productive interdisciplinary research. The heuristic rubric of the Second Sophistic is by no means the only one through which to advance such work. Nevertheless, the inclusion of Philo within comparative studies of postclassical Greek authors has already yielded progress, and we are now well positioned to pursue Nock's observation that Philo's writings deserve a place alongside Plutarch and other Greek writers in the Roman Empire.

31.2 Classical *Paideia*: Reading and Writing with Philo

The Roman period gave rise to new and reconfigured literary genres. For example, biographical writing, though not unattested earlier, emerged in different ways in the first century CE. It has been argued by Simon Swain, among others, that during the Roman Empire there was "a great increase in the portraiture of the individual in writing and art," and that this should be understood in conjunction with the distinctive political and intellectual contexts of the period.[24] Naturally and for good reason, pride of place goes to Plutarch whose *Lives* offer the most prolific evidence. Surveys often omit Philo, however, even though he produced biographical accounts of legendary heroes prior to Plutarch (extant *Lives* are of Abraham, Joseph, and Moses), as well as, in a very different mode, a recent emperor (in *Legatio ad Gaium*). Indeed, as Niehoff has demonstrated, Philo's writings anticipate the concerns of Plutarch: together, they "are the first writers in the Imperial period who advance a moralizing and anecdotal approach to biography."[25]

Biography is not the only classical genre in which Philo's treatises participate; he was well versed in the practices of rhetoric that were established in Athens and came to flourish afresh in the Second Sophistic. Thomas Conley offers a concise survey of the techniques of rhetoric exhibited in Philo's writings: style, sentence construction, use of amplification, and topoi, such as "commonplace similes, exempla, and themes."[26]

---

[23] M. R. Niehoff, *Philo of Alexandria: An Intellectual Biography*, ABRL (New Haven: Yale University Press, 2018), at 21–22. On Niehoff's application of the designation "Second Sophistic," see also my review in *JTS* 67 (2018): 777–81.

[24] S. Swain, "Biography and Biographic in the Literature of the Roman Empire," in *Portraits: Biographical Representation in the Greek and Latin Literature of the Roman Empire*, ed. M. J. Edwards and S. Swain (Oxford: Clarendon, 1997), 1–38, at 2. Also important is P. Cox Miller, *Biography in Late Antiquity: A Quest for the Holy Man*, Transformation of Classical Heritage 5 (Berkeley: University of California Press, 1983). Although she is concerned primarily with the third and fourth centuries, she helpfully surveys the genre in earlier periods (3–16).

[25] M. R. Niehoff, "Philo and Plutarch as Biographers—Parallel Responses to Roman Stoicism," *GRBS* 52 (2012): 361–92, at 384; see also Niehoff, *Philo of Alexandria*, 109–30.

[26] T. M. Conley, "Philo of Alexandria," in *Handbook of Classical Rhetoric in the Hellenistic Period (330 B.C.–A.D. 400)*, ed. S. Porter (Leiden: Brill, 1997), 695–713, at 706–7; cf. T. M. Conley, "Philo's Rhetoric: Argumentation and Style," *ANRW* 2.21.1 (1984): 343–71; also M. Alexandre, Jr, "Philo of Alexandria and Hellenic *Paideia*," *Euphrosyne* 37 (2009): 121–30.

As with biography, however, the study of Philo's use of rhetoric also exposes a disciplinary chasm: Conley's treatment belongs to a *Handbook* intended for New Testament specialists; by contrast, a comparable *Companion* aimed at classicists has no sustained attention to Jewish authors.[27]

In short, Philo has been an underappreciated resource among classicists as a *writer*, participating as he did in the ever-changing landscape of classical genres, such as biography and rhetoric. At the same time, Philo as a *reader* can provide valuable insights into the ongoing popularity of classical texts and the working methods of Greek intellectuals. While Philonic scholars have long been attentive to his broad knowledge of Greek literature, recent research has made important advancements in this area. David Lincicum's "Preliminary Index to Philo's Non-Biblical Citations and Allusions" is an invaluable resource, giving ready access to relevant textual data, and this is complemented by numerous relevant studies published in recent years.[28] These developments correspond in a timely fashion to a paradigm shift within classics toward reception history as an increasingly prominent interpretive lens. This phenomenon is well described by Charles Martindale in an introductory essay to the volume *Classics and the Uses of Reception*. As he observes, whereas classical scholarship was once dominated by historical positivism, which aimed at recovering final meanings, now it is broadly recognized that texts are not fixed and stable entities. Consequently, "the sharp distinction between antiquity itself and its reception over the centuries is dissolved .... The complex chain of receptions has the effect that a work can operate across history obliquely in unexpected ways."[29] This process begins in antiquity itself and can be studied through various modes—for example, performance, education, textual transmission, imitation—evident in Philo's corpus.[30]

Unfortunately, Philo tells us almost nothing about how he gained access to the classical texts which he cites. Others, such as Pliny the Younger, are much more explicit in detailing what William Johnson describes as the "Pragmatics of Reading."[31] For Philo,

---

[27] E. Gunderson, ed., *The Cambridge Companion to Ancient Rhetoric* (Cambridge: Cambridge University Press, 2009). Its Epilogue does include a chapter on Christianity: T. Penner and C. Vander Stichele, "Rhetorical Practice and Performance in Early Christianity," 245–60. The "Jewish Roots" of Christian "missionary preaching" are discussed briefly, but this is limited to the consistent recourse to scripture. Paul's so-called Areopagus speech in Acts 17 is characterized as the "perhaps the least 'Jewish' speech in the book of Acts" apparently because "Paul cites a Greek source as well" (at 249). Importantly, however, the line of poetry quoted by Paul (Aratus, *Phaen.* 5) had already been quoted by the Jewish apologist Aristobulus in the second century BCE.

[28] D. Lincicum, "A Preliminary Index to Philo's Non-Biblical Citations and Allusions," *SPhiloA* 25 (2013): 139–67; see now also J. R. Royse, "Some Overlooked Classical References in Philo," *SPhiloA* 32 (2020): 249–55; and n. 6 above for a representative list of studies.

[29] C. Martindale, "Introduction: Thinking through Reception," in *Classics and the Uses of Reception*, ed. C. Martindale and R. F. Thomas (Oxford: Blackwell, 2006), 1–13, at 4.

[30] On reception in antiquity, see L. Hardwick, *Reception Studies*, Greece and Rome: New Surveys in the Classics 33 (Oxford: Oxford University Press, 2003), 12–31. Philo is often overlooked, however. For instance, the volume, *Beyond the Fifth Century: Interactions with Greek Tragedy from the Fourth Century BCE to the Middle Ages*, ed. I. Gildenhard and M. Revermann (Berlin: de Gruyter, 2010), an outstanding treatment of the reception of tragedy from the fourth century BCE to the medieval period, does not take Judaism into consideration. But see more recently, C. J. P. Friesen, "Attending Euripides: Philo of Alexandria's Dramatic Appropriations," in *Euripides-Rezeption in Kaiserzeit und Spätantike*, ed. M. Schramm, Millennium Studies 83 (Berlin: de Gruyter, 2020), 259–74.

[31] W. A. Johnson, *Readers and Reading Culture in the High Roman Empire: A Study of Elite Communities* (Oxford: Oxford University Press, 2010), esp. 17–62.

however, we are left to speculation. The possibilities for his encounters with texts have been well summarized by Lincicum: through his own education, in the audience at performances, doxographical handbooks, collections of excerpts (made by himself or others), philosophical readings in private religious settings, and, finally, through direct use of complete volumes.[32] It seems certain that Philo had access to a private book collection (probably limited to philosophical texts), and it is also tempting to imagine him visiting the famous Library of Alexandria, even though he only makes passing reference to "libraries" (βιβλιοθῆκαι) at the Sebasteum (*Legat.* 151). A recent volume on the Library devotes an entire chapter to Philo, though it is concerned almost exclusively with a negative: that is, why Philo says nothing about this famous Alexandrian institution.[33]

In spite of these uncertainties Philo can offer insights into the historical fortunes of classical texts. Here, one example may be sufficient—his deployment of the *Syleus*, a satyr play by Euripides.[34] Though clearly not one of Euripides' best-known works, Philo quotes from it on four occasions in three separate treatises (*Leg.* 3.202; *Ios.* 78; *Prob.* 25, 99–104). Three of these have all the hallmarks of a gnomic citation prevalent among ancient writers and used elsewhere by Philo. Each time he quotes the same four-line fragment (*TrGF* 5.687) detached from any reference to the dramatic context, and with the same basic moralizing application—namely, as an expression of the virtuous person's courage in the face of suffering or slavery.[35] Moreover, this particular fragment is attested in other authors, also with disjunction from context (Artemidorus 4.59; Eusebius, *Praep. evang.* 6.6.2; and Michael Psellus, *Poemata* 21.275–76). It is highly probable, therefore, that these lines were accessible through some common anthologized source.[36] In *Probus* 99–104, however, things appear differently: Philo deploys the same gnomic passage, but now identifies the speaker and the playwright:

---

[32] D. Lincicum, "Philo's Library," *SPhiloA* 26 (2014): 99–114; see also G. E. Sterling, "'The School of Sacred Laws': The Social Setting of Philo's Treatises," *VC* 53 (1999): 148–64.

[33] E. Friedheim, "Quelques notes sur la signification historique du silence philonien à propos de la Bibliothèque d'Alexandrie," in *The Library of Alexandria: A Cultural Crossroads of the Ancient World: Proceedings of the Second Polis Institute Interdisciplinary Conference*, ed. C. Rico and A. Dan (Jerusalem: Polis Institute Press, 2017), 245–55. On the Library, see also R. S. Bagnall, "Alexandria: Library of Dreams," *PAPhS* 146 (2002): 348–62; more broadly, J. König, K. Oikonomopoulou, and G. Woolf, eds., *Ancient Libraries* (Cambridge: Cambridge University Press, 2013); G. W. Houston, *Inside Roman Libraries: Book Collections and Their Management in Antiquity* (Chapel Hill: University of North Carolina Press, 2014).

[34] I have discussed Philo and the *Syleus* in greater detail elsewhere; see C. J. F. Friesen, *Playing Gods, Acting Heroes, and the Interaction between Judaism, Christianity, and Greek Drama in the Early Common Era* (London: Routledge, 2024), 67–84.

[35] Note the introductory formulae: "the tragic expression in the face of suffering" (τὸ τραγικὸν πρὸς τὴν ἀλγηδόνα, *Leg.* 3.202); "as the tragedian says," (ὡς ὁ τραγικός φησιν, *Ios.* 78); "acting with youthful vigor, [the free person] proclaims in response" (νεανιευσάμενος δὲ ἀντικηρύξει, *Prob.* 25). For similar uses of Euripides by Philo, see e.g. *Aet.* 5, 30, 144; *Leg.* 1.7 (*TrFG* 5.839); *Prob.* 22 (*TrGF* 5.958); *Prob.* 145 (*TrGF* 5.893.1); *Prob.* 116 (*Hec.* 548–51); *Prob.* 141 (*TrGF* 5.275.3–4). And for a comparison of introductory formulae for Euripides across Philo's corpus, see S. Marculescu, "'Comme dit l'auteur tragique': la présence d'Euripide chez Philon d'Alexandrie," in *Les illusions de l'autonymie: la parole rapportée de l'Autre dans la littérature*, ed. M.-F. Marein et al. (Paris: Éditions Hermann, 2019), 133–48, esp. 141–45.

[36] On gnomic anthologies, or florilegia, see H. Chadwick, "Florilegium," *RAC* 7 (1969): 1131–59; D. Konstan, "Excerpting as a Reading Practice," in *Deciding Culture: Stobaeus' Collection of Excerpts of Ancient Greek Authors*, ed. G. Reydams-Schils and C. Lévy (Turnhout: Brepols, 2009), 9–22.

> ἴδε γοῦν οἷα παρ' Εὐριπίδῃ φησὶν ὁ Ἡρακλῆς·
> πίμπρα, κάταιθε σάρκας, ἐμπλήσθητί μου
> πίνων κελαινὸν αἷμα· πρόσθε γὰρ κάτω
> γῆς εἶσιν ἄστρα γῆ τ' ἄνεισ' εἰς αἰθέρα,
> πρὶν ἐξ ἐμοῦ σοι θῶπ' ἀπαντῆσαι λόγον.
>
> See, then, what kinds of things Heracles says in Euripides:
> Ignite and burn up my flesh, be filled with drinking my dark blood;
> for the stars will come down to earth, and the earth ascend to the sky
> before a flattering word from me meets you. (*Prob.* 99; *TrGF* 5.687)

He follows with an extensive summary of the play's plot together with four additional excerpts which are unattested elsewhere (*TrGF* 5.688–91). The nature of Philo's source for this otherwise obscure play and the additional fragments is of considerable interest, though it must remain a matter of speculation. One possibility is that he acquired an *hypothesis*, that is, a narrative summary of the drama. Collections of these were relatively widespread, and they provided summaries and backgrounds for a range of classical works. For Attic drama, Monique van Rossum-Steenbeek has cataloged and analyzed twenty-eight papyri, several of which date to Philo's period. The *Syleus* is found once—on a second-century alphabetical collection treating Euripidean plays—but unfortunately it is too fragmentary to assess its relationship to Philo's description of the play.[37] In view of the minimal detail generally preserved in other such *hypotheses*, however, Philo's research likely extended beyond this.[38] Rossum-Steenbeek theorizes that these papyri "do not seem to have been intended as independent reading matter" but rather functioned to help "the readers to acquire information on or form a picture of the literature they were reading or about to read," that is, "as a kind of reference book."[39] Perhaps the most likely explanation, therefore, is that Philo, interested in learning more about the dramatic context of his initial gnomic fragment, went to the additional effort of consulting an *hypothesis* as well as a text of the play itself.[40] Of course, Philo is frustratingly silent on the matter; but we might imaginatively compare the comments of Galen, who, when looking for a particular volume of one Archigenes, reports that "I went running around to all the libraries, all the booksellers, and all the doctors ... to get hold of this book" (*Loc. Aff.* 3.5).[41]

---

[37] M. van Rossum-Steenbeek, *Greek Readers' Digests? Studies on a Selection of Subliterary Papyri*, Mnemosyne, bibliotheca classica Batava 175 (Leiden: Brill, 1998), 1–52, esp. 20–21, 213–15.

[38] As Rossum-Steenbeek notes, the *hypotheses* often correspond roughly to the information found in mythographers, such as Pseudo-Apollodorus (*Greek Readers' Digests*, 25–30). In the case of the *Syleus*, however, Philo's detail is much more extensive than what is in the *Bibliotheca* (2.6.3).

[39] Rossum-Steenbeek, *Greek Readers' Digests*, 161.

[40] See similarly Marculescu, "Comme dit l'auteur tragique," 139–41.

[41] Quoted in Houston, *Inside Roman Libraries*, at 18.

31.3 Philo, Greek Identity, and the Politics of the Roman Empire

Greek sophists in the Roman Empire were frequently found in ambassadorial roles, representing their communities before the emperor.[42] Philo's leadership of a Jewish delegation to Rome places him squarely in this sphere. Moreover, his narration of this experience in the *Legatio* employs sophistic strategies, as for instance in his ridicule of Gaius' emulations of demigods and gods (*Legat.* 76–113), taken by Anderson to be the leading example of Philo's sophistic style: "[t]he gods serve as the cast-list for bitterly sarcastic sophistic *psogos*," which is akin to "the sophistic practice of writing sabre-rattling invectives after the victim's death, as in the case of Aelian's attack on Elagabalus."[43] Anderson's cursory observations merit further inspection. The correlations between Philo's comments and broader sophistic techniques can be seen through a comparison with Dio Chrysostom's first *Kingship Oration*, addressed to Trajan in Rome, enumerating the qualities of an ideal ruler for the benefit of the recently ascendant emperor. Dio's oration deploys a second-person address (e.g. *Or.* 1.9, 36), even though it remains uncertain whether it was actually delivered before an imperial audience. In Philo's case, it is clear that he did not deliver his scathing critique in the presence of Gaius, and thus it is all the more striking that at several points he shifts into second person (esp. *Legat.* 81–92), even calling upon the emperor with the vocative Γάιε (81, 86, 91). These moves function to construct a fiction of a genuine imperial audience for his speech, as Dio later would for his.

Perhaps the most striking correlation between the *Legatio* and Dio's first *Kingship Oration* is the function of Heracles as a potential model for imperial emulation.[44] Philo reports that the emperor adorned himself with Heracles' best-known attributes: "as in a theater (ὥσπερ ἐν θεάτρῳ), he took up different apparel at different times, sometimes a lion skin and a club, both gold-gilded, adorning himself as Heracles (διακοσμούμενος εἰς Ἡρακλέα)" (79; cf. Cassius Dio 59.26.7).[45] Gaius was neither the first nor the last emperor to liken himself (or be likened) to Heracles.[46] Trajan also, it seems, had a fondness for him and a desire to model himself after this son of Zeus (Pliny, *Pan.* 14.5).[47]

---

[42] See Bowersock, *Greek Sophists*, 43–58.

[43] Anderson, *The Second Sophistic*, 204.

[44] In addition to Heracles, according to Philo, Gaius impersonated the demigods Dionysus and the Dioscuri (78–92) as well as the full deities, Hermes, Apollo, and Ares (93–113). Cassius Dio likewise notes that Gaius impersonated a similar range of demigods and gods including Heracles, Dionysus, and Apollo, although his list adds Neptune and the goddesses Juno, Diana, or Venus (59.26.5–27.2). See also Suetonius, *Cal.* 22; Athenaeus, *Deipn.* 4.148d. For discussion, see A. A. Barrett, *Caligula: The Corruption of Power* (London: B. T. Batsford, 1989); E. S. Gruen, "Caligula, the Imperial Cult, and Philo's *Legatio*," *SPhiloA* 24 (2012): 135–47; Niehoff, *Philo of Alexandria*, 63–65.

[45] For a more complete discussion of Heracles in Philo's corpus, see my "Heracles and Philo of Alexandria: The Son of Zeus between Torah and Philosophy, Empire and Stage," in *Philo and Greek Myth: Narratives, Allegories, and Arguments*, ed. F. Alesse and L. De Luca, SPhA 10 (Leiden: Brill, 2019), 176–99.

[46] For Alexander and Commodus, see Athenaeus, *Deipn.* 12.537f; for Nero, Suetonius, *Nero* 21.1; for Mark Antony, Plutarch, *Ant.* 4.2; see also Appian, *Bell. civ.* 3.16; and A. R. Anderson, "Heracles and His Successors: A Study of a Heroic Ideal and the Recurrence of a Heroic Type," *HSCP* 39 (1928): 7–58, esp. 42–44.

[47] See O. Hekster, "Propagating Power: Hercules as an Example for Second-Century Emperors," in *Herakles and Hercules: Exploring a Greco-Roman Divinity*, ed. L. Rawlings and H. Bowden (Swansea: Classical Press of Wales, 2005), 205–21.

Thus, the comments of Philo and Dio depend upon the common knowledge that the respective emperors both aspired to imitate the demigod. More than this, however, both draw on a shared application of Heracles' heroic achievements as a measure of virtuous statesmanship. In the fourth century, in an address to Philip of Macedon, Isocrates had appealed to the potentate's Heraclean lineage. Contrary to much mythology, Heracles' virtue consists "in his wisdom, ambition, and justice," more than "in his strength of body" (τῇ φρονήσει καὶ τῇ φιλοτιμίᾳ καὶ τῇ δικαιοσύνῃ ... τῇ ῥώμῃ τῇ τοῦ σώματος, *Or.* 5.110); and his lasting achievement was establishing peace in Hellas and leaving the inhabitants free to rule themselves (111–12), a model which Isocrates now urges Philip to emulate. In Philo's lifetime, Tiberius, in his eulogy of Augustus, according to Cassius Dio, similarly compared his predecessor to Heracles, even claiming that the achievements of Augustus were greater in that "he, not among beasts but among men, willingly, by both waging wars and framing laws, saved the state completely and became distinguished himself" (56.36.5).[48]

In his *Kingship Oration*, Dio invents an elaborate legend concerning Heracles in which he is faced with a choice between two women sitting atop two mountains, the one is Royalty (Βασιλεία), the other Tyranny (Τυραννίς) (*Or.* 1.69–83).[49] For Dio, Heraclean labors become a political allegory, concerned not with monstrous beasts, but rather the eradication of tyrants and the protection of good government throughout the world: "wherever [Heracles] sees tyranny and a tyrant, he punishes and destroys them, both among Greeks and barbarians.... Indeed, it is because of this that he is savior of the earth and people, not because he repelled beasts for them" (84). This perspective on the Heraclean labors—that they were above all for the good of human civilization—is precisely the one adopted by Philo in his own address to Gaius: "Heracles purged land and sea, having undertaken labors most necessary and useful (ἄθλους ἀναγκαιοτάτους καὶ ὠφελιμωτάτους) for all people for the sake of destroying the harmful and destructive aspects of each nature" (*Legat.* 91). Philo asks: "but indeed, did you emulate Heracles with your own tireless labors (τοῖς ἀκαμάτοις σαυτοῦ πόνοις) and unceasing acts of courage, having filled mainlands and islands with good law and justice, plenty and thriving, and the abundance of all other good things?" (90).

Thus, in his efforts as an ambassador to Rome on behalf of his community in Alexandria, Philo takes on a role that would later become increasingly prominent among Greek intellectuals in the period of the Second Sophistic. His account of the events reported in the *Legatio* deploy appropriate literary strategies, evident, for

---

[48] Cf. Horace, *Carm.* 1.12.25, 3.3.9–12, 4.4.61–65; *Ep.* 2.1.5–13; Virgil, *Aeneid* 6.788–807.

[49] The parable of the Choice of Heracles is first attested most famously in Xenophon where it is recited by Socrates and attributed to the fifth-century sophist Prodicus (*Mem.* 2.1.21–34). The young hero, coming of age, reaches a crossroads and is faced with the choice of two women, one represented as Vice (Κακία) the other as Virtue (Ἀρετή). The former is richly decorated, but soft and plump, promising an easy road to all the pleasures of life; the latter is pure and modest, offering the greatest honor, but only by means of "toil and effort" (πόνου καὶ ἐπιμελείας, 2.1.28). This parable remained popular throughout antiquity, and was even adapted by Philo; see Friesen, "Heracles and Philo," 177–80. His version replaces Vice with Pleasure (ἡδονή), and rather than explicitly naming Heracles as its protagonist he applies it universally "each one of us" (ἡμῶν ἑκάστῳ) (*Sacr.* 20–33; see also Justin, *2 Apol.* 11; Athenaeus, *Deipn.* 12.510c; Philostratus, *VS* 496; Lucian, *Somn.*; Maxiumus, *Diss.* 14.1); the most complete comparative analysis is J. Alpers, *Hercules in bivio* (PhD diss., University of Göttingen, 1912).

instance, in his use of Heracles as a heroic model to be followed by a just ruler.[50] Indeed, in his political application of Heraclean labors, Philo participates in a widely attested rhetorical tradition used also by Isocrates, Dio Chrysostom, and Tiberius.

31.4 Philo Playing with Plays: Theater and Metatheater

Greek literature has, from its inception, been inseparable from public performance. This is most obvious in the theater, a prominent institution which, in various ways, came to represent broader collective and social experiences. While most commonly associated with fifth-century Athens, classical plays continued to be performed throughout the Greek-speaking world, and were also translated into Latin for Roman audiences.[51] Theater served ideological and political purposes: emperors, for instance, took to the stage (sometimes literally) to act, recite lines, or express their relationship to their subjects.[52] At Rome, so-called *fabulae praetextae* were performed as celebrations of military victories. These developments in the area of drama correspond to a wider cultural phenomenon of theatricality. In her brilliant study of Neronian Rome, Shadi Bartsch defines "theatricality" as that which "makes actors out of human beings placed in situations in which they feel themselves watched, in which their performance is subject to the evaluation of a superior who must be watched in turn to gauge his reactions; and in those contexts in which there exists a well-defined, self-conscious audience ... , it entails a reversal of the normal one-way direction of the spectator's gaze."[53] For Bartsch, a decisive shift in this regard occurs under Nero because now the emperor himself would perform on stage and frequently the response of the audience was scrutinized. In Tacitus especially, "the interaction of emperor and audience in the theater provides ... a dramatic parallel to the insidious relations obtaining between the emperor and his subjects when the stage was far from sight."[54]

If attention is paid to Philo, however, greater continuity between Nero and Gaius is evident.[55] As noted above, according to Philo (*Legat.* 79), Gaius was in the habit of playing the roles of divinities "as in a theater." Later in the same treatise he likens

---

[50] Philo's attention to the political tasks of sophists can also be seen in his account of Joseph's interaction with the pharaoh. He contrasts the biblical patriarch with others who populated the court. The pharaoh immediately recognized him as a "model of wisdom" who would "reveal the truth" and get rid of "the ignorance of the sophists among us (τῶν παρ' ἡμῖν σοφιστῶν)" (*Ios.* 106). As a true *politikos*, Joseph was capable of interpreting dreams (*oneirokritikos*), setting him apart from those who "deliver wisdom for a wage" (125). See Anderson, *The Second Sophistic*, 204–5; cf. Winter, *Philo and Paul*, 91–94.

[51] See F. I. Zeitlin, "Thebes: Theater of Self and Society in Athenian Drama," in *Greek Tragedy and Political Theory*, ed. J. P. Euben (Berkeley: University of California Press, 1986), 101–41; S. Goldhill, "The Great Dionysia and Civic Ideology," in *Nothing to Do with Dionysos? Athenian Drama in Its Social Context*, ed. J. J. Winkler and F. I. Zeitlin (Princeton: Princeton University Press, 1990), 97–129; I. Gildenhard, "Buskins & SPQR: Roman Receptions of Greek Tragedy," in *Beyond the Fifth Century*, 153–85.

[52] See H. von Hesberg, "The King on Stage," in *Art of Ancient Spectacle*, ed. B. Bergmann and C. Kondoleon, Studies in the History of Art 56 (Washington, DC: National Gallery, 1999), 65–75.

[53] S. Bartsch, *Actors in the Audience: Theatricality and Doublespeak from Nero to Hadrian*, Revealing Antiquity 6 (Cambridge, MA: Harvard University Press, 1994), 10–11.

[54] Bartsch, *Actors in the Audience*, 3–10, at 10.

[55] See similarly E. Muehlberger, "The Representation of Theatricality in Philo's *Embassy to Gaius*," *JSJ* 39 (2008): 46–67.

the experience of the Alexandrian delegation's imperial audience to a theatrical spectacle: "upon us who were there, a dramatic production was about to be staged (ἔμελλε σκηνοβατεῖσθαι δραματοποιία) against the entire nation" (351). After being ridiculed "as in theatrical mimes" (ὡς ἐν θεατρικοῖς μίμοις, 359), "they had fled such a theater (θέατρον) and also a prison rather than a court of law; for as in a theater (ὡς ... ἐν θεάτρῳ) there was a sound of clucking from people hissing, mocking, and jeering without measure" (368).[56] While Philo's theatrical language is highly rhetorical, it may correspond to his actual experience in Rome. Philo indicates that the meeting occurred in two "gardens" (κῆποι), those of Maecenas and Lamia (*Legat.* 351), and, as Annewies van den Hoek and John Herrmann, Jr., have recently discussed, the Gardens of Maecenas include archaeological remains of an auditorium dating to the Augustan period.[57] While we cannot be certain that this was the site of the meeting between Gaius and Philo's Jewish delegation, such a theatrical structure would bear striking coherence with Philo's description of events.

While Philo's experience with theatricality in relation to Gaius was uniformly negative, elsewhere in his corpus his attitude toward drama is much more positive. On numerous occasions, he quotes from plays in support of philosophical arguments (see above on the *Syleus*, pp. 524–25). Of all his treatises, the highest concentration of such quotations is in the *Probus*, where he also issues a programmatic explanation for his use of poetry in general: "Poets and prose writers (ποιηταὶ καὶ συγγραφεῖς) are witnesses of the freedom of good people; on their ideas Greeks and barbarians alike are reared nearly from their swaddling-clothes and as a result become better in their character" (98).[58] While these were clearly textual appropriations, later in the *Probus* he claims to have attended the theater himself and recounts his experience:

πρῴην ὑποκριτῶν τραγῳδίαν ἐπιδεικνυμένων καὶ τὰ παρ' Εὐριπίδῃ τρίμετρα διεξιόντων ἐκεῖνα
    τοὐλεύθερον γὰρ ὄνομα παντὸς ἄξιον,
    κἂν σμίκρ' ἔχῃ τις, μεγάλ' ἔχειν νομιζέτω,
τοὺς θεατὰς ἅπαντας εἶδον ἐπ' ἄκρων ποδῶν ὑπ' ἐκπλήξεως ἀναστάντας καὶ φωναῖς μείζοσι καὶ ἐκβοήσεσιν ἐπαλλήλοις ἔπαινον μὲν τῆς γνώμης, ἔπαινον δὲ καὶ τοῦ ποιητοῦ συνείροντας, ὃς οὐ μόνον τὴν ἐλευθερίαν ἔργοις ἀλλὰ καὶ τοὔνομα αὐτῆς ἐσέμνυνεν.

---

[56] For related discussion, see F. Calabi, "Theatrical Language in Philo's *In Flaccum*," in *Italian Studies on Philo of Alexandria*, ed. F. Calabi, SPhA 1 (Boston: Brill, 2003), 91–116; R. Bloch, "Von Szene zu Szene: Das jüdische Theater in der Antike," in *Juden in ihrer Umelt: Akkulturation des Judentums in Antike und Mittelalter*, ed. M. Konradt and R. C. Schwinges (Basel: Schwabe, 2009), 57–86, esp. 73–74; C. J. P. Friesen, "Virtue and Vice on Stage: Philo of Alexandria's Theatrical Ambivalences," *JAJ* 8 (2017): 241–56, esp. 242–49.

[57] A. van den Hoek and J. H. Herrmann, Jr., "Chasing the Emperor: Philo in the *Horti* of Rome," *SPhiloA* 28 (2016): 171–204.

[58] See similarly Philo's comments toward the end of the treatise: it is "fitting to heed poets" (ποιηταῖς προσέχειν ἄξιον): "Why shouldn't we? They are educators (παιδευταί) through our entire life, just as parents train their children in moderation (σωφρονίζοντες) privately, so also they do for their cities publicly (δημοσίᾳ τὰς πόλεις)" (*Prob.* 143). On the public value of dramatic poets, see also Aristophanes, *Ran.* 1054–55; Dio Chrysostom, *Or.* 32.6.

> Recently when actors were performing a tragedy and they went through these trimeters by Euripides—
>> Freedom is a name worthy of everything, even if someone has little, let him understand that he has much— (*TrGF* 5.275.3–4)
>
> I saw all the audience members standing up on their tip-toes from amazement, and with great voices and responsive shouts jointly declaring their praise of the maxim and praise also of the poet, who revered not only freedom in actions but also its very name. (*Prob.* 141; cf. *Ebr.* 177)

Two points concerning Philo's relationship with the theater and theatricality here are worth noting.[59] First, he identifies the playwright as Euripides. While this is not unexpected given that he was by far the most popular tragedian across antiquity, there may be more at stake.[60] Euripides had a well-known reputation as the "philosopher of the stage" (Clement, *Strom.* 5.11.70.2; Origen, *Cels.* 4.77; Vitruvius, 8 praef. 1; Dio Chrysostom, *Or.* 18.7), and was thought to have a had a close relationship with Socrates, a nearly universally celebrated intellectual hero (Aristophanes, *Ran.* 1491–99; *TrGF* T 5.1A.3; *TrGF* T 47a; Diog. Laert. 2.18).[61] In fact, Diogenes Laertius (2.22) reports that Socrates attended the very same tragedy (*Auge*) quoted here by Philo. It is also striking that the same two lines that Philo reports having heard in the theater appear elsewhere in a florilegium, that is, in the collected excerpts of Stobaeus in the fifth century (4.8.3).[62] While not decisive, this concurrence raises the possibility that Philo acquired them from some similar source and retroactively inserted them into a "recollection" of their performance.[63]

Second, the manner in which Philo presents his experience in the theater is of interest, that is, he subordinates the content of the drama on stage to his observations of the audience. This is evident grammatically: the quotation is imbedded within a genitive absolute (ὑποκριτῶν τραγῳδίαν ἐπιδεικνυμένων), whereas the main clause is introduced as, "I saw all the audience members" (τοὺς θεατὰς ἅπαντας εἶδον), and thereafter Philo dwells at greater length on their reaction.[64] Philo is, of course, not alone in his attention to the audience. As Horace observed regarding Democritus, he would "watch the people more carefully than the shows themselves" (*spectaret populum ludis attentius ipsis*, *Ep.* 2.1.197). Similarly, Epictetus instructed his pupils to maintain a

---

[59] See also Friesen, "Attending Euripides," 269–71.
[60] Philo quotes Euripides as many as twenty-one times compared with six for Aeschylus and once for Sophocles (tabulated from Lincicum, "A Preliminary Index"). This relative frequency is roughly consistent with what is preserved on papyri: according to Robert Garland there are 176 with Euripides, thirty-eight with Sophocles, and thirty-five with Aeschylus; R. Garland, *Surviving Greek Tragedy* (London: Duckworth, 2004), 53).
[61] For this, see T. Irwin, "Euripides and Socrates," *CP* 78 (1983): 183–97; J. M. Dillon, "Euripides and the Philosophy of His Time," *Classics Ireland* 11 (2004): 47–73, esp. 70–73.
[62] Twice elsewhere Philo's gnomic quotations of Euripides are also in Stobaeus: *TrGF* 5.200 in *Spec.* 4.47 and Stob. 4.13.3; *TrGF* 5.420 in *Somn.* 1.154; *Mos.* 1.31; and Stob. 4.41.1.
[63] Cf. the confidence of Koskenniemi: "this passage proves that he was present when Euripides' drama was performed, and he witnessed the strong feeling in the audience"; Koskenniemi, *Greek Writers and Philosophers*, 64.
[64] See also J. Jay, "The Problem of the Theater in Early Judaism," *JSJ* 44 (2013): 218–53, esp. 226. In Philo's other mention of attending the theater, his concern is also with the audience more than the play, as he uses it to illustrate the various ways in which people are affected by stimuli (*Ebr.* 177).

detached position with respect to a tragic performance; in contrast to the common theater-goer who is caught up in emotional reactions, his students were to view tragedy as illustrating the consequences of over-valuing externals (Arrian, *Epict.* 1.4.26).

Thus, Philo's interest in the theater goes beyond merely citing gnomic fragments; he was attentive to the political dynamics involved in theatricality, and through his attendance of the theater he positioned himself as a meta-observer in the manner of a philosopher.

31.5 Conclusion

As an Alexandrian Jew with the education of an elite Greek living under the Roman Empire, Philo poses distinct opportunities for the modern academy to transgress its conventional disciplinary configurations. At a time when leading classicists are reevaluating the hierarchies of their canon, Philo's oeuvre offers a range of resources to be explored. With such an objective in view, this chapter suggested that the Second Sophistic is one promising rubric under which Philonic studies and classics can be productively integrated. Philo was an active participant within his own contemporary literary culture: he contributed to the development and evolution of conventional genres, and his own engagement with classical texts provides a valuable perspective on the working methods a Greek intellectual. In addition, Philo's role in the Jewish delegation to Rome firmly situates him within the sphere of other sophists, and his rhetorical strategies in the *Legatio ad Gaium* deploy common topoi known from Isocrates to Dio Chrysostom. Finally, Philo's evocation of theatricality with its breakdown of distinctions between actor and audience situations him firmly within the world of Greco-Roman elites and their cultural self-positioning. These foci are intended to be illustrative not exhaustive, aimed at thematizing potential areas for further cross-disciplinary engagement and opening avenues for future research.

32

Contemporary Receptions and Future Prospects among Historians of Philosophy

Gretchen Reydams-Schils

Recent events suggest that research on Philo's position in the history of philosophy remains strong: in May 2019 Michael Cover and Lutz Doering organized an international conference on "Philo and Philosophical Discourse," the contributions of which will be published as a collection of essays.[1] To give some more examples, in *Trascendenza e cambiamento in Filone di Alessandria: la chiave del paradosso* (2019) published with Brepols in the series Monothéismes et Philosophie, Francesca Simeoni examines the role of paradoxes in Philo's thinking. And in her monograph *Virtue and Law in Plato and Beyond* (2017), Julia Annas devotes a chapter to Philo of Alexandria.[2] So where do we stand now on the questions of Philo's relation to the ancient philosophical tradition and his place in research on the history of philosophy, and especially on that strand of Platonism commonly referred to as Middle Platonism? Philo remains a very rich and rewarding author, who keeps pushing back against overly narrow conceptions of philosophy on the part of his readers and interpreters.

32.1 Overview of Scholarship

With John Dillon's inclusion of Philo in his groundbreaking overview of Middle Platonism,[3] David Runia's magisterial study of the importance of Plato's *Timaeus* for Philo's worldview,[4] and the issue of the *Studia Philonica Annual* containing contributions by Gregory Sterling and David Runia and responses by David Winston, Thomas Tobin, and John Dillon on the question of whether Philo can be considered a Middle Platonist,[5] Philo became the subject of renewed interest by scholars of the history of

---

[1] M. B. Cover and L. Doering, eds., *Philo of Alexandria and Philosophical Discourse*, Ioudaioi 14 (Göttingen: Vandenhoeck & Ruprecht, 2024).
[2] F. Simeoni, *Trascendenza e cambiamento in Filone di Alessandria: la chiave del paradosso*, Monothéismes et Philosophie 25 (Turnhout: Brepols, 2019); J. Annas, *Virtue and Law in Plato and Beyond* (Oxford: Oxford University Press, 2017).
[3] J. Dillon, *The Middle Platonists (80 B.C. to A.D. 220)* (Ithaca: Cornell University Press, 1977).
[4] D. T. Runia, *Philo of Alexandria and the Timaeus of Plato*, PhA 44 (Leiden: Brill, 1986).
[5] *SPhiloA* 5 (1993).

ancient philosophy.[6] Sterling compares Philo's method of reading scripture to the stances of contemporaneous philosophers who attempted to bridge east and west, namely the Stoic Chaeremon and the Platonists Plutarch and Numenius, in order to argue that for Philo the Jewish tradition and Platonism were two sides of the same coin. Runia revisits his earlier claims, in the light of research published after his study on the role of Plato's *Timaeus* in Philo's writings,[7] to argue for the centrality of Platonizing features while simultaneously stressing the differences between Philo and Middle Platonism and calling Philo a "philosophically oriented exegete" rather than a (Middle Platonist) philosopher.

Yet to date there are also major monographs on Middle Platonism or overviews published that still do not take Philo into account. Thus, when Federico Petrucci constructs his compelling case for Taurus' contribution to the debates about how to interpret Plato's *Timaeus* and its cosmogony, he explicitly leaves aside Philo, except for a brief treatment of his *De aeternitate mundi*, 30–31.[8] George Boys-Stones, however, does include Philo as a source in his overview of Platonist philosophy from 80 BCE to 250 CE,[9] as does the collection of sources *Der Platonismus in der Antike*, started by Heinrich Dörrie and continued by Matthias Baltes, Marie-Luise Lakmann, and Christian Pietsch.[10]

Another pivotal phase in the more recent treatments of Philo in scholarly circles of the history of ancient philosophy is represented by the work of Carlos Lévy and by the year-long seminars on Hellenistic and Roman philosophy which he started, together with Bernard Besnier, in Paris-Créteil in 1992 (as a collaboration between Paris XII-Val de Marne and the École Normale Supérieure de Fontenay-Saint Cloud), which continue to this day. In 1995 Lévy organized a colloquium on Philo and the language of philosophy, which paid tribute to Valentin Nikiprowetzky and led to the publication of a collection of articles by the latter called *Études philoniennes*,[11] but also revalorized Philo's pursuit of philosophy as not exclusively in service of the exegesis of scripture (more on this below, p. 534).[12] Crucial was Lévy's own contribution "Le concept de *doxa* des Stoïciens à Philon d'Alexandrie: essai d'étude diachronique" in 1989 to the Symposium Hellenisticum (published in 1993),[13] a closed and by-invitation-only

---

[6] In this contribution I focus on Philo's reception among scholars working more broadly on the history of ancient philosophy. But a number of Philo scholars such as F. Calabi (see e.g. *God's Acting, Man's Acting: Tradition and Philosophy in Philo of Alexandria* [Leiden: Brill, 2008]), D. Winston (e.g. *Logos and Mystical Theology in Philo of Alexandria* [Cincinnati: Hebrew Union College Press, 1985]), and R. Radice (e.g. *Platonismo e creazionismo in Filone di Alessandria: Metafisica del Platonismo nel suo sviluppo storico e nella filosofia patristica* [Milan: Catholic University of Milan, 1989]) have, of course, also greatly enhanced our understanding of Philo's philosophical positions.

[7] D. T. Runia, "Was Philo a Middle Platonist? A Difficult Question Revisited," *SPhiloA* 5 (1993): 112–40.

[8] F. Petrucci, *Taurus of Beirut: The Other Side of Middle Platonism* (London: Routledge; Taylor & Francis Group, 2018), 139 n. 171.

[9] G. Boys-Stones, *Platonist Philosophy 80 BC to AD 250: An Introduction and Collection of Sources in Translation* (Cambridge: Cambridge University Press, 2018).

[10] H. Dörrie, M. Baltes, M.-L. Lakmann, and C. Pietsch, *Der Platonismus in der Antike. Grundlagen–System–Entwicklung* (Stuttgart: Frommann-Holzboog, 1987–ongoing).

[11] V. Nikiprowetzky, *Études philoniennes* (Paris: Cerf, 1996), selected and edited by J. Riaud.

[12] The contributions of this colloquium were published in 1998 as C. Lévy and B. Besnier, *Philon d'Alexandrie et le langage de la philosophie: actes du colloque international organisé par le Centre d'études sur la philosophie hellénistique et romaine de l'Université de Paris XII-Val de Marne (Créteil, Fontenay, Paris, 26–28 octobre 1995)* (Turnhout: Brepols, 1998). See also the introduction Lévy wrote for F. Calabi et al., eds, *Pouvoir et puissances chez Philon d'Alexandrie* (Turnhout: Brepols, 2015).

[13] C. Lévy, "Le concept de *doxa* des Stoïciens à Philon d'Alexandrie: essai d'étude diachronique," in *Passions and Perceptions: Studies in Hellenistic Philosophy of Mind*, ed. J. Brunschwig and M. Nussbaum (Cambridge: Cambridge University Press, 1993), 250–84.

seminar that has been taking place since 1976 (the first one was in Chantilly, France, on Stoic logic) and has a significant influence on the scholarly agenda in post-Aristotelian philosophy through the publication of its proceedings. This contribution represents two of the main themes in Lévy's research on Philo, one, the kind of "scepticism" Philo invokes, the other, his creative adaptation of Greek philosophical notions and terminology. Inspired by this line of research and under Lévy's mentorship, as well as that of Winston and Sterling, my own research on the emergence of the notion of providence in the Platonist and Stoic receptions of Plato's *Timaeus* included a chapter on Philo of Alexandria (more on this below, p. 538).[14] Henceforth Philo would also figure regularly and prominently on the agenda of the Notre Dame Workshop on Ancient Philosophy, established officially in 2001.

The collection of essays edited and published by Francesca Alesse on Philo's role and position in post-Aristotelian philosophy[15] provides a good indication of how far the interest in Philo in ancient philosophy circles has come (even if the progress needs to be maintained), with contributions by, among others, Graziano Ranocchia on the critique of Epicureanism, the late Robert Sharples on possible influences by Aristotle and the Peripatetic tradition, Mauro Bonazzi on method and Platonism, Anthony A. Long and Margaret Graver on Stoicism, and Roberto Radice and myself on the interaction between Platonism and Stoicism (as well as other strands of ancient thought). Alesse's introduction to the volume gives a good and succinct overview of previous scholarship, and also highlights the work that Runia and Mansfeld have carried out together on the doxographical tradition, and its implications for our interpretations of Philo of Alexandria.[16]

32.2 The Role of Philosophy in Philo's Works

One can study the works of Philo of Alexandria as witnesses to the ancient philosophical traditions, and as such he can provide his readers with fragments of views not otherwise attested. This approach, in turn, can be linked to the question of his sources. Yet while Philo is indeed a valuable witness to the philosophical views circulating in Alexandria and Rome during his lifetime (*c.*15 BCE–*c.*50 CE), in a period for which other sources are relatively scarce, one cannot assess the value of the evidence without addressing first *how* Philo makes use of this material. Philo's own approach is quite distinctive, and this feature implies, too, that we cannot use his work as a mere depository of other, older and contemporaneous, philosophical views. So, this query naturally leads one to the question of the *role* of philosophical views and terminology in Philo's writings.

---

[14] G. Reydams-Schils, *Demiurge and Providence: Stoic and Platonist Readings of Plato's* Timaeus, MON 2 (Turnhout: Brepols, 1999).
[15] F. Alesse, ed., *Philo of Alexandria and Post-Aristotelian Philosophy*, SPhA 5 (Leiden: Brill, 2008).
[16] See now J. Mansfeld and D. T. Runia, *Aetiana V: An Edition of the Reconstructed Text of the Placita with a Commentary and a Collection of Related Texts*, 4 vols (Leiden: Brill, 2020).

The reception of Philo's work in the ancient philosophical tradition has been something of an enigma, and therefore difficult to assess. In his contribution to this volume (Chapter 7), Sterling revisits some of his earlier work to explore parallels between Philo, on the one hand, and Plutarch, Numenius, and Plotinus, on the other. Of these three possibilities, Numenius appears to present the most promising case, also because of his well-attested interest in the Jewish tradition. Sterling focuses on Numenius' association of the "cultivator and planter" with the divine, his use of ὁ ὤν/τὸ ὄν to designate the First God, and his understanding of the stability of this God (also shared by Plotinus).

But an even more foundational issue is the role philosophy played in Philo's own oeuvre. In his *De congressu* (*On the Preliminary Studies*) Philo reflects on his own educational trajectory (74–76) and puts Greek learning in the position of handmaid, as Hagar in relation to Sarah, who stands for true wisdom. Among these different types of learning Philo includes grammar (as the study of language and literature in antiquity), music, geometry, rhetoric, and logic (11, λογικὴ θεωρία), or what he also calls 'dialectical science' (18, διαλεκτικὴ ἐπιστήμη), here presented as the twin sister of rhetoric and as the ability to distinguish true from false arguments.[17] This ability would allow one to refute sophists, but Philo also cautions, in a negative view of the "sceptics" (52, σκεπτικοί), that one can become entangled in this kind of ability and never rise above "petty quibbles and trifling disputes" to the "best things in nature, whether perceived by the senses or the mind." Such an attitude is hardly any better than sophistry.

Philosophy, however, cannot be reduced, according to Philo, to logic or the ability to distinguish between true and false arguments, but also pertains to wisdom and virtue, to which the other types of learning are handmaidens. Thus, a central question for the interpretation of Philo's work is how he sees the relation between the Greek and Roman philosophical tradition, philosophy, and wisdom and virtue. (One needs to keep in mind here that "philosophy" in Philo's writings is not necessarily limited to the Greek and Roman philosophical tradition, but could also contain, for instance, aspects of the Jewish wisdom tradition.) At first glance Philo establishes a clear hierarchy in this case too, which does not map easily onto the Sarah-Hagar binary distinction:

> And indeed just as the school subjects contribute to the acquirement of philosophy, so does philosophy to the getting of wisdom. For philosophy is the practice or study of wisdom, and wisdom is the knowledge of things divine and human and their causes. And therefore just as the culture of the schools is the bond-servant of philosophy, so must philosophy be the servant of wisdom. Now philosophy teaches us the control of the belly and the parts below it, and control also of the tongue. Such powers of control are said to be desirable in themselves, but they will assume a grander and loftier aspect if practiced for the honor and service of God. (*Congr.* 79–80)[18]

---

[17] For an overview of Philo's use of Greek writers and philosophers, see E. Koskenniemi, *Greek Writers and Philosophers in Philo and Josephus: A Study of Their Secular Education and Educational Ideals* (Leiden: Brill, 2019); and D. Lincicum, "A Preliminary Index to Philo's Non-Biblical Citations and Allusions," *SPhiloA* 25 (2013): 139–67.

[18] Unless otherwise indicated I use the translations of Colson and Whitaker.

The image of philosophy as a handmaid to wisdom would allow one to subjugate Philo's interest in philosophy neatly to his exegesis and commitment to the (Greek-)Jewish tradition. And Nikiprowetzky was right in emphasizing the (exegetical) context of Philo's application of philosophical notions.[19] A contextualized reading goes a long way to account for the sometimes bewildering range of views represented in Philo, and their apparently loosely associative structure. But even the passage quoted above already indicates that the relation between philosophy and "wisdom" in Philo's sense is more complex than one of subjugation. First, philosophy is also valuable in its own right and does not fulfill a merely instrumental function; and, second, in *some sense* philosophy is also *constitutive of* wisdom as long as one, according to Philo, realizes the limits of human knowledge, thereby acknowledging the "nothingness" of the human being (*Congr.* 107) in relation to God, and cultivates wisdom for the sake of honoring God. The question of the relation between philosophy and "wisdom" becomes concrete in the figure of Moses, as Philo depicts him, and so one also needs to investigate the importance of philosophy for Moses' attitudes towards God and the world (see e.g. *Opif.* 8).[20]

More importantly, one could make the case that the relation between scripture and philosophy in Philo's works operates in both directions. It is not just scripture that provides the framework for Philo's views; philosophy, Greek and Roman (more on this below, p. 538), also shapes his relation to scripture and the non-Greek aspects of the wisdom tradition, as recently highlighted again by Sharon Weisser[21] in the introduction to her analysis of Philo's treatment of the passions.[22] As Weisser has emphasized, given that Philo considers scripture to be providing unadorned philosophy (φιλοσοφία γυμνή, *Post.* 102), he is reading scripture itself as a *philosophical text*, albeit one that requires the deciphering of its message, beyond its surface meaning. There is no need to posit an a priori contradiction between exegesis and philosophy.

So, while it may not be possible to derive a fully coherent system of philosophical views from Philo's writings, as Harry Wolfson (1947) or Erwin Goodenough (1940) attempted to do (with many insights, however, that are still valuable today),[23] this challenge does not imply that one could not derive any consistent themes from his expositions. Thus Weisser, for instance, reassesses the scarlet threads that run through Philo's treatment of the passions and his views on *apatheia* vs *metriopatheia*.[24] Similarly, I have argued that the different models for the structure of the soul which Philo uses in different contexts center around a simpler model of an opposition between soul and body,

---

[19] V. Nikiprowetzky, *Le commentaire de l'écriture chez Philon d'Alexandrie, son caractère et sa portée; observations philologiques* (Leiden: Brill: 1977).

[20] On this issue, see G. E. Sterling, "Platonizing Moses: Philo and Middle Platonism," *SPhiloA* 5 (1993): 99–103.

[21] S. Weisser, *Éradication ou modération des passions? Histoire de la controverse chez Cicéron, Sénèque et Philon d'Alexandrie* (Turnhout: Brepols, 2022).

[22] On this issue, see also D. Winston, "Response to Runia and Sterling," *SPhiloA* 5 (1993): 141–46.

[23] H. A. Wolfson, *Philo: Foundations of Religious Philosophy in Judaism, Christianity, and Islam*, 4th edn (Cambridge, MA: Harvard University Press, 1976); E. R. Goodenough, *An Introduction to Philo Judæus*, 2nd edn (New Haven: Yale University Press; Oxford: Oxford University Press, 1962 [orig. 1940]).

[24] Weisser, *Éradication ou modération des passions?*

and between rational and irrational aspects of the soul.[25] For this purpose he attempts to create as much common ground as possible between models from different schools of thought, doing so, I submit, for two complementary reasons: on the one hand, because he realizes that as human beings we cannot fully know the specific nature of the soul or the mind (as in *Leg.* 1.91; *Mut.* 10), but on the other, because he does want to overcome the negative, potentially paralyzing aspect of a skeptical approach and avoid getting stuck in "petty quibbles and trifling disputes" (*Congr.* 52).

Philo's method of interpreting scripture beyond the surface meaning of the text (without, however, systematically rejecting the literal meaning), or his allegorical method, as it is commonly called, also raises the question of the exact relation between the "physical" level of readings, by which I mean interpretations derived from natural philosophy, and the "ethical" ones. Again, at first glance, Philo is rather cautious about physical interpretations because he rejects the kind of stance, which in his work is presented primarily by the "Chaldeans," that would see the order of the universe and the heavens as its own final point of reference—a critique aimed at the immanent view of the divine in Stoicism, as well as related beliefs in, for instance, astronomy. The positive side to Philo's skepticism again reveals itself here. It is impossible to derive truth from the physical world through the senses, and thus Philo, like the skeptical Academics before him, questions the possibility of the firm epistemological grasp (κατάληψις) of nature and heaven via the senses in the Stoics. For Philo, this visible order in nature itself refers to a higher agency and cause, that of a transcendent God, who, however, cannot be known by human beings in his essence. The ethical level of interpretation, which focuses on the virtues and piety towards this God, describes the human condition in terms of a struggle between soul and body, between reason and the passions, and between the allurements of the sensible realm and the priority of the intelligible one.

Yet, in this instance too, we need finer distinctions. Generally speaking, Philo actually integrates physical readings into his soul allegory.[26] Physics in this sense is at least conducive to ethics. But there are instances in which the physical reading can even rank higher than the ethical one, as in *Mos.* 2.96, where σύμβολον φυσικώτερον ("a symbol in a more natural sense") stands for the mercy and power of God, while ἠθικώτερον ("in a more ethical sense") stands for the human mind repressing vanity. Philo also distinguishes between different levels within the physical mode of interpretation, and this distinction allows him to criticize those who, because of their naive trust in sense-perception, "do not have much precision in their natural philosophy" (*Leg.* 3.61). People who declare "that nothing exists beyond the world of sight and senses … gave themselves to studies directed against nature or rather against their own soul" (*Somn.* 2.283). In other words, the inability to look beyond the physical realm undermines even natural philosophy itself, and thus Philo can reclaim natural philosophy from the "Chaldeans" and the Stoics. Moreover, people "who are unversed in allegory and the

---

[25] G. Reydams-Schils, "Philo of Alexandria on Stoic and Platonist Psycho-Physiology: The Socratic Higher Ground," *Ancient Philosophy* 22 (2002): 125–47.
[26] Reydams-Schils, *Demiurge and Providence*, 141–45.

nature-truth which loves to conceal its meaning" (*Fug.* 179) give Moses grounds for accusing them of atheism and, among other things, preferring the body over the soul. On the other hand, there are φυσικοὶ ἄνδρες (the natural philosophers, or people pursuing that line of inquiry) whose allegorizing in terms of soul, virtue, and God Philo clearly approves (*Abr.* 99; *Post.* 7).

This evidence indicates a strong connection between the "true" physical readings and the allegory of the soul, that is of the soul in quest of virtue and God. Hence, we do find many passages in which Philo uses φυσικῶς/φυσικώτερον/φυσικώτατον (as referring to the mode of interpretation in the key of natural philosophy) in connection with his soul-allegory and/or God. If we expand the semantic field to include expressions such as τῶν τῆς φύσεως [πραγμάτων]/ἐν τῇ φύσει/περὶ φύσιν (nature, matters pertaining to nature), physics is even more elevated. Moses becomes the ἑρμηνεύς (interpreter) of nature, and Heraclitus is dependent on him (*Her.* 213; cf. also *QG* 4.152). The powerful description of the Therapeutae at the end of the *De vita contemplativa* combines the inquiry into nature with all the themes that matter most to Philo. Engaging in this kind of inquiry is nothing short of the task of wisdom (*Prov.* 1).

32.3 Platonism and Stoicism

The question of the exact relation between the "physical" and the "ethical" readings of scripture leads us naturally to the relation between the Platonist and the Stoic elements in Philo's work. This combination (unlike the integration of certain Peripatetic elements that are easier to reconcile with a Platonist perspective) may come as a surprise given the considerable tensions between these two currents of thought. Hans von Arnim's collection of fragments of the early Stoics includes many passages from Philo,[27] but given the methodological concerns discussed above, such a procedure is no longer tenable: Philo adapts this material to his own purposes. In an older strand of scholarship, combinations of Stoic and seemingly Platonist features were often attributed to Posidonius, even if the latter was not mentioned explicitly as a source, because of his alleged leanings towards Platonism. This position has been challenged too. Philo's Stoic affiliation has been endorsed most strongly by Émile Bréhier.[28] Hans-Friedrich Weiss claims that Philo could just as well be called a Platonizing Stoic;[29] according to Roberto Radice, the Stoic influences outnumber the Platonist ones, but the latter are more fundamental;[30] Mansfeld emphasizes that some texts of Philo are really more Stoic than anything else.[31] The current consensus, however, appears to locate Philo in

---

[27] H. von Arnim and M. Adler, *Stoicorum veterum fragmenta* (Stuttgart: Teubner, 1964; [orig. 1903–24]).
[28] E. Bréhier, *Les idées philosophiques et religieuses de Philon d'Alexandrie*, 2nd edn (Paris: J. Vrin, 1925).
[29] H.-F. Weiss, *Untersuchungen zur Kosmologie des hellenistischen und palästinischen Judentums* (Berlin: Akademie-Verlag, 1966).
[30] Radice, *Platonismo e creazionismo in Filone di Alessandria*.
[31] J. Mansfeld, "Philosophy in the Service of Scripture: Philo's Exegetical Strategies," in *The Question of "Eclecticism": Studies in Later Greek Philosophy*, ed. J. Dillon and A. A. Long (Berkeley: University of California Press, 1988), 70–102.

the context of Middle Platonism, broadly construed—as covering a variety of modes of philosophical discourse from the first century BCE to the end of the second century CE, and it cannot be denied that Plato's *Timaeus* appears to be one of Philo's main frames of reference.

But rather than relying on some kind of method of triage—whereby one would label certain features as Platonist and others as Stoic—and in addition to the work championed by scholars such as Lévy that focuses on how philosophical notions and terminology are repurposed in very specific ways by Philo,[32] it would be fruitful to explore further how the Platonist and Stoic features actually relate to one another. In his introduction to the French translation and edition of Philo's works, Roger Arnaldez already noted that "even in the midst of phrases borrowed from Plato's *Timaeus* we can detect Stoic language."[33] In other words, as I have argued,[34] Stoic elements had grafted themselves onto Plato's *Timaeus* itself by the time Philo came into contact with the text and its reception history, primarily because in the Hellenistic period the early Stoics had co-opted many aspects of the *Timaeus* for their own purpose. (In antiquity to engage with an account meant also to engage with the tradition of its interpretation.)

A major break-through on the question of the relation between Platonism and Stoicism in Philo's works has occurred recently in the monograph of Maren Niehoff, *Philo of Alexandria: An Intellectual Biography*.[35] She asks us to think through the possible impact of Philo's embassy to Rome and his encounter with the kind of Stoicism of the Roman imperial period represented by Seneca. This hypothesis would explain why in the historical and the philosophical works, and especially in the works of the Exposition of the Law Stoicism comes more strongly to the fore, and Philo moves away from the more radical transcendental perspective in the Allegorical Commentary. Her approach is thus reverse of that of Richard Goulet,[36] who has argued that the more immanentist Stoic features came to Philo from previous exegeses, on which he superimposed his more Platonist perspective. Niehoff's thesis also has implications for the dating of Philo's works, and she argues that the philosophical works as a group are to be dated to the phase of Philo's involvement with Rome. The *Questions and Answers* on Genesis and Exodus would constitute a transition in Philo's attempt to reach broader audiences. In addition to the question of the chronology of Philo's work, Niehoff's thesis also allows her to compare Philo's undertaking with other attempts to negotiate the reality of Roman imperial culture and power in early Christianity and the Second Sophistic.

---

[32] See above, §32.1.

[33] R. Arnaldez, *Philon d'Alexandrie*, Vol. 1: *Introduction generale, De opificio mundi*, Oeuvres de Philon d'Alexandrie (Paris: Éditions du Cerf, 1961), 73: "nous pouvons remarquer la langue stoïcienne au milieu même des phrases empruntées au *Timée*." I owe this reference to Maren Niehoff. See also G. Reydams-Schils, "Natural Philosophy and Stoicism in Philo of Alexandria," in *Philo of Alexandria and Philosophical Discourse*.

[34] Reydams-Schils, *Demiurge and Providence*, 135–65. See also C. Lévy, "Cicero and the *Timaeus*," in *Plato's Timaeus as Cultural Icon*, ed. G. Reydams-Schils (Notre Dame: University of Notre Dame Press, 2003), 95–110.

[35] M. R. Niehoff, *Philo of Alexandria, An Intellectual Biography* (New Haven: Yale University Press, 2018).

[36] R. Goulet, *La philosophie de Moïse: essai de reconstitution d'un commentaire philosophique préphilonien du Pentateuque* (Paris: Vrin, 1987).

As I have argued elsewhere,[37] Niehoff's thesis invites further research into what I call the "bridge concepts" between the work from before Philo's embassy to Rome, primarily the Allegorical Commentary, and the later writings. A first bridge could be constituted by Plato's *Timaeus*, the influence of which makes itself felt throughout Philo's writings, especially in light of the thesis that Stoic readings of that work predate Philo (see above, p. 539). In this light, it might also be worthwhile to engage in a comparative study of Seneca's and Philo's reception of the *Timaeus*. And in other contexts in so-called Middle Platonism, too, we can detect a tension between the more transcendental and noetic aspect of Plato's Demiurge, as *nous* and insofar as he turns his attention to intelligible reality, and his more relational aspect, as manifested in his ordering of the world.

Second, we have evidence that Plato's *Laws* may have been important for the Stoics as well, and that work, in an echo of the *Theaetetus*, revisits the theme of "man being the measure of all things" in connection with a critique of self-love (715e–716d and 731d6–732b4) that has many features in common with Philo's rejection of that attitude especially in the Allegorical Commentary.[38]

Third, one could argue that it is precisely the system of God, his Logos, and his powers, fully developed in the Allegorical Commentary (see esp. *Fug.* 94), that also paves the way for the expression of human beings' piety through imitating the Logos and these powers as modes of being active in the world. And while it is true that this way of relating to the divine, rather than the radically transcendent one, gets emphasized in the later Exposition of the Law (as well as in the historical and philosophical works), the kernel of this notion, that one expresses piety also through imitating the beneficial and kingly powers of God, can already be found in the Allegorical Commentary (as in *Leg.* 1.58, *Post.* 181, *Ebr.* 91–92).

Finally, as Niehoff also notes, even in the Allegorical Commentary Philo combines the Platonic motif of "becoming like God" with the Stoic injunction of "living according to nature."[39] This pairing is not a random juxtaposition, but indicates that Philo is prepared to integrate key aspects of the Stoic perspective into his dominant view of the relation between the ordered world, human beings, and God.

32.4 Conclusion

Where do we go from here? Future work on the role of philosophy in Philo's works could address other core notions in his work and examine how he reshapes terminology. The

---

[37] See my review of M. R. Niehoff, *Philo of Alexandria, An Intellectual Biography*, Bryn Mawr Classical Review 2018.05.36.
[38] G. Reydams-Schils, "Philautia, Self-Knowledge, and *oikeiôsis* in Philo of Alexandria and Plutarch," in *Plutarch and the New Testament in Their Religio-Philosophical Contexts. Bridging Discourses in the World of the Early Roman Empire*, ed. R. Hirsch-Luipold (Leiden: Brill, 2022), 125–40.
[39] Niehoff, *Philo of Alexandria*, 158, 238–39; see also W. E. Helleman, "Deification and Assimilation to God," SPhiloA 2 (1990): 51–71; G. Reydams-Schils, "'Unsociable Sociability': Philo on the Active and the Contemplative Life," in *Pouvoir et puissances chez Philon d'Alexandrie*, ed. F. Calabi et al. (Turnhout: Brepols, 2015), 305–18; and Annas, *Virtue and Law in Plato and Beyond*, 206–13.

notion of "bridge concepts" opens new avenues for research as well. We could devote more research to sorting out the role of Philo's "philosophical treatises" as a sub-corpus (including the Armenian dialogues), paying attention, again, also to the *forms* of philosophy in late antiquity.[40] And last but not least, we could make significant progress by comparing Philo's undertaking to similar interactions with Roman culture and the Second Sophistic.

If one wants to avoid the rather awkward (to put it mildly!) historical irony of Philo of Alexandria's position in the history of ancient philosophy mirroring that of the Jewish community in Alexandria,[41] a number of conditions for future research need to be met. First, we need a notion of (the history of) philosophy that is broad enough to recognize and capture Philo's undertaking, and this approach in turn will require an openness to the hermeneutical and historical aspects of ancient philosophy. Such an approach takes modes of discourse and textuality into account and covers the full range of themes, whereas the so-called analytic approach tends to focus on the structures of arguments and to privilege certain aspects of ancient philosophy, such as epistemology and skepticism, or action theory and ethics. In this respect scholars who are working on Philo from the perspective of religious studies (and who continue to make significant contributions to our understanding of Philo's philosophical undertaking too) are currently far ahead. Moreover, Niehoff's recent monograph clearly demonstrates the value of re-integrating philosophy with other modes of discourse prevalent in the cultural circles with which Philo came into contact, just as she did in her prior monograph[42]—on the relation between Jewish exegesis and the modes of interpreting Homer in Alexandria, a tradition that is a crucial component of the philosophical discourse as well.[43]

Second, one should take the self-avowed structures of hierarchy and subordination in Philo's works with a grain of salt. Philosophy is not that easy to subordinate to the interpretation of the Torah in Philo's approach, nor is Stoicism easy to subordinate to Platonism. In order to discern more clearly which views actually emerge from Philo, we first and foremost need to continue to refine our categories for reading and interpreting him. But for now it might be useful to emphasize again that he is indeed indispensable for a full and correct understanding of philosophy in his era, and not just as a witness to different currents of thought. Perhaps we should even keep open the possibility of considering him a philosopher who expressed some, though not all, of his views, through scriptural exegesis.[44]

---

[40] I owe this point to Michael Cover.

[41] Lévy, "Le concept de *doxa* des Stoïciens à Philon d'Alexandrie," 250, as quoted also by Weisser, *Éradication ou modération des passions?*, 272 n. 19: "Les études philoniennes ont toujours eu un statut spécial par rapport aux recherches sur l'histoire de la philosophie ancienne. Le 'philonien' est quelqu'un qui étudie un corpus où tout est exprimé en fonction de concepts philosophiques mais auquel on a dénié, pour des raisons parfois contradictoires la qualité du texte philosophique." See also D. T. Runia, "The Rehabilitation of the Jackdaw: Philo of Alexandria and Ancient Philosophy," in *Greek and Roman Philosophy 100 BC–200 AD*, ed. R. Sorabji and R. W. Sharples (London: Institute of Classical Studies, 2007), 483–500.

[42] M. R. Niehoff, *Jewish Exegesis and Homeric Scholarship in Alexandria* (Cambridge: Cambridge University Press, 2011).

[43] On this point, see also Runia, "The Rehabilitation of the Jackdaw," 489.

[44] Pace Runia, *Philo of Alexandria and the Timaeus of Plato*, 545, who presents Philo as a "philosophically oriented exegete"; in his 1993 (see above p. 533) and 2007 contributions he revisits this issue. I would like to thank Michael Cover, Maren Niehoff, and Sharon Weisser for their comments on earlier drafts of this chapter.

33
Contemporary Receptions and Future Prospects among Scholars of Judaism

Ellen Birnbaum

From the late first century CE to the time of the Italian Renaissance, one finds barely a trace of Philo in any known, extant Jewish source. After a brief report by Josephus about Philo's participation in an embassy to Caligula, it is not until the 1500s that other Jews begin to mention Philo explicitly by name and engage earnestly with his writings.[1] If contemporary scholars of Judaism cannot make up for these almost fifteen centuries of neglect, these scholars are nonetheless ensuring that Philo's rightful place will be secured as a devoted Jew and seminal Jewish thinker and exegete. They are accomplishing this by seeking to understand Philo as a Jew on his own terms, in the context of his Jewish contemporaries, and in relation to Jews of later times.

Decades ago, it was typical for authors to evaluate Philo's standing as a Jew by viewing him in connection with rabbinic Judaism. Indeed, this kind of assessment is very much in line with that of Azariah de' Rossi, now perhaps the most acknowledged Jew to have reintroduced Philo to a Jewish audience hundreds of years earlier.[2] While all of these authors contributed profoundly to our understanding of Philo, however, their approach left room for further probing of his self-perception as a Jew.

Recognition of this opportunity, along with a growing interest in the variety of expressions of Judaism during the Second Temple period, has allowed later students of Philo to pursue a more nuanced comprehension of his Jewish identity and of his place among other Jews of his time. Indeed, some pursuits from the late 1980s on might be seen as a response to the approach of the preceding decades. So that we may fully appreciate the nature of the more recent efforts, let us begin by considering some pivotal studies from the last century.

---

[1] Josephus, *A.J.* 18.259–60. The best-known discussion of Philo's work by a Jew from the Renaissance period is found in Azariah de' Rossi's *The Light of the Eyes*. See J. Weinberg, *Azariah de' Rossi: The Light of the Eyes. Translated from the Hebrew with an Introduction and Annotations*, YJS 31 (New Haven: Yale University Press, 2001). In the present volume, see also the chapters on Josephus, by Katell Berthelot, and on the Jewish rediscovery of Philo in early modern Europe, by Joanna Weinberg. It is possible that Philo's ideas were known during the intervening centuries, but he is almost never mentioned by name. For details, see, in this volume, the chapters on rabbinic Judaism, by Steven Fraade, and on post-rabbinic medieval Judaism, by Elke Morlok and Ze'ev Strauss.

[2] See the previous note.

33.1 Mid-Twentieth Century Debates about Philo's Judaism

While Philo was no stranger to European scholars before the twentieth century, it was only in the 1900s that he began to attract the attention of North American writers, whether Jewish or not. Three of these writers—Erwin Ramsdell Goodenough, Harry Austryn Wolfson, and Samuel Belkin—were particularly influential and helped to shape the agenda in Philonic research for many years.[3] Their studies, though, may be best understood against the backdrop of a work by yet another American scholar, George Foote Moore. In 1927 and 1930, Moore produced a three-volume set entitled *Judaism in the First Centuries of the Christian Era*.[4] Especially in light of the views of many Christians that Judaism was superseded by Christianity, Moore, a Christian scholar himself, offered a deeply learned and sympathetic presentation of Palestinian Tannaitic (or early rabbinic) Judaism, which he preferred to call "normative Judaism." While Moore undoubtedly wished to emphasize the eventual "supremacy of the type of Judaism represented by the Tannaim," the value-laden term "normative Judaism" carried notable consequences for the treatment of earlier, diverse, and divergent forms of Judaism, including that of Philo.[5]

Interested in the origins of Christianity, Goodenough, a student of Moore, turned to the Hellenistic Jewish background, whose most salient representative was Philo. This Alexandrian thinker, Goodenough believed, provided literary evidence for a widespread form of Judaism that was informed and inspired by pagan mysteries and was represented in art found in Palestine and throughout the diaspora. While never questioning Philo's devotion, commitment, and adherence to Jewish tradition, Goodenough was primarily interested in what he called Philo's "religiosity" and he discerned in Philo a mystical Judaism that differed from Judaism in its normative expression.[6]

Wolfson and Belkin, by contrast, regarded Philo to be very much in harmony with "normative" Judaism. Although Wolfson, who had also studied with Moore, used

---

[3] For titles and other bibliographic details of works by these authors, see below, nn. 6–8. A 2018 conference in Lyon, France, on the reception of Philo from the sixteenth to eighteenth centuries (http://ihrim.ens-lyon.fr/IMG/pdf/2018progphilon-web72.pdf) highlights the longstanding place of Philo in European scholarship, as do the chapters in this volume on the Jewish rediscovery of Philo in early modern Europe, by Joanna Weinberg; on Philo in German philosophy, by Dirk Westerkamp; and on Philo and the *Wissenschaft des Judentums*, by Görge Hasselhoff. Although our focus in this chapter will be on scholarship primarily since the late 1980s, several distinguished scholars from an earlier period have occasionally taken similar approaches to those described here. For helpful surveys of this earlier literature, see L. H. Feldman, *Studies in Judaica: Scholarship on Philo and Josephus (1937–1962)* (New York: Yeshiva University, 1963); E. Hilgert, "Philo Judaeus et Alexandrinus: The State of the Problem," in *The School of Moses: Studies in Philo and Hellenistic Religion In Memory of Horst R. Moehring*, ed. J. P. Kenney, BJS 304; SPhiloM 1 (Atlanta: Scholars Press, 1995).

[4] G. F. Moore, *Judaism in the First Centuries of the Christian Era*, 3 vols (Cambridge, MA: Harvard University Press, 1927–30; repr. 3 vols in 2 (New York: Schocken Books, 1971). (The citation in the next note is from the original edition.)

[5] Moore, *Judaism*, 3:vi.

[6] E. R. Goodenough, *An Introduction to Philo Judaeus*, Brown Classics in Judaica, 2nd edn (Oxford: Blackwell, 1962; repr., Lanham, MD: University Press of America, 1986), 13 (the 1st edn was published in 1940 by Yale University Press); E. R. Goodenough, *By Light, Light: The Mystic Gospel of Hellenistic Judaism* (New Haven: Yale University Press, 1935; repr., Amsterdam: Philo Press, 1969); E. R. Goodenough, *Jewish Symbols in the Greco-Roman Period*, 13 vols (New York: Pantheon Books, 1953–68).

different terminology, he nonetheless declared that "Alexandrian Judaism at the time of Philo was of the same stock as Pharisaic Judaism, which flourished in Palestine at that time."[7] Wolfson associated Palestinian Pharisaic Judaism with rabbinic literature and also spoke of "native Jewish tradition" (e.g. 1:181; 2:195), "native Judaism" (e.g. 2:128, 415), or simply "Jewish tradition" (e.g. 1:185; 2:410). His primary task, however, was not to establish similarities between Philo and this tradition but instead to bring relevant parallels to bear in the different enterprise of examining Philo "as a critic of Greek philosophy" (1:93). Indeed, Wolfson's chief aim was to illuminate Philo's system of ideas—especially "in relation to his Greek and scriptural sources" (1:93)— a system that Wolfson claimed prevailed throughout the Middle Ages. In stark contrast to Goodenough's mystic, Wolfson's Philo was a Jewish philosopher who, standing firmly in accord with "native Judaism" and being thoroughly familiar with Platonic, Aristotelian, Stoic, and other Greek currents of thought, forged an innovative method of reconciling the truths of reason and revelation.

Yet another approach to the relationship between Philo and native, or normative, Judaism was taken by Samuel Belkin. Rather than focusing on Philo's religiosity or system of thought, however, Belkin undertook to study Philo as a "master of Jewish law," or *halakha*. In his volume *Philo and the Oral Law: The Philonic Interpretation of Biblical Law in Relation to the Palestinian Halakah*, Belkin examined several categories of law, which Philo discusses in his four books of *De specialibus legibus*, and concluded that "Philo's Halakah is based upon the Palestinian Oral Law as it was known in Alexandria."[8]

This trio of American authors, then, offered three different portraits of Philo—as mystic, philosopher, and halakhic Jew—and of his standing in connection with rabbinic tradition. Before leaving this trio, let us consider one more noteworthy scholar, Samuel Sandmel. In a 1949 Yale University dissertation devoted to presentations of Abraham in Jewish literature, Sandmel, a student of Goodenough, brought into sharp focus the notion of two different kinds of Judaism; his dissertation was tellingly entitled *Abraham in Normative and Hellenistic Jewish Tradition*.[9] Sandmel later revised this study to discuss more comprehensively Philo's portrayal of Abraham and entitled the work *Philo's Place in Judaism: A Study of Conceptions of Abraham in Jewish Literature*.[10]

Although Sandmel also surveyed depictions of the patriarch in biblical, apocryphal, pseudepigraphical, Greco-Jewish, and rabbinic literature, at the book's end he concentrated only on Philo and the rabbis. Sandmel concluded that Philo either did not know

---

[7] H. A. Wolfson, *Philo: Foundations of Religious Philosophy in Judaism, Christianity, and Islam*, 2 vols (Cambridge, MA: Harvard University Press, 1947; repr., 1982), 1:56. Parenthetical references in this discussion of Wolfson are to volumes and pages in this edition.

[8] S. Belkin, *Philo and the Oral Law: The Philonic Interpretation of Biblical Law in Relation to the Palestinian Halakah*, HSS 11 (Cambridge, MA: Harvard University Press, 1940; repr., New York: Johnson Reprint Corp, 1968), vii, x.

[9] S. Sandmel, "Abraham in Normative and Hellenistic Jewish Tradition," PhD diss., Yale University, 1949.

[10] S. Sandmel, *Philo's Place in Judaism: A Study of Conceptions of Abraham in Jewish Literature*, augmented edn (New York: Ktav, 1971), xxix. This work was originally published in two installments in *HUCA* 25 (1954): 209–37 and 26 (1955): 151–332.

or else rejected rabbinic exegesis; that his Judaism differed from that of the rabbis as "philosophical mysticism based on the Bible differs from halakic legalism"; that Philo's Judaism was thoroughly hellenized; and that "Philo and his associates reflect a marginal, aberrative version of Judaism which existed at the time when there were many versions of Judaism...."[11] Sandmel, then, left us with a distinct portrait of normative, or rabbinic, Judaism, on one hand, and, on the other, Hellenistic Judaism, whose foremost proponent was Philo.

33.2 Philo Judaeus on His Own Terms

In 1995, Earle Hilgert published a bibliographic essay entitled "Philo Judaeus et Alexandrinus: The State of the Problem," in which he reviewed various attempts, similar to those described above, to situate Philo in relation to Judaism, on one hand, and Hellenism, on the other. Toward the end of his essay, Hilgert called attention to the need to understand "Philo's personal *Sitz im Leben* in Roman Alexandria as significant for understanding his cultural and religious orientation."[12] In the last sentence, he applauded "an important contribution" in this area by Alan Mendelson.[13]

Mendelson's monograph *Philo's Jewish Identity* is indeed a splendid point of departure from which to explore more recent and contemporary approaches to Philo as a Jew. A full-length study devoted entirely to Philo, its focus is on Philo for his own sake and in his own Alexandrian context rather than in comparison with other either Jewish or non-Jewish sources. This focus necessarily gives rise to new questions that pertain to Philo's self-understanding and his understanding of others—both Jews and non-Jews. Since the publication of Mendelson's book in 1988, several other studies have appeared whose concern has been to illuminate aspects of Philo's Jewish identity. Such aspects have included descriptions of the beliefs and practices that constitute Philo's Judaism; examination of the balance or tension in his thought between his particular, Jewish loyalties and his universal, cosmopolitan impulses; comparisons with other kinds of Judaism that shed light on Philo's own way of being a Jew; consideration of factors—such as the purpose of and intended audiences for specific works—that may shape Philo's presentation of Jews and Judaism; investigation of Philo's attitudes toward Jews and non-Jews; and attention to social circumstances that may affect Philo's identity or be reflected in his discussions of Jews and Judaism. Because of limited space we will restrict our discussion primarily to seven book-length studies that address one or more of these aspects of Philo's Jewish identity, even as we recognize that other books

---

[11] Sandmel, *Philo's Place in Judaism*, 211.
[12] Hilgert, "Philo Judaeus et Alexandrinus," 13–14.
[13] Hilgert, "Philo Judaeus et Alexandrinus," 15. The book by Mendelson is *Philo's Jewish Identity*, BJS 161 (Atlanta: Scholars Press, 1988). In n. 67 on p. 14, Hilgert also cites an article in which the author similarly pays attention to Philo's Alexandrian setting, namely, P. Borgen, "Philo of Alexandria. A Critical and Synthetical Survey of Research since World War II," in *Religion (Hellenistisches Judentum in römischer Zeit: Philon und Josephus)*, ANRW II.21.1 (Berlin: de Gruyter, 1984), 98–154. We will discuss a 1997 monograph by Borgen below.

and articles may also be relevant.[14] As it happens, most of these studies are in English, although they were produced by scholars not only from the Anglophone countries of North America but also from Israel, Germany, France, and Norway.

Mendelson himself begins by asking what, according to Philo, would be the minimal requirements for one to be considered a Jew and also what qualities an ideal Jew would possess. The latter kind of Jew, who would belong to Philo's elite circle, would share his conviction that allegorical interpretation best uncovers the truth of scripture. Defining the minimal requirements for one to be considered a Jew, however, is rather more complicated. In chapters entitled "Orthodoxy" and "Orthopraxy" respectively, Mendelson delineates the specific beliefs and practices that Philo would regard as essential. As for beliefs, "the alpha and the omega of orthodoxy was a belief in monotheism."[15] Mendelson also discusses five fundamental tenets about God that Philo presents in *Opif*. 170–72. Turning to practices, Mendelson then highlights Philo's treatment of circumcision; the Sabbath; festivals, sacrifice, and the Day of Atonement; dietary laws; and the prohibition against intermarriage.

Another dimension of Philo's Jewish identity is his self-perception and response to the way outsiders viewed Jews and Judaism. In a chapter called "Philo's Apologetic," Mendelson shows how Philo replies—usually implicitly—to such charges as that the Sabbath inculcates laziness; that circumcision signals a lustful, immoderate nature; and that Mosaic laws, including dietary restrictions, reflect a misanthropic stance toward outsiders. In a final chapter, Mendelson considers Philo's mostly contemptuous attitude toward Egyptians and his more positive attitude toward Greeks, whom he nonetheless recognized to be politically opposed to the Jews. In conclusion, Mendelson asserts that Philo was convinced of the "spiritual supremacy of the Jews" and observes that while this "sense of spiritual superiority may have helped to preserve the Alexandrian Jews' religious identity ... as in other times and places, the Jews of Alexandria paid a heavy price for this sense of themselves."[16]

As a graduate student influenced and deeply impressed by all the scholars mentioned above, I too wished to gain a better grasp of what it meant to Philo to be a Jew. Noting that he regards the goal of seeing God to be the height of happiness, I wondered what role he thought being a Jew plays in helping one to achieve this goal. In my 1992 dissertation, published as a book in 1996, I focused on two relationships to the divine—the goal or quest to see God and the covenant described in the Bible between God and Israel.[17] Because Philo understands "Israel" to mean "the one who sees God," I examined how he uses the terms "Israel" and "Jews" to learn whether or not he always

---

[14] For references to some of these other books and articles, see E. Birnbaum, "Two Millennia Later: General Resources and Particular Perspectives on Philo the Jew," *CurBR* 4 (2006): 241–76, in which I discuss some of the same material as here but with a focus on the various approaches just described.

[15] Mendelson, *Philo's Jewish Identity*, 49.

[16] Mendelson, *Philo's Jewish Identity*, 128, 138. This last quotation appears to refer indirectly to the anti-Jewish sentiments and acts of violence described by Philo in *Flacc*. and *Legat*. The implication seems to be that the Jewish attitudes identified by Mendelson led to these reactions.

[17] E. Birnbaum, *The Place of Judaism in Philo's Thought: Israel, Jews, and Proselytes*, BJS 290; SPhiloM 2 (Atlanta: Scholars Press, 1996).

equates the two groups and what the implications of this usage are for who he believes can see God.

As my research progressed, I noticed a pattern in Philo's different works: he frequently speaks of the Jews in his exegetical series known as the Exposition of the Law but never (or almost never) in the other two series, the Allegorical Commentary and *Questions and Answers on Genesis and Exodus*. Conversely, he liberally mentions "Israel" in the Allegorical Commentary and occasionally in QGE but does so only twice in the Exposition. This observation led me to reflect on Philo's possible aims and audiences for his different sets of works and to organize my research according to these different works.

I concluded that Philo speaks of Israel and the Jews rather separately. For him, the Jews are the empirical, historical nation that believes in and worships God, while Israel constitutes a collectivity that has the ability to see God. Philo does not directly address whether he equates Israel and the Jews precisely or whether non-Jews can see God and should thus be counted as part of Israel. According to him, non-Jews can, however, become proselytes and join the Jewish nation. As for the covenant relationship between God and biblical Israel, Philo redefines this so that one may understand that the relationship can apply to any virtuous person or soul. Moreover, believing that the Exposition—in which Philo speaks often about the Jews—is directed toward a mixed audience of Jews and non-Jews, I argued that Philo there wishes to present his people as much as possible as an open and welcoming group.

Despite our different perspectives, like Mendelson, I too focused primarily on Philo himself instead of placing him in relation to other sources. In so doing, I very consciously shifted my approach from that of Sandmel's book *Philo's Place in Judaism* and titled my own study *The Place of Judaism in Philo's Thought*. In this work, I sought to understand why being Jewish was important to Philo and how he balanced his loyalty to the particular Jewish nation and its tradition, on one hand, and his ideal cosmopolitan vision of a virtuous, spiritual community, on the other.

Another monograph dedicated to Philo's Jewish dimensions is Naomi Cohen's *Philo Judaeus: His Universe of Discourse*. Sympathetic to Belkin's approach to Philo, Cohen sets out "to show how thoroughly Jewish (in the traditional sense) this highly sophisticated, and highly cultured man was."[18] Although her work has much in common with earlier attempts to understand Philo in relation to rabbinic sources, one may categorize her efforts as part of the more recent approach in that her primary aim is to illuminate Philo's own Jewishness and to understand him on his own terms rather than to place him on the normative-Hellenistic continuum.

To structure her study, Cohen focuses on *Spec.* 4.132–50, a passage whose topics, she argues, provide key indicators of Philo's Judaism. Chapters are devoted to Philo's understanding of the Decalogue as a framework for Mosaic laws; Judaism as a philosophy; the Greek virtues and the Mosaic laws; the notion of δικαιοσύνη as observance of the commandments; "Philo's Shema," including such subjects as priestly vestments,

---

[18] N. G. Cohen, *Philo Judaeus: His Universe of Discourse*, BEATAJ 24 (Frankfurt am Main: Peter Lang, 1995), xv.

phylacteries, Torah study, the mezuzah, and absence of reference to the paragraph on ritual fringes; examples of Philo's "Judeo-Greek vocabulary"—i.e. words or phrases that carry specifically Jewish connotations in addition to their commonly accepted meanings; and Philo's understanding of such biblical injunctions as not to add or subtract from the law (Deut 4:2; 13:1) and not to remove a neighbor's landmarks (Deut 19:14; cf. Prov 22:28).

In concluding, Cohen asserts that Philo's references to "*agraphos nomos* [unwritten law] and its synonyms ... , on the one hand, and the rabbinic 'Oral Law' on the other, indicate the same body of tradition, which was already clearly identifiable in Philo's day, and it was this body of tradition which was in the course of time sifted and codified by the Sages."[19] While not all scholars would agree with Cohen's assessment of this and other issues, her observations accord with a more generally accepted argument that runs throughout her volume that a shared treasury of oral traditions—both legal and non-legal—existed in Philo's day and that he himself drew upon these traditions. Cohen thus situates Philo squarely within prevailing Jewish currents of his own time and later.[20]

In 2001, Maren Niehoff published one of the first books of the new millennium on Philo as a Jew; it was entitled *Philo on Jewish Identity and Jewish Culture*. An important aspect of the book pertains to Philo's views of others: Egyptians, Greeks, and Romans. Niehoff contends that these views as well as his approach to the importance of the mother in determining Jewish descent, the status of Jerusalem as "mother city," and Jewish values of religion and self-restraint were largely shaped by what she calls "contemporary Roman discourse." Believing that, for the most part, Philo addresses his works toward wealthy, well-educated Jews like himself, Niehoff argues that one of his goals is to foster the identification of these elite Jews with the Roman ruling class.[21] Thus, Philo's understanding of the mother's role in the ascertainment of Jewish descent aligns with Roman law. His disdain for Egyptians as the "ultimate Other" and his ambivalence toward Greeks, which combines admiration for and a sense of superiority to them, likewise reflects Roman attitudes. The notion of Roman influence fades somewhat into the background in the latter part of the book, where Niehoff explores such topics as the raising of children as Jews, the role of scripture in Jewish culture, Philo's use of parables to convey Jewish culture, and his inscription of Jewish culture into nature. As in other studies that we have discussed so far, Niehoff's primary focus on Philo leads her to consider for their own sake Philo's attitudes toward other groups

---

[19] Cohen, *Philo Judaeus*, 284.

[20] For other views of Philo's understanding of "unwritten law," see J. Martens, *One God, One Law: Philo of Alexandria on the Mosaic and Greco-Roman Law*, SPhAMA 2 (Leiden: Brill, 2003), esp. 175–85; H. Najman, *Seconding Sinai: The Development of Mosaic Discourse in Second Temple Judaism*, JSJSup 77 (Leiden: Brill, 2003), esp. 126–37. For a different approach to the notion of shared exegetical traditions, see J. L. Kugel, *Traditions of the Bible: A Guide to the Bible As It Was at the Start of the Common Era* (Cambridge, MA: Harvard University Press, 1998).

[21] M. R. Niehoff, *Philo on Jewish Identity and Culture*, TSAJ 86 (Tübingen: Mohr Siebeck, 2001), e.g. 9, 13. The author has since changed her mind and now believes that Philo wrote different works for different audiences, some of which included non-Jews; see M. R. Niehoff, *Philo of Alexandria: An Intellectual Biography*, AYBRL (New Haven: Yale University Press, 2018).

and toward issues related to Jewish life. She emphasizes Roman influence not to characterize Philo as separate from Jewish tradition, but rather to illustrate the very nature of his Jewish identity.

Just as Niehoff carries forward Mendelson's earlier examination of Philo's attitudes toward other groups, so too does Jutta Leonhardt pursue in more depth many aspects of Philo's worship, some of which Mendelson also discusses. In *Jewish Worship in Philo of Alexandria*, which, like Niehoff's book, also appeared in 2001, Leonhardt investigates Philo's description of the ten festivals that he presents in *Spec.* 2 as well as two other festivals contemporary to him: the celebration of the Greek translation of the Bible and the banquet of the Therapeutae. She also sets forth Philo's treatment of the Sabbath and Sabbath assemblies. Other chapters are dedicated to prayer and praise; psalms, hymns, and praise; thanksgiving; and temple tax, sacrifices, and purifications.[22]

Leonhardt adds much to our knowledge of these aspects of Philo's worship. She concludes that Philo finds in the particular Jewish rites a universal significance, which "opens them up to every human being who understands and accepts their meaning."[23] As for Philo's relationship with other contemporary Jewish traditions, Leonhardt regards him as "more frustrating than helpful";[24] because his descriptions are based on biblical customs, we cannot infer with certainty about practices from his own day. Moreover, according to her, Philo rarely distinguishes between Judaism in the homeland and in the diaspora. Despite our inability to pinpoint certain details, however, Philo does appear to be familiar with "a wide variety of groups and regional differences"[25] and seems to share with other Jews an approach that integrates Jewish and Greek cultures. Indeed, she suggests that Philo's presentation has commonalities with Plato's *Laws* and that Philo appears to have seen Jewish worship as a concrete expression of Plato's ideal state.

Similar features and others related to Philo's Jewish identity are also addressed in two additional monographs that highlight Philo's situation as a first-century CE diaspora Jew. An interesting contrast to Leonhardt's discussion, for example, is found in *Philon d'Alexandrie: un penseur en diaspora* by Mireille Hadas-Lebel.[26] Whereas Leonhardt observes that Philo hardly ever makes a distinction between Judaism in the homeland and in the diaspora, Hadas-Lebel takes every opportunity to emphasize the role of the diaspora in Philo's understanding of his Jewish heritage. Thus, she begins her book with a lively description of Alexandria and then turns to the realities of "being Jewish in Alexandria in Philo's day" and the fraught political situation in that city. By the time she addresses "Judaism according to Philo: Practice and Ethics," Hadas-Lebel can declare that "[t]he point of view maintained by a diaspora Jew ... reflects, implicitly or explicitly, an echo of the incomprehension, if not hostility, that Jewish practices

---

[22] J. Leonhardt, *Jewish Worship in Philo of Alexandria*, TSAJ 84 (Tübingen: Mohr Siebeck, 2001).
[23] Leonhardt, *Jewish Worship in Philo of Alexandria*, 277.
[24] Leonhardt, *Jewish Worship in Philo of Alexandria*, 278.
[25] Leonhardt, *Jewish Worship in Philo of Alexandria*, 280.
[26] M. Hadas-Lebel, *Philon d'Alexandrie: un penseur en diaspora* (Paris: Fayard, 2003).

might have provoked within a pagan environment."²⁷ According to her, then, Philo discusses three primary indicators of Jewish identity—circumcision, dietary laws, and the Sabbath—with an acute awareness of how they were perceived by the surrounding culture, namely, as strange, unfriendly, and/or lazy. Hadas-Lebel also addresses the peculiarity of Jews' celebrating the Exodus from Egypt while they were living in Egypt and notes that with this and other festivals Philo stresses the universal significance over the national, as reflected in his omission of reference to the covenant.

Peder Borgen is another author who has long shown great sensitivity to Philo's situation in the diaspora. In his book *Philo of Alexandria: An Exegete for His Time*, Borgen provides background on Philo's family and the city of Alexandria.²⁸ While much of the book is devoted to the forms and other characteristics of Philo's exegetical works, in the latter half Borgen turns to several topics relevant to Philo's Jewish identity, with special attention to social and political factors. Thus, Borgen believes that Philo proclaims the meaning of the Mosaic laws for the Greek-speaking world and in doing so emphasizes several levels, including the particular, the universal, and "the beyond," the last of which pertains to the divine realm. Borgen also argues that Philo's exegetical and historical works should be read in light of each other, as one can detect hints of social and political realities in some of Philo's interpretations (e.g. in his apologetic presentations of circumcision and dietary restrictions) and reflections of exegetical ideas in some of his historical accounts (e.g. in *Legat.* 3–7, in his portrayal of the Jews as having been taken as God's portion; as being able to see God, in accordance with the meaning of the name "Israel"; and as benefitting from God's providence).²⁹

Despite tensions between Alexandrian Jews and their non-Jewish neighbors, Borgen claims that Philo projects an open and welcoming attitude toward non-Jews in his description of the celebration on Pharos of the translation of the Hebrew Bible into Greek and also in his discussion of proselytes. Philo's treatment of the theme of *philanthrōpia* (love of humanity) also reflects in part a motivation to defend his people against accusations of misanthropy and a wish to blend Jewish and Greek ideas. Finally, Borgen presents some ideas about Philo's eschatological vision, which signals "the realization of the universal aspect of Moses's kingship and the universal role of the Hebrew nation and its laws."³⁰ Central to Borgen's understanding of Philo as a Jew, then, is the awareness of the Jews' situation among their non-Jewish neighbors and a related awareness of Philo's interpretations of particular biblical narratives and laws in universal terms that might appeal to a Greek-reading audience.

Besides these books on Philo's Jewish identity and position as a diaspora Jew, the new millennium has seen the publication of several introductions, guides, or handbooks to Philo. Two single-authored introductions have brief chapters related to

---

[27] M. Hadas-Lebel, *Philo of Alexandria: A Thinker in the Jewish Diaspora*, SPhA 7, trans. Robyn Fréchet (Leiden: Brill, 2012), 91. Originally published in French in 2003 (see the previous note), the book was translated into Hebrew (2006) and later into English. The quotation here is from the latter translation.
[28] P. Borgen, *Philo of Alexandria, An Exegete for His Time*, NovTSup 86 (Leiden: Brill, 1997).
[29] Borgen, *Philo of Alexandria*, esp. 140–93.
[30] Borgen, *Philo of Alexandria*, 271.

Philo as a Jew, while two other, multi-authored guides contain fuller chapters related to Philo as a Jew within his own context and then in relation to other kinds of Judaism.[31] In *Reading Philo: A Handbook to Philo of Alexandria*, edited by Torrey Seland, I myself contributed a chapter on "Philo's Relevance for the Study of Jews and Judaism in Antiquity." I framed the chapter with a much-debated question in the study of antiquity about whether we can speak of a "common Judaism," with a core set of features, or only of multiple "Judaisms," represented by different groups of Jews with their own distinctive views and ways of life. To show how Philo may shed light on the issue, I reviewed evidence from his writings that pertain to seven areas: Jewish practices, beliefs and ideas, community institutions, the Bible and biblical interpretation, Jews and Jewish identity, Jews' interactions with and attitudes toward non-Jews and their culture, and historical events that pertain to Jews. I concluded that "Philo occasionally shows strong commonalities with what we know about other Jews, but he also displays important differences and distinctive features. Rather than attempting to characterize Philo generally as representative or not representative of Jews and Judaism in antiquity, it is best to consider individual issues in all their complexity."[32]

Just as Mendelson's book presented a felicitous starting-place for our consideration of receptions of Philo by contemporary scholars of Judaism, I offer the article just mentioned as a point of transition to studies of Philo among Jews of his time. The shift that Mendelson made from assessing where Philo might stand on a continuum between "normative" and "Hellenistic" Judaism to considering him on his own terms heralded the possibility of reaching a new and more profound understanding of this complex Alexandrian Jew. On the basis of the works surveyed above, while scholars do not agree on every detail, a picture emerges of Philo as practitioner of a Judaism that had much in common with other expressions of Judaism but that was also well suited for an educated, cosmopolitan diaspora Jew like himself.

In the earlier endeavor to assess Philo as a Jew primarily in comparison with rabbinic Judaism, he was often viewed as somewhat of an outlier. By contrast, the question of what he can teach us about Jews and Judaism in antiquity is based on the assumption that he is instead an important representative of a legitimate kind of Judaism that itself can illuminate other contemporary ways of being Jewish. In the studies to which we now turn, Philo is fully appreciated both on his own terms and as an integral part of the era between the Bible and the Mishnah during which Judaism was characterized by great variety and creativity.

---

[31] K. Schenck, *A Brief Guide to Philo* (Louisville: Westminster John Knox Press, 2005), esp. 29–48; O. Kaiser, *Philo von Alexandrien: Denkender Glaube—Eine Einführung*, FRLANT 259 (Göttingen: Vandenhoeck & Ruprecht, 2015), esp. 142–48; C. Termini, "Philo's Thought within the Context of Middle Judaism," and D. Winston, "Philo and Rabbinic Literature," in *The Cambridge Companion to Philo*, ed. A. Kamesar (Cambridge: Cambridge University Press, 2009), 95–123 and 231–53, respectively; K.-G. Sandelin, "Philo as a Jew," and E. Birnbaum, "Philo's Relevance for the Study of Jews and Judaism in Antiquity," in *Reading Philo: A Handbook to Philo of Alexandria*, ed. T. Seland (Grand Rapids: Eerdmans, 2014), 19–46 and 200–225, respectively.

[32] Birnbaum, "Philo's Relevance for the Study of Jews and Judaism in Antiquity," 225.

33.3 Philo and His Jewish Contemporaries

In recent decades the burgeoning interest in Philo in particular should be seen as part of a larger interest in Second Temple Judaism in general, both in the homeland and the diaspora. The mid-twentieth-century discovery of the Dead Sea Scrolls contributed in no small part to this growing interest. Scholars who formerly viewed what was called "Intertestamental Judaism" as valuable background to the New Testament also began to recognize that the varieties of Judaism that flourished during the Second Temple period are fascinating in themselves and constitute an important, but largely overlooked, chapter in Jewish history.[33] Below we will consider four examples of scholarship that illustrate how Philo has been and can be integrated into a larger picture of Judaism in antiquity and also how Philonic evidence has contributed and can contribute to our understanding of this larger picture.

33.3.1 *Outside the Bible*

Especially significant is the massive three-volume work *Outside the Bible: Ancient Jewish Writings Related to Scripture*, edited by Louis Feldman, James Kugel, and Lawrence Schiffman. This is an extensive collection of Jewish writings that were produced "between the end of the Babylonian exile (538 BCE) and the transmission of the Mishnah (200 CE) ... in a variety of languages in the places where Jews lived during that period—in Judea, Egypt, Asia Minor, Syria, and elsewhere."[34] Encompassing selections from the Greek translation of the Hebrew Bible as well as from the apocrypha, pseudepigrapha, Philo, Josephus, and the Dead Sea Scrolls, the volumes present English translations along with introductions and detailed commentaries.

Acknowledging that with the rise of rabbinic Judaism, these works were "taken off the official Jewish bookshelf" and preserved primarily by Christians, the editors declare that "*Outside the Bible* puts these ancient books back into their original Jewish context" (1:xv). Contributors, both Jews and Christians, "have intentionally sought to trace heretofore neglected connections to other Jewish writings from the Hebrew Bible itself to the vast body of Rabbinic writings ..." (1:xv–xvi). To highlight the connection of these texts to the Hebrew Bible, the editors organized them according to style and theme. Philonic writings are presented in sections on his biblical interpretations and his philosophical treatises. Rather than facing the rabbis on his own—as in other, especially earlier, studies—here Philo takes his place among other similarly neglected but

---

[33] For other factors contributing to interest in this period, see e.g. J. M. G. Barclay, *Jews in the Mediterranean Diaspora from Alexander to Trajan (323 BCE–117 CE)*, HCS 33 (Berkeley: University of California Press, 1996), 4–9.

[34] L. H. Feldman, J. L. Kugel, and L. H. Schiffman, eds, *Outside the Bible: Ancient Jewish Writings Related to Scripture*, 3 vols (Philadelphia: The Jewish Publication Society; Lincoln: University of Nebraska Press, 2013), 1:xv. Here and in the rest of the chapter, after initial references to a work, parentheses will contain page numbers from the work under discussion.

very important sources. In setting forth this literature, the editors express their hope that "*Outside the Bible* will offer *all* readers an entirely new perspective on a fascinating body of material deriving from one of Judaism's most significant and fruitful periods of creativity" (1:xvi, their emphasis).

33.3.2 *Jews in the Mediterranean Diaspora*

In *Jews in the Mediterranean Diaspora from Alexander to Trajan (323 BCE–117 CE)*, John Barclay takes a different approach to some of the same material. Barclay divides his presentation into three parts: (1) the diaspora in Egypt; (2) the diaspora in other Mediterranean sites, including Cyrenaica, Syria, Asia, and Rome; and (3) a synthetic analysis of Jewish identity in the Mediterranean diaspora. Wishing to offer "a *comprehensive* and *multi-faceted* survey" (his emphasis), Barclay blends analyses of history, literature, and social attitudes for all regions.[35] Philonic evidence amply informs his discussions. The treatises *Flacc.* and *Legat.*, for example, are important sources for Barclay's historical interpretations, especially of the violence in Alexandria against the Jews in 38 CE, but these works inform his treatment of other parts of the diaspora as well. As for literary sources from Egypt, Barclay discusses Philo along with Artapanus, Ezekiel the Tragedian, the Letter of Aristeas, Aristobulus, the Wisdom of Solomon, 3 Maccabees, Joseph and Aseneth, and the Egyptian Sibylline Oracles.

In connection with social attitudes, sensitive to earlier debates regarding normative and divergent or non-normative Judaism, Barclay introduces a different approach that takes into account degrees of social integration (what he calls "assimilation") and of immersion in such cultural elements as language, values, and intellectual traditions ("acculturation"). He also recognizes that Jews who were thoroughly familiar with Greek culture "could use their training either to defend or attack Judaism, either to justify or to undermine its peculiar customs" (96). Accordingly, he proposes a third category, "accommodation," "to measure *how*, not *how much*, Jews used their acculturation" (97, his emphasis): At one extreme, Jews could submerge Jewish uniqueness in the larger culture; at the other extreme, they might express antagonism to the larger culture (96–98). The middle ground, where Barclay places Philo, involves a reinterpretation of Judaism with some preservation of its uniqueness. Because Philo was considerably involved with non-Jews yet retained his distinctive Jewish identity, Barclay characterizes his level of assimilation as medium—i.e. in the middle between the two extremes.

Instead of a supposed tension between "Jew" and "Greek," Barclay detects in Philo a different conflict—between philosophical contemplation and social activism. Ultimately, however, Philo was drawn to the latter because of his commitment to the Jewish community. Similarly, his universalistic tendencies served to bolster the particular teachings of Moses. Indeed, Barclay contends that Philo's loyalty to the Jewish community and its Mosaic tradition was so strong that it kept him "from spinning into

---

[35] Barclay, *Jews in the Mediterranean Diaspora*, 9.

philosophical abstraction and coupled his universalist vision to the practical and social interests of Alexandrian Jews" (163).

Finally, evidence from Philo also contributes to a synthetic sketch of Jewish identity in the Mediterranean diaspora. Here Barclay discusses such social, symbolic, and practical features as the ethnic bond; the local community; links with Jerusalem, the homeland, and other diaspora communities; the Law/Jewish scriptures and the figure of Moses; rejection of alien, pluralist, and iconic cults; separatism at meals; male circumcision; and Sabbath observance. Although Barclay draws copiously from Philo—and, for that matter, Josephus—to construct a wide-ranging portrait of the entire Mediterranean diaspora, he does not allow either author to dominate this portrait. Integrated among his contemporaries, Philo emerges as one of several Jewish writers—albeit a very important one—in the Egyptian diaspora.

33.3.3 Specific Topics: *Judaism and the Gentiles*

While the works mentioned above take a broad perspective on the Second Temple era—through presenting either a wide collection of literature or an extensive historical, literary, and social portrait—below we will consider two more books that focus on this period from the narrower perspective of individual topics. A fine example is Terence L. Donaldson's *Judaism and the Gentiles: Jewish Patterns of Universalism (to 135 CE)*.[36] With his interest in studying Jewish attitudes toward non-Jews from the beginning of the Hellenistic era through the Bar Kokhba revolt, Donaldson examines evidence from an impressive range of sources: scripture, Septuagint, and apocrypha; pseudepigrapha; Qumran; Philo; Josephus; Greco-Roman literature; early Christian literature; and inscriptions.

Acknowledging that universalism is generally associated with Christianity and particularism with Judaism, Donaldson aims to expand our understanding of universalism and to show that "[d]uring this period Judaism was in its own ways just as 'universalistic' as was Christianity—indeed, in some ways even more so" (1). He accomplishes his aim by suggesting four "patterns of universalism." These include: (1) sympathization, which involves gentile participation in activities—such as worship at the Jerusalem Temple—that show a sympathetic stance toward Jews; (2) conversion, which involves the full adoption by gentiles of the Jewish way of life and the incorporation of gentiles into the Jewish community; (3) ethical monotheism, which involves aligning Torah religion and Greek philosophy through understanding "the Torah as a particular expression of a natural law accessible to everyone through reason and by seeing Torah religion and Greek philosophy as parallel paths to the same goal" (14); and, finally, (4) participation in eschatological redemption, which involves inclusion of gentiles along with Israel as beneficiaries of the end-time redemption (13–14).

---

[36] T. L. Donaldson, *Judaism and the Gentiles: Jewish Patterns of Universalism (to 135 CE)* (Waco, TX: Baylor University Press, 2007).

Of 221 passages analyzed throughout, Donaldson analyzes twenty-four passages from Philo and assigns some to more than one category of universalism. Accordingly, sixteen passages reflect conversion; five, sympathization; four, ethical monotheism; and one, eschatological participation. Donaldson concludes that Philo "presents us with two quite distinct patterns of universalism" (275)—one through the welcoming of proselytes to the Mosaic law and the other through recognizing value in the path of philosophy and reason. At different points, moreover, Philo can assert that the path of Mosaic law is superior to philosophy or that the two paths are equal. Accordingly, Donaldson declares "the tension between these two patterns of universalism must be allowed to stand" (276).

Donaldson's rich and insightful discussion of Philo is but one chapter in a long, detailed consideration of many more sources. At the end, Donaldson synthesizes his results and reflects on some larger questions. Among these is the issue, mentioned above (p. 551), of whether it is more fitting in relation to this era to speak of "Judaism" or "Judaisms." While recognizing that the "range of diversity is striking," Donaldson nonetheless gives more weight to the "elements of unity" and concludes that "the singular (Judaism) continues to be more appropriate than the plural (Judaisms)" (512-13).

33.3.4 Specific Topics: *Judaisms and Their Messiahs*

By contrast, a different conclusion is set forth in an earlier, multi-authored work entitled *Judaisms and Their Messiahs at the Turn of the Christian Era*. This collection is based on the premise that one must speak of a plurality of Judaisms, each of which "comprises a world view and a way of life that together come to expression in the social world of a group of Jews."[37] In an introductory chapter, William Scott Green observes that belief in the messiah was once widely held to be a fundamental aspect of "a preconceived and synthetic Judaism." He declares, however, that "[t]he evidence in this book shows that preoccupation with the messiah was not a uniform or definitive trait, nor a common reference point, of early Jewish writings or the Jews who produced them."[38] Besides a chapter on Philo, other chapters are devoted to wisdom literature, Enochic writings, 1-2 Maccabees, the Maccabean period, Qumran covenanters, New Testament writings, 4 Ezra, other Jewish pseudepigrapha, and the Mishnah.

Writing on Philo, Richard Hecht begins by showing that Harry Wolfson and Erwin Goodenough, "the two great Philo interpreters of [the twentieth] century,"[39] both affirmed—though in different ways—that Philo maintained the traditional Jewish messianic belief: "For Wolfson, Philo's Messiah is the nationalist Messiah of the 'native'

---

[37] J. Neusner, Preface to *Judaisms and Their Messiahs at the Turn of the Christian Era*, ed. J. Neusner, W. S. Green, and E. Frerichs (Cambridge: Cambridge University Press, 1987), ix–xiv; the quotation appears on p. ix.

[38] W. S. Green, "Introduction: Messiah in Judaism: Rethinking the Question," in *Judaisms and Their Messiahs at the Turn of the Christian Era*, 1–13; the quotation appears on p. 10. Cf. Donaldson's assignment of only one Philonic passage (*Mos.* 2.43–44) to the category of eschatological participation (*Judaism and the Gentiles*, 231–35).

[39] R. D. Hecht, "Philo and Messiah," in *Judaisms and Their Messiahs at the Turn of the Christian Era*, 139–68; the quotation appears on p. 140.

Judaism of the Land of Israel; for Goodenough it is a pre-Christian figure who anticipates his full realization in the New Testament" (148). Hecht himself proposes to demonstrate the error of these positions by examining several Philonic passages that pertain either to a messianic figure or age (*Conf.* 62–63; *Virt.* 75; *Mos.* 2.44, 288; *Opif.* 79–81; *Praem.* 79–172). He concludes that in one category of texts, messianic terminology is used allegorically to indicate the Logos, and in a second category, which includes only the long *Praem.* passage, messianic terminology describes historical or political processes in a spiritualized way without reference to a Jewish national destiny. To account for Philo's understanding, Hecht then considers the contemporary social and political unrest in Alexandria and concludes that Philo's approach was a way for him to neutralize potential messianic activity against the Romans. By allegorizing the messianic belief as applicable to the inner life of the soul and shearing this belief of its historical and national features, "Philo gave it a new life apart from the particular political energies it might release" (163).

The works just discussed on the specific topics of universalism and messianism illustrate two aspects of the approach to Philo adopted by many scholars from the past three or four decades: First, both Donaldson and Hecht study the Philonic passages on their own terms rather than through a lens tinted by assumptions about normative and non-normative kinds of Judaism. Indeed, by presenting the views of Wolfson and Goodenough, Hecht is quite explicit about the dangers of using such a lens. Second, the results of each chapter on Philo are used—whether by a single author or several editors—to contribute to a larger understanding of the time in which he lived.

Evidence from Philo has been similarly studied and applied in many other works about antiquity. Examples of topics include the Sabbath, dietary laws, the covenant, the meaning of "Israel," artistic imagery and its prohibition, the Temple, the synagogue, interpretation of various exegetical themes, reception of individual Pentateuch books, Mosaic authority, proselytism, Jewish attitudes toward gentiles, and Jewish life among Greeks and Romans.[40]

---

[40] These topics correspond roughly to the seven areas outlined in my above-mentioned essay, "Philo's Relevance." For works on these topics in which studies of Philo contribute to the larger picture of religious life during Philo's time, see e.g. references in that essay and the following sources (some of which are also included there): L. Doering, *Schabbat: Sabbathalacha und -praxis im antiken Judentum und Urchristentum*, TSAJ 78 (Tübingen: Mohr Siebeck, 1999); H. Weiss, *A Day of Gladness: The Sabbath among Jews and Christians in Antiquity* (Columbia: University of South Carolina Press, 2003); J. D. Rosenblum, *The Jewish Dietary Laws in the Ancient World* (Cambridge: Cambridge University Press, 2016); L. L. Grabbe, "Did All Jews Think Alike? 'Covenant' in Philo and Josephus in the Context of Second Temple Judaic Religion," in *The Concept of the Covenant in the Second Temple Period*, ed. S. E. Porter and J. C. R. de Roo, JSJSup 71 (Leiden: Brill, 2003), 251–66; A. M. Schwemer, "Zum Verhältnis von Diatheke und Nomos in den Schriften der jüdischen Diaspora Ägyptens in hellenistisch-römischer Zeit," in *Bund und Tora: Zur theologischen Begriffsgeschichte in alttestamentlicher, frühjüdischer und urchristlicher Tradition*, ed. F. Avemarie und H. Lichtenberger, WUNT 92 (Tübingen: Mohr Siebeck, 1996), 67–109; C. T. R. Hayward, *Interpretations of the Name Israel in Ancient Judaism and Some Early Christian Writings: From Victorious Athlete to Heavenly Champion* (Oxford: Oxford University Press, 2005); J. A. Staples, *The Idea of Israel in Second Temple Judaism: A New Theory of People, Exile, and Israelite Identity* (Cambridge: Cambridge University Press, 2021); S. Pearce, "Philo of Alexandria on the Second Commandment," in *The Image and Its Prohibition in Jewish Antiquity*, ed. S. Pearce, JJSSS 2 (Oxford: Journal of Jewish Studies, 2013), 49–76; C. T. R. Hayward, *The Jewish Temple: A Non-Biblical Sourcebook* (London: Routledge, 1996); J. R. Trotter, *The Jerusalem Temple in Diaspora Jewish Practice and Thought during the Second Temple Period*, JSJSup 192 (Leiden: Brill, 2019); L. I. Levine, *The Ancient Synagogue: The First Thousand Years*, 2nd edn (New Haven: Yale University Press, 2005); A. Runesson, D. D. Binder, and B. Olsson, *The Ancient Synagogue from Its*

33.4 Philo and Jews of Later Times

The previous two sections have shown how contemporary scholars of Judaism have integrated Philo and Jewish tradition in at least two ways: first, scholars have recognized that, within his own thought, Philo's ideas are an inseparable blend of Jewish and other—for example, Greek and/or universalistic—components. Philo's way of being Jewish, then, is no longer seen as resulting from a patchwork of elements, each from a different cultural current, but rather as an *integration* of these elements. Second, scholars have incorporated Philo into studies of other Jews of his own time and have thus brought him into relation with these Jews to highlight similarities and differences between them. Instead of standing apart from or being compared with a mainstream, rabbinic standard, then, Philo is being considered as one of many different representatives of Jews from the Second Temple period. In the present section, we will briefly explore other ways in which scholars have been and are integrating Philo and Jewish tradition by including him in broad surveys of topics from the Bible to later periods of Jewish history and thought, studying him in relation to subsequent eras of Judaism, and translating his works into the language of the Jewish homeland.

As for broad surveys, discussions of Philo have been included in works on such topics as Jewish spirituality, Jewish leadership, the interpretation of Tamar, and reasons for the commandments.[41] In a recent publication aimed at a somewhat more popular readership, Philo's "Exposition of the Laws" (*sic*) is presented as one of "18 Classics of Jewish Literature" that range from the Bible to the twentieth century.[42]

Origins to 200 C.E.: A Source Book, AGJU 72 (Leiden: Brill, 2008); Kugel, *Traditions of the Bible*; P. M. Sherman, *Babel's Tower Translated: Genesis 11 and Ancient Jewish Interpretation*, BibInt 117 (Leiden: Brill, 2013); G. E. Sterling, "When the Beginning Is the End: The Book of Genesis in the Commentaries of Philo," in *The Book of Genesis: Composition, Reception, and Interpretation*, ed. C. A. Evans, J. N. Lohr, and D. L. Petersen, VTSup 152 (Leiden: Brill, 2012), 427–46; G. E. Sterling, "The People of the Covenant or the People of God: Exodus in Philo of Alexandria," in *The Book of Exodus: Composition, Reception, and Interpretation*, ed. T. B. Dozeman, C. A. Evans, and J. N. Lohr, VTSup 164 (Leiden: Brill, 2014), 404–39; D. Lincicum, *Paul and the Early Jewish Encounter with Deuteronomy*, WUNT 2.284 (Tübingen: Mohr Siebeck, 2010); S. J. K. Pearce, *The Words of Moses: Studies in the Reception of Deuteronomy in the Second Temple Period*, TSAJ 152 (Tübingen: Mohr Siebeck, 2013); Najman, *Seconding Sinai*; M. F. Bird, *Crossing Over Sea and Land: Jewish Missionary Activity in the Second Temple Period* (Peabody, MA: Hendrickson, 2010); D. T. Runia, "Philo and the Gentiles," in *Attitudes to Gentiles in Ancient Judaism and Early Christianity*, ed. D. C. Sim and J. S. McLaren, LNTS 499 (London: Bloomsbury, 2013), 28–45; A. Ophir and I. Rosen-Zvi, *Goy: Israel's Multiple Others and the Birth of the Gentile*, Oxford Studies in the Abrahamic Religions (Oxford: Oxford University Press, 2018); E. S. Gruen, *Diaspora: Jews amidst Greeks and Romans* (Cambridge, MA: Harvard University Press, 2002); K. Berthelot, *Jews and Their Roman Rivals: Pagan Rome's Challenge to Israel* (Princeton: Princeton University Press, 2021). Readers are also encouraged to consult the annotated bibliographies published in the *Studia Philonica Annual* as well as the cumulative bibliographic volumes referenced there.

[41] D. Winston, "Philo and the Contemplative Life," in *Jewish Spirituality: From the Bible through the Middle Ages*, ed. A. Green, World Spirituality 13 (New York: Crossroad, 1986), 198–231; E. Birnbaum, "A Leader with Vision in the Ancient Jewish Diaspora: Philo of Alexandria," in *Jewish Religious Leadership: Image and Reality*, ed. J. Wertheimer (New York: The Jewish Theological Seminary, 2004), 1:57–90; E. Blachman, *The Transformation of Tamar (Genesis 38) in the History of Jewish Interpretation*, Contributions to Biblical Exegesis & Theology 71 (Leuven: Peeters, 2013). While these works were published from the late twentieth century onward, a study originally published in the 1940s in Hebrew by Isaac Heinemann was recently translated into English: I. Heinemann, *The Reasons for the Commandments in Jewish Thought from the Bible to the Renaissance*, trans. L. Levin (Boston: Academic Studies Press, 2009).

[42] A. Kirsch, *The People and the Books: 18 Classics of Jewish Literature* (New York: Norton, 2016), esp. 45–74.

Besides fitting Philo into surveys of topics or themes across Jewish history, scholars of later periods have also incorporated him, for different purposes, into discussions of particular subjects. Aiming "to give a full account of the rabbinic construction of divine law as a crucial, if often overlooked, partner in the Western conversation about law,"[43] for example, Christine Hayes includes Philo in a presentation of first-century CE attitudes regarding Mosaic law. Unlike earlier approaches that put him forward as a lone subject of comparison with the rabbis, Hayes discusses Philo within the context of other Second Temple sources in order to present a contrasting position to that of the rabbis. Here, then, Philo is one representative among others of a different perspective on Mosaic law—a perspective, in fact, of which the rabbis seem to have been aware, even if they did not necessarily know Philo's position directly.[44]

As another example from a subsequent period, in a study of the language of mystical union in medieval and later Jewish thinkers, Adam Afterman argues that "the religious idea of mystical union primarily originated in Philo," whose ideas may have influenced Plotinus, Platonism, "and the entire Western mystical tradition."[45] Afterman believes that Philo's ideas about mystical union had their source in his comments on biblical verses that mention "cleaving" to God. Here, then, Philo is understood to have developed a notion that was eventually transmitted and reintroduced in "an Arab-Muslim garb" to Jewish thinkers only centuries later.[46]

While Philo's influence on later Jewish writers regarding mystical union thus appears to have been indirect, his role in the thought of some modern Jewish thinkers is decidedly more explicit. Benjamin Pollock, for example, details how Franz Rosenzweig (1886–1929) grappled with Philo as he (Rosenzweig) forged his own ideas about Judaism.[47] In her dissertation on Hermann Cohen (1842–1918), Shira Billet argues that Philo was centrally important for this proponent of *Wissenschaft des Judentums*.[48] Scholars have recognized that other figures in the *Wissenschaft* movement were likewise drawn to Philo and the Alexandrian Jewish community and saw them as models for how to live as Jews in the diaspora.[49]

---

[43] C. Hayes, *What's Divine about Divine Law? Early Perspectives* (Princeton: Princeton University Press, 2015), 5.

[44] Hayes, *What's Divine about Divine Law?*, 222–45. See also Steven Fraade, Chapter 8 in this volume.

[45] A. Afterman, *"And They Shall Be One Flesh": On the Language of Mystical Union in Judaism*, SJJTP 26 (Leiden: Brill, 2016), 2.

[46] Afterman, *"And They Shall Be One Flesh,"* 26; cf. E. R. Wolfson, "Traces of Philonic Doctrine in Medieval Jewish Mysticism: A Preliminary Note," *SPhiloA* 8 (1996): 99–106. The Hebrew words related to "cleaving," are formed from the root *d-b-q*; the Greek translates these words with three different verbs. See Afterman, *"And They Shall Be One Flesh,"* 29, 37. For other ways in which Philo's influence was perceived in medieval Judaism, see Elke Morlok and Ze'ev Strauss, Chapter 17 in this volume.

[47] B. Pollock, "Philosophy's Inquisitor: Franz Rosenzweig's Philo between Judaism, Paganism, and Christianity," *SPhiloA* 27 (2015): 111–27.

[48] S. Billet, "The Philosopher as Witness: Hermann Cohen's Philosophers and the Trials of *Wissenschaft des Judentums*," PhD diss., Princeton University, 2019. (The author is currently preparing this work for publication.)

[49] See e.g. M. R. Niehoff, "Alexandrian Judaism in 19th Century *Wissenschaft des Judentums*: Between Christianity and Modernization," in *Jüdische Geschichte in hellenistisch-römischer Zeit: Wege der Forschung: Vom alten zum neuen Schürer*, ed. A. Oppenheimer (Munich: Oldenbourg, 1999), 9–28. See also Görge Hasselhoff, Chapter 29 in this volume and, for the earlier reception of Philo among Jewish Hegelians, see Dirk Westerkamp, Chapter 26 in this volume.

The studies mentioned above show the ways in which Philo is being integrated into discussions of later periods of Jewish history and thought—and indeed into the thought of some later Jewish thinkers themselves.[50] The same phenomenon was illustrated at a 2014 conference at Yale University on "Philo's Readers: Affinities, Reception, Transmission, and Influence." Of thirteen presentations directly related to Philo's reception, six pertained to his reception in later Jewish sources.[51] Finally, in a development not unrelated to Philo's reintegration into the history of Jews and Judaism, his works have been translated into modern Hebrew.[52] This multi-volume translation will ensure that Philo's writings will be accessible to scholars in the Jewish homeland who are bringing—and will undoubtedly continue to bring—their own perspectives to the great diaspora thinker from Alexandria.

33.5 Conclusion

Over the past three or four decades, Philo has emerged from the shadow of the rabbis to stand in his own light and to illuminate other areas in the study of Jews and Judaism. Several authors have produced works in which they consider Philo's Jewish identity in its own right from a variety of angles. In turn, Philo too has shed light on his Jewish contemporaries. His contributions to our knowledge of his time are apparent, for example, in a collection of literature from the period, a study of Jewish life in the Mediterranean diaspora, and treatments of specific topics in such areas as Jewish worship, beliefs and ideas, community institutions, the Bible and its interpretation, Jewish identity, Jews' interactions with and attitudes toward non-Jews and their culture, and historical events. Finally, Philo is increasingly being incorporated into wider surveys of Judaism from antiquity to the present, recognized as an influence—whether direct or indirect—on later Jewish sources, appreciated as a model for how to live as a Jew in the diaspora, and studied in the language of the Jewish homeland.

These developments hold much promise for the future. While Philo's overall Jewish identity has already been considered from several perspectives, we lack knowledge on many specific questions that pertain to the areas listed above. As scholars continue to explore and fill in gaps in our knowledge in these areas, we stand to learn more not only about Philo but also about other Jews and Judaism during his time and about differences between the homeland and the diaspora.

---

[50] As a recent example, Arthur Green speaks admiringly of Philo at several points in his (Green's) construction of "a Jewish mystical theology": A. Green, *Seek My Face, Speak My Name: A Contemporary Jewish Theology* (Northvale, NJ: Jason Aronson Inc., 1992), esp. 129, 195, 197; A. Green, *Seek My Face: A Jewish Mystical Theology*, 2nd edn (Woodstock, VT: Jewish Lights Publishing, 2003), esp. 124, 189, 191. See also D. Winston, "Philo and the Hellenistic Jewish Encounter," *SPhiloA* 7 (1995): 124–42, esp. 135–42.

[51] For a summary of the conference, see E. Birnbaum, "Philo at Yale," *Adamantius* 20 (2014): 632–35.

[52] S. Daniel-Nataf, Y. Amir, and M. Niehoff, eds, *Philo of Alexandria: Writings*, 5 vols (Jerusalem: Bialik Institute and the Israel Academy of Sciences and Humanities, 1986–2012).

Scholars of later periods of Judaism face different kinds of challenges. With little evidence of direct knowledge of Philo by Jews during the nearly fifteen centuries between Josephus and Jews in the time of the Italian Renaissance, researchers can nonetheless probe further into affinities, contrasts, and possible lines of influence between Philo and his descendant co-religionists. The reintroduction of Philo by Jews in the 1500s opens up additional avenues of investigation pertaining to later Jewish thinkers' direct familiarity with him, their evaluations of him as a Jew, and their attitudes toward him as a possible model. Although it took hundreds of years for Philo to be acknowledged by fellow Jews, he has been and is being re-embraced by Jews and scholars of Judaism. One hopes that recognition of his vital place within the Jewish tradition will only continue to grow.

34

Contemporary Receptions and Future Prospects among Scholars of Christianity

Mark Edwards

If Christianity is the rebellious child of Judaism and the fosterling of Greek philosophy, under which of these rubrics should we look for signs of the influence of Philo? The battle for his soul has raged since the end of the nineteenth century, and almost every participant has opined that the Hellenism, the Judaism, or the hybridity which is being ascribed to Philo will determine whether his legacy to Christian thought was slight or copious, toxic or benign. For the purpose of this chapter it will therefore be necessary to take into account the classic studies of Philo which have been produced in the course of the twentieth century, whether or not they took the Christian use of Philo as their principal topic of interest. We shall find in fact that studies which aim at nothing but the classification of Philo in his own time have been as pregnant as those that expressly set out to review his fortunes after death.

34.1 Some Early Investigations

At the end of the nineteenth century, the common opinion of Philo was that, notwithstanding his conspicuous piety, he read the Torah in Greek without the assistance of that incipient tradition of commentary that we have come to call rabbinic.[1] The rabbis find no place in the Jewish milieu which James Drummond reconstructs for Philo in the fullest and most empirical study hitherto published in English.[2] For Drummond he represents a "Jewish Alexandrian" school, which blended the ancestral faith with Greek thought to give it a speculative character that is quite at odds with the masterful and assertoric style of the Hebrew scriptures. His devotion to the Septuagint, which frequently administers a philosophic corrective to the Hebrew, may have rendered him more susceptible to the intellectual climate of Alexandria, but the air that he inhaled

---

[1] See D. Winston, "Philo and Rabbinic Literature," in *The Cambridge Companion to Philo*, ed. A. Kamesar (Cambridge: Cambridge University Press, 2009), 231–53, at 231. I owe much of the information in this paragraph to Winston's article.

[2] J. Drummond, *Philo Judaeus, or the Jewish Alexandrian Philosophy in Its Development and Completion* (London: Williams and Norgate, 1888).

was wholly Greek. More than half a century later the learned Talmudist E. E. Urbach took up the same position, protesting that even Jewish notions of God as a divine architect consulting his scrolls offered no true parallel to the Philonic notion of the Logos as the seat of divine ideas.[3]

Drummond had little to say of Philo's supposed anticipations of Christianity, although Carl Siegfried had already compiled a rambling and eclectic inventory of patristic borrowings from the Alexandrian, much of which would now be thought to invite the charge of parallelomania (see below, p. 566).[4] In 1908 Paul Heinisch achieved a more orderly arrangement of select passages in a monograph on Philo as a precursor to the Christian practice of allegory.[5] When Adolf von Harnack, the eminent historian of the church, undertook his prodigious *History of Christian Doctrine*, he was in no doubt that Philo set the example of subordinating the word of God to the teaching of the world which was followed with deadly effect by every "catholic" writer after Paul.[6] Philo's claim to be a church father, however, is not directly addressed in a work which set the benchmark for English scholarship, F. C. Conybeare's edition of the *De vita contemplativa*.[7] Conybeare's collation of the Greek with an Armenian version reinforced the case for the authenticity of the treatise, which had recently been impugned. While this result is currently accepted by the majority of scholars, the question of Philo's role as a witness to or influence on the development of monasticism has receded, while debate has turned instead on the presence of women among his Therapeutae and the possible relation of this sect to the community of Qumran.[8]

"Born a Jew, taught as a Greek" is the leitmotif of Henri Guyot's *L'Infinité divin depuis Philon le Juif jusqu' à Plotin*,[9] the title of which gives Philo his due as the first to declare that even the intellect cannot apprehend God by its native powers. Behind this philosophical innovation Guyot discerns that inveterate horror of idolatry which was expressed with equal vigour by the rabbis. A thoroughly amphibious picture of Philo had been drawn two years before by Edward Caird, sometime professor of moral philosophy at Glasgow, in his second series of Gifford lectures in defence of natural theology.[10] In the tradition of Hegel, Caird maintains that Greek philosophy exhibits a progressive approximation to the true idea of God, which, without divesting him of the higher traits of personality, acknowledges both his absolute transcendence and his omnipresence in the phenomenal world. Platonism accentuates the transcendence of the first principle, while acknowledging the operation of an immanent principle in the

---

[3] E. E. Urbach, *The Sages: Their Concepts and Beliefs*, trans. I. Abrahams (Jerusalem: Hebrew University Press, 1979), 200.

[4] C. Siegfried, *Philo von Alexandria als Ausleger des alten Testaments* (Jena: Dufft, 1875).

[5] P. Heinisch, *Der Einfluss Philo auf die älteste christliche Exegese (Barnabas, Justin und Clement von Alexandria)* (Münster: Aschendorff, 1908).

[6] A. von Harnack, *Lehrbuch der Dogmengeschichte* (Tübingen: Mohr, 1909-10), 1:20, 124-25. The relevant passages are quoted in D. T. Runia, *Philo in Early Christian Literature: A Survey* (Assen: van Gorcum, 1993), to whom I also owe the references to Siegfried and Heinisch.

[7] F. C. Conybeare, *Philo about the Contemplative Life* (Oxford: Clarendon, 1895).

[8] J. Taylor, *Jewish Women Philosophers of First-Century Alexandria* (Oxford: Oxford University Press, 2003); G. Vermes, *Post-Biblical Jewish Studies* (Leiden: Brill, 1975), 30-36.

[9] H. Guyot, *L'Infinité divin depuis Philon le Juif jusqu' à Plotin* (Paris: Alcan, 1906).

[10] E. Caird, *The Evolution of Theology in the Greek Philosophers* (Glasgow: MacLehose, 1904), 2:184-209.

lower orders of reality; by contrast, the Stoics conceived of God as an all-pervading Logos, or rational principle, which guided and sustained the natural realm yet remained inseparable from it. Philo, as the heir to both schools of thought, had the further advantage, as a Jew, that he was not bound to follow either where he could not reconcile it to the infallible teachings which had been vouchsafed to his people through the prophets, and above all through the inspired legislation of Moses. Being at once believer and philosopher, he was under the obligation of marrying two incongruous modes of thinking, one concrete and vivid, the other discursive and analytical, bringing under the microscope of philosophy the truths which were glimpsed in Israel only through the stained glass of poetry and myth.

34.2 Goodenough: Bridging the Mysteries

Caird was one of the first, and for some years also the last, to strike an even balance between the Greek and the Jewish elements in Philo. The Jewish scholar Isaac Heinemann declared that neither the oral Torah nor the written one in its Hebrew form was known to this prince of the tribe of Hellas.[11] Philo did indeed assert the pre-eminence of the Torah over all the Greek schools, but, rather than believe by faith what could not be proved by reason, he subjects the Torah to a process of allegorical decipherment, which proves it to be a treasury of the best that had been taught in any of the Greek traditions. At the opposite pole to Heinemann stands Goodenough's monograph *By Light, Light*[12] in which the celebrated student of Jewish symbolism contends that Hellenized Judaism acted as a bridge between the gospel and philosophy, facilitating the imposition of systematic rigor and logical clarity on a faith that had entered the world by a lightning-stroke of revelation. Philo, in Goodenough's view, is above all a man enraptured by the sense of God, as is evidenced by his frequent descriptions of ecstasy, far outnumbering those of any Greek precursor, even in the Platonic tradition. He imitates this tradition in appropriating the language of pagan mysteries, but the God who awaits the devotee at the terminus of his ascent is no Olympian, nor even the Platonic form of the Good, but the loving and personal creator who set the tongues of his prophets alight in the days when Israel lived by inspiration.

In his critique of Goodenough Walter Völker, a German protestant, accused him of mishandling the term "mysticism" and of impugning Philo's loyalty to his own ancestral faith.[13] On the one hand, he is not to be convicted of any borrowing from the Greek mysteries, and the essence of his own faith can be found in the sapiential literature of the Septuagint; on the other hand, the term "mysticism" denotes not merely a sense of exaltation above the mundane, but a real and intimate communion with the

---

[11] I. Heinemann, *Philons jüdische und griechische Bildung* (Breslau: Marcus, 1932).
[12] E. R. Goodenough, *By Light, Light: The Mystic Gospel of Hellenistic Judaism* (New Haven: Yale University Press, 1935).
[13] W. Völker, *Fortschritt und Vollendung bei Philo von Alexandrien. Eine Studie zur Geschichte der Frömmigkeit* (Leipzig: Hinrichs, 1938).

Godhead, which is possible only in Christ. In his subsequent *Introduction to Philo Judaeus* Goodenough retorts that Völker can justify his simplification of Philo only by dismissing every text that he cannot bully into his service.[14] In the introduction he reiterates his belief that Philo's adoption of Greek thought facilitated the Hellenization of Christianity, and challenges those who hold that his religion was cosmetic to explain the frequency of the mystical passages in his corpus. At the same time, he ascribes to him a compendious philosophy which teaches the reader how to combine a provisional existence in this world with the preparation of the soul for the future life.

Thus Goodenough suggests that Philo imbibed the thought of Greece in a Jewish decoction, but denies that the rabbinic substitution of Memra, or word, for the name of God presents a true analogue to his doctrine of the Logos (99). The Jewish notion of virtue is irreconcilable with the civic ethic of the Greeks, and in his literal observance of the Torah Philo remains a "Jew of the Jews" (101). By contrast, his metaphysics is informed by the ambient culture of Alexandria. God is both the abstract good and the donor of grace, absolutely free of the world and yet omnipresent within it; being the source of all that exists, he is not circumscribed by a body or by an independent law of nature, as the Stoics imagine. Yet neither is his prepotence incompatible with delegation of power to the Logos and the angels, so long as there is no idolatry or division of worship. Hence we are not surprised that his mysticism, far from being merely Platonic, redeems the "failure of the Hellenistic scientist to be a spiritual leader" (181). Where myth "vivified the abstract" and the mysteries decanted the higher doctrines from the head to the heart, the elevation of the soul above the world is exemplified in scripture by the visions of Moses and the patriarchs. Thus he bequeathed to the church an example of religious probity, all the more luminous because he could hold his own with the most pure-blooded Greek.

34.3 Wolfson: Philo, Philosophy, and the Rabbis

No wonder then that to classicists in the first half of the twentieth century Philo was a dilettante who took himself for a philosopher. Their scorn served as the whetstone for an article by Harry Austryn Wolfson, first holder of the Nathan Littauer Chair of Jewish Studies at Harvard from 1925 to 1958, in which he maintained that scholars were accustomed to misread Philo as an eclectic (and a poor one at that) because they failed to grasp that he aimed above all at a coherent vindication of the scriptures. This was a popular summary of his prodigious study of Philo, published initially in 1947, which contended, in the teeth of all previous scholarship, that the doctrines ascribed to Moses by the Jewish philosopher correspond in detail not to the Stoic or Platonic teachings of his day but to those of his near-contemporaries among the rabbis.[15] Wolfson had

---

[14] Goodenough, *An Introduction to Philo Judaeus* (New Haven: Yale University Press, 1940). Page references in the next paragraph are supplied parenthetically in the main text.

[15] H. A. Wolfson, *Philo: Foundations of Religious Philosophy in Judaism, Christianity and Islam*, 2 vols (Cambridge, MA: Harvard University Press, 1948, 1st ed. 1947).

surprised the world by maintaining a similar thesis with regard to Spinoza in 1934, and the book on Philo completed a project, commencing with his study of Maimonides in 1912, of reducing the history of western thought to three epochs, the two turning points of which were each inaugurated by a Jew at the margins of a gentile world.

Only, however, by taking up a firm position on topics that still divide scholarship is Wolfson able to justify his estimate of Philo's originality.[16] He asserts, for example, that Philo held creation out of nothing to be a necessary corollary of divine omnipotence;[17] nevertheless, the fashion in recent years has been to doubt that any clear statement of it is to be found in the Bible or in Jewish and Christian interpretation of it before the late second century.[18] On the other hand, Wolfson was right to nominate Philo as the first writer in Greek to predicate infinity of God, this being for Plato and Aristotle a term that signifies only deficit of form rather than a superabundance of power. The concomitant beliefs that God remains unknowable even to the liberated intellect and is not to be described except by negatives were to find their way from Philo to Clement of Alexandria, who agrees with Wolfson in treating him as a representative spokesman of Judaism. Origen, by contrast, hesitated to embrace either of these opinions, and when Plotinus, a generation after him, asserts the infinity of the highest principle for the first time in Greek philosophy, he simultaneously strips it of any power of willing or knowing, two inalienable properties of God in Philo's scheme of providence.[19]

When Gregory of Nyssa clothes the infinite God in a darkness which can be penetrated only by the surrender of reason to love, we cannot assume that he owes to Philo everything that he has not drawn from Plotinus. We may also wonder, with Irénée Hausherr, how many Christians adhere to Philo's doctrine of divine unknowability without some complementary doctrine of plenary knowledge through the incarnation.[20] In his celebration of God's unfathomable goodness, Gregory of course maintains with Philo, and with all Christians between Philo's day and his own, that God was free to create another world than this, or no world at all; this secession from the prevailing assumptions of the Greek schools, however, was forced upon all Christians by the scriptures, and need not be traced to any philosophical antecedent. The most distinctive features of Philo's thought anticipate the ripening of a new cosmology and a new metaphysic in the Christian world, but we cannot be confident that he was their source if this implies that the church could not have got so far without him. All this being said, however, there is one postulated borrowing which appears to be undeniable—the qualification of God's inscrutability in Gregory, Basil the Great, and Evagrius Ponticus by a distinction between the essence of God, which remains for ever hidden, and the energies by which he condescends to be known on earth.

---

[16] The case is set out in five points by H. A. Wolfson, "The Philonic God of Revelation and his Latter-Day Deniers," *HTR* 53 (1960): 101–24.
[17] "The Philonic God of Revelation," 108.
[18] See, however, J. C. O'Neill, "How Early Is the Doctrine of Creation out of Nothing?" *JTS* 53 (2002): 449–65.
[19] See further C. de Vogel, "La théorie de l'*apeiron* chez Platon et la tradition platonicienne," *Revue philosophique de la France et de l'Étranger* 149 (1959): 21–39.
[20] See e.g. I. Hausher, "Ignorance infinie ou science infinie?," *OCP* 25 (1959): 44–52.

34.4 Circumscribing Philo: Sandmel and Dillon

Wolfson remains an authority on imperial Platonism and the evolution of Christian philosophy; many concurred, however, when Samuel Sandmel, a Jewish student of the New Testament, taxed him with "parallelomania" in his use of rabbinic matter.[21] This endemic vice of biblical scholarship (as Sandmel opines) is the multiplication of specious similarities without regard to the essence of the things that are being compared. 259 rabbinic apophthegms in Paul would not have reconciled a Jew to his conviction that the fullness of the Godhead dwelt in the one man, Jesus of Nazareth; likewise the peculiar timbre of Philo's thought eludes us in a whole thesaurus of quotations from the synagogue. In his later *Introduction to Philo*[22] he admits that "two-way" traffic between Alexandria and Palestine is a possible explanation of "overlaps in halakhic and haggadic elements" (132), but warns us not to confuse Pythagorean and rabbinic speculations on the symbolism of numbers (23), and above all not to forget the fixed antipathy of the rabbis to allegorical exegesis (22). Thus it appears that, even if rabbinic thought were more commensurable with that of Paul than Sandmel allows, a reading of Philo would throw no light on the emergence of Christianity; on the other hand, critics of Sandmel have adduced texts from the Cairo Genizah which suggest that a strict dichotomy between the two modes of exegesis cannot be sustained.

Of course, it is not Mishnaic legislation but Greek philosophy that is conventionally held to have been the stepmother of gentile Christianity. Substance and definition were added to the description of Philo as an Alexandrian Platonist by the French scholar Pierre Boyancé; definitive proof that, judged as a philosopher, he deserves this label rather than the disparaging "eclectic" has been provided by the classicist John Dillon in his imposing survey of Middle Platonism.[23] This is not to deny, but rather to explain, his espousal of teachings that were extrinsic to the thought of Plato himself. Thus there is nothing anomalous in his blending of Stoic with Peripatetic logic, in his apparent vacillation between Platonic and Aristotelian divisions of the soul, or in his attempts to reconcile a deterministic understanding of natural law with a belief in the divine tutelage of individual souls (166–69 and 174–80). Philo's personification of Sophia, or Wisdom, as God's executor in the physical cosmos finds its analogue in the Pythagorean dyad and in Plutarch's figure of Isis (163–64); Stoic in its basis, his ethics also takes on a Pythagorean color (151). Most evidently Pythagorean in origin is the equation of the Platonic Forms with numbers; on the other hand, it is his own reading of the *Timaeus* that enables him to identify the Logos, in one of its aspects, with the eternal paradigm of the contingent order (155–62). Philo thus exemplifies,

---

[21] S. Sandmel, "Parallelomania," *JBL* 81 (1962): 1–13.
[22] S. Sandmel, *Philo of Alexandria: An Introduction* (New York: Oxford University Press, 1979). Page numbers are given parenthetically in the main text. Note that he does not follow his tutor Goodenough in giving Philo the epithet Judaeus.
[23] J. M. Dillon, *The Middle Platonists* (London: Duckworth, 1977), 139–83. Page numbers given parenthetically in the main text.

but did not create, that tendency which came to dominate the Platonic schools of late antiquity—a tendency recognized, as David Runia notes, by the Christians who styled him a Pythagorean.[24] At the same time, had Wolfson read Dillon, he would have observed that he falls well short of proving that every tenet in Philo's system could have been espoused by a Platonist of his own day, in Alexandria or elsewhere.

34.5 Philo and Christian Mysticism

If Sandmel were right, we could not accept Philo's claim to be a biblical theologian, and it would consequently be hard to disagree with Harnack's judgment that his influence on Christianity was malign. Again, if Dillon's proof of his integrity as a Platonist excluded any other description of him, Goodenough's thesis that he served as a bridge between the schools and the church would be untenable. But Dillon is also the co-author of a commentary on the treatise *On the Giants*,[25] in which Philo divides the human race into sons of earth, sons of heaven, and sons of God. Platonic models for this trichotomy were easily marshalled; another classicist, Christoph Riedweg,[26] has shown in his study of the terms *mustērion* and *teletē* (rite) in Philo that, although he was no initiate, he imitates Plato's adaptation of mystical nomenclature to the pilgrimage of the soul. While Riedweg doubts that the Torah is the true source of the lessons that Philo ostensibly derives from it, he concedes the originality of his precept that God must be sought in the unfathomable darkness where he hides himself from all but the pure in heart. Hans Lewy had already collated the texts in which the ecstatic state is characterized as a sober drunkenness transcending vision and intellection.[27] James Miller's *Measures of Wisdom*, a study of the perennial image of the cosmic dance, allots a whole chapter to Philo's pursuit of "Corybantic ecstasy" and its relation to the four "interlocking" systems of law (Mosaic, natural, Roman, and Greek) to which he found himself beholden.[28] Others have proposed Philo as a Jewish exemplar of gnosis, a widespread quest for knowledge of the kind that could not be attained by the exercise of discursive reason; it is agreed, however, that he was at most a satellite of this movement, which in its most egregious form denies the highest god a role in creating the world.[29]

Nevertheless, for much of the twentieth century Christian students of mysticism made only passing mention of Philo, notwithstanding their acknowledgment of the seminal role of Plato in occidental literature. Andrew Louth has filled the lacuna,

---

[24] D. T. Runia, "Why Does Clement of Alexandria call Philo 'the Pythagorean'?," *VC* 49 (1995): 1–22.
[25] D. Winston and J. Dillon, *Two Treatises of Philo: A Commentary on* De Gigantibus *and* Quod deus sit Immutabilis (Chico, CA: Scholars Press, 1983).
[26] C. Riedweg, *Mysterienterminologie bei Platon, Philon und Klemens von Alexandrien* (Berlin: de Gruyter, 1986).
[27] H. Lewy, *Sobria Ebrietas. Untersuchungen zur Geschichte der antiken Mystik* (Giessen: Töpelmann, 1929).
[28] J. L. Miller, *Measures of Wisdom: The Cosmic Dance in Classical and Christian Antiquity* (Toronto: University of Toronto Press, 1986), 85.
[29] H. Jonas, *Gnosis und die spätantiker Geist* (Gottingen: Vandenhoeck and Ruprecht, 1954), 2:70–121; R. McL. Wilson, "Philo and Gnosticism," *Kairos* 14 (1972): 213–19; B. A. Pearson, *Gnosticism, Judaism and Egyptian Christianity* (Minneapolis: Fortress, 1990), 165–92.

demonstrating that Philo prefigures Christian thought not only by proclaiming the unknowability of God but also by enjoining constant perusal of the scriptures as a means of drawing out the soul from its passions and submitting it to the guidance of the Word.[30] Clement of Alexandria's adoption of this mysticism of darkness, illustrated once again by the ascent of Moses on Sinai, is the subject of the next chapter in Louth's book, as in that of Riedweg; the relation between the two men is treated at length in a monograph by Annewies van den Hoek, while Henny Hägg, in a study of apophatic theology in Clement, lays stress on Philo's contrast between the inscrutable *ousia* or essence of God and the *energeiai* or operations and hints that, whether or not he inspired the prologue to the Fourth Gospel, his doctrine of the Logos was one factor which shaped the Christian understanding of this text.[31]

34.6 Runia and After

Few scholars postulate any direct influence of Philo on the New Testament, though it is common enough to notice at least some kinship between his doctrine of the Logos and the prologue to the Fourth Gospel. Parallels between Philo and Paul are collected by Henry Chadwick, doyen of English patristic scholarship in the second half of the twentieth century. Paul and Philo share a nascent concept of natural law and agree that our knowledge of God in the present world is a mere adumbration; on the other hand, the parallels are too vague to indicate more than a common background, and Philo has stopped his ears in advance to the gospel when he scoffs that it is as impossible for a human to become God as for God to make himself a man (*Legat.* 118). In his contribution to the Cambridge *History of Later Greek and Early Medieval Philosophy*, Chadwick admits that the history of Christian thought begins with a Jew, and one who was both faithful and representative enough to resist the "totalitarian" claims of Hellenism.[32] Yet David Winston, superseding Chadwick in the new *Cambridge History of Philosophy in Late Antiquity*, avers that Dillon's Platonist Philo has ousted all his Stoic, eclectic, and Gnostic rivals.[33] Philo the Jew does not even merit a place in this gallery of rejected portraits, and the case is supposed to be sealed by David Runia's monograph *Philo of Alexandria and the* Timaeus *of Plato*.[34] But Runia, who may have written more about Philo than anyone in history, has never failed to set *Philo Judaeus* side to side with *Philo Alexandrinus*, and is perhaps best known for his study of the blending of the two into the posthumous figure of *Philo Christianus*.

---

[30] A. Louth, *The Origins of the Christian Mystical Tradition* (Oxford: Clarendon, 1983), 18–35.

[31] A. van den Hoek, *Clement of Alexandria and His Use of Philo in the Stromateis: An Early Christian Reshaping of a Jewish Model* (Leiden: Brill, 1988); H. F. Hägg. *Clement of Alexandria and the Beginnings of Christian Apophaticism* (Oxford: Oxford University Press, 2006), 125 and 182.

[32] H. Chadwick, "St Paul and Philo of Alexandria," *BJRL* 48 (1966): 286–307; "Philo and the Beginnings of Christian Thought," in *The Cambridge History of Later Greek and Early Medieval Philosophy*, ed. A. H. Armstrong (Cambridge: Cambridge University Press, 1967), 137–57.

[33] D. Winston, "Philo," in *The Cambridge History of Philosophy in Late Antiquity*, ed. L. P. Gerson (Cambridge: Cambridge University Press, 2015), 235–57 at 235.

[34] D. T. Runia, *Philo of Alexandria and the* Timaeus *of Plato* (Leiden: Brill, 1986).

In the review of scholarship which prefaces his *Philo and Early Christian Literature*,[35] he observes that theologians are less willing than historians of philosophy to admit the salutary influence of Philo on Christian thought: they will either assert, with Harnack, that his influence was pernicious, or deny, with Eric Osborn,[36] that his exegesis played any part in the church's reflection on its axial doctrines. Runia adds that the difficulties of his investigation are compounded by the absence of direct reference to Philo in sources that have clearly made use of his work at first or at second hand: Ambrose, for example, offers copious parallels without a single avowed citation. When he is cited by name, he is sometimes a representative Jew, sometimes a Platonist, and sometimes, as in Eusebius, a rare witness to the nascent institutions of the church. Alexandrian Christians, who are peculiarly apt to base their reasoning on scripture, and peculiarly inventive in their discovery of its hidden sense, are as liberal as we might expect in the use of their Philonic patrimony. For all that, they would not disagree with Augustine's judgment (perhaps on a second-hand report of Philo's exegesis) that no scriptural text is fully understood by those who fail to discern its application to Christ. Runia does not purport to determine whether the fundamental beliefs of Philo can be harmonized with the gospel or the creeds, although he comments that in some passages from the fourth century he is cited without approval because his Judaism is patently inconsistent with orthodoxy.

While it would be hard for any scholar to outdo Runia in his close examination of Philo's reasoning and of his debts to both his Greek and his Jewish precursors, some new paths have been struck in both the appreciation and the historiography of the allegorical method in exegesis. Many scholars now concur that Valentin Nikiprowetzky has demonstrated the predominantly exegetical character of Philo's thought in a series of articles culminating in his *Le commentaire de l'Écriture selon Philon d'Alexandrie*.[37] Without questioning the presence of both a Stoic and a Platonic strain in Philo, Nikiprowetzky finds the scarlet thread in his careful parsing of the Law, conceived not only as a set of positive ordinances but as the appointed means of raising the soul from the slough of error and passion to the throne of God. As Maren Niehoff observes, this conclusion requires us to acknowledge the salience of the Jewish tradition; Niehoff herself regards the synthesis of Plato and the Stoics as a productive "contribution to Platonism," and has shown that Philo ought to command the interest of scholars not only as a subject for biography but as an early practitioner of this literary form.[38]

Nikiprowetzky pointed out the cardinal place of the Law in Philo's thinking within a few years of the rise of the *nouvelle théologie*, which had shown that the early Christian use of allegory is not a charter for arbitrary reasoning, since its tendency is always to put Christ himself at the heart of revelation. Philo's role in teaching this device to Clement and Origen is acknowledged in classic studies of patristic exegesis by Henri de Lubac

---

[35] Runia, *Philo in Early Christian Literature*, 47–58. See also his "Platonism, Philonism and the Beginnings of Christian Thought," translated from the Dutch in his *Philo and the Church Fathers* (Leiden: Brill, 1995), 1–24.
[36] E. Osborn, *The Beginning of Christian Philosophy* (Cambridge: Cambridge University Press, 1982).
[37] V. Nikiprowetzky, *Le commentaire de l'Écriture selon Philon d'Alexandrie* (Leiden: Brill, 1977).
[38] M. Niehoff, *Philo of Alexandria: An Intellectual Biography* (New Haven: Yale University Press, 2018).

and Jean Daniélou,[39] who remind the purported advocates of biblical Christianity that no text can retain its sanctity unless each new generation finds some means of palliating the words that have come to seem contradictory, immoral, or obscure. It is fair to say, however, that they notice, rather than justify, his engagement with the scriptures; nor has either of them pre-empted Ilaria Ramelli in identifying Philo as the "one before us" whom Origen cites as a witness to some of his more audacious readings.[40] The charge of fanciful interpretation is rebutted, astutely though briefly, by a great theologian of the Reformed tradition, T. F. Torrance, who remarks that Philo often described the hidden sense as a physiological one because it points to the truth underlying the objects of everyday perception.[41] A cogent demonstration that the world itself is the proper subject of Philo's exegesis has been offered by David Dawson in a book which deserves much praise for its intercalation of Valentinus the Gnostic between Philo and Clement, and still more for its recognition that Philo's aim is not to Hellenize his own faith but to subordinate the teaching of the schools to the wisdom of Moses: "Philo uses just this sort of allegorical reading of scripture to reinterpret the cosmos, world history and Alexandrian social reality, as well as classical philosophy and literary wisdom, by viewing them all through the lens of Moses' original Pentateuch."[42] Nevertheless, although the modern academy has witnessed and sanctioned a great profusion of hermeneutic strategies, it does so because it no longer demands a correlation of meaning with reality, or even with the intention of the author. A recent book by Baudouin Decharneux, a prolific author on Philo, restores to him his fundamental principle that different senses of scripture correspond to different levels of vision and these in turn to more or less elevated planes of being.[43] Hence the angels whom we encounter with some fatigue in his work are not superfluous, but form a bridge between the noetic and the phenomenal order which is comparable to the commentator's use of allegory as a bridge between poetic and philosophic modes of speech. In his recent monograph Jang Ryu, without neglecting the Stoic and Platonic elements in Philo's epistemology, shows that he works out a minute itinerary of the soul's ascent to God through an internally coherent reading of biblical texts, adducing men whom he takes to have been historical figures as spiritual paradigms, and extolling the Pentateuch as a perfect mirror to the natural world whose origin and constitution Moses alone had been privileged to discern.[44]

Some mention of Philo, therefore, ought to preface the many discussions of contemplation through the spiritual senses which have been inspired by the *nouvelle théologie*. In the last few decades, both Roman Catholic and Protestant theologies have been

---

[39] H. de Lubac, *Exégèse médiévale* (Paris: Aubier, 1959), 1:200–8 and 376–80; J. Daniélou, *The Theology of Judaeo-Christianity*, trans. John Austin Baker (London: Dartman, Longman and Todd, 1964), 80, 137–39; *Philo of Alexandria*, trans. J. Colbert (Eugene, OR: Cascade, 2014).

[40] I. L. E. Ramelli, "Philo as Origen's Declared Model: Allegorical and Historical Exegesis of Scripture," *Studies in Jewish-Christian Relations* 7 (2012): 1–17, esp. 7.

[41] T. F. Torrance, *Divine Meaning: Studies in Patristic Hermeneutics* (London: T. and T. Clark, 1995).

[42] D. Dawson, *Allegorical Readers and Cultural Revision in Ancient Alexandria* (Berkeley: University of California Press, 1992), 74.

[43] B. Decharneux, *L'ange, le devin et le prophète* (Brussels: University of Brussels, 1994).

[44] J. Ryu, *Knowledge of God in Philo of Alexandria* (Tübingen: Mohr Siebeck, 2015).

more hospitable to the cognate notion of *theōsis* or deification, properly understood as the consummation of God's image and likeness in humanity. The deification of Moses in Philo has long been a subject of scholarly contention: in the days before the term was widely entertained in Christian thought, such scholars as Donald Hagner, Carl Holladay, and Louis Feldman protested that a true apotheosis of any man would be inconsistent with his rigorous monotheism:[45] had he not said, after all, that a human being can no more become god than God can become a man?[46] More recently, however, scholars who took more account of Philo's Platonic heritage have observed that the Greek world recognized gradations of transcendence, while Philo himself was willing to speak of higher and lower aspects of the divine and even of a "second god." David Litwa supports this view in the wake of studies by Runia and Winston, in opposition to the theologian Richard Bauckham.[47] Theology has its own province and history another: denizens of the latter will welcome the recognition in Runia, Winston, and Litwa of Philo's double ancestry.

34.7 Conclusion

With the foundation of the *Studia Philonica Annual* in 1989 and the appearance in 2000 of a comprehensive index to Philo's writings, it can be said scholars now possess the tools for a greater mastery of Philo than has ever been possible. On the other hand, the proliferation of scholarship encourages specialization, and minds that can grasp the whole of Philo's work as both philosopher and exegete, together with all the precedents and analogues that the Greek or Jewish traditions can afford, will no doubt continue to be as rare as they were in Wolfson's day—if only because it is less common now to be equally fluent in Greek and in Hebrew. More and more, perhaps, we shall resemble the blind men in an Indian parable, each handling only one portion of the elephant; but at least we shall not mistake our portion for the whole animal, nor will theologians or philosophers be taxed, in a homelier phrase, with treating Philo like the elephant in the room.

---

[45] D. A. Hagner, "The Vision of God in Philo and John: A Comparative Study," *JETS* 14 (1971): 81–93; C. Holladay, *Theios Anêr in Hellenistic Judaism: A Critique of the Use of this Category in New Testament Studies* (Missoula, MT: Scholars Press, 1977), 108–29; L. Feldman, *Philo's Portrayal of Moses in the Context of Ancient Judaism* (Notre Dame: University of Notre Dame Press, 2007), 339–48. These references are taken from Litwa (see n. 47 below).

[46] See *Legat.* 118.

[47] D. M. Litwa, "The Deification of Moses in Philo of Alexandria," *SPhiloA* 26 (2014): 1–27, citing D. T. Runia, "God and Man in Philo of Alexandria," *JTS* 39 (1988): 48–75; D. Winston, "Philo's Conception of the Divine Nature," in *Neoplatonism and Jewish Thought*, ed. L. E. Goodman (New York: SUNY, 1992), 21–42; R. Bauckham, "Moses as God: A Precedent for Christology?" in *The Spirit of Christ in the New Testament and Theology. Essays in Honour of Max Turner*, ed. I. H. Marshall, V. Rabens, and C. Bennema (Grand Rapids: Eerdmans, 2012), 246–65.

35

Bibliographies on Philo

David T. Runia

It may seem unusual to devote a final chapter of this volume to an account of bibliographical studies on Philo. But it can hardly be denied that such studies form an essential aspect of the reception of his life and thought. Everything that we know about the Alexandrian has reached us via the written word. First his writings were preserved and transmitted to later generations. Then in the nearly twenty centuries since his death, but especially in the last two centuries, a massive amount of scholarship has been produced on those writings and other sources of information about him. It has been the task of bibliographers to keep track of this literature and organize it so that all those who wish to know about Philo and study his works can find their way. The aim of this chapter is to give an overview of bibliographical work that has been carried out on Philo from its beginnings in the ancient world up to the present day.

35.1 Ancient Beginnings

During the course of his career as a writer Philo produced at least seventy-five treatises and about two-thirds of them survived.[1] Scholars have plausibly assumed that he had a library where he kept copies of his writings together with other literature which he used for study and for composing his works.[2] This library must have played a role in the survival of his writings, though we have no idea how this occurred. Two centuries later copies of most of Philo's works had found their way to the Episcopal Library of Caesarea Maritima, where a catalog was drawn up by Pamphilus, priest of the Church of Caesarea, later continued by his adopted son Eusebius.[3] This catalog of the holdings of the Library was the basis for what might be called the first Philonic bibliography.

---

[1] For Philo's lost treatises, see my list in D. T. Runia, *SPhiloA* 4 (1992): 78–79.

[2] See G. E. Sterling, "'The School of Sacred Laws': The Social Setting of Philo's Treatises," *VC* 53 (1999): 148–64; D. Lincicum, "Philo's Library," *SPhiloA* 26 (2014): 99–114.

[3] For the catalog, see Eusebius, *Hist. eccl.* 6.32.3 (using the term *pinakes*, "lists"); see further A. J. Carriker, *The Library of Eusebius of Caesarea*, VCSup 67 (Leiden: Brill, 2003), 1–25; A. Grafton and M. Williams, *Christianity and the Transformation of the Book: Origen, Eusebius, and the Library of Caesarea* (Cambridge, MA: Harvard

Early in the fourth century Eusebius began to write his *Ecclesiastical History*.[4] In book 2 he refers to Philo and uses his evidence when describing the very beginnings of the Christian church. Appended to this account is a section on Philo himself, described as being "copious in his speech and wide-ranging in his thoughts, sublime and elevated in his studies on the divine scriptures."[5] He then proceeds to give a detailed list of Philo's writings, as he will later do for the early Christian writers who occur in his narrative. An examination of the list shows that Eusebius has taken the trouble to impose order on the collection of works that he knew about.[6] He observes that most of Philo's writings are focused on the text of the Pentateuch, so he first lists the works on Genesis, followed by those on Exodus, and the remaining "single works," which include the philosophical treatises and other historical-apologetic writings. The list is not structured in the way that we now organize the Philonic corpus. Eusebius did not recognize the division into the three main biblical commentaries. But it gives enough detail to justify the conclusion that the main survival route for Philo's writings was their presence in the library of Caesarea. Through Eusebius' account bibliographical labors on Philo got off to an early and promising start.

About a century after Eusebius first wrote his *History*, the presbyter Rufinus produced a Latin translation as part of his project to make significant writings of the Greek church fathers accessible to a western audience.[7] This work had a broad dissemination in the west during the medieval period.[8] The chapter on Philo's writings was part of that translation and so, through Rufinus' work, readers could have the benefit of Eusebius' account of Philo's writings, though there is little evidence that the list of writings was studied. After all, most of the works to which it refers were not available to Latin readers.

A little earlier than Rufinus, Jerome had also made use of Eusebius' labors when writing the brief biographical sketch of Philo as part of his work *De viris illustribus*.[9] Proceeding more systematically than Eusebius, Jerome includes details about literary activity where known in his treatment of all 135 famous men, and Philo is no exception. His list of over thirty works is clearly taken over from Eusebius, and not without errors.[10] When he writes at the end of his lists that "there are also many other memorials to his [Philo's] ability which have not come into our hands," this is probably meant to give the impression that he had seen all the writings in his list, which can hardly have

---

University Press, 2006). On the transmission of Philo's writings in general, see D. T. Runia, *Philo in Early Christian Literature: A Survey*, CRINT III.3 (Assen: Van Gorcum, 1993), 16–31.

[4] On Eusebius' reception of Philo, see Sabrina Inowlocki, Chapter 9 in this volume.

[5] *Hist. eccl.* 2.18.

[6] On this list, see D. T. Runia, "Caesarea Maritima and the Survival of Hellenistic-Jewish Literature," in *Caesarea Maritima: A Retrospective after Two Millenia*, ed. A. Raban and K. G. Holum, Documenta et Monumenta Orientis Antiqui 21 (Leiden: Brill, 1996), 476–95; Carriker, *The Library of Eusebius*, 164–77; J. Otto, *Philo of Alexandria and the Construction of Jewishness in Early Christian Writings*, OECS (Oxford: Oxford University Press, 2018), 175–81.

[7] Printed with the same numbering beside Eusebius' Greek text in Eusebius Pamphili, *Eusebius Werke: 2. Kirchengeschichte*, ed. E. Schwartz, T. Mommsen, F. Winkelmann, GCS N.F. 6.1–3 (Berlin: Akademie Verlag, 1999 [1st edn, 1903–9]). For the date after 402 CE, see Mommsen in vol. 3, p. ccli.

[8] On Philo in the Latin west, see David Runia and Frans van Liere, Chapter 21 in this volume.

[9] *De vir. ill.* 11. Text in A. Ceresa-Gastaldo, *Gerolamo Gli Uomini Illustri*, Biblioteca Patristica 12 (Florence: EDB, 1988), 96–99. On Jerome, see Matthew Kraus, Chapter 14 in this volume. Philo is among only three non-Christians in the work. The other two are Seneca and Josephus.

[10] For a brief discussion of this list, see Runia, "Caesarea Maritima," 482–84.

574   THE RECEPTION OF PHILO OF ALEXANDRIA

been the case.[11] Jerome's work was widely distributed in the medieval west, but his list too does not appear to have received much attention.

Some time after the publication of Jerome's work a Greek translation was made, attributed pseudonymously to Jerome's companion, Sophronius of Bethlehem.[12] This translation forms the basis of the list of Philo's works in the massive Byzantine encyclopedia, the *Souda*, to be dated to about 1000 CE but compiled from earlier writings.[13] About a century earlier the patriarch Photius compiled his celebrated *Bibliotheca*. This work might be regarded as a kind of predecessor of an annotated bibliography. But the section on Philo mentions and makes brief comments on only a small selection of Philo's writings.[14] The chapter on Philo in the *Sententious notes* of Theodore Metochites (1270–1332) remarks that Philo was a prolific writer, but does not include any bibliographical information.[15] The information available on Philo during the Byzantine period thus seems not to have increased beyond the few patristic texts discussed above.

35.2 Early Modern Bibliographical Labors

In the age of printed books, commencing with the Gutenberg Bible in 1455, Philo's writings got off to a very slow start. It was not until 1552, nearly a century later, that the first edition of his Greek treatises by Adrian Turnebus saw the light of day.[16] After this there was a flurry of activity, including various Latin translations, all of which was distilled in the major edition of Philo's *Opera omnia*, first published in 1613, with further editions in 1640, 1691, and 1729.[17] On this textual basis Philonic scholarship gradually expanded, so that in the course of time it could be collected together and become the object of bibliographical labors.

As a first milestone, though it is not a bibliography proper, we might take the *Bibliotheca Graeca* of the astonishing German polymath Johann Albertus Fabricius (1668–1734). Published in fourteen volumes from 1705 to 1728, it exhaustively covers all known scholarship on classical authors up to that time. The section on Philo

---

[11] This statement has often drawn sharp criticism, e.g. in J. N. D. Kelly, *Jerome: His Life, Writings, and Controversies* (London: Duckworth, 1975), 177. But a kinder interpretation is also possible; see Runia, "Caesarea Maritima," 484.

[12] Text in O. von Gebhardt, *Hieronymus. Liber de viris inlustribus in griechischer Übersetzung (der sogenannte Sophronius)*, TU 14.1b (Leipzig: J. C. Hinrichs, 1896), 14–16; also in C-W 1.CI–CII.

[13] Text in A. Adler, ed., *Suidae Lexicon*, 5 vols (Leipzig: Teubner, 1928–38), Φ 448; on Byzantium, see also David Runia, Chapter 20 in this volume.

[14] *Bibl.* 103–5. See further discussion in Chapter 20 in this volume (pp. 336–38).

[15] Ch. 16. See further discussion in Chapter 20 in this volume (pp. 342–43).

[16] Adrianus Turnebus, *Philonis Iudaei in libros Mosis, de mundi opificio, historicos, de legibus; eiusdem libri singulares* (Paris, 1552). This work is no. 398 in the bibliography of Goodhart and Goodenough (G-G), to be introduced in the following section; for full details, see n. 39 below. On this edition, see the study of G. E. Sterling, "The First Critical Edition of Philo," *SPhiloA* 33 (2021): 133–60. On the very limited number of Philonic texts published before Turnebus, see chapter 22, pp. 367–69.

[17] Adrianus Turnebus, David Hoeschel, and Sigismundus Gelenius, Φίλωνος Ἰουδαίου ἐξηγητικὰ συγγράμματα. *Philonis Iudaei opera ...* (Geneva, 1613) (G-G 398). Subsequent editions published in Paris (1640, G-G 402), Frankfurt-an-der-Oder (1691, G-G 402a, 1729 not in G-G). On these so-called Vulgate editions, see D. T. Runia, "When the Old and the New Overlap: The 1729 Edition of Philo's *Opera omnia*" (forthcoming). See Chapter 22 in this volume on early printed editions.

Judaeus is found in vol. 4 published in 1717.[18] It describes Philo's life and times, gives a catalog of his works, lists the editions and translations of the corpus, and distinguishes him from other ancient authors with the same name. Numerous compactly formulated references to scholarship are interspersed with this information. What is missing is a discussion of Philo's thought, a subject which Fabricius had investigated in his early dissertation of 1693. A revised version of the work, edited by Gottlieb Christophorus Harles (1738–1815) and published in 1795, considerably expands the account and adds references to theological and philosophical discussions.[19]

In the nineteenth century classical and biblical studies continued to progress, and it was in Germany, with its great tradition of *Altertumswissenschaft*, where the most impressive bibliographical activity took place. As an example we might mention the *Bibliotheca scriptorum classicorum et Graecorum et Latinorum* published by the Leipzig publisher Wilhelm Engelmann (1808–78).[20] This work commences its references with the year 1700 and was deliberately planned as a continuation of Fabricius' work, but giving bibliographical references only, with the authors listed in alphabetical order. In the 6th edition published in 1847 only a page is devoted to Philo. By the time of the 7th edition of 1878 edited by Emil Preuss (b. 1845), this had expanded to three pages, while in the 8th edition in 1911 by Rudolf Klussmann (1846–1925) it had become six pages. This bibliographical work was compiled from the viewpoint of classical studies, so focused on only part of Philo's legacy, with most attention paid to textual and interpretative studies.

With the rise of the *Wissenschaft des Judentums* in Germany there was scope for bibliographical works specifically treating Jewish authors. Among such works pride of place should be given to the *Bibliotheca Judaica* of the distinguished scholar of Judaism, Julius Fürst (1805–73), published in three volumes by the same firm of Wilhelm Engelmann.[21] As the subtitle indicates, this work aimed to be a bibliographical handbook of the whole of Jewish literature and related studies, presented in alphabetical order of authors. A section of seven pages is devoted to Philo,[22] first presenting a thorough list of all texts and translations of his works, including translations into Hebrew, followed by three pages of studies from the seventeenth century onwards. In the same final volume Fürst included an exhaustive account of the history of Jewish bibliography, but under this title he does not include any references to Hellenistic Judaism.[23]

---

[18] J. A. Fabricius, *Bibliotheca Graeca*, 14 vols (Hamburg, 1714–28); on Philo, vol. 4 (1717), 104–22 (G-G 566). This account was added to the 1729 edition of Philo's works; see my article cited in the previous note.

[19] Revised edition by G. C. Harles (Leipzig 1790–1812); on Philo (1795), 4:721–50. This edition was reprinted by Georg Olms, Hildesheim, in 1966.

[20] *Bibliotheca scriptorum classicorum et graecorum et latinorum. Alphabetisches Verzeichniss der Ausgaben, Uebersetzungen und Erläuterungsschriften der griechischen und lateinischen Schriftsteller, welche vom Jahre 1700 bis zu Ende des Jahres 1846 besonders in Deutschland gedruckt worden sind* (Leipzig: Wilhelm Engelmann, 1847). We have not had access to earlier editions.

[21] J. Fürst, *Bibliotheca Judaica. Bibliographisches Handbuch der gesammten jüdischen Literatur mit Einschluss der Schriften über Juden und Judenthum und einer Geschichte der jüdischen Bibliographie. Nach alfabetischer Ordnung der Verfasser*, 3 vols (Leipzig: Wilhelm Engelmann, 1849–63).

[22] Fürst, *Bibliotheca Judaica*, 3:87–94 (G-G 528).

[23] Fürst, *Bibliotheca Judaica*, 3:ix–civ.

The culmination of the nineteenth-century German-language handbook literature on what is now called Second Temple Judaism is without doubt the work of the Protestant theologian Emil Schürer (1844–1910).[24] The first two volumes treat the general history and culture of the Jewish people during this period. Volume 3 presents first the Palestinian-Jewish literature (§32), followed by the Hellenistic-Jewish literature (§33). Philo then has the distinction of taking up an entire section on his own (§34).[25] This section is divided into two parts, the former and more extensive on Philo's writings, with each treatise separately discussed, the latter on his doctrine. Both parts are preceded by bibliographical lists of relevant literature, augmented by copious further references in the footnotes to the text. This work thus provides a well-rounded picture of Philonic studies at the end of the nineteenth century, with the proviso that there is clear bias towards scholarship in the German language, which admittedly was the dominant force at that time. Remarkably the work was translated into English and republished in 1973–89.[26] It was of course thoroughly updated, also in bibliographical terms, but the very fact of its republication is a clear indication of the excellence of the original work.

Appearing in 1908, almost simultaneously with the last volume of Schürer's revised Handbook, Émile Bréhier's monograph on Philo's philosophical and religious ideas exerted a strong influence on Philonic scholarship far beyond the French linguistic area. It contains at the beginning of the work a well-compiled list of manuscripts and editions and a bibliography divided into seven categories ranging from general studies to studies on the relation between Philo and Christianity.[27] This serviceable bibliography was not, however, updated in subsequent editions of the work.[28] Almost two decades later in 1926 the French Latinist Jules Marouzeau (1878–1964) founded the bibliographical research tool for classical scholars *L'Année philologique* publishing in the following year an overview of the years 1914 to 1924.[29] It contains a page of items on Philo, so almost joining up with the bibliography in Bréhier's monograph.[30] The repertory has continued ever since and remains a valuable instrument for Philonists, giving references to items that relate to classical studies, including ancient history.[31] A similar

---

[24] E. Schürer, *Geschichte des jüdischen Volkes im Zeitalter Jesu Christi*, 4th edn, 3 vols in 4 (Leipzig: J. C. Hinrichs, 1901–9). The first edition in a single volume, entitled *Lehrbuch der neutestamentlichen Zeitgeschichte* (Leipzig: J. C. Hinrichs, 1874) had a much shorter section (§32) on Philo.

[25] E. Schürer, *Geschichte des jüdischen Volkes*, 3:633–716 (G-G 593).

[26] E. Schürer, G. Vermes, F. Millar, and M. Black, *The History of the Jewish People in the Age of Jesus Christ (175 B.C.–A.D. 135)*, 3 in 4 vols (Edinburgh: T. & T. Clark, 1973–87). The section on Philo was updated by J. Morris, 3.2:809–99. An earlier English translation of the 2nd edition of the German work was published by the same Edinburgh firm in 1890–93.

[27] É. Bréhier, *Les idées philosophiques et religieuses de Philon d'Alexandrie*, Études de philosophie médiévale 8 (Paris: Vrin, 1908), virtually unaltered reprints 1925, 1950 (G-G 626).

[28] The only items added are some items from 1909 to 1912, including Bréhier's French translation of the *Legum allegoriae*.

[29] J. Marouzeau, *Dix années de bibliographie classique: bibliographie critique et analytique de l'antiquité greco-latine pour la période 1914–24*, Vol. 1: *Auteurs et Textes* (Paris: Les belles lettres, 1927), 276–77 (G-G 540).

[30] The years 1896–1914 were subsequently covered in the additional volume by S. Lambrino, *Bibliographie de l'antiquité classique, 1896–1914* (Paris: Les belles lettres, 1951), 441–42.

[31] From 2014 onwards it has been available online. The database is made available to libraries by Brepols Publishers.

repertory, *Elenchus bibliographicus biblicus*, was commenced for biblical studies in 1920. It too contained regular listings of publications on Philo.[32]

35.3 The Bibliography of Goodhart and Goodenough

In 1938 a landmark in bibliographical studies on Philo saw the light of day. Few ancient authors, if any, have been blessed with such a comprehensive bibliography. It was the product of the collaboration between two men, the one a bibliophile and amateur scholar, the other an academic at one of the great American universities. Howard Lehman Goodhart (1884–1951) was born in New York into a prominent Jewish banking family.[33] He studied first at Yale, graduating in 1905, then during a year abroad in Berlin and Amsterdam, thereafter joining his father's Wall Street firm. Business appears to have flourished, for in 1925 he retired, allowing him to devote his time to his passion of book-collecting. Goodhart amassed two major collections, one of incunabula, shared with his daughter Phyllis Goodhart Gordan,[34] the other of Philonica. For the latter he collected all the books of and about Philo that he could find.

Erwin Ramsdell Goodenough (1893–1965) was also born in New York, but had a very different background, growing up in a devout Methodist family.[35] After a somewhat chequered career in various theological institutions and universities and brief stints as a minister, he was offered in 1923 the position of Instructor at Yale University, where he rose to the position of Professor of the History of Religion by 1934. The following year he published his chief work on Philo, the celebrated, if controversial, *By Light, Light: The Mystic Gospel of Hellenistic Judaism*.[36] Writing in 1951 just before Goodhart's death, he described their collaboration as follows:[37]

> Fifteen years ago began one of the most pleasant experiences I have ever had, for at that time I came to know Howard L. Goodhart, '05, and to coöperate in a project of great meaning to both of us. It appeared that he had for some years been "collecting Philo Judaeus." This meant to him at first buying all the fifteenth-century books in which Philo was mentioned, as well as all the early editions of Philo's writing. Then he had bought a number of "secondary works" on Philo, as well as later editions and translations. From this he had gone on to consider publishing a catalogue of his collection. It was at this stage that I came to know him and to work with him.... As Mr Goodhart and I came to influence each other, he taught me to appreciate the beauty

---

[32] G-G 545. Published in Rome as part of the journal *Biblica*.

[33] For details of Goodhart's life, see the obituary in the *New York Times*, August 11, 1951.

[34] Now in the special collections of the Bryn Mawr College Library in Philadelphia. There are virtually no incunabula of relevance to Philo, so there was little overlap between the two collections.

[35] On the life and writings of Goodenough, see R. S. Eccles, *Erwin Ramsdell Goodenough: A Personal Pilgrimage*, Society of Biblical Literature: Biblical Scholarship in America (Chico, CA: Scholars Press, 1985).

[36] E. R. Goodenough, *By Light, Light: The Mystic Gospel of Hellenistic Judaism* (New Haven: Yale University Press, 1935; reprinted Amsterdam: Philo Press, 1969).

[37] E. R. Goodenough, "A Collection of Philo Judaeus," *Yale University Library Gazette* 25 (1951): 155.

of early printing, and I made him see the value for scholarly use of as complete as possible a collection of the editions of Philo, and of the literature about him. [He was] stimulated ... to greater activity, so that he ... bought Philo items of all sorts and had articles in periodicals photostated,[38] until he had made by far the best assembly in existence of material for research in Philo.

The result of this mutual encouragement and collaboration was "A General Bibliography of Philo Judaeus," published by Yale University Press in 1938.[39]

Consisting of no less than 1,603 items, the bibliography is remarkably complete. In the preface the authors note that completeness was one of the chief aims, but that did not mean that it should include all incidental references to Philo in popular works. On the other hand, a "Philo item" is not always obvious from the title of a study, so knowledge of the field is required. This dilemma faces all bibliographers of Philo, given the broad scope of his contributions to so many differing fields. The two authors were certainly very thorough in their survey, and the number of items of any importance that escaped their notice is likely to be very small.

Unusually for a bibliography of an ancient author, the first section with 386 items lists all the known manuscripts of Philo's writings in Greek, Latin, and Armenian. The list of Greek manuscripts, divided into fourteen groups, contains not only those with complete treatises of Philo (consisting of twenty-three families based on Cohn-Wendland's edition), but also those many catenae and florilegia in which Philonic fragments occur, as well manuscripts of authors such as Eusebius and Procopius in which important Philonic material is present. For the first category they indicate the treatises that are present in each case, for the remaining two categories the contents are less fully described. There is no doubt that the catalog contains many errors and imperfections,[40] and after eighty years there will be quite a number of additions that could be made. It would certainly benefit from being updated or even redone. But for the present it still remains the best available.

The second section, with 130 items, lists all the editions of Philo's works extant in Greek, followed by translations, first into Latin and Armenian, and then into ten modern languages. Next there are two sections with 30 and 118 items respectively which contain bibliographies and general studies on Philo, of which I have made good use in my discussion above of the period preceding the authors' work. Hereafter the rest of the bibliography is divided into twenty-eight sections which cover all the various

---

[38] This is a reference to use of the photostat process. This machine was invented in 1907 by Oscar T. Gregory. Each copy took two minutes to produce through a photographic process which resulted in a negative, i.e. white on black, copy. Too costly for general use, by the 1950s it was overtaken by the invention of the process of xerography, though the term "photostat" is still often used.

[39] H. L. Goodhart and E. R. Goodenough, "A General Bibliography of Philo Judaeus," in E. R. Goodenough, *The Politics of Philo Judaeus: Practice and Theory* (New Haven: Yale University Press 1938), 125–321. The chronology that Goodenough gives in the quotation cited above may be doubted. The date of completion of the bibliography is given as September 1937 (p. 128). The process which he describes must have taken a number of years at the least (unless he exaggerates his own influence).

[40] As the leading contemporary expert on Philonic manuscripts, James Royse, informs me.

themes, general and more particular, which relate to Philo's historical and intellectual context and his own thought, all items being ordered on the basis of their date of publication.[41] In the Preface the authors admit that this arrangement has arbitrary elements, and they include numerous cross-references in order to guide the user further. The bibliography's major defect is that it does not have a subject index, only an index of manuscripts and of authors, so this relatively granular division of topics is what readers need to rely on in order to find what they are looking for. Of particular note is §30, Philo in Later Christian Tradition, which provided a guide to the references to Philo in authors from the second century up to the Reformation.[42] The following §31, Mention of Philo in Printed Books of the Fifteenth Century (seventy-two items), falls outside the scope of the bibliography proper and is evidently based on the collection of incunabula that Goodhart and his daughter had acquired. Two further features of the bibliography that should not be overlooked are that it notes the many reprintings of the books that it lists, and that it has also assembled all the book reviews of major items from the nineteenth century onwards.[43]

Throughout the bibliography two markers are used. All items marked with an asterisk (*) were present in Goodhart's collection of works of and on Philo. Of those marked with a dagger (†) he was in possession of a photostat copy. The extent of his collection can be gauged from the following statistics: 385 items are listed with an asterisk and another 168 with a dagger, amounting to 553 items in total. If we exclude the items in the bibliography which could not be collected, the total is about 1,072.[44] This means that Goodhart's collection embraced more than half of all the items that the bibliography contained, and of course well over half the items that were most important for the study of Philo. It was without doubt the most extensive private collection of Philonica ever assembled.

In the Preface the two bibliographers stated that they "would try to keep the Bibliography growing through the years," but this did not happen. No addenda were ever published. Goodhart died in August 1951. But he had made provisions for the preservation of significant parts of his collection. In a brief article written by Goodenough in the year of Goodhart's death we learn that "during the autumn of 1950 … he transferred to Yale those many items of his Philo collection which Yale did not already have, with the result that the combined collections have made the [Yale Sterling] Library permanently the best place in the world for research in Philo."[45]

---

[41] The sections are listed in the table of contents on pp. 129–30.
[42] This provided a valuable starting-point for the author when commencing his work on Philo in the Christian tradition; see above n. 3.
[43] Sometimes indicating the source for more esoteric items which they had probably not seen.
[44] Excluded are §1 (manuscripts), §§30 and 31 (described in the text above), and most of §33 (Pseudo-Philonic writings). The total number is approximate and does not include additional items placed at the end of sections (numbers with letters, e.g. 664a).
[45] Goodenough, "A Collection," 156. The gift did not include the incunabula bequeathed to his daughter; see above n. 34. The copy of the *editio princeps* of Philo by A. Turnebus now in the Bryn Mawr Library no doubt belonged to Goodhart. Yale already had a copy donated by the class of 1877. One would like to know what happened to his copy of the 1613 Geneva edition of Philo's works, which was "bound for Louis XIII [of France] and bearing his rare coat of arms," mentioned by Goodenough in *The Politics of Philo Judaeus* (above n. 39), 121 n. 1. It is not in Yale or Bryn Mawr.

Fig. 35.1 The personal bookplate of Howard Lehman Goodhart with the Dutch motto "Beidt uw tijd" (Bide your time). Located on the flyleaf of the 1691 edition of Philo's *opera omnia* in the Beinecke Library, Yale University, New Haven, United States. Image by David T. Runia. On this edition see also chapter 22, section 5.

Further information is supplied in an article by W. V. Jackson in an article on library resources for classical studies in American university libraries. He notes that Goodhart's gift consisted of 228 volumes of monographs, eighty-six volumes of periodicals and twenty-seven volumes of photostats.[46] At the present time rarer items of the benefaction are housed in the Yale Beinecke Rare Book & Manuscript Library, some with Goodhart's personal bookplate or with recognition that they are gifts from his library (see Figs 35.1–2).[47] The remainder have been interspersed in the Sterling Library's collections, including the bound collections of pamphlets and photostats.[48] They remain available for scholarly consultation.

35.4 Continuations: Feldman, Hilgert, Radice, and Runia

From 1937 onwards Philonic scholars can no longer rely on Goodhart and Goodenough's bibliography for a complete listing of studies on Philo. For the period up to 1986, i.e. the next fifty years, three bibliographies deserve mention. Each of these portray themselves as a continuation of the earlier work.

The first of these, published in 1963, is Louis Feldman's *Scholarship on Philo and Josephus (1937–1962)*.[49] Strictly speaking, it falls outside the scope of this article, since

---

[46] W. V. Jackson, "Library Resources for Classical Studies," *College and Research Libraries* (1959): 466.
[47] The book plate is from the copy of Philo's 1691 *opera omnia* (G-G 402a). The motto is in Dutch and means "bide your time," an appropriate aphorism for a collector of rare books.
[48] Based on the author's personal experience while a Visiting Professor at the Yale Divinity School in 2018.
[49] Studies in Judaica 1 (New York, n.d. but published in 1963). The contents had largely appeared in four installments in *Classical World* in 1961–62, but was updated for this separate publication.

Fig. 35.2 Bookplate of the Yale University Library in the same volume, indicating that it was a gift from the Library of Howard Lehman Goodhart. Beinecke Library, image David T. Runia.

it is presented as a critical bibliography and does indeed include critiques of many of the items it contains, usually attached to a summary of their contents. Since, however, it aims to be a complete account of scholarship during the stated period, it should be briefly mentioned. The unnumbered bibliography is organized by means of a well devised subdivision into twenty-two sections, beginning with editions and translations and ending with an interesting section on desiderata for the study of Philo. A separate section at the beginning discusses bibliographical sources of information. The debt to *L'Année philologique* is stated at the outset. But the author, one of the foremost twentieth-century scholars of ancient Judaism,[50] is particularly keen to ensure that a full account of the Jewish side of Philonic scholarship is included, including journal articles written in Hebrew, which were starting to appear during this period.

The next work, "Bibliographia Philoniana 1935–1981," compiled by the American New Testament scholar and Philonist Earle Hilgert was published in 1984 in a volume dedicated to Philo in the German book series Aufstieg und Niedergang der römischen

---

[50] On Feldman (1926–2017), see the obituary in *Yeshiva University News*, March 27, 2017. Though trained as a classicist and specializing in Hellenistic Judaism, Feldman was thoroughly versed in the many traditions of Second Temple and Rabbinic Judaism.

Welt.[51] It was partly based on yearly bibliographies that he had compiled for the journal *Studia Philonica*, published by the Philo Institute in Chicago.[52] Comprising a little under 1,100 items, the bibliography basically follows the method of Goodhart and Goodenough, except that its items are not numbered and it does not include book reviews. It is very comprehensive and well organized. The division into twenty-one sections is closer to Feldman than the more detailed division of Goodhart and Goodenough. Hilgert's theological background can perhaps be seen in the separate sections on the Old Testament and the New Testament. An impressive aspect of this bibliography is its completeness. It eschews any linguistic restrictions and contains many items in less well-known languages, sensibly citing such items in the original with an English translation in brackets. The number of items in Hebrew is particularly striking. Its one defect is the lack of indices.[53]

The third bibliography was produced by the Italian scholar Roberto Radice and published in Italian in 1983.[54] It covers the years 1937 to 1982, with an Appendix on current research at the time of publication. Like Feldman and Hilgert, Radice takes as his point of departure the bibliography of Goodhart and Goodenough. In his Introduction he acknowledges the assistance that he received from both compilations, as well as two other works.[55] In comparison with his predecessors, Radice made two important innovations. He divided the mass of material into two parts. The first focused on Philo's actual writings, grouping together all bibliographical studies, editions, translations, commentaries, and lexica. The second contained all other "critical literature," i.e. secondary studies on Philo, listed per year of publication (and in alphabetical order within years). The second and more important innovation was that he provided a compact summary of every item, together with a list of reviews of monograph items. This gave the user a brief indication of their contents, without giving a full critique as Feldman had done. Radice carried out his work with admirable thoroughness. The bibliography contains 1,118 items. It also includes excellent indices of texts, subjects, and both ancient and modern authors' names, allowing quick and efficient orientation for the user. Its chief disadvantage was hardly its own fault, namely the fact that it was written in Italian and so had limited impact on scholarship in other languages.

---

[51] E. Hilgert, "Bibliographia Philoniana 1935–1981," in *Hellenistisches Judentum in römischer Zeit: Philon und Josephus*, ed. W. Haase, ANRW II 21.1 (Berlin: de Gruyter, 1984), 47–97. On its author (1923–2020), see C. S. Dudley and M. M. Mitchell, "Earle Hilgert: Scholar, Teacher, Librarian, Administrator and Colleague," in *Heirs of the Septuagint. Philo, Hellenistic Judaism and Early Christianity: Festschrift for Earle Hilgert*, ed. D. T. Runia, D. M. Hay, and D. Winston, BJS 230 [= SPhiloA 3 (1991)] (Atlanta: Scholars Press, 1991), 11–17.

[52] Vols 1–6 (1971–80). Hilgert's bibliographies cover the years 1963–78. On the Institute and its journal, see E. Hilgert, "The Philo Institute, *Studia Philonica* and Their *Diadochoi*," in *In the Spirit of Faith: Studies in Philo and Early Christianity in Honor of David Hay*, ed. D. T. Runia and G. E. Sterling [= SPhiloA 13 (2001)], BJS 332 (Providence, RI, 2001), 13–24.

[53] Perhaps these were not permissible in the format of an article within an edited volume of a larger series.

[54] R. Radice, *Filone di Alessandria: bibliografia generale 1937–1982*, Elenchos: Collana di testi e studi sul pensiero antico 8 (Naples: Bibliopolis, 1983). Radice (1947–), a prolific scholar specializing in ancient philosophy, has spent his entire career at the Catholic University of Milan. He retired from the chair of ancient philosophy in 2017.

[55] G. Delling, *Bibliographie zur jüdisch-hellenistischen und intertestamentarischen Literatur 1900–1970*, TUGAL 106/2 (Berlin: Akademie-Verlag, 1975), esp. 56–80 on Philo; A. V. Nazzaro, *Recenti Studi Filoniani (1963–70)* (Naples: Loffredo Editore, 1971).

35.5 The International Philo Bibliography Project

In compiling his bibliography Radice had received valuable assistance from the great French Philonist Valentin Nikiprowetzky.[56] Before his untimely death Nikiprowetzky had also been in contact with the Dutch-Australian scholar David Runia (author of the present article), whom he introduced to Radice. In discussions between the two younger scholars the suggestion arose that they could produce together an updated English version of the Italian bibliography. This work, covering exactly a half century of Philonic scholarship from 1937 to 1986, was published in 1988.[57] Its method closely follows that of Radice's bibliography, consisting of the same two parts together with comprehensive indices. The practice of including summaries of all items and reviews of monographs was also continued. Importantly, the coverage was expanded, with works written in Hebrew and Dutch added with the assistance of a team of Israeli and Dutch scholars.[58] The main innovation of this new version, apart from the increased coverage, was that the items in the second part were numbered per year, using an ingenious numbering system.[59] This meant that the year of publication could be immediately deduced from the item's number. In total this bibliography contained 1,666 items, considerably more than the 1,072 of Goodhart and Goodenough[60] and the 1,118 of Radice's Italian work. This is an indication of the remarkable increase in Philonic scholarship during the fifty years of coverage. The Introduction to the bibliography presents some "Brief observations on fifty years of Philonic scholarship," which give an analysis of the 1,666 studies in terms of quantity, language and subject matter, both as a whole and in terms of figures per decade.[61]

In the meantime, during the 1980s, the journal *Studia Philonica* had lapsed. In 1989 it was restarted with the new title the *Studia Philonica Annual* under the editorship of David Runia.[62] In the first volume a bibliography for 1981–86 was published as a continuation of Hilgert's work in the ANRW volume. It was basically a reprint of information already available in the 1988 bibliography of Radice and Runia, but without the summaries. The following year, in vol. 2, a supplementary list of items for 1986 was published, followed by a list of all publications in 1987. Now the items were again accompanied by summaries prepared by the compilers. New was the additional Supplement, containing a provisional bibliography of studies published in 1988–90. The 1990 bibliography set the scene for annual bibliographies which have appeared in

---

[56] On Nikiprowetzky (1922–83), see A. Caquot, M. Hadas-Lebel, and J. Riaud, eds, *Hellenica et Judaica: hommage à Valentin Nikiprowetzy* (Leuven: Peeters, 1986), esp. the "In memoriam" by the first two editors on pp. 1–9.

[57] R. Radice and D. T. Runia, *Philo of Alexandria: An Annotated Bibliography 1937–1986*, VCSup 8 (Leiden: Brill, 1988) (abbreviated R-R). A lightly revised 2nd edition appeared in 1992. The translation from Italian was carried out by Anthony P. Runia (Groningen).

[58] Team members were Rudolf Bitter, Naomi Cohen, Michael Mach, David Satran, and Daniel Schwartz.

[59] E.g. the studies in 1937 were numbered from 3701 (S. Belkin) to 3717 (M. Stein), etc.

[60] On this number, see above n. 44.

[61] Radice and Runia, *Philo of Alexandria*, xxiii–xxix.

[62] Vols 1–35, 1989–2022 (latest volume); from vol. 11 (1999) under joint editorship with Gregory E. Sterling.

the *Studia Philonica Annual* up to the present time. Each year the studies are collected for the year preceding the journal's publication by three years, together with a supplementary bibliography up to the year of publication. The latest bibliography published in 2023 thus covers the year 2020, together with a supplementary section for the years 2021–23.

At first these bibliographies were produced by Radice, Runia, and Satran, who had been the key figures for the 1937–88 bibliography published in 1988. In 1995 David Runia took the initiative to establish The International Philo Bibliography Project (IPBP), gathering together an international team of scholars who have worked together to produce the yearly bibliographies ever since then. All told, twenty-six scholars have participated in the thirty-four bibliographies from 1990 to 2023.[63] For these bibliographies all language restrictions have been lifted, so they contain items in languages such as Portuguese, Swedish, Norwegian, Danish, Polish, Russian, Chinese, Korean, and so on. However, the coverage of scholarship in all these languages is irregular and incomplete, since the team lacks all the information to collect it, not to speak of the linguistic expertise to process them adequately. The total number of items in these thirty-four annual bibliographies amounts to 3,876 publications, thus considerably more than in all the years up to 1986.[64]

During this period David Runia has also published three additional collected bibliographies as continuations of the 1988 collective volume. The first covered the years 1987–96, the second the years 1997–2006, the third the years 2007–16.[65] They are based on the annual bibliographies, but follow the format of the earlier volume by Radice and Runia. The items are thus divided into two parts, and book reviews for monographs are also included. There are also extensive indices, which are lacking in the annual bibliographies.

35.6 The Internet Revolution

During the period just described a highly significant event occurred which has radically changed the science and practice of bibliography. In 1989 Tim Berners-Lee

---

[63] They are: Marta Alesso (Argentina), Maureen Attali (Switzerland), Katell Berthelot (France), Ellen Birnbaum (USA), Anne Boiché (France), Paul Cathey (Germany), Kenneth Fox (Canada), Albert Geljon (The Netherlands), Heleen Keizer (Italy), Jutta Leonhardt-Balzer (UK/Germany), José Pablo Martín† (Argentina), Olivier Munnich (France), Maren Niehoff (Israel), Sarah Pearce (UK), Roberto Radice (Italy), Jean Riaud† (France), Justin Rogers (USA), David Runia (The Netherlands/Australia), Karl-Gustav Sandelin (Finland), David Satran (Israel), Gottfried Schimanowski (Germany), Torrey Seland (Norway), Bert Van den Berg (The Netherlands), Sharon Weisser (Belgium/Israel), Sami Yli-Karjanmaa (Finland), Dieter Zeller† (Germany).

[64] The most prolific year so far has been 2017, with 149 items (not including later addenda).

[65] D. T. Runia (with the assistance of H. M. Keizer), *Philo of Alexandria: An Annotated Bibliography 1987–1996 with Addenda for 1937–1986*, VCSup 57 (Leiden: Brill, 2000) (abbreviated RRS1); D. T. Runia, *Philo of Alexandria: An Annotated Bibliography 1997–2006 with Addenda for 1987–1996*, VCSup 109 (Leiden: Brill, 2012) (abbreviated RRS2); D. T. Runia, *Philo of Alexandria: An Annotated Bibliography 2007–2016 with Addenda for 1980–2006*, VCSup 174 (Leiden: Brill, 2022) (abbreviated RRS3). These bibliographies are slightly more complete than the yearly bibliographies, since the opportunity was taken to add items missing in the latter. They continue the numbering system of the earlier 1988 work. It should be noted that R-R, RRS1, and RRS2 are all available for free download on the Brill website.

invented the World Wide Web. Previous to this the internet was used mainly by the military and scientists, but from the end of the millennium onwards it started to supersede many kinds of communication that used to be the preserve of the printed word. The disruptive effect of this digital revolution on the newspaper and magazine industry is well known. Book publishing has also experienced its effects, but they have so far been much less drastic. Many scholarly publications are now published digitally. Books are now often available both in hard copy and as e-books, though hardly any in electronic form only.[66] The situation for journals differs. Not only are many journals distributed electronically, but quite a few are now published in electronic format only and made available via the internet. This has led to an increase in the number of journals, which are now much easier and cheaper to produce. The digital revolution has thus led to a greater proliferation of research. For bibliographers it is quite a challenge to keep track of these developments. Fortunately the internet itself offers various tools allowing bibliographers to cope with the new flood of material.

As an example we may take the French repertory *L'Année philologique* which, as we saw,[67] was founded in 1926. Although still available in a print edition published annually (with considerable delays), the main form in which this most valuable resource is consulted is now the online database, which contains the entire contents of the repertory from its beginnings nearly a century ago and can be searched by digital means.[68] In more general terms, the digital database has thus become an essential tool for the bibliographer. Various databases can be consulted for listings of publications on Philo and related subjects. Among these we can mention, in addition to the example just given, RAMBI (studies on Judaism), Academic Search, Philosopher's Index, Religion Index, Index Theologicus/Bildi, Worldcat (books only), Dissertation Abstracts, and numerous others.[69] All these databases, which we cannot possibly discuss in detail in the present context, can be used to locate publications on Philo. They have proved highly valuable in drawing up the annual lists of publications to be processed by the International Philo Bibliography Project.[70]

A difficulty is that the information on Philo is scattered across many different databases. This is inevitable because research on Philo extends across many scholarly subdomains, each of which may be best served by a particular electronic resource. Indeed it regularly occurs that the potential bibliographer is confronted with a surfeit of information, which becomes rather tedious to process. At present there is no online database which specializes in scholarly literature on Philo in particular.[71]

---

[66] It is particularly useful when texts are made available in digital form. The text of Philo's Greek works is available on the TLG database. The entire Loeb Classical Library, including the volumes on Philo, can now be consulted online. This is invaluable for searching and for consulting texts when traveling.

[67] See above text at n. 29.

[68] Now published by the publishing house Brepols (Turnhout, Belgium) and available via subscription.

[69] There is no need to give references. These databases can easily be located on the internet. Many are freely available. Some require subscriptions and can be consulted via libraries. Of these probably the most comprehensive is RAMBI, the database on Jewish studies produced at the Hebrew University of Jerusalem.

[70] Expertly searched for many years by Marten Hofstede (Leiden), a member of the Project team.

[71] In fact, online bibliographies specializing on individual figures from the ancient world are as yet uncommon.

But there is another development in the digital realm which can provide a valuable resource for scholars studying Philo. Specific bibliographies are being compiled which provide guides in electronic form for the study of particular authors or subjects. Prominent among such initiatives is the *Oxford Bibliographies Online*.[72] Very recently three prominent Philo scholars have produced such specialized bibliographies on Philo, from the viewpoints of biblical studies, Jewish studies, and classical studies respectively.[73] In each case the subject is divided into sub-sections, for which a limited number of references (usually eight) is selected. In addition, there are brief evaluative comments on each reference and an indication of how access can be obtained to them. These thus amount to curated critical "bibliographies raisonées" not dissimilar to that produced fifty years ago by Feldman,[74] but now using the resources of the internet, which has the advantage of enabling them to be easily updated at regular intervals. Many other bibliographies developed as part of the same resource touch on subjects that are relevant to Philonic studies.[75]

35.7 Conclusion

By consulting the bibliographical labors of Philonic scholars throughout the ages—starting with Eusebius in antiquity and going right through to the International Philo Bibliography Project at the present time—scholars and all others seeking to know about Philo and the scholarship produced about him have been very well served. Special mention should be made of the work of Goodhart and Goodenough, which covered early research up to the year 1937 with a thoroughness seldom matched for other ancient authors. When to their bibliography is added the subsequent ones of Radice and Runia and of the International Philo Bibliography Project, the result is a total number of well over 7,000 items, all of which have been collected, listed, organized, and—for those published since 1937—summarized.[76] Through the combined labors of many scholars, and also the generous facilitation provided by a number of publishers,[77] the bibliographical resources available for the study of Philo are more extensive than for virtually any other ancient author.

---

[72] Commercially available at www.oxfordbibliographies.com.
[73] D. T. Runia, "Philo of Alexandria (Subject Area: Biblical Studies)," in *Oxford Bibliographies Online* (Oxford: Oxford University Press, 2010, updated 2015); M. R. Niehoff, "Philo of Alexandria (Subject Area: Jewish Studies)," in *Oxford Bibliographies Online* (Oxford: Oxford University Press, 2014, updated 2015); G. E. Sterling, "Philo of Alexandria (Subject: Classics)," in *Oxford Bibliographies Online* (Oxford: Oxford University Press, 2015).
[74] See above text at n. 49.
[75] For more information, see the note in *SPhiloA* 27 (2015): 259.
[76] Based on G-G 1,072 items, R-R 1,118, additions to R-R 160, RRS1 953 + 40, RRS2 1,082 + 29, RRS3 1,217 = 6,219 in total, plus approximately 1050 published since 2016 (based on an average of about 150 items a year). Summaries are not yet available for items published after 2018.
[77] Notably the publishing houses of Brill (Leiden) and SBL Press (Atlanta).

Bibliography

Abbamonte, G., M. Laureys, and L. Miletti, eds. *I paratesti nelle edizioni a stampa dei classici greci e latini (XV–XVIII sec.)*. Pisa: Edizioni ETS, 2020.

ʿAbd al-Raḥmān Badawī, ed. *Ūrūsiyūs, Tārīkh al-ʿālam: al-tarjama al-ʿarabiyya al-qadīma*. Beirut: al-Muʾassasa al-ʿarabiyya li-l-dirāsāt wa-l-nashr, 1982.

Abeghyan, M. *History of Old Armenian Literature*, Book 1, *Collected Writings* 3. Erevan: Academy of Science of ArmSSR, 1968 (in Armenian).

Abrahamyan, A. G., ed. *The Works by Yovhannēs the Philosopher*. Erevan: Erevan State University Press, 1956 (in Armenian).

Abrams, D. "The Boundaries of Divine Ontology: The Inclusion and Exclusion of Metatron in the Godhead." *HTR* 87 (1994): 291–321.

Adelmann, D. *"Reinige dein Denken": Über den jüdischen Hintergrund der Philosophie von Hermann Cohen*. Aus dem Nachlass herausgegeben, ergänzt und mit einem einleitenden Vorwort versehen von G. K. Hasselhoff. Würzburg: Königshausen & Neumann, 2010.

Adkin, N. "Jerome on Ambrose: The Preface to the Translation of Origen's Homilies on Luke." *Revue Benedictine* 107 (1997): 5–14.

Adler, A., ed. *Suidae Lexicon*. 5 vols. Leipzig: Teubner, 1928–38.

Afterman, A. *"And They Shall Be One Flesh": On the Language of Mystical Union in Judaism*. Supplements to the Journal of Jewish Thought and Philosophy 26. Leiden: Brill, 2016.

Afterman, A. "From Philo to Plotinus: The Emergence of Mystical Union." *JR* 93 (2013): 177–96.

Akhiezr, G. *Historical Consciousness, Haskalah, and Nationalism among the Karaites of Eastern Europe*. Leiden: Brill, 2018.

Akinean, N. "Die theologische Schule von Bitlis." Pages 3–7 in *Handes Amsorya, Zeitschrift für Armenische Philologie*. Vienna: Mechitarist Order, 1951 (in Armenian).

Akinean, N. "Hellenists' School (572–603)." *Handes Amsorya (Monthly Magazine), Zeitschrift für Armenische Philologie* 5–6 (1932): 284–92 (in Armenian).

Akinean, N. *The School of Baghesh [Bitlis] 1500-1704. A Contribution to the History of Armenian Church and Literature*. Vienna: Mkhitarists' Press, 1952 (in Armenian).

Albeck, H. and J. Theodor, eds. *Midrash Bereshit Rabba: Critical Edition with Notes and Commentary*. Jerusalem: Wahrmann Books, 1965.

Albert, B.-S. "Adversus Iudaeos in the Carolingian Empire." Pages 119–42 in *Contra Iudaeos: Ancient and Medieval Polemics between Christians and Jews*. Edited by Ora Limor and Guy G. Stroumsa. Tübingen: Mohr Siebeck, 1996.

Albert, J. "Annotationum philologicarum in Novum Testamentum ex Philone Judaeo collectarum specimen." Pages 104–26 in *Museum Historico-Philologico-Theologicum* 1.1. Bremen: H. Jaeger, 1728.

Aldus Manutius. *The Greek Classics*. Edited and translated by N. G. Wilson. The Tatti Renaissance Library 70. Cambridge, MA: Harvard University Press, 2016.

Aleknienė, T. "L'extase mystique' dans la tradition platonicienne: Philon d'Alexandrie et Plotin." *SPhiloA* 22 (2010): 53–82; repr. as pages 203–45 in T. Aleknienė, *A l'approche du divin: Dialogues de Platon et tradition Platonicienne*. Vestigia 42. Fribourg: Academic Press, 2016.

Alesse, F., ed. *Philo of Alexandria and Post-Aristotelian Philosophy*. SPhA 5. Leiden: Brill, 2008.

Alexander, P. J. "A Neglected Palimpsest of Philo Judaeus: Preliminary Remarks *editorum in usum*." Pages 1–14 in *Studia Codicologica*. Edited by K. Treu. TU 124. Berlin: Akademie-Verlag, 1977.

Alexandre, Jr., M. "Philo of Alexandria and Hellenic *Paideia*." *Euphrosyne* 37 (2009): 121–30.

Alexandre, Monique. "Apologétique judéo-hellénistique et premières apologies chretiennes." Pages 1–40 in *Les apologistes chrétiens et la culture grecque*. Edited by B. Pouderon and J. Doré. Théologie historique 105. Paris: Beauchesne, 1998.

Alexandre, Monique. "Du grec au latin: les titres des oeuvres de Philon d'Alexandrie." Pages 255–86 in *Titres et articulations du texte dans les oeuvres antiques: actes du colloque international de Chantilly 13–15 Décembre 1994*. Edited by J.-Cl. Fredouille et al. Paris: Études augustiniennes, 1997.

Alexandre, Monique. "L'approche des vies d'écrivains dans l'Histoire Ecclésiastique." Pages 117–44 in *Vies anciennes d'auteurs grecs: mythe et biographie*. Edited by Ph. Brunet and M.-P. Noël. Tours: Université François Rabelais, 1998.

Alexandre, Monique. "La culture profane chez Philon." Pages 105–29 in *Philon d' Alexandrie*. Edited by R. Arnaldez, C. Mondésert, and J. Poilloux. Paris: Cerf, 1967.

Alexandre, Monique. "La théorie de l'exégèse dans le *De hominis opificio* et l'*In Hexaemeron*." Pages 87–110 in *Écriture et culture philosophique dans la pensée de Grégoire de Nysse*. Edited by M. Harl. Leiden: Brill, 1971.

Alkier, S. *Urchristentum: Zur Geschichte und Theologie einer exegetischen Disziplin*. BHT 83. Tübingen: Mohr Siebeck, 1993.

Alpers, J. *Hercules in bivio*. PhD diss. University of Göttingen, 1912.

Altaner, B. "Augustinus und Philo von Alexandrien: eine quellenkritische Untersuchung." *ZKT* 65 (1941): 81–90; repr. as pages 181–93 in *Kleine patristische Schriften*. TU 83. Berlin: Akademie, 1967.

Altmann, A. "A Note on the Rabbinic Doctrine of Creation." *JJS* 7 (1956): 195–96.

Altmann, A. "Ars Rhetorica as Reflected in Some Jewish Figures of the Italian Renaissance." Pages 1–22 in *Jewish Thought in the Sixteenth Century*. Edited by B. D. Cooperman. Cambridge, MA: Harvard University Press, 1983.

Altmann, A. "Heʿarot ʿal ha-neo-ʾaplaṭoniyut šel šelomo ʾibn-gabirol." Pages 91–97 in *Faces of Judaism: Selected Essays*. Edited by A. Shapira. Tel Aviv: Am Oved Publishers, 1983.

Altmann, A. *Moses Mendelssohn: A Biographical Study*. Tuscaloosa, AL: University of Alabama Press, 1973.

Altmann, A. "Saadya's Theory of Revelation: Its Origin and Background." Pages 4–25 in *Saadya Studies: In Commemoration of the One Thousandth Anniversary of the Death of R. Saadya Gaon*. Edited by E. I. J. Rosenthal. Manchester: Manchester University Press, 1943.

Amadouni, G. "Le role historique des Hiéromoines arméniens." *OCA* 153 (1958): 279–306.

Amand de Mendieta, E. "La préparation et la composition des neuf 'Homélies sur l'Hexaéméron' de Basile de Césarée." *StPatr* 16.2 (1985): 349–67.

Amir, Y. "Die Zehn Gebote bei Philon von Alexandrien." Pages 131–63 in Y. Amir, *Die hellenistische Gestalt des Judentums bei Philon von Alexandrien*. Neukirchen-Vluyn: Neukirchener Verlag, 1983.

Amir, Y. "The Transference of Greek Allegories to Biblical Motifs in Philo." Pages 15–25 in *Nourished with Peace: Studies in Hellenistic Judaism in Memory of Samuel Sandmel*. Edited by F. E. Greenspahn, E. Hilgert, and B. L. Mack. Chico, CA: Scholars Press, 1984.

Ammann, A. *Josephus Frobenianus. Editions- und Rezeptionsgeschichte des Flavius Josephus im Basler Humanismus*. Basel: Schwabe Verlag, 2020.

Amolo von Lyon, *Liber de Perfidia Judaeorum*. Edited by Cornelia Herbers-Rauhut. Monumenta Germaniae Historica. Quellen zur Geistesgeschichte des Mittelalters, 29. Wiesbaden: Harrassowitz, 2017.

Anderson, A. R. "Heracles and His Successors: A Study of a Heroic Ideal and the Recurrence of a Heroic Type." *HSCP* 39 (1928): 7–58.

Anderson, G. *The Second Sophistic: A Cultural Phenomenon in the Roman Empire*. London: Routledge, 1993.

Andia, Y. de *Henosis: L'union à Dieu chez Denys l'Aréopagite*. PhA 71. Leiden: Brill, 1996.

Anetsʿi, S. and Continuators. *The Chronicle from Adam to 1776*: Critical Text, Study and Commentary by K. Matevosyan. Erevan: Nayiri, 2014.

Annas, J. *Virtue and Law in Plato and Beyond*. Oxford: Oxford University Press, 2017.

Antʿapyan, Pʿ. "On the Text of the 'Scholia to the Philo's Seven Writings' by Yovhannēs Sarkawag." *Historical-Philological Journal* 1 (1983): 177–90.

Appelbaum, A. "A Fresh Look at Philo's Family." *SPhiloA* 30 (2018): 93–114.

Arduini, M. L. "Il tema 'vir' e 'mulier' nell'esegesi patristica e medievale di *Eccli*., XLII,14: a proposito di una interpretazione di Ruperto di Deutz." *Aev* 54 (1980): 315–30.

Arevshatyan, S. *The Formation of the Philosophical Science in Ancient Armenia (V-VI cc.)*. 2nd edn. Erevan: National Academy of Sciences, 2016 (in Russian).

Aristotelis opera, 5 vols. Venice: Aldus Manutius, 1495–98.

Arlenius, A. P. and S. Gelenius, eds. *Flavii Josephi opera*. Basel: H. Frobenium, 1544.

Arnaldez, R. *Philon d'Alexandrie*, Vol. 1: *Introduction generale, De opificio mundi*. Les oeuvres de Philon d'Alexandrie. Paris: Cerf, 1961.

Arnim, H. F. A. von and M. Adler. *Stoicorum veterum fragmenta*. Stuttgart: Teubner, 1964.

Artsruni, T. *History of the House of the Artsrunik*. Translation and commentary by Robert W. Thomson. Detroit: Wayne State University Press, 1985.

Arzhanov, Y. *Syriac Sayings of Greek Philosophers: A Study in Syriac Gnomologia with Edition and Translation*. CSCO 669 / Subsidia 138. Louvain: Peeters, 2019.

Ashwin-Siejkowski, P. *Clement of Alexandria on Trial: The Evidence of "Heresy" from Photius' Bibliotheca*. VCSup. Leiden: Brill, 2010.

Assmann, J. "The Mosaic Distinction: Israel, Egypt, and the Invention of Paganism." *Representations* 56 (1996): 48–67.

Assmann, J. *Moses the Egyptian. The Memory of Egypt in Western Monotheism*. Cambridge, MA: Harvard University Press, 1998.
Ast, F. *Grundriss der Geschichte der Philosophie*. Landshut: Joseph Thomann, 1807.
Athanassiadi, P. and M. Frede, eds. *Pagan Monotheism in Late Antiquity*. Oxford: Clarendon Press, 1999.
Attridge, H. W. *The Epistle to the Hebrews: A Commentary*. Hermeneia. Philadelphia: Fortress Press, 1989.
Attridge, H. W. "Philo and John: Two Riffs on One Logos." *SPhiloA* 17 (2005): 103–17.
Attridge, H. W. "Training Eyes to See Rightly: Educational Principles in Philo and the Fourth Gospel." *SPhiloA* 32 (2020): 41–54.
Aubineau, M. *Grégoire de Nysse, Traité de la Virginité*. SC 119. Paris: Cerf, 1966.
Aucher, J.-B. *Eusebii Pamphili Caesariensis episcopi Chronicon bipartitum, nunc primum ex armeniaco textu in latinum conversum, adnotationibus auctum, graecis fragmentis exornatum, opera P. Jo. Baptistae Aucher Ancyrani, pars II*. Venice: typis coenobii armenorum in insula S. Lazari, 1818.
Aucher, J.-B. *Philonis Judaei Paralipomena Armena*. Venice: L. Lazarus, 1826.
Aucher, J.-B. *Philonis Judaei Sermones Tres Hactenus Inediti, I. et II. De Providentia, et III. De Animalibus*. Venice: Typis Coenobii PP. Armenorum in insula S. Lazari, 1822.
Aziza, C. Review of H. Savon, *Saint Ambroise devant l'exégèse de Philon le Juif*. *Latomus* 39.1 (1980): 241–42.
Azkoul, M. *St. Gregory of Nyssa and the Tradition of the Fathers*. Lewiston: Mellen Press, 1995.
Bacher, W. "The Church Father Origen and Rabbi Hoshaya." *JQR* 3 (1891): 357–60.
Bacher, W. *Die Agada der palästinensischen Amoräer*, vol. 1. Strasbourg: Trübner, 1892.
Baer, R. A. *Philo's Use of the Categories Male and Female*. Leiden: Brill, 1970.
Bagnall, R. S. "Alexandria: Library of Dreams." *PAPhS* 146 (2002): 348–62.
Baird, W. *History of New Testament Research*, Vol. 3: *From C. H. Dodd to Hans Dieter Betz*. Minneapolis: Fortress, 2013.
Baker, K., S.J., trans. *Controversies of the Christian Faith*. Ramsey, NJ: Keep the Faith, 2016.
Balch, D. L. "Two Apologetic Encomia: Dionysius on Rome and Josephus on the Jews." *JSJ* 13 (1982): 102–22.
Ball, W. E. "St. John and Philo Judaeus." *Contemporary Review* 73 (1898): 219–34.
Ballenstedt, H. C. *Philo und Johannes oder fortgesetzte Anwendung des Philo zur Interpretation der Johannes Schriften, mit besondrer Hinsicht auf der Frage: ob Johannes der Verfasser der ihm zugeschriebenen Schriften seyn könne*. Göttingen: Heinrich Dieterich, 1812.
Balsam-Geld, O. "Atticism, Judaism, and Luzzatto's Relationship to Philosophy and Philosophers." *Daat: A Journal of Jewish Philosophy & Kabbala* 84 (2017): 262–69.
Baltes, M. "Idee (Ideenlehre)." *RAC* 17 (1998): 213–46.
Baltes, M. "Plutarchus [2] C. Philosophical Work." *Brill's New Pauly* 11 (2007): 416–23.
Balthasar, H. Urs von. *Origen: Spirit and Fire: A Thematic Anthology of His Writings*. Translated by R. J. Daly. 2nd edn. Washington, DC: Catholic University of America Press, 1984.
Balthasar, H. Urs von. "Patristik, Scholastik und Wir." *Theologie der Zeit* 3 (1939): 65–104.
Balthasar, H. Urs von. "Wendung nach Osten." *Stimmen der Zeit* 136 (1939): 32–46.
Bamberger, B. J. "Philo and the Aggadah." *HUCA* 48 (1977): 153–85.
Bandy, A. C. *On the Months (De mensibus): Three Works of Ioannes Lydus 1*. Lewiston: Mellon Press, 2013.
Bar Hebraeus. *Tārīkh mukhtaṣar al-duwal*. Edited by A. Ṣāliḥānī. Beirut: al-Maṭbaʿa al-kāthūlīkiyya, 1890.
Bar-Kochva, B. *The Image of the Jews in Greek Literature*. Berkeley: University of California Press, 2010.
Barbàra, M. A. "L'esegesi patristica del 'Vino' del Cantico dei Cantici." *Aug* 57 (2017): 569–91.
Barclay, J. M. G. *Flavius Josephus: Against Apion*. Leiden: Brill, 2007.
Barclay, J. M. G. "Hostility to Jews as a Cultural Construct: Egyptian, Hellenistic, and Early Christian Paradigms." Pages 365–86 in *Josephus und das Neue Testament: Wechselseitige Wahrnehmungen*. Edited by C. Böttrich and J. Herzer. Tübingen: Mohr Siebeck, 2007.
Barclay, J. M. G. *Jews in the Mediterranean Diaspora from Alexander to Trajan (323 BCE–117 CE)*. HCS 33. Berkeley: University of California Press, 1996.
Barclay, J. M. G. "Judaism in Roman Dress: Josephus' Tactics in the *Contra Apionem*." Pages 231–45 in *Internationales Josephus-Kolloquium Aarhus 1999*. Münsteraner Judaistische Studien 6. Edited by J. U. Kalms. Münster: LIT, 2000.
Barclay, J. M. G. "The Politics of Contempt. Judeans and Egyptians in Josephus' *Against Apion*." Pages 277–300 in his *Pauline Churches and Diaspora Jews*. Tübingen: Mohr Siebeck, 2011.
Barclay, J. M. G. and B. G. White, eds. *The New Testament in Comparison: Validity, Method and Purpose in Comparing Traditions*. LNTS 600. London: Bloomsbury, 2020.
Bardy, G. *Didyme l'Aveugle*. Paris: Beauchesne, 1910.
Bargès, J.-J.-L. *Homélie sur St Marc, apôtre et évangéliste par Anba Sévère, évêque de Nestéraweh*. Paris: Ernest Leroux, 1877.
Barnard, J. A. *The Mysticism of Hebrews: Exploring the Role of Jewish Apocalyptic Mysticism in the Epistle to the Hebrews*. WUNT 2.331. Tübingen: Mohr Siebeck, 2012.

Barnard, L. W. *Justin Martyr: His Life and Thought*. Cambridge: Cambridge University Press, 1967.

Barnard, P. M., ed. *Clement of Alexandria, Quis Dives Salvetur*. Cambridge: Cambridge University Press, 1897.

Barnes, M. R. "Eunomius of Cyzicus and Gregory of Nyssa: Two Traditions of Transcendent Causality." *VC* 52 (1998): 59–87.

Barnes, T. D. *Constantine and Eusebius*. Cambridge, MA: Harvard University Press, 1981.

Barnes, T. D. "The Election of Ambrose of Milan." Pages 39–60 in *Episcopal Elections in Late Antiquity*. Edited by J. Leemans. Arbeiten zur Kirchengeschichte 119. Berlin: de Gruyter, 2011.

Barnes, T. D. "Methodius, Maximus, and Valentinus." *JTS* 30 (1979): 47–55.

Baronio, C. *Annales Ecclesiastici*. Vol. 1. Rome: Typographia Vaticana, 1588.

Barrett, A. A. *Caligula: The Corruption of Power*. London: B. T. Batsford, 1989.

Barthélemy, D. *Études d'histoire du texte de l'Ancien Testament*. Orbis Biblicus et Orientalis 21. Göttingen: Editions Universitaires Fribourg, 1978.

Barthélemy, D. "Est-ce Hoshaya Rabba qui censura le 'Commentaire allégorique'? À partir des retouches faites aux citations bibliques, étude sur la tradition textuelle du Commentaire allégorique de Philon." Pages 45–78 in *Philon d'Alexandrie, Lyon 11–15 Septembre 1966: colloques nationaux du Centre National de la Recherche Scientifique*. Edited by R. Arnaldez et al. Paris: Editions du Centre National de la Recherche Scientifique, 1967.

Barthold, C., ed. *Hieronymus: De viris illustribus = Berühmte Männer*. Mülheim: Carthusianus, 2010.

Bartsch, S. *Actors in the Audience: Theatricality and Doublespeak from Nero to Hadrian*. Revealing Antiquity 6. Cambridge, MA: Harvard University Press, 1994.

Barzilay, I. E. *Shlomo Yehudah Rapoport (Shir) (1790–1867) and His Contemporaries: Some Aspects of Jewish Scholarship of the Nineteenth Century*. Tel Aviv: Massada Press, 1969.

Bauckham, R. "Moses as God: A Precedent for Christology?" Pages 246–65 in *The Spirit of Christ in the New Testament and Theology. Essays in Honour of Max Turner*. Edited by I. H. Marshall, V. Rabens, and C. Bennema. Grand Rapids: Eerdmans, 2012.

Bauer, B. *Kritik der evangelischen Geschichte der Synoptiker*. 2 vols. Leipzig: Otto Wigand, 1841.

Bauer, B. *Philo, Strauss und Renan und das Urchristenthum*. Berlin: Gustav Hempel, 1874.

Bauer, W. *Orthodoxy and Heresy in Earliest Christianity*. Edited by R. Kraft and G. Krodel. Philadelphia: Fortress, 1971.

Baur, F. C. *Christianity and the Christian Church in the First Three Centuries*. Edited by P. C. Hodgson. Translated by R. F. Brown and P. C. Hodgson. Eugene, OR: Cascade, 2019.

Baur, F. C. *History of Christian Dogma*. Translated by R. F. Brown and P. C. Hodgson. Oxford: Oxford University Press, 2014.

Bay, C., A. Ellis, J. Mania, S. Moscone, and L Tröger, eds. *The Medieval Afterlife of Hellenistic Judaism: Reception and Reinvention in Western Europe*. Basel: Schwabe, 2024.

Bayer, L. *Isidors von Pelusium klassische Bildung*. Paderborn: F. Schöningh, 1915.

Bayliss, Grant D. *The Vision of Didymus the Blind: A Fourth-Century Virtue-Origenism*. Oxford: Oxford University Press, 2016.

Becker, G. *Catalogi bibliothecarum antiqui*. Bonn: Max. Cohen, 1895.

Bedjan, P., ed. *Gregorii Barhebraei Chronicon Syriacum*. Paris, 1890. English translation: E. A. W. Budge, trans. *The Chronography of Abû'l Faraj, the Son of Aaron, the Hebrew Physician, Commonly Known as Bar Hebraeus*. 2 vols. Oxford: Oxford University Press, 1932.

BeDuhn, J. *Augustine's Manichaean Dilemma*. 2 vols. Divinations. Philadelphia: University of Pennsylvania, 2010–13.

Begg, C. T. "Josephus' and Philo's Retelling of Numbers 31 Compared." *ETL* 83 (2007): 81–106.

Beiser, F. C. *The German Historicist Tradition*. Oxford: Oxford University Press, 2011.

Bekken, P. J. "Philo's Relevance for the Study of the New Testament." Pages 226–67 in *Reading Philo: A Handbook to Philo of Alexandria*. Edited by T. Seland. Grand Rapids: Eerdmans, 2014.

Belkin, S. "The Alexandrian Source for *Contra Apionem* II." *JQR* 27 (1936–37): 1–32.

Belkin, S. *Philo and the Oral Law: The Philonic Interpretation of Biblical Law in Relation to the Palestinian Halakah*. HSS 11. Cambridge, MA: Harvard University Press, 1940.

Bellarmine, R., S.J. *De scriptoribus ecclesiasticis*. Vol. 1. Lyons: Horatius Cardon, 1613.

Bellarmine, R., S.J. *Disputationum Roberti Bellarmini Politiani, S.J., S.R.E. Cardinalis, De controversiis christianae fidei adversus hujus temporis haereticos*. 4 vols. Ingolstadt: Adam Sartori, 1601.

Bellier, P. *Les œuvres de Philon Iuif, autheur tres-eloquent, et philosophe tres-graue. Contenans l'interpretation de plusieurs diuins & sacrez mysteres, & l'instruction d'un chacun en toutes bonnes & sainctes moeurs. Mises de grec en françois, par Pierre Bellier*. Paris: Nicolas Chesneau, also Michel Sonnius, 1575.

Bendova, M. "The Influence of Philo's *De Abrahamo* on Gregory of Nyssa's *De Vita Moysis*." *AUC Theologica* 8 (2018): 91–109.

Benedetto, G., ed. *J. H. Withof. Callimaco e I Telchini*. Palermo: Sellerio Editore, 1995.
Bennett, J. "August Neander and the Religion of History in the Nineteenth-Century 'Priesthood of Letters.'" *Historical Journal* 63.3 (2020): 633–59.
Bentley, J. H. *Humanists and Holy Writ: New Testament Scholarship in the Renaissance*. Princeton: Princeton University Press, 1983.
Bentley, R., ed. *P. Terentii Afri Comoediae. Recensuit, notasque suas et Gabrielis Faerni addidit Richardus Bentleius. Editio altera denuo recensita, ac Indice amplissimo [...] aucta*. Amsterdam: R. & J. Wetstein & G. Smith, 1727.
Berger, K. and C. Colpe. *Religionsgeschichtliches Textbuch zum Neuen Testament*. Göttingen: Vandenhoeck & Ruprecht, 1987.
Berkmüller, S. *Schriftauslegung und Bildgebrauch bei Isidor von Pelusium*. AKG 143. Berlin: de Gruyter, 2020.
Bernard, J. P., T. Birch, and J. Lockman, eds. *A General Dictionary, Historical and Critical*. London: J. Bettenham, 1736.
Bernays, J. "Philon's Hypothetika und die Verwünschungen des Buzyges in Athen." Pages 262–82 in his *Gesammelte Abhandlungen, Volume 1*. Berlin: W. Hertz, 1885.
Bernays, J. "Über die Herstellung des Zusammenhanges in der unter Philo's Namen gehenden Schrift περὶ ἀφθαρσίας κόσμου durch Blätterversetzung." Pages 34–40 in *Monatsberichte der Königlich Preußischen Akademie der Wissenschaften zu Berlin 1863*. Berlin: Verlag der Königlichen Akademie der Wissenschaften, 1864.
Berner, U. *Origenes*. EdF 147. Darmstadt: Wissenschaftliche Buchgesellschaft, 1981.
Berns, A. *The Bible and Natural Philosophy in Renaissance Italy*. Cambridge: Cambridge University Press, 2019.
Berthelot, K. "The Canaanites who 'Trusted in God': An Original Interpretation of the Fate of the Canaanites in Rabbinic Literature." *JJS* 62.2 (2011): 233–61.
Berthelot, K. *In Search of the Promised Land? The Hasmonean Dynasty between Biblical Models and Hellenistic Diplomacy*. Göttingen: Vandenhoeck & Ruprecht, 2018.
Berthelot, K. *Jews and Their Roman Rivals: Pagan Rome's Challenge to Israel*. Princeton: Princeton University Press, 2021.
Berthelot, K. *L'"humanité de l'autre homme" dans la pensée juive ancienne*. Leiden: Brill, 2004.
Berthelot, K. *Philanthrôpia Judaica: le débat autour de la "misanthropie" des lois juives dans l'Antiquité*. Leiden: Brill, 2003.
Berthelot, K. "Philo and the Allegorical Interpretation of Homer in the Platonic Tradition (with an Emphasis on Porphyry's *De antro nympharum*)." Pages 155–74 in *Homer and the Bible in the Eyes of Ancient Interpreters*. Edited by M. R. Niehoff. Jerusalem Studies in Religion and Culture 16. Leiden: Brill, 2012.
Berthelot, K. "Philo and the Conquest of Canaan." *JSJ* 38 (2007): 39–56.
Berthelot, K. "Philo's Perception of the Roman Empire." *JSJ* 38 (2007): 166–87.
Berthelot, K. "Philon d'Alexandrie, lecteur d'Homère: quelques éléments de réflexion." Pages 145–57 in *Prolongements et renouvellements de la tradition classique*. Edited by A. Balansard, G. Dorival, and M. Loubet. Aix-en-Provence: Publications de l'Université Provence, 2011.
Bettan, I. *Studies in Jewish Preaching: Middle Ages*. Cincinnati: Hebrew Union College Press, 1939.
Biblia Patristica: Index des Citations et Allusions Bibliques dans la Littérature Patristique. 6 vols and supplement. Paris: Centre National de la Recherche Scientifique, 1991.
Bibliotheca scriptorum classicorum et graecorum et latinorum. Alphabetisches Verzeichniss der Ausgaben, Uebersetzungen und Erläuterungsschriften der griechischen und lateinischen Schriftsteller, welche vom Jahre 1700 bis zu Ende des Jahres 1846 besonders in Deutschland gedruckt worden sind. Leipzig: Wilhelm Engelmann, 1847.
Bienert, W. A. *"Allegoria" und "Anagoge" bei Didymos dem Blinden von Alexandria*. PTS 13. Berlin: de Gruyter, 1972.
Bietenhard, H. "Logos-Theologie im Rabbinat: Ein Beitrag zur Lehre vom Worte Gottes im rabbinischen Schrifttum." *ANRW* 2.19.2 (1979): 580–618.
Bietz, W. K. *Paradiesesvorstellungen bei Ambrosius und seinen Vorgängern*. PhD diss. University of Giessen, 1974.
Billet, S. "The Philosopher as Witness: Hermann Cohen's Philosophers and the Trials of *Wissenschaft des Judentums*." PhD diss. Princeton University, 2019.
Billings, T. H. *The Platonism of Philo Judaeus*. Chicago: University of Chicago Press, 1919.
Bird, M. F. *Crossing over Sea and Land: Jewish Missionary Activity in the Second Temple Period*. Peabody, MA: Hendrickson, 2010.
Birnbaum, E. "A Leader with Vision in the Ancient Jewish Diaspora: Philo of Alexandria." Pages 57–90 in *Jewish Religious Leadership: Image and Reality*. Edited by J. Wertheimer. New York: The Jewish Theological Seminary, 2004.
Birnbaum, E. "Philo at Yale." *Adamantius* 20 (2014): 632–35.

Birnbaum, E. "Philo's Relevance for the Study of Jews and Judaism in Antiquity." Pages 200–25 in *Reading Philo: A Handbook to Philo of Alexandria*. Edited by T. Seland. Grand Rapids: Eerdmans, 2014.

Birnbaum, E. *The Place of Judaism in Philo's Thought: Israel, Jews, and Proselytes*. BJS 290. Atlanta: Scholars Press, 1996.

Birnbaum, E. "Two Millennia Later: General Resources and Particular Perspectives on Philo the Jew." *CurBR* 4 (2006): 241–76.

Biron, J. "La *Sacra Bibliotheca Sanctorum Patrum* (1589) de Marguerin de La Bigne et la Compagnie de la Grand-Navire." Pages 127–44 in *Le Livre médiéval et humaniste dans les Collections de l'UQAM*. Edited by B. Dunn-Lardeau and J. Biron. Quebec: Figura, 2006.

Bischoff, B. and V. Brown. "Additions to *Codices Latini Antiquiores*." *Medieval Studies* 47 (1985): 317–66.

Blachman, E. *The Transformation of Tamar (Genesis 38) in the History of Jewish Interpretation*. Contributions to Biblical Exegesis & Theology 71. Leuven: Peeters, 2013.

Blanchet, M.-H. *Georges-Gennadios Scholarios (vers 1400-vers 1472): un intellectuel orthodoxe face à la disparition de l'empire byzantine*. Archives de l'Orient chrétien 20. Paris: Institut Français d'Etudes Byzantines, 2008.

Bloch, H. *Die Quellen des Flavius Josephus in seiner Archäologie*. Stuttgart: Teubner, 1879.

Bloch, R. "Bringing Philo Home: Responses to Harry A. Wolfson's *Philo* (1947) in the Aftermath of World War II." *HTR* 116:3 (2023): 466–89.

Bloch, R. *Moses und der Mythos: Die Auseinandersetzung mit der griechischen Mythologie bei jüdischen-hellenistischen Autoren*. JSJSup 145. Leiden: Brill, 2011.

Bloch, R. "Mose und die Scharlatane: Zum Vorwurf γόης καὶ ἀπατεών in *Contra Apionem* 2:145.161." Pages 142–57 in *Internationales Josephus-Kolloquium Brüssel 1998*, Münsteraner Judaistische Studien 4. Edited by F. Siegert and J. U. Kalms. Münster: LIT, 1999.

Bloch, R. "Von Szene zu Szene: Das jüdische Theater in der Antike." Pages 57–86 in *Juden in ihrer Umelt: Akkulturation des Judentums in Antike und Mittelalter*. Edited by M. Konradt and R. C. Schwinges. Basel: Schwabe, 2009.

Bloom, H. *The Anxiety of Influence: A Theory of Poetry*. 2nd edn. Oxford: Oxford University Press, 1997.

Bobichon, P. *Dialogue avec Tryphon, Volume II: Notes de la traduction, appendices, indices*. Fribourg: Academic Press, 2003.

Bøhm, C. *Die Rezeption der Psalmen in den Qumranschriften, bei Philo von Alexandrien und im Corpus Paulinum*. WUNT 2.437. Tübingen: Mohr Siebeck, 2017.

Böhm, T. *Theoria Unendlichkeit Aufstieg: Philosophische Implikationen zu De Vita Moysis von Gregor von Nyssa*. VCSup 35. Leiden: Brill, 1996.

Bollack, J. *Jacob Bernays. Un homme entre deux mondes*. Villeneuve d'Ascq, Nord: Presses universitaires du Septentrion, 1998.

Bonmariage, C. and S. Moureau. "*Corpus Dionysiacum Arabicum*: Étude, édition critique et traduction des *Noms Divins* IV, §1–9." *Le Muséon* 124 (2011): 181–227.

Borgeais, C. "La Personnalité de Jérôme dans son *De Viris Illustribus*." Pages 283–93 in *Jérôme entre l'Occident et l'Orient*. Edited by Yves-Marie Duval. Paris: Études augustiniennes, 1988.

Borgen, P. *Bread from Heaven: An Exegetical Study of the Concept of Manna in the Gospel of John and the Writings of Philo*. 2nd edn. NovTSup 10. Leiden: Brill, 1981.

Borgen, P. "Observations on the Theme 'Paul and Philo': Paul's Preaching of Circumcision in Galatia (Gal 5:11) and Debates on Circumcision in Philo." Pages 85–102 in *Die Paulinische Literatur und Theologie*. Edited by S. Pedersen. Arhus: Forlaget Aros, 1980.

Borgen, P. "Philo of Alexandria: Reviewing and Rewriting Biblical Material." *SPhiloA* 9 (1997): 37–53.

Borgen, P. "Philo of Alexandria: A Critical and Synthetical Survey of Research since World War II." *Religion (Hellenistisches Judentum in römischer Zeit: Philon und Josephus)*. ANRW II.21.1. (1984): 98–154.

Borgen, P. *Philo of Alexandria: An Exegete for His Time*. NovTSup 86. Leiden: Brill, 1997.

Borgen, P. "The Prologue of John: An Exposition of the Old Testament." Pages 75–96 in *Philo, John and Paul: New Perspectives on Judaism and Early Christianity*. Edited by P. Borgen. BJS 131. Atlanta: Scholars Press, 1987.

Borgen, P. "Response Concerning the Jewish Sources." *NTS* 23 (1976): 67–75.

Borgen, P. "Some Hebrew and Pagan Features in Philo's and Paul's Interpretation of Hagar and Ishmael." Pages 151–64 in *The New Testament and Hellenistic Judaism*. Edited by P. Borgen and S. Giversen. Aarhus: Aarhus University Press, 1995.

Boring, M. E., K. Berger, and C. Colpe. *Hellenistic Commentary to the New Testament*. Nashville: Abingdon, 1995.

Bourgogne, A. de. *Lapis lydius sive vanitas per veritatem falsi*. Antwerp, 1639.

Bowersock, G. W. *Greek Sophists in the Roman Empire*. Oxford: Clarendon Press, 1969.

Bowman, S. B. "Philo." Page 1655 in vol. 3 of *The Oxford Dictionary of Byzantium*. Edited by A. P. Kazdhan. New York: Oxford University Press, 1991.

Boyancé, P. "Études Philoniennes." *REG* 76 (1963): 64–110.

Boyarin, D. *Border Lines: The Partition of Judeo-Christianity*. Philadelphia: University of Pennsylvania Press, 2004.

Boyarin, D. "The Gospel of the *Memra*: Jewish Binitarianism and the Prologue to John." *HTR* 94 (2001): 243–84.

Boyarin, D. *A Radical Jew: Paul and the Politics of Identity*. Berkeley: University of California Press, 1994.

Boys-Stones, G. *Platonist Philosophy 80 BC to AD 250: An Introduction and Collection of Sources in Translation*. Cambridge: Cambridge University Press, 2018.

Boys-Stones, G. *Post-Hellenistic Philosophy: A Study of Its Development from the Stoics to Origen*. Oxford: Oxford University Press, 2001

Boys-Stones, G. "Time, Creation, and the Mind of God." *OSAPh* 40 (2011): 319–37.

Brakke, D. *The Gnostics: Myth, Ritual, and Diversity in Early Christianity*. Cambridge, MA: Harvard University Press, 2010.

Brämer, A. *Rabbiner Zacharias Frankel. Wissenschaft des Judentums und conservative Reform im 19. Jahrhundert*. Netiva 3. Hildesheim et al.: Olms, 2000.

Brann, M. *Geschichte des jüdisch-theologischen Seminars (Fraenkel'sche Stiftung) in Breslau. Festschrift zum fünfzigjährigen Jubiläum der Anstalt*. Breslau: Schatzky, 1904.

Bréhier, E. *Les idées philosophiques et religieuses de Philon d'Alexandrie*. 2nd edn. Paris: J. Vrin, 1925.

Brenk, F. E. "Plutarch's Middle-Platonic God: About to Enter (or Remake) the Academy." Pages 121–43 in F. E. Brenk, *With Unperfumed Voice: Studies in Plutarch, in Greek Literature, Religion and Philosophy, and in the New Testament Background*. Postdamer Altertumswissenschaftliche Beiträge 21. Stuttgart: Steiner, 2007.

Breuer, E. *The Limits of Enlightenment: Jews, Germans, and the Eighteenth-Century Study of Scripture*. Cambridge, MA: Harvard University Press, 1996.

Brink, F. E. "Philo and Plutarch on the Nature of God." *SPhiloA* 26 (2014): 79–92.

Brock, S. *Studies in Syriac Christianity*. Ashgate: Variorum, 1992.

Broek, R. van den. "Jewish and Platonic Speculations in Early Alexandrian Theology: Eugnostus, Philo, Valentinus, and Origen." Pages 190–203 in *The Roots of Egyptian Christianity*. Edited by B. Pearson and J. E. Goehring. Philadelphia: Fortress, 1986.

Brown, R. E. *The Gospel of John I*. AB 29. Garden City, NY: Doubleday, 1966.

Brucker, J. J. *Kurtze Fragen aus der philosophischen Historie*. 9 vols. Ulm: Daniel Bartholomai und Sohn, 1734.

Bruns, J. E. "Philo Christianus: The Debris of a Legend." *HTR* 66 (1973): 141–45.

Bucur, B. G. "'Early Christian Binitarianism': From Religious Phenomenon to Polemical Insult to Scholarly Concept." *Modern Theology* 27.1 (2011): 102–20.

Budde, J. F. *Introductio ad historiam philosophia ebraeorum*. Halle: Orphanotrophium Glavcha-Halensis, 1702.

Budé, G. *Aristotelis philosophi nobilissimi de mundo libellus*. Paris: Ascensianis, 1526.

Buell, D. K. *Making Christians: Clement of Alexandria and the Rhetoric of Legitimacy*. Princeton: Princeton University Press, 1999.

Buell, D. K. *Why This New Race? Ethnic Reasoning in Early Christianity*. New York: Columbia University Press, 2008.

Buhle, J. G. *Geschichte der neueren Philosophie*. 9 vols. Göttingen: Johann Friedrich Röwer, 1796–1805.

Bultmann, C. "Historical-Critical Inquiry." Pages 431–54 in *The Hebrew Bible: A Critical Companion*. Edited by J. Barton. Princeton: Princeton University Press, 2016.

Bultmann, R. *Primitive Christianity in Its Contemporary Setting*. Translated by R. H. Fuller. London and New York: Thames and Hudson, 1956.

Bursian, C. *Geschichte der classischen Philologie in Deutschland von den Anfängen bis zur Gegenwart*. 2 vols. Munich: Oldenbourg, 1883.

Bussnich, J. "Mystical Elements in the Thought of Plotinus." *ANRW* 2.36.7 (1994): 5300–5330.

Byers, S. *Perception, Sensibility, and Moral Motivation in Augustine: A Stoic-Platonic Synthesis*. Cambridge: Cambridge University Press, 2013.

Cain, A. *The Letters of Jerome: Asceticism, Biblical Exegesis, and the Construction of Christian Authority in Late Antiquity*, Oxford Early Christian Studies. Oxford and New York: Oxford University Press. 2009.

Cain, A. and J. Lössl, *Jerome of Stridon: His Life, Writings and Legacy*. Farnham; Burlington, VT: Ashgate. 2009.

Caird, E. *The Evolution of Theology in the Greek Philosophers*. Glasgow: MacLehose, 1904.

Calabi, F. *God's Acting, Man's Acting: Tradition and Philosophy in Philo of Alexandria*. Leiden: Brill, 2008.
Calabi, F. "Theatrical Language in Philo's *In Flaccum*." Pages 91–116 in *Italian Studies on Philo of Alexandria*. Edited by F. Calabi. SphA 1. Boston: Brill, 2003.
Calabi, F. et al., eds. *Pouvoir et puissances chez Philon d'Alexandrie*. Turnhout: Brepols, 2015.
Cameron, A. and S. G. Hall. *Eusebius*, Life of Constantine: *Introduction, Translation and Commentary*. Clarendon Ancient History Series. Oxford: Clarendon Press, 1999.
Canellis, A. *Jerome, Préfaces aux livres de la Bible*. SC 592. Paris: Cerf, 2017.
Canellis, A. "La Lettre 64 de Saint Jérôme et le symbolisme des couleurs." *VC* 72 (2018): 235–54.
Canfora, L. *Ellenismo*. Bari: Laterza, 1987.
Canfora, L. *Il Fozio ritrovato: Juan de Mariana e André Schott*. Bari: Edizioni Dedalo, 2001.
Canons and Decrees of the Council of Trent. Translated by H. J. Schroeder, O.P. St. Louis: Herder, 1941.
Capone, A. "*Stoici, qui nostro dogmati in plerisque concordant*: Gerolamo e lo stoicismo." *Adamantius* 24 (2018): 435–50.
Caquot, A., M. Hadas-Lebel, and J. Riaud, eds. *Hellenica et Judaica: hommage à Valentin Nikiprowetzy*. Leuven: Peeters, 1986.
Carabine, D. "Gregory of Nyssa on the Incomprehensibility of God." Pages 79–99 in *The Relationship between Neoplatonism and Christianity*. Edited by T. Finan and V. Twomey. Dublin: Four Courts Press, 1992.
Carasik, M. "To See a Sound: A Deuteronomic Rereading of Exodus 20:15." *Proof* 19 (1999): 257–76.
Carleton Paget, J. *The Epistle of Barnabas: Outlook and Background*. Tübingen: Mohr Siebeck, 1994.
Carleton Paget, J. "Judaism in the Second Century." Pages 383–425 in J. Carleton Paget, *Jews, Christians and Jewish Christians*. Tübingen: Mohr Siebeck, 2010.
Carleton Paget, J. "Some Observations on Josephus and Christianity." *JTS* 52 (2001): 539–624.
Carlier, C. *La cité de Moïse: le peuple juif chez Philon d'Alexandrie*. Turnhout: Brepols, 2008.
Carlucci, G. *I Prolegomena di André Schott alla* Biblioteca *di Fozio*. Bari: Edizioni Dedalo, 2012.
Carpzov, I. B. *Dissertatio inauguralis critico theologica de* λόγῳ *Philonis non Iohanneo adversus Thomam Mangey Anglum*. Helmstadt: Paul. Dieteric. Schnorr, 1749.
Carras, G. P. "Dependence or Common Tradition in Philo *Hypothetica* VIII.6.10–7.20 and Josephus *Contra Apionem* 2.190–219." *SPhiloA* 5 (1993): 24–47.
Carras, G. P. "Philo's *Hypothetica*, Josephus' *Contra Apionem* and the Question of Sources." Pages 431–50 in *SBL 1990 Seminar Papers*. Edited by D. Lull. Atlanta: Scholars Press, 1990.
Carrier, R. "Origen, Eusebius, and the Accidental Interpolation in Josephus' *Jewish Antiquities* 20.200." *JECS* 20 (2012): 489–514.
Carrière, F. *Commentarius in universam scripturam*. Lyons: Horatius Boissat & Georgius Remeus, 1663.
Carriker, A. J. *The Library of Eusebius of Caesarea*. VCSup 67. Leiden: Brill, 2003.
Cassin, M. "'Plumer Isocrate': usage polémique du vocabulaire comique chez Grégoire de Nysse." *REG* 121 (2008): 783–96.
Cassuto, U. *A Commentary on the Book of Exodus*. Translated by I. Abrahams. Jerusalem: Magnes, 1967.
Cavadini, J. C. "Exegetical Transformation: The Sacrifice of Isaac in Philo, Origen, and Ambrose." Pages 35–49 in *In Dominico Eloquio: In Lordly Eloquence: Essays on Patristic Exegesis in Honor of Robert Louis Wilken*. Edited by P. Blowers et al. Grand Rapids: Eerdmans, 2002.
Cavarnos, J. P. *Gregorii Nysseni Opera*. VIII/1. Leiden: Brill, 1952.
Ceresa-Gastaldo, A. *Gerolamo Gli Uomini Illustri*. Biblioteca Patristica 12. Florence: EDB, 1988.
Chadwick, H. "Christian Platonism in Origen and Augustine." Pages 217–30 in *Origeniana Tertia*. Edited by R. Hanson and H. Crouzel. Rome: Ateneo, 1985.
Chadwick, H. "Florilegium." *RAC* 7 (1969): 1131–59.
Chadwick, H. "Philo and the Beginnings of Christian Thought." Pages 137–57 in *The Cambridge History of Later Greek and Early Medieval Philosophy*. Edited by A. H. Armstrong. Cambridge: Cambridge University Press, 1967.
Chadwick, H. "St. Paul and Philo of Alexandria." *BJRL* 48 (1966): 286–307.
Charles, R. H., ed. *The Apocrypha and Pseudepigrapha of the Old Testament*. 2 vols. Oxford: Clarendon Press, 1913.
Cheikho, L., ed., *Agapius Episcopus Mabbugensis, Historia Universalis*. CSCO ser. III, t. 5. Beirut: E typographeo catholico, 1912.
Chesne, Léger du. *Oratio funebris* in Adrien Turnèbe, *Viri clariss. Adriani Turnebi … Opera, nunc primum ex bibliotheca amplissimi viri: Stephani Adriani f. Turnebi … in unum collecta, emendata, aucta et tributa in tomos III … Additi sunt singulis tomis singuli indices rerum et verborum locupletissimi*. 3 vols. Strasbourg: Lazare Zetzneri, 1600.
Chidester, D. *Word and Light: Seeing, Hearing, and Religious Discourse*. Urbana, IL: University of Illinois Press, 1992.

Chiesa, B. "Yaqub al Qirqisani come fonte storiografica." Pages 11–49 in *Yaqub al Qirqisani on Jewish Sects and Christianity*. Edited by B. Chiesa and W. Lockwood. Frankfurt: Peter Lang, 1984.

Christopherson, J. *Philonis Judaei scriptoris eloquentissimi gravissimique libri quatuor, quorum primus est, De mundi fabricatione, quae est a Moyse descripta, secundus, De decem praeceptis, quae capita legum sunt, tertius, De magistratu seu principe deligendo, quartus, De officio Iudicis, iam primum de Graeco in Latinum conversi: Ioanne Christophorsono Anglo, interprete*. Antwerp: Ioannes Vervvithaghen, 1553.

Christopherson, J. *Libri quatuor. I. De mundi fabricatione, quae est à Moyse descripta. II. De decem praeceptis, quae capita legum sunt. III. De magistratu seu principe deligendo. IV. De officio Iudicis, iam primum de graeco in latinum conuersi*. Antwerp: Joannes Verwithaghen 1553.

Church, P. *Hebrews and the Temple: Attitudes to the Temple in Second Temple Judaism and in Hebrews*. NovTSup 171. Leiden: Brill, 2017.

Ciholas, K. *The Lighthouse*. Austin, TX: Atmosphere Press, 2022.

Clarke, M. L. *Greek Studies in England 1700-1830*. Cambridge: Cambridge University Press, 1945.

Clerc, J. Le. *A Supplement to Dr. Hammond's Paraphrase and Annotations on the New Testament*. London: Sam. Buckley, 1699.

Coakley, D. "Stearne [Sterne], John." *Oxford Dictionary of National Biography* (2004), online. https://doi.org/10.1093/ref:odnb/26410.

Cohen, H. *Der Begriff der Religion im System der Philosophie*. Gießen: Töpelmann, 1915.

Cohen, H. *Ethik des reinen Willens*. Berlin: Bruno Cassirer, 1904.

Cohen, H. *Ethik des reinen Willens*. 2nd edn. Berlin: Bruno Cassirer, 1907.

Cohen, H. *Religion der Vernunft aus den Quellen des Judentums*. 2nd edn. Frankfurt am Main: Kauffmann, 1929.

Cohen, N. G. "Philo Judaeus and the Torah True Library." *Tradition: A Journal of Orthodox Jewish Thought* 41 (2008): 31–48.

Cohen, N. G. *Philo Judaeus: His Universe of Discourse*. BEATAJ 24. Frankfurt am Main: Peter Lang, 1995.

Cohen, N. G. *Philo's Scriptures: Citations from the Prophets and Writings: Evidence for a Haftarah Cycle in Second Temple Judaism*. JSJSup 123. Leiden: Brill, 2007.

Cohen, S. J. D. "Adolf Harnack's 'The Mission and Expansion of Judaism': Christianity Succeeds Where Judaism Fails." Pages 163–69 in *The Future of Early Christianity: Essays in Honor of Helmut Koester*. Edited by B. A. Pearson. Minneapolis: Fortress, 1991.

Cohen, S. J. D. "Respect for Judaism by Gentiles According to Josephus." *HTR* 80 (1987): 409–30.

Cohen, Y. "The Reception of Classical World in Modern Hebrew Culture: From the Late Eighteenth-Century to the Early Twentieth-Centuries" (in Hebrew). PhD diss. Ben-Gurion University of the Negev, Beersheba, 2018.

Cohn, L. "Ein Philo-Palimpsest (Vaticanus gr. 316)." *SPAW* 1 (1905): 36–52.

Cohn, L. "Einteilung und Chronologie der Schriften Philos." *Philologus, Supplementband* 7 (1899): 387–436.

Cohn, L. "The Latest Researches on Philo of Alexandria." *JQR* 5 (1892): 24–50.

Cohn, L. "Philo von Alexandria." *NJKA* 1 (1898): 514–540.

Cohn, L. "Zur Lehre vom Logos bei Philo." Pages 303–31 in *Judaica: Festschrift zu Hermann Cohens siebzigstem Geburtstag*. Berlin: Bruno Cassirer, 1912.

Cohn, L., ed. *Die Werke Philos von Alexandria in deutscher Übersetzung*. Vols. 1–5. Breslau: M. & H. Marcus, 1909–29.

Cohn, L., ed. *Die Werke Philos von Alexandria in deutscher Übersetzung*. Vol. 6. Breslau: Stefan Münz, 1938.

Cohn, L., ed. *Die Werke Philos von Alexandria in deutscher Übersetzung*. Vol. 7. Berlin: de Gruyter, 1964.

Cohn, L., ed. *Philonis Alexandrini Libellus de opificio mundi*. Breslauer Philologische Abhandlungen, vol. IV.4. Breslau: M. & H. Marcus, 1889.

Cohn, L. and P. Wendland, ed. *Philonis Alexandrini opera quae supersunt*. 7 vols in 8. Berlin: Reimer, 1896–1930.

Colish, M. L. *Ambrose's Patriarchs: Ethics for the Common Man*. Notre Dame, IN: University of Notre Dame Press, 2005.

Collard, C. "Markland, Jeremiah (1693–1776)." Pages 629–30 in vol. 2 of *Dictionary of British Classicists*. Edited by R. B. Todd. London: Thoemmes Continuum, 2004.

Collins, J. J. *Jewish Wisdom in the Hellenistic Age*. Louisville, KY: Westminster John Knox, 1997.

Colson, F. H., G. H. Whitaker, and R. Marcus, ed. and trans. *Philo in Ten Volumes (and Two supplementary Volumes)*. 12 vols. LCL. Cambridge, MA: Harvard University Press, 1929–62.

Coman, J. *Utilisation des Stromates de Clément par Eusèbe dans la Préparation Evangélique: Überlieferungsgeschichtliche untersuchungen*. Berlin: Akademie, 1981.

Conley, T. M. "Philo of Alexandria." Pages 695–713 in *Handbook of Classical Rhetoric in the Hellenistic Period (330 B.C.–A.D. 400)*. Edited by S. Porter. Leiden: Brill, 1997.

Conley, T. M. "Philo's Rhetoric: Argumentation and Style." *ANRW* 2.21.1 (1984): 343–71.
Constantinidou, N. "Constructions of Hellenism through Printing and Editorial Choices: The Case of Adrien de Turnèbe. Royal Lecturer and Printer in Greek (1512–1565)." *IJCT* 25 (2018): 262–84.
Constas, N. P. "Weaving the Body of God: Proclus of Constantinople, the Theokotos, and the Loom of the Flesh." *JECS* 3 (1995): 169–94.
Conway-Jones, A. *Gregory of Nyssa's Tabernacle Imagery in Its Jewish and Christian Contexts.* Oxford: Oxford University Press, 2014.
Conybeare, F. C. *Philo about the Contemplative Life.* Oxford: Clarendon Press, 1895.
Corke-Webster, J. *Eusebius and Empire: Constructing Church and Rome in the Ecclesiastical History.* Cambridge: Cambridge University Press, 2019.
Courcelle, P. *Late Latin Writers and Their Greek Sources.* Cambridge, MA: Harvard University Press, 1969.
Courcelle, P. *Les Confessions de Saint Augustin dans la tradition littéraire: antécédents et postérité.* Paris: Études augustiniennes, 1963.
Courcelle, P. *Les lettres grecques en Occident.* Paris: Boccard, 1948.
Courcelle, P. "Saint Augustin a-t-il lu Philon d'Alexandrie?" *REA* 63 (1961): 78–85.
Courtney, E. *A Commentary on the Satires of Juvenal.* London: Athlone Press, 1980.
Cover, M. B. "A New Fragment of Philo's *Quaestiones in Exodum* in Origen's Newly Discovered *Homilies on the Psalms*? A Preliminary Note." *SPhiloA* 30 (2018): 15–29.
Cover, M. B. "Of Dreams and Editions: Emendations, Conjectures, and Marginal Summaries in David Hoeschel's Copy of *De somniis* 2." Pages 243–68 in *Ancient Texts, Papyri, and Manuscripts.* Edited by A. T. Farnes, S. Mackie, and D. T. Runia. Leiden: Brill, 2022.
Cover, M. B. "Paris and Augsburg Revisited: David Hoeschel, Bürgerhumanimus, and the Ecumenical Completion of Turnèbe's Philo" (forthcoming).
Cover, M. B. "Philo's Poetics of Association: The Exegetical Structure of Philo's *On the Cherubim*." Paper presented in the Philo of Alexandria Seminar, SBL Annual Meeting, 18–21 November 2017, Boston, MA.
Cover, M. B. "Reconceptualizing Conquest: Colonial Narratives and Philo's Roman Accuser in the Hypothetica." *SPhiloA* 22 (2010): 183–207.
Cover, M. B. "The Sun and the Chariot: The *Republic* and the *Phaedrus* as Sources for Rival Platonic Paradigms of Psychic Vision in Philo's Biblical Commentaries." *SPhiloA* 26 (2014): 151–67.
Cover, M. B. and L. Doering, eds. *Philo of Alexandria and Philosophical Discourse.* Ioudaioi 14. Göttingen: Vandenhoeck & Ruprecht, 2024.
Cox, R. *By the Same Word: Creation and Salvation in Hellenistic Judaism and Early Christianity.* BZNW 145. Berlin: de Gruyter, 2007.
Cramer, A. *Catenae Graecorum patrum in Novum Testamentum* 7. Oxford: Typographeo Academico, 1843.
Crouzel, H. *Origène.* Paris: Lethielleux, 1985.
Dahm, K. H. "Commotion, Rebellion, and War: Eusebius of Caesarea's Narrative of Jewish Revolts against Roman Rule in His Ecclesiastical History." *JECS* 29 (2021): 495–523.
Daley, B. E. "Balthasar's Reading of the Church Fathers." Pages 187–206 in *The Cambridge Companion to Hans Urs von Balthasar.* Edited by E. T. Oakes. Cambridge: Cambridge University Press, 2006.
Daley, B. E. "The Giant's Twin Substances: Ambrose and the Christology of Augustine's *Contra sermonem Arianorum*." Pages 477–95 in *Augustine: Presbyter Factus Sum.* Edited by J. T. Lienhard et al. New York: Peter Lang, 1993.
Daley, B. E. *Gregory of Nazianzus.* The Early Church Fathers. London: Routledge, 2006.
Daniel-Nataf, S., et al., eds. *Philo of Alexandria: Writings.* 6 vols. Jerusalem: Bialik Institute and the Israel Academy of Sciences and Humanities, 1986–2012.
Daniel-Nataf, S., Y. Amir, and M. Niehoff, eds. *Philo of Alexandria: Writings.* 5 vols. Jerusalem: Bialik Institute and the Israel Academy of Sciences and Humanities, 1986–2012 (in Hebrew).
Daniel, R. "Literary and Sub-Literary Papyri from Berlin." Pages 284–94 in *Proceedings of the 20th International Congress of Papyrologists.* Edited by A. Bülow-Jacobsen. Copenhagen: University of Copenhagen Press, 1994.
Daniélou, J. "*Akolouthia* chez Grégoire de Nysse." *RevSR* 27 (1953): 219–49.
Daniélou, J. *Grégoire de Nysse, La vie de Moïse.* SC 1. Paris: Cerf, 1968.
Daniélou, J. *L'être et le temps chez Grégoire de Nysse.* Leiden: Brill, 1970.
Daniélou, J. "La notion de confins (*methorios*) chez Grégoire de Nysse." *RSR* 49 (1961): 161–87.
Daniélou, J. "La typologie d'Isaac dans le Christianisme primitif." *Bib* 28 (1974): 363–93.
Daniélou, J. "Moïse: exemple et figure chez Grégoire de Nysse." *Cahiers Sioniens* 8 (1954): 267–82.
Daniélou, J. "Philo et Grégoire de Nysse." Pages 333–45 in *Philon d'Alexandrie: Lyon 11–15 Septembre 1966.* Edited by R. Arnaldez, C. Mondésert, and J. Poilloux. Paris: CNRS, 1967.
Daniélou, J. *Philo of Alexandria.* Translated by J. Colbert. Eugene, OR: Cascade, 2014.
Daniélou, J. *Théologie du judéo-christianisme.* Tournai: Desclée, 1958.

Daniélou, J. *The Theology of Judaeo-Christianity*. Translated by John Austin Baker. London: Dartman, Longman and Todd, 1964.
Dassmann, E. *Ambrosius von Mailand: Leben und Werk*. Stuttgart: Kohlhammer, 2004.
Davidson, I. J. *Ambrose, De Officiis: Edited with an Introduction, Translation, and Commentary*. 2 vols. Oxford: Oxford University Press, 2001.
Dawson, D. *Allegorical Readers and Cultural Revision in Ancient Alexandria*. Berkeley: University of California Press, 1992.
de' Rossi, A. *The Light of the Eyes*. Translated by J. Weinberg. New Haven: Yale University Press, 2001.
de' Rossi, A. *Me'or Einayim*. Edited by D. Cassel. Vilna: Yosef Reuven Rom, 1866.
Decharneux, B. *L'ange, le devin et le prophète*. Brussels: University of Brussels, 1994.
Decock, P. B. "Migration as a Basic Image for the Life of Faith: The Letter to the Hebrews, Philo and Origen." *Neot* 51 (2017): 129–50.
DeConick, A. D. "Crafting Gnosis: Gnostic Spirituality in the Ancient New Age." Pages 287–305 in *Gnosticism, Platonism and the Late Ancient World: Essays in Honour of John D. Turner*. Edited by K. Corrigan and T. Rasimus. Nag Hammadi and Manichaean Studies 82. Leiden: Brill, 2013.
DeConick, A. D. "The Countercultural Gnostic: Turning the World Upside Down and Inside Out." *Gnosis* 1 (2016): 7–35.
DeConick, A. D. *The Gnostic New Age: How a Countercultural Spirituality Revolutionized Religion from Antiquity to Today*. New York: Columbia University Press, 2016.
Deconinck-Brossard, F. "Mangey, Thomas." *Oxford Dictionary of National Biography* 36 (2004): 412–413.
DelCogliano, M. "Phinehas the Zealot and the Cappadocians: Philo, Origen, and a Family Legacy of Anti-Eunomian Rhetoric." *Annali di storia dell'esegesi* 34 (2017): 107–23.
Delitzsch, F. "The Logos in John and Philo." *American Presbyterian and Theological Review* 2 (1864): 506–15.
Delling, G. *Bibliographie zur jüdisch-hellenistischen und intertestamentarischen Literatur 1900-1970*. TUGAL 106/2. Berlin: Akademie-Verlag, 1975.
Delling, G. *Studien zum Neuen Testament und zum hellenistichen Judentum. Gesammelte Aufsätze, 1950-1968*. Göttingen: Vandenhoeck & Ruprecht, 1970.
Delling, G. "Zum Corpus Hellenisticum Novi Testamenti." *ZNW* 54 (1963): 1–15.
DeMeuse, E. J. "*Nostre Philon*: Philo after Trent." *SPhiloA* 29 (2017): 87–109.
DeMeuse, E. J. "Spanish Jesuits and 'the Greeks': Reception and Perception of the Eastern Church in Luis de Molina, Francisco Suárez, and Gabriel Vásquez." *JTS* 69.1 (2018): 133–69.
Des Places, É. *Etudes platoniciennes 1929-1979*. Etudes préliminaires aux Religions orientales dans l'Empire romain 90. Leiden: Brill, 1981.
Destinon, J. von. *Die Quellen des Flavius Josephus*. Kiel: Lipsius & Tischer, 1881.
DeVore, D. J. *Eusebius' Ecclesiastical History and Classical Culture: Philosophy, Empire, and the Formation of Christian Identity*. Cambridge: Cambridge University Press, forthcoming.
DeVore, D. J. "Eusebius' Un-Josephan History: Two Portraits of Philo of Alexandria and the Sources of Ecclesiastical Historiography." *StPatr* 66 (2013): 161–79.
DeVore, D. J. *Greek Historiography, Roman Society, Christian Empire: The Ecclesiastical History of Eusebius of Caesarea*. PhD diss. University of California Berkeley, 2013.
Dienstfertig, M. *Die Prophetologie in der Religionsphilosophie des ersten nachchristlichen Jahrhunderts, unter besonderer Beachtung der Verschiedenheit in den Auffassungen des Philon von Alexandrien und des Flavius Josephus*. PhD diss. Erlangen. Breslau: Schatzky, 1892.
Dihle, A. "Das Streben nach Vollkommenheit nach Philon und Gregor von Nyssa." Pages 329–35 in *Stimuli: Exegese und ihre Hermeneutik in Antike und Christentum: Festschrift für Ernst Dassmann*. JAC Ergänzungsband 23. Edited by G. Schöllgen and C. Scholten. Münster: Aschendorffsche Verlagsbuchhandlung, 1996.
Dijkhuis, H. *Kaïns Kinderen: over Kaïn en de oorsprong van het kwaad*. Amsterdam: Boom, 1999.
Dillon, J. "Euripides and the Philosophy of His Time." *Classics Ireland* 11 (2004): 47–73.
Dillon, J. *The Middle Platonists: A Study of Platonism 80 B.C. to A.D. 220*. London: Duckworth, 1977.
Dillon, J. "Plutarch and God: Theodicy and Cosmogony in the Thought of Plutarch." Pages 223–37 in *Traditions of Theology: Studies in Hellenistic Theology, Its Background and Aftermath*. Edited by D. Frede and A. Laks. Philosophia Antiqua 89. Leiden: Brill, 2001.
Dinan, A. "Another Citation of Philo in Clement of Alexandria's *Protrepticus* (10, 93, 1–2)." *VC* 64 (2010): 435–44.
Dixon, S. "Urban Order and Religious Coexistence in the German Imperial City: Augsburg and Donauwörth, 1548–1608." *Central European History* 40.1 (2007): 1–33.
Dodd, C. H. *The Interpretation of the Fourth Gospel*. Cambridge: Cambridge University Press, 1953.
Dodds, E. R. *Les sources de Plotin*. Entretiens sur l'Antiquité Classique 5. Geneva: Fondation Hardt, 1960.

Dodds, E. R. "Numenius and Ammonius." Pages 3–33 in *Entretiens sur l'Antiquité Classique*, Volume 5: *Les sources des Plotin*. Geneva: Fondation Hardt, 1957.

Dodwell, H. *Dissertationes in Irenaeum. Auctore Henrico Dodwello A.M. Historices in Academia Oxoniensi Praelectore Cambdeniano. Accedit fragmentum Philippi Sidetae, hactenus ineditum, De Catechistarum Alexandrinorum Successione, cum notis*. Oxford: E Theatro Sheldoniano, 1689.

Dodwell, H. "Prolegomena Apologetica." Pages 1–282 in J. Stearne, *De obstinatione. Opus posthumum, pietatem Christiano-Stoicam, scholastico more, suadens*. Dublin: Benjamin Tooke, Typographus Regius, 1672.

Doering, L. "Philon im Kontext des palästinischen Judentums." Pages 147–66 in *Abrahams Aufbruch: Philon von Alexandria, De migration Abrahami*. Edited by M. R. Niehoff and R. Feldmeier. SAPERE 30. Tübingen: Mohr Siebeck, 2017.

Doering, L. *Schabbat: Sabbathalacha und -praxis im antiken Judentum und Urchristentum*. TSAJ 78. Tübingen: Mohr Siebeck, 1999.

Dohrmann, N. B. and D. Stern. *Jewish Biblical Interpretation and Cultural Exchange: Comparative Exegesis in Context*. Jewish Culture and Contexts. Philadelphia: University of Pennsylvania Press, 2008.

Donaldson, T. L. *Judaism and the Gentiles: Jewish Patterns of Universalism (to 135 CE)*. Waco, TX: Baylor University Press, 2007.

Dorn, J. C. *Ioannis Ionsii Holsati de scriptoribus historiae philosophicae libri IV. Nunc denuo recogniti atque ad praesentem aetatem usque perducti cura Io. Christophori Dornii cum praefatione Burcardi Gotthelfii Struvii*. Jena: viduam Meyerianam, 1716.

Dörrie, H., M. Baltes, M.-L. Lakmann, and C. Pietsch. *Der Platonismus in der Antike. Grundlagen–System–Entwicklung*. Stuttgart: Frommann-Holzboog, 1987–ongoing.

Dozy, R. *Supplément aux dictionnaires arabes*. 2 vols. Leiden: Brill, 1881.

Drobner, H. R. *Gregorii Nysseni Opera* IV/1. Leiden: Brill, 2009.

Druille, P. and D. Asade. "Filón de Alejandría y la embajada a Gayo en el *Chronicon Syriacum* y *Historia Dynasticarum* de Bar Hebraeus. Transmisión, texto y traducción." *Circe de clásicos y modernos* 23.2 (2019): 73–101.

Drummond, J. *Philo Judaeus, or the Jewish Alexandrian Philosophy in Its Development and Completion*. London: Williams and Norgate, 1888.

Dubie, N. "Simple Philo of Alexandria." Pages 47–48 in his *Radio Sky*. New York: Norton, 1991.

Dudley, C. S. and M. M. Mitchell. "Earle Hilgert: Scholar, Teacher, Librarian, Administrator and Colleague." Pages 11–17 in *Heirs of the Septuagint. Philo, Hellenistic Judaism and Early Christianity: Festschrift for Earle Hilgert*. Edited by D. T. Runia, D. M. Hay, and D. Winston. BJS 230. Atlanta: Society of Biblical Literature, 1991.

Dunderberg, I. *Gnostic Morality Revisited*. Tubingen: Mohr Siebeck, 2015.

Dunn, J. D. G. *Christology in the Making: An Inquiry into the Origins of the Doctrine of the Incarnation*. London: SCM Press, 1980.

Duval, Y.-M. "L'originalité du *De virginibus* dans le mouvement ascétique occidental: Ambroise, Cyprien, Athanase." Pages 15–66 in *Ambroise de Milan: XVIe centenaire de son élection épiscopale*. Edited by T.-M. Duval. Paris: Études augustiniennes, 1974.

Duvick, B., trans. *Proclus, On Plato's Cratylus*. Ithaca: Cornell University Press, 2007.

Eccles, R. S. *Erwin Ramsdell Goodenough: A Personal Pilgrimage*. Biblical Scholarship in America. Chico, CA: Scholars Press, 1985.

Edwards, M. J. *Image, Word, and God in the Early Christian Centuries*. Ashgate Studies in Philosophy and Theology in Late Antiquity. Farnham: Ashgate, 2013.

Edwards, M. J. "Justin's Logos and the Word of God." *JECS* 3 (1995): 261–80.

Eghishē. *History of Vardanides*. Translated into Modern Armenian by E. Ter-Minasyan. Erewan: Armenian State Press, 1946.

Egmond, B. van. *Augustine's Early Thought on the Redemptive Function of Divine Judgement*. Oxford: Oxford University Press, 2018.

Ehrman, B. D. *Forgery and Counterforgery: The Use of Literary Deceit in Early Christian Polemics*. Oxford: Oxford University Press, 2013.

Einatean, J. "Yovhannēs Sarkawag's Treatise On Polygonal Numbers." *Bulletin of Matenadaran* 23 (2016): 260–90 (in Armenian).

Elbaum, J. "*Yalqut Shim'oni* and the Medieval Midrashic Anthology." Pages 159–75 in *The Anthology in Jewish Literature*. Edited by D. Stern. New York: Oxford University Press, 2004.

Elishe. *History of Vardan and the Armenian War*. Translation and Commentary by R. W. Thomson. Cambridge, MA: Harvard University Press, 1982.

Elliott, P. M. C. "Ambrose of Milan and His Use of Philo of Alexandria in His Letters on the *Hexameron*." PhD diss. Hebrew Union College, 2018.

Elliott, P. M. C. *Creation and Literary Re-Creation: Ambrose's Use of Philo in the Hexameral Letters.* Piscataway, NJ: Gorgias Press, 2019.

Engberg-Pedersen, T. "Philo's *De vita contemplativa* as a Philosopher's Dream." *JSJ* 30 (1999): 40–64.

Engels, F. "Bruno Bauer und das Urchristentum" (1882). Pages 297–305 in vol. 19 of *Marx-Engels Werke* Berlin: Dietz, 1962.

Erikson, A., ed. *Letters to Erik Benzelius the Younger from Learned Foreigners.* 2 vols. Göteborg: Kungl. Vetenskaps- och Vitterhets-Samhället, 1980.

Erikson, A. and N. E. Nilsson, eds. *Erik Benzelius' Letters to His Learned Friends.* Göteborg: Kungl. Vetenskaps- och Vitterhets-Samhället, 1983.

Ernesti, J. A. *Principles of Biblical Interpretation.* 2 vols. Translated by C. H. Terrot. Edinburgh: T&T Clark, 1832.

Etienne, S. "Réflexion sur l'apostasie de Tibérius Julius Alexander." *SPhiloA* 12 (2000): 122–42.

Eusebius of Caesarea. *Ecclesiastica Historia.* Basel: Joannes Oporinus, 1562.

Évieux, P. *Isidore de Péluse.* ThH 99. Paris: Beauchesne, 1995.

Fabricius, J. A. *Bibliotheca Graeca.* 14 vols. Hamburg: Liebezeit & Felginer, 1714–28.

Fabricius, J. A. *Exercitatio de platonismo Philonis Judaei Viro doctissimo Johanni Jonsio opposita, Et indultu Amplissimae Facultatis Philosophicae pro loco Dissertationis argumentum proponenda a M. Joh. Alberto Fabricio.* Leipzig: Zeidler, 1693.

Fabricius, J. A. *Opusculorum historico-critico-literariorum sylloge quae sparsim viderant lucem nunc recensita denuo et partim aucta.* Hamburg: Sumptibus viduae Felgineriae, 1738.

Fabricius, J. A. and G. C. Harles. "De Philone Iudaeo." Pages 721–50 in *Ioannis Alberti Fabricii Bibliotheca Graeca sive notitia scriptorum veterum Graecorum […] editio nova variorum curis emendatior atque auctior curante Gottlieb Christophoro Harles.* Hamburg: Carolum Ernestum Bohn, 1795.

Fackenheim, E. "Samuel Hirsch and Hegel." Pages 21–40 in E. Fackenheim, *Jewish Philosophers and Jewish Philosophy.* Edited by M. L. Morgan. Bloomington, IN: Indiana University Press, 1996.

Farandos, G. D. *Kosmos und Logos nach Philon von Alexandria.* Amsterdam: Rodopi, 1976.

Favrelle, G. *Eusèbe de Césarée: Préparation évangélique.* Livre XI. SC 292. Paris: Cerf, 1982.

Fedwick, P. J. "A Chronology of the Life and Works of Basil of Caesarea." Pages 3–19 in *Basil of Caesarea: Christian, Humanist, Ascetic. A Sixteen-Hundredth Anniversary Symposium.* Edited by P. J. Fedwick. 2 vols. Toronto: Pontifical Institute of Mediaeval Studies, 1981.

Feiner, S. *Haskalah and History: The Emergence of a Modern Jewish Historical Consciousness.* Oxford: Littman Library of Jewish Civilization, 2001.

Feldman, L. H. *Flavius Josephus: Judean Antiquities 1–4.* Leiden: Brill, 2000.

Feldman, L. H. "Josephus' Portrayal of the Hasmoneans Compared with 1 Maccabees." Pages 41–68 in *Josephus and the History of the Greco-Roman Period.* Edited by F. Parente and J. Sievers. Leiden: Brill, 1994.

Feldman, L. H. "Philo, Pseudo-Philo, Josephus, and Theodotus on the Rape of Dinah." *JQR* 94 (2004): 253–77.

Feldman, L. H. *Philo's Portrayal of Moses in the Context of Ancient Judaism.* Notre Dame, IN: University of Notre Dame Press, 2008

Feldman, L. H. *Scholarship on Philo and Josephus (1937–1962).* Studies in Judaica 1. New York: Yeshiva University, 1963.

Feldman, L. H., J. L. Kugel, and L. H. Schiffman, eds. *Outside the Bible: Ancient Jewish Writings Related to Scripture.* 3 vols. Philadelphia: The Jewish Publication Society; Lincoln: University of Nebraska Press, 2013.

Ferentilli, M. A., trans. *De opificio mundi: La creatione del mondo descritta da Filone Hebreo.* Venice: Gabriel Giolito di Ferrarii, 1572.

Ferentilli, M. A. *Discorso universale di M. Agostino Ferentilli … Aggiuntavi La Creatione del Mondo, descritta da Filone Hebreo.* Venice: Gabriel Giolito di Ferrarii, 1570.

Fernandez, B., S.J. *Commentaria atque observationes morales in Genesim.* 3 vols. Lyons: Horatius Cardon, 1618–27.

Ferro, R. *Federico Borromeo ed Ericio Puteano: Cultura e letteratura a Milano agli inizi del Seicento.* Milan: Biblioteca Ambrosiana; Rome: Bulzoni, 2007.

Feuerbach, L. *Das Wesen des Christentums.* Ch. 8 in *Gesammelte Werke.* Edited by W. Schuffenhauer. Berlin: Akademie, 1967.

Fleteren, F. van. "Principles of Augustine's Hermeneutics." Pages 1–32 in *Augustine: Biblical Exegete.* Edited by F. van Fleteren. Frankfurt am Main: Peter Lang, 2001.

Fludd, R. *Philosophia Moysaica.* Gouda: Petrus Rammazenius, 1638.

Flusser, D. *The Josippon [Josephus Gorionides].* Jerusalem: Bialik, 1978 (in Hebrew).

Foakes Jackson, F. J. and K. Lake. *The Beginnings of Christianity, Part I: The Acts of the Apostles.* London: Macmillan and Co., 1920.

Formstecher, S. *Die Religion des Geistes: Eine wissenschaftliche Darstellung des Judenthums nach seinem Charakter, Entwicklungsgange und Berufe in der Menschheit.* Frankfurt am Main: J. C. Hermann, 1841.

Forrai, R. "The Interpreter of the Popes: The Translation Project of Anastasius Bibliothecarius." PhD diss. Central European University, Budapest, 2008.

Forrai, R. "The Notes of Anastasius on Eriugena's Translation of the *Corpus Dionysiacum*." *Journal of Medieval Latin* 18 (2008): 74–100.

Förster, T. *Ambrosius, Bischof von Mailand: Eine Darstellung seines Lebens und Wirkens.* Halle: Eugen Strien, 1884.

Fraade, S. D. "Ancient Jewish Law and Narrative in Comparative Perspective: The Damascus Document and the Mishnah." *Diné Israel: Studies in Halakhah and Jewish Law* 24 (2007): 65*–99*.

Fraade, S. D. "Before and after Babel: Linguistic Exceptionalism and Pluralism in Early Rabbinic Literature." *Diné Israel* 28 (2011): 31*–68*.

Fraade, S. D. "Between Rewritten Bible and Allegorical Commentary: Philo's Interpretation of the Burning Bush." Pages 221–32 in *Rewritten Bible after Fifty Years: Texts, Terms, or Techniques? A Last Dialogue with Geza Vermes.* Edited by J. Zsengellér. JSJSup 166. Leiden: Brill, 2014.

Fraade, S. D. "Early Rabbinic Midrash between Philo and Qumran." Pages 281–93 in *Strength to Strength: Essays in Appreciation of Shaye J. D. Cohen.* Edited by M. L. Satlow. Providence: Brown Judaic Studies, 2018.

Fraade, S. D. *From Tradition to Commentary: Torah and Its Interpretation in the Midrash Sifre to Deuteronomy.* Albany: State University of New York Press, 1991.

Fraade, S. D. "Hearing and Seeing at Sinai: Interpretive Trajectories." Pages 247–68 in *The Significance of Sinai: Traditions about Sinai and Divine Revelation in Judaism and Christianity.* Edited by G. J. Brooke, H. Najman, and L. T. Stuckenbruck. TBN 12. Leiden: Brill, 2008.

Fraade, S. D. "'A Heart of Many Chambers': The Theological Hermeneutics of Legal Multivocality." *HTR* 108 (2015): 113–28.

Fraade, S. D. "Language Mix and Multilingualism in Ancient Palestine: Literary and Inscriptional Evidence." *Jewish Studies* 48 (2012): 1*–40*.

Fraade, S. D. "Looking for Legal Midrash at Qumran." Pages 59–79 in *Biblical Perspectives: Early Use and Interpretation of the Bible in Light of the Dead Sea Scrolls.* Edited by M. E. Stone and E. G. Chazon. Leiden: Brill, 1998.

Fraade, S. D. "Rabbinic Midrash and Ancient Jewish Biblical Interpretation." Pages 99–120 in *The Cambridge Companion to the Talmud and Rabbinic Literature.* Edited by C. E. Fonrobert and M. S. Jaffee. Cambridge: Cambridge University Press, 2007.

Fraade, S. D. "Rabbinic Polysemy and Pluralism Revisited: Between Praxis and Thematization." *AJS Review* 31 (2007): 1–40.

Fraade, S. D. "The Temple Scroll as Rewritten Bible: When Genres Bend." Pages 136–54 in *Hā-'îsh Mōshe: Studies in Scriptural Interpretation in the Dead Seas and Related Literature: Studies in Honor of Moshe J. Bernstein.* Edited by B. Y. Goldstein, M. Segal, and G. J. Brooke. STDJ 122. Leiden: Brill, 2018.

Fraisse, O. "Einleitung." Pages 7–50 in Ibn Gabirol, *Fons vitae. Lebensquelle: Kapitel I und II.* Edited by O. Fraisse. Herders Bibliothek der Philosophie des Mittelalters 21. Freiburg: Herder, 2009.

Frankel, Z. *Programm zur Eröffnung des jüdisch-theologischen Seminars zu Breslau "Fraenkel'sche Stiftung" den 16. Ab 5614 / 10. August 1854.* Breslau: Korn, 1854.

Frankel, Z. *Ueber den Einfluss der palästinischen Exegese auf die alexandrinische Hermeneutik.* Leipzig: Joh. Ambr. Barth, 1851.

Frankel, Z. "Zur Ethik des jüdisch-alexandrinischen Philosophen Philo." *MGWJ* 16 (1867): 241–52.

Frede, M. "Numenius." *ANRW* 2.36.2 (1987): 1034–75.

Frede, M. "Numenius [6] of Apameia." *Brill's New Pauly* 9 (2006): 896–98.

Fredriksen, P. *Augustine and the Jews.* New York: Doubleday, 2008.

Fredriksen, P. *Jesus of Nazareth, King of the Jews.* New York: Alfred A. Knopf, 1999.

Freudenthal, J. *Hellenistische Studien.* Breslau: H. Skutsch, 1875.

Freudenthal, J. "Zur Geschichte der Anschauungen über die jüdisch-hellenistische Religionsphilosophie." *MGWJ* 18 (1869): 399–421.

Freudenthal, M. *Die Erkenntnislehre Philos von Alexandria.* Berliner Studien für classische Philologie und Archäologie 13.1. Berlin: Calvary, 1891.

Friedenberg, D. M. *Tiberius Julius Alexander: A Historical Novel.* Amherst, NY: Prometheus Books, 2010.

Friedheim, E. "Quelques notes sur la signification historique du silence philonien à propos de la Bibliothèque d'Alexandrie." Pages 245–55 in *The Library of Alexandria: A Cultural Crossroads of the Ancient World: Proceedings of the Second Polis Institute Interdisciplinary Conference.* Edited by C. Rico and A. Dan. Jerusalem: Polis Institute Press, 2017.

Friesen, C. J. P. *Acting Gods, Playing Heroes, and the Interaction between Judaism, Christianity, and Greek Drama in the Early Common Era*. London: Routledge, 2024.
Friesen, C. J. P. "Attending Euripides: Philo of Alexandria's Dramatic Appropriations." Pages 259–74 in *Euripides-Rezeption in Kaiserzeit und Spätantike*. Edited by M. Schramm. Millennium Studies 83. Berlin: de Gruyter, 2020.
Friesen, C. J. P. "Dying Like a Woman: Euripides' Polyxena as Exemplum between Philo and Clement of Alexandria." *GRBS* 56 (2016): 623–45.
Friesen, C. J. P. "Hannah's 'Hard Day' and Hesiod's 'Two Roads': Poetic Wisdom in Philo's *De ebrietate*." *JSJ* 46 (2015): 44–64.
Friesen, C. J. P. "Heracles and Philo of Alexandria: The Son of Zeus between Torah and Philosophy, Empire and Stage." Pages 176–99 in *Philo and Greek Myth: Narratives, Allegories, and Arguments*. Edited by F. Alesse and L. De Luca. SPhA 10. Leiden: Brill, 2019.
Friesen, C. J. P. "Virtue and Vice on Stage: Philo of Alexandria's Theatrical Ambivalences." *JAJ* 8 (2017): 241–56.
Früchtel, E. "Philon und die Vorbereitung der christlichen Paideia und Seelenleitung." Pages 19–33 in *Frühchristentum und Kultur*. Edited by F. R. Prostmeier. Freiburg: Herder, 2007.
Früchtel, L. "Isidoros von Pelusion als Benützer des Clemens Alexandrinus und anderer Quellen." *Philologische Wochenschrift* 58 (1938): 61–64.
Früchtel, L. "Neue Quellennachweise zu Isidoros von Pelusion." *Philologische Wochenschrift* 58 (1938): 764–68.
Früchtel, L. "Zum Oxyrhynchos-Papyrus des Philon (Ox.-Pap. XI 1356)." *Philologische Wochenschrift* 58 (1938): 1437–39.
Fuks, G. "Josephus and the Hasmoneans." *JJS* 41 (1990): 166–76.
Funkenstein, A. *Perceptions of Jewish History*. Berkeley: University of California Press, 1993.
Furher, T. "Augustine's Moulding of the Manichaean Idea of God in the *Confessiones*." *VC* 67 (2013): 531–47.
Fürst, A. "Acktuelle Tendenzen der Hieronymus-Forschung: Impressionen von einer Tagung über Hieronymus in Cardiff." *Adamantius* 13 (2007): 144–51.
Fürst, A. *Hieronymus: Askese und Wissenschaft in der Spätantike*. Freiburg: Herder. 2003.
Fürst, A., ed. *Origenes in Frankreich: Die Origeniana Pierre-Daniel Huets*. Adamantiana 10. Münster: Aschendorff, 2017.
Fürst, A. *Origenes: Grieche und Christ in römischer Zeit*. SAC 9. Stuttgart: Hiersemann, 2017.
Fürst, A. *Von Origenes und Hieronymus zu Augustinus: Studien zur antiken Theologiegeschichte*. Berlin: de Gruyter, 2011.
Fürst, J. *Bibliotheca Judaica. Bibliographisches Handbuch der gesammten jüdischen Literatur mit Einschluss der Schriften über Juden und Judenthum und einer Geschichte der jüdischen Bibliographie. Nach alfabetischer Ordnung der Verfasser*. 3 vols. Leipzig: Wilhelm Engelmann, 1849–63.
Gabriel, F. and S. Marculescu, eds. *Philon d'Alexandrie dans l'Europe moderne: réceptions d'un corpus judéo-hellénistique (xvie–xviiie s.)*. Forthcoming.
Gafni, I. M. "Josephus and 1 Maccabees." Pages 116–31 in *Josephus, The Bible, and History*. Edited by L. H. Feldman. Leiden: Brill, 1989.
Galen. *On the Usefulness of the Parts of the Body*. Translated by M. Tallmadge May. 2 vols. Ithaca: Cornell University Press, 1968.
Gambetti, S. *The Alexandrian Riots of 38 C.E. and the Persecution of the Jews: A Historical Reconstruction*. JSJSup 135. Leiden: Brill, 2009.
Gamble, H. Y. *Books and Readers in the Early Church*. New Haven: Yale University Press, 1995.
Gandzakets'i, K. *History of Armenia*. Edited by K. Melik'-Ohanjanyan. Erevan: Academy of Science of ArmSSR, 1961.
Garb, J. "Powers of Language in Kabbalah: Comparative Reflections." Pages 233–69 in *The Poetics of Grammar and the Metaphysics of Sound and Sign*. Edited by S. La Porta and D. D. Shulman. Leiden: Brill, 2007.
Garland, R. *Surviving Greek Tragedy*. London: Duckworth, 2004.
Garnsey, P. "The Middle Stoics and Slavery: Hellenistic Constructs." Pages 159–74 in *Hellenistic Constructs: Essays in Culture, History and Historiography*. Edited by P. Cartledge, P. Garnsey, and E. S. Gruen. Berkeley: University of California Press, 1997.
Gautier, P. "Eloge inédit du lecteur Jean Kroustoulas par Michel Psellos." *Rivista di studi bizantini e neoellenici* 17–19 (1980–82): 119–47.
Gebhardt, O. von. *Hieronymus. Liber de viris inlustribus in griechischer Übersetzung (der sogenannte Sophronius)*. TU 14.1b. Leipzig: J. C. Hinrichs, 1896.
Geerard, M. *Clavis Patrum Graecorum*. 5 vols. Turnhout: Brepols, 1974–87.

Gelenius, S. *Philonis Iudaei, scriptoris eloquentissimi, ac philosophi summi, lucubrationes omnes quotquot haberi potuerunt, nunc primum Latinae ex Graecis factae.* Basel: apud Nicolaum Episcopium iuniorem, 1554.

Geljon, A. C. "Divine Infinity in Gregory of Nyssa and Philo of Alexandria." *VC* 59 (2005): 152–77.

Geljon, A. C. "Philo of Alexandria and Gregory of Nyssa on Moses at the Burning Bush." Pages 225–36 in *The Revelation of the Name YHWH to Moses.* Themes in Biblical Narrative 9. Edited by G. H. van Kooten. Leiden: Brill, 2006.

Geljon, A. C. "Philo's Influence on Didymus the Blind." Pages 357–72 in *Philon d'Alexandrie: Un penseur à l'intersection des cultures Gréco-Romaine, Orientale, Juive et Chrétienne.* Edited by S. Inowlocki and B. Decharneux. Monothéismes et Philosophie. Turnhout: Brepols, 2011.

Geljon, A. C. "Philonic Elements in Didymus the Blind's Exegesis of the Story of Cain and Abel." *VC* 61 (2007): 282–312.

Geljon, A. C. *Philonic Exegesis in Gregory of Nyssa's* De vita Moysis. BJS 333. SPhiloM 5. Providence: Brown Judaic Studies, 2002.

Geljon, A. C. and D. T. Runia. *Philo of Alexandria,* On Planting: *Introduction, Translation, and Commentary.* PACS 5. Leiden: Brill, 2019.

Geller, S. A. "Fiery Wisdom: Logos and Lexis in Deuteronomy 4." *Proof* 14 (1994): 103–39.

Gerber, C. *Ein Bild des Judentums für Nichtjuden von Flavius Josephus.* Leiden: Brill, 1997.

Gerhard, J. "On Creation and Angels." in *Theological Commonplaces VIII.* Translated by R. J. Dinda. Edited by B. T. G. Mayes. St. Louis: Concordia, 2013.

Gerhard, J. "On the Church." in *Theological Commonplaces XXV.* Translated by R. J. Dinda. Edited by B. T. G. Mayes. St. Louis: Concordia, 2010.

Gfrörer, A. F. *Philo und die judisch-alexandrinische Theosophie.* 2 vols. Stuttgart: E. Schweizerbart's Verlagsbuchhandlung, 1831.

Ghellinck, J. de. "Note sur l'expression 'Geminae Gigas substantiae'." *RSR* 5 (1914): 416–21.

Gibson, R. "'Cf. e.g.': A Typology of 'Parallels' and the Function of Commentaries on Latin Poetry." Pages 331–57 in *The Classical Commentary: Histories, Practices, Theory.* Edited by R. Gibson and C. Shuttleworth Kraus. Mnemosyne Supplements 232. Leiden: Brill, 2002.

Giet, S. *Basile de Césarée, Homélies sur l'Hexaéméron.* SC 26. Paris: Cerf, 1968.

Gildenhard, I. "Buskins & SPQR: Roman Receptions of Greek Tragedy." Pages 153–85 in *Beyond the Fifth Century: Interactions with Greek Tragedy form the Fourth Century BCE to the Middle Ages.* Edited by I. Gildenhard and M. Revermann. Berlin: de Gruyter, 2010.

Gildenhard, I. and M. Revermann, eds. *Beyond the Fifth Century: Interactions with Greek Tragedy from the Fourth Century BCE to the Middle Ages.* Berlin: de Gruyter, 2010.

Giulea, D. A. *Pre-Nicene Christology in Paschal Contexts: The Case of the Divine Noetic Anthropos.* Leiden: Brill, 2014.

Gleason, M. "Mutilated Messengers: Body Language in Josephus." Pages 50–85 in *Being Greek under Rome: Cultural Identity, the Second Sophistic and the Development of Empire.* Edited by S. Goldhill. Cambridge: Cambridge University Press, 2001.

Gobry, I. "La ténèbre (γνόφος): l'héritage alexandrin de Saint Grégoire de Nysse." *Diotima: Revue de recherche philosophique* 19 (1991): 79–82.

Goetschel, R. "Philon et le Judaïsme hellénistique au miroir de Nachman Krochmal." Pages 371–83 in *Hellenica et Judaica. Hommage à Valentin Nikiprowetzky.* Edited by A Caquot et al. Leuven and Paris: Peeters, 1986.

Goldhill, S. "The Great Dionysia and Civic Ideology." Pages 97–129 in *Nothing to Do with Dionysos? Athenian Drama in Its Social Context.* Edited by J. J. Winkler and F. I. Zeitlin. Princeton: Princeton University Press, 1990.

Goldhill, S. "What Is Local Identity? The Politics of Cultural Mapping." Pages 46–68 in *Local Knowledge and Microidentities in the Imperial Greek World.* Edited by T. Whitmarsh. Greek Culture in the Roman World. Cambridge: Cambridge University Press, 2010.

Goldkorn, G. *Hommage à Philon d'Alexandrie.* Paris: Manuel Bruker, 1964.

Goldstein, J. A. *I Maccabees: A New Translation with Introduction and Commentary.* New York: Doubleday, 1976.

Goodenough, E. R. *By Light, Light: The Mystic Gospel of Hellenistic Judaism.* New Haven: Yale University Press, 1935.

Goodenough, E. R. "A Collection of Philo Judaeus." *Yale University Library Gazette* 25 (1951): 155–56.

Goodenough, E. R. *An Introduction to Philo Judæus.* 2nd edn. New Haven: Yale University Press. Oxford: Oxford University Press, 1962.

Goodenough, E. R. *Jewish Symbols in the Greco-Roman Period.* 13 vols. New York: Pantheon Books, 1953–68.

Goodenough, E. R. *The Theology of Justin Martyr*. Jena: Biedermann, 1923.
Goodhart, H. L. and E. R. Goodenough. "A General Bibliography of Philo Judaeus." Pages 125–321 in *The Politics of Philo Judaeus: Practice and Theory*. Edited by E. R. Goodenough. New Haven: Yale University Press, 1938.
Goodman, M. "Josephus' Treatise *Against Apion*." Pages 45–58 in *Apologetics in the Roman Empire: Pagans, Jews, Christians*. Edited by M. J. Edwards, M. Goodman, and S. Price. Oxford: Oxford University Press, 1999.
Gori, F. *Tutte le opere di Sant'Ambrogio: Verginità e vedovanza*. Biblioteca Ambrosiana 14.1. Rome: Biblioteca Ambrosiana, 1989.
Gossel, W. *Quibus ex fontibus Ambrosius in describendo corpore humano hauserit (Ambrosius Exam. VI. 54–74)*. PhD diss. Leipzig, 1908.
Goulet, R. *La philosophie de Moïse: essai de reconstitution d'un commentaire philosophique préphilonien du Pentateuque*. Paris: J. Vrin, 1987.
Grabbe, L. L. "Did All Jews Think Alike? 'Covenant' in Philo and Josephus in the Context of Second Temple Judaic Religion." Pages 251–66 in *The Concept of the Covenant in the Second Temple Period*. Edited by S. E. Porter and J. C. R. de Roo. JSJSup 71. Leiden: Brill, 2003.
Grabbe, L. L. *Etymology in Early Jewish Interpretation*. BJS 115. Atlanta: Scholars Press, 1988.
Grabbe, L. L. "Philo of Alexandria and the Origins of the Stoic ΠΡΟΠΑΘΕΙΑΙ." Pages 197–221 in *Philo of Alexandria and Post-Aristotelian Philosophy*. Edited by F. Alesse. Studies in Philo of Alexandria 5. Leiden: Brill, 2008.
Graetz, H. *Geschichte der Judäer von dem Tode Juda Makkabi's bis zum Untergange des jüdischen Staates*. Dritte verbesserte und stark vermehrte Auflage. Leipzig: Oskar Leiner, 1878.
Graetz, H. *Geschichte der Judäer von dem Tode Juda Makkabi's bis zum Untergange des jüdischen Staates*. Vierte verbesserte und stark vermehrte Auflage. Leipzig: Oskar Leiner, 1888.
Graetz, H. *Geschichte der Juden von dem Tode Juda Makkabi's bis zum Untergang des jüdischen Staates*. Leipzig: Leopold Schnauß, 1856.
Graetz, H. *Geschichte der Juden von dem Tode Juda Makkabi's bis zum Untergang des jüdischen Staates*. Zweite verbesserte und stark vermehrte Auflage. Leipzig: Oskar Leiner, 1863.
Graf, G. *Geschichte der christlichen arabischen Literatur*. 5 vols. Vatican: Biblioteca Apostolica Vaticana, 1944–53.
Grafton, A. "Christian Hebraism and the Rediscovery of Hellenistic Judaism." Pages 169–80 in *Jewish Culture in Early Modern Europe: Essays in Honor of David B. Ruderman*. Edited by R. J. Cohen, N. B. Dohrmann, A. Shear, and E. Reiner. Pittsburgh: University of Pittsburgh Press; Cincinnati: Hebrew Union College Press, 2014.
Grafton, A. *Joseph Scaliger: A Study in the History of Classical Scholarship*. Oxford: Clarendon Press, 1993.
Grafton, A. "Joseph Scaliger et l'histoire du Judaïsme Hellénistique." Pages 51–63 in *La république des letters et l'histoire du Judaïsme antique XVIe-XVIIe siècles*. Edited by C. Grell and F. Laplanche. Paris: Presses de l'Université de Paris-Sorbonne, 1992.
Grafton, A. *Worlds Made by Words: Scholarship and Community in the Modern West*. Cambridge, MA: Harvard University Press, 2009.
Grafton, A. and J. Weinberg. *"I have always loved the Holy Tongue": Isaac Casaubon, the Jews, and a Forgotten Chapter in Renaissance Scholarship*. Cambridge, MA: Harvard University Press, 2011.
Grafton, A. and M. Williams. *Christianity and the Transformation of the Book: Origen, Eusebius, and the Library of Caesarea*. Cambridge, MA: Harvard University Press, 2006.
Grant, R. M. "The Appeal to the Early Fathers." *JTS* 11 (1960): 13–24.
Grant, R. M. *Eusebius as Church Historian*. Oxford: Clarendon Press, 1980.
Grant, R. M. "Eusebius, Josephus and the Fate of the Jews." *SBL Seminar Papers* 115 (1979): 69–86.
Grant, R. M. *Greek Apologists of the Second Century*. Philadelphia: Fortress Press, 1988.
Grant, R. M. "Theophilus of Antioch to Autolycus." *HTR* 40 (1947): 237–41.
Grätz, H. "Die Construction der jüdischen Geschichte: Eine Skizze." *Zeitschrift für die religiösen Interessen des Judenthums* 3 (1846): 81–97.
Graver, M. "Philo of Alexandria and the Origins of the Stoic ΠΡΟΠΑΘΕΙΑΙ." Pages 197–221 in *Philo of Alexandria and Post-Aristotelian Philosophy*. Edited by F. Alesse. Studies in Philo of Alexandria 5. Leiden: Brill, 2008.
Graves, R. *Claudius the God*. London: Arthur Barker, 1935.
Graves, R. *I, Claudius*. London: Arthur Barker, 1934.
Green, A. *Seek My Face: A Jewish Mystical Theology*. 2nd edn. Woodstock, VT: Jewish Lights Publishing, 2003.
Green, A. *Seek My Face, Speak My Name: A Contemporary Jewish Theology*. Northvale, NJ: Jason Aronson Inc., 1992.

Green, T. H. "Lectures on the Fourth Gospel." Pages 135–88 in *Unpublished Manuscripts in British Idealism: Political Philosophy, Theology and Social Thought, I*. Edited by C. Tyler; London: Thoemmes, 2005.

Green, W. S. "Introduction: Messiah in Judaism: Rethinking the Question." Pages 1–13 in *Judaisms and Their Messiahs at the Turn of the Christian Era*. Edited by J. Neusner, W. S. Green, and E. Frerichs. Cambridge: Cambridge University Press, 1987.

Greer, R. *Origen: An Exhortation to Martyrdom, Prayer and Selected Works*. Classics of Western Spirituality. Mahwah, NJ: Paulist Press, 1979.

Gregerman, A. *Building on the Ruins of the Temple: Apologetics and Polemics in Early Christianity and Rabbinic Judaism*. TSAJ 165. Tübingen: Mohr Siebeck, 2016.

Griffin Jr., M. I. J. *Latitudinarianism in the Seventeenth-Century Church of England*. Edited by Lila Freedman. Leiden: Brill, 1992.

Grigoryan, G. "The Armenian Commentaries to Philo's Works." *Bulletin of Matenadaran* 5 (1960): 95–110.

Grimm, C. L. W. *Das erste Buch der Maccabäer*. Leipzig: S. Hirzel, 1853.

Grossberg, M., trans. *Sefer Yetzirah Ascribed to the Patriarch Abraham with Commentary by Dunash Ben Tamim*. London: E. Z. Rabbinoviṭsh, 1902.

Grote. U. *Der Schatz von Münster*. Münster: Aschendorff, 2019.

Grotius, H. *Annotationes in Novum Testamentum*. 9 vols. Groningen: W. Zuideman, 1826–34.

Gruen, E. S. "Caligula, the Imperial Cult, and Philo's *Legatio*." *SPhiloA* 24 (2012): 135–47.

Gruen, E. S. *Diaspora: Jews amidst Greeks and Romans*. Cambridge, MA: Harvard University Press, 2002.

Gruen, E. S. "Jewish Literature and the Second Sophistic." Pages 639–54 in *The Oxford Handbook of the Second Sophistic*. Edited by D. S. Richter and W. A. Johnson. Oxford: Oxford University Press, 2017.

Grypeou, E. and H. Spurling, eds. *The Exegetical Encounter between Jews and Christians in Late Antiquity*. Leiden: Brill, 2009.

Gryson, R. "Le vêtement d'Aaron interprété par saint Ambroise." *Muséon* 92 (1979): 273–80.

Gryson, R. "Les Lévites, figure du sacerdoce véritable, selon Saint Ambroise." *ETL* 56 (1980): 89–112.

Guazzelli, G. A. "Cesare Baronio and the Roman Catholic Vision of the Early Church." Pages 52–71 in *Sacred History: Uses of the Christian Past in the Renaissance World*. Edited by K. Van Liere et al. Oxford: Oxford University Press, 2012.

Guillaumont, A. "Philon et les origines du monachisme." Pages 361–73 in *Philon d'Alexandrie: Lyon 11–15 Septembre 1966*. Edited by R. Arnaldez, C. Mondésert, and J. Pouilloux. Paris: CNRS, 1967.

Gunderson, E., ed. *The Cambridge Companion to Ancient Rhetoric*. Cambridge: Cambridge University Press, 2009.

Guttmann, J. *Trauerrede an der Bahre des Professor Dr. Leopold Cohn, Oberbibliothekar an der Königlichen Universitätsbibliothek zu Breslau am 21. November 1915*. Breslau: Verein für jüdische Geschichte und Literatur zu Breslau, 1915.

Gutzwiller, K. J. "Cleopatra's Ring." *GRBS* 36 (1995): 383–98.

Haaland, G. "Josephus and the Philosophers of Rome: Does *Contra Apionem* Mirror Domitian's Crushing of the 'Stoic Opposition'?" Pages 297–316 in *Josephus and Jewish History in Flavian Rome and Beyond*. Edited by J. Sievers and G. Lembi. Leiden: Brill, 2005.

Hadas-Lebel, M. *Philo of Alexandria: A Thinker in the Jewish Diaspora*. SPhA 7. Translated by R. Fréchet. Leiden: Brill, 2012.

Hadas-Lebel, M. *Philon d'Alexandrie: un penseur en diaspora*. Paris: Fayard, 2003.

Hadas-Lebel, M. "Voltaire lecteur de Flavius Josèphe," *Revue des études juives* 150.3–4 (1991): 529–34.

Hadot, P. "Plotinus." *Brill's New Pauly* 11 (2007): 395–403.

Häfner, R. "Fabricius, Johann Albert." Pages 383–85 in *Geschichte der Altertumswissenschaften. Biographisches Lexicon*. Der Neue Pauly, Supplemente 6. Edited by P. Kuhlmann and H. Schneider. Stuttgart: J. B. Metzler, 2012.

Hagendahl, H. *Latin Fathers and the Classics: A Study on the Apologists, Jerome and Other Christian Writers*. Studia Graeca et Latina Gothoburgensia. Göteborg: Institute of Classical Studies. 1958.

Hagendahl, R. and J. H. Waszink. "Hieronymus." *RAC* 15 (1989): 117–39.

Hägg, H. F. *Clement of Alexandria and the Beginnings of Christian Apophaticism*. Oxford: Oxford University Press, 2006.

Hagner, D. A. "The Vision of God in Philo and John: A Comparative Study." *JETS* 14 (1971): 81–93.

Haimson Lushkov, A. "Citation, Spoliation, and Literary Appropriation in Livy's AUC." Pages 30–46 in *Rome, Empire of Plunder: The Dynamics of Cultural Appropriation*. Edited by M. P. Loar et al. Cambridge: Cambridge University Press, 2018.

Hannah, D. D. *Michael and Christ: Michael Traditions and Angel Christology in Early Christianity*. Tübingen: Mohr Siebeck, 1999.

Harding, P. "Taylor, John (1704–66)." Pages 951–52 in vol. 3 of *Dictionary of British Classicists*. Edited by R. B. Todd. London: Thoemmes Continuum, 2004.

Hardwick, L. *Reception Studies*. Greece and Rome: New Surveys in the Classics 33. Oxford: Oxford University Press, 2003.
Hardwick, M. E. *Josephus as a Historical Source in Patristic Literature through Eusebius*. Brown Judaic Studies 128. Atlanta: Scholars Press, 1989.
Hariulf. *Chronique de l'Abbaye de Saint-Riquier (Ve Siècle–1104)*. Edited by F. Lot. Paris: Picard, 1894.
Harker, A. *Loyalty and Dissidence in Roman Egypt: The Case of the* Acta Alexandrinorum. Cambridge: Cambridge University Press, 2008.
Harl, M. *Philon d'Alexandrie,* Quis rerum divinarum heres sit: *introduction, traduction et notes*, Les oeuvres de Philon d'Alexandrie 15. Paris: Cerf, 1966
Harles, G. C. *Biblioteca Graeca*. Revised Edition. Leipzig, 1790–1812.
Harmsen, T. "Dodwell, Henry." In *Oxford Dictionary of National Biography* (2004), online. https://doi.org/10.1093/ref:odnb/7763.
Harnack, A. von. *Lehrbuch der Dogmengechichte*. Tübingen: Mohr, 1909–10.
Harnack, A. von. *The Mission and Expansion of Christianity in the First Three Centuries*. Translated by James Moffatt. London: Williams & Norgate, 1908.
Harrington, D. J. *Pseudo-Philon, Les Antiquités Bibliques*. SC 229. Paris: Cerf, 1976.
Harris, J. M. *Nachman Krochmal: Guiding the Perplexed of the Modern Age*. New York: New York University Press, 1991.
Harris, J. R., ed. *Fragments of Philo Judaeus*. Cambridge: Cambridge University Press, 1886.
Harris, J. R. "The Influence of Philo upon the New Testament." *ExpT* 37 (1926): 565–66.
Harut'yunyan, E. *Mxit'ar Ayrivanets'i: Life and Works*. Erewan: Academy of Science of Armenian SSR, 1985.
Harvey, W. Z. "Hebraism and Western Philosophy in Harry Austryn Wolfson's Theory of History." *Daat* 4 (1980): 103–9 (in Hebrew).
Hasselhoff, G. K. "Idee und Leitgedanken des Bandes." Pages 3–16 in *Die Entdeckung des Christentums in der Wissenschaft des Judentums*. Edited by G. K. Hasselhoff. Studia Judaica 54. Berlin: de Gruyter, 2010.
Hasselhoff, G. K. "Manuel Joel and the Neo-Maimonidean Discovery of Kant." Pages 289–307 in *The Cultures of Maimonideanism. New Approaches to the History of Jewish Thought*. Edited by J. T. Robinson. Supplements to the Journal of Jewish Thought and Philosophy 9. Leiden: Brill, 2009.
Hasselhoff, G. K. "Philosophie und Rabbinat: Manuel Joel." Pages 285–313 in *Religion und Rationalität*. Edited by G. K. Hasselhoff and Michael Meyer-Blanck. Studien des Bonner Zentrums für Religion und Gesellschaft 4. Würzburg: Ergon, 2008.
Hasselhoff, G. K. "'Ueber den wissenschaftlichen Einfluss des Judenthums auf die nichtjüdische Welt' (M. Joel)—Zu einem Forschungsprogramm des Breslauer Jüdisch-Theologischen Seminars." *Kalonymos* 22.3 (2019): 4–8.
Hata, G. "The Abuse and Misuse of Josephus in Eusebius' Ecclesiastical History, Books 2 and 3." Pages 91–102 in *Studies in Josephus and the Varieties of Ancient Judaism*. Edited by S. J. D. Cohen and J. J. Schwartz. Leiden: Brill, 2006.
Hata, G. "Eusebius and Josephus: The Way Eusebius Misused and Abused Josephus." *Patristica: Proceedings of the Colloquia of the Japanese Society for Patristic Studies*. Supplement 1 (2001): 49–66.
Hausher, I. "Ignorance infinie ou science infinie?" *OCP* 25 (1959): 44–52.
Hay, D. M. "References to Other Exegetes." Pages 81–97 in *Both Literal and Allegorical: Studies in Philo of Alexandria's Questions and Answers on Genesis and Exodus*. Edited by D. M. Hay. Providence: Brown University Press, 1991.
Hayes, C. *What's Divine about Divine Law? Early Perspectives*. Princeton: Princeton University Press, 2015.
Hayward, C. T. R. *Interpretations of the Name Israel in Ancient Judaism and Some Early Christian Writings: From Victorious Athlete to Heavenly Champion*. Oxford: Oxford University Press, 2005.
Hayward, C. T. R. *Saint Jerome's Hebrew Questions on Genesis*. Oxford Early Christian Studies. Oxford: Clarendon Press, 1995.
Hayward, C. T. R. "St. Jerome and the Meaning of the High-Priestly Vestments." Pages 90–105 in *Hebrew Study from Ezra to Ben-Yehuda*. Edited by W. Horbury. Bloomsbury Academic, 1999.
Hayward, C. T. R. *The Jewish Temple: A Non-Biblical Sourcebook*. London: Routledge, 1996.
Hecht, R. D. "Philo and Messiah." Pages 139–68 in *Judaisms and Their Messiahs at the Turn of the Christian Era*. Edited by J. Neusner, W. S. Green, and E. Frerichs. Cambridge: Cambridge University Press, 1987.
Heckel, T. K. *Der Innere Mensch: Die paulinische Verarbeitung eines platonischen Motivs*. Tübingen: Mohr Siebeck, 1993.
Hedley, D. and D. J. Tolan, eds., *Participation in the Divine: A Philosophical History, From Antiquity to the Modern Era*. Cambridge Studies in Religion and Platonism. Cambridge: Cambridge University Press, 2024.
Heemstra, M. *Fiscus Iudaicus and the Parting of the Ways*. Tübingen: Mohr Siebeck, 2010.
Hegel, G. W. F. *Encyklopädie der philosophischen Wissenschaften*. Gesammelte Werke, vol. IX. Edited by W. Bonsiepen and H.-C. Lucas. Hamburg: Meiner, 1992.

Hegel, G. W. F. "The Lectures of 1831 (Excerpts)." Pages 721–60 in vol. 2 of *Lectures on the Philosophy of Religion*. Edited by P. C. Hodgson. Berkeley: University of California Press, 1987.

Hegel, G. W. F. "Religionsphilosophie (1831)." Pages 611–48 in vol. 1 of *Vorlesungen über die Philosophie der Religion*. Edited by W. Jaeschke. Hamburg: Meiner, 1985.

Hegel, G. W. F. *The Philosophy of History*. Translated by T. Knox. Chicago: Encyclopedia Britannica, 1952.

Hegel, G. W. F. *Vorlesungen über die Geschichte der Philosophie*. Berlin: Duncker and Humblot, 1835; repr. Stuttgart: Fromann-Holzboog 1959.

Hegel, G. W. F. *Vorlesungen über die Philosophie der Religion*. Edited by H. Glockner. Stuttgart: Fromann-Holzboog, 1927–39.

Hegermann, H. *Die Vorstellung von Schöpfungsmittler im hellenistichen Judentum und Urchristentum*. TU 82. Berlin: Akademie, 1961.

Heidl, G. *Origen's Influence on the Young Augustine*. Piscataway, NJ: Gorgias, 2003.

Heil, G. and A. M. Ritter, eds. *Corpus Dionysiacum II*. 2nd edition. Berlin: de Gruyter, 2012.

Heinemann, I. *Philons griechische und jüdische Bildung: Kultuvergleichende Untersuchungen zu Philons Darstellung der jüdischen Gesetze*. Breslau: M. & H. Marcus, 1932; repr. Hildesheim: G. Olms, 1962.

Heinemann, I. "Philos Lehre vom Eid." Pages 109–18 in *Judaica: Festschrift zu Hermann Cohens siebzigstem Geburtstag*. Berlin: Bruno Cassirer, 1912.

Heinemann, I. *The Reasons for the Commandments in Jewish Thought from the Bible to the Renaissance*. Translated by L. Levin. Boston: Academic Studies Press, 2009.

Heinisch, P. *Der Einfluss Philo auf die älteste christliche Exegese (Barnabas, Justin und Clement von Alexandria)*. Münster: Aschendorff, 1908.

Heinrici, C. F. G. "Instruktionstext fur Mitarbeiter am Corpus Hellenisticum Novi Testamenti." Pages 303–10 in *Fruhjudentum und Neues Testament im Horizont Biblischer Theologie. Mit einem Anhang zum Corpus Judaeo-Hellenisticum Novi Testamenti*. Edited by W. Kraus and K.-W. Niebuhr. WUNT 162. Tubingen: Mohr Siebeck, 2003.

Heinze, M. *Die Lehre vom Logos in der griechischen Philosophie*. Oldenburg: Schmidt, 1872.

Hekster, O. "Propagating Power: Hercules as an Example for Second-Century Emperors." Pages 205–21 in *Herakles and Hercules: Exploring a Greco-Roman Divinity*. Edited by L. Rawlings and H. Bowden. Swansea: Classical Press of Wales, 2005.

Helleman, W. E. "Deification and Assimilation to God." SPhiloA 2 (1990): 51–71.

Helleman-Elgersma, W. "Augustine and Philo of Alexandria's Sarah as a Wisdom Figure." StPatr 18 (2013): 105–15.

Helm, R., ed. *Eusebius Werke 7: Die Chronik des Hieronymus*. GCS 47. Berlin: Akademie Verlag, 1956.

Helmbold, W. C. and E. N. O'Neill. *Plutarch's Quotations*. Philological Monographs 19. London: American Philological Association, 1959.

Henke, R. von. *Basilius und Ambrosius über das Sechstagewerk: Eine vergleichende Studie*. Chrêsis VII. Basel: Schwabe, 2000.

Henrichs, A. "Philosophy, the Handmaiden of Theology." GRBS 9 (1968): 437–50.

Henry, P. *Recherches sur la Préparation Evangélique d'Eusèbe et l'édition perdue des Œuvres de Plotin publiée par Eustochius*. Paris: Bibliothèque de l'Ecole des Hautes Etudes, Sciences religieuses, 1935.

Henry, R. *Photius Bibliothèque*. 8 vols. Paris: Les belles lettres, 1959–77.

Henten, J. W. van "Commonplaces in Herod's Commander Speech in Josephus *A.J.* 15.127–146." Pages 183–206 in *Josephus and Jewish History in Flavian Rome and Beyond*. Edited by J. Sievers and G. Lembi. Leiden: Brill, 2005.

Hermann, M.-L. *Die 'Hermeneutische Stunde' des Hebräerbriefs: Schriftauslegung in Spannungsfeldern*. Herders Biblische Studien 72. Freiburg: Herder, 2013.

Hernández, P. N. "Philo and Greek Poetry." SPhiloA 26 (2014): 135–49.

Hertog, C. den. *The Other Face of God: 'I Am That I Am' Reconsidered*. Hebrew Bible Monographs 32. Sheffield: Sheffield Phoenix Press, 2012.

Hesberg, H. von. "The King on Stage." Pages 65–75 in *Art of Ancient Spectacle*. Edited by B. Bergmann and C. Kondoleon. Studies in the History of Art 56. Washington, DC: National Gallery, 1999.

Hess, M. *Die heilige Geschichte der Menschheit: Von einem Jünger Spinoza's*. Stuttgart: Hallbergische Verlagshandlung, 1837.

Hester, C., ed. *Ferdinand Christian Baur. Die frühen Briefe (1814–1835)*. Contubernium 38. Sigmaringen: Jan Thorbecke, 1993.

Heumann, C. A. *Acta Philosophorum*. Halle: Rengerische Buchhandlung, 1715.

Heyden, K. "Die *Christliche Geschichte* des Philippos von Side. Mit einem kommentierten Katalog der Fragmente." Pages 210–43 in *Julius Africanus und die christliche Weltchronik. Julius Africanus und die christliche Weltchronistik*. Edited by M. Wallraff. Berlin: de Gruyter, 2006.

Heyne, C. G., trans. *Philo vom Leben Moses, das ist: von der Gottesgelahrtheit und dem prophetischen Geiste*. Dresden: Waltherische Buchhandlung, 1778.

Hilgert, E. "Bibliographia Philoniana 1935–1981." Pages 47–97 in *Hellenistisches Judentum in römischer Zeit: Philon und Josephus*. Edited by W. Haase. ANRW II 21.1. Berlin: de Gruyter, 1984.

Hilgert, E. "Philo Judaeus et Alexandrinus: The State of the Problem." Pages 1–15 in *The School of Moses: Studies in Philo and Hellenistic Religion In Memory of Horst R. Moehring*. Edited by J. P. Kenney. BJS 304. Atlanta: Scholars Press, 1995.

Hilgert, E. "The Philo Institute, *Studia Philonica* and Their *Diadochoi*." Pages 13–24 in *In the Spirit of Faith: Studies in Philo and Early Christianity in Honor of David Hay*. Edited by D. T. Runia and G. E. Sterling. BJS 332. Providence, RI: Brown Judaic Studies, 2001.

Hill, R. C. *Didymus the Blind: Commentary on Genesis*. FC 132. Washington, DC: Catholic University of America Press, 2016.

Hill, R. C. *Didymus the Blind: Commentary on Zechariah*. FC 111. Washington, DC: Catholic University of America Press, 2006.

Hinchliff, P. and J. Prest. "Jowett, Benjamin. 1817–1893." *Oxford Dictionary of National Biography*, (2004). https://doi.org/10.1093/ref:odnb/15143.

Hirsch-Luipold, R. "Der eine Gott bei Philon von Alexandrien und Plutarch." Pages 141–68 in *Gott und die Götter bei Plutarch: Götterbilder–Gottesbilder-Weltbilder*. Edited by R. Hirsch-Luipold. RVV 54. Berlin: de Gruyter, 2005.

Hirsch, S. *Die Religionsphilosophie der Juden oder das Prinzip der jüdischen Religionsanschauung und sein Verhältnis zum Heidenthum, Christenthum und zur absoluten Philosophie*. Leipzig: H. Hunger, 1841.

Hirschfeld, H. "The Arabic Portion of the Cairo Genizah at Cambridge." *JQR* 16 (1904): 573–78.

Hirshman, M. *Torah for the Entire World*. Tel Aviv: Hakibbutz Hameuchad, 1999 (in Hebrew).

Hobbs, R. G. "Reading the Old Testament after Trent: Cardinal Robert Bellarmine and His Italian Predecessors on Psalm Four." *Reformation & Renaissance Review* 12 (2010): 207–34.

Hoek, A. van den. "Assessing Philo's Influence in Christian Alexandria: The Case of Origen." Pages 223–39 in *Shem in the Tents of Japheth: Essays on the Encounter of Judaism and Hellenism*. Edited by J. Kugel, JSJSup 74. Leiden: Brill, 2002.

Hoek, A. van den. "The Catechetical School of Early Christian Alexandria and Its Philonic Heritage." *HTR* 90 (1997): 59–87.

Hoek, A. van den: *Clément d'Alexandrie, Les Stromates, Stromates IV: Introduction, texte critique et notes*. Translated by C. Mondésert. SC 463. Paris: Cerf, 2001.

Hoek, A. van den. "Clement of Alexandria and His Use of Philo in the *Protrepticus and Paedagogue*." *SPhiloA* 36 (forthcoming).

Hoek, A. van den. *Clement of Alexandria and His Use of Philo in the* Stromateis: *An Early Christian Reshaping of a Jewish Model*. VCSup 3. Leiden: Brill, 1988.

Hoek, A. van den. "How Alexandrian Was Clement of Alexandria? Reflections on Clement and His Alexandrian Background." *HeyJ* 31 (1990): 179–94.

Hoek, A. van den. "Origen and the Intellectual Heritage of Alexandria: Continuity or Disjunction?" Pages 40–50 in *Origeniana Quinta*. Edited by R. J. Daly. Peeters: Leuven, 1992.

Hoek, A. van den. "Philo and Origen: A Descriptive Catalogue of Their Relationship." *SPhiloA* 12 (2000): 44–121.

Hoek, A. van den. "Techniques of Quotation in Clement of Alexandria: A View of Ancient Literary Working Methods." *VC* 50 (1996): 223–43.

Hoek, A. van den and J. H. Herrmann, Jr. "Chasing the Emperor: Philo in the *Horti* of Rome." *SPhiloA* 28 (2016): 171–204.

Hoenig, C. *Plato's Timaeus and the Latin Tradition*. Cambridge: Cambridge University Press, 2018.

Hoeschel, D. *Philo Judaeus De Septenario: Eiusdem fragmenta II. E libro de Providentia: omnia e codicibus nunc primum edita*. Augsburg: Ad insigne pinus, 1614.

Hoeschel, D. *Philonis Iudaei opuscula tria: 1, Quare quorundam in sacris literis mutata sint nomina; 2, De formatione Euae ex Adami latere; & de utriusque lapsu; 3, Somniorum Iosephi, Pharonis, picernaeque ac pistoris, allegorica expositio: Graeca nunc primum edita, studio & opera Davidis Hoeschelii A. M. eiusdemque Notatiunculis alicubi illustrata*. Frankfurt: Joannes Wechelus, 1587.

Hoeschel, D. Ὁμιλίαι θεοφόρων τινῶν πατέρων: *Homiliae quaedam sacrae, Basilii M., Gregorii Nysseni, Nazianzeni, Ioan. Chrysostomi, Cyri Germani; in praecipuas anni ferias: cum fragmento Cyrilli Alexandrini*. Augsburg: Manger, 1587.

Holladay, C. R., ed. *Fragments from Hellenistic Jewish Authors*, Vol. III: *Aristobulus*. Atlanta: Scholars Press, 1995.

Holladay, C. R. *Theios Anēr in Hellenistic Judaism: A Critique of the Use of this Category in New Testament Studies*. Missoula, MT: Scholars Press, 1977.

Hollerich, M. J. *Eusebius of Caesarea's Exegesis in the Age of Constantine*. Oxford: Oxford University Press, 1999.

Hollerich, M. *Making Christian History: Eusebius of Caesarea and His Readers*. Berkeley: University of California Press, 2021.
Holzhausen, J. *Der Mythos vom Menschen im hellenistischen Agypten: Eine Studie zum 'Poimandres' (=CH 1), zu Valentin und dem gnostischen Mythos*. Bodenheim: Athenäum Hain Hanstein, 1994.
Homes Dudden, F. *The Life and Times of St. Ambrose*. Oxford: Clarendon Press, 1935.
Horn, G. *Historia philosophica*. Lyon: apud Johannem Elsevirium, 1655.
Horowitz, J. "Entwicklung des alexandrinischen Judentums unter dem Einflusse Philos." Pages 535–67 in *Judaica: Festschrift zu Hermann Cohens siebzigstem Geburtstag*. Berlin: Bruno Cassirer, 1912.
Horst, P. W. van der. "Johann Jakob Wettstein nach 300 Jahren: Erbe und Anfang." *TZ* 49 (1993): 267–80.
Horst, P. W. van der. *Philo's Flaccus: The First Pogrom: Introduction, Translation, and Commentary*. PACS 2. Leiden: Brill, 2003.
Houston, G. W. *Inside Roman Libraries: Book Collections and Their Management in Antiquity*. Chapel Hill: University of North Carolina Press, 2014.
Hubbard, J. M. "Does Justin Argue with Jews? Reconsidering the Relevance of Philo." *VC* 75 (2022): 237–56.
Hult, K. *Theodore Metochites on Ancient Authors and Philosophy: Semeioseis gnomikai 1–26 & 71*. Studia Graeca et Latina Gothoburgensia 65. Goteburg: Acta Universitatis Gothoburgensis, 2002.
Humphrey, L. *Interpretatio linguarum, seu de ratione convertendi et explicandi autores tam sacros quàm prophanos, libri tres*. Basel: Hieronymus Frobenius and Nicolaus Episcopius, 1559.
Humphrey, L. *Optimates, sive de nobilitate. Adiunctus est propter utilitatem et affinitatem argumenti, Philo Iudaeus De nobilitate*. Basel: Ioannes Oporinus, 1560.
Humphrey, L. *The Nobles, or the Nobilitye. The original nature, dutyes, right, and Christian Institucion thereof three bookes. Fyrste eloquentlye written in Latine by Lawrence Humphrey … late englished. Whereto, for the readers commodititye, and matters affinitye, is coupled the small treatyse of Philo, a Jewe. By the same Author out of the Greeke Latined, nowe also Englished*. London: Thomas Marshe, 1563.
Hunger, H. and O. Kresten. *Katalog der griechischen Handschriften der Österreichischen Nationalbibliothek. Teil 3/1. Codices Theologici 1–100*. Vienna: Verlag Brüder Hollinek, 1976.
Hurst, L. D. *The Epistle to the Hebrews: Its Background of Thought*. SNTSMS 65. Cambridge: Cambridge University Press, 1990.
Hurst, L. D. "How 'Platonic' are Heb. Viii.5 and ix.23f?," *JTS* 34 (1983): 156–68.
Huss, B. *The Zohar: Reception and Impact*. Oxford: Littman Library of Jewish Civilization, 2016.
Ibn Gabirol, S. *The Font of Life (Fons vitae)*. Translated by J. A. Laumakis. Milwaukee: Marquette University Press, 2014.
Ibn Gabirol, S. *Selected Poems of Solomon Ibn Gabirol*. Translated by P. Cole. Lockert Library of Poetry in Translation. Princeton: Princeton University Press, 2001.
Idel, M. *Ben: Sonship and Jewish Mysticism*. New York: Continuum, 2007.
Idel, M. "Judah Moscato: A Late Renaissance Jewish Preacher." Pages 41–66 in *Preachers of the Italian Ghetto*. Edited by D. Ruderman. Berkeley: University of California Press, 1992.
Idel, M. *Language, Torah and Hermeneutics in Abraham Abulafia*. Albany: SUNY Press; 1989.
Idel, M. "On Kabbalah in R Judah Moscato's Qol Yehuda." Pages 57–77 in *Rabbi Judah Moscato and the Jewish Intellectual World of Mantua in the 16th–17th Centuries*. Edited by G. Veltri and M. Gianfranco. Leiden: Brill, 2012.
Idel, M. "On Transmission in Jewish Culture." Pages 138–65 in *Transmitting Jewish Traditions: Orality, Textuality, and Cultural Diffusion*. Edited by Y. Elman and I. Gershoni. New Haven: Yale University Press, 2000.
Idel, M. *The Privileged Divine Feminine in Kabbalah*. Berlin: de Gruyter, 2019.
Idel, M. "Rabbinism versus Kabbalism: On G. Scholem's Phenomenology of Judaism." *Modern Judaism* 11 (1991): 281–96.
Ihm, M. "Philo und Ambrosius." *Neue Jahrbücher für Philologie und Paedagogik* 142 (1890): 282–88.
Ihm, S. *Ps.-Maximus Confessor: Erste kritische Edition einer Redaktion des sacroprofanen Florilegiums Loci communes nebst einer vollständigen Kollation einer zweiten Redaktion und weiterem Material*. Palingenesia 73. Stuttgart: Steiner, 2001.
Image, I. *The Human Condition in Hilary of Poitiers: The Will and Original Sin between Origen and Augustine*. Oxford: Oxford University Press, 2018.
Inowlocki, S. *Eusebius and the Jewish Authors: His Citation Technique in an Apologetic Context*, AGJU 64. Leiden: Brill, 2006.
Inowlocki, S. "Eusebius of Caesarea's *interpretatio christiana* of Philo's *De vita contemplativa*." *HTR* 97 (2004): 305–28.
Inowlocki, S. "From the Church to the Monastery: Philo's *Vita Contemplativa* in Late Ancient Christian Literature." In Jerusalem *Studies in Jewish Thought*. Edited by M. Niehoff and S. Weisser (forthcoming) (Hebrew).

Inowlocki, S. "The Hand of the Slave and the Hand of the Martyr: Pamphilus of Caesarea, Autography, and the Rise of Textual Relics." *Journal of Late Antiquity* 16 (2023): 289–23.

Inowlocki, S. "Les enjeux idéologiques de la réception des extraits philoniens sur la cause seconde dans la *Préparation évangélique*." In *Eusèbe de Césarée et la philosophie*. Edited by in S. Morlet. Turnhout: Brepols, forthcoming.

Inowlocki, S. "The Reception of Philo's *Legatio ad Gaium* in Eusebius of Caesarea's Works." *SPhiloA* 16 (2004): 30–49.

Inowlocki, S. "What Caesarea Has to Do with Alexandria? The Christian Library between Myth and Reality." *Scripta Classica Israelica* 43 (2024): 1–19.

Inowlocki, S. and C. Zamagni, eds. *Reconsidering Eusebius: A Fresh Look at His Life, Work, and Thought*. Leiden: Brill, 2011.

Iricinschi, E. "Good Hebrew, Bad Hebrew: Christians as Triton Genos in Eusebius' Apologetic Writings." Pages 69–86 in *Reconsidering Eusebius: Collected Papers on Literary, Historical, and Theological Issues*. Edited by S. Inowlocki and C. Zamagni. Leiden: Brill, 2011.

Irshai, O. "Jews and Judaism in Early Church Historiography: The Case of Eusebius of Caesarea (Preliminary Observations and Examples)." Pages 799–828 in *Jewish Life in Byzantium: Dialectics of Minority and Majority Cultures*. Edited by R. Bonfil et al. Leiden: Brill, 2011.

Irwin, T. "Euripides and Socrates." *CP* 78 (1983): 183–97.

Jackson, W. V. "Library Resources for Classical Studies." *College and Research Libraries* (1959): 459–68.

Jacobs, A. S. *Remains of the Jews: The Holy Land and Christian Empire in Late Antiquity*. Stanford: Stanford University Press, 2004.

Jacobson, H. *A Commentary on Pseudo-Philo's* Liber antiquitatem biblicarum, *with Latin Text and English Translation*. 2 vols. Leiden and New York: Brill, 1996.

Jaeger, W. *Gregorii Nysseni Opera*. Vols 1–2. Leiden: Brill, 1960.

Jahukyan, G. *Grammatical and Orthographical Works in Ancient and Medieval Armenia*. Erevan: Erevan State University, 1954 (in Armenian).

Jaitner-Hahner, U. *Humanismus im Umbrien und Rom. Lilius Tifernas, Kanzler und Gelehrter des Quattrocento*. Saecula Spiritalia 25. Baden-Baden: Valentin Koerner, 1993.

Jansen, C. *Pentateuchus sive commentarius in quinque libros Moysis*. Louvain: Jacob Zegerius, 1641.

Jay, J. "The Problem of the Theater in Early Judaism." *JSJ* 44 (2013): 218–53.

Joël, M. *Beiträge zur Geschichte der Philosophie*. Breslau: H. Skutsch, 1876.

Joël, M. *Blicke in die Religionsgeschichte zu Anfang des zweiten christlichen Jahrhunderts*. 2 vols. Breslau: Schottlaender, 1880–83.

Joël, M. "Ueber einige geschichtliche Beziehungen des Philonischen Systems." *MGWJ* 12 (1863): 19–31.

Joël, M. "Ueber Philo, den hervorragendsten Vertreter der jüdisch-alexandrinischen Geistesrichtung." *Jahrbuch für Israeliten* 5624 (1863–64): 24–57.

Johnson, A. P. *Ethnicity and Argument in Eusebius'* Praeparatio Evangelica. Oxford: Oxford University Press, 2006.

Johnson, A. P. "Philonic Allusions in *PE* 7.7.8." *ClQ* 56 (2006): 239–48.

Johnson, A. P. and J. Schott, eds. *Eusebius of Caesarea: Tradition and Innovation*. Hellenic Studies Series 60. Cambridge, MA: Harvard University Press, 2013.

Johnson, W. A. *Readers and Reading Culture in the High Roman Empire: A Study of Elite Communities*. Oxford: Oxford University Press, 2010.

Johnson, W. A. and D. S. Richter. "Periodicity and Scope." Pages 3–10 in *The Oxford Handbook to the Second Sophistic*. Edited by D. S. Richter and W. A. Johnson. Oxford: Oxford University Press, 2017.

Johnson Hodge, C. *If Sons Then Heirs: A Study of Kinship and Ethnicity in the Letters of Paul*. Oxford: Oxford University Press, 2007.

Jonas, H. *Gnosis und spätantiker Geist*. Vol. 2. Göttingen: Vandenhoeck & Ruprecht, 1954.

Jones, M. "Philo Judaeus and Hugo Grotius's Modern Natural Law." *JHI* 74 (2013): 339–59.

Jonsius, J. *De scriptoribus historiae philosophicae libri IV*. 2nd edn. Jena: apud Viduam Meyerianam, 1716.

Jonsius, J. *De scriptoribus historiae philosophicae libri IV*. Frankfurt: Götzius, 1659.

Jowett, B. *The Epistles of St. Paul to the Thessalonians, Galatians, Romans; with Critical Notes and Dissertations*. 2nd edn. London: J. Murray, 1859.

Jughaetsʻi, S. *Book of Logic*. Constantinople: Yovhannēs and Poghos Press, 1794.

Justinianus, A., ed. *Philonis Judaei Centum et duae Quaestiones, et totidem responsiones morales super Genesim*. Paris: Prelum Ascensianum, 1520.

Kaiser, O. *Philo von Alexandrien: Denkender Glaube—Eine Einführung*. FRLANT 259. Göttingen: Vandenhoeck & Ruprecht, 2015.

Kalinowska-Wójcik, B. "Jüdische Geschichtsforschung im Schlesien des 19. Und frühen 20. Jahrhunderts: Jacob Caro (1835–1904), Markus Brann (1849–1920) und Ezechiel Zivier (1868–1925)." Pages 331–66 in *Gelehrte—Schulen—Netzwerke. Geschichtsforscher in Schlesien im langen 19. Jahrhundert.* Edited by J. Bahlcke and R. Gehrke. Neue Forschungen zur schlesischen Geschichte 28. Vienna: Böhlau, 2020.

Kalvesmaki, J. *The Theology of Arithmetic: Number Symbolism in Platonism and Early Christianity.* Hellenic Studies 59. Cambridge, MA: Center for Hellenic Studies, 2013.

Kamesar, A. "Ambrose, Philo, and the Presence of Art in the Bible." *JECS* 9 (2001): 73–103.

Kamesar, A., ed. *The Cambridge Companion to Philo.* Cambridge: Cambridge University Press, 2009.

Kamesar, A. *Jerome, Greek Scholarship, and the Hebrew Bible: A Study of the Quaestiones Hebraicae in Genesim.* Oxford Classical Monographs. Oxford: Clarendon Press. 1993.

Kamesar, A. "Philo, the Presence of 'Paideutic' Myth in the Pentateuch, and the 'Principles' or *Kephalaia* of Mosaic Discourse." *SPhiloA* 10 (1998): 34–65.

Kamesar, A. "San Basilio, Filone, e la tradizione ebraici." *Henoch* 17 (1995): 129–40.

Kamlah, E. "Frömmigkeit und Tugend: Die Gesetzesapologie des Josephus in C. Apion 2, 145–295." Pages 220–32 in *Josephus-Studien: Untersuchungen zu Josephus, dem antiken Judentum und dem Neuen Testament.* Edited by O. Betz, K. Haacker, and M. Hengel. Göttingen: Vandenhoeck & Ruprecht, 1974.

Kasher, A. *Against Apion.* Jerusalem: Zalman Shazar Center, 1997.

Katz, P. *Philo's Bible: The Aberrant Text of Bible Quotations in Some Philonic Writings and Its Place in the Textual History of the Greek Bible.* Cambridge: Cambridge University Press, 1950

Kaufmann, D. *Die Sinne: Beiträge zur Geschichte der Physiologie und Psychologie im Mittelalter aus hebräischen und arabischen Quellen.* Leipzig: F. A. Brockhaus, 1884.

Kayser, C. L. *Flavii Philostrati opera*, vol. 1. Leipzig: Teubner, 1870; repr. Hildesheim: Olms, 1964.

Keech, D. *The Anti-Pelagian Christology of Augustine of Hippo, 396–430.* Oxford: Oxford University Press, 2012.

Keim, K. T. *The History of Jesus of Nazara.* Translated by Arthur Ransom. 2nd edn. London: Williams and Norgate, 1876.

Keizer, H. *Life, Time, Eternity: A Study of AIΩN in Greek Literature and Philosophy and Philo.* PhD diss. Amsterdam, 1999.

Kellner, J. B. *Der heilige Ambrosius, Bischof von Mailand, als Erklärer des alten Testaments: Ein Beitrag zur Geschichte der biblischen Exegese.* Regensburg: Manz, 1893.

Kelly, J. N. D. *Jerome: His Life, Writings, and Controversies.* London: Duckworth, 1975.

Kennedy, H. A. A. *Philo's Contribution to Religion.* London: Hodder and Stoughton, 1919.

Keoseyan, H. "Some Sources of the Sermons by *Eghishē*." *Historical-Philological Journal* 4 (1988): 108–12.

Kerns, L. "Soul and Passions in Philo of Alexandria." *StPatr* 11 (2013): 141–54.

Khachikyan, L. *Commentary on Genesis by Eghishē.* Edited by L. Ter-Petrosyan. Erewan: Zvart'nots', 1992.

Khachikian, L. "Gladzor University and Its Students' Graduation Theses." Pages 302–26 in vol. 1 of L. Khachikian, *Works.* Erevan: Nayiri, 2012.

Khorenatsi, M. *History of the Armenians.* New revised edition of the 1978 Harvard University Press edition. Translation and Commentary on Literary Sources by R. W. Thomson. Ann Arbor: Caravan Books, 2006.

Khosrov Bishop of Andzewkʽ. *Commentary on the Breviary.* Edited by Mowsēs, erudite vardapet. Ortaköy: Poghos Arapean Apuchekhts'i & Sons Publishing House, 1840.

King, K. L. "The Body and Society in Philo and the *Apocryphon of John*." Pages 82–97 in *The School of Moses: Studies in Philo and Hellenistic Religion in Memory of Horst R. Moehring.* Edited by J. P. Kenney. Atlanta: Scholars Press, 1995.

King, K. L. *What Is Gnosticism?* Cambridge, MA: Belknap Press, 2003.

Kingsley, C. *Hypatia, or Old Foes with a New Face.* London: Thomas Nelson and Sons, 1903.

Kirsch, A. *The People and the Books: 18 Classics of Jewish Literature.* New York: Norton, 2016.

Kiwleserean, B. *Eghishē, a Critical Study.* Vienna: Mkitarists' Press, 1909.

Klayets'i, Y. (Catholicos). "Beginning and cause of the Lections, saying by Yakob." Pages 177–79 in *Philo the Alexandrian in Perception of Armenian Middle Ages.* Edited by O. Vardazaryan. Erewan: "Lusabats'" Publishing House, 2006.

Klein, M. *Meletemata Ambrosiana: mythologica de Hippolyto doxographica de Exameri fontibus.* Königsberg: Lankeit, 1927.

Klein, M. L., ed. and trans. *The Fragment-Targums of the Pentateuch According to Their Extant Sources.* 2 vols. Rome: Biblical Institute Press, 1980.

Knight, F. "Greek Apologists of the Second Century." Pages 81–104 in *Apologetics in the Roman Empire.* Edited by M. J. Edwards, M. Goodman, and S. Price. Oxford: Oxford University Press, 1999.

Köckert, C. *Christliche Kosmologie und kaiserzeitliche Philosophie.* STAC 36. Tübingen: Mohr Siebeck, 2009.

Koester, H. *Introduction to the New Testament*, Vol. 1: *History and Literature of Early Christianity.* 2nd edn. Berlin: de Gruyter, 2000.

Kofsky, A. *Eusebius of Caesarea against Paganism.* Leiden: Brill, 2000.

Kohler, G. Y. "Heinrich Graetz and the Kabbalah." *Kabbalah. Journal for the Study of Jewish Mystical Texts* 40 (2017): 107–30.

König, J., K. Oikonomopoulou, and G. Woolf, eds. *Ancient Libraries*. Cambridge: Cambridge University Press, 2013.
Konstan, D. "Excerpting as a Reading Practice." Pages 9–22 in *Deciding Culture: Stobaeus' Collection of Excerpts of Ancient Greek Authors*. Edited by G. Reydams-Schils and C. Lévy. Turnhout: Brepols, 2009.
Konstan, D. and I. L. E. Ramelli. "The Use of XAPA in the New Testament and Its Background in Hellenistic Moral Philosophy." *Exemplaria Classica* 14 (2010): 185–204.
Kooten, G. H. van. *Paul's Anthropology in Context: The Image of God, Assimilation to God, and Tripartite Man in Ancient Judaism, Ancient Philosophy and Early Christianity*. Tübingen: Mohr Siebeck, 2008.
Koskenniemi, E. *Greek Writers and Philosophers in Philo and Josephus: A Study of Their Secular Education and Educational Ideals*. SPhA 9. Leiden: Brill, 2019.
Koskenniemi, E. "Philo and Classical Drama." Pages 137–51 in *Ancient Israel, Judaism, and Christianity in Contemporary Perspective: Essays in Memory of Karl-Johan Illman*. Edited by J. Neusner et al. Studies in Judaism. Lanham, MD: University Press of America, 2006.
Koskenniemi, E. "Philo and Classical Education." Pages 102–28 in *Reading Philo: A Handbook to Philo of Alexandria*. Edited by T. Seland. Grand Rapids: Eerdmans, 2014.
Koskenniemi, E. "Philo and Greek Poets." *JSJ* 41 (2013): 301–22.
Kraft, R. "Philo on Seth: Was Philo Aware of Traditions which Exalted Seth and His Progeny?" Pages 457–58 in vol. 2 of *The Rediscovery of Gnosticism*. Edited by B. Layton. Supplements to Numen 41. Leiden: Brill, 1981
Kramer, B. and J. Kramer. "Les éléments linguistiques hébreux chez Didyme l'Aveugle." Pages 313–23 in Ἀλεξανδρῖνα: *Hellénisme, judaïsme, et christianisme à Alexandrie. Mélanges offerts au P. Claude Mondésert*. Paris: Cerf, 1987.
Kratz-Ritter, B. *Salomon Formstecher: Ein deutscher Reformrabbiner*. Hildesheim: Olms, 1991.
Kraus, M. A. *Jewish, Christian, and Classical Exegetical Traditions in Jerome's Translation of the Book of Exodus: Translation Technique and the Vulgate*. VCSup. Leiden: Brill. 2017.
Krikones, Christos Th. [Χρῖστος Θ. Κρικώνης], Συναγωγὴ Πατέρων εἰς τὸ κατὰ Λουκᾶν Εὐαγγέλιον ὑπὸ Νικήτα Ἡρακλείας (κατὰ τὸν κώδικα Ἰβήρων 371), Βυζάντινα Κείμενα καὶ Μελέται 9. Thessaloniki: Κέντρον Βυζαντινῶν Ἐρευνῶν, 1973.
Krochmal, N. *Führer der Verwirrten der Zeit*. Translated and edited by A. Lehnhardt. 2 vols. Hamburg: Meiner 2012.
Krochmal, N. *More Nevuchim ha-Sman*. Edited by Leopold Zunz. Lemberg, 1851.
Krochmal, N. *Moreh nevokhei ha-zeman*. Edited by Yehoyada Amir. Jerusalem: Carmel Publishing House, 2010.
Krochmal, N. *The Writings of Nachman Krochmal*. Edited by S. Rawidowicz. 2nd edn. Waltham, MA: Ararat, 1971 (in Hebrew).
Krochmalnik, D. "Das Andachtshaus der Vernunft. Zur sakralen Poesie und Musik bei Moses Mendelssohn." *Mendelssohn-Studien* 11 (1999): 21–47.
Krüger, P. *Philo und Josephus als Apologeten des Judentums*. Leipzig: Verlag der Dürr'schen Buchhandlung, 1906.
Kuehn, C. A. and J. D. Baggarly. *Anastasius of Sinai, Hexaemeron*. Rome: Pontificio Istituto Orientale, 2007.
Kugel, J. L. *Traditions of the Bible: A Guide to the Bible as It Was at the Start of the Common Era*. Cambridge, MA: Harvard University Press, 1998.
Kühnius, A. F. *Spicilegium Christophori Friderici Loesneri observationum ad Novum Testamentum e Philone Alexandrino*. Pforten: E. C. Benek, 1785.
Kümmel, W. G. *Il Nuovo Testamento: Storia dell'indagine scientifica sul problema neotestamentario*. Translated by V. Benassi. Bologna: EDB, 2010.
Kund, S. *Commentary on the Catholic Epistles (attributed to Athanasios of Alexandria)*. Edited by Y. Kʻeoseyean and G. Tēr-Vardanean. Commentaries on the New Testament 17. Vagharshapat: Holy See of Edjmiadzin, 2003.
La Porta, S. "Monasticism and the Construction of the Armenian Intellectual Tradition." Pages 339–42 in *Monasticism in Eastern Europe and the Former Soviet Republics*. Edited by I. A. Murzaku. London: Routledge, 2015.
Lachower, F. "Nigleh ve-nistar be-mišnato šel ranaq." Pages 296–332 in *ʿAl gevul ha-yašan ve-hahadaš: Massot sifrutiyot*. Jerusalem: Bialik Institute, 1951.
Lachter, H. "Kabbalah, Philosophy, and the Jewish-Christian Debate: Reconsidering the Early Works of Joseph Gikatilla." *JJTP* 16 (2008): 1–58.
Ladner, G. B. "The Philosophical Anthropology of Saint Gregory of Nyssa." *DOP* 12 (1958): 59–94.
Lambrino, S. *Bibliographie de l'antiquité classique, 1896–1914*. Paris: Les belles lettres, 1951.
Lamirande, E. "Le masculin et le feminin dans la tradition alexandrine: le commentaire de Didyme l'Aveugle sur la 'Genèse.'" *Science et Esprit* 41 (1989): 137–65.
Lane, W. L. *Hebrews 1–8*. WBC 47A. Dallas: Word, 1998.

Lang, B. *Wisdom and the Book of Proverbs: An Israelite Goddess Redefined*. New York: Pilgrim Press, 1986.
Langermann, Y. T. "Dunash ibn Tamim." Page 315 in *The Biographical Encyclopedia of Astronomers*. Edited by T. Hockey et al. New York: Springer, 2007.
Langermann, Y. T. "On the Beginnings of Hebrew Scientific Literature and on Studying History through 'Maqbiloṯ' (Parallels)." *Aleph* 2 (2002): 169–89.
Lanzillotta, F. L. R. "Devolution and Recollection, Deficiency and Perfection: Human Degradation and the Recovery of the Primal Condition according to some Early Christian Texts." Pages 443–60 in *The Wisdom of Egypt: Jewish, Early Christian, and Gnostic Essays in Honour of Gerard P. Luttikhuizen*. Edited by A. Hilhorst and G. H. van Kooten. Leiden: Brill, 2005.
Laporte, J. "The High Priest in Philo of Alexandria." *SPhiloA* 3 (1991): 71–82.
Larcher, C. *Études sur le Livre de la Sagesse*. Études bibliques. Paris: Gabalda, 1969.
Latomus, J. *Libellus de fide et operibus, et de votis atque institutis monasticis*. Antwerp: 1530.
Lattès, J.-C. *Le dernier roi des Juifs*. Paris: NiL éditions, 2012.
Laughton, A. B. *Virginity Discourse and Ascetic Politics in the Writings of Ambrose of Milan*. PhD diss. Duke University, 2010.
Lauro, E. A. D. *The Soul and Spirit of Scripture within Origen's Exegesis*. The Bible in Ancient Christianity 3. Leiden: Brill, 2005.
Layton, R. A. *Didymus the Blind and His Circle in Late-Antique Alexandria*. Urbana, IL: University of Illinois Press, 2004.
Layton, R. A. "*Propatheia*: The Origins of the Passions in the Exegesis of Origen and Didymus." *VC* 54 (2000): 242–62.
Le Boulluec, A. "Aux origines, encore, de l' 'école' d'Alexandrie." *Adamantius* 5 (1999): 8–36.
Le Boulluec, A. "Clément d'Alexandrie lecteur de Philon." Pages 422–40 in *Les études philoniennes: regards sur cinquante années de recherche (1967–2017)*. Edited by S. Morlet and O. Munnich. SPhA 13. Leiden: Brill, 2021
Leben, C. "Hebrew Sources in the Doctrine of the Law of Nature and Nations in Early Modern Europe." *European Journal of International Law* 27.1 (2016): 79–106.
Leclerc, J. *Genesis sive Mosis prophetæ*. Amsterdam: Henric Schelte, 1710.
Ledegang, F. "The Interpretation of the Decalogue by Philo, Clement of Alexandria and Origen." Pages 245–53 in *Origeniana Nona: Origen and the Religious Practice of His Time: Papers of the 9th International Origen Congress, Pécs, Hungary, 29 August-2 September 2005*. Edited by G. Heidl and R. Somos. Leuven: Peters, 2009.
Lefort, L.-T. "Athanase, Ambroise et Chenoute 'sur la virginité." *Muséon* 48 (1935): 55–73.
Legaspi, M. C. *The Death of Scripture and the Rise of Biblical Studies*. OSHT. Oxford: Oxford University Press, 2010.
Legh Allen, N. P. *Christian Forgery in Jewish Antiquities: Josephus Interrupted*. Newcastle: Cambridge Scholars Publishing, 2020.
Lehnardt, A. "Einleitung." Pages vii–lxxvi in *Nachman Krochmal: Führer der Verwirrten der Zeit*. Edited and translated by A. Lehnhardt. Hamburg: Meiner, 2012.
Lehnus, L. "Callimaco redivivo tra Thomas Stanley e Richard Bentley." *Eikasmos* 2 (1991): 285–309.
Lehnus, L. *Incontri con la filologia del passato*. Milan: Dedalo, 2012.
Leighton, C. D. A. "Ancienneté Among the Non-Jurors: A Study of Henry Dodwell." *History of European Ideas* 31 (2005): 1–16.
Leighton, C. D. A. "The Religion of the Non-Jurors and the Early British Enlightenment: A Study of Henry Dodwell." *History of European Ideas* 28 (2002): 247–62.
Leipoldt, Johannes. *Didymus der Blinde*. TU 29. Leipzig: J. C. Hinrichs, 1905.
Lemerle, P. *Le premier humanisme Byzantin: notes et remarques sur enseignement et culture à Byzance des origines au Xe siècle*. Paris: PUF, 1971.
Lenk, L. "Höschel, David." Pages 368–69 in *Neue Deutsche Biographie* 9. Berlin: Dunker and Humboldt, 1972.
Lenox-Conyngham, A. "The Judgment of Ambrose the Bishop on Ambrose the Roman Governor." *StPatr* 17 (1982): 62–65.
Leonas, A. "Philo's Chronology and Social Position." *Adamantius* 24 (2018): 334–48.
Leonhardt, J. *Jewish Worship in Philo of Alexandria*. TSAJ 84. Tübingen: Mohr Siebeck, 2001.
Leopold, J. "Philo's Vocabulary and Word Choice." Pages 137–40 in *Two Treatises of Philo of Alexandria: A Commentary on De Gigantibus and Quod Deus Sit Immutabilis*. Edited by D. Winston and J. Dillon. Brown Judaic Studies 25. Chico, CA: Scholars Press, 1983.
Lerousseau, A. *Le judaïsme dans la philosophie allemande 1770–1850*. Paris: Presses Universitaires de France, 2001.
Levine, L. I. *The Ancient Synagogue: The First Thousand Years*. 2nd edn. New Haven: Yale University Press, 2005.

Levitan, W. *Abelard and Heloise: The Letters and Other Writings*. Indianapolis: Hackett, 2007.
Lévy, C. "Cicero and the *Timaeus*." Pages 95–110 in *Plato's* Timaeus *as Cultural Icon*. Edited by G. Reydams-Schils. Notre Dame, IN: University of Notre Dame Press, 2003.
Lévy, C. "Le concept de doxa des Stoïciens à Philon d' Alexandrie: essai d'étude diachronique." Pages 250–84 in *Passions and Perceptions: Studies in Hellenistic Philosophy of Mind*. Edited by J. Brunschwig and M. Nussbaum. Cambridge: Cambridge University Press, 1993.
Lévy, C. and B. Besnier, eds. *Philon d'Alexandrie et le langage de la philosophie: actes du colloque international organisé par le Centre d'études sur la philosophie hellénistique et romaine de l'Université de Paris XII-Val de Marne. (Créteil, Fontenay, Paris, 26–28 octobre 1995)*. Turnhout: Brepols, 1998.
Lévy, I. *La légende de Pythagore de Grèce en Palestine*. Paris: Champion, 1927.
Lewis, J. *Adrien Turnèbe (1512–1565): A Humanist Observed*. Travaux d'Humanisme et Renaissance 320. Geneva: Libraire Droz S.A., 1998.
Lewy, H. *Neue Philontexte in der Überarbeitung des Ambrosius, mit einem Anhang: neu gefundene griechische Philonfragmente. Sonderausgabe aus den Sitzungsberichten der Preussischen Akademie der Wissenschaften, Phil.-Hist. Klasse*, IV. Berlin: Verlag der Akademie der Wissenschaften, 1932.
Lewy, H. *The Pseudo-Philonic De Jona. Part I. The Armenian Text with a Critical Introduction*. Studies and Documents 7. London: Christophers, 1936.
Lewy, H. *Sobria Ebrietas. Untersuchungen zur Geschichte der antiken Mystik*. Giessen: Töpelmann, 1929.
Liebes, Y. *Ars Poetica in Sefer Yetsira*. Tel Aviv: Schocken, 2000 (in Hebrew).
Liebes, Y. "The Work of the Chariot and the Work of Creation as Mystical Teachings in Philo of Alexandria." Pages 105–20 in *Scriptural Exegesis: The Shapes of Culture and the Religious Imagination. Essays in Honour of Michael Fishbane*. Edited by D. A. Green and L. S. Lieber. Oxford: Oxford University Press, 2009.
Lienhard, J., ed. *Origen: Homilies on Luke*. Washington, DC: Catholic University of America Press, 1996.
Liere, F. van. "Josephus at Saint Victor: A First Edition of Andrew of Saint Victor's *Principatum Israelitice Gentis*." *Journal of Medieval Latin* 26 (2016): 1–29.
Liere, F. van. "Twelfth-Century Christian Scholars and the Attribution of the Talmud." *Medieval Perspectives* 17.2 (2002): 93–104.
Lilla, S. *Clement of Alexandria: A Study in Christian Platonism and Gnosticism*. Oxford Theological Monographs. Oxford: Oxford University Press, 1971.
Lincicum, D. *Paul and the Early Jewish Encounter with Deuteronomy*. Grand Rapids: Baker Academic, 2013.
Lincicum, D. "Philo's Library." *SPhiloA* 26 (2014): 99–114.
Lincicum, D. "A Preliminary Index to Philo's Non-Biblical Citations and Allusions." *SPhiloA* 25 (2013): 139–67.
Lipsius, J. *Iusti Lipsii Opera*. Lyon: Horatium Cardon, 1613.
Littlewood, A. R. *Michaelis Pselli Oratoria Minora*. Leipzig: Teubner, 1985.
Litwa, M. D. "The Deification of Moses in Philo of Alexandria." *SPhiloA* 26 (2014): 1–27.
Litwa, M. D. "Did 'the Gnostic Heresy' Influence Valentinus? An Investigation of Irenaeus *Against Heresies* 1.11.1 and 1.29." *VC* 78 (2024): 138–60.
Litwa, M. D. *Early Christianity in Alexandria: From Its Beginnings to the Late Second Century*. Cambridge: Cambridge University Press, 2024.
Litwa, M. D. *The Evil Creator: Origins of an Early Christian Idea*. New York: Oxford University Press, 2021.
Litwa, M. D. "The God 'Human' and Human Gods: Models of Deification in Irenaeus and the Apocryphon of John." *ZNW* 18 (2013): 70–94.
Litwa, M. D. *Posthuman Transformation in Ancient Mediterranean Thought: Becoming Angels and Demons*. Cambridge: Cambridge University Press, 2020.
Loader, W. *Philo, Josephus, and the Testaments on Sexuality*. Grand Rapids: Eerdmans, 2011.
Loesner, C. F. *Observationes ad Novum Testamentum e Philone Alexandrino*. Leipzig: A. F. Boehmium, 1777.
Löfstedt, B. "Zu den lateinischen Übersetzungen von (Ps.) Philons Schriften." *Eranos* 89 (1991): 101–6.
Logan, A. H. B. *Gnostic Truth and Christian Heresy*. London: T&T Clark, 1996.
Löhr, W. "Gnostic Determinism Reconsidered." *VC* 46 (1992): 381–90.
Loisy, A. *Le Quatrième Évangile*. Paris: Alphonse Picard et Fils, 1903.
Lona, H. E. *Der erste Clemensbrief*. Göttingen: Vandenhoeck und Ruprecht, 1998.
Longenecker, R. N. *Galatians*. WBC 41. Dallas: Word, 1998.
Louth, A. *The Origins of the Christian Mystical Tradition: From Plato to Denys*. Oxford: Oxford University Press, 1981.
Lubac, H. de. *Exégèse médiévale*. Vol. 1. Paris: Aubier, 1959.
Lubac, H. de. "Origen: Man of the Church." Pages 51–102 in *History and Spirit: The Understanding of Scripture According to Origen*. Translated by A. Englund Nash. San Francisco, Ignatius, 2007.
Lucchesi, E. *L'usage de Philon dans l'oeuvre exégétique de Saint Ambroise*. Leiden: Brill, 1977.
Lucci, D. "Ante-Nicene Authority and the Trinity in Seventeenth-Century England." *Intellectual History Review* 28 (2018): 101–24.

Lührmann, D. "Alttestamentliche Pseudepigraphen bei Didymos von Alexandrien." *ZAW* 104 (1992): 231–49.
Lund, J. *Die alten Jüdischen Heiligthümer, Gottesdienste und Gewohnheiten, in gründlicher Beschreibung, des ganzen Levitischen*. Hamburg: Johann Wolfgang Fickweiler, 1722.
Luther, M. D. *Martin Luthers Werke: Kritische Gesamtausgabe*. Weimar: Hermann Boehlau, 1883–1983.
Luzzatto, S. *Discorso*. Venice: Gioanne Calleoni, 1638.
Machielsen, J. "Sacrificing Josephus to Save Philo: Cesare Baronio and the Jewish Origins of Christian Monasticism." *IJCT* 23 (2016): 239–45.
MacMullen, R. *Enemies of the Roman Order: Treason, Unrest, and Alienation in the Empire*. Cambridge, MA: Harvard University Press, 1966.
MacRae, G. "The Jewish Background of the Gnostic Sophia Myth." *NovT* 12 (1970): 86–101.
Mahler, R. *A History of Modern Jewry: 1780–1815*. New York: Schocken Books, 1971.
Mai, A. *Philonis Iudaei de cophini festo et de colendis parentibus, cum brevi scripto de Iona*. Milan, Regiis Typis, 1818.
Malherbe, A. and E. Ferguson. *Gregory of Nyssa: The Life of Moses*. New York: Paulist Press, 1978.
Manandean, Y. *The Hellenizing School and the Periods of Its Development*. Vienna: Mekhitharists' Press, 1928 (in Armenian).
Mancini Lombardi, S. and P. Pontani, eds. *Studies on the Ancient Armenian Version of Philo's Works*. SPhA 6. Leiden: Brill, 2011.
Mangey, T. *Eight Sermons Preach'd on Several Occasions. By Thomas Mangey, D.D. Rector of St. Mildred's, Breadstreet, and Prebendary of Durham*. London: W. Innys, 1732.
Mangey, T., ed. *Philonis Judaei opera quae reperiri potuerunt omnia*. 2 vols. London: William Bowyer, 1742.
Mann, J. *Texts and Studies in Jewish Literature*. Philadelphia: Hebrew Press of the Jewish Publication Society of America for the Author, 1935.
Mansfeld, J. "Philosophy in the Service of Scripture: Philo's Exegetical Strategies." Pages 70–102 in *The Question of "Eclecticism": Studies in Later Greek Philosophy*. Edited by J. Dillon and A. A. Long. Berkeley: University of California Press, 1988.
Mansfeld, J. *The Pseudo-Hippocratean Tract Περὶ ἑβδομάδων, ch. 1–11 and Greek Philosophy*. Philosophical Texts and Studies 20. Assen: Van Gorcum, 1971.
Mansfeld, J. and D. T. Runia. *Aetiana V: An Edition of the Reconstructed Text of the Placita with a Commentary and a Collection of Related Texts*. 4 vols. Leiden: Brill, 2020.
Marculescu, S. "'Comme dit l'auteur tragique': la présence d'Euripide chez Philon d'Alexandrie." Pages 133–48 in *Les illusions de l'autonymie: la parole rapportée de l'Autre dans la littérature*. Edited by M.-F. Marein et al. Paris: Éditions Hermann, 2019.
Marcus, R. "A Sixteenth Century Hebrew Critique of Philo (Azariah dei Rossi's 'Meor Eynayim,' Pt. I, cc. 3–6)." *HUCA* 21 (1948): 29–71.
Markschies, C. *Kaiserzeitliche christliche Theologie und ihre Institutionen: Prolegomena zu einer Geschichte der antiken christlichen Theologie*. Tübingen: Mohr Siebeck, 2007.
Markys, R. A. *Saint Cicero and the Jesuits: The Influence of the Liberal Arts on the Adoption of Moral Probabilism*. Burlington, VT: Ashgate, 2008.
Marouzeau, J. *Dix années de bibliographie classique, bibliographie critique et analytique de l'antiquité greco-latine pour la période, 1914–24*. Vol. 1. *Auteurs et Textes*. Paris: Les belles lettres, 1927.
Martens, J. *One God, One Law: Philo of Alexandria on the Mosaic and Greco-Roman Law*. SPhAMA 2. Leiden: Brill, 2003.
Martens, P. W. "*On the Confusion of Tongues* and Origen's Allegory of the Dispersion of the Nations." *SPhiloA* 24 (2012): 107–27.
Martens, P. W. *Origen and Scripture: The Contours of the Exegetical Life*. Oxford Early Christian Studies. Oxford: Oxford University Press, 2012.
Martín, J. P. "El platonismo medio y Filón geún un studio de David Runia." *Methexis* 5 (1992): 135–43.
Martín, J. P. "Filón y las ideas christianas del siglo II: estado de la cuestión." *RevistB* 50 (1998): 263–94.
Martín, J. P. "L'interpretazione allegorica nella lettura di Barnaba nel giudaismo alessandrino." *Studi Storico-religiosi* 6 (1982): 177–78.
Martín, J. P. "La antropología de Filón y la de Teófilo de Antioquia: sus lecturas de Genesis 2–5." *Salmanticensis* 36 (1989): 23–71.
Martín, J. P. "La presencia de Filón en el Exáemeron de Teófilo de Antioquía." *Salamaticensis* 33 (1986): 144–77.
Martín, J. P. "Philo and Augustine: *De Civitate Dei* XIV 28 and XV: Preliminary Observations." *SPhiloA* 3 (1991): 283–94.
Martín, J. P. "Prima Clementis: estoicismo o filonismo." *Salmanticensis* 41 (1994): 5–11.
Martin, L. H. "Genealogy and Sociology in the Apocalypse of Adam." Pages 25–36 in *Gnosticism & the Early Christian World in Honor of James M. Robinson*. Edited by J. E. Goehring et al. Sonoma: Polebridge, 1990.

BIBLIOGRAPHY 615

Martindale, C. "Introduction: Thinking through Reception." Pages 1–13 in *Classics and the Uses of Reception*. Edited by C. Martindale and R. F. Thomas. Oxford: Blackwell, 2006.
Mason, S. *Josephus and the New Testament*. Peabody, MA: Hendrickson, 1992.
Massebieau, L. "Le classement des oeuvres de Philon." *Bibliothèque de l'École des Hautes Études*, Section des Sciences religieuses, 1 (1889): 1–91.
Matt, D., ed. *The Zohar. Pritzker Edition*. 12 vols. Stanford: Stanford University Press, 2003–17.
Matusova, E. "Allegorical Interpretation of the Pentateuch in Alexandria: Inscribing Aristobulus and Philo in a Wider Literary Context." *SPhiloA* 22 (2010): 1–51.
May, G. "Die Chronologie des Lebens und der Werke des Gregor von Nyssa." Pages 51–67 in *Écriture et culture philosophique dans la pensée de Grégore de Nysse*. Edited by M. Harl. Leiden: Brill, 1971.
McCuaig, W. "The Tridentine Ruling on the Vulgate and Ecclesiastical Censorship in the 1580s." *Renaissance and Reformation* 18.3 (1994): 43–55.
McLynn, N. *Ambrose of Milan: Church and Court in a Christian Capital*. Los Angeles: University of California Press, 1994.
Méhat, A. *Étude sur les 'Stromates' de Clément d'Alexandrie*. Paris: Seuil, 1966.
Meier, J. P. *A Marginal Jew: Rethinking the Historical Jesus*, Vol. 1: *The Roots of the Problem and the Person*. ABRL. Garden City, NY: Doubleday, 1991.
Mélèze Modrzejewski, J. *The Jews of Egypt: From Rameses II to Emperor Hadrian*. Princeton: Princeton University Press, 1997.
Melikset-Bek, L. *Armenian Vardapets of the Northern Regions and Their Identity*. Holy Etchmiadzin: Publishing House of Mother See of Holy Etchmiadzin, 2016.
Melkonyan, A. "Newly Found Commentary on David the Invincible's *Barjracʻucʻēkʻ* by Vardan Areweḷʻi." *Bulletin of Matenadaran* 22 (2015): 390–401.
Mendelson, A. *Philo's Jewish Identity*. BJS 161. Atlanta: Scholars Press, 1988.
Mendelson, A. *Secular Education in Philo of Alexandria*. HUCM 7. Cincinnati: Hebrew Union College Press, 1982.
Mendelson, A. "Two Glimpses of Philo in Modern English Literature: Works by Charles Kingsley and Francis Warner." Pages 328–43 in *Heirs of the Septuagint. Philo, Hellenistic Judaism and Early Christianity: Festschrift for Earle Hilgert*. Edited by D. T. Runia, D. M. Hay, and D. Winston. BJS 230. Atlanta: Scholars Press, 1991.
Mendelssohn, M. *Moses Mendelssohn's Hebrew Writings*. Translated by E. Breuer. Introduced and annotated by E. Breuer and D. Sorkin. Yale Judaica Series 33. New Haven: Yale University Press, 2018.
Mendelssohn, M. *Sefer Netivot ha- Šalom*. Edited by I. Elbogen et al. Gesammelte Schriften. Jubiläumsausgabe 15.1. Bad Cannstatt: Frommann-Holzboog, 1983.
Mendelssohn, M. *Writings on Judaism, Christianity & the Bible*. Edited by M. Gottlieb. Translated by E. Sacks, C. Bowman, and A. Arkush. Brandeis Library of Modern Jewish Thought. Waltham, MA: Brandeis University Press, 2011.
Menegoz, E. *La théologie de l'Epitre aux Hebreux*. Paris: Librairie Fischbacher, 1894.
Mercati, G. "Appunti dal palinsesto Vaticano di Filone." *RB* 12 (1915): 540–55.
Mercier, C. and F. Petit. *Quaestiones et solutiones in Genesim I et II–III, IV, V, VI e versione armeniaca: complément de l'ancienne version latine*. Les oeuvres de Philon d'Alexandrie 34B. Paris: Cerf, 1984.
Merri, P. "La vita di Mosè di Filone Alessandrino e di Gregorio Nissene: note sull' uso dell' allegoria." *Annali della Facoltà di Lettere e Filosofia della Università di Perugia* 20 (1982): 31–53.
Messadié, G. *La fortune d'Alexandrie*. Paris: JC Lattès, 1996.
Messana, V. "Caino ed Abele come εἴδη archetipali della città terrena secondo Agostino ed Ambrogio." *Sileno* 4 (1976): 269–302.
Metzler, K. *Die Kommentierung des Buches Genesis*. Berlin: de Gruyter, 2010.
Metzler, K., ed. *Epitome* of Exodus: *Prokop von Gaza: Eclogarum in libros historicos Veteris Testamenti epitome, 2: Der Exoduskommentar*. GCS N.F. 27. Berlin: de Gruyter, 2020.
Metzler, K. *Eustathios von Thessalonike und das Mönchtum: Untersuchungen und Kommentar zur Schrift De emendanda vita monachica*. Corpus fontium historiae Byzantinae 45. Berlin: de Gruyter, 2006.
Metzler, K. *Prokop von Gaza: Der Genesiskommentar. Aus den "Eclogarum in libros historicos Veteris Testamenti epitome" übersetzt und mit Anmerkungen versehen*. GCS N.F. 23. Berlin: de Gruyter, 2016.
Metzler, K., ed. *Prokop von Gaza: Eclogarum in libros historicos Veteris Testamenti epitome*, Vol. 1: *Der Genesiskommentar*. GCS N.F. 22. Berlin: de Gruyter, 2015.
Meyer, H. *Verzeichniß der auserlesenen Büchersammlung des seeligen Herrn Moses Mendelssohn*. Berlin: Soncino, 1786.
Michaelis, J. D. *Introduction to the New Testament*. Translated by H. Marsh. 4th edn. London: Rivington, 1823.
Miletto, G. "Judah Moscato: Biographical Data and Writings." Pages 1–13 in *Rabbi Judah Moscato and the Jewish Intellectual World of Mantua in the 16th–17th Centuries*. Edited by G. Veltri and G. Miletto. Leiden: Brill, 2012.

Miletto, G. *Glauben und Wissen im Zeitalter der Reformation.* Berlin: de Gruyter, 2004.
Miletto, G. "The Teaching Program of David ben Abraham and His Son Abraham Provenzali in Its Historical-Cultural Context." Pages 127–48 in *Cultural Intermediaries: Jewish Intellectuals in Early Modern Italy.* Edited by D. B. Ruderman and G. Veltri. Philadelphia: University of Pennsylvania Press, 2004.
Miller, E. *Portrait of a College: A History of the College of Saint John the Evangelist in Cambridge.* Cambridge: Cambridge University Press, 1961.
Miller, J. L. *Measures of Wisdom: The Cosmic Dance in Classical and Christian Antiquity.* Toronto: University of Toronto Press, 1986.
Miller, M. *Rabbis and Revolution: The Jews of Moravia in the Age of Emancipation.* Stanford: Stanford University Press, 2011.
Miller, P. C. *Biography in Late Antiquity: A Quest for the Holy Man.* Transformation of Classical Heritage 5. Berkeley: University of California Press, 1983.
Minasyan, T. "Arakʻel Vardapet (Arkhimandrite) and the Scriptorium of Deghdzut." *Bulletin of Matenadaran* 29 (2020): 298–308.
Mira, M. "Philo of Alexandria." Pages 601–3 in *The Brill Dictionary of Gregory of Nyssa.* Edited by L. F. Mateo-Seco and G. Maspero. VCSup 99. Leiden: Brill, 2010.
Mitchell, S. and P. van Nuffelen, ed. *One God: Pagan Monotheism in the Roman Empire.* Cambridge: Cambridge University Press, 2010.
Moffatt, J. *An Introduction to the Literature of the New Testament.* Edinburgh: T&T Clark, 1911.
Mohring, H. "Arithmology as an Exegetical Tool in the Writings of Philo of Alexandria." Pages 141–76 in *The School of Moses: Studies in Philo and Hellenistic Religion in Memory of Horst R. Moehring.* Edited by J. P. Kenney. BJS 304. SPhiloM 1. Atlanta: Scholar's Press, 1995.
Momigliano, A. *Prime linee di storia della tradizione maccabaica.* Rome: Foro italiano, 1930.
Momigliano, A. "Prologue in Germany." Pages 543–62 in A. Momigliano, *Nono contributo alla storia degli studi classici e del mondo antico.* Edited by Riccardo di Donato. Rome: Edizioni di storia e letteratura, 1992.
Momigliano, A. *Quinto contributo alla storia degli studi classici e del mondo antico.* Rome: Edizioni di storia e letteratura, 1975.
Momigliano, A. "Un' apologia del giudaismo: il *Contro Apione* di Flavio Giuseppe." Pages 63–71 in *Pagine Ebraiche.* Turin: Einaudi, 1987.
Monk, J. H. *The Life of Richard Bentley, D. D.* 2 vols. London: J. G. & F. Rivington, 1833.
Montepaone, O. *Auctorem producere. L'Apocolocyntosis nelle edizioni a stampa dall'Umanesimo sino alla rifondazione scientifica di inizio Ottocento.* Milan: Ledizioni, 2021.
Montes-Peral, L. A. *Akataleptos Theos: Der unfassbare Gott.* ALGHJ 16. Leiden: Brill, 1987.
Montgomery, J. W. "Sixtus of Sienna and Roman Catholic Biblical Scholarship in the Reformation Period." *Archiv für Reformationgeschichte* 54 (1963): 214–34.
Moore, G. F. *Judaism in the First Centuries of the Christian Era.* 3 vols. Cambridge, MA: Harvard University Press, 1927–30; repr. 3 vols. in 2. New York: Schocken Books, 1971.
More, H. *Henrici Mori Scriptorum Philosophicorum.* London: J. Martyne and G. Kettilby, 1679.
Morel, F. *Les œuvres de Philon Iuif… Reueuës, corrigées & augmentées de trois liures, traduits sur l'original Grec, Par Fed. Morel.* Paris: David Gilles, 1612.
Morel, F. *Philonis Judaei liber singularis, quare quorundam in scripturis sacris mutata sint nomina. Ex interpretatione F. Morelli.* Paris: F. Morellum, 1593.
Morelli, F. "Philo Vindobonensis restitutus. No c'è due senza tre: P/ Vindob. G 30531 + 60584 + 21649." *ZPE* 173 (2010): 167–74.
Moreschini, C. *Filosofia e Letterature in Gregorio di Nazianzio.* Milan: Vita e Pensiero, 1997.
Moreschini, C. "Further Considerations on the Philosophical Background of *Contra Eunomium* III." Pages 595–612 in *Gregory of Nyssa, Contra Eunomium III: An English Translation and Supporting Studies.* Edited by J. Leemans and M. Cassin. VCSup 124. Leiden: Brill, 2014.
Moreschini, C. and P. Gallay. *Grégoire de Nazianze: Discours 38–41.* SC 358. Paris: Cerf, 1990.
Morford, M. *Stoics and Neostoics: Rubens and the Circle of Lipsius.* Princeton: Princeton University Press, 1991.
Morlet, S. *La Démonstration évangélique d'Eusèbe de Césarée.* Paris: Études augustiniennes, 2009.
Morlet, S. "Les recherches sur Philon et Eusèbe de Césarée depuis 1967." Pages 441–72 in *Les études philoniennes: Regards sur cinquante ans de recherche (1967–2017).* Edited by S. Morlet and O. Munnich. Leiden: Brill, 2021.
Morlet, S. and L. Perrone. *Eusèbe de Césarée, Histoire ecclésiastique: Commentaire.* Vol. 1. Paris: Cerf, 2012.
Morlok, E. *Rabbi Joseph Gikatilla's Hermeneutics.* Tübingen: Mohr Siebeck, 2011.
Morris, J. "The Jewish Philosopher Philo, I. Life and Works." Pages 809–70 in vol. 3.1 of E. Schürer, *The History of the Jewish People in the Age of Jesus Christ (175 B.C.–A.D. 135).* Revised edition by G. Vermes, F. Millar, and M. Goodman. London: T&T Clark, 1973.
Moscato, J. *Nefutsot Yehudah.* Venice: Giovanni di Gara, 1589.

Moscato, J. *Qol Yehuda*. Venice: Giovanni di Gara, 1594.
Mosikyan, K. "Nemesius of Emessa's *On the Nature of Man* in Medieval Armenian Literature." *Bulletin of Matenadaran* 26 (2018): 177–206 (in Armenian).
Mott, S. C. "Greek Ethics and Christian Conversion: The Philonic Background of Titus II 10–14 and III 3–7." *NovT* 20.1 (1978): 22–48.
Motzo, B. "Le ΥΡΟΘΕΤΙΚΑ di Filone." *Atti della Reale Accademia delle Scienze di Torino* 47 (1911): 556–73.
Mras, K. *Eusebius Werke, Band 8: Die Praeparatio evangelica*. GCS 43.1, 43.2. Berlin: Akademie, 1954–56.
Muehlberger, E. "The Representation of Theatricality in Philo's *Embassy to Gaius*." *JSJ* 39 (2008): 46–67.
Mühlenberg, E. *Die Unendlichkeit Gottes bei Gregor von Nyssa: Gregors Kritik am Gottesbegriff der klassischen Metaphysik*. Forschungen zur Kirchen- und Dogmengeschichte 16. Göttingen: Vandenhoeck & Ruprecht, 1966.
Munk, S. *Philosophie und philosophische Schriftsteller der Juden: Eine historische Skizze*. Translated by B. Beer. Leipzig: Heinrich Hunger, 1852.
Munnich, O. "Les retouches faites aux lemmes bibliques dans le Commentaire allégorique de Philon d'Alexandrie: bilan et proposition." Pages 137–83 in *Les études philoniennes: Regards sur cinquante ans de recherche (1967–2017)*. Edited by S. Morlet and O. Munnich. Leiden: Brill, 2021.
Muradyan, G. *Grecisms in Ancient Armenian*. Hebrew University Armenian Studies 13. Leuven: Peeters, 2012.
Muradyan, G. "Le style hellénisant des *Progymnasmata* arméniens dans le contexte d'autres écrits originaux." In *Actes du Sixième Colloque international de Linguistique arménienne*. Edited by A. Donabédian and A. Ouzounian = *Slovo* 26–27 (1999): 83–94.
Muradyan, G. "The Hellenizing School." Pages 321–48 in *Armenian Philology in the Modern Era: From Manuscript to Digital Text*. Edited by V. Calzolari and M. E. Stone. HdO Section 8 Uralic & Central Asian Studies, 23/1. Leiden: Brill, 2014.
Muradyan, G. "On the Date of Two Sources of Movsēs Khorenats'i." *Historico-Philological Journal of the Armenian Academy* 4 (1990): 94–104 (in Armenian).
Musurillo, H. *Gregorii Nysseni Opera*, VII.1. Leiden: Brill, 1964.
Najman, H. *Seconding Sinai: The Development of Mosaic Discourse in Second Temple Judaism*. JSJSup 77. Leiden: Brill, 2003.
Nasrallah, J. *Histoire du mouvement littéraire dans l'église melchite du Ve au XXe siècle*. Vol. IV/1. Louvain: Peeters and Paris: Chez l'auteur, 1979.
Nautin, P. *Lettres et écrivains chrétiens des IIe et IIIe siècles*. Paris: Cerf, 1961.
Nazzaro, A. V. *Recenti Studi Filoniani (1963–70)*. Naples: Loffredo Editore, 1971.
Neander, A. *General History of the Christian Religion and Church*. Translated by J. Torrey. 13th American edn. Boston: Houghton, Mifflin and Company, 1871.
Necker, G. "Hans Blumenberg's Metaphorology and the Historical Perspective of Mystical Terminology." *JSQ* 22 (2015): 184–203.
Nele Jansen, K. *Die Rabbiner im Deutschen Reich 1871–1945*. 2 parts. Biographisches Handbuch der Rabbiner 2. Munich: K. G. Saur, 2009.
Nelson, A. B. "The Classroom of Didymus the Blind." PhD diss. University of Michigan, 1995.
Neubauer, A. *Aus der Petersburger Bibliothek. Beiträge und Documente zur Geschichte des Karäerthums und der karäischen Literatur*. Leipzig: O. Leiner, 1866.
Neubauer, A. *Catalogue of the Hebrew Manuscripts in the Bodleian Library*. Edited by A. Neubauer and A. E. Cowley. Oxford: Clarendon Press, 1906.
Neumark, D. *Geschichte der jüdischen Philosophie des Mittelalters nach Problemen dargestellt*. 3 vols. Berlin: Georg Reimer, 1907.
Neuschäfer, B. *Origenes als Philologe*. Schweizerische Beiträge zur Altertumswissenschaft 18. Basel: Friedrich Reinhardt, 1987.
Neusner, J. "Preface." Pages ix–xiv in *Judaisms and Their Messiahs at the Turn of the Christian Era*. Edited by J. Neusner, W. S. Green, and E. Frerichs. Cambridge: Cambridge University Press, 1987.
Neville Birdsall, J. "The Continuing Enigma of Josephus' Testimony about Jesus." *BJRL* 67 (1985): 609–22.
Newman, H. "Jerome and the Jews." PhD diss. Hebrew University, 1997.
Nickelsburg, G. W. E. "The Bible Rewritten and Expanded." Pages 89–156 in *Jewish Writings of the Second Temple Period: Apocrypha, Pseudepigrapha, Qumran Sectarian Writings, Philo, Josephus*. Edited by M. E. Stone. Philadelphia: Fortress, 1984.
Niehoff, M. R. "Abraham in the Greek East: Faith, Circumcision, and Covenant in Philo's Allegorical Commentary and Paul's Letter to the Galatians." *SPhiloA* 32 (2020): 227–48.
Niehoff, M. R. "Alexandrian Judaism in 19th Century *Wissenschaft des Judentums*: Between Christianity and Modernization." Pages 9–28 in *Jüdische Geschichte in hellenistisch-römischer Zeit: Wege der Forschung: Vom alten zum neuen Schürer*. Edited by A. Oppenheimer. Schriften des Historischen Kollegs 44. Munich: Oldenbourg, 1999.

Niehoff, M. R. "Colonizing and Decolonizing the Creation: A Dispute between Rabbi Hoshaya and Origen." Pages 113–29 in *Scriptures, Sacred Traditions, and Strategies of Religious Subversion: Studies in Discourse with the Work of Guy G. Stroumsa*. Edited by M. Blidstein, S. Ruzer, and D. Stökl Ben Ezra. STAC 112. Tübingen: Mohr Siebeck, 2018.
Niehoff, M. R. "*Creatio ex Nihilo* Theology in *Genesis Rabbah* in Light of Christian Exegesis." *HTR* 99 (2006): 60–61.
Niehoff, M. R. "Die 'Sapientia Salomonis' und Philon—Vertreter derselben alexandrinisch-jüdischen Religionspartei?" Pages 257–71 in *Sapientia Salomonis (Weisheit Salomos), eingeleitet, übersetzt und mit interpretierenden Essays versehen*. Edited by K.-W. Niebuhr. SAPERE 27. Tübingen: Mohr Siebeck, 2015.
Niehoff, M. R. "Eusebius as a Reader of Philo." *Adamantius* 21 (2015): 185–94.
Niehoff, M. R., ed. *Homer and the Bible in the Eyes of Ancient Interpreters*. Jerusalem Studies in Religion and Culture 16. Leiden: Brill, 2012.
Niehoff, M. R. *Jewish Exegesis and Homeric Scholarship in Alexandria*. Cambridge: Cambridge University Press, 2011.
Niehoff, M. R. "Josephus and Philo in Rome." Pages 135–46 in *A Companion to Josephus*. Edited by H. Howell Chapman and Z. Rodgers. Chichester, West Sussex, UK: John Wiley & Sons, 2016.
Niehoff, M. R. "Justin's *Timaeus* in Light of Philo's." *SPhiloA* 28 (2016): 375–92.
Niehoff, M. R. "Origen's Commentaries on the Old Testament." Pages 195–210 in *The Oxford Handbook to Origen*. Edited by R. Heine. Oxford: Oxford University Press, 2022.
Niehoff, M. R. "Origen's *Commentary on Genesis* as a Key to *Genesis Rabbah*." Pages 129–53 in *Genesis Rabbah in Text and Context*. Edited by S. K. Gribetz et al. Tübingen: Mohr Siebeck, 2016.
Niehoff, M. R. "Philo and Plutarch as Biographers—Parallel Responses to Roman Stoicism." *GRBS* 52 (2012): 361–92.
Niehoff, M. R. *Philo of Alexandria: An Intellectual Biography*. New Haven: Yale University Press, 2018.
Niehoff, M. R. "Philo of Alexandria (Subject Area: Jewish Studies)." In *Oxford Bibliographies Online*. Oxford: Oxford University Press, 2014, updated 2015. https://doi.org/10.1093/OBO/9780199840731-0061.
Niehoff, M. R. *Philo on Jewish Identity and Culture*. TSAJ 86. Tübingen: Mohr Siebeck, 2001.
Niehoff, M. R. "Philo's Exposition in a Roman Context." *SPhiloA* 23 (2011): 1–21.
Niehoff, M. R. "Philo's Role as a Platonist in Alexandria." *Études platoniciennes* 7 (2010): 35–62.
Niehoff, M. Review of M. Hadas-Lebel, *Philo of Alexandria: A Thinker in the Jewish Diaspora*. BMCR 2013.04.13.
Niehoff, M. R. "What Is in a Name? Philo's Mystical Philosophy of Language." *JSQ* 2 (1995): 220–52.
Nikiprowetzky, V. *Études philoniennes*. Paris: Cerf, 1996.
Nikiprowetzky, V. *Le commentaire de l'écriture chez Philon d'Alexandrie, son caractère et sa portée; observations philologiques*. Leiden: Brill: 1977.
Nikiprowetzky, V. "Saint Ambroise et Philon." *REG* 94 (1981): 193–99.
Noble, S. "A Byzantine Bureaucrat and Arabic Philosopher: Ibrāhīm ibn Yuḥannā al-Anṭākī and His Translation of *On the Divine Names* 4.18–35." Pages 276–312 in *Caught in Translation: Studies on Versions of Late Antique Christian Literature*. Edited by M. Toca and D. Batovici. Leiden: Brill, 2020.
Nock, A. D. *Conversion: The Old and the New in Religion from Alexander the Great to Augustine of Hippo*. Oxford: Oxford University Press, 1933.
Nock, A. D. "Philo and Hellenistic Philosophy." Pages 559–65 in *Essays on Religion and the Ancient World*. Edited by Z. Stewart. 2 vols. Oxford: Clarendon Press, 1972.
Nongbri, B. *God's Library: The Archaeology of the Earliest Christian Manuscripts*. New Haven: Yale University Press, 2018.
Nuß, M. "Ernesti, Johann August." Pages 372–74 in *Geschichte der Altertumswissenschaften: Biographisches Lexikon*. Edited by P. Kuhlmann and H. Schneider. Stuttgart: Metzler, 2012.
O'Malley, J. W. *Trent: What Happened at the Council*. Cambridge, MA: Belknap, 2013.
O'Neill, J. C. "How Early Is the Doctrine of Creation out of Nothing?" *JTS* 53 (2002): 449–65.
Oates, W. J. and E. O'Neill, Jr., ed. *Euripides: The Complete Greek Drama*. Vol. 1. *Iphigenia in Tauris*. Translated by R. Potter. New York: Random House, 1938.
Obermeier, F. "Thevet, André, OFM, später säkularisiert." *Biographisch-Bibliographisches Kirchenlexikon* 22 (2003): 1348–58.
Odorico, P. *Il prato e l'ape*. Wiener Byzantinistische Studien 17. Vienna: Austrian Academy of Sciences, 1986.
Ohanjanyan, A., ed. *Collection Tōnapatchaṙ*. Part 1. Vagharshapat: Holy See of Edjmiadzin, 2016.
Olivier, J.-M. *Répertoire des bibliothèques et des catalogues de manuscrits grecs de Marcel Richard*. 3rd edn. Turnhout: Brepols, 1995.
Olivier, J.-M. *Supplément au répertoire des bibliothèques et des catalogues de manuscrits grecs*. 2 vols. Turnhout: Brepols, 2018.

Olson, K. "Eusebian Reading of the *Testimonium Flavianum*." Pages 169–202 in *Eusebius of Caesarea: Tradition and Innovations*. Edited by A. Johnson and J. Schott. Hellenic Studies Series 60. Washington, DC: Center for Hellenic Studies, 2013.

Olson, K. "Eusebius and the *Testimonium Flavianum*." *CBQ* 61 (1999): 305–22.

Oort, J. van. "Augustin und der Manichäismus." *ZRGG* 46 (1994): 126–42.

Oort, J. van. *Jerusalem and Babylon: A Study into Augustine's City of God and the Sources of the Doctrine of the Two Cities*. Leiden: Brill, 1991.

Oort, J. van. "The Young Augustine's Knowledge of Manichaeism." *VC* 62 (2008): 441–66.

Ophir, A. and I. Rosen-Zvi. *Goy: Israel's Multiple Others and the Birth of the Gentile*. Oxford Studies in the Abrahamic Religions. Oxford: Oxford University Press, 2018.

Opsomer, J. "M. Annius Ammonius, a Philosophical Profile." Pages 123–86 in *The Origins of the Platonic System: Platonisms of the Early Empire and Their Philosophical Contexts*. Edited by M. Bonazzi and J. Opsomer. Collections des études Classiques 23. Leuven: Peeters, 2009.

Origen. *Homilies on Jeremiah and 1 Kings 28*. Translated by J. C. Smith. FOTC 97. Washington, DC: Catholic University of America Press, 1998.

Osborn, E. *The Beginning of Christian Philosophy*. Cambridge: Cambridge University Press, 1982.

Osborn, E. *Justin Martyr*. Tübingen: Mohr Siebeck, 1973.

Osborn, E. "Philo and Clement." *Prudentia* 19 (1987): 35–49.

Otto, J. "Philo, Judaeus? A Re-evaluation of Why Clement Calls Philo 'the Pythagorean.'" *SPhiloA* 25 (2013): 115–38.

Otto, J. "Origen's Criticism of Philo of Alexandria." *StPatr* 92 (2017): 121–30.

Otto, J. *Philo of Alexandria and the Construction of Jewishness in Early Christian Writings*. Oxford: Oxford University Press, 2018.

Papaioannou, S. "Encomium for the Monk Ioannes Kroustoulas Who Read Aloud at the Holy Soros." Pages 218–44 in *Michael Psellos on Literature and Art: A Byzantine Perspective on Aesthetics*. Edited by C. Barber and S. Papaioannou. Notre Dame, IN: Notre Dame University Press, 2017.

Papy, J. "Justus Lipsius." *The Stanford Encyclopedia of Philosophy* (Spring 2019 Edition), online version.

Paramelle, J., E. Lucchesi, and J. Sesiano. *Philon d'Alexandrie: Questions sur la Genèse II, 1–7: text grec, version arménienne, parallèles latins*. Geneva: Patrick Cramer, 1984.

Parker, E. and A. Treiger. "Philo's Odyssey into the Medieval Jewish World: Neglected Evidence from Arab Christian Literature." *Dionysius* 30 (2012): 117–46.

Parvan, A. "Genesis 1–3: Augustine and Origen." *VC* 66 (2012): 56–92.

Pasquali, G. "Biblioteca." *Enciclopedia Italiana di scienze, lettere ed arti* 6 (1938): 942–47.

Passarella, R. "Medicina in allegoria: Ambrogio, Filone e l'arca di Noè." Pages 113–39 in *Tra IV e V secolo: Studi sulla cultura latina tardoantica*. Edited by I. Gualandri. Quaderni di Acme 50. Milan: Cisalpino, 2002.

Payne Smith, R. *Thesaurus Syriacus*. 2 vols. Oxford: Clarendon Press, 1879–1901.

Paz, Y. *From Scribes to Scholars: Rabbinic Biblical Exegesis in Light of the Homeric Commentaries*. Culture, Religion, and Politics in the Greco-Roman World 6. Tübingen: Mohr Siebeck, 2022.

Pearce, S. J. K. *The Land of the Body: Studies in Philo's Representation of Egypt*. WUNT 208. Tübingen: Mohr Siebeck, 2007.

Pearce, S. J. K. "Philo of Alexandria on the Second Commandment." Pages 49–76 in *The Image and Its Prohibition in Jewish Antiquity*. Edited by S. Pearce. JJSSS 2. Oxford: Journal of Jewish Studies, 2013.

Pearce, S. J. K. *The Words of Moses: Studies in the Reception of Deuteronomy in the Second Temple Period*. TSAJ 152. Tübingen: Mohr Siebeck, 2013.

Pearson, B. A. *Gnosticism, Judaism, and Egyptian Christianity*. Minneapolis: Fortress, 1990.

Pearson, B. A. "Philo and Gnosticism." *ANRW* 21.1.2 (1984): 295–342.

Pearson, B. A. and J. E. Goehring, eds. *The Roots of Egyptian Christianity*. Philadelphia: Fortress, 1986.

Peerbolte, B. J. L. "The *Wisdom of Solomon* and the Gnostic Sophia." Pages 97–114 in *Wisdom of Egypt: Jewish, Early Christian and Gnostic Essays in Honour of Gerard P. Luttikhuizen*. Edited by A. Hilhorst and G. H. van Kooten. Leiden: Brill, 2005.

Pelikan, J. and H. T. Lehman, ed. *Luther's Works*. St. Louis: Concordia Publishing House, 1955–67.

Pelletier, A. *La Lettre d'Aristée à Philocrate: introduction, texte critique, traduction et notes*. SC 89. Paris: Cerf, 1962.

Pelli, M. *"Bikurei Ha'itim" the "First Fruits" of Haskalah: An Annotated Index to "Bikurei Ha'itim." The Hebrew Journal of the Haskalah in Galicia (1820–1831)*. Jerusalem: Magnes Press, 2005 (Hebrew).

Penelas, M., ed. *Kitāb Hurūšiyūš: Traducción árabe de las Historiae adversus paganos de Orosio*. Madrid: Consejo superior de investigaciones científicas, 2001.

Penland, L. "The History of the Caesarean Present: Eusebius and Narratives of Origen." Pages 148–68 in *Eusebius of Caesarea: Tradition and Innovations*. Edited by A. Johnson and J. Schott. Hellenic Studies Series 60. Washington, DC: Center for Hellenic Studies, 2013.

Penner, T. and C. Vander Stichele. "Rhetorical Practice and Performance in Early Christianity." Pages 245–60 in *The Cambridge Companion to Ancient Rhetoric*. Edited by E. Gunderson. Cambridge: Cambridge University Press, 2009.

Pépin, J. "Exégèse de *In principio* et théorie des principes dans l'*Exameron* (I 4,12–16)." Pages 427–82 in vol. 1 of *Ambrosius Episcopus: Atti del Congresso internazionale di studi ambrosiani di Milano 1974*. Edited by G. Lazzati. Studia Patristica Mediolanensia 6. Milan: Vita et Pensiero, 1976.

Pépin, J. "Recherches sur le sens et les origines de l'espression *caelum caeli* dans le livre XII des Confessions de S. Augustin." *Archivum Latinitatis Medii Aevi* 23 (1953): 185–274.

Pépin, J. "Saint Augustin et le symbolisme néoplatonicien de la vêture." Pages 293–306 in *Augustinus Magister*, vol. 1. Paris: Études augustiniennes, 1954.

Pépin, J. *Théologie cosmique et théologie chrétienne (Ambroise, Exam. I 1, 1–4)*. Paris: Presses Universitaires de France, 1964.

Pererius, B., S.J. *Commentarii et disputationes in Genesim*. Ingolstadt: David Sartorius, 1590.

Perrone, L. "Doctrinal Traditions and Cultural Heritage in the Newly Discovered Homilies of Origen on the Psalms (Codex Monacensis Graecus 314)." *Phasis* 18 (2015): 191–212.

Perrone, L. "Eusebius of Caesarea as a Christian Writer." Pages 515–30 in *Caesarea Maritima: A Retrospective after Two Millenia*. Edited by A. Raban and K. G. Holum. Documenta et Monumenta Orientis Antiqui 21. Leiden: Brill, 1996.

Perrone, L. "Origen's 'Confessions': Recovering the Traces of a Self-Portrait." *StPatr* 56 (2011): 3–27.

Peronne, L., ed. *Origenes XIII: Die neuen Psalmenhomilien: eine kritische Edition des Codex Monacensis Graecus 314*. GCS. Berlin: de Gruyter, 2015.

Pessin, S. *Ibn Gabirol's Theology of Desire: Matter and Method in Jewish Medieval Neoplatonism*. Cambridge: Cambridge University Press, 2013.

Petavius, D. *Opus de theologicis dogmatibus, auctius in hac nova editione. Tomus tertius. In quo de Angelis, de Mundi opificio, de Pelagianis ac Semipelagianis, deque Tridentini Concilii interpretatione, et S. Augustini doctrina disseritur*. Antwerp: G. Gallet, 1700.

Petersen, S. *"Zertstört die Werke der Weiblichkeit!" Maria Magdalena, Salome und andere Jüngerinnen Jesu in christlich-gnostischen Schriften*. Leiden: Brill, 1999.

Petit, F. *L'ancienne version latine des Questions sur la Genèse de Philon d'Alexandrie*, Vol. 1: *Édition critique*, Vol. 2: *Commentaire*. TU 113–14. Berlin: Akademie-Verlag, 1973.

Petit, F. "La chaîne grecque sur la Genèse, miroir de l'exégèse ancienne." Pages 243–53 in *Stimuli. Exegese und ihre Hermeneutik in Antike und Christentum*. Edited by G. Schöllgen and C. Scholten. Münster: Achendorff, 1996.

Petit, F. *La Chaîne sur la Genèse*. 4 vols. Leuven: Peeters, 1992–96.

Petit, F. *La Chaîne sur l'Exode*. 4 vols. Leuven: Peeters, 1999–2001.

Petit, F. "Le fragment 63 de la Bibliothèque de l'Université de Fribourg-en-Brisgau." *Codices Manuscripti* 9 (1983): 164–72.

Petit, F. *Quaestiones in Genesim et in Exodum: Fragmenta Graeca*. Les oeuvres de Philon d'Alexandrie 33. Paris: Cerf, 1978.

Petit, P. "Émerveillement, prière, et esprit chez saint Basile le Grand." *Collectanea Cisterciensia* 35 (1973): 81–107, 218–38.

Petitmengin, P. "Gelenius (Sigismundus) (1497–1554)." Pages 337–51 in *Centuriæ latinæ II. Cent une figures humanistes de la Renaissance aux Lumières*. Edited by C. Nativel. Geneva: Droz, 2006.

Petrei, R., ed. *Epistolae duae, una: Q. Ciceronis ad M. Tullium: De petitione consulatus ... His accesserunt eiusdem Petreii notae quoddam Προλεγόμενον Philonis, de officio iudicis*. Paris: Andream Wechelum, 1564.

Pétrement, S. *A Separate God: The Christian Origins of Gnosticism*. Translated by C. Harrison. London: Darton, Longman and Todd, 1990.

Petrosyan, G. B. *Mathematics in Armenia in Ancient and Middle Ages*. Erevan: Erevan State University Press, 1959 (in Armenian).

Pfeiffer, R. *History of Classical Scholarship From 1300 to 1850*. Oxford: Oxford University Press, 1976.

Pfleiderer, O. *Christian Origins*. Translated by D. A. Huebsch. New York: B. W. Huebsch, 1906.

Pieper, P. and W. Rösch. *Der Domschatz zu Münster*. Münster: Aschendorf, 1981.

Pines, S. *An Arabic Version of the Testimonium Flavianum and Its Implications*. Jerusalem: Israel Academy of Sciences and Humanities, 1971.

Pizzolato, L. F. "La coppia umana in S. Ambrogio." Pages 180–211 in *Etica sessuale nel Cristianesimo delle origini*. Edited by R. Catalamessa. Studia Patristica Mediolanensia 5. Milan: Vita e Pensiero, 1976.

Pizzolato, L. F. *La dottrina esegetica di sant'Ambrogio*. Studia Patristica Mediolanensia 9. Milan: Vita e Pensiero, 1978.

Places, É. des. *Numenius of Apameia, Fragments: text établi et traduit*. Collection des universités de France. Paris: Les belles lettres, 1973.

Pollock, B. "Philosophy's Inquisitor: Franz Rosenzweig's Philo between Judaism, Paganism, and Christianity." *SPhiloA* 27 (2015): 111–27.

Portaleone, A. *Shiltei ha-Gibborim*. Mantua, 1612.

Possevino, A. *Bibliotheca selecta de ratione studiorum*. Cologne: Joannes Gymnicus, 1607.

Potter, J. *Archaeologia Graeca, sive veterum Graecorum, praecipue vero Atheniensium, ritus civiles, religiosi, militares et domestici, fusius explicati per Joannem Potterum*. Lugduni Batavorum: Excudit Petrus Vander Aa, 1702.

Potter, J. *Clementis Alexandrini Opera quae extant, recognita et illustrata per Joannem Potterum, episcopum Oxoniensem*. Oxford: E Theatro Sheldoniano, 1715.

Praag, H. van. *Deference to Doubt: A Young Man's Quest for Religious Identity in First Century Judea*. Jerusalem: Urim publications, 2020.

Prévost, G. *L'Assassin et le Prophète*. Paris: NiL éditions, 2002.

Prinzivalli, E. *Didimo il Cieco: Lezioni sui Salmi. Il Commento ai Salmi scoperto a Tura*. Milan: Paoline, 2005.

Prinzivalli, E. *Magister Ecclesiae: il Dibattito su Origene fra III e IV Siecolo*. SEAug 82. Rome: Institutum Patristicum Augustinianum, 2002.

Prosperi, A. "Religion." Pages 276–97 in *The Cambridge Companion to the Italian Renaissance*. Edited by M. Wyatt. Cambridge: Cambridge University Press, 2014.

Prostmeier, F. *Der Barnabasbrief*. KAV. Göttingen: Vandenhoeck und Ruprecht, 1999.

Pucci, P. *Odysseus Polytropos: Intertextual Readings of the Odyssey and the Iliad*. Ithaca: Cornell University Press, 1993.

Pyka, M. *Jüdische Identität bei Heinrich Graetz*. Jüdische Religion, Geschichte und Kultur 5. Göttingen: Vandenhoeck & Ruprecht, 2009.

Radice, R. *Filone di Alessandria: bibliografia generale 1937–1982*. Elenchos: Collana di testi e studi sul pensiero antico 8. Naples: Bibliopolis, 1983.

Radice, R. "La 'ricezione' di Filone nella cultura cristiana dei primi quattro secoli: aspetti storici e metodologici di questo tema nell'opera di D.T. Runia *Filone di Alessandria e la prima letteratura cristiana*." Pages v–xxvii in D. T. Runia, *Filone di Alessandria nella prima letteratura cristiana: uno studio d'assieme*. Translated by R. Radice. Milan: Vita e Pensiero, 1999.

Radice, R. "Le judaïsme alexandrine et la philosophie grecque: influences probables et points de contact." Pages 483–92 in *Philon d'Alexandrie et le langage de la philosophie*. Edited by C. Lévy. Monothéismes et Philosophie. Turnhout: Brepols, 1998.

Radice, R. "The 'Nameless Principle' from Philo to Plotinus: An Outline of Research." Pages 167–82 in *Italian Studies on Philo of Alexandria*. Edited by F. Calabi. SPhAMA 1. Boston: Brill, 2003.

Radice, R. *Platonismo e creazionismo in Filone di Alessandria: Metafisica del Platonismo nel suo sviluppo storico e nella filosofia patristica*. Milan: Catholic University of Milan, 1989.

Radice, R. and D. T. Runia. "Appendice: *Testimonia de Philone* da Giuseppe Flavio al 1000 d.C." Pages 380–81 in D. T. Runia, *Filone di Alessandria nella prima letteratura cristiana: uno studio d'assieme*. Translated by R. Radice. Milan: Vita e Pensiero, 1999.

Radice, R. and D. T. Runia. *Philo of Alexandria: An Annotated Bibliography 1937–1986*. VCSup 8. Leiden: Brill, 1988.

Rahmer, M. *Die Hebräischen Traditionen in den Werken des Hieronymus: Die Commentarii zu den XII Kleinen Propheten*. Vol. 2. Berlin: M. Poppelauer, 1902.

Rajak, T. "The *Against Apion* and the Continuities in Josephus' Political Thought." Pages 222–46 in *Understanding Josephus: Seven Perspectives*. Edited by S. N. Mason. Sheffield: Sheffield Academic Press, 1998.

Rajak, T. "Friends, Romans, Subjects: Agrippa II's Speech in Josephus' *Jewish War*." Pages 122–34 in *Images of Empire*. Edited by L. Alexander. Sheffield: Sheffield Academic Press, 1991.

Rajak, T. "Philo's Knowledge of Hebrew: The Meaning of the Etymologies." Pages 173–87 in *The Jewish-Greek Tradition in Antiquity and the Byzantine Empire*. Edited by J. K. Aitken and J. Carleton Paget. Cambridge: Cambridge University Press, 2014.

Ramelli, I. L. E. "Alexander of Aphrodisias: A Source of Origen's Philosophy?" *Philosophie antique* 14 (2014): 237–90.

Ramelli, I. L. E. *Bardaiṣan of Edessa: A Reassessment of the Evidence and a New Interpretation*. Piscataway, NJ: Gorgias, 2009.

Ramelli, I. L. E. "Bardaisan of Edessa, Origen, and Imperial Philosophy: A Middle Platonic Context?" *Aram* 30 (2018): 1–26.

Ramelli, I. L. E. "The Birth of the Rome-Alexandria Connection: The Early Sources on Mark and Philo, and the Petrine Tradition." *SPhiloA* 23 (2011): 69–95.

Ramelli, I. L. E. *The Christian Doctrine of* Apokatastasis: *A Critical Assessment from the New Testament to Eriugena*. Leiden: Brill, 2013.

Ramelli, I. L. E. "The *Dialogue of Adamantius*: A Document of Origen's Thought? Part One." *StPatr* 52 (2012): 71–98.

Ramelli, I. L. E. "The *Dialogue of Adamantius*: A Document of Origen's Thought? Part Two." *StPatr* 56.4 (2013): 227–73.

Ramelli, I. L. E. "The Logos/Nous One-Many between 'Pagan' and Christian Platonism." *StPatr* 102 (2021): 11–44.

Ramelli, I. L. E. "Matter in the Dialogue of Adamantius: Origen's Heritage and Hylomorphism." Pages 74–124 in *Platonism and Christianity in Late Ancient Cosmology: God, Soul, Matter*. Edited by J. Zachhuber and A. Schiavoni. Leiden: Brill, 2022.

Ramelli, I. L. E. "Origen in Augustine: A Paradoxical Reception." *Numen* 60 (2013): 280–307.

Ramelli, I. L. E. *Origen the Philosophical Theologian*. Berlin: de Gruyter, 2024.

Ramelli, I. L. E. "Osservazioni circa il *Testimonium Flavianum*." *Sileno* 24 (1998): 219–35.

Ramelli, I. L. E. "Philo and Paul on Soteriology and Eschatology." Forthcoming.

Ramelli, I. L. E. "Philo as One of the Main Inspirers of Early Christian Hermeneutics and Apophatic Theology." *Adamantius* 24 (2018): 276–92.

Ramelli, I. L. E. "Philo as Origen's Declared Model: Allegorical and Historical Exegesis of Scripture." *Studies in Christian-Jewish Relations* 7 (2012): 1–17.

Ramelli, I. L. E. "Philo's Doctrine of *Apokatastasis*: Philosophical Sources, Exegetical Strategies, and Patristic Aftermath." *SPhiloA* 26 (2014): 29–55.

Ramelli, I. L. E. "Philosophical Allegoresis of Scripture in Philo and Its Legacy in Gregory of Nyssa." *SPhiloA* 20 (2008): 55–99.

Ramelli, I. L. E. "The Philosophical Stance of Allegory in Stoicism and Its Reception in Platonism, 'Pagan' and Christian." *IJCT* 18 (2011): 335–71.

Ramelli, I. L. E. "A Pseudepigraphon Inside a Pseudepigraphon? The Seneca-Paul Correspondence and the Letters Added Afterwards." *JSP* 23 (2014): 259–89.

Ramelli, I. L. E. "The Reception of Paul in Origen: Allegoresis of Scripture, *Apokatastasis*, and Women's Ministry." In *The Pauline Mind*. Edited by S. Porter and D. Yoon. Routledge Philosophical Minds. New York: Routledge, forthcoming.

Ramelli, I. L. E. "The Relevance of Greco-Roman Literary Themes for New Testament Interpretation." In *The Cambridge Handbook of Historical Biblical Exegesis*. Edited by S. E. Porter and D. J. Fuller. Cambridge: Cambridge University Press, forthcoming.

Ramelli, I. L. E. "Seneca the Younger." Pages 6145–48 in *The Blackwell Encyclopedia of Ancient History*. Edited by A. Erskine. Oxford: Wiley-Blackwell, 2013.

Ramelli, I. L. E. "Simon Son of John, Do You Love Me? Some Reflections on John 21:15." *NovT* 50 (2008): 332–50.

Ramelli, I. L. E. *Social Justice and the Legitimacy of Slavery: The Role of Philosophical Asceticism from Ancient Judaism to Late Antiquity*. Oxford: Oxford University Press, 2016.

Ramelli, I. L. E. "Spiritual Weakness, Illness, and Death in 1 Cor 11:30." *JBL* 130 (2011): 145–63.

Ramelli, I. L. E. "Time and Eternity." Pages 41–54 in *The Routledge Handbook to Early Christian Philosophy*. Edited by M. Edwards. London: Routledge, 2021.

Ramelli, I. L. E. and D. Konstan. *Terms for Eternity*: Αἰώνιος *and* ἀίδιος *in Classical and Christian Authors*. Piscataway, NJ: Gorgias, 2007.

Rapoport, S. L. "Alexandria." Pages 98–103 in *Sefer ʿErekh Milin*. Prague: Moshe ha-Levi Landau, 1852.

Rapoport, S. L. *S. L. Rapoport's hebräische Briefe an S. D. Luzzatto (1833–1860)*. Vol. 2. Edited by E. Gräber. Przemysl: gr. Kat. Domkapitels, 1885.

Rappaport, S. *Agada und Exegese bei Flavius Josephus*. Vienna: Alexander Kohut Memorial Foundation, 1930.

Rasimus, T. *Paradise Reconsidered in Gnostic Mythmaking: Rethinking Sethianism in Light of the Ophite Evidence*. Leiden: Brill, 2009.

Rauschenbach, S. *Judentum für Christen. Vermittlung und Selbstbehauptung Menasse ben Israels in den gelehrten Debatten des 17. Jahrhunderts*. Frühe Neuzeit 164. Berlin: de Gruyter, 2012.

Reardon, B. P. *Courants littéraires grecs des IIe et IIIe siècles après J.-C*. Paris: Les belles lettres, 1971.

Reinach, T. *Contre Apion*. 2nd edn. Paris: Les belles lettres, 1972.

Reinach, T. and L. Blum. *Flavius Josèphe: Contre Apion*. Paris: Les belles lettres, 1930.

Reinhold, E. *Lehrbuch der Geschichte der Philosophie*. Jena: Friedrich Mauke, 1839.

Renoux, A. *Le codex arménien Jérusalem 121*, Vol. I: *Introduction aux origines de la Liturgie Hiérosolymitaine: lumières Nouvelles*. Patrologia Orientalis 35. Brepols, Turnhout, 1969.

Renoux, A. *Le codex arménien Jérusalem 121*, Vol. II: *Édition compare du texte et de deux autres manuscrits. Introduction, textes, traduction et notes*. Patrologia Orientalis 36. Brepols, Turnhout, 1971.

Renoux, A. *Le codex arménien Jérusalem 121*, Vol. III: *Le Lectionnaire de Jérusalem en Arménie: Le Čašoc'. I. Introduction et liste des manuscrits*. Patrologia Orientalis 44. Brepols, Turnhout, 1989.

Réville, J. *La doctrine du Logos dans le quatrieme évangile et dans les oeuvres de Philon*. Paris: G. Fischbacher, 1881.

Reydams-Schils, G. *Demiurge and Providence: Stoic and Platonist Readings of Plato's Timaeus*. MON 2. Turnhout: Brepols, 1999.

Reydams-Schils, G. "Philautia, Self-Knowledge, and Oikeiôsis in Philo of Alexandria and Plutarch." Pages 125–40 in *Plutarch and the New Testament in Their Religio-Philosophical Contexts: Bridging Discourses in the World of the Early Roman Empire*. Edited by R. Hirsch-Luipold. Leiden: Brill, 2022.

Reydams-Schils, G. "Philo of Alexandria on Stoic and Platonist Psycho-Physiology: The Socratic Higher Ground." *Ancient Philosophy* 22 (2002): 125–47.

Reydams-Schils, G. "'Unsociable Sociability': Philo on the Active and the Contemplative Life." Pages 305–18 in *Pouvoir et puissances chez Philon d'Alexandrie*. Edited by F. Calabi et al. Turnhout: Brepols, 2015.

Reynolds, L. D. and N. G. Wilson. *Scribes and Scholars: A Guide to the Transmission of Greek & Latin Literature*. 4th edn. Oxford: Clarendon Press, 2013.

Riaud, J. "Les Thérapeutes d'Alexandrie dans la tradition et dans la recherche critique jusqu'aux découvertes de Qumran." *ANRW* 2.20.2 (1987): 1189–1296.

Rice, A. *Christ the Lord: Out of Egypt*. New York: Alfred A. Knopf, 2005.

Rice, A. *Christ the Lord: The Road to Cana*. New York: Alfred A. Knopf, 2008.

Richard, M. "Florilèges grecs." *DSpir* 4: 475–512. Paris: Beauchesne, 1964.

Riedweg, C. *Mysterienterminologie bei Platon, Philon und Klemens von Alexandrien*. Berlin: de Gruyter, 1986.

Riel, G. van. "Augustine's Exegesis of 'Heaven and Earth' in *Conf*. XII: Find Truth amidst Philosophers, Heretics and Exegetes." *Quaestio* 7 (2007): 191–228.

Riel, G. van. "Augustine's Plato." Pages 448–69 in *Brill's Companion to the Reception of Plato in Antiquity*. Edited by H. Tarrant et al. Leiden: Brill, 2018.

Rippner, B. "Ueber die Ursprünge des Philonischen Logos." *MGWJ* 21 (1872): 289–305.

Rist, J. M. *Plotinus: The Road to Reality*. Cambridge: Cambridge University Press, 1967.

Ritter, B. *Philo und die Halacha. Eine vergleichende Studie unter steter Berücksichtigung des Josephus*. Leipzig: J. C. Hinrichs, 1879.

Roberts, A. M. *Reason and Revelation in Byzantine Antioch: The Christian Translation Program of Abdallah ibn al-Fadl*. Berkeley Series in Postclassical Islamic Scholarship. Oakland, CA: University of California Press, 2020.

Roberts, C. *Buried Books in Antiquity: Habent Sua Fata Libelli*. London: The Library Association, 1963.

Robinson, J. M., ed. *The Coptic Gnostic Library: A Complete Edition of the Nag Hammadi Codices*. 5 vols. Leiden: Brill, 2000.

Rogers, J. M. *Didymus the Blind and the Alexandrian Christian Reception of Philo*. SPhiloM 8. Atlanta: Society of Biblical Literature, 2017.

Rogers, J. M. "Origen in the Likeness of Philo: Eusebius of Caesarea's Portrait of the Model Scholar." *Studies in Jewish-Christian Relations* 12 (2017): 1–13.

Rogers, J. M. "Origen's Use of Philo Judaeus." Pages 83–99 in *The Oxford Handbook of Origen*. Edited by R. Heine and K. J. Torjesen. Oxford: Oxford University Press, 2022.

Rogers, J. M. "The Philonic and the Pauline: Hagar and Sarah in the Exegesis of Didymus the Blind." *SPhiloA* 26 (2014): 57–77.

Roggema, B. and A. Treiger, eds. *Patristic Literature in Arabic Translations*. Leiden: Brill, 2020.

Rorem, P. and J. C. Lamoreaux. *John of Scythopolis and the Dionysian Corpus: Annotating the Areopagite*. Oxford: Clarendon Press, 1998.

Rosenblum, J. D. *The Jewish Dietary Laws in the Ancient World*. Cambridge: Cambridge University Press, 2016.

Roskam, G. "Nutritious Milk from Hagar's School: Philo's Reception of Homer." *SPhiloA* 29 (2017): 1–32.

Rossum-Steenbeek, M. van. *Greek Readers' Digests? Studies on a Selection of Subliterary Papyri*. Mnemosyne, bibliotheca classica Batava 175. Leiden: Brill, 1998.

Royse, J. R. "The Biblical Quotations in the Coptos Papyrus of Philo." *SPhiloA* 28 (2016): 49–76.

Royse, J. R. "The Cohn-Wendland Critical Edition of Philo of Alexandria." *SPhiloA* 33 (2021): 197–207.

Royse, J. R. "Did Philo Publish His Works?" *SPhiloA* 25 (2013): 74–100.

Royse, J. R. "Fragments of Philo of Alexandria Preserved in Pseudo-Eustathius." *SPhiloA* 30 (2018): 1–14.

Royse, J. R. "Further Greek Fragments of Philo's *Quaestiones*." Pages 143–53 in *Nourished with Peace: Studies in Hellenistic Judaism in Memory of Samuel Sandmel*. Edited by F. E. Greenspahn, E. Hilgert, and B. L. Mack. Chico, CA: Scholars Press, 1984.
Royse, J. R. "Jeremiah Markland's Contribution to the Textual Criticism of Philo." *SPhiloA* 16 (2004): 50–60.
Royse, J. R. "The Original Structure of Philo's *Quaestiones*." *SPhilo* 4 (1976–77): 41–78.
Royse, J. R. "The Oxyrhynchus Papyrus of Philo." *BASP* 17 (1980): 155–65.
Royse, J. R. "Philo." Pages 741–46 in *Textual History of the Bible*, Vol. 1: *The Hebrew Bible*, Part 1C: *Writings*. Edited by A. Lange and E. Tov. Leiden: Brill, 2016.
Royse, J. R. "Philo of Alexandria at New College." *New College Notes* 13.4 (2020): 1–9.
Royse, J. R. "Philo of Alexandria, *Quaestiones in Exodum* 2.62–68: Critical Edition." *SPhiloA* 24 (2012): 1–72.
Royse, J. R. "Philo's Division of His Works into Books." *SPhiloA* 13 (2001): 59–85.
Royse, J. R. "Reverse Indexes to Philonic Texts in the Printed Florilegia and Collections of Fragments." *SPhiloA* 5 (1993): 156–79.
Royse, J. R. Review of J. Paramelle, *Philon d'Alexandrie*, in *SPhiloA* 1 (1989): 134–44.
Royse, J. R. "Some Overlooked Classical References in Philo." *SPhiloA* 32 (2020): 249–55.
Royse, J. R. *The Spurious Texts of Philo of Alexandria: A Study of Textual Transmission and Corruption with Indexes to the Major Collections of Greek Fragments*. ALGHJ 22. Leiden: Brill, 1991.
Royse, J. R. "The Text of Philo's *De Abrahamo*." *SPhiloA* 20 (2008): 151–65.
Royse, J. R. "The Text of Philo's *De Decalogo* in Vaticanus gr. 316." *SPhiloA* 27 (2015): 133–42.
Royse, J. R. "The Text of Philo's *De plantatione*." *SPhiloA* 29 (2017): 139–58.
Royse, J. R. "The Text of Philo's *De virtutibus*." *SPhiloA* 18 (2006): 73–101.
Royse, J. R. "The Text of Philo's *Legum Allegoriae*." *SPhiloA* 12 (2000): 1–28.
Royse, J. R. "The Text of Philo's *Quis rerum divinarum heres* 167–173 in Vaticanus 379." *Theokratia* 3 (1979): 217–23.
Royse, J. R. "The Text of Stobaeus: The Manuscripts and Wachsmuth's Edition." Pages 156–73 in *Aëtiana IV: Papers of the Melbourne Colloquium on Ancient Doxography*. Edited by J. Mansfeld and D. T. Runia. PhA 148. Leiden: Brill, 2018.
Royse, J. R. "The Works of Philo." Pages 32–64 in *The Cambridge Companion to Philo*. Edited by A. Kamesar. Cambridge: Cambridge University Press, 2009.
Royse, J. R. "Three More Spurious Fragments of Philo." *SPhiloA* 17 (2005): 95–98.
Rudberg, S. Y. *Basilius von Caesarea: Homilien zum Hexaemeron*. Berlin: Akademie Verlag, 1997.
Ruderman, D. B. and G. Veltri, eds. *Cultural Intermediaries: Jewish Intellectuals in Early Modern Italy*. Philadelphia: University of Pennsylvania Press, 2004.
Runesson, A., D. D. Binder, and B. Olsson. *The Ancient Synagogue from Its Origins to 200 C.E.: A Source Book*. AGJU 72. Leiden: Brill, 2008.
Runia, D. T. "Ancient Philosophy and the New Testament: 'Exemplar' as Example." Pages 347–61 in *Method and Meaning: Essays on New Testament Interpretation in Honor of Harold W. Attridge*. Edited by A. B. McGowan and K. H. Richards. Resources for Biblical Literature 67. Atlanta: Society of Biblical Literature, 2011.
Runia, D. T. "A Brief History of the Term *Kosmos Noētos* from Plato to Plotinus." Pages 151–72 in *Traditions of Platonism: Essays in Honour of John Dillon*. Edited by J. J. Cleary. Aldershot: Ashgate, 1999.
Runia, D. T. "Caesarea Maritima and the Survival of Hellenistic-Jewish Literature." Pages 476–95 in *Caesarea Maritima: A Retrospective after Two Millenia*. Edited by A. Raban and K. G. Holum. Documenta et Monumenta Orientis Antiqui 21. Leiden: Brill, 1996.
Runia, D. T. "Confronting the Augean Stables: Royse's *Fragmenta Spuria Philonica*." *SPhiloA* 4 (1992): 78–86.
Runia, D. T. "Cosmos, Logos, and Nomos: The Alexandrian Jewish and Christian Appropriation of the Genesis Creation Account." Pages 179–209 in *Cosmologie et cosmogonie dans la littérature antique*. Edited by P. Derron. Vadoeuvres-Geneva: Hardt, 2015.
Runia, D. T. "From Stoicism to Platonism: The Difficult Case of Philo of Alexandria's *De Providentia* I." Pages 159–78 in *From Stoicism to Platonism: The Development of Philosophy, 100 BCE–100 CE*. Edited by T. Engberg-Pedersen. Cambridge: Cambridge University Press, 2017.
Runia, D. T. "God and Man in Philo of Alexandria." *JTS* 39 (1988): 48–75.
Runia, D. T. "History of Philosophy in the Grand Manner: The Achievement of H. A. Wolfson." *Philosophia Reformata* 49 (1984): 112–33.
Runia, D. T. "The Idea and the Reality of the City in the Thought of Philo of Alexandria." *JHI* 61 (2000): 361–79.
Runia, D. T. "An Index to Cohn-Wendland's *Apparatus Testimoniorum*." *SPhiloA* 4 (1992): 87–96.
Runia, D. T. "Is Philo Committed to the Doctrine of Reincarnation?" *SPhiloA* 31 (2019): 107–25.

Runia, D. T. "The Late-Byzantine Philonic Treatise *De Mundo*: Analysis of Its Method and Contents." Pages 303–28 in *Ancient Texts, Papyri, and Manuscripts: Studies in Honor of James R. Royse*. Edited by A. T. Farnes, S. D. Mackie, and D. T. Runia. NTTSD 64. Leiden: Brill, 2022.

Runia, D. T. "L'exégèse philosophique et l'influence de la penseé philonienne dans la tradition patristique." Pages 327–48 in *Philon d'Alexandrie et le langage de la philosophie*. Edited by Carlos Lévy. Monothéismes et Philosophie. Turnhout: Brepols, 1998.

Runia, D. T. "Naming and Knowing: Themes in Philonic Theology with Special Reference to *De mutatione nominum*." Pages 69–91 in *Knowledge of God in the Graeco-Roman World*. Edited by R. B. van den Broek. Leiden: Brill, 1988.

Runia, D. T. "One of Us or One of Them? Christian Reception of Philo the Jew in Egypt." Pages 203–22 in *Shem in the Tents of Japheth: Essays on the Encounter of Judaism and Hellenism*. Edited by J.L. Kugel. JSJSup 74. Leiden: Brill, 2002.

Runia, D. T. "Philo Alexandrinus." Pages 716–19 in *Augustinus-Lexicon* 4. Schwabe: Basel, 2016.

Runia, D. T. "Philo and Origen: A Preliminary Survey." Pages 333–39 in *Origeniana Quinta: Papers of the 5th International Origen Congress Boston College 14–18 August 1989*. Edited by R. J. Daly. BETL 105. Leuven: Peeters, 1992.

Runia, D. T. *Philo and the Church Fathers*. VCSup 32. Leiden: Brill, 1995.

Runia, D. T. "Philo and the Early Christian Fathers." Pages 210–30 in *The Cambridge Companion to Philo*. Edited by A. Kamesar. Cambridge: Cambridge University Press, 2009.

Runia, D. T. "Philo and the Gentiles." Pages 28–45 in *Attitudes to Gentiles in Ancient Judaism and Early Christianity*. Edited by D. C. Sim and J. S. McLaren. LNTS 499. London: Bloomsbury, 2013.

Runia, D. T. "Philo in Byzantium: An Exploration." *VC* 70 (2016): 259–81.

Runia, D. T. *Philo in Early Christian Literature: A Survey*. Compendia rerum Iudaicarum ad Novum Testamentum III.3. Assen: Van Gorcum; Minneapolis: Fortress Press, 1993.

Runia, D. T. "Philo in the Patristic Tradition." Pages 268–86 in *Reading Philo: A Handbook to Philo of Alexandria*. Edited by T. Seland. Grand Rapids: Eerdmans, 2014.

Runia, D. T. "Philo of Alexandria." Pages 77–84 in *The First Christian Theologians: An Introduction to Theology in the Early Church*. Edited by G.R. Evans. Malden, MA: Blackwell, 2004.

Runia, D. T. "Philo of Alexandria (Subject area: Biblical Studies)." In *Oxford Bibliographies Online*. Oxford: Oxford University Press, 2010, updated 2015. https://doi.org/10.1093/OBO/9780195393 361-0095.

Runia, D. T. with the assistance of H. M. Keizer. *Philo of Alexandria: An Annotated Bibliography 1987–1996 with Addenda for 1937–1986*. VCSup 57. Leiden: Brill, 2000.

Runia, D. T. *Philo of Alexandria: An Annotated Bibliography 1997–2006 with Addenda for 1987–1996*. VCSup 109. Leiden: Brill, 2012.

Runia, D. T. *Philo of Alexandria: An Annotated Bibliography 2007–2016 with Addenda for 1980–2006*. VCSup 174. Leiden: Brill, 2022.

Runia, D. T. *Philo of Alexandria and the* Timaeus *of Plato*. PhA 44. Leiden: Brill, 1986.

Runia, D. T. *Philo of Alexandria, On the Creation of the Cosmos according to Moses: Introduction, Translation and Commentary*. PACS 1. Leiden: Brill, 2001.

Runia, D. T. "Philon von Alexandria," *RAC* 27 (2015): 605–27.

Runia, D. T. "Philo, *Quaestiones In Genesim* 2.62 and the Problem of Deutero-Theology." Pages 259–69 in *Armenian, Hittite and Indo-European Studies: A Commemoration Volume for Jos J. S. Weitenberg*. Edited by U. Bläsing. Hebrew University Armenian Studies 15. Leuven: Peeters, 2019.

Runia, D. T. "Philo's De Aeternitate Mundi: The Problem of Its Interpretation." *VC* 35.2 (1981): 105–51.

Runia, D. T. "Philonic Nomenclature." *SPhiloA* 6 (1994): 1–27.

Runia, D. T. "Philonica in the *Catena in Genesim*." *SPhiloA* 11 (1999): 113–20.

Runia, D. T. "*Polis* and *Megalopolis*: Philo and the Founding of Alexandria." *Mnemosyne* 42 (1989): 398–412.

Runia, D. T. "References to Philo from Josephus up to 1000 AD." *SPhiloA* 6 (1994): 111–21.

Runia, D. T. "The Rehabilitation of the Jackdaw: Philo of Alexandria and Ancient Philosophy." Pages 483–500 in *Greek and Roman Philosophy 100 BC–200 AD*. Edited by R. Sorabji and R. W. Sharples. London: Institute of Classical Studies, 2007.

Runia, D. T. "The Structure of Philo's Allegorical Treatises: A Review of Two Recent Studies and Some Additional Comments." *VC* 38 (1984): 209–56.

Runia, D. T. "Verba Philonica, ΑΓΑΛΜΑΤΟΦΟΡΕΙΝ, and the Authenticity of the *De Resurrectione* Attributed to Athenagoras." *VC* 46 (1992): 313–27.

Runia, D. T. "When the Old and the New Overlap: The 1729 Edition of Philo's *opera omnia*." Forthcoming.

Runia, D. T. "'Where, Tell Me, Is the Jew …': Basil, Philo and Isidore of Pelusium." *VC* 46 (1992): 172–89.

Runia, D. T. "Why Does Clement of Alexandria Call Philo 'The Pythagorean'?" *VC* 49 (1995): 1–22.

Runia, D. T. "Why Philo of Alexandria Is an Important Writer and Thinker." Pages 13–33 in *Philon d'Alexandrie: un penseur à l'intersection des cultures gréco-romaine, orientale, juive et chrétienne*. Edited by S. Inowlocki and B. Decharneux. Monothéismes et philosophie. Turnhout: Brepols, 2011.

Runia, D. T. "Witness or Participant? Philo and the Neoplatonic Tradition." Pages 36–56 in *The Neoplatonic Tradition: Jewish, Christian and Islamic Themes*. Edited by A. Vanderjagt and D. Pätzold. Dialectica Minora 3. Cologne: Dinter, 1991.

Runia, D. T., Y. Arzhanov, and A. Treiger. "References to Philo of Alexandria in Greek, Latin, Syriac and Arabic Literature up to 1500 C.E." *SPhiloA* 35 (2023): 231–59.

Rybińska, A. *Manuel Joël (1826–1890). Biografia kulturowa wrocławskiego rabina z kręgu* Wissenschaft des Judentums. Lublin: Wydawnictwo Uniwersytetu Marii Curie-Skłodowskiej, 2020.

Ryu, J. *Knowledge of God in Philo of Alexandria*. Tübingen: Mohr Siebeck, 2015.

Sachsen, M. von, ed. and trans. *Nerses von Lampron, Erklärung der Sprichwörter Salomos*. 3 vols. Leipzig: O. Harrassowitz, 1919–26.

Sack, V. "Fundbericht zu Fragment 63 der Universitätsbibliothek Freiburg i. Br." *CM* 9 (1983): 173–74.

Salmerón, A., S.J. *Comentarii in evangelicam historiam, & in Acta Apostolorum, in duodecim tomos distributi*. Madrid: Ludovico Sanchez, 1598.

Sandbach, F. H. *Plutarch's Moralia XV*. LCL. Cambridge, MA: Harvard University Press, 1987.

Sandelin, K.-G. *Die Auseinandersetzung mit der Weisheit in 1. Korinther 15*. Åbo: Åbo Akademi, 1976.

Sandelin, K.-G. "The Letter of Eudaemon: An Exercise in Historical Fiction." Pages 281–92 in *Voces Clamantium in Deserto: Essays in Honor of Kari Syreeni*. Edited by S.-O. Back and M. Kankaanniemi. Studier i exegetik och judaistik utgivna av Teologiska fakulteten vid Åbo Akademi 11. Åbo: Åbo Akademi, 2012.

Sandelin, K.-G. "Philo as a Jew." Pages 19–46 in *Reading Philo: A Handbook to Philo of Alexandria*. Edited by T. Seland. Grand Rapids: Eerdmans, 2014.

Sanders, E. P. *Paul and Palestinian Judaism*. Philadelphia: Fortress, 1977.

Sandler, P. *Mendelssohn's Edition of the Pentateuch*. Jerusalem: R. Mass, 1940 (in Hebrew).

Sandmel, S. "Abraham in Normative and Hellenistic Jewish Tradition." PhD diss. Yale University, 1949.

Sandmel, S. "Parallelomania." *JBL* 81 (1962): 1–13.

Sandmel, S. *Philo of Alexandria: An Introduction*. New York: Oxford University Press, 1979.

Sandmel, S. *Philo's Place in Judaism: A Study of Conceptions of Abraham in Jewish Literature*. New York: Ktav, 1971.

Sandys, J. E. *A History of Classical Scholarship*. 3 vols. Cambridge: Cambridge University Press, 1903–8.

Sandys, J. E. *A Short History of Classical Scholarship from the Sixth Century B.C. to the Present Day*. Cambridge: Cambridge University Press, 1915.

Santos, B. S. "A natureza do homem como fronteira (methórios) em Fílon de Alexandria e Gregório de Nissa." *Revista de Filosofia Aurora* 24 (2012): 597–613.

Savon, H. *Ambroise de Milan*. Paris: Desclée, 1997.

Savon, H. "Remploi et transformation de thèmes philoniens dans la première lettre d'Ambroise à Just." Pages 83–95 in *"Chartae caritatis": Études de patristique et d'Antiquité tardive offertes à Yves-Marie Duval*. Edited by B. Gain, G. Nauroy, and P. Jay. Paris: Études augustiniennes, 2004.

Savon, H. "Saint Ambroise critique de Philon dans le *De Cain et Abel*." *StPatr* 13.2 (1975): 273–79.

Savon, H. "Saint Ambroise et saint Jérôme, lecteurs de Philon." *ANRW* 2.21.1 (1984): 731–59.

Savon, H. *Saint Ambroise devant l'exégèse de Philon le Juif*. Paris: Études augustiniennes, 1977.

Sbath, P. *Bibliothèque de manuscrits Paul Sbath: Catalogue*. Cairo: H. Friedrich et Co., 1928.

Scaliger, J. A. *Scaligerana*. The Hague, 1666.

Schäfer, P. *Judeophobia: Attitudes toward the Jews in the Ancient World*. Cambridge, MA: Harvard University Press, 1997.

Schaller, B. "Zur Überlieferungsgeschichte des ps.-Philonischen 'Liber Antiquitatum Biblicarum' im Mittelalter." *JSJ* 10 (1979): 64–73.

Schamp, J. *Photios historien des lettres: la Bibliothèque et ses notices biographiques*. Paris: Les belles lettres, 1987.

Schäublin, C. "Homerum ex Homero." *MH* 34.4 (1977): 221–27.

Scheffer, W. *Quaestionum Philonianarum, part. 2: De usu Philonis in interpretatione Novi Testamenti*. Marburg: Chr. Garthe, 1831.

Scheil, V. *Deux traités de Philon. Traités réédités d'après un papyrus du VIe siècle environ*. Mémoires publiés par les membres de la Mission archéologique française au Caire 9. Fasc. 2. Paris: Ernest Leroux, 1893.

Schelling, F. W. J. *Philosophie der Offenbarung 1841/42*. Edited by M. Frank. Frankfurt am Main: Suhrkamp 1993.

Schelling, F. W. J. *Urfassung der Philosophie der Offenbarung*. Edited by W. E. Ehrhardt. Hamburg: Meiner 1992.
Schenck, K. L. *A Brief Guide to Philo*. Louisville, KY: Westminster John Knox Press, 2005.
Schenck, K. L. "Philo and the Epistle to the Hebrews: Ronald Williamson's Study after Third Years." *SPhiloA* 14 (2002): 112–35.
Schenke, H.-M. *Der Gott "Mensch" in der Gnosis*. Göttingen: Vandenhoeck & Ruprecht, 1962.
Schenke, H.-M. "The Phenomenon and Significance of Gnostic Sethianism." Pages 588–616 in vol. 2 of *The Rediscovery of Gnosticism*. Edited by B. Layton. 2 vols. Leiden: Brill, 1981.
Schenkl, K. *Sancti Ambrosii Opera: Pars Prima qua continentur libri Hexameron, De paradiso, De Cain et Abel, De Noe, De Abraham, De Isaac, De bono mortis*. CSEL 32.1. Vienna: P. Tempsky, 1866.
Scheuchzer, J. J. *Kupfer-Bibel*. Augsburg: Christian Ulrich Wagner, 1731.
Schiffman, L. H. and J. C. VanderKam, eds. *Encyclopedia of the Dead Sea Scrolls*. 2 vols. Oxford: Oxford University Press, 2000.
Schimanowski, G. "Die jüdische Integration in die Oberschicht Alexandriens und die angebliche Apostasie des Tiberius Julius Alexander." Pages 111–35 in *Jewish Identity in the Greco-Roman World*. Edited by J. Frey, D. R. Schwartz, and S. Gripentrog. AJEC 71. Leiden: Brill, 2007.
Schimanowski, G. "Philo als Prophet, Philo als Christ, Philo als Bischof." Pages 36–49 in *Grenzgänge. Menschen und Schicksale zwischen jüdischer, christlicher und deutscher Identität: Festschrift für Diethard Aschoff*. Edited by F. Siegert. Münsteraner Judaistische Studien 11. Münster: LIT Verlag, 2002.
Schlanger, J. *The Philosophy of Solomon Ibn Gabirol*. Jerusalem: Magnes Press, 1980.
Schmitz, T. *Bildung und Macht: Zur sozialen und politischen Funktion der zweiten Sophistik in der griechischen Welt der Kaiserzeit*. Zetemata 97. Munich: Beck, 1997.
Schoedel, W. R. "Enclosing, not Enclosed: The Early Christian Doctrine of God." Pages 75–86 in *Early Christian Literature and the Classical Intellectual Tradition*. Edited by W. R. Schoedel and R. L. Wilken. Paris: Beauchesne, 1979.
Schoedel, W. R. "Theophilus of Antioch: Jewish Christian?" *ICS* 18 (1993): 279–97.
Schoettgen, C. "Praefatio ad Lectorem." Pages 1–4 in *Philonis Judaei omnia quae extant Opera ex accuratissima Sigismundi Gelenii, et aliorum interpretation, partim ab Adriano Turnebo, partim a Davide Hoeschelio, ex Augustana, edita et illustrata [...] Accedunt noviter Notitia vitae et operum Philonis, ex viri celeberrimi Joannis Alberti Fabricii Bibliotheca Graeca, et Praefatio Christiani Schoettgenii*. Frankfurt: Jeremiam Schrey et J.G. Conradi, 1729.
Scholem, G. "'Iqbotaw shel Gebirol be-Qabbalah." Pages 160–78 in *Me'assef Sofere 'Ereṣ Yisra'el*. Edited by A. Kabak and E. Steinman. Tel Aviv: Keren ha-Tarbut, 1940.
Scholem, G. *Die Geheimnisse der Schöpfung. Ein Kapitel aus dem kabbalistischen Buche Sohar*. Frankfurt: Suhrkamp, 2018.
Scholem, G. *Origins of the Kabbalah*. Edited by R. J. Z. Werblowsky. Translated by A. Arkush. Princeton: Princeton University Press, 1987.
Scholem, G. *Sefer ha-Zohar shel Gershom Shalom*. 6 vols. Jerusalem: Magnes Press, 1992.
Scholtz, G. "The Notion of Historicism and 19th Century Theology." Pages 149–67 in *Biblical Studies and the Shifting of Paradigms, 1850–1914*. Edited by H. G. Reventlow and W. Farmer. JSOTSup 192. Sheffield: Sheffield Academic Press, 1995.
Schorch, G. *Moses Mendelssohns Sprachpolitik*. Studia Judaica 67. Berlin: de Gruyter, 2012.
Schott, J. *Christianity, Empire, and the Making of Religion in Late Antiquity*. Philadelphia: University of Pennsylvania Press, 2008.
Schreckenberg, H. *Die Flavius-Josephus-Tradition in Antike und Mittelalter*. Leiden: Brill, 1972.
Schroeder, F. M. "Ammonius Saccas." *ANRW* 2.36.1 (1987): 493–536.
Schulte, C. *Von Moses bis Moses... : Der jüdische Mendelssohn*. Hannover: Wehrhahn, 2020.
Schürer, E. *Geschichte des jüdischen Volkes im Zeitalter Jesu Christi*. 4th edn. 3 vols. Leipzig: J. C. Hinrichs, 1901-9.
Schürer, E. *A History of the Jewish People in the Time of Jesus Christ*. 2nd edn. 5 vols. Translated by J. Macpherson, S. Taylor, and P. Christie. Edinburgh: T&T Clark, 1898–1910.
Schürer, E. *Lehrbuch der neutestamentlichen Zeitgeschichte*. Leipzig: J. C. Hinrichs, 1874.
Schürer, E., G. Vermes, F. Millar, and M. Black. *The History of the Jewish People in the Age of Jesus Christ (175 B.C.–A.D. 135)*. 4 vols. Edinburgh: T& T Clark, 1973–87.
Schwartz, D. R. "Philo and Josephus on the Violence in Alexandria in 38 C.E." *SPhiloA* 24 (2012): 149–66.
Schwartz, D. R. "Philo, His Family, and His Times." Pages 9–31 in *The Cambridge Companion to Philo*. Edited by A. Kamesar. Cambridge: Cambridge University Press, 2009.
Schwartz, D. R. "Philo's Priestly Descent." Pages 144–71 in *Nourished with Peace: Studies in Hellenistic Judaism in Memory of Samuel Sandmel*. Edited by F. E. Greenspahn, E. Hilgert, and B. L. Mack. Chico, CA: Scholars Press, 1984.

Schwartz, D. R. "Philonic Anonyms of the Roman and Nazi Periods: Two Suggestions." *SPhiloA* 1 (1989): 63–73.
Schwartz, D. R. *Reading the First Century: On Reading Josephus and Studying Jewish History of the First Century*. Tübingen: Mohr Siebeck, 2013.
Schwartz, E., T. Mommsen, and F. Winkelmann. *Eusebius Werke*, Vol. 2: *Kirchengeschichte*. GCS N.F. 6.1–3. Berlin: Akademie Verlag, 1999.
Schwartz, J. "Quelques réflexions à propos de trois catastrophes." Pages 21–29 in *Les juifs au regard de l'histoire: mélanges en l'honneur de Bernhard Blumenkranz*. Edited by G. Dahan. Paris: Picard, 1985.
Schwartz, S. "The Rabbi in Aphrodite's Bath: Palestinian Society and Jewish Identity in the High Roman Empire." Pages 335–61 in *Being Greek under Rome: Cultural Identity, the Second Sophistic and the Development of Empire*. Edited by S. Goldhill. Cambridge: Cambridge University Press, 2001.
Schweitzer, A. *Paul and His Interpreters: A Critical History*. Translated by W. Montgomery. London: Adam & Charles Black, 1912.
Schwemer, A.-M. "Zum Verhältnis von Diatheke und Nomos in den Schriften der jüdischen Diaspora Ägyptens in hellenistisch-römischer Zeit." Pages 67–109 in *Bund und Tora: Zur theologischen Begriffsgeschichte in alttestamentlicher, frühjüdischer und urchristlicher Tradition*. Edited by F. Avemarie und H. Lichtenberger. WUNT 92. Tübingen: Mohr Siebeck, 1996.
Scully, E. "Jerusalem's Lost Etymology." *VC* 70 (2016): 1–30.
Searby, D. M. *The Corpus Parisinum: A Critical Edition of the Greek Text with Commentary and English Translation*. 2 vols. Lewiston, NY: The Edwin Mellen Press, 2007.
Segal, A. F. *Two Powers in Heaven: Early Rabbinic Reports about Christianity and Gnosticism*. Leiden: Brill, 1977.
Seibel, W. *Fleisch und Geist beim heiligen Ambrosius*. Münchner Theologische Studien 11/14. Munich: Zink, 1958.
Sela, Y. "The Voice of the Psalmist: On the Performative Role of Psalms in Moses Mendelssohn's *Jerusalem*." Pages 109–34 in *Psalms in/on Jerusalem*. Edited by I. Pardes and O. Münz-Manor. Berlin: de Gruyter, 2019.
Seland, T., ed. *Reading Philo: A Handbook to Philo of Alexandria*. Grand Rapids: Eerdmans, 2014.
Sementchenko, L. V. "On the Two Conceptions of Just War in the 'Jewish Antiquities' of Flavius Josephus." *REA* 103 (2001): 485–95.
Septimus, B. "Biblical Religion and Political Rationality in Simone Luzzatto, Maimonides and Spinoza." Pages 399–443 in *Jewish Thought in the Seventeenth-Century*. Edited by B. Septimus and I. Twersky. Cambridge, MA: Harvard University Press, 1987.
Sferlea, O. "À propos de l'infinité divine dans le débat trinitaire du *Contra Eunome* III: le noyau de la réfutation est-il philosophique ou bien scripturarie?" Pages 675–85 in *Gregory of Nyssa, Contra Eunomium III. An English Translation with Commentary and Supporting Studies*. Edited by J. Leemans and M. Cassin. Leiden: Brill, 2014.
Shavit, Y. *Athens in Jerusalem: Classical Antiquity and Hellenism in the Making of the Modern Secular Jew*. Oxford: Littman Library of Jewish Civilization, 1997.
Shear, A. *The Kuzari and the Shaping of Jewish Identity 1167–1900*. Cambridge: Cambridge University Press, 2008.
Sherman, P. M. *Babel's Tower Translated: Genesis 11 and Ancient Jewish Interpretation*. BibInt 117. Leiden: Brill, 2013.
Shirinian, M. E. "Philo and the *Book of Causes* by Grigor Abasean." Pages 155–89 in *Studies on the Ancient Armenian Version of Philo's Works*. Edited by S. Mancini Lombardi and P. Pontani. Studies in Philo of Alexandria 6. Leiden: Brill, 2011.
Shnorhali, S. *Commentary on the Catholic Epistles*. Constantinople: Abraham Terzean's Publishing House, 1828.
Shotwell, W. A. *The Biblical Exegesis of Justin Martyr*. London: SPCK, 1965.
Sichardus, J., ed. *Philonis Iudaei Alexandrini, libri antiquitatum. Quaestionum et solutionum in Genesim. De essaeis. De nominibus Hebraicis. De mundo, Gvlielmo Bvdaeo interprete*. Basel: Adamus Petrus, 1527.
Sicherl, M. *Griechische Erstausgaben des Aldus Manutius: Druckvorlagen, Stellenwert, kultureller Hintergrund*. Studien zur Geschichte und Kultur des Altertums 1.10. Paderborn: Ferdinand Schöningh, 1997.
Sickenberger, J. *Die Lukaskatene des Niketas von Herakleia*. TU NS 7.4. Leipzig: J. C. Hinrichs, 1902.
Sidaway, J. *The Human Factor: "Deification" as Transformation in the Theology of Hilary of Poitiers*. Louvain, Peeters, 2016.
Siegert, F. "Der Armenische Philo: Textbestand, Editionen, Forschungsgeschichte." *ZKG* 100.3 (1989): 353–69.

Siegert, F. "Griechische Mythen im hellenistischen Judentum." Pages 132–52 in *Griechische Mythologie und frühes Christentum*. Edited by R. von Haehling. Darmstadt: Wissenschaftliche Buchgesellschaft, 2005.

Siegert, F. "Philo and the New Testament." Pages 175–209 in *The Cambridge Companion to Philo*. Edited by A. Kamesar. Cambridge: Cambridge University Press, 2009.

Siegfried, C. "Carpzov, Johann Benedict." *Allgemeine Deutsche Biographie* 4 (1876): 22–23.

Siegfried, C. *Philo von Alexandria als Ausleger des Alten Testaments an sich selbst und nach seinem geschichtlichen Einfluss betrachtet. Nebst Untersuchungen über die Graecitaet Philo's*. Jena: Dufft, 1875.

Sigonio, C. *Opera omnia*. Edited by F. Argelati. Milan, 1737.

Sills, D. R. "Re-Inventing the Past: Philo and the Historiography of Jewish Identity." PhD diss. University of California, Santa Barbara, 1984.

Silvas, A. M. *Gregory of Nyssa: The Letters*. VCSup 83. Leiden: Brill, 2007.

Simeoni, F. *Trascendenza e cambiamento in Filone di Alessandria: la chiave del paradosso*. Monothéismes et Philosophie 25. Turnhout: Brepols, 2019.

Simon, M. "Éléments gnostiques chez Philon." Pages 359–76 in *The Origins of Gnosticism / Le Origini dello gnosticismo*. Edited by U. Bianchi. Leiden: Brill, 1967.

Simonetti, M. "Lettera e allegoria nell'esegesi veterotestamentaria di Didimo." *Vetera Christianorum* 20 (1983): 341–89.

Singer, I. B. *Old Love*. New York: Farrar, Strauss, and Giroux, 1979.

Singer, I. B. "The Safe Deposit." *The New Yorker*. April 16, 1979, 36–42.

Singer, I. B. "The Spinoza of Market Street." Pages 3–24 in I. B. Singer, *The Spinoza of Market Street*. New York: Farrar, Strauss, and Giroux, 1961.

Sirinian, A. "'Armenian Philo': A Survey of the Literature." Pages 10–16 in *Studies on the Ancient Armenian Version of Philo's Works*. Edited by S. Mancini Lombardi and P. Pontani. Studies in Philo of Alexandria 6. Leiden: Brill, 2011.

Sirota, B. S. "The Trinitarian Crisis in Church and State: Religious Controversy and the Making of the Postrevolutionary Church of England, 1687–1702." *Journal of British Studies* 52 (2013): 26–54.

Sixtus of Sienna. *Bibliotheca sancta*. Lyons: Sumptibus, 1593.

Skarsaune, O. *The Proof from Prophecy: A Study in Justin Martyr's Proof-Text Tradition: Text-type, Provenance, Theological Profile*. Leiden: Brill, 1987.

Skeat, T. C. "The Oldest Manuscript of the Four Gospels?" *NTS* 43 (1997): 1–34.

Sly, D. *Philo's Alexandria*. London: Routledge, 1996.

Smallwood, E. M. *Philonis Alexandrini Legatio ad Gaium: Edited with an Introduction, Translation, and Commentary*. Leiden: Brill, 1961.

Smallwood, E. M. *The Jews under Roman Rule from Pompey to Diocletian*. Leiden: Brill, 1976.

Smart, H. *Pierrot*. London: Faber, 1991.

Smith, C. B. *No Longer Jews: The Search for Gnostic Origins*. Peabody: Hendrickson, 2004.

Smith, G. S. *Guilt by Association: Heresy Catalogues in Early Christianity*. Oxford: Oxford University Press, 2014.

Smith, J. W. *Christian Grace and Pagan Virtue: The Theological Foundation of Ambrose's Ethics*. Oxford: Oxford University Press, 2011.

Smith, J. Z. "*Adde parvum parvo magnus acervus erit*." *History of Religions* 11 (1971): 67–90.

Smith, J. Z. *Drudgery Divine: On the Comparison of Early Christianities and the Religions of Late Antiquity*. Chicago: University of Chicago Press, 1990.

Smith, J. Z. "In Comparison a Magic Dwells." Pages 23–44 in *A Magic Still Dwells: Comparative Religion in the Postmodern Age*. Edited by K. C. Patton and B. C. Ray. Berkeley: University of California Press, 2000.

Smith, R. "Sex Education in the Gnostic Schools." Pages 345–60 in *Images of the Feminine in Gnosticism*. Edited by K. L. King. Minneapolis: Fortress, 1988.

Smits, E. "A Contribution to the History of Pseudo-Philo's 'Liber Antiquitatum Biblicarum' in the Middle Ages." *JSJ* 23 (1992): 197–216.

Sodano, A. R. "Ambrogio e Filone: leggendo il *De paradiso*." *Annali della Facoltà di Lettere e Filosofia, Università di Macerata* 8 (1975): 65–82.

Solignac, A. "Philon d'Alexandria: II Influence sur les Pères de l'Eglise," *Dictionnaire de spiritualité ascétique et mystique, doctrine et histoire* 12 (Paris: Beauchesne, 1984): 1366–74

Solomon ibn Gabirol, *Avencebrolis (Ibn Gabirol), Fons vitae, ex arabico in latinum translatus ab Johanne Hispano et Dominico Gundissalino*. Edited by C. Baeumker and G. von Hertling. Beiträge zur Geschichte der Philosophie des Mittelalters, Texte und Untersuchungen 1.2. 2nd edn. Münster: Aschendorff, 1995.

Spicq, C. *L'Epître aux Hébreux*. Paris: Gabalda, 1952–53.

Spicq, C. *L'Epitre aux Hébreux*. SB. Paris: Libraire Lecoffre, 1977.
Spicq, C. "Le Philonisme de l'Épitre aux Hébreux." *RB* 56 (1949): 542–72.
Spilsbury, P. "Flavius Josephus on the Rise and Fall of the Roman Empire." *JTS* 54 (2003): 1–24.
Srigley, R. D. "Albert Camus on Philo and Gnosticism." *SPhiloA* 7 (1995): 103–6.
Staden, H. von. "'A Woman Does Not Become Ambidextrous': Galen and the Culture of Scientific Commentary." Pages 109–39 in *The Classical Commentary: Histories, Practices, Theory*. Edited by R. K. Gibson and C. Shuttleworth Kraus. Supplements to Mnemosyne 232. Leiden: Brill, 2002.
Staehle, K. *Die Zahlenmystik bei Philon von Alexandreia*. Leipzig: Teubner, 1931.
Stanley, T. *The History of Philosophy*. London: Humphrey Moseley and Thomas Dring, 1655. Latin Translation: *Historia philosophiae*. Leipzig: Thomas Fritsch, 1711.
Staples, J. A. *The Idea of Israel in Second Temple Judaism: A New Theory of People, Exile, and Israelite Identity*. Cambridge: Cambridge University Press, 2021.
Starobinski-Safran, E. "Exode 3, 14 dans l'œuvre de Philon d'Alexandrie." Pages 47–55 in *Dieu et l'être: exégèses d'Exode 3, 14 et de Coran 20, 11–24*. Centre d'études des religions du Livre 152. Paris: Études augustiniennes, 1978.
Stearne, J. *Aphorismi de Foelicitate*. Dublin: Typis Johannis Crooke, Typographi Regii, 1664.
Stefaniw, B. *Christian Reading: Language, Ethics, and the Order of Things*. Berkeley: University of California Press, 2019.
Stefano, S. *Exempla tria insignia naturae, legis, et gratiae, cùm in vita Iosephi patriarchae, & magni Mosis à Philone Hebraeo; tum à D. Gregorio Nyssae Pontifice, in forma perfecti hominis Christiani ad Olympium Monachum; eleganter expressa*. Venice: Bologninus Zalterius 1575.
Stefano, S. *Il ritratto del vero e perfetto gentiluomo espresso da Filone Ebreo nella vita di Giuseppe Patriarca, e fatto volgare da Piet. Franc. Zino*. Venice: Giolito, 1574.
Stefano, S. *Iosephi patriarchae vita a Philone Hebraeo graecè composita; et a Petro Francisco Zino Canonico Veronensi in latinum conuersa: In qua optimi viri civilis forma describitur*. Venice: Christophorus Zanetus, 1574.
Steinheim, S. L. *Die Offenbarung nach dem Lehrbegriffe der Synagoge*. 4 vols. Frankfurt and Altona: Siegmund Schmerber et al., 1835–65.
Sterling, G. E. "Adrianus Turnebus and the Editio Princeps of Philo (1552)." Forthcoming.
Sterling, G. E. "*Creatio Temporalis, Aeterna, vel Continua*? An Analysis of the Thought of Philo of Alexandria." *SPhiloA* 4 (1992): 15–41.
Sterling, G. E. "Different Traditions or Emphases: The Image of God in Philo's *De opificio mundi*." Pages 41–56 in *New Approaches to the Study of Biblical Interpretation in Judaism of the Second Temple Period and in Early Christianity: Proceedings of the Eleventh International Symposium of the Orion Center for the Study of the Dead Sea Scrolls and Related Literature, June 2007*. Edited by G. Anderson, R. Clements, and D. Satran. Leiden: Brill, 2013.
Sterling, G. E. "The First Critical Edition of Philo: Thomas Mangey and the 1742 Edition." *SPhiloA* 33 (2021): 133–60.
Sterling, G. E. "'The Jewish Philosophy': Reading Moses via Hellenistic Philosophy According to Philo." Pages 129–54 in *Reading Philo: A Handbook to Philo of Alexandria*. Edited by T. Seland. Grand Rapids: Eerdmans, 2014.
Sterling, G. E. "'A Man of the Highest Repute': Did Josephus Know the Writings of Philo?" *SPhiloA* 25 (2013): 101–13.
Sterling, G. E. "Ontology versus Eschatology: Tensions between Author and Community in Hebrews." *SPhiloA* 13 (2001): 190–211.
Sterling, G. E. "The People of the Covenant or the People of God: Exodus in Philo of Alexandria." Pages 404–39 in *The Book of Exodus: Composition, Reception, and Interpretation*. Edited by T. B. Dozeman, C. A. Evans, and J. N. Lohr. VTSup 164. Leiden: Brill, 2014.
Sterling, G. E. "Philo and the Logic of Apologetics: An Analysis of the *Hypothetica*." Pages 412–30 in *SBL 1990 Seminar Papers*. Edited by D. J. Lull. Atlanta: Scholar Press, 1990.
Sterling, G. E. "'Philo Has Not Been Used Half Enough': The Significance of Philo of Alexandria for the Study of the New Testament." *PRSt* 30.3 (2003): 251–69.
Sterling, G. E. "Philo of Alexandria." Pages 299–316 in *A Guide to Early Jewish Texts and Traditions in Christian Transmission*. Edited by A. Kulik. Oxford: Oxford University Press, 2019.
Sterling, G. E. "Philo of Alexandria (Subject: Classics)." In *Oxford Bibliographies Online*. Oxford: Oxford University Press, 2015. https://doi.org/10.1093/OBO/9780195389661-0205.
Sterling, G. E. "Philo of Alexandria's Life of Moses: An Introduction to the Exposition of the Law." *SPhiloA* 30 (2018): 31–45.
Sterling, G. E. "The Place of Philo of Alexandria in the Study of Christian Origins." Pages 21–52 in *Philo und das Neue Testament, Wechselseitige Wahrnehmungen*, Vol. 1: *Internationales Symposium*

zum *Corpus Judaeo-Hellenesticum*. Edited by K.-W. Niebuhr and R. Deines. Tübingen: Mohr Siebeck, 2004.
Sterling, G. E. "Platonizing Moses: Philo and Middle Platonism." *SPhiloA* 5 (1993): 96–111.
Sterling, G. E. "The Queen of the Virtues: Piety in Philo of Alexandria." *SPhiloA* 18 (2006): 103–23.
Sterling, G. E. "Recherché or Representative? What Is the Relationship between Philo's Treatises and Greek-Speaking Judaism?" *SPhiloA* 11 (1999): 1–30.
Sterling, G. E. "The School of Moses in Alexandria: An Attempt to Reconstruct the School of Philo." Pages 141–66 in *Second Temple Jewish Paideia in Context*. Edited by J. M. Zurawski and G. Bocaccini. Berlin: de Gruyter, 2017.
Sterling, G. E. "'The School of Sacred Laws': The Social Setting of Philo's Treatises." *VC* 53 (1999): 148–64.
Sterling, G. E. "The *Studia Philonica*, The *Studia Philonica Annual*, and the Study of Philo of Alexandria (1972-2017)." Pages 37–81 in *Les études philoniennes: Regards sur cinquante ans de recherche (1967-2017)*. Edited by S. Morlet and O. Munnich. SPA 13. Leiden: Brill, 2021.
Sterling, G. E. "The Theft of Philosophy: Philo of Alexandria and Numenius of Apamea." *SPhiloA* 27 (2015): 71–85.
Sterling, G. E. "When East and West Meet: Eastern Religions and Western Philosophy in Philo of Alexandria and Plutarch of Chaeronea." *SPhiloA* 28 (2016): 137–50.
Sterling, G. E. "When the Beginning Is the End: The Book of Genesis in the Commentaries of Philo." Pages 427–46 in *The Book of Genesis: Composition, Reception, and Interpretation*. Edited by C. A. Evans, J. N. Lohr, and D. L. Petersen. VTSup 152. Leiden: Brill, 2012.
Stern, D. *Parables in Midrash: Narrative and Exegesis in Rabbinic Literature*. Cambridge, MA: Harvard University Press, 1991.
Stern, M. *Greek and Latin Authors on Jews and Judaism*. 3 vols. Jerusalem: The Israel Academy of Sciences and Humanities, 1974–84.
Stinger, C. L. *Humanism and the Church Fathers: Ambrogio Traversari, 1386–1439 and Christian Antiquity in the Italian Renaissance*. Albany, NY: SUNY Press, 1977.
Stone, M. E. with additional annotations by Sh. Efrati. *The Genesis Commentary by Step'anos of Siwnik' (Dub.):. Edition, Translation and Comments*. CSCO 695 = Scriptores armeniaci 32. Leuven: Peeters, 2021.
Strauss, D. F. *The Life of Jesus Critically Examined*. Translated by Maryann Evans [George Eliot]. London: Chapman Brothers, 1846; repr. Philadelphia: Fortress, 1972.
Strauss, Z. "Jüdische Pädagogik, hebräische Dichtkunst und jüdisch-hellenistische Religionsästhetik in Mendelssohns *Bi'ur*." *Trumah* 25 (2022): 166–72.
Strauss, Z. "Solomon Judah Rapoport's Maskilic Revival of Philo of Alexandria: Rabbi Yedidya ha-Alexandri as a Pioneer of Jewish Philosophy." *SPhiloA* 31 (2019): 201–26.
Strauss, Z. "Yedidyah Ha-Alexandri and the Crisis of the Modern Jewish Age: Philo of Alexandria as an Exemplary Ḥasid in Naḥman Krochmal's Thought." *Religions* 12.6.337 (2021): 1–27.
Strecker, G. "Das Göttinger Project 'Neuer Wettstein'." *ZNW* 83 (1992): 245–52.
Strecker, G. and U. Schnelle, eds. *Neuer Wettstein: Texte zum Neuen Testament aus Griechentum und Hellenismus*. Berlin: de Gruyter, 1996–.
Stroumsa, G. A. *Another Seed: Studies in Gnostic Mythology*. Leiden: Brill, 1984.
Stroumsa, G. G. *Barbarian Philosophy: The Religious Revolution of Early Christianity*. Tübingen: Mohr Siebeck, 1999.
Stroumsa, G. G. "Christ's Laughter: Docetic Origins Reconsidered." *JECS* 12 (2004): 267–88.
Stroumsa, G. G. "*Paradosis*: Esoteric Traditions in Early Christianity." Pages 27–45 in G. G. Stroumsa, *Hidden Wisdom: Esoteric Traditions and the Roots of Christian Mysticism*. 2nd edn. Leiden: Brill, 2005.
Suárez, F., S.J. *Opera omnia*. Edited by M. André and C. Berton. Paris: Ludovicus Vivès, 1856–78.
Suchla, B. R., ed. *Ioannis Scythopolitani Prologus et Scholia in Dionysii Areopagitae Librum De Divinis Nominibus cum additamentis interpretum aliorum*. Corpus Dionysiacum IV/1. Berlin: de Gruyter, 2011.
Svendsen, S. N. *Allegory Transformed: The Appropriation of Philonic Hermeneutics in the Letter to the Hebrews*. WUNT 2.269. Tübingen: Mohr Siebeck, 2009.
Swain, S. "Biography and Biographic in the Literature of the Roman Empire." Pages 1–38 in *Portraits: Biographical Representation in the Greek and Latin Literature of the Roman Empire*. Edited by M. J. Edwards and S. Swain. Oxford: Clarendon Press, 1997.
Swain, S. *Hellenism and Empire: Language, Classicism, and Power in the Greek World AD 50-250*. Oxford: Clarendon Press, 1996.
Sychowski, S. von. *Hieronymus als Litterarhistoriker: Eine quellenkritische Untersuchung der Schrift des H. Hieronyms "De viris illustribus."* Kirchengeschichtliche Studien 2.2. Münster: Heinrich Schöninch, 1894.
Szilágyi, K. "Christian Books in Jewish Libraries: Fragments of Christian Arabic Writings from the Cairo Genizah." *Ginzei Qedem* 2 (2006): 107*–62*.

Tal, A. *The Samaritan Pentateuch Edited According to MS 6 (C) of the Shekhem Synagogue.* Texts and Studies in the Hebrew Language and Related Subjects 8. Tel Aviv: Chaim Rosenberg School for Jewish Studies, Tel Aviv University, 1994.

Tamrazyan, A. "The Reinterpretation of the Theory of Human Constitution in the Armenian Medieval Exegetic Tradition." Pages 3–502 in *Essays and Studies.* Edited by A. Tamrazyan. Erevan: Nayiri, 2013 (in Armenian).

Taylor, A. W. "Humanist Philology and Reformation Controversy: John Christopherson's Latin Translations of Philo Judaeus and Eusebius of Caesarea." Pages 79–100 in *Tudor Translation.* Edited by F. Schurink. Basingstoke: Palgrave Macmillan, 2011.

Taylor, J. E. *Jewish Women Philosophers of First-Century Alexandria: Philo's "Therapeutae" Reconsidered.* Oxford: Oxford University Press, 2003.

Tchekhanovets, Y. *The Caucasian Archaeology of the Holy Land: Armenian, Georgian and Albanian Communities between the Fourth and Eleventh Centuries CE.* HdO 1.123. Leiden: Brill, 2018.

Teller, R. *Die Heilige Schrift des Alten und Neuen Testaments.* Leipzig: Bernhard Christoph Breitkopf, 1749.

Tennemann, W. G. *Grundriß der Geschichte der Philosophie.* Leipzig: Johann Ambrosius Barth, 1829.

Terian, A. "Armenian Philonic Corpus." Pages 317–30 in *A Guide to Early Jewish Texts and Traditions in Christian Transmission.* Edited by A. Kulik. Oxford: Oxford University Press, 2019.

Terian, A. "Back to Creation: The Beginning of Philo's Third Commentary." *SPhiloA* 9 (1997): 19–36.

Terian, A. *The Festal Works of St. Gregory of Narek: Annotated Translation of the Odes, Litanies, and Encomia.* Collegeville, MN: Liturgical Press, 2016.

Terian, A. *From the Depths of the Heart: Annotated Translation of the Prayers of St. Gregory of Narek.* Collegeville, MN: Liturgical Press Academic, 2021.

Terian, A. "The Hellenizing School, Its Time, Place, and Scope of Activities Reconsidered." Pages 175–86 in *East of Byzantium: Syria and Armenia in the Formative Period.* Edited by N. G. Garsoïan, T. F. Mathews and R. W. Thomson. Washington, DC: Dumbarton Oaks, 1980.

Terian, A. *Opera Selecta Teriana: A Scholarly Retrospective.* New Rochelle, NY: St Nersess Armenian Seminary, 2008.

Terian, A., ed. and trans. *Philo, Alexander vel de ratione quam habere etiam bruta animalia (De animalibus) e versione armeniaca.* PAPM 36. Paris: Cerf, 1988.

Terian, A. "A Philonic Fragment on the Decad." Pages 173–82 in *Nourished with Peace: Studies in Hellenistic Judaism in Memory of Samuel Sandmel.* Edited by F. E. Greenspahn, E. Hilgert, and B. L. Mack. Scholars Press Homage Series 9. Chico, CA: Scholars Press, 1984.

Terian, A. "Philonic Precursors of Certain Images in St. Gregory of Narek." *Bulletin of Matenadaran* 26 (2018): 14–29 (in Armenian).

Terian, A. *Philonis Alexandrini De Animalibus: The Armenian Text with an Introduction, Translation and Commentary.* Studies in Hellenistic Judaism, Supplement to Studia Philonica 1. Chico, CA: Scholars Press, 1981.

Terian, A. "Some Stock Arguments for the Magnanimity of the Law in Hellenistic Jewish Apologetics." Pages 141–49 in *Jewish Law Association Studies I.* Edited by B. S. Jackson. Chico, CA: Scholars Press, 1985.

Termini, C. "Philo's Thought within the Context of Middle Judaism." Pages 95–123 in *The Cambridge Companion to Philo.* Edited by A. Kamesar. Cambridge: Cambridge University Press, 2009.

Teske, R. "Origen and St. Augustine's First Commentaries on Genesis." Pages 179–85 in *Origeniana V.* Edited by R. J. Daly. Leuven: Peeters, 1992.

Thackeray, H. St. J. et al. *Josephus.* 10 vols. LCL. Cambridge, MA: Harvard University Press, 1926–65.

Theiler, W. "Sachweiser zu Philo." Pages 386–411 in *Die Werke Philos von Alexandria in deutscher Übersetzung,* vol. 7. Edited by L. Cohn, I. Heinemann, and M. Adler. Berlin: de Gruyter, 1962.

Theissen, G. *The Shadow of the Galilean: The Quest of the Historical Jesus in Narrative Form.* SCM Press: London, 1987.

Theissen, G. and A. Merz. *The Historical Jesus: A Comprehensive Guide.* London: SCM Press, 1998.

Thevet, A. *Vrais pourtraits et vies des hommes illustres.* Paris: Vesve Kervert et Guillaume Chaudière, 1584.

Thompson, J. L. *Writing the Wrongs: Women of the Old Testament among Biblical Commentators from Philo through the Reformation.* Oxford: Oxford University Press, 2001.

Thomson, R. W. *The Lawcode [Datastanagirkʻ] of Mxitʻar Goš.* Dutch Studies in Armenian Language and Literature 6. Amsterdam and Atlanta, GA: Rodopi, 2000.

Tiedemann, D. *Geist der spekulativen Philosophie.* Marburg: Neuen Akademischen Buchhandlung, 1793.

Tiktin, S. *Die Lehre von den Tugenden und Pflichten bei Philo von Alexandrien.* Breslau: Schatzky, 1895.

Tishby, I. "Rabbi Moses Cordovero as He Appears in the Treatise of Rabbi Mordekhai Dato." *Sefunot: Studies and Texts on the History of the Jewish Community in Safed* 7 (1963): 119–66 (in Hebrew).

Tobin, T. H. *The Creation of Man: Philo and the History of Interpretation.* Washington, DC: Catholic Biblical Association, 1983.

Tobin, T. H. "Logos." *ABD* 4 (1992): 348–56.
Tobin, T. H. "The Prologue of John and Hellenistic Jewish Speculation." *CBQ* 52 (1990): 252–69.
Too, Yun Lee. *The Idea of the Library in the Ancient World*. Oxford: Oxford University Press, 2010.
Torrance, T. F. *Divine Meaning: Studies in Patristic Hermeneutics*. London: T&T Clark, 1995.
Touati, C. "Judaïsme talmudique et rabbinique: la découverte par le judaïsme de la Renaissance de Flavius Josèphe et de Philon le Juif." *Annuaire École Pratique des Hautes Études*, Ve. section: *Sciences Religieuses* 97 (1988–89): 214–17.
Toussaint, C. *L'Hellénisme et L'Apôtre Paul*. Paris: Ê. Nourry, 1921.
Trakatellis, D. C. *The Pre-Existence of Christ in the Writings of Justin Martyr*. Missoula, MT: Scholars Press, 1976.
Treadgold, W. T. *The Nature of the Bibliotheca of Photius*. Washington, DC: Dumbarton Oaks Center, 1980.
Treiger, A. "Arabic [Translations of Byzantine Literature]." Pages 642–61 in *The Oxford Handbook of Byzantine Literature*. Edited by S. Papaioannou. Oxford: Oxford University Press, 2021.
Treiger, A. "The Arabic Version of Pseudo-Dionysius the Areopagite's *Mystical Theology*, Chapter 1." *Le Muséon* 120 (2007): 365–93.
Treiger, A. "Christian Graeco-Arabica: Prolegomena to a History of the Arabic Translations of the Greek Church Fathers." *Intellectual History of the Islamicate World* 3 (2015): 188–227.
Treiger, A. *The Church Fathers in Arabic Translations*. Leiden: Brill, 2025.
Treiger, A. "Greek into Arabic in Byzantine Antioch: ʿAbdallāh ibn al-Faḍl's *Book of the Garden* (*Kitāb ar-Rawḍa*)." Pages 227–38 in *Ambassadors, Artists, Theologians: Byzantine Relations with the Near East from the Ninth to the Thirteenth Centuries*. Edited by Z. Chitwood and J. Pahlitzsch. Mainz: Verlag des Römisch-Germanischen Zentralmuseums, 2019.
Treiger, A. "New Evidence on the Arabic Versions of the *Corpus Dionysiacum*." *Le Muséon* 118 (2005): 219–40.
Treitel, L. "Agada bei Philo." *MGWJ* 53 (1909): 28–45, 159–73, 286–91.
Treitel, L. "Die alexandrinische Lehre von den Mittelwesen oder göttlichen Kräften, insbesondere bei Philo, geprüft auf die Frage, ob und welchen Einfluß sie auf das Mutterland Palästina gehabt. Beitrag zur Geschichte der jüdischen Religionsphilosophie." Pages 177–84 in *Judaica: Festschrift zu Hermann Cohens siebzigstem Geburtstage*. Berlin: Bruno Cassirer, 1912.
Treitel, L. "Die Bedeutung der jüdischen Feste nach Philo." *Das Jüdische Literaturblatt* 1 (1872): 19–21.
Treitel, L. "Die religions- und kulturgeschichtliche Stellung Philos." *Theologische Studien und Kritiken* 77 (1904): 380–401.
Treitel, L. "Der Nomos, insonderheit Sabbat und Feste, in philonischer Beleuchtung, an der Hand von Philo's Schrift De Septenario." *MGWJ* 47 (1903): 214–31.
Treitel, L. *Gesamte Theologie und Philosophie Philo's von Alexandria*. Berlin: Schwetschke, 1923.
Treitel, L. *Philonische Studien*. Edited by M. Brann. Breslau: Marcus, 1915.
Treitel, L. "Ursprung, Begriff und Umfang der allegorischen Schrifterklärung." *MGWJ* 55 (1911): 543–54.
Treu, U. "Isidor II (von Pelusium)." *RAC* 18 (1998): 982–1002.
Tripaldi, D. "From Philo to Areimanios: Jewish Traditions and Intellectual Profiles in First-Third Century Alexandria in the Light of the *Apocryphon of John*." Pages 101–20 in *Jews and Christians in Antiquity: A Regional Perspective*. Edited by P. Lanfranchi and J. Verheyden. Leuven: Peeters, 2018.
Trisoglio, F. "Filone Alessandrino e l'esegesi Christina." *ANRW* 2.21.1 (1984): 588–730.
Troiani, L. *Commento storico al "Contro Apione" di Giuseppe*. Pisa: Giardini, 1977.
Tropper, A. "Tractate Avot and Early Christian Succession Lists." Pages 159–88 in *The Ways that Never Parted: Jews and Christians in Late Antiquity and the Early Middle Ages*. Edited by A. H. Becker and A. Yoshiko Reed. Tübingen: Mohr Siebeck, 2003.
Trotter, J. R. *The Jerusalem Temple in Diaspora Jewish Practice and Thought during the Second Temple Period*. JSJSup 192. Leiden: Brill, 2019.
Turnebus, A. *Adversariorum, tomus primus duodecim libros continens Cum indice copiosissimo*, 2 vols. Paris: Gabriel Ruoni, 1564–65.
Turnebus, A., ed. *Philonis Iudaei in libros Mosis de mundi opificio, historicos, de legibus. Eiusdem libri singulares. Ex Bibliotheca Regia*. Paris: Adrianus Turnebus, 1552.
Turnebus, A., D. Hoeschel, and S. Gelenius. Φίλωνος Ἰουδαίου ἐξηγητικὰ συγγράμματα. *Philonis Iudaei opera*. Geneva, 1613.
Turner, J. D. *Sethian Gnosticism and the Platonic Tradition*. Leuven: Peeters, 2001.
Tzvetkova-Glaser, A. *Pentateuchauslegung bei Origenes und den frühen Rabbinen*. Frankfurt am Main: Peter Lang, 2010.
Ulrich, J. *Euseb von Caesarea und die Juden: Studien zur Rolle der Juden in der Theologie des Eusebius von Caesarea*. Berlin: de Gruyter, 1999.

Uluhogean, G. "'Guidance for Hermits' by Eghishē and Its Interrelations with Surrounding Culture (Endeavor of Interpretation)." Pages 341–46 in *Armenia and Christian Orient*. Edited by P. M. Muradyan. Erewan: "Gitutiun" Publishing House of NAS RA, 2000.

Unnik, W. C. van. "'Tiefer Friede" (1 Klemens 2.2)." *VC* 24 (1970): 261–79.

Urbach, E. E. *The Sages: Their Concepts and Beliefs*. Translated by I. Abrahams. Jerusalem: Hebrew University Press, 1979.

Vaeuraeus, I., ed. *Philonis Iudaei de divinis decem oraculis, quae summa sunt legum capita, Liber Iohanne Vaeuraeo interprete*. Paris: Carolus Stephanus 1554.

Vajda, G. *Le commentaire sur le "Livre de la Création" de Dūnaš ben Tāmīm de Kairouan (Xe siècle)*. Revised and edited by P. B. Fenton. Collection de la Revue des Études Juives. Leuven: Peeters, 2002.

Vannier, M.-A. "Origène et Augustin, interprètes de la création." Pages 723–36 in *Origeniana Sexta: Origène et la Bible = Origen and the Bible. Actes du Colloquium Origenianum Sextum, Chantilly, 30 Août–3 Septembre 1993*. Edited by G. Dorival and A. Le Boulluec. Leuven: Peeters, 1995.

Vardan Arewelts'i. *Sermons & Panegyrics*. Edited by H. Kyoseyan. Erevan: Erevan State University Publishing House, 2000 (in Armenian).

Vardazaryan, O. "An Application of the Dionysian *Ars* in Armenian Medieval Scholiography." *REArm* 39 (2020): 73–90.

Vardazaryan, O. "The 'Armenian Philo': A Remnant of an Unknown Tradition." Pages 195–98 in *Studies on the Ancient Armenian Version of Philo's Works*. Edited by S. Mancini Lombardi and P. Pontani. Studies in Philo of Alexandria 6. Leiden: Brill, 2011.

Vardazaryan, O. "The Armenian Scholia to the Works of Philo of Alexandria." *Historical-Theological Journal* 185.1 (2005): 203–4.

Vardazaryan, O. "The 'Causes' to the Writings by Philo. Texts and Studies." *Proceedings of the "V. Brusov" Erevan State University of Linguistics, Social Studies* 3 (2005): 185–233 (in Armenian).

Vardazaryan, O. "Colophons on the Manuscript Tradition of 'Armenian Philo'." Pages 261–72 in *Levon Khachikian 9. Proceedings of the International Conference dedicated to the 90th Anniversary of the Founder-director of the Matenadaran (October 9-11, 2008)*. Edited by G. Ter-Vardanean. Erevan: Nayiri, 2010 (in Armenian).

Vardazaryan, O. "Yovhan Orotnets'i's *Sylloge of the Exposition on Philo the Sage's* De providentia." *Bulletin of Matenadaran* 17 (2006): 213–59.

Vardazaryan, O. and deacon Th. Eranyan, "An Anonymous Commentary on Exodus 12." *Etchmiadzin* 9 (2010): 86–112 (in Armenian).

Vasiliev, A., ed. and trans. *Kitāb al-ʿunvān, Histoire universelle, écrite par Agapius (Mahboub) de Menbidj*. Seconde partie (I), Patrologia Orientalis 7.4. Paris: Firmin-Didot, 1911.

Veltri, G. "The Humanist Sense of History and the Jewish Idea of Tradition: Azaria de' Rossi's Critique of Philo Alexandrinus." *JSQ* 2.4 (1995): 372–93.

Veltri, G. "Von Faszination und Irrtum des Humanismus: Jüdisches Denken in der italienischen Renaissance." Pages 1–21 in *An der Schwelle zur Moderne: Juden in der Renaissance*. Edited by G. Veltri and A. Winkelmann. Leiden: Brill, 2003.

Veltri, G. *Gegenwart der Tradition: Studien zur jüdischen Literatur und Kulturgeschichte*. Leiden: Brill, 2002.

Veltri, G. and A. Lissa. *Discourse on the State of the Jews*. Berlin: de Gruyter, 2019.

Verdoner, M. *Narrated Reality: The* Historia ecclesiastica *of Eusebius of Caesarea*. Frankfurt am Main: Peter Lang, 2011.

Vermes, G. "The Jesus Notice of Josephus Re-Examined." *JJS* 38 (1987): 1–10.

Vermes, G. *Post-Biblical Jewish Studies*. Leiden: Brill, 1975.

Vogel, C. de. "La théorie de l'*apeiron* chez Platon et la tradition platonicienne." *Revue philosophique de la France et de l'Étranger* 149 (1959): 21–39.

Vogüé, A. de. "Échos de Philon dans la Vie de Saint Sulpice de Bourges et dans la Règle d'Abélard pour le Paraclet." *Analecta Bollandiana* 103 (1985): 359–65.

Völker, W. *Fortschritt und Vollendung bei Philo von Alexandrien. Eine Studie zur Geschichte der Frömmigkeit*. Leipzig: J. C. Hinrichs, 1938.

Vollmer, H. *Die alttestamentlichen Citate bei Paulus*. Freiburg im Breisgau and Leipzig: Mohr Siebeck, 1895.

Wall, W. *Critical Notes on the Old Testament*. London: C. David, 1734.

Walpole, A. S. *Early Latin Hymns*. Cambridge: Cambridge University Press, 1922.

Weigert, S. *Hebraica veritas Übersetzungsprinzipien und Quellen der Deuteronomiumübersetzung des Hieronymus*. BWANT. Stuttgart: Kohlhammer, 2016.

Weinberg, J. "Azariah de' Rossi and Septuagint Traditions." *Italia* 5:1–2 (1985): 7–35.

Weinberg, J. *The Light of the Eyes* of Azariah de' Rossi. *An English Translation with Introduction and Notes*. New Haven: Yale University Press, 2001.

Weinberg, J. "Pagan, Church Father or Rabbi: The Debate over Philo of Alexandria in Early Modern Europe." Forthcoming.

Weinberg, J. "The Quest for Philo in Sixteenth-Century Jewish Historiography." Pages 163–88 in *Jewish History: Essays in Honour of Chimen Abramsky*. Edited by A. Rapoport-Albert and S. J. Zipperstein. London: Peter Halban, 1988.

Weinfeld, M. *The Anchor Bible: Deuteronomy 1–11, A New Translation with Introduction and Commentary*. New York: Doubleday, 1991.

Weinfeld, M. *Deuteronomy and the Deuteronomic School*. Oxford: Clarendon Press, 1972.

Weiss, H. *A Day of Gladness: The Sabbath among Jews and Christians in Antiquity*. Columbia: University of South Carolina Press, 2003.

Weiss, H.-F. *Untersuchungen zur Kosmologie des hellenistischen und palästinischen Judentums*. Berlin: Akademie Verlag, 1966.

Weisse, S. *Philo von Alexandrien und Moses Maimonides: Ein vergleichender Versuch*. Dessau: Herzogl. Hof-Buchdruckerei, 1884.

Weisser, S. *Éradication ou modération des passions? Histoire de la controverse chez Cicéron, Sénèque et Philon d'Alexandrie*. Turnhout: Brepols, 2022.

Weisser, S. "Why Does Philo Criticize the Stoic Ideal of Apatheia in On Abraham 257: Philo and Consolatory Literature." *ClQ* 62 (2012): 242–59.

Wendland, P. "Die Therapeuten und die philonische Schrift vom beschaulichen Leben." *Neue Jahrbücher für classische Philologie*. Supplementband 22 (1896): 695–771.

Wendland, P. *Neu entdeckte Fragmente Philos: Nebst einer Untersuchung über die ursprüngliche Gestalt der Schrift De sacrificiis Abelis et Caini*. Berlin: Georg Reimer, 1891.

West, M. L. "The Cosmology of 'Hippocrates,' De Hebdomadibus." *ClQ* 21 (1971): 365–88.

Westeinde, J. van 't. "Teach and Transform: Education and (Re)constructing Identity in Jerome's letters." *StPtr* 74 (2016): 223–37.

Westerkamp, D. *Die philonische Unterscheidung: Aufklärung, Orientalismus und die Konstruktion der Philosophie*. Munich: Fink, 2009.

Westerkamp, D. "The Philonic Distinction: German Enlightenment Historiography of Jewish Thought." *History and Theory* 47 (2008): 533–59.

Westerkamp, D. "Platon in Moses. Hegels Kritik der Substanzmetaphysik und die *philosophia hebraeorum*." *Hegel-Jahrbuch* (2005): 106–13.

Wettstein, J. *Novum Testamentum Graecum*. 2 vols. Amsterdam: Ex Officina Dommeriana, 1751–52.

Whealey, A. "Josephus, Eusebius of Caesarea, and the Testimonium Flavianum." Pages 73–116 in *Josephus und das Neue Testament*. Edited by C. Böttrich and J. Herzer. Tübingen: Mohr Siebeck, 2007.

Whealey, A. "The *Testimonium Flavianum*." Pages 345–55 in *A Companion to Josephus*. Edited by H. H. Chapman and Z. Rogers. Oxford: Wiley-Blackwell, 2016.

White, L. M. and J. T. Fitzgerald. "Quod est comparandum: The Problem of Parallels." Pages 13–39 in *Early Christianity and Classical Culture: Comparative Studies in Honor of Abraham J. Malherbe*. Edited by J. T. Fitzgerald, T. H. Olbricht, and L. M. White. NovTSup 110. Leiden: Brill, 2003.

Whitmarsh, T. *Beyond the Second Sophistic: Adventures in Greek Postclassicism*. Berkeley: University of California Press, 2013.

Whitmarsh, T. "Greece: Hellenistic and Early Imperial Continuities." Pages 11–24 in *The Oxford Handbook to the Second Sophistic*. Edited by D. S. Richter and W. A. Johnson. Oxford: Oxford University Press, 2017.

Whitmarsh, T. *Greek Literature and the Roman Empire: The Politics of Imitation*. Oxford: Oxford University Press, 2001.

Whittaker, J. "Ammonius on the Delphic E." *ClQ* 19 (1969): 185–92.

Whittaker, J. "Moses Atticizing." *Phoenix* 21 (1967): 196–201.

Whittier, J. G. *The Pennsylvania Pilgrim and Other Poems*. Boston: J. R. Osgood and Company, 1872.

Wilbrand, W. *S. Ambrosius quos auctores quaeque exemplaria in epistulis componendis secutus sit*. Münster: Aschendorff, 1909.

Wilke, C. *"Den Talmud und den Kant": Rabbinerausbildung an der Schwelle zur Moderne*. Netiva 4. Hildesheim et al.: Olms, 2003.

Williams, D. H. *Ambrose of Milan and the End of the Nicene-Arian Conflicts*. New York: Oxford University Press, 1995.

Williams, F. *The Panarion of Epiphanius of Salamis, Books II and III: De Fide*. Leiden: Brill, 2013.

Williams, M. A. "The Demonizing of the Demiurge: The Innovation of Gnostic Myth." Pages 73–107 in *Innovations in Religious Traditions*. Edited by M. A. Williams, C. Cox, and M. S. Jaffe. Berlin: de Gruyter, 1992.

Williams, M. A. *The Immovable Race: A Gnostic Designation and the Theme of Stability in Late Antiquity.* Leiden: Brill, 1985.
Williams, M. A. *Rethinking "Gnosticism": An Argument for Dismantling a Dubious Category.* Princeton: Princeton University Press, 1996.
Williams, M. A. "Variety in Gnostic Perspectives on Gender." Pages 2–22 in *Images of the Feminine in Gnosticism.* Edited by K. L. King. Harrisburg, PA: Trinity Press International, 2000.
Williams, M. H. "Lessons from Jerome's Jewish Teachers: Exegesis and Cultural Interaction in Late Antique Palestine." Pages 66–86 in *Jewish Biblical Interpretation and Cultural Exchange: Comparative Exegesis in Context.* Edited by N. B. Dohrmann and D. Stern. Philadelphia: University of Pennsylvania Press, 2008.
Williams, M. H. *The Monk and the Book: Jerome and the Making of Christian Scholarship.* Chicago: University of Chicago Press, 2006.
Williams, T. "The Curses of Bouzyges: New Evidence." *Mnemosyne* 15 (1962): 396–98.
Williamson, R. *Jews in the Hellenistic World: Philo.* Cambridge: Cambridge University Press, 1989.
Williamson, R. *Philo and the Epistle to the Hebrews.* ALGHJ 4. Leiden: Brill, 1970.
Wilpert, P. "Philon bei Nikolaus von Kues." Pages 69–79 in *Antike und Orient im Mittelalter: Vorträge der Kölner Mediaevistentagungen 1956–1959.* Edited by P. Wilpert. Miscellanea mediaevalia 1. Berlin: de Gruyter, 1962.
Wilson, R. McL. "Philo and Gnosticism." *SPhiloA* 5 (1993): 84–92.
Wilson, R. McL. "Philo of Alexandria and Gnosticism." *Kairos* 14 (1972): 213–19.
Wilson, W. T. *Philo of Alexandria, On Virtues: Introduction, Translation, and Commentary.* Philo of Alexandria Commentary Series 3. Leiden: Brill, 2011.
Wilson, W. T. *The Sentences of Pseudo-Phocylides.* Berlin: de Gruyter, 2005.
Winden, J. C. M. van. "In the Beginning: Some Observations on the Patristic Interpretation of Genesis 1,1." *VC* 17 (1963): 105–21.
Winden, J. C. M. van. "Quotations from Philo in Clement of Alexandria's *Protrepticus*." *VC* 32 (1978): 208–13.
Winston, D. *Logos and Mystical Theology in Philo of Alexandria.* Cincinnati: Hebrew Union College Press, 1985.
Winston, D. "Philo." Pages 235–57 in *The Cambridge History of Philosophy in Late Antiquity.* Edited by L. P. Gerson. Cambridge: Cambridge University Press, 2015.
Winston, D. "Philo and Rabbinic Literature." Pages 231–53 in *The Cambridge Companion to Philo.* Edited by A. Kamesar. Cambridge: Cambridge University Press, 2009.
Winston, D. "Philo and the Contemplative Life." Pages 198–231 in *Jewish Spirituality: From the Bible through the Middle Ages.* World Spirituality 13. Edited by A. Green. New York: Crossroad, 1986.
Winston, D. "Philo and the Hellenistic Jewish Encounter." *SPhiloA* 7 (1995): 124–42.
Winston, D. "Philo and the Rabbis on Sex and the Body." *Poetics Today* 19 (1998): 41–62.
Winston, D. "Philo's Conception of the Divine Nature." Pages 21–42 in *Neoplatonism and Jewish Thought.* Edited by L. E. Goodman. New York: SUNY, 1992.
Winston, D. "Philo's *Nachleben* in Judaism." *SPhiloA* 6 (1994): 103–10.
Winston, D. "Philo's Theory of Eternal Creation: *De Prov.* 1.6–9." *PAAJR* 46–47 (1980): 593–606.
Winston, D. "Response to Runia and Sterling." *SPhiloA* 5 (1993): 141–46.
Winston, D. "Theodicy and the Creation of Man in Philo of Alexandria." Pages 105–11 in *Hellenica et Judaica: Hommage à Valentin Nikiprowetzky.* Edited by A. Caquot, M. Hadas-Lebel, and J. Riaud. Leuven: Peeters, 1986.
Winston, D. "Two Types of Mosaic Prophecy According to Philo." Pages 448–52 in *Society of Biblical Literature 1988 Seminar Papers, 1988.* Edited by D. J. Lull. Atlanta: Scholars Press, 1988.
Winston, D. *The Wisdom of Solomon.* AB 43. New York: Doubleday, 1979.
Winston, D. and J. Dillon. *Two Treatises of Philo of Alexandria: A Commentary on De Gigantibus and Quod Deus Sit Immutabilis.* Chico, CA: Scholars Press, 1983.
Winter, B. W. *Philo and Paul among the Sophists: Alexandrian and Corinthian Responses to a Julio-Claudian Movement.* 2nd edn. Grand Rapids: Eerdmans, 2002.
Winter, P. "Josephus on Jesus and James." Pages 428–41 in E. Schurer, *The History of the Jewish People in the Age of Jesus Christ.* Revised and edited by G. Vermes and F. Millar. Edinburgh: T&T Clark, 1973.
Wisse, F. "Flee Femininity: Antifemininity in Gnostic Texts and the Question of Social Milieu." Pages 297–307 in *Images of the Feminine in Gnosticism.* Edited by K. L. King. Harrisburg, PA: Trinity Press International, 2000.
Wolf, I. "Ueber den Begriff einer Wissenschaft des Judenthums." *Zeitschrift für die Wissenschaft des Judenthums* 1 (1823): 1–24.
Wolfson, E. R. "Heading the Law beyond the Law: Transgendering Alterity and the Hypernomian Perimeter of the Ethical." *EJJS* 14 (2020): 215–63.

Wolfson, E. R. "Inscribed in the Book of the Living: *Gospel of Truth* and Jewish Christology." *JSJ* 38 (2007): 234–71.
Wolfson, E. R. *Through A Speculum That Shines: Vision and Imagination in Medieval Jewish Mysticism.* Princeton: Princeton University Press, 1997.
Wolfson, E. R. "Traces of Philonic Doctrine in Medieval Jewish Mysticism: A Preliminary Note." *SPhiloA* 8 (1996): 99–106.
Wolfson, H. A. "Hallevi and Maimonides on Prophecy (Continued)." *JQR* 33 (1942): 49–82.
Wolfson, H. A. *Philo: Foundations of Religious Philosophy in Judaism, Christianity and Islam.* 2 vols. Cambridge, MA: Harvard University Press, 1948.
Wolfson, H. A. "The Philonic God of Revelation and His Latter-Day Deniers." *HTR* 53 (1960): 101–24.
Wolfson, H. A. *The Philosophy of the Church Fathers: Faith, Trinity, Incarnation.* Cambridge, MA: Harvard University Press, 1956.
Wolfson, H. A. *Religious Philosophy: A Group of Essays.* Cambridge, MA: Harvard University Press, 1961.
Wong, C.-K. "Philo's Use of Chaldaioi." *SPhiloA* 4 (1992): 1–14.
Wright, J. "Christopherson, John." In *Oxford Dictionary of National Biography* (2004). https://doi.org/10.1093/ref:odnb/5373.
Wright, R. A. "Plutarch on Moral Progress." Pages 136–50 in *Passions and Moral Progress in Greco-Roman Thought.* Edited by J. T. Fitzgerald. Routledge Monographs in Classical Studies. London and New York: Routledge, 2008.
Wuensch, R. *Ioannis Laurentii Lydi liber de mensibus.* Leipzig: Teubner, 1898
Yadin, A. *Scripture as Logos: Rabbi Ishmael and the Origins of Midrash.* Philadelphia: University of Pennsylvania Press, 2004.
Yakobean, A. "The Newly Discovered [Preamble to the] Festal Calendar: *Lord Yovhannēs the Lector's Preliminary Summary of the History of These Words*." Pages 91–99 in *Handes Amsorya, Zeitschrift für Armenische Philologie.* Vienna: Mechitarist Order, 2006 (in Armenian).
Yarbro Collins, A. "Numerical Symbolism in Jewish and Early Christian Apocalyptic Literature." *ANRW* 2.21.2 (1984): 1221–87.
Yli-Karjanmaa, S. "Philo of Alexandria." Pages 116–29 in *Brill's Companion to the Reception of Plato in Antiquity.* Edited by H. Tarrant, F. Renaud, D. Baltzly, and D. A. Layne. Leiden: Brill, 2018.
Yli-Karjanmaa, S. *Reincarnation in Philo of Alexandria.* SPhiloAMS 7. Atlanta: Society of Biblical Literature, 2015.
Yonge, C. D. *The Works of Philo Judaeus, the Contemporary of Josephus, Translated from the Greek.* 2nd edn. London: George Bell & Sons, 1890.
Yovhannēs Erznkatsʻi. *Compilative Commentary on Grammar.* Edited by L. Khachʻerean. Los Angeles: Alco Printing Company, 1983.
Zacuto, A. *Sefer Yuḥaśin.* Amsterdam: Shlomo ben Yosef Proops, 1717.
Zahn, T. "Die Dialoge des 'Adamantius' mit den Gnostikern." *ZKG* 9 (1888): 193–239.
Zedelmaier, H. *Der Anfang der Geschichte: Studien zur Ursprungsdebatte im 18. Jahrhundert.* Hamburg: Felix Meiner, 2003.
Zeegers, N. "Les trois cultures de Théophile d'Antioche." Pages 135–76 in *Les apologistes chrétiens et la culture grecque.* Edited by B. Pouderon and J. Doré. Théologie historique 105. Paris: Beauchesne, 1998.
Zeitlin, F. I. "Thebes: Theater of Self and Society in Athenian Drama." Pages 101–41 in *Greek Tragedy and Political Theory.* Edited by J. P. Euben. Berkeley: University of California Press, 1986.
Zeller, D. "Philons spiritualisierende Eschatologie und ihre Nachwirkung bei den Kirchenvätern." Pages 19–35 in *Vom Jenseits: Jüdisches Denken in der europäischen Geistesgeschichte.* Edited by E. Goodman-Thau. Berlin: de Gruyter, 1997.
Zeller, E. *Die Philosophie der Griechen: Eine Untersuchung über Charakter, Gang und Hauptmomente ihrer Entwicklung, Dritter Theil: Die nacharistotelische Philosophie, Zweite Hälfte.* Tübingen: Ludwig Friedrich Fues, 1852.
Zeller, E. *Die Philosophie der Griechen in ihrer geschichtlichen Entwicklung.* 3rd edn. Leipzig: L. F. Fues, 1881.
Zimmermann, M. *Schriftsinn und Theologisches Verstehen: Die heutige hermeneutische Frage in Ausgang von Origenes.* Adamantiana 9. Münster: Aschendorff, 2017.
Zino, P. F., ed. *Example tria insignia naturae, legis, et gratiae, cùm in vita Iosephi patriarchae, & magni Mosis à Philone Hebraeo...* Venice: Bologninus Zalterius, 1575.
Zino, P. F. *Il ritratto del vero e perfetto gentiluomo espresso da Filone Ebreo nella vita di Giuseppe Patriarca.* Venice: Giolito, 1574.
Zino, P. F., ed. *Iosephi patriarchae vita a Philone Hebraeo graecè composita.* Venice: Christophorus Zanetus, 1574.

Ziolkowski, J. M. *Letters of Peter Abelard: Beyond the Personal.* Washington, DC: Catholic University of America Press, 2008.
Zoepfl, F., ed. *Der Kommentar des Pseudo-Eustathius zum Hexaëmeron.* ATA 10. Münster: Aschendorff, 1927.
Zunz, L. *Die Monatstage des Kalenderjahres, ein Andenken an Hingeschiedene.* Berlin: M. Poppelauer, 1872.
Zunz, L. *Zur Geschichte und Literatur.* Vol. 1. Berlin: Veit und Comp., 1845.
Zurawski, J. M. "Mosaic Torah as Encyclical Paideia: Reading Paul's Allegory of Hagar and Sarah in Light of Philo of Alexandria's." Pages 283–307 in *Pedagogy in Ancient Judaism and Early Christianity.* Edited by K. Martin Hogan, M. Goff, and E. Wasserman. Atlanta: Society of Biblical Literature Press, 2017.

Index Locorum

For the benefit of digital users, indexed terms that span two pages (e.g., 52–53) may, on occasion, appear on only one of those pages.

Tables are indicated by an italic *t* following the page number.

Philo of Alexandria

De opificio mundi
general: 267–68, 268n.52, 334–35, 338, 373, 375, 404, 410, 414–15, 536
1–12: 198
2: 25
4–6: 56n.60
7: 181, 198, 375
8: 536
8–9: 181
8–13: 216*t*
13: 56n.59, 174
15: 181
15–25: 125n.94
17: 44
17–20: 286
18: 253–54, 286–87
19: 61n.88, 286–87
20 433
21: 190, 447–48
24: 44, 61, 286, 363–64
24–27: 158n.68
25: 174, 433–34
27: 57
28: 186
31: 174
33: 44, 52
33–35: 52
35: 181
36: 57, 58, 61n.88
38: 57
43: 52
45–46: 57
47: 173n.68
50: 57
51: 57
54: 52
56–57: 57, 58n.70
65: 186
69: 53, 54n.44, 58n.69, 96, 96n.23, 100, 174n.70
69–71: 186
69–86: 216*t*
71: 191n.62
72: 57
72–75: 63
73–75: 182
74: 58n.69

74–75: 94n.10
77–78: 186
79–81: 555–56
82: 55n.47
87–88: 174
89: 54n.43, 173
89–100: 173
89–127: 173n.60
91: 173
97: 192
99: 173n.67, 173n.68
100: 117n.48, 173n.66, 296n.100
100–26: 216*t*
103–5: 233
105: 114
131: 186
134: 58n.69
134–35: 57, 58–59, 58n.67, 186
134–37: 54n.45
135: 100, 191–92
137–71: 216*t*
139: 61
146: 96, 100, 101
147: 216*t*
148: 58n.69
152: 104
157: 104
170–72: 48n.5, 56, 546
171: 117

Legum allegoriae
general: 279–80, 303, 337
1: 259–60, 265, 340–41, 376–77
1–2: 8–9, 301, 337–38
1.12–2.18: 214
1.15: 296n.100
1.2–3: 174
1.3: 57, 309n.66
1.31: 53n.36, 54n.44
1.31–2.53: 54n.45
1.32: 100n.48
1.42: 100n.46
1.43–44: 119n.68
1.43–47: 315
1.44: 190
1.45: 57, 101
1.47–48: 119n.65
1.48: 119n.68

1.51: 234n.36
1.53–54: 57
1.56–62: 305
1.58: 540
1.63: 314
1.72: 314–15
1.72–73: 168
1.73: 330
1.80: 119n.65
1.84: 191n.62
1.88–89: 57
1.91: 536–37
1.94: 57
1.102: 341n.51
1.103: 172n.54
1.105–7: 252n.59
1.108: 99, 192

2: 259–60, 265, 372, 376–77, 384
2.1: 97n.27
2.1–2: 117
2.3: 70–71
2.5–8: 102
2.12: 56n.59
2.24: 102, 172n.54
2.29: 102
2.31: 102
2.34: 102, 236n.53
2.49: 97–98
2.49–50: 102
2.55–56: 297–98
2.59: 54n.44
2.70: 102
2.73: 104
2.74: 104
2.77: 104
2.77–79: 188
2.78–81: 54–55
2.84: 70n.15
2.86: 61
2.87: 104
2.88: 70n.15
2.92: 104
2.103–4: 89*t*
2.104: 164
2.105: 70, 104

3.4: 184
3.12–13: 188
3.18: 89*t*
3.42: 94n.12, 99
3.53: 57
3.61: 70, 70n.15, 537–38
3.64: 57
3.66: 70n.15, 104
3.67: 172n.54
3.68: 104
3.69: 192
3.71: 99
3.72: 192

3.75–76: 104
3.80: 89*t*
3.82: 191n.62
3.88–93: 54n.40
3.96: 96, 433
3.99: 287n.43
3.102: 41
3.102–3: 41
3.118: 89*t*
3.121: 89*t*
3.128: 168
3.132: 240n.74
3.140: 240n.74
3.175: 61, 184
3.180–81: 184
3.202: 524
3.212: 188
3.244–45: 188

4 (Harris fr. 8.1): 85n.58

De cherubim
general: 340–41
3: 38
5: 233n.31
6: 38
7: 233n.31
8: 38
12: 171
18–19: 95n.16, 123n.86
36: 61, 89*t*
41: 233n.31
42: 184
43: 184
48: 184
49: 97–98
50: 103
57: 102–3
63: 341n.51
73: 38
125: 57
127: 44
145: 38

De sacrificiis Abelis et Caini
general: 263–65, 267
1–4: 167n.35
3: 104–5
8: 259–60
11–12: 167–68
11–45: 176n.82
19–20: 216*t*
32: 265–66
35: 341n.51
40: 341n.51
45: 168
49: 168
51: 89*t*
59: 62n.102, 190
78: 138n.33

INDEX LOCORUM 641

82–85: 297n.110
94: 85n.58, 86t
101: 85n.58, 86t
106: 172n.54
118: 62n.96, 216t
126: 62n.96

Quod deterius potiori insidiari soleat
general 265, 267
13: 196–97
18: 188
22–23: 96n.23
28: 103
82: 190–91
86: 100
89: 52–53
90: 100
105: 119n.65
122: 107n.70
139: 116n.43
150–66: 115–16
160: 115–16, 120n.74
160–66: 115–16

De posteritate Caini
general: 265, 267–68, 372, 416–17
5–18: 68n.11
7: 537–38
10–11: 171
14: 189–90
15: 52–53
19–30: 95n.16
22–31: 121n.75, 123n.89
27: 123n.86
28: 123n.87
29–30: 123n.88
32: 57, 171
43: 104–5
60: 192
66–75: 168
69: 190–91
98: 168
102: 536
115: 188
145: 341n.51
148–50: 55n.50
150: 52
167–69: 190
169: 52–53
170: 104–5
171: 119n.68
173: 104–5
174: 341n.51
181: 540

De gigantibus
general: 259–60, 267, 344, 373
6–15: 391n.28
19–57: 51n.26
48–49: 95n.16
49: 123n.87
60: 54n.44, 253–54, 341n.51
65: 217n.36

Quod Deus sit immutabilis
general: 266, 267, 373
14: 99
39: 52
52: 196–97
52–54: 85n.58, 86t
53: 97
57: 63n.106
69: 85n.58, 86–87, 86t
76–77: 89t
78: 54–55, 54n.39
134–35: 61
150: 99
162–64: 188
298: 433–34

De agricultura
general: 267
1: 119n.65
1–25: 164n.20, 168n.40
24: 341n.51
25: 119n.65
41: 168n.39
42: 168
51: 52, 62n.96, 433–34
66: 168n.39
67–76: 164
67–83: 89t
80–81: 185
95–101: 54–55
101: 188
132: 55n.50

De plantatione
general: 373–74, 376–77
1: 119n.65
1–27: 119
3: 181
8: 270
8–10: 159
9: 53n.34
10: 270
14: 391n.28
18: 433
28–72: 119
36–37: 193
38: 57
42: 96n.23
44: 54n.45
50: 94n.8
121: 52
140: 119n.65

De ebrietate
general: 265, 267, 373
19: 188

30: 97–98, 97n.34
41–55: 89t
45: 89t
67–71: 216t
85: 297–98
91–92: 540
101: 99
148: 191n.62
177: 529–30
208–9: 188
223: 265–66

De sobrietate
general: 259–60, 267, 328n.34, 341–42, 373
36: 119n.65

De confusione linguarum
general: 259–60, 267, 344
22–23: 294n.82
30: 123n.87
30–32: 95n.16
32: 294n.82
40–41: 96
41: 433
60–63: 44
62–63: 96, 164, 555–56
63: 62n.96
97: 62n.103
126: 102
138: 52–53
145–46: 44
145–47: 292–93
145–48: 292–93
146: 44, 61, 61n.89, 62n.96, 190–91
146–47: 96, 292n.71
147: 61
167: 260n.5
169–82: 63
174–75: 391n.28
177: 99
182: 52

De migratione Abrahami
general: 267
1–4: 165
2: 54n.44, 99
9: 99, 101
16: 99
33: 98–99
47–48: 293
47–49: 136–37
48: 133n.21
67: 89t, 168
77: 185
89–93: 37, 506–7
183: 184
187–91: 171–72
188: 171–72
190–91: 101–2
193: 192

Quis rerum divinarum heres sit
general: 263–65, 268
14: 264–65
31: 190
48: 89t
53: 97n.35
55: 101
57: 54n.45
69: 54n.44
70: 116n.43
82: 185
92: 192
119: 61
134: 251
136: 57
140: 251
141–43: 216t
147: 52
161: 54n.41
168–70: 54–55
183–85: 216t
186–92: 216t
188: 53n.34
213: 538
225: 89t
231: 96
257: 101–2
264: 94n.9
274: 94n.11

De congressu eruditionis gratia
general: 342
2: 233n.31
6: 38n.26
11: 38, 535
18: 535
52: 535, 536–37
64–66: 38
70: 38
74: 38n.26
74–76: 38n.26, 535
74–80: 517–18
79: 372n.19
79–80: 535
90: 173n.68
96–97: 168
107: 536
117: 231n.23

De fuga et inventione
4–24: 216t
16: 216t
32: 191n.62
44: 216t
45: 171–72
50–52: 97–98, 433–34
55: 193
68–70: 94n.10
68–72: 96n.23
94: 196–97, 540

108–9: 97–98
109: 97–98
112: 53n.34
132–37: 216t
143: 216t
150: 105
157–60: 216t
161–65: 190
165: 54–55, 189–90
166: 191n.62
168–71: 216t
179: 537–38

De mutatione nominum
general: 372, 376–77, 378–79, 402–3
1–15: 120–21
7: 189n.53
7–15: 125n.95
10: 536–37
11: 116, 120–21, 120n.74
11–14: 252n.65
12: 120–21
13–14: 120–21
15: 62n.102
17: 201, 208, 208n.42
77: 233n.31
87: 63n.106
194–200: 394–95
255: 38

De somniis
general: 464
1: 267, 334–35
1.17–18: 57
1.34: 100
1.41: 171–72
1.41–60: 171–72
1.67: 94n.7
1.68–74: 62n.104
1.75: 44, 289
1.77: 234
1.85: 62n.101
1.123: 101
1.129: 63n.106
1.138–46: 391n.28
1.203–8: 296–97
1.205: 188
1.215: 52, 62n.96
1.228–30: 44
1.229: 89t
1.231: 120n.74
1.237: 85, 85n.58, 86t, 87
1.238: 62n.103
1.241: 95n.16, 123n.85
1.244: 89t

2: 259–60, 279–80, 372
2.24: 208
2.36: 236n.53
2.48–63: 101

2.67: 105–6
2.70: 101n.51
2.147: 199, 208n.42
2.164–65: 198–99, 208
2.185: 103
2.192: 265–66
2.201: 89t
2.204: 52
2.215–302: 123–24
2.219: 123–24
2.219–20: 123n.88
2.221: 97n.33, 123–24, 123n.85
2.221–30: 95n.16
2.222: 123–24, 123n.85
2.223–24: 123n.85
2.223–25: 123–24
2.226–27: 123–24, 123n.86
2.227–28: 123–24, 123n.87
2.228–30: 123n.86
2.229–33: 123–24
2.234–36: 123–24, 123n.88
2.237: 99, 123–24
2.240: 38
2.242: 97–98, 101
2.250: 253–54
2.283: 537–38

De Abrahamo
general: 8–9, 267, 301, 303, 373, 522
1–2: 198
3–4: 147
5–6: 312
51: 252n.65
69–71 304
72: 171–72
76: 54–55, 54n.39
99: 233n.31, 537–38
101–2: 342
107–41: 62n.102
121: 313, 318
171: 196–97
236: 285
256–57: 175n.72
271: 314

De Iosepho
general: 267, 271–72, 337, 373, 376–77, 404, 522
2: 168n.39
5: 200, 208n.42
40–48: 216t
78: 524
80–124: 113
82: 197–98
123: 216t
125–47: 113
126: 216t
127–29: 113, 114
144: 216t
175–76: 205
176: 205–6, 208, 209n.43

De vita Moysis
general: 187–89, 279–80, 334n.8, 335–36, 373, 404, 464, 468–69, 471, 522
1: 267
1–2: 268n.52, 271–72
1.10–12: 234n.36
1.27: 96
1.29: 185
1.31: 199–200, 208, 208n.42
1.32: 180
1.44–47: 269
1.48: 180
1.59: 187–88
1.60: 168n.39
1.62: 330
1.65: 187–88
1.65–70: 62n.103
1.75: 120n.74
1.75–76: 252n.65
1.84–88: 469
1.87: 234
1.109: 89*t*
1.122: 239–40n.71
1.140–42: 204, 269
1.141: 204, 208, 209n.43
1.149: 26n.37
1.177: 187–88
1.187: 191n.62
1.207: 54n.43
1.255–57: 472–74
1.256–57: 469
1.264–304: 216*t*
1.280: 196–97

2: 259–60, 267
2.2: 166
2.26–40: 469–71
2.26–44: 232n.30
2.27: 201, 208, 208n.42
2.28–33: 60n.84
2.37–40: 60–61n.85
2.40: 129n.11
2.44: 555–56
2.45–53: 198
2.48: 198
2.51: 198
2.71–end: 267
2.74: 41, 112n.26
2.74–76: 41
2.76: 112n.26
2.84–88: 471–72
2.88: 238n.59
2.96: 537–38
2.97: 234n.36
2.109–35: 231–32, 232n.30
2.112: 238n.61
2.113: 240n.74
2.115: 172
2.118: 230–31, 238n.60
2.119: 238n.61
2.122: 187, 238n.61
2.125: 238n.61
2.128: 187, 238n.61
2.128–29: 240n.74
2.131: 237–38
2.182: 187
2.195: 110n.11, 125n.97
2.210: 54n.43
2.213: 137
2.288: 94n.13, 101, 555–56
2.291: 234n.36

De Decalogo
general: 8–9, 267–68, 274, 300, 301, 303, 312, 341–42, 375
2–17: 283
20–31: 173n.68
32–49: 135–36
33: 298n.114
35–36: 293–94
45–49: 293–94
47: 310–11
49: 137, 140
100: 56n.59
105: 61
154–74: 130–31

De specialibus legibus
general: 341–42, 373, 379, 391, 402–3, 416–17, 464, 475
1: 267, 404–5
1–4: 259–60, 381n.55
1.13–20: 198
1.16ff: 234n.36
1.18ff: 234n.36
1.32–50: 189–90
1.40: 54–55
1.41: 198
1.50: 189–90
1.51–53: 29–30
1.53: 475
1.79–81: 8–9, 300, 301
1.81: 61, 62n.103
1.82–97: 234–35
1.83–99: 231–32
1.85: 230–31
1.86–88: 238n.61
1.97: 26n.37, 475
1.131–61: 8–9, 300, 301
1.145–47: 234–35
1.147: 234–35
1.168: 26n.37
1.168–69: 475
1.190: 26n.37
1.262: 54n.42
1.269: 54n.42
1.275: 54–55
1.285–345: 8–9, 300, 301, 312

1.305: 119n.65
1.339: 201, 208, 208n.42
2: 372
2–4: 274
2.1–95: 267
2.147: 185
2.162 478–79
2.167: 26n.37
2.211: 54n.43
2.262: 478–79

3: 266
3–4: 267–68
3.1–6: 99
3.1–7: 8–9, 300, 301
3.8–64: 8–9, 300, 301
3.57: 235n.42
3.76: 208
3.77: 57
3.77–78: 201n.23
3.93–95: 30n.55
3.147–49: 30n.55
3.189: 234n.36
3.195: 392n.30

4: 266, 372, 375
4.30–34: 30n.55
4.69: 240n.74
4.100–31: 55n.50
4.101–2: 55n.50
4.106–8: 55n.50
4.116: 55n.50
4.123: 100, 100n.50, 101
4.132–50: 547–48
4.133–35: 131
4.188: 102
4.219–25: 22
4.227: 234n.36
4.233: 89*t*

De virtutibus
general: 260n.7, 266, 267, 372, 373, 381n.55
52: 259–60
59–60: 205, 206, 208
75: 555–56
82–101: 27
82–160: 27–28
102–8: 27, 28n.48
108: 29–30
109: 21
109–20: 27
125–47: 27
129: 52
140: 27n.42
141: 26n.37
154: 234n.36
203: 53n.36, 58n.69
222: 105–6
212–16: 344n.73

De praemiis et poenis
1–3: 198, 372
23: 57
39–40: 117n.48
40: 70n.16
51: 89*t*
79–172: 555–56
85: 190
132: 216*t*

Quod omnis probus liber sit
general: 337, 487–88
2: 296n.100
2–8: 216*t*
13: 191n.62
17–117: 216*t*
25: 524
43: 216*t*
75–87: 231–32
98: 529
99–104: 524–25
141: 529–31

De vita contemplativa
general: 6–10, 150–51, 158, 184–85, 259–60, 260n.10, 277–78, 279, 322–27, 331, 337, 339, 359–60, 389–90, 406–8, 409, 487–88, 538, 562
1–41: 9–10, 277, 350–51, 368
2: 70n.16, 117n.48
10–13: 138n.33
11: 184–85
13: 301
21–22: 284n.17, 325
25: 284n.17, 325, 360n.65
28–29: 284n.17, 325
29: 325
30: 360n.65
34–35: 284n.17, 326
45: 304
68: 284n.17, 326
78: 83–84, 158, 269, 284n.17, 326
87: 185
88: 184
90: 185

De aeternitate mundi
general: 268n.52, 344, 533
12: 296n.100
30–31: 533
33–34: 294n.82
66: 52
86–87: 294n.82
92: 294n.82
134: 96

In Flaccum
general: 17n.2, 19, 337, 487–88, 496
Legatio ad Gaium

general: 4–5, 9, 259–60, 327–29, 337, 362, 475, 487–88, 522, 523–24, 527
3–7: 550
4: 236n.53
76–113: 526–27
79: 526–27, 528–29
81–92: 526
84: 527
90: 527
91: 527
99: 433
118: 568
151: 523–24
156–57: 475
162–64: 149n.22
181–83: 33n.3
279–80: 475
294–98: 475
306: 475
306: 26n.37
311–18: 475
346: 149
349–72: 33n.3
351: 528–29
351–368: 528–29
352: 528–29
355: 20–21
359: 528–29
368: 528–29

Quaestiones et solutiones in Genesin
general 8, 9–10, 260n.5, 267–68, 269, 274–75, 276, 277, 278, 303, 305n.41, 306, 350–51, 352–53, 400–1
1–3 301
1–4: 8–9, 300
1.1–3: 306–7
1.2: 314
1.3: 314
1.4: 96
1.6: 317
1.7: 101
1.8: 101
1.8–47: 214
1.9: 314
1.12: 305
1.12–13: 58, 306–7, 314–15
1.14: 57
1.14: 306, 315
1.15: 57, 106
1.16: 252n.59
1.17: 296n.100
1.24: 101–2
1.28: 201, 208, 209n.43
1.31: 104
1.32: 307
1.36: 57
1.47–48: 104
1.48: 309
1.50–51: 100n.48

1.51: 104
1.54: 94n.8
1.55: 85, 85n.58, 86–87, 86*t*, 97, 106
1.56: 101
1.59: 168n.38
1.62: 274
1.64–77: 214
1.78: 167n.35
1.79: 175
1.87–2.82: 214, 250–51
1.92: 317–18
1.93: 106
1.94: 96n.23
1.99: 296n.100

2.1–7: 248, 249–51, 269
2.5: 310–11
2.6: 91–92, 101, 250–51
2.54: 85n.58, 86*t*, 97
2.56: 96n.23
2.58: 63n.113
2.60: 199, 208n.42
2.62: 61, 97, 159, 270, 307, 434

3: 214
3–4: 253
3.1: 304–6
3.5: 313
3.16: 296n.100
3.38: 312
3.42: 28n.48
3.47: 312
3.48: 198–99, 201, 208, 208n.42
3.49: 296n.100, 312
3.53: 233n.31
3.62: 28n.48

4: 301
4.2: 57
4.4: 57
4.8: 57
4.23: 309n.66
4.30: 309
4.92: 314
4.99: 202–3, 208, 209n.44, 309
4.110: 172
4.138: 506–7
4.152: 236, 538
4.154–245: 250, 368
4.195: 277
4.198: 269
4.200: 269
4.202: 269
4.245: 277–78

Quaestiones et solutiones in Exodum
general: 269, 274–75, 276, 303, 316, 341–42, 547
1–2: 8–9, 300, 301
1.8: 103
1.9: 305

1.15: 308
1.19: 274

2.11: 207
2.12: 207
2.17: 89t
2.49: 103
2.52: 41, 112n.26
2.62: 234n.36
2.62–68: 268
2.68: 70n.16, 174–75
2.82: 41, 112n.26
2.85: 238n.59
2.90: 41, 112n.26
2.110: 200–1, 208, 208n.42
2.110–16: 238n.61
2.112: 238–40
2.116: 238–40
2.117: 230–31

frag. 27: 200n.18

Hypothetica
general: 24–28, 259–60, 270, 279–80, 372
6.2–3: 25
7.6–7: 26
7.8: 26
7.9: 27n.42
11.2: 27n.42

De providentia
general: 268n.52, 274–75, 276, 311–12, 313, 316, 379
1: 537–38
1–2: 8–9, 300, 301
1.2–3: 319
1.6–7: 310

2: 270, 271, 279–80, 379
2.18: 312
2.64: 33

De animalibus
general: 8–9, 203, 274–75, 276, 300, 301, 303, 312, 313
61: 317
100: 198–99, 203, 208, 208n.42

De Deo
general: 8–9, 95n.16, 123n.86, 300, 301, 312
3: 103n.53

Bible

Genesis
1: 43, 56, 174, 216t, 294n.86
1–2: 216t
1–3: 56, 57
1:1: 44, 289–90, 294
1:1–2: 251
1:1–2:3: 174–75
1:3: 291–92, 293

1:5: 181
1:14–19: 174
1:26: 53, 56n.61, 57, 58, 63, 96, 99, 174, 181
1:26–28: 174
1:27: 186
1:28: 104n.57
2–3: 216t
2:1: 289–90
2:4: 174–75
2:6–7: 340–41
2:7: 53, 56n.61, 58–59, 100, 186
2:8: 317
2:8–3:19: 214
2:14: 330
2:15: 306
2:16: 106
2:17: 107
2:18: 117
2:21: 101–2
2:23: 201, 202
3:20: 102–3
3:22: 63, 86t, 106, 107
3:24: 171
4: 214
4:2a: 167
4:4: 86t
4:14: 115–16
4:16: 171
4:25: 104–5
4:26: 175
5:1–2: 168–69
6–10: 214
6:1–4: 217, 373
6:1–5: 51n.26
6:4–12: 373
6:6: 106, 107
6:7: 86t
6:14–16: 250–51
6:17: 217
8:21: 86t
9:3: 63n.113
9:6: 307
9:21: 373
9:11: 123–24, 123n.85
9:20: 119
9:24–27: 260n.5, 373
9:28–29: 260n.5
9:28–10:32: 260n.5
11:1–9: 260n.5
12–15:6: 218
12:1: 165
12:4: 171–72
12:11–19: 199–200
12:27–18:16: 214
12:27–25:10: 214
14:9: 285
14:20: 274
17:1: 120–21
18: 62–63, 62n.99, 62n.101, 62n.102, 244
18:11: 103

18:22: 95n.16, 123–24, 123n.86, 125–26
19:24: 62n.101
22:6: 165
22:7: 216t
23:6: 166
24:16: 202–3
25:20: 352–53
25:22–25: 54–55
26:32: 352–53
28–35: 62–63
28:9: 352–53
28:11: 62n.102
31–35: 62n.99
31:13: 86t, 89t, 95n.16
32:22–31: 63n.106
34: 394–95
35:20: 89t
37:8–11: 200
38: 105
39:20–41:45: 113
41:7: 123n.88
41:17: 123–24
41:17–24: 123–24
42:11: 96
42:25: 205
46:4: 123n.88
48:13–19: 54–55

Exodus
2:3: 234n.36
2:11–15: 180
3: 62n.103, 120–21, 190–91
3:2–3: 62–63
3:3: 88–91, 89t
3:4–15: 254–55
3:14: 5–6, 70–71, 115–16, 119–21, 120n.74, 125–26, 252–53, 281, 293
3:14–15: 252–53
3:22: 204
4:4: 104
5:1: 234
6:3: 120–21
7:15: 95n.16
8:26: 216t
12:23: 102
14:10–14: 199–200
15:15: 131–32
15:21: 88, 89t
16: 130n.13
16:1: 130n.13
17:6: 95n.16, 123–24, 123n.85
18:11: 89t
19:18: 293–94
19:19: 132n.17
19:5: 132n.17
19:6: 166
20:2–14: 130–31
20:15: 132–34, 135
20:15: 134, 137, 138

20:17: 132n.18
20:18: 136, 293
20:19: 132, 137, 138, 139–40
20:21: 189–90
20:22: 136
21–24: 130–31
21:24: 391
23:4–5: 207
23:20–24: 292–93
24:5–6: 216t
24:10: 95n.16, 123–24, 123n.85
24:17: 134n.27
25:4: 468–69, 471–72, 473
25:40: 41, 42, 112n.26
25:8: 112n.26
25:9: 41
26–28: 71
26:1: 234n.36
26:30: 41, 112n.26
27:8: 41
28: 238–40
30:12–16: 216t
32:2–7: 216t
33: 55
33:1: 54–55
33:3: 54–55
33:7: 115–16
33:12–32: 189–90
33:20: 134n.24, 189–90

Leviticus
8: 238–40
10:1–2: 105–6
10:16–20: 216t
11:22 LXX: 70n.15
14:34: 23n.23
16:17: 123–24
19:14: 27n.46
23:15: 478–79

Numbers
12:8: 134n.24
14:44: 95n.16
16:48: 123–24, 123n.88
17:13 LXX: 123–24, 123n.88
20:17: 188
21:4–8: 54–55
21:4–9: 188
21:17–18: 472
21:18: 469, 472, 473–74
21:22: 188
22–24: 216t
23:19: 85, 86–87, 86t
27:16–17: 206, 207

Deuteronomy
general: 353
1:31: 85, 86–88, 86t
4: 133n.21

INDEX LOCORUM 649

4:2: 547–48
4:12: 133n.21, 136, 137–38
4:15–19: 133n.21
4:17: 234n.36
4:19: 155n.49
4:36: 133n.21
5: 133n.21
5:5: 95n.16, 123–24, 123n.86, 124n.90
5:20–24: 133n.21
5:31: 95, 95n.16, 123–24, 123n.87
6:4: 117
8:5: 85, 86–88, 86*t*
8:11: 313
8:15: 123–24
13:1: 547–48
16–18: 129
16:18–22: 131
16:18–18:22: 130–31
16:21–22: 234n.36
16:22: 89*t*
18:3: 234–35
19:4: 547–48
20: 21
20:1: 21
20:10: 23n.23
20:10–14: 22, 23
20:10–15: 21
20:10–19: 22
20:11: 22–23
20:16–18: 23n.23
20:20: 234n.36
21:16: 216*t*
22:27: 201n.23
23:8–9: 29–30
27:18: 27n.46
28:23: 216*t*
30:15: 85n.59
32: 129
32:46–47: 43
33:2: 133n.23, 140
34: 129
34:6: 234n.36

1 Samuel
2:5: 99

4 Kingdoms
2:12: 88, 89*t*

Job
10:8a: 53n.35
28: 43–44

Psalms
15: 89*t*
17:12: 189–90
19:8: 43
29:7: 132, 133–34, 137

36:23a: 89*t*
62:12: 138n.32
74:9: 89*t*
75:5: 89*t*
75:7: 88, 89*t*
76:14: 92
76:14b: 89*t*
107:20: 43
118:73a: 53n.35
119:105: 43
119:130: 43
138:4: 139
147:15: 43
147:18: 43

Proverbs
1: 538
1:20–23: 43–44
5:18: 165
8: 97
8–9: 43–44
8:22–23: 97–98, 101
8:22–24: 43–44
8:27: 43–44
8:30: 287n.40
9:9: 89*t*, 91
9:9a: 88–91
21:16: 317–18
22:28: 547–48

Ecclesiastes
9:9: 165
10:7: 166

Isaiah
6:10: 102, 196–97
40:11: 43
42:16: 27n.46

Jeremiah
3:4: 97n.32
18:8: 86–87, 86*t*
20:7: 91
23:29: 138n.32

Ezekiel
1:26–28: 96
27:7: 231n.22
40–48: 42n.41

Daniel
6:3: 200

Hosea
10:12: 239n.66

Amos
6:2–6: 233
6:5: 233

Zechariah
6:12: 96, 164
10:5 LXX: 164
11:17 LXX: 164–65

Malachi
3:6: 295–96

Wisdom of Solomon
general: 348–50, 354–58
2:1–20: 355–58
2:10: 355–58
2:16: 355–58
2:20: 355–58
7–9: 43–44
7:26: 101
8:2: 97n.31
8:3: 97
8:9: 97n.31
8:16: 97n.31
10:1: 54n.45
11:17: 355
11:17–19: 89t
13:1: 181
16:20–21: 179

Sirach (Ecclesiasticus)
18:1: 355
19:13: 196–97
24: 43–44, 97

Baruch
3:9–4:4: 43–44

Matthew
4:23: 454
13:15: 196–97
22:2: 85, 86–87, 86t
26:37: 175n.76

Mark
10:27: 199–200

Luke
3:11: 239n.70
22:1: 341–42

John
1: 43–44
1:1: 44
1:1–2: 44
1:1–3: 454
1:1–5: 43
1:3: 44
1:1–18: 43
1:10–12b: 43
1:12: 44
1:14: 43

1:16: 43
7:25–26: 196–97
10:8: 91–92
14:6: 92
16:1–4: 32–33
17:21: 70n.17
17:21–23: 70–71

Acts
general: 358–59
2:45: 151n.31
4:34–35: 151n.31
6:9: 32–33
7:20–22: 180
13:5: 32–33
13:14: 32–33
14:1: 32–33
17:13: 307–8
17:34: 327n.29
18:24–19:1: 33
18:27–19:1: 33

Romans
1:20: 179–80
8:29: 62n.96
13:13–14: 244

1 Corinthians
1:12: 33
3:4–6:22: 33
7:23: 216t
12:22–23: 250–51
16:12: 33

2 Corinthians
3:6: 305
11:24: 32–33

Galatians
2:3: 37
2:11–16: 37
3:24–25: 87
3:28: 186
4: 39
4:4–7: 37
4:21–31: 36–37, 38
4:22–31: 165–66
4:24: 37, 253–54, 455–56
5:2–4: 37
5:6: 37
6:12–15: 37

Philippians
3:13: 88–91, 89t

Colossians
1:15: 62n.96
1:15–20: 36–37

2 Timothy
2:24–25: 196–97

Titus
3:13: 33

Hebrews
4:12: 89t
8:1–6: 36–37, 42
8:2: 41
8:5: 41–43
8:6: 41, 42
8:6–13: 42
8:13: 42
9:11: 41
9:11–15: 42
9:23–24: 41, 42
9:24: 42
9:26: 42
10:1: 42, 84
10:1–18: 42
11:10: 181
11:16: 42

Revelation
1:4: 338

Greco-Roman Authors

Alcinous, *Handbook*
10.1–4: 94n.7
15–17: 94n.8
23: 94n.10
23–24: 94n.9
23.1: 94n.11

Anatolius
35.14–21: 173

Anthologia Palatina
9.752: 191n.62

Aristophanes, *Ranae*
1491–99: 530

Aristotle *Nicomachean Ethics*
5.4.7: 164n.21

Arrian, *Epicteti dissertationes*
1.4.26: 531

Cassius Dio
56.36.5: 527
59.26.7: 526–27

Cicero
De officiis
1.11.34–36: 23n.24
1.16.51–52: 26n.39

De republica
3.23.34–35: 23n.24

Clitarchus, *Sententiae*
81: 201n.22

Corpus hermeticum
10.14: 95n.15
2.12: 95n.15

Demosthenes
De falsa legatione
195: 197–98

Fragmenta
13 frag. 27: 199

Olynthiaca
2.12: 200–1

Dio Chrysostom, *Orationes*
1.9: 526
1.36: 526
1.69–83: 527
76.5: 26n.40
18.7: 530

Dionysius, *Antiquitates romanae* 28–29
14.6.1–6: 28n.51
2.17.1: 28n.51

Diogenes Laertius
2.18: 530
2.22: 530

Eunapius, *Vitae Sophistarum*
6: 121n.77

Euripides
Iphigenia Taurica
895: 199n.14

Syleus
TrGF 5.687–691: 524–25

Supplices
531: 26n.40

Troades
887–88: 138n.33

Galen, *On the Usefulness of the Parts of the Body*
14.7: 98n.40

Heliodorus, *Aethiopica*
9.9: 110n.11

Heraclitus
frag. 76: 112–13
frag. 91: 113n.32

Herodorus of Heraclea, FGH 31
frag. 14: 104

Hesiod, *Theogony*
924–29: 98–99

Homeric Hymn to Pythian Apollo
300–26: 98–99

Horace
Carmina
1.12.25: 527n.48
3.3.9–12: 527n.48
4.4.61–65: 527n.48

Epistulae
2.1.5–13: 527n.48
2.1.197: 531

Isocrates, *Orationes*
5.110–12: 527

Juvenal, *Satires*
14.96–107: 26n.39

Libanius, *Epistulae*
1352: 201n.22

Menander, *Dyskolos*
510–11: 26n.38
641–42: 26n.38

Numenius
frag. 1a: 118
frag. 2.19: 120n.72
frag. 2.23: 120n.72
frag. 3.1: 120n.72
frag. 3.8: 120n.72
frag. 3.9: 120n.72
frag. 4: 121n.75, 124n.91
frag. 4.7: 120n.72
frag. 4.9: 120n.72
frag. 4.12: 120n.72
frag. 5.5: 120n.72
frag. 5.6: 120n.72
frag. 5.13–14: 120n.72
frag. 5.18: 120n.72
frag. 5.19: 120n.72
frag. 5.25: 120n.72
frag. 6.7: 120n.72
frag. 6.8: 120n.72
frag. 6.15: 120n.72
frag. 7.2: 120n.72
frag. 7.13: 120n.72
frag. 7.14: 120n.72

frag. 8: 372n.20
frag. 8.2: 120n.72
frag. 13: 118–19
frag. 15: 121n.75, 124n.91
frag. 57: 118n.59

Philostratus, *Vitae sophistarum*
481: 519
511: 519

Pindar, *Pythian Odes*
7.14–15: 200

Plato
Cratylus
400c: 94n.12
414a: 202

Leges
715e–716d: 540
731d6–732b4: 540

Parmenides
130c: 96
142a: 438–39

Phaedo
64c: 94n.13
81e: 94n.12

Phaedrus
274–75: 296–97

Respublica
473d: 166
6.506e–509a: 94n.7

Sophista
248e: 124
249c–d: 124

Theaetetus
715e–716d: 540
731d6–732b4: 540

Timaeus
27d: 119–20
27d–28a: 115–16
34b: 119
36e: 119
40d: 94n.8
41a–b: 94n.8, 94n.10
41b–c: 296–97
41d–e: 94n.11
69d–e: 94n.9

Pliny, *Panegyricus*
14.5: 526–27

Plotinus, *Enneads*
2.9.15: 122
3.2–3: 125n.94
3.7.1: 122n.81
3.7.7: 122n.81
5.1.7: 122–23
5.1.8: 122n.81
5.3.13: 125n.95
5.3.14: 125n.95
5.6.6: 125n.95
5.8.6: 121
6.3.27: 122–23
6.4.16: 122n.81
6.8.17: 122–23
6.9.11: 122–23
6.9.3: 122–23

Plutarch
De adulatore et amico
70E: 111n.13

Amatorius
762A: 111–12
764A: 111–12

De defectu oraculorum
426E: 112
431A: 111n.13

Demetrius
2.2–3: 110–11, 111n.17
19.2: 110–11

De E apud Delphos
384F: 112
385A–B: 111n.13
385D–386A: 112
387F: 111n.13
388F: 115n.38, 115n.39
392A: 112–13
392B: 113n.32
392C: 112–13
392D: 112–13
392E: 115
393A: 115
393A–C: 116
393B: 115
393C: 115n.39, 117n.50

Fragmenta
frag. 157: 112n.23
frag. 190: 112n.23

De Iside et Osiride
354F: 115n.38
374E–F: 112n.24
377F–378A: 112n.24
381B: 138n.33
381F: 115n.38

Moralia
1007C: 138n.33

Quaestionum convivialum
628A: 111n.13
678C: 110–11
700E: 110–11

De sera numinis vindicta
559C: 113n.32

Sulla
16.8: 110–11

Themistocles
32.5: 111n.13

Porphyry
De abstinentia
4.2.2: 156

Vita Plotini
1: 122
3: 118n.60, 121
4–5: 122
7: 122n.80
9: 122
10: 121
14: 118n.60, 122
17: 118n.60, 122
18: 122n.80
19: 122n.80
20: 122n.80
24–26: 122n.80

Ps-Plato, *Axiochus*
366a: 94n.12

Pseudo-Hippocrates, *De hebdomadibus*
5: 114, 114t

Seneca
De beneficiis
4.29.1: 26n.39

Epistulae morales
58.22–23: 114–15, 117–18
75.9: 175n.74

Sententiae Pythagoreorum
no. 193: 199

Sextus Empiricus, *Adversus mathematicos*
6.13: 201n.22

Sophocles, *Antigone*
255: 26n.40

Stobaeus
Anthology
2.7.13: 26–27n.41
4.8.3: 530

Florilegium
2.33.12: 199

Strabo, *Geographica*
16.2.10: 118n.58

Suetonius, *Divus Claudius*
25: 153

Tacitus
Annales
11.24: 28–29

Germania
7: 30n.54
12: 30n.54

Historiae
5.5.1–2: 28n.50
5.2–13: 395n.46

Valerius Maximus, *Memorable Deeds and Sayings*
2.6.1: 30n.54

Vergil, *Aeneid*
6.365: 26n.40
6.788–807: 527n.48
6.852–53: 23n.24

Vita Aesopi
109: 201n.22

Vitruvius, *De architectura*
8 praef. 1: 530

Dead Sea Scrolls

Temple Scroll
51:11–66:7: 131

Pseudepigrapha

1 Enoch
42: 43–44

Ezekiel Tragicus, *Exagoge*
37: 180

Jubilees
2:25–33: 130n.13
49:1: 130n.13
49:1–23: 130n.13
50:1: 130n.13
50:1–13: 130n.13
50:6: 130n.13

Letter of Aristeas
144.2: 55n.49
145–48: 55n.49
153–54: 55n.49
163.2–3: 55n.49
165–67: 55n.49
169: 55n.49

Liber antiquitatum biblicarum
general: 9–10, 350–51, 352–53, 368,
   390–91, 404
5.8: 352–53
6: 352–53
7.5: 352–53
8.8: 352–53

Ps-Phocylides, *Sentences*
22–30: 27n.46
24: 27n.46
99–102: 27n.46

Sibylline Oracles
5: 59n.74

Josephus

Antiquitates Judaicae
1.18–25: 24
1.24: 24n.27, 197
1.24–25: 30
2.269: 234n.34
2.286: 25n.33
2.320: 25n.33
3.81: 132–33
3.163: 238n.61
3.183: 238n.59
3.184: 238n.60
3.184–85: 238n.61
3.185: 231n.23
4.74: 234–35
4.102: 23n.22
4.196–98: 129
4.279: 30n.55
4.283–84: 30n.55
4.285–86: 30n.55
4.296–97: 22
4.296–98: 23
4.298: 22–23
18.18–23: 392n.29
18.159–60: 18
18.257: 20–21
18.257–59: 20–21
18.257–60: 18, 33n.3, 149n.22
18.259: 17, 18–19, 109
18.259–60: 48–49
18.260: 19, 502n.15
19.276: 18
19.276–77: 18
20.100: 18

Bellum Judaicum
1.3: 150
2.8: 231–32
2.154–58: 392n.29
2.169–74: 149
2.586: 24n.26

5.205: 18
5.213: 231n.23

Contra Apionem
general: 17
1.73–105: 107n.67
1.228–52: 107n.67
1.304–11: 107n.67
2.40: 29
2.145: 24–25
2.146: 27n.42
2.148: 26n.37
2.161: 25
2.175–78: 25n.34
2.190–208: 27
2.190–214: 27–28
2.206–7: 30n.54
2.209: 25–26
2.209–10: 27, 28n.48
2.211: 25–26, 27
2.211–12: 27
2.213: 25–26, 27, 27n.42
2.214–17: 30n.54
2.232–35: 23n.21
2.255–61: 26n.37, 28n.51
2.260–61: 29
2.261: 27n.42
2.272: 22–23
2.276–77: 30n.54
2.291: 26n.37

Rabbinic Works and Later Jewish Writings

Mishnah
'Abot 1:1: 297n.105
'Abot 2:10: 136n.30
'Abot 5:1: 294n.86
Sotah 2.1: 235n.42

Tosefta
Ḥag. 2:5: 136n.30

Babylonian Talmud
Avodah Zarah 17b: 234n.35
Ḥag. 10b: 234n.34
Ḥag. 13a–b: 136n.30
Šabb 88b: 138n.32
Sanh. 34a: 138n.32
Zevahim 88b: 235n.46

Jerusalem Talmud
Ḥag. 2:1: 136n.30
Ned. 3:2: 138n.32
Shevi'it 6:1: 23n.23

Fathers According to Rabbi Nathan
A 18: 130
28: 136n.30

Sifra
Qedoshim parashah 10:1: 138n.32

Sifre Numbers
102: 138n.32
103: 134n.24
112: 138n.32

Sifre Deuteronomy
343: 133n.23, 136n.30, 140

Genesis Rabbah
1.1: 57n.64, 286–87, 288–89
3.4: 289
7.1: 57n.64
9.3: 287
12.12: 287

Leviticus Rabbah
17.5–6: 23n.23
21.7: 235n.46

Deuteronomy Rabbah
5.14: 23n.23

Mekhilta of R. Ishmael
Baḥodesh 3: 136n.30, 140
Baḥodesh 4: 136n.30
Baḥodesh 9: 132, 138–39

Mekhilta of R. Shim'on bar Yoḥai
Exod 15:2: 134n.26
Exod 19:8: 136n.30
Exod 20:15: 134

Pirqe Rabbi Eleazer
41: 132n.16

Tanḥuma
Ha'azinu 4: 138n.35

Midrash Leqaḥ Ṭov
Deut 4:12: 138n.35

Midrash Samuel
9:4: 132n.16

Midrash Tadshe
1, p. 88: 57n.64

Pesiqta de Rab Kahana
Supplement 7: 138n.35

Ibn Ezra, *Sefer ha-Yashar*
On Exod 5:21: 132n.18
On Exod 20:15: 132n.18
On Deut 4:12: 133n.21, 138n.35

Maimonides, *Guide for the Perplexed*
1:63: 281

Sefer Yeṣirah
2:6: 295n.93

Solomon ibn Gabirol, *Fons vitae*
3:45: 289
4:8: 288n.49
4:20: 288n.49
5:17: 288n.49
5:42: 289n.53
5:43: 295n.91

Zohar
1:15a: 294
3:48b: 294–95

Early Christian Writings

1 Clement
2.2: 52–53
20: 52
20.1: 52
20.10: 52
20.2: 52
20.3: 52
20.4: 52
20.9: 52
33.3: 52–53
33.4–5: 53, 58n.66
49.2: 52–53

Ambrose
De Abraham
general: 214
II.1–48: 218

De Cain et Abel
general: 214

Congra sermonem Arianorum
8.6: 217n.35

Epistulae
1: 215n.29, 216t, 223–24
2: 215n.29, 216t
3: 215n.27, 215n.29, 216t
4: 215n.27, 215n.29, 216t
6: 215n.29, 216t
7: 215n.29, 216t
10: 215n.27, 215n.29, 216t
14: 215n.29, 216t
28: 215n.29, 216t
29: 215n.29, 216t, 224
31: 215n.29, 216t, 224
34: 215n.29, 216t, 224
36: 215n.29, 216t
44: 215n.29, 216t
48: 215n.29, 216t
55: 215n.27, 215n.29, 216t, 223–24

De fuga saeculi
general: 214–15

Hexaemeron
6.9.72: 217n.33

De Noe et Arca
general: 214
8.24: 217n.34, 250–51

De officiis
1.1.3–4: 210

De paenitentia
2.67: 210n.2

De Paradiso
general: 214
1.1: 214n.24
4.25: 250–51

Veni, redemptor gentium
217n.35

Augustine
De civitate Dei
14.28: 253–54
21.17: 243
21.23: 243

Confessionum libri XIII
1–3: 251
1.13: 242–43
5.13.23–24: 211n.6
7.9.3: 244n.14
8.2.3: 213n.20
8.12.29: 244
9.2.3: 245–46
12: 251

Contra Academicos
2.2.5: 244

Contra Faustum
general: 409–10
12.39: 91–92, 247, 248, 372n.20, 410n.65

Enarrationes in Psalmos
Enarrat. Ps. 9.12: 253–54
Enarrat. 2 in Ps. 31: 243–44
Enarrat. Ps. 101.2.10: 252n.65
Enarrat. Ps. 121.5: 252n.65
Enarrat. Ps. 134.6: 252n.65

Epistulae
28.2: 243n.6

De Genesi ad litteram
4–5: 252
6.22.33: 251–52

De Genesi contra Manichaeos
2.21.32: 245n.20

De haeresibus
43: 243

De libero arbitrio
3.217: 245n.20

De ordine
1.8.24: 244
1.11.31: 244
1.11.32: 244

Retractionum libri II
1.7.6: 243

Sermones
2.5: 252–53, 252n.65
7.7: 252–53, 252n.65
45.10: 245n.20

De vita beata
1.4: 244

Basil of Caesarea
Enarratio in propheta Esaiam
433C: 180n.20

Epistulae
190.3: 179, 227n.1

Homilies on the Hexaemeron
1.1: 180
1.6: 179–80
1.7: 181
1.10: 181
1.20–24: 180
2.3: 181
2.5: 179–80
2.8: 181
3.9: 179–80
3.10: 179–80
4.1: 181
9.1: 179–80
9.6: 181, 182

De legendis gentilium libris
3: 180n.20

Clement of Alexandria
Eclogae Propheticae
38: 73n.27
56.2: 73–74
frag. 48: 73–74

Paedagogus
general: 69–71
1.5.1–2: 69n.14, 72
1.21.3–4: 69n.14
1.57.1–4: 69n.14
1.71.1–2: 69n.14, 70–71
1.71.2: 71n.19
1.77.2: 69n.14
2.75.1: 69n.14
2.92.1: 69n.14

Protrepticus
general: 69–71
5.1–2: 69n.13, 72
22.3: 69n.13
25.1: 69n.13
67.2: 69n.13
69.1–2: 69n.13
93.1–2: 69n.13
94.3: 69n.13
109.2: 69n.13
111.1: 69n.13, 70

Stromateis
general: 71–73
1.1.11: 49n.15
1.2.2: 67n.7
1.5.29.4: 253n.70
1.9.1: 67n.7
1.101–2: 73n.27
1.11.2: 66, 73–74
1.13.2: 67n.7
1.13.57.5: 89t
1.28–32: 71n.20
1.31.1: 47n.2, 73–74
1.72.4: 47n.2, 48–49, 73–74
1.74.2–75.1: 73n.27
1.150–82: 71n.20
1.151.2: 47n.2, 73–74
1.153.2–3: 166n.26
1.153.23: 180n.20
2.5–6: 71n.20
2.5.3–2.6.3: 68n.11
2.6.1: 189–90
2.46–52: 71n.20
2.78–100: 67–68, 71n.20
2.100.3: 47n.2, 73–74
3.81–82: 73n.27
3.92: 73n.27
4.100.3: 70
4.105–19: 67–68
5.32–40: 71n.20, 239–40n.71
5.67–68: 71n.20
5.71–74: 71n.20
5.93.4–94.5: 155
5.11.70.2: 530

6.7.57: 435–36
6.11.86–87: 249–50

Didymus
Commentarii in Ecclesiasten
general: 165–66
7.34: 163n.7
276.20–22: 165
276.22–24: 165–66
300.15: 166n.25
300.18–19: 166
300.20: 166n.29

Commentarii in Genesim
general: 166–69
31.16–18: 174–75
34.2–29: 174
34.24–29: 174
56.15–16: 174
70.13: 167n.36
70.15–21: 174
91.13–22: 175n.71
118.24–25: 167
119.2–4: 167
119.19–21: 167–68
119.24: 168
135.26–136.2: 171
136.11–12: 171
139.10–14: 168, 168n.43, 171
139.12: 167n.36
146.2–22: 169n.44
147.15–18: 168–69, 168n.43, 171, 172
168.10–27: 165n.23
183.27–184.23: 173
213.4: 171n.53
213.4–6: 172
235.25–30: 169
236.5–9: 169

Commentarii in Psalmos
43.23–25: 176
226.9–11: 175n.71

Commentarii in Zachariam
general: 164–65
1.48: 253n.70
3.273: 164
4.167: 164–65
123.21: 164n.21
364.18: 167n.36
377.20: 167n.36

Fragmenta in Epistulam i ad Corinthios
fr. in 1 Cor 16:17–18: 163n.7

Epiphanius, *Panarion*
1.9.11: 202n.26
3.416: 200

Epistle of Barnabas
4.11: 55n.50
5.10: 54–55
6: 55
6.8–19: 54–55
6.12–13: 54n.44
7: 55n.48
7.10: 54n.41
8: 54–55, 55n.48
10: 54–55
10.3: 55n.50
10.4: 55n.49, 55n.50
10.8: 55n.49
10.11: 55n.51
10.11d: 55n.49
12.5–7: 54–55
13: 54–55
13.2–6: 54n.40
15: 54–55, 55n.53
15.1: 54–55
15.5: 54n.43

Eusebius
Chronicon
general 349
203: 230
204: 230
213: 230
213–15: 149n.24
214: 230

Contra Hieroclem
374: 159n.78

Demonstratio evangelica
1.6.17a–19d: 161
6.18: 154n.47
6.24.7: 253n.70
8.2: 149n.23

Historia ecclesiastica
general: 148–53
2.4.1–6 372n.21
2.4.2: 147, 230–31
2.4.2–3: 109
2.4.2–6.4 349
2.5.1: 149
2.5.2–5: 149n.22
2.5.4: 155
2.5.6: 149–50
2.6: 152, 161
2.6.3: 149–50
2.16–18 349
2.16.1: 150–51
2.17: 9, 150, 170n.48, 230–31, 322–23, 406–7
2.17–18: 148
2.17.1: 33, 152
2.17.1–18.8 372n.21
2.17.2: 151
2.17.6: 151n.31
2.17.7–8 325
2.17.9 325, 360n.65
2.17.10–11 325

2.17.13 325
2.17.14: 151n.30
2.17.16–17 326
2.17.19 326
2.17.19–20: 158
2.17.20, 326
2.17.23: 2.18, 150–52, 151n.30, 166n.26, 227n.3, 228–29, 263, 270, 327–28, 573n.5
2.18.1: 77n.7, 152
2.18.6 372n.23
2.18.8 348
2.18.8: 48n.10, 152
3.9: 150
3.17.1: 150–51
3.23 322–23
3.31 322–23
4.6: 161
4.18.1–10: 60n.79
4.24.1: 56n.54
5.10: 66, 74
5.10.1–4: 48–49
5.11.2: 73–74
6.3.9: 74–75
6.6: 66, 74
6.13–14: 66, 74
6.13.7: 149n.21
6.14.8: 66, 74n.29
6.15: 152n.38
6.15.1: 67n.7
6.19.13: 74n.29
6.20: 74–75
7.32.2–4: 152n.38
7.32.6: 152n.38
7.32.22: 152n.38
7.32.25–28: 152n.38

Laus Constantini
12.7.1: 159n.78

De martyribus Palaestinae
4.5–6: 152n.38
5.2: 152n.38
7.4–5: 152n.38
11.1: 152n.38
27: 161n.85

Praeparatio evangelica
general: 153–56, 372
1.9.20: 157n.58
1.10.49: 157n.58
2.2.52: 157n.58
3.1.1: 112n.23
3.7.2: 157n.58
4.15.9: 157n.58
5.1.11: 157n.58
6.6.2: 524
6.10.50: 152n.38
7: 158
7.6.1–2: 147
7.7.4: 147

7.8.20–21: 147
7.8.37: 147
7.8.37–40: 161
7.8.40: 147
7.12.14: 147, 154
7.13.1–2: 159
7.13.4–6: 159
7.17.4: 147, 154
7.20.9: 147, 154
7.21.5: 154
8: 155, 156
8–10: 147–48
8.1.7: 161
8.6–7: 156
8.6.1: 155
8.7.21: 24–25
8.8: 156
8.9: 156
8.10: 156
8.10.19: 156
8.11–12: 156
8.11.1–19: 155n.52
8.12.20–22: 155
8.12.21: 155
8.14: 156
8.14.72: 155
8.18: 147, 379
10.6.15: 157n.58
10.9.26: 152n.38
11: 155, 158
11.9.8: 155
11.14.10: 155n.49
11.15–19: 155
11.18.20–21: 121n.75, 124n.91
11.18.26: 157n.58
11.20: 95n.15
11.23.12: 155n.49
11.24: 155
11.24.1–6: 158n.68
11.24.12: 155
11.25: 155
13.18.12: 155n.49

Gregory of Nazianzus
Funebris oratio in laudem Basilii
42.3: 200–1
43.3: 208

Orationes
14 865A: 192
14 865B: 192
14 868A: 192
14 869A: 193
14 869B: 192
14 900C: 192
38.12: 193

Gregory of Nyssa
De anima et resurrectione
78.1–6: 186n.45

Apologia in Hexaemeron
general: 185–86
6.4–6: 186n.44
14.11–12: 186n.44
18.13–19.12: 186n.44
23.13–24.3: 186n.44
37.7–13: 186n.44
72.7–10: 186n.44

Contra Eunomium
general: 183–84
1.167–71: 190n.55
1.179: 190–91
1.359–69: 190n.55
1.574: 190n.55
2.85–105: 190
2.95–98: 190
2.236: 190n.55
2.246–68: 190n.55
3.1.103–7: 190n.55
3.5.24: 183
3.7.8–9: 183
3.7.9: 190–91
3.9.37: 190–91

Homiliae in Canticum Canticorum
5: 186n.45
5.156.18: 191n.63
5.157.14–21: 190n.55
10.308–9: 191n.63
11.33.13–15: 191–92
12.362.12: 191n.63
181.4–21: 189n.53
322.11–323.9: 189n.53

De hominis opificio
general: 185–86
128B: 186n.44
132D–133B: 186
144C: 186n.44
181A–D: 186

In ascensionem Christi
324.18–20: 191n.63

Orationes de beatitudinibus
8.164.16–17: 191–92

Psalmorum tituli
44.18–19: 189n.53
118.1–4: 186n.45

De virginitate
general: 184–85
pr. 1: 184
4.6: 185
4.8: 185
14.3: 184
19: 185
20.4: 184–85

De vita Moysis
general: 187–89
1.2: 187
1.17–18: 180n.20
1.19: 187–88
1.20: 187–88
1.31: 187–88
2.7: 188
2.12: 188
2.20–23: 190–91
2.26: 188
2.35: 188
2.163–64: 189n.53
2.185: 187
2.191: 187, 239n.66, 239–40n.71
2.199: 187
2.200: 239n.67
2.201: 239n.66
2.219–55: 189–90
2.236–38: 189–90
2.239: 189–90
2.276–77: 188
2.288–89: 188
2.290: 188

Irenaeus, *Against Heresies*
1.20.1–2: 292n.69

Isidore of Pelusium, *Epistulae*
2.143: 307
3.81: 372n.20
47: 207
609: 198–99, 208
642: 196
643: 196, 207, 209
715: 201n.23, 208
770: 196–97, 207, 209
819: 197, 207, 209
881: 197–98, 207, 209
904: 199, 208n.42
915: 205–6, 208, 209n.43
960: 199–200, 208, 208n.42
979: 203, 209n.44
1043: 201, 208, 209n.43
1088: 202, 208, 209n.44
1089: 205, 206, 208
1156: 200, 208n.42
1162: 200–1, 208, 208n.42
1225: 199, 208n.42
1450: 201, 208, 208n.42
1618: 200n.20
1631: 198–99, 203, 208, 208n.42
1647: 198–99, 201, 208, 208n.42
1723: 204, 208, 209n.43
1757: 198, 209
1809: 201, 208, 208n.42

Jerome
Adversus Jovinianum libri II
2.14: 230

Adversus Pelagianos dialogi III
3.6: 230

Chronicon Eusebii a Graeco Latine redditum et continuatum
203: 230
213: 230

Commentariorum in Amos libri III
2.9: 230
3.6: 230–31

Commentariorum in Danielem
1.1.4a: 230, 232n.30

Commentariorum in Ezechielem libri XVI
Praef.: 247–48
4.16.10b: 230, 232n.30
8:7: 231n.22
16:10: 230–31

Commentariorum in Osee libri III
3.2–3: 234–35

Commentariorum in Zachariam libri III
Praef.: 164n.17

Epistulae
22.35: 403n.23
6: 243n.6
22: 230–31
22.35.8: 230, 231–32
29.7: 234–35
29.7.1: 230, 231–32, 232n.30
64: 232n.30, 234–35, 237–38
64.2: 234–35
64.5: 235n.42
64.9: 234–35
64.9.2: 237–38
64.14: 235n.46
64.18: 234–35, 237–38
64.18.1: 237–38
64.18.6–8: 238n.61
64.18.8: 237–38
64.19: 238–40
64.19.1: 237–38
64.19.2: 238–40
64.19.3: 239n.66
64.20.3: 238–40
64.20.4: 238–40
64.20.5–6: 239n.66
64.21.3: 238–40
70.3.3: 230, 232–33
78.3: 235n.42
78.3.2: 233

De nominibus hebraicis, praef.: 170n.48, 230, 232

Praefatio in libros Salomonis: 227, 230

Praefatio in Librum Iob: 230
Praefatio in Pentateuchum: 232n.30

Quaestionum hebraicarum liber in Genesim
4:25: 236–37
17:15: 233
25:8: 235–37
26:12: 236–37
32:28–29: 236–37
35:18: 236–37

De viris illustribus
general: 227–28
8: 247–48
8.4: 230
11: 9–10, 247, 348–49, 360n.66, 363n.88, 372n.20, 392–93, 398, 573n.9
11.1–3: 230
11.1–7: 227–29, 230
11.4–7: 230
13.2: 230
54: 247–48
109.2: 163n.15, 164n.16
113: 146n.8

John Chrysostom
Ad Stagirium
47:438: 200n.15

Homiliae in Genesim
15: 202n.26
32.7: 199–200, 208
51.3: 199–200

De Sacerdotio
1.4: 200n.15
1.7: 200n.15

John of Damascus, *Sacra parallela*
PG 96: 60: 204
PG 96: 88: 204
PG 96: 284: 203n.29

Justin Martyr
Apologia i
31.2–4: 60n.84
58.3: 62n.96
59: 435–36
63: 62–63

Apologia ii
10: 61
13: 61

Dialogus cum Tryphone
20.2: 63n.113
40: 63
56: 62n.101
56–57: 62n.99
56.11: 61n.92

57.3: 63n.106
58: 62n.99, 62n.104
58.3: 63n.106
59: 62–63, 63n.107
59–60: 62n.99
61.2: 61
62.1–3: 63
62.4: 62n.95
68: 60–61n.85
112–13: 60n.83
128: 61, 62–63
128.2: 61–62n.94
138.2: 62n.95

Nag Hammadi
Eugnostus
76.14–24: 97n.29

Nature of the Rulers
89.8–9: 102
89.10–11: 102–3
89.13–15: 102–3
90.6: 104
94.5–7: 99n.41

Norea
28.30–29.1: 96–97

On the Origin of the World
120.3–4: 104

Revelation of Adam
64.8: 102n.52
73.13–74.26: 105n.62
75–76: 105

Second Discourse of Great Seth
65.18–31: 103n.54

Secret Book of John
5.7: 97n.29
6.10–33: 98
9.28–35: 99
14.23: 99
14.24: 99
15.3: 99
19.10–20.28: 101
19.25–26: 100
20.9: 98n.36
21.4–5: 99
21.10: 99
21.12: 99
21.18–21: 101
22.12–15: 104, 104n.57
23.12–13: 102–3
24.26–29: 104n.57
28.21: 104
29.11–12: 105
29.6–7: 102

31.5–6: 102
48.2–3: 97n.29

Three Steles of Seth
118.26: 96n.25
119.4: 95
121.9–15: 95
123.16–17: 98n.36

Wisdom of Jesus Christ
104.17–19: 98n.37

Zostrianos
1.10–13: 103
24.4: 103
131.3–8: 103

Niles of Ancyra, *Ep.* 1.257: 200

Origen of Alexandria
Commentarii in Romanos
1.1: 74, 74n.29
3.8.4: 173–74
4.2–3: 190
4.5.171–83: 252–53

Commentarius in Canticum
general: 88–91, 89t
2.4.28–30: 244

Commentarii in evangelium Joannis
1.30.206: 191
2.25: 74, 74n.29
2.172: 189–90

Commentarium in evangelium Matthaei
general: 85–88
11.16: 171n.53
12.31: 74, 74n.29
14.2: 74, 74n.29
15.3: 74n.29
17.17: 85, 86–87, 86t, 88–91
17.18: 87n.62
26.37: 176n.77

Contra Celsum
4.51: 74n.29
4.71: 165n.23
4.77: 530
6.2: 165n.23
6.17: 189–90
6.21: 74n.29

Epistula ad Africanum
7: 91n.69

Homiliae in Exodum
9: 238n.65
9.4: 238n.65

Homiliae in Genesim
2.1: 249
2.2: 248
2.3–5: 249
2.5: 248

Homiliae in Jeremiam
13.2: 253n.70
18.4: 86–87
18.6: 85, 86–87, 86t
20.2–3: 91
20.3: 91

Homiliae in Leviticum
6: 238–40
6.2: 238–40, 245n.20
6.3: 239n.70
6.4: 238–40
6.6: 238–40

Homiliae in Lucam
16: 76n.1, 76n.2

Homiliae in Numeros
20.5: 234n.35
22.4: 206n.36, 207
27.9: 234n.33

Homiliae in Psalmos
15.1.1: 89t
36.4.1: 88–91, 89t
67.1.5: 89t
67.2.4: 89t
73.1.5: 89t
73.3.8: 89t
74.1.5: 89t
75.1.6: 88–91, 89t, 92
76.1.5: 89t
77.2.7: 89t
77.7.3: 89t

De principiis
1.2.2: 252
1.4.5: 252
4.2.4: 83–84

Selecta in Genesim
PG 12:97 l.13: 70n.15

Selecta in Psalmos
Ps 4:5: 176n.77

Pamphilus, *Apologia pro Origene*
12: 245–46

Paulinus of Milan, *Life of Ambrose*
3.6–9: 211n.5

Ps.-Athanasius, *Homilia de passione et cruce domini* PG 28:233 l. 41: 70n.15

Ps.-Clementine Homilies 4–6: 59n.74

Rufinus, *Apologia* 2.26: 213n.19

Theodore Metochites, Σημειώσεις γνωμικαί
16: 248n.35

Theodoret, *Quaestiones in Numeros* 47: 205

Theophilus of Antioch, *Ad Autolycum*
2.10: 57n.64
2.12: 56
2.13: 56, 57, 57n.64, 58
2.14: 56n.61
2.15: 56n.61, 57, 57n.64, 58n.70
2.16: 56n.61
2.17: 56n.61
2.18: 57, 58–59
2.19: 56n.61
2.20: 202n.26
2.24: 57, 58
2.25: 57
2.27: 57, 58–59
2.28: 57
2.30: 57
2.36: 59
3.23: 59
3.9: 56

Subject Index

For the benefit of digital users, indexed terms that span two pages (e.g., 52–53) may, on occasion, appear on only one of those pages.

1 Clement 5, 51–53
1 Maccabees 555
2 Maccabees 555
4 Ezra 555

abortion, image of 98–99
acculturation 553
Adam 57, 306, 317–18
Adam, and Seth 168–69
Adler, Maximilian 496–97
Aeschylus 517–18
aggadah 491
Albert, Johannes 454
Alesse, Francesca 534
Alexandria, philosophy in 534
Allegorical Commentary 30–31, 65–66, 77–78, 84–85, 127–28, 168, 169–70, 177, 188–89, 335–36, 340–41, 372, 373, 539–40, 547
allegory 2, 3, 4–5, 7–8, 10, 11, 37, 47–48, 53–55, 56, 58, 63, 65, 67, 69–70, 71, 83–84, 91–92, 98, 102–3, 104–5, 111–12, 113, 135, 156, 158, 165–69, 170–74, 176–77, 178, 179–80, 187, 188–89, 193, 197, 209, 214–15, 218, 220, 228–29, 230, 234–35, 237–40, 241, 246–47, 248, 250–51, 253–54, 281–82, 285, 290–91, 305, 337–38, 343, 345, 347–48, 362, 371–72, 384–85, 391, 393, 395, 396, 405–6, 416–17, 418–19, 431–32, 437, 443–44, 455–56, 457–58, 460–61, 467, 478–79, 484–86, 488–89, 491–92, 537–38, 546, 555–56, 563, 566, 569–70
Ambrose of Milan 7–8, 9–10, 210–26, 276, 348–49, 350–51
    Ambrose, education of 210–11
    Ambrose, Letters of 215
    Ambrose, views on gender and sexuality 224–25
Ammonius 110–18, 121–22, 126, 336
Anderson, Graham 519–20, 526
Annas, Julia 532
Apollos 33, 36–37
apologetic discourse 28, 47–64, 546
Apostolic Fathers 5, 47–64
Arabic literature, Philo in 3–4, 9, 284, 322–32
arithmology 7, 172–74, 334–35, 342, 345
Armenian literature, Philo in 1, 8–9, 259, 261, 262, 270–73, 277, 279–80, 299–321
assimilation 553
Athanasius 197, 224–25, 404–5
Augustine 8, 9–10, 242–55, 276, 348–49, 350–51, 389–90, 410–11, 500–1

Augustine, conversion of 244
Augustine, knowledge of Origen 244–46
Augustine, knowledge of Philo 246–49
Augustine, use of Latin translations of Philo 249–54

Balthasar, Hans Urs von 79
Barclay, John 24–25, 27, 553–54
Barnabas, *see* Epistle of Barnabas
Basil of Caesarea 7, 179–82, 185, 192, 193, 194, 217, 565
Baur, Ferdinand Christian 461–62
becoming 112–13
Bede, the Venerable 9–10, 349–50, 358–59, 363–64
being 115–18, 252–53
Belkin, Samuel 12, 24–25, 543–44, 547
Bernay, Jacob 490
bibliographies of Philo 12–13, 572–86
biography as genre 522
Bloom, Harold 82–83
body 38, 58–59, 83–84, 91–92, 94, 99–100, 115–16, 164–65, 185, 192, 202–3, 217, 248, 313, 318, 326, 360, 409–10, 509, 536–37
Book of Enoch 317–18, 552
Borgen, Peder 24–25, 35, 38, 550
Bowersock, Glenn 19, 519
Budé, Guillaume 368, 400–1
Bultmann, Rudolf 462–63
Byzantium 1, 9–10, 195–96, 302, 332, 333–46, 420, 574

Cain and Abel 167–68, 223, 253–54
Cain, descendants of 168
Cappadocians 7, 178–93
Carpzov IV, Johann Benedict 454–55
Cassiodorus 9–10, 349–50, 354
Catenae 8, 262, 267–68, 269, 271–72, 273–74, 276, 306, 335–36, 341–42
Catholic 3–4, 10, 375, 377, 378, 400–13, 414–15, 419, 422, 423–35, 459–60, 504–5, 570–71
Chadwick, Henry 242–43, 568
Christopherson, John 10, 11, 375, 414–16, 424–25
classical studies, Philo and 9–10, 12, 229, 517–31, 575–77, 586
    reception history 523
Claudius 18, 28, 152, 153, 328, 501
Clement of Alexandria 5, 65–75, 263, 322, –24, 335, 336–38, 340–41, 418, 426–27, 435–36
    Clement of Alexandria, works of 66

666 SUBJECT INDEX

codices of Philo 8, 266–70
Cohen, Hermann 11, 491–92, 494–96, 558
Cohen, Naomi 547–48
Cohn, Leopold 374, 380, 461, 491–92, 495, 496
Cohn-Wendland edition 11, 205–7, 260–61, 264, 266, 270, 370–71, 373–74, 484, 496–97, 578
colors, in the Bible 294–95, 471–72
commentary on Scripture 127–28, 141
comparative method 465
Constantinople 179, 192, 301–2, 341–42
Corpus Hellenisticum Novi Testamenti project 463–64
Counter-Reformation, *see* Reformation
Cover, Michael 532
creation 174, 186, 252, 283, 285–87
 creation of humanity 53, 186

Day of Atonement 54–55, 546
de' Rossi, Azariah 10, 76, 387–95, 396, 397, 398–99, 412, 467–68, 469–71, 472, 476–78, 479–80, 481, 512, 542
Decalogue 130–31, 133–34, 295, 547–48
diaspora 32–33, 38–39, 45, 49–50, 419–20, 469, 543, 549–50, 552, 559
 diaspora, Philo and 553–54
Didymus the Blind 7, 162–77, 335, 339
 Didymus, Commentaries of 163–70
Dillon, John 70–71, 532–33, 566–67, 568
Dio Chrysostom 520–22, 526–27, 530, 531
Dionysius the Areopagite 9, 271, 279, 322–27, 332
divine, participation in 100–1
divine image 99–100
divine intermediaries 94
divine transcendence 94
Doering, Lutz 532
Donaldson, Terence L. 554–55
doxography, Philo and 523–24, 534
drama, Attic 525
 drama, Philo and 529
Dunash ibn Tamim 288–91

Eden, Garden of 57, 212, 305, 306, 317–18, 330
 as metaphor for luxury 101
Elliott, Paul M. C. 224
Embassy to Emperor Gaius 526–28
epistemology 124–25, 494, 541, 569–70
Epistle of Barnabas 5, 53–55, 107
Ernesti, Johann August 416–17, 455–56, 463–64
ethical commandments 26
etymology 7, 170–72, 201, 230, 233–34, 253–54
Eudorus 117–18, 122
Eunomius 7, 183–84, 190–91, 193
Euripides 329–30, 334–35, 517–18, 524–25, 529–30
Eusebius 3–4, 6–8, 12–13, 109, 145–61, 259–60, 263, 267–68, 270–71, 279–80, 306, 311, 322–27, 339, 348–49, 352, 358, 362, 375, 389–90, 406–7, 416–17, 423, 425–26, 572–73, 578
 Eusebius, citation practices 157–60
 Eusebius, views on Judaism 147–56
 Eusebius as mediator of Philo 3–4

Eustathius, Pseudo- 8, 272–73
Eve 54–55, 57, 99, 104, 225
 Eve, as means of knowledge 102–3
exegete, Philo as 47–48, 106, 146, 151–52, 230, 345, 363–64, 532–33, 540, 541, 542, 550, 571
exegetical inversion 105–6
exegetical method 5, 7, 32–33, 60, 83, 170–76, 298, 569
Exposition of the Law 30–31, 65–66, 127–28, 177, 188–89, 334–35, 372, 373, 376–77, 539, 540, 547

Fabricius, Johann Albert 12–13, 383–85, 415, 420–26, 427, 574–75
family of Philo 18, 501–2, 504–5, 550
Feldman, Louis 12–13, 23, 552, 570–71, 580–82, 586
Flesch, Josef 11, 397, 467–68, 481–82
florilegium 8, 9, 194, 261, 267–68, 269–70, 273, 274–76, 279–80, 329–30, 331, 345, 530, 578
Frankel, Zacharias 11, 478–79, 484–86, 488–89, 490, 498
Freudenthal, Jacob 490–91
Freudenthal, Max 494
Früchtel, Ludwig 194, 198–204, 274–75

Gaius Caligula 4–5, 18, 19, 20–21, 48–49, 149–50, 152, 311, 327–29, 339–40, 349, 354, 358–59, 389–90, 501–2, 519–20, 526–27, 528–29
Galatians 37
Genesis Rabbah 286–87, 289–90
gentiles 362, 554–55
German idealism 11, 429, 438–42
Gfrörer, August Friedrich 461
gnosticism 5–6, 93–108, 245–46, 292–93, 441, 569–70
God
 incomprehensibility of 189–90
 infinity of 190
 invisibility of 189–90
 names of 174–75
 as Self-Existent 119–20
 as Standing One 95, 122–24
Goodenough, E. R. 12, 50–51, 159, 536–37, 543–44, 555–56, 563–64, 567
Goodhart and Goodenough 12–13, 261, 400–1, 577–80, 581–82, 583, 586
Graetz, Heinrich 11, 486–88, 490
Grecism 299–300
Greek literature, Philo's knowledge of 523
Gregory of Nazianzus 7, 179, 192–93, 194
Gregory of Nyssa 7, 166, 170, 178, 182–92, 193, 246, 565
Grotius, Hugo 3–4, 454
Gruen, Erich 521

Hadas-Lebel, Mireille 549–50
Halacha 433–34, 478–79, 491–93, 544
Harnack, Adolf von 462–63, 491–92, 562, 567, 569
Haskalah, Philo and 11, 467–83
hearing 131–41
heavenly sanctuary 41

SUBJECT INDEX 667

Hebrews (epistle) 4–5, 11, 35–36, 39–43, 84, 453, 458
Hecht, Richard 555–56
Hegel 11, 429, 438–41
Heracles 526–27
Heraclitus 113, 114–15, 117–18, 538
Hesiod 517–18
Hexaemeron 56, 180–81, 244–45
Hilgert, Earle 12–13, 545, 580–82
Hoek, Annewies van den 48–49, 81–82, 88, 528–29, 567–68
Hoeschel, David 10, 11, 377–85, 415–16, 427
Homer 38, 72–73, 182, 313, 378, 517–18, 541
Huet, Pierre-Daniel 79

Ibn Ezra 480
Idel, Moshe 292–93
identity, Philo's 545–50
injustice 203–4
interpretation, physical and ethical 537–38
Isidore of Pelusium 7, 194–209, 307, 339–40, 345
   Isidore of Pelusium, *Epistulae* 196–98
Isidore of Seville 9–10, 349–50, 354, 355–58
Isocrates 183, 526–27
Israel 22, 139, 464, 477, 546–47, 556

Jerome 7–8, 9–10, 12–13, 227–41, 263, 277, 348–49, 350, 352–53, 358–59, 362–63, 389–90, 402–3, 404–5, 573–74
   Jerome, *De nominibus hebraicis* 232
   Jerome, on Philo's treatises 228–29
Jewish Enlightenment, *see* Haskalah
Jewish Hellenism 49–50, 64
Jewish Theological Seminary, Breslau 484–98
Joel, Manuel 11, 437, 488–90
John (Gospel) 4–5, 11, 43–45, 46, 416–17, 418–19, 432–33, 441–42, 456, 458–60
John Chrysostom 194, 199–200, 208, 306, 308, 332, 339, 377
John of Damascus (*Sacra parallela*) 274–75, 332, 335–36, 416–17
Joseph Gikatilla
   Ginnat 'Egoz 291–92, 295–97
   Sha'are 'Orah 291–92, 297–98
Josephus 4–5, 17–31, 274–75, 328, 339–40, 341–42, 358–59, 361–62, 368–69, 372, 388–89, 391–92, 396, 401, 402, 406–9, 421, 508
Jowett, Benjamin 457–58, 459–60
Judaism, of Philo 542–45, 551–53
Judaism, Orthodoxy 546
Judaism, Orthopraxy 546
Judaism, universalist view of 475–76, 491–92, 554–55, 556
Justin Martyr 5, 60–63, 338, 404–5, 435–36

Kabbalah 281–82, 291–98, 394, 395, 396, 429, 430, 431, 437, 449, 472, 480, 501
Karaite Judaism 10, 283, 290–91, 386, 397–99
Keim, Karl Theodor 462
Krochmal, Naḥman 11, 429, 443–47, 467–68, 476–82

Latin translation of Philo 1, 8, 10, 259, 262, 277–79, 350–52, 368, 374–77, 379, 381–82, 385, 386, 389–90, 400–1, 402–3
law
   as Mosaic constitution 129
   oral and unwritten 548
   Philo and rabbis on 558
   topical arrangements of 128–31
Leonhardt, Jutta 549–50
Letter of Aristeas 24, 55, 60, 156, 157, 388–89, 469, 553
Lévy, Carlos 533–34
Liber Philonis 9–10, 350, 351–53, 359–60, 362, 363, 368
Libraries, Philo and 523–24
library in Caesarea 6–7, 12–13, 263, 335–36, 572, 573
library in Jerusalem 74–75
Logos (λόγος) 2, 4–5, 11, 44–45, 61, 62–63, 67, 96, 100, 119, 154, 159, 190–91, 292–93, 307, 309, 363, 418–19, 432–34, 436, 439–42, 444, 446–49, 454, 457–59, 467–68, 480–81, 482–83, 484–86, 495–96, 509–10, 511–12, 540, 555–56, 561–62, 564, 566–67, 568
Lucchesi, Enzo 212, 218–21, 225–26
Luther, Martin 384–85, 406–7
Luzzatto, Samuel D. 480
Luzzatto, Simone 10, 395–97

Maimonides 281–82, 283–84, 437, 471, 480–81, 493, 564–65
Mangey, Thomas 11, 218, 260–61, 276, 385, 414–28
manuscripts of Philo 7–8, 10, 74, 75, 146, 159, 219, 259–80, 299–321, 333, 337–38, 344, 350–52, 367–85, 386–87, 414–15, 417–18, 576–77, 578
Marcion 58–59, 71, 73–74
maskilim 482–83
medieval Jewish Mysticism 281–98
medieval Jewish Philosophy 281–98
Menasseh ben Israel 397, 475–76
Mendelson, Alan 499–500, 508, 545–46, 549, 551
Mendelssohn, Moses 11, 468–76, 482
messiah/messianism 444, 458, 486–87, 501–2, 555–56
Middle Platonism, *see* Platonism
midrash 6, 8–9, 36, 43, 84, 127–28, 131–41, 282, 285–87, 298, 393, 446, 491–92
Mishnah 127, 130, 131, 141, 285–86, 398–99, 430, 479–80, 491–93, 551, 555, 566–67
monasticism 10, 162, 179, 185, 228–29, 326–27, 342, 349–50, 358–64, 389–90, 402, 406–9, 562
monotheism 112, 117, 196, 439, 441–42, 446, 462, 546, 554, 570–71
Moore, George Foote 543–44
Moses 5–6, 12, 54–55, 67, 71, 95, 101, 111–12, 123–24, 129, 147, 161, 166, 180, 187–89, 198, 205–6, 293, 307–8, 313, 334, 536, 538, 569–70
   Moses, law of 24–28, 30–31, 38–39, 156, 326–27, 328, 562–63
mystery cults 5–6, 111–12, 543, 563–64

Neander, Alexander 460–61
Neoplatonism 5–6, 8–9, 110, 122, 220–21, 282, 288–89, 438–39, 484–86
   see also Platonism

SUBJECT INDEX

Nero, emperor 508, 519, 528
New Testament
   New Testament, and Alexandrian Judaism 460–61
   New Testament criticism, Philo and 453–66
   New Testament reception of Philo 4–5, 32–46
   New Testament scholarship 11
Niehoff, Maren 83, 440, 521–22, 539–40, 541, 548–49, 569
Nikiprowetzky, Valentin 533–34, 536, 569–70, 583
Noah 57, 91–92, 105, 119, 214, 217, 222, 249, 306, 348–49, 352–53, 362, 409–10
nouvelle théologie 3–4, 569–71
number symbolism, *see* arithmology
Numenius of Apamea 5–6, 60, 95, 110, 118–21, 124–26, 421–22, 535

Origen of Alexandria 5, 6–7, 8, 74–75, 118, 128, 146, 162–64, 170–71, 172–74, 178, 189–90, 207, 211, 229, 232, 238–40, 263, 286–87, 339, 384–85, 396, 426–27, 565, 569–70
   Origen, absorption of Philo 82–91
   Origen, chronology of 77–78
   Origen, exegesis of 83–84
   Origen, influence on Augustine 242–46
Otto, Jennifer 82
Oxyrhynchus Papyrus 263, 265–66, 274–75, 279–80

paideia 5, 12, 38–39, 67, 70–71, 165, 194, 522–25
Pamphilus 74, 146, 151, 245–46, 572
Pantaenus 48–49, 65, 66, 73–74, 81, 151, 336, 425–27
papyrus 8, 259–60, 263–66
parallelomania 36, 45, 463, 562, 566
parallels, use of 463
Paul (Apostle) 4–5, 11, 33, 35, 83–84, 165–66, 169, 307–8, 326–27, 508, 566
   Paul, Philo and 436, 448, 456–58, 568
pax Romana 23
Perrone, Lorenzo 88–91
pesharim 83, 127–28
Peter (Apostle) 33, 150–51, 152, 153, 159–60, 228–29, 247–48, 358–59, 508, 510–11
Petit, Françoise 207, 262, 271–72, 273, 274–75, 276, 278, 350–52
philanthrōpia 24–28, 29–30, 550
Philo of Alexandria
   De mundo 261, 269, 344, 367–68
   as ecclesiastical author 151–53
   ethics of 253
   as Hebrew 154–55, 159
   originality of 125–26
   Philo's writings, critical edition 496
   Philo's writings, dissemination 48–49, 263
   Philo's writings, German translation 496–97
   Philo's writings, Hebrew translation 388–89, 559
   Philo's writings, preservation 8, 75, 146, 425–26
   Quaestiones 271–72, 273, 274–75, 276, 334–36
   scholarly approaches to 80–82
   as witness for ecclesiastical way of life 150–51
philosophy
   philosophy, ancient 12, 109–26, 532–41

philosophy, and scripture 536, 541
philosophy, and wisdom 536, 541
philosophy, in Philo's writings 534–38
philosophy, Jewish 282–85
Phocylides, Pseudo- 24, 27
Photius 9–10, 336–41, 343, 345, 346, 415–16, 574
Plato 47–48, 248, 343, 409–10
   Plato, *Laws* 540, 549
   Plato, *Theaetetus* 540
   Plato, *Timaeus* 115–16, 119–20, 250–51, 288–89, 348, 394, 421–22, 532–33, 539–40, 566–67
Platonism 11, 41–42, 58, 72, 94, 96, 109–26, 247, 269–70, 337–38, 358–59, 362–63, 371–72, 384–85, 387, 402–4, 416–17, 421–23, 431, 435–36, 453, 488–89, 538–40, 563, 566–71
   Middle Platonism 5–6, 432–33, 532–33
Plotinus 6, 121–125, 155, 243–44, 535, 558, 565
   Plotinus, *Enneads* 122
Plutarch 5–6, 110–18, 125–26, 522, 532–33, 566–67
   knowledge of Jews and Judaism 111
poetry, biblical 472–75
Porphyry 121, 122, 156, 230–31, 243–44
pre-passion (προπάθεια) 175–76
priestly vestments 71, 187, 231–32, 237–40, 547–48
Procopius 8, 9–10, 207, 271–72, 335–36, 578
Protestant 3–4, 377, 378, 406, 412, 419, 422, 442, 570–71
Psellus, Michael 9–10, 340–42
Pythagoreanism 47–49, 64, 73–74, 109, 114, 117, 118, 173–74, 295–96, 298, 349–50, 358–59, 362–63, 387, 421, 423, 431, 488–89, 566–67

Qirqisani, Jacob 283
Qumran 6, 503–4, 509, 510–11, 554, 555, 562
quotation practices 34–35, 67–68, 271–72

rabbi, rabbinic, etc.
Rabbi 'Akiba 133–34
Rabbi Hoshaya 77–78, 84–85, 286–87
Rabbinic Judaism 5, 6, 10, 56, 77–78, 82, 127–42, 234, 281, 285–87, 386, 388–89, 390–95, 432–33, 437, 476, 482–83, 484–90, 544–45, 552–53, 558, 561–62, 564–65, 566
Radice, Roberto 12–13, 110, 534, 538–39, 582–84
Rapoport, Solomon J. L. 11, 281–82, 467–68, 476–82
reception, modes of 2–3, 34–36
Reformation 10, 225, 402, 406–9, 423–24, 578–79
Religionsgeschichtliche School 463–64
revelation 131–41, 291–93, 294, 298, 431, 436, 441, 495, 543–44
rhetoric, classical 179, 182, 519, 520, 522–23, 535
Ritter, Bernard Loebel 11, 493–94
Rome 7–8, 28–30, 60, 149–50, 247–48, 348
   Rome, Philo and 33, 48–49, 65–66, 228–29, 230, 358–59, 389–90, 519–20, 521–22, 526–28, 539
Rosenzweig, Franz 558
   Rome, philosophy in 110, 534

Runia, David T. 3, 76–77, 78–82, 195–98, 211–12, 230–31, 284, 532–33, 566–67, 568–71, 580–84

Sandmel, Samuel 36, 463, 544–45, 566–67
Sarah and Hagar 37–38, 67, 71, 165–66, 169, 188, 253–54, 342, 371–72, 535
Savon, Hervé 212, 218–21, 234–35, 237–38
Scheffer, Wilhelm 455
Schelling, Friedrich 11, 429, 441–42
scholia 267, 300–1, 302, 308, 310–11, 312, 313, 315–16, 318, 320, 321, 323–24
Schürer, Emil 462–63, 576–77
scripture, interpretation of 7, 10, 47–48, 53–54, 127–28, 141, 154, 237–38, 248, 337, 354, 431–32, 455, 461, 484–86
second century 48–49
Second Sophistic 519–22, 527–28
secondary lemmata 84–91, 115–16
Secret Book of John 98, 99, 104
seeing 131–41
Sefer ha-Zohar 291–92
Sefer Yeṣirah 289–91, 294–95, 298, 430, 431, 437, 479–81
Seneca 114–15, 117–18, 247, 423–24, 539–40
senses of scripture 83–84
Septuagint 10, 32–33, 47–48, 51, 60, 68, 77, 137, 169–70, 233, 388–89, 391, 392, 396, 404–5, 433, 469, 484–86, 561–62
serpent 54–55, 70, 104, 188, 306, 309
Seth, family of 104–5
Sethianism 5–6, 93–108
Simeoni, Francesca 532
Simplicianus 213, 245–46
Sinai 131–41, 291–92, 294–95, 567–68
skepticism, Philo and 533–34, 537, 541
sleep of Adam 101–2
sober drunkenness 191, 567
Solomon ibn Gabirol 282, 288–91
    Solomon ibn Gabirol, *Fons vitae* 288–90
sophists, Philo and 526–28
Souda 9–10, 338–40, 345, 372, 389–90, 574
Spinoza 109–10, 432, 444, 511–12, 564–65
spirit 83–84, 100–1, 106, 165–66, 305, 442, 445, 458
stages of life 112–15
Sterling, Gregory 24–25, 32–33, 532–33
Stoicism 11, 12, 51, 52, 83, 176, 283, 423–27, 488–89, 538–40, 562–63

Stoicism, Philo and 167, 169, 203–4, 253–54, 538–40
Strauss, David Friedrich 448, 461–62
supersessionism 146–47

Talmud 284, 285–86, 353, 394–95, 396, 398–99, 430, 484–86, 491–92, 561–62
Terian, Abraham 300–2, 309
theanthropy 5–6, 95–97
theater, Philo and 12, 528–31
Theiler, Willy 496–97
theophany 61, 62–63
Theophilus of Antioch 5, 56–59
Therapeutae 6–8, 150–51, 184, 247, 271, 305–6, 323–24, 339–40, 349, 393, 406–7, 409, 436–37, 479–80, 486–87, 538, 549, 562
Thesaurus Linguae Graecae 195–96, 333–34
Torah, *see* law; Moses, law of
translation 234–41
Treitel, Leopold 11, 491–93
Trinity 7, 11, 181, 196, 307, 309, 313, 330, 339–40, 345, 418–20, 421–22, 445, 488–89
Trisoglio, Francesco 192–93
Turnebus, Adrianus (Adrien Turnèbe) 10, 11, 268, 369–83, 385, 400–1, 414–16, 419, 574

warfare, laws of 21–24
Weisser, Sharon 536–37
Wendland, Paul 271–72, 496
Wettstein, Johann Jakob 454–55
Whitmarsh, Tim 520–21
Winter, Bruce 33, 520
wisdom 43–45, 91, 252, 288, 305, 435–36, 484–86, 535–492, 566–67
    as God's wife 97–98
Wissenschaft des Judentums 11, 281, 285, 443, 448, 467–68, 476–77, 484–98, 558, 575
Wolfson, Harry A. 8–9, 12, 78–79, 109–10, 252, 282–85, 432, 536–37, 543–44, 555–56, 564–65
womanhood, forsaking of 103
word of God 43–45, 307, 439, 455–56, 562

Yedidyah, Philo as 10, 388–89, 394, 468–76, 482

Zeller, Eduard 486–87, 489–90
Zohar 282, 294–95, 298, 430, 437, 471